Essentials of Psychology
Second Edition *offers an integrated pedagogical system designed to help students get the most out of their reading. Based on the proven PQ4R study system, it includes an outline, a preview statement, preview questions, instructional captions,* In Review *charts, and a marginal glossary. Each chapter ends with an Active Review *that includes a* Linkages *diagram, chapter summary,* Learn by Doing *and* Step into Action *sections, a review of key terms, and multiple-choice questions.*

1

Introduction to the Science of Psychology

An Integrated Pedagogical System

Each chapter opens with a full **outline,** a brief **preview statement,** and a list of **preview questions** related to each main section of the chapter. The preview questions are repeated at the start of each section and within the chapter summary.

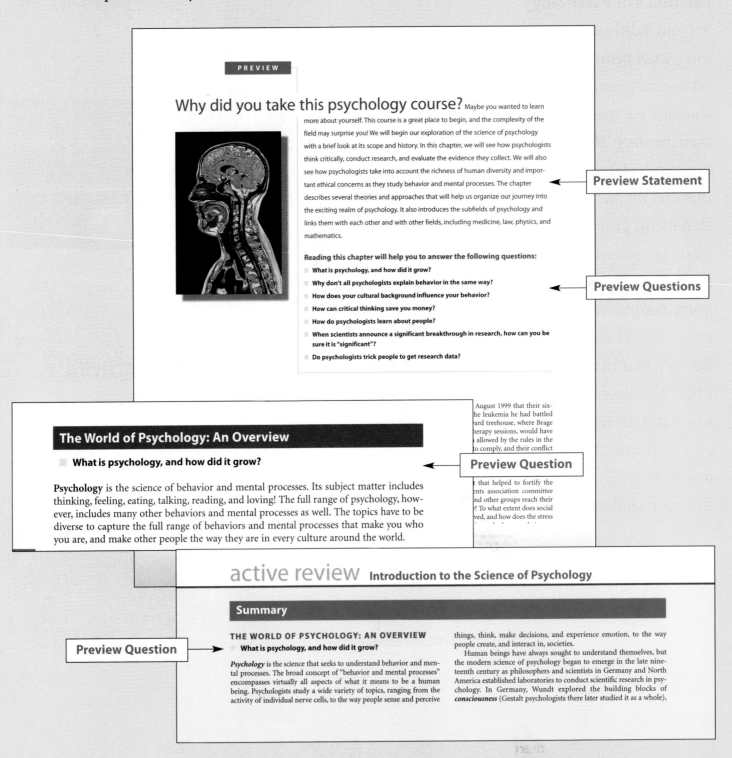

PREVIEW

Why did you take this psychology course? Maybe you wanted to learn
more about yourself. This course is a great place to begin, and the complexity of the field may surprise you! We will begin our exploration of the science of psychology with a brief look at its scope and history. In this chapter, we will see how psychologists think critically, conduct research, and evaluate the evidence they collect. We will also see how psychologists take into account the richness of human diversity and important ethical concerns as they study behavior and mental processes. The chapter describes several theories and approaches that will help us organize our journey into the exciting realm of psychology. It also introduces the subfields of psychology and links them with each other and with other fields, including medicine, law, physics, and mathematics.

→ **Preview Statement**

Reading this chapter will help you to answer the following questions:

- What is psychology, and how did it grow?
- Why don't all psychologists explain behavior in the same way?
- How does your cultural background influence your behavior?
- How can critical thinking save you money?
- How do psychologists learn about people?
- When scientists announce a significant breakthrough in research, how can you be sure it is "significant"?
- Do psychologists trick people to get research data?

→ **Preview Questions**

The World of Psychology: An Overview

- **What is psychology, and how did it grow?**

→ **Preview Question**

Psychology is the science of behavior and mental processes. Its subject matter includes thinking, feeling, eating, talking, reading, and loving! The full range of psychology, however, includes many other behaviors and mental processes as well. The topics have to be diverse to capture the full range of behaviors and mental processes that make you who you are, and make other people the way they are in every culture around the world.

August 1999 that their six-
he leukemia he had battled
ard treehouse, where Brage
herapy sessions, would have
allowed by the rules in the
to comply, and their conflict

that helped to fortify the
nts association committee
nd other groups reach their
? To what extent does social
ved, and how does the stress

active review Introduction to the Science of Psychology

Summary

Preview Question →

THE WORLD OF PSYCHOLOGY: AN OVERVIEW
- **What is psychology, and how did it grow?**

Psychology is the science that seeks to understand behavior and mental processes. The broad concept of "behavior and mental processes" encompasses virtually all aspects of what it means to be a human being. Psychologists study a wide variety of topics, ranging from the activity of individual nerve cells, to the way people sense and perceive

things, think, make decisions, and experience emotion, to the way people create, and interact in, societies.

Human beings have always sought to understand themselves, but the modern science of psychology began to emerge in the late nineteenth century as philosophers and scientists in Germany and North America established laboratories to conduct scientific research in psychology. In Germany, Wundt explored the building blocks of **consciousness** (Gestalt psychologists there later studied it as a whole),

An Integrated Pedagogical System

Instructional captions for all figures, tables, photographs, and cartoons reiterate core concepts and help to interpret visual material.

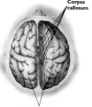

Corpus callosum

Hemispheres

FIGURE 2.11

The Brain's Left and Right Hemispheres

The brain's two hemispheres are joined by a core bundle of nerve fibers known as the corpus callosum; in this figure the corpus callosum has been cut, and the hemispheres are separated. The two cerebral hemispheres look nearly the same but perform somewhat different tasks. For one thing, the left hemisphere receives sensory input from, and controls movement on, the right side of the body. The right hemisphere senses and controls the left side of the body.

sphere interfered with the use or comprehension of language. Corresponding damage to the right hemisphere usually did not. Could it be that the right and left hemispheres of the brain serve different functions?

This is not a new idea. It has long been understood that most sensory and motor pathways cross over from one hemisphere to the other as they enter or leave the brain. As a result, the *left hemisphere* receives information from and controls movements of, the *right* side of the body. The *right hemisphere* receives input from and controls the *left* side of the body. Figure 2.11 shows the two hemispheres. The fact that language centers such as Broca's area and Wernicke's area almost always occur on the left side of the brain suggests that each hemisphere might be specialized to perform some functions almost independently of the other hemisphere.

In the late 1800s there was great interest in the idea that the hemispheres might be specialized, but no techniques were available for testing it. Renewed interest grew out of studies during the 1960s by Roger Sperry, Michael Gazzaniga, and their colleagues.

Split-Brain Studies Sperry studied *split-brain* patients—people who had undergone surgery in an attempt to control the severe seizures of epilepsy. Before the surgery, their seizures began in one hemisphere and then spread throughout the brain. As a last resort, surgeons isolated the two hemispheres from each other by cutting the corpus callosum.

After the surgery, researchers used a special device like the one shown in Figure 2.12 to present visual images to only one side of these patients' split brains. They found that cutting the tie between the hemispheres had dramatically affected the way these people thought about and dealt with the world. For example, when the image of a spoon was presented to the left, language-oriented side of patient N.G.'s split brain, she could say what the spoon was. But when the spoon was presented to the right side of her brain, she could not describe the spoon in words. She still knew what the object was, because she could pick it out from a group of objects by feeling its shape with her left hand (controlled by the right hemisphere). When asked what she had just grasped, she replied, "A pencil." The right hemisphere recognized the object, but the patient could not say what it was because the left (language) half of her brain did not see or feel it (R. W. Sperry, 1968).

Although the right hemisphere has no control over spoken language in split-brain patients, it does have important capabilities related to nonspoken language. For example, a split-brain patient's right hemisphere can guide the left hand in spelling out words with Scrabble tiles (Gazzaniga & LeDoux, 1978). Thanks to this finding, researchers concluded that split-brain patients have self-awareness and normal learning abilities in their

FIGURE 2.12

Apparatus for Studying Split-Brain Patients

When the person stares at the dot on the screen, images briefly presented on one side of the dot go to only one side of the brain. For example, a picture of a spoon presented on the left side of the screen goes to the right side of the brain. The right side of the brain can find the spoon and direct the left hand to touch it; but because the language areas on the left side of the brain did not see it, the person is not able to say what it is.

Statistical Analysis of Research Results

in review

Methods of Psychological Research			
Method	Features	Strengths	Pitfalls
Naturalistic observations	Observation of human or animal behavior in the environment where it typically occurs	Provide descriptive data about behavior presumably uncontaminated by outside influences	Observer bias self-conscious distort results
Case studies	Intensive examination of the behavior and mental processes associated with a specific person or situation	Provide detailed descriptive analyses of new, complex, or rare phenomena	May not provi representative of phenomena
Surveys	Standard sets of questions asked of a large number of participants	Gather large amounts of descriptive data relatively quickly and inexpensively	Sampling erro phrased quest response biases distort results
Experiments	Manipulation of an independent variable and measurement of its effects on a dependent variable	Can establish a cause-effect relationship between independent and dependent variables	Confounding variables may prevent valid conclusions
Quasi-experiments	Measurement of dependent variables when random assignment to groups is impossible or unethical	Can provide strong evidence suggesting cause-effect relationships	Lack of random assignment may weaken conclusions
All of the above	Choosing among alternative hypotheses; sometimes generating theories	Can expand our understanding of behavior and mental processes	Errors, limitations, and biases in research evidence can lead to incorrect or incomplete explanations

***In Review* Charts** summarize information in a convenient format.

A truer comparison would sample men and women of equal status. Similarly, researchers who use a male-only sample should give this fact the same emphasis in their report as is customarily the case when only females are studied (Ader & Johnson, 1994). To do otherwise would imply that males provide a standard against which females' behavior and mental processes are to be compared. Finally, researchers must report whatever results appear. It is just as valuable to know that men and women, or African Americans and European Americans, did *not* differ on a test of leadership ability as to know that they did. Stephanie Riger (1992) suggests that one of psychologists' greatest challenges is to "disengage themselves sufficiently from commonly shared beliefs so that those beliefs do not predetermine research findings" (p. 732). For a recap of the strategies research psychologists use in their studies, see "In Review: Methods of Psychological Research."

Statistical Analysis of Research Results

■ When scientists announce a significant breakthrough in research, how can you be sure it is "significant"?

data Numbers that represent research findings and provide the basis for conclusions.

Regardless of the research methods used, any study usually generates a large amount of data. **Data** are numbers that represent research findings and provide the basis for conclusions. Researchers use *statistical analyses* to summarize and analyze data. These

The **marginal glossary** found throughout the text defines key terms on the appropriate pages.

Active Review

The **Active Review** *at the end of each chapter acts as a built-in study guide.*

A ***Linkages Diagram*** illustrates how material in the chapter is connected to other chapters. A ***Chapter Summary,*** two ***Learn by Doing*** activities, an opportunity to ***Step into Action,*** a ***Review of Key Terms,*** and a ***Multiple-Choice Self-Test*** all help students master the chapter material successfully.

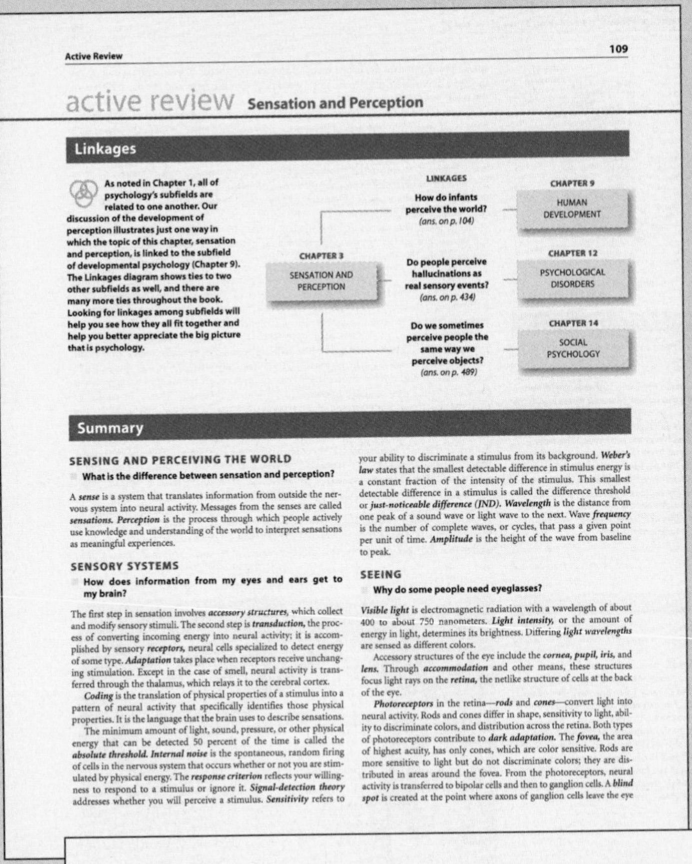

Active Review 109

active review **Sensation and Perception**

Linkages

As noted in Chapter 1, all of psychology's subfields are related to one another. Our discussion of the development of perception illustrates just one way in which the topic of this chapter, sensation and perception, is linked to the subfield of developmental psychology (Chapter 9). The Linkages diagram shows ties to two other subfields as well, and there are many more ties throughout the book. Looking for linkages among subfields will help you see how they all fit together and help you better appreciate the big picture that is psychology.

LINKAGES
CHAPTER 3
SENSATION AND PERCEPTION
How do infants perceive the world? (ans. on p. 104)
CHAPTER 9
HUMAN DEVELOPMENT
Do people perceive hallucinations as real sensory events? (ans. on p. 434)
CHAPTER 12
PSYCHOLOGICAL DISORDERS
Do we sometimes perceive people the same way we perceive objects? (ans. on p. 489)
CHAPTER 14
SOCIAL PSYCHOLOGY

Summary

SENSING AND PERCEIVING THE WORLD

What is the difference between sensation and perception?

A *sense* is a system that translates information from outside the nervous system into neural activity. Messages from the senses are called *sensations. Perception* is the process through which people actively use knowledge and understanding of the world to interpret sensations as meaningful experiences.

SENSORY SYSTEMS

How does information from my eyes and ears get to my brain?

The first step in sensation involves *accessory structures,* which collect and modify sensory stimuli. The second step is *transduction,* the process of converting incoming energy into neural activity; it is accomplished by sensory *receptors,* neural cells specialized to detect energy of some type. *Adaptation* takes place when receptors receive unchanging stimulation. Except in the case of smell, neural activity is transferred through the thalamus, which relays it to the cerebral cortex.

Coding is the translation of physical properties of a stimulus into a pattern of neural activity that specifically identifies those physical properties. It is the language that the brain uses to describe sensations.

The minimum amount of light, sound, pressure, or other physical energy that can be detected 50 percent of the time is called the *absolute threshold. Internal noise* is the spontaneous, random firing of cells in the nervous system that occurs whether or not you are stimulated by physical energy. The *response criterion* reflects your willingness to respond to a stimulus or ignore it. *Signal-detection theory* addresses whether you will perceive a stimulus. *Sensitivity* refers to your ability to discriminate a stimulus from its background. *Weber's law* states that the smallest detectable difference in stimulus energy is a constant fraction of the intensity of the stimulus. This smallest detectable difference in a stimulus is called the difference threshold or *just-noticeable difference (JND). Wavelength* is the distance from one peak of a sound wave or light wave to the next. Wave *frequency* is the number of complete waves, or cycles, that pass a given point per unit of time. *Amplitude* is the height of the wave from baseline to peak.

SEEING

Why do some people need eyeglasses?

Visible light is electromagnetic radiation with a wavelength of about 400 to about 750 nanometers. *Light intensity,* or the amount of energy in light, determines its brightness. Differing *light wavelengths* are sensed as different colors.

Accessory structures of the eye include the *cornea, pupil, iris,* and *lens.* Through *accommodation* and other means, these structures focus light rays on the *retina,* the netlike structure of cells at the back of the eye.

Photoreceptors in the retina—*rods* and *cones*—convert light into neural activity. Rods and cones differ in shape, sensitivity to light, ability to discriminate colors, and distribution across the retina. Both types of photoreceptors contribute to *dark adaptation.* The *fovea,* the area of highest acuity, has only cones, which are color sensitive. Rods are more sensitive to light but do not discriminate colors; they are distributed in areas around the fovea. From the photoreceptors, neural activity is transferred to bipolar cells and then to ganglion cells. A *blind spot* is created at the point where axons of ganglion cells leave the eye

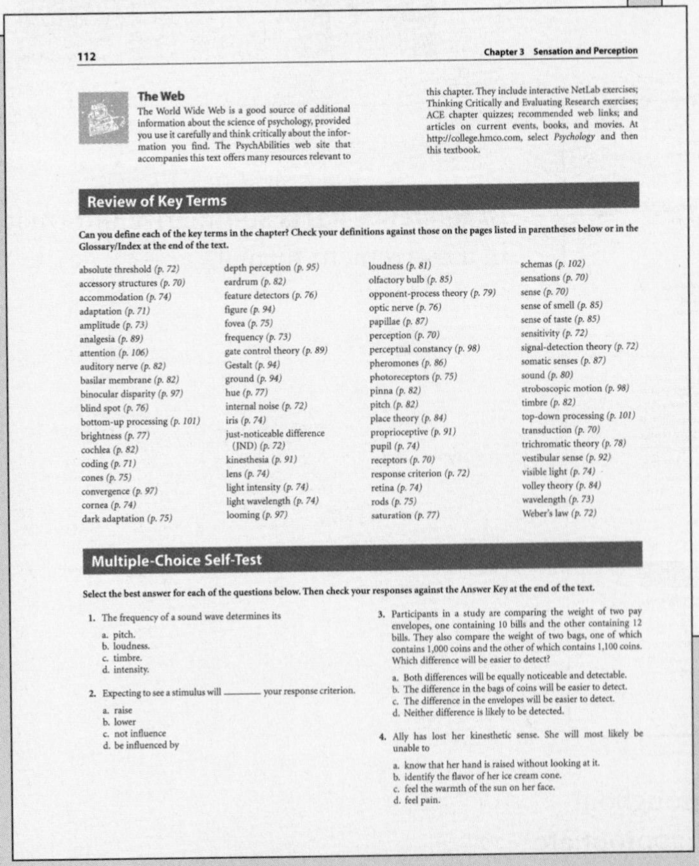

112 Chapter 3 Sensation and Perception

The Web

The World Wide Web is a good source of additional information about the science of psychology, provided you use it carefully and think critically about the information you find. The PsychAbilities web site that accompanies this text offers many resources relevant to this chapter. They include interactive NetLab exercises; Thinking Critically and Evaluating Research exercises; ACE chapter quizzes; recommended web links; and articles on current events, books, and movies. At http://college.hmco.com, select *Psychology* and then this textbook.

Review of Key Terms

Can you define each of the key terms in the chapter? Check your definitions against those on the pages listed in parentheses below or in the Glossary/Index at the end of the text.

absolute threshold *(p. 72)*
accessory structures *(p. 70)*
accommodation *(p. 74)*
adaptation *(p. 71)*
amplitude *(p. 73)*
analgesia *(p. 89)*
attention *(p. 106)*
auditory nerve *(p. 82)*
basilar membrane *(p. 82)*
binocular disparity *(p. 97)*
blind spot *(p. 76)*
bottom-up processing *(p. 101)*
brightness *(p. 77)*
cochlea *(p. 82)*
coding *(p. 71)*
cones *(p. 75)*
convergence *(p. 97)*
cornea *(p. 74)*
dark adaptation *(p. 75)*
depth perception *(p. 95)*
eardrum *(p. 82)*
feature detectors *(p. 76)*
figure *(p. 94)*
fovea *(p. 75)*
frequency *(p. 73)*
gate control theory *(p. 89)*
Gestalt *(p. 94)*
ground *(p. 94)*
hue *(p. 77)*
internal noise *(p. 72)*
iris *(p. 74)*
just-noticeable difference (JND) *(p. 72)*
kinesthesia *(p. 91)*
lens *(p. 74)*
light intensity *(p. 74)*
light wavelength *(p. 74)*
looming *(p. 97)*
loudness *(p. 81)*
olfactory bulb *(p. 85)*
opponent-process theory *(p. 79)*
optic nerve *(p. 76)*
papillae *(p. 87)*
perception *(p. 70)*
perceptual constancy *(p. 98)*
pheromones *(p. 86)*
photoreceptors *(p. 75)*
pinna *(p. 82)*
pitch *(p. 82)*
place theory *(p. 84)*
proprioceptive *(p. 91)*
pupil *(p. 74)*
receptors *(p. 70)*
response criterion *(p. 72)*
retina *(p. 74)*
rods *(p. 75)*
saturation *(p. 77)*
schemas *(p. 102)*
sensations *(p. 70)*
sense *(p. 70)*
sense of smell *(p. 85)*
sense of taste *(p. 85)*
sensitivity *(p. 72)*
signal-detection theory *(p. 72)*
somatic senses *(p. 87)*
sound *(p. 80)*
stroboscopic motion *(p. 98)*
timbre *(p. 82)*
top-down processing *(p. 101)*
transduction *(p. 70)*
trichromatic theory *(p. 78)*
vestibular sense *(p. 92)*
visible light *(p. 74)*
volley theory *(p. 84)*
wavelength *(p. 73)*
Weber's law *(p. 72)*

Multiple-Choice Self-Test

Select the best answer for each of the questions below. Then check your responses against the Answer Key at the end of the text.

1. The frequency of a sound wave determines its
   a. pitch.
   b. loudness.
   c. timbre.
   d. intensity.

2. Expecting to see a stimulus will ______ your response criterion.
   a. raise
   b. lower
   c. not influence
   d. be influenced by

3. Participants in a study are comparing the weight of two pay envelopes, one containing 10 bills and the other containing 12 bills. They also compare the weight of two bags, one of which contains 1,000 coins and the other of which contains 1,100 coins. Which difference will be easier to detect?
   a. Both differences will be equally noticeable and detectable.
   b. The difference in the bags of coins will be easier to detect.
   c. The difference in the envelopes will be easier to detect.
   d. Neither difference is likely to be detected.

4. Ally has lost her kinesthetic sense. She will most likely be unable to
   a. know that her hand is raised without looking at it.
   b. identify the flavor of her ice cream cone.
   c. feel the warmth of the sun on her face.
   d. feel pain.

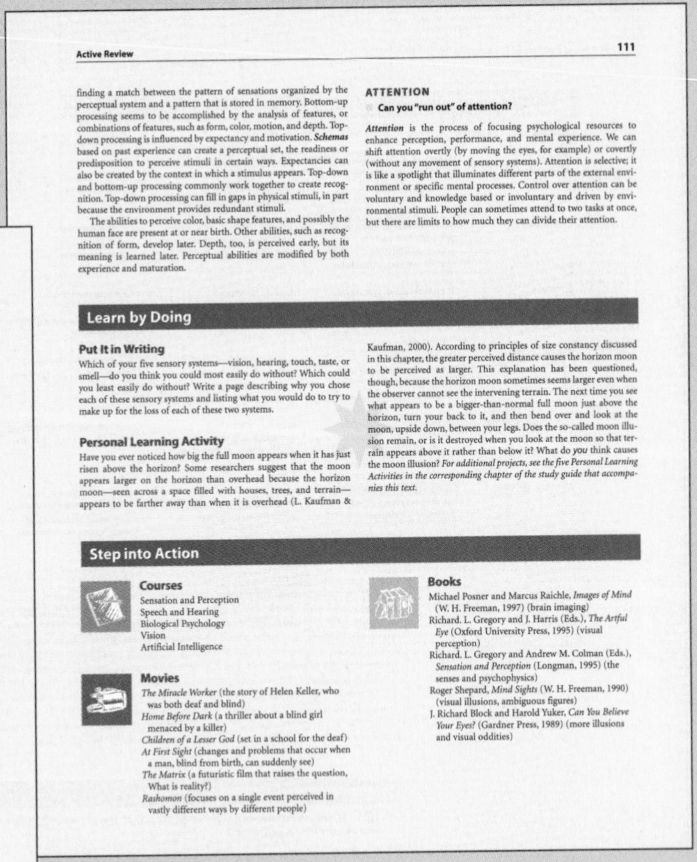

Active Review 111

finding a match between the pattern of sensations organized by the perceptual system and a pattern that is stored in memory. Bottom-up processing seems to be accomplished by the analysis of features, or combinations of features, such as form, color, motion, and depth. Top-down processing is influenced by expectancy and motivation. *Schemas* based on past experience can create a perceptual set, the readiness or predisposition to perceive stimuli in certain ways. Expectancies can also be created by the context in which a stimulus appears. Top-down and bottom-up processing commonly work together to create recognition. Top-down processing can fill in gaps in physical stimuli, in part because the environment provides redundant stimuli.

The abilities to perceive color, basic shape features, and possibly the human face are present at or near birth. Other abilities, such as recognition of form, develop later. Depth, too, is perceived early, but its meaning is learned later. Perceptual abilities are modified by both experience and maturation.

ATTENTION

Can you "run out" of attention?

Attention is the process of focusing psychological resources to enhance perception, performance, and mental experience. We can shift attention overtly (by moving the eyes, for example) or covertly (without any movement of sensory systems). Attention is selective; it is like a spotlight that illuminates different parts of the external environment or specific mental processes. Control over attention can be voluntary and knowledge based or involuntary and driven by environmental stimuli. People can sometimes attend to two tasks at once, but there are limits to how much they can divide their attention.

Learn by Doing

Put It in Writing

Which of your five sensory systems—vision, hearing, touch, taste, or smell—do you think you could most easily do without? Which could you least easily do without? Write a page describing why you chose each of these sensory systems and listing what you would do to try to make up for the loss of each of these two systems.

Personal Learning Activity

Have you ever noticed how big the full moon appears when it has just risen above the horizon? Some researchers suggest that the moon appears larger on the horizon than overhead because the horizon moon—seen across a space filled with houses, trees, and terrain—appears to be farther away than when it is overhead (L. Kaufman & Kaufman, 2000). According to principles of size constancy discussed in this chapter, the greater perceived distance causes the horizon moon to be perceived as larger. This explanation has been questioned, though, because the horizon moon sometimes seems larger even when the observer cannot see the intervening terrain. The next time you see what appears to be a bigger-than-normal full moon just above the horizon, turn your back to it, and then bend over and look at the moon, upside down, between your legs. Does the so-called moon illusion remain, or is it destroyed when you look at the moon so that terrain appears above it rather than below it? What *do* you think causes the moon illusion? *For additional projects, see the five Personal Learning Activities in the corresponding chapter of the study guide that accompanies this text.*

Step into Action

Courses

Sensation and Perception
Speech and Hearing
Biological Psychology
Vision
Artificial Intelligence

Movies

The Miracle Worker (the story of Helen Keller, who was both deaf and blind)
Home Before Dark (a thriller about a blind girl menaced by a killer)
Children of a Lesser God (set in a school for the deaf)
At First Sight (changes and problems that occur when a man, blind from birth, can suddenly see)
The Matrix (a futuristic film that raises the question, What is reality?)
Rashomon (focuses on a single event perceived in vastly different ways by different people)

Books

Michael Posner and Marcus Raichle, *Images of Mind* (W. H. Freeman, 1997) (brain imaging)
Richard. L. Gregory and J. Harris (Eds.), *The Artful Eye* (Oxford University Press, 1995) (visual perception)
Richard. L. Gregory and Andrew M. Colman (Eds.), *Sensation and Perception* (Longman, 1995) (the senses and psychophysics)
Roger Shepard, *Mind Sights* (W. H. Freeman, 1990) (visual illusions, ambiguous figures)
J. Richard Block and Harold Yuker, *Can You Believe Your Eyes?* (Gardner Press, 1989) (more illusions and visual oddities)

Learn by Doing

Three new **Learn by Doing** *features throughout the text promote active learning.*

Figure and Photo Captions

Dozens of new figure and photo captions identified with a "Learn by Doing" symbol reinforce concepts by suggesting ways in which students can demonstrate the concepts for themselves.

BON APPÉTIT! The definition of *delicacy* differs from culture to culture. At this elegant restaurant in Mexico, diners pay to feast on baby alligators, insects, and other dishes that some people from other cultures would not eat even if the restaurant paid *them*. To appreciate your own food culture, make a list of foods that are traditionally valued by your family or cultural group but that people from other groups do not, or might even be unwilling, to eat.

Bolivian highlands but illegal in the United States (Burchard, 1992). And insects called *palm weevils*, a delicacy for people in Papua New Guinea (Paoletti, 1995), are regarded by many Westerners as disgusting (Springer & Belk, 1994). Even within the same general culture, different groups may have sharply contrasting food traditions. Thus, squirrel brains won't be found on most dinner tables in the United States, but some people in the rural South consider them to be a tasty treat. In short, eating serves functions beyond nutrition—functions that help to remind us of who we are and with whom we identify.

Eating Disorders

Problems in the processes regulating hunger and eating may cause an *eating disorder*. The most common and dangerous examples are obesity, anorexia nervosa, and bulimia nervosa.

Obesity The World Health Organization defines **obesity** as a condition in which a person's body-mass index, or BMI, is greater than 30 (WHO, 1995). BMI is determined by dividing a person's weight (in kilograms) by the square of the person's height (in meters). Thus, someone who is 5 feet 2 inches and weighs 164 pounds would be classified as obese, as would someone 5 feet 10 inches who weighs 207 pounds. (You will find quick BMI calculators at web sites such as www.consumer.gov/weightloss/bmi.htm.) Using this BMI criterion, 27 percent of adults in the United States are obese (USDHHS, 2000). And obesity appears to be on the rise, not only in the United States but also in regions as diverse as Asia, South America, and Africa (Kopelman, 2000; Lewis et al., 2000; Mokdad et al., 2000; Taubes, 1998). Obesity is associated with health problems such as diabetes, high blood pressure, and increased risk of heart attack; nearly 300,000 deaths in the United States alone are attributed to obesity (Allison et al., 1999). Caring for people with obesity-related health problems costs about $51 billion each year (Wolf & Colditz, 1998).

Learn by Doing Marginal Callout

A symbol appears in the page margin where active learning opportunities occur in the narrative.

The Process of Attention

To experience attention as a process, try "moving it around" a bit. When you finish reading this sentence, look at something behind you, then face forward and notice the next sound you hear, then visualize your best friend, then focus on how your tongue feels. You just used attention to direct your perceptual systems toward different aspects of your external and internal environments. When you looked behind you, shifting attention involved *overt orienting*—pointing sensory systems at a particular stimulus. But you were able to shift attention to an image of your friend's face without having to move a muscle. This is called *covert orienting*.

Put It in Writing and *Personal Learning Activity*

As part of the Active Review section, ***Put It in Writing*** invites readers to write about a specific chapter topic, and ***Personal Learning Activity*** provides another opportunity to *do* psychology—not just read about it.

Learn by Doing

Put It in Writing

Try writing your own definition of intelligence. Make a list of at least seven behaviors or characteristics that you feel represent "intelligence," and then decide how they could best be tested in children and adults from your own culture and other cultures. Describe the kinds of difficulties you encountered in making your list and designing your assessment devices.

Personal Learning Activity

Consider a problem that you are facing at the moment, or one that is being faced by someone you know. In accordance with the problem-solving section of this chapter, write down all the alternative solutions you can think of to solve this problem; then list the pros and cons of each option. Which alternative comes out on top? Does the alternative that seems best on paper also strike you as the best solution to try? Why or why not? *For additional projects, see the five Personal Learning Activities in the corresponding chapter of the study guide that accompanies this text.*

Thinking Critically

A dedicated section in each chapter helps improve this vital skill.

Structured around five questions, these sections encourage readers to analyze material before drawing conclusions:

- What am I being asked to believe or accept?
- Is there evidence available to support the claim?
- Can that evidence be interpreted another way?
- What evidence would help to evaluate the alternatives?
- What conclusions are most reasonable?

In short, the question of whether psychotherapy "works" is difficult or impossible to answer scientifically in a way that applies across the board. However, several research reviews (E. M. Anderson & Lambert, 1995; Galatzer-Levy et al., 2000; Shadish et al., 2000; M. L. Smith, Glass, & Miller, 1980; Weisz & Jensen, 1999) and personal experience leave psychotherapists convinced that it *does* work (see Figure 13.2). Further, most of them believe that the theoretical approach and treatment methods *they* use are superior to those of other therapists (e.g., Giles, 1990). They can't all be right, of course, so what is going on?

What am I being asked to believe or accept?

Some researchers argue that theories of behavior disorder and the specific treatment methods based on them don't have much to do with the success of psychotherapy. All approaches, they say, are equally effective. This has been called the "Dodo Bird Verdict," after the *Alice in Wonderland* creature who, when called upon to judge who had won a race, answered, "Everybody has won and all must have prizes" (Luborsky, Singer, & Luborsky, 1975).

Is there evidence available to support the claim?

Some evidence does suggest that there are no significant differences in the overall effectiveness of the psychodynamic, phenomenological, and behavioral approaches to therapy. Statistical analyses that combine the results of a large number of therapy studies show that the three approaches are associated with about the same degree of success (M. J. Lambert & Bergin, 1994; M. L. Smith, Glass, & Miller, 1980).

Thinking Critically

Focus on Research

Highlighting a particular study, these sections emphasize the value of research and the creativity with which it is often conducted.

These sections are organized around five questions:

- What was the researcher's question?
- How did the researcher answer the question?
- What did the researcher find?
- What do the results mean?
- What do we still need to know?

Problem-Solving Strategies in the Real World

The problem-solving strategies we have described were identified by laboratory studies in which psychologists observed volunteers wrestling with, and perhaps "thinking aloud" about, various types of problems. However, we do not yet know how well the strategies seen in these studies reflect the problem-solving methods that people use in the real world. To explore this question, researchers have reconstructed problem-solving strategies associated with major inventions and scientific discoveries (Klahr & Simon, 1999; Weber, 1992).

What was the researcher's question?

On December 17, 1903, Wilbur and Orville Wright successfully flew the first heavier-than-air flying machine. Gary Bradshaw (1993a, 1993b) was interested in identifying the problem-solving strategies that led to this momentous event. He found that forty-nine individuals or teams had worked on the problem of heavier-than-air flight, but only the Wright brothers were successful. In fact, it took them only four years to develop the airplane, whereas others worked for decades without success. Bradshaw asked, How did the Wright brothers solve the problem of creating a heavier-than-air flying machine when so many others had failed?

How did the researcher answer the question?

Bradshaw compared the written records left by all the individuals and teams who had worked on an airplane design. Using this "comparative case study" method, he was able

Focus on Research

Linkages

*The **Linkages** feature reflects the relationships among the subfields of psychology.*

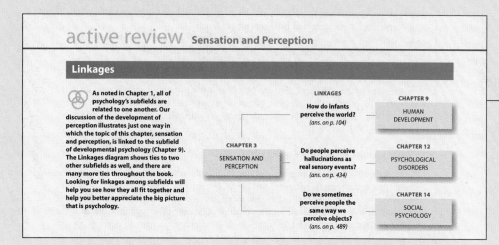

Linkages Diagram

In the *Active Review* section at the end of each chapter, a **Linkages diagram** presents three questions to illustrate how material in the chapter is related to other chapters in the book.

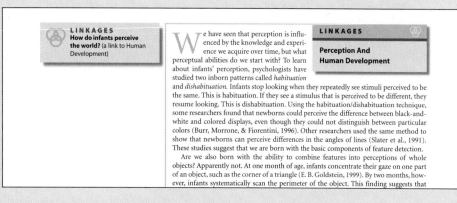

Linkages Sections

One of the questions in the Linkages diagram is discussed at length in the chapter's special section titled ***Linkages.***

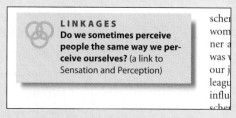

Marginal Callouts

The Linkages diagram directs students to the pages that carry further discussion of each question, where a **marginal callout** appears.

Linkages

ESSENTIALS *of* PSYCHOLOGY

SECOND EDITION

Douglas A. Bernstein
University of South Florida
University of Surrey

Peggy W. Nash
Broward Community College

with

Alison Clarke-Stewart
University of California, Irvine

Louis A. Penner
University of South Florida

Edward J. Roy
University of Illinois at Urbana-Champaign

Houghton Mifflin Company   Boston   New York

To my dear wife, Miss Lindsay N. Kennedy
     Doug Bernstein

To my family and sons, Rob and Jeff, with love
     Peggy Nash

Editor-in-Chief: Kathi Prancan
Senior Sponsoring Editor: Kerry Baruth
Senior Development Editor: Jane Knetzger
Senior Project Editor: Aileen Mason
Editorial Assistant: Rachel Levison
Senior Production/Design Coordinator: Sarah Ambrose
Senior Manufacturing Coordinator: Priscilla Bailey
Marketing Manager: Ros Kane

Photo Researcher: Ann Schroeder
Cover Illustration: Andy Powell

CREDITS *Chapter opening photos:* **p. 1:** © David Job/Stone. **p. 37:** © Cleo/PhotoEdit. **p. 68:** © Peter Cade/Stone. **p. 114:** © Doug Martin/Photo Researchers. **p. 144:** © Jack Monnier/Stone. **p. 178:** © Lawrence Migdale/Stock Boston. **p. 212:** © Michael Newman/PhotoEdit. **p. 256:** © Bob Daemmrich/Stock Boston. **p. 298:** © Myrleen Ferguson/PhotoEdit. **p. 347:** © Esbin/Anderson/The Image Works. **p. 376:** © Michael Busselle/Stone. **p. 408:** © Bruce Ayres/Stone. **p. 450:** © Zigy Kaluzny/Stone. **p. 485:** © Robert Ginn/PhotoEdit.

(Credits continue following references.)

Printed in the U.S.A.

Library of Congress Catalog Card Number: 2001086738

ISBN: 0-618-12296-6 (student text)
     0-618-12297-4 (AIE)

1 2 3 4 5 6 7 8 9—VH—05 04 03 02 01

BRIEF CONTENTS

CONTENTS

4 CONSCIOUSNESS 114

5 LEARNING 144

8 MOTIVATION AND EMOTION 256

9 HUMAN DEVELOPMENT 298

10 HEALTH, STRESS, AND COPING 347

11   PERSONALITY   376

12   PSYCHOLOGICAL DISORDERS   408

13   TREATMENT OF PSYCHOLOGICAL DISORDERS   450

14 SOCIAL PSYCHOLOGY   485

PREFACE

PSYCHOLOGY IS A RICH and varied science, covering the breadth and depth of human behavior—everything from fleeting reflexes to enduring memories, from falling asleep to falling in love. In our experience, most students enter the introductory course thinking that psychology concerns itself mainly with personality, psychological testing, mental disorders, psychotherapy, and other aspects of clinical psychology. Many of these students are surprised, then, when we ask them to read about such topics as the structure of the brain, optical illusions, the effect of jet lag on Olympic athletes, AIDS and the immune system, and prenatal risk factors, to name just a few. Yet these are all topics under the umbrella that is psychology.

For all its diversity, psychology is also a remarkably integrated discipline whose subfields are linked to one another through common interests and overarching research questions. As psychologists and scholars, we wrote this book to portray the wide range of topics that make up the science of psychology. As teachers, we focused on the essentials of the discipline, the core concepts of psychology that we hope will be especially accessible and interesting to students. We also tried to present these topics through an integrated, active pedagogical system designed to help students get the most out of the text.

In revising *Essentials of Psychology,* we rededicated ourselves to presenting a textbook that not only is clear and enjoyable to read, but that also provides features to support the learning process in all students, regardless of their academic background. Specifically, we set these goals:

- To focus on topics that represent the full range of psychology, from cell to society, without overwhelming the reader with details.

- To provide lots of active learning exercises that invite students to work with the text material in ways that can help them understand and remember it.

- To help students develop their ability to think critically and scientifically by examining the ways that psychologists have solved, or failed to solve, fascinating puzzles of behavior and mental processes.

- To explain the content of psychology with an emphasis on the *doing* of psychology, grounding all discussions in current and classic research studies. (We help students appreciate the importance of research by exploring one study in detail in a special feature in each chapter.)

Our discussion of research in psychology is also designed to remind students that although, in some ways, "people are people wherever you go," sociocultural factors, including gender, ethnicity, cultural background, and geography, often shape human behavior and mental processes. We repeatedly point out, therefore, that psychological research on the thinking styles, perceptual habits, psychological disorders, social pressures, and other phenomena seen in North America or Europe, for example, may or may not apply to other cultures, or even to subcultures within Western countries.

Rather than isolating discussion of sociocultural material in boxed features, we have woven it into every chapter so that students will encounter it repeatedly as they read. We introduce the importance of sociocultural factors in Chapter 1 and continue to reinforce it through coverage of such topics as the impact of culture and experience on perception (Chapter 3), classrooms across cultures (Chapter 5), ethnic differences in IQ (Chapter 7), social and cultural factors in sexuality (Chapter 8), gender differences in stress responses (Chapter 10), personality, culture, and human development (Chapter 11), gender and cultural differences in depression and suicide (Chapter 12), and cultural factors in aggression (Chapter 14), to cite just a few examples. (In the annotated instructor's version of the book, each discussion of sociocultural factors is marked in the margin of the page where the discussion appears.)

WHAT'S NEW IN THE NEW EDITION?

Guided by feedback from faculty colleagues and students, and by our own teaching experiences, we have made a number of changes in *Essentials*. We believe that this new edition retains the best features of the first edition, and offers even more of what faculty and students want and need.

Improved Organization

Designed for presentation in a single semester, the book's fourteen-chapter organization has been retained. It has also been slightly revised. We now cover psychological disorders and treatment of psychological disorders in separate chapters, and we have combined the topics of thought, language, and intelligence into a single chapter. Have we arranged our fourteen chapters in an ideal sequence? That sequence reflects the way we teach our introductory courses, but we know that each instructor has his or her own preferences for sequencing that may not match ours. Accordingly we have again written each of the fourteen chapters as a freestanding unit so that you may assign it in whatever order you wish. For example, many instructors prefer to teach the material on human development relatively late in the course, which is why it appears as Chapter 9. However, the chapter can be just as comfortably assigned earlier in the course.

An Emphasis on Learning by Doing

To help promote active learning, we have placed three kinds of "Learn by Doing" features throughout the book.

- First, we have created dozens of new figure and photo captions that help students understand and remember a psychological principle or phenomenon by suggesting ways in which they can demonstrate it for themselves. In the memory chapter, for example, a photo caption suggests that students show the photo to a friend, and then ask questions about it to illustrate the operation of constructive memory. These captions are all identified with a Learn by Doing symbol.

- Second, we have placed a Learn by Doing symbol in page margins at the many places where active learning opportunities occur in the narrative. At these points, we ask students to stop reading and try *doing something* to illustrate or highlight the psychological principle or phenomenon under discussion. For example, in the sensation and perception chapter, we ask the student to focus attention on various targets as a way of appreciating the difference between overt and covert attention shifts.

- Finally, we have carried the active learning theme through to the end of each chapter, where—as part of the built-in study guide we call "Active Review"—students will find new sections called "Put It in Writing" and "Personal Learning Activity." These sections invite students to (a) write about a specific chapter-related topic, and (b) collect, analyze, and discuss some data on a chapter-related principle or phenomenon.

Improved Active Review

The new Put It in Writing and Personal Learning Activity sections are just one part of our effort to add educational value to the built-in study guide that we call Active Review. Other changes include the following:

- To help students understand and appreciate the ways in which the chapter they have just read relates to other subfields of psychology, the Active Review opens with a *Linkages* diagram.

- As in the first edition, the Active Review contains a chapter summary organized around the chapter's main topic headings. However, we have made the summary more accessible by breaking up the longer paragraphs into more manageable segments.

- We have revised the twenty-item multiple-choice self-tests that appear at the end of each chapter to make them somewhat less detail-oriented, and somewhat more focused on the application, not just the definition, of principles, concepts, and phenomena.

- To highlight our emphasis on active learning, the "To Learn More" section of the Active Review has been renamed "Step into Action." As before, it lists the courses in which students can pursue further chapter-related study, and it provides an annotated list of movies and books related to each chapter. However, where we previously listed only search words for seeking chapter-related information on the World Wide Web, we now refer students to Houghton Mifflin's *PsychAbilities* web site. This site is continuously updated and expanded to provide the latest, most interesting, and most valuable web addresses related to chapter content, as well as a range of interactive activities and self-quizzes for each chapter.

- The "Review of Key Terms," which invites students to write their own definitions of the most important terms presented in the chapter, has been updated to include all the key terms discussed in the new edition.

New "Applying Psychology" Photos

As in the first edition, we continue to emphasize the many ways in which psychological theory and research results are being applied to benefit human welfare. In this edition, we further highlight the diversity of applied psychology by including in each chapter at least one Applying Psychology photo that offers a memorable example. In the learning chapter, for example, a photo illustrates the use of classical conditioning principles in the humane control of predators that once threatened sheep ranchers' livelihoods. In the health, stress, and coping chapter, the Applying Psychology photo illustrates health psychologists' use of health-belief models and persuasive communication principles to promote behavior that protects people from the threat of AIDS.

Updated Content

As in the first edition, our goal in preparing this new edition of *Essentials* was to present the latest, as well as the most established, results of basic and applied research on topics that are both important to psychology and of high interest to students. Accordingly, we offer updated coverage of research on how drugs affect the brain (Chapter 2), the basis for optical illusions (Chapter 3), the effects of subliminal messages (Chapter 4), the importance of active learning in the classroom (Chapter 5), the accuracy of eyewitness testimony (Chapter 6), the origins of intelligence (Chapter 7), sources of sexual orientation (Chapter 8), the development of morals (Chapter 9), the effects of stress on health (Chapter 10), what determines and shapes our personalities (Chapter 11), the causes of multiple personality disorder (Chapter 12), the effects of psychotherapy (Chapter 13), and the development of ethnic prejudice (Chapter 14).

In this new edition, students will also encounter the latest evidence on topics such as

- Stem cell growth and transplant technology, and their potential for treating Alzheimer's disease and repairing brain damage (Chapter 2)

- Individual differences in taste abilities, including how to determine if one is a "supertaster" (Chapter 3)

- Resetting biological clocks by shining light on the backs of the knees (Chapter 4)

- Use of conditioned eyeblink responses to identify people at risk for the development of Alzheimer's disease (Chapter 5)

- Factors that may make people more susceptible to reporting false memories (Chapter 6)

- Cultural differences in how people think (Chapter 7)

- Factors that influence subjective well-being, and why (Chapter 8)

- Whether there are gender differences in moral reasoning (Chapter 9)

- The "tend and befriend" response to stressors, and how it relates to the traditional "fight or flight" syndrome (Chapter 10)

- The validity of projective tests (Chapter 11)

- The origins of schizophrenia, depression, and anxiety (Chapter 12)

- A proposal to have psychotherapists follow procedure manuals when treating some clients (Chapter 13)

- The unconscious nature of some aspects of ethnic stereotyping and prejudice (Chapter 14)

SPECIAL FEATURES

The second edition of *Essentials of Psychology* contains improved versions of a number of special features found in its predecessor. Designed to promote efficient learning and mastery of the material, these include, in each chapter, an integrated pedagogical system, as well as sections called "Thinking Critically," "Focus on Research," and "Linkages," along with an expanded Active Review.

An Integrated Pedagogical System

Our integrated pedagogical system is designed to help students get the most out of their reading. In keeping with the PQ4R study system (discussed in detail in Chapter 6, "Memory"), learning aids in each chapter include the following elements.

Preview Questions To help students survey and question the material, each chapter opens with a full outline, a brief preview statement, and a list of questions related to the key topic of each main section of the chapter. Those questions are repeated within the chapter at the start of each corresponding main section, and

they appear again in the Active Review, where they help to organize the chapter summary. For the second edition, many of these questions have been revised to make them more engaging and to refer to topics covered early in the related section of the chapter.

Margin Glossary Key terms are defined in the margin of the page where they appear, or on the facing page, reinforcing core concepts without interrupting the flow of reading. (For the second edition, we have revised many of our phonetic guides to make it easier than ever for students to correctly pronounce unfamiliar key terms—as well as other terms whose pronunciation is not immediately obvious.) In the Active Review section at the end of each chapter, a definition exercise encourages students to restate these core concepts in their own words.

Instructional Captions Captions to all figures, tables, photographs, and cartoons reiterate core concepts and help students learn to interpret visual information. And, as mentioned earlier, many of these captions prompt students to engage in various kinds of active learning experiences.

In Review Charts In Review study charts summarize information in a convenient tabular format. We have placed two or three In Review charts strategically in each chapter to help students synthesize and assimilate large chunks of information—for example, on drug effects, key elements in personality theories, and stress responses and mediators.

Active Review As mentioned earlier, we have expanded and improved the built-in study guide at the end of each chapter. This Active Review section now includes:

- A *Linkages diagram* containing questions that illustrate three of the ways in which material in each chapter is connected to other chapters in the book.

- A *chapter summary* organized, as before, around major topic headings and the related preview questions, but now presented in an easier-to-read format containing paragraphs that are shorter, and focused on subheadings.

- *Learn by Doing,* a new feature designed to promote active learning. Here, students will find Put It in Writing and Personal Learning Activity sections that invite them to (a) write about a specific chapter-related topic, and (b) collect, analyze, and discuss some data on a chapter-related principle or phenomenon. For example, in the personality chapter, the Put It in Writing section suggests that students list a celebrity's personality traits, and then summarize how various personality theories would account for the development of those traits. In the biology and behavior chapter, students are asked to write about how research on brain development might affect one's choice of an infant day-care center. These Put It in Writing suggestions might be helpful as writing-across-the-curriculum assignments. The Personal Learning Activities suggest ways in which students can *do* psychology as well as read about it. In the motivation and emotion chapter, for example, the Personal Learning Activity section suggests a way in which students can collect data on lie-detection skills. In the social psychology chapter, students are invited to test some assumptions of evolutionary theories of mate selection by analyzing personals ads in a local newspaper. Each Personal Learning Activity section ends by referring the student to additional projects listed in the study guide that accompanies the book.

■ A *Step into Action* section, which (a) suggests courses that students can take to pursue further chapter-related study, (b) presents an annotated list of movies and books related to each chapter, and (c) encourages students to visit Houghton Mifflin's *PsychAbilities* web site for resources related to the chapter in the form of interactive activities, self-quizzes, and web links.

■ A *Review of Key Terms,* which invites students to write their own definitions of the most important terms presented in the chapter. These lists have been updated to include all the key terms discussed in the new edition, and the pronunciation guides for the more difficult terms have been improved.

■ A twenty-item *Multiple-Choice Self-Test* designed to help students assess their understanding of the chapter's key points prior to taking quizzes and exams. As before, we provide an answer key at the back of the book that identifies and briefly explains each correct answer, and refers students to the page on which the tested material was first discussed.

Thinking Critically

A special Thinking Critically section in each chapter helps students hone their abilities in this vital skill. Our approach to writing centers on describing research on psychological phenomena in a way that reveals the logic of the scientific method, identifies possible flaws in design or interpretation, and leaves room for more questions and further research. In other words, as author-teachers, we try to model critical thinking processes for our readers. The Thinking Critically sections are designed to make these processes more explicit and accessible by providing readers with a framework for analyzing evidence before drawing conclusions. The framework is built around five questions that the reader should find useful in analyzing not only psychological research studies, but other forms of communication as well, including political speeches, advertising claims, and appeals for contributions. These five questions first appear in Chapter 1, when we introduce the importance of critical thinking, and they are repeated in every chapter's Thinking Critically section:

1. What am I being asked to believe or accept?

2. Is there evidence available to support the claim?

3. Can that evidence be interpreted another way?

4. What evidence would help to evaluate the alternatives?

5. What conclusions are most reasonable?

Using this simple yet powerful framework, we explore issues such as subliminal persuasion, pornography and aggression,

recovered memories, and acupuncture, to name just a few. Page viii includes a complete list of the Thinking Critically features.

Focus on Research

Scientists in psychology have helped us to better understand behavior and mental processes through their commitment to empirical research. They have posed vital questions about psychological phenomenon and designed research that is capable of answering, or at least illuminating, those questions. In Chapter 1 we introduce readers to the methods of scientific research and to basic research designs in psychology. Every subsequent chapter features a Focus on Research section that highlights a particular research study to help students appreciate the value of research and the creativity with which psychologists have conducted it. Like the Thinking Critically sections, the Focus on Research features are organized around five questions designed to help readers organize their thinking about research questions and research results:

1. What was the researcher's question?

2. How did the researcher answer the question?

3. What did the researcher find?

4. What do the results mean?

5. What do we still need to know?

These Focus on Research sections help students to see how psychologists have used experiments, surveys, observations, and other designs to explore phenomena, such as learned helplessness, infant cognition, and evolutionary theories of helping. A full list of the Focus on Research features appears on page ix.

Linkages

In our experience, introductory psychology students are better able to appreciate the scope of our discipline when they look at it not as a laundry list of separate topics but as an interrelated set of subfields, each of which contributes to and benefits from the work going on in all of the others. To help students see these relationships, we have built into the book an integrating tool called Linkages. There are three elements in the Linkages program.

■ *Linkages diagrams*   The first element of each chapter's Active Review is a Linkages diagram, which presents a set of questions that illustrate three of the ways in which material in the chapter is related to other chapters in the book. For example, the Linkages diagram in Chapter 2, "Biology and Behavior," contains questions that show how biological psychology is related to consciousness ("Does the brain shut down when we sleep?"), human development ("How do our brains change over a lifetime?"), and treatment of psychological disorders ("How do drugs help people who suffer from schizophrenia?"). These diagrams are designed to help students keep in mind how the content of each chapter fits into psychology as a whole. To introduce the concept of Linkages, the diagram in Chapter 1 appears within the body of the chapter.

■ *Cross-references*   The page numbers following each question in the Linkages diagrams direct the student to pages that carry further discussion of that question. There, the linking question is repeated in the margin next to the discussion.

■ *Linkages sections*   One of the questions in each chapter's Linkages diagram reminds the student of the chapter's discussion of that question in a special section titled, appropriately enough, Linkages (see page x for a complete list of Linkages sections).

These three elements combine with the text narrative to highlight the network of relationships among psychology's subfields. This Linkages program is designed to help students see the "big picture" that is psychology—no matter how many chapters their instructor assigns, or in what sequence.

TEACHING AND LEARNING SUPPORT PACKAGE

Many useful instructional and pedagogical materials have been developed to support the *Essentials of Psychology* textbook and the introductory course. Designed to enhance the teaching and learning experience, the components of the supplemental package are remarkably well integrated with the text and include some of the latest technologies. New features of several supplements reflect the text's emphasis on active learning and writing across the curriculum.

For the Instructor

Annotated Instructor's Edition   To help instructors coordinate the many print, video, and software supplements available with the text, the *Annotated Instructor's Edition* shows which materials apply to the content on each page of the student text. The annotations coordinate learning objectives, test questions, discussion and lecture ideas, handouts, overhead transparencies, PowerPoint slides, active learning activities, video segments, and the like. New to the second edition are annotations marking passages in the text that cover sociocultural topics. A key to the annotations appears on the inside front cover.

Instructor's Resource Manual   For each chapter of the textbook, the *Instructor's Resource Manual* includes learning objectives, a lecture outline, and numerous classroom "supplements," that is, discussion, activity, and lecture suggestions and related handouts. The revised manual includes new Thinking Critically and Put It in Writing supplements similar to the exercises that appear in the textbook. The manual also includes a video guide and a pedagogical strategy section that covers active learning, critical thinking, using the Linkages feature, using the Research Focus supplements, and new to this edition, writing across the curriculum. For instructors switching from the first to the second edition of the text, the manual includes a detailed transition guide for each chapter, outlining the key changes between editions.

Test Bank   The *Test Bank,* available in print or within a testing software program, includes 125 multiple-choice questions per chapter, 25 percent more than in the first edition. Half of these are new, as are one-third of the essay questions. Each multiple-choice question is keyed to pages in the student text and to the learning objectives that appear in the *Instructor's Resource Manual* and *Study Guide* and that are now printed in the test bank, too. Each question is identified by whether it tests simple factual recall or deeper conceptual understanding. Over sixty percent of the items have been class-tested with between 400 and 2,500 students. A statistical performance analysis is provided for those items. The computerized version allows instructors to edit questions, integrate their own, and generate paper or online exams.

PowerPoint Slides   A new and extensive set of PowerPoint slides is available with the second edition. Each chapter's show includes dozens of slides featuring a lecture sequence that includes tables, figures, and photos from the textbook and other sources. The slides are available on the *PsychAbilities* web site and the *Essentials* instructor CD.

Overhead Transparencies   The *Essentials* transparency acetates include one hundred four-color images from the text and other sources, organized by chapter.

Instructor's Resource CD-ROM   Instructors may obtain a CD that includes the PowerPoint slides, learning objectives, lecture outlines, *Instructor's Resource Manual* activities and handouts, selected *Study Guide* materials, the video guide, and the second-edition transition guide.

PsychAbilities Web Site   On the full-service, interactive web site accompanying *Essentials,* instructors have access to the PowerPoint slides and most elements of the *Instructor's Resource Manual,* as previously described, as well as an online guide offering tips on how to use and assign the student activities available on the site. To view a sampling of instructor materials, point to **http://college.hmco.com** and select *Psychology* and then this textbook.

Content for Course Management Software   A Blackboard course cartridge and a Web CT e-Pack are available with this text, allowing instructors to create a virtual classroom on either of these two distributed learning systems. Features of the course management systems include grading, calendar, and communication tools that allow instructors to create a web site for their course without any knowledge of HTML. The customized *Essentials* cartridges feature quizzes, study materials, and exercises related to the text.

Lecture Starter Videos   Four videotapes featuring brief clips designed to launch lectures or discussions are available with *Essentials of Psychology.* The *Introductory Psychology Lecture Starter Video* includes approximately sixty-five short (two- to seven-minute) videoclips organized into thirty-four topical areas. An accompanying guide resides on the *PsychAbilities* web site. Also available are lecture starter videotapes covering child development, social psychology, and abnormal psychology.

The Psychology Show   This video supplement is available in both videodisc and VHS format. Featuring nineteen brief segments and numerous still images, *The Psychology Show* is designed to expand on the text's coverage of major topical areas and stimulate class discussion. The accompanying guide offers information on each motion segment and provides bar codes for videodisc use.

Media Policy   Ask your Houghton Mifflin representative about additional videos available for rental or purchase, including, among others, *The Brain* modules, *The Mind* modules, and *Discovering Psychology*.

For the Student

PsychAbilities Web Site   For each chapter, the *PsychAbilities* web site offers students, among other things, interactive NetLab exercises, Thinking Critically and Evaluating Research exercises, ACE self-quizzes, learning objectives, recommended web links, and articles on current events, books, and movies.

PsychAbilities CD-ROM   The CD that accompanies every copy of the student text at no extra charge features study outlines corresponding to each chapter of the textbook, embedded with relevant interactive NetLab exercises, Evaluating Research and Critical Thinking exercises, ACE self-quizzes, a glossary, and a link to the *PsychAbilities* web site.

Study Guide   The *Study Guide* augments the Active Review study materials built into every chapter of the textbook. Introductory sections in the guide provide tips on developing critical thinking skills, studying Linkages, reading a textbook, and new to this edition, developing writing skills. For each chapter of the text, the guide includes learning objectives, key-term hints and examples, a Concepts and Exercises section that shows students how to apply their knowledge of psychology to everyday issues and concerns, a Critical Thinking exercise, and several Personal Learning Activities like those in the text. In addition, each chapter concludes with two multiple-choice quizzes with wrong-answer rejoinders and a self-diagnostic quiz analysis to pinpoint weak topic and cognitive skill areas. A new section of each chapter, called "What Should I Write About?", provides advice on how to choose an appropriate term-paper topic related to the chapter.

Internet Guide for Psychology   Houghton Mifflin's *Internet Guide for Psychology*, which can also be shrinkwrapped for free with new copies of *Essentials of Psychology*, introduces students to electronic mail, discussion groups, the World Wide Web, and Usenet news groups. It provides students with step-by-step exercises and a wealth of addresses and sites relevant to psychology.

Psychology in Context: Voices and Perspectives   The second edition of this exceptional reader, edited by David N. Sattler and Virginia Shabatay, may be shrinkwrapped with the text. It features engaging first-person narratives and essays by noted writers, with each article keyed to major psychological concepts.

Psychology: Fields of Application   This unique reader, edited by Astrid Stec and Douglas Bernstein, explores the most prominent areas of applied psychology. Each chapter features an expert's account of one area of application, including a brief history of the area's development, examples of research and how it has been applied, and the challenges facing the field.

ACKNOWLEDGMENTS

Many people provided us with the help, criticism, and encouragement we needed to create *Essentials of Psychology,* and to revise it into this second edition. We are of course indebted to our colleagues Alison Clarke-Stewart, Louis Penner, Ed Roy, and Chris Wickens, who, as co-authors of the Bernstein, Clarke-Stewart, Penner, Roy, and Wickens textbook, *Psychology,* provided invaluable assistance in reviewing the revised *Essentials* manuscript as it developed.

Special thanks are also due to our dear friend and valued colleague, Sandra Goss Lucas, director of Introductory Psychology at the University of Illinois, who worked closely with us as we shaped and organized the new edition of *Essentials,* and who helped us to revise and improve the multiple-choice self-tests at the end of each chapter.

We also want to offer heartfelt thanks to our friends and colleagues who did such a wonderful job in creating revised versions of the ancillary materials for *Essentials.* Most of these people have worked with us for years, and many of them had been graduate student instructors in the University of Illinois Introductory Psychology program out of which this book emerged. They include Kelly Bouas Henry, Missouri Western State College; Sandra Goss Lucas, Amanda Allman, and Jonathan Nall, all of the University of Illinois; Elaine Cassel, Marymount University; Billa R. Reiss, St. Johns University; and David B. Strohmetz, Monmouth University.

We also extend our deep appreciation to the *Essentials'* Board of Consultants, eight dedicated instructors whose involvement in focus groups and surveys, comments on manuscript chapters, and answers to development queries shaped the first edition of this text.

Charles Blair-Broeker, Cedar Falls High School

Ken LeSure, Cuyahoga Community College

Barbara Lusk, Collin County Community College

Malinda Jo Muzi, Community College of Philadelphia

Maggie Sokolik, University of California, Berkeley

Nancy Simpson, Trident Technical College

Fred Whitford, Montana State University

Robert Wildblood, Northern Virginia Community College

We wish to thank several of our colleagues who helped us get the new edition off to a good start by reviewing and commenting on the strengths and weaknesses of the first edition.

Patricia Abbott, D'Youville College

Gerry Altmann, York University, U.K.

Robin A. Anderson, St. Ambrose University

James F. Calhoun, University of Georgia

Yiwei Chen, Bowling Green State University

Samuel Clay, Heartland Community College

Anne M. Cooper, St. Petersburg Junior College

Laura Freberg, California Polytechnic State University,
San Luis Obispo

John R. Foust, Parkland College

Lynn Haller, Morehead State University

Wen Harris, Lane Community College

John S. Klein, Castleton State College

Ronald Kleinknecht, Western Washington University

Janet L. Kottke, California State University, San Bernardino

Joseph A. Mayo, Gordon College

Sheila M. Murphy, Mount Wachusett Community College

Steve A. Nida, Franklin University

Christine Offutt Lingenfelter, Lock Haven University

James S. Previte, Victor Valley College

Wayne J. Robinson, Monroe Community College

Kenneth M. Rosenberg, State University of New York, Oswego

Cynthia J. Smith, Wheeling Jesuit University

Mitchell Speaks, Keene State College

Linda K. Swindell, Anderson University

Parsram S. Thakur, Community College of Rhode Island

Inger Thompson, Glendale Community College

Michael J. Wenger, University of Notre Dame

Gordon Whitman, Sandhills Community College

Jean M. Wynn, Manchester Community College

Grace Galliano, Kennesaw State University

Christopher Gilbert, Bristol Community College

Craig W. Gruber, Walt Whitman High School

Debra Hollister, Valencia Community College

Gene Indenbaum, SUNY Farmingdale

David Murphy, Waubonsee College

Randall E. Osborne, Indiana University East

Ralph G. Pifer, Sauk Valley Community College

John L. Romanek, Jefferson Community College

Holly Straub, University of South Dakota

M. Lisa Valentino, Seminole Community College

C. Van Youngman, Art Institute of Philadelphia

We owe an enormous debt as well to the colleagues listed next for their thoughtful reviews of the first-edition manuscript as it was being developed. Their advice and suggestions for improvement were responsible for many of the good qualities you will find in this book. If you have any criticisms, they probably involve areas our reviewers warned us about!

Grace Auyang, University of Cincinnati

Alan Baxter, Technical Career Institutes, New York

Beth Benoit, University of Massachusetts, Lowell and
Middlesex Community College

Joseph J. Benz, University of Nebraska at Kearney

Winfield Brown, Florence Darlington Technical College

Saundra Ciccarelli, Gulf Coast Community College

Nat DeAnda, Los Madanos College

The process of creating *Essentials of Psychology* was greatly facilitated by the work of many dedicated people in the College Division at Houghton Mifflin Company. From the sales representatives and sales managers who reinforced our colleagues' requests for the text, to the marketing staff who worked to tell our colleagues what *Essentials* has to offer, it seems everyone in the division had a hand in shaping this book, and now in revising it. Several people in the editorial and production areas at Houghton Mifflin deserve special mention, however, because they did an absolutely outstanding job in helping us develop and revise the *Essentials* manuscript and turning that manuscript into the beautiful book you are now holding. Senior Development Editor Jane Knetzger was involved in the shaping and development of *Essentials* from day one; her advice and suggestions were invariably helpful. For this revised edition, Jane did a great job "on the front lines" as we worked on the new manuscript and tried to meet the goal of focusing on the essentials of psychology. Thanks for all your help, Jane. And many thanks to Aileen Mason, for coordinating the myriad production tasks associated with this project and for keeping them, and us, on schedule. We appreciate it very much. We also want to thank Ann Schroeder and Charlotte Miller for their outstanding work in the creation of the art and photo program for *Essentials,* and many thanks, too, to Mary Berry for her flawless copyediting of the final manuscript, and to Sarah Ambrose for her work as Senior Production/Design Coordinator. Without these people, and those who worked with them, the second edition of *Essentials of Psychology* would still be just an idea.

Finally, we want to express our thanks to our friends and our families who helped sustain us as we worked on this new edition. Your love and support mean more to us than we can ever express in words.

Doug Bernstein

Peggy Nash

Introduction to the Science of Psychology

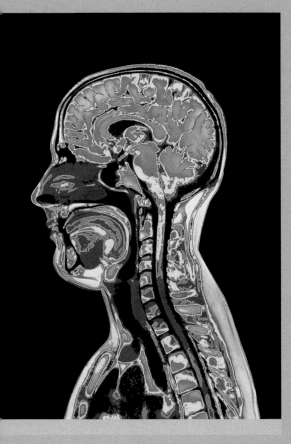

Why did you take this psychology course?

Maybe you wanted to learn more about yourself. This course is a great place to begin, and the complexity of the field may surprise you! We will begin our exploration of the science of psychology with a brief look at its scope and history. In this chapter, we will see how psychologists think critically, conduct research, and evaluate the evidence they collect. We will also see how psychologists take into account the richness of human diversity and important ethical concerns as they study behavior and mental processes. The chapter describes several theories and approaches that will help us organize our journey into the exciting realm of psychology. It also introduces the subfields of psychology and links them with each other and with other fields, including medicine, law, physics, and mathematics.

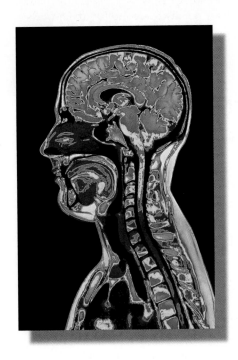

Reading this chapter will help you to answer the following questions:

- **What is psychology, and how did it grow?**
- **Why don't all psychologists explain behavior in the same way?**
- **How does your cultural background influence your behavior?**
- **How can critical thinking save you money?**
- **How do psychologists learn about people?**
- **When scientists announce a significant breakthrough in research, how can you be sure it is "significant"?**
- **Do psychologists trick people to get research data?**

It was bad enough when Brage Sassin's parents learned in August 1999 that their six-year-old son had only a 25 percent chance of surviving the leukemia he had battled since the age of two. Then came word that his new backyard treehouse, where Brage found relief from the stress of hospital visits and chemotherapy sessions, would have to come down because it had been built six feet higher than allowed by the rules in the family's Tampa, Florida, neighborhood. The Sassins refused to comply, and their conflict with the local residents association soon received nationwide media coverage. Among the hundreds of people expressing outrage at the situation were a local attorney, who took the Sassins' case at no charge, and two of Brage's doctors, who certified that the treehouse provided medically necessary psychological comfort that helped to fortify the boy's resistance to disease. On January 11, 2000, a residents association committee decided that the treehouse could stay. How do committees and other groups reach their decisions, and what role did outside pressure play in this one? To what extent does social pressure influence you? How are interpersonal conflicts resolved, and how does the stress of conflict affect the health of those involved? What determines whether people ignore other people's problems or go out of their way to help?

Source: Botwinick (1961).

FIGURE 1.1

Husband and Father-in-Law

 Look carefully at this figure, called "Husband and Father-in-Law" (Botwinick, 1961). You should be able to see it as two different people, depending upon how you mentally organize the features of the drawing. The elderly "father-in-law" faces to your right and is turned slightly toward you. He has a large nose, and the dark areas represent a coat pulled up to his chin. However, the tip of his nose can also be seen as the tip of a younger man's chin. The "husband" is in profile, also looking to your right, but away from you. The old man's mouth is the young man's neck band. Both men are wearing broad-brimmed hats. Can you see them? Your ability to see two different figures in a drawing that does not physically change—and to choose which one to see at any given moment—demonstrates that you actively manipulate incoming information rather than just passively receive it.

psychology   The science that seeks to understand behavior and mental processes.

Psychologists study questions like these because psychology is the science that seeks to understand behavior and mental processes, and to apply that understanding to serve human welfare. Psychologists have still not traced all the causes and effects of interpersonal conflict, nor have they found sure-fire ways to prevent it, but in later chapters, you will see that research in areas such as motivation, aggression, stress and health, personality, psychological disorders, and social psychology offers some important clues. That research tells part of the story of psychology, but there is much more. We hope this book will give you a better understanding of what psychology is, what psychologists study, where and how they work, what they have and have not discovered so far, and how their discoveries are being put to practical use.

The World of Psychology: An Overview

■ What is psychology, and how did it grow?

Psychology is the science of behavior and mental processes. Its subject matter includes thinking, feeling, eating, talking, reading, and loving! The full range of psychology, however, includes many other behaviors and mental processes as well. The topics have to be diverse to capture the full range of behaviors and mental processes that make you who you are, and make other people the way they are in every culture around the world.

Behavior and Mental Processes

How would you answer the question "Who are you?" For one thing, you are a collection of cells that make up your bones and muscles, your skin and hair, your brain and other organs. Part of what we mean by behavior and mental processes is the activity of these cells, especially as they communicate with one another. Your heart beats, your lungs breathe, and you stay alive all thanks to the activity of cells in your brain and body. It was your cells' ability to divide and carry out specific functions that allowed you to blossom from the single fertilized cell you once were into the complex being you are today.

Specialized cells give you the ability to sense information coming from the outside world and from inside your body. As we will see in Chapter 2, cells in your sense organs provide your brain with information that allows you to see, hear, smell, taste, and feel your world. Cells in your brain and motor system allow you to move and produce the coordinated patterns of behavior we call walking, dancing, talking, and the like.

Are you, then, just a bundle of cells that passively receives information and automatically reacts to it? You know you are much more than that, and we can help you prove it. Look at Figure 1.1. Although the drawing does not change, two different images emerge, depending on which of the features you emphasize. Obviously, you don't just take in raw information. You also interpret it and give it meaning. Chapter 3, on sensation and perception, discusses this fascinating aspect of behavior and mental processes.

In addition to interpreting information, you can think about it and decide how to respond. Suppose you see someone standing in front of you with a knife. You recognize the knife as dangerous. You understand the meaning of the words "Give me your money." You decide to comply. However, if the person with the knife smiles and says, "Happy birthday," you will probably reach for the knife to cut your cake. Immediate circumstances and your capacity for learning, memory, and thought guide your decision about what to do in these two situations, as we will see in Chapters 5, 6, and 7. If you could not understand the words you hear, or you could not recall the faces of your family or what you have learned about muggers and birthdays, you would be at a loss.

So far, you seem to be an utterly rational being, capable of coolly processing information under any circumstances. But would you experience only logical thought in the knife situations we described? Probably not. Chances are, you would also experience an emotion—maybe fear or happiness. Where do these emotions come from? Why are they

UNDERSTANDING THE SCOPE OF PSYCHOLOGY
Make a list of the questions that you think psychologists might ask about each of these photos. To help you get started, the wedding picture might prompt a psychologist to ask about the physical and personality characteristics that attracted this couple to each other, about how they went about deciding to marry, and about whether their relationship is strong enough to survive. Try to think of at least three more questions for that photo. What might psychologists ask about the picture of the woman whose home was suddenly destroyed by a tornado? The list you compile will represent just a few of the behaviors and mental processes that psychologists seek to understand. Throughout this book you will see how research by psychologists has provided knowledge and insights that are being used every day to promote human welfare.

sometimes so difficult to control? You might ask the same questions about your wants and needs. Perhaps you do volunteer work, love to read, compete fiercely, work two jobs, skydive, knit, or have a bad habit. In Chapter 8 we will explore why you behave as you do, how your behavior makes you feel, and how your feelings influence your behavior. Feelings add yet other dimensions to your being and reflect yet other aspects of behavior and mental processes.

Above all, you are an individual. In many ways you are unlike anyone else on earth. You have your own personality, attitudes, beliefs, and probably a special set of problems of one kind or another. Your individuality comes partly from the unique set of physical characteristics and behavioral tendencies you inherited from your parents. Another part comes from the experiences you had while growing up in your particular family and culture. The kaleidoscope of individual differences in behavior and mental processes is discussed throughout this book, particularly in the chapters on health, stress, and coping (10); personality (11); and psychological disorders (12).

Finally, you are an individual in a social world. So, your answer to the question "Who are you?" would probably include something about how and where you fit into that world. You might mention the size of your family, the groups you belong to, or your attitudes about government. As we'll see in Chapter 14, no definition of behavior and mental processes is complete without some reference to how people think about, and relate to, other people. And no wonder. Great human achievements—from the performance of beautiful music to the exploration of space—can result when people work together. And great human tragedies—from the Holocaust to terrorism and war—can occur when prejudice and hatred turn people against one another.

A Brief History of Psychology

The roots of psychology can be traced through centuries. Caveman and cavewoman probably wondered why each behaved as they did. Since at least the time of Socrates, Plato, and Aristotle in ancient Greece, psychological topics have inspired lively curiosity. Debate has long raged about the source of human knowledge, the nature of mind and soul, the relationship of mind to body, and the possibility of scientifically studying these matters (Wertheimer, 1987).

Scientific psychology has its roots in philosophy, and especially in a philosophical approach called **empiricism.** To empiricists, knowledge comes through experience and

empiricism   The view that knowledge comes from experience and observation.

consciousness   The awareness of external stimuli and our own mental activity.

WILHELM WUNDT (1832–1920) In a classic experiment on the speed of mental processes, Wundt (third from left) first measured how quickly people could respond to a light by releasing a button they had been holding down. He then determined how much longer the response took when they held down one button with each hand and had to decide—based on the color of the light—which one to release. Wundt reasoned that the additional time taken reflected how long it took to perceive the color and decide which hand to move.

observation, not through speculation. In the 1600s, empiricists like John Locke, George Berkeley, and David Hume challenged philosophers from Plato to René Descartes who believed that we are born with some knowledge. Empiricists said that at birth, our minds are like a blank slate (*tabula rasa* in Latin) upon which experience writes a lifelong story.

By 1859, English naturalist Charles Darwin had published *The Origin of Species*. Darwin (1809–1882) argued that the forms of life we see today are the result of *evolution*, of changes in life forms that occur over many generations. Indeed, through *natural selection*, individuals whose behavior and appearance allow them to withstand the elements, to avoid predators, and to mate are able to survive and produce offspring with similar characteristics. Those less successful at adjusting, or *adapting*, to changing conditions die out of the species. Notice that Darwin included humans as one of the forms of life that evolved. His revolutionary ideas moved the entire field of biology into the forefront of research. When biological research expanded, psychology as a science was not far behind.

Wundt and the Structuralism of Titchener   The birth date of modern, scientific psychology is usually given as 1879. This is the year in which Wilhelm Wundt (pronounced "Voont") established the first formal psychology research laboratory, at the University of Leipzig, in Germany. Wundt was a physiologist, studying sensory-perceptual systems. At that time, physiologists measured sensory and perceptual ability and limits. However, Wundt's goal was to use the methods of laboratory science to study **consciousness**—the mental experience that arises from these systems. In doing so, Wundt changed psychology from the *philosophy* of mental processes to the *science* of mental processes.

Wundt wanted to describe the basic elements of consciousness, their organization, and their relation to one another (Schultz & Schultz, 2000). In an attempt to study conscious experience, Wundt used the technique of *introspection*, which means "inward looking." Edward Titchener, an American who had been a student of Wundt, used introspection in his own laboratory at Cornell University to study sensations, feelings, and images associated with conscious experience. Look at the object in Figure 1.2. Try to describe *not* what it is but only how intensely and clearly you experience the sensations and images (such as redness, brightness, and roundness). This was the difficult task that Wundt and Titchener set for carefully trained "introspectors" in a search for the building

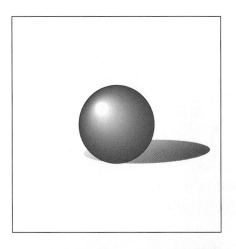

FIGURE 1.2

A Stimulus for Introspection

 Look at this object and try to describe not what it is but only the intensity and clarity of the sensations and images (such as redness, brightness, and roundness) that make up your experience of it. If you succeeded, you would have been an excellent participant in Titchener's laboratory.

blocks of consciousness. The term *structuralism* was used to describe Titchener's efforts to define the structure of consciousness. Wundt and Titchener were not the only scientific researchers in psychology, and their work was not universally accepted. Other scientific psychologists in Europe were studying sensory limits and the capability for learning and memory. They saw the structuralists' work as too simplistic.

Gestalt Psychology   Around 1912, another group of European psychologists led by Max Wertheimer, Kurt Koffka, and Wolfgang Köhler also argued against the value of trying to break down human experience or consciousness into its component parts. They were called *Gestalt psychologists* because they pointed out that the whole (or *Gestalt,* in German) of conscious experience is not the same as the sum of its parts. Wertheimer pointed out, for example, that when two lights are placed near each other in a dark room and go on and off in just the right sequence, we experience not two lights but a single light "jumping" back and forth. You have probably seen this *phi phenomenon* at night in advertising signs that create the impression of a series of lights racing around the display. Similarly, consider how boring it would be to browse slowly through the thousands of still images that are the component parts of movies. Yet when those images are projected onto a screen at just the right speed, they combine to create a rich emotional experience. In other words, said the Gestaltists, consciousness should be studied in its entirety, not piece by piece.

Freud and Psychoanalysis   While Wundt, in Germany, was conducting scientific research on consciousness, Sigmund Freud (1856–1939) was in Vienna, Austria, exploring the unconscious. Freud, a physician, began to question the basic assumption that biological factors were behind all behavior and mental processes. Using hypnosis and other methods, Freud suggested that the cause of some people's physical ailments was not physical. The real cause, he said, was shocking experiences in the distant past that the patients had pushed out of consciousness (Breuer & Freud, 1896). He eventually came to believe that *psychological processes,* especially hidden conflicts within the mind, motivated much of our behavior. He said that sexual and aggressive instincts, clashing with society's rules, generated many of these hidden conflicts. For nearly fifty years, Freud revised and expanded his ideas into a body of work known as *psychoanalysis.* This theory included his views on personality and mental disorder, as well as a set of treatment methods. Freud's ideas were (and still are) controversial. Even so, he was a groundbreaker who has had a huge influence on psychology and many other fields.

William James and Functionalism   Psychologists in North America began their scientific inquiry into psychology at about the same time as Wundt was doing his work in Germany. In the late 1800s, William James (1842–1910) founded the first psychology laboratory in the United States, at Harvard University. At the University of Toronto, James Mark Baldwin established the first Canadian laboratory in 1889.

William James rejected Wundt's approach and Titchener's structuralism. Influenced by Charles Darwin's theory of evolution, James was more interested in understanding how consciousness *functions* to help people adapt to their environments (James, 1890, 1892). This idea came to be called *functionalism.* It focused on the ongoing "stream" of consciousness, the ever-changing pattern of images, sensations, memories, and other mental events that people experience. James wanted to know how the functions of consciousness could be applied, how they worked for the individual. He asked, for example, why most people remember recent events better than things that happened in the distant past. Other functionalists measured individual differences in learning, memory, and intelligence. They recommended improving educational practices in the schools, even assisting teachers with programs tailored to children with special needs (Nietzel, Bernstein, & Milich, 1998).

John B. Watson and Behaviorism   Darwin's theory also led psychologists, especially in North America after 1900, to study animals as well as humans. If all species evolved in adaptive ways, perhaps their behavior and mental processes would follow the same, or similar, laws. Psychologists observed animal behavior in mazes and other experimental

JOHN B. WATSON (1878–1958) **The founder of behaviorism, Watson argued that by focusing on observable behavior—such as this baby's grasping reflex—psychologists would not have to rely on people's potentially distorted reports about themselves.**

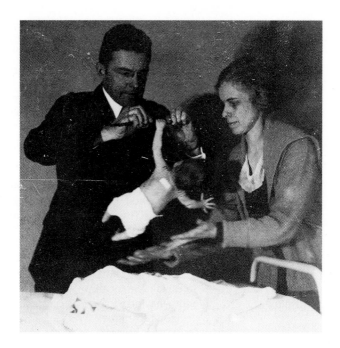

situations. From their observations, they drew conclusions about conscious experience, learning, memory, intelligence, and other mental processes in animals and humans.

John B. Watson, a psychology professor at Johns Hopkins University, agreed that obvious or overt behavior in animals *and* humans was the most important source of scientific information for psychology. In 1913, Watson wrote an article called "Psychology as the Behaviorist Views It." In it, he argued that psychologists should concern themselves only with observable, overt behavior, not mental events (J. B. Watson, 1913, 1919). His *behaviorism* did not address consciousness, as structuralism and functionalism did, let alone consider the unconscious, as Freudians did. Preoccupation with consciousness, said Watson, would prevent psychology from ever being a true science. Watson believed that *learning* is the most important cause of behavior. He was famous for claiming that if he had enough control over the environment, he could create learning experiences that would turn any infant into a doctor, a lawyer, or even a criminal.

The American psychologist B. F. Skinner was another early champion of behaviorism. From the 1930s until his death in 1990, Skinner studied how rewards and punishments shape, maintain, and change behavior through what he termed "operant conditioning." His *functional analysis of behavior* helped explain, for example, how parents and teachers can unknowingly encourage children's tantrums by rewarding them with attention. In functional analysis, you first discover what rewards or punishers shape the behavior. Then you can change the consequences to change the behavior. Watson's and Skinner's vision of psychology as the learning-based science of observable behavior found favor with many psychologists. Behaviorism dominated psychological research in North America from the 1920s through the 1960s.

Psychology Today "In Review: The Development of Psychology" summarizes the schools of thought that have influenced psychologists over the years. By the 1960s, the fact that behaviorism ignored mental processes was seen as a serious limitation (e.g., Ericsson & Simon, 1994). As the computer age dawned, psychologists began to think about mental activity in a new way—as information processing. At the same time, progress in biotechnology began to offer psychologists new ways to study the biological bases of mental processes. Armed with ever more sophisticated research tools, many psychologists today are trying to do what Watson thought was impossible: to study mental processes and even watch the brain perform them. So, psychology has come full circle, once again accepting consciousness, in the form of cognitive processes, as a legitimate topic for research (R. W. Robins, Gosling, & Craik, 1999).

in review

The Development of Psychology

Approach	Founders	Goals	Methods	Applications
Structuralism	Edward Titchener, trained by Wilhelm Wundt	To study conscious experience and its structure	Experiments; introspection	"Pure scientific research": spurred development of psychological laboratories
Gestalt psychology	Max Wertheimer	To describe organization of mental processes: "The whole is greater than the sum of its parts."	Observation of sensory/perceptual phenomena	Understanding of visual illusions; laid some of the groundwork for humanistic and cognitive psychology
Psychoanalysis	Sigmund Freud	To explain personality and behavior; to develop techniques for treating mental illness	Study of individual cases	Development of psychotherapy; emphasis on childhood as important in personality development
Functionalism	William James	To study how the mind works in allowing an organism to adapt to the environment	Naturalistic observation of animal and human behavior	Child psychology; educational and industrial psychology; study of individual differences
Behaviorism	John B. Watson, B. F. Skinner	To study only observable behavior and explain behavior via learning principles	Observation of the relationship between environmental stimuli and behavioral responses	Behavior modification methods; improved teaching methods

Approaches to the Science of Psychology

▪ Why don't all psychologists explain behavior in the same way?

biological approach   The view that behavior is the result of physical processes, especially those relating to the brain, to hormones, and to other chemicals.

evolutionary approach   A view that emphasizes the inherited, adaptive aspects of behavior and mental processes.

psychodynamic approach   A view developed by Freud emphasizing unconscious mental processes in explaining human thought, feelings, and behavior.

behavioral approach   A view based on the assumption that human behavior is determined mainly by what a person has learned in life, especially by rewards and punishments.

If you were a psychologist and wanted to understand a particular behavior or mental process, where would you look for answers? Would you study genes, parenting styles, brain cells, or hormones? The direction of your research would be determined largely by your *approach* to psychology—that is, by the set of assumptions, questions, and methods that you believe would be most helpful for understanding the things you wish to explore. Some psychologists adopt one particular approach, whereas many others are *eclectic*, combining features of two or more approaches. Eclectics believe that no single perspective can account for all aspects of psychological phenomena.

Many Approaches, One Theme

Psychologists no longer refer to themselves as structuralists or functionalists, but the psychodynamic and behavioral approaches remain, along with others known as the biological, evolutionary, cognitive, and humanistic approaches. For all the differences, a commitment to empiricism and scientific research unifies psychology (Kimble, 1999).

AN ETHOLOGIST AT WORK Konrad Lorenz, one of the founders of ethology, observed and described many examples of inborn but environmentally triggered behaviors. One of the most delightful of these behaviors is shown here. Baby geese follow their mother because her movement and honking provide signals that are naturally attractive. After Lorenz squatted and made mother-goose noises in front of newborn geese whose real mother was not present, the goslings began following him wherever he went, much to the amusement of his neighbors.

cognitive approach A view that emphasizes research on how the brain takes in information, creates perceptions, forms and retrieves memories, processes information, and generates integrated patterns of action.

Psychologists perform experiments and other scientific procedures to systematically gather and analyze information about psychological phenomena. However, they approach behavior and mental processes in many different ways. Some approaches are currently more influential than others, but the essential features of all of them deserve review.

The Biological Approach   As its name implies, the **biological approach** assumes that behavior and mental processes are largely shaped by biological processes. Researchers who follow this approach might investigate whether aggressive behavior or schizophrenia, for example, could be due to a chemical imbalance. These psychologists study the psychological effects of hormones, genes, and the activity of the nervous system, especially the brain. New techniques for "seeing" the brain have led to new theories of disorder. And today, treatment interventions include an array of therapeutic drugs from Antabuse to Zoloft. Research discussed in nearly every chapter of this book reflects the enormous influence of the biological approach on psychology today.

The Evolutionary Approach   Darwin's ideas on evolution and adaptation of species laid the foundation for an evolutionary approach to psychology. He attempted to establish universal laws of biology and behavior, especially animal behavior. Scientists who study animal behavior in the natural environment are called *ethologists*. They examine the effects of natural selection on inherited physical qualities, such as camouflage coloration that aids survival. Instinctive or *species-specific* behaviors, such as maternal retrieval of babies to the nest, also help a species to endure. Psychologists who take an **evolutionary approach** say that the behavior of animals and humans today is the result of evolution through natural selection. They see aggression, for example, as a form of territory protection, and gender differences in mate selection preferences as reflecting different ways of helping genes to survive in future generations (D. M. Buss, 1999). You will see the influence of the evolutionary approach in later chapters in relation to topics as diverse as helping, mental disorders, temperament, and interpersonal attraction.

The Psychodynamic Approach   The **psychodynamic approach** offers a different slant. Rooted in Freud's theory, this approach maintains that all behavior and mental processes reflect the constant and mostly unconscious psychological struggles that rage silently within each person. Usually, these struggles involve dynamic conflict between the impulse to satisfy instincts or wishes and the need to play by the rules in a society. Anxiety, depression, and other disorders are outward signs of this inner turmoil. The strictly Freudian perspective is far less influential in psychology now than in the past (R. W. Robins, Gosling, & Craik, 1999). Aspects of Freud's theory are still the focus of research on such topics as repressed memory and psychological defense mechanisms, but most psychologists who take a psychodynamic approach prefer revised versions of Freud's original theories (Westen & Gabbard, 1999). We'll explore these versions in Chapter 11.

The Behavioral Approach   As founded by John Watson, the **behavioral approach** views behavior and mental processes as primarily the result of learning. Psychologists who take this approach see rewards and punishments acting on the raw materials provided by genes, evolution, and biology to shape each individual. So, whether they are considering a person's aggression, parenting, or drug abuse, behaviorists would look at that person's learning history. They also believe that because people learn problem behaviors, they can also learn to change or prevent them by unlearning old habits and developing new ones.

The Cognitive Approach   The **cognitive approach** focuses on how people take in, mentally represent, and store information. Cognitive psychologists then relate perception and information processing to patterns of behavior. They hope to discover the building blocks of cognition and to determine how they produce complex behaviors such as remembering a fact, naming an object, or writing a word (Reisberg, 1997). Cognitive psychologists study such areas as decision making, problem solving, interpersonal attraction, and intelligence. Aggression, for instance, might be viewed as a result of poor

in review

Approaches to Psychology	
Approach	**Characteristics**
Biological	Emphasizes activity of the nervous system, especially the brain; the action of hormones and other chemicals; and genetics.
Evolutionary	Emphasizes the ways in which behavior and mental processes are adaptive for survival.
Psychodynamic	Emphasizes internal conflicts, mostly unconscious, which usually pit sexual or aggressive instincts against environmental obstacles to their expression.
Behavioral	Emphasizes learning, especially each person's experience with rewards and punishments.
Cognitive	Emphasizes mechanisms through which people receive, store, retrieve, and otherwise process information.
Humanistic	Emphasizes individual potential for growth and the role of unique perceptions in guiding behavior and mental processes.

problem solving. Some psychologists work in *cognitive science,* a multidisciplinary field in which researchers from computer science, biology, engineering, linguistics, and philosophy study intelligent systems in humans and computers.

The Humanistic Approach   According to the **humanistic approach,** our capacity to choose how to think and act determines our behavior. Each person's unique perceptions—not instincts, biological processes, or rewards and punishments—dictate the cognitive choices made. If you perceive the world as a friendly place, you are likely to feel happy and secure. If you view it as dangerous and hostile, you will probably be defensive and anxious. Carl Rogers (1902–1987) was a major proponent of this approach. Rogers had been trained in psychodynamic theory but rejected it in favor of a more humanistic view. Abraham Maslow also helped to shape the humanistic movement in North America. Humanistic psychologists believe that people are essentially good, that they are in control of themselves, and that they seek to grow toward their fullest potential. Instead of searching for universal laws of behavior, humanists focus on immediate, individual experience. Carl Rogers developed a distinctive approach to psychotherapy, as described in Chapter 13. Certain humanistic concepts and predictions remain vague and difficult to test scientifically, but many of them are still influential among some psychologists. The humanistic approach, and the others we have described, are summarized in "In Review: Approaches to Psychology."

Subfields of Psychology

Have you ever taken a career test, called a crisis hotline, been coached in a visualization exercise before a big sports contest, or volunteered to take part in a research study? If so, you've seen just a few of the many activities that the world's approximately half-million psychologists engage in. Most have chosen to focus on one or two of the many specialty areas, or *subfields,* within psychology.

Wundt and other early psychologists called themselves *experimental psychologists.* They wanted to separate from their colleagues in philosophy who thought about mental processes but did not do experimental research on them. Today, psychologists in all the subfields listed below also rely on experiments and other empirical methods to conduct their research or guide their work.

humanistic approach   A view of behavior as controlled by the decisions that people make about their lives based on their perceptions of the world.

cognitive psychologists Psychologists whose research focus is analysis of the mental processes underlying judgment, decision making, problem solving, imagining, and other aspects of human thought or cognition.

biological psychologists Psychologists who analyze the biological factors influencing behavior and mental processes.

personality psychologists Psychologists who focus on the unique characteristics that influence individuals' behavior.

developmental psychologists Psychologists who seek to understand, describe, and explore how behavior and mental processes change over the course of a lifetime.

quantitative psychologists Psychologists who develop statistical methods for evaluating and analyzing data from psychological research.

clinical and counseling psychologists Psychologists who seek to assess, understand, and modify abnormal behavior.

community psychologists Psychologists who work to obtain psychological services for underserved client groups, and to prevent psychological disorders by working for changes in social systems.

educational psychologists Psychologists who study methods by which instructors teach and students learn, and who apply their results to improving such methods.

school psychologists Psychologists who test IQ, diagnose students' academic problems, and set up programs to improve students' achievement.

social psychologists Psychologists who study how people influence one another's behavior and attitudes, especially in groups.

industrial-organizational psychologists Psychologists who examine how social factors influence people's performance in the workplace.

Cognitive psychologists, for example, study basic mental processes and form hypotheses about their relation to behavior in areas such as sensation, perception, learning, memory, judgment, decision making, and problem solving.

Biological psychologists, also called *physiological psychologists* or *neuroscientists,* study questions such as what role is played by genetics and brain anatomy in schizophrenia, how brain cells communicate, whether patterns of brain activity can reveal when a person is lying, or how hormones associated with stress can suppress the body's immune system.

Personality psychologists study individuality—the uniqueness of each person. Your personality traits, like your fingerprints, are different from those of all other people. However, some combinations of personality traits may predict patterns of behavior. For instance, personality psychologists study shy and bold children over many years. They hope to discover factors that might predict the appearance of alcoholism, drug abuse, aggressiveness, or other problems in later life.

Developmental psychologists study and describe changes in behavior and mental processes over the life span, trying to understand their causes and effects. They explore areas such as the development of thought, friendship patterns, parenting styles, and whether a midlife crisis is inevitable.

Quantitative psychologists develop statistical methods for analyzing vast amounts of data collected by their colleagues in other subfields. We'll soon examine one tool they use to evaluate the validity of tests, as well as the mathematical methods they have developed to separate the effects of heredity and environment. Are people born brilliant, or is their brilliance created by their environment? This is one of the hottest topics in psychology today, and quantitative psychologists are right in the middle of it.

Clinical, counseling, and community psychologists study the causes of behavior disorders and offer services to help troubled people overcome these disorders. Each state, province, or country specifies the qualifications for titles in this subfield. Generally, a **clinical psychologist** has a Ph.D. in psychology; most provide therapy services, and many do research as well. A **counseling psychologist** might work as a mental health counselor, for example, and would have either a Ph.D. or a master's degree in psychology. **Community psychologists** offer psychological services to the homeless and others who need help but tend not to seek it. By working for changes in schools and other social systems, they also try to prevent poverty and other stressful conditions that so often lead to disorder. All these groups differ from *psychiatrists,* who are medical doctors with a specialty in abnormal behavior (psychiatry) and are licensed to prescribe medications.

Educational psychologists conduct research and develop theories about teaching and learning. They see the results of their work applied to improving teacher training, refining school curricula, reducing dropout rates, and helping students learn more efficiently (Hoy, 1999). **School psychologists** specialize in IQ testing, diagnosing learning disabilities and other academic problems, and setting up programs to improve students' achievement and satisfaction in school.

Social psychologists study the ways that people influence one another. They conduct research on social-influence strategies such as the effectiveness of advertising in the safe-sex campaign to halt the spread of AIDS. They explore topics such as prejudice and other attitudes, peer pressure, and interpersonal attraction—whom we like, and why. **Industrial-organizational psychologists** seek to improve the efficiency, productivity, and satisfaction of workers and the organizations that employ them. They conduct research on topics such as increasing the motivation of current employees and helping companies select the best new workers.

The field of psychology is as diverse as the behaviors and processes it considers (Stec & Bernstein, 1999). It also includes *health psychologists,* who study the effects of

Applying Psychology

DEFUSING PREJUDICE IN THE CLASSROOM   Social psychologists such as Eliot Aronson have worked to develop classroom activities that allow children from various ethnic groups to work cooperatively with one another. Research indicates that these cooperative learning experiences help generate mutual respect and minimize prejudicial attitudes (Aronson, Wilson, & Akert, 1999).

TABLE 1.1	Typical Activities and Work Settings for Psychologists

The fact that psychologists can work in such a wide variety of settings and perform such a wide range of functions helps account for the popularity of psychology as an undergraduate major (APA, 2000; National Center for Education Statistics, 1998). Psychology courses also provide excellent background for students planning to enter medicine, law, business, and many other fields.

Percentage of Psychologists	Work Setting	Typical Activities
22.8%	Colleges, universities, and professional schools	Teaching, research, and writing, often in collaboration with colleagues from other disciplines
27.5%	Mental health facilities (e.g., hospitals, clinics, counseling centers)	Testing and treatment of children and adults
31.5%	Private practice (alone or in a group of psychologists)	Testing and treatment of children and adults; consultation to business and other organizations
6.1%	Business, government, and organizations	Testing potential employees; assessing employee satisfaction; identifying and resolving conflicts; improving leadership skills; offering stress management and other employee assistance programs; improving equipment design to maximize productivity and prevent accidents
4.5%	Schools (including those for developmentally disabled and emotionally disturbed children)	Testing mental abilities and other characteristics; identifying problem children; consulting with parents; designing and implementing programs to improve academic performance
7.6%	Other	Teaching prison inmates; research in private institutes; advising legislators on educational, research, or public policy; administering research funds; research on effectiveness of military personnel; etc.

Source: Data from 1998 APA Directory Survey.

behavior on health and the impact of illness on behavior and emotion; *sport psychologists,* who search for the keys to maximum athletic performance; *environmental psychologists,* who explore the effects of the physical environment on behavior and mental processes; and *forensic psychologists,* who create criminal profiles, assist in jury selection, and are involved in the legal aspects of insanity and psychology. *Engineering psychologists* study the relationships of human beings to the computers and other machines they use. For example, they have designed new computer keyboards to ease stress on wrists. Radar screens, seat belts, and controls for adjustable hospital beds have also been researched and modified by engineering psychologists. (See Table 1.1 for a summary of the typical activities and work settings of psychologists.)

Linkages Within Psychology and Beyond

Perhaps you're thinking that there's a lot of overlap among psychology's subfields. If so, you're right. What links psychologists' interests? Sometimes they are investigating a common topic, such as violence or language. At other times they are dealing with a crossover issue, such as how biological and cultural influences interact to shape personality (Plomin, 1997). Even when psychologists are not conducting research across subfields, they often draw on and contribute to the knowledge developed in other subfields. Their theories, methods, findings, and applications to daily life are woven closely together.

Recognizing the links among psychology's subfields that appear time and again in this book is an important part of understanding psychology as a whole. To help you identify some of these linkages, we have provided a diagram similar to the one in Figure 1.3 near the end of each chapter. The questions in these diagrams illustrate some of the relationships between the topics discussed in one chapter and the topics of other chapters. The page numbers after each question indicate where discussions related to them appear. Of course, there are many more linkages than could be included in the diagrams. We hope that the diagrams will prompt you to look for these additional linkages. This kind of detective work can be enjoyable and useful. You may find it easier to remember material in one chapter by relating it to linked material in other chapters. You might also want to use the questions as a self-testing device when studying for quizzes and exams.

Psychology itself is linked to other disciplines. Some of these connections occur because of common interests across disciplines, as in the case of cognitive science or neuroscience. Other links occur because of crossover applications. For example, psychologists apply chaos theory from physics and mathematics to detect underlying order in seemingly random patterns of violence, drug abuse, depression, or family conflict (e.g., Vallacher & Novak, 1997). Genetic counselors use psychological knowledge about decision making and stress management to help clients with a risky gene profile decide

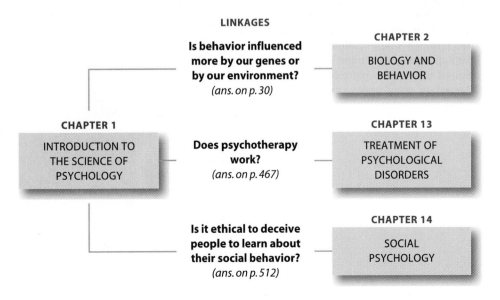

FIGURE 1.3

Linkages to the Science of Psychology

By staying alert to linkages as you read this book, you will come away not only with threads of knowledge about each subfield but also with an appreciation of the fabric of psychology as a whole. We discuss one linkage in detail in each chapter in a special Linkages section.

LINKAGES

Is behavior influenced more by our genes or by our environment?
(ans. on p. 30)

CHAPTER 2
BIOLOGY AND BEHAVIOR

CHAPTER 1
INTRODUCTION TO THE SCIENCE OF PSYCHOLOGY

Does psychotherapy work?
(ans. on p. 467)

CHAPTER 13
TREATMENT OF PSYCHOLOGICAL DISORDERS

Is it ethical to deceive people to learn about their social behavior?
(ans. on p. 512)

CHAPTER 14
SOCIAL PSYCHOLOGY

whether to have children (Shiloh, 1996), and psychologists' memory research has influenced how lawyers and judges question witnesses and instruct juries (U.S. Department of Justice, 1999). Throughout this book you'll encounter examples of other ways in which psychological theories and research have been applied to fields as diverse as medicine, dentistry, law, business, engineering, architecture, aviation, public health, and sports.

Human Diversity and Psychology

How does your cultural background influence your behavior?

It used to be that psychologists assumed all people were essentially the same. They thought that whatever principles emerged from research with one group of people would apply to people everywhere. Because about 90 percent of psychological researchers worked at universities in North America and Europe, they tended to study local college students. These students were mostly white and middle-class, and more often men than women (M. Crawford & Marecek, 1989; Graham, 1992). Most of the psychologists, too, tended to be white, middle-class, and male (L. Walker, 1991). However, women and people of color made important early contributions to psychology as well (Schultz & Schultz, 2000). Their contributions continue to increase, as does their growing representation in the field. In the United States, women now constitute about 44 percent of all psychologists holding doctoral degrees (National Science Foundation, 1997), and they are earning about 67 percent of the new psychology doctorates awarded each year (National Science Foundation, 1998). Moreover, nearly 16 percent of new doctoral degrees are being earned by members of ethnic minorities (National Science Foundation, 1998).

The Impact of Culture on Psychology

Each person is different from everyone else, yet in some ways, people are very much alike. They tend to live in groups; develop religious beliefs; and create rules, music, and games. Similarly, the principles of nerve cell activity or reactions to heat or a sour taste are the same in men and women the world over, as is their recognition of a smile. This is not true of *all* characteristics, however. It turns out that the forces that motivate people, the devel-

Applying Psychology

PREPARATION FOR SURGERY
Health psychologists have learned that when patients are mentally prepared for a surgical procedure, they are less stressed by it and recover more rapidly. Their research is now routinely applied in hospitals through programs in which children and adults are given clear information about what to expect before, during, and after their operations.

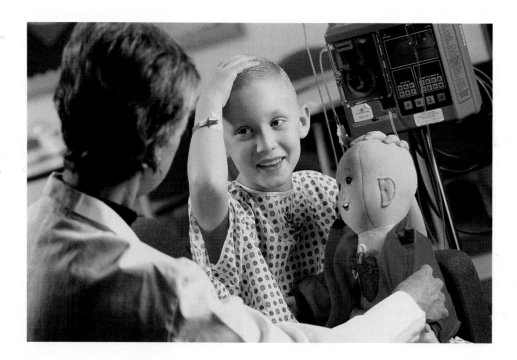

opment of moral thought, and patterns of interpersonal communication are not universal. **Sociocultural variables** shape people's experiences and what they learn from them. These variables include social identity, gender, ethnicity, social class, and culture. They lead to many significant differences in behavior and mental processes, especially across cultures (Cross & Markus, 1999; Sue, 1999).

Culture has been defined as the accumulation of values, rules of behavior, forms of expression, religious beliefs, occupational choices, and the like for a group of people who share a common language and environment (A. P. Fiske et al., 1998). As such, culture is an organizing and stabilizing influence. It encourages or discourages particular behaviors and mental processes; it also allows people to understand and anticipate the behavior of others in that culture. It is a kind of group adaptation, passed on by tradition and example rather than by genes from one generation to the next. Culture determines, for example, whether children's education will focus on skill at hunting or reading, how close people stand when they talk to each other, and whether or not they form lines in public places (Munroe & Munroe, 1994).

Psychologists as well as anthropologists have isolated many respects in which cultures differ (Triandis, 1998). Table 1.2 outlines one way of analyzing these differences. It shows that many cultures can be described as either individualist or collectivist. *Individualist* cultures tend to encourage people to place personal goals ahead of the goals of the collective, such as the family or work group. *Collectivist* cultures tend to encourage collective (group) goals over personal ones (P. B. Smith & Bond, 1999). Some cultures have loose rules for social behavior; others have tight ones. Some value achievement; others, self-awareness. One culture may seek dominance over nature; another, harmony with it. Time may be of the essence in one culture and not emphasized in another.

Many people in individualist cultures, such as those typical of North America and Western Europe, tend to focus on and value personal rather than group goals and achievement. Competitiveness to distinguish oneself from others is common, as is a sense of isolation. By contrast, in collectivist cultures such as Japan, people tend to think of themselves mainly as part of family or work groups. Cooperative effort aimed at advancing the welfare of those groups is highly valued. And although loneliness is rarely a problem, fear of rejection by the group is common. Though we seldom think about it, many aspects of U.S. culture—from self-reliant cowboy heroes and bonuses for "top"

MARY WHITON CALKINS (1863–1930) When Mary Whiton Calkins studied psychology at Harvard University with William James, he described her as brilliant. Because she was a woman, however, Harvard refused to grant her a doctoral degree; when they offered her the degree through Radcliffe, an affiliated school, she refused it. Nevertheless, her research on memory helped her to be named, in 1905, the first woman president of the American Psychological Association (APA). Margaret Washburn (1871–1939) encountered similar sex discrimination at Columbia University, so she transferred to Cornell, became the first woman to earn a doctorate in psychology, and in 1921 was elected the second woman president of the APA.

GILBERT HAVEN JONES (1883–1966) When Gilbert Haven Jones graduated from the University of Jena in Germany in 1909, he became one of the first African Americans to earn a doctorate in psychology. Many others were to follow, including J. Henry Alston, who was the first African American to publish research in a major U.S. psychology journal (Alston, 1920).

sociocultural variables Social identity and other background factors, such as gender, ethnicity, social class, and culture.

culture The accumulation of values, rules of behavior, forms of expression, religious beliefs, and occupational choices for a group of people who share a common language and environment.

THE IMPACT OF CULTURE Culture helps shape virtually every aspect of our behavior and mental processes, from how we dress to what we think is important. Because we grow up immersed in our culture, it is easy to forget its influence, until—like these participants at a United Nations World Conference on Women—we encounter people whose culture has shaped them differently.

employees to the invitation to "help yourself" at a buffet table—reflect its tendency toward an individualist orientation (see Table 1.3).

We often associate cultures with particular countries, but in reality, most countries are *multicultural* (Phinney, 1996). In other words, they host many subcultures within their borders. For instance, the United States encompasses African Americans, Hispanic Americans, Asian Americans, and American Indians, as well as European Americans with Italian, German, English, Polish, Irish, and other origins. In each of these groups, the individuals who identify with their cultural heritage tend to share behaviors, values, and beliefs based on their culture of origin. In other words, they form a *subculture*.

Like fish unaware of the water they swim in, we often fail to notice how our culture or subculture has shaped our patterns of thinking and behaving. We may notice it only when we come in contact with people whose culture or subculture has shaped different

TABLE 1.2		
Some Characteristics of Behavior and Mental Processes Typical of Individualist vs. Collectivist Cultures **Cultural factors do not act as cookie cutters that make everyone in a culture the same, but certain broad tendencies in behavior and mental processes have been associated with particular kinds of cultures (A. P. Fiske et al., 1998; Triandis, 1996).**		

Variable	Individualist	Collectivist
Personal identity	Separate from others	Connected to others
Major goals	Self-defined; be unique; realize your personal potential; compete with others	Defined by others; belong; occupy your proper place; meet your obligations to others; be like others
Criteria for self-esteem	Ability to express unique aspects of the self; ability to be self-assured	Ability to restrain the self and be part of a social unit; ability to be self-effacing
Sources of success and failure	Success comes from personal effort; failure, from external factors	Success is due to help from others; failure is due to personal faults
Major frame of reference	Personal attitudes, traits, and goals	Family, work group

TABLE 1.3

Cultural Values as Seen in Advertising

 The statements listed here appeared in advertisements in Korea and the United States. The statements from Korea reflect collectivist values, whereas those from the United States emphasize a more individualist orientation (Han & Shavitt, 1994). Can you tell which are which? (The answers are at the bottom of this page.) How did you do? To follow up on this exercise, try to identify cultural values in the ads you see in newspapers and magazines and on billboards and television. If possible, compare the values in those ads with the values in ads from other cultures that might be found on Internet sites or in international newspapers.

1. "She's got a style all her own."
2. "You, only better."
3. "A more exhilarating way to provide for your family."
4. "We have a way of bringing people closer together."
5. "Celebrating a half-century of partnership."
6. "How to protect the most personal part of the environment: Your skin."
7. "Our family agrees with this selection of home furnishings."
8. "A leader among leaders."
9. "Make your way through the crowd."
10. "Your business success: Harmonizing with (company name)."

Source: Brehm, Kassin, & Fein (1999).

patterns. For example, an American teaching in Korea discovered that some people there believe it is in poor taste to write a student's name in red ink (Stevens, 1999). He was told that doing so conveys a prediction or wish that the person will die, because red ink was traditionally used to record new names in official death registers. Even some of the misunderstandings between people in the same culture are traceable to subtle, culturally influenced differences in communication patterns (Tannen, 1994). In the United States, for instance, women's efforts to connect with others by talking may be perceived by many men as "pointless" unless the discussion is geared to solving a particular problem. Thus, women often feel frustrated and misunderstood by men, who tend to offer well-meant, but unwanted, advice instead of conversation.

Psychology and Sociocultural Variables Today

For decades, psychologists interested in cross-cultural research have studied cultural differences (Triandis, 1964). Now, the influence of sociocultural variables is of growing interest to psychologists in general (J. G. Miller, 1999). As psychology strives to be the science of *all* behavior and mental processes, its research will increasingly look at ethnicity, gender, and other sociocultural variables (D. W. Sue et al., 1999). We'll see this trend in much of the research we explore in the chapters to come.

Thinking Critically About Psychology (or Anything Else)

How can critical thinking save you money?

Often, people simply accept what they are told because it comes from a believable source or because "everyone knows" it is true. How many of the myths in Table 1.4 have you heard and believed? Some advertisers, politicians, TV evangelists, and social activists hope for this kind of easy acceptance when they want your money, vote, or loyalty. They want you to believe their promises or claims without careful thought. They don't want you to think critically. Uncritically accepting claims for the value of astrologers' predictions, "get-rich-quick" investments, new therapies, or proposed government policies can be embarrassing, expensive, and sometimes dangerous. Critical thinkers carefully evaluate evidence for *and against* such claims before reaching a conclusion about them.

Answer key for Table 1.3: U.S. ads are numbers 1, 2, 6, 8, and 9.

TABLE 1.4	Some Myths About Human Behavior

Many people believe that the statements listed here are true, but critical thinkers who take the time to investigate them will discover that they are not.

Myth	Fact
Many children are injured each year in the United States when razor blades, needles, or poisons are put in Halloween candy.	Reported cases are rare, most turn out to be hoaxes, and in the only documented case of a child dying from poisoned candy, the culprit was the child's own parent (Brunvald, 1989).
If your roommate commits suicide during the school term, you automatically get A's in all your classes for that term.	No college or university anywhere has ever had such a rule.
If you visit the Microsoft Corporation homepage on the Internet, your computer will be infected by a virus that wipes out all your files.	This is not true, but word of this virus kept thousands of people from visiting the Microsoft homepage in 1996.
People have been known to die from fire erupting from within their own bodies.	In rare cases, human bodies have been totally consumed by fire that causes relatively little damage to the surrounding area. However, each alleged "spontaneous human combustion" case has been traced to an external source of ignition (Benecke, 1999). The same phenomenon was duplicated in a laboratory demonstration in 1998.
Most big-city police departments rely on the advice of psychics to help them solve murders, kidnappings, and missing-persons cases.	Only about 35 percent of urban police departments ever seek psychics' advice, and that advice is virtually never more helpful than other means of investigation (Nickell, 1997; Wiseman, West, & Stemman, 1996).
Murders, suicides, and mental disorders are more likely to occur when the moon is full.	Crime statistics and mental hospital admissions data show no evidence to support this common belief (Bickis, Kelly, & Byrnes, 1995; Culver, Rotton, & Kelly, 1988).
You can't fool a lie detector.	Lie detectors can be helpful in solving crimes, but they are not perfect; their results can free a guilty person or send an innocent person to jail (see Chapter 8).
Viewers never see David Letterman walking to his desk after the opening monologue because his contract prohibits him from showing his backside on TV.	When questioned about this story on the air, Letterman denied it and, to prove his point, lifted his jacket and turned a full circle in front of the cameras and studio audience (Brunvald, 1989).

critical thinking The process of assessing claims and making judgments on the basis of well-supported evidence.

THINKING CRITICALLY

Is EMDR an Effective Treatment for Anxiety?

Critical thinking is the process of assessing claims and making judgments on the basis of well-supported evidence (C. Wade, 1988). Consider the following example. Francine Shapiro, a clinical psychologist in northern California, had an odd experience one day. While she was walking and thinking about some distressing events, she noticed her emotional reaction to them was fading away. What had caused this fading? Thinking back, she realized she had been involuntarily moving her eyes back and forth. To see if the eye movements had caused the emotion-reducing effect, she tried it deliberately. The effect was even stronger. Curious, she examined the effect in friends and colleagues, and then in clients who had suffered traumas such as childhood sexual abuse, military combat, or rape. As these people thought about these events, they followed her finger with their eyes as she moved it back and forth in front of their faces. Like her, they said that their reactions to the memories faded. And her clients reported that other trauma-related problems such as nightmares, fears, and emotional flashbacks dropped dramatically, often after only one session (F. Shapiro, 1989a).

Shapiro called her new treatment *eye movement desensitization and reprocessing*, or *EMDR* (F. Shapiro, 1991). Today, Shapiro and other therapists are using EMDR to treat a wide range of anxiety-related problems in children and adults, from simple phobias to disorders caused by the trauma of military combat (e.g., Greenwald, 1999; Manfield, 1998; P. Smith & Yule, 1999). Psychologists did not know what to make of EMDR. Is it a breakthrough or a coincidence?

To scientifically examine any aspect of behavior and mental processes, you must think critically. First determine what questions to ask. Making progress toward answers depends on translating critical thinking into scientific research methods. One strategy for applying critical thinking to EMDR or any other topic is to ask the following five questions:

What am I being asked to believe or accept?

In this case, you are asked to believe that EMDR reduces or eliminates anxiety-related problems.

Is there evidence available to support the claim?

Shapiro began her EMDR research on herself. When she found the same effects in others, coincidence became an unlikely explanation for the observed changes.

Can that evidence be interpreted another way?

The dramatic effects that Shapiro's friends and clients experienced might have been due to their motivation to change or their desire to please her, not to EMDR. Even the most remarkable evidence cannot be accepted as confirming an assertion until all reasonable alternative explanations have been ruled out.

What evidence would help to evaluate the alternatives?

The ideal method for testing the EMDR theory would be to identify three groups of people who are identical in every way except for the anxiety treatment they receive. One group receives EMDR. The second group gets an equally motivating but useless treatment. The third group gets no treatment at all. If the group receiving EMDR improves much more than the other two groups do, then the mere passage of time or clients' motivation are less likely explanations.

What conclusions are most reasonable?

The evidence available so far has not yet ruled out alternative explanations for the effects of EMDR (e.g., Lohr et al., 1999). So, the only reasonable conclusions to be drawn at this point are that (1) EMDR remains a controversial treatment, (2) it seems to have an impact on some clients, and (3) further research is needed in order to understand it (DeJongh, Ten Broeke, & Renssen, 1999). Does that sound wishy-washy? Critical thinking sometimes does seem indecisive, but that's because scientific conclusions must be guided by the evidence available. Yet, critical thinking also opens the way to understanding. To help you sharpen your critical thinking skills, we have included a critical thinking example like this one in every chapter of the book.

Research Designs in Psychology

How do psychologists learn about people?

Like other scientists, psychologists try to achieve four main goals in their research: to *describe* a phenomenon, to *make predictions* about it, and to introduce enough *control* in their research to allow them to *explain* the phenomenon with some degree of confidence. They not only gather evidence but also assess its quality. As scientists, psychologists evaluate the quality of evidence in terms of two characteristics: reliability and validity. **Reliability** is the degree to which the evidence can be repeated. **Validity** is the degree to which the evidence accurately assesses the topic being studied. For example, if Francine Shapiro had not been able to repeat, or replicate, the eye movement effects with others, or if only a few clients had shown improvement, she would question the reliability of the evidence. If the clients' reports of improvement were not checked for accuracy through, say, supporting reports from family members, she would doubt their validity.

The Role of Theories

After gathering evidence from research on a particular phenomenon, scientists may organize their explanations into a theory. A **theory** is an integrated set of statements designed to account for, predict, and even suggest ways of controlling certain phenomena. Shapiro's theory about EMDR suggests that the eye movements activate parts of the brain where traumatic or unpleasant information has been stored but never fully processed (F. Shapiro, 1994, 1995, 1999). Theories are tentative explanations that must be subjected to scientific evaluation based on critical thinking. For example, Shapiro's theory about EMDR has been criticized as vague, lacking in supportive evidence, and having less plausibility than alternative explanations (e.g., Armstrong & Vaughan, 1996; Muris & Merckelbach, 1999). In other words, theories are based on research results, but they also generate questions to be asked in further research. Many psychologists will test predictions from a single theory. That theory will be revised or even abandoned if research does not support it. Without research results, there would be nothing to explain. Without explanatory theories, the results might never be organized in a useful way. This continual interaction between theory and research lies at the heart of all that we've found out about psychology over the past century.

   The constant formulating, evaluating, reformulating, and abandoning of theories has generated many competing explanations of behavior and mental processes. And because human behavior is so complex, general conclusions drawn from one set of research results or offered by one theory cannot be considered definitive "answers." Although such conclusions may be correct overall, they often need to be qualified. Perhaps they apply only in certain situations, or to only a particular group. Perhaps the most accurate conclusion is that we need further research. Keep this point in mind the next time you hear self-proclaimed experts—called "pop" (for *popular*) psychologists by the scientific community—giving easy answers and simple formulas for complex problems. They tend to oversimplify issues, cite evidence for their views without concern for reliability or validity, and ignore good evidence that contradicts their pet theories. Psychological scientists must be more cautious, often suspending final judgments about behavior and mental processes until they have collected better data. Nevertheless, tentative conclusions based on today's knowledge form the foundation for the research that will increase understanding tomorrow. Let's look at how research goals and methods are blended in psychologists' work.

Naturalistic Observation

The process of watching and recording a phenomenon as it naturally occurs, without interfering with it, is called **naturalistic observation.** This method gathers descriptive data in cases where other techniques might be disruptive. For example, much of what we

reliability   The degree to which test results or other research evidence occurs repeatedly.

validity   The degree to which evidence from a test or other research method measures what it is supposed to measure.

theory   An integrated set of propositions used to account for, predict, and even control behavior and mental processes.

naturalistic observation   The process of watching without interfering as a phenomenon occurs in the natural environment.

NATURALISTIC OBSERVATION Observing people in natural settings can provide important clues to understanding social interaction and other aspects of behavior and mental processes. It is harder than it might seem. Imagine you are studying these children at play, and make a list of the *exact* behaviors you would count as "aggressive," "cooperative," and "competitive."

know about gender differences in how children play and communicate with one another has come from psychologists' observations in classrooms and playgrounds. Observations of adults, too, have suggested that childhood gender differences might underlie some of the conflict and miscommunication seen in marriages and other male-female intimate relationships (e.g., Bradbury, Campbell, & Fincham, 1995). Understanding gender differences that first came to light through observational research helps therapists who work with couples in conflict.

Naturalistic observation can provide a lot of rich information, but it is not without its problems (Nietzel, Bernstein, & Milich, 1998). For one thing, people tend to act differently when they know they are being observed (and research ethics usually requires that they do know). To minimize this problem, researchers typically observe people long enough for them to get used to the situation and begin behaving more naturally. But the observations themselves can be distorted or incomplete if the observers are not well trained or are biased about what they expect to see. In addition, researchers cannot draw conclusions about cause and effect from observation alone, although what they see can provide many testable ideas about what is causing what.

Case Studies

A **case study** intensively examines some event or phenomenon in a particular individual, group, or situation. Often, case studies combine observations, tests, interviews, and analysis of written records. Case studies are especially useful when a phenomenon is new, complex, or rare. They have a long tradition in clinical psychology. Freud's development of psychoanalysis, for example, was based on case studies of people whose paralysis or other physical symptoms disappeared when they were hypnotized or asleep.

Case studies have played a special role in neuropsychology, which focuses on the relationships among brain activity, thinking, and behavior. Consider the case of Dr. P., a patient described by neurologist Oliver Sacks (1985). Dr. P. was a distinguished musician who began to show odd symptoms. He could not recognize familiar people or distinguish between people and things. For instance, while he and his wife were at the neurologist's office, Dr. P. mistook his foot for his shoe. When he rose to leave, he tried to lift off his wife's head as if it were a hat and put it on his own head. He could not name common objects, but he could describe them. When handed a glove, for example, he said, "A continuous surface, infolded on itself. It appears to have . . . five outpouchings, if this is the word . . . a container of some sort." Only later, when he put it on his hand, did he

case study A research design involving the intensive examination of some phenomenon in a particular individual, group, or situation.

DESIGNING SURVEY RESEARCH Whether gay men and lesbians should be allowed to serve openly in the U.S. military is a controversial issue. To appreciate the difficulty of conducting survey research on such topics, try writing a question about this issue that you think is clear enough and neutral enough to generate valid data. Show your question to some friends. Do they agree that it would be a good survey question?

exclaim, "My God, it's a glove!" (Sacks, 1985, p. 13). Using case studies like this one, pioneers in neuropsychology noted the symptoms suffered by people with particular kinds of brain damage or disease. Eventually, neuropsychologists were able to tie specific disorders to certain types of injuries, poisons, and other causes. In Dr. P.'s case, it was probably a large brain tumor that caused his symptoms.

Case studies do have their limitations. They may not represent people in general, and they may contain only the evidence a particular researcher considered important. Nonetheless, case studies provide valuable raw material for further research and can serve as the testing ground for new treatments, training programs, and other applications of research.

Surveys

Whereas case studies give a close-up view of an individual, **surveys** give broad portraits of large groups. A survey uses interviews or questionnaires to ask people about their behavior, attitudes, beliefs, opinions, or intentions. Just as politicians and advertisers rely on opinion polls to test the popularity of policies or products, psychologists use surveys to gather descriptive data on just about any behavior or mental process. However, the validity of survey data depends partly on the wording of survey questions (Schwarz, 1999). This point was vividly illustrated in a nationwide survey of Americans' opinion of President Bill Clinton in August 1998, just after he admitted to having an adulterous affair with a young White House intern. Only 40 percent of those responding said their opinion was favorable—suggesting a 20-point drop from his previous popularity surveys. However, the wording used in the new survey had been changed. The August 1998 poll asked people to say what they thought of Bill Clinton *as a person*, but pollsters in the previous surveys had named famous individuals, including Mr. Clinton, one by one and asked people whether they had a favorable or unfavorable opinion *of this person*. When this original wording was used again just a day after the August 1998 survey, 55 percent of respondents said they had a favorable opinion of President Clinton, a drop of only 5 percentage points.

A survey's validity also depends on who is surveyed and who chooses to respond (Rogelberg & Luong, 1998). If the particular people surveyed do not fairly represent the views of the population you are interested in, it is easy to be misled by survey results. If

surveys A research design that involves giving people questionnaires or interviews designed to describe their attitudes, beliefs, opinions, and intentions.

only Clinton supporters had been included in the August 1998 survey, his popularity would have been far higher than if only his opponents had been polled. In either case, the results would only reflect the views of a biased subset of people, not Americans in general.

Other limitations of the survey method are more difficult to avoid. For example, people may be reluctant to admit undesirable or embarrassing things about themselves. They may say what they believe they *should* say about an issue. This is called the *social desirability effect.* Survey results and the conclusions drawn from them can be distorted by these concerns (C. F. Turner, Miller, & Rogers, 1998). They may also be distorted by who *doesn't* respond. Let's say a researcher sends a survey to office workers to find out about workloads. Most likely, the busiest workers would not have time to fill out and return the survey. Thus, the results would underestimate the average workload. Still, surveys provide an efficient way to gather large amounts of data about people's attitudes, beliefs, or other characteristics.

Experiments

Naturalistic observation, case studies, and surveys are valuable for describing and making predictions about behavior and mental processes, but they cannot offer explanations for the results. To make the best choice among alternative explanations and to determine what causes the phenomena they observe, psychological scientists must take control over certain factors, or **variables,** in their research. Controlled research usually takes the form of an experiment.

In an **experiment,** the researcher manipulates one variable and then observes the effect of that manipulation on another variable, while holding all other variables constant. The variable manipulated by the experimenter is called the **independent variable.** The variable that is measured following this manipulation is called the **dependent variable,** because it *depends* on the independent variable. The group that receives the experimental treatment is called the **experimental group.** The group that receives no treatment, or some other treatment, is called the **control group.** Control groups provide baselines against which to compare the performance of the experimental group. If everything about the two groups is exactly the same except for exposure to treatment, then any difference between the groups at the end of the experiment should be due to the treatment.

variables Specific factors or characteristics that can take on different numerical values in research.

experiment A situation in which the researcher manipulates one variable and observes the effect of that manipulation on another variable, while holding all other variables constant.

independent variable In an experiment, the variable manipulated by the researcher.

dependent variable In an experiment, the factor affected by the independent variable.

experimental group The group that receives the experimental treatment. Its performance or response is compared with that of one or more control groups.

control group The group that receives no treatment or provides some other baseline against which to compare the performance or response of the experimental group.

hypothesis In scientific research, a specific, testable proposition about a phenomenon.

FOCUS ON RESEARCH

Studying EMDR

You have probably asked yourself questions such as "What caused that accident?" or "Why did she get so upset?" These are the kinds of questions that scientists ask, too. Curiosity frequently starts the questioning process. For example, Francine Shapiro wanted to know whether, and why, her eye movements caused a reduction in her emotional reactions. The first questions are often too general to be scientifically investigated, but critical thinking can help scientists (and you) narrow the questions enough to clarify the assertion to be evaluated. In the Focus on Research section in each chapter, we will examine a particular study to illustrate how researchers in psychology pose and answer questions about behavior and mental processes. For example,

■ What was the researcher's question?

Psychologists and other scientists typically phrase their questions in terms of a **hypothesis**—a specific, testable statement about something they want to study. Researchers state hypotheses to establish in clear, precise terms what they think may be true, and how they will know if it is not. Shapiro's hypothesis was *EMDR treatment causes significant reduction in anxiety.*

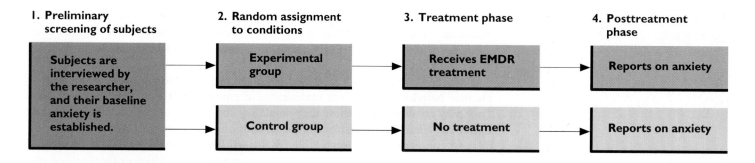

1. Preliminary screening of subjects	2. Random assignment to conditions	3. Treatment phase	4. Posttreatment phase
Subjects are interviewed by the researcher, and their baseline anxiety is established.	Experimental group	Receives EMDR treatment	Reports on anxiety
	Control group	No treatment	Reports on anxiety

FIGURE 1.4

A Simple Two-Group Experiment

Ideally, the only difference between the experimental and control group in experiments like this one is whether the participants receive the treatment the experimenter wishes to evaluate. Under such ideal circumstances, at the end of the experiment any difference in the two groups' reported levels of anxiety (the dependent variable) should be attributable to whether or not they received treatment (the independent variable).

operational definitions   Statements that define phenomena or variables by describing the exact research operations or methods used in measuring them.

confounding variable   Any factor that affects the dependent variable along with, or instead of, the independent variable.

random variables   Confounding variables—specifically, uncontrolled or uncontrollable factors that affect the dependent variable along with, or instead of, the independent variable.

▦ How did the researcher answer the question?

To understand and evaluate hypotheses, scientists use **operational definitions,** which are statements describing the exact operations or methods used in their research. In Shapiro's hypothesis, *EMDR treatment* was operationally defined as having a certain number of back-and-forth eye movements per second for a particular period of time. And *significant reduction in anxiety* was defined as a certain amount of reduction in clients' self-reported discomfort.

Shapiro performed an experiment in an attempt to better understand the effects of EMDR. She first identified twenty-two people suffering the ill effects of traumas such as rape or military combat. These were her research participants, as you can see in Figure 1.4. She assigned the participants to two groups. The first group received a single session of EMDR for about fifty minutes. The second group focused on their unpleasant memories for eight minutes, but without moving their eyes back and forth (F. Shapiro, 1989b). The experimenter controlled whether EMDR treatment was given to each participant, so the presence or absence of treatment was the independent variable. The participants' anxiety level was the dependent variable. In Shapiro's experiment, having a control group allowed her to measure how much change in anxiety might be expected from exposure to bad memories without EMDR treatment.

▦ What did the researcher find?

The results of F. Shapiro's (1989b) experiment showed that participants receiving EMDR treatment experienced a complete and nearly immediate reduction in anxiety related to their traumatic memories. Those in the control group showed no such change.

▦ What do the results mean?

At this point, you might be ready to believe that the treatment caused the difference. Before coming to that conclusion, though, look again at the structure, or *design*, of the experiment. The treatment group's session lasted about fifty minutes. The control group focused on their memories for only eight minutes. Would the people in the control group have improved if they had also spent fifty minutes focusing on their memories? We do not know, because the experiment did not compare methods of equal length. It is all too easy for people, scientists included, to look only for evidence that supports their hypothesis, especially if they expect or hope the hypothesis is true. This common human failing is called *confirmation bias*. Scientists have a responsibility to combat confirmation bias by looking for contradictory as well as supporting evidence for even their most cherished hypotheses.

▦ What do we still need to know?

Experiments are now being conducted that introduce enough control into the treatment situation to evaluate alternative explanations for the EMDR effect. Most of the controlled studies completed so far cast doubt on whether the eye movements in EMDR are causing clients' improvement (e.g., Carrigan & Levis, 1999; Cusack & Spates, 1999; G. M. Rosen, 1999), but we still don't know for sure what *is* producing the effects that EMDR proponents report.

Anyone who conducts or relies on research must be on guard for flaws in experimental design and control. Before drawing any conclusions from research, experimenters need to consider other factors, especially variables that could confuse, or *confound,* interpretation of the results.

Any factor that might have affected the dependent variable, along with or instead of the independent variable, may operate as a **confounding variable.** When confounding variables are present, the experimenter cannot know whether the independent variable or the confounding variable produced the results. Let's consider three sources of confounding variables: random variables, participants' expectations, and experimenter bias.

Random Variables   Uncontrolled, and sometimes uncontrollable, factors such as differences among the participants' backgrounds, personalities, physical health, or vulnerability to stress are examples of **random variables.** Experimenters cannot create groups that are alike on all random variables. To solve this problem, or at least control it, they do all they can to keep constant the temperature, noise, and other environmental circumstances that might affect participants' behavior. They also flip a coin or use some other random process to assign each participant to experimental or control groups. Such procedures, called **random assignment,** tend to spread the effects of uncontrolled variables randomly (and probably about evenly) across groups. This minimizes the chance that they will distort the results of the experiment.

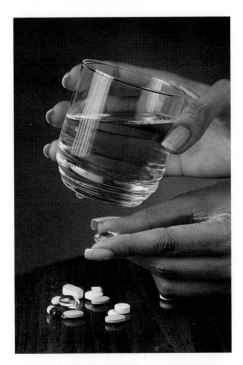

I FEEL BETTER, I THINK   Millions of people spend billions of dollars on shark cartilage, rice-bran extracts, and dozens of equally ineffective "cures" for cancer, arthritis, and other serious diseases. Whatever benefits these remedies might bring appear to arise from placebo effects, the positive expectations generated in patients who believe in them. Placebo effects must be controlled for in research on psychological, as well as medical, treatments.

Expectations: The Placebo Effect   Differences in what participants think about the experimental situation can act as another confounding variable. If participants expect that a treatment will help them, they may try harder to improve than those in a control group who receive no treatment or a less impressive one. Improvement created by a participant's expectations is called the *placebo effect.* A **placebo** (pronounced "plah-SEE-boe") contains nothing known to be helpful, but nevertheless produces benefits because a person *believes* it will do so.

How can researchers determine whether the independent variable or a placebo effect caused a result? Often they include a special control group that receives *only* a placebo. Then they compare results for the experimental group, the placebo group, and those participants receiving no treatment. In one stop-smoking study, for example, participants in a placebo group took sugar pills that the experimenter said would help them endure the stress of giving up cigarettes (D. A. Bernstein, 1970). These participants did as well at quitting as those in the experimental group, who had received extensive treatment. This result suggested that the experimental group's success may have been due largely to the participants' expectations, not to the treatment methods. Some studies suggest the same conclusion about the effects of EMDR, because significant anxiety reduction has been observed in clients who get a version of the treatment that does not involve eye movements or even focusing on traumatic memories (S. P. Cahill, Carrigan, & Frueh, 1999; Cusack & Spates, 1999). Obviously, additional placebo-controlled experiments will have to be done before final conclusions about the value of EMDR can be reached.

Experimenter Bias   Sometimes experimenters can unintentionally affect their results. This **experimenter bias** may introduce another potential confounding variable. Robert Rosenthal (1966) was one of the first to demonstrate the power of experimenter bias. His participants were laboratory assistants who were asked to place rats in a maze. Rosenthal told some of the assistants that their rats were "maze-bright." He told the others that their rats were "maze-dull." In fact, both groups of rats were randomly drawn from the same population and had equal maze-learning capabilities. Surprisingly, the so-called maze-bright animals learned the maze significantly faster than the "maze-dull" ones. Why? Rosenthal concluded that the result had nothing to do with the rats and everything to do with the experimenters. He suggested that the assistants' expectations about their rats' supposedly superior (or inferior) capabilities caused them to slightly alter their training and handling techniques. This alteration, in turn, speeded or slowed the animals' learning.

To prevent experimenter bias from confounding results, experimenters often use a **double-blind design.** In this design, the participants *and* those giving the treatments are

random assignment   The procedure by which random variables are evenly distributed in an experiment—specifically, through placement of participants in experimental and control groups by means of a coin flip or some other random process.

placebo   A physical or psychological treatment that contains no active ingredient but produces an effect because the person receiving it believes it will.

experimenter bias   A confounding variable that occurs when an experimenter unintentionally encourages participants to respond in a way that supports the hypothesis.

double-blind design   A research design in which neither the experimenter nor the participants know who is in the experimental group and who is in the control group.

unaware of, or "blind" to, who is receiving a placebo, and do not know the expected results of the various treatments. Only the director of the study, who makes no contact with participants, has this information, and the director does not reveal it until the end of the experiment. Double-blind studies have not been conducted with EMDR yet, which is another reason for caution in drawing conclusions about this treatment.

In summary, experiments are vital tools for examining cause-effect relationships between variables, but they are also vulnerable to error. To maximize the value of their experiments, scientists try to eliminate as many confounding variables as possible, repeat their work to ensure consistent results, and then carefully interpret results to take into account the limitations or problems that remain.

Quasi-Experiments   Sometimes it is impossible or unethical to create the conditions for a controlled experiment. Consider the problem of studying the hypothesis that drugs taken by a pregnant woman harm her developing baby. A controlled experimental design would randomly assign newly pregnant women to one of two groups. One group would be given the "treatment"—taking cocaine, for example. The other group would get no "treatment." Then, the researchers would observe the condition of the babies delivered by the women in both groups. Such an experiment would be unthinkable, however. To evaluate hypotheses like this one, psychologists might conduct a **quasi-experiment.** A quasi-experiment is designed to approximate the control of a true experiment (*quasi* means "resembling"), but it does not include random assignment of participants to groups or other elements of true experimental control (Shadish, Cook, & Campbell, in press). For example, researchers could measure differences in the characteristics of children whose mothers did or did not use drugs during pregnancy, but they could not firmly state the cause of those differences.

Selecting Human Participants for Research

Psychological research attempts to describe, explain, predict, and control behavior and mental processes. Achieving these goals depends first on the way samples of participants are selected. Psychologists cannot draw conclusions about a population unless they have access to a sample of participants that accurately represents it. **Sampling,** the process of selecting research participants, is a very important component of the research enterprise. Conclusions based on results from a sample can be applied, or *generalized,* only to a population that is like the sample population. In other words, the sample of participants studied must be representative of people in general if the researcher wants results that reveal something about people in general.

If every member of a population to be studied has an equal chance of being chosen as a research participant, the individuals selected constitute a **random sample.** If everyone does not have an equal chance of participating, those selected constitute a **biased sample.** In reality, few researchers are likely to succeed in drawing a random sample from the general population. One practical alternative is to randomly draw a sample from a population that is typical, or *representative,* of some specific population of interest—such as female college students, middle-aged musicians, or members of Britain's Labour Party. If drawn at random, the larger these samples are, the more likely it is that they will represent the population of interest to the researcher.

In fact, a representative sample of the general population may not be necessary or even desirable in some cases. For example, studying language development in the average child may be less valuable than studying the unfortunate child raised in solitary confinement by parents who provided no language instruction (Rymer, 1992). Also, if you want to learn about a specific group (male Asian American accountants, say), your participants should be selected from that group, not from the general population.

Psychologists must also guard against allowing preconceptions about gender, ethnicity, and other variables to influence the questions they ask, the research designs they create, and the way they analyze, interpret, and report their data (Denmark et al., 1988; C. C. I. Hall, 1997). For instance, comparing how long male executives and female secretaries have been at their jobs might create a false impression of greater male job commitment if people in lower-status positions change jobs more often, regardless of gender.

quasi-experiments   Research studies whose designs approximate the control of a true experiment but do not include all elements of experimental control.

sampling   The process of selecting participants who are members of the population that the researcher wishes to study.

random sample   A group of research participants selected from a population each of whose members had an equal chance of being chosen for study.

biased sample   A group of research participants selected from a population each of whose members did not have an equal chance of being chosen for study.

in review

Methods of Psychological Research

Method	Features	Strengths	Pitfalls
Naturalistic observations	Observation of human or animal behavior in the environment where it typically occurs	Provide descriptive data about behavior presumably uncontaminated by outside influences	Observer bias and participant self-consciousness can distort results
Case studies	Intensive examination of the behavior and mental processes associated with a specific person or situation	Provide detailed descriptive analyses of new, complex, or rare phenomena	May not provide representative picture of phenomena
Surveys	Standard sets of questions asked of a large number of participants	Gather large amounts of descriptive data relatively quickly and inexpensively	Sampling errors, poorly phrased questions, and response biases can distort results
Experiments	Manipulation of an independent variable and measurement of its effects on a dependent variable	Can establish a cause-effect relationship between independent and dependent variables	Confounding variables may prevent valid conclusions
Quasi-experiments	Measurement of dependent variables when random assignment to groups is impossible or unethical	Can provide strong evidence suggesting cause-effect relationships	Lack of random assignment may weaken conclusions
All of the above	Choosing among alternative hypotheses; sometimes generating theories	Can expand our understanding of behavior and mental processes	Errors, limitations, and biases in research evidence can lead to incorrect or incomplete explanations

A truer comparison would sample men and women of equal status. Similarly, researchers who use a male-only sample should give this fact the same emphasis in their report as is customarily the case when only females are studied (Ader & Johnson, 1994). To do otherwise would imply that males provide a standard against which females' behavior and mental processes are to be compared. Finally, researchers must report whatever results appear. It is just as valuable to know that men and women, or African Americans and European Americans, did *not* differ on a test of leadership ability as to know that they did. Stephanie Riger (1992) suggests that one of psychologists' greatest challenges is to "disengage themselves sufficiently from commonly shared beliefs so that those beliefs do not predetermine research findings" (p. 732). For a recap of the strategies research psychologists use in their studies, see "In Review: Methods of Psychological Research."

Statistical Analysis of Research Results

■ **When scientists announce a significant breakthrough in research, how can you be sure it is "significant"?**

data Numbers that represent research findings and provide the basis for conclusions.

Regardless of the research methods used, any study usually generates a large amount of data. **Data** are numbers that represent research findings and provide the basis for conclusions. Researchers use *statistical analyses* to summarize and analyze data. These

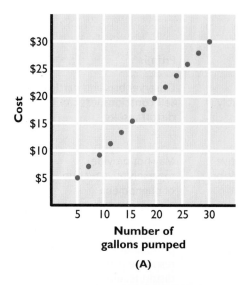

(A)

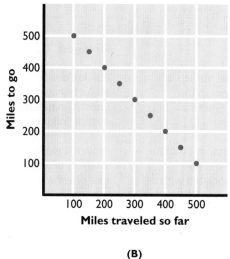

(B)

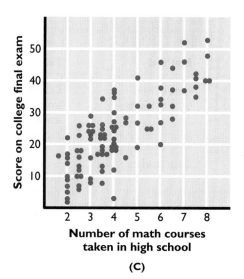

(C)

FIGURE 1.5

Three Correlations

The strength and direction of the correlation between variables can be seen in a graph called a *scatterplot*. In Part A, we have plotted the cost of gasoline against the number of gallons pumped. Because the number of gallons is *positively* and perfectly correlated with their cost, the scatterplot appears as a straight line, and you can predict the value of either variable from a knowledge of the other. Part B shows a perfect *negative* correlation between the number of miles traveled toward a destination and the distance remaining. Again, one variable can be exactly predicted from the other. Part C illustrates a correlation of +.81 between the number of high school math courses students had taken and their scores on a college-level final exam in math (Hays, 1981). As correlations decrease, they are represented by less and less organized scatterplots. A correlation of 0.00 would appear as a shapeless cloud.

correlation   The degree to which one variable is related to another. The strength and direcon of the relationship are measured by a correlation coefficient. Correlation does *not* guarantee causation.

methods include *descriptive statistics* and *inferential statistics*. As the name implies, descriptive statistics describe a set of data. Inferential statistics are mathematical procedures used to draw conclusions from data and to make assumptions about what they mean (these are described in the "Statistics in Psychological Research" Appendix). One important statistical concept that we explore here is *correlation*.

Let's begin with a research question: Do the number of fears people have tend to decrease with age? In general, the answer is yes (Kleinknecht, 1991). To test hypotheses about questions such as this, psychologists must have a way to measure how, and to what extent, variables such as age and fearfulness are related, or correlated. **Correlation** means just what it says: "co-relation." In statistics, it refers both to the strength of the relationship between two variables *and* to the direction of the relationship. A *positive correlation* means that the two variables increase together or decrease together. A *negative correlation* means that the variables move in opposite directions. When one increases, the other decreases. For example, James Schaefer observed 4,500 customers in 65 bars and found that the tempo of the jukebox music was negatively correlated with the rate at which the customers drank alcohol. The slower the tempo, the faster the drinking (Schaefer et al., 1988).

Does this mean Schaefer could wear a blindfold and predict exactly how fast people are drinking by timing the music? Could he plug his ears and determine the musical tempo by watching people's sip rates? No, and no, because the accuracy of predictions about one variable from knowing the other depends on the *strength* of the correlation. Only a perfect correlation between two variables would allow you to predict the exact value of one from a knowledge of the other. The weaker the correlation, the less one variable can tell you about the other.

To describe the strength of a correlation, psychologists calculate a statistic called the *correlation coefficient* (see the appendix on statistics). The correlation coefficient can vary from +1.00 to −1.00. The sign of a correlation coefficient indicates direction. A plus sign signifies a *positive* correlation. A minus sign signifies a *negative* correlation. The *absolute value* of a correlation indicates the strength of the relationship. A perfectly predictable relationship between two variables is indicated by +1.00 or −1.00 (see Figure 1.5). A correlation of 0.00 between people's shoe size and the age of their cars, for example, indicates that there is virtually no relationship between the variables.

Psychologists use correlation coefficients to help them describe and predict phenomena, to evaluate existing hypotheses, and to generate new hypotheses. However, scientists are careful when interpreting correlations. Consider, for example, the positive correlation

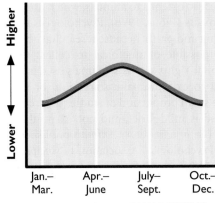

(A) ICE CREAM CONSUMPTION

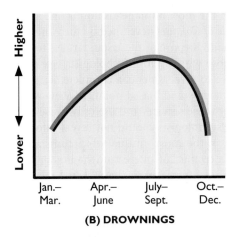

(B) DROWNINGS

FIGURE 1.6

Correlation and Causation

These graphs show that in the United States, ice cream consumption and drownings tend to rise and fall together. However, this positive correlation does not mean that eating ice cream causes drowning. In this case, the correlation probably reflects a third variable—time of year—that affects both ice cream sales and the likelihood of swimming and boating.

statistically significant Referring to a correlation, or a difference between two groups, that is larger than would be expected by chance.

that has been found between watching violent television programs and behaving violently. Does seeing violence on TV cause viewers to be violent, or does being violent to begin with cause a preference for violent shows? Perhaps neither causes the other; violent behavior *and* TV choices could both be due to a third factor, such as personality. The mere fact that two variables are correlated does not mean that one is causing an effect on the other. And even if one *is* causing an effect on the other, a correlation coefficient cannot say which variable is influencing which. In short, correlations can reveal and describe relationships, but correlations alone cannot explain them. Remember, correlation does not guarantee causation (see Figure 1.6).

When a correlation coefficient is larger than would be expected by chance alone, it is said to be **statistically significant** (see the appendix on statistics). Statistical significance alone does not constitute final "proof" (J. N. Hunter, 1997), but scientists pay more attention to correlations or other research findings that are statistically significant, especially when those results are repeated, or *replicated,* in separate studies (Rosenthal, 1996). So, when thinking critically about research, part of the process of evaluating evidence about hypotheses is to ask whether a researcher's results are statistically significant and repeatable.

Ethical Guidelines for Psychologists

Do psychologists trick people to get research data?

Statistics can easily be misunderstood. They can also be manipulated. A few years ago newspaper headlines stated, "Hair dye causes cancer." Hairdressers were alarmed at first, then angry. The information given to the public was less than accurate. In the actual study, rats—not humans—had been used. The rats *drank* the hair dye, and yes, they developed cancer.

Spectacular headlines sell newspapers, but scientific psychologists have an ethical obligation not to manipulate, distort, or sensationalize their research results. The obligation to analyze and report research fairly and accurately is just one of the ethical standards that guide psychologists. Preservation of the welfare and dignity of their research participants is another. Although researchers *could* measure anxiety by putting a loaded gun to people's heads, or study marital conflicts by telling one partner that the other has been unfaithful, such methods are potentially harmful and therefore unethical.

In each of these examples, the ethical course of action is obvious: The psychologist must find another way to conduct the research. In practice, ethical choices are often more complicated. Many experiments reflect a compromise between the need to protect participants from harm and the need to learn about the unknown. In cases where a study is likely to create risks or discomfort for participants, researchers must present the study to a research review committee whose members have no connection to the research. The committee weighs the potential benefits of the work in terms of knowledge and human welfare against any potential harm. They ensure that the researcher has minimized any discomfort and risk to the participants and that they will not suffer any long-term negative consequences. Researchers must also inform potential participants about every aspect of the study that might influence their decision to participate and ensure that each individual's involvement is voluntary. Can a researcher withhold information about a study because full disclosure in advance would bias a participant's behavior? Can participants be given inaccurate information to create mild annoyance, a sense of time urgency, or some other temporary condition essential to the study? Review committees may allow such deceptions but require the researcher to "debrief" the participants as soon as the study is over by revealing all relevant information about the research and correcting any false impressions it created. If these protections and ethical obligations have been observed, the committee is likely to allow the research to be done.

CARING FOR RESEARCH ANIMALS
Psychologists are careful to protect the welfare of the animals they study. They take no pleasure in animals' suffering, and besides, inflicting undue stress on research animals can create reactions that can act as confounding variables. For example, in a study of how learning is affected by the size of food rewards, the researcher could starve animals to make them hungry enough to want the rewards. But this would introduce discomfort that would make it impossible to separate the effects of the reward from the effects of starvation.

The obligation to protect participants' welfare also extends to animals, which are used in about 8 percent of psychological research projects (Plous, 1996). Psychologists study animals partly because their behavior is interesting and partly because research with animals can yield information that would be impossible or unethical to collect using humans. Contrary to the allegations of some animal-rights activists, animals used in psychological research are not routinely subjected to extreme pain, starvation, or other inhumane conditions (Novak, 1991). Even in the small proportion of studies that require the use of electric shock, the discomfort created is mild, brief, and not harmful. The Animal Welfare Act, the *Guide for the Care and Use of Laboratory Animals* published by the National Institutes of Health, the American Psychological Association's *Principles on Animal Use,* and other laws and regulations set high standards for the care and treatment of animals in research. In those relatively rare studies that require animals to undergo short-lived pain, legal and ethical standards require the psychologist to persuade funding agencies and local animal research–monitoring committees that the discomfort is justified by the expected benefits to human welfare.

The responsibility for conducting research in the most humane fashion is one aspect of the *Ethical Principles of Psychologists and Code of Conduct* developed by the American Psychological Association (APA, 1992b). The main purpose of these standards is to protect and promote the welfare of society and those with whom psychologists work. For example, as teachers, psychologists should strive to give students a complete, accurate, and up-to-date view of each topic. Presenting narrow and biased points of view would be unethical. Psychologists should perform only those services and use only those techniques for which they are adequately trained. Psychologists should not reveal information obtained from clients or students, except in the most unusual of circumstances. Finally, they should avoid situations in which a conflict of interest might impair their judgment or harm someone else. They should not, for example, have sexual relations with their clients, students, or employees.

Despite these guidelines, doubt and controversy arise in some cases about whether a proposed experiment or a particular practice, such as deceiving participants, is ethical (e.g., Kimmel, 1998; Ortmann & Hertwig, 1997). Indeed, ethical principles for psychologists will continue to evolve as psychologists face new and more complex ethical issues (Biaggio, Paget, & Chenoweth, 1997; S. Martin, 1999).

LINKAGES
Is behavior influenced more by our genes or by our environment? (a link to Biology and Behavior)

M ark and John were identical twins separated at birth. The separation occurred because their parents were unmarried and poor. They offered the children to an immigrant couple, but the couple could care for only one of the twins. John grew up with them, secure and loved. Mark went from orphanage to foster home to hospital and, finally, back to his natural father's second wife. The boys' environments had been completely different, yet their genes were the same.

They met for the first time at twenty-four years of age. They were physically alike. The same molars were giving them toothaches. There were also similarities in their behavior and mental processes. They used the same aftershave, smoked the same brand of cigarettes, brushed with the same imported brand of toothpaste, and liked the same sports. Both had served in the military, having joined within eight days of each other. Testing by a psychologist found they had nearly identical overall IQ scores.

Our genes intertwine with our environment to shape behavior and mental processes. Genetic inheritance is often called our biological *nature*. The environmental conditions and events before and after birth are referred to as *nurture*. Exploring the influences of nature and nurture in relation to perception, personality, mental ability, mental disorders, and other phenomena has taken psychologists into the field of *behavioral genetics*. Most behavioral tendencies can be influenced by many different genes, but also by the environ-

LINKAGES

Psychological Research and Behavioral Genetics

Separated at birth, the Mallifert twins meet accidentally.

ment. Researchers in behavioral genetics explore the *relative roles* of genetic and environmental factors in creating differences among behavioral tendencies in *groups* of people.

Early research in behavioral genetics relied on the selective breeding of animals. For example, Robert Tryon (1940) mated rats who were fast maze learners with other fast learners and mated slower learners with other slow learners. After repeating this process for several generations, he found that the offspring of the fast learners were significantly better at maze learning than those of the slow learners.

Selective-breeding studies must be interpreted with caution, though, because it is not specific behaviors that are inherited. What *are* inherited are differing sets of physical structures, capacities, and the like, which in turn make certain behaviors more or less likely. These behavioral tendencies are often very specific, and they can be altered by the environment (Gottlieb, 2000). For example, selectively bred "maze-dull" rats performed just as well as "maze-bright" rats on many tasks other than maze learning (Searle, 1949). And, when raised in an environment containing tunnels and other stimulating features, "dull" animals did as well at maze learning as "bright" ones. Both groups did equally poorly in the maze after being raised in an environment that lacked stimulating features (R. M. Cooper & Zubek, 1958).

Research on behavioral genetics in humans must be interpreted with even greater care. First, environmental influences have an enormous impact on human behavior. Second, legal, moral, and ethical considerations prohibit manipulations such as selective breeding, so research in human behavioral genetics depends on studies in which control is imperfect. Some of the most important research designs are family studies, twin studies, and adoption studies (Pike & Plomin, 1996; N. L. Segal, 1993).

In *family studies,* researchers look at whether close family relatives are more likely than distant ones to show similarities in behavior and mental processes. If increasing similarity is associated with closer family ties, the similarities might be inherited. For example, data from family studies suggest a genetic basis for schizophrenia, as Figure 1.7 shows. Remember, though, that correlation does not guarantee causation. Family studies alone cannot establish the role of genetic factors in mental disorders or other characteristics. Close relatives tend to share environments as well as genes. Therefore, similarities in close relatives might stem from environmental factors instead of, or in addition to, genetic ones.

Twin studies explore the nature-nurture mix by comparing similarities seen in identical twins with those of nonidentical twins. Twins usually share the same environment

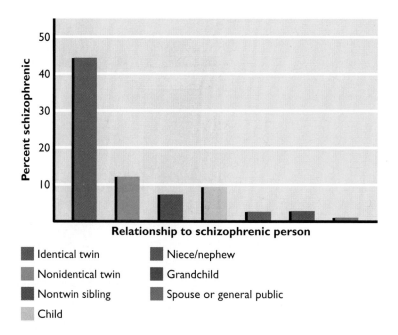

FIGURE 1.7

Family Studies of Schizophrenia

Data from family studies show that the risk of developing schizophrenia, a severe mental disorder described in Chapter 12, is highest for the siblings and children of schizophrenics and is lowest for people with no genetic relationship to a schizophrenic. Does this mean that schizophrenia is inherited? The data are certainly consistent with that interpretation, but the question cannot be answered through family studies alone.

- Identical twin
- Nonidentical twin
- Nontwin sibling
- Child
- Niece/nephew
- Grandchild
- Spouse or general public

and may also be treated very much the same by parents and others. So, if identical twins—whose genes are the same—are more alike on some characteristics than nonidentical twins (whose genes are no more similar than those of other siblings), those characteristics may have a significant genetic component.

Adoption studies take advantage of the naturally occurring quasi-experiments that happen when babies are adopted. The logic of these studies is that if adopted children's characteristics are more like those of their biological parents than those of their adoptive parents, genetics probably plays a clear role in those characteristics. In fact, the personalities of young adults who were adopted at birth tend to be more like those of their biological parents than those of their adoptive parents. Especially valuable are adoption studies of identical twins who, like Mark and John, were separated soon after birth. If identical twins show similar characteristics after years of living in very different environments, the role of heredity in those characteristics is highlighted. Adoption studies of intelligence tend to support the role of genetics in variations in mental ability. However, environmental influences are important, too.

Remember that behavioral genetics research looks at the relative roles of heredity and environment that underlie group differences. It cannot determine the degree to which a *particular* person's behavior is due to heredity or environment.

active review   Introduction to the Science of Psychology

Summary

THE WORLD OF PSYCHOLOGY: AN OVERVIEW

■ **What is psychology, and how did it grow?**

Psychology is the science that seeks to understand behavior and mental processes. The broad concept of "behavior and mental processes" encompasses virtually all aspects of what it means to be a human being. Psychologists study a wide variety of topics, ranging from the activity of individual nerve cells, to the way people sense and perceive

things, think, make decisions, and experience emotion, to the way people create, and interact in, societies.

Human beings have always sought to understand themselves, but the modern science of psychology began to emerge in the late nineteenth century as philosophers and scientists in Germany and North America established laboratories to conduct scientific research in psychology. In Germany, Wundt explored the building blocks of *consciousness* (Gestalt psychologists there later studied it as a whole), and in Vienna, Freud explored the unconscious. At the same time in the United States, James was applying Darwin's theory of evolution to the exploration of human behavior. In the early twentieth century, Watson argued that to be truly scientific, psychologists should focus only on observable behavior. He founded behaviorism, which dominated psychology for decades. Today, consciousness—in the form of cognitive processes—is being intensively studied once again.

APPROACHES TO THE SCIENCE OF PSYCHOLOGY
Why don't all psychologists explain behavior in the same way?

Psychologists are unified by their commitment to *empirical* research and scientific methods, by their linked interests, and by the legacy of psychology's founders. Psychologists differ in their approaches to psychology—that is, in the assumptions, questions, and methods they believe will be most helpful in their work. Those psychologists adopting a *biological approach* examine how physiological factors shape behavior and mental processes. Research by ethologists helped stimulate the *evolutionary approach,* which emphasizes the inherited, adaptive aspects of behavior and mental processes. The *psychodynamic approach* sees behavior and mental processes as a struggle to resolve conflicts between impulses and the demands made by society to control those impulses. Psychologists who take the *behavioral approach* consider behavior to be determined primarily by learning based on experiences with rewards and punishments. The *cognitive approach* assumes that behavior can be understood through analysis of the basic mental processes that underlie it. And the *humanistic approach* views behavior as controlled by the decisions that people make about their lives based on their perceptions of the world.

Because the subject matter of psychology is so diverse, most psychologists work in particular subfields within the discipline. For example, *cognitive psychologists* focus on basic psychological processes such as learning, memory, and perception. *Personality psychologists* focus on characteristics that set people apart from one another. *Developmental psychologists* specialize in trying to understand the development of behavior and mental processes over a lifetime. *Quantitative psychologists* develop methods for statistical analysis of research data. *Clinical* and *counseling psychologists* provide direct service to troubled people and conduct research on abnormal behavior. *Community psychologists* work to prevent mental disorders and extend mental health services to those who need it. *Educational psychologists* conduct and apply research on teaching and learning, whereas *school psychologists* specialize in assessing and alleviating children's academic problems. *Social psychologists* examine questions regarding how people influence one another; *industrial-organizational* psychologists investigate ways to improve satisfaction and performance in the workplace. Health psychologists, sport psychologists, environmental psychologists, and forensic psychologists exemplify some of psychology's many other subfields. Psychologists often work in more than one subfield, share knowledge with colleagues in other subfields, and contribute to knowledge in other disciplines.

HUMAN DIVERSITY AND PSYCHOLOGY
How does your cultural background influence your behavior?

Most of the prominent figures in psychology's history were white males, but women and members of ethnic minority groups made important contributions from the start, and they continue to do so. Psychologists are increasingly taking into account the influence of *culture* and other *sociocultural variables* such as gender and ethnicity in shaping human behavior and mental processes.

THINKING CRITICALLY ABOUT PSYCHOLOGY (OR ANYTHING ELSE)
How can critical thinking save you money?

Critical thinking is the process of assessing claims and making judgments on the basis of well-supported evidence. This process can unfold by asking five questions: What am I being asked to believe? Is there evidence available to support the claim? Can that evidence be interpreted another way? What evidence would help to evaluate the alternatives? What conclusions are most reasonable?

RESEARCH DESIGNS IN PSYCHOLOGY
How do psychologists learn about people?

Research in psychology, as in other sciences, focuses on four main goals: description, prediction, control, and explanation.

Often, questions about psychological phenomena are phrased in terms of *hypotheses* about *variables* that are operationally defined. Evidence for hypotheses must be evaluated for *reliability* and *validity.* Explanations of phenomena often take the form of *theories,* which are integrated sets of propositions that can be used to account for, predict, and even control certain phenomena. Theories must be subjected to rigorous evaluation.

Naturalistic observation entails watching without interfering as behavior occurs in the natural environment. *Case studies* are intensive examinations of a particular individual, group, or situation. *Surveys* ask questions, through interviews or questionnaires, about behavior, attitudes, beliefs, opinions, and intentions. In *experiments,* researchers manipulate an *independent variable* and observe the effect of that manipulation on a *dependent variable. Operational definitions* describe each variable by the way it is measured. Participants receiving experimental treatment are called the *experimental group.* Participants in comparison conditions are called *control groups.*

Experiments can reveal cause-effect relationships between variables, but only if researchers use *random assignment, placebo* conditions, *double-blind designs,* and other strategies to avoid being misled by *random variables, experimenter bias,* and other *confounding variables.* When ethics or other concerns prevent full experimental control, researchers sometimes employ *quasi-experiments.*

Psychologists' research can be limited if their *sampling* procedures do not give them a representative cross-section of the population they want to study and about which they want to draw conclusions. Anything other than a *random sample* is said to be a *biased sample* of participants.

STATISTICAL ANALYSIS OF RESEARCH RESULTS
When scientists announce a significant breakthrough in research, how can you be sure it is "significant"?

Psychologists use descriptive and inferential statistical analyses to summarize and analyze *data,* the numbers that represent research findings and provide the basis for conclusions. A *correlation* is the degree to which one variable is related to another. Although often valuable to research, correlations alone cannot establish that two variables are causally related; nor can they determine which variable might affect which, or why. When a correlation coefficient is larger than would be expected by chance alone, it is said to be *statistically significant.*

ETHICAL GUIDELINES FOR PSYCHOLOGISTS

■ **Do psychologists trick people to get research data?**

Ethical guidelines promote the protection of human and animal participants in psychological research, and set the highest standards for behavior in all other aspects of psychologists' professional lives.

Learn by Doing

Put It in Writing

Choose one or two recent newspaper or magazine articles describing a research study in psychology, and then, based on the article alone, try to answer the five critical thinking questions we described earlier (*What am I being asked to believe or accept?, Is there evidence available to support the claim?, Can that evidence be interpreted another way?, What evidence would help to evaluate the alternatives?*, and *What conclusions are most reasonable?*). When you have finished, write a paragraph or two describing how well you think the popular press covers the results of scientific research in psychology, and how such coverage could be improved.

Personal Learning Activity

Try designing an experiment on a hypothesis of your choice. First, state your hypothesis as specifically as possible, being sure to include operational definitions of the independent and dependent variables. Then tell where you will get your research participants, what the experimental and control groups will experience, and what all your research procedures will be. For example, if your hypothesis is that rock music played during studying improves students' memory for the material, then you should decide what you mean by *rock music* and *improved memory,* what the experimental and control groups will hear while studying, what they will study, and how you will measure the students' memory for what they learned. *For additional projects, see the Personal Learning Activities in the corresponding chapter of the study guide that accompanies this text.*

Step into Action

Courses

History and Systems of Psychology
Experimental Psychology

Movies

Gorillas in the Mist (naturalistic observation)
The Joy Luck Club (cultural influences on behavior)

Books

Roger Baker and Herbert Wright, *One Boy's Day* (Harper, 1951) (naturalistic observation)
Michael B. Thorne and Tracy B. Henley, *Connections in the History and Systems of Psychology* (2nd ed.)

(Houghton Mifflin, 2001) (approaches to the science of psychology)

The Web

The World Wide Web is a good source of additional information about the science of psychology, provided you use it carefully and think critically about the information you find. The PsychAbilities web site that accompanies this text offers many resources relevant to this chapter. These resources include interactive NetLab exercises; Thinking Critically and Evaluating Research exercises; ACE chapter quizzes; recommended web links; and articles on current events, books, and movies. At http://college.hmco.com, select *Psychology* and then this textbook.

Review of Key Terms

Can you define each of the key terms in the chapter? Check your definitions against those on the pages listed in parentheses below or in the Glossary/Index at the end of the text.

behavioral approach *(p. 9)*

biased sample *(p. 26)*

biological approach *(p. 9)*

biological psychologists *(p. 11)*

case study *(p. 21)*

clinical and counseling
 psychologists *(p. 11)*

cognitive approach *(p. 9)*

cognitive psychologists *(p. 11)*

community psychologists
 (p. 11)

confounding variable *(p. 25)*

consciousness *(p. 5)*

control group *(p. 23)*

correlation *(p. 28)*

critical thinking *(p. 18)*

culture *(p. 15)*

data *(p. 27)*

dependent variable *(p. 23)*

developmental psychologists
  (p. 11)

double-blind design *(p. 26)*

educational psychologists
  (p. 11)

empiricism *(p. 4)*

evolutionary approach *(p. 9)*

experiment *(p. 23)*

experimental group *(p. 23)*

experimenter bias *(p. 25)*

humanistic approach *(p. 10)*

hypothesis *(p. 23)*

independent variable *(p. 23)*

industrial-organizational
  psychologists *(p. 11)*

naturalistic observation *(p. 20)*

operational definitions *(p. 24)*

personality psychologists
  (p. 11)

placebo *(p. 25)*

psychodynamic approach *(p. 9)*

psychology *(p. 3)*

quantitative psychologists *(p. 11)*

quasi-experiments *(p. 26)*

random assignment *(p. 25)*

random sample *(p. 26)*

random variables *(p. 25)*

reliability *(p. 20)*

sampling *(p. 26)*

school psychologists *(p. 11)*

social psychologists *(p. 11)*

sociocultural variables *(p. 15)*

statistically significant *(p. 29)*

survey *(p. 22)*

theory *(p. 20)*

validity *(p. 20)*

variables *(p. 23)*

Multiple Choice Self-Test

Select the best answer for each of the questions below. Then check your response against the Answer Key at the end of the text.

1. Introspection was a research method used primarily by _____ to discover the elements of consciousness.

   a. structuralists
   b. behaviorists
   c. functionalists
   d. ethologists

2. To understand what rewards a child receives for bullying other children, a behaviorist would use

   a. cognitive science.
   b. functional analysis of behavior.
   c. introspection.
   d. psychoanalysis.

3. Psychologists who emphasize the role of mental processes in explaining behavior take a(n) _____ approach.

   a. evolutionary
   b. biological
   c. cognitive
   d. deterministic

4. Sue purchased what a breeder claims are two purebred Abyssinian cats, Chessie and Baby. She hypothesizes that Baby is not really pure in breed because she doesn't act like Chessie. According to the critical thinking steps in your text, what does Sue need to do?

   a. Restate her hypothesis.
   b. Ignore the behavioral differences between her two cats.
   c. Compare the behavior of other Abyssinians to her cats' behavior.
   d. Conclude that one of her cats is not purebred.

5. A hypothesis is a

   a. method of control used in experiments.
   b. method of describing a psychological phenomenon.
   c. specific, testable proposition about a phenomenon.
   d. theory in its final form.

6. Dr. McMarty has collected data by doing case studies and naturalistic observation on a phenomenon never studied before. Her next step will probably be to

   a. design an experiment.
   b. examine the data for patterns or relationships among the variables.
   c. check for statistical significance.
   d. form an explanation that will lead to a theory.

7. Case studies are used to

   a. avoid a placebo effect.
   b. determine the effects of an independent variable.
   c. collect descriptive data.
   d. provide control in an experiment.

8. Before using survey results to support a hypothesis, we must be sure that

   a. the questions are properly worded.
   b. the sample used is representative of the population of interest.
   c. the responses are not biased by efforts to appear "socially acceptable."
   d. all of the above

9. Dr. Daneli believes that memory is aided by an increase in the neurotransmitter serotonin. To avoid confounding the results of his experiment aimed at testing this hypothesis, he should use a(n) _____ design.

   a. operational
   b. naturalistic
   c. random
   d. double-blind

10. In Dr. Daneli's experiment, Group A receives serotonin before being given a memory test, while Group B takes the same test without being given serotonin. In this experiment, performance on the memory test is the _____ variable.

    a. dependent
    b. independent
    c. control
    d. random

11. José believes that growing up in an abusive family causes children to become physically violent. He wants to draw the strongest possible conclusions about causality with the fewest ethical concerns; therefore, he should use

    a. case studies.
    b. an experiment.
    c. a quasi-experiment.
    d. a survey.

12. Jeremy designed an experiment to test the effects of praise on the sharing behavior of children. Children in Group A will be praised after they share; children in Group B will only be observed. Group A is the _____ group.

    a. control
    b. experimental
    c. operational
    d. random

13. Correlation coefficients are said to be statistically significant if they are

    a. greater than .30.
    b. positive.
    c. larger than would be expected by chance.
    d. greater than .30 and positive.

14. Choose the strongest correlation coefficient.

    a. +.75
    b. −.99
    c. +.01
    d. −.01

15. A correlation coefficient can tell us all of the following, except the _____ of a relationship between two variables.

    a. strength
    b. direction
    c. existence
    d. cause

16. Larry says that people act the way they learned to act. He believes that if others stop rewarding a person's annoying behavior, that behavior will lessen. Larry most likely takes a(n) _____ approach to psychology.

    a. behavioral
    b. cognitive
    c. evolutionary
    d. humanistic

17. Species-specific behaviors are

    a. instinctive.
    b. learned.
    c. probably not adaptive.
    d. seen in birds, but not mammals.

18. Which of the following is the correct list of scientific research goals?

    a. adjudication, prediction, control, and explanation
    b. random guessing, understanding, reasoning, and control
    c. description, uncritical thinking, control, and explanation
    d. description, prediction, control, and explanation

19. Which of the following is not a possible random variable?

    a. treatment given to participants
    b. room temperature
    c. time of day
    d. participants' personalities

20. Why do psychologists follow ethical guidelines?

    a. Psychologists would not want the cost of participating in an experiment to be too high in comparison with the information to be gained.
    b. The American Psychological Association has set standards for psychologists to follow when conducting research and treating clients.
    c. Stress and pain could act as confounding variables in an experiment.
    d. all of the above

2

Biology and Behavior

Everything we do, from blinking at a bright light to falling in love, has a biological

basis. Why and how we behave and think is, in large part, the story of how the brain and body work. In this chapter we tell that story, beginning with a basic biological unit of the body, a specialized cell called the *neuron*. Collections of neurons form the systems that receive information from our senses; process that information; and translate it into behavior, thoughts, and biochemical changes. Chemicals in our bodies activate our nervous systems and maintain our hormones in delicate balance.

Reading this chapter will help you to answer the following questions:

- **What are neurons, and what do they do?**
- **How do biochemicals affect my mood?**
- **How is my nervous system organized?**
- **How is my brain "wired"?**
- **How can my hormones help me in a crisis?**

W hat do Ronald Reagan, Muhammad Ali, Michael J. Fox, and Christopher Reeve all have in common? Each of these men has a nervous system disorder that affects his behavior. Former president Reagan has severe Alzheimer's disease; former heavyweight boxing champ Ali has Parkinson's syndrome; and Fox, who recently gave up his role in the TV show *Spin City,* is in the early stages of Parkinson's disease. Reeve, who starred in the *Superman* movies, is paralyzed as a result of damage to his spinal cord. Medical research has not yet found cures for these disorders, although it has developed treatments that attempt to reverse or minimize the symptoms and suffering. You may know others whose behavior has changed because of a devastating biological condition.

Indeed, biological factors are intimately related to all behavior and mental processes. It is not a question of *whether* biology has an impact on behavior, but a question of *how.* This is the realm of **biological psychology**—the study of cells, genes, and organs of the body and the physical, hormonal, and chemical changes involved in behavior and mental processes. All behavior and mental processes are *based* on biological processes, but those processes are also influenced by the environment. In this chapter we begin to consider the relationship between the body and mind, the brain and behavior.

Understanding how we think, feel, act, and react requires knowledge of our body and how it works. Two primary systems—the nervous system and the endocrine system—direct the activities of the body. The nervous system receives information, sends messages from one part of the body to another, and initiates action. The endocrine system regulates internal activity of the body with glands that secrete chemicals, called *hormones*, into the bloodstream to control metabolism, reactions to stress, sexual functioning, and the like. These are the basic pieces of the puzzle of the body. Putting the pieces together is the next step in understanding our complex behavior.

biological psychology The study of physical and chemical changes involved in behavior and mental processes.

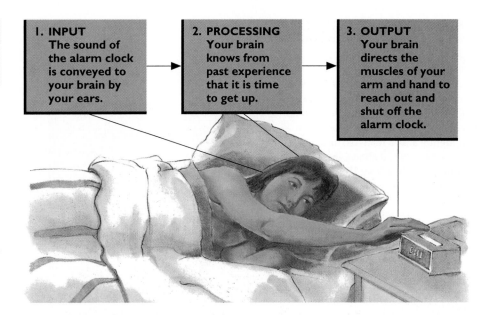

FIGURE 2.1

Three Functions of the Nervous System

The nervous system's three main functions are to receive information (input), integrate that information with past experiences (processing), and guide actions (output). When the alarm clock goes off, this person's nervous system, like yours, gets the message, recognizes what it means, and takes action—to get out of bed or perhaps just hit the snooze button!

1. **INPUT** The sound of the alarm clock is conveyed to your brain by your ears.

2. **PROCESSING** Your brain knows from past experience that it is time to get up.

3. **OUTPUT** Your brain directs the muscles of your arm and hand to reach out and shut off the alarm clock.

Cells of the Nervous System

What are neurons, and what do they do?

The nervous system is a vast network of cells that work together to let us see and hear, think about things, and move. Scientists are exploring the nervous system at many levels—from the individual cell to the most complex networks of cells. We begin our exploration of the nervous system at the "bottom," with a description of its individual cells. Then we consider how these cells are organized to form the structures of the human nervous system.

Neurons

Every thought, every feeling, and every action are somehow represented in the nervous system. The nervous system is a complex combination of cells that allows you to gain information about what is going on inside and outside your body and to respond appropriately. As Figure 2.1 shows, it is an information-processing system with three functions: input, processing, and output. The nervous system is able to do what it does partly because it is made up of cells that communicate with each other. Two major types of cells, neurons and glial cells, allow the nervous system to carry out its complex signaling tasks efficiently. The specialized cells that send and receive signals are called **neurons.** Neurons are basically alike in structure but differ in length, shape, size, and function. The neuron from your big toe to your spine is more than three feet long, whereas neurons in the brain may extend no more than a tiny fraction of an inch.

Glial cells (from the Greek word meaning "glue") hold neurons together, direct growth, keep the chemical environment stable, secrete chemicals to help restore damage, and even modify signals sent between neurons (Araque et al., 1999). Without the "glue" of glial cells, the neurons could not function.

Every cell in the body has a skin called an *outer membrane,* a cell body that contains a core called the *nucleus,* and tiny "engines," called *mitochondria* (pronounced "my-toh-CON-dree-uh"). Neurons are no different. A neuron's outer membrane acts like a screen, letting some substances pass in and out while blocking others. In the neuron's cell body, the nucleus (or center) carries genetic information that tells the cell what to do. Neurons have many mitochondria that turn oxygen and glucose into energy. This process is especially vital to brain cells, because while the brain accounts for only 2 percent of the body's weight, it uses more than 20 percent of the body's oxygen. Defects in mitochondria are

neurons Specialized cells of the nervous system that send and receive messages.

glial cells Cells that hold neurons together, direct growth, and help restore damaged neurons.

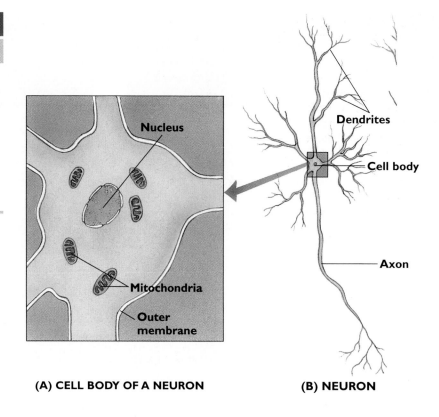

(A) CELL BODY OF A NEURON　　　　　**(B) NEURON**

seen in Alzheimer's disease, a condition most common in elderly people that causes a devastating loss of memory (K. D. Davis et al., 1997).

Neurons have special structural and chemical features that allow them to communicate with each other. Let's first examine their structure. Although neurons come in many shapes and sizes, they all have long, thin fibers that reach outward from the cell body like arms. When these fibers get close to other neurons, communication between the cells can occur. The interweaving of these fibers with fibers from other neurons allows each neuron to be close to thousands or even hundreds of thousands of other neurons.

Fibers extending from the cell body are called *axons* and *dendrites*. Each neuron generally has only one **axon,** whose function is to carry signals away from the cell body. The axon may have many branches along its stem. At the end of each axon are *terminal branches* with pouch-like sacs called *vesicles*. **Dendrites** are the fibers that receive signals from the axons of other neurons and carry those signals to the cell body. As you can see in Figure 2.2, a neuron can have many dendrites, each of which usually has many branches, much like a tree. Remember that *a*xons carry signals *a*way from the cell body, and *d*endrites *d*etect those signals.

Action Potentials

The communication signal between neurons begins with an electrochemical pulse called an **action potential,** which shoots down the axon. Figure 2.3 shows this process. This is an *all-or-nothing* affair: The cell either fires its action potential at full strength or it does not fire at all. Once a cell has fired, there is a short recovery time called the **refractory period,** during which the cell cannot fire again. The speed of an action potential ranges from about 5 to about 260 miles per hour and depends on the thickness or diameter of the axon—larger ones are faster—and on the presence of myelin. *Myelin* is a fatty substance that wraps around some axons like a stocking and speeds up action potentials. When a neuron fires, dendrites in the next cell detect the message and send the signal to their cell body.

axon A fiber that carries signals away from the cell body.

dendrites Fibers that receive signals from the axons of other neurons.

action potential The electrochemical impulse or message that is sent down an axon and stimulates release of a neurotransmitter.

refractory period A short recovery time after cell firing, during which the cell cannot fire again.

FIGURE 2.3

FIGURE 2.3

Communication Between Neurons

When stimulation of a neuron reaches a certain level, the neuron fires, sending an action potential shooting to the end of its axon and triggering the release of a neurotransmitter into the synapse. This process stimulates neighboring neurons and may cause them to fire their own action potentials.

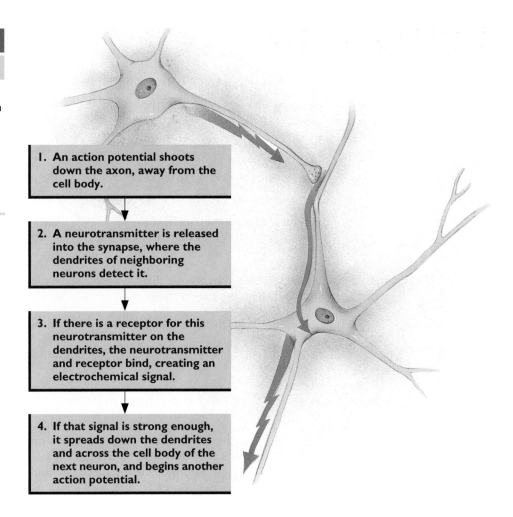

1. **An action potential shoots down the axon, away from the cell body.**

2. **A neurotransmitter is released into the synapse, where the dendrites of neighboring neurons detect it.**

3. **If there is a receptor for this neurotransmitter on the dendrites, the neurotransmitter and receptor bind, creating an electrochemical signal.**

4. **If that signal is strong enough, it spreads down the dendrites and across the cell body of the next neuron, and begins another action potential.**

Synapses and Communication Between Neurons

How do the dendrites detect a signal from another neuron? It works a little like the game of tag you played as a child. In this neural communication tag game, however, one neuron "sends" a tag without actually touching the next neuron. When the action potential reaches the axon's terminal branches, the vesicles located there release a chemical substance called a **neurotransmitter.** Between the axon of one neuron and the dendrites of another is a tiny gap less than a millionth of an inch wide. This is the *synaptic gap*, often referred to simply as the **synapse.** The neurotransmitters flow across the gap. On the dendrite of the next cell, the neurotransmitters reach places where they chemically fit, or bind, to proteins called *receptors*. Like a key fitting into the right lock, a neurotransmitter snugly binds to its own receptors but not to receptors for other neurotransmitters. The receptors "recognize" only one type of neurotransmitter. In the dendrite, this binding creates an electrochemical signal that is called a *postsynaptic potential* because it occurs *after* the neurotransmitter has crossed the synapse. The postsynaptic potential, in turn, passes the message to the cell body for the signaling process to continue.

Generally, more than one message must go to a cell to make it fire. Signals from groups of cells often arrive at the same postsynaptic cell at about the same time. The messages from these many cells may conflict with one another. Some messages tell the cell to fire, whereas others tell the cell not to fire. Whether it actually does fire depends on which kind of signals are most numerous. So axons, neurotransmitters, synapses, and dendrites allow cells of the nervous system to communicate. If these components are damaged or disordered, however, serious problems can result. In the case of Christopher Reeve, for example, a spinal cord injury suffered in a riding accident damaged his nervous system

neurotransmitter   A chemical that transfers messages across synapses.

synapse   The tiny gap between the axon of one neuron and the dendrite of another.

in review

Neurons, Neurotransmitters, and Receptors

Part	Function	Type of Signal Carried
Axon	Carries signals away from the cell body	The action potential, an all-or-nothing electrochemical signal that shoots down the axon to vesicles at the tip of the axon, releasing neurotransmitters
Dendrite	Detects and carries signals to the cell body	The postsynaptic potential, an electrochemical signal moving toward the cell body
Synapse	Provides an area for the transfer of signals between neurons, usually between axon and dendrite	Chemicals that cross the synapse and reach receptors on another cell
Neurotransmitter	A chemical released by one cell that binds to the receptors on another cell	A chemical message telling the next cell to fire or not to fire its own action potential
Receptor	Proteins on the cell membrane that receive chemical signals	Recognizes certain neurotransmitters, thus allowing it to begin a postsynaptic potential in the dendrite

to the point that its axons and dendrites can no longer send or receive the signals that had allowed him to feel most of his body and to move most of his muscles. ("In Review: Neurons, Neurotransmitters, and Receptors" summarizes the process of neural communication.)

The Chemistry of Behavior: Neurotransmitters

How do biochemicals affect my mood?

Different sets of neurons use different neurotransmitters. A group of neurons that communicate using the same neurotransmitter is called a *neurotransmitter system.* Chemical neurotransmission was first demonstrated, in frogs, by Otto Loewi in 1921. Since then, about 100 different neurotransmitters have been identified. Let's explore where these neurotransmitters operate and how they affect behavior.

Seven Major Neurotransmitters

Of all the neurotransmitters, seven are particularly important: acetylcholine, norepinephrine, serotonin, dopamine, GABA, glutamate, and endorphins.

Acetylcholine   The first compound to be identified as a neurotransmitter was acetylcholine (pronounced "uh-see-tull-KO-leen"). Some of the neurons that communicate using acetylcholine control the contraction of muscles by releasing acetylcholine onto muscle tissue. Acetylcholine is also the neurotransmitter used by neurons that slow the heartbeat and activate the digestive system. Disruption of acetylcholine systems can result in a wide variety of problems, including the memory loss and eventual loss of all mental powers seen in Alzheimer's disease.

Norepinephrine   Norepinephrine (pronounced "nor-eppa-NEF-rin") systems affect arousal, wakefulness, learning, and mood. This neurotransmitter is involved when your

PROMOTING PARKINSON'S DISEASE RESEARCH Former heavyweight boxing champion Muhammad Ali suffers from Parkinson's disease. Even though his shakiness is getting worse, he appeared before these U.S. senators and representatives and encouraged them to sponsor bills to fund more research on curing, and perhaps even preventing, Parkinson's disease.

nervous system prepares you to fight or run away from a threat; changes in norepinephrine systems have also been implicated in depression.

Serotonin The neurotransmitter serotonin (pronounced "sair-ah-TOE-nin") is similar to norepinephrine in that it affects both sleep and mood. Serotonin has also been implicated in aggression and impulsive behaviors (Lyons et al., 1999). Unlike norepinephrine, though, what you eat can affect the amount of serotonin in your brain. For example, eating carbohydrates can increase serotonin, and the increase in serotonin normally reduces the desire for carbohydrates. Some researchers suspect that malfunctions in this serotonin feedback system can result in the mood and appetite problems seen in some types of obesity, premenstrual tension, and depression (Wurtman & Wurtman, 1995). Antidepressant medications such as Prozac, Zoloft, and Paxil appear to relieve some of the symptoms of depression by acting on serotonin systems to maintain optimal levels of this neurotransmitter.

Dopamine Dopamine (pronounced "DOPE-uh-meen") is a neurotransmitter that is important for movement. Malfunctions of dopamine systems contribute to movement disorders such as the shakiness experienced by people with Parkinson's disease. Parkinson's has been treated with some success using drugs that enable neurons to make more dopamine or that stimulate dopamine receptors (Chase, 1998). Other dopamine systems are involved in the experiencing of reward, or pleasure, which is vital in shaping and motivating behavior (Spanagel & Weiss, 1999). Animals will work very hard to receive a direct dose of dopamine to a portion of the brain. These dopamine systems play a role in the rewarding properties of many drugs, including cocaine (Wise, 1998). Certain dopamine systems are also suspected to be partly responsible for the perceptual, emotional, and thought disturbances associated with schizophrenia, a severe mental disorder (Breier et al., 1997).

GABA GABA stands for *gamma-aminobutyric acid.* Whereas most neurotransmitters excite neurons to fire action potentials, GABA *reduces* the likelihood that a neuron will fire. Drugs that enhance GABA activity will thus inhibit neural firing. In the case of alcohol, for example, the result is an impairment of thinking, judgment, and motor skills. Malfunctions of GABA systems contribute to severe anxiety and to Huntington's disease, an inherited disorder. Normally, GABA systems inhibit dopamine systems. Therefore, when GABA systems are lost through Huntington's disease, the dopamine systems may run wild. The effects are somewhat opposite those of Parkinson's disease. Instead of the slow and shaky movements of Parkinson's, the Huntington's victim suffers uncontrollable movement of the arms and legs, along with a progressive loss of thinking abilities. Woody Guthrie, the legendary folksinger, was a famous victim of Huntington's disease.

Drugs that block GABA receptors produce intense repetitive electrical discharges, known as *seizures*. Researchers suspect that impaired GABA systems probably contribute to epilepsy, a brain disorder associated with seizures and convulsive movements. Repeated or sustained seizures can result in permanent brain damage. Drug treatments can reduce seizure frequency and severity, but completely effective drugs are not yet available.

Glutamate   Glutamate (pronounced "GLOO-tuh-mate") is used by more neurons than any other neurotransmitter. Glutamate's importance comes from its role in enabling the brain to "strengthen" its synaptic connections. Such strengthening allows messages to cross the synapse more easily. This process is necessary for normal development and may be at the root of learning and memory. Yet overactivity of glutamate synapses can cause neurons to die. This overactivity is the main cause of the brain damage that occurs when oxygen is cut off from neurons during a stroke. Glutamate can "excite neurons to death." Blocking glutamate receptors immediately after a brain trauma can prevent permanent brain damage (Bittigau & Ikonomidou, 1997). Glutamate may also contribute to the cell loss that occurs in Alzheimer's disease (Olney, Wozniak, & Farber, 1997).

Endorphins   Substances called *opiates*, such as morphine and heroin, can relieve pain, produce intense feelings of happiness, and, in high doses, bring on sleep. After marking morphine with a radioactive substance, researchers traced where it becomes concentrated in the brain. They found that opiates bind to receptors that are not associated with any previously identified neurotransmitter. Because it was unlikely that the brain had developed opiate receptors just in case a person might want to use morphine or heroin, researchers reasoned that the body must contain a substance similar to opiates. This hypothesis led to the search for a naturally occurring, or *endogenous*, morphine. (*Endogenous* is pronounced "en-DODGE-uh-niss.") *Endorphin* is a contraction of the words *endogenous morphine*. As it turns out, there are many natural opiate-like compounds, and new ones are still being discovered. Thus, the term *endorphin* refers to any neurotransmitter that can bind to the same receptors stimulated by opiates. Endorphins reduce pain and produce feelings of pleasure.

Neurotransmitters link biochemistry to behavior and mental processes. ("In Review: Major Neurotransmitters" summarizes our discussion of seven of them.) Many drugs, like heroin and Prozac, have effects on various neurotransmitters or receptor sites. The intimate relationships among neurotransmitters, drugs, behavior, and mental processes

in review

Major Neurotransmitters

Neurotransmitter	Normal Function	Disorder Associated with Malfunctioning
Acetylcholine	Movement, memory	Alzheimer's disease
Norepinephrine	Sleep, learning, mood	Depression
Serotonin	Mood, appetite, aggression	Depression
Dopamine	Movement, reward	Parkinson's disease, schizophrenia
GABA	Movement	Huntington's disease; epilepsy
Glutamate	Memory	Neuron loss after stroke
Endorphins	Modulation of pain	No established disorder

suggest exciting research questions. For instance, can drugs be used to improve mental functioning?

Are There Drugs That Can Make You Smarter?

Drugs intended to improve cognitive functioning are called *nootropics* (pronounced "no-oh-TROH-pix"), a word that comes from *noos*, which is Greek for "mind." In some circles, nootropics are seen as "smart drugs" and sold at "smart bars." Are smart drugs really effective, or are they modern-day snake oil, giving only an illusion of a sharpened mind?

What am I being asked to believe or accept?

The belief that certain drugs can improve memory was popularized in the 1990s by John Morgenthaler and Ward Dean, who wrote two books, *Smart Drugs and Nutrients* and a sequel called *Smart Drugs II: The Next Generation.* One on-line reviewer of the second book wrote, "And the results have been nothing less than a total transformation. My life has come together finally and I am advancing in my work" (Anonymous, 1998).

Is there evidence available to support the claim?

Some drugs can improve mental performance under some conditions. For instance, animals given the drugs that Morgenthaler and Dean wrote about show improvements in performance on tasks requiring attention and memory. These drugs have also been shown to facilitate recalling old memories and forming new ones (Mondadori, 1996). Nootropic drugs also have biochemical effects on brain metabolism in elderly people: Some increase blood flow in the brain, and others affect specific neurotransmitters (Dormehl et al., 1999).

One study of elderly people with general brain impairment found improvement after twelve weeks of treatment with smart drugs. Other studies have shown memory improvement in elderly people with memory problems due to poor blood circulation to the brain (Balestreri, Fontana, & Astengo, 1987). Some studies have also found positive effects on memory in normal persons. For example, young adult college students improved on tests of memory after taking some of these drugs (File, Fluck, & Fernandes, 1999).

Can that evidence be interpreted another way?

Glowing testimonials from people who feel that these drugs helped them may reflect their *belief* in the drugs, not the effectiveness of the drugs themselves. For example, in 1894, when the scientist Charles Édouard Brown-Séquard was feeling old and tired, he gave himself injections of extract of ground-up dog testicles. He reported a return to youthful energy and sharpened cognitive abilities. It was all probably a placebo effect. Only carefully controlled double-blind studies can separate the effect of a participant's expectations from the specific effects of drugs or other treatments.

Some of the controlled studies previously cited show that nootropic drugs have positive effects on memory and cognitive ability, but the effects tend to be small and inconsistent. Often, the drugs primarily affect attentiveness, and the improvements are no greater than those caused by drinking a cup of coffee (Service, 1994). Overall, evidence from well-designed studies shows nootropic drugs to be a major disappointment (Riedel & Jolles, 1996).

What evidence would help to evaluate the alternatives?

Researchers are testing several promising new categories of nootropic drugs in animals (e.g., Hirouchi et al., 2000). It will take years of study to determine which ones are truly effective, and under what circumstances. Research on side effects will also be needed. For example, one of the more effective drugs for Alzheimer's patients was found to cause serious liver damage in about a third of those who took it (Molloy et al., 1991). And one of the chemicals occasionally found to improve memory in humans may create nausea and increased blood pressure (Goodman-Gilman et al., 1990).

What conclusions are most reasonable?

In spite of their unimpressive showing overall, nootropic drugs are sometimes used with Alzheimer's patients, mainly for lack of better alternatives (Sramek & Cutler, 1999). As for the drinks you can buy in smart bars, be sure they taste good, because their effect on your mental powers is likely to be minimal. Instead of smart drugs, try education: Educational achievement and a life of working at a job that engages your mind are more likely to lower the risk for Alzheimer's disease (D. A. Evans et al., 1997).

The Peripheral Nervous System: Keeping in Touch with the World

How is my nervous system organized?

There are two main parts to the human nervous system—the *central nervous system* and the *peripheral nervous system*. They are called nervous *systems* because they are composed of billions of neurons. The **central nervous system (CNS)** consists of the brain and spinal cord, which are encased in bone for protection. Like the chief executive officer in a company, the CNS receives information, processes it, and determines what actions should result.

The **peripheral nervous system** sends sensory information from the eyes, ears, and other sense organs to the CNS. Messages from the brain and spinal cord are also carried by the peripheral nervous system to the muscles, glands, and other parts of the body. In essence, the peripheral nervous system is an information relay system to and from the CNS. Unlike the CNS, it is not protected by bone. To accomplish its relay tasks, the peripheral nervous system has two subsystems—the autonomic nervous system and the somatic nervous system. Figure 2.4 shows the organization of the nervous system.

The Somatic Nervous System

Imagine that you are at the beach. It is hot, and the ocean smells salty. An attractive stranger approaches, catching your eye. The stranger smiles. You smile in return. The stranger continues walking away. In these few seconds, your nervous system has been busy. You feel the warmth of the sun and smell the ocean because your **somatic nervous system** takes in these pieces of sensory information and sends them to the central nervous system for processing. The CNS evaluates the warmth and the smells, sending messages through the somatic nervous system to the muscles that allow you to turn over, sit up, or put on more sunscreen. Sensory neurons bring information into the brain. Motor neurons carry information from the part of the brain that directs motion.

The Autonomic Nervous System

The **autonomic nervous system** carries messages back and forth between the CNS and the heart, lungs, and other organs and glands (Janig, 1996). The autonomic nervous system takes the stranger's "attractive" rating from the CNS and translates it into an increase in heart rate, pupil dilation, and perhaps a little blushing. This system is called "autonomic" because such activities are generally autonomous, or independent of your control. With training and practice, some people can use a technique called *biofeedback* to bring some of their involuntary responses, such as heart rate, under conscious (CNS) control.

As shown in Figure 2.4, the autonomic system also has two subsystems of its own—the *sympathetic nervous system* and the *parasympathetic nervous system*. These two sys-

central nervous system (CNS)   The brain and spinal cord.

peripheral nervous system   The part of the human nervous system that sends messages to and from the central nervous system.

somatic nervous system   The subsystem of the peripheral nervous system that transmits information from the senses to the central nervous system and carries signals from the CNS to the muscles that move the skeleton.

autonomic nervous system   The subsystem of the peripheral nervous system that carries messages between the central nervous system and the heart, lungs, and other organs and glands in the body.

FIGURE 2.4

Organization of the Nervous System

The brain and spinal cord make up the bone-encased central nervous system (CNS), the body's central information processor, decision maker, and director of actions. The peripheral nervous system, which is not housed in bone, functions mainly to carry messages. The somatic subsystem of the peripheral nervous system transmits information to the CNS from the outside world and conveys instructions from the CNS to the muscles. The autonomic subsystem conveys messages from the CNS that alter the activity of organs and glands, and it sends information about that activity back to the brain.

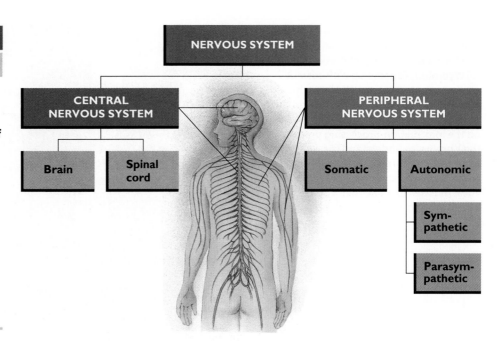

tems work like a seesaw on a playground. Generally, the **sympathetic nervous system** readies your body for action in the face of stress. The **parasympathetic nervous system** calms you down once the crisis has passed. The sympathetic nervous system *spends* energy, whereas the parasympathetic nervous system *conserves* energy.

The Central Nervous System: Making Sense of the World

▪ How is my brain "wired"?

Comparing the central nervous system (CNS) to the central processor in a computer, *computational neuroscientists* have created neural networks on computers to better understand how the brain works and how it relates to sensory and motor systems and learning (Voegtlin & Verschure, 1999). In these computer models, information is processed at different places at the same time. This arrangement is known as *parallel distributed processing.* In the brain, sensation, perception, learning, and memory all rely on parallel distributed processing, too.

The central nervous system, however, does not simply function as a high-powered computer. It certainly isn't laid out as neatly, either. The layout of the brain is more like what you would see on a college campus. There are clusters of offices for the administrators in one place, clusters of faculty offices in another place, and classrooms in yet another. Some of the sidewalks or hallways that connect these clusters are large; others are narrow. There are many different but connected ways to get to the same place. Like campus office clusters, the CNS has clusters of neuron cell bodies called **nuclei** (pronounced "NUKE-lee-eye"; *nuclei* is the plural of *nucleus*). The sidewalks and hallways of the CNS are axons that travel together in bundles called **fiber tracts** or *pathways.* The axon (hallway) from any given cell (office) may merge with and leave many fiber tracts (sidewalks) and send branches out to other tracts. Let's consider a practical example of nervous system functioning to begin learning our way around the "campus" of the brain.

It is cold and dark outside but warm under the blankets as your alarm clock goes off. The time is 6 A.M. In this simple case of information processing, which was illustrated in Figure 2.1, your ears receive sensory input in the form of sound from the alarm. The sound is converted into neural signals and sent to the brain. Your brain compares these

sympathetic nervous system   The subsystem of the autonomic nervous system that readies the body for action in the face of crisis.

parasympathetic nervous system   The subsystem of the autonomic nervous system that calms the body and influences activity related to its protection, nourishment, and growth.

nuclei   Clusters of nerve cell bodies in the central nervous system.

fiber tracts   Bundles of axons that travel together; also called *pathways.*

signals with previous experiences stored in memory and correctly associates the sound with "alarm clock." Your output is not yet at peak performance, though. Brain activity has not yet reached the waking state. Your muscles are directed poorly as you fumble to turn off the alarm. Shuffling to the kitchen, you touch the coffee pot's heating element. Things get more lively now. Heat energy activates sensory neurons in your fingers, generating action potentials that speed along fiber tracts going into the spinal cord. Motor (body movement) neurons are reflexively activated by the CNS, causing muscles in your arm to contract and quickly withdraw your hand.

The Spinal Cord

The **spinal cord** receives signals like pain and touch from the senses and passes those signals to the brain. Neuron fibers within the cord also carry signals downward from the brain to the muscles. Some cells of the spinal cord can direct simple behaviors without instructions from the brain. These behaviors are called **reflexes,** because the response to the incoming signal is directly "reflected" back out, as shown in Figure 2.5. Spinal reflexes, like the one that pulled your hand away from the heat, are very fast because they make few time-consuming synaptic links. Because a reflex occurs without instructions from the brain, it is called *involuntary.* At the same time, though, action potentials are being sent along fiber tracts to the brain. So, you officially "know" you have been burned a fraction of a second after your reflex got you out of trouble. The spinal cord is an example of a *feedback system.* When touching something hot sets off a simple reflex, it causes one set of arm muscles to contract and an opposing set of muscles to relax. If this did not happen, the arm would go rigid. The muscles also have receptors that send information to the spinal cord to let it know how extended they are so that adjustments can be made for a smooth contracting motion. Information about the consequences of an action goes back to the source of the action for further adjustment. That is a feedback system.

The Brain

Have you ever been bothered by a tune or a phrase that you "couldn't get out your head"? New techniques for monitoring the activity of various brain regions can actually "see" inside your head to locate where such persistent thoughts occur (Zungu-Dirwayi et al., 1999). The same techniques can be used to determine which parts of the brain are active

spinal cord The part of the central nervous system that receives information from the senses, passes these signals to the brain, and sends messages from the brain to the body.

reflexes Simple, involuntary, and unlearned behaviors directed by the spinal cord without instructions from the brain.

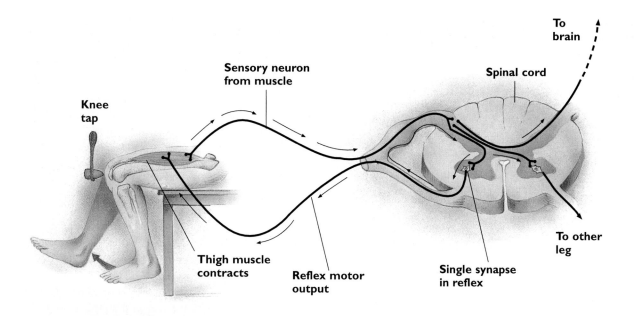

To brain

Sensory neuron from muscle

Spinal cord

Knee tap

Thigh muscle contracts

Reflex motor output

Single synapse in reflex

To other leg

FIGURE 2.5

A Reflex Pathway

LEARN BY DOING **Sit on a chair; cross one leg over the other; and then use the handle of a butter knife or some other solid object to gently tap your top knee, just below the joint, until you get a "knee jerk" reaction. Tapping the knee at just the right spot sets off an almost instantaneous sequence of events that begins with stimulation of sensory neurons that respond to stretch. When those neurons fire, their axons, which end within the spinal cord, cause spinal neurons to fire. This in turn stimulates the firing of motor neurons with axons ending in the thigh muscles. The result is a contraction of the thigh muscles and a kicking of the lower leg and foot. Information about the knee tap and about what the leg has done also goes to the cerebral cortex, but the reflex is completed without waiting for guidance from the brain.**

hindbrain The portion of the brain that lies just inside the skull and is a continuation of the spinal cord.

medulla The area of the hindbrain that controls vital autonomic functions such as heart rate, blood pressure, and breathing.

when people are excited by sexually explicit images (Stoleru et al., 1999). These new techniques, combined with older techniques, have opened new doors to studying brain function in humans (see Table 2.1). Each technique can indirectly measure the activity of neurons firing, and each has different advantages and disadvantages. One of the earliest of these techniques, called the *electroencephalograph (EEG)*, measures general electrical activity of the brain. Electrodes are pasted on the scalp to detect the electrical fields resulting from the activity of billions of neurons. Although this tool can associate rapidly changing electrical activity with changes in the activity of the brain, it cannot tell us exactly *where* the active cells are.

A newer technique, called the *PET scan*, can locate cell activity by recording where radioactive substances become concentrated when injected into the bloodstream. *PET* stands for *positron emission tomography*. It records images from the brain that indicate the location of the radioactivity as the brain performs various tasks. For instance, PET studies have revealed that specific brain regions are activated when we look at fearful facial expressions (J. S. Morris et al., 1998). PET scans can tell us a lot about where changes in brain activity occur, but they can't reveal details of the brain's physical structure.

A detailed structural picture of the brain can be seen, however, using magnetic resonance imaging, or MRI. MRI exposes the brain to a magnetic field and measures the resulting radiofrequency waves to get amazingly clear pictures of the brain's anatomical details (see Figure 2.6). The newest technique, called functional MRI, or fMRI, combines the advantages of PET and MRI and is capable of detecting changes in blood flow that reflect ongoing changes in the activity of neurons—providing a sort of "moving picture" of the brain (e.g., Engel, 1999).

These tools have opened new frontiers for biological psychology and medicine. Much of our growing understanding of how and why behavior occurs comes from research with these techniques. Let's now explore some of the structures highlighted by these techniques, starting with three major subdivisions of the brain: the hindbrain, the midbrain, and the forebrain.

The Hindbrain

Figure 2.7 shows the major structures of the brain. The **hindbrain** lies just inside the skull and is actually a continuation of the spinal cord. Incoming signals from the spinal cord first reach the hindbrain. Many vital autonomic functions, such as heart rate, blood pressure, and breathing, are controlled by nuclei in the hindbrain, particularly in an area called the **medulla.**

TABLE 2.1	Nonsurgical Techniques for Studying Human Brain Function and Structure	
Technique	**What It Shows**	**Advantages (+) and Disadvantages (−)**
EEG (electroencephalograph): Multiple electrodes are pasted to the outside of the head	Lines that chart the summated electrical fields resulting from the activity of billions of neurons	+ Detects very rapid changes in electrical activity, allowing analysis of stages of cognitive processing − Provides poor spatial resolution of the source of electrical activity
PET (positron emission tomography) and SPECT (single photon emission computed tomography): Positrons and photons are emissions from radioactive substances	An image of the amount and localization of any molecule that can be injected in radioactive form, such as neurotransmitters, drugs, or tracers for blood flow or glucose use (which indicates specific changes in neuronal activity)	+ Allows functional and biochemical studies + Provides visual image corresponding to anatomy − Requires exposure to low levels of radioactivity − Provides spatial resolution better than that of EEG but poorer than that of MRI − Cannot follow rapid changes (faster than 30 seconds)
MRI (magnetic resonance imaging): Exposes the brain to a magnetic field and measures radiofrequency waves	The traditional MRI provides a high-resolution image of brain anatomy, and the newer functional MRI (fMRI) provides images of changes in blood flow (which indicate specific changes in neuronal activity)	+ Requires no exposure to radioactivity + Provides high spatial resolution of anatomical details (<1 mm) + Provides high temporal resolution ($<\frac{1}{10}$ second)

FIGURE 2.6

Combining a PET Scan and Magnetic Resonance Imaging

Researchers have superimposed images from PET scans and MRI to construct a three-dimensional view of the living brain. This figure shows the brain of a young epileptic girl. The picture of the outer surface of the brain is from the MRI; the pink area is from the PET scan and shows the source of epileptic activity. The images at the right are the MRI and PET images at one plane, or "slice," through the brain (indicated by the line on the brain at the left).

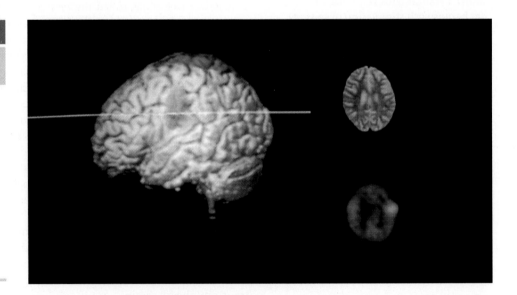

reticular formation A collection of cells and fibers in the hindbrain and midbrain that are involved in arousal and attention.

Weaving throughout the hindbrain and into the midbrain is a meshlike collection of cells called the **reticular formation** (*reticular* means "net-like"). This network is involved in arousal and attention. Cutting off fibers of the reticular system from the rest of the brain would put a person into a permanent coma. Some of the fibers carrying pain signals from the spinal cord connect in the reticular formation and immediately arouse the brain from sleep. Within seconds, the hindbrain causes your heart rate and blood pressure to increase. You are awake and aroused.

Major Structures of the Brain

This side view of a section cut down the middle of the brain reveals the forebrain, midbrain, hindbrain, and spinal cord. Many of these subdivisions do not have clear-cut borders, because they are all interconnected by fiber tracts. The brain's anatomy reflects its evolution over millions of years. Newer structures (such as the cerebral cortex, which is the outer surface of the forebrain) that handle higher mental functions were built on older ones (such as the medulla) that coordinate heart rate, breathing, and other, more basic functions.

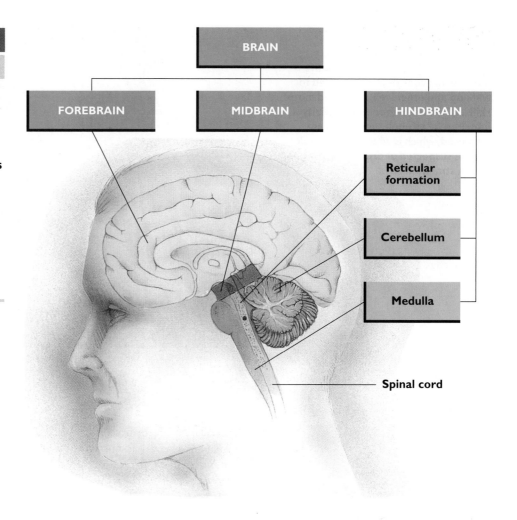

The **cerebellum** is also part of the hindbrain. Its primary function is to control finely coordinated movements, such as writing or threading a needle. When you catch a thrown ball, it is the cerebellum that allows your eyes to track the moving ball accurately (Krauzlis & Lisberger, 1991). Activities like sports, dancing, and playing piano are made up of well-rehearsed movements that are stored in the cerebellum. Recent MRI studies reveal that the cerebellum also participates in cognitive tasks such as reading (Cabeza & Nyberg, 2000; Fulbright et al., 1999).

Reflexes and feedback systems are important in the hindbrain. For example, if blood pressure drops, heart action reflexively increases to make up for that decrease. If you stand up very quickly, your blood pressure can drop so suddenly that you feel lightheaded until the hindbrain reflexively "catches up." You will faint if the hindbrain does not activate the autonomic nervous system to increase your blood pressure.

The Midbrain

A small structure called the **midbrain** lies above the hindbrain. If you focus your eyes on another person and then move your head, midbrain circuits allow you to move your eyes smoothly in the direction opposite from your head movement so you never lose focus. Did you ever swing a bat, swat a mosquito, or jump rope? Part of the midbrain and its connections to the forebrain allowed you to produce those movements smoothly. When a car backfires, causing you to reflexively turn your head and look in the direction of the sound, it is again the midbrain at work. Together, the midbrain and parts of the hindbrain other than the cerebellum are called the *brainstem*.

cerebellum The part of the hindbrain that controls finely coordinated movements.

midbrain A small structure between the hindbrain and the forebrain that helps produce smooth movements.

A FIELD SOBRIETY TEST The cerebellum is heavily involved in the balance and coordination required for walking and other well-rehearsed motor skills. When the cerebellum's activity is impaired by alcohol, these skills are disrupted, which is why the police ask people suspected of drunken driving to walk a straight line.

The Forebrain

In humans, the **forebrain** controls the most complex aspects of behavior and mental life. It folds back over and completely covers the rest of the brain. The outer surface of the forebrain is called the *cerebral cortex.* Figure 2.8 shows some structures of the forebrain.

Two structures deep within the forebrain, the *hypothalamus* and the *thalamus,* help operate basic drives, emotion, and sensation. The **thalamus** acts as a relay station for pain and sense-organ signals (except smell) from the body to the upper levels of the brain. The thalamus also processes and makes sense of these signals. The **hypothalamus** lies under the thalamus (*hypo* means "under") and helps regulate hunger, thirst, and sex drives. The hypothalamus is well-connected to the autonomic nervous system and to other parts of the brain. Damage to parts of the hypothalamus upset normal appetite, thirst, and sexual behavior.

Can you set an "internal alarm clock" to wake up in the morning at whatever time you want? Some people can, with the help of a remarkable part of the hypothalamus that contains the brain's own clock: the *suprachiasmatic nuclei.* The suprachiasmatic (pronounced "soo-pra-kye-as-MAT-ik") nuclei operate on approximately a twenty-four-hour cycle, controlling *circadian rhythms* (biological rhythms such as waking and sleeping) and body temperature. Some of us are morning people and others are night people. Studies of the suprachiasmatic nuclei in animals suggest that having different night or morning energy times is biological and stable throughout a lifetime (Cofer et al., 1992).

Other parts of the forebrain, especially the *amygdala* (pronounced "ah-MIG-duh-luh") and the *hippocampus,* help to regulate memory and emotion. The **amygdala** links different kinds of sensory information in memory, such as the shape and feel of objects (E. A. Murray & Mishkin, 1985). If you close your eyes and pick up an object, your amygdala helps you recognize it. The amygdala also plays a role in fear and other emotions (LeDoux, 1995; Whalen, 1998), connecting emotion to sensation. People who suffer from posttraumatic stress disorder have unusual amygdala activity (Shin et al., 1997). The amygdala, hippocampus, and some portions of the cerebral cortex are part of a group of brain structures called the *limbic system,* which is activated when emotions are being generated.

The **hippocampus** also helps you form new memories. In one case, a patient known as R.B. suffered a stroke (an interruption of blood flow to the brain) that damaged only his hippocampus. Although his intelligence remained above average and he could recall

forebrain   The part of the brain responsible for the most complex aspects of behavior and mental life.

thalamus   A forebrain structure that relays messages from sense organs to higher brain parts.

hypothalamus   A forebrain structure that regulates hunger, thirst, and sex drives, with many connections to and from the autonomic nervous system and other parts of the brain.

amygdala   A forebrain structure that links information from various systems and plays a role in emotions.

hippocampus   A forebrain structure associated with the formation of new memories.

FIGURE 2.8

Major Structures of the Forebrain

The structures of the forebrain are covered by an outer "bark" known as the *cerebral cortex*. This diagram shows some of the structures that lie deep within the forebrain. The amygdala, the hippocampus, and portions of the cerebral cortex are part of the limbic system.

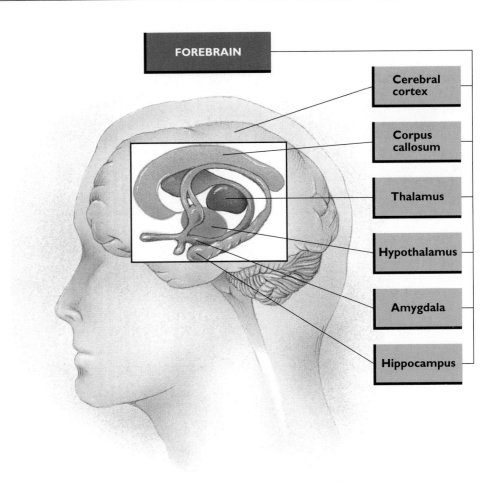

FOREBRAIN

- Cerebral cortex
- Corpus callosum
- Thalamus
- Hypothalamus
- Amygdala
- Hippocampus

old memories, he was almost totally unable to build new memories (Squire, 1986). Damage to the hippocampus within a day of a mildly painful event seems to erase memories of the experience. However, if the damage occurs several days after the event, the memory remains. It seems that memories are not permanently stored in the hippocampus but instead are transferred from there to somewhere else in the brain.

The hippocampus becomes smaller with age, and research shows that this shrinkage relates to the declining memory function that many elderly people experience (Golomb et al., 1994). On average, the hippocampus of a person with Alzheimer's disease has been found to be 40 percent smaller than that of a person without the disease. Alzheimer's disease is a major cause of senile dementia, which involves the decay of cognitive capabilities. About 10 percent of people over age sixty-five and 47 percent of people over eighty-five suffer from this disease (G. W. Small et al., 1997; U.S. Surgeon General, 1999). The financial cost of Alzheimer's disease is more than $100 billion a year in the United States (G. W. Small et al., 1997). The cost in human suffering is incalculable.

The Cerebral Cortex

On the surface of the forebrain is the **cerebral cortex.** The total area of the cerebral cortex is one to two square feet, but it fits into the skull because it is somewhat wrinkled and folded. You can wad up a T-shirt and fit it into a bowl in much the same way. The cerebral cortex is much larger in humans than in other animals (with a few exceptions, such as dolphins). Like a computer's central processing unit, the cerebral cortex is our primary processing area. It analyzes all information from the senses and controls voluntary movement, abstract thinking, and the other most complex aspects of our behavior and mental processes. The cerebral cortex looks somewhat round, with a long groove down the middle creating two halves, called *cerebral hemispheres*. The **corpus callosum,** a massive bundle of more than a million fibers, connects the two hemispheres.

cerebral cortex The outer surface of the forebrain.

corpus callosum A massive bundle of fibers that connects the left and right cerebral hemispheres.

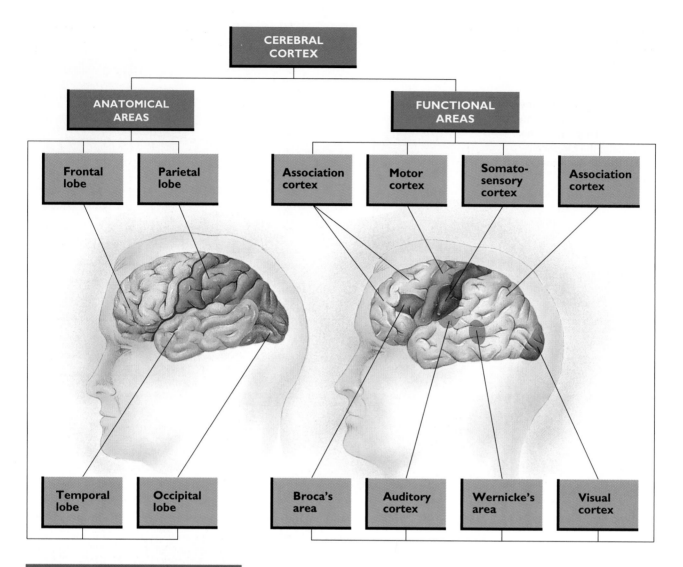

FIGURE 2.9

The Cerebral Cortex (viewed from the left side)

The brain's ridges (gyri) and valleys (sulci) are landmarks that divide the cortex into four lobes: the frontal, parietal, occipital, and temporal. These terms describe where the regions are (the lobes are named for the skull bones that cover them), but the cortex is also divided in terms of function. These functional areas include the motor cortex (which controls movement), sensory cortex (which receives information from various senses), and association cortex (which integrates information). Also labeled are Wernicke's area and Broca's area, two regions that are found only on the left side of the cortex and that are vital to the interpretation and production of speech.

The folds of the cerebral cortex give the surface of the human brain its wrinkled appearance, its ridges and valleys. The ridges are called *gyri* (pronounced "ji-rye"), and the valleys are known as *sulci* (pronounced "sulk-eye") or *fissures.* As you can see in Figure 2.9, several deep sulci divide the cortex into four areas: the frontal (front), parietal (top), occipital (back), and temporal (side) lobes. The gyri and sulci provide landmarks for describing the structure of the cortex, but the *functions* of the cortex do not follow these boundaries. When divided according to function, the cortex includes areas of sensory cortex, motor cortex, and association cortex. ("In Review: Organization of the Brain" summarizes the major structures and functions of the brain.)

Sensory and Motor Cortex

The **sensory cortex** lies in the parietal, occipital, and temporal lobes. Different regions of the sensory cortex receive information from different senses. Occipital lobe cells called the *visual cortex* receive visual information. Temporal lobe cells called the *auditory cortex* receive information from the ears. And information from the skin, such as touch, pain, and temperature, is received by cells in the parietal lobe. These skin-related areas are called the *somatosensory cortex* (*soma* is Greek for "body"). Information about skin sensations from neighboring parts of the body comes to neighboring parts of the somatosensory cortex. It is as if the outline of a tiny person, dangling upside down, determined the location of the information (see Figure 2.10). This pattern is called the *homunculus* (Latin for "little man").

Organization of the Brain		
Major Division	**Some Major Structures**	**Some Major Functions**
Hindbrain	Medulla	Regulates breathing, heart rate, and blood pressure
	Reticular formation (also extends into midbrain)	Regulates arousal and attention
	Cerebellum	Controls finely coordinated movements
Midbrain	Various nuclei	Relays sensory signals to forebrain; creates automatic responses to certain stimuli; initiates smooth movement
Forebrain	Thalamus	Interprets and relays sensory information
	Hypothalamus	Regulates hunger, thirst, and sex drives
	Amygdala	Connects sensations and emotions
	Hippocampus	Forms new memories
	Cerebral cortex	Analyzes sensory information; controls voluntary movements, abstract thinking, and other complex cognitive activity
	Corpus callosum	Transfers information between the two cerebral hemispheres

sensory cortex The part of the cerebral cortex located in the parietal, occipital, and temporal lobes that receives stimulus information from the skin, eyes, and ears, respectively.

motor cortex The part of the cerebral cortex that controls voluntary movement.

In the frontal lobe, specific neurons of the **motor cortex** control voluntary movements in specific parts of the body. The motor cortex's arrangement mirrors that of the somatosensory cortex. Thus, the parts of the motor cortex that control hand movement are near parts of the sensory cortex that receive sensory information from the hands.

Seems easy, doesn't it? You have a map of your body parts in the cortex, and you activate cells in the hand region of the cortex if you want to move your hand. In fact, the actual process is quite complex. Recall again your sleepy reach for the coffee pot. The cortex must first translate the coffee pot's location into a location relative to your body. Next, the cortex must determine which muscles must be contracted to produce the desired movement toward that location. Populations of neurons work together to produce just the right combinations of direction and force in particular muscle groups. Making these determinations involves many interconnected areas of the cortex. Computer models of neural networks are showing how these complex problem-solving processes might occur.

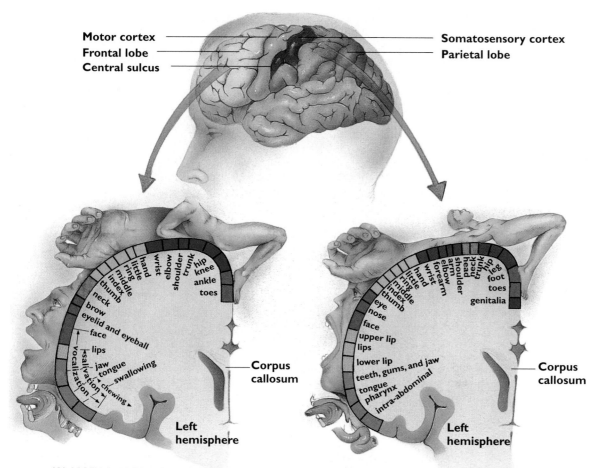

Motor cortex
Frontal lobe
Central sulcus

Somatosensory cortex
Parietal lobe

Corpus callosum

Corpus callosum

Left hemisphere

Left hemisphere

(A) MOTOR AREAS (END VIEW)

(B) SOMATOSENSORY AREAS (END VIEW)

Note: Did you notice the error in this classic drawing? (The figure shows the right side of the body, but the left hand and left side of the face.)

Source: Penfield & Rasmussen, 1968.

FIGURE 2.10

Motor and Somatosensory Cortex

The areas of cortex that move parts of the body (motor cortex) and receive sensory input from body parts (somatosensory cortex) appear in both hemispheres of the brain. Here we show cross-sections of only those on the left side, looking from the back of the brain toward the front. Areas controlling movement of neighboring parts of the body, such as the foot and leg, occupy neighboring parts of the motor cortex. Areas receiving input from neighboring body parts, such as the lips and tongue, are near one another in the sensory cortex. Notice that the size of these areas is uneven; the larger the area devoted to each body part, the larger that body part appears on the "homunculus."

FOCUS ON RESEARCH

The Case of the Disembodied Woman

The well-known neurologist Oliver Sacks described the case of "Christina," a woman who had somehow lost the ability to feel the position of her own body (Sacks, 1985). This case study led to important insights about biological psychology that could not be studied through controlled experiments. One such insight was the realization that the sense known as kinesthesia (pronounced "kin-es-THEE-see-uh") not only tells us where our body parts are but also plays an important role in our sense of self.

In 1977, Christina was a healthy young woman who entered a hospital in preparation for some minor surgery. Before the surgery could be performed, however, she began to have difficulty holding onto objects. Then she had trouble moving. She would rise from bed and flop onto the floor like a rag doll. Christina seemed to have "lost" her body. She felt disembodied, like a ghost. On one occasion, for example, she became annoyed at a visitor she thought was tapping her fingers on a tabletop. But it was she, not the visitor, who was doing it. Her hands were acting on their own. Her body was doing things she did not know about.

■ **What was the researcher's question?**

Christina could not walk or use her hands and arms. Why was a seemingly normal, healthy young woman falling and dropping things?

THE FAR SIDE   By GARY LARSON

"Whoa! *That* was a good one! Try it, Hobbs —
just poke his brain right where my finger is."

How did the researcher answer the question?

A psychiatrist at the hospital thought that Christina was suffering from a psychological disorder that produced physical symptoms (see conversion disorder, described in Chapter 12). But Dr. Sacks decided to conduct an intense and careful case study of Christina. (Recall from Chapter 1 that the case-study method is an intensive investigation of a phenomenon in a particular individual, group, or situation.)

What did the researcher find?

It turned out that the psychiatrist's diagnosis was wrong. Dr. Sacks's examinations and tests revealed that Christina had lost all sensory feedback about her joints, muscle tone, and the position of her limbs. Christina had suffered a breakdown, or degeneration, of the sensory neurons that normally bring in kinesthetic information. In other words, there was a biological reason why Christina could not walk or control her hands and arms.

What do the results mean?

In his analysis of this case, Dr. Sacks noted that the sense we have of our bodies is provided partly through our experience of seeing it, but also partly through proprioception (sensing the self). Christina herself put it this way: "Proprioception is like the eyes of the body, the way the body sees itself. And if it goes, it's like the body's blind." With great effort and determination, Christina was ultimately able to regain some of her ability to move about. If she looked intently at her arms and legs, she could coordinate their movement somewhat. Eventually, she left the hospital and resumed many of her normal activities. But Christina never recovered her sense of self. She still feels like a stranger in her own body.

What do we still need to know?

Notice that Christina's case study did not confirm any hypotheses about kinesthesia in the way an experiment might. It did, however, focus attention on what it feels like to have lost this sense. It also highlighted a rare condition that, though almost unknown when Dr. Sacks reported it, has been observed more often in recent years, especially among people taking megadoses of vitamin B6, also known as pyridoxine (Sacks, 1985). These high doses—or even lower doses taken over a long period of time—can damage sensory neurons (Dordain & Deffond, 1994). How and why vitamin B6 does such damage still needs to be determined. Are there other causes of this kinesthetic disorder? What treatments might best combat it? Much research remains to be done, and pursuing that work is how psychologists and other scientists begin to unravel the mysteries of behavior and mental processes.

Association Cortex

Parts of the cortex that do not directly receive specific sensory information or control specific movements are referred to as **association cortex.** The term *association* describes these areas well, because they receive input from more than one sense or input that combines sensory and motor information. For instance, these areas associate words with images. Association cortex appears in all of the lobes and forms a large part of the cerebral cortex in humans. For this reason, damage to association areas can create serious problems in a wide range of mental abilities.

Consider language. Language information comes from the auditory cortex for spoken language or from the visual cortex for written language. Areas of the motor cortex produce speech (Geschwind, 1979). Putting it all together in the complex activity known as language involves activity in association cortex. In the 1860s, Paul Broca described the effects of damage to association cortex in the frontal lobe near motor areas that control

association cortex The parts of the cerebral cortex that integrate sensory and motor information and perform complex cognitive tasks.

LANGUAGE AREAS OF THE BRAIN Have you ever tried to write notes while you were talking to someone? Like this teacher, you can probably write and talk at the same time, because each of these language functions uses different areas of association cortex. However, stop reading for a moment, and try writing one word with your left hand and a different word with your right hand. If you had trouble, it is partly because you asked the same language area of your brain to do two things at once.

 LINKAGES
Where are the brain's language centers? (a link to Biology and Behavior)

face muscles. This part of the cortex is on the left side of the brain and is called *Broca's area* (see Figure 2.9). Damage to Broca's area disrupts speech organization, a condition called *Broca's aphasia*. Victims have difficulty speaking, often making errors in grammar. Each word comes out slowly. One patient was asked about a dental appointment and said haltingly, "Yes . . . Monday . . . Dad and Dick . . . Wednesday 9 o'clock . . . doctors . . . and . . . teeth" (Geschwind, 1979). The patient had the ideas of *dentist* and *teeth* right but could not express them clearly. Surprisingly, when a person with Broca's aphasia sings, the words come easily and correctly. Apparently, words set to music are handled by a different part of the brain.

Other language problems result from damage to a portion of association cortex described in the 1870s by Carl Wernicke. Like Broca's area, *Wernicke's area* is on the left side of the brain (see Figure 2.9). It is in the temporal lobe, near the area of the sensory cortex that receives information from the ears. Wernicke's area also receives input from the visual cortex and is involved in the interpretation of both speech and written words. Damage to Wernicke's area produces complicated symptoms. It can leave patients with the ability to speak but disrupts the ability to understand the meaning of words or to speak *understandably*. One patient, having been asked to describe a picture of two boys stealing cookies behind a woman's back, said, "Mother is away here working her work to get her better, but when she's looking the two boys looking in the other part. She's working another time" (Geschwind, 1979).

It appears that written language and spoken language require the use of different areas of association cortex. So does language involving specific grammatical or conceptual categories. For example, two women—H.W. and S.J.D.—each had a stroke in 1985, causing damage to different language-related parts of their association cortex. Neither woman has difficulty speaking or writing nouns, but both have difficulty with verbs (Caramazza & Hillis, 1991). H.W. can write verbs but cannot speak them. S.J.D. can speak verbs but has difficulty writing them. Interestingly, H.W. has difficulty pronouncing *watch* when it is used as a verb in the sentence "I watch TV," but she speaks the same word easily when it appears as a noun in "My watch is slow."

The Divided Brain: Lateralization

A striking suggestion emerged from observations of people with damage to the language centers of the brain. Researchers noticed that damage to specific areas of the left hemi-

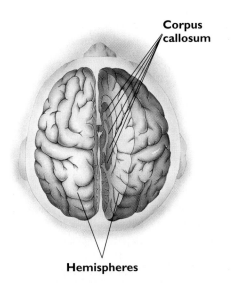

Corpus callosum

Hemispheres

FIGURE 2.11

The Brain's Left and Right Hemispheres

The brain's two hemispheres are joined by a core bundle of nerve fibers known as the corpus callosum; in this figure the corpus callosum has been cut, and the hemispheres are separated. The two cerebral hemispheres look nearly the same but perform somewhat different tasks. For one thing, the left hemisphere receives sensory input from, and controls movement on, the right side of the body. The right hemisphere senses and controls the left side of the body.

sphere interfered with the use or comprehension of language. Corresponding damage to the right hemisphere usually did not. Could it be that the right and left hemispheres of the brain serve different functions?

This is not a new idea. It has long been understood that most sensory and motor pathways cross over from one hemisphere to the other as they enter or leave the brain. As a result, the *left hemisphere* receives information from and controls movements of, the *right* side of the body. The *right hemisphere* receives input from and controls the *left* side of the body. Figure 2.11 shows the two hemispheres. The fact that language centers such as Broca's area and Wernicke's area almost always occur on the left side of the brain suggests that each hemisphere might be specialized to perform some functions almost independently of the other hemisphere.

In the late 1800s there was great interest in the idea that the hemispheres might be specialized, but no techniques were available for testing it. Renewed interest grew out of studies during the 1960s by Roger Sperry, Michael Gazzaniga, and their colleagues.

Split-Brain Studies Sperry studied *split-brain* patients—people who had undergone surgery in an attempt to control the severe seizures of epilepsy. Before the surgery, their seizures began in one hemisphere and then spread throughout the brain. As a last resort, surgeons isolated the two hemispheres from each other by cutting the corpus callosum.

After the surgery, researchers used a special device like the one shown in Figure 2.12 to present visual images to only one side of these patients' split brains. They found that cutting the tie between the hemispheres had dramatically affected the way these people thought about and dealt with the world. For example, when the image of a spoon was presented to the left, language-oriented side of patient N.G.'s split brain, she could say what the spoon was. But when the spoon was presented to the right side of her brain, she could not describe the spoon in words. She still knew what the object was, because she could pick it out from a group of objects by feeling its shape with her left hand (controlled by the right hemisphere). When asked what she had just grasped, she replied, "A pencil." The right hemisphere recognized the object, but the patient could not say what it was because the left (language) half of her brain did not see or feel it (R. W. Sperry, 1968).

Although the right hemisphere has no control over spoken language in split-brain patients, it does have important capabilities related to nonspoken language. For example, a split-brain patient's right hemisphere can guide the left hand in spelling out words with Scrabble tiles (Gazzaniga & LeDoux, 1978). Thanks to this finding, researchers concluded that split-brain patients have self-awareness and normal learning abilities in their

FIGURE 2.12

Apparatus for Studying Split-Brain Patients

When the person stares at the dot on the screen, images briefly presented on one side of the dot go to only one side of the brain. For example, a picture of a spoon presented on the left side of the screen goes to the right side of the brain. The right side of the brain can find the spoon and direct the left hand to touch it; but because the language areas on the left side of the brain did not see it, the person is not able to say what it is.

right hemispheres. In addition, these patients' right hemispheres showed superiority over their left hemispheres at tasks involving spatial relationships, drawing three-dimensional shapes, and recognizing human faces.

Having these two somewhat specialized hemispheres allows the normal brain to perform some tasks more efficiently, particularly difficult ones (Hoptman & Davidson, 1994). But the differences between the hemispheres should not be exaggerated. Remember, the corpus callosum usually integrates the functions of the "two brains." As a result, the hemispheres work closely together, each making up well for whatever lack of ability the other may have (Banich & Heller, 1998).

Plasticity in the Brain

The brain has the remarkable ability to strengthen neural connections at synapses and to establish new synapses. This ability, called **synaptic plasticity,** is what allows us to form memories and learn from experiences. However, the brain's plasticity is severely limited when it comes to repairing damage.

Why does the brain have such a hard time repairing itself? For one thing, neurons divide and multiply during prenatal development, but as the brain matures after birth, most of its neurons stop dividing. Indeed, new neurons are produced so slowly in adult animals, including humans, that until recently the production of new neurons was thought to be impossible. Actually, learning new things and facing stress do cause new neurons to appear in a small area of the hippocampus in rats, rabbits, monkeys, and humans (Blakeslee, 2000; Gould et al., 1999). However, the brain normally responds to experience or injury mainly by changing the connections between axons and dendrites, not by making more neurons. Second, the axons and dendrites of any new neurons grown in the brain would have the difficult task of "rewiring" all the lost communication links with neighboring neurons. In the peripheral nervous system, glial cells guide the regrowth of axons. In the central nervous system, however, communication links cannot be reconnected, because the glial cells "clean up" after brain damage by consuming the injured neurons and forming a barrier to new connections (I. H. Robertson & Murre, 1999).

Nevertheless, the brain does try to restore itself. Healthy neurons attempt to take over for damaged ones by changing their own function and by sprouting axons whose connections help nearby regions take on new functions (Cao et al., 1994). These changes rarely result in complete restoration of lost functions, though new research with animals and humans suggests that there might yet be hope for patients who have suffered severe injuries to the brain or spinal cord. For example, special mental and physical exercise programs appear helpful in "re-wiring" the brains of stroke victims so as to reverse some forms of paralysis and improve some cognitive abilities (Liepert et al., 2000; I. H. Robertson & Murre, 1999). Scientists have also discovered a protein called Nogo that prevents newly sprouted axons from making connections with other neurons in the central nervous system. Blocking the action of Nogo in rats allowed surviving neurons to make new axonal connections and actually repair spinal cord damage (M. S. Chen et al., 2000). Much more research is needed, of course, but if it is successful and is found to apply to humans, it might someday help make it possible for patients like Christopher Reeve to walk again.

Other new methods are also being devised to help people recover from brain damage. One approach is to replace lost tissue with tissue from another brain. Scientists have transplanted, or grafted, tissue from a still-developing fetal brain onto the brain of an adult animal of the same species. If the receiving animal does not reject the graft, it sprouts axons that make some functional connections in the brain. This treatment has reversed animals' learning difficulties, movement disorders, and other results of brain damage. It has also been used to treat a small number of Parkinson's disease patients, with very encouraging results that have been maintained for years after the transplant (Kordower et al., 1995). Exciting new work with animals has shown that the effectiveness of brain-tissue grafts can be greatly increased by adding proteins called *growth factors,* which promote neuron survival (Takayama et al., 1995). One of the most effective of these proteins is glial cell line–derived neurotrophic factor, or GDNF (Lapchak et al., 1997). The brain-tissue transplant procedure shows promise, but because its use with humans requires tissue from aborted fetuses, it is very controversial. An alternative trans-

synaptic plasticity   The brain's ability to create, and change the strength of, synapses.

(A) AT BIRTH

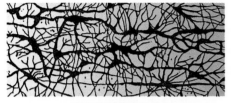

(B) SIX YEARS OLD

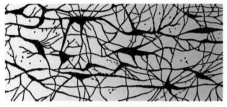

(C) FOURTEEN YEARS OLD

Source: Conel (1939/1967).

FIGURE 2.13

Changes in Neurons of the Cerebral Cortex During Development

During childhood, the brain overproduces neural connections, establishes the usefulness of certain connections, and then "prunes" the extra connections. Overproduction of synapses, especially in the frontal cortex, may be essential for infants to develop certain intellectual abilities. Some scientists believe that connections that are used survive, whereas others die.

LINKAGES
How do our brains change over a lifetime? (a link to Human Development)

plantation approach to repairing spinal cord injury is offered by the newly developing field of *tissue engineering.* In one preliminary study, immature cells from an adult rat's spinal cord were stimulated to grow and then implanted into the gap in other rats' severed spinal cords. Within a few months, some of these previously paralyzed rats were able to stand and walk (Noble, 2000).

It has recently been discovered that growth factors can also promote the appearance of new neurons by stimulating *stem cells* found in the brain, the bone marrow, and elsewhere in the body (Takahashi, Palmer, & Gage, 1999). As their name suggests, stem cells can develop into many kinds of cells, including neurons. In fact, new cells that appear in the adult hippocampus grow from these stem cells (Gould et al., 1999). Research with stem cells raises the hope that injured adult brains can be stimulated to form significant numbers of new neurons (Magavi, Leavitt, & Macklis, 2000; Takahashi et al., 1999). It may even be possible that patients suffering from Parkinson's disease and Alzheimer's disease might be cured by replacing dying neurons with new ones from their own brains or bone marrow, or from transplants of stem cells that were harvested from fetal tissue and converted into neurons (Kondo & Raff, 2000; Lennard & Jackson, 2000; Phillips et al., 2000; Sanchez-Ramos et al., 2000; Woodbury et al., 2000).

LINKAGES

Human Development and the Changing Brain

How does the human brain change as we develop? Researchers are using PET scans and MRI to begin to answer that question. They have discovered interesting correlations between changes in neural activity and the behavior of newborns and infants. Among newborns, PET scans show that activity is relatively high in the thalamus but low in a portion of the forebrain related to smooth movement. This finding may be related to the way newborns move. They make random, sweeping movements of the arms and legs—much like patients with Huntington's disease, who have a hyperactive thalamus and a withering of the portion of the forebrain that controls smooth movement (Chugani & Phelps, 1986). During the second and third months of life, activity increases in many regions of the cortex. This change is correlated with the loss of reflexes not under cortical control, such as the grasping reflex. At eight or nine months of age, infants exhibit increased frontal cortex activity, which correlates well with the apparent beginnings of cognitive activity (Chugani & Phelps, 1986). The brain continues to mature even through adolescence, showing evidence of ever more efficient neural communication in its major fiber tracts (Paus et al., 1999).

As noted earlier, most of these changes reflect changes in axons and synapses, not the appearance of new cells. After birth, the number of dendrites and synapses increases. Although different areas of the cortex sprout at different rates, the number of synapses can increase tenfold in the first year after birth (Huttenlocher, 1990). In fact, by the time children are six or seven years old, their brains have more dendrites than those of adults, and they use twice as much energy. In early adolescence, the number of dendrites and neural connections actually drops, so the adult level is reached by about the age of fourteen. During childhood, the brain overproduces neural connections and then "prunes" the extra connections. Figure 2.13 shows the changes in neural connections during development.

In spite of dendrite pruning, the brain retains its plasticity and "rewires" itself to form new connections throughout life. Genes apparently determine the basic pattern of growth and the major lines of connections. However, the details of the connections seem to depend on factors such as how interesting the environment is. For example, researchers have compared the brains of rats raised in individual cages with only a boring cage-side view to the brains of rats raised with toys and playmates. The cerebral cortex of those from the enriched environment had more and longer dendrites, as well as more synapses, than did the cortex of animals raised alone in bare cages (A. M. Turner & Greenough, 1985). Furthermore, the number of synapses increased when old animals

Some Major Glands of the Endocrine System

Each of the glands shown releases its hormones into the bloodstream. Even the hypothalamus, a part of the brain, regulates the nearby pituitary gland by secreting hormones.

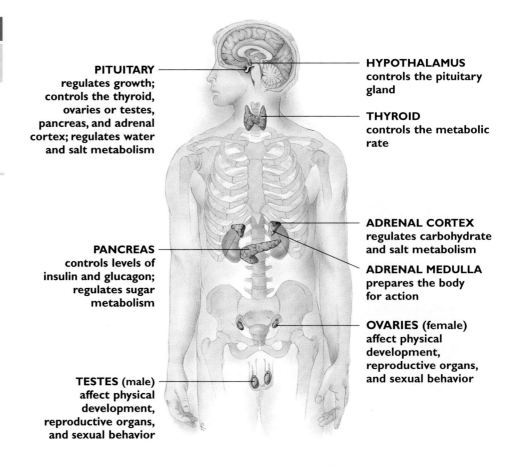

PITUITARY regulates growth; controls the thyroid, ovaries or testes, pancreas, and adrenal cortex; regulates water and salt metabolism

HYPOTHALAMUS controls the pituitary gland

THYROID controls the metabolic rate

ADRENAL CORTEX regulates carbohydrate and salt metabolism

ADRENAL MEDULLA prepares the body for action

PANCREAS controls levels of insulin and glucagon; regulates sugar metabolism

OVARIES (female) affect physical development, reproductive organs, and sexual behavior

TESTES (male) affect physical development, reproductive organs, and sexual behavior

who had always lived in boring cages were moved to an enriched environment (E. J. Green, Greenough, & Schlumpf, 1983). Environmentally influenced neuronal changes may help explain why the maze-learning ability of genetically "maze-dull" rats raised in stimulating cages can equal that of genetically "maze-bright" animals.

Researchers have not yet determined whether an enriched environment stimulates the development of new connections or slows down normal pruning. Also not known is whether animals moved from a stimulating environment to a boring one will lose synaptic connections. If existing findings apply to humans, however, they hold implications for raising children and treating the elderly (see Chapters 7 and 9). It is surely the case that within the limits set by genetics, interactions with the world mold the brain itself.

endocrine system   Cells that form organs called *glands* and that communicate with each other by secreting hormones.

glands   Organs that secrete hormones into the bloodstream.

hormones   Chemicals secreted by glands into the bloodstream, allowing stimulation of cells that are not directly connected.

fight-or-flight syndrome   Physical reactions initiated by the sympathetic nervous system that prepare the body to fight or to run from a threatening situation.

The Endocrine System: Coordinating the Internal World

How can my hormones help me in a crisis?

Neurons are not the only cells that use chemicals to communicate with one another in ways that affect behavior and mental processes. Another kind of cell with this ability is found in the **endocrine system** (pronounced "EN-doh-krinn"). Operating on orders from the brain, the endocrine system regulates growth, metabolism, and sexual behavior, and it readies the body for action. The cells of the endocrine organs, or **glands,** communicate by secreting chemicals, much as neurons do. Figure 2.14 shows some major glands of the endocrine system. The chemicals that these glands secrete are called **hormones.**

Hormones from endocrine organs are similar to neurotransmitters. In fact, many such chemicals, including norepinephrine and endorphins, act both as hormones and as neurotransmitters. However, whereas neurons secrete neurotransmitters into synapses, endocrine organs put their chemicals into the bloodstream to be carried throughout the body. In this way, endocrine glands can stimulate cells with which they have no direct connection. Not all cells receive the hormonal message. Hormones, like neurotransmitters, can influence only those cells with receptors capable of receiving them (McEwen, 1991). *Target organs* are those whose cells have receptors for a particular hormone.

Each hormone acts on many target organs, producing coordinated effects throughout the body. For example, when a woman's ovaries secrete the sex hormone estrogen, it activates her reproductive system, causing the uterus to grow in preparation for nurturing an embryo. It enlarges the breasts to prepare them for nursing. It stimulates the brain to increase interest in sexual activity. And it stimulates the pituitary gland to release another hormone that causes a mature egg to be released by the ovary for fertilization. The brain, as a kind of "boss," has ultimate control over the secretion of hormones. The hypothalamus controls the pituitary gland, which in turn controls endocrine organs in the body. The brain is also a target organ for most hormones. In short, the endocrine system typically involves the brain, the pituitary gland, the endocrine organ, and the target organs (which include the brain). Each part in the system uses hormones to signal the next.

The secretion of each hormone is increased or decreased by other hormones. Let's look, for example, at stress-hormone systems. When the brain interprets a situation as threatening, it stimulates the pituitary to release adrenocorticotropic hormone (ACTH), which causes the adrenal glands to release the hormone cortisol into the bloodstream. Cortisol, in turn, acts on cells throughout the body, including the brain. One effect of cortisol is to activate the emotion-related limbic system, making it more likely that you will remember stressful or traumatic events (L. Cahill & McGaugh, 1998). The combined effects of the adrenal hormones and the activation of the sympathetic nervous system result in the **fight-or-flight syndrome.** This set of responses prepares us for action in response to danger or other stress. The heart beats faster, the liver releases glucose into the bloodstream, fuels are mobilized from fat stores, and the body as a whole is placed in a state of high arousal. Without the endocrine system and the effects of its hormones on the brain, your life would not only be much less emotional, but you also would be less able to escape or avoid threatening experiences.

active review Biology and Behavior

Linkages

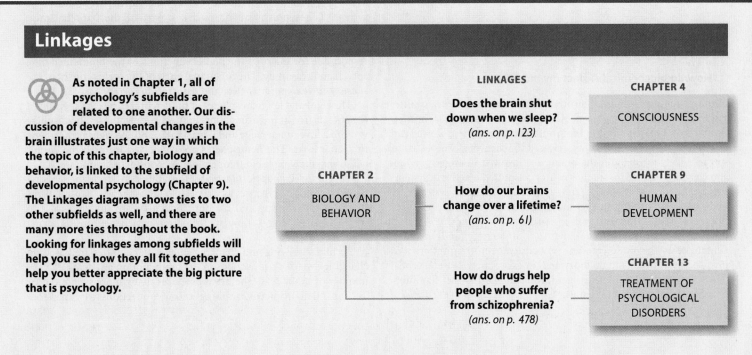

As noted in Chapter 1, all of psychology's subfields are related to one another. Our discussion of developmental changes in the brain illustrates just one way in which the topic of this chapter, biology and behavior, is linked to the subfield of developmental psychology (Chapter 9). The Linkages diagram shows ties to two other subfields as well, and there are many more ties throughout the book. Looking for linkages among subfields will help you see how they all fit together and help you better appreciate the big picture that is psychology.

LINKAGES

Does the brain shut down when we sleep?
(ans. on p. 123)

CHAPTER 4
CONSCIOUSNESS

CHAPTER 2
BIOLOGY AND BEHAVIOR

How do our brains change over a lifetime?
(ans. on p. 61)

CHAPTER 9
HUMAN DEVELOPMENT

How do drugs help people who suffer from schizophrenia?
(ans. on p. 478)

CHAPTER 13
TREATMENT OF PSYCHOLOGICAL DISORDERS

Summary

Biological psychology focuses on the biological aspects of our being, which provide the physical basis for behavior and mental processes. Included among these aspects is the nervous system, which is composed of billions of cells that allow humans and other organisms to gain information about what is going on inside and outside the body and to respond appropriately.

CELLS OF THE NERVOUS SYSTEM

What are neurons, and what do they do?

Much of our understanding of the biological aspects of psychology has stemmed from research on animal and human nervous systems at levels ranging from single cells to complex organizations of cells, including the brain. The fundamental units of the nervous system are cells called *neurons* and *glial cells.* Neurons are especially good at receiving signals from, and transmitting signals to, other neurons. Neurons have cell bodies and two types of fibers, called *axons* and *dendrites.* Axons usually carry signals away from the cell body, whereas dendrites usually carry signals to the cell body.

Neurons can transmit signals because of the structure of the axons and dendrites, the excitable surface of some of these fibers, and the *synapses,* or gaps, between cells. A neuron can transmit, or fire, an *action potential* from one end of its axon to the other. The speed of the action potential is fastest in neurons sheathed in myelin. Between firings there is a very brief rest, called a *refractory period.*

When an action potential reaches the end of an axon, the axon releases a chemical called a *neurotransmitter.* It crosses the synapse and interacts with the postsynaptic cell at receptors that make the postsynaptic cell either more likely or less likely to fire its own action potential. Because the fibers of neurons have many branches, each neuron can interact with thousands of other neurons. Each neuron constantly integrates signals received at its many synapses; the result of this integration determines how often the neuron fires an action potential.

THE CHEMISTRY OF BEHAVIOR: NEUROTRANSMITTERS

How do biochemicals affect my mood?

Neurons that use the same neurotransmitter form a neurotransmitter system. There are seven particularly important neurotransmitters. Acetylcholine systems in the brain influence memory processes and movement. Norepinephrine is released by neurons whose axons spread widely throughout the brain; it is involved in arousal, mood, and learning. Serotonin, another neurotransmitter, is active in systems regulating mood, attention, and appetite. Dopamine systems are involved in movement and reward; Parkinson's disease, drug addiction, and schizophrenia involve dopamine systems. GABA is an inhibitory neurotransmitter involved in anxiety and epilepsy. Glutamate is the most common excitatory neurotransmitter; it is involved in learning and memory and, in excess, may cause neuronal death. Finally, endorphins are neurotransmitters that act like morphine by modulating pain pathways.

THE PERIPHERAL NERVOUS SYSTEM: KEEPING IN TOUCH WITH THE WORLD

How is my nervous system organized?

Neurons are organized in networks of connected cells, forming sensory systems, which receive information from the environment, and motor systems, which influence the actions of muscles and other organs. The two major divisions of the nervous system are the *central nervous system (CNS),* which includes the brain and spinal cord, and the *peripheral nervous system.* The peripheral nervous system has two components. The first is the *somatic nervous system,* which transmits information from the senses to the CNS and carries signals from the CNS to muscles that move the skeleton. The second is the *autonomic nervous system,* whose subsystems, the *sympathetic nervous system* and the *parasympathetic nervous system,* carry messages back and forth between the CNS and the heart, lungs, and other organs and glands.

THE CENTRAL NERVOUS SYSTEM: MAKING SENSE OF THE WORLD

How is my brain "wired"?

The CNS is laid out in interconnected groups of neuron cell bodies called *nuclei,* whose collections of axons travel together in *fiber tracts* or pathways. The *spinal cord* receives information from the peripheral senses and sends it to the brain; it also relays messages from the brain to the rest of the body. In addition, cells of the spinal cord can direct simple behaviors, called *reflexes,* without instructions from the brain. The brain's major subdivisions are the *hindbrain, midbrain,* and *forebrain.* The hindbrain includes the *medulla* and the *cerebellum.* The *reticular formation* is found in both the hindbrain and the midbrain.

The forebrain is the largest and most highly developed part of the brain. Its structures include the *hypothalamus* and *thalamus,* as well as the *hippocampus* and the *amygdala,* which form part of the limbic system. The suprachiasmatic nuclei, a part of the hypothalamus, maintain a clock that determines biological rhythms. The outer surface of the cerebral hemispheres is called the *cerebral cortex;* it is responsible for many of the higher functions of the brain, including speech and reasoning. The functional areas of the cortex consist of the *sensory cortex, motor cortex,* and *association cortex.*

The right and left hemispheres of the cerebral cortex are specialized to some degree in their functions. In most people, the left hemisphere is more active in language and logical tasks and the right hemisphere, in spatial tasks. The hemispheres are connected through the *corpus callosum,* allowing them to operate in a coordinated fashion.

The brain's *synaptic plasticity,* the ability to strengthen neural connections at its synapses as well as to establish new synapses, forms the basis for learning and memory. Scientists are studying ways to increase plasticity and stimulate formation of new neurons following brain damage.

A child's growing and changing intellectual abilities are based on changing synaptic connections in the brain, not on an increase in the number of brain cells. The brain produces many more synaptic connections than it needs, pruning extra connections as experience strengthens useful connections. The ability to form new synapses continues even into old age.

THE ENDOCRINE SYSTEM: COORDINATING THE INTERNAL WORLD

How can my hormones help me in a crisis?

Like nervous system cells, the cells of the *endocrine system* communicate by releasing a chemical that signals other cells. However, the chemicals released by endocrine organs, or *glands,* are called *hormones* and are carried by the bloodstream to remote target organs. The brain is the main controller: Through the hypothalamus, it controls the pituitary gland, which in turn controls endocrine organs in the body. The brain is also a target organ for most endocrine secretions. The target organs often produce a coordinated response to hormonal stimulation. One of these responses is the *fight-or-flight syndrome,* which is set off by adrenal hormones that prepare for action in times of stress.

Learn by Doing

Put It in Writing

You want to help your sister choose an infant care center for your one-year-old nephew that will be most likely to stimulate his brain development. Write a page about what biological psychology research tells you about the role of environment on brain development. Does that research provide a useful guide for choosing the best day-care center? Why or why not?

Personal Learning Activity

To get a rough measure of the role of your brain's left hemisphere in language, try the following test. First, see how long you can balance a yardstick on the tip of your right index finger, and then try the same task with your left hand. The difference in how long you can keep the stick balanced will probably be determined by whether you are right-handed or left-handed. Now try this balancing act eight more times, alternating hands on each trial so that you use your left index finger four times and your right index finger four times. Now here's where language might come in: On two of the four trials with each hand, count backwards from 100 by 3s (100, 97, 94, 91, etc.) out loud while you try to keep the stick balanced. It has been suggested that this language task might interfere with your balancing skill, especially when you are using your right hand (Kemble, Filipi, & Gravlin, 1985; Kinsbourne & Cook, 1971). Why? If the left side of your brain is more involved with language, then trying to count backwards while balancing with your right hand requires the left hemisphere to do two things at once. When counting while balancing with the left hand, the right hemisphere is handling the balancing, and the left hemisphere is dealing with the language task. Is this what happened in your case? Try the same tests on your friends, and summarize the results. *For additional projects, see the five Personal Learning Activities in the corresponding chapter of the study guide that accompanies this text.*

Step into Action

Courses

Biological Bases of Behavior, Physiological Psychology, Biological Psychology, Brain and Behavior, Introduction to Neuroscience, Anatomy and Physiology

Movies

Awakenings (neurotransmitters and mental functioning)

Books

Steven Pinker, *How the Mind Works* (Norton, 1997) (brain and behavior)

William Calvin, *The Throwing Madonna: Essays on the Brain* (Bantam, 1991) (brain and behavior)

Jimmy Breslin, *I Want to Thank My Brain for Remembering Me: A Memoir* (Little, Brown, 1997) (brain and behavior)

William Calvin and George Ojemann, *Conversations with Neil's Brain: The Neural Nature of Thought and Language* (Addison-Wesley, 1994) (the brain's role in thought and language, as illustrated through the case of brain surgery on an epileptic patient)

Robert Ornstein, *The Right Mind: Making Sense of the Hemispheres* (Harcourt, 1997) (hemispheric laterality)

Ross Pelton, *Mind Food and Smart Pills* (T & R Publishers, 1997) (foods and drugs that may affect mental functioning)

The Web

The World Wide Web is a good source of additional information about the science of psychology, provided you use it carefully and think critically about the information you find. The PsychAbilities web site that accompanies this text offers many resources relevant to this chapter. They include interactive NetLab exercises; Thinking Critically and Evaluating Research exercises; ACE chapter quizzes; recommended web links; and articles on current events, books, and movies. At http://college.hmco.com, select *Psychology* and then this textbook.

Review of Key Terms

Can you define each of the key terms in the chapter? Check your definitions against those on the pages listed in parentheses below or in the Glossary/Index at the end of the text.

action potential *(p. 40)*

amygdala *(p. 52)*

association cortex *(p. 57)*

autonomic nervous system *(p. 46)*

axon *(p. 40)*

biological psychology *(p. 38)*

central nervous system *(p. 46)*

cerebellum *(p. 51)*

cerebral cortex *(p. 53)*

corpus callosum *(p. 53)*

dendrites *(p. 40)*

endocrine system *(p. 62)*

fiber tracts *(p. 47)*

fight-or-flight syndrome *(p. 63)*

forebrain *(p. 52)*

glands *(p. 62)*

glial cells *(p. 39)*

hindbrain *(p. 49)*

hippocampus *(p. 52)*

hormones *(p. 62)*

hypothalamus *(p. 52)*

medulla *(p. 49)*

midbrain *(p. 51)*

motor cortex *(p. 55)*

neurons *(p. 39)*

neurotransmitter *(p. 41)*

nuclei *(p. 47)*

parasympathetic nervous system *(p. 47)*

peripheral nervous system *(p. 46)*

reflexes *(p. 48)*

refractory period *(p. 40)*

reticular formation *(p. 50)*

sensory cortex *(p. 54)*

somatic nervous system *(p. 46)*

spinal cord *(p. 48)*

sympathetic nervous system *(p. 47)*

synapse *(p. 41)*

synaptic plasticity *(p. 59)*

thalamus *(p. 52)*

Multiple-Choice Self-Test

Select the best answer for each of the questions below. Then check your responses against the Answer Key at the end of the text.

1. A woman was rushed into an emergency room with severely burned hands. She had picked up an iron because she couldn't tell it was hot, and she currently doesn't feel pain from the burns. The neurologist who examined her concluded that the woman's _____ system was malfunctioning.

   a. sensory
   b. motor
   c. autonomic
   d. parasympathetic

2. Dr. Frankenstein has given up on creating a human and is trying to build King Kong's cousin. However, he forgot to install the motor nerves of the somatic system. What will Kong's kin be unable to do?

   a. climb skyscrapers
   b. hear people scream
   c. digest skyscrapers
   d. see people run from him

3. Kalli finishes her exam and hurries home. When she arrives, she flops down on her bed to relax. As Kalli relaxes, her _____ nervous system becomes less active, whereas her _____ nervous system becomes more active.

   a. central; somatic
   b. somatic; central
   c. parasympathetic; sympathetic
   d. sympathetic; parasympathetic

4. The _____ is located in the hindbrain and helps to regulate heart rate, blood pressure, and breathing.

   a. medulla
   b. hypothalamus
   c. thalamus
   d. cerebellum

5. Broca's area and Wernicke's area are located in the _____ cerebral hemisphere and are involved in _____.

   a. right; language
   b. left; language
   c. right; movement
   d. left; biological rhythms

6. A friend has asked you for help with her history homework. She must be able to recognize and name famous people. Which cerebral hemisphere is most likely to become activated while she does her homework?

   a. the right
   b. the left
   c. both
   d. either

7. A nurse has mixed up some test results on neurotransmitter function for several patients at the hospital where you work. To help her out, you tell her that the Huntington's patient's chart will show malfunctions in _____ systems, and the Parkinson's patient's chart will show malfunctions in _____ systems.

   a. dopamine; norepinephrine
   b. dopamine; acetylcholine
   c. GABA; dopamine
   d. acetylcholine; norepinephrine

8. Ted is trying to make a study sheet to help him learn the differences between neurotransmitters and hormones. Which of the following statements on his list is not correct?

   a. Neurotransmitters travel via the bloodstream, and hormones travel across synapses.
   b. Both hormones and neurotransmitters stimulate only those cells and organs that have receptors for them.
   c. Hormones and neurotransmitters regulate complex behaviors and mental processes.
   d. Hormones operate mainly in the endocrine system; neurotransmitters operate mainly in the nervous system.

9. George is experiencing a tingling sensation in his left foot. Which area of the brain has most likely been affected?

   a. left temporal lobe
   b. left striatum
   c. right frontal lobe
   d. right parietal lobe

10. Karena accidentally touched a hot stove, and she instantly jerked her hand away. This automatic response was directed by neurons entering and leaving the _____, which is part of the _____ nervous system.

    a. spinal cord; central
    b. spinal cord; autonomic
    c. hypothalamus; central
    d. hypothalamus; autonomic

11. In today's episode of your favorite soap opera, a doctor charges through the emergency room doors and tells a worried spouse that her husband has a neurological problem. "The nerves that carry signals to his muscles are not functioning," the doctor says, "because the _____ nervous system has been damaged."

    a. central
    b. autonomic
    c. somatic
    d. sympathetic

12. Venus is playing volleyball. She is running, hitting the ball, and shouting encouragement to her teammates. As a consequence, her heart rate is high, her breathing is rapid, and she is sweating. Which subdivision of her autonomic nervous system has been activated?

    a. parasympathetic
    b. peripheral
    c. somatic
    d. sympathetic

13. Riley was an excellent pianist until he suffered brain damage. Now, problems with fine motor skills make it impossible for him to play the piano. Riley most likely had damage to his _____.

    a. cerebellum
    b. hippocampus
    c. hypothalamus
    d. reticular formation

14. People with severed spinal cords cannot receive sensory information from, or send signals to, the muscles below the level of damage because

    a. the brain can no longer decipher incoming sensory information.
    b. the information going to and from the brain must travel through the spinal cord.
    c. the thalamus's relay station for sensory information degenerates after spinal cord injuries.
    d. neurotransmitters in sensory neurons dry up.

15. Lily had surgery on her hindbrain, because damage in that area caused her to lapse into a coma. The damage most likely occurred in the

    a. cerebellum.
    b. hippocampus.
    c. hypothalamus.
    d. reticular formation.

16. The occipital lobe receives sensory information concerning

    a. pain.
    b. body movement.
    c. vision.
    d. body temperature.

17. Roberto, an actor, is recovering following a freak accident on the set of his latest movie. When asked about the accident, Roberto, once a confident and fluent speaker, can now only say, "Noise . . . acting . . . hurts." The part of Roberto's brain most likely involved in this type of speech problem is _____ area.

    a. Broca's
    b. Sperry's
    c. Wernicke's
    d. Sylva's

18. The hippocampus has been found to be significantly smaller in patients who are suffering from which of the following problems?

    a. Parkinson's disease
    b. Alzheimer's disease
    c. depression
    d. eating disorder

19. When Mitch saw a woman who appeared to be drowning, he grabbed his life preserver and ran to save her. To prepare his body for running, Mitch's _____ released cortisol and other chemicals into his bloodstream.

    a. glands
    b. neurotransmitter systems
    c. synapses
    d. target organs

20. Almyra has a brain tumor that has caused her to be unable to move her left leg. Her _____ lobe on the _____ side of the brain is the one most likely affected.

    a. frontal; left
    b. frontal; right
    c. parietal; left
    d. parietal; right

3

Sensation and Perception

Simply reading and understanding this sentence is a feat of immense proportions as lines and squiggles (letters) become meaningful words. This is what sensation and perception are all about. You translate outside stimulation, such as the light bouncing off this page, into neural activity called *sensations*. Then you interpret these sensations as meaningful perceptual experiences—in this case, as letters and words. These processes are so quick and automatic that you might take them for granted. In this chapter, you will learn about how our sensory systems receive stimulation and how that stimulation is coded into patterns of nerve activity for the brain to decode. The sensory systems include vision, hearing, taste, smell, and touch. Next, you will discover how the brain interprets, or perceives, this information from your senses. Principles for organizing the perceptual world allow you to recognize what you have seen, heard, tasted, smelled, or felt.

Reading this chapter will help you to answer the following questions:

- **What is the difference between sensation and perception?**
- **How does information from my eyes and ears get to my brain?**
- **Why do some people need eyeglasses?**
- **How would my voice sound on the moon?**
- **Why can't I taste anything when I have a cold?**
- **Which is the largest organ in my body?**
- **How do sensations become perceptions?**
- **What determines how I perceive my world?**
- **How do I recognize familiar people?**
- **Can you "run out" of attention?**

Years ago, Fred Aryee lost his right arm below the elbow in a boating accident, yet he still "feels" sensations from his missing arm and hand. His doctor asked Aryee to reach for a cup on the table in front of him with his right arm. When asked what he felt, Aryee said, "I feel my fingers clasping the cup" (Shreeve, 1993). People like Fred may also feel intense pain that seems to be coming from a lost limb (Merzenich, 1998). Where do these "phantom limb" sensations and perceptions come from? Fred no longer has fingers to send messages to the brain, yet he experienced his "feeling" of the cup as real.

The question, then, is, What is reality? We tend to assume that everyone experiences the same reality, but sensory psychologists tell us that reality is not that simple. Every

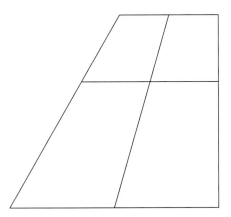

FIGURE 3.1

What Do You See?

individual's senses actively shape information about the outside world to create a *personal* reality. Psychologists distinguish between sensation (the initial message coming from the senses) and perception (the process of giving meaning to that message). So you do not actually sense a *cat* lying on the sofa. You sense shapes and colors, the visual sensations. You then use your knowledge of the world to interpret, or perceive, these sensations as a cat. However, it is impossible to draw a clear line between sensation and perception, because the process of interpreting sensations begins in the sense organs themselves.

Sensing and Perceiving the World

What is the difference between sensation and perception?

To understand how sensory systems help us create reality, we need basic information about the senses. A **sense** is a system that translates outside information into activity in the nervous system. For example, your eyes convert light into neural activity that tells the brain something about the source of the light or about the objects reflecting the light. Messages from the senses are called **sensations.** Sensations shape behaviors and mental processes by providing the vital link between the self and the world outside the brain.

Perception is the process of using information and your understanding of the world so that sensations become meaningful experiences. Perception is more than a passive process of absorbing and decoding incoming sensations. For example, the stimuli (plural for *stimulus*) in Figure 3.1 convey only raw sensory information about a series of intersecting lines. But your perceptual system automatically interprets this image as a rectangle (or window frame) lying on its side. Perception is so quick and familiar that it is difficult to appreciate the processes that allow you to turn sensory signals into your personal experience of reality. By shaping experience, perceptions influence thoughts, feelings, and actions. But before something can be perceived, it must be sensed.

Sensory Systems

How does information from my eyes and ears get to my brain?

Your senses gather information about the world by detecting various forms of energy, such as sound, light, heat, and physical pressure. Your eyes detect light energy, your ears detect the energy of sound, and your skin detects the energy of heat and pressure. Humans depend mainly on vision, hearing, and the skin senses to gain information about the world. We depend less than other animals on smell and taste. To your brain, "the world" also includes the rest of your body, so specific sensory systems provide information about the location and position of your body parts.

All of these senses must detect stimuli, encode them into neural activity, and transfer this coded information to the brain. Figure 3.2 illustrates these basic steps in sensation. At each step, sensory information is "processed" in some way. So the information that arrives at one point in the system is not exactly the same information that goes to the next step.

In some sensory systems, the first step in sensation involves **accessory structures,** which modify the incoming stimulus. For example, the lens of the eye is an accessory structure that changes incoming light by focusing it. The outer part of the ear is an accessory structure that collects sound.

The second step in sensation is **transduction,** which is the process of converting incoming energy into neural activity. Your radio receives electromagnetic energy from your favorite station and transduces it into sounds. In much the same way, your ears receive sound energy and transduce it into neural activity that you recognize as voices and music. Transduction takes place at structures called **receptors,** specialized cells that

sense   A system that translates data from outside the nervous system into neural activity.

sensations   Raw information from the senses.

perception   The process through which people take raw sensations from the environment and give them meaning, using knowledge, experience, and understanding of the world.

accessory structures   Structures, such as the outer part of the ear, that modify a stimulus.

transduction   The process of converting incoming physical energy into neural activity.

receptors   Cells specialized to detect certain types of energy and convert it into neural activity.

adaptation   Decreasing responsiveness to an unchanging stimulus over time.

coding   Translation of the physical properties of a stimulus into a specific pattern of neural activity.

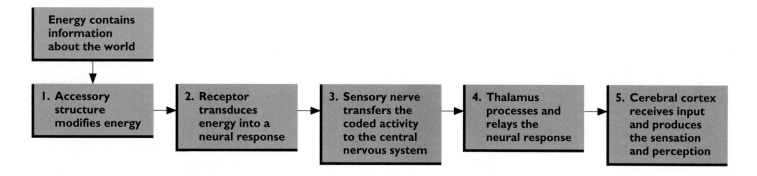

FIGURE 3.2

Elements of a Sensory System

Objects in the world generate energy that is focused by accessory structures and detected by sensory receptors, which convert the energy into neural signals. The signals are then relayed through parts of the brain, which processes them into perceptual experiences.

detect certain forms of energy. These receptors respond to incoming energy by firing an action potential and releasing neurotransmitters that send signals to neighboring cells. Sensory receptors respond best to *changes* in energy. A constant level of stimulation usually produces **adaptation,** a decreasing responsiveness to the stimulus over time. This is why the touch sensations you get from your glasses or your watch disappear shortly after you have put them on.

Sensory nerves carry information from receptors to the brain. For all the senses except smell, this information goes first to the thalamus, which then relays it to the cerebral cortex. The most complex processing occurs in the cortex. (You may want to review the discussion of brain structures in Chapter 2.)

Coding Sensations: Did You Feel That?

When receptors transduce or convert energy, they must somehow *code* the physical properties of the stimulus into patterns of neural activity. When organized by the brain, those neural patterns allow us to make sense of the stimulus. This processing lets you determine whether you are looking at a cat, a dog, or your friend.

Each psychological dimension of a sensation, such as brightness or color, has a corresponding physical dimension that is encoded by the sensory receptors. In other words, **coding** translates the physical properties of a stimulus, such as the loudness of sound, into a pattern of neural activity that tells us what those physical properties are.

Absolute Thresholds: Is Something Out There?

How much stimulus energy is needed to trigger a conscious perceptual experience? Not much at all. Normal human vision can detect the light equivalent to a candle flame burning in the dark thirty miles away. The minimum detectable amount of light, sound, pressure, or other physical energy is called the *absolute threshold.* Table 3.1 lists absolute thresholds for human vision, hearing, taste, smell, and touch.

TABLE 3.1

Some Absolute Thresholds

LEARN BY DOING **Absolute thresholds can be amazingly low. Here are examples of the stimulus equivalents at the absolute threshold for the five primary senses. Set up the conditions for testing the absolute threshold for sound, and see if you can detect this minimal amount of auditory stimulation. If you couldn't hear it, the signal-detection theory we discuss in this section may help explain why.**

Human Sense	Absolute Threshold Is Equivalent to:
Vision	A candle flame seen at 30 miles on a clear night
Hearing	The tick of a watch under quiet conditions at 20 feet
Taste	One teaspoon of sugar in 2 gallons of water
Smell	One drop of perfume diffused into the entire volume of air in a 6-room apartment
Touch	The wing of a fly falling on your cheek from a distance of 1 centimeter

Source: Galanter (1962).

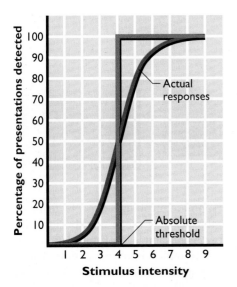

FIGURE 3.3

The Absolute Threshold

The curve shows the relationship between the physical intensity of a signal and the likelihood that it will be detected. If the absolute threshold were truly absolute, all signals at or above a particular intensity would always be detected, and no signal below that intensity would ever be detected (see red line). But this response pattern almost never occurs, so the "absolute" threshold is defined as the intensity at which the signal is detected with 50 percent accuracy.

---

absolute threshold   The minimum amount of stimulus energy that can be detected 50 percent of the time.

internal noise   The spontaneous, random firing of nerve cells that occurs because the nervous system is always active.

response criterion   The internal rule a person uses to decide whether or not to report a stimulus.

signal-detection theory   A mathematical model of what determines a person's report of a near-threshold stimulus.

sensitivity   The ability to detect a stimulus.

Weber's law   A law stating that the smallest detectable difference in stimulus energy (just-noticeable difference) is a constant fraction of the intensity of the stimulus.

just-noticeable difference (JND)   The smallest detectable difference in stimulus energy; also called *difference threshold.*

Psychologists discovered these thresholds by exploring *psychophysics,* the relationship between *physical energy* in the environment and your *psychological experience* of that energy. In a typical absolute threshold experiment, you would be seated in a darkened laboratory. After your eyes got used to the darkness, the researcher would show you brief flashes of light. These flashes would differ in brightness, or stimulus intensity. Each time, you'd be asked if you saw the light. Averaged over a large number of trials, your responses would probably form a curve like the one shown in Figure 3.3. As you can see, the absolute threshold is not an all-or-nothing phenomenon. A stimulus at an intensity of 3, which is below the absolute threshold in the figure, will still be detected 20 percent of the time it occurs. Because of such variability, psychophysicists redefined the **absolute threshold** as the smallest amount of energy that can be detected 50 percent of the time. Why does an "absolute" threshold vary? The two most important reasons have to do with internal noise and our response criterion.

Internal noise is the spontaneous, random firing of cells in the nervous system that happens (to varying degrees) whether or not you are stimulated by physical energy. This constant neural activity is a little like "snow" on a television screen or static between radio stations. If the amount of internal noise happens to be high at a particular moment, your sensory systems may mistakenly interpret the noise as an external stimulus.

The second source of variation in absolute threshold, the **response criterion,** reflects a person's willingness to respond to a stimulus. A person's *motivation*—wants and needs—as well as *expectancies* affect the response criterion. For example, if you were punished for reporting that a faint light appeared when it did not, then you might be motivated to raise your response criterion. That is, you would report the light only when you were quite sure you saw it. Similarly, expecting a faint stimulus to occur lowers the response criterion. Expecting the stimulus makes it more likely that you will detect it than if it is unexpected.

Signal-Detection Theory   Whether you detect a stimulus depends on its physical energy, the effects of internal noise, and your response criterion. Because all human beings experience these effects, researchers realized the measurement of absolute thresholds could never be more precise than the 50 percent rule mentioned earlier. So they abandoned the effort to determine absolute thresholds and turned to signal-detection theory.

Signal-detection theory presents a mathematical model of how your personal sensitivity and response criterion combine to determine your decision about whether or not a near-threshold stimulus occurred (D. M. Green & Swets, 1966). **Sensitivity** refers to your ability to discriminate a stimulus from its background. It is influenced by internal noise, the intensity of the stimulus, and the capacity of your sensory systems. The response criterion is the internal rule, also known as *bias,* that you use in deciding whether to report a signal. Will a lab technician notice the presence of cancer cells in a Pap smear? Will an airport security guard spot the weapon in a passenger's x-rayed luggage? Signal-detection theory provides a way to understand and predict such responses, because it allows precise measurement of sensitivity to stimuli of any kind (Swets, 1992).

Judging Differences Between Stimuli   In many situations, you have to detect a stimulus *and* determine whether two stimuli are the same or different. When tuning up for a concert, musicians must decide if notes played by two instruments are the same. When repainting part of a wall, you need to decide if the new paint matches the old.

Your ability to judge differences between stimuli depends on the strength of the stimuli you are dealing with. The weaker the stimuli are, the easier it is to detect small differences between them. For example, if you are comparing the weight of two oranges, you will be able to detect a difference of as little as a fraction of an ounce. But if you are comparing two boxes weighing around fifty pounds, you may not notice a difference unless it is a pound or more. One of the oldest laws in psychology, named after German physiologist Ernst Weber (pronounced "VAY-ber"), gives a precise description of this relationship. **Weber's law** states that the smallest detectable difference in stimulus energy is a constant fraction of the intensity of the stimulus. The smallest detectable difference in the stimulus is called the *difference threshold* or **just-noticeable difference (JND).** According to this law, if an object weighs 25 pounds, the JND is only half a pound. So, if you added

DETECTING VITAL SIGNS   According to signal detection theory, the likelihood that security personnel will detect the outline of a bomb or other weapon in a passenger's luggage depends partly on the sensitivity of their visual systems as they look at x-ray images, and partly on their response criterion, which is affected by their expectations that weapons might appear, and by how motivated they are to look carefully for them. To help keep inspectors' response criteria sufficiently low, those responsible for airport security occasionally attempt to smuggle a simulated weapon through a checkpoint. This procedure serves to assess the quality of security, and also prevents guards from becoming complacent.

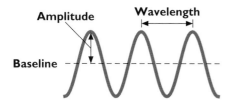

FIGURE 3.4

The Dimensions of a Wave

Wavelength is the distance from one peak of a wave to the next. Frequency is the number of complete waves, or cycles, that pass a given point in a given amount of time, such as one second. Amplitude is the height of a wave from baseline to peak.

a container of yogurt to a grocery bag with three gallons of milk in it, you could not tell the difference. But candy snatchers beware. It takes a change of only two-thirds of an ounce to determine that someone has been into a two-pound box of chocolates! Different senses have different JNDs. Vision, for instance, is very sensitive. Only a small change in the intensity of light is needed for a difference in its brightness to be noticeable.

Sensory Energy   The sensory energies of light and sound vibrate as waves passing through space. These waves result from reflected light or vibrations that cause fluctuations in air pressure such as movement of vocal cords. The eye and ear detect the waves as light and sound. These waves of light and sound can be described in terms of wavelength, frequency, and amplitude, and it is these properties that determine what is sensed and perceived. **Wavelength** is the distance from one peak of the wave to the next. Wave **frequency** is the number of complete waves, or cycles, that pass a given point per unit of time. **Amplitude** is the height of the wave from baseline to peak (see Figure 3.4). Different wavelengths, frequencies, and amplitudes create different visual and sound experiences. Let's now consider how these physical properties of light and sound waves become sights and sounds.

Seeing

▪ Why do some people need eyeglasses?

Soaring eagles have the incredible ability to see a mouse move in the grass from a mile away. Cats have special "reflectors" at the back of their eyes that help them to see even in very dim light. Nature has provided each species with a visual system uniquely adapted to its way of life. The human visual system is also adapted to do many things well. It combines great sensitivity with great sharpness, enabling people to see objects near and far, during the day and night. Our night vision is not as good as that of some animals, but our color vision is excellent. Not a bad tradeoff; after all, being able to experience a sunset's splendor seems worth an occasional stumble in the dark.

Light

Light is a form of energy known as *electromagnetic radiation*. Most electromagnetic radiation, including x-rays, radio waves, television signals, and radar, passes through space

wavelength   The distance from one peak to the next in a wave of light or sound.

frequency   The number of complete waves, or cycles, that pass a given point per unit of time.

amplitude   The distance between the peak and the baseline of a wave.

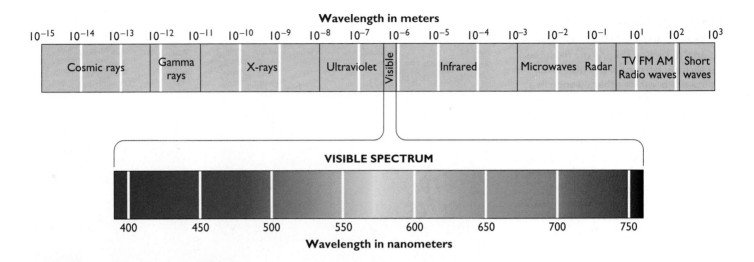

VISIBLE SPECTRUM

FIGURE 3.5

The Spectrum of
Electromagnetic Energy

The human eye is sensitive to only a narrow range of electromagnetic wavelengths. To detect energy outside this range, we rely on radios, TV sets, radar detectors, infrared night-vision scopes, and other electronic instruments that can "see" their own kind of light, just as the eye sees visible light.

visible light   Electromagnetic radiation that has a wavelength of about 400 nanometers to about 750 nanometers.

light intensity   A physical dimension of light waves that refers to how much energy the light contains and that determines its brightness.

light wavelength   A physical dimension of light waves that refers to their length and that produces sensations of different colors.

cornea   The curved, transparent, protective layer through which light rays enter the eye.

pupil   An opening in the eye, just behind the cornea, through which light passes.

iris   The part of the eye that gives it its color and adjusts the amount of light entering it.

lens   The part of the eye directly behind the pupil.

retina   The surface at the back of the eye onto which the lens focuses light rays.

accommodation   The ability of the lens to change its shape and bend light rays so that objects are in focus.

undetected by the human eye. You can see in Figure 3.5 that visible light is but a small portion of the spectrum, or range, of electromagnetic radiation. In fact, **visible light** is electromagnetic radiation with a wavelength ranging from just under 400 nanometers to about 750 nanometers. (A *nanometer* is one-billionth of a meter.) Light waves vibrate with a certain wavelength as they pass, like particles, through space. Light has some properties of waves and some properties of particles. It is correct to refer to light as either *light waves* or *light rays*.

Sensations of light depend on the intensity and wavelength of light waves. **Light intensity,** which refers to how much energy the light contains, determines the brightness of light. And what color you sense depends mainly on **light wavelength.** At a given intensity, different wavelengths produce sensations of different colors. For instance, 440-nanometer light appears violet blue, and 600-nanometer light appears orangish red.

Focusing Light

The eye transduces light energy into neural activity. First, accessory structures of the eye focus light rays into a sharp image. The light rays enter the eye by passing through the curved, transparent protective layer called the **cornea.** As shown in Figure 3.6, the light then passes through the **pupil,** the opening just behind the cornea. The **iris,** which gives the eye its color, adjusts the amount of light allowed into the eye by constricting to reduce the size of the pupil or relaxing to enlarge it. Directly behind the pupil is the **lens.** Both the cornea and lens of the eye are curved so that they bend light rays. (A camera lens works the same way.) The light rays focus into an image on the surface at the back of the eye. This surface is called the **retina.**

Light rays from the top of an object are focused at the bottom of the image on the retinal surface. Light rays from the right side of the object end up on the left side of the retinal image. The brain rearranges this upside-down and reversed image so that we can see the object as it is (see Figure 3.7).

If the rays meet either in front of the retina (nearsightedness) or behind it (farsightedness), the image will be out of focus. The muscles that hold the lens adjust its shape so that either near or far objects can be focused on the retina. Let's say that you are peering at something very close. To obtain a focused image, your muscles must tighten the lens, making it more curved. This ability to change the shape of the lens to bend light rays is called **accommodation.** Over time, the lens loses some of its flexibility, and accommodation becomes more difficult. This is why most older people need glasses for reading or close work.

Converting Light into Images

The conversion of light energy into neural activity takes place in the retina, which contains neurons that actually constitute an extension of the brain. The word *retina* is Latin for "net," and the retina is in fact an intricate network of cells.

FIGURE 3.6

Major Structures of the Eye

As shown in this top view of the eye, light rays bent by the combined actions of the cornea and the lens are focused on the retina, where the light energy is converted into neural activity. Nerve fibers from the retina combine to form the optic nerve, which leaves the back of the eye and continues to the brain.

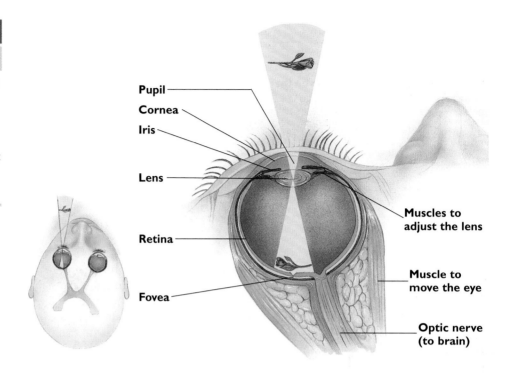

Pupil

Cornea

Iris

Lens

Retina

Fovea

Muscles to adjust the lens

Muscle to move the eye

Optic nerve (to brain)

Rods and Cones Specialized cells in the retina called **photoreceptors** convert light energy into neural activity. There are two basic types of photoreceptors: rods and cones. **Rods** and **cones** are retinal cells that are named for their shapes and contain chemicals that respond to light. When light strikes these chemicals, they break apart, creating a signal that can be transferred to the brain.

The process of rebuilding these light-sensitive chemicals after they break down takes a little time. This explains why you cannot see when you first come from bright sunshine into a dark room. In the dark, as your rods build up their light-sensing chemicals, your ability to see gradually increases. This increasing ability to see in the dark over time is called **dark adaptation.** You become about 10,000 times more sensitive to light after about half an hour in a darkened room.

There are three kinds of light-sensing chemicals in cones, and they provide the basis for color vision. Rods have only one kind of chemical, so they cannot discriminate colors. However, rods are more sensitive to light than cones. Rods allow you to see when there is only dim light, as on a moonlit night. But if you have trouble trying to match a pair of socks in a darkened room, you now know the reason. In dim light you are seeing with your rods, which cannot discriminate colors. It's at higher light intensities that the cones, with their ability to detect colors, become most active.

Cones are concentrated in the center of the retina, in a circular region called the **fovea,** which is where the eye focuses incoming light. Differences in the density of cones in the fovea probably account for differences in various people's visual *acuity,* or ability to see details. There are no rods in the human fovea. With increasing distance from the fovea, though, the number of cones gradually decreases, and the proportion of rods gradually increases. So, if you are trying to detect a small amount of light, like that from a faint star, it is better to look slightly away from where you expect to see it. This focuses the weak light on the very light-sensitive rods outside the fovea. Because cones do not work well in low light, looking directly at the star will make it seem to disappear.

From the Retina to the Brain If the eye simply transferred to the brain the stimuli focused on the retina, the images would look like a blurry TV picture. Instead, the eye sharpens visual images. How? The key lies in the interactions among cells of the retina.

Light rays pass through several layers of retinal cells before striking the rods and cones. Signals generated by the rods and cones then go back toward the surface of the retina, making connections with *bipolar cells* and *ganglion cells,* which allow the eye to

photoreceptors Specialized cells in the retina that convert light energy into neural activity.

rods Photoreceptors in the retina that allow sight even in dim light, but that cannot discriminate colors.

cones Photoreceptors in the retina that are less light-sensitive than rods, but that can distinguish colors.

dark adaptation The increasing ability to see in the dark as time passes.

fovea A region in the center of the retina.

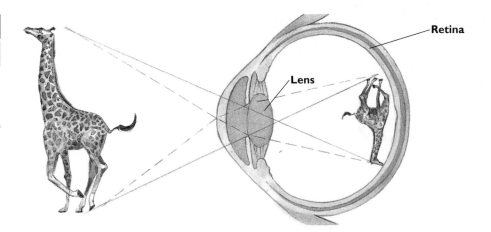

FIGURE 3.7

The Lens and the Retinal Image

Upside-down and reversed images on the retina are rearranged by the brain so that you see objects as they are.

begin analyzing visual information even before that information leaves the retina. Ganglion cells in the retina have axons that form the **optic nerve,** which then goes to the brain. Because there are no receptors for visual stimuli at the point where the optic nerve exits the eyeball, a **blind spot** is created, as Figure 3.8 demonstrates.

After leaving the retina, about half the optic nerve fibers cross over to the opposite side of the brain at a structure called the *optic chiasm.* (*Chiasm* means "cross" and is pronounced "KYE-az-um.") Fibers from the inside half of each eye, nearest to the nose, cross over. Fibers from the outside half of each eye do not. This arrangement brings all the visual information about the right half of the visual world to the left hemisphere of the brain and all the visual information from the left half of the visual world to the right hemisphere of the brain.

The optic chiasm is part of the bottom surface of the brain. Beyond this chiasm, the fibers extend into the brain itself. The axons from most of the ganglion cells form synapses in the thalamus. Neurons there send the visual input to the primary visual cortex in the occipital lobe at the back of the brain. The primary visual cortex sends visual information to many association areas of the brain for processing (see Figures 2.8 and 2.9).

Certain cells in the brain's cerebral cortex are called **feature detectors** because they respond to specific characteristics of objects in the visual field (Hubel & Wiesel, 1979). For example, one type of feature detector specializes in responding to straight lines. Others respond to corners, to angles, or to some other feature. The combined responses of several types of feature-detecting cells allow us to sense the shapes of objects, such as rectangles or triangles. Most people can also detect color. Let's explore how color vision works.

Seeing Color

Like beauty, color is in the eye of the beholder. Many animals see only shades of gray even when they look at a rainbow, but for humans, color is an important feature of vision.

RODS AND CONES This electron microscope view of rods (blue) and cones (aqua) shows what your light receptors look like. Rods are more light-sensitive, but they do not detect color. Cones can detect color, but they require more light in order to be activated. To experience the difference in how these cells work, try looking at an unfamiliar color photograph in a room where there is barely enough light to see. Even this dim light will activate your rods and allow you to make out images in the picture. But because there is not enough light to activate your cones, you will not be able to see colors in the photo.

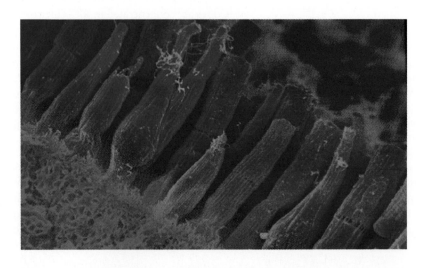

FIGURE 3.8

Find Your Blind Spot

There is a blind spot where the optic nerve exits the eye. To "see" your blind spot, cover your left eye and stare at the cross inside the circle. Move the page closer and farther away, and at some point the dot to the right should disappear from view. However, the vertical lines around the dot will probably look continuous, because the brain tends to fill in visual information at the blind spot. We are normally unaware of this "hole" in our vision because the blind spot of one eye is in the normal visual field of the other eye.

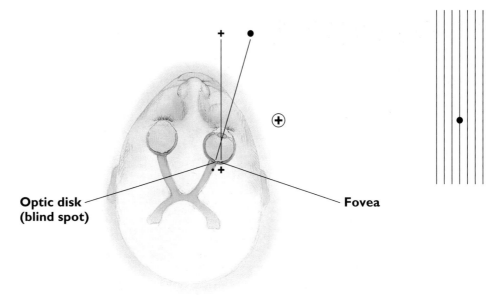

Optic disk (blind spot)   Fovea

Wavelengths and Color Sensations   At a given intensity, each wavelength of light is sensed as a certain color. However, the eye rarely, if ever, encounters pure light of a single wavelength. Sunlight, for example, is a mixture of all wavelengths of light. When sunlight passes through a droplet of water, the droplet acts like a prism. It bends different wavelengths of light to different degrees, separating them into a colorful rainbow. The spectrum of color found in the rainbow illustrates an important concept: The sensation produced by a *mixture* of different wavelengths of light is not the same as the sensations produced by separate wavelengths.

The sensation of a color results from features of the wavelength mixtures striking the eye. The three separate aspects of this sensation are hue, saturation, and brightness. These are *psychological* dimensions that correspond roughly to the physical properties of light. **Hue,** the essential "color," is determined by the dominant wavelength in the mixture of the light. Black, white, and gray are not considered hues, because they do not have a dominant wavelength. **Saturation** is related to the purity of the color. A color is more saturated (purer) if just one wavelength is more intense—contains more energy—than other wavelengths. The yellow of a school bus and the red of a stop sign are saturated colors. Add in many other wavelengths, and the color is said to be *desaturated*. Pastels are colors that have been desaturated by the addition of whiteness. **Brightness** refers to the overall intensity of the wavelengths making up light.

The color circle shown in Figure 3.9 arranges hues by perceived similarities. Mix two different light wavelengths of equal intensity, and the color you sense is midway between the two original colors. This process is known as *additive color mixing,* because the effects of the wavelengths are added together. Keep adding different colored lights and you eventually get white, which is the combination of all wavelengths. You are probably more familiar with a different form of color mixing, called *subtractive color mixing,* which occurs when paints are combined. Paint, like other physical objects, reflects certain wavelengths and absorbs others. Grass is green because it absorbs all wavelengths *except* wavelengths perceived as green. White objects appear white because they reflect all wavelengths.

Theories of Color Vision

Psychologists have long tried to explain how color vision works, but only two theories have stood the test of time: trichromatic (or "three-color") theory and opponent-process theory.

The Trichromatic Theory of Color Vision   In the early 1800s, Thomas Young and, later, Hermann von Helmholtz proved that by mixing pure versions of blue, green, and red

optic nerve   A bundle of fibers that carries visual information to the brain.

blind spot   The point at which the optic nerve exits the eyeball.

feature detectors   Cells in the cortex that respond to a specific feature of an object.

hue   The essential color determined by the dominant wavelength of a light.

saturation   The purity of a color.

brightness   The overall intensity of the wavelengths making up light.

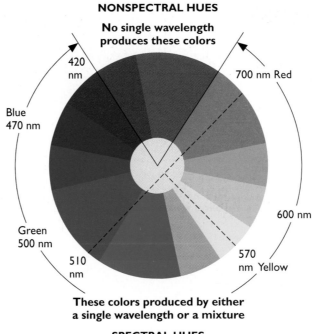

FIGURE 3.9

The Color Circle

Ordering colors according to their psychological similarities creates a color circle that predicts the result of additive mixing of two colored lights. For example, mixing equal amounts of pure green and pure red light will produce yellow, the color that lies at the midpoint of the line connecting red and green. (Note: *Nm* stands for *nanometers,* the unit in which light wavelengths are measured.)

NONSPECTRAL HUES

No single wavelength produces these colors

420 nm

700 nm Red

Blue 470 nm

600 nm

Green 500 nm

570 nm Yellow

510 nm

These colors produced by either a single wavelength or a mixture

SPECTRAL HUES

light in different ratios, they could produce *any* other color. Their theory of color vision is called the **trichromatic theory.**

Recall that cones make color vision possible. But how? There are three types of cones, and each is *most* sensitive to particular wavelengths. *Short-wavelength* cones respond most to light in the blue range. *Medium-wavelength* cones are most sensitive to light in the green range. Finally, *long-wavelength* cones respond best to light in the yellow range (by tradition, though, these are known as "red" cones). No single cone, by itself, can signal the color of a light. It is the *ratio* of the activities of the three types of cones that determines what color will be sensed. As you can see in Figure 3.10, the exact mixture of

THE SENSATION OF COLOR The vivid array of colored powders offered by this vendor in India allows him to create virtually any combination of hue (color), saturation (purity), and brightness that a customer might request.

trichromatic theory A theory of color vision stating that information from three types of visual elements combines to produce the sensation of color.

opponent-process theory A theory of color vision stating that the visual elements sensitive to color are grouped into three pairs: a red-green element, a blue-yellow element, and a black-white element.

FIGURE 3.10

Individual Differences in Cone Types

These photographs show that people can differ widely from one another in the distribution of blue, green, and red cones in their retinas (Roorda & Williams, 1999). J.W., whose retina is shown in Part A, has an especially high population of red cones, whereas green cones predominate in A.N., whose retina is shown in Part B. Both have normal color vision, but J.W. will be somewhat more sensitive to long wavelengths of light, while A.N. will be somewhat more sensitive to light of medium wavelengths.

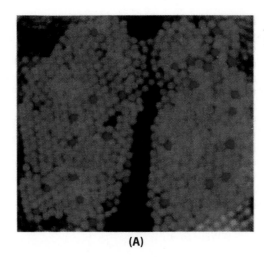 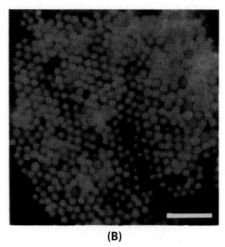

(A)   (B)

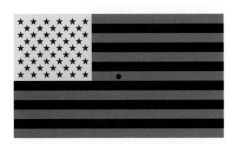

FIGURE 3.11

Afterimages Produced by the Opponent-Process Nature of Color Vision

 Stare at the dot in the figure for at least thirty seconds, and then focus on the dot in the white space below it. The afterimage you will see can be explained by the opponent-process theory of color vision. What colors appeared in the afterimage you saw?

these three cone types can differ from person to person. The trichromatic theory was applied in the creation of color television screens, which contain microscopic elements of red, green, and blue. A television broadcast excites these elements to varying degrees, mixing their colors to produce many other colors. You see color mixtures, not patterns of red, green, and blue dots, because the dots are too small and close together to be seen individually.

The Opponent-Process Theory of Color Vision   Although essentially correct, the trichromatic theory cannot explain some aspects of color vision, such as afterimages. If you stare at Figure 3.11 for thirty seconds and then look at the blank white space below it, you will see an afterimage. What was yellow in the original image will be blue in the afterimage. What was green before will appear red, and what was black will now appear white.

This type of observation led Ewald Hering to offer another theory of color vision, called the **opponent-process theory.** Hering suggested that color-sensitive visual elements in the eye are arranged into three kinds of pairs and that the members of each pair oppose, or inhibit, each other. Each element signals one color or the other (red or green, blue or yellow, black or white), but never both. This theory explains color afterimages. When one member of an opponent pair is no longer stimulated, the other is activated. So, in Figure 3.11, if the original image you look at is green, the afterimage will be red.

Summing Up   Together, the trichromatic and opponent-process theories encompass most of what we now know about the complex process of color vision. We see color because our three types of cones have different sensitivities to different wavelengths. We sense different colors when the three cone types are stimulated in different ratios. Because there are three types of cones, any color can be produced by mixing three pure wavelengths of light. But there is more to it than that. The cones connect to ganglion cells containing pairs of opposing elements that respond to different colors and inhibit each other. This arrangement provides the basis for afterimages. Therefore, the trichromatic theory explains color vision as it relates to rods and cones, whereas the opponent-process theory explains color vision as it relates to the ganglion cells. Both theories are needed to account for the complexity of our visual sensations of color. ("In Review: Seeing" summarizes our discussion of vision.)

Colorblindness

Cones normally contain three kinds of chemicals, each of which responds best to a particular wavelength of light. People who have cones containing only two of these three color-sensitive chemicals are described as *colorblind.* They are not really blind to all color, but they discriminate fewer colors than do other people, as Figure 3.12 shows. Red-green colorblindness, for example, means that reds and greens look the same brownish gray color. Colorblindness is more common in men than in women.

in review

Seeing		
Aspect of Sensory System	**Elements**	**Key Characteristics**
Energy	Visible light: electromagnetic radiation with a wavelength of about 400 nm to about 750 nm	The intensity, wavelength, and complexity of light waves determine the brightness, hue, and saturation of visual sensations.
Accessory structures of the eye	Cornea, pupil, iris, lens	Light rays are bent to focus on the retina.
Conversion of visual stimuli to neural activity	Photoreceptors (rods and cones) in the retina	Rods are more sensitive to light than cones, but cones discriminate among colors. Sensations of color depend first on the cones, which respond differently to different light wavelengths, and then on processing by ganglion cells.
Pathway to the brain	Optic nerve to optic chiasm to thalamus to primary visual cortex	Neurons in the brain respond to particular aspects of the visual stimulus, such as shape.

FIGURE 3.12

Are You Colorblind?

 At the upper left is a photo as it appears to people whose cones have all three types of color-sensitive chemicals. The other photos simulate how colors appear to people who are missing chemicals for short wavelengths (lower left), long wavelengths (upper right), or medium wavelengths (lower right). If any of these photos look to you just like the one at the upper left, you may have a form of colorblindness.

Hearing

How would my voice sound on the moon?

When Neil Armstrong stepped onto the moon in 1969, millions of people back on earth heard his radio transmission: "That's one small step for man, one giant leap for mankind." But if Armstrong had taken off his space helmet and shouted, "Whoo-ee! I can moonwalk," not even an astronaut three feet away could have heard him. Why? Because he would have been speaking into airless, empty space. **Sound** is a repetitive fluctuation in the pressure of a substance, such as air. Because the moon has almost no atmosphere and almost no air pressure, sound cannot exist there.

sound A repetitive fluctuation in the pressure of a medium such as air.

loudness A psychological dimension of sound determined by the amplitude of a sound wave.

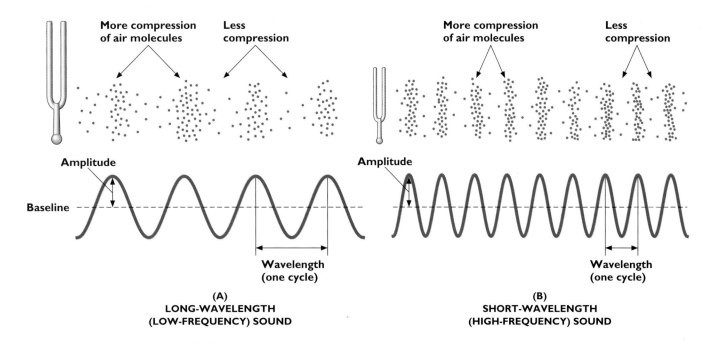

More compression of air molecules   Less compression

Amplitude

Baseline

Wavelength (one cycle)

(A) LONG-WAVELENGTH (LOW-FREQUENCY) SOUND

More compression of air molecules   Less compression

Amplitude

Wavelength (one cycle)

(B) SHORT-WAVELENGTH (HIGH-FREQUENCY) SOUND

Sound

Vibrations of an object produce the fluctuations in pressure that make sound. When you speak, your vocal cords vibrate, causing fluctuations in air pressure that spread as waves. A *wave* is a repetitive change in pressure that spreads out in three dimensions. Waves can move great distances, but the air itself barely moves. Imagine a jam-packed line of people waiting to get into a movie. If someone at the rear of the line shoves the next person, a wave of people jostling against people may spread all the way to the front of the line. However, the person who shoved in the first place is still no closer to getting into the theater. Sound is represented on a graph by waveforms like those in Figure 3.13. A waveform representation shows two dimensions, but remember that the wave actually moves through the air in three dimensions.

Several characteristics of waves are important in understanding sounds. The psychological dimension of **loudness** is determined by the amplitude, or height, of the sound wave. The greater the amplitude, the louder the sensation of sound. Loudness is described in units called *decibels* (abbreviated *dB*). By definition, 0 decibels is the minimum detectable sound for normal hearing. Table 3.2 gives examples of the intensity, or loudness, of some common sounds.

FIGURE 3.13

Sound Waves and Waveforms

Sound is produced when objects, such as a tuning fork, vibrate. The vibration creates alternating regions of greater and lesser compression of air molecules, which can be represented as a waveform. The point of greatest compression is the peak of the wave. The lowest point of the wave is where compression is least.

TABLE 3.2

Intensity of Sound Sources

Sound intensity varies across an extremely wide range. A barely audible sound is, by definition, 0 decibels; every increase of 20 dB reflects a tenfold increase in the amplitude of sound waves. Thus, the 40-dB sounds of an office are actually 10 times as intense as a 20-dB whisper; and traffic noise of 100 dB is 10,000 times as intense as that whisper.

Source	Sound Level (decibels)
Spacecraft launch (from 45 meters)	180
Loudest rock band on record	160
Pain threshold (approximate)	140
Large jet motor (at 22 meters)	120
Loudest human shout on record	111
Heavy auto traffic	100
Conversation (at about 1 meter)	60
Quiet office	40
Soft whisper	20
Threshold of hearing	0

Source: M. W. Levine & Schefner (1981).

FIGURE 3.14

Structures of the Ear

The outer ear (pinna and ear canal) channels sound waves into the middle ear, where the vibrations of the eardrum are amplified by the delicate bones that stimulate the cochlea. In the cochlea, in the inner ear, the vibrations are converted, or transduced, into changes in neural activity, which are sent along the auditory nerve to the brain.

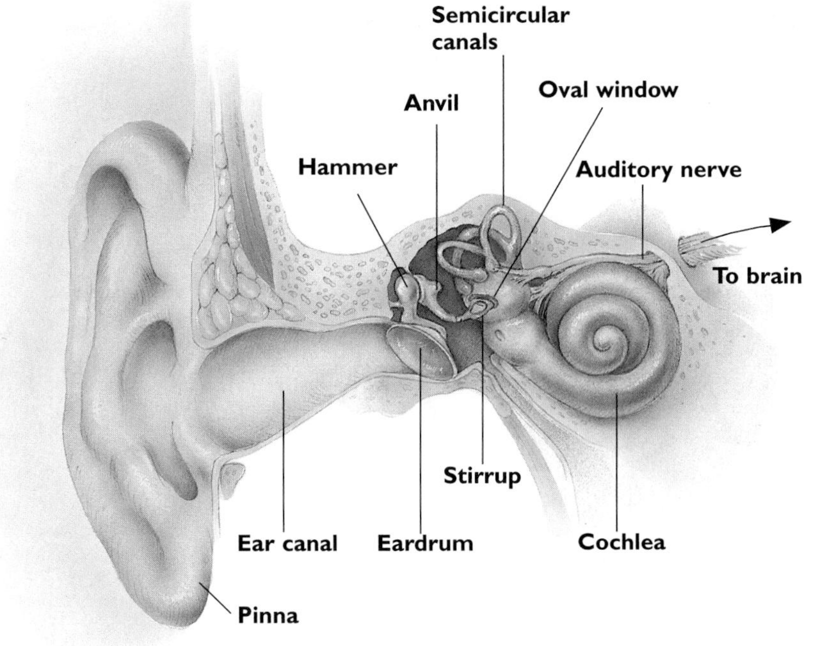

pitch   How high or low a tone sounds. The psychological dimension of pitch depends on the frequency of a sound wave.

timbre   The quality of a sound that identifies it.

pinna   The crumpled part of the outer ear that collects sound waves.

eardrum   A tightly stretched membrane in the middle ear that generates vibrations that match the sound waves striking it; also known as the *tympanic membrane*.

cochlea   A fluid-filled spiral structure in the inner ear in which auditory transduction occurs.

basilar membrane   The floor of the fluid-filled duct that runs through the cochlea.

auditory nerve   The bundle of axons that carries messages from the hair cells of the cochlea to the brain.

The distance from one wave peak to the next is the sound's wavelength. The number of complete waves or cycles that pass a given point in one second is the frequency, described in units called *hertz,* abbreviated *Hz* (for Heinrich Hertz, a nineteenth-century physicist). One cycle per second is 1 hertz. The speed of sound is constant in a given medium, such as air, so wavelength and frequency are related. The longer the wavelength, the lower the sound frequency. The psychological dimension of **pitch**—how high or low a tone sounds—depends on the frequency of the sound wave. High-frequency waves are sensed as sounds of high pitch. The highest note on a piano has a frequency of about 4,000 hertz, and the lowest note has a frequency of about 50 hertz. Humans can hear sounds ranging from about 20 to 20,000 hertz.

Most sounds are a mixture of many frequencies and amplitudes, and this mixture creates a sound's **timbre** (pronounced "tamber"), the psychological dimension of sound quality. Complex wave patterns added to the *fundamental,* or lowest, frequency of sound determine its timbre. The extra waves allow you to tell the difference between, say, a note played on a flute and the same note played on a clarinet.

The Ear

The human ear converts sound energy into neural activity through a series of accessory structures and transduction mechanisms. The crumpled part of the ear on the side of the head, called the **pinna,** collects sound waves in the outer ear. The pinna then funnels sound down through the ear canal. At the end of the ear canal, the sound waves reach the middle ear (see Figure 3.14). There they strike the **eardrum,** a tightly stretched membrane also known as the *tympanic membrane.* The sound waves set up vibrations in the eardrum. The *hammer,* the *anvil,* and the *stirrup,* three tiny bones named for their shapes, amplify these vibrations and direct them onto a smaller membrane called the *oval window.*

The Inner Ear   Sound vibrations passing through the oval window enter the inner ear, reaching the **cochlea** (pronounced "COK-lee-ah"), where transduction occurs. The cochlea is rolled into a coiled spiral. (*Cochlea* comes from the Greek word for "snail.") A fluid-filled tube runs down its length. The **basilar membrane** forms the floor of this tube, as you can see in Figure 3.15. When a sound wave passes through the fluid in the tube, it moves the basilar membrane. This movement, in turn, deforms *hair cells* on the membrane. These hair cells make connections with fibers from the **auditory nerve,** a bundle of axons that goes into the brain. Deformation of the hair cells stimulates the

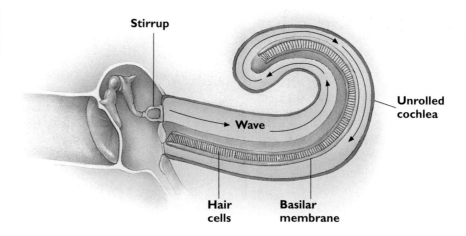

FIGURE 3.15

The Cochlea

The vibrations of the stirrup set up vibrations in the fluid inside the cochlea. The coils of the cochlea are unrolled in this illustration to show the path of the fluid waves along the basilar membrane. Movements of the basilar membrane stimulate hair cells, which transduce the vibrations into changes in neural firing patterns.

auditory nerve, which sends coded signals to the brain about the amplitude and frequency of the sound waves. These signals allow you to sense loudness, pitch, and timbre.

Deafness The middle and inner ear are among the most delicate structures in the body, and damage to them can lead to deafness. One form of deafness is caused by problems with the bones of the middle ear. Over time they can fuse together, preventing accurate reproduction of vibrations. This condition is called *conduction deafness*. Surgical treatment may involve breaking the bones apart or replacing the natural bones with plastic ones; a hearing aid that amplifies vibrations can also be helpful.

Damage to the auditory nerve or the hair cells results in *nerve deafness*. Hair cell damage can be caused by very loud sounds, including amplified rock music (E. B. Goldstein, 1999). High-intensity sound can actually rip off the hair cells of the inner ear. Generally, any sound loud enough to produce ringing in the ears causes some damage. In humans, small amounts of damage accumulate to produce significant hearing loss by middle age—as many older rock musicians, and their fans, are finding out (S. Levine, 1999).

Hair cells can be regenerated in chickens' ears (Cotanche, 1997), and recently, scientists have succeeded in getting hair cells to regenerate in mammals (Malgrange et al., 1999). Eventually, this procedure may be possible in humans, too. Scientists are also perfecting an artificial cochlea to stimulate the auditory nerve (Lee et al., 2001).

Auditory Pathways to the Brain Before sounds can be heard, the information coded in the auditory nerve fibers must be conveyed to the brain and processed further. The auditory nerve is the bundle of axons that conveys this information to the thalamus. From there, the information is relayed to the *primary auditory cortex*, an area in the temporal lobe of the brain (see Figure 2.9). Cells in the auditory cortex have preferred frequencies. That is, individual cells respond most vigorously to sounds of a particular frequency. Each neuron in the auditory nerve also has a "favorite," or characteristic, frequency. Yet each responds to some extent to a range of frequencies, so the cortex must examine the pattern of activity of many neurons to determine the frequency of a sound. Some parts of the auditory cortex are devoted to processing certain types of sounds. One part, for example, specializes in information coming from human voices (Belin et al., 2000). The auditory cortex receives information from other senses as well. Studies show that the primary auditory cortex is activated when you *watch* someone say words (but not when the person makes other facial movements). This is the biological basis for the lip reading that helps you to hear what people say (Calvert et al., 1997).

Coding Sounds

Most people can hear a wide range of sound intensities. The faintest sound that can be heard barely moves the ear's hair cells. Sounds more than a trillion times more intense can also be heard. Between these extremes, the auditory system codes intensity in a rather simple way: The more intense the sound, the more rapid the firing of a given neuron. How do people tell the difference between sound frequencies and thus sense differences

SHAPING THE BRAIN The brain region known as *primary auditory cortex* is larger in trained musicians than in people whose jobs are less focused on fine gradations of sound. How much larger this area becomes is correlated with how long the musicians have studied their art. This finding reminds us that, as described in Chapter 2, the brain can literally be shaped by experience and other environmental factors (Pantev et al., 1998).

in review

Hearing		
Aspect of Sensory System	**Elements**	**Key Characteristics**
Energy	Sound: pressure fluctuations of air produced by vibrations	Amplitude, frequency, and complexity of sound waves determine the loudness, pitch, and timbre of sounds.
Accessory structures of the ear	Pinna, eardrum, hammer, anvil, stirrup, oval window, basilar membrane	Changes in pressure produced by the original wave are amplified.
Conversion of sound frequencies into neural activity	Hair cells in the inner ear	Frequencies are coded by the location of the hair cells receiving the greatest stimulation (place theory) and by the combined firing rate of neurons (volley theory).
Pathway to the brain	Auditory nerve to thalamus to primary auditory cortex	Auditory cortex examines patterns of information from the auditory nerve, allowing us to sense loudness, pitch, and timbre.

in pitch? Frequency differences appear to be coded in two ways: by their location on the basilar membrane and by the rate at which the auditory neurons fire.

The place on the basilar membrane where the wave peaks depends on the sound frequency. High-frequency sounds produce a wave that peaks soon after it starts down the basilar membrane. Lower-frequency sounds produce a wave that peaks farther down the basilar membrane. According to **place theory,** the greatest response by hair cells occurs at the peak of the wave. Because the location of the peak varies with the frequency of sound, it follows that hair cells at a particular place on the basilar membrane are most responsive to a particular frequency of sound. When cells with a particular characteristic frequency fire, we sense a sound of that frequency.

Place theory cannot explain the encoding of very low frequencies, such as deep bass notes, because there are no auditory nerve fibers that have very low preferred frequencies. Humans can hear frequencies as low as twenty hertz, though, so they must be encoded somehow. The answer seems to be *frequency matching,* a process in which the firing rate of a neuron in the auditory nerve matches the frequency of a sound wave. Frequency-matching theory is sometimes called the **volley theory** of frequency coding, because the outputs of many cells can combine to create a *volley* of firing.

The nervous system apparently uses more than one way to code the range of audible frequencies. The lowest frequencies are coded by frequency matching. Low to moderate frequencies are coded by frequency matching, as well as by the place on the basilar membrane where the wave peaks. And high frequencies are coded solely by the place where the wave peaks. ("In Review: Hearing" summarizes the coding process and other aspects of the auditory system.)

place theory   A theory of hearing stating that hair cells at a particular place on the basilar membrane respond most to a particular frequency of sound.

volley theory   A theory of hearing stating that the firing rate of an auditory nerve matches a sound wave's frequency; also called *frequency-matching theory.*

The Chemical Senses: Taste and Smell

Why can't I taste anything when I have a cold?

There are animals without vision and animals without hearing, but there are no animals without some form of chemical sense. Chemical senses arise from the interaction of chemicals and receptors. Our **sense of smell** (olfaction) detects chemicals that are airborne, or *volatile*. Our **sense of taste** (gustation) detects chemicals in solution that come into contact with receptors inside the mouth. These systems are connected.

Smell, Taste, and Flavor

If you have a stuffy nose, everything tastes like cardboard. Why? Because smell and taste act as two components of a single system, known as *flavor* (Rozin, 1982). Most of the properties that make food taste good are actually odors detected by the olfactory system, not activities of the taste system. The scent and taste pathways converge in the cerebral cortex (Rolls et al., 1998), which is how smell and taste come to seem like one sensation.

Both tastes and odors prompt strong emotional responses. People have an inborn dislike of bitter flavors, but we have to learn to associate emotions with odors (Bartoshuk, 1991). Many animals easily learn taste aversions to particular foods when the taste is associated with nausea, but humans learn aversions to odors more readily than to tastes (Bartoshuk & Wolfe, 1990).

Variations in our nutritional state also affect our experience of taste and flavor, as well as our motivation to eat particular foods. Food deprivation or salt deficiency makes sweet or salty things taste better. Influences on protein and fat intake are more indirect. Protein and fat molecules have no particular taste or smell. Thus, preferring or avoiding foods that contain these nutrients is based on associations between scent cues from other volatile substances in food and on the nutritional consequences of eating the foods (Bartoshuk, 1991; Schiffman et al., 1999).

We experience warm foods as sweeter, but temperature does not alter our experience of saltiness (Cruz & Green, 2000; Frankmann & Green, 1987). Warming releases aromas that rise from the mouth into the nose and create more flavor sensations. This is why some people find hot pizza delicious and cold pizza disgusting. Spicy "hot" foods actually stimulate pain fibers in the mouth, because they contain a substance called *capsaicin* (pronounced "kap-SAY-uh-sin").

Our Sense of Smell

People sense odors in the upper part of the nose (see Figure 3.16). Receptors there detect molecules that pass into the moisture lining of the nose, called the mucous membrane. Odor molecules then bind to receptors on the dendrites of olfactory neurons, causing a biochemical change. This change, in turn, leads to changes in the firing rates of the neurons. The axons of these olfactory neurons combine to form the olfactory nerve (Dionne & Dubin, 1994). A single molecule of an odorous substance can cause a change in the activity of an olfactory neuron, but detection of the odor by a human requires about fifty such molecules (Menini, Picco, & Firestein, 1995). There are thousands of different receptors for odors, but there are even more possible odors in the world. Any particular odor is sensed as a particular *pattern* of responses by these *odorant receptors* (Duchamp-Viret, Chaput, & Duchamp, 1999). Thus, a rose, a pizza, and your favorite cologne each have a different smell because they stimulate their own unique pattern of activity in your odorant receptors.

Odor molecules can reach olfactory receptors either through the nose or through an opening in the palate at the back of the mouth. This opening allows us to sample odors from food as we eat. Eating slowly not only prolongs taste sensations but also exposes your nose to a wider variety of food odors (McGee, 1999). Unlike every other sense, our sense of smell does not send its messages through the thalamus. Instead, axons from olfactory neurons in the nose extend through a bony plate and directly into the brain, where they have a synapse in a structure called the **olfactory bulb.** Connections from the

sense of smell The sense that detects chemicals that are airborne; also called *olfaction.*

sense of taste The sense that detects chemicals in solution that come into contact with receptors inside the mouth; also called *gustation.*

olfactory bulb A brain structure that receives messages regarding smell.

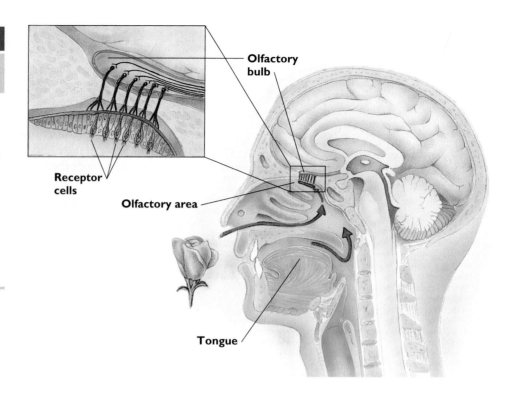

The Olfactory System: The Nose and the Rose

Are there smells that bring back vivid memories of your childhood or a loved one? Airborne chemicals from flowers, food, cologne, or other sources reach the olfactory area through the nostrils and through the back of the mouth. Fibers pass directly from the olfactory area to the olfactory bulb in the brain, and from there signals pass to areas that are involved in emotion. This arrangement helps explain why odors often trigger strong emotional memories.

pheromones   Chemicals that are released by one animal and detected by another, shaping the second animal's behavior or physiology.

papillae   Structures in the mouth, on which taste buds are grouped.

somatic senses   Senses that are spread throughout the body rather than located in a specific organ; also called *somatosensory systems*. The somatic senses include touch, temperature, pain, and kinesthesia.

olfactory bulb spread throughout the brain, but they are especially plentiful in the amygdala, a part of the brain involved in emotional experience. In humans, the amygdala is especially active in response to disgusting odors (Zald & Pardo, 1997).

The unique anatomy of the olfactory system may help account for the unique relationship between smells and memory. Associations between a certain experience and a particular odor are not weakened much by time or later experiences (Lawless & Engen, 1977). So catching a whiff of the cologne once worn by a lost loved one can reactivate intense feelings of love or sadness associated with that person. Odors can also be better than sights or sounds at bringing back accurate memories of significant experiences linked with them (Engen, Gilmore, & Mair, 1991).

Species ranging from humans to worms have remarkably similar neural mechanisms for sensing smell. Different species vary considerably, however, in their sensitivity to odor and in the degree to which they depend on it for survival. Whereas humans have about 9 million olfactory neurons, dogs have about 225 million. No wonder dogs are so dependent on smell to identify food, territory, and receptive mates. Dogs and many other species also have an accessory olfactory system that detects pheromones. **Pheromones** (pronounced "FAIR-oh-mohns") are chemicals that, when released by one animal and detected by another, can shape the second animal's behavior. For example, when a male snake detects a chemical on the skin of a female snake, it is stimulated to "court" the female (Mason et al., 1989).

In humans, pheromones released by women can influence other women's menstrual cycles, so that women living together eventually tend to menstruate at about the same time (K. Stern & McClintock, 1998). Furthermore, odorants that cannot be consciously detected have been shown to influence mood, suggesting a pheromone-like action (Jacob & McClintock, 2000). There is not yet any solid evidence that humans give off or can detect pheromones that act as sexual attractants. However, learned associations between certain odors and emotional experiences probably enhance a person's readiness for sex. People also use olfactory information in other situations. For instance, after just a few hours of contact with their newborn babies, mothers can usually identify them by the infants' smell. And if infants are breastfed, they can discriminate their own mother's odor from that of other breastfeeding women and appear to be comforted by it (Porter, 1998/1999).

in review

Smell and Taste		
Aspect of Sensory System	**Elements**	**Key Characteristics**
Energy	Smell: volatile chemicals Taste: chemicals in solution	The amount, intensity, and location of the chemicals determine taste and smell sensations.
Structures of taste and smell	Smell: chemical receptors in the mucous membrane of the nose Taste: taste buds grouped in papillae in the mouth	Odor and taste molecules stimulate chemical receptors.
Pathways to the brain	Olfactory bulb and taste buds	Axons from the nose and mouth bypass the thalamus and extend directly to the olfactory bulb.

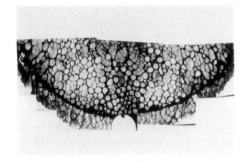

FIGURE 3.17

Are You a Supertaster?

This photo shows papillae on the tongue of a "supertaster." If you don't mind a temporary stain on your mouth and teeth, you can look at your own papillae by painting the front of your tongue with a cotton swab soaked in blue food coloring. Distribute the dye by moving your tongue around and swallowing; then look into a magnifying mirror as you shine a flashlight on your tongue. The pink circles you see against the blue background are papillae, each of which has about six taste buds buried in its surface. Get several friends to do this test, and you will see that genes create wide individual differences in taste bud density.

Our Sense of Taste

Our receptors for taste are in the taste buds, which are grouped together in structures called **papillae** (pronounced "puh-PILL-ee"). Normally, there are about ten thousand taste buds in a person's mouth, mostly on the tongue but also on the roof of the mouth and on the back of the throat.

The human taste system detects only a few basic sensations: sweet, sour, bitter, and salty. Each taste bud responds best to one or two of these categories, but it also responds weakly to others. Monosodium glutamate (MSG) produces a possible fifth taste, called *umami,* which enhances other tastes (Hettinger, Frank, & Myers, 1996). Scientists have only recently begun to identify how chemical interactions between foods and taste receptors signal various tastes (Herness & Gilbertson, 1999). They do know, however, that about 25 percent of the population are "supertasters"—individuals whose genes have given them an especially large number of papillae on their tongues (Bartoshuk, 2000; see Figure 3.17). Supertasters are more sensitive than other people to bitterness, as revealed in their reaction to foods such as broccoli, soy products, and grapefruit. ("In Review: Smell and Taste" summarizes our discussion of these senses.)

Sensing Your Body

▪ **Which is the largest organ in my body?**

Some senses are not located in a specific organ, such as the eye or the ear. These are the **somatic senses,** also called *somatosensory systems,* which are spread throughout the body. The somatic senses include the skin senses of touch, temperature, and pain, as well as a body sense, called *kinesthesia,* that tells the brain where the parts of the body are. Kinesthesia is closely related to our sense of balance. Although balance is not strictly a somatosensory system, we will describe it here.

THE SENSE OF TOUCH   Touch provides information about the world that is vital to survival. Its importance is revealed in many other aspects of behavior as well. For example, this software developer can work without his sight, but not without touch.

Touch and Temperature

People can function and prosper without vision, hearing, or smell. But a person without a sense of touch would have difficulty surviving. Without this sense, you could not even swallow food because you could not tell where it was in your mouth and throat. You receive touch sensations through your skin, which is often called the body's largest organ. The skin covers nearly two square yards of surface area, weighs more than twenty pounds, and has hair virtually everywhere on it. The hairs on your skin do not sense anything directly. However, when the hairs are bent, they push against the skin beneath them. Receptors in, and just below, the skin send the "touch" message to the brain.

Coding Touch Information   The sense of touch codes information about two aspects of an object contacting the skin: its weight and its location. The *intensity* of the stimulus—how heavy it is—is coded both by the firing rate of individual neurons and by the number of neurons stimulated. A heavy object triggers a higher rate of firing and stimulates more neurons than a light object. The brain "knows" where the touch occurs based on the *location* of the nerves that sense the touch information.

Adapting to Touch Stimuli   Constant input from all your touch neurons would provide too much unnecessary information. Once you get dressed, you do not need to be constantly reminded that you are wearing clothes. Partly because of the process of adaptation, you do not continue to feel your clothes against your skin.

    Changes in touch (as when a shoelace breaks and your shoe suddenly feels loose) provide the most important sensory information. The touch sense emphasizes these changes and filters out the excess information. How? Typically, a touch neuron responds with a burst of firing when a stimulus is applied, then quickly returns to its baseline firing rate, even though the stimulus may still be in contact with the skin. If the touch pressure increases, the neuron again responds by increasing its firing rate, then slowing down. A few neurons adapt more slowly, however, continuing to fire as long as pressure is applied. By attending to this input, you can sense a constant stimulus (try doing so by focusing on touch sensations from your glasses or shoes).

Sensing Temperature   Some of the skin's sensory neurons respond to a change in temperature but not to simple contact. "Warm fibers" and "cold fibers" respond to specific temperature changes only. However, many fibers that respond to temperature also respond to touch, so these sensations sometimes interact. For example, if you touch an object made up of alternating warm and cool sections, you will have the sensation of intense heat (Thunberg, 1896, cited in Craig & Bushnell, 1994). Different firing patterns in a single nerve fiber in the skin can code different stimuli, but just how these different stimuli can create differing patterns of firing is not yet known.

Pain

Touch can feel pleasurable, but if the intensity of stimulation increases too much, it can turn into a pain sensation. Pain tells you about the impact of the world on your body. It also has a distinctly negative emotional component that interrupts whatever you are doing (Eccleston & Crombez, 1999).

Pain as an Information Sense   The information-carrying aspect of pain is very similar to that of touch and temperature. The receptors for pain are free nerve endings, which come from the spinal cord, enter the skin, and then simply end. Painful stimuli cause the release of chemicals that fit into these specialized receptors in pain neurons, causing them to fire. The axons of pain-sensing neurons release neurotransmitters not only near the spinal cord (thus sending pain information to the brain) but also near the skin (causing swelling).

    Two types of nerve fibers carry pain signals from the skin to the spinal cord. One carries sharp, pricking pain sensations, and the other carries continuous, dull aches and burning sensations. When pain impulses reach the spinal cord, they form synapses with neurons that relay the pain signals to the thalamus and other parts of the brain. Different pain neurons are activated by different degrees of painful stimulation.

THE COMPLEX NATURE OF PAIN **If pain were based only on the nature of incoming stimuli, this participant in a purification ceremony in Singapore would be hurting. However, the experience of pain is a complex phenomenon that is affected by psychological and biological variables that can make it more or, as in this case, less intense.**

Emotional Aspects of Pain   There are specific pathways that carry the emotional component of a painful stimulus to areas of the hindbrain, reticular formation, and cortex via the thalamus (Craig et al., 1994). However, our overall emotional response to pain depends greatly on how we think about it (Keefe & France, 1999). In one study, some participants were told about the kind of painful stimulus they were to receive and when to expect it. Others were not informed. Those who knew what to expect objected less to the pain, even though the sensation was reported to be equally noticeable in both groups (D. J. Mayer & Price, 1982). People can lessen their emotional responses to pain by using pain-reducing strategies (such as distracting thoughts), especially if they expect these strategies to succeed (Young et al., 1995).

Modulating Pain: The Gate Control Theory   Pain is useful because it can protect you from harm. There are times, though, when enough is enough. Fortunately, the nervous system has several mechanisms for controlling the experience of pain. One theory about how these mechanisms work is called the **gate control theory** (Melzack & Wall, 1965). This theory suggests that there is a "gate" in the spinal cord that either allows pain signals to reach the brain or prevents their passage. Some details of the original theory were incorrect, but more recent work supports the idea that natural mechanisms can indeed block pain sensations (Stanton-Hicks & Salamon, 1997).

For example, input from other skin senses can come into the spinal cord at the same time the pain gets there and "take over" the pathways that the pain impulses would have used. This appears to be the reason we can relieve pain by rubbing the skin around a wound, applying mild electrical stimulation, or using creams that produce temperature sensations. It also explains why scratching relieves itching. (Itching is actually low-level activity in pain fibers.)

Alternatively, the brain can close the gate to pain impulses by sending signals down the spinal cord. These messages from the brain block incoming pain signals at spinal cord synapses. The result is **analgesia** (pronounced "ann-nuhl-JEE-zhah"), a reduction in pain sensation in the presence of a normally painful stimulus. Drugs that dull pain sensations, such as aspirin, are called *analgesics*.

gate control theory   A theory suggesting the presence of a "gate" in the spinal cord that either permits or blocks the passage of pain impulses to the brain.

analgesia   Reduction in the sensation of pain in the presence of a normally painful stimulus.

NATURAL ANALGESIA   The stress of athletic exertion causes the release of endorphins, natural painkillers that have been associated with pleasant feelings called "runner's high."

Natural Analgesics   As we saw in Chapter 2, natural opiates called *endorphins* play a role in the brain's ability to block pain signals. Endorphins are natural painkillers that act as neurotransmitters at many levels of the pain pathway. In the spinal cord, for example, they block the synapses of the fibers that carry pain signals. Endorphins may also relieve pain when the adrenal and pituitary glands secrete them into the bloodstream as hormones. The more endorphin receptors a person has inherited, the more pain tolerance that person has (Benjamin, Wilson, & Mogil, 1999; Uhl, Sora, & Wang, 1999).

Several conditions can cause the body to ease its own pain. During the late stages of pregnancy, a spinal cord endorphin system develops to reduce the mother's labor pains (Dawson-Basoa & Gintzler, 1997). For both infant rats and infant humans, sucking sweet water or milk releases endorphins and decreases sensitivity to pain (E. M. Blass, 1996). For humans, it reduces crying, too. An endorphin system may also be activated when we eat spicy chili peppers. People who like "hot" foods can no longer tolerate them when they receive *naloxone,* a drug that blocks the action of endorphins (Estcorn, 1992, cited in J. Stern & Stern, 1992). An endorphin system is activated when people *believe* they are receiving a painkiller, even when they are not. This is one basis for the placebo effect described in Chapter 1. Interestingly, the resulting pain inhibition is experienced in the part of the body where it was expected to occur, but not elsewhere (Benedetti, Arduino, & Amanzio, 1999). Physical or psychological stress can also activate natural analgesic systems. Stress-induced release of endorphins may account for the fact that injured soldiers and athletes sometimes continue to perform in the heat of battle or competition with no apparent pain.

There are also mechanisms for restoring pain sensitivity once a crisis is past. Studies with animals show that they can learn that certain situations signal "safety," prompting the release of a neurotransmitter that counteracts endorphins' painkilling effects (Wiertelak, Maier, & Watkins, 1992). Blocking these "safety signals" increases the painkilling effects brought on by a placebo (Benedetti & Amanzio, 1997).

THINKING CRITICALLY

Does Acupuncture Relieve Pain?

*A*cupuncture is an ancient and widely used treatment in Asian medicine that is alleged to relieve pain. The method is based on the idea that body energy flows along lines called *channels* (Vincent & Richardson, 1986). According to this approach, there are fourteen main channels, and a person's health depends on the balance of energy flowing in them. Stimulating the channels by inserting fine needles into the skin and twirling them is said to restore a balanced flow of energy. The needles produce an aching and tingling sensation called *Teeh-ch'i* at the site of stimulation, and they relieve pain at distant, seemingly unrelated parts of the body.

■ What am I being asked to believe or accept?

Acupuncturists assert that twirling needles in the skin can relieve pain caused by everything from tooth extraction to cancer.

■ Is there evidence available to support the claim?

Numerous studies show positive results in 50 to 80 percent of patients treated by acupuncture for various kinds of pain (Richardson & Vincent, 1986). In one controlled study of headache pain, 53 percent of the participants reported reduced pain following real acupuncture, whereas only 33 percent of those in a placebo group improved following fake electrical stimulation (Dowson, Lewith, & Machin, 1985). This latter figure is about the usual proportion of people responding to a placebo.

Another headache study found both acupuncture and drugs to be superior to a placebo. Each reduced the frequency of headaches, but the drugs were more effective than acupuncture at reducing the severity of headache pain (Hesse, Mogelvang, &

Simonsen, 1994). Unfortunately, such well-controlled studies are rare, and their results are often contradictory (Ter Riet, Kleijnen, & Knipschild, 1990).

Drugs that slow the breakdown of opiates also prolong the analgesia produced by acupuncture (He, 1987). The pain-reducing effects of acupuncture during electrical stimulation of a tooth can be reversed by naloxone, a substance that blocks the painkilling effects of endorphins and other opiate drugs. These findings suggest that acupuncture somehow activates endorphins, the body's natural painkillers. Is this activation brought about only by a placebo effect? Probably not entirely, because acupuncture produces naloxone-reversible analgesia even in monkeys and rats, who obviously have no expectations about acupuncture (Ha et al., 1981; Kishioka et al., 1994).

▪ Can that evidence be interpreted another way?

Yes. Evidence about acupuncture might be interpreted as simply confirming that the body's painkilling system can be stimulated by external means. Acupuncture may merely provide one activating method. There may be other, even more efficient methods for doing so. We already know, for example, that successful placebo treatments for human pain appear to operate by activating the endorphin system.

In studies of acupuncture, it is very difficult to control for the placebo effect, especially in double-blind fashion. How could a therapist *not* know whether the treatment being given is acupuncture or some other procedure? And from the patient's perspective, what placebo treatment could look and feel like having a needle inserted and twirled in the skin?

▪ What evidence would help to evaluate the alternatives?

Scientists do not yet know what factors govern whether acupuncture will activate the endorphin system. Other important unknowns include the types of pain for which acupuncture is most effective, the types of patients who respond best, and the precise procedures that are most effective. Knowing more about the general relationship between internal painkilling systems and external methods for stimulating them would also be valuable.

▪ What conclusions are most reasonable?

There seems little doubt that, in some circumstances, acupuncture relieves pain. Acupuncture is not a cure-all, however. For example, committees convened in the U.S. and the U.K. have concluded that acupuncture can be useful in the treatment of pain and nausea (British Medical Association, 2000; National Institutes of Health, 1998), but more than $2 million in research has failed to show that acupuncture is better than new anti-nausea drugs or conventional painkilling procedures (Taub, 1998).

Sensing Body Position

Most sensory systems receive information from the external world, such as the light reflected from a sunflower or the feeling of cool water. But as far as the brain is concerned, the rest of the body is "out there," too. You know about the position of your body and what each of its parts is doing only because sensory systems provide this information to your brain. These sensory systems are described as **proprioceptive** ("received from one's own," pronounced "pro-pree-oh-SEP-tiv").

Kinesthesia   Remember Christina, the woman we met in Chapter 2 who did not recognize her own body? She had lost her sense of **kinesthesia** (pronounced "kin-es-THEE-zhah"), which tells us where the parts of the body are in relation to one another. Try this: Close your eyes; then hold your arms out in front of you and touch your two index fingers together. You probably did this well because your kinesthetic sense told you where each finger was with respect to your body. You also depend on kinesthetic information to guide all

proprioceptive   Referring to sensory systems that allow us to know about the location of our body parts and what each is doing.

kinesthesia   The proprioceptive sense that tells us where the parts of the body are with respect to one another.

in review

Body Senses			
Sense	**Energy**	**Conversion of Physical Energy to Nerve Activity**	**Pathways and Characteristics**
Touch	Mechanical deformation of skin	Skin receptors (may be stimulated by hair on the skin)	Nerve endings respond to changes in weight (intensity) and location of touch.
Temperature	Heat	Sensory neurons in the skin	Changes in temperature are detected by warm-sensing and cool-sensing fibers. Temperature interacts with touch.
Pain	Increases with intensity of touch or temperature	Free nerve endings in or near the skin surface	Changes in intensity cause the release of chemicals detected by receptors in pain neurons. Some fibers convey sharp pain; others convey dull aches and burning sensations.
Kinesthesia	Mechanical energy of joint and muscle movement	Receptors in muscle fibers	Information from muscle fibers is sent to the spinal cord, thalamus, cerebellum, and cortex.

your movements, from walking to complex athletic actions such as running down a basketball court while dribbling a ball and avoiding an opposing player. These movement patterns become simple and fluid because, with practice, the brain uses kinesthetic information automatically. Normally, kinesthetic information comes primarily from the joints and muscles. Receptors in muscle fibers send information to the brain about the stretching of muscles. When the position of the bones changes, receptors in the joints set off neural activity. This coded information goes to the spinal cord and then to the thalamus, along with sensory information from the skin. Finally it goes to the cerebellum and to the somatosensory cortex, both of which help coordinate movements.

Balance   Have you ever been on a roller coaster? How did you feel when the ride ended? The **vestibular sense** tells the brain about the position of the head (and therefore the body) in space and about its general movements. You have probably heard it referred to as the *sense of balance*. People usually become aware of the vestibular sense only when they overstimulate it and become dizzy or motion sick.

The inner ear contains the organs for the vestibular sense. Each ear has two *vestibular sacs* filled with fluid and containing small crystals called *otoliths* ("ear stones") that rest on hair endings. Three arc-shaped tubes called the *semicircular canals* are also fluid filled (see Figure 3.14). Tiny hairs extend into the fluid in the canals. When your head moves, the otoliths shift in the vestibular sacs and the fluid moves in the semicircular canals, stimulating hair endings. This process activates neurons that travel along the auditory nerve, signaling the brain about the amount and direction of head movement.

Neural connections from the vestibular system to the cerebellum help coordinate bodily movements. Connections to the part of the autonomic nervous system that affects the digestive system help create the nausea that may follow overstimulation of the vestibular system—by a roller coaster ride, for instance. Finally, connections to the eye muscles produce *vestibular-ocular reflexes,* which cause your eyes to move opposite to your head movements. These reflexes allow you to focus on one spot even when your head is moving. You can dramatize these reflexes by having a friend spin you around on a stool for a while. When you stop, try to fix your gaze on one point in the room. You'll be unable to do so, because the excitation of the vestibular system will cause your eyes to move repeat-

vestibular sense   The proprioceptive sense that provides information about the position of the head and about its general movements.

edly in the direction opposite from the way you were spinning. (See "In Review: Body Senses" for a summary of our discussion of touch, temperature, pain, and kinesthesia.)

Perception

▉ **How do sensations become perceptions?**

So far, we have explored how sensory information reaches the brain. Let's now consider the processes of perception that allow the brain to make sense of that information. These perceptual processes can sometimes make the difference between life and death. For example, at a traffic circle in Scotland, fourteen fatal accidents occurred in one year, partly because drivers did not slow down as they approached the circle. After warning signs failed to solve the problem, Gordon Denton, a British psychologist, found a clever solution. He recommended that white lines be painted across the road leading to the circle, in a pattern something like this:

/   /   /   / / / ///

Crossing these lines, which were spaced progressively more closely, gave drivers the impression that they were speeding up, so their automatic response was to slow down. During the fourteen months after Denton's idea was implemented, there were only two fatalities at the traffic circle! The same striping is now being used to slow drivers on roads approaching small towns in the United States (Associated Press, 1999). Denton's solution depended partly on his knowledge of *sensation*, but mostly on the principles of human *perception*.

Some perceptual tasks take attention and effort, as when a child struggles to recognize printed letters. But as experienced readers know, a lot of the perceptual work that transforms sensory information into meaningful experiences happens automatically, without conscious awareness. To illustrate the workings of these complex processes, psychologists draw attention to *perceptual failures*—cases in which we perceive stimuli incorrectly. Just as drivers at the traffic circle incorrectly perceived themselves as speeding up, you will probably perceive the two lines in Figure 3.18 as differing in length, even though they are the same.

FIGURE 3.18

Misperceiving Reality

LEARN BY DOING **Measure lines A-C and A-B. They are exactly the same length, but you probably perceived A-C as longer. Why? Partly because your visual system tries to interpret all stimuli as three-dimensional, even when they are not. A three-dimensional interpretation of this drawing would lead you to see the two lines as the edges of two parallel paths, one of which ends closer to you than the other. Your eyes tell you that the two paths originate from about the same point (the castle entrance), so you assume that the closer line must be the longer of the two.**

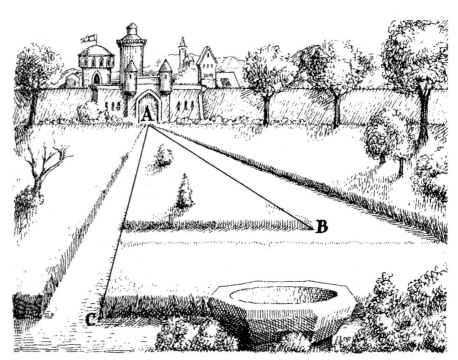

Source: Gardner (1988).

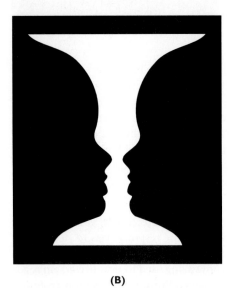

(A)

(B)

Reversible Images

These *reversible images* can be organized by your perceptual system in two ways. Try perceiving Part A as the word *figure*, and the space around the letters becomes meaningless background. Now emphasize the word *ground,* and what had stood out a moment ago now becomes background. You can do the same in Part B. When you emphasize the vase, the faces become background; if you organize the faces as the figure, what had been a vase now becomes background.

figure   The part of the visual field that has meaning.

ground   The contourless part of the visual field; the background.

Gestalt   Principles for organizing stimuli into shapes and patterns. *Gestalt* is the German word meaning (roughly) "whole figure."

depth perception   Perception of distance, allowing us to experience the world in three dimensions.

Organizing the Perceptual World

What determines how I perceive my world?

To further appreciate the wonder of the complicated perceptual work you do every day, imagine yourself driving on a busy road searching for Barney's Diner, an unfamiliar restaurant where you are to meet a friend. The roadside is crammed with signs of all shapes and colors, some flashing, some rotating. If you are ever to recognize the sign that says "Barney's Diner," you must impose some sort of organization on this overwhelming mixture of visual information. How do you do this? How do you know where one sign ends and another begins? And how do you know that an apparently tiny sign is not too small to read but is just far away?

Principles of Perceptual Organization

Before you can recognize the "Barney's Diner" sign, your perceptual system must separate that sign from its background of lights, colors, letters, and other competing stimuli. Two basic principles—*figure-ground perception* and *grouping*—guide this initial organization.

Figure and Ground   When you look at a complex scene or listen to a noisy environment, your perceptual apparatus automatically picks out certain features, objects, or sounds to emphasize. The emphasized features become the **figure.** This part of the visual field has meaning, stands in front of the rest, and always seems to include contours or edges. These contours and edges separate the figure from the less relevant background, called the **ground** (E. Rubin, 1915). So, as you drive toward an intersection, a stop sign becomes a figure, standing out clearly against the background of trees, houses, and cars.

To experience how perception creates figure and ground, look at Figure 3.19. Notice that *you* can decide how to organize the stimuli in the drawings. You can repeatedly reverse figure and ground to see faces, then a vase, then faces again, or to see the word *figure* or the word *ground.* These "reversible" images show that your perceptual systems are not just video cameras or tape machines that passively record incoming sensations; you play an active part in organizing what you perceive. However, you usually organize sensory stimulation into only one perceptual category at a time. This is why it is difficult to see both a vase and two faces—or the words *figure* and *ground*—at the same time.

Grouping   Why is it that certain parts of the world become figure and others become ground, even when nothing in particular stands out in the pattern of light that falls on the retina? The answer is that certain properties of stimuli lead you to group them together, more or less automatically.

In the early 1900s, several German psychologists described the principles behind this grouping of stimuli. They argued that people perceive sights and sounds as organized wholes. These wholes, they said, become different from, and more than, the sum of the individual sensations, just as water becomes something more than just an assortment of hydrogen and oxygen atoms. Because the German word meaning (roughly) "whole figure" is **Gestalt** (pronounced "ge-SHTALT"), these researchers became known as *Gestalt psychologists.* They proposed a number of principles that describe how the perceptual system "glues" raw sensations together in particular ways:

1. *Proximity.*   The closer objects or events are to one another, the more likely they are to be perceived as belonging together, as Figure 3.20(A) illustrates.

2. *Similarity.*   Similar elements are perceived to be part of a group, as in Figure 3.20(B). This is why students wearing the same school colors at a stadium will be perceived as belonging together even if they are not seated close together.

3. *Continuity.*   Sensations that appear to create a continuous form are perceived as belonging together, as in Figure 3.20(C).

Gestalt Principles of
Perceptual Grouping

We tend to perceive Part A as two groups
of two circles plus one single circle, rather
than as, say, five circles. In Part B, we see
two columns of Xs and two columns of
Os, not four rows of XOXO. We see the X in
Part C as being made out of two continuous lines, not a combination of the odd
forms shown. In Part D, we fill gaps so as
to perceive a hollow cube. In Part E, the
different angle of the lines in one part of
the rectangle makes it stand out from the
other parts. In Part F, we see the same
three-dimensional cube from different
angles, but the one on the left is normally
perceived as a two-dimensional hexagon
with spokes; the other, as a three-
dimensional cube. In Part G, we tend to
pair up dots in the same oval even
though they are far apart.

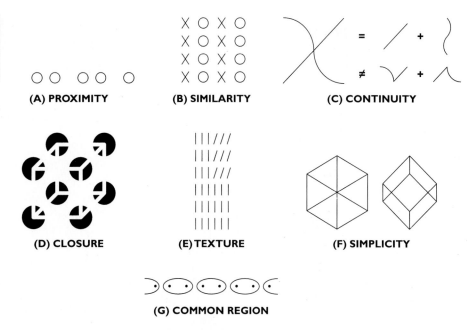

(A) PROXIMITY   (B) SIMILARITY   (C) CONTINUITY

(D) CLOSURE   (E) TEXTURE   (F) SIMPLICITY

(G) COMMON REGION

THE FAR SIDE   By GARY LARSON

The deadly couch cobra — coiled and alert in its
natural habitat.

4. *Closure.* We tend to mentally "fill in" missing parts of incomplete objects, as in
Figure 3.20(D). The gaps are easy to see, but the tendency to link disconnected parts can
be so strong that you may perceive faint connections that are not actually there.

5. *Texture.* When basic features of stimuli have the same texture (such as the
angle of several elements), we tend to group those stimuli together, as in Figure 3.20(E).
Thus, we group standing trees together and perceive them as separate from their fallen
neighbors.

6. *Simplicity.* We tend to group features of a stimulus in a way that provides the
simplest interpretation of the world. In Figure 3.20(F), perceiving the image on the left
as a two-dimensional hexagon with six spokes is much simpler than perceiving it as a
three-dimensional cube. So the two-dimensional perception usually prevails. However,
perceiving the image on the right as two-dimensional would be complicated (try describing it in words!), so we are likely to see it as a cube.

7. *Common fate.* Sets of objects that move in the same direction at the same speed
are perceived together. Thus, a flock of birds, though separated in space, will be perceived
as a group. Choreographers and marching-band directors use the principle of common
fate when they arrange for groups of dancers or musicians to move identically, causing
the audience to perceive waves of motion or large moving objects.

8. *Common region and synchrony.* Stephen Palmer (1999) has proposed some additional grouping principles. One of these, called *common region*, states that elements
located within some boundary tend to be grouped together. The boundary can be created by an enclosing perimeter, as in Figure 3.20(G), a region of color, or other factors.
The principle of synchrony highlights the fact that stimuli that occur at the same time
are likely to be perceived as coming from the same source. For example, if you see a car
up ahead stop violently at the same instant you hear a crash, you will probably perceive
these visual and auditory stimuli as part of the same event.

Perception of Depth and Distance

We are able to experience the world in three-dimensional depth even though the visual
information we receive from it is projected onto two-dimensional retinas. This is possible because of **depth perception,** our ability to perceive distance. Depth perception, in
turn, is made possible partly by *stimulus cues* provided by the environment and partly by
the properties of our visual system.

Stimulus Cues   To some extent, people perceive depth through the same cues that artists use to create the impression of depth and distance on a two-dimensional canvas. Figure 3.21 demonstrates several of these cues:

▪ The two people at the far left of Figure 3.21 illustrate the principle of *relative size*: If two objects are assumed to be the same size, the object producing a larger image on the retina is perceived as closer than the one producing a smaller image.

▪ Another cue comes from *height in the visual field:* On the ground, more distant objects are usually higher in the visual field than those nearby. Because the buildings in Figure 3.21 are higher than the people in the foreground, the buildings appear to be farther away from you.

▪ The person walking near the car in the middle of Figure 3.21 illustrates another depth cue called *interposition.* Closer objects block the view of things farther away.

▪ The tiny figure near the dotted center line of the road in Figure 3.21 is seen as very far away because she is near a point in the road where its edges, like all parallel lines that recede into the distance, appear to converge toward a single point. This apparent convergence provides a cue called *linear perspective.* The closer together two converging lines are, the greater the perceived distance.

▪ Notice that the road in Figure 3.21 disappears into a hazy background. Because increased distance usually produces less clarity, *reduced clarity* is interpreted as a cue for greater distance.

A CASE OF DEPTH MISPERCEPTION
The runner in this photo is actually farther away than the man on the pitcher's mound. But because he is lower, not higher, in the visual field—and because his leg can be seen as in front of, not behind, the pitcher's leg—the runner appears smaller than normal rather than farther away.

■ *Light and shadow* also contribute to the perception of three dimensions (Ramachandran, 1988). The buildings in the background of Figure 3.21 are seen as three-dimensional, not flat, because of the shadows on their right faces.

■ An additional stimulus-based depth cue comes from continuous changes across the visual field, called gradients. For example, a *textural gradient* is a graduated change in the texture, or "grain," of the visual field, as you can see in the sidewalk, the grass, and the road in Figure 3.21. Texture appears finer as distance increases. So, as the texture of a surface changes across the retinal image, you perceive a change in distance.

Cues Based on Properties of the Visual System   Some depth cues result from the way human eyes are built and positioned. Recall that to bring an image into focus on the retina, the lens of the eye changes shape, or *accommodates*. Information about the muscle activity involved is relayed to the brain, and this accommodation cue helps create the perception of distance.

Two other depth cues are produced by the relative location of our two eyes. One is **convergence.** Each eye is located at a different place on the skull so that the eyes must converge, or rotate inward, to project the same image on each retina. The closer the object, the more the eyes must converge. Eye muscles send information about this convergence to the brain, which processes it as a distance cue.

Second, because they are in slightly different locations, each eye sees the world from a slightly different angle. The difference between these different retinal images is called **binocular disparity.** The difference, or disparity, between images gets smaller for objects that are far away, and larger for objects that are nearby. The brain not only combines the two images of an object but also takes into account how much they differ. This information helps to generate the impression of a single object located at a particular distance. View-Master slide viewers, 3-D movies, and virtual reality devices also use binocular disparity cues to create the appearance of depth in a two-dimensional stimulus. They show each eye a picture of a scene that was taken from slightly different angles.

In short, many cues—some present in the environment and in retinal images, others arising from the structure of the visual system—combine to give us a powerful and accurate sense of depth and distance.

Perception of Motion

Sometimes the most important property of an object is its motion—how fast it is going and where it is heading. Usually motion perception occurs as visual patterns from objects move across the surface of the retina. As in the case of depth perception, you automatically translate this two-dimensional information into a three-dimensional experience. One example is the response to **looming,** which is a rapid expansion in the size of an image so that it fills the retina. When an image looms, there is an automatic tendency to perceive it as an approaching stimulus. If the expansion is as fast to the right as to the left, and as fast above as below, this information signals that the object is directly approaching the eyes. In other words: Duck!

We are lucky that movement of the retinal image is not the only factor contributing to motion perception. If it were, everything in sight would appear to move every time you moved your eyes and head. This does not happen because, as noted earlier, the brain receives and processes information about the motion of the eyes and head. So if head or eye movements occur while images of fixed objects move across the retina, you will perceive those objects as stationary. If the images move but the eyes and head do not, you will perceive the objects as moving. To demonstrate this, scan the room with your eyes. Stationary objects will not appear to move. Now close one eye and carefully move your open eyeball by gently pushing on its lower eyelid. Because your brain receives no signals that your eye is being moved by its own muscles, you will perceive objects in the room as moving.

When you *are* moving, as in a car, the flow of visual information across the retina combines with information from the vestibular and touch senses to give you the experience of being in motion. So if you accelerate in a car, you feel pressure from the back of

convergence   A depth cue resulting from rotation of the eyes so that the image of an object can be projected on each retina.

binocular disparity   A depth cue based on the difference between the retinal images received by each eye.

looming   A motion cue whereby rapid expansion in the size of an image fills the available space on the retina.

BINOCULAR DISPARITY CUES The difference between each eye's view of an object is smaller for distant objects and greater for closer ones. These binocular disparity cues help to create our perception of a three-dimensional world using only two-dimensional retinas. To see for yourself how binocular disparity changes with distance, hold a pencil vertically about six inches in front of your nose; then close one eye and notice where the pencil is in relation to the background. Now open that eye, close the other one, and notice how much the pencil "shifts." These are the two different views your eyes have of the pencil. Repeat this procedure while holding the pencil at arm's length. Notice that there is now less disparity or "shift," because there is less difference in the angles from which your two eyes see the pencil.

the seat and feel your head tilting backward. If visual flow is perceived *without* appropriate sensations from other parts of the body, particularly the vestibular senses, motion sickness may result. This explains why you might feel nauseous while operating motion simulators or playing some video games, especially those with virtual reality technology. The images suggest that you are moving through space when there is no real motion.

Other illusions of motion are far less unpleasant. The most important of these, called **stroboscopic motion,** occurs because we tend to perceive movement when a series of still images appear, one at a time, in rapid succession. Stroboscopic motion allows us to see movement in the still images presented by films and videos. Films consist of sequences of snapshots presented at a rate of twenty-four per second. Each snapshot is slightly different from the preceding one, and each is separated by a brief blank-out produced by the projector's shutter. Videotapes show thirty snapshots per second. As we watch, the "sensory memory" of each image lasts long enough in the brain to bridge the gap until the next image appears. Thus, we are usually unaware that we are seeing a series of still pictures and that, about half the time, there is actually no image on the screen!

Perceptual Constancy

Suppose that one sunny day you are watching someone walking toward you along a tree-lined sidewalk. The visual sensations produced by this person are actually very strange. The size of the image on your retinas keeps getting larger as the person gets closer. To see this for yourself, hold out a hand at arm's length and look at someone far away. The retinal image of that person will be so small that you can cover it with your hand. If you do the same thing when the person is three feet away, the retinal image will be too large to be covered by your hand, yet you perceive the person as being closer now, not bigger. Similarly, if you watch a person pass from bright sunshine through the shadows of trees, your retinas receive images that shift back and forth from dark to light. Still, you perceive the person's coloring as staying the same.

These examples illustrate **perceptual constancy,** the perception that objects maintain their size, shape, color, and other properties despite changes in their retinal image. Without this aspect of perception, you would experience the world as a place where solid objects continuously change their properties.

Size Constancy Why does an object's perceived size stay more or less constant, regardless of changes in the size of its retinal image? One reason is that the brain perceives a

stroboscopic motion An illusion in which lights or images flashed in rapid succession are perceived as moving.

perceptual constancy The perception of objects as retaining the same size, shape, color, and other properties despite changes in their retinal image.

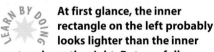

At first glance, the inner rectangle on the left probably looks lighter than the inner rectangle on the right. But carefully examine the inner rectangles alone (covering their surroundings), and you will see that both are of equal intensity. The brighter surround in the right-hand figure leads you to perceive its inner rectangle as relatively darker.

change in the distance of an object and automatically adjusts the perception of size. Thus, the *perceived size* of an object is equal to the size of the retinal image multiplied by the perceived distance (Holway & Boring, 1941). As an object moves closer, the size of its retinal image increases, but the perceived distance decreases at the same rate. So, the perceived size remains constant. If a balloon is inflated in front of your eyes, perceived distance remains constant, and the perceived size (correctly) increases as the size of the retinal image increases.

Shape Constancy   The principles behind shape constancy are closely related to those of size constancy. To see shape constancy at work, remember what page you are on, close this book, and tilt it toward and away from you several times. The book will continue to look rectangular, even though the shape of its retinal image changes dramatically as you move it. Your brain automatically integrates information about retinal images and distance as movement occurs. In this case, the distance information had to do with the difference in distance between the near and far edges of the book.

Brightness Constancy   Even with dramatic changes in the amount of light striking an object, the object's perceived brightness remains relatively constant. Place a piece of charcoal in sunlight and a piece of white paper in nearby shade. The charcoal will look very dark and the paper very bright, yet a light meter would tell you that much more light energy is reflected from the sun-bathed coal than from the shaded paper. Why? Partly because the charcoal is the darkest object *relative* to its sunlit background, and the paper is the brightest object *relative* to its background of shade. As shown in Figure 3.22, the brightness of an object is perceived in relation to its background.

Optical Illusions

Usually, the perceptual system works automatically and perfectly to create correct perceptions of depth, distance, and size. Sometimes, though, it can fail, resulting in *optical illusions* such as the ones shown in Figure 3.23. Why does the monster that is placed higher in Figure 3.23(A) look larger than the lower one, even though they are equal in size? The converging lines in the tunnel provide depth cues telling you that the higher

These illusions are named for the scientists who described them. In Part A, a version of the *Ponzo illusion,* the upper monster looks bigger but is actually the same size as the lower one. In the *Müller-Lyer illusion* (Part B), both vertical lines are actually of equal length; in the *Ebbinghaus illusion* shown in Part C, both center circles are exactly the same size. To prove that you can't always believe your eyes, measure these drawings for yourself.

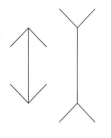

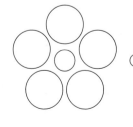

(A)   (B)   (C)

in review

Principles of Perceptual Organization and Constancy

Principle	Description	Example
Figure-ground	Certain objects or sounds automatically become identified as figure, whereas others become meaningless background.	You see a person standing against a building, not a building with a person-shaped hole in it.
Grouping	Properties of stimuli lead us to automatically group them together. These include proximity, similarity, continuity, closure, texture, simplicity, common fate, common region, and synchrony.	People who are sitting together, or who are dressed similarly, are perceived as a group.
Depth perception	The world is perceived as three-dimensional, with help from stimulus cues (such as relative size, height in the visual field, interposition, linear perspective, reduced clarity, light and shadow, and gradients) and from visual system cues (such as accommodation, convergence, and binocular disparity).	A person who looks tiny and appears high in the visual field will be perceived as being of normal size, but at a great distance.
Perceptual constancy	Objects are perceived as constant in size, shape, color, and other properties despite changes in their retinal images.	A train coming toward you is perceived as getting closer, not larger; a gas station sign is perceived as rotating, not changing shape.

monster is farther away. Because the retinal image of the "distant" monster is the same size as the "closer" one, your perceptual system calculates that the more distant monster must be bigger. This is the principle of size constancy at work: When two objects have retinal images of the same size, you perceive the one that seems farther away as larger. Now look at Figure 3.23(B). The two vertical lines are the same length, but the one on the right looks longer. Why? One possible reason is that the perceived length of an object is based on what frames it. When the frame is perceived as larger, as on the right side of Figure 3.23(B), so is the line segment within it (Rock, 1978). In Figure 3.23(C), the inner circle at the left looks smaller than the one at the right because, like the brightness of the center rectangles in Figure 3.22, the inner circles are judged in relation to what surrounds them. Because perception is based on many principles, illusions like these probably reflect the violation of more than one of them. (See "In Review: Principles of Perceptual Organization and Constancy.")

Culture, Experience, and Perception

We have talked as if all aspects of perception appear at birth and work or fail in the same way for everyone, everywhere. However, some perceptual abilities appear later than others (see this chapter's Linkages section), and virtually all of them are honed by experience in the world.

For example, people are better at judging the size and distance of familiar objects than those of unfamiliar ones. This phenomenon suggests that size constancy depends not only on judging image sizes and distances but also on knowledge and experience that tell us that most objects (aside from balloons) do not suddenly change size. As with size constancy, much of the ability to judge shape constancy depends on automatic processes, but our expectations that books and other solid objects do not suddenly change shape also play a role. The knowledge-based nature of perception can also be seen in brightness constancy: Part of the reason you perceive charcoal to be darker than a sheet of paper, no matter how much light it reflects, is that you *know* charcoal is black.

If experience can affect perception, *differing* experiences can, too. For example, people in cultures that do and do not use pictures and paintings to represent reality show

top-down processing   Aspects of recognition guided by higher-level cognitive processes and psychological factors such as expectations.

bottom-up processing   Aspects of recognition that depend first on information about stimuli that come up to the brain from the sensory systems.

Source: Hudson (1960).

FIGURE 3.24

Culture and Depth Cues

In research on the influence of experience on perception, people are shown drawings like these and asked to judge which animal is closer to the hunter. Those in cultures where pictured depth cues are familiar choose the antelope, which is at the same distance from the viewer as the hunter. Those in cultures less familiar with such cues may choose the elephant, which, though closer on the page, is more distant when depth cues are considered.

FIGURE 3.25

Categorizing Perceptions

What do you see here? For the identity of this figure, turn to page 102.

differing responses to pictures containing depth cues (Derogowski, 1989). People in the Me'n or the Nupa cultures of Africa, who have little experience with pictorial representation, have a more difficult time judging distances shown in pictures than do people in picture-oriented cultures (see Figure 3.24). These individuals also tend to have a harder time sorting *pictures* of three-dimensional objects into categories, even though they can easily sort the objects themselves (Derogowski, 1989). So, although the structure and principles of human perceptual systems tend to create generally similar views of the world for all of us, our perception of reality is also shaped by experience, including the experience of living in a particular culture.

Recognizing the Perceptual World

How do I recognize familiar people?

So far, we have ignored a vital question about perception: How do you recognize what objects are? If you are driving in search of Barney's Diner, exactly what happens when your eyes finally locate the pattern of light that spells out its name? How do you recognize it as the place you are seeking?

In essence, your brain must analyze the incoming pattern of information and compare that pattern to information stored in your memory. If it finds a match, recognition takes place, and the stimulus is put into a *perceptual category.* Once recognition occurs, your perception of the stimulus may never be the same again. Look at Figure 3.25. Do you see anything familiar? If not, turn to Figure 3.26; then look at Figure 3.25 again. You should now see it in an entirely new light. The difference between your "before" and "after" experiences is the difference between the sensory world before and after a perceptual match occurs and recognition takes place.

How does this matching process occur? Some aspects of recognition begin at the "top." That is, they are guided by knowledge, expectations, and other psychological factors. This phenomenon is called **top-down processing,** because it involves high-level, knowledge-based information. Other aspects of recognition begin at the "bottom," relying on specific, detailed information from the sensory receptors and assembling them into a whole. This latter phenomenon is called **bottom-up processing,** because it begins with basic information units that serve as a foundation for recognition.

FIGURE 3.26

Another Version of Figure 3.25

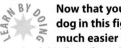 **Now that you can identify a dog in this figure, it should be much easier to recognize when you look back at the original version.**

Bottom-Up Processing

All along the path from the eye to the brain, certain cells respond to selected features of a stimulus. The stimulus is first analyzed into these *basic features*, which are then recombined to create the perceptual experience.

What are these features? As mentioned earlier, certain cells specialize in responding to lines, edges, corners, and stimuli having specific orientations in space (Hubel & Wiesel, 1979). For example, cells in the cerebral cortex that fire only in response to a diagonal line act as feature detectors for diagonal lines. The analysis by such feature detectors, early in the sensation-perception sequence, may contribute to recognition of letters or judgments of shape. Color and motion are other sensory features that appear to be analyzed separately, in different parts of the brain, prior to full perceptual recognition (Beatty, 1995; Cowey, 1994).

The brain also apparently analyzes patterns of light and darkness in the visual scene. Analyzing these patterns may help us to perceive textural gradients, which in turn help us to judge depth and recognize the general shape of blurry images.

Top-Down Processing

Bottom-up feature analysis can explain why you recognize the letters in a sign for Barney's Diner. But why is it that you can recognize the sign more easily if it appears where you were told to expect it rather than a block earlier? And why can you recognize it even if a few letters are missing from the sign? Top-down processing seems to be at work in those cases. In top-down processing, people rely on their knowledge in making inferences, or "educated guesses," that help them recognize objects, words, or melodies, especially when sensory information is vague or ambiguous (DeWitt & Samuel, 1990; Rock, 1983). For example, once you knew that there was a dog in Figure 3.25, it became much easier for you to perceive one. Similarly, police officers find it easy to recognize familiar people on blurry security camera videos, but it is much more difficult for them to recognize strangers (Burton et al., 1999).

Top-down processing illustrates that our experiences create **schemas,** mental representations of what we know and expect about the world. Schemas can bias our perception toward one recognition or another by creating a *perceptual set*—that is, a readiness to perceive a stimulus in a certain way. Expectancy may also be shaped by the immediate *context* in which a stimulus occurs. For example, people are more likely to perceive the image in Figure 3.25 as a dog if it appears in a set of clearer pictures of dogs. Context and

schemas Mental representations of what we know and expect about the world.

Mechanisms of Pattern Recognition

Mechanism	Description	Example
Bottom-up processing	Raw sensations from the eye or the ear are analyzed into basic features, such as edges, color or movement; these features are then recombined at higher brain centers, where they are compared to stored information about objects or sounds.	You recognize a dog as a dog because its physical features—four legs, barking, panting—match your perceptual category for "dog."
Top-down processing	Knowledge of the world and experience in perceiving allow people to make inferences about the identity of stimuli, even when the quality of raw sensory information is low.	On a dark night, a small, vaguely seen blob pulling on the end of a leash is recognized as a dog because the stimulus occurs at a location where we would expect a dog to be.

expectancy have biasing effects for sounds as well as sights. The raw sound "eye screem" takes on a different meaning when heard in the context of "I scream when I am angry" versus "I love ice cream."

Motivation is another aspect of top-down processing that can affect perception. A hungry person, for example, might initially mistake a sign for "Burger's Body Shop" as indicating a place to eat. Similarly, you may remember a time when an obviously incompetent referee incorrectly called a penalty on your favorite sports team. You knew the call was wrong because you clearly saw the other team's player at fault. But suppose you had been cheering for that other team. The chances are good that you would have seen the referee's call as the right one. (See "In Review: Mechanisms of Pattern Recognition" for a summary of bottom-up versus top-down processing.)

Top-Down and Bottom-Up Processing Together

Bottom-up and top-down processing usually work together to help us recognize the perceptual world. This interaction is beautifully illustrated by the process of reading. When the quality of the raw stimulus on the page is poor, as in Figure 3.27, top-down processes compensate to make continued reading possible. They allow you to fill in where words are not well perceived and processed, thus giving you a general idea of the meaning of the text.

You can fill in the gaps because the world is *redundant;* it provides multiple clues about what is going on. If you lose or miss one stimulus in a pattern, others can help so that you still recognize the pattern. There is so much redundancy in written language, for instance, that many of the words and letters you see are not needed. Fo- ex-mp-e, y-u c-n r-ad -hi- se-te-ce -it- ev-ry -hi-d l-tt-r m-ss-ng. Similarly, vision in three dimensions normally provides multiple cues to depth, making recognition of distance easy and clear.

WHAT DOES IT LOOK LIKE TO YOU? Many people in Clearwater, Florida, see the pattern of light reflected from this office building as an image of the Virgin Mary. Their perceptual categorization results from a combination of bottom-up and top-down recognition processes. Feature detectors automatically register the edges and colors of the images, whereas knowledge, beliefs, and expectancies give meaning to these features. A person from a Muslim or Hindu culture might not see this Christian image, however. Try showing this photo to people of different faiths (don't mention what it might be), and make note of who recognizes what.

FIGURE 3.27	Interaction of Top-Down and Bottom-Up Processing

Which obscured line do you find easier to read: the one on the top or the one on the bottom? Top-down processing should help you read the obscured text on the top line. However, in the bottom line, the words are not related, so top-down processing cannot operate.

it is very easy to read this redundant sentence
BUT NOT
butter resist poodle act grandad also way(sting)

It is when many of these cues are eliminated that ambiguous stimuli create the sorts of depth illusions discussed earlier.

In hearing, too, top-down processing can compensate for ambiguous stimuli. In one experiment, participants heard strings of five words in meaningless order, such as "wet brought who socks some." There was so much background noise, however, that only about 75 percent of the words could be recognized (G. A. Miller, Heise, & Lichten, 1951). The words were then read to a second group of participants in a meaningful order (for example, "who brought some wet socks"). The second group was able to recognize almost all of the words, even under the same noisy conditions. In fact, it took twice as much noise to reduce their performance to the level of the first group. Why? When the words were in meaningless order, only bottom-up processing was available. Recognizing one word was no help in identifying the next. Meaningful sentences, however, provided a more familiar context and allowed for some top-down processing. Hearing one word helped the listener make a reasonable guess (based on knowledge and experience) about the others.

 LINKAGES
How do infants perceive the world? (a link to Human Development)

 LINKAGES

Perception And Human Development

We have seen that perception is influenced by the knowledge and experience we acquire over time, but what perceptual abilities do we start with? To learn about infants' perception, psychologists have studied two inborn patterns called *habituation* and *dishabituation*. Infants stop looking when they repeatedly see stimuli perceived to be the same. This is habituation. If they see a stimulus that is perceived to be different, they resume looking. This is dishabituation. Using the habituation/dishabituation technique, some researchers found that newborns could perceive the difference between black-and-white and colored displays, even though they could not distinguish between particular colors (Burr, Morrone, & Fiorentini, 1996). Other researchers used the same method to show that newborns can perceive differences in the angles of lines (Slater et al., 1991). These studies suggest that we are born with the basic components of feature detection.

Are we also born with the ability to combine features into perceptions of whole objects? Apparently not. At one month of age, infants concentrate their gaze on one part of an object, such as the corner of a triangle (E. B. Goldstein, 1999). By two months, however, infants systematically scan the perimeter of the object. This finding suggests that they are perceiving the pattern, or shape, of the object, not just its component features.

The ability to recognize more complex patterns seems to come only with experience. However, infants may be innately tuned to perceive at least one important complex pattern: the human face. In one study of newborns, patterns like those in Figure 3.28 were

FIGURE 3.28

Infants' Perceptions of Human Faces

Newborns show significantly greater interest in the face-like pattern at the far left than in any of the other patterns. Evidently, some aspects of face perception are innate.

  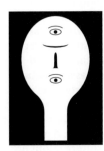 

Face   **Configuration**   **Linear**   **Scrambled**

Source: Johnson et al. (1991).

The Visual Cliff

The *visual cliff* is a glass-topped table that creates the impression of a sudden drop-off. A ten-month-old placed at what looks like the edge will calmly crawl across the shallow side to reach a parent but will hesitate and cry rather than crawl over the "cliff" (E. J. Gibson & Walk, 1960).

moved slowly past the infants' faces (M. A. Johnson et al., 1991). The infants moved their heads and eyes to follow these patterns. But they tracked the face-like pattern shown on the left side of Figure 3.28 significantly farther than any of the nonfaces. The difference in tracking indicates that infants can tell faces from nonfaces and are more interested in faces. In a more recent experiment, infants looked more at a face-like pattern drawn especially for the newborn visual system (Valenza et al., 1996). Why should this be? Investigators suggest that interest in human faces is adaptive, in evolutionary terms. It helps newborns focus on their only source of food and care.

Our ability to accurately perceive depth and distance develops more slowly than our ability to recognize shapes. Infants' ability to use binocular disparity and motion cues to judge depth appears to develop sometime after about three months of age. And infants do not use textural gradients and linear perspective as cues to depth until they are five to seven months old (Arterberry, Craton, & Yonas, 1993).

These conclusions are based partly on research with the *visual cliff,* a glass-topped table that creates the impression of a sudden drop-off (see Figure 3.29). A ten-month-old placed at what looks like the edge will calmly crawl across the shallow side to reach a parent, but will hesitate and cry rather than crawl over the "cliff." Changes in heart rate show that infants too young to crawl also perceive the depth but are not frightened by it. Here again, nature and nurture interact adaptively: Depth perception appears shortly after birth, but fear and avoidance of dangerous depth do not develop until an infant is old enough to crawl into trouble.

In summary, there is little doubt that many of the basic building blocks of perception are present within the first few days after birth. The basics include such organ-based cues to depth as accommodation and convergence. Maturation of the visual system adds to these basics as time goes by. Over the first few months after birth, the eye's fovea gradually develops the number of cone cells necessary for high visual acuity and perception of fine details (E. B. Goldstein, 1999). Visual experience is also necessary. Experience teaches the infant to recognize unified patterns and objects, to interpret depth and distance cues, and to use them in moving safely through the world. Like so many aspects of human psychology, perception is the result of a blending of heredity and environment. From infancy onward, the perceptual system creates a personal reality.

Attention

Can you "run out" of attention?

You still haven't found Barney's Diner! By now, you understand *how* you will recognize the right sign when you perceive it. But how can you be sure you *will* perceive it? The diner's sign will appear as one ingredient in a sensory soup that also includes road signs, traffic lights, sirens, talk radio, and dozens of other stimuli. You can't perceive all of them at once. So, to find Barney's, you are going to have to be sure that the information you process includes the stimuli that will help you reach your goal. In short, you are going to have to pay attention.

Attention is the process of directing and focusing certain psychological resources to enhance perception, performance, and mental experience. We use attention to *direct* our sensory and perceptual systems toward certain stimuli, to *select* specific information for further processing, to *allocate* the mental energy required to do that processing, and to *regulate* the flow of resources necessary for performing a task or coordinating several tasks at once (Wickens & Carswell, 1997).

Psychologists have discovered three important characteristics of attention. First, it *improves mental processing*. You often need to concentrate attention on a task to do your best at it. Second, attention takes *effort*. Prolonged concentration of attention can leave you drained. When you are tired, focusing attention on anything becomes more difficult. Third, attention is *limited*. When your attention is focused on your reading, for instance, you will have less attention left over to listen to a conversation in the next room.

The Process of Attention

To experience attention as a process, try "moving it around" a bit. When you finish reading this sentence, look at something behind you, then face forward and notice the next sound you hear, then visualize your best friend, then focus on how your tongue feels. You just used attention to direct your perceptual systems toward different aspects of your external and internal environments. When you looked behind you, shifting attention involved *overt orienting*—pointing sensory systems at a particular stimulus. But you were able to shift attention to an image of your friend's face without having to move a muscle. This is called *covert orienting*.

Your search for Barney's Diner will be aided by your ability to overtly allocate attention to a certain part of the environment. It would be made even easier if Barney's had the only flashing sign on the road. As the most intense stimulus around you, it would attract your attention automatically. Psychologists describe this ability to search for targets rapidly and automatically as *parallel processing*. It is as if you can examine all nearby locations at once (in parallel) and rapidly detect the target no matter where it appears.

Dividing and Focusing Attention

Often you can divide your attention efficiently enough to allow you to perform more than one activity at a time (Damos, 1992). You can drive a car, listen to the radio, sing along, and keep a beat by drumming on the steering wheel. However, your attention cannot be divided beyond a certain point without a loss in performance and mental-processing ability. The reason is that attention is a limited resource. If you try to spread it over too many targets, you "run out" of attention.

Still, it can sometimes be hard to keep your attention focused rather than divided. Look at the list of words in Figure 3.30 and, as rapidly as possible, call out the *color of the ink* in which each word is printed. This *Stroop task* (Stroop, 1935) is not easy, because

attention   The process of directing and focusing certain psychological resources, usually by voluntary control.

BLUE GREEN

GREEN ORANGE

PURPLE ORANGE

GREEN BLUE

RED RED

GRAY GRAY

RED BLUE

BLUE PURPLE

FIGURE 3.30

The Stroop Task

 Look at this list of words and, as rapidly as possible, call out the *color of the ink* in which each word is printed. How did you do?

your brain automatically processes the *meanings* of the familiar words in the list. These meanings then compete for attention with the responses you are supposed to give. To do well, you must focus on the ink color and not allow your attention to be divided between color and meaning. Children just learning to read have far less trouble with this task, because they do not yet process the meanings of words as automatically as experienced readers do.

Attending to some stimuli makes us less able to attend to others. In other words, attention is selective. It is like a spotlight that can illuminate only a part of the external or internal environment at any particular moment. So if you focus intently on your reading or a video game, you may fail to perceive even dramatic changes in other parts of your environment. This phenomenon has been called *inattentional blindness* (Mack & Rock, 1998). In one study, a researcher asked college students for directions to a campus building (Simons & Levin, 1997). During each conversation, two other researchers dressed as workmen passed between the first researcher and the student, carrying a large door. As the door hid the researcher from the student's view, one of the "workmen" took his place. This new person then resumed the conversation with the student as though nothing had happened. Amazingly, only half of the students noticed that they were suddenly talking to a new person! The rest had apparently been paying so much attention to the researcher's question, or to the map he was showing, that they did not notice his appearance. Magicians take advantage of inattentional blindness when they use sudden movements or other attention-grabbing stimuli to draw our attention away from the actions that lie behind their tricks.

How do you control, or allocate, your attention? Research shows that control over attention can be voluntary or involuntary (Yantis, 1993). *Voluntary,* or goal-directed, control over attention occurs when you purposely focus so that you can perform a task. Voluntary control reflects top-down processing, because attention is guided by knowledge-based factors such as intention, beliefs, expectations, and motivation. As people learn certain skills, they voluntarily direct their attention to information they once ignored. For example, the experienced driver looks farther down the road than the first-time driver does.

When some aspect of the environment—such as a loud noise—diverts your attention, control is said to be *involuntary,* or stimulus driven. Stimulus characteristics that tend to capture attention include abrupt changes in lighting or color (such as flashing signs), movement, and the appearance of unusual shapes (Folk, Remington, & Wright, 1994). Engineering psychologists' research on which stimuli are most likely to attract attention—and distract attention—has been used in the design of everything from Internet web sites to operator warning devices for airliners, nuclear power plants, and other complex systems (Clay, 2000b; Laughery, 1999).

Although you can walk while talking, or drive while listening to music, you would find it virtually impossible to read and talk at the same time. Why is it sometimes so easy and at other times so difficult to do two things at once? When one task is so automatic as to require little or no attention, it is usually easy to do something else at the same time (B. Schneider, 1985). Even when two tasks require attention, it may still be possible to perform them simultaneously, as long as each taps into different kinds of attention (Wickens et al., 1992). Some types of attention are devoted to perceiving incoming stimuli. Others handle making responses. This specialization of attention allows a skilled pianist to read musical notes and press keys simultaneously the first time through a piece. Apparently, the human brain can manage more than one type of attention and more than one spotlight of attention (Wickens, 1989). This notion of different types of attention also helps explain why an experienced driver can listen to the radio while steering safely.

W e have seen that if you divide your attention among too many tasks, you may not do equally well at all of them. Some researchers have documented this phenomenon by looking at what happens in the brain as people attend to more than one source of information at once.

■ What was the researchers' question?

If directing attention to more than one task causes extra mental work to be done, there should be evidence of that work in brain activity. One possibility is that information-processing activity in the brain should slow down. Does it? This was the question asked by one research team.

■ How did the researchers answer the question?

Allan J. Nash and Mercedes Fernandez (1996) examined brain processing speed as participants engaged in various tasks. Sixteen college students heard high and low tones and saw red and green light flashes. They were asked to respond as quickly as possible to the identified target stimulus. On some trials they were to ignore tones and respond only to one of the lights, and on other trials they were to respond to one light and keep a running count of one of the tones. In short, the participants either attended to one task (responding to a light) or split their attention between two tasks (responding to a light and counting tones). The speed of the participants' reactions to the flashing light was measured throughout the experiment.

■ What did the researchers find?

When attention had to be shared between information required for two tasks, reaction times were slower than they were in response to the single-attention task.

■ What do the results mean?

The finding that reaction times were slower on split-attention trials suggests that information processing in the brain was slower, too. Further evidence for this conclusion has been provided by positron-emission tomography (PET) scans. They reveal increased blood flow to regions of the brain where mental processing is taking place (Corbetta et al., 1991). When attention is focused on only one stimulus feature, increased blood flow appears only in the part of the brain where that feature is analyzed. But when attention is divided, the added supply of blood is shared between two locations.

■ What do we still need to know?

Still to be determined are the limits of attention and processing; the means by which attention is shared; and the specific parts of the brain that are involved in attention, whether divided or undivided. Other research using PET scans, surgery on animals, and case studies of humans with brain damage has shown that switching the spotlight of visual attention involves at least three different parts of the brain (e.g., Posner & Raichle, 1994). Attention appears to be a linked set of resources that improve mental processing at several levels and locations in the brain. No single brain region has yet been identified as an "attention center" (Posner & Peterson, 1990).

active review Sensation and Perception

Linkages

As noted in Chapter 1, all of psychology's subfields are related to one another. Our discussion of the development of perception illustrates just one way in which the topic of this chapter, sensation and perception, is linked to the subfield of developmental psychology (Chapter 9). The Linkages diagram shows ties to two other subfields as well, and there are many more ties throughout the book. Looking for linkages among subfields will help you see how they all fit together and help you better appreciate the big picture that is psychology.

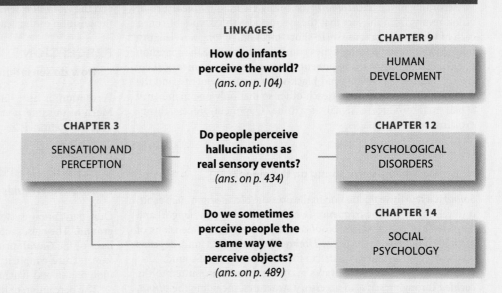

LINKAGES

How do infants perceive the world?
(ans. on p. 104)

CHAPTER 9
HUMAN DEVELOPMENT

CHAPTER 3
SENSATION AND PERCEPTION

Do people perceive hallucinations as real sensory events?
(ans. on p. 434)

CHAPTER 12
PSYCHOLOGICAL DISORDERS

Do we sometimes perceive people the same way we perceive objects?
(ans. on p. 489)

CHAPTER 14
SOCIAL PSYCHOLOGY

Summary

SENSING AND PERCEIVING THE WORLD

What is the difference between sensation and perception?

A *sense* is a system that translates information from outside the nervous system into neural activity. Messages from the senses are called *sensations. Perception* is the process through which people actively use knowledge and understanding of the world to interpret sensations as meaningful experiences.

SENSORY SYSTEMS

How does information from my eyes and ears get to my brain?

The first step in sensation involves *accessory structures,* which collect and modify sensory stimuli. The second step is *transduction,* the process of converting incoming energy into neural activity; it is accomplished by sensory *receptors,* neural cells specialized to detect energy of some type. *Adaptation* takes place when receptors receive unchanging stimulation. Except in the case of smell, neural activity is transferred through the thalamus, which relays it to the cerebral cortex.

Coding is the translation of physical properties of a stimulus into a pattern of neural activity that specifically identifies those physical properties. It is the language that the brain uses to describe sensations.

The minimum amount of light, sound, pressure, or other physical energy that can be detected 50 percent of the time is called the *absolute threshold. Internal noise* is the spontaneous, random firing of cells in the nervous system that occurs whether or not you are stimulated by physical energy. The *response criterion* reflects your willingness to respond to a stimulus or ignore it. *Signal-detection theory* addresses whether you will perceive a stimulus. *Sensitivity* refers to

your ability to discriminate a stimulus from its background. *Weber's law* states that the smallest detectable difference in stimulus energy is a constant fraction of the intensity of the stimulus. This smallest detectable difference in a stimulus is called the difference threshold or *just-noticeable difference (JND). Wavelength* is the distance from one peak of a sound wave or light wave to the next. Wave *frequency* is the number of complete waves, or cycles, that pass a given point per unit of time. *Amplitude* is the height of the wave from baseline to peak.

SEEING

Why do some people need eyeglasses?

Visible light is electromagnetic radiation with a wavelength of about 400 to about 750 nanometers. *Light intensity,* or the amount of energy in light, determines its brightness. Differing *light wavelengths* are sensed as different colors.

Accessory structures of the eye include the *cornea, pupil, iris,* and *lens.* Through *accommodation* and other means, these structures focus light rays on the *retina,* the netlike structure of cells at the back of the eye.

Photoreceptors in the retina—*rods* and *cones*—convert light into neural activity. Rods and cones differ in shape, sensitivity to light, ability to discriminate colors, and distribution across the retina. Both types of photoreceptors contribute to *dark adaptation.* The *fovea,* the area of highest acuity, has only cones, which are color sensitive. Rods are more sensitive to light but do not discriminate colors; they are distributed in areas around the fovea. From the photoreceptors, neural activity is transferred to bipolar cells and then to ganglion cells. A *blind spot* is created at the point where axons of ganglion cells leave the eye as a bundle of fibers called the *optic nerve.* Half of these fibers cross over at the optic chiasm. *Feature detectors* are cells in the cerebral cortex that respond to specific characteristics of objects in the visual field. The color of an object depends on which of the wavelengths striking it are absorbed and which are reflected. The sensation of color has three psychological dimensions: *hue, saturation,* and *brightness.*

According to the *trichromatic* (or Young-Helmholtz) *theory,* color vision results from the fact that the eye includes three types of cones, each of which is most sensitive to short, medium, or long wavelengths; information from the three types combines to produce the sensation of color. According to the *opponent-process* (or Hering) *theory,* there are red-green, blue-yellow, and black-white visual elements, and the members of each pair inhibit each other so that only one member of a pair may produce a signal at a time. Opponent-process theory explains color afterimages.

HEARING

How would my voice sound on the moon?

Sound is a repetitive fluctuation in the pressure of a medium such as air; it travels in waves. The *frequency* (which is related to *wavelength*) and *amplitude* of sound waves produce the psychological dimensions of *pitch* and *loudness,* respectively. *Timbre,* the quality of sound, depends on complex wave patterns added to the basic frequency of sound.

The energy from sound waves is collected and transmitted to the *cochlea* through a series of accessory structures, including the *pinna, eardrum,* hammer, anvil, stirrup, and oval window. Transduction occurs when sound energy stimulates hair cells on the *basilar membrane* of the cochlea, which in turn stimulate the *auditory nerve.* Auditory information is relayed through the thalamus to the primary auditory cortex.

The intensity of a sound stimulus is coded by the firing rate of auditory neurons. *Place theory* describes the coding of high frequencies. They are coded by the place on the basilar membrane where the wave peaks. Each neuron in the auditory nerve is most sensitive to a specific frequency (its preferred frequency). According to *volley theory,* some frequencies may be matched by the firing rate of a group of neurons.

THE CHEMICAL SENSES: TASTE AND SMELL

Why can't I taste anything when I have a cold?

The chemical senses include smell (olfaction) and taste (gustation). Our *sense of smell* detects volatile chemicals that come into contact with olfactory receptors in the nose. Olfactory signals are sent to the *olfactory bulb* in the brain without passing through the thalamus. *Pheromones* are odors from one animal that change the physiology or behavior of another animal. Our *sense of taste* detects chemicals that come into contact with taste receptors in *papillae* on the tongue. The basic taste sensations are sweet, sour, bitter, and salty. The senses of smell and taste interact to produce flavor.

SENSING YOUR BODY

Which is the largest organ in my body?

The *somatic senses,* also called somatosensory systems, include the skin senses and the *proprioceptive* senses. The skin senses detect touch, temperature, and pain. Nerve endings in the skin generate touch sensations when they are mechanically stimulated. Some nerve endings are sensitive to temperature, and some respond to both temperature and touch.

Pain provides information about intense stimuli. Sharp pain and dull, chronic pain are carried by different nerve fibers. The emotional response to pain depends on how the painful stimulus is interpreted.

According to the *gate control theory,* pain signals can be blocked on their way to the brain, sometimes by messages sent from the brain down the spinal cord, resulting in *analgesia.* Endorphins act at several levels in pain systems to reduce sensations of pain.

The proprioceptive senses are *kinesthesia,* which provides information about the position of body parts with respect to one another, and the *vestibular sense* (balance), which provides information about the position of the head in space.

PERCEPTION

How do sensations become perceptions?

Perception is the knowledge-based interpretation of sensations. Much of this interpretation takes place automatically, but sometimes conscious effort is required to translate sensations into meaningful experience.

ORGANIZING THE PERCEPTUAL WORLD

What determines how I perceive my world?

Our perceptual systems automatically discriminate *figure* from *ground.* They also automatically group stimuli into patterns on the basis of the *Gestalt* principles of proximity, similarity, continuity, closure, texture, simplicity, common fate, and two others known as common region and synchrony.

The perception of distance, or *depth perception,* depends partly on stimulus cues and partly on the physical structure of the visual system. Stimulus cues include relative size, height in the visual field, interposition, linear perspective, reduced clarity, light and shadow, and textural gradients. Cues based on the structure of the visual system include *convergence* of the eyes (the fact that the eyes must move to focus on the same object), *binocular disparity* (the fact that the eyes are set slightly apart), and accommodation (changes in the shape of the lenses as objects are brought into focus).

The perception of motion results, in part, from the movement of stimuli across the retina. Expanding or *looming* stimulation is perceived as an approaching object. Movement of the retinal image is interpreted along with information about movement of the head, eyes, and other parts of the body, so that one's own movement can be discriminated from the movement of external objects. *Stroboscopic motion* is a movement illusion arising when a series of slightly different still images are seen in rapid succession.

Because of *perceptual constancy,* the brightness, size, and shape of objects can be seen as constant despite changes in the sensations received from those objects. Size constancy and shape constancy depend on the relationship between the retinal image of the object and the knowledge-based perception of its distance. Brightness constancy depends on the perceived relationship between the brightness of an object and its background.

Optical illusions are distortions of reality that result when principles of perception are applied inappropriately. Many illusions are caused by misreading depth cues and by evaluating stimuli in the context of their surroundings.

To the extent that the visual environments of people in different cultures differ, their perceptual experiences—and their responses to perceptual illusions—may differ as well.

RECOGNIZING THE PERCEPTUAL WORLD

How do I recognize familiar people?

Both *bottom-up processing* and *top-down processing* contribute to recognition of the world. The ability to recognize objects is based on finding a match between the pattern of sensations organized by the perceptual system and a pattern that is stored in memory. Bottom-up processing seems to be accomplished by the analysis of features, or combinations of features, such as form, color, motion, and depth. Top-down processing is influenced by expectancy and motivation. *Schemas* based on past experience can create a perceptual set, the readiness or predisposition to perceive stimuli in certain ways. Expectancies can also be created by the context in which a stimulus appears. Top-down and bottom-up processing commonly work together to create recognition. Top-down processing can fill in gaps in physical stimuli, in part because the environment provides redundant stimuli.

The abilities to perceive color, basic shape features, and possibly the human face are present at or near birth. Other abilities, such as recognition of form, develop later. Depth, too, is perceived early, but its meaning is learned later. Perceptual abilities are modified by both experience and maturation.

ATTENTION
Can you "run out" of attention?

Attention is the process of focusing psychological resources to enhance perception, performance, and mental experience. We can shift attention overtly (by moving the eyes, for example) or covertly (without any movement of sensory systems). Attention is selective; it is like a spotlight that illuminates different parts of the external environment or specific mental processes. Control over attention can be voluntary and knowledge based or involuntary and driven by environmental stimuli. People can sometimes attend to two tasks at once, but there are limits to how much they can divide their attention.

Learn by Doing

Put It in Writing

Which of your five sensory systems—vision, hearing, touch, taste, or smell—do you think you could most easily do without? Which could you least easily do without? Write a page describing why you chose each of these sensory systems and listing what you would do to try to make up for the loss of each of these two systems.

Personal Learning Activity

Have you ever noticed how big the full moon appears when it has just risen above the horizon? Some researchers suggest that the moon appears larger on the horizon than overhead because the horizon moon—seen across a space filled with houses, trees, and terrain—appears to be farther away than when it is overhead (L. Kaufman &

Kaufman, 2000). According to principles of size constancy discussed in this chapter, the greater perceived distance causes the horizon moon to be perceived as larger. This explanation has been questioned, though, because the horizon moon sometimes seems larger even when the observer cannot see the intervening terrain. The next time you see what appears to be a bigger-than-normal full moon just above the horizon, turn your back to it, and then bend over and look at the moon, upside down, between your legs. Does the so-called moon illusion remain, or is it destroyed when you look at the moon so that terrain appears above it rather than below it? What do *you* think causes the moon illusion? *For additional projects, see the five Personal Learning Activities in the corresponding chapter of the study guide that accompanies this text.*

Step into Action

Courses

Sensation and Perception
Speech and Hearing
Biological Psychology
Vision
Artificial Intelligence

Movies

The Miracle Worker (the story of Helen Keller, who was both deaf and blind)
Home Before Dark (a thriller about a blind girl menaced by a killer)
Children of a Lesser God (set in a school for the deaf)
At First Sight (changes and problems that occur when a man, blind from birth, can suddenly see)
The Matrix (a futuristic film that raises the question, What is reality?)
Rashomon (focuses on a single event perceived in vastly different ways by different people)

Books

Michael Posner and Marcus Raichle, *Images of Mind* (W. H. Freeman, 1997) (brain imaging)
Richard. L. Gregory and J. Harris (Eds.), *The Artful Eye* (Oxford University Press, 1995) (visual perception)
Richard. L. Gregory and Andrew M. Colman (Eds.), *Sensation and Perception* (Longman, 1995) (the senses and psychophysics)
Roger Shepard, *Mind Sights* (W. H. Freeman, 1990) (visual illusions, ambiguous figures)
J. Richard Block and Harold Yuker, *Can You Believe Your Eyes?* (Gardner Press, 1989) (more illusions and visual oddities)

The Web

The World Wide Web is a good source of additional information about the science of psychology, provided you use it carefully and think critically about the information you find. The PsychAbilities web site that accompanies this text offers many resources relevant to this chapter. They include interactive NetLab exercises; Thinking Critically and Evaluating Research exercises; ACE chapter quizzes; recommended web links; and articles on current events, books, and movies. At http://college.hmco.com, select *Psychology* and then this textbook.

Review of Key Terms

Can you define each of the key terms in the chapter? Check your definitions against those on the pages listed in parentheses below or in the Glossary/Index at the end of the text.

absolute threshold *(p. 72)*
accessory structures *(p. 70)*
accommodation *(p. 74)*
adaptation *(p. 71)*
amplitude *(p. 73)*
analgesia *(p. 89)*
attention *(p. 106)*
auditory nerve *(p. 82)*
basilar membrane *(p. 82)*
binocular disparity *(p. 97)*
blind spot *(p. 76)*
bottom-up processing *(p. 101)*
brightness *(p. 77)*
cochlea *(p. 82)*
coding *(p. 71)*
cones *(p. 75)*
convergence *(p. 97)*
cornea *(p. 74)*
dark adaptation *(p. 75)*

depth perception *(p. 95)*
eardrum *(p. 82)*
feature detectors *(p. 76)*
figure *(p. 94)*
fovea *(p. 75)*
frequency *(p. 73)*
gate control theory *(p. 89)*
Gestalt *(p. 94)*
ground *(p. 94)*
hue *(p. 77)*
internal noise *(p. 72)*
iris *(p. 74)*
just-noticeable difference
  (JND) *(p. 72)*
kinesthesia *(p. 91)*
lens *(p. 74)*
light intensity *(p. 74)*
light wavelength *(p. 74)*
looming *(p. 97)*

loudness *(p. 81)*
olfactory bulb *(p. 85)*
opponent-process theory *(p. 79)*
optic nerve *(p. 76)*
papillae *(p. 87)*
perception *(p. 70)*
perceptual constancy *(p. 98)*
pheromones *(p. 86)*
photoreceptors *(p. 75)*
pinna *(p. 82)*
pitch *(p. 82)*
place theory *(p. 84)*
proprioceptive *(p. 91)*
pupil *(p. 74)*
receptors *(p. 70)*
response criterion *(p. 72)*
retina *(p. 74)*
rods *(p. 75)*
saturation *(p. 77)*

schemas *(p. 102)*
sensations *(p. 70)*
sense *(p. 70)*
sense of smell *(p. 85)*
sense of taste *(p. 85)*
sensitivity *(p. 72)*
signal-detection theory *(p. 72)*
somatic senses *(p. 87)*
sound *(p. 80)*
stroboscopic motion *(p. 98)*
timbre *(p. 82)*
top-down processing *(p. 101)*
transduction *(p. 70)*
trichromatic theory *(p. 78)*
vestibular sense *(p. 92)*
visible light *(p. 74)*
volley theory *(p. 84)*
wavelength *(p. 73)*
Weber's law *(p. 72)*

Multiple-Choice Self-Test

Select the best answer for each of the questions below. Then check your responses against the Answer Key at the end of the text.

1. The frequency of a sound wave determines its

   a. pitch.
   b. loudness.
   c. timbre.
   d. intensity.

2. Expecting to see a stimulus will —————— your response criterion.

   a. raise
   b. lower
   c. not influence
   d. be influenced by

3. Participants in a study are comparing the weight of two pay envelopes, one containing 10 bills and the other containing 12 bills. They also compare the weight of two bags, one of which contains 1,000 coins and the other of which contains 1,100 coins. Which difference will be easier to detect?

   a. Both differences will be equally noticeable and detectable.
   b. The difference in the bags of coins will be easier to detect.
   c. The difference in the envelopes will be easier to detect.
   d. Neither difference is likely to be detected.

4. Ally has lost her kinesthetic sense. She will most likely be unable to

   a. know that her hand is raised without looking at it.
   b. identify the flavor of her ice cream cone.
   c. feel the warmth of the sun on her face.
   d. feel pain.

5. As Bart listens to his favorite CD, his auditory system is translating sound information into neural impulses. Which of the following represents the correct sequence of structures through which that information passes?

   a. auditory nerve, basilar membrane, primary auditory cortex, thalamus
   b. eardrum, ear canal, auditory nerve, cochlea
   c. outer ear, cochlea, eardrum, basilar membrane
   d. pinna, eardrum, basilar membrane, auditory nerve

6. In an experiment, Dante raises his hand each time he hears a tone through a set of headphones. The tone gets quieter and quieter until he fails to hear it half the time. After repeating the same procedure many times, the researcher ends the experiment, because she has found Dante's

   a. absolute threshold.   b. difference threshold.
   c. internal noise.   d. response criterion.

7. Which of these light stimuli would be sensed as the most saturated color?

   a. wavelengths ranging from 400 to 700 nanometers
   b. wavelengths of very high intensity
   c. wavelengths that are all 600 nanometers
   d. wavelengths ranging from 600 to 700 nanometers

8. A projection-screen TV aims green, red, and blue lights at a screen. Because the TV can show a full range of colors by combining the green, red, and blue lights in differing amounts, it best illustrates the _____ theory of color vision.

   a. convergence   b. frequency-matching
   c. opponent-process   d. trichromatic

9. Roberta suddenly lost her sense of vision and hearing, but her sense of smell is intact. These symptoms suggest that Roberta has experienced damage to her

   a. occipital lobe.   b. temporal lobe.
   c. thalamus.   d. hypothalamus.

10. Four swimmers practicing their synchronized swimming routine are perceived as a group, because they are performing the same movements at the same speed. This is an example of

    a. closure.   b. common fate.
    c. orientation.   d. interposition.

11. Shanelle is planning to take a group of children on a field trip to a big-city museum. She wants all the children to wear identical T-shirts. That way, a stray child will still be recognized as part of the group. This example demonstrates the principle of

    a. similarity.   b. proximity.
    c. orientation.   d. textural gradients.

12. When you perceive an object as closer to you because it blocks out part of the background, you are using the depth cue called

    a. linear perspective.
    b. reduced clarity.
    c. interposition.
    d. movement gradient.

13. As soon as Jocelyn stepped on a tack, she reflexively pulled her foot away. Jocelyn primarily used _____ processing to sense and react reflexively.

    a. bottom-up   b. parallel
    c. serial   d. top-down

14. As Cliff walks out his front door, he sees a snowball coming straight at him. Although the retinal image of the snowball is increasing, he realizes that the snowball is approaching, not getting larger. This example illustrates

    a. induced motion.   b. looming.
    c. the movement gradient.   d. reduced clarity.

15. The perceptual principle that allows Cliff to perceive the snowball as remaining the same size despite a change in the size of its retinal image is

    a. looming.   b. proximity.
    c. size constancy.   d. movement gradient.

16. At football games, people in the stands sometimes hold up colored cards. The fans on the other side of the stadium see these cards as spelling a word because of which of the following principles?

    a. proximity
    b. similarity
    c. interposition
    d. both similarity and proximity

17. After tying one hundred yellow ribbons into bows for party decorations, Aparna saw blue afterimages. "I had no idea that would happen," she said. "My _____ processing must have been most active in creating the perception."

    a. bottom-up   b. simultaneous
    c. network   d. top-down

18. Although José appears to be listening as Rich talks about his new clothes, vacation plans, and exercise routine, José is thinking about the list of errands he has to run. José is

    a. covertly orienting.
    b. overtly orienting.
    c. using parallel distributed processing.
    d. using serial processing.

19. In cooking school, Natalie studied flavor. She learned that the flavor of food can be altered by

    a. changing its color.
    b. changing its temperature.
    c. asking people to hold their noses when tasting it.
    d. both b and c.

20. Rashid rated the taste of several liquids on the basis of how salty, sweet, or sour each one was. This procedure most likely tested Rashid's

    a. analgesia.
    b. gustation.
    c. kinesthesia.
    d. vestibulation.

4

Consciousness

"I felt like I was watching myself from across the room." "I was so self-

conscious." "Sorry—I spaced out for a minute there!" As these statements suggest, we are aware of ourselves as we interact with the world—even aware that sometimes we "space out." But what does it mean to be self-conscious or detached or daydreaming? In this chapter, we delve into both "normal" and altered states of consciousness. Most of the altered states—sleep, dreaming, hypnosis, meditation—differ psychologically and physiologically from normal waking consciousness. We'll examine how they differ, and we'll look at the effects of psychoactive drugs, which, in addition to altering consciousness, have complex physiological effects.

Reading this chapter will help you to answer the following questions:

- **Can unconscious thoughts affect your behavior?**
- **Does your brain go to sleep when you do?**
- **Can you be hypnotized against your will?**
- **How do drugs affect the brain?**

KEEPING AN EYE OUT Humans are not the only creatures capable of processing information while apparently unconscious. Recent research shows that while ducks sleep, one hemisphere of their brains can process visual information from an eye that remains open. Birds positioned where they are most vulnerable to predators, such as at the end of a row, may spend twice as much time in this kind of "alert" sleep than do birds in more protected positions (Rattenborg, Lima, & Amlaner, 1999).

There is an old *Sesame Street* episode in which Ernie is trying to find out whether Bert is asleep or awake. In other words, Ernie is trying to determine Bert's state of consciousness. Ernie observes that Bert's eyes are closed, and he comments that Bert *usually* closes his eyes when he is asleep. Ernie also notes that when Bert is asleep, he does not respond to pokes, so naturally, he delivers a few pokes. At first, Bert does not respond; but after being poked a few times, he awakes, very annoyed, and yells at Ernie for waking him. Ernie then informs Bert that he just wanted to let him know it was time for his nap.

Doctors face a similar situation in dealing with the more than 30 million people each year who receive general anesthesia during surgery. All these patients certainly appear to go to sleep, but there is no reliable way of knowing whether they are actually unconscious. It turns out that about 1 percent of them retain some degree of consciousness during the surgical procedure (Ranta, Jussila, & Hynynen, 1990; Sandin et al., 2000). In rare cases, patients have conscious awareness of pain and remember the trauma. Although their surgical wounds heal, these people may be psychologically scarred by the experience and may even show symptoms of posttraumatic stress disorder (Schwender et al., 1995).

The fact that people can be conscious while "asleep" under the influence of powerful anesthetic drugs obviously makes defining *consciousness* quite difficult. Indeed, after decades of discussion and research by philosophers, psychologists, and even physicists, some believe that consciousness is still not yet understood well enough to be precisely defined (F. Crick & Koch, 1998; King & Pribram, 1995). Given the ethical and legal concerns raised by the need to ensure that patients are not subjected to pain during surgery, doctors tend to define *consciousness* as awareness that is demonstrated by either explicit or implicit recall (Schwender et al., 1995). In psychology, the definition is somewhat

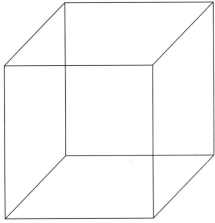

FIGURE 4.1

The Necker Cube

Each of the two squares in the Necker cube can be perceived as either the front or rear surface of the cube. Try to make the cube switch back and forth between these two orientations. Now try to hold only one orientation. You probably cannot maintain the whole cube in consciousness for longer than about 3 seconds before it "flips" from one orientation to the other.

consciousness The awareness of external stimuli and our own mental activity.

state of consciousness The characteristics of consciousness at any particular moment.

conscious level The level of consciousness at which mental activities accessible to awareness occur.

nonconscious level The level of consciousness at which reside processes that are totally inaccessible to conscious awareness, such as blood flowing through veins.

broader: **Consciousness** is generally defined as your awareness of the outside world and of your mental processes, thoughts, feelings, and perceptions (Metzinger, 2000). Let's see how this definition applies as we explore the scope of consciousness and various states of consciousness.

The Scope of Consciousness

◼ **Can unconscious thoughts affect your behavior?**

Mental activity changes constantly. The features of consciousness at any instant—what reaches your awareness, the decisions you are making, and so on—make up your **state of consciousness** at that moment. Possible states include coma, deep sleep, hypnosis, meditation, daydreams, and alert wakefulness. Consciousness can also be altered by drugs and other influences.

States of Consciousness

States of consciousness can be viewed as different points on a continuum of consciousness. Consider, for example, the varying states of consciousness that might occur aboard an airliner flying from New York to Los Angeles. In the cockpit, the pilot calmly scans instrument displays while talking to an air-traffic controller. In seat 9B, a lawyer has just finished her second cocktail while planning a courtroom strategy. Nearby, a young father gazes out a window, daydreaming, while his small daughter sleeps in his lap, dreaming dreams of her own. All these people are experiencing different states of consciousness. Some states are active, and some are passive. The daydreaming father lets his mind wander, passively noticing images, memories, and other mental events that come to mind. The lawyer actively directs her mental processes, evaluating various options and considering their likely outcomes, all the while altering her state of consciousness by sipping alcohol.

Generally, people spend most of their time in a *waking* state of consciousness. Mental processing in this state varies with changes in attention or arousal. While reading, you may temporarily ignore sounds around you. Similarly, if you are upset or bored, you may tune out important cues from the environment, making it dangerous to perform complex activities like driving a car.

Levels of Consciousness

At any moment, the events and mental processes that you are aware of exist at the **conscious level.** For example, look at the *Necker cube* in Figure 4.1. If you are like most people, you can hold the cube in one orientation for only a few seconds before the other version "pops out" at you. The version that you experience at any moment is at your conscious level of awareness for that moment.

Some events, however, cannot be experienced consciously. For example, you are not directly aware of your brain regulating your blood pressure. Such mental processing occurs at the **nonconscious level,** totally removed from conscious awareness. Some people can learn to alter a nonconscious process through *biofeedback training.* In this training, you receive information about your biological processes and try to change them. Usually, special equipment is required, but you can approximate a biofeedback session by having a friend take your pulse, at thirty-second intervals, while you sit quietly. First, establish a baseline pulse; then imagine a peaceful scene, or think about lowering your pulse rate. After each thirty-second period, ask your friend to softly say whether your pulse is higher or lower compared with the baseline. After four or five minutes of having this information "fed back" to you, you will probably be able to keep your pulse below the original baseline. Yet the pulse-regulating processes themselves remain out of consciousness.

Evidence for subconscious mental processing includes research showing that some surgery patients later comply with instructions or suggestions given while they were under anesthesia and that they do not recall hearing that information (Bennett, Giannini, & Davis, 1985). Another study found that people displayed physiological arousal to emotionally charged words even when they were not paying attention to them (Von Wright, Anderson, & Stenman, 1975).

BLOOM COUNTY by Berke Breathed

Reprinted by permission of International Creative Management, Inc. Copyright © 1996 by Berke Breathed

Some mental events are not conscious but can become so or can influence conscious experience. These mental events make up the *cognitive unconscious* (Reber, 1992), which includes the preconscious and the subconscious. Mental events that are outside awareness, but can easily be brought into awareness, exist at the **preconscious level.** What did you have for dinner last night? The information you needed to answer this question was probably not in your conscious awareness at the moment, but it was at the preconscious level. So when you read the question, you could answer it immediately. Similarly, when you play trivia games, you draw on your large storehouse of preconscious memories to come up with obscure facts.

Other mental activities can alter thoughts, feelings, and actions but are more difficult to bring into awareness (Ratner, 1994). Freud suggested that these **unconscious** activities, especially those involving unacceptable sexual and aggressive urges, are actively kept out of consciousness. Most psychologists do not accept Freud's view, but they still use the term *unconscious,* or **subconscious,** to describe mental activity that influences us in various ways but occurs outside of awareness.

Mental Processing Without Awareness

Research with surgery patients provided one demonstration of mental processing without awareness. After their operations, but while the patients were still unconscious from the anesthesia, an audiotape of fifteen word pairs was played over and over for them in the recovery room. After regaining consciousness, the patients could not say what words were on the tape, or even if a tape had been played at all. However, when given one word from each of the word pairs and asked to say the first word that came to mind, the patients were able to come up with the other member of the word pair from the tape (Cork, Kihlstrom, & Hameroff, 1992).

Even when conscious and alert, you can sometimes process and use information without being aware of it (L. M. Ward, 1997). In one study, participants watched a computer screen as an X flashed in one of four locations. The task was to indicate where the X appeared. The X's location *seemed* to vary randomly but was actually determined by a set of complex rules. Participants' responses became progressively faster and more accurate. Then, unknown to the participants, the rules were abandoned, and the X appeared in *truly* random locations. Participants' accuracy and speed deteriorated instantly. Apparently, the participants had learned the rules without being aware of them and had applied them to improve their performance. However, even when offered $100 to state the rules that had guided the location sequence, they could not do so, nor were they sure any such rules existed (Lewicki, 1992).

Visual processing without awareness may even occur in certain cases of blindness. In cases of blindness caused by damage only to the primary visual cortex, fibers from the eyes are still connected to other brain areas that process visual information. Some of these surviving pathways may permit visual processing, but without visual awareness—a condition known as *blindsight* (Gazzaniga, Fendrich, & Wessinger, 1994). Thus, even though such patients say they see nothing, if forced to guess, they can still locate visual targets, identify the direction and orientation of moving images, reach for objects, and name the color of lights.

preconscious level The level of consciousness at which reside mental events that are not currently conscious but can become conscious at will.

unconscious The term used to describe a level of mental activity said by Freud to contain sexual, aggressive, and other impulses, as well as once-conscious but unacceptable thoughts and feelings of which an individual is unaware.

subconscious Another term used to describe the mental level at which influential, but normally inaccessible, mental processes take place.

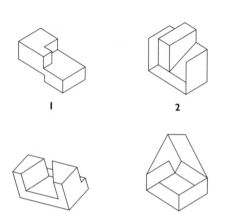

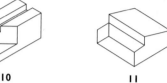

Source: D. L. Schacter et al. (1991).

Priming research also demonstrates mental processing without awareness. In a typical priming study, people tend to respond faster or more accurately to stimuli they have seen before. This is true even when they cannot consciously recall having seen those stimuli (R. L. Abrams & Greenwald, 2000; Arndt et al., 1997; Bar & Biederman, 1998; D. L. Schacter & Cooper, 1993). In one study, for example, people looked at figures like those in Figure 4.2. They had to decide which figures could actually exist in three-dimensional space and which figures could not. The participants were better at classifying pictures they had seen before, even when they could not remember having seen them (L. A. Cooper et al., 1992; D. L. Schacter et al., 1991).

Similar results occur in experiments on the *mere-exposure effect,* the tendency for people to like previously encountered stimuli more than new ones. In one such experiment, participants first viewed a series of unfamiliar block figures similar to those in Figure 4.2. Next, they were shown several pairs of figures and asked to say which member came from the series they had seen earlier. They also stated which figure in each pair they liked better. Their choice about the previously seen figure was correct about half the time, as would be expected by chance alone. However, they tended to *like best* the figures they had seen before, even when they did not remember having seen them. These responses demonstrated the mere-exposure effect, revealing a memory of their prior experience with the figures that was not reflected in their conscious awareness (Seamon et al., 1995).

Can something you perceive at a *subliminal* level—that is, below your conscious awareness—affect your thoughts, emotions, and actions? In 1957, an adman named James Vicary claimed that a New Jersey theater flashed messages such as "buy popcorn" and "drink Coke" on a movie screen, too briefly to be noticed, while customers watched the movie *Picnic.* He said that these subliminal messages caused a 15 percent rise in sales of Coca-Cola and a 58 percent increase in popcorn sales. Can such "mind control" really work? Many people seem to think so. Millions of dollars are spent each year on audiotapes and videos that promise subliminal help to people who want to lose weight, raise self-esteem, quit smoking, make more money, or achieve other goals.

What am I being asked to believe or accept?

The claim underlying the alleged value of subliminal tapes is that information can be detected, perceived, and acted upon without our being aware of it. The strong version of this claim implies that people's buying habits, political decisions, and other actions can be secretly influenced without their awareness.

Is there evidence available to support the claim?

Studies that present visual stimuli too briefly to be perceived consciously provide some evidence that subliminal messages can affect conscious judgments. In one such study, participants viewed slides showing people performing ordinary acts like washing dishes. Unknown to the participants, each slide was preceded by a subliminal exposure to a photo of "positive" stimuli (such as a child playing) or "negative" stimuli (such as a monster). Later, participants rated the people on the visible slides as more likable, polite, friendly, successful, and reputable when their images had been preceded by a positive subliminal photo (Krosnick et al., 1992). The subliminal photos not only affected participants' liking of the people they saw but also shaped beliefs about their personalities.

In another study, participants were shown written messages at subliminal speed while researchers recorded their physiological arousal. Although the slides were flashed too quickly to be consciously perceived, the participants exhibited more physiological arousal after messages such as "no one loves me," but not after nonemotional messages such as "no one lifts it" (Masling & Bornstein, 1991). Researchers have also exposed participants to subliminal presentations of slides showing snakes, spiders, flowers, and mushrooms. Even though the slides were impossible to perceive at a conscious level, participants who were afraid of snakes or spiders exhibited physiological arousal (and reported feeling fear) in response to slides of snakes and spiders (Öhman & Soares, 1994).

The results of studies like these confirm that subliminal information can have an impact on judgments and emotion, but they say little or nothing about the value of subliminal tapes for achieving self-help goals. Indeed, no laboratory evidence exists to support the effectiveness of these tapes. Their promoters offer only the reports of satisfied customers (McGarvey, 1989).

Can that evidence be interpreted another way?

Many commercial claims for subliminal persuasion—including the New Jersey theater case mentioned earlier—have turned out to be publicity stunts using phony data (Pratkanis, 1992). Other claims may reflect what statisticians call a *Type 1 error,* which occurs when researchers collect so much data that the desired result finally appears by chance. But it is misleading to publicize one positive result without mentioning all the negative results.

Further, testimonials from satisfied customers could be biased by what these people would *like* to believe about the subliminal tapes they bought. There are studies that support this interpretation. In one of those studies, half the participants were told that they would be listening to tapes containing subliminal messages for improving memory. The other half were told that the subliminal messages would promote self-esteem. However, the participants were not necessarily exposed to the subliminal messages they were expecting. Half the participants in the memory group got self-esteem messages, and half of the self-esteem group got memory messages. Regardless of which version they actually got, participants who *thought* they had heard memory enhancement messages reported improved memory; those who *thought* they had received self-esteem messages said their self-esteem had improved (Pratkanis, Eskenazi, & Greenwald, 1994). In other words, the effects of the tapes were determined by the listeners' expectations—not by the tapes' subliminal content. This result suggests that customers' reports about the value of subliminal self-help tapes may reflect placebo effects based on optimistic expectations rather than on the effects of subliminal messages.

What evidence would help to evaluate the alternatives?

The effects of subliminal messages must be assessed through controlled experiments like the ones described in Chapter 1. Those advocating the development and use of subliminal methods must provide supporting evidence from such research.

What conclusions are most reasonable?

The available evidence suggests that subliminal perception occurs but has no potential for "mind control" (Greenwald, Klinger, & Schuh, 1995). Subliminal effects are usually small and short-lived, and they affect only general measures of overall arousal. Most researchers agree that subliminal messages have no special power to create needs, goals, skills, or actions (Pratkanis, 1992). Indeed, advertisements, political speeches, and other messages that people can perceive consciously have far stronger persuasive effects.

Subliminal Messages in Rock Music

Numerous Internet web sites present claims that satanic or drug-related messages have been embedded in the recorded music of rock bands such as Marilyn Manson, Nine Inch Nails, Judas Priest, Led Zeppelin, and the Rolling Stones. These alleged messages are subliminal, the story goes, because they are recorded backward, but they are said to have influenced listeners to commit suicide or murder. For this assertion to be true, however, the content of the subliminal backward message would have to be perceived at some level of consciousness.

What was the researchers' question?

There is no compelling evidence that backward messages are actually present in most of the music cited. However, John R. Vokey and J. Don Read (1985) asked whether any backward messages that *might* exist could be perceived and understood when the music was playing forward. They also asked whether such messages have any effect on behavior.

How did the researchers answer the question?

Vokey and Read conducted a series of studies of the impact of backward-recorded messages. They first recorded readings of portions of the Twenty-third Psalm and Lewis Carroll's poem "The Jabberwocky." This poem includes many nonsense words, but it follows grammar rules (for example, " 'Twas brillig and the slithy toves . . . "). These recordings were then played backward to groups of college students. The students were asked to judge whether what they heard would have been nonsensical or meaningful if played forward.

What did the researchers find?

When the students heard the material played backward, they could not discriminate sense from nonsense. They could not tell the difference between declarative sentences and questions. They could not even identify the original material on which the recordings were based. In short, the participants could not make sense of the backward messages at a conscious level. Could they do so subconsciously? To find out, the researchers asked the participants to sort the backward statements they heard into one of five categories: nursery rhymes, Christian, satanic, pornographic, or advertising. They reasoned that if some sort of meaning could be subconsciously understood, the participants would be able to sort the statements nonrandomly. As it turned out, however, the accuracy of the participants' category judgments was no better than chance.

Can even *unperceived* backward messages unconsciously shape behavior? To answer this question, Vokey and Read presented a backward version of a message whose sentences contained homophones (words that sound alike but have two spellings and two different meanings, such as *feat* and *feet*). When heard in the normal forward direction, such messages affect people's spelling of ambiguous words that are read aloud to them at a later

Answer key for Figure 4.2: Figures 1, 4, 5, 7, 10, and 12 can exist in three-dimensional space.

time. (For example, they tend to spell out *f-e-a-t* rather than *f-e-e-t* if they previously heard the sentence "It was a great feat of strength.") This example of priming occurs even if people do not recall having heard the message. After hearing a *backward* version of the message, however, the participants in this study did not produce the expected spelling bias.

What do the results mean?

Obviously, it wasn't possible for the participants to subconsciously understand meaning in the backward messages. Backward messages are evidently not consciously or unconsciously understood, nor do they influence behavior.

What do we still need to know?

Researchers would like to understand why the incorrect idea persists that backward messages *can* influence behavior. Beliefs and suspicions do not simply disappear in the face of contrary scientific evidence (Vyse, 1997). Perhaps such evidence needs to be publicized more widely in order to lay the misconceptions to rest, but it seems likely that some people so deeply *want* to believe in the existence and power of backward messages in rock music that such beliefs will forever hold the status of folk myths in Western culture.

Altered States of Consciousness

When changes in mental processes are great enough for you or others to notice significant differences in how you function, you have entered an **altered state of consciousness** (Glicksohn, 1991). In an altered state, mental processing shows distinct changes unique to that state. Cognitive processes or perceptions of yourself or the world may change, and normal inhibitions or self-control may weaken (Martindale, 1981).

The phrase *altered states of consciousness* recognizes waking consciousness as the most common state, a baseline against which "altered" states are compared. However, this is not to say that waking consciousness is universally considered more normal, proper, or valued than other states. In fact, value judgments about different states of consciousness vary considerably across cultures (C. Ward, 1994).

Consider, for instance, *hallucinations*, which are perceptual experiences (such as hearing voices) that occur without sensory stimuli. In the United States, hallucinations are viewed as undesirable. Mental patients who hallucinate often feel stress and self-blame. They may avoid reporting their hallucinations, and they tend to receive poorer prognoses and more drastic treatments than patients who do not hallucinate (G. T. Wilson et al., 1996). Among the Moche of Peru, however, hallucinations have a culturally approved place. When someone experiences illness or misfortune, a healer conducts an elaborate ritual to find causes

altered state of consciousness A condition that exists when changes in mental processes are extensive enough to produce noticeable differences in psychological and behavioral functioning.

ALTERED STATES AND CULTURAL VALUES   Different cultures define which altered states of consciousness are approved and which are inappropriate. The top photo shows members of a Brazilian spirit possession cult in various stages of trance. The bottom photo depicts a Moche *curandero,* or "curer," in Peru who is attempting to heal an ailing patient by using fumes from a potion—and a drug derived from the San Pedro cactus—to put himself in an altered state of consciousness.

and treatments. During the ceremony, the healer ingests mescaline, a drug that causes hallucinations. These hallucinations are thought to give the healer spiritual insight into the patient's problems (de Rios, 1989). In the context of many other tribal cultures, too, purposeful hallucinations are respected, not disapproved (Grob & Dobkins-de-Rios, 1992).

In short, states of consciousness differ not only in terms of their characteristics but also in their value to members of particular cultures. In the sections that follow, we describe some of the most interesting altered states of consciousness, beginning with the most common one: sleep.

Sleeping and Dreaming

Does your brain go to sleep when you do?

According to ancient myths, sleepers lose control of their minds and flirt with death as their souls wander freely. Early researchers thought sleep was a time of mental inactivity. In fact, sleep is an active, complex state.

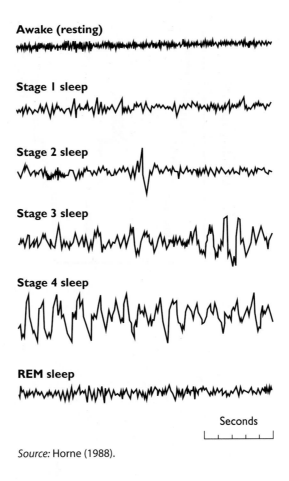

Source: Horne (1988).

FIGURE 4.3

EEG During Sleep

EEG recordings of brain wave activity disclose four relatively distinct stages of slow-wave sleep. Notice the regular patterns of brain waves that occur just before a person goes to sleep, followed by the slowing of brain waves as sleep becomes deeper (stages 1 through 4). In REM (rapid eye movement) sleep, the frequency of brain waves increases dramatically. In some ways the brain waves of REM sleep resemble those of people who are awake.

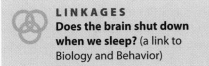

LINKAGES
Does the brain shut down when we sleep? (a link to Biology and Behavior)

slow-wave sleep Sleep stages 1 through 4, which are accompanied by slow, deep breathing; a calm, regular heartbeat; and reduced blood pressure.

rapid eye movement (REM) sleep The stage of sleep during which the EEG resembles that of someone who is awake, but muscle tone decreases dramatically.

Stages of Sleep

Sleep researchers use an *electroencephalograph*, or *EEG,* to record the brain's electrical activity during sleep. EEG recordings, often called *brain waves,* vary in height (amplitude) and speed (frequency) as behavior or mental processes change. The brain waves of an awake, alert person have high frequency and low amplitude. They appear as small, closely spaced, irregular EEG spikes. A relaxed person with closed eyes shows slower, rhythmic brain waves at speeds of eight to twelve cycles per second (cps). During a normal night's sleep, brain waves show distinctive and systematic changes in amplitude and frequency as you pass through various stages of sleep (Guevara et al., 1995).

Slow-Wave Sleep   Imagine that you are participating in a sleep study. You are hooked up to an EEG and various monitors, and filmed as you sleep through the night. If you were to watch that film, here's what you'd see: At first, you are relaxed, with eyes closed, but awake. At this point, your muscle tone and eye movements are normal, and your EEG shows the slow brain waves associated with relaxation. You then drift into what is called **slow-wave sleep,** which is named for the fact that your EEG shows even slower brain waves. Your breathing deepens, your heartbeat slows, and your blood pressure drops. Over the next half hour, you descend ever deeper into stages of sleep that are characterized by even slower brain waves with even higher amplitude (see Figure 4.3). When you reach stage 4, the deepest stage of slow-wave sleep, it is quite difficult to be awakened. If you *were* roused from this stage of deep sleep, you would be groggy and confused.

REM Sleep   After thirty to forty-five minutes in stage 4, you quickly return to stage 2 and then enter a special stage in which your eyes move rapidly under your closed eyelids. This is called **rapid eye movement (REM) sleep,** or *paradoxical sleep.* It is called *paradoxical* because its characteristics contain a paradox, or contradiction. In REM sleep, your EEG resembles that of an awake, alert person, and your physiological arousal—heart rate,

A Night's Sleep

During a typical night a sleeper goes through this sequence of EEG stages. Notice that sleep is deepest during the first part of the night and more shallow later on, when REM sleep becomes more prominent.

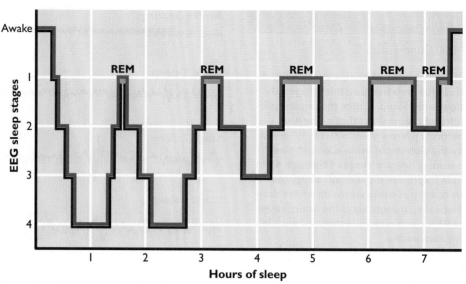

Source: Cartwright (1978).

breathing, and blood pressure—is also similar to when you are awake. However, your muscles are nearly paralyzed. Sudden, twitchy spasms appear, especially in your face and hands, but your brain actively suppresses other movements (Blumberg & Lucas, 1994). In other words, there are two distinctly different types of sleep, REM sleep and slow-wave sleep (which is sometimes called *non-REM,* or *NREM, sleep*).

A Night's Sleep   Most people pass through the cycle of sleep stages four to six times each night. Each cycle lasts about ninety minutes, but with a somewhat changing pattern of stages and stage duration. Early in the night, most of the time is spent in the deeper stages of slow-wave sleep, with only a few minutes in REM (see Figure 4.4). As sleep continues, though, it is dominated by stage 2 and REM, from which sleepers finally awaken.

Sleep patterns change with age. The average infant sleeps about sixteen hours a day, and the average seventy-year-old sleeps only about six hours (Roffwarg, Muzio, & Dement, 1966). The composition of sleep changes, too. REM accounts for half of total sleep at birth but less than 25 percent in young adults. Sometime in life, most people experience sleep-related problems. These can range from occasional nights of tossing and turning to more serious and long-term sleep disorders.

Sleep Disorders

The most common sleep disorder is **insomnia,** in which one feels daytime fatigue due to trouble falling asleep or staying asleep. If you have difficulty getting to sleep or staying asleep that persists for longer than one month at a time, you may be suffering from insomnia. Besides being tiring, insomnia is tied to mental distress and impairment of functioning. Insomnia is especially associated with depressive and anxiety disorders (Ball, Buchwald, & Waddell, 1995). Overall, insomniacs are three times more likely to show a mental disorder than those with no sleep complaints (Ford & Kamerow, 1989). It is unclear from such correlations, however, whether insomnia causes mental disorders, mental disorders cause insomnia, or some other factor causes both.

Sleeping pills can relieve insomnia. However, they interact dangerously with alcohol, disturb REM sleep, and may eventually lead to *increased* sleeplessness (Ashton, 1995). In the long run, learning-based treatments may be more helpful (Lichstein & Riedel, 1994). Stress management techniques such as relaxation training have been shown to help insomniacs reduce tension and other stress reactions, thus allowing sleep (D. A. Bernstein, Borkovec, & Hazlett-Stevens, 2000).

Narcolepsy is a disturbing daytime sleep disorder that is typically first seen in people who are from fifteen to twenty-five years old (Choo & Guilleminault, 1998). People with

insomnia   A sleep disorder in which a person feels tired during the day because of trouble falling asleep or staying asleep at night.

narcolepsy   A daytime sleep disorder in which a person switches abruptly and without warning from an active waking state into several minutes of REM sleep.

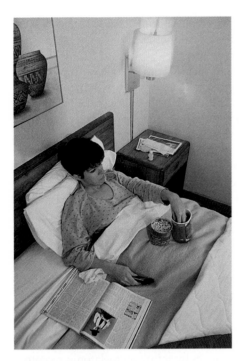

Applying Psychology

SLEEP RESTRICTION THERAPY Insomnia can often be reduced through *sleep restriction therapy,* in which the person goes to bed only when sleepy and gets out of bed if sleep does not come (Spielman, Saskin, & Thorpy, 1987). The goal for insomniacs is to learn to associate their bed with sleeping, not reading, eating, watching television, or worrying.

---

sleep apnea   A sleep disorder in which people briefly but repeatedly stop breathing during the night.

sudden infant death syndrome (SIDS) A disorder in which a sleeping baby stops breathing but does not awaken and suffocates.

sleepwalking   A phenomenon that starts primarily in non-REM sleep, especially in stage 4, and involves walking while one is asleep.

nightmares   Frightening dreams that take place during REM sleep.

night terrors   Horrific dream images during stage 4 sleep, followed by a rapid awakening and a state of intense fear.

REM behavior disorder   A sleep disorder in which a person fails to show the decreased muscle tone normally seen in rapid eye movement sleep, thus allowing the person to act out dreams, sometimes with dangerous results.

circadian rhythm   A cycle, such as waking and sleeping, that repeats about once a day.

narcolepsy abruptly enter REM sleep directly from the waking state, usually as they are laughing or experiencing some other emotional state. Because of the loss of muscle tone in REM, the narcoleptic collapses and remains briefly immobile even after awakening. The cause of narcolepsy may involve genetic factors and lack of a hormone called hypocretin (Peyron et al., 2000; Sinton & McCarley, 2000). Napping, stimulants, and other drugs are often helpful treatments.

People who suffer from **sleep apnea** briefly stop breathing hundreds of times each night, waking each time long enough to resume breathing. In the morning, victims do not recall the awakenings. However, they feel tired and tend to show impaired attention and learning ability (Naëgelé et al., 1995). Apnea has many causes, including obesity and compression of the windpipe. It has also been related to snoring. Effective treatments include weight loss and use of a mask that provides a steady stream of air (R. J. Davies & Stradling, 2000).

In cases of **sudden infant death syndrome (SIDS),** sleeping infants stop breathing and die. In the United States, SIDS strikes about two of every thousand infants, usually when they are two to four months old (J. A. Hirschfeld, 1995). Some SIDS cases may stem from problems with brain systems regulating breathing or from exposure to cigarette smoke (Harper et al., 1988; Klonoff-Cohen & Edelstein, 1995). Because SIDS is less common in cultures where infants and parents sleep in the same bed, it may also be that sleeping position is involved in sudden infant death (McKenna et al., 1993). It has been estimated that about half of apparent SIDS cases might actually be accidental suffocations caused when infants sleep face down on a soft surface (Guntheroth & Spiers, 1992). Since doctors began advising parents to be sure their babies sleep face-up, the number of infants dying from SIDS in the United States has dropped by 40 percent (E. Gibson et al., 2000).

Sleepwalking occurs in non-REM sleep, usually in childhood (Masand, Popli, & Welburg, 1995). By morning, most sleepwalkers have forgotten their travels. Despite myths to the contrary, waking a sleepwalker is not harmful. Drugs help, but most children simply outgrow the problem. One adult sleepwalker was cured when his wife blew a whistle whenever he began a nighttime stroll (R. G. Meyer, 1975).

Nightmares are frightening REM dreams (Zadra & Donderi, 2000). **Night terrors** are horrific dream images during stage 4 sleep. Sleepers often awaken from a night terror with a bloodcurdling scream and remain intensely afraid for up to thirty minutes. Yet they may not recall the episode in the morning. Night terrors are especially common in boys, but adults can suffer milder versions. The condition is sometimes treatable with drugs (Lillywhite, Wilson, & Nutt, 1994).

People with **REM behavior disorder** do not experience the near-paralysis that normally accompanies rapid eye movement sleep. They move as if acting out their dreams (T. Watanabe & Sugita, 1998). If the dreams are violent, the disorder can be dangerous to the dreamer or those nearby. Indeed, many sufferers attack sleeping partners. One man grabbed his wife's throat because, he claimed, he was dreaming about breaking a deer's neck. The disorder sometimes occurs along with daytime narcolepsy (Schenck & Mahowald, 1992). Fortunately, drug treatments are usually effective.

Why Do People Sleep?

People clearly need a certain amount of uninterrupted sleep to function normally. In fact, most living creatures sleep. In trying to understand why people sleep, psychologists have studied both the functions of sleep and the ways in which brain mechanisms shape its characteristics.

Sleep as a Circadian Rhythm   Humans and almost all animals display cycles of behavior and physiology that repeat about every 24 hours. This pattern is called a **circadian rhythm.** (*Circadian* is pronounced "sir-KAY-dee-en." It comes from the Latin *circa dies,* meaning "about a day.") Longer and shorter rhythms also occur, but they are less common. These rhythms are linked to signals such as the light of day and the dark of night.

Some rhythms continue without such time cues, though. Volunteers living for months without external light and dark cues maintain daily rhythms in sleeping and waking,

**SUDDEN INFANT DEATH SYNDROME
(SIDS)** In SIDS cases, seemingly healthy
infants stop breathing while asleep in
their cribs. All the causes of SIDS are not
known, but health authorities now suggest that infants should sleep on their
backs, as this baby demonstrates.

eating, urination, hormone release, and other physiological functions. Under such conditions, these cycles repeat about every 24 hours (Czeisler et al., 1999). The sleep-wake
cycle is just one example of the rhythmic nature of life.

Disruption of the sleep-wake cycle can create problems. For example, air travel across
several time zones often causes **jet lag,** a pattern of fatigue, irritability, inattention, and
sleeping problems. The traveler's body feels ready to sleep at the wrong time for the new
location. Similar problems affect workers who repeatedly change between day and night
shifts. It tends to be easier to stay awake longer than usual than to go to sleep earlier than
usual. If you've ever had a hard time adjusting to daylight savings time (when clocks are
set forward an hour), you've seen that sleep-wake rhythms readjust more easily when
sleep is shifted to a later rather than an earlier time. That's why changing time zones
causes more intense symptoms of jet lag after eastward travel (when time is lost) than
after westward travel (when time is gained) (A. N. Nicholson et al., 1986).

Because circadian rhythms continue without external cues, an internal "biological
clock" must keep track of time. This clock is in the *suprachiasmatic nuclei (SCN)* of the
hypothalamus, as shown in Figure 4.5. When animals with SCN damage receive transplanted SCN cells, their circadian rhythms become like those of the donor animal
(Menaker & Vogelbaum, 1993). Signals from the SCN reach hindbrain areas that initiate
sleep or wakefulness (Moore, 1997). SCN neurons also regulate the release of the hormone *melatonin.* Melatonin, in turn, appears to be important in maintaining circadian
rhythms. Taken about an hour before you want to fall asleep, melatonin reduces disori-
entation from jet lag or other sleep-wake cycle changes by acting on melatonin receptors
in the SCN (C. Liu et al., 1997; Sack et al., 1997).

You can also reduce the disruptive effects of jet lag or changes in work shifts through
exposure to bright light during waking hours. It was once thought that this procedure
speeds the resetting of the body's circadian rhythms only through the eyes' connections
to the SCN. However, researchers have recently discovered that light shining on the back
of the knees can have the same effect! A possible explanation for this phenomenon is that
light passing through the thin skin there causes changes in the blood that convey signals
to the brain (Campbell & Murphy, 1998).

The Functions of Sleep   Examining the effects of sleep deprivation may help explain why
people sleep at all. People who go without sleep for as long as a week usually do not suffer serious long-term effects. However, extended sleeplessness leads to fatigue, irritability, and inattention (Drummond et al., 2000; A. P. Smith & Maben, 1993). Short-term
sleep deprivation can also be dangerous. Most fatal auto accidents in the United States
occur during the "fatigue hazard" hours of midnight to 6 A.M. (Coleman, 1992), leading

DISRUPTED CIRCADIAN RHYTHMS
The 2000 Olympic games brought contestants from around the world to compete in Sydney, Australia. Coming from
different countries and time zones, some
competitors' circadian rhythms were
disrupted.

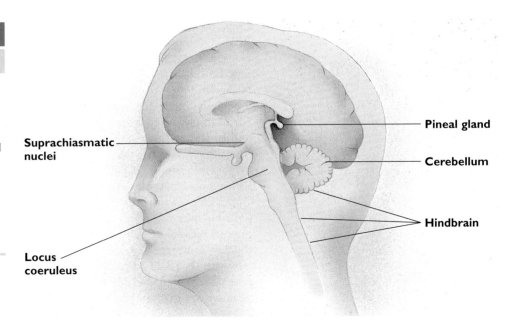

FIGURE 4.5

Sleep, Dreaming, and the Brain

This diagram shows the location of some of the brain structures thought to be involved in sleep and dreaming, as well as in other altered states discussed later in the chapter. Scientists have discovered that cells in a region near the suprachiasmatic nuclei may act as a "master switch" for sleep by sending signals that shut down arousal systems in the hindbrain (Gallopin et al., 2000; Sherin et al., 1996).

some researchers to consider "sleepy driving" as dangerous as drunk driving. Fatigue may be the primary cause of up to 25 percent of all auto accidents (Summala & Mikkola, 1994). During extended wakefulness, the brain's level of a sleep-inducing neurotransmitter (adenosine) increases to the point where people find it very difficult to stay awake (Porkka-Heiskanen et al., 1997).

Some researchers believe that non-REM sleep helps to restore the body and the brain's energy stores for the next day's activity (Porkka-Heiskanen et al., 1997). Indeed, most people get their non-REM sleep first (Hartman, Baekeland, & Zwilling, 1972). After total sleep deprivation, people do not make up lost sleep hour for hour. Instead, they sleep about 50 percent more than usual, then wake up feeling rested. But if people are deprived *only* of REM sleep, they later compensate more directly. In one study, participants were awakened whenever their EEG showed REM. When allowed to sleep uninterrupted the next night, they "rebounded," nearly doubling the percentage of time spent in REM (Dement, 1960). This apparent need for REM sleep suggests that REM has special functions.

What these special functions might be is still unclear, but there are several interesting possibilities. First, REM may improve the functioning of neurons that use norepinephrine (Siegel & Rogawski, 1988). Norepinephrine is a neurotransmitter released by cells in the *locus coeruleus* (pronounced "lo-kus seh-ROO-lee-us"; see Figure 4.5.) During waking hours, it affects alertness and mood. But the brain's neurons do not fully respond to norepinephrine if it is released continuously for too long. The locus coeruleus is almost completely inactive during REM sleep, leading researchers to suggest that REM helps restore sensitivity to norepinephrine and thus its ability to keep us alert (Steriade & McCarley, 1990). Animals deprived of REM show unusually high norepinephrine levels and decreased daytime alertness (J. W. Brock et al., 1994).

REM sleep may also be a time for developing, checking, and expanding the brain's nerve connections (Roffwarg, Muzio, & Dement, 1966). This notion would explain why, as mentioned earlier, infants—whose brains are still developing—spend so much time in REM. In contrast, guinea pigs and other animals born with well-developed brains spend very little sleep time in REM early in their lives (Cartwright, 1978). REM sleep may also help to solidify and absorb the day's experiences. In one study, people who were REM deprived showed poorer retention of a skill learned the day before when compared with people who were either deprived of non-REM sleep or allowed to sleep normally (Karni et al., 1994).

Dreams and Dreaming

The brain is active in all sleep stages, and some of this activity is experienced as the sensations and perceptions known as **dreams.** Some dreaming occurs during non-REM

jet lag   Fatigue, irritability, inattention, and sleeping problems caused by air travel across several time zones.

dreams   Story-like sequences of images, sensations, and perceptions that last from several seconds to many minutes and occur mainly during REM sleep.

sleep, but most dreams—and the most bizarre and vivid dreams—occur during REM (Casagrande et al., 1996; Dement & Kleitman, 1957; Stickgold, Rittenhouse, & Hobson, 1994). Dreams may be as short as a few seconds or last for many minutes. They may be organized or chaotic, realistic or fantastic, boring or exciting (Hobson & Stickgold, 1994).

Although they may seem senseless, dreams often contain a certain amount of logic. For example, when people read dream reports whose segments had been randomly reordered, they could correctly say which had been rearranged and which were intact. And although dreams often involve one person transforming into another or one object turning into another object, it is rare that objects become people or vice versa (Stickgold, Rittenhouse, & Hobson, 1994).

Daytime activities may have some influence on dream content, though their impact is probably minor (Foulkes, 1985). In one study, people wore red-tinted goggles for a few minutes just before going to sleep. Although they didn't know the purpose of the study, the next morning they reported more red images in their dreams than people who had not worn the goggles (Roffwarg, Hermann, & Bowe-Anders, 1978). It is also sometimes possible to intentionally direct dream content. This is called **lucid dreaming,** because the sleeper is aware of dreaming while a dream is occurring (LaBerge, 1993).

Research leaves little doubt that everyone dreams during every night of normal sleep. Even blind people dream, although their perceptual experiences are usually not visual. Whether you remember a dream depends on how you sleep and wake up. Recall is better if you awaken abruptly and lie quietly while writing or tape-recording your recollections.

Why do we dream? Theories abound. Some see dreaming as a fundamental process through which all species with complex brains analyze and consolidate information (Porte & Hobson, 1996). This view is supported by the fact that dreaming appears to occur in most mammals, as indicated by the appearance of REM sleep. For example, after researchers disabled the neurons that cause REM sleep paralysis, sleeping cats ran around and attacked, or seemed alarmed by, unseen objects, presumably the images from dreams (Winson, 1990).

According to Sigmund Freud (1900), dreams are a disguised form of *wish fulfillment.* They are a way to satisfy unconscious urges or resolve unconscious conflicts that are too upsetting to deal with consciously. Thus, sexual desires might appear in a dream as the rhythmic motions of a horseback ride. Conflicting feelings about a parent might appear as a dream about a fight. Seeing his patients' dreams as a "royal road to a knowledge of the unconscious," Freud interpreted their meaning as part of his psychoanalytic treatment of psychological disorders (see Chapter 13).

In contrast, the *activation-synthesis* theory sees dreams as the meaningless, random byproducts of REM sleep (Hobson, 1997). According to this theory, hindbrain arousal during REM creates random messages that *activate* the brain, especially the cerebral cortex. Dreams result as the cortex connects, or *synthesizes,* these random messages as best as it can, using stored memories and current feelings to translate random brain activity into something more coherent. From this perspective, dreams represent the brain's attempt to make sense of meaningless stimulation during sleep, much as we might try to find meaningful shapes in cloud formations (D. M. Bernstein & Roberts, 1995; Rittenhouse, Stickgold, & Hobson, 1994).

Even if dreams arise from random brain activity, their content may still have psychological significance. For example, the mental style or current concerns of the dreamer can affect the ways in which dreams are organized and recalled (Domhoff, 1996; Stevens, 1996). There are also similarities between the emotions and thoughts experienced in dreams and in recent waking life (Domhoff, 1999). However, research using brain imaging techniques shows that while we are asleep, brain areas involved in emotion tend to be overactivated, whereas those areas controlling logical thought tend to be suppressed (Braun, Balkin, & Wesensten, 1998; Hobson et al., 1998). This is probably why dreams rarely provide realistic, logical solutions to our problems (Blagrove, 1996).

lucid dreaming   Having the awareness that a dream is a dream while it is occurring.

INDUCING HYPNOSIS In the late 1700s, Austrian physician Franz Anton Mesmer used a forerunner of hypnosis to treat physical disorders. His procedure, known as *mesmerism,* included elaborate trance-induction rituals, but we now know that hypnosis can be induced far more easily, often simply by staring at an object, as this woman did.

Hypnosis

Can you be hypnotized against your will?

In the late 1700s, an Austrian physician, Franz Anton Mesmer, became famous for his ability to treat various physical disorders using *mesmerism.* His procedure began with patients touching afflicted body parts to magnetized metal rods extending from a tub of water. Upon then being touched by Mesmer, the patients would fall into a curative "crisis" or trance, sometimes accompanied by convulsions. Mesmer's technique was an early form of hypnosis. We now know that hypnosis can be induced without such elaborate rituals, often simply by asking a person to stare at an object.

The word *hypnosis* comes from the Greek word *hypnos,* meaning "sleep." However, hypnotized people are not sleeping. Describing their hypnotic experiences, these people say that although their bodies were deeply relaxed, their minds were active and alert. **Hypnosis** has been defined as an altered state of consciousness brought on by special techniques and producing responsiveness to suggestions for changes in experience and behavior (Kirsch, 1994a). Most hypnotized people do not feel forced to follow the hypnotist's instructions. They simply see no reason to refuse (Hilgard, 1965).

Experiencing Hypnosis

Usually, hypnosis begins with suggestions that the person feels relaxed and sleepy. The hypnotist then gradually focuses the person's attention on a restricted, often monotonous set of stimuli, such as a swinging pendant. The hypnotist suggests that the individual ignore everything else and imagine certain feelings.

Not everyone can be hypnotized. Special tests measure **hypnotic susceptibility,** the degree to which people respond to hypnotic suggestions (Gfeller, 1994). These tests show that about 10 percent of adults are difficult or impossible to hypnotize (Hilgard, 1982). People who can easily be hypnotized typically differ from others in having a better ability to focus attention and ignore distraction (H. W. Crawford, Brown, & Moon, 1993). They have more active imaginations (Spanos, Burnley, & Cross, 1993), a tendency to fantasize (Lynn & Rhue, 1986), a capacity for processing information quickly and easily (Dixon, Brunet, & Lawrence, 1990), and more positive attitudes toward hypnosis (Gfeller, 1994). Your *willingness* to be hypnotized is the most important factor. You cannot be hypnotized against your will.

The results of hypnosis can be fascinating. People told that their eyes are locked shut may struggle unsuccessfully to open them. They may appear deaf or blind or insensitive to pain. They may forget their own names. Some appear to remember forgotten things. Others show *age regression,* apparently recalling or reenacting their childhood (see Figure 4.6). Hypnotic effects can last for hours or days through *posthypnotic suggestions,* which are instructions about how to behave after hypnosis has ended (such as smiling whenever someone says "England"). Some individuals show *posthypnotic amnesia,* an inability to recall what happened while they were hypnotized, even after being told what happened.

Ernest Hilgard (1965, 1992) described the main changes that people display during hypnosis. First, hypnotized people *tend not to begin actions on their own,* waiting instead for the hypnotist's instructions. One participant said, "I was trying to decide if my legs were crossed, but I couldn't tell, and didn't quite have the initiative to move to find out" (Hilgard, 1965). Second, hypnotized people tend to ignore all but the hypnotist's voice and whatever it points out: Their *attention is redistributed.* Third, hypnosis enhances the ability to *fantasize.* Participants more vividly imagine a scene or relive a memory. Fourth, hypnotized people *readily take on roles.* They more easily act like a person of a different age or a member of the opposite sex than nonhypnotized people do. Fifth, hypnotized individuals show *reduced reality testing.* They tend not to question whether statements are true, and they are more willing to accept apparent distortions of reality. Thus, a hypnotized person might shiver in a warm room if a hypnotist says it is snowing.

hypnosis An altered state of consciousness brought on by special techniques, characterized by varying degrees of responsiveness to suggestions for changes in experience and behavior.

hypnotic susceptibility The degree to which a person responds to hypnotic suggestion.

Source: Hilgard (1965).

FIGURE 4.6

Hypnotic Age Regression

Here are the signatures of two adults before hypnotically induced age regression (top) and while age regressed (bottom). The lower signatures look less mature, but was the change due to hypnosis? To find out, ask a friend to write his or her name on a blank sheet of paper, first as usual, and then as if he or she were five years old. If the two signatures look significantly different, what does this say about the cause of certain age-regression effects?

Explaining Hypnosis

Hypnotized people look and act different from nonhypnotized people (Hilgard, 1965). Do these differences indicate an altered state of consciousness?

Advocates of **state theory** say that they do. They point to the dramatic effects that hypnosis can produce, including insensitivity to pain and the disappearance of warts (Noll, 1994). They also note that there are subtle differences in the way hypnotized and nonhypnotized people carry out suggestions. In one study, hypnotized people and those who had been asked to simulate hypnosis were told to run their hands through their hair whenever they heard the word *experiment* (Orne, Sheehan, & Evans, 1968). Simulators did so only when the hypnotist said the cue word. Hypnotized participants complied no matter who said it. Another study found that hypnotized people complied more often than simulators with a posthypnotic suggestion to mail postcards to the experimenter (Barnier & McConkey, 1998).

In contrast to traditional beliefs, **role theory** maintains that hypnosis is not a special state of consciousness. Rather, hypnotized people are said to be merely complying with social demands and acting in accordance with a special social role (Kirsch, 1994b). In other words, hypnosis provides a socially acceptable reason to follow someone's suggestions.

Support for role theory comes from several sources. First, nonhypnotized people sometimes display behaviors usually associated with hypnosis. For example, on television game shows contestants do lots of odd or silly things, and they're not under hypnosis. Second, laboratory studies show that motivated but nonhypnotized volunteers can duplicate many aspects of hypnotic behavior, from arm rigidity to age regression (Dasgupta et al., 1995; Orne & Evans, 1965).

Hilgard (1979, 1992) has proposed a **dissociation theory** to blend role and state theories. He suggests that hypnosis is not one specific state but a general condition that temporarily reorganizes or breaks down our usually centralized control of thoughts and actions. Hypnosis activates a process called *dissociation,* meaning a split in consciousness (Hilgard, 1979). Dissociation allows body movements normally under voluntary control to occur on their own, and normally involuntary processes (such as overt reactions to pain) to be controlled voluntarily.

Hilgard argues that this relaxation of central control is possible because of a *social agreement* between the hypnotized person and the hypnotist to share control. In other words, people usually decide for themselves how to act or what to attend to, perceive, or remember. During hypnosis, the hypnotist is given permission to control some of these experiences and actions. Compliance with a social role may tell part of the story, Hilgard says, but hypnosis also leads to significant changes in mental processes.

FIGURE 4.7

Reports of Pain in Hypnosis

This graph compares the average reports of pain when participants' hands were immersed in ice water. The red line shows the reports by nonhypnotized participants. The blue line shows the reports by hypnotized participants who were told they would feel no pain. The purple line shows responses made by hypnotized participants who were told they would feel no pain but were asked to press a key if "any part of them" felt pain. The key pressing by this "hidden observer" suggests that under hypnosis, the experience of pain was dissociated from conscious awareness.

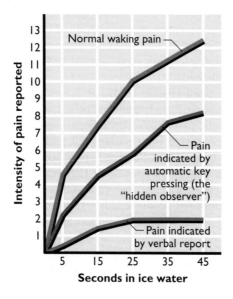

SURGERY UNDER HYPNOSIS
Bernadine Coady, of Wimblington, England, has a condition that makes it dangerous for her to have general anesthesia. So in April 1999, when a hypnotherapist failed to show up to help her through a foot operation, she used self-hypnosis as her only anesthetic. The surgery involved cutting through skin, muscle, and bone, and it would have been extremely painful without anesthesia. She said, though, that she imagined the pain as "waves lashing against a sea wall . . . [and] going away, like the tide." Coady said she had no discomfort and that "if I ever need another operation, I won't be using anesthetics."

LINKAGES
Does meditation relieve stress? (a link to Health, Stress, and Coping)

state theory A theory proposing that hypnosis creates an altered state of consciousness.

role theory A theory proposing that hypnotized people act in accordance with a social role that demands compliance.

dissociation theory A theory proposing that hypnosis is a socially agreed-upon opportunity to display one's ability to let mental functions become dissociated.

Support for dissociation theory comes from a study in which hypnotized participants immersed one hand in ice water after being told that they would feel no pain (Hilgard, Morgan, & MacDonald, 1975). They were asked to press a key with the other hand, to indicate if "any part of them" felt pain. The participants told the researchers that they felt almost no pain. But their key pressing told a different story, as Figure 4.7 shows. Hilgard concluded that a "hidden observer" was reporting on pain that was reaching the person but that had been separated, or dissociated, from conscious awareness (Hilgard, 1977).

Much remains to be learned about the nature of hypnosis as contemporary research continues to test the various explanatory theories (J. P. Green & Lynn, 1995). However, traditional distinctions between state and role theories have become less important as researchers focus on larger questions, such as why people are susceptible to hypnosis and what roles social and cognitive factors may play in it.

Applications of Hypnosis

Whatever hypnosis is, it has proven useful, especially in relation to pain (Clay, 1996). Hypnosis seems to be the only anesthetic some people need to block the pain of dental work, childbirth, burns, and surgery (Van Sickel, 1992). For others, hypnosis relieves chronic pain from arthritis, burns, nerve damage, migraine headaches, and cancer (Nolan et al., 1995; Patterson, Goldberg, & Ehde, 1996). Hypnotic suggestion can reduce nausea and vomiting due to chemotherapy (Redd, 1984). It can also help reduce surgical bleeding (Gerschman, Reade, & Burrows, 1980).

Other applications of hypnosis are more controversial, especially the use of hypnosis to aid memory. For example, hypnotic "age regression" is sometimes used in an attempt to help people recover lost memories. However, "age-regressed" memories may actually be *less* accurate than those of nonhypnotized individuals (Lynn et al., 1997). Similarly, it is doubtful that hypnosis can help witnesses to recall a crime (Lynn, Myers, & Malinoski, in press). Their expectations about, and confidence in, hypnosis may cause them to unintentionally distort information or reconstruct memories for the events in question (Garry & Loftus, 1994; Spanos, 1996; Weekes et al., 1992).

LINKAGES

Meditation, Health, and Stress

Meditation provides a set of techniques intended to create an altered state of consciousness characterized by inner peace and tranquillity (D. H. Shapiro & Walsh, 1984). Some people claim that meditation increases their awareness and understanding of themselves and their environment. Others claim that it reduces anxiety, improves health, and aids performance in everything from work to tennis (Bodian, 1999; Mahesh Yogi, 1994).

Techniques to achieve a meditative state differ, depending on belief and philosophy (for example, Eastern meditation, Sufism, yoga, or prayer). However, in the most common meditation methods, attention is focused on just one thing until the meditator stops thinking about anything else and experiences nothing but "pure awareness" (Benson, 1975). In this way, the individual becomes more fully aware of the present moment rather than being caught up in the past or the future.

To organize their attention, meditators may focus on the sound or tempo of their breathing, or slowly repeat a mantra, which is a soothing word or phrase. During a typical meditation session, breathing, heart rate, muscle tension, blood pressure, and oxygen consumption decrease (Wallace & Benson, 1972). Most forms of meditation induce EEG activity similar to that seen in a relaxed, eyes-closed, waking state (see Figure 4.3).

Meditators often report significant reductions in stress-related problems such as general anxiety, high blood pressure, and insomnia (Beauchamp-Turner & Levinson, 1992). More generally, meditators' scores on personality tests indicate increases in overall mental health, self-esteem, and social openness (Janowiak & Hackman, 1994; Sakairi, 1992). Exactly how meditation produces its effects is unclear. Many of its effects can also be achieved by biofeedback, hypnosis, and just relaxing (Beyerstein, 1999; Holmes, 1984).

Psychoactive Drugs

How do drugs affect the brain?

The altered states we have discussed so far serve a biological need (sleep) or rely on the chemistry of the brain and body (hypnosis and meditation). Other altered states can be brought on only by outside agents: drugs. Every day, most people in the world use drugs that alter brain activity and consciousness (Levinthal, 1996). For example, 80 to 90 percent of people in North America use caffeine, the stimulant found in coffee, tea, chocolate, and cola. A drug is a chemical that is not required for normal physiological functioning, yet has an effect on the body. You may say that you "need" a cup of coffee in the morning, but you will wake up without it; accordingly, the caffeine in coffee is defined as a drug. Drugs that affect the brain, changing consciousness and other psychological processes, are called **psychoactive drugs.** The study of psychoactive drugs is called **psychopharmacology.**

| FIGURE 4.8 | Agonists and Antagonists |

In Part A, a molecule of neurotransmitter interacts with a receptor on a neuron's dendrites by fitting into and stimulating it. Part B shows a drug molecule acting as an *agonist,* affecting the receptor in the same way a neurotransmitter would. Part C depicts an *antagonist* drug molecule blocking a natural neurotransmitter from reaching and acting upon the receptor.

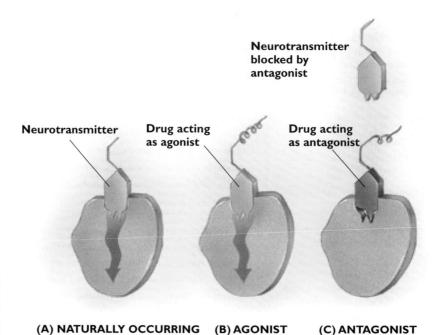

(A) NATURALLY OCCURRING NEUROTRANSMITTER   **(B) AGONIST**   **(C) ANTAGONIST**

psychoactive drugs   Chemical substances that act on the brain to create psychological effects.

psychopharmacology   The study of psychoactive drugs and their effects.

The definition of inappropriate drug use can vary across cultures and over time (S. Weiss & Moore, 1990). For example, in the United States cocaine was once a respectable, commercially available drug; today, it is illegal.

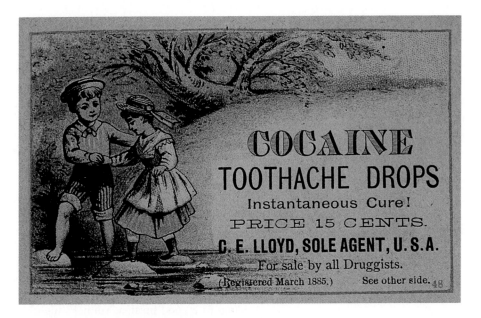

Psychopharmacology

Most psychoactive drugs affect the brain by altering the interactions between neurotransmitters and their receptors, as described in Chapter 2. To create their effects, these drugs must cross the **blood-brain barrier,** a feature of blood vessels in the brain that prevents some substances from entering brain tissue. Once past this barrier, a psychoactive drug's effects depend on several factors: With which neurotransmitter systems does the drug interact? How does the drug affect those neurotransmitters or their receptors? What physiological functions are performed by the brain systems that use those neurotransmitters?

Drugs can affect neurotransmitters or their receptors through several mechanisms. Neurotransmitters fit into their own receptors, as Figure 4.8 shows. Some drugs, such as morphine, are similar enough to a particular neurotransmitter to fool its receptors. These drugs, called **agonists,** bind to receptors and mimic the effects of the normal neurotransmitter. Other drugs, called **antagonists,** are similar enough to a neurotransmitter to occupy its receptors but cannot mimic its effects. When they bind to receptors they prevent the normal neurotransmitter from binding. Still other drugs work by increasing or decreasing the release of a specific neurotransmitter. Finally, some drugs work by speeding or slowing the *removal* of a neurotransmitter from synapses.

Predicting a drug's behavioral effects is complicated. Some drugs interact with many neurotransmitter systems. Also, the nervous system may compensate for a given drug's effects. For instance, repeated exposure to a drug that blocks receptors for a certain neurotransmitter often leads to an increase in the number of receptors available to accept that neurotransmitter.

The Varying Effects of Drugs

Unfortunately, chemical properties that give drugs their medically desirable main effects, such as pain relief, often create undesirable side effects as well.

Substance Abuse   One side effect may be the potential for abuse. **Substance abuse** is a pattern of use that causes serious social, legal, or interpersonal problems for the user (American Psychiatric Association, 1994). Of course, as a culture changes, the drugs that cause a person social and legal problems may also change, as Figure 4.9 illustrates.

Substance abuse can lead to psychological or physical dependence. People displaying **psychological dependence** on a drug will continue to use it despite its adverse effects. They need the drug for a sense of well-being and become preoccupied with getting the drug if it is no longer available. However, they can still function without the drug. Psychological dependence can occur with or without *physical dependence,* also known as

blood-brain barrier   A feature of blood vessels in the brain that prevents some substances from entering brain tissue.

agonists   Drugs that bind to a receptor and mimic the effects of the neurotransmitter that normally fits that receptor.

antagonists   Drugs that bind to a receptor and prevent the normal neurotransmitter from binding.

substance abuse   The use of psychoactive drugs in ways that deviate from cultural norms.

psychological dependence   A condition in which a person continues drug use despite adverse effects, needs the drug for a sense of well-being, and becomes preoccupied with obtaining the drug if it is unavailable.

addiction. **Addiction** is a physiological state in which there is not only a strong craving for the drug, but in which using the drug becomes necessary to prevent an unpleasant **withdrawal syndrome.** Withdrawal symptoms vary depending on the drug, but they often include an intensification of craving for the drug and physical effects generally opposite to those of the drug itself.

Physical dependence can develop gradually, without a person's awareness. As the addiction progresses, the person may also develop drug **tolerance,** a condition in which increasingly larger drug doses are required to produce the same effect (Gilman et al., 1985). Scientists now believe that the changes in the brain that underlie addiction may be similar to those that occur during learning (Overton et al., 1999). With the development of tolerance, many addicts need the drug just to prevent the negative effects of not taking it. However, most researchers believe that a craving for the positive effects of drugs is what keeps addicts coming back to drug use (Schulteis et al., 2000; Wise, 1996).

The potential for "normal" people to develop drug dependence should not be underestimated. (If you're a coffee drinker, think about how you'd feel without that morning "jolt.") All addictive drugs stimulate the brain's "pleasure centers," regions that are sensitive to the neurotransmitters dopamine and endorphin. Neuron activity in these areas of the brain produces intensely pleasurable feelings. It also helps generate the pleasant feelings of a good meal, a "runner's high," or sex (Grunberg, 1994; G. C. Harris & Aston-Jones, 1995). Thus, addictive drugs have the capacity for creating tremendously rewarding effects in most people.

Expectations and Drug Effects   Drug effects are determined by more than biochemistry. *Learned expectations* also play a role (Cumsille, Sayer, & Graham, 2000; Goldman, Del Boca, & Darkes, 1999; K. D. Stein, Goldman, & Del Boca, 2000). Expectations about drug effects develop in part as people watch other people react to drugs (Sher et al., 1996). Because what they see can differ from one individual and culture to the next, researchers have concluded that drug effects vary considerably throughout the world (MacAndrew & Edgerton, 1969). In the United States, for example, loss of inhibition, increased anger and violence, and sexual promiscuity are commonly associated with drinking alcohol. These effects are not seen in all cultures, however. In Bolivia's Camba culture, people sometimes engage in extended bouts of drinking a brew that is 89 percent alcohol (178 proof). During their binges, the Camba repeatedly pass out, wake up, and start drinking again—all the while maintaining tranquil social relations. Other studies have shown that learned expectancies also contribute to the effects of heroin, cocaine, and marijuana (T. W. Robbins & Everitt, 1999; Schafer & Brown, 1991; S. S. Smith et al., 1992).

In short, the effects of psychoactive drugs are complex and variable. Here, we consider several major categories of psychoactive drugs that people use primarily to produce altered states of consciousness. They include depressants, stimulants, opiates, and hallucinogens.

Depressants

Depressants, such as alcohol and barbiturates, reduce or depress central nervous system activity, partly by increasing activity of the *inhibitory* neurotransmitter GABA (see Chapter 2). Because GABA itself reduces neuron activity, drugs that enhance GABA's functions heighten its inhibitory effects, creating feelings of relaxation, drowsiness, and sometimes depression.

Alcohol   The most common depressant drug by far is alcohol. In the United States, more than 100 million people drink alcohol. It is equally popular worldwide (Alvarez, Delrio, & Prada, 1995). Alcohol's physiological effects involve the neurotransmitters GABA, endorphins, and dopamine, among others (Koob et al., 1998). The GABA effect is notable; drugs that interact with GABA receptors can block some of alcohol's effects (Suzdak et al., 1986).

Alcohol also enhances the effect of endorphins, the body's natural painkillers. The fact that endorphins produce a sense of well-being may explain why people initially feel "high"

---

addiction   Development of a physical need for a psychoactive drug.

withdrawal syndrome   A set of symptoms associated with discontinuing the use of an addictive substance.

tolerance   A condition in which increasingly larger drug doses are needed to produce a given effect.

depressants   Psychoactive drugs that inhibit the functioning of the central nervous system.

when drinking alcohol. It may also explain why endorphin antagonists are better than placebos at reducing alcohol cravings and relapse rates in recovering alcoholics (Salloum et al., 1998). Alcohol also interacts with dopamine systems. Prolonged alcohol use can have lasting effects on the brain's ability to regulate dopamine levels (Tiihonen et al., 1995). Dopamine agonists reduce alcohol cravings and withdrawal effects (Lawford et al., 1995).

Alcohol affects specific brain regions. It depresses activity in the locus coeruleus, an area that helps activate the cerebral cortex (Koob & Bloom, 1988). This reduced activity, in turn, tends to cause cognitive changes and a release of culturally prescribed inhibitions. Some drinkers begin talking loudly, acting silly, or telling others what they think of them. Emotional reactions range from euphoria to despair. Normally shy people may become impulsive or violent. Alcohol also impairs the hippocampus, making it more difficult to process information and form new memories (Givens, 1995). And it suppresses the cerebellum, causing poor motor coordination, stumbling, and falling (J. Rogers et al., 1986). Alcohol's ability to depress hindbrain mechanisms required for breathing and heartbeat can make overdoses fatal.

Some effects of alcohol—such as anger and aggressiveness—depend both on biochemical factors and on learned expectations (Goldman, Darkes, & Del Boca, 1999; Kushner et al., 2000). Disruptions in motor coordination, speech, and thought result mainly from biochemical factors. These biological effects depend on the amount of alcohol the blood carries to the brain. Because it takes the liver about an hour to break down one ounce of alcohol (the amount in one typical drink), alcohol has milder effects if consumed slowly. Faster drinking or drinking on an empty stomach speeds absorption of alcohol into the blood and heightens its effects. Even after allowing for differences in average male and female body weight, researchers have found metabolic differences that make male bodies able to tolerate somewhat greater amounts of alcohol. A given quantity of alcohol may thus affect a woman more than a man (York & Welte, 1994).

Genetics also seems to play a role in determining the biochemical effects of alcohol. Evidence suggests that particular ethnic groups have a genetic predisposition toward alcohol dependence (Agarwal, 1997), though the genes involved have not yet been identified (Holden, 1998). Other groups (the Japanese, for example) may have inherited metabolic characteristics that enhance alcohol's adverse effects, possibly inhibiting the development of alcohol abuse (Iwahashi et al., 1995).

Barbiturates Sometimes called "downers" or sleeping pills, *barbiturates* are very addictive. In small doses, they have psychoactive effects that include relaxation, mild pleasure, loss of muscle coordination, and lowered attention. Higher doses cause deep sleep, but continued use actually distorts sleep patterns (Kales & Kales, 1973). Thus, long-term use of barbiturates as sleeping pills is unwise. Overdoses can be fatal. Withdrawal symptoms are among the most severe for any drug and can include intense agitation, violent outbursts, convulsions, hallucinations, and even sudden death.

Stimulants

Whereas depressants slow down central nervous system activity, **stimulants** speed it up. Amphetamines, cocaine, caffeine, and nicotine are all examples of stimulants.

Amphetamines Often called "uppers" or "speed," *amphetamines* increase the release of norepinephrine and dopamine into synapses, affecting sleep, learning, and mood. Amphetamines also decrease the *removal* of both substances at synapses, leaving more of them in the synapse, ready to work. The increased activity at these neurotransmitters' receptors results in alertness, arousal, and appetite suppression. Amphetamines' rewarding properties are probably associated with dopamine activity, because taking dopamine antagonists reduces amphetamine use (Holman, 1994).

People who abuse amphetamines usually want to lose weight, stay awake, or obtain a "high." Continued use leads to anxiety, insomnia, heart problems, confusion, paranoia, nonstop talking, and psychological and physical dependence. In some cases, the symptoms of amphetamine abuse appear virtually identical to those of paranoid schizophrenia, a serious mental disorder linked to dopamine malfunction.

stimulants Psychoactive drugs that have the ability to increase behavioral and mental activity.

Cocaine Like amphetamines, *cocaine* increases norepinephrine and dopamine activity, and thus produces many amphetamine-like effects. Cocaine's particularly powerful and rapid effect on dopamine activity may underlie its remarkably addictive nature (Holman, 1994). Indeed, drugs with rapid onset and short duration are generally more addictive than others (Kato, Wakasa, & Yamagita, 1987). Cocaine can be smoked, injected, or inhaled nasally (Gossop et al., 1994). Because it is so addictive and dangerous, it is one of the most intensely studied of all psychoactive drugs.

Cocaine stimulates self-confidence, a sense of well-being, and optimism. Continued use brings nausea, overactivity, insomnia, paranoia, a sudden depressive "crash," hallucinations, sexual dysfunction, and seizures (Lacayo, 1995). Overdoses, especially of the purified cocaine known as "crack," can be deadly. Even small doses can cause a fatal heart attack or stroke (Marzuk et al., 1995). There is now little doubt that a pregnant woman who uses cocaine harms her fetus (Hurt et al., 1995). However, many of the severe, long-term behavioral problems in "cocaine babies" may have as much to do with poverty and neglect after birth as with the mother's cocaine use beforehand. Indeed, some research suggests that early intervention can reduce the effects of both cocaine and the hostile environment that confronts most cocaine babies (Wren, 1998).

Caffeine *Caffeine* may be the world's most popular drug. It works by blocking receptors for the sleep-inducing neurotransmitter *adenosine.* Caffeine reduces drowsiness, improves problem solving, increases the capacity for physical work, and raises urine production (Warburton, 1995). At high doses it causes anxiety and tremors. People can develop tolerance to caffeine, and it can be physically addictive (Strain et al., 1994). Withdrawal symptoms—including headache, fatigue, anxiety, shakiness, and craving— appear on the first day of abstinence and last about a week (Silverman et al., 1992). Caffeine may make it harder for women to become pregnant and may increase the risk of miscarriage (Alderete, Eskenazi, & Sholtz, 1995; Cnattingius et al., 2000). Overall, however, moderate daily caffeine use appears to have few, if any, negative effects (Kawachi, Colditz, & Stone, 1994; W. G. Thompson, 1995).

Nicotine A powerful autonomic nervous system stimulant, *nicotine* is the psychoactive ingredient in tobacco. It is an acetylcholine agonist that also increases the availability of glutamate, the brain's primary excitatory neurotransmitter (McGehee et al., 1995). Nicotine has many psychoactive effects, including elevated mood and improved memory and attention (Pomerleau & Pomerleau, 1992). Like heroin and cocaine, nicotine can be physically addictive (F. J. White, 1998). The nicotine withdrawal syndrome includes craving, anxiety, irritability, lowered heart rate, and weight gain (Epping-Jordan et al., 1998; Hughes, Higgins, & Bickel, 1994). Some smokers appear to develop only a psychological dependence on nicotine (Robinson & Pritchard, 1995), but whichever is the case, there is no doubt that tobacco smoking is usually a difficult habit to break (Shiffman et al., 1997). It is also clearly recognized as a major risk factor for cancer, heart disease, and respiratory disorders (National Center for Health Statistics, 1999).

MDMA "Ecstasy," or MDMA (short for 3,4-methylenedioxymethamphetamine), is a stimulant that causes visual hallucinations and a feeling of greater closeness to others, but also dry mouth, hyperactivity, and jaw muscle spasms resulting in "lockjaw." On the day after using MDMA—also known as "XTC," "clarity," "essence," "E," and "Adam"— people often experience muscle aches, fatigue, depression, and poor concentration (Peroutka, Newman, & Harris, 1988). Because MDMA increases the activity of dopamine-releasing neurons, it leads to some of the same effects as those produced by cocaine and amphetamines (T. D. Steele, McCann, & Ricaurte, 1994). MDMA is a serotonin agonist and also causes neurotransmitter release, thus possibly accounting for the drug's hallucinatory effects (R. A. Green, Cross, & Goodwin, 1995). Although it does not appear to be physically addictive, MDMA is a dangerous, potentially deadly drug with many negative effects (National Institute on Drug Abuse, 2000). Ecstasy permanently damages the brain, killing serotonin-sensitive neurons (R. A. Green, Cross, & Goodwin, 1995). The damage increases with higher doses and continued use (Battaglia, Yeh, & De Souza, 1988). MDMA users may also develop symptoms of *panic disorder,* which include intense anxiety and a sense of impending death (see Chapter 12).

DEADLY DRUG USE In his short career as a comedian, Chris Farley starred on *Saturday Night Live* and in several movies. At the age of thirty-three, he died from an overdose of cocaine and opium.

Opiates

The **opiates** (opium, morphine, heroin, and codeine) are unique in their capacity for inducing sleep and relieving pain (Julien, 1997). Opium, derived from the poppy plant, relieves pain and causes feelings of well-being and dreamy relaxation. One of its most active ingredients, *morphine,* was first isolated in the early 1800s. It is used worldwide for pain relief. Percodan and Demerol are some common morphine-like drugs. *Heroin* is derived from morphine but is three times more powerful, causing intensely pleasurable reactions. Opiates have complex effects on consciousness. Drowsy, cloudy feelings occur because opiates depress activity in some areas of the cerebral cortex. They also create excitation in other parts, causing some users to experience euphoria (Bozarth & Wise, 1984). Opiates exert many of their effects by stimulating the receptors normally stimulated by endorphins, the body's naturally occurring painkillers. This action "tricks" the brain into activating its painkilling and mood-altering systems (Julien, 1997).

Opiates are highly addictive, partly because they stimulate a type of glutamate receptor in the brain's neurons that causes physical changes in these neurons. It may be, then, that opiates alter neurons so that they come to require the drug to function properly. Beyond the hazard of addiction itself, heroin addicts risk death through overdoses, contaminated drugs, or AIDS contracted by sharing needles (National Institute on Drug Abuse, 1997).

Hallucinogens

Hallucinogens, also called *psychedelics,* create a loss of contact with reality and alter other aspects of emotion, perception, and thought. They can cause distortions in body image (one may feel gigantic or tiny), loss of identity (confusion about who one actually is), dream-like fantasies, and hallucinations. Because these effects resemble many severe forms of mental disorder, hallucinogens are also called *psychotomimetics* ("mimicking psychosis").

LSD   One of the most powerful hallucinogens is *lysergic acid diethylamide,* or *LSD.* It was first synthesized from a rye fungus by a Swiss chemist, Albert Hofmann. In 1938, after Hofmann accidentally ingested a minuscule amount of the substance, he discovered the drug's strange effects in the world's first LSD "trip" (Julien, 1997). LSD hallucinations can be quite bizarre. Time may seem distorted, sounds may cause visual sensations, and users may feel as if they have left their bodies. These experiences probably result from LSD's action as a serotonin agonist, because serotonin antagonists greatly reduce LSD's hallucinatory effects (N. R. Carlson, 1998; Leonard, 1992).

The precise effects of LSD are unpredictable. Unpleasant hallucinations and delusions can occur during a person's first—or two hundredth—LSD experience. Although LSD is not addictive, tolerance to its effects does develop. Some users suffer lasting side effects, including severe short-term memory loss, paranoia, violent outbursts, nightmares, and panic attacks (Gold, 1994). Sometimes "flashbacks" can occur, in which a person suddenly returns to an LSD-like state of consciousness weeks or even years after using the drug.

Marijuana   A mixture of crushed leaves, flowers, and stems from the hemp plant (*Cannabis sativa*) makes up *marijuana.* The active ingredient is *tetrahydrocannabinol,* or *THC.* When inhaled, THC is absorbed in minutes by many organs, including the brain, and it continues to affect consciousness for a few hours. THC tends to collect in fatty deposits of the brain and reproductive organs, where it can be detected for weeks. Low doses of marijuana may initially create restlessness and hilarity, followed by a dreamy, carefree relaxation, an expanded sense of space and time, more vivid sensations, food cravings, and subtle changes in thinking (Kelly et al., 1990).

Recent studies have added fuel to the ongoing discussion about whether or not marijuana is safe (Iversen & Snyder, 2000; Strang, Witten, & Hall, 2000). One study with rats found a physiological basis for a marijuana withdrawal syndrome (Rodriguez de Fonseca et al., 1997). If these results can be applied to humans, they would suggest that withdrawal from marijuana might be accompanied by anxiety and depression. A second study found that marijuana interacts with the same dopamine and opiate receptors that heroin acts on (Tanda, Pontieri, & Di Chiara, 1997), implying that marijuana might be a "gateway" to the use of opiates. However, other highly respected researchers have

opiates   Psychoactive drugs that have the ability to produce both sleep-inducing and pain-relieving effects.

hallucinogens   Psychoactive drugs that alter consciousness by producing a temporary loss of contact with reality and changes in emotion, perception, and thought.

in review

Major Classes of Psychoactive Drugs

Drug	Trade/Street Name	Main Effects	Potential for Physical/ Psychological Dependence
Depressants			
Alcohol	"booze"		High/High
Barbiturates	Seconal, Tuinal ("downers"), Nembutal	Relaxation, anxiety reduction, sleep	High/High
Stimulants			
Amphetamines	Benzedrine, Dexedrine, Methadrine ("speed," "uppers," "ice")		Moderate/High
Cocaine	"coke," "crack"	Alertness, euphoria	Moderate to high/High
Caffeine		Alertness	Moderate/Moderate
Nicotine	"smokes," "coffin nails"	Alertness	High (?)/High
MDMA	ecstasy, clarity	Hallucinations	Low/(?)
Opiates			
Opium		Euphoria	High/High
Morphine	Percodan, Demerol	Euphoria, pain control	High/High
Heroin	"junk," "smack"	Euphoria, pain control	High/High
Psychedelics			
LSD	"acid"	Altered perceptions, hallucinations	Low/Low
Marijuana (cannabis)	"pot," "dope," "reefer"	Euphoria, relaxation	Low/Moderate

cautioned that the interpretation of these results is not clear-cut (Grinspoon, 1999), because sex and chocolate have their rewarding effects by activating those same neurotransmitter receptors—and few people would want to outlaw those pleasures!

Regardless of whether marijuana is addicting, leads to use of opiates, or is less potent than other drugs, it can create a number of problems. It disrupts memory formation, making it difficult to carry out mental or physical tasks (Pope & Yurgelun-Todd, 1996). And because marijuana disrupts muscle coordination, driving while under its influence can be dangerous. In fact, motor impairment continues well after the subjective effects of the drug have worn off. As one study demonstrated, pilots had difficulty landing a simulated aircraft even a full day after smoking a single marijuana cigarette (Yesavage et al., 1985). Marijuana easily reaches a developing fetus and therefore should not be used by pregnant women (Fried, Watkinson, & Gray, 1992). Finally, long-term use can lead to psychological dependence (Stephens, Roffman, & Simpson, 1994), as well as to lasting impairments in reasoning and memory. Research has shown that adults who frequently used marijuana scored lower than equal-IQ nonusers on a twelfth-grade academic achievement test (R. I. Block & Ghoneim, 1993).

Marijuana may have considerable value in some domains, however. Doctors have successfully used it in the treatment of asthma, glaucoma, epilepsy, chronic pain, and nausea from cancer chemotherapy (Grinspoon & Bakalar, 1995). Critics of this practice say that medical legalization of marijuana should not occur until controlled research more firmly establishes its medicinal value (Bennet, 1994). With encouragement from bodies such as the National Institute of Medicine (Joy, Watson, & Benson, 1999), such research is now under way. A British company is working on new cannabis-based medicines (Altman, 2000), and the United Nations has encouraged governments to sponsor additional work on the medical uses of marijuana (Wren, 1999). ("In Review: Major Classes of Psychoactive Drugs" summarizes our discussion of these substances.)

active review Consciousness

Linkages

As noted in Chapter 1, all of psychology's subfields are related to one another. Our discussion of meditation, health, and stress illustrates just one way in which the topic of this chapter, consciousness, is linked to the subfield of health psychology (Chapter 10). The Linkages diagram shows ties to two other subfields as well, and there are many more ties throughout the book. Looking for linkages among subfields will help you see how they all fit together and help you better appreciate the big picture that is psychology.

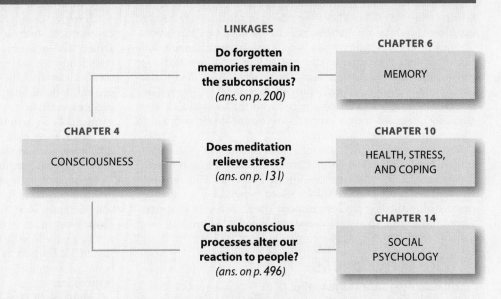

LINKAGES

Do forgotten memories remain in the subconscious? (ans. on p. 200)

CHAPTER 6 MEMORY

CHAPTER 4 CONSCIOUSNESS

Does meditation relieve stress? (ans. on p. 131)

CHAPTER 10 HEALTH, STRESS, AND COPING

Can subconscious processes alter our reaction to people? (ans. on p. 496)

CHAPTER 14 SOCIAL PSYCHOLOGY

Summary

Consciousness can be defined as awareness of the outside world and of one's own thoughts, feelings, perceptions, and other mental processes.

THE SCOPE OF CONSCIOUSNESS

Can unconscious thoughts affect your behavior?

A person's *state of consciousness* is constantly changing. When the changes are particularly noticeable, they are called *altered states of consciousness.* Examples include sleep, hypnosis, meditation, and some drug-induced states. Cultures vary considerably in the value placed on different states of consciousness.

Variations in how much awareness you have for a mental function are described by different levels of consciousness. The *preconscious level* includes mental activities that are outside of awareness but can easily be brought to the *conscious level. Subconscious* and *unconscious* mental activity involves thoughts, memories, and processes that are more difficult to bring to awareness. Mental processes that cannot be brought into awareness occur at the *nonconscious level.*

Awareness is not always required for mental operations. For example, the priming phenomenon shows that people's responses to stimuli speed up and improve as stimuli are repeated, even when the people have no conscious memory of which stimuli are old and which are new. And the mere-exposure effect shows that people tend to judge previously encountered stimuli more favorably, even when they are unaware of having seen those stimuli before.

SLEEPING AND DREAMING

Does your brain go to sleep when you do?

Sleep is an active and complex state. Different stages of sleep are defined on the basis of changes in brain activity (as measured by an electroencephalograph, or EEG) and physiological arousal. Sleep normally begins with stage 1 sleep and progresses gradually to stage 4 sleep. Sleep stages 1 through 4 constitute *slow-wave sleep,* or non-REM sleep. After passing back to stage 2, people enter *rapid eye movement (REM) sleep,* or paradoxical sleep. The sleeper cycles through these stages several times each night, gradually spending more time in stage 2 and REM sleep later in the night.

Sleep disorders can disrupt the natural rhythm of sleep. Among the most common is *insomnia,* in which one feels tired because of trouble falling asleep or staying asleep. *Narcolepsy* produces sudden daytime sleeping episodes. In cases of *sleep apnea,* people briefly but repeatedly stop breathing during sleep. *Sudden infant death syndrome (SIDS)* may be due to brain abnormalities or accidental suffocation. *Sleepwalking* happens most frequently during childhood. *Nightmares* and *night terrors* are different kinds of frightening dreams. *REM behavior disorder* is potentially dangerous because it allows people to act out REM dreams. The cycle of waking and sleeping is a natural *circadian rhythm,* controlled by the suprachiasmatic nuclei of the brain. *Jet lag* can be one result of disrupting the normal sleep-wake cycle.

The purpose of sleep is still unclear. Non-REM sleep may aid bodily rest and repair. REM sleep may help maintain activity in brain areas that provide daytime alertness, or it may allow the brain to "check circuits," eliminate useless information, and solidify learning from the previous day.

Most dreaming occurs during REM sleep. *Dreams* are story-like sequences of images, sensations, and perceptions that occur during sleep. Evidence from research on *lucid dreaming* suggests that people may be able to control their own dreams. Some claim that dreams are the meaningless by-products of brain activity, but one's recall of dreams may still have psychological significance.

HYPNOSIS

Can you be hypnotized against your will?

Hypnosis is a well-known but still poorly understood phenomenon. Tests of *hypnotic susceptibility* suggest that some people cannot be hypnotized. Hypnotized people tend to focus attention on the hypnotist and passively follow instructions. They become very good at fantasizing and role taking. They may exhibit apparent age regression, experience posthypnotic amnesia, and obey posthypnotic suggestions.

State theory sees hypnosis as a special state of consciousness. *Role theory* suggests that hypnosis creates a special social role that gives people permission to act in unusual ways. *Dissociation theory* combines aspects of role and state theories, suggesting that hypnotized individuals enter into a social contract with the hypnotist to allow normally integrated mental processes to become dissociated and to share control over these processes.

Hypnosis is useful in the control of pain and the reduction of nausea associated with cancer chemotherapy. Meditation is a set of techniques designed to create an altered state of consciousness characterized by inner peace and increased awareness. The consistent practice of meditation has been associated with reductions in stress-related problems such as anxiety and high blood pressure.

PSYCHOACTIVE DRUGS

How do drugs affect the brain?

Psychoactive drugs affect the brain, changing consciousness and other psychological processes. *Psychopharmacology* is the field that studies drug effects and their mechanisms. Psychoactive drugs exert their effects primarily by influencing specific neurotransmitter systems and, hence, certain brain activities. To reach brain tissue, drugs must cross the *blood-brain barrier.* Drugs that mimic the receptor effects of a neurotransmitter are called *agonists;* drugs that block the receptor effects of a neurotransmitter are called *antagonists.* Some drugs alter the release or inactivation of specific neurotransmitters, thus affecting the amount of neurotransmitter available for receptor effects.

Adverse effects such as *substance abuse* often accompany the use of psychoactive drugs. *Psychological dependence, addiction* (physical dependence), *tolerance,* and a *withdrawal syndrome* may result. Drugs that produce dependence share the property of directly stimulating certain dopamine-sensitive areas of the brain known as pleasure centers. The consequences of using a psychoactive drug depend both on how the drug affects neurotransmitters and on the user's expectations.

Alcohol and barbiturates are *depressants.* They reduce activity in the central nervous system, often by enhancing the action of inhibitory neurotransmitters. They have considerable potential for producing both psychological and physical dependence.

Stimulants, such as amphetamines and cocaine, increase behavioral and mental activity mainly by increasing the action of dopamine and norepinephrine. These drugs can produce both psychological and physical dependence. Caffeine, one of the world's most popular stimulants, may also create dependence. Nicotine is a potent stimulant. And MDMA, which has both stimulant and hallucinogenic properties, is one of several psychoactive drugs that can permanently damage brain tissue.

Opiates such as opium, morphine, and heroin are highly addictive drugs that induce sleep and relieve pain.

LSD and marijuana are examples of *hallucinogens,* or psychedelics. They alter consciousness by producing a temporary loss of contact with reality and changes in emotion, perception, and thought.

Learn by Doing

Put It in Writing

Watch a prime time television program, and make notes on the role that alcohol, nicotine, and other drugs play in the story. Now think about what you saw, and write a one-page paper describing the messages the show sent to viewers about drugs. Did it directly or indirectly approve or disapprove of drug use? Did it lead viewers to expect particular effects from particular drugs? Conclude your paper by considering what effects these drug-related messages might have on viewers, especially young children.

Personal Learning Activity

For the next two weeks, keep a note pad or tape recorder by your bed, and write down or record your dreams as soon as you awaken. During this same period, use a diary or calendar to jot down significant events, problems, and emotional reactions in your waking life. Then compare the two sets of information. Do you see any correlation? For example, did any of your life events appear in your dreams? Did any dreams contain wished-for solutions to the problems or challenges you were facing at the time? What do you think your own data might say about the meaning of dreams in general? *For additional projects, see the five Personal Learning Activities in the corresponding chapter of the study guide that accompanies this text.*

Step into Action

Courses
History of Psychology
Neuropsychology
Cognitive Psychology
Psychopharmacology
Computational Neuroscience
Sleep

Movies
Rush; Trainspotting; Basketball Diaries (drug addiction)

Boyz N the Hood (role of drugs and alcohol in adolescent development)

Stir of Echoes; Hypnosis (myths and misconceptions about hypnosis)

Sacred Sleep: The Power of Dreams (various cultures view the meaning of dreams)

Deadly Dreams (portrayal of dreams as glimpses of the future)

Books
Nicholas Humphrey, *A History of the Mind: Evolution and the Birth of Consciousness* (Copernicus, 1999) (description of how consciousness has arisen from brain activity)

Ernest Keen, *Chemicals for the Mind: Pharmacology and Human Consciousness* (Praeger, 2000) (theories of consciousness and drugs' effects on it)

Robert M. Julien, *A Primer of Drug Action: A Concise, Nontechnical Guide to the Actions, Uses, and Side Effects of Psychoactive Drugs* (8th ed.) (W. H. Freeman, 1997) (the title says it all)

Daniel Goleman, *The Meditative Mind: Varieties of Meditative Experience* (J. P. Tarcher, 1996) (meditation and its effects)

Steven J. Lynn, Irving Kirsch, and Judith W. Rhue (Eds.), *Casebook of Clinical Hypnosis* (American Psychological Association, 1996) (summary of clinical cases by distinguished hypnotherapists)

Joseph Barber (Ed.), *Hypnosis and Suggestion in the Treatment of Pain* (Norton, 1996) (case studies in pain management using hypnosis)

Stanley Coren, *Sleep Thieves: An Eye-Opening Exploration into the Science and Mysteries of Sleep* (Free Press, 1996) (an introduction to sleep research)

Mary A. Carskadon (Ed.), *Encyclopedia of Sleep and Dreaming* (Macmillan, 1996) (a comprehensive set of research articles on sleep and dreaming)

The Web
The World Wide Web is a good source of additional information about the science of psychology, provided you use it carefully and think critically about the information you find. The PsychAbilities web site that accompanies this text offers many resources relevant to this chapter. These resources include interactive NetLab exercises; Thinking Critically and Evaluating Research exercises; ACE chapter quizzes; recommended web links; and articles on current events, books, and movies. At http://college.hmco.com, select *Psychology* and then this textbook.

Review of Key Terms

Can you define each of the key terms in the chapter? Check your definitions against those on the pages listed in parentheses below or in the Glossary/Index at the end of the text.

addiction *(p. 134)*

agonists *(p. 133)*

altered state of consciousness *(p. 121)*

antagonists *(p. 133)*

blood-brain barrier *(p. 133)*

circadian rhythm *(p. 125)*

conscious level *(p. 116)*

consciousness *(p. 116)*

depressants *(p. 134)*

dissociation theory *(p. 130)*

dreams *(p. 127)*

hallucinogens *(p. 137)*

hypnosis *(p. 129)*

hypnotic susceptibility *(p. 129)*

insomnia *(p. 124)*

jet lag *(p. 126)*

lucid dreaming *(p. 128)*

narcolepsy *(p. 124)*

night terrors *(p. 125)*

nightmares *(p. 125)*

nonconscious level *(p. 116)*

opiates *(p. 137)*

preconscious level *(p. 117)*

psychoactive drugs *(p. 132)*

psychological dependence *(p. 133)*

psychopharmacology *(p. 132)*

rapid eye movement (REM) sleep *(p. 123)*

REM behavior disorder *(p. 125)*

role theory *(p. 130)*

sleep apnea *(p. 125)*

sleepwalking *(p. 125)*

slow-wave sleep *(p. 123)*

state theory *(p. 130)*

state of consciousness *(p. 116)*

stimulants *(p. 135)*

subconscious *(p. 117)*

substance abuse *(p. 133)*

sudden infant death syndrome (SIDS) *(p. 125)*

tolerance *(p. 134)*

unconscious *(p. 117)*

withdrawal syndrome *(p. 134)*

Multiple-Choice Self-Test

Select the best answer for each of the questions below. Then check your responses against the Answer Key at the end of the text.

1. During her first semester at college, Zandra never noticed the framed Rembrandt prints in the hallway of her classroom building. Then, in an art appreciation class the next semester, she found that she liked Rembrandt paintings more than those by other artists, although she'd never had a preference for his work before. Zandra has experienced

   a. the prosopagnosia effect.
   b. the mere-exposure effect.
   c. binocular priming.
   d. visual masking.

2. Lisa always forgets to take off her watch before she steps into the shower, probably because the sensation of the watch on her arm occurs at the _____ level.

   a. nonconscious
   b. preconscious
   c. subconscious
   d. unconscious

3. Denisha is not acting her usual self tonight. Because she's had too much alcohol, she readily accepts her friends' suggestion that they use an alley as a restroom. Denisha is not considering the consequences of her actions; therefore, she is most likely

   a. in an altered state of consciousness.
   b. in a preconscious state.
   c. under the influence of priming.
   d. under the influence of a stimulant.

4. Ruby has had a terrible evening. Just as her boyfriend, Kato, started to propose to her, he fell asleep. Ruby would feel better if she knew that Kato suffers from

   a. hypersomnia.
   b. narcolepsy.
   c. insomnia.
   d. night terrors.

5. Edie has purchased a tape that supposedly contains subliminal messages to help her lose weight. According to the Thinking Critically section in this chapter, Edie's success in losing weight most likely depends on

   a. the content of the subliminal messages.
   b. her expectation that the subliminal messages will help.
   c. how relaxed the subliminal messages make her feel.
   d. the number of times the subliminal messages occur.

6. Benjamin Franklin said, "Early to bed and early to rise, makes a man healthy, wealthy, and wise." A psychologist who knows about circadian rhythms would probably make which statement instead?

   a. "Whenever you bed, whenever you rise, a change in your rhythm will be your demise."
   b. "Bed when you will, rise when you wish, it just doesn't make that big of a diff."
   c. "Early to bed, early to rise, makes a man grisly and grumpy, but wise."
   d. "Bed after midnight will make you uptight."

7. Sylandra hates her brother, but her therapist suggests that she is unable to let herself experience this unacceptable feeling. According to Freud, Sylandra's hatred for her brother most likely resides at the _____ level.

   a. conscious
   b. unconscious
   c. nonconscious
   d. preconscious

8. Hypnosis has been especially effective in

   a. connecting with past lives.
   b. improving memory.
   c. pain control.
   d. lowering cholesterol.

9. Norman has found himself a quiet spot, settled into a comfortable position, started using his mantra, and assumed a passive attitude. He is most likely about to

   a. meditate.
   b. enter self-hypnosis.
   c. go to sleep.
   d. daydream.

10. In an experiment, Leroy is connected to an EEG machine and a muscle tension monitor as he sleeps. When he shows brain waves similar to those of an awake person, but near-paralysis in his muscles, the researcher can conclude that Leroy is in _____ sleep.

    a. stage 1
    b. stage 2
    c. stage 4
    d. REM

11. Dr. Lyman has developed a new drug that treats movement disorders by blocking dopamine receptors. Dr. Lyman's new drug is a dopamine

    a. agonist.
    b. antagonist.
    c. reuptake blocker.
    d. placebo.

12. A young man experiencing hallucinations is brought to a hospital emergency room. Which of the following drugs could his doctor rule out as a likely cause of the hallucinations?

    a. MDMA
    b. cocaine
    c. caffeine
    d. LSD

13. Lavonne volunteered to participate in a hypnosis study. After being hypnotized, she put her hand in painfully cold ice water. She orally reported no pain, but she pressed a button indicating that "some part of her" felt pain. This result supports the _____ theory of hypnosis.

    a. role
    b. state
    c. dissociation
    d. James-Lange

14. Noel has taken a drug that increases the activity of the neurotransmitter norepinephrine. Which of the following drugs has Noel taken?

    a. alcohol
    b. LSD
    c. cocaine
    d. opium

15. Tolerance is defined as

    a. a need for larger amounts of a drug to achieve the same effect.
    b. a physical need for a drug.
    c. dependence on a drug.
    d. a drug buildup that prevents overdosing.

16. Abel took a drug to reduce the pain in his broken arm. The drug mimicked endorphins, because it bound itself to endorphin receptors and caused the same response as endorphins do. Abel took an endorphin

    a. agonist.
    b. antagonist.
    c. reuptake blocker.
    d. protagonist.

17. The drug Abel took to reduce his pain would be classified as a(n)

    a. depressant.
    b. opiate.
    c. psychedelic.
    d. stimulant.

18. Which of the following is not an opiate?

    a. cocaine
    b. heroin
    c. morphine
    d. opium

19. Delta had a dream in which an evil butcher was chasing her with a knife and urging her to do aerobics. The dream became very scary, but because it took place in REM sleep, she had the feeling that she couldn't move or scream. Delta's dream would be classified as a

    a. sign of REM behavior disorder.
    b. narcoleptic vision.
    c. nightmare.
    d. night terror.

20. Which of the following is true about alcohol?

    a. A given amount of alcohol will affect a man more than a woman.
    b. Alcohol's effects are the same whether it is consumed slowly or quickly.
    c. There are no genetic predispositions toward alcohol abuse.
    d. Dopamine agonists reduce alcohol cravings.

5

Learning

Live and learn. This simple phrase captures the idea that learning is a lifelong process that affects our behavior every day. Understanding how learning takes place is thus an important part of understanding ourselves. Sometimes, learning involves linking signals, as when we learn to associate wailing sirens with ambulances. Other times, learning depends on what happens after we do something—whether we are praised or punished, for example. But learning is more than these kinds of associations. What we think and how we feel about life's signals and consequences also have an impact on what we learn to do, and not do. Blend in practice and feedback, mix well, and you have all the ingredients of the learning process.

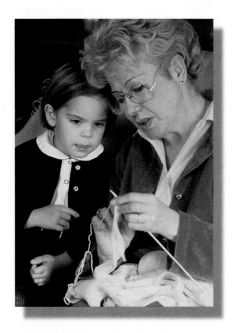

Reading this chapter will help you to answer the following questions:

- **How did Russian dogs teach psychologists about learning?**
- **How do reward and punishment work?**
- **Can people learn to be helpless?**
- **What should teachers learn about learning?**

ike most newborn babies, Jeffrey cried until he was fed. He awakened at 3 A.M. nearly every day, hungry and crying for food. And as she had done every day since he was born, his mother would put on her slippers and walk down the tile hallway to his bedroom. After a quick change of his diaper came the feeding. By the time he was four months old, Jeffrey would cry for about a minute and then quietly wait a few more minutes for his mother to arrive for his feeding. One particular morning, as his mother was halfway down the hall, she stopped in her tracks as she felt a sneeze coming. She pinched her nostrils together, and the urge to sneeze passed. However, she noticed that Jeffrey had begun to cry again. This was unusual. She began to walk again, and he quieted. Her scientific curiosity aroused, she walked a few steps, then stopped, then started, then stopped. She discovered that Jeffrey stopped crying when he heard her footsteps but resumed crying when he did not hear her coming.

Jeffrey had learned many things in his four short months. He could anticipate events and predict outcomes based on the meaning of certain sounds. Like all of us, he showed an ability to learn about relationships in the environment and to adjust to them. This adjustment to changes in the environment is called *adaptation*. Along with adaptation comes expectations and predictions about what is and what is not likely to occur in our world. The entire process of development, from birth to death, involves adapting to increasingly complex, ever-changing environments, using continuously updated knowledge and skills gained through experience.

All species exhibit, to some degree, the ability to adapt to changing environments. Individual variability in this ability shapes the evolution of behavior and appearance in animals and humans. As Charles Darwin noted, individuals who don't adapt may not survive to reproduce. Many forms of adaptation follow the principles of learning.

Learning is a relatively permanent change in behavior or knowledge due to experience. We are born with some behaviors and knowledge, acquire others through maturation, and learn still others. Some of our sayings, such as "Once burned, twice shy" and "Fool me once, shame on you; fool me twice, shame on me," reflect this vital learning process. Indeed, learning plays a central role in most aspects of human behavior. If you want to know who you are and how you became the person you are today, examining what and how you have learned is a good place to start.

You learn primarily by identifying relationships between events and noting the regularity of patterns in the world around you. When two events repeatedly take place together, you can predict that one will occur based on what you know about the other. Jeffrey predicted his feeding from hearing his mother's footsteps. You have learned that a clear blue sky means dry weather, that too little sleep makes you irritable, that you can reach someone on the telephone by pressing certain numbers, and that yelling orders motivates some people and angers others.

What determines whether and how you learn? Which patterns of relationships do you identify, and how do you do it? One form of learning focuses on the importance of rewards and punishments in altering the frequency of observable behavior. Another aspect of learning focuses on the signals that trigger behavior. These automatic associations don't tell the whole story, though. Research on learning and on the role of cognitive processes in learning have thrown open the doors to studying the most complex learning processes that help make you who you are. This chapter describes what psychologists now know about the fundamental principles of learning.

Classical Conditioning: Learning Signals and Associations

How did Russian dogs teach psychologists about learning?

At the first notes of the national anthem, a young athlete's heart may begin to pound. Those sounds signal that the game is about to begin. Similarly, a low-fuel light on your car's instrument panel might make your adrenaline flow, because it means that you are almost out of gas. People are not born with these reactions. They have learned them from associations between events in the world. The experimental study of this kind of learning was begun, almost by accident, by Ivan Petrovich Pavlov.

Pavlov's Discovery

Although Pavlov is one of the best-known figures in psychology, he was not a psychologist. He was a Russian physiologist who won the Nobel Prize in 1904 for his research on the digestive system of dogs. In the course of this research, Pavlov noticed a strange phenomenon. His dogs sometimes salivated when no food was present. For instance, they salivated when they saw the assistant who normally brought their food.

Pavlov devised a simple experiment to determine how salivation could occur without an obvious physical cause, such as food. First he performed an operation to divert a dog's saliva into a container, allowing him to measure precisely how much was secreted. Next he placed the dog in an apparatus similar to the one shown in Figure 5.1.

The experiment had three phases. In the first phase, Pavlov and his associates confirmed that when meat powder was placed on the dog's tongue, the dog automatically salivated (Anrep, 1920). They also confirmed that the dog did not automatically salivate in response to neutral stimuli, such as a white lab coat or a tone. The researchers thus established the existence of the two basic components for Pavlov's experiment: (1) a natural reflex (in this case, automatic salivation to meat powder placed on the dog's tongue) and (2) a neutral stimulus (the sound of a tone, which by itself would cause no saliva-

learning   The modification of pre-existing behavior and understanding.

classical conditioning   A procedure in which a neutral stimulus is paired with a stimulus that elicits a reflexive response until the neutral stimulus alone comes to elicit a similar response.

unconditioned stimulus (UCS)   A stimulus that elicits a response without conditioning.

unconditioned response (UCR)   The automatic, unlearned, reflexive reaction to a stimulus.

Apparatus for Measuring
Conditioned Responses

In this more elaborate version of Pavlov's original apparatus, the amount of saliva flowing from a dog's cheek is measured and then recorded on a slowly revolving drum of paper.

Pen recording
on cylinder

tion). A *reflex* is the swift, automatic response to a stimulus, such as shivering in the cold or jumping when you are jabbed with a needle. A neutral stimulus is one that does not elicit the reflex being studied.

In the second phase of Pavlov's experiment, the tone sounded, and meat powder was placed in the dog's mouth. The dog salivated. This *pairing* of the tone followed by the meat powder was repeated several times. Then, in the third phase, the tone was sounded, and no meat powder was presented. The dog again salivated. The tone by itself now made the dog salivate. The tone had come to predict the presentation of the meat powder. You may have seen the same principle in action when you open a can of pet food with an electric can opener. The sound of the can opener may bring your pet running. It means that food is coming.

Pavlov's experiment demonstrated what we now call **classical conditioning.** In this procedure, a neutral stimulus is repeatedly paired with a stimulus that already triggers a reflexive response, until the previously neutral stimulus alone provokes a similar response. Figure 5.2 shows the basic elements of classical conditioning. The stimulus that naturally elicits a response *without* conditioning, such as the meat powder in Pavlov's experiment, is called the **unconditioned stimulus (UCS).** The automatic, unlearned, reflexive response to this stimulus is called the **unconditioned response (UCR).** The

Classical Conditioning

Before classical conditioning has occurred, meat powder on a dog's tongue produces salivation, but the sound of a tone—a neutral stimulus—does not. During the process of conditioning, the tone is repeatedly paired with the meat powder. After classical conditioning has taken place, the sound of the tone alone acts as a conditioned stimulus, producing salivation.

PHASE I: Before conditioning has occurred

| UCS (meat powder) | → | UCR (salivation) |

| Neutral stimulus (tone) | → | No salivation |

PHASE II: The process of conditioning

| Neutral stimulus (tone) followed by UCS (meat powder) | → | UCR (salivation) |

PHASE III: After conditioning has occurred

| CS (tone) | → | CR (salivation) |

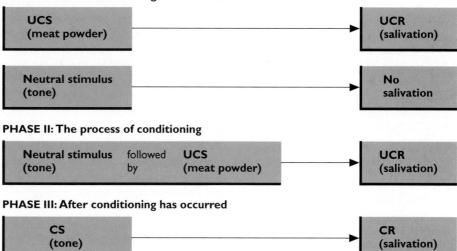

Applying Psychology

PREDATOR CONTROL THROUGH CONDITIONING In the western United States, some ranchers lace a sheep carcass with enough lithium chloride to make wolves and coyotes nauseous. The predators associate nausea with the taste of sheep and afterward stay away from the ranchers' flocks. A similar program supported by the government of India has greatly reduced the human death toll from tiger attacks. Stuffed dummies are connected to a shock generator and placed in areas where tigers have killed people. When the animals approach the dummies, they receive a shock (UCS). After learning to associate shock with the human form (CS), the tigers tend to avoid people (CR).

neutral stimulus (tone), after being paired with the unconditioned stimulus (meat powder), is called the **conditioned stimulus (CS),** and the response it comes to trigger is a learned or **conditioned response (CR).**

Conditioned Responses over Time: Extinction and Spontaneous Recovery

If a barking dog bit you in the past, you may be afraid whenever you hear a dog barking now. The more bad experiences you have had with dogs, the stronger will be your learned distress in response to the sound of barking. In the language of classical conditioning, continued pairings of a conditioned stimulus (CS/bark) with an unconditioned stimulus (UCS/bite) strengthen the conditioned response (CR/distress). The curve on the left side of Figure 5.3 shows an example: Repeated associations of a tone (CS) with meat powder (UCS) caused Pavlov's dogs to increase their salivation (CR) to the tone alone.

What if the meat powder (UCS) is no longer given? In general, the conditioned response will gradually disappear through a process known as *extinction* (see the center section of Figure 5.3). **Extinction** is the result of eliminating the UCS (meat powder) and repeatedly presenting the CS (tone) alone. Eventually, the CS (tone) will no longer elicit the CR (salivation). If the CS (tone) and the UCS (meat powder) are again paired after the conditioned response has been extinguished, the conditioned response returns to its original strength very quickly. This quick relearning of a conditioned response after extinction is called **reconditioning.** Because reconditioning takes much less time than the original conditioning, extinction must not have completely erased the association between the conditioned stimulus and the conditioned response.

The right side of Figure 5.3 illustrates additional evidence for this conclusion. An extinguished conditioned response will temporarily reappear if, after some time delay, the conditioned stimulus occurs without the unconditioned stimulus. This is called **spontaneous recovery,** the temporary reappearance of a conditioned response after extinction (and without further CS-UCS pairings). In general, the longer the time between extinction and the reappearance of the CS, the stronger the recovered conditioned response. However, unless the UCS is again paired with the CS, extinction rapidly occurs again. So, when you hear a song or smell the cologne associated with a former love, there is a ripple of emotion—a conditioned response. Through its association with that person, the song or fragrance, which once had no particular significance, has become a conditioned stimulus. Even years later, it can provoke conditioned emotional reactions.

conditioned stimulus (CS) An originally neutral stimulus that now elicits a conditioned response.

conditioned response (CR) The response elicited by the conditioned stimulus.

extinction The gradual disappearance of a conditioned response.

reconditioning The relearning of a conditioned response following extinction.

spontaneous recovery The reappearance of a conditioned response after extinction.

stimulus generalization A process in which a conditioned response is elicited by stimuli similar to the original conditioned stimulus.

stimulus discrimination A process through which people learn to differentiate among similar stimuli and respond appropriately to each one.

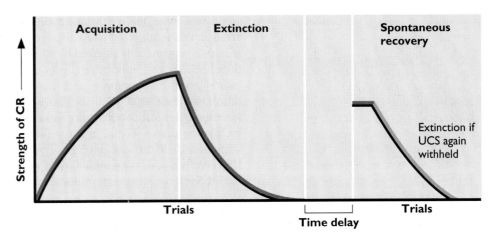

FIGURE 5.3

Changes over Time in the Strength of a Conditioned Response

As the conditioned stimulus (CS) and the unconditioned stimulus (UCS) are repeatedly paired during initial conditioning, the strength of the conditioned response (CR) increases. During extinction, the strength of the CR decreases as more trials occur in which the CS is presented without the UCS. Eventually the CR disappears. However, after a brief period, the CR reappears if the CS is again presented.

Stimulus Generalization and Discrimination

After a conditioned response is acquired, stimuli similar to the conditioned stimulus also elicit the response. This phenomenon is called **stimulus generalization.** Thus, even though only one dog bit you, you may now show some fear of *all* dogs. Usually the greater the similarity between a new stimulus and the original conditioned stimulus, the stronger the conditioned response will be. So, if you were bitten by a small, curly-haired dog, your fear response would be strongest to other small dogs with similar hairstyles. Figure 5.4 shows an example involving varying sounds.

Stimulus generalization has important advantages. It is important for survival that you respond quickly to a whole range of danger cues after exposure to just one. For instance, if you became sick after drinking sour-smelling milk, it would be adaptive for you to avoid all dairy products with a similar odor. Generalization, however, would be paralyzing if it had no limits. Imagine how inconvenienced you'd be if your fear response to dogs were generalized to the point where you could not look at pictures of dogs and avoided all people, even friends, who owned a dog.

Stimulus generalization does not run wild because it is usually balanced by a process called *stimulus discrimination.* Through **stimulus discrimination** you learn to differentiate among similar stimuli. You should be afraid of the dog that bit you, but not necessarily of every other dog in the world.

The Signaling of Significant Events

Classical conditioning allows one stimulus (the conditioned stimulus, or CS) to substitute for another (the unconditioned stimulus, or UCS) in producing a reflexive response. In this way, an animal or person can prepare for the arrival of the UCS. It is certainly adaptive to prepare for the arrival of food, for example. Having saliva automatically flowing in advance makes it easier to swallow food. Early research on classical conditioning focused on its role in controlling such automatic, involuntary behavior. However, psychologists now recognize the wider implications of classical conditioning. They argue that organisms acquire conditioned responses when one event reliably predicts, or *signals,* the appearance of another. In other words, classical conditioning does not simply produce robot-like, reflexive responses. It provides a means through which animals and people develop *mental representations* of the relationships between events in their environment. These representations aid in adaptation and survival.

What determines whether and how a conditioned response is learned? Some important factors are the timing, predictability, and strength of signals. Others include how much attention signals receive and how easily they can be associated with other stimuli.

Timing   A signal that comes *after* an event cannot prepare you for that event. If your teacher dismisses class every day at 9:59 and a bell rings at 10:00, the bell cannot prepare you for the dismissal. It comes too late to be a useful signal. So classical conditioning

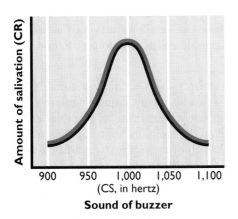

FIGURE 5.4

Stimulus Generalization

The strength of a conditioned response (CR) is greatest when the original conditioned stimulus (CS) occurs, but the CR also appears following stimuli that closely resemble the CS. Here, the CS is the sound of a buzzer at 1,000 hertz (Hz), and the CR is salivation. Notice that the CR generalizes well to stimuli at 990 or 1,010 Hz, but that it gets weaker and weaker following stimuli that are less and less similar to the CS.

works best when the conditioned stimulus precedes the unconditioned stimulus. This arrangement is adaptive. Normally, the presence of food, predators, or other significant stimuli is most reliably signaled by smells, sounds, or other events that come just before their appearance (Einhorn & Hogarth, 1982). So it is logical that the brain should be "wired" to form associations most easily between things that occur at about the same time. How close together do they have to be? There is no single "best" interval for every situation. Classical conditioning can occur when the interval between the CS and the UCS is less than a second or more than a minute. It all depends on the particular CS, UCS, and UCR that are involved (Longo, Klempay, & Bitterman, 1964; Pavlov, 1927). However, classical conditioning will always be weaker if the interval between the CS and the UCS is longer than what is ideal for the stimuli and responses in a given situation.

Predictability   It is not enough for the CS merely to come before the UCS. Suppose your dogs, Moxie and Fang, have very different personalities. When Moxie growls, she sometimes bites, but sometimes she doesn't. Fang growls *only* before biting. Your conditioned fear response to Moxie's growl will probably occur slowly, because her growl is a stimulus that does not *reliably* predict or signal the danger of a bite. However, you are likely to quickly develop a classically conditioned fear response to Fang's growl. It *always* means that you are in danger of being bitten. Classical conditioning proceeds most rapidly when the CS *always* signals the UCS, and *only* the UCS. Even if both dogs provide the same number of pairings of the CS (growl) and the UCS (bite), it is only with Fang that the CS *reliably* predicts the UCS (R. A. Rescorla, 1968).

Signal Strength   A conditioned response will be learned more rapidly if the UCS is strong than if it is weak. Thus, for example, a CS that acts as a predictive signal will be more rapidly associated with a strong shock (UCS) than with a weak one. The effect of signal strength on classical conditioning makes adaptive sense. It is more important to be prepared for major events than for those that have little impact.

The same principle holds true for the strength of the conditioned stimulus. A conditioned response will be learned more quickly if the cue or CS attracts your attention. Louder tones, brighter lights, or other more noticeable events tend to get attention, so they are more rapidly associated with a UCS.

Attention   Attention can influence *which* of several possible conditioned stimuli actually becomes associated with an unconditioned stimulus. Many stimuli may precede a UCS in the natural environment. For instance, suppose you are at the beach eating a tasty plum, reading a magazine, listening to Elton John on the radio, and enjoying the smell of suntan lotion just before being stung by a bee. Which of these stimuli is most likely to become a conditioned stimulus for fear? It depends partly on where you were focusing your attention when you were stung. The stimulus you most closely attended to—the one you most fully perceived—is most likely to become a CS that later triggers a conditioned response.

Second-Order Conditioning   In some cases, a learned signal (CS) can function as if it were an unlearned signal (UCS). For instance, a painful medical procedure (UCS) at the doctor's office can be associated with the doctor's white coat (CS). The white coat (CS) then evokes a conditioned fear response. And once the white coat (CS) has the power to trigger fear, the coat might become associated with the doctor's office. Eventually, the doctor's office itself might evoke a fear response. Why? Because the CS (white coat) has taken on the properties of the UCS (pain). The doctor's office signals the white coat, which in turn signals pain. When a conditioned stimulus (CS) acts like a UCS, creating conditioned stimuli out of events associated with it, the phenomenon is called **second-order conditioning.** This process is an adaptive "early warning system." It prepares us for damaging or life-threatening events (UCS) that are signaled not only by a CS but also by events that precede, and thus predict, that CS.

Second-order conditioning can result in incorrect diagnoses of high blood pressure (hypertension). For some patients, the mere presence of a doctor or nurse becomes a conditioned stimulus for fear, and their blood pressure rises as part of a conditioned fear response. Doctors call these people *white coat hypertensives* (M. G. Myers et al., 1996).

second-order conditioning   A process in which a conditioned stimulus acts like an unconditioned stimulus, creating conditioned stimuli out of events associated with it.

TASTE AVERSIONS Humans can develop classically conditioned taste aversions, even to preferred foods. For example, Ilene Bernstein (1978) gave one group of cancer patients Mapletoff ice cream an hour before they received nausea-provoking chemotherapy. A second group ate this same distinctively flavored ice cream on a day they did not receive chemotherapy. A third group got no ice cream. Five months later, the patients were asked to taste several ice cream flavors. Those who had never tasted Mapletoff and those who had not eaten it in association with chemotherapy chose it as their favorite. Those who had eaten Mapletoff before receiving chemotherapy found it very distasteful.

Biopreparedness Certain signals or events are especially suited to form associations with other events (Logue, 1985). For example, some signals are more easily associated with an unconditioned stimulus than others. This natural affinity for certain events to become linked suggests that organisms are "biologically prepared" or "genetically tuned" to develop certain conditioned associations. For example, people are much more likely to develop a conditioned fear of dogs, snakes, and rats than of doorknobs or stereos (Kleinknecht, 1991). And experiments with animals suggest that they tend to learn the type of associations that are most relevant to their environment (Staddon & Ettinger, 1989). Birds of prey, which strongly depend upon their vision in finding food, may develop taste aversions on the basis of appearance. Coyotes and rats depend more on their sense of smell, so they tend to develop aversions related to odor.

Conditioned taste aversion offers a dramatic example of this *biopreparedness* phenomenon. In one study, rats were either shocked or made nauseous in the presence of a light, a buzzer, and flavored water. The rats formed only certain conditioned associations. Those that had been shocked developed a conditioned fear response to the light and the buzzer, but not to the flavored water. And those that had been made nauseous developed a conditioned avoidance of the flavored water, but they showed no particular response to the light or buzzer (Garcia & Koelling, 1966). These results reflect an adaptive process. Something we eat or drink will more likely produce nausea than will a noise or light. Thus, nausea is more likely to become a conditioned response to an internal stimulus, such as a flavor, than to an external stimulus. In contrast, the sudden pain of a shock is more likely to have been caused by an external stimulus, so it makes evolutionary sense that the organism should be "tuned" to associate shock or sudden pain with a sight or sound.

Conditioned taste aversion illustrates that for certain kinds of stimuli, classical conditioning can occur even when there is a considerable delay between the CS (taste) and the UCS (nauseous sensations). Poisons do not usually produce their effects until minutes or hours after being ingested. However, people who have experienced food poisoning may never again eat the type of food that made them ill. Organisms that are biologically prepared to link taste signals with illness, even a delayed illness, are more likely to survive than organisms not so prepared.

Some Applications of Classical Conditioning

The principles of classical conditioning are summarized in "In Review: Basic Processes of Classical Conditioning." These principles have proven useful in many areas, including overcoming fears and diagnosing Alzheimer's disease.

Phobias Phobias are intense, irrational fears of objects or situations. Either the objects or situations are not dangerous, or they are less dangerous than the fear response would suggest. Classical conditioning often plays a role in the development of such fears (Bouton, Mineka, & Barlow, 2001). As noted earlier, a person bitten by a dog may learn a dog phobia that is so intense and generalized that it leads the person to avoid *all* dogs and all situations where dogs might be encountered. Dangerous situations can also produce classical conditioning of very long-lasting fears. Decades after their war experiences, some military veterans still respond to simulated battle sounds with pronounced changes in heart rate and blood pressure and other signs of emotional arousal (Edwards & Acker, 1972).

Classical conditioning has also been used to treat phobias (see Chapter 13). Joseph Wolpe (1958) pioneered the development of this methodology. He showed that irrational fears could be relieved through *systematic desensitization,* a procedure that associates a new response (CR), such as relaxation, with a feared stimulus. To treat a thunderstorm phobia, for instance, a therapist might first teach the client to relax deeply and then associate that relaxation with increasingly intense sights and sounds of thunderstorms (CS) presented on videotape (Öst, 1978). Because, as Wolpe noted, a person cannot be relaxed and afraid at the same time, the new CR (relaxation) replaces the old one (fear).

in review

Basic Processes of Classical Conditioning

Process	Description	Example
Acquisition	A neutral stimulus and an unconditioned stimulus (UCS) are paired. The neutral stimulus becomes a conditioned stimulus (CS), eliciting a conditioned response (CR).	A child learns to fear (conditioned response) the doctor's office (conditioned stimulus) by associating it with the reflexive emotional reaction (unconditioned response) to a painful injection (unconditioned stimulus).
Stimulus generalization	A conditioned response is elicited not only by the conditioned stimulus but also by stimuli similar to the conditioned stimulus.	A child fears most doctors' offices and places that smell like them.
Stimulus discrimination	Generalization is limited so that some stimuli similar to the conditioned stimulus do not elicit the conditioned response.	A child learns that his mother's doctor's office is not associated with the unconditioned stimulus.
Extinction	The conditioned stimulus is presented alone, without the unconditioned stimulus. Eventually the conditioned stimulus no longer elicits the conditioned response.	A child visits the doctor's office several times for a checkup, but does not receive a shot. Fear may eventually cease.

Diagnosis of Alzheimer's Disease   A puff of air directed at your eye is an unconditioned stimulus that causes a reflexive unconditioned response, namely an eye blink (Hilgard & Marquis, 1936). If each air puff is preceded by a flash of light, the light will become a conditioned stimulus that can cause an eye blink on its own. Recent research with animals has demonstrated that the hippocampus, a brain structure that is damaged in the early stages of Alzheimer's disease, is involved in the development of this type of conditioned response (J. T. Green & Woodruff-Pak, 2000). That research is now being applied in the identification of those people who are at high risk for this devastating brain disorder. One study found that elderly people whose eye blink conditioning was impaired were the ones most likely to develop Alzheimer's disease within two or three years (Downey-Lamb & Woodruff-Pak, 1999). Knowing who is at high risk for Alzheimer's is important because it allows doctors to offer these people medication that might delay the emergence of the disease.

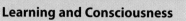

LINKAGES

Learning and Consciousness

People appear to be genetically "wired" to attend to, and orient toward, certain kinds of events. Loud noises and pain attract immediate attention. *New* stimuli are also very likely to attract attention. When a new stimulus is repeated often, though, it isn't new anymore. It no longer grabs our attention, and we stop focusing on it. We learn not to respond. This reduced responsiveness to a repeated stimulus, called **habituation**, is perhaps the simplest form of learning. It has been observed in organisms ranging from sea snails to humans (Pinel, 1993). It provides another example of how learning helps organisms adapt to their environments (B. Schwartz & Reisberg, 1991). Habituation has a direct connection to classical conditioning and to certain drug effects, according to a theory proposed by Richard Solomon.

According to R. L. Solomon's (1980) *opponent-process theory*, habituation is the result of two processes. These processes balance each other, like a seesaw. The first process is a relatively automatic, involuntary response, essentially an unconditioned response (UCR). The second, or opponent, process is a learned or conditioned response (CR) that follows and counteracts the first. For example, an injection of adrenaline produces an

habituation Reduced responsiveness to a repeated stimulus.

increase in heart rate (UCR), the first process. Then the opponent process decreases the heart rate somewhat. This second, counterbalancing process is a learned response (CR). If the UCS (injection) is repeated many times, the learned opposing response, or CR (slowed heart rate), occurs more quickly and with greater intensity. As the CR more strongly counteracts the UCR over time, the rise in heart rate caused by the injection gets smaller and smaller, resulting in what we call *habituation*.

What would you expect to happen in the case of extended use of heroin, according to Solomon's theory? Initially, the first process (UCR) produces an intensely pleasurable "high." But with repeated use of the drug, the high is countered or neutralized as the opponent process (unpleasantness) becomes quicker and stronger. Thus, progressively larger doses of the drug are required to obtain the same drug high. According to Solomon, opponent processes could be the basis for the development of drug tolerance and addiction, described in Chapter 4.

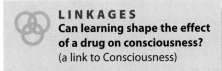

LINKAGES
Can learning shape the effect of a drug on consciousness?
(a link to Consciousness)

Instrumental and Operant Conditioning: Learning the Consequences of Behavior

How do reward and punishment work?

Classical conditioning is an important form of learning, but it cannot explain most of what you learn on a daily basis. In classical conditioning, neutral and unconditioned stimuli are predictably paired. The result is an association of the two. This association is reflected in the fact that the conditioned stimulus now triggers the conditioned response. Notice that both stimuli occur before, or along with, the conditioned response. But you also learn many associations between responses and the stimuli that *follow* them, between behavior and its consequences (Colwill, 1994). A child learns to say "please" to get a piece of candy. A headache sufferer learns to take a pill to escape the pain. A dog learns to "shake hands" to get a treat.

From the Puzzle Box to the Skinner Box

Edward L. Thorndike, an American psychologist, did much of the fundamental research on the consequences of behavior. Whereas Pavlov explored classical conditioning, Thorndike studied the ability of animals to think and reason. For example, he placed a hungry cat in a *puzzle box* like the one in Figure 5.5. The cat had to learn some response—say, stepping on a pedal—to unlock the door and get food. During the first few trials in the puzzle box, the cat explored and prodded until it finally hit the pedal.

FIGURE 5.5

Thorndike's Puzzle Box

This drawing illustrates the kind of puzzle box used in Thorndike's research. His cats learned to open the door and reach food by stepping on the pedal, but the learning occurred gradually. Some cats actually took longer to get out of the box on one trial than on a previous trial.

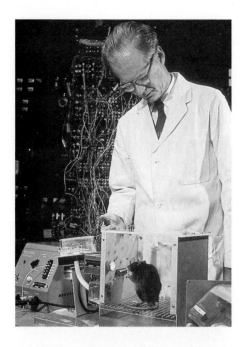

law of effect   A law stating that if a response made in the presence of a particular stimulus is rewarded, the same response is more likely to occur when that stimulus is encountered again.

operant conditioning   A process in which responses are learned on the basis of their rewarding or punishing consequences.

operant   A response that has some effect on the world.

reinforcer   A stimulus event that increases the probability that the response immediately preceding it will occur again.

positive reinforcers   Stimuli that strengthen a response if they follow that response.

The animal eventually solved the puzzle, but very slowly. It did not appear to understand, or suddenly gain *insight* into, the problem (E. L. Thorndike, 1898). After many trials, though, the cat learned to solve the puzzle quickly each time it was placed in the box. What was it learning? Thorndike argued that any response (such as pacing or meowing) that did not produce a satisfying effect (opening the door) gradually became weaker. And any response (pressing the pedal) that did have a satisfying effect gradually became stronger. The cat's learning, said Thorndike, is governed by the **law of effect.** According to this law, if a response made to a particular stimulus is followed by satisfaction (such as food or some other reward), that response is more likely to occur the next time the stimulus is present. Conversely, responses that produce discomfort are less likely to be performed again. Thorndike described this kind of learning as *instrumental conditioning.* Responses are strengthened when they are instrumental in producing rewards (E. L. Thorndike, 1905).

About forty years after Thorndike published his work, B. F. Skinner extended and formalized many of Thorndike's ideas. During instrumental conditioning, said Skinner, an organism learns a response by *operating on* the environment. He thus called the process of learning these responses **operant conditioning.** His primary aim was to analyze *how* behavior is changed by its consequences. To study operant conditioning, Skinner devised new tools. One was a chamber that came to be known as the *Skinner box* (see Figure 5.6).

Basic Components of Operant Conditioning

The Skinner box allowed researchers to arrange relationships between a particular response and its consequences. They could then analyze how those consequences affected behavior. The phenomena seen in classical conditioning (stimulus generalization, stimulus discrimination, extinction, and spontaneous recovery) also appear in operant conditioning. In operant conditioning, however, the focus is on operants, reinforcers, and discriminative stimuli.

Operants and Reinforcers   Skinner coined the term *operant* or *operant response* to distinguish the responses in operant conditioning from those in classical conditioning. In classical conditioning, the conditioned response does not affect whether or when the stimulus occurs. Pavlov's dogs salivated when a buzzer sounded. The salivation had no effect on the buzzer or on whether food was presented. In contrast, an **operant** has some effect on the world. It is a response that operates on the environment. When a child says, "Momma, I'm hungry" and is then fed, the child has made an operant response that influences when food will appear.

A **reinforcer** is a stimulus event that increases the probability that the operant behavior will occur again. There are two main types of reinforcers: positive and negative. **Positive reinforcers** strengthen a response if they are *presented* after that response occurs. The food given to a hungry pigeon after it pecks a key is a positive reinforcer for key pecking. Among people, positive reinforcers can include food, smiles, money, and other desirable outcomes. Presentation of a positive reinforcer after a response is called *positive reinforcement.* **Negative reinforcers** are the *removal* of unpleasant stimuli, such as pain or noise. For example, the disappearance of headache pain after you take a pain reliever acts as a negative reinforcer that strengthens the taking of that pain reliever in the future. The process of strengthening behavior (taking pain relievers) through the removal of an aversive stimulus (pain) is called *negative reinforcement.* Notice that reinforcement always *increases* the likelihood of the behavior that precedes it, whether the reinforcer is adding something pleasant or removing something unpleasant. Figure 5.7 shows this relationship.

Escape and Avoidance Conditioning   The effects of negative reinforcement can be studied through either escape conditioning or avoidance conditioning. **Escape conditioning** occurs when you learn to make a response to *end* an aversive stimulus. As Figure 5.8 shows, a dog can learn to jump over the barrier in a shuttle box to escape shock; parents often learn to give in to their children's demands because doing so stops an unpleasant behavior. For example, if a child throws a tantrum in a toy store, the parents may buy a

FIGURE 5.7

Positive and Negative Reinforcement

 List two examples of situations in which your behavior was affected by positive reinforcement and two in which you were affected by negative reinforcement. Remember that behavior is strengthened through positive reinforcement when something pleasant or desirable occurs following the behavior. Behavior is strengthened through negative reinforcement when the behavior results in the removal or termination of something unpleasant.

POSITIVE REINFORCEMENT

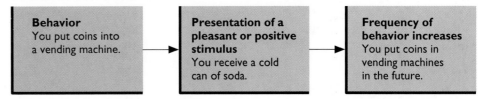

NEGATIVE REINFORCEMENT

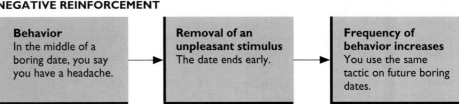

negative reinforcers　The removal of unpleasant stimuli, such as pain, that strengthens responses that precede the removal.

escape conditioning　The process of learning responses that terminate an aversive stimulus.

avoidance conditioning　The process of learning responses that avoid an aversive stimulus.

discriminative stimuli　Stimuli that signal whether reinforcement is available if a certain response is made.

toy for the child, thus stopping the tantrum. What behaviors have been reinforced? On the one hand, the child has been positively reinforced for throwing tantrums. On the other hand, the child has trained the parents through negative reinforcement—escape conditioning, in this case. The parents escape the tantrum by buying the toy. In the future, they may do so again.

Look again at Figure 5.8, and imagine that a buzzer sounds a few seconds before the shock occurs. In this situation, the dog can learn to jump the barrier at the sound of the buzzer and avoid the shock. Children, too, sometimes avoid being scolded by apologizing for misdeeds as soon as they see a parent's frown. When an animal or person responds to a signal in a way that *avoids* exposure to an impending aversive stimulus, **avoidance conditioning** has occurred.

These examples show that avoidance conditioning often represents a marriage of classical and operant conditioning. If a buzzer predicts shock (an unconditioned stimulus), the buzzer becomes a conditioned stimulus (CS). Through classical conditioning, the buzzer (now a CS) elicits a conditioned fear response (CR). Like the shock itself, conditioned fear is an unpleasant internal sensation. The animal then learns the instrumental response of jumping the barrier. The instrumental response (jumping) is reinforced because it terminates the unpleasant fear stimulus.

Avoidance conditioning is an important influence on everyday behavior. You go to work even when you would rather stay in bed. You stop at red lights even when you are in a hurry. Each of these behaviors reflects avoidance conditioning. They allow you to avoid a negative consequence, such as lost pay or a traffic ticket.

Avoidance is a difficult habit to break, partly because reduced fear reinforces avoidance responses (R. L. Solomon, Kamin, & Wynne, 1953). Avoidance responses, in turn, prevent the opportunity to learn that the "rules" may have changed and that avoidance is no longer necessary. If you fear elevators and avoid them, you will never discover that they are safe. Avoidance conditioning may also prevent people from learning new, more desirable behaviors. Fear of doing something embarrassing may cause people with limited social skills to shy away from social situations, but it also prevents them from learning how to be successful in those situations.

Discriminative Stimuli and Stimulus Control　Even if you have been reinforced for telling jokes, you are not likely to do so when you are alone. Pigeons show similar wisdom. If they are reinforced for pecking a key when a red light is on, but there is no reinforcement when a green light is on, they will eventually peck only when they see a red light. This behavior demonstrates the effect of **discriminative stimuli,** which are stimuli that signal whether reinforcement is available if a certain response is made. *Stimulus discrimination* occurs when an organism learns to make a particular response in the presence of one

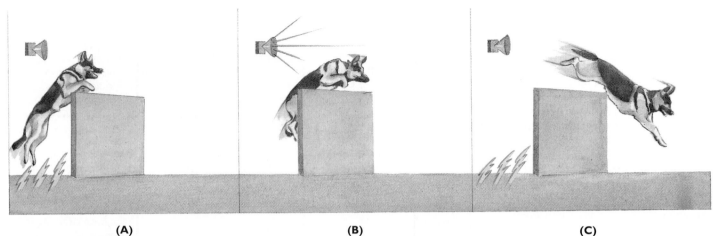

(A) **(B)** **(C)**

Source: Adapted from Hintzman (1978).

FIGURE 5.8

A Shuttle Box

A shuttle box has two compartments, usually separated by a barrier, and its floor is an electric grid. Shock can be administered through the grid to either compartment. In escape conditioning (A), the animal can get away from shock by jumping over the barrier when the shock occurs. In avoidance conditioning, a buzzer signals the onset of shock (B), and the animal can avoid the shock if it jumps as soon as the buzzer sounds (C).

stimulus but not another (see Figure 5.9). The response is then said to be under *stimulus control*. Stimulus discrimination allows people or animals to learn what is appropriate (reinforced) and inappropriate (not reinforced) in particular situations.

Stimulus generalization also occurs in operant conditioning. That is, an animal or person will perform a response in the presence of a stimulus that is similar to, but not exactly like, a stimulus that has signaled reinforcement in the past. The more similar the new stimulus is to the old one, the more likely it is that the response will be performed. Suppose you ate a wonderful meal at a restaurant built in the style of an Italian country house. The next time you go out, you might be attracted to another restaurant that looks like the one where you had that great meal.

Stimulus generalization and stimulus discrimination complement each other. In one study, for example, pigeons received food for pecking a key when they saw only certain works of art (Watanabe, Sakamoto, & Wakita, 1995). As a result, these birds learned to *discriminate* the works of the impressionist painter Claude Monet from those of the cubist painter Pablo Picasso. Later, when the birds were shown new paintings by other impressionist and cubist artists, they were able to *generalize* from the original artists to other artists who painted in the same style, as if they had learned the conceptual categories of "impressionism" and "cubism." We humans learn to place people and objects into even more finely detailed categories, such as "honest" or "dangerous." We discriminate one stimulus from

FIGURE 5.9

Stimulus Discrimination

In this experiment the rat could jump from a stand through any of three doors, but it was reinforced only if it jumped through the door that differed from the other two. The rat learned to do this quite well: On this trial, it discriminated vertical from horizontal stripes.

"Oh, not bad. The light comes on, I press the bar, they write me a check. How about you?"

another and then, through generalization, respond similarly to all those we perceive to be in a particular category. As we'll see in Chapter 14, on social psychology, prejudice is an example of category discrimination and then generalization about categories of people.

Forming and Strengthening Operant Behavior

Your daily life is full of examples of operant conditioning. You go to movies, parties, classes, and jobs primarily because doing so brings reinforcement. What is the effect of the type or timing of your reinforcers? How do you learn new behaviors? How can you get rid of old ones?

Shaping   Let's say you want to train your dog, Sugar, to sit and "shake hands." You figure that positive reinforcement should work, so you decide to give Sugar a treat every time she sits and shakes hands. But there's one small problem. Smart as Sugar is, she may never spontaneously make the desired response, in which case you'd never be able to give the reinforcer. The way around this problem is to shape Sugar's behavior. **Shaping** is the process of reinforcing *successive approximations* to the target behavior. For example, you might first give Sugar a treat whenever she sits down. Next, you might reinforce her only when she sits and partially lifts a paw. Finally, you might reinforce only complete paw lifting. Eventually, you would require Sugar to perform the entire sit-lift-shake sequence before giving the treat. Shaping is a powerful tool. Animal trainers have used it to teach chimpanzees to roller-skate, dolphins to jump through hoops, and pigeons to play Ping-Pong (Coren, 1999).

Secondary Reinforcement   **Primary reinforcers** are events or stimuli that satisfy needs basic to survival. Food and water are examples of primary reinforcers. Operant conditioning often begins using primary reinforcers, because their effects are powerful and automatic. But constantly giving Sugar food as a reward can be disruptive to training, because she will stop to eat after every response. Also, once she gets full, food will no longer act as an effective reinforcer. To avoid these problems, parents and animal trainers capitalize on the principle of secondary reinforcement.

Secondary reinforcers are previously neutral stimuli that take on reinforcing properties if paired with stimuli that are already reinforcing. In short, they are rewards that people or animals learn to like. If you say "Good girl!" just before feeding Sugar, those words will become reinforcing after a few pairings. "Good girl!" can then be used alone to reinforce Sugar's behavior. It helps if the words are again paired with food every now and then. This process is actually another application of classical conditioning. The primary

shaping   The reinforcement of responses that come successively closer to some desired response.

primary reinforcers   Events or stimuli that satisfy physiological needs basic to survival.

secondary reinforcers   Rewards that people or animals learn to like.

SECONDARY REINFORCEMENT A touch, a smile, or a loving look are among the many social stimuli that can serve as positive reinforcers for humans.

reinforcer (food) is the unconditioned stimulus. And because "Good girl!" has been repeatedly paired with the food, these sounds become a predictable signal for food. In other words, the sound of the words becomes a conditioned stimulus (CS). For this reason, secondary reinforcers are sometimes called *conditioned reinforcers*. As you might imagine, parents have used such reinforcers for generations.

Secondary reinforcement greatly expands the power of operant conditioning (B. Schwartz & Reisberg, 1991). The most obvious secondary reinforcer is money. As suggested by the plots of many movies and books, some people will do almost anything for it. Its reinforcing power lies in its association with the many rewards it can buy. What becomes a secondary reinforcer can vary a great deal from person to person and culture to culture. Tickets to a rock concert may be an effective secondary reinforcer for some people, but not for all. A ceremony honoring outstanding job performance might be strongly reinforcing in an individualist culture, but the same honor might be embarrassing for a person in a collectivist culture, where group cooperation is given greater value than personal distinction (A. P. Fiske et al., 1998). When carefully chosen, however, secondary reinforcers can build or maintain behavior, even when primary reinforcement is absent for long periods.

Delay and Size of Reinforcement   Much of our behavior is learned and maintained because it is regularly reinforced. But many of us overeat, smoke, drink too much, or procrastinate, even though we know these behaviors are bad for us. We may want to eliminate them, but they are hard to change. We seem to lack "self-control." But if behavior is controlled by its consequences, why do we perform acts that are ultimately self-defeating?

Part of the answer lies in the timing of reinforcers. The good feelings (positive reinforcers) that follow, say, excessive drinking are immediate. But hangovers and other negative consequences are usually delayed, weakening their impact. Operant conditioning is stronger when there is little delay in receiving a reinforcer. Thus, under some conditions, delaying a positive reinforcer for even a few seconds can decrease the effectiveness of positive reinforcement. (An advantage of praise and other secondary reinforcers is that they can easily be delivered immediately after the desired response occurs.) The size of the reinforcer is also important. In general, conditioning is faster when the reinforcer is large than when it is small.

Schedules of Reinforcement   A *continuous reinforcement schedule* is a procedure in which a reinforcer is delivered every time a particular response occurs. Although this arrangement is an effective way to begin the learning process, it can be impractical in the long run. More often, reinforcement is given only some of the time. The result is a *partial*, or *intermittent, reinforcement schedule*. Intermittent schedules determine when and how the reinforcer will be given. "When" refers to the number of responses that have to occur, or the amount of time that has to pass, before a reinforcer will occur. "How" refers to whether the reinforcer will be delivered on a predictable or unpredictable basis. There are four basic partial reinforcement schedules, as shown in Figure 5.10:

1. *Fixed-ratio (FR) schedules* provide reinforcement following a fixed (unchanging) number of responses. Rats might receive food after every tenth time they press a bar (FR 10) or after every twentieth time (FR 20). Assembly workers might be paid for every five computers they produce.

2. *Variable-ratio (VR) schedules* also call for reinforcement after a given number of responses. However, that number varies from one reinforcement to the next, so the particular response after which a reinforcement will be given cannot be predicted. On a VR 30 schedule, a rat will sometimes be reinforced after ten bar presses, and sometimes after fifty bar presses; but overall, the reinforcement will occur after an *average* of thirty responses. Gambling offers a variable-ratio schedule. Slot machines, for example, pay off only after a frustratingly unpredictable number of lever pulls, averaging perhaps one in twenty.

Schedules of Partial Reinforcement

These curves illustrate the patterns of behavior typically seen under different reinforcement schedules. The steeper the curve, the faster the response rate; the thin diagonal lines crossing the curves show when reinforcement was given. In general, the rate of responding is higher under ratio schedules than under interval schedules.

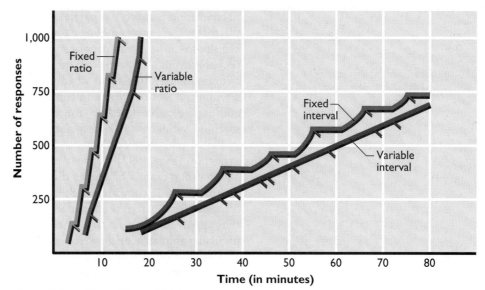

Source: Adapted from Skinner (1961).

Applying Psychology

REINFORCEMENT SCHEDULES ON THE JOB Workers at the Lincoln Electric Company, in Cleveland, Ohio, are paid for every piece of welding equipment they produce. This fixed-ratio reinforcement schedule results in very high production rates and in annual incomes of up to $85,000. While most of the employees like the reward system, they are not necessarily satisfied with their jobs. This may be because job satisfaction is usually based on factors other than high pay (see Chapter 8, on motivation and emotion).

3. *Fixed-interval (FI) schedules* provide reinforcement for the first response that occurs after some fixed time has passed since the last reward. On an FI 60 schedule, for instance, the first response after sixty seconds have passed will be rewarded, regardless of how many responses have been made during that interval. You may have noticed that some radio stations make use of fixed-interval schedules. Listeners who have won a call-in contest might have to wait at least ten days before they are eligible to win again.

4. *Variable-interval (VI) schedules* reinforce the first response after some period of time, but the amount of time varies unpredictably. So, on a VI 60 schedule, the first response that occurs after an average of 60 seconds is reinforced, but the actual time between reinforcements might vary anywhere from 1 to 120 seconds or more. Police in Illinois once used a VI schedule by stopping drivers at random times and awarding prizes to those who were buckled up (Mortimer et al., 1988). This strategy successfully encouraged seat belt use.

Different schedules of reinforcement produce different patterns of responding (Skinner, 1961a), but both fixed- and variable-ratio schedules produce high response rates overall. The reason, in both cases, is that the frequency of reward depends directly on the rate of responding. Under a fixed-interval schedule, it does not matter how many responses are made during the time between rewards. Because the timing of the reinforcement is so predictable, the rate of responding typically drops immediately after reinforcement, then increases as the time for another reward approaches. When teachers schedule quizzes on the same day each week, most students will study just before each quiz and then almost cease studying immediately afterward. By contrast, the possibility of unpredictable "pop" quizzes (on a variable-interval schedule) typically generates more consistent studying patterns.

Schedules and Extinction   Ending the relationship between an operant response and its consequences weakens that response. In fact, failure to reinforce a response eventually *extinguishes* it. The response occurs less and less often and eventually may disappear. If you repeatedly send e-mail to someone who never replies, you stop trying after a while. Extinction in operant conditioning does not totally erase learned relationships, though. If a discriminative stimulus for reinforcement reappears some time after an operant response has been extinguished, that response may recur (spontaneously recover). And if again reinforced, the response will be relearned rapidly.

In general, behaviors learned under a partial reinforcement schedule are far more difficult to extinguish than those learned on a continuous reinforcement schedule. This phenomenon is called the **partial reinforcement extinction effect.** Imagine, for example, that you are in a gambling casino, standing near a broken candy machine and a broken slot machine. If you deposit money in the broken candy machine, this behavior will probably extinguish (stop) very quickly. The candy machine should deliver its goodies on a continuous reinforcement schedule, so you can easily tell that it is not going to provide a reinforcer. Slot machines, in contrast, are known to offer rewards on an intermittent and unpredictable schedule. You might put in coin after coin, unsure of whether the machine is broken or is simply not paying off at that particular moment.

Partial reinforcement helps to explain why superstitious behavior is so resistant to extinction (Vyse, 1997). Suppose you take a shower just before hearing that you passed an important exam. The shower did nothing to cause this outcome. The reward followed it through sheer coincidence. Still, for some people, this *accidental reinforcement* can function like a partial reinforcement schedule, strengthening actions that precede, and thus *appear* to cause, reward. Therefore, someone who wins a lottery while wearing a particular shirt may begin wearing the "lucky shirt" all the time. Of course, if you wear a lucky shirt often enough, a rewarding event is bound to follow every now and then, on a very sparse, partial schedule.

Why Reinforcers Work

What makes a reinforcer reinforcing? For primary reinforcers, at least, the reason could be that they satisfy basic physiological needs for survival. Yet stimuli like saccharin, which have no nutritional value, can be as powerfully reinforcing as sugar, which is nutritious. And what about addictive drugs, which are also powerful reinforcers, even though they threaten the health of those who use them?

Research by biological psychologists suggests that reinforcers may work by exerting particular effects on the brain. In their classic study on this point, James Olds and Peter Milner (1954) discovered that mild electrical stimulation of certain areas of the hypothalamus can be a powerful reinforcer. Hungry rats will ignore food if they can press a lever that stimulates these "pleasure centers" in the brain (Olds, 1973). It is not yet clear whether physiological mechanisms underlie the power of all reinforcers, but evidence available so far certainly suggests that these mechanisms are important components of the process. We already know, for example, that activation of dopamine systems is associated with the pleasure of many stimuli, including food, sex, and some addictive drugs such as cocaine (Bardo, 1998).

Punishment and Learning

Positive and negative reinforcement *increase* the frequency of a response, either by presenting something pleasurable or by removing something unpleasant. In contrast, **punishment** presents an aversive stimulus or removes a pleasant one and *decreases* the frequency of the immediately preceding response. Swatting your dog with a newspaper when it begins chewing on your shoe presents an aversive stimulus following a response. And taking away a child's TV privileges because of rude behavior is a kind of punishment—sometimes called *penalty*—that removes a positive stimulus (see Figure 5.11).

Punishment and negative reinforcement are often confused, but they are quite different. Just remember that reinforcement of any type always *strengthens* behavior, whereas punishment always *weakens* behavior. If shock is *turned off* when a rat presses a lever, that is negative reinforcement. It increases the probability that the rat will press the lever when shock occurs again. But if shock is *turned on* when the rat presses the lever, that is punishment. The rat will be less likely to press the lever again. Now you decide: When a toddler reaches toward an electric outlet and her father says "NO!" and gently taps her hand, is that punishment or negative reinforcement? It is punishment, because it will reduce the likelihood of the behavior that preceded it.

Although punishment can change behavior, it has drawbacks. First, it does not "erase" an undesirable habit. It merely lowers the probability of its immediate recurrence. Children often repeat punished acts when they think they can do so without getting

partial reinforcement extinction effect A phenomenon in which behaviors learned under a partial reinforcement schedule are more difficult to extinguish than those learned on a continuous reinforcement schedule.

punishment The presentation of an aversive stimulus or the removal of a pleasant one following some behavior.

FIGURE 5.11

Two Kinds of Punishment

In one form of punishment, a behavior is followed by an aversive or unpleasant stimulus. In a second form of punishment, sometimes called *penalty,* **a pleasant stimulus is** *removed* **following a behavior. In either case, punishment decreases the chances that the behavior will occur in the future.**

PUNISHMENT I

| **Behavior**
You touch a hot iron. | → | **Presentation of an unpleasant stimulus**
Your hand is burned. | → | **Frequency of behavior decreases**
You no longer touch hot irons. |

PUNISHMENT II (Penalty)

| **Behavior**
You're careless with your ice cream cone. | → | **Removal of a pleasant stimulus**
The ice cream falls on the ground. | → | **Frequency of behavior decreases**
You're not as careless with the next cone. |

caught. Second, punishment can produce unwanted side effects. If you punish a child for swearing, the child may associate the punisher with the punishment and end up simply fearing you. Third, punishment is often ineffective unless it is given immediately after the response and each time the response is made. If a child gets into the cookie jar and enjoys a few cookies before being discovered and punished, the effect of the punishment will be greatly reduced. Fourth, physical punishment can become aggression, even abuse, when given in anger. Because children tend to imitate what they see, frequent punishment may lead them to behave aggressively themselves (S. Gilbert, 1997). Finally, although punishment signals that inappropriate behavior has occurred, it does not specify correct alternative behavior. An "F" on a term paper indicates that the assignment was poorly done, but the grade alone tells the student nothing about how to improve.

When used properly, however, punishment can work. As shown in Figure 5.12, for example, it can help children who suffer from certain developmental disorders or who engage in self-injurious behavior (J. E. Flavell et al., 1982). Punishment is especially effective when a few guidelines are followed. First, to prevent the development of a general fear of the punisher, specify why punishment is being given. Second, emphasize that the behavior, not the person, is being punished. Third, without being abusive, make sure the punishment is immediate and noticeable enough to eliminate the undesirable response. A half-hearted "Quit it" may actually reinforce a child's pranks, because almost any attention is rewarding to some children. Finally, identify and positively reinforce more appropriate responses.

FIGURE 5.12

Life-Saving Punishment

This child suffered from chronic ruminative disorder, a condition in which he regurgitated all food. At left, the boy was approximately one year old and had been vomiting for four months. At right is the same child thirteen days after punishment with electric shock had eliminated the vomiting response; his weight had increased 26 percent. He was physically and psychologically healthy when tested six months, one year, and two years later (Lang & Melamed, 1969).

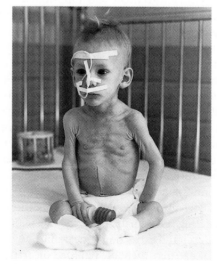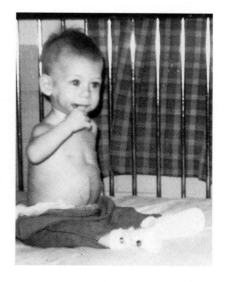

Source: Lang & Melamed (1969).

in review

Reinforcement and Punishment

Concept	Description	Example or Comment
Positive reinforcement	Increasing the frequency of behavior by following it with the presentation of a positive reinforcer—a pleasant, positive stimulus or experience	Saying "Good job" after someone works hard to perform a task.
Negative reinforcement	Increasing the frequency of behavior by following it with the removal of an unpleasant stimulus or experience	Pressing the "mute" button on a TV remote control removes the sound of an obnoxious commercial.
Escape conditioning	Learning to make a response that removes an unpleasant stimulus	A little boy learns that crying will cut short the time that he must stay in his room.
Avoidance conditioning	Learning to make a response that avoids an unpleasant stimulus	You slow your car to the speed limit when you spot a police car, thus avoiding being stopped and reducing the fear of a fine. Very resistant to extinction.
Punishment	Decreasing the frequency of behavior by either presenting an unpleasant stimulus (punishment I) or removing a pleasant one (punishment II, or penalty)	Swatting the dog after she steals food from the table, or taking a favorite toy away from a child who misbehaves. A number of cautions should be kept in mind before using punishment.

When these guidelines are not followed, the beneficial effects of punishment may be wiped out or may be only temporary (Hyman, 1995). As demonstrated in the U.S. prison system, punishment alone does not usually lead to rehabilitation. Following their release, about two-thirds of prison inmates are rearrested for felonies or serious misdemeanors within three years, and about 40 percent will go back to prison (U.S. Department of Justice, 1997).

Operant Conditioning of Human Behavior

Although the principles of operant conditioning were originally worked out with animals in the laboratory, they are valuable for understanding human behavior. ("In Review: Reinforcement and Punishment" summarizes some key concepts of operant conditioning.) Effective use of reinforcements and punishments by parents, teachers, and peers is vital to helping children learn what is and is not appropriate behavior at the dinner table, in the classroom, or at a birthday party. People learn how to be "civilized" in their own particular culture partly through experiencing positive and negative responses from others. For example, the prevalence of aggressive behavior varies considerably from culture to culture, in part because some cultures reward it more than others. In some Inuit cultures, for example, aggressive behavior is actively discouraged and extremely rare (Banta, 1997). It is much more common among the Yanomamo, a South American Indian group in which a male's status is based on his ability to fight and even kill. Differing patterns of rewards and punishments for boys and girls also underlie the development of behavior that fits culturally approved *gender roles,* a topic explored in more detail in Chapter 9, on human development.

The scientific study of operant conditioning has led to numerous treatment programs for altering problematic behavior. Behavior modification programs that combine the use of rewards and extinction (or carefully administered punishment) have helped countless mental patients, mentally retarded or brain-damaged individuals, autistic children, and hard-to-manage youngsters to develop the behavior patterns they need to live happier and more productive lives (e.g., Ayllon, 1999; Kazdin, 1977). These programs include establishing goal behaviors, choosing reinforcers and punishers, and developing a systematic plan for applying them to achieve desired changes. Many self-help books also incorporate principles of positive reinforcement, recommending self-reward following each small victory in people's efforts to lose weight, stop smoking, avoid procrastination, or reach other goals (Seligman, 1995).

When people cannot do anything to alter the consequences of a behavior, discriminative stimuli may hold the key to changing that behavior. For example, people trying to quit smoking often find it easier to abstain if, at first, they stay away from bars and other places where there are discriminative stimuli for smoking. Old cues can trigger old behavior, so they should avoid the old cues until new behavior can be established. Stimulus control can also help alleviate insomnia. Insomniacs tend to use their beds for nonsleeping activities such as watching television, writing letters, reading magazines, worrying, and so on. Soon the bedroom becomes a discriminative stimulus for so many activities that relaxation and sleep become less and less likely. Sleep restriction therapy strongly encourages insomniacs to use their beds *only* for sleeping, which makes it more likely that they will sleep better (Morin et al., 1993).

Cognitive Processes in Learning

■ **Can people learn to be helpless?**

In the first half of the twentieth century, psychologists tended to regard classical and operant conditioning as resulting from the automatic, unthinking formation or modification of associations between observable stimuli and observable responses. Little consideration was given to the role of mental activity that might accompany the learning process.

This strictly behavioral view of classical and operant conditioning is challenged by the cognitive approach, which has become increasingly influential in recent decades. Cognitive psychologists see a common thread in these two forms of learning. Both classical and operant conditioning, they argue, help animals and people to detect and understand what causes what (Young, 1995). By extension, both types of conditioning may result not only from automatic associations but also from the *mental processes* that underlie adaptation to, and understanding of, the world around us. Certainly there is evidence that cognitive processes play an important role in learning. The importance of how people represent, store, and use information has been demonstrated in research on learned helplessness, latent learning, cognitive maps, insight, and observational learning.

Learned Helplessness

Babies learn that crying attracts attention. Children learn how to make the TV louder. Adults learn what it takes to succeed in the workplace. In short, people learn to expect that certain actions on their part predict certain consequences. If this learning is disrupted, problems may result. One such problem is **learned helplessness,** a tendency to give up any effort to control the environment (Seligman, 1975).

Learned helplessness was first demonstrated in animals. As described earlier, dogs placed in a shuttle box will learn to jump over a partition to escape a shock (see Figure 5.8). But if the dogs are first placed in a restraining harness and receive shocks that they cannot escape, they later do not even try to escape when the shock is turned on in the shuttle box (Overmier & Seligman, 1967). It is as if the animals had learned that "shock happens, and there is nothing I can do about it." Do people learn the same lesson?

learned helplessness A process in which a person or animal stops trying to exert control after experience suggests that no control is possible.

What lessons do abused and neglected children learn about their ability to get what they need from the environment? Do they learn that even their best efforts result in failure? Do they give up even trying? Why would a student with above-average ability tell a counselor, "I can't do math"? How do people develop an "I can't do it" attitude?

What was the researcher's question?

Can lack of control over the environment lead to helplessness in humans? Donald Hiroto (1974) conducted an experiment to test the hypothesis that people develop learned helplessness either after experiencing lack of control or after simply being told that their control is limited.

How did the researcher answer the question?

Hiroto assigned research participants to one of three groups. One group heard a series of thirty random bursts of loud, obnoxious noise and, like dogs receiving inescapable shock, had no way to stop it. A second group could control the noise by pressing a button to turn it off. The third group heard no noise at all. After this preliminary phase, all three groups were exposed to eighteen additional bursts of noise, each preceded by a red warning light. During this second phase, *all* participants could stop the noise by moving a lever. However, they did not know whether to push the lever left or right on any given trial. Still, they could prevent the noise if they acted quickly enough. Before these new trials began, the experimenter told half the participants in each group that avoiding or escaping the noise depended on their *skill*. The other half were told that their success would be a matter of *chance*.

What did the researcher find?

The people who had previously experienced lack of control now failed to control noise on about four times as many trials (50 percent versus 13 percent) as did those who had earlier been in control. This finding was similar to that of the research with dogs and inescapable shock. When the dogs were later placed in a situation where they could escape or avoid shock, they did not even try. Humans, too, seem to use prior experiences to guide later efforts to try, or not to try, to control their environment.

Expectation of control, whether accurate or not, also had an effect on behavior. In Hiroto's study, those participants who expected that *skill* could control the noise exerted control on significantly more trials than did those who expected chance to govern the result. This outcome occurred regardless of whether the participants had experienced control before.

What do the results mean?

These results support Hiroto's hypothesis that people, like animals, tend to make less effort to control their environment when prior experience suggests that those efforts will be in vain. But unlike animals, humans need only be *told* that they have no control or are powerless in order for this same effect to occur.

Hiroto's (1974) results appear to reflect a general phenomenon. When prior experience leads people to *believe* that there is nothing they can do to change their lives or control their destiny, they may stop trying to improve their lot (Dweck, Chiu, & Hong, 1995; C. Peterson, Maier, & Seligman, 1993). Instead, they may passively endure painful situations. Has this ever happened to you?

◼ What do we still need to know?

Further research is needed on when and how learned helplessness affects people's thoughts, feelings, and actions. For example, could learned helplessness help explain why some battered women remain with abusive partners? We do know that learned-helplessness experiences are associated with the development of a generally pessimistic way of thinking that can produce depression and other mental disorders (Peterson & Seligman, 1984). People with this *pessimistic explanatory style* see the good things that happen to them as temporary and due to chance, and the bad things as permanent and due to internal factors (e.g., lack of ability). This explanatory style has, in fact, been associated with poor grades, inadequate sales performance, health problems, and other negative outcomes (C. Peterson & Barrett, 1987; Seligman & Schulman, 1986; S. E. Taylor, 1998a). However, the mechanism responsible for this connection remains unknown (Wiebe & Smith, 1997); understanding how pessimistic (or optimistic) explanatory styles can lead to negative (or positive) consequences will be an important new focus of research (Salovey, Rothman, & Rodin, 1998). Research is also needed to determine how best to minimize learned helplessness and maximize learned optimism in areas such as education, parenting, and psychotherapy.

Latent Learning and Cognitive Maps

Decades ago, Edward Tolman studied cognitive processes in learning by watching rats try to solve mazes. The rats' task was to find the goal box where food awaited. As shown in Figure 5.13, the rats at first took many wrong turns. Over time, though, they made fewer and fewer mistakes. The behavioral interpretation of this result was that the rats learned a long chain of turning responses that were reinforced by food. Tolman disagreed and offered evidence for a cognitive interpretation.

In one of Tolman's studies, three groups of rats were placed in the same maze once a day for several consecutive days (Tolman & Honzik, 1930). For Group A, food was placed in the goal box of the maze on each trial. These rats gradually improved their performance. Group B also ran the maze once a day, but there was never any food in the goal box. The animals in Group B continued to make many errors. Neither of these results is surprising.

FIGURE 5.13

Latent Learning

This graph shows the average number of wrong turns rats made on their way to the goal box of a maze. Notice that when rats in Group C did not receive food reinforcement, they continued to make many errors. The day after first finding food there, however, they took almost no wrong turns! The reinforcement, argued Tolman, affected only the rats' *performance;* they must have *learned* the maze earlier, without reinforcement.

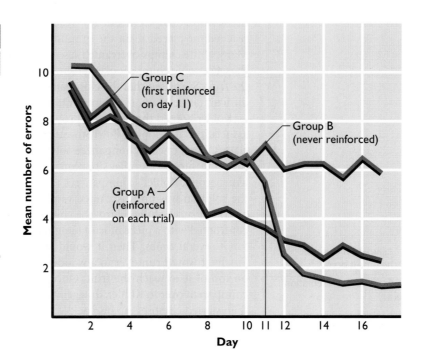

The third group of rats, Group C, was the critical one. For the first ten days, they received no reinforcement for running the maze and continued to make many mistakes. On the eleventh day, food was placed in the goal box for the first time. What do you think happened? On the day after receiving reinforcement, these rats made almost no mistakes (again, see Figure 5.13). In fact, their performance was as good as that of the group that had been reinforced every day. The single reinforcement trial on day 11 produced a dramatic change in their performance the next day.

Tolman argued that these results support two conclusions. First, because the rats in Group C improved their performance the *first time* they ran the maze after being reinforced, the reinforcement on day 11 could not have significantly affected their *learning* of the maze. Rather, the reinforcement simply changed their subsequent *performance*. They must have learned the maze earlier as they wandered around making mistakes on their way to the end of the maze. These rats demonstrated **latent learning**—learning that is not evident when it first occurs. Second, the rats' sudden improvement in performance after the first reinforcement trial could have occurred only if the rats had earlier developed a cognitive map of the maze. A **cognitive map** is a mental representation of some physical arrangement—in this case, a maze.

Tolman concluded that cognitive maps develop naturally through experience, even in the absence of any overt response or reinforcement. Research on learning in the natural environment has supported this view. We develop mental maps of shopping malls and city streets, even when we receive no direct reward for doing so (A. Tversky & Kahneman, 1991).

Much as Gestalt psychologists believe that a whole perception is more than the sum of its parts (see Chapter 3), cognitive psychologists see learning as more than the sum of reinforcement effects and automatic associations. And just as our perceptions depend on the meaning we attach to sensations, some forms of learning require higher mental processes and depend on how the learner attaches meaning to events.

Insight and Learning

Wolfgang Köhler was a psychologist whose work on the cognitive aspects of learning happened almost by accident. He was visiting the Atlantic island of Tenerife when World War I broke out in 1914. As a German on an island controlled by Germany's enemy, Britain, Köhler was confined there until the war ended in 1918. He devoted his time to studying problem solving in a colony of local chimpanzees (Köhler, 1924).

For example, Köhler would put a chimpanzee in a cage and place a piece of fruit where the chimp could see it but not reach it. He sometimes hung the fruit too high to be reached, or placed it on the ground too far outside the animal's cage to be retrieved. Many of the chimps overcame these obstacles easily. If the fruit was out of reach outside the cage, some chimps looked around the cage, found a long stick, and used it to rake in the fruit. Surprised that the chimpanzees could solve these problems, Köhler tried more difficult tasks. Again, the chimps quickly got to the fruit, as Figure 5.14 illustrates.

Köhler argued that animals' problem solving does not have to depend on automatic associations developing slowly through trial and error. Three observations supported his claims. First, once a chimpanzee solved a particular problem, it would immediately do the same thing in a similar situation. In other words, it acted as if it understood the problem. Second, Köhler's chimpanzees rarely tried a solution that did not work. Apparently, the solution was not discovered randomly, but "thought out" ahead of time and then acted out successfully. Third, the chimps often reached a solution quite suddenly. When confronted with a piece of fruit hanging from a string, for instance, a chimp would jump for it several times. Then it would stop jumping, look up, and pace back and forth. Finally it would run over to a wooden crate, place it directly under the fruit, and climb on top of it to reach the fruit. Once, when there were no other objects in the cage, a chimp went over to Köhler, dragged him by the arm until he stood beneath the fruit, and then started climbing up his back!

Köhler believed that the only explanation for these results was that the chimpanzees suddenly had **insight** into the problem as a whole. They did not, he said, solve the prob-

latent learning Learning that is not demonstrated at the time it occurs.

cognitive map A mental representation of the environment.

insight A sudden understanding about what is required to produce a desired effect.

(A) (B) (C)

Source: Köhler (1976).

FIGURE 5.14

Insight

Here are three impressive examples of problem solving by chimpanzees. In Part A the animal fixed a fifteen-foot pole in the ground, climbed to the top, and dropped down after grabbing the fruit. In Part B the chimp stacked two boxes from different areas of the compound, climbed to the top, and used a pole to knock down the fruit. The chimp in Part C stacked three boxes and climbed them to reach the fruit.

lem simply through forming associations between responses and consequences. Some psychologists have argued that insight does not develop as quickly as Köhler's descriptions suggest. They see insight as the result of actual trial and error experimentation (Harlow, 1949) or of an extended "mental trial-and-error" process in which people (and some animals) envision a course of action, mentally simulate its results, compare it with the imagined outcome of other alternatives, and then settle on the course of action most likely to aid complex problem solving and decision making (D. N. Klein, 1993).

Observational Learning: Learning by Imitation

People learn a lot from personal experience, but they can also learn by observing what others do, and what happens to them when they do it. Learning by watching others—a process called **observational learning,** or *social learning*—is efficient and adaptive. We don't have to find out for ourselves that a door is locked or an iron is hot if we have just seen someone else try the door or suffer a burn.

Modeling and Vicarious Conditioning   Children are particularly influenced by the adults and peers who act as *models* for appropriate behavior. In a classic experiment, Albert Bandura showed nursery school children a film starring an adult and a large, inflatable, bottom-heavy "Bobo" doll (Bandura, 1965). The adult in the film punched the Bobo doll in the nose, kicked it, threw things at it, and hit its head with a hammer while saying things like "sockeroo!" There were different endings to the film. Some children saw an ending in which the aggressive adult was called a "champion" by a second adult and rewarded with candy and soft drinks. Some saw the aggressor scolded and called a "bad person." Some saw a neutral ending in which there was neither reward nor punishment. After the film, each child was allowed to play alone with a Bobo doll. How the children played in this and similar studies led to some important conclusions about learning and the role of cognitive factors in it.

observational learning   Learning by watching the behavior of others.

LEARNING BY IMITATION Much of our behavior is learned by imitating others, especially those who serve as role models. To appreciate the impact of social learning in your life, list five examples of how your own actions, speech, appearance, or mannerisms have come to match those of a parent, a sibling, a friend, a teacher, or even a celebrity.

Bandura found that children who saw the adult rewarded for aggression showed the most aggressive acts in play (see Figure 5.15). They had received **vicarious conditioning,** a kind of observational learning through which a person is influenced by watching or hearing about the consequences of others' behavior. The children who had seen the adult punished for aggressive acts initially showed less aggression, but they still learned something. When later offered rewards for all the filmed aggressive acts they could perform, these children displayed just as many of these acts as the children who watched the

FIGURE 5.15

Observational Learning

Albert Bandura found that after observing an aggressive model, many children imitate the model's acts precisely, especially if the model's aggression was rewarded.

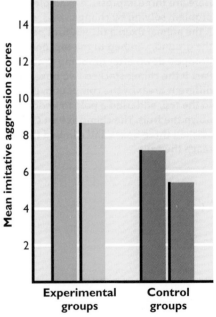

Aggressive model rewarded
Aggressive model punished
Non-aggressive model
No model

Source: Bandura, Ross, & Ross (1963).

adult being rewarded. Observational learning can occur even when there are no vicarious consequences; many children in the neutral condition also imitated the model's aggression.

Observational learning is a powerful source of human socialization throughout development (Bandura, 1999). Experiments show that children are more willing to help and share after seeing a demonstration of helping by an impressive model. This effect is observed even when several months have elapsed since the demonstration (Schroeder et al., 1995). Fears, too, can be learned by watching fearfulness in others (Cook & Mineka, 1987; Kleinknecht, 1991).

THINKING CRITICALLY

Does Watching Violence on Television Make People More Violent?

If observational learning is important, then surely television—and televised violence—must teach children a great deal. It is estimated that the average child in the United States spends more time watching television than attending school (Hepburn, 1995; Nielsen Media, 1990). Much of what children see is violent (Seppa, 1997). Prime-time programs in the United States present an average of 5 violent acts per hour. Some Saturday morning cartoons include more than 20 per hour (American Psychological Association, 1993; Gerbner, Morgan, & Signorielli, 1994). As a result, the average child will have witnessed at least 8,000 murders and more than 100,000 other acts of televised violence *before finishing elementary school* (Kunkel et al., 1996).

Psychologists have long speculated that watching so much violence might be emotionally arousing, making viewers more likely to react violently to frustration (Huston & Wright, 1989). Indeed, there is evidence that exposure to media violence can trigger or amplify viewers' aggressive thoughts and feelings, thus increasing the likelihood that they will act aggressively (C. A. Anderson & Dill, 2000; Bushman, 1998). Televised violence might also provide models that viewers imitate, particularly if the violence is carried out by the "good guys" (Bandura, 1983). Finally, prolonged viewing of violent TV programs might "desensitize" viewers, making them less distressed when they see others suffer and less disturbed about inflicting pain on others (Aronson, 1999b; Donnerstein, Slaby, & Eron, 1995). Concern over the influence of violence on television has recently led to the development of a violence-blocking "V-Chip" for new television sets in the United States.

What am I being asked to believe or accept?

Many have argued that watching violence on television *causes* violent behavior in viewers (Eron et al., 1996; Huesmann, 1998). In 1993, a National Academy of Science report concluded that "overall, the vast majority of studies, whatever their methodology, showed that exposure to television violence resulted in increased aggressive behavior, both contemporaneously and over time" (Reiss & Roth, 1993, p. 371). An American Psychological Association Commission on Violence and Youth reached the same conclusion (American Psychological Association, 1993).

Is there evidence available to support the claim?

Three types of evidence back up the claim that watching violent television programs increases violent behavior. First, there are anecdotes and case studies. Children have poked one another in the eye after watching the Three Stooges appear to do so on television. And adults have claimed that watching TV shows prompted them to commit murders or other violent acts matching those seen on the shows.

Second, many correlational studies have found a strong link between watching violent television programs and later acts of aggression and violence. One such study tracked people from the time they were six or seven (in 1977) until they reached their early twenties (in 1992). Those who watched more violent television as children were significantly more aggressive as adults (Huesmann et al., 1997) and more likely to engage in criminal activity (Huesmann, 1995). They were also more likely to use physical punishment on

vicarious conditioning A kind of observational learning through which a person is influenced by watching or hearing about the consequences of others' behavior.

their own children, who themselves tended to be much more aggressive than average. These latter results were found not only in the United States, but also in Israel, Australia, Poland, the Netherlands, and even Finland, where the number of violent TV shows is very small (Centerwall, 1990; Huesmann & Eron, 1986).

Finally, the results of numerous experiments support the view that TV violence increases aggression among viewers (American Psychological Association, 1993; Paik & Comstock, 1994; Reiss & Roth, 1993). In one study, groups of boys watched violent or nonviolent programs in a controlled setting and then played floor hockey (Josephson, 1987). Boys who had watched the violent shows were more likely than those who had watched nonviolent programs to behave aggressively on the hockey floor. This effect was greatest for boys who had the most aggressive tendencies to begin with. More extensive experiments in which children are exposed for long periods to carefully controlled types of television programs also suggest that exposure to large amounts of violent activity on television results in aggressive behavior (Eron et al., 1996).

Can that evidence be interpreted another way?

Anecdotal reports and case studies are certainly open to different interpretations. If people face imprisonment or execution for their violent acts, how much credibility can we give to their claims that their actions were triggered by television programs? How many other people might say that the same programs made them *less* likely to be violent? Anecdotes alone do not provide a good basis for drawing solid scientific conclusions.

What about the correlational evidence? Recall that a *correlation* between two variables does not necessarily mean that one *caused* the other. Both might be caused by a third factor. Why are certain people watching so much television violence in the first place? This question suggests two possible "third factors" that might account for the observed relationship between watching TV violence and acting aggressively.

First, people who tend to be aggressive may prefer to watch more violent TV programs *and* behave aggressively toward others. So personality may partly account for the observed correlations (e.g., Aluja-Fabregat & Torrubia-Beltri, 1998). Second, perhaps poverty, unemployment, or the effects of drugs and alcohol leave certain people more time to watch television and leave them with frustration or other stressors that trigger aggressive behavior.

Finally, some researchers question whether the results of controlled experiments on the effects of televised violence extend beyond the experimental situation (C. A. Anderson, Lindsay, & Bushman, 1999). Who is to say, for example, whether an increase in aggressive acts during a hockey game has any later bearing on a child's tendency to commit an act of violence?

What evidence would help to evaluate the alternatives?

By their nature, correlational studies of the role of TV violence in violent behavior can never be conclusive. As we've pointed out, a third, unidentified causal variable could always be responsible for the results. More important would be further evidence from controlled experiments in which equivalent groups of people were given different, long-term "doses" of TV violence, and its effects on their subsequent behavior were observed. Such experiments could also explore the circumstances under which different people (for example, children versus adults) are affected by various forms of violence. However, studies like these create an ethical dilemma. If watching violent television programs *does* cause violent behavior, are psychologists justified in creating conditions that might lead some people to be more violent? If such violence occurred, would the researchers be partly responsible to the victims and to society? If some participants commit violent acts, should the researchers continue the experiment to establish a pattern, or should they terminate the participation of those individuals? Difficulty in answering questions like these is partly responsible for the use of short-term experiments and correlational designs in this research area, as well as for some of the remaining uncertainty about the effects of television violence.

What conclusions are the most reasonable?

The evidence collected so far makes it reasonable to conclude that watching TV violence may be one cause of violent behavior (Huesmann et al., 1997; S. L. Smith & Donnerstein, 1998). But any cause-effect relationship between watching TV violence and acting violently is not an inevitable one. There are many circumstances in which the effect does not occur (Charleton, Gunter, & Coles, 1998; Freedman, 1992). Parents, peers, and other environmental influences, along with personality factors, may dampen or amplify the effect of watching televised violence. Indeed, not every viewer interprets violence in the same way, and not every viewer is equally vulnerable (Wood, Wong, & Chachere, 1991). The most vulnerable may be those who are most aggressive or violence-prone in the first place, a trait that could well have been acquired by observing the behavior of parents or peers (Huesmann et al, 1997).

Still, the fact that violence on television *can* have a causal impact on violent behavior is reason for serious concern. This issue continues to influence public debate about what should, and should not, be aired on television (Glod, 1998).

Using Research on Learning to Help People Learn

What should teachers learn about learning?

Teaching and training—explicit efforts to assist learners in mastering a skill—are major aspects of socialization in virtually every culture. The study of how people learn thus has important implications for improved teaching in our schools (N. M. Lambert, 1999; Woolfolk-Hoy, 1999) and for helping people develop skills.

Classrooms Across Cultures

Many people believe that schools in the United States are not doing a very good job (Associated Press, 1997; Carnegie Task Force, 1996; Penner et al., 1994). The average performance of U.S. students on tests of reading, math, and other basic academic skills has tended to fall short of that of youngsters in other countries, especially Asian countries (International Association for the Evaluation of Education Achievement, 1999). In one comparison study, Harold Stevenson (1992) followed a sample of pupils in Taiwan, Japan, and the United States from first grade, in 1980, to eleventh grade, in 1991. In the first grade, the Asian students scored no higher than their U.S. peers on tests of mathematical aptitude and skills, nor did they enjoy math more. However, by the fifth grade the U.S. students had fallen far behind. Corresponding differences were seen in reading skills.

Important potential causes of these differences were found in the classroom itself. In a typical U.S. classroom session, teachers talked to students as a group; then students worked at their desks independently. Reinforcement or other feedback about performance on their work was usually delayed until the next day or, often, not provided at all. In contrast, the typical Japanese classroom placed greater emphasis on cooperative work between students (Kristof, 1997). Teachers provided more immediate feedback on a one-to-one basis. And there was an emphasis on creating teams of students with varying abilities, an arrangement in which faster learners help teach slower ones. However, before concluding that the differences in performance are the result of social factors alone, we must consider another important distinction: The Japanese children practiced more. They spent more days in school during the year and, on average, spent more hours doing homework. Interestingly, they were also given longer recesses than U.S. students and had more opportunities to get away from the classroom during a typical school day.

Although the significance of these cultural differences in learning and teaching is not yet clear, the educational community in the United States is paying attention to them. Indeed, psychologists and educators are considering how principles of learning can be applied to improve education (Bransford, Brown, & Cocking, 1999; Woolfolk-Hoy, 1999). For

Applying Psychology

RECIPROCAL TEACHING Ann Brown and her colleagues (1992) have demonstrated the success of *reciprocal teaching,* in which children take turns teaching each other. This technique is similar to the cooperative arrangements seen in Japanese education.

LEARNING FROM MISTAKES Good coaches provide enough feedback to help budding athletes develop their skills, but not so much that the coaching interferes with the learning process. Striking this delicate balance is one of the greatest challenges faced by coaches, and by all teachers.

example, anecdotal and experimental evidence suggests that some of the most successful educational techniques are those that apply basic principles of operant conditioning, offering frequent testing, positive reinforcement for correct performance and immediate corrective feedback following mistakes (Kass, 1999; Oppel, 2000; Walberg, 1987).

Active Learning

The importance of cognitive processes in learning is apparent in instructional methods that emphasize *active learning.* These methods take many forms, including, for example, small-group problem-solving tasks, discussion of "one-minute essays" written in class, use of "thumbs up" or "thumbs down" to indicate agreement or disagreement with the instructor's assertions, and multiple-choice questions that give students feedback about their understanding of the previous fifteen minutes of a lecture. Students typically find classes that include active learning experiences to be interesting and enjoyable (Mehta, 1995; Moran, 2000; B. Murray, 2000). In addition, active learning methods help students go beyond memorizing isolated facts; these methods encourage students to think more deeply, consider how new material relates to what they already know, and apply it in new situations. This kind of thinking also makes the material easier to remember, which is why we have included so many opportunities for you to actively learn, rather than just passively read, the material in this book.

Active learning strategies have been found to be superior to passive teaching methods in a number of experiments with children and adults (Meyers & Jones, 1993). In one study, a fifth-grade teacher spent some days calling only on those students whose hands were raised. The rest listened passively. On other days, *all* students were required to answer every question by holding up a card with their response written on it. Scores on next-day quizzes and biweekly tests showed that students remembered more of the material covered on the active learning days than on the "passive" days (R. Gardner, Heward, & Grossi, 1994). In another study of two consecutive medical school classes taught by the same instructor, scores on the final exam were significantly higher when students learned mainly through small-group discussions and case studies than mainly through lectures (Chu, 1994). Similarly, among adults being taught to use a new computer program, active learning with "hands-on" practice was more effective than passively watching a demonstration video (Kerr & Payne, 1994). Finally, high school and college students who passively listened to a physics lecture received significantly lower scores on a test of lecture content than did those who participated in a virtual reality lab that allowed them to "interact" with the physical forces covered in the lecture (Brelsford, 1993). Rigorous experimental research is still needed, however, to compare the short- and long-term effects of active learning with those of more traditional methods.

Skill Learning

The complex action sequences, or *skills,* that people learn to perform in everyday life develop through learning processes that include feedback and, of course, lots of practice. Indeed, *practice*—the repeated performance of a skill—is critical to mastery. For perceptual-motor skills such as billiards or piano, both physical and mental practice are beneficial (Druckman & Bjork, 1994). To be most effective, practice should continue past the point of correct performance until the skill can be performed automatically, with little or no attention. Feedback about the correctness of the response is also necessary. As with any learning process, the feedback should come soon enough to be effective, but not so quickly that it interferes with the learner's efforts to learn independently.

Large amounts of guidance may produce very good performance during practice, but too much guidance may impair later performance (Kluger & DeNisi, 1998; Wickens, 1992). For instance, coaching students about correct responses in math may impair their ability later to retrieve the correct response from memory on their own. Independent practice at retrieving previously learned responses or information requires more effort, but it is critical for skill development (Ericsson & Charness, 1994). There is little or no evidence to support "sleep learning" or similar schemes designed to make learning effortless (Druckman & Bjork, 1994). In short, "no pain, no gain."

active review   Learning

Linkages

As noted in Chapter 1, all of psychology's subfields are related to one another. Our discussion of opponent process theory and drug effects illustrates just one way in which the topic of this chapter, learning, is linked to the subfield of consciousness (Chapter 4). The Linkages diagram shows ties to two other subfields as well, and there are many more ties throughout the book. Looking for linkages among subfields will help you see how they all fit together and help you better appreciate the big picture that is psychology.

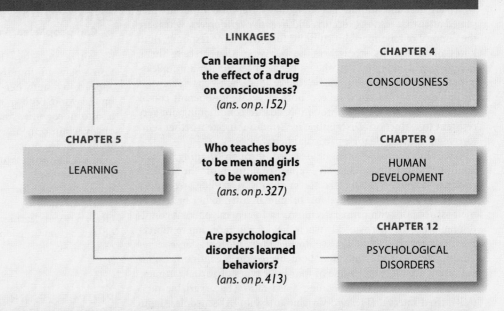

LINKAGES

CHAPTER 5

LEARNING

Can learning shape the effect of a drug on consciousness?
(ans. on p. 152)

CHAPTER 4

CONSCIOUSNESS

Who teaches boys to be men and girls to be women?
(ans. on p. 327)

CHAPTER 9

HUMAN DEVELOPMENT

Are psychological disorders learned behaviors?
(ans. on p. 413)

CHAPTER 12

PSYCHOLOGICAL DISORDERS

Summary

Individuals adapt to changes in the environment through the process of *learning,* which is the modification through experience of preexisting behavior and understanding.

CLASSICAL CONDITIONING: LEARNING SIGNALS AND ASSOCIATIONS
How did Russian dogs teach psychologists about learning?

One form of learning is *classical conditioning.* It occurs when a *conditioned stimulus,* or *CS* (such as a tone), is repeatedly paired with an *unconditioned stimulus,* or *UCS* (such as meat powder on a dog's tongue), which naturally brings about an *unconditioned response,* or *UCR* (such as salivation). Eventually the conditioned stimulus will elicit a response, known as the *conditioned response,* or *CR,* even when the unconditioned stimulus is not presented.

In general, the strength of a conditioned response grows as CS-UCS pairings continue. If the UCS is no longer paired with the CS, the conditioned response eventually disappears; this is *extinction.* After extinction, the conditioned response often reappears if the CS is presented after some time; this is *spontaneous recovery.* In addition, if the conditioned and unconditioned stimuli are paired once or twice after extinction, *reconditioning* occurs; that is, the conditioned response reverts to its original strength.

Because of *stimulus generalization,* conditioned responses occur to stimuli that are similar, but not identical to, conditioned stimuli. Generalization is limited by *stimulus discrimination,* which prompts conditioned responses to some stimuli but not to others.

Classical conditioning involves learning that the CS is an event that predicts the occurrence of another event, the UCS. The conditioned response is not just an automatic reflex but a means through which animals and people develop mental representations of the relation-

ships between events. Classical conditioning works best when the conditioned stimulus precedes the unconditioned stimulus by intervals ranging from less than a second to a minute or more, depending on the stimuli involved. Conditioning is also more likely when the CS reliably signals the UCS. In general, the strength of a conditioned response and the speed of conditioning increase as the intensity of the UCS—and the strength of the CS—increases. The particular stimulus likely to become a CS linked to a subsequent UCS depends in part on which stimulus was being attended to when the UCS occurred. *Second-order conditioning* occurs when a conditioned stimulus becomes powerful enough to make CSs out of stimuli associated with it. Some stimuli are easier to associate than others; organisms seem to be biologically prepared to learn certain associations, as exemplified by taste aversions.

Classical conditioning plays a role in the development and treatment of phobias and in procedures for identifying people at risk for Alzheimer's disease.

Habituation is reduced responsiveness to a repeated stimulus. According to Solomon's opponent-process theory, habituation is the result of two processes that balance each other. The first process is a relatively automatic, involuntary response—essentially a UCR. The second, or opponent, process is a learned or conditioned response that follows and counteracts the first. This theory may help explain drug tolerance.

INSTRUMENTAL AND OPERANT CONDITIONING: LEARNING THE CONSEQUENCES OF BEHAVIOR
How do reward and punishment work?

Learning occurs not only through associating stimuli but also through associating behavior with its consequences. Thorndike's *law of effect* holds that any response that produces satisfaction becomes more likely to occur again, and any response that produces discomfort becomes less likely. Thorndike referred to this type of learning as instrumental conditioning. Skinner called the process *operant conditioning.*

An *operant* is a response that has some effect on the world. A *reinforcer* increases the probability that the operant preceding it will occur again. There are two types of reinforcers: *positive reinforcers,* which are desirable stimuli that strengthen a response if they are presented after that response occurs, and *negative reinforcers,* which are the removal of an unpleasant stimulus following some response. Both kinds of reinforcers strengthen the behaviors that precede them. *Escape conditioning* results when a behavior terminates an unpleasant stimulus. *Avoidance conditioning* results when behavior avoids an unpleasant stimulus; it reflects both classical and operant conditioning. Behaviors learned through avoidance conditioning are very resistant to extinction. *Discriminative stimuli* indicate whether reinforcement is available for a particular behavior.

Complex responses can be learned through *shaping,* which involves reinforcing successive approximations of the desired response. *Primary reinforcers* are inherently rewarding; *secondary reinforcers* are rewards that people or animals learn to like because of their association with primary reinforcers. In general, operant conditioning proceeds more quickly when the delay in receiving reinforcement is short rather than long, and when the reinforcer is large rather than small. Reinforcement may be delivered on a continuous reinforcement schedule or on one of four basic types of partial, or intermittent, reinforcement schedules: fixed-ratio (FR), variable-ratio (VR), fixed-interval (FI), and variable-interval (VI) schedules. Ratio schedules lead to a rapid rate of responding. Behavior learned through partial reinforcement is very resistant to extinction; this phenomenon is called the *partial reinforcement extinction effect.* Partial reinforcement is involved in superstitious behavior, which results when a response is coincidentally followed by a reinforcer.

Psychologists are not certain what makes reinforcers rewarding, but activity in the brain's "pleasure centers" is one possibility.

Punishment decreases the frequency of a behavior by following it either with an unpleasant stimulus or with the removal of a pleasant one. Punishment modifies behavior but has several drawbacks. It only suppresses behavior; fear of punishment may generalize to the person doing the punishing; it is ineffective when delayed; it can be physically harmful and may teach aggressiveness; and it teaches only what not to do, not what should be done to obtain reinforcement.

The principles of operant conditioning have been applied in many areas, from teaching social skills to treating sleep disorders.

COGNITIVE PROCESSES IN LEARNING
Can people learn to be helpless?

Cognitive processes—how people represent, store, and use information—play an important role in learning. *Learned helplessness* appears to result when people believe that their behavior has no effect on the world. Both animals and humans display *latent learning.* They also form *cognitive maps* of their environments, even in the absence of any reinforcement for doing so. Experiments on *insight* also suggest that cognitive processes play an important role in learning, even by animals. The process of learning by watching others is called *observational learning,* or social learning. Some observational learning occurs through *vicarious conditioning,* in which one is influenced by seeing or hearing about the consequences of others' behavior. Observational learning is more likely to occur when the person observed is rewarded for the observed behavior. It is a powerful source of socialization.

USING RESEARCH ON LEARNING TO HELP PEOPLE LEARN
What should teachers learn about learning?

Research on how people learn has implications for improved teaching and for the development of a wide range of skills. The degree to which learning principles, such as immediate reinforcement, are used in teaching varies considerably from culture to culture. The importance of cognitive processes in learning is seen in active learning methods designed to encourage people to think deeply about and apply new information instead of just memorizing isolated facts. Observational learning, practice, and corrective feedback play important roles in the learning of skills.

Learn by Doing

Put It in Writing

Imagine that you have inherited a circus from a long-lost relative, but you discover that all of the animal acts are stale and out of date. At a meeting with the employees, you explain that the principles of classical and operant conditioning could be used to improve these acts. Write a one-page paper describing how classical conditioning could be used to teach elephants a new trick, and how operant conditioning could be used to spice up a trained seal act. Be sure to label all the concepts and principles you use (such as conditioned stimulus, conditioned response, shaping, and the like).

Personal Learning Activity

Select a pair of friends or relatives of about the same age and intelligence, and try teaching each of them something that is new to them but that you know well—perhaps the words to a song; a popular dance; or how to use e-mail, tie a tie, hit a tennis ball, or use roller blades. Teach one person simply by telling or showing what you want him or her to learn, but work out a set of active learning methods to use with the second person. (Recall that active learning requires the learner to get involved in the learning process by doing something other than just listening to a lesson.) Keep a record of which student did better at this learning task and how long it took each student to learn. Which method was more efficient, and which student do you think enjoyed the learning process more? Did your results confirm or conflict with research on active learning in the classroom? *For additional projects, see the five Personal Learning Activities in the corresponding chapter of the study guide that accompanies this text.*

Step into Action

Courses

Learning
Animal Behavior
Behavior Modification

Movies

The Miracle Worker (shaping and reinforcement)
A Clockwork Orange; The Manchurian Candidate (misconceptions about the power of classical conditioning)
Free Willy (reinforcement and animal behavior)

Books

Kieran Egan, *The Educated Mind: How Cognitive Tools Shape Our Understanding* (University of Chicago Press, 1997) (how children learn)
Linda Metcalf, *Parenting Toward Solutions: How Parents Can Use Skills They Already Have to Raise Responsible, Loving Kids* (Prentice-Hall, 1996) (learning-based parenting skills)

Martin Seligman, *What You Can Change and What You Can't: The Complete Guide to Successful Self-Improvement* (Fawcett Books, 1995) (using learning principles for self-improvement)
Martin Seligman, with Karen Reivich, Lisa Jaycox, and Jane Gillham, *The Optimistic Child* (Harper Perennial Library, 1996) (the role of cognitive processes in learning and behavior)

The Web

The World Wide Web is a good source of additional information about the science of psychology, provided you use it carefully and think critically about the information you find. The PsychAbilities web site that accompanies this text offers many resources relevant to this chapter. These resources include interactive NetLab exercises; Thinking Critically and Evaluating Research exercises; ACE chapter quizzes; recommended web links; and articles on current events, books, and movies. At http://college.hmco.com, select *Psychology* and then this textbook.

Review of Key Terms

Can you define each of the key terms in the chapter? Check your definitions against those on the pages listed in parentheses below or in the Glossary/Index at the end of the text.

avoidance conditioning (*p. 155*)
classical conditioning (*p. 147*)
cognitive map (*p. 166*)
conditioned response (CR) (*p. 148*)
conditioned stimulus (CS) (*p. 148*)
discriminative stimuli (*p. 155*)
escape conditioning (*p. 154*)
extinction (*p. 148*)
habituation (*p. 152*)

insight (*p. 166*)
latent learning (*p. 166*)
law of effect (*p. 154*)
learned helplessness (*p. 163*)
learning (*p. 146*)
negative reinforcers (*p. 154*)
observational learning (*p. 167*)
operant (*p. 154*)
operant conditioning (*p. 154*)

partial reinforcement extinction effect (*p. 160*)
positive reinforcers (*p. 154*)
primary reinforcers (*p. 157*)
punishment (*p. 160*)
reconditioning (*p. 148*)
reinforcer (*p. 154*)
second-order conditioning (*p. 150*)
secondary reinforcers (*p. 157*)
shaping (*p. 157*)

spontaneous recovery (*p. 148*)
stimulus discrimination (*p. 149*)
stimulus generalization (*p. 149*)
unconditioned response (UCR) (*p. 147*)
unconditioned stimulus (UCS) (*p. 147*)
vicarious conditioning (*p. 168*)

Multiple-Choice Self-Test

Select the best answer for each of the questions below. Then check your responses against the Answer Key at the end of the text.

1. The fact that you didn't notice the feeling of your watch until you read this sentence is an example of

   a. habituation.
   b. stimulus generalization.
   c. stimulus discrimination.
   d. spontaneous recovery.

2. In a classical conditioning experiment, a puff of air was blown into Ralph's eye, and he reflexively blinked. The experimenter then began flashing a green light just before presenting the puff of air. After many pairings of the green light and the puff of air, Ralph began to blink as soon as the green light was presented, whether or not the air puff followed. In this experiment the green light is the

   a. unconditioned stimulus.
   b. conditioned stimulus.
   c. conditioned response.
   d. unconditioned response.

3. To best obtain classical conditioning in the experiment described in the previous question, the experimenter should present the puff of air _____ presenting the green light.

   a. after
   b. just before
   c. at the same time as
   d. hours before

4. Suppose that the experimenter in Question 2 continues presenting the green light, but never again follows it with the puff of air. Ralph will soon _____ through the process of _____.

   a. blink faster; reconditioning
   b. stop blinking in response to the green light; extinction
   c. blink slower; stimulus control
   d. stop blinking; spontaneous recovery

5. Reconditioning refers to the

   a. automatic appearance of a conditioned response following extinction.
   b. re-pairing of the conditioned stimulus with the conditioned response.
   c. creation of spontaneous recovery.
   d. re-pairing of the conditioned stimulus and the unconditioned stimulus after extinction.

6. Laverne lost control and ate an entire coconut cream pie. Later that day she got the flu, complete with nausea and vomiting. After this experience Laverne associated coconut cream pie with being sick, and now she can't even stand the smell of it. This is an example of _____, which supports the concept of _____.

   a. escape conditioning; spontaneous recovery
   b. discriminative conditioning; biopreparedness
   c. aversive conditioning; biopreparedness
   d. latent learning; spontaneous recovery

7. After being bitten by a dog at a young age, Najla became fearful of all types of dogs. Now, when Najla sees a dog, her heart races and she feels like running away. Which of the following is a conditioned stimulus for Najla?

   a. dog bite
   b. fear
   c. running away
   d. seeing a dog

8. After watching a number of people petting and playing with a dog, Najla decides that dogs aren't as scary as she'd thought. The next day, at her neighbors' house, she pets their dog. Najla's fear has been reduced through

   a. classical conditioning.
   b. operant conditioning.
   c. spontaneous recovery.
   d. observational learning.

9. Manuel has learned that every time he cleans his room, his mother makes his favorite dessert. This is an example of

   a. classical conditioning.
   b. negative reinforcement.
   c. operant conditioning.
   d. extinction.

10. Jodi is angry at her boss and would like to tell him exactly how she feels about him. But when Jodi did something like that at her previous job, she was fired. Now she is afraid of losing her job, as well as her temper, so she keeps quiet. What kind of learning does this example represent?

    a. escape conditioning
    b. classical conditioning
    c. avoidance conditioning
    d. discriminative stimuli

11. Ten minutes before a movie starts, the theater is filled with people who are talking or laughing. As soon as the lights go out, everyone becomes quiet. Sudden darkness serves as a _____ in this example of operant conditioning.

    a. positive reinforcer
    b. negative reinforcer
    c. punishment
    d. discriminative stimulus

12. Craig wanted to teach his dog, JoJo, to sit up and beg using operant conditioning principles. He started by giving JoJo a treat when she was simply standing. Then he gave her a treat only if she was sitting. Next, he only gave her a treat if she was sitting and had raised one paw, and so on. This is an example of

    a. stimulus discrimination.
    b. stimulus generalization.
    c. negative reinforcement.
    d. shaping.

13. Loretta gets a backache every day, but if she sits in a tub of hot water, the pain goes away. So she decides to sit in a hot tub every day. She has learned to do this through

    a. positive reinforcement.
    b. negative reinforcement.
    c. stimulus discrimination.
    d. shaping.

14. Nancy stole money out of her mother's purse. If punishment is to have the most effect, Nancy's mother should

    a. say nothing to Nancy about it until her father comes home, and let him handle the situation.
    b. tell Nancy how angry she is, and punish her by spanking her hard and taking away all of her privileges for the rest of the year.
    c. tell Nancy that she still loves her, but also immediately give a punishment that is significant, but not harmful.
    d. tell Nancy that she knows she stole the money and urge her not to do it again.

15. Learned helplessness results when people observe or believe that

    a. their behavior is unrelated to the consequences that occur.
    b. certain behaviors always result in negative consequences.
    c. positive consequences are rare.
    d. certain behaviors provide escape from negative stimuli.

16. Every fifth time Jamey washes the dishes, his mom gives him a candy bar. Once a week, on average, Susan's dad gives her a cookie for washing the dishes. What schedules of reinforcement are Jamey and Susan on, respectively?

    a. fixed-interval, variable-interval
    b. fixed-ratio, variable-interval
    c. variable-ratio, fixed-interval
    d. variable-interval, fixed-ratio

17. Kenyatta's grandmother came to visit recently for the first time. In the middle of the night she got up to use the bathroom, but she took a wrong turn in the dark and bumped into a wall. This incident is an example of

    a. an incorrect cognitive map.
    b. reverse insight.
    c. latent learning.
    d. vicarious learning.

18. Just as Baby Albert was shown a white lab rat, a loud noise startled him and made him cry. After several such incidents, Albert cried whenever he saw the white rat. Later, when his mother took him to a petting zoo, Albert cried when he saw a white rabbit. This is an example of

    a. stimulus generalization.
    b. stimulus discrimination.
    c. vicarious learning.
    d. observational learning.

19. Leroy and Jared were coloring in their coloring books. When Jared started coloring on the walls, his mother spanked him and put him in a boring time-out room. Leroy decided that it wasn't a good idea to color on the walls. Leroy learned this lesson through

    a. insight.
    b. latent learning.
    c. vicarious learning.
    d. observational extinction.

20. According to this chapter, teachers should do which of the following to bring about the most improvement in students' recall of material?

    a. lecture more slowly
    b. hand out lecture outlines before class begins
    c. encourage students to recopy their notes
    d. have students work in groups to solve problems

6

Memory

Have you ever forgotten where you parked

your car? Have you ever felt that a name you were trying to remember was on the tip of your tongue? Researchers in the field of memory explore these common experiences. *Memory* is a complex process of encoding, storing, and retrieving information. You use different kinds of memory for different types of information, such as personal experiences, specific skills, and abstract concepts. Once information is stored in your memory, recalling it can sometimes be difficult. In this chapter, you will learn about some techniques that can help you to retrieve memories. What psychologists have learned about memory has been used to create study techniques that really work!

Reading this chapter will help you to answer the following questions:

- **How does information turn into memories?**
- **What am I most likely to remember?**
- **How do I retrieve stored memories?**
- **How accurate are my memories?**
- **What causes me to forget things?**
- **How does my brain change when I store a memory?**
- **How can I remember more information?**

"I'll make him an offer he can't refuse." "I'll be back." "Trust no one." "Life is like a box of chocolates." "I see dead people." "Show me the money." "Is that your final answer?" Do you remember where you heard these words? They are memorable lines from *The Godfather, The Terminator, The X-Files, Forrest Gump, The Sixth Sense, Jerry McGuire,* and *Who Wants to Be a Millionaire.* Can you say who Private Ryan was and why he needed to be saved? And do you know which classic film character said "Play it again, Sam"? (If you don't, ask a friend who knows about old movies.) The most common answer is Rick, the café owner played by Humphrey Bogart in *Casablanca.* Bogart, however, never actually said this often-quoted line, though many people are sure they "remember" it.

Your memory stores vast amounts of useful and not-so-useful information from all of your experiences. This chapter will help you understand the nature of memory—how you form memories, how memory errors happen, and how you forget.

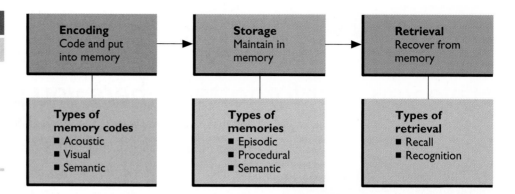

The Nature of Memory

How does information turn into memories?

Memory is a funny thing. You might be able to remember the name of your first-grade teacher, but not the name of someone you met just five minutes ago. Mathematician John Griffith estimated that in an average lifetime, a person stores roughly five hundred times as much information as can be found in all the volumes of the *Encyclopaedia Britannica* (M. Hunt, 1982). Keep in mind, however, that although we retain a great deal of information, we also lose a great deal (Bjork & Vanhuele, 1992).

Memory plays a critical role in your life. Without memory, you would not know how to shut off your alarm, take a shower, get dressed, recognize objects, or communicate. You would be unaware of your own likes and dislikes. You would have no idea of who you are (Craik et al., 1999). The impressive capacity of human memory depends on the operation of a complex mental system (Schacter, 1999).

Basic Memory Processes

A psychology professor we know sometimes drives to work and sometimes walks. He once drove to his office, forgot that he had driven, and walked home. When he didn't see his car in its normal spot the next morning, he reported the car stolen. The police soon called to say that "some college kids" had probably stolen the car, because it was found on campus (next to the psychology building!). What went wrong? There are several possibilities. Memory depends on three basic processes: encoding, storage, and retrieval (see Figure 6.1). Our absent-minded professor might have had problems with any one of these.

First, information must be put into memory, a step that requires encoding. **Encoding** is a process that puts information to be remembered into a form that our memory system can accept and use. We use *memory codes* to translate information from the senses into mental representations of that information. **Acoustic codes** represent information as sequences of sounds, such as a tune or a rhyme. **Visual codes** represent stimuli as pictures, such as the image of a person's face. **Semantic codes** represent the general meaning of an experience. Thus, if you see a billboard that reads "Huey's Going-Out-of-Business Sale," you might encode the sound of the words as if they had been spoken (acoustic coding), the image of the letters as they were arranged on the sign (visual coding), or the fact that you recently saw an ad for Huey's (semantic coding). The type of coding we use influences what we remember. Semantic coding might allow you to remember that an unfamiliar car was parked in your neighbors' driveway just before their house was robbed. If there were little or no other coding, however, you might not be able to remember the make, model, or color of the car.

The second basic memory process is storage. **Storage** refers to the holding of information in your memory over time. When you recall a vacation taken in childhood or find it possible to use a pogo stick many years after you last played with one, you are depending on the storage capacity of your memory.

encoding The process of putting information into a form that the memory system can accept and use.

acoustic codes Mental representations of stimuli as sounds.

visual codes Mental representations of stimuli as pictures.

semantic codes Mental representations of experiences by their general meaning.

storage The process of maintaining information in the memory system over time.

NEXT STOP, CARNEGIE HALL As she practices, this young violinist is developing procedural memories of how to play her instrument that may be difficult to put into words. To appreciate the special nature of procedural memory, try writing a step-by-step description of *exactly* how you tie a shoe.

retrieval The process of recalling information stored in memory.

episodic memory A person's recall of a specific event that happened while he or she was present.

semantic memory A type of memory containing generalized knowledge of the world.

procedural memory A type of memory containing information about how to do things.

explicit memory The process through which people deliberately try to remember something.

implicit memory The unintentional recollection and influence of prior experiences.

The third process, **retrieval,** occurs when you find information stored in memory and bring it into consciousness. Retrieving stored information such as your address or telephone number is usually so fast and effortless that it seems automatic. The search-and-retrieval process becomes more noticeable, however, when you read a quiz question but cannot quite recall the answer. Retrieval involves both recall and recognition. To *recall* information, you have to retrieve it from memory without much help; this is what is required when you answer an essay test question or play *Jeopardy!* In *recognition,* retrieval is aided by clues, such as the response alternatives given on multiple-choice tests and the questions on *Who Wants to Be a Millionaire.* Accordingly, recognition tends to be easier than recall.

Types of Memory

In which hand does the *Statue of Liberty* hold her torch? When was the last time you made a phone call? What part of speech is used to modify a noun? Your attempt to answer the first question is likely to elicit a visual image. To answer the second, you must remember a particular event in your life. The third question requires general knowledge that is unlikely to be tied to a specific event. Some psychologists suggest that answering each of these questions requires a different type of memory (Baddeley, 1998). How many types of memory are there? No one is sure, but most research suggests that there are at least three basic types. Each is named for the kind of information it handles: episodic, semantic, and procedural (J. B. Best, 1999).

Any memory of a specific event that happened while you were present is an **episodic memory.** It is a memory of an episode in your life. What you had for dinner yesterday, what you did last summer, or where you were last Friday night are episodic memories. **Semantic memory** contains generalized knowledge of the world—such as that twelve items make a dozen—that does not involve memory of a specific event. So you would answer the question "Are wrenches pets or tools?" using your semantic memory, because you don't have to remember a specific episode in which you learned that wrenches are tools. As a general rule, people convey episodic memories by saying, "I remember when, . . ." whereas they convey semantic memories by saying, "I know that . . ." (Tulving, 1995). **Procedural memory** involves knowledge of how to do things, such as riding a bike, reading a map, or playing tennis. A procedural memory often consists of a complicated sequence of movements that cannot be described adequately in words. For instance, a gymnast might find it impossible to describe the exact motions in a particular routine.

Many activities require all three types of memory. Consider the game of tennis. Knowing the official rules or the number of sets needed to win a match involves semantic memory. Remembering which side served last requires episodic memory. And knowing how to hit the ball involves procedural memory.

Recalling all three kinds of memories can be either intentional or unintentional. When you deliberately try to remember something, such as where you went on your last vacation, you are relying on **explicit memory.** In contrast, **implicit memory** involves the unintentional recollection and influence of prior experiences (D. L. Nelson, 1999; D. L. Schacter, Chiu, & Ochsner, 1993). For instance, while watching a movie about a long car trip, you might begin to feel slightly anxious because you subconsciously recall a time you had engine trouble on such a trip. Implicit memory operates automatically and without conscious effort. In fact, people are often unaware that their actions have been influenced by previous events. Because some influential events cannot be recalled even when people try to do so, implicit memory has been said to involve "retention without remembering" (Roediger, Guynn, & Jones, 1995).

Models of Memory

Your explicit memory for some information is far better and lasts far longer than for other information. Suppose your friends throw a surprise party for you. When you enter the room, you might barely notice the flash of a camera. Later, you cannot recall it at all. And you might forget in a few seconds the name of a person you met at the party. But if you live to be a hundred, you will never forget where the party took place or how surprised and pleased you were. Why do some things stay in memory forever, whereas others barely make an impression? Each of four models of memory provides a somewhat different explanation. Let's see how the levels-of-processing, transfer-appropriate processing, parallel distributed processing, and information-processing models look at memory.

Levels of Processing   The **levels-of-processing model** suggests that memory depends on the extent to which you encode and process information when you first receive it. Consider, for example, the task of remembering a phone number you just saw on television. If you were unable to write it down, you would probably repeat the number over and over to yourself until you could get to the phone. This repetition process is called **maintenance rehearsal.** It can be an effective method for encoding information temporarily, but what if you need to remember something for hours, months, or years? In such cases, you would be better off using **elaborative rehearsal,** a process in which you relate new material to information you already have stored in memory. For example, instead of trying to remember a new person's name by simply repeating it to yourself, try thinking about how the name is related to something you know well. Let's say you are introduced to a man named John Crews. You might think, "He is as tall as my Uncle John, who always wears a crew cut."

Study after study has shown that memory is improved when people use elaborative rather than maintenance rehearsal (Jahnke & Nowaczyk, 1998). Why? According to the levels-of-processing model, the reason is that material is processed more "deeply" when elaborative rehearsal is used. The more you think about new information, organize it, and relate it to something you already know, the "deeper" the processing, and the better your memory of the information becomes. Reading teachers use this idea when they ask their students not only to define a new word but also to use it in a sentence. Figuring out how to use the new word takes deeper processing than merely defining it. (The next time you come across an unfamiliar word in this book, don't just read its definition. Try to use the word in a sentence by coming up with an example of the concept that relates to your knowledge and experience.)

Transfer-Appropriate Processing   Level of processing is not the only factor that affects memory (Baddeley, 1992). Another critical factor, suggested by the **transfer-appropriate processing model** of memory, is how the encoding process matches up with what is later retrieved. In one study, for example, half the students in a class were told that an upcoming exam would be multiple choice. The other half of the students were told to expect a series of essay questions. Only half the students got the type of exam they expected, however. These students did much better on the exam than those who took an unexpected type of exam. Apparently, in studying for the exam, the two groups used encoding strategies that were most appropriate to the type of exam they expected. Those who tried to retrieve the information in a way that did not match their encoding method had a harder time (d'Ydewalle & Rosselle, 1978). Results like these indicate that how well the encoding method transfers to the retrieval task is just as important as the depth of processing.

Parallel Distributed Processing   A third approach to memory is based on **parallel distributed processing (PDP) models** of memory (Rumelhart & McClelland, 1986). These models suggest that new experiences do more than store facts that are later retrieved individually. These experiences also change your knowledge base in ways that alter your *overall understanding* of the world and how it operates. For example, when you first arrived at college, you learned specific facts, such as where classes are held, what time the library closes, and where to get the best pizza. Over time, these and many other facts of college life form a network of information that creates a more general understanding of how the whole college system works. Developing this network makes experienced students not only more knowledgeable but also more sophisticated. It allows them to, say, allocate their study time so as to do well in their most important classes, and to plan a schedule that avoids conflicts between work and recreational activities.

This network idea is reflected in PDP models of memory, which see each unit of knowledge as ultimately connected with every other unit. The connections between units

levels-of-processing model   A model of memory suggesting that differences in how well something is remembered reflect the degree or depth of mental processing.

maintenance rehearsal   A memorization method that involves repeating information over and over to keep it active in memory.

elaborative rehearsal   A memorization method that relates new information to information already stored in memory.

transfer-appropriate processing model   A model suggesting that memory depends on how the encoding process matches up with what is ultimately retrieved.

parallel distributed processing (PDP) models   Models of memory suggesting that new experiences not only provide specific information but also become part of, and alter, a whole network of associations in people's overall knowledge base.

information-processing model   A model suggesting that information must pass through sensory memory, short-term memory, and long-term memory in order to become firmly embedded in memory.

in review

Models of Memory	
Model	**Assumptions**
Levels of processing	The more deeply material is processed, the better our memory of it.
Transfer-appropriate processing	Retrieval is improved when we try to recall material in a way that matches how the material was encoded.
Parallel distributed processing (PDP)	New experiences add to and alter our overall knowledge base; they are not separate, unconnected facts. Networks of associations allow us to draw inferences and make generalizations about the world.
Information processing	Information is processed in three stages: sensory memory, short-term memory, and long-term memory.

become stronger as they are experienced together more frequently. "Knowledge" is distributed across a network of associations that allows you to quickly and efficiently draw inferences and generalizations. For example, because of your network of associations, just seeing the word *chair* allows you to know immediately what a chair looks like, what it is used for, where it tends to be located, who might buy one, and the like. PDP models of memory explain this process very effectively.

Information Processing   The **information-processing model** is probably the most influential and comprehensive model of memory. It suggests that for information to be firmly implanted in memory, it must pass through three stages of mental processing: sensory memory, short-term memory, and long-term memory (see Figure 6.2).

In *sensory memory,* information from the senses—sights or sounds, for example—is held in sensory registers very briefly, often for less than one second. Information in the sensory registers may be attended to, analyzed, and encoded as a meaningful pattern; this is the process of *perception* discussed in Chapter 3. If the information in sensory memory is perceived, it can enter *short-term memory.* If nothing further is done, the information will disappear in less than twenty seconds. But if the information in short-term memory is further processed, it may be encoded into *long-term memory,* where it may remain indefinitely.

The act of reading illustrates all three stages of memory processing. As you read any sentence in this book, for example, light energy reflected from the page reaches your eyes, where it is converted to neural activity and registered in your sensory memory. If you pay attention to these visual stimuli, your perception of the patterns of light can be held in short-term memory. This stage of memory holds the early parts of the sentence so that they can be integrated and understood as you read the rest of the sentence. As you read, you are constantly recognizing words by matching your perceptions of them with the patterns and meanings you have stored in long-term memory. Thus, all three stages are necessary for you to understand a sentence. ("In Review: Models of Memory" summarizes the four memory models we have discussed.)

FIGURE 6.2

Three Stages of Memory

This traditional information-processing model describes memory as consisting of three storage systems.

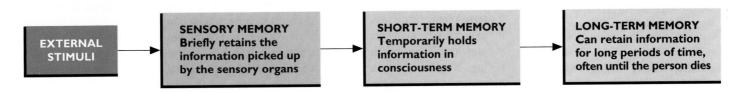

SENSORY MEMORY AT WORK In a darkened room, ask a friend to hold a small flashlight and move it very slowly in a circle. You will see a single point of light moving in a circle. If it appears to have a "tail," like a comet, that is your sensory memory of the light before it fades. Now ask your friend to speed up the movement. This time, you should see a complete circle of light, because as the light moves, its impression on your sensory memory does not have time to fade before the circle is completed. A similar process allows us to see still images "move" when we watch a film or video (see our discussion of stroboscopic motion in Chapter 3).

sensory memory A type of memory that is very brief, but lasts long enough to connect one impression to the next.

sensory registers Memory systems that briefly hold incoming information.

selective attention The process of focusing mental resources on only part of the stimulus field.

short-term memory (STM) A stage of memory in which information normally lasts less than twenty seconds. Also called *working memory*.

working memory See *short-term memory*.

Storing New Memories

■ **What am I most likely to remember?**

All the models and types of memory we've been discussing give us different ways to think about the three basic memory processes of encoding, storage, and retrieval. We code information in order to store it, and we can retrieve only information that has been stored. Obviously, the storage of information is critical to memory. According to the information-processing model, sensory memory, short-term memory, and long-term memory each provide a different type of storage. Let's take a closer look at these three memory systems in order to better understand how they work—and sometimes fail.

Sensory Memory

To recognize incoming stimuli, the brain must analyze and compare them with what is already stored in long-term memory. Although this process is very quick, it still takes time. The major function of **sensory memory** is to hold information long enough for it to be processed further. This "holding" function is the job of the **sensory registers,** which act as temporary storage bins. There is a separate register for each of the five senses. Every register is capable of storing an almost complete representation of a sensory stimulus (J. B. Best, 1999). However, the sensory registers hold this representation for only a very brief period of time, often less than one second.

Sensory memory helps us experience a constant flow of information, even if that flow is interrupted. To appreciate this fact, move your head and eyes slowly from left to right. Although it seems to you that your eyes are moving smoothly, like a movie camera scanning a scene, this is not what happens. Your eyes fixate at one point for about one-fourth of a second and then rapidly jump to a new position. You perceive smooth motion because you hold the scene in your visual sensory register until your eyes fixate again. Similarly, when you listen to someone speak, your auditory sensory register allows you to experience a smooth flow of information, even though there are actually short silences between or within words.

The fact that sensory memories fade quickly if they are not processed further is actually an adaptive characteristic of this memory system (Baddeley, 1998). You simply cannot deal with all of the sights, sounds, odors, tastes, and touch sensations that come to your sense organs at any given moment. Using **selective attention,** you focus your mental resources on only part of the stimuli around you, thus controlling what information is processed further in short-term memory.

Short-Term, or Working, Memory

The sensory registers allow your memory system to develop a representation of a stimulus. However, they do not allow the more thorough analysis needed if the information is going to be used in some way. That function is accomplished by **short-term memory (STM),** the part of your memory system that stores limited amounts of information for up to about eighteen seconds. When you check *TV Guide* for the channel number of a show and then switch to that channel, you are using short-term memory.

Many researchers refer to short-term memory as **working memory,** because it helps you to do much of your mental work, from punching in a phone number to solving a math problem (Baddeley, 1992). Suppose you are buying something for 83 cents. You go through your change and pick out two quarters, two dimes, two nickels, and three pennies. To do this you must remember the price, retrieve the rules of addition from long-term memory, *and* keep a running count of how much change you have so far. Now try to recall how many windows there are on the front of the house or apartment where you grew up. To answer this question, you will probably form a mental image of the building. Here, too, you are using a working-memory process that allows you to keep that image in your mind while you count the windows.

```
9 2 5
8 6 4 2
3 7 6 5 4
6 2 7 4 1 8
0 4 0 1 4 7 3
1 9 2 2 3 5 3 0
4 8 6 8 5 4 3 3 2
2 5 3 1 9 7 1 7 6 8
8 5 1 2 9 6 1 9 4 5 0
9 1 8 5 4 6 9 4 2 9 3 7
```

Source: Howard (1983).

FIGURE 6.3

The Capacity of Short-Term Memory

 Here is a test of your immediate, or short-term, memory span. Ask someone to read to you the numbers in the top row at the rate of about one per second; then try to repeat them back in the same order. Then try the next row, and the one after that, until you make a mistake. Your immediate memory span is the maximum number of items you can repeat back perfectly.

immediate memory span   The maximum number of items a person can recall perfectly after one presentation of the items.

chunks   Stimuli that are perceived as units or meaningful groupings of information.

Encoding in Short-Term Memory   The encoding of information in short-term memory is much more elaborate and varied than encoding in the sensory registers (Brandimonte, Hitch, & Bishop, 1992). Acoustic coding (by sound) seems to dominate short-term memory. This conclusion comes from research on the mistakes people make when encoding information in short-term memory. These mistakes tend to involve the substitution of similar sounds. For instance, Robert Conrad (1964) showed people strings of letters and asked them to repeat the letters immediately. Among their most common mistakes was the replacement of the correct letter with another that sounded like it. For example, the correct letter *C* was replaced with a *D, P,* or *T.* The participants made these mistakes even though the letters were presented visually, without any sound. Studies in several cultures have also shown that items are more difficult to remember if they sound similar. For example, native English speakers perform more poorly when they must remember a string of letters like *ECVTGB* (which all have similar sounds) than when asked to remember one like *KRLDQS* (which have distinct sounds).

Although encoding in short-term memory is usually acoustic, it is not *always* acoustic. Information in short-term memory can be also coded visually, semantically, and even kinesthetically, in terms of physical movements (J. B. Best, 1999). In one study, deaf people were shown a list of words and then asked to immediately write down all they could remember (Shand, 1982). When these participants made errors, they wrote words that are expressed through similar *hand movements* in American Sign Language, rather than words that *sounded* similar to the correct words. Apparently, these individuals had encoded the words on the basis of the movements they would use when signing them.

Storage Capacity of Short-Term Memory   How much information can you hold in short-term memory? You can easily determine the answer by conducting the simple experiment shown in Figure 6.3 (Howard, 1983). Your **immediate memory span** is the maximum number of items you can recall perfectly after one presentation. If your memory span is like most people's, you can repeat six or seven items from the test in this figure. You should come up with about the same result whether you use digits, letters, words, or virtually any type of unit (Hayes, 1952; I. Pollack, 1953). George Miller (1956) noticed that many studies using a variety of tasks showed the same limit on the ability to process information. This "magic number," which is seven plus or minus two, appears to be the immediate memory span or capacity of short-term memory, at least in laboratory settings. It is generally considered to be somewhat less in more naturalistic settings (Martindale, 1991). The "magic number" refers to meaningful *groupings* of information, called **chunks,** not to a certain number of discrete elements.

To see the difference between discrete elements and chunks, read the following letters to a friend, pausing at each dash: *FB-IAO-LM-TVI-BMB-MW.* The chances are very good that your friend will not be able to repeat this string of letters perfectly. Why? There are fifteen letters, which exceeds most people's immediate memory span. Now, give your friend the test again, but group the letters like this: *FBI-AOL-MTV-IBM-BMW.* Your friend will probably repeat the string easily (Bower, 1975). Although the same fifteen letters are involved, they will be processed as only five meaningful chunks of information.

The Power of Chunking   Chunks of information can be quite complex. If you heard someone say, "The boy in the red shirt kicked his mother in the shin," you could probably repeat the sentence easily. Yet, it contains twelve words and forty-three letters. How can you repeat the sentence so effortlessly? The answer is that you are able to build bigger and bigger chunks of information (Ericsson & Staszewski, 1989). In this case, you might represent "the boy in the red shirt" as one chunk of information rather than as six words or nineteen letters. Similarly, "kicked his mother" and "in the shin" represent separate chunks of information. You can also create chunks by using elaborative rehearsal, as discussed earlier. To do this, you would find a set of rules or associations in long-term memory that you could use to group several items together. Thus, you might represent "the boy in the red shirt" as a single visual image.

Learning to use bigger and bigger chunks of information can greatly benefit short-term memory. This effect can easily be seen in children. Their short-term memories

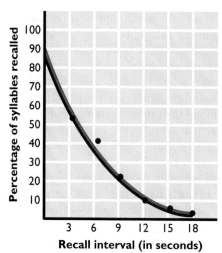

Source: Data from L. R. Peterson & Peterson (1959).

FIGURE 6.4

Forgetting in Short-Term Memory

This graph shows the percentage of nonsense syllables recalled after various intervals during which rehearsal was prevented. Notice that virtually complete forgetting occurred after a delay of eighteen seconds.

Brown-Peterson procedure   A method for determining how long unrehearsed information remains in short-term memory.

long-term memory (LTM)   The stage of memory for which the capacity to store new information is believed to be unlimited.

improve partly because they become able to hold as many as seven chunks in memory, but also because they get better at grouping information into chunks (Servan-Schreiber & Anderson, 1990). Adults also can greatly increase the capacity of their short-term memory by using more appropriate chunking. For example, after extensive training, one college student increased his immediate memory span from seven to eighty digits (Neisser, 2000b). So although the capacity of short-term memory is more or less constant (from five to nine chunks of meaningful information), the size of those chunks can vary tremendously.

Duration of Short-Term Memory   Why don't you remember every phone number you ever dialed or every conversation you ever had? The answer is that you usually forget information in short-term memory quickly. Although this adaptive feature of short-term memory gets rid of a lot of useless information, it can be inconvenient. You may have discovered this if you ever looked up a phone number, got distracted before you could call it, and then forgot the number.

How long does information remain in short-term memory if you don't keep rehearsing it? John Brown (1958) and Lloyd and Margaret Peterson (1959) devised the **Brown-Peterson procedure** to measure the duration of short-term memory when no rehearsal is allowed. In this procedure, participants are presented with a group of three letters, such as *GRB*. They then count backward by threes from some number until they get a signal. Counting prevents the participants from rehearsing the letters. At the signal, they stop counting and try to recall the letters. By varying the number of seconds spent counting backward, the experimenter can determine how much forgetting takes place over time. As you can see in Figure 6.4, information in short-term memory is forgotten gradually until, after only eighteen seconds, participants can remember almost nothing. Evidence from other such experiments also suggests that *unrehearsed* information can be held in short-term memory for no more than about eighteen seconds. However, if the information is rehearsed or processed further in some other way, it may be encoded into long-term memory.

Long-Term Memory

When people talk about memory, they are usually referring to long-term memory. **Long-term memory (LTM)** is the part of the memory system whose encoding and storage capabilities can produce memories that last a lifetime.

Encoding in Long-Term Memory   Some information is encoded into long-term memory automatically, without any conscious attempt to memorize it (N. R. Ellis, 1991). However, placement of information into long-term memory is often the result of more elaborate and conscious processing that usually involves *semantic coding*. As we mentioned earlier, semantic encoding often leaves out details in favor of the more general, underlying meaning of the information.

The notion that semantic encoding dominates in LTM was demonstrated in a classic study by Jacqueline Sachs (1967). Her participants first listened to tape recordings of people reading from books. Then Sachs showed them sets of sentences with the same meaning and asked whether each exact sentence had been read on the tape. Participants did very well when tested *immediately*, using mainly short-term memory. After only twenty-seven seconds, though, they could not be sure which of two sentences they had heard. For example, they could not remember whether they had heard "He sent a letter about it to Galileo, the great Italian scientist" or "A letter about it was sent to Galileo, the great Italian scientist." Why did this happen? It occurred because the delay was long enough that the participants had to recall the information from long-term memory, where they had encoded the *general meaning* of what they had heard, but not the exact wording.

Counterfeiters depend on the fact that people encode the general meaning of visual stimuli rather than specific details. For example, look at Figure 6.5, and find the correct drawing of a U.S. penny (Nickerson & Adams, 1979). Most people from the United States

FIGURE 6.5

Encoding into Long-Term Memory

Which is the correct image of a U.S. penny? (See p. 189 for the answer.)

(A)   (B)   (C)   (D)   (E)

Source: Nickerson & Adams (1979).

are unsuccessful at this task. People from Great Britain do poorly at recognizing their country's coins, too (G. V. Jones, 1990).

Storage Capacity of Long-Term Memory   The capacity of long-term memory is extremely large. Indeed, many psychologists believe that it is literally unlimited (Matlin, 1998). There is no way to prove this, but we do know that people store vast quantities of information in long-term memory that can be remembered remarkably well after long periods of time. For example, people are amazingly accurate at recognizing the faces of their high school classmates after having not seen them for over twenty-five years (Bruck, Cavanagh, & Ceci, 1991). They also do surprisingly well on tests of a foreign language or high school algebra fifty years after having formally studied these subjects (Bahrick et al., 1994; Bahrick & Hall, 1991). And college students are fairly accurate in remembering their high school grades—especially if they were good grades (Bahrick, Hall, & Berger, 1996).

But long-term memories are also subject to distortion. In one study illustrating this point, students were asked to describe where they were and what they were doing at the moment they heard about the verdict in the O. J. Simpson murder trial (Schmolck, Buffalo, & Squire, 2000). The students reported their recollections three times, first just three days after the verdict, and then again after fifteen and thirty-two months. At the final reporting, almost all the students claimed they could still remember accurately where they were and what they were doing, but more than 70 percent of their memories were distorted and/or inaccurate. For example, three days after the verdict, one student said he heard about it while in a campus lounge with many other students around him. Thirty-two months later, this same student recalled hearing the news in the living room of his home with his father and sister. Most of the students whose memories had been substantially distorted over time were unaware that this distortion had occurred; they

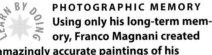

PHOTOGRAPHIC MEMORY Using only his long-term memory, Franco Magnani created amazingly accurate paintings of his hometown in Italy even though he had not seen it for more than thirty years (see comparison photo, at right; Sacks, 1992). People like Magnani display *eidetic imagery,* commonly called *photographic memory.* About 5 percent of all school-age children have photographic memory, but it is very rare among adults (Haber, 1979). You can test yourself for eidetic imagery by drawing a detailed picture or map of a place that you know well but have not seen recently. How did you do?

Storing New Memories			
Storage System	**Function**	**Capacity**	**Duration**
Sensory memory	Briefly holds representations of stimuli from each sense for further processing	Large: absorbs all sensory input from a particular stimulus	Less than 1 second
Short-term, or working, memory	Holds information in awareness while it is being processed	Five to nine distinct items or chunks of information	About 18 seconds
Long-term memory	Stores new information indefinitely	Unlimited	Unlimited

were very confident that the reports were accurate. Later, we will see that such overconfidence can also appear in courtroom testimony by eyewitnesses to crime.

Distinguishing Between Short-Term and Long-Term Memory

Some psychologists argue that short-term memory and long-term memory have different features and obey different laws (N. Cowan, 1988). ("In Review: Storing New Memories" summarizes the characteristics of these systems.) Evidence that information is transferred from short-term memory to a distinct storage system comes primarily from experiments on recall.

You can conduct your own recall experiment. Look at the following list of words for thirty seconds, and then look away and write down as many of the words as you can, in any order: *desk, chalk, pencil, chair, paperclip, book, eraser, folder, briefcase, essays*. Which words you recall depends in part on their serial position, or where the words are in the list. The *serial-position curve* in Figure 6.6 shows this effect. From this curve you can see the chances of recalling words appearing in each position in a list. For the first two or three words in a list, recall tends to be very good. This phenomenon is called the **primacy effect.** The probability of recall decreases for words in the middle of the list and

FIGURE 6.6	A Serial-Position Curve

The probability of recalling an item is plotted here as a function of its serial position in a list of items. Generally, the first several items and the last several items are most likely to be recalled.

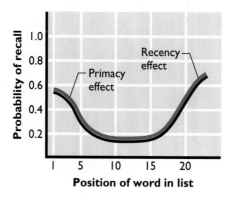

FIGURE 6.7

Separating Short-Term from Long-Term Memory

The results of two studies by Murray Glanzer and Anita Cunitz support the idea that short- and long-term memory are distinct systems. Part A shows that doing arithmetic before trying to recall a list of words destroys the recency effect but does not alter the primacy effect. Part B shows that presenting words at a faster rate—which keeps people from rehearsing the early words enough to put them into long-term memory—reduces the primacy effect but does not change the recency effect.

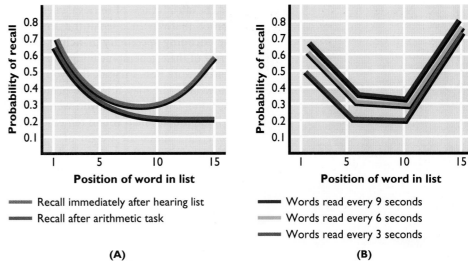

(A)

- ▬▬ Recall immediately after hearing list
- ▬▬ Recall after arithmetic task

(B)

- ▬▬ Words read every 9 seconds
- ▬▬ Words read every 6 seconds
- ▬▬ Words read every 3 seconds

Source: Part A: data from Glanzer & Cunitz (1966); part B: data from Koppenaal & Glanzer (1990).

then rises dramatically for the last few words. The ease of recalling words near the end of the list is called the **recency effect.** The primacy effect may reflect the rehearsal that puts early words into long-term memory. The recency effect may occur because the last few words are still in short-term memory when you try to recall the list (Glanzer & Cunitz, 1966; Koppenaal & Glanzer, 1990; see Figure 6.7).

K. Anders Ericsson and Walter Kintsch (1995) proposed a different way of thinking about the relationship between short-term and long-term memory. Studying people who display unusually good memory abilities, they suggested the operation of a "long-term, working memory." By this they mean that people who are skilled at remembering a list of items may be especially capable of rapidly transferring information from working (or short-term) memory into long-term memory. Once the transfer occurs, networks of related information already in long-term memory are activated to help the person remember the items. Many people with excellent memories appear to operate this way. In one study, researchers tested a waiter who was famous for remembering up to twenty dinner orders without writing anything down. He didn't do as well as that under laboratory conditions, but he was still able to remember five complex dinner orders almost to perfection. College students who tried the same task got about 20 percent of the orders wrong (Ericsson & Polson, 1988).

Retrieving Memories

▓ **How do I retrieve stored memories?**

Like those college students taking dinner orders, most people have trouble remembering things at one time or another. Have you ever been unable to recall the name of a musical group or movie star, only to think of it the next day? Remembering requires not only the appropriate coding and storing of information but also the ability to bring it into consciousness. In other words, you have to be able to *retrieve* it.

Retrieval Cues and Encoding Specificity

Retrieval cues are stimuli that help you retrieve information from long-term memory. As mentioned earlier, retrieval cues are what make recognition tasks (such as multiple-choice tests) easier than recall tasks (such as essay exams).

primacy effect   A phenomenon whereby recall for the first two or three items in a list is particularly good.

recency effect   A phenomenon whereby recall for the last few items in a list is particularly good.

retrieval cues   Stimuli that allow or help people to recall information.

Answer key to Figure 6.5: Drawing A shows the correct penny image.

CONTEXT-DEPENDENT MEMORIES
Some parents find that being in their child's schoolroom for a teacher conference provides context cues that bring back memories of their own school days.

The effectiveness of retrieval cues depends on the extent to which they tap into information that was encoded at the time of learning (Tulving, 1983). This rule is known as the **encoding specificity principle.** Because long-term memories are often encoded in terms of their general meaning, cues that trigger the meaning of the stored information tend to work best. Imagine that you have learned a long list of sentences, one of which is either (1) "The man lifted the piano" or (2) "The man tuned the piano." Now suppose that on a later recall test, you were given the retrieval cue "something heavy." This cue would probably help you to remember the first sentence (because you probably encoded something about the weight of a piano as you read it) but not the second sentence (because it has nothing to do with weight). Similarly, the cue "makes nice sounds" would probably help you recall the second sentence, but not the first (Barclay et al., 1974).

Context and State Dependence

Have you ever taken a test in a classroom other than the one in which you learned the material for that test? If so, your performance may have been affected. Research has shown that people tend to recall more of what they have learned when they are in the place in which they learned it. Why? Because if they have encoded features of the environment where the learning occurred, these features can later act as retrieval cues (Richardson-Klavehn & Bjork, 1988). In one experiment, people studied a series of photos while in the presence of a particular odor. Later, they reviewed a larger set of photos and tried to recognize the ones they had seen earlier. Half of the people were exposed to the original odor while taking the recognition test. The other half were tested in the presence of another odor. Those who smelled the same odor during learning and testing did significantly better on the recognition task than those tested in the presence of a different odor. The matching odor served as a powerful retrieval cue (Cann & Ross, 1989).

Context-dependent memories are those that are helped or hindered by similarities or differences in environmental context. This context-dependency effect is not always strong (Smith, Vela, & Williamson, 1988), but some students do find it helpful to study for a test in the classroom where the test will be given.

Sometimes, we also encode information about how we were feeling during a learning experience, and this information, too, can act as a retrieval cue. When our internal state influences retrieval, we have a **state-dependent memory.** For example, if people learn new material while under the influence of marijuana, they tend to recall it better if they are also tested under the influence of marijuana (J. E. Eich et al., 1975). Similar effects have been found with alcohol (Overton, 1984), other drugs (E. Eich, 1989), and various mood states (Eich & Macaulay, 2000). College students are more likely to remember positive incidents from the past when they are feeling good at the time of recall (G. H. Bower, 1981; Ehrlichman & Halpern, 1988). Negative events are more likely to be recalled when people are feeling sad or angry (Lewinsohn & Rosenbaum, 1987). These *mood congruency effects* are strongest when people try to recall personally meaningful episodes (E. Eich & Metcalfe, 1989). The more meaningful the experience, the more likely it is that the memory has been colored by their mood. (See "In Review: Factors Affecting Retrieval from Long-Term Memory.")

Retrieval from Semantic Memory

What factors affect our ability to retrieve information from semantic memory, where general knowledge about the world is stored? Researchers studying this question typically ask participants general-knowledge questions, such as (1) Are fish minerals? (2) Is a beagle a dog? (3) Do birds fly? and (4) Does a car have legs? As you might imagine, most people virtually always respond correctly to such questions. But by measuring *how long* it takes to answer them, psychologists gain important clues about how semantic memory is organized and how we retrieve information from it.

Semantic Networks One explanation of semantic memory suggests that concepts such as "bird" or "animal" are represented in a dense network of associations (Churchland,

encoding specificity principle A principle stating that the ability of a cue to aid retrieval depends on whether it taps into information that was encoded at the time of the original learning.

context-dependent memories Memories that are helped or hindered by similarities or differences between the contexts in which they are learned and recalled.

state-dependent memory Memory that is helped or hindered by similarities or differences in a person's internal state during learning versus recall.

spreading activation In semantic network theories of memory, a principle that explains how information is retrieved.

Factors Affecting Retrieval from Long-Term Memory	
Process	**Effect on Memory**
Encoding specificity	Retrieval cues are effective only to the extent that they tap into information that was originally encoded.
Context dependence	Retrieval is most successful when it occurs in the same environment in which the information was originally learned.
State dependence	Retrieval is most successful when people are in the same psychological state as when they originally learned the information.

1989). Figure 6.8 presents a fragment of what a semantic memory network might look like. In general, semantic network theories suggest that information is retrieved from memory through the principle of **spreading activation** (Medin & Ross, 1997). In other words, when you think about some concept, it becomes activated in the network, and this activation begins to "spread" down all the paths related to it. For example, if you are asked whether the statement "A robin is a bird" is true or false, the concepts of both "robin" and "bird" will become activated, and the spreading activation from each will intersect somewhere in these paths.

Some associations within the network are stronger than others, and spreading activation travels more quickly along stronger paths than along weaker ones. For instance, you probably have a stronger association between "bat" and "wings" than between "bat" and "mammal." Accordingly, you'd respond more quickly to "Can a bat fly?" than to "Is a bat a mammal?"

Because of the tight organization of semantic networks and the speed at which activation spreads through the network, people gain access to an enormous body of knowledge about the world quickly and effortlessly. They retrieve not only facts that they have learned directly but also knowledge that allows them to infer other facts about the world (Matlin, 1998). For example, imagine answering the following two questions: (1) Is a robin a bird? and (2) Is a robin a living thing? You can probably answer the first question "directly," because you probably learned this fact at some point in your life. However, you

FIGURE 6.8

Semantic Networks

This drawing represents just a small part of a network of semantic associations. These networks allow people to retrieve specific pieces of previously learned information and to make new inferences about concepts.

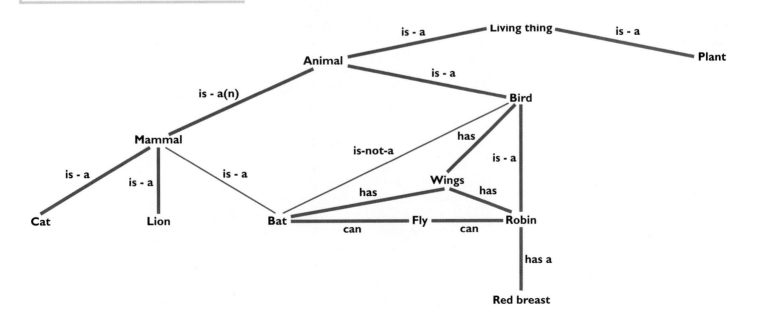

may never have consciously thought about the second question, so answering it requires some inference. Figure 6.8 illustrates the path to that inference. Because you know that a robin is a bird, a bird is an animal, and animals are living things, you infer that a robin must be a living thing. As you might expect, however, it takes slightly longer to answer the second question than the first.

Retrieving Incomplete Knowledge   Concepts are represented in semantic memory as unique sets of features or attributes. But what if you can retrieve some features of a concept from your semantic network, but not enough of them to identify what the concept is? For example, you might know that there is an animal that has wings, can fly, and is *not* a bird, and yet be unable to retrieve its name (Connor, Balota, & Neely, 1992). When this happens, you are retrieving *incomplete knowledge*. (The animal in question is a bat.)

The *tip-of-the-tongue phenomenon* is a common example of incomplete knowledge. In a typical experiment on this phenomenon, participants listen as dictionary definitions are read to them. They are then asked to identify the word being defined (R. Brown & McNeill, 1966). If they cannot recall a defined word, they are asked if they can recall any feature of it, such as its first letter or how many syllables it has. People are surprisingly good at this task, indicating that they are able to retrieve at least some knowledge of the word (Brennen et al., 1990). Most people experience the tip-of-the-tongue phenomenon about once a week (A. S. Brown, 1991).

Constructing Memories

▦ **How accurate are my memories?**

Our memories are affected not only by what we perceive but also by generalized knowledge about the world (D. L. Schacter, Norman, & Koutstaal, 1998). We use that existing knowledge to organize new information as we receive it, and we fill in gaps in the information that we encode and retrieve (Sherman & Bessennoff, 1999). This process is called *constructive memory.*

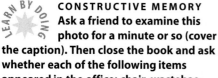

CONSTRUCTIVE MEMORY
Ask a friend to examine this photo for a minute or so (cover the caption). Then close the book and ask whether each of the following items appeared in the office: chair, wastebasket, bottle, typewriter, coffeepot, and book. If your friend reports having seen a wastebasket or book, you will have demonstrated constructive memory.

In one study of constructive memory, undergraduates were asked to wait for several minutes in the office of a graduate student (W. F. Brewer & Treyens, 1981). Later, they were asked to recall everything that was in the office. Most of the students mistakenly "remembered" seeing books, even though there were none. Apparently, the general knowledge that graduate students read many books influenced the participants' memory of what was in the room.

By constructing our own versions of what we have seen and heard, we may experience an event differently from the way it actually happened. These errors, called *false memories,* can occur in relation to anything from the objects present in a room to the identity of an armed robber (Clancy et al., 2000). Later, we discuss how false memories might color eyewitness testimony and reports of sexual abuse in childhood. For now, though, let's take a look at how researchers study false memories about less dramatic everyday experiences.

What was the researchers' question?

How easy is it for people to form false memories? Henry Roediger and Kathleen McDermott (1995) addressed this question in an experiment to test for false memories as people recalled lists of words that had been read to them.

How did the researchers answer the question?

College students heard sixteen lists of words. Each word list related to a particular theme. For example, the snow list featured fifteen words such as *sleet, slush, frost, white, cold,* and so on. Yet the list's theme word—in this case, *snow*—was never included. After hearing half the lists, the students were simply asked to recall as many words as they could. But after hearing the other half, the students did math problems before trying to recall the words. Working the math problems prevented them from rehearsing the words, as they had been able to do with the previous lists. When all sixteen lists had been presented, the students were given a new list of words and asked to say which of them had been on the lists they had heard earlier and which had not. Some of the words on this new list were theme words, such as *snow,* that had never been presented. Would the students "remember" having heard the theme words? How confident would they be about their "memory" of these words?

What did the researchers find?

The students falsely, but confidently, recalled hearing the theme words on 55 percent of the lists. In fact, theme words were falsely remembered as often as listed words were correctly remembered. As you might expect, accurate recall of the listed words was greater when the students had been allowed to say them shortly after hearing them rather than after first doing math problems. However, false memory of never-presented theme words occurred in both conditions.

What do the results mean?

The results of this study suggest that the participants could not always distinguish words they had heard from those they had not heard. Why? The never-presented theme words "belonged" with the lists of presented words and apparently were "remembered" because they fit logically into the gaps in the students' memories. In short, the students' knowledge of words that "should" have been included on the lists created a "memory" that they *were* presented.

Given that rehearsal is known to improve short-term memory, why did these false memories appear even when the participants could both rehearse the listed words and quickly try to recall them? Perhaps the association between the never-presented theme words and the listed words was strong enough that rehearsing the listed words "pulled" the theme words along with them.

▧ What do we still need to know?

Studies like this one make it clear that memory is constructive, and that memory distortion and inaccuracy are commonplace (D. L. Schacter, Norman, & Koutstaal, 1998; Schmolck, Buffalo, & Squire, 2000). We still need to identify the processes behind such distortion. In addition, we are not yet sure why false memories can seem as real to us as our memories of actual events. Perhaps the more frequently we recall an event (as when students were allowed to rehearse some lists), the stronger is our belief that we have accurately recalled it. There is also evidence that merely thinking about or hearing sounds associated with certain objects or events appears to make false memories of them more likely (Henkel, Franklin, & Johnson, 2000). Questions about how false memories are created lead to even deeper questions about the degree to which our imperfect memory processes might distort our experiences of reality. Is there an objective reality, or do we each experience our own version of it?

Constructive Memory and PDP Models

Parallel distributed processing models offer one way of explaining how semantic and episodic information become integrated in constructive memories. As noted earlier, PDP models suggest that newly learned facts alter our general knowledge of the world. In these network models, learned associations between specific facts come together. Let's say, for example, that your own network "knows" that your friend Joe is a male European American student who is a business major. It also "knows" that Claudia is a female African American student. However, your network has never learned Claudia's major. Now suppose that *every other* student you know is a business major. In this case, the connection between "students you know" and "business majors" would be so strong that you would conclude that Claudia is a business major, too. You would be so confident in this belief that it would take overwhelming evidence for you to change your mind (Rumelhart & McClelland, 1986). In short, you would have constructed a memory about Claudia.

PDP networks also produce *spontaneous generalizations.* Thus, if your friend tells you that she just bought a new car, you would know without asking that, like all other cars you have experienced, it has four wheels. This is a spontaneous generalization from your knowledge base. However, spontaneous generalizations can create significant errors if the network is based on limited or biased experience with a class of objects or people.

If it occurs to you that ethnic prejudice can result from such spontaneous generalization errors, you are right (Greenwald & Banaji, 1995). But ironically, researchers are encouraged by this prejudicial aspect of PDP networks, because it is an accurate reflection of human thought and memory. Virtually all people make spontaneous generalizations about males, females, European Americans, African Americans, the young, the old, and many other categories (Rudman et al., 1999). Is prejudice, then, a process that we have no choice in or control over? Not necessarily. Relatively unprejudiced people tend to recognize that they are making generalizations and consciously try to ignore or suppress them (Monteith, Sherman, & Devine, 1998).

Schemas   PDP models also help us understand constructive memory by explaining the operation of the schemas that guide it. As described in Chapters 7 and 14, **schemas** are mental representations of categories of objects, events, and people. For example, most Americans have a schema for *baseball game,* so simply hearing these words is likely to

schemas   Mental representations of what we know and expect about the world.

FIGURE 6.9

The Effect of Schemas on Recall

In a classic study, people were shown figures like these, along with labels designed to activate certain schemas (Carmichael, Hogan, & Walter, 1932). For example, when showing the top figure, the experimenter said either "This resembles eyeglasses" or "This resembles a dumbbell." When the participants were asked to reproduce the figures from memory, their drawings tended to resemble the items mentioned by the experimenter. In other words, their memory had been altered by the schema-activating labels.

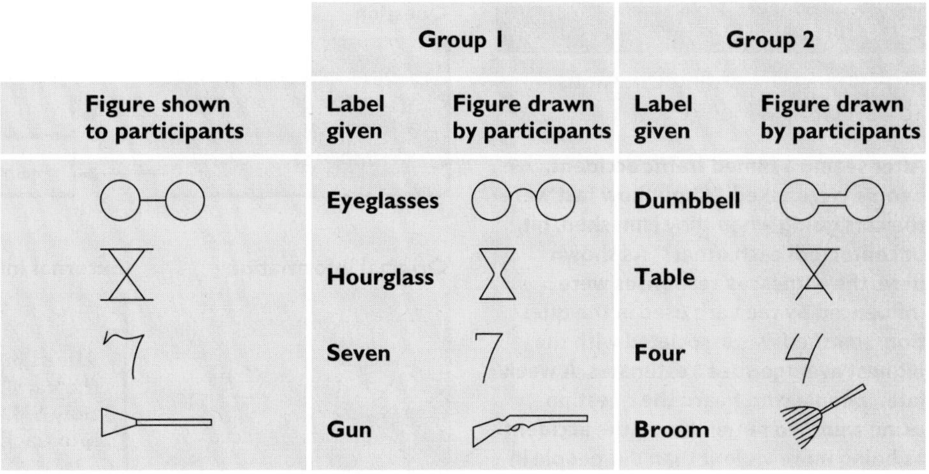

		Group 1		Group 2	
Figure shown to participants		**Label given**	**Figure drawn by participants**	**Label given**	**Figure drawn by participants**
○—○		Eyeglasses	○○	Dumbbell	○—○
⋈		Hourglass	⋈	Table	⋈
7		Seven	7	Four	4
⊐—		Gun	⟍	Broom	⟋

activate whole clusters of information in long-term memory, including the rules of the game, images of players, bats, balls, a green field, summer days, and perhaps hot dogs and stadiums. The generalized knowledge contained in schemas provides a basis for making inferences about incoming information during the encoding stage. So if you hear that a baseball player was injured, your schema about baseball might prompt you to encode the incident as game related, even though the cause was not mentioned. As a result, you are likely to recall the injury as having occurred during a game (see Figure 6.9 for another example).

LINKAGES

How accurate is eyewitness testimony? (a link to Sensation and Perception)

LINKAGES

Memory and Perception in the Courtroom

There are few situations in which accurate retrieval of memories is more important—and constructive memory is more dangerous—than when an eyewitness testifies in court about a crime. Let's consider the accuracy of eyewitness memory and how it can be distorted (E. F. Loftus, 1993). The most compelling evidence a lawyer can provide is that of an eyewitness, but eyewitnesses make many mistakes (E. F. Loftus & Ketcham, 1991). In 1984, for example, North Carolina college student Jennifer Thompson confidently identified Ronald Cotton as the man who had raped her at knifepoint. Mainly on the basis of Thompson's eyewitness testimony, Cotton was convicted of rape and sentenced to life in prison. He was released eleven years later, when DNA evidence revealed that he was innocent (and identified another man as the rapist). The eyewitness-victim's certainty had convinced a jury, but her memory had been faulty (O'Neill, 2000).

Like the rest of us, eyewitnesses can remember only what they perceived, and they can perceive only what they attended to (Backman & Nilsson, 1991). The witnesses' task is to report as accurately as possible what they saw or heard. But no matter how hard they try to be accurate, there are limits to how valid their reports can be (Kassin, Rigby, & Castillo, 1991). For example, hearing new information about a crime, including the form of a lawyer's question, can alter a witness's memory (Belli & Loftus, 1996). Experiments show that when witnesses are asked, "How fast was the blue car going when it *slammed into* the truck?" they are likely to recall a higher speed than when asked, "How fast was the blue car going when it *hit* the truck?" (E. F. Loftus & Palmer, 1974; see Figure 6.10). There is also evidence that an object mentioned after the fact is often mistakenly remembered as having been there in the first place (Dodson & Reisberg, 1991). For example, if a lawyer says that a screwdriver was lying on the ground (when it was not), witnesses often recall with great certainty having seen it (Ryan & Geiselman, 1991). Some theorists have speculated that mentioning an object makes the original memory more difficult to retrieve

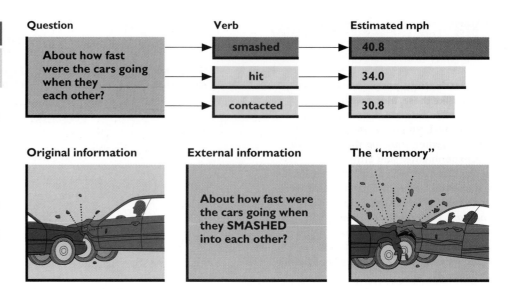

FIGURE 6.10

The Impact of Leading Questions on Eyewitness Memory

After seeing a filmed traffic accident, people were asked, "About how fast were the cars going when they (smashed, hit, or contacted) each other?" As shown here, the witnesses' responses were influenced by the verb used in the question; *smashed* was associated with the highest average speed estimates. A week later, people who heard the question using *smashed* remembered the accident as being more violent than did people in the other two groups (E. F. Loftus & Palmer, 1974).

Applying Psychology

EXPLORING MEMORY PROCESSES Research by cognitive psychologist Elizabeth Loftus has demonstrated mechanisms through which information received after the fact—including information contained in questions asked by attorneys—can alter the memory of eyewitnesses to accidents and crimes. These constructive memory processes can sometimes lead witnesses to "remember" things that did not actually happen, or that did not happen exactly as recalled.

(B. Tversky & Tuchin, 1989). However, there is now considerable evidence that when objects are mentioned later, they are integrated into the old memory and are not distinguished from what was originally seen (E. F. Loftus, 1992).

Jurors' belief in a witness's testimony often depends as much (or even more) on *how* the witness presents evidence as on the content or relevance of that evidence. For example, many jurors are particularly impressed by witnesses who give lots of details about what they saw. Detailed testimony from prosecution witnesses is especially likely to lead to guilty verdicts, even when the details reported are irrelevant (B. E. Bell & Loftus, 1989). Apparently, when a witness reports details, such as the exact time of the crime or the color of the criminal's shoes, jurors assume that the witness paid especially close attention or has a particularly good memory. This assumption seems reasonable, but there are limits on how much people can pay attention to, particularly when they are emotionally aroused and there is not much time to scan the scene. So especially when crimes happen quickly, witnesses whose attention was drawn to details such as shoe color might not have accurately perceived the criminal's facial features (Backman & Nilsson, 1991). The fact that an eyewitness reports many details does not guarantee that all of them were remembered correctly. Similarly, although jurors tend to believe witnesses who are confident about their testimony (Leippe, Manion, & Romanczyk, 1992), research shows that witnesses' confidence is frequently much higher than the accuracy of their reports (Sporer et al., 1995). In other words, as in the Jennifer Thompson case, even witnesses who are confident about their testimony are not always correct.

Many of the potential problems in eyewitness memory were revealed by a study that asked participants to watch a videotaped crime and then try to identify the criminal from a set of photographs (Wells & Bradfield, 1999). None of the photos showed the person who had committed the crime, but some participants nevertheless identified one of them as the criminal they saw on tape. When these mistaken participants were led to believe that they had correctly identified the criminal, they became even more confident in the accuracy of their false identification. These incorrect, but confident, witnesses became more likely than other participants to claim that it had been easy for them to identify the criminal from the photos because they had had a good view of him and had paid careful attention to him.

Many safeguards are built into the U.S. judicial system to minimize the chances that an innocent person will be falsely convicted. Nevertheless, experimental evidence on eyewitness perception, attention, and memory suggests that the system is far from perfect. Taking this evidence into account, the federal government recently published procedural guidelines for police and prosecutors who deal with eyewitnesses (U.S. Department of Justice, 1999). These guidelines warn that asking witnesses leading questions about what they saw can distort memory, and they note that false identifications are less likely if witnesses viewing suspects in a lineup are told that the real perpetrator might not be included (Foxhall, 2000). Application of the guidelines may eventually lead to a court system that provides added protection of the rights and welfare of all citizens (Wells et al., 2000).

Forgetting

■ **What causes me to forget things?**

The frustrations of forgetting—where you left your keys, the answer to a test question, an anniversary—are apparent to most people nearly every day (Neisser, 2000a). Let's look more closely at the nature of forgetting and what causes it.

How Do We Forget?

Hermann Ebbinghaus, a German psychologist, began the systematic study of memory and forgetting about a hundred years ago, using only himself as a research participant. He read aloud a list of nonsense syllables, such as *POF, XEM,* and *QAL,* at a constant pace, and then tried to recall the syllables.

Ebbinghaus devised the **method of savings** to measure how much was forgotten over time. This method computes the difference between the number of repetitions (or trials) needed to learn a list of items and the number of repetitions needed to relearn it after some period of time has elapsed. This difference represents the *savings* from one learning to the next. If it took Ebbinghaus ten trials to learn a list and ten more trials to relearn it, there would be no savings. Forgetting would have been complete. If it took him ten trials to learn the list and only five trials to relearn it, there would be a savings of 50 percent.

Ebbinghaus's research produced two lasting discoveries. One is the shape of the forgetting curve shown in Figure 6.11. Even when psychologists have substituted words, sentences, and stories for nonsense syllables, the forgetting curve shows the same strong

| FIGURE 6.11 | Ebbinghaus's Curve of Forgetting |

LEARN BY DOING **Select thirty words at random from a dictionary, and spend a few minutes memorizing them. After an hour has passed, write down as many words as you can remember, but don't look at the original list again. Do the same self-test eight hours later, a day later, and two days later. Now look at the original list, and see how well you did on each recall test. Ebbinghaus found that most forgetting occurs during the first nine hours after learning, and especially during the first hour. If this was not the case for you, why do you think you got different results?**

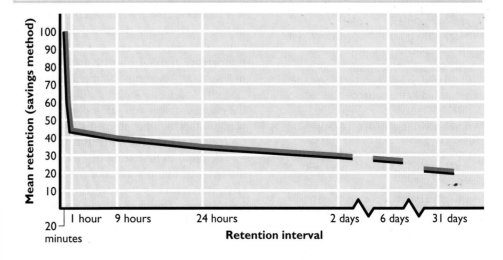

method of savings A method for measuring forgetting.

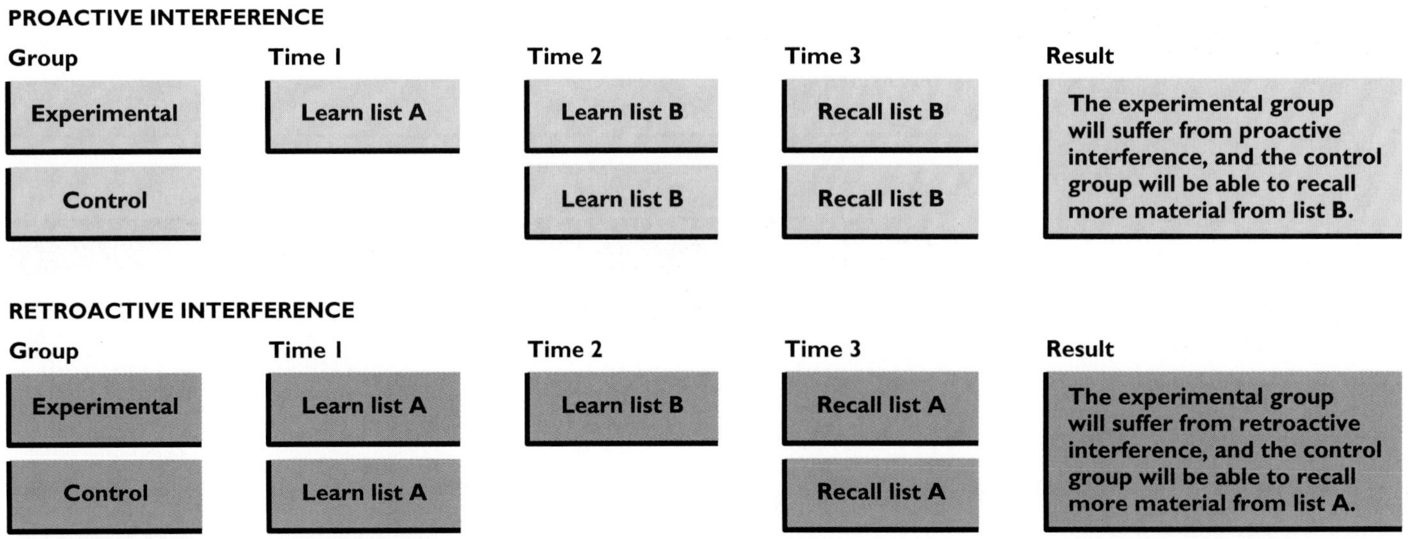

PROACTIVE INTERFERENCE

Group	Time 1	Time 2	Time 3	Result
Experimental	Learn list A	Learn list B	Recall list B	The experimental group will suffer from proactive interference, and the control group will be able to recall more material from list B.
Control		Learn list B	Recall list B	

RETROACTIVE INTERFERENCE

Group	Time 1	Time 2	Time 3	Result
Experimental	Learn list A	Learn list B	Recall list A	The experimental group will suffer from retroactive interference, and the control group will be able to recall more material from list A.
Control	Learn list A		Recall list A	

FIGURE 6.12

Procedures for Studying Interference

To recall the difference between the two types of interference, remember that the prefixes—*pro* and *retro*—indicate directions in time. *Pro* means "forward," and *retro* means "backward." In *proactive* interference, previously learned material interferes with *future* learning; *retroactive* interference occurs when new information interferes with the recall of *past* learning.

decay The gradual disappearance of the mental representation of a stimulus.

interference The process through which storage or retrieval of information is impaired by the presence of other information.

retroactive interference A cause of forgetting whereby new information placed in memory interferes with the ability to recall information already in memory.

proactive interference A cause of forgetting whereby previously learned information interferes with the ability to remember new information.

initial drop in memory, followed by a more moderate decrease over time (Slamecka & McElree, 1983). Of course, we remember sensible stories better than nonsense syllables, but the *shape* of the curve is the same no matter what type of material is involved (R. A. Davis & Moore, 1935). Even the forgetting of events from daily life tends to follow Ebbinghaus's forgetting curve (Thomson, 1982).

Ebbinghaus also discovered just how long-lasting "savings" in long-term memory can be. Psychologists now know from the method of savings that information about everything from algebra to bike riding is often retained for decades (Matlin, 1998). So, although you may forget something you have learned if you do not use the information, it is very easy to relearn the material if the need arises, indicating that the forgetting was not complete (L. K. Hall & Bahrick, 1998).

Why Do We Forget?

We have seen *how* forgetting occurs, but *why* does it happen? In principle, one of two processes can be responsible (J. B. Best, 1999). One process is **decay,** the gradual disappearance of the information from memory. Decay occurs in memory in much the same way as the inscription on a ring or bracelet wears away and becomes less distinct over time. Forgetting might also occur because of interference. Through **interference,** either the storage or the retrieval of information is impaired by the presence of other information. Interference might occur because one piece of information actually displaces other information, pushing it out of memory. It might also occur because one piece of information makes storing or recalling other information more difficult.

In the case of short-term memory, if an item is not rehearsed or thought about, memory of it decreases consistently over the course of eighteen seconds or so. Simple decay appears to play a big role in the forgetting of information in short-term memory. But interference through displacement can also be operating. Like a desktop, short-term memory can hold only so much. When additional items are added, the old ones tend to "fall off" and are no longer available (Haberlandt, 1999). Displacement is one reason why the phone number you just looked up is likely to drop out of short-term memory if you read another number immediately afterward. Rehearsal prevents displacement by continually reentering the same information into short-term memory.

The cause of forgetting from long-term memory appears to be more directly tied to interference, but it is also more complicated. In long-term memory there can be **retroactive interference,** in which learning of new information interferes with recall of older information. There can also be **proactive interference,** in which old information interferes with learning or remembering new information. Retroactive interference would help explain why studying French vocabulary this term might make it more difficult to

FIGURE 6.13

Retrieval Failures and Forgetting

On the initial test in Tulving and Psotka's experiment, people's ability to recall a list of items was strongly affected by the number of other lists they learned before being tested on the first one. When item-category (retrieval) cues were provided on a second test, however, retroactive interference from the intervening lists almost disappeared.

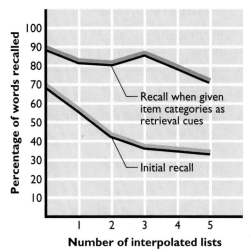

Recall when given item categories as retrieval cues

Initial recall

Number of interpolated lists

Source: Tulving & Psotka (1971).

remember the Spanish words you learned last term. And because of proactive interference, the French words you are learning now might make it harder to learn German next term. Figure 6.12 outlines the types of experiments used to study the influence of each form of interference in long-term memory.

Does interference push information out of memory, or does it merely hinder the ability to retrieve the information? To find out, Endel Tulving and Joseph Psotka (1971) presented people with different numbers of word lists. Each list contained words from six categories, such as types of buildings *(hut, cottage, cabin, hotel)* or earth formations *(cliff, river, hill, volcano)*. Some people learned a list and then recalled as many of the words as possible. Other groups learned the first list and then learned different numbers of other lists before trying to recall the first one.

The results were dramatic. As the number of additional lists increased, the number of words that people could recall from the original list consistently decreased. This finding reflected strong retroactive interference. Then the researchers gave a second test, in which they provided people with a retrieval cue by telling the category of the words (such as "types of buildings") to be recalled. Now the number of additional lists had almost no effect on the number of words recalled from the original list, as Figure 6.13 shows. These results indicate that the words were still represented in long-term memory; they had not been pushed out, but the participants could not remember them without appropriate retrieval cues. In short, faulty retrieval caused the original forgetting. Putting more and more information in long-term memory may be like placing more and more CDs in a storage case. Although none of the CDs disappears, it becomes increasingly difficult to find the one you are looking for.

Some theorists have concluded that all forgetting from long-term memory is due to some form of retrieval failure (Ratcliff & McKoon, 1989). Does this mean that everything in long-term memory remains there until death, even if you cannot always, or ever, recall it? No one yet knows for sure.

IT'S ALL COMING BACK TO ME NOW This grandfather has not fed an infant for decades, but his memory of how to do it is not entirely gone. He showed some "savings"; it took him less time to relearn the skill than it took to learn it initially.

While looking into her young daughter's eyes one day in 1989, Eileen Franklin-Lipsker suddenly had a vivid memory. She remembered seeing her father kill her childhood friend more than twenty years earlier. On the basis of her testimony about this memory, her father, George Franklin, Sr., was sent to prison for murder (E. F. Loftus & Ketcham, 1994).

THINKING CRITICALLY

Can Traumatic Memories Be Repressed, Then Recovered?

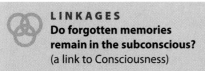

LINKAGES
Do forgotten memories remain in the subconscious?
(a link to Consciousness)

What am I being asked to believe or accept?

The prosecution in the Franklin case successfully argued that Eileen had recovered a *repressed memory*. Similar arguments in other cases tried in the early 1990s also resulted in imprisonment as now-adult children claimed to have recovered childhood memories of physical or sexual abuse at the hands of their parents. The juries in these trials accepted the assertion that all memory of shocking events can be repressed, or pushed into an inaccessible corner of the mind where, for decades, subconscious processes keep it out of awareness, yet potentially subject to recall (I. E. Hyman, 2000). And juries are not the only believers. A few years ago a large American news organization reported that the United States had illegally used nerve gas during the war in Vietnam. This story was based, in part, on a Vietnam veteran's account of recovered memories of having been subjected to a nerve gas attack.

Is there evidence available to support the claim?

Proponents of the repressed memory argument point to several lines of evidence to support their claims. First, as discussed in Chapter 4, on consciousness, a substantial amount of mental activity occurs outside of awareness (Kihlstrom, 1999). Second, research on implicit memory shows that our behavior can be influenced by information of which we are unaware (Schacter, Chiu, & Ochsner, 1993). Third, retrieval cues can help people recall memories that had previously been inaccessible to conscious awareness (Andrews et al., 2000; Landsdale & Laming, 1995). For example, carefully documented cases report that these cues have helped soldiers remember for the first time the circumstances under which they had been wounded many years before (Karon & Widener, 1997). Fourth, research on *motivated forgetting* suggests that people may be more likely to forget unpleasant events than pleasant ones. In one study, a psychologist kept a detailed record of his daily life over a six-year period. When he later tried to recall these experiences, he remembered more than half of the positive events but only one-third of the negative ones (Waagenaar, 1986). In another study, 38 percent of women who, as children, had been brought to a hospital because of sexual abuse did not recall—or at least did not report—the incident as adults (L. M. Williams, 1994).

Can that evidence be interpreted another way?

Those who are skeptical about repressed memories do not deny that subconscious memory and retrieval processes exist (Kihlstrom, 1999). They also recognize that, sadly, child abuse and other traumas are all too common. But these facts do not eliminate the possibility that any given "recovered" memory may actually be a distorted, or constructed, memory (Clancy et al., 2000). Our recall of past events is affected by what happened at the time, what we knew beforehand, and everything we experienced since. The people who "remembered" nonexistent books in an office constructed that memory based on what prior knowledge led them to *assume* was there.

As we saw in the Focus on Research section, false memories—distortions of actual events and the recall of events that didn't actually happen—can be just as vivid as real, accurate memories, and people can be just as confident in them (Pezdek, Finger, & Hodge, 1997; Roediger & McDermott, 2000). In one case study, for example, a teenager named Chris was given descriptions of four incidents from his childhood and asked to write about each of them every day for five days (E. F. Loftus, 1997a). One of these incidents—being lost in a shopping mall at age five—never really happened. Yet Chris eventually "remembered" this event, and he even added many details about the mall and the stranger whose hand he was supposedly found holding. He also rated this (false) memory as being more vivid than two of the other three (real) incidents he wrote about. A more recent study found similar results in about half of seventy-seven child participants (Porter, Yuille, & Lehman, 1999). Experiments, too, show that children who are repeatedly asked about a nonexistent trauma (getting a hand caught in a mousetrap) eventually develop a vivid and unshakable false memory of experiencing it (Ceci et al., 1994). Some people appear more likely than others to develop false memories. For example, two studies have found that women who have suffered physical or sexual abuse are more likely to falsely remember words on the recall test described in the Focus on Research section of this chapter (Bremner, Shobe, & Kihlstrom, 2000; Zoellner et al., 2000). This tendency appears strongest among abused women who show signs of posttraumatic stress disorder (Bremner, Shobe, & Kihlstrom, 2000). Another study found that susceptibility to false memory in the word-recall task was greater in women who reported recovered memories of sexual abuse than in nonabused women or those who had always remembered the abuse they suffered (Clancy et al., 2000).

Why would anyone remember a trauma that did not actually occur? Elizabeth Loftus (1997a) suggests that for one thing, popular books such as *The Courage to Heal* (Bass & Davis, 1994) and *Secret Survivors* (Blume, 1998) may lead people to believe that anyone who experiences guilt, depression, low self-esteem, overemotionality, or any of a long list of other problems is harboring repressed memories of abuse. According to Loftus, this message is reinforced by some therapists, particularly those who specialize in using guided imagination, hypnosis, and other methods to "help" clients recover repressed memories (Polusny & Follette, 1996; Poole et al., 1995). In so doing, these therapists may inadvertently influence people to construct false memories (Olio, 1994). As one client described her therapy, "I was rapidly losing the ability to differentiate between my imagination and my real memory" (E. F. Loftus & Ketcham, 1994, p. 25). To such therapists, a client's failure to recover memories of abuse, or refusal to accept that they exist, is evidence of "denial" (E. F. Loftus, 1997a).

The possibility that recovered memories might actually be false memories has led to dismissed charges or not-guilty verdicts for defendants in some repressed memory cases. In other cases, previously convicted defendants have been released. (George Franklin's conviction was overturned, but only after he spent five years in prison.) Concern over the potential damage resulting from false memories has prompted the establishment of the False Memory Syndrome Foundation, a support group for families affected by abuse accusations stemming from allegedly repressed memories. More than 100 of these families (including George Franklin) have filed lawsuits against hospitals and therapists (False Memory Foundation, 1997). One recent suit led to a $2 million judgment against a Minnesota therapist whose client discovered that her "recovered" memories of childhood were false; a similar case in Illinois resulted in a $10.6 million settlement and the suspension of the license of the psychiatrist who had "found" his patient's lost memories.

What evidence would help to evaluate the alternatives?

Evaluating reports of recovered memories would be easier if we had more information about how common it is for people to forget traumatic memories *and* how accurate their memories of such events are, if and when they recall them. So far, we know that some people apparently forget intense emotional experiences, but that most have vivid and long-lasting memories of them (H. G. Pope et al., 1998; Strongman & Kemp, 1991). Especially valuable is research like the sexual abuse survey mentioned earlier in which women were interviewed long after documented incidents of sexual abuse had occurred. Further research of this kind will yield better estimates of the prevalence of repressed memories, and might also offer clues as to the kinds of people and events most likely to be associated with this kind of forgetting.

It would also be valuable to know more about the processes through which repression might occur. Is there a mechanism that specifically pushes traumatic memories out of awareness, then keeps them at a subconscious level for long periods? Thus far, cognitive psychologists have not found evidence for such a mechanism (E. F. Loftus, 1997a; H. G. Pope et al., 1998).

What conclusions are most reasonable?

An objective reading of the research evidence supports the view that recovery of traumatic memories is at least possible. But the implantation of false memories is also possible and has been demonstrated experimentally.

The intense conflict between organizations such as the False Memory Syndrome Foundation and people who believe in recovered memories reflects a fundamental disagreement about evidence. To many therapists who deal daily with victims of sexual abuse and other traumas, clients' reports constitute stronger "proof" of recovered memories than do the results of laboratory experiments. Those reports are viewed with considerably more skepticism by psychologists who engage in, or rely on, empirical research on the processes of memory and forgetting (K. S. Pope, in press).

In short, whether one believes a claim of recovered memory may be determined by the relative weight one assigns to evidence based on personal experiences and intuition versus evidence that comes from controlled experiments. Still, the apparent ease with which false memories can be created should lead judges, juries, and the general public to exercise great caution before accepting unverified memories of traumatic events as the truth. At the same time, we should not uncritically reject the claims of people who appear to have recovered memories (Nadel & Jacobs, 1998). Perhaps the wisest course is to use all the scientific and circumstantial evidence available to carefully and critically examine claims of recovered memories while keeping in mind the possibility that constructive memory processes *might* have influenced them. This careful, scientific approach is vital if we are to protect the rights of those who report recovered memories, as well as those who face accusations arising from them.

Biological Bases of Memory

■ **How does my brain change when I store a memory?**

Many psychologists who study memory focus on explicit and implicit mental processes. Others explore the physical, electrical, and chemical changes that take place in the brain when people encode, store, and retrieve information (Cabeza & Nyberg, 2000; E. E. Smith, 2000).

The Biochemistry of Memory

As described in Chapter 2, communication among brain cells takes place at the synapses between axons and dendrites, using chemicals called *neurotransmitters* that are released at the synapses. The formation and storage of new memories are associated with at least two kinds of changes in synapses.

The first kind of change occurs as new experiences alter the functioning of *existing* synapses. For example, when two neurons fire at the same time and together stimulate a third neuron, that other neuron will later be more responsive than before to stimulation by either neuron alone. This process of "sensitizing" synapses is called *long-term potentiation.* The second kind of change occurs when stimulation from the environment promotes the formation of *new* synapses. Scientists have now actually seen this process occur. As shown in Figure 6.14, repeatedly sending signals across a particular synapse increases the number of special little branches, called *spines,* that appear on the receiving cell's dendrites (Toni et al., 1999).

In the hippocampus (see Figure 6.15), these changes appear to occur at synapses that use the neurotransmitter *glutamate* (Malenka & Nicoll, 1999). Other neurotransmitters, such as *acetylcholine,* also play important roles in memory formation. The memory problems seen in Alzheimer's patients are related to a deficiency in neurons that use acetylcholine and send fibers to the hippocampus and the cortex (Muir, 1997). Drugs that interfere with the action of acetylcholine impair memory, and drugs that increase the amount of acetylcholine in synapses improve memory in aging animals and humans (Sirvio, 1999).

In summary, research has shown that the formation of memories is associated with changes in many individual synapses that, together, strengthen and improve the communication in networks of neurons (Rosenzweig & Bennett, 1996).

anterograde amnesia   A loss of memory for events that occur after a brain injury.

FIGURE 6.14

Building Memories

These models of synapses are based on electron microscope images of neurons in the brain. Notice that before the synapse has been "sensitized," just one spine (shown in white) appears on this part of the dendrite. Afterward, there are two spines. The creation and changing of many individual synapses in the brain appears to underlie the formation and storage of new memories.

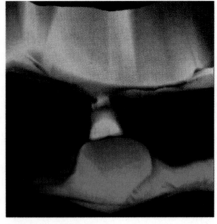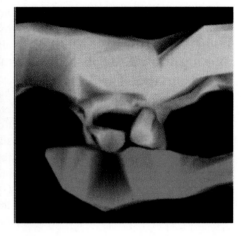

Source: Barinaga (1999).

 LINKAGES
Where are memories stored?
(a link to Biology and Behavior)

Location of Memories in the Brain

Are the biochemical processes involved in memory concentrated in certain regions, or are they distributed throughout the brain? The latest research suggests that memory involves both specialized regions for various types of memory formation and widespread areas for storage.

The Impact of Brain Damage   Studies of how brain injuries affect memory provide evidence about which parts of the brain are involved in various kinds of memory. For example, damage to the hippocampus, nearby parts of the cerebral cortex, and the thalamus often results in **anterograde amnesia,** a loss of memory for any event occurring *after* the injury. People who suffer this kind of damage are unable to form new memories.

The case of H.M. provides a striking example of anterograde amnesia (B. Milner, 1966). When H.M. was twenty-seven years old, part of his hippocampus was removed to end his severe epileptic seizures. After the operation, both his long-term and short-term memory appeared normal, but something was wrong. Two years later, he still believed that he was twenty-seven. When his family moved into a new house, he could not remember the new address or how to get there. When his uncle died, he grieved in a

FIGURE 6.15

Brain Structures Involved in Memory

Combined neural activity in many parts of the brain allows us to encode, store, and retrieve memories. The complexity of the biological bases of these processes is underscored by research showing that different aspects of a memory—such as the sights and sounds of some event—are stored in different parts of the cerebral cortex.

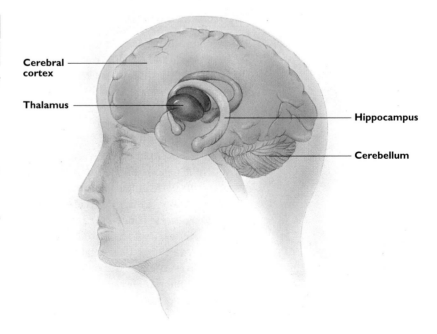

normal way; but soon after, he began to ask why his uncle had not visited him. He had to be repeatedly reminded of the death and, each time, H.M. began the mourning process all over again. The surgery had apparently destroyed the mechanism that transfers information from short-term to long-term memory.

Patients like H.M. can't form new episodic memories, but they can use procedural memory and perform tasks that require other kinds of memory. For example, using procedural memory, H.M. learned how to solve a complicated puzzle, but at each daily practice session, he insisted he was seeing the puzzle for the first time. A musician with a similar kind of brain damage was able to use his procedural memory to continue leading choral groups (Vattano, 2000).

Retrograde amnesia involves loss of memory for events *prior* to some brain injury (N. Kapur, 1999). Often, a person with this type of amnesia can't remember anything that took place in the months or years before the injury. For example, in 1994, in England, head injuries from a car crash left Perlene Griffith-Barwell, thirty-six, with retrograde amnesia so severe that she forgot virtually everything she had learned about everything and everybody over the previous twenty years. She thought she was still sixteen and did not recognize her husband, Malcolm, or her four children. She said, "The children were sweet, but they didn't seem like mine," and she "didn't feel anything" for Malcolm. Her memories of the last twenty years have never fully returned. She is divorced, but she still lives with her children and holds a job in a bank (Weinstein, 1999).

Unlike Perlene, most victims of retrograde amnesia gradually recover their memories. The most distant events are recalled first; then the person gradually regains memory for events leading up to the injury. Recovery is seldom complete, however, and the person may never remember the last few seconds before the injury. One man received a severe blow to the head after being thrown from his motorcycle. After regaining consciousness, he claimed that he was eleven years old. Over the next three months, he slowly recalled more and more of his life. He remembered when he was twelve, thirteen, and so on— right up until the time he was riding his motorcycle the day of the accident. But he was never able to remember what happened just before the accident (Baddeley, 1982). Those final events were probably encoded into short-term memory, but apparently they were never transferred into long-term memory. Conditions that suppress neural activity in the brain—including strong electrical impulses, anesthetics, and poisoning by carbon monoxide or other toxins—can also disrupt the transfer of information from short-term to long-term memory. The damage to memory in these cases and others is consistent with the view that short-term memory and long-term memory are distinct systems.

Multiple Storage Areas   Obviously, the hippocampus does not permanently store long-term memories (Rosenbaum et al., 2000). (If it did, H.M. would not have retained memories from the years before part of his hippocampus was removed.) The hippocampus and thalamus send nerve impulses to the cerebral cortex, and it is in the cortex that long-term semantic and episodic memories are probably stored (Gabrieli, 1998)—but not just in one place. As we saw in Chapter 2, different regions of the cortex receive messages from different senses. Specific aspects of an experience are probably stored near these regions. For example, damage to the auditory association cortex disrupts memory for sounds (Colombo et al., 1990). A memory, however, involves more than one sensory system. Even in the simple case of a rat remembering a maze, the experience of the maze involves vision, smell, specific movements, and emotions, each of which may be stored in different regions of the brain (Gallagher & Chiba, 1996). Thus memories are both localized and distributed. Certain brain areas store specific aspects of each remembered event, but many brain systems are involved in experiencing a whole event. For example, the cerebellum (see Figure 6.15) is involved in the storage of procedural memories, such as dance steps and other movements. Finally, recent research with animals suggests that when an emotional (fear-related) memory is recalled, it appears to be subject to a biological re-storage process during which it is open to alteration (Nader, Schafe, & Le Doux, 2000). Future research on this phenomenon may one day shed additional light on the processes of constructive memory and the bases for false memories.

retrograde amnesia   A loss of memory for events that occurred prior to a brain injury.

Improving Your Memory

■ **How can I remember more information?**

Although many basic questions about what memory is and how it works remain, psychologists know a great deal about how people can improve their memories (Neisser, 2000a).

Mnemonics

One way in which almost anyone can improve his or her memory is to employ mnemonics (pronounced "nee-MON-ix"). **Mnemonics** are strategies for putting information into an organized *context* in order to remember it more easily. To remember the names of the Great Lakes, for example, you could use the acronym HOMES (for Huron, Ontario, Michigan, Erie, and Superior). Verbal organization is the basis for many mnemonics. You can link items by weaving them into a story, a sentence, or a rhyme. To help customers remember where they have parked their cars, some large garages have replaced section designations such as "A1" or "G8" with the names of colors, months, or animals. Customers can then tie the location of their cars to information already in long-term memory—for example, "I parked in the month of my mother's birthday."

One simple but powerful mnemonic is called the *method of loci* (pronounced "LOW-sigh"), or the "method of places." To use this method, first think about a set of familiar locations. Use your home, for example. You might imagine walking through the front door, around all four corners of the living room, and through each of the other rooms. Next, imagine each item to be remembered in one of these locations. Whenever you want to remember a list, use the same locations, in the same order. Creating vivid or unusual images of how the items appear in each location seems to be particularly effective (Kline & Groninger, 1991). For example, tomatoes smashed against the front door or bananas hanging from the bedroom ceiling might be helpful in recalling these items on a grocery list.

Guidelines for More Effective Studying

The success of mnemonic strategies demonstrates again the importance of relating new information to knowledge already stored in memory. All mnemonic systems require that you have a well-learned body of knowledge (such as locations) that can be used to provide a context for organizing incoming information (Hilton, 1986).

When you want to remember more complex material, such as a textbook chapter, the same basic principle applies (Palmisano & Herrmann, 1991). Indeed, you can improve your memory for text material by first creating an outline or other overall context for learning, rather than by just reading and rereading (Glover et al., 1990). For retaining information over long periods, maintenance rehearsal alone tends to be ineffective, no matter how much time you spend on it (Bjorklund & Green, 1992). In short, "work smarter, not harder."

In addition, spend your time wisely. *Distributed practice* is much more effective than *massed practice* for learning new information. If you are going to spend ten hours studying for a test, you will be much better off studying for ten 1-hour blocks, separated by periods of sleep and other activity. "Cramming" for one 10-hour block will not be as successful. By scheduling more study sessions, you will stay fresh and be able to think about the material from a new perspective during each session. This method will help you elaborate on the material, as in elaborative rehearsal, and thus remember it better.

Reading a Textbook   More specific advice for remembering textbook material comes from a study that examined how successful and unsuccessful college students approached their reading (Whimbey, 1976). Unsuccessful students tended to read the material straight through. They did not slow down when they reached a difficult section. They kept going even when they did not understand what they were reading. In contrast, successful college students monitored their understanding, reread difficult sections, and

mnemonics   Strategies for organizing information in order to remember it.

periodically stopped or reviewed what they had learned. In short, effective learners engage in a very deep level of processing. They are active learners. They think of each new fact in relation to other material, and they develop a context in which many new facts can be organized effectively.

Research on memory suggests two specific guidelines for reading a textbook. First, make sure that you understand what you are reading before moving on (Herrmann & Searleman, 1992). Second, use the *PQ4R method* (E. L. Thomas & Robinson, 1972), which is one of the most successful strategies for remembering textbook material (J. R. Anderson, 1990b; Chastain & Thurber, 1989). PQ4R stands for six activities to engage in when you read a chapter: preview, question, read, reflect, recite, and review. These activities are designed to increase the depth to which you process the information you read:

1. *Preview.*   Take a few minutes to skim the chapter. Look at the section headings and any boldfaced or italicized terms. Obtain a general idea of what material will be discussed, the way it is organized, and how its topics relate to one another and to what you already know. Some people find it useful to survey the entire chapter once and then survey each major section in a little more detail before reading it.

2. *Question.*   Before reading each section, ask yourself what content will be covered and what information should be extracted from it.

3. *Read.*   Read the text, but think about the material as you read. Are the questions you raised earlier being answered? Do you see the connections between the topics?

4. *Reflect.*   As you read, think of your own examples—and create visual images—of the concepts and phenomena you encounter. Ask yourself what the material means, and consider how each section relates to other sections in the chapter, and other chapters in the book (this book's Linkages features are designed to promote this kind of reflection).

5. *Recite.*   At the end of each section, recite the major points. Resist the temptation to be passive and say, "Oh, I remember that." Be active. Put the ideas into your own words by reciting them aloud.

6. *Review.*   Finally, at the end of the chapter, review all the material. You should see connections not only within each section but also among sections. The objective is to see how the material is organized. Once you grasp the organization, the individual facts will be far easier to remember.

By following these procedures, you will learn and remember the material better. You will also save yourself considerable time.

Lecture Notes   As a student or businessperson, you will often have to learn and remember material from lectures or presentations. Taking notes will help, but doing so *effectively* is an acquired skill. Research on memory suggests some simple strategies for taking and using notes effectively.

Realize first that in note taking, more is not necessarily better. Taking detailed notes on everything requires that you pay close attention to unimportant as well as important content, leaving little time for thinking about the material. Note takers who concentrate on expressing the major ideas in relatively few words remember more than those who try to catch every detail (Pauk & Fiore, 2000). In short, the best way to take notes is to think about what is being said. Draw connections with other material in the presentation. Then summarize the major points clearly and concisely.

Once you have a set of lecture notes, review them as soon as possible after the lecture so that you can fill in missing details. (Remember: Most forgetting from long-term memory occurs during the first hour after learning.) When the time comes for serious study, use your notes as if they were a chapter in a textbook. Write a detailed outline. Think about how various points are related. Once you have organized the material, the details will make more sense and will be much easier to remember. ("In Review: Improving Your Memory" summarizes tips for studying.)

in review | Improving Your Memory

Goal	Helpful Techniques
Remembering lists of items	Use mnemonics. Look for meaningful acronyms. Try the method of loci.
Remembering textbook material	Follow the PQ4R system. Allocate your time to allow for distributed practice. Read actively, not passively.
Taking lecture notes	Take notes, but record only the main points. Think about the overall organization of the material. Review your notes as soon after the lecture as possible in order to fill in missing points.
Studying for exams	Write a detailed outline of your lecture notes rather than passively reading them.

active review Memory

Linkages

As noted in Chapter 1, all of psychology's subfields are related to one another. Our discussion of eyewitness testimony illustrates just one way in which the topic of this chapter, memory, is linked to the subfield of sensation and perception (Chapter 3). The Linkages diagram shows ties to two other subfields as well, and there are many more ties throughout the book. Looking for linkages among subfields will help you see how they all fit together and help you better appreciate the big picture that is psychology.

LINKAGES

CHAPTER 6

MEMORY

How accurate is eyewitness testimony? *(ans. on p.195)*

CHAPTER 3

SENSATION AND PERCEPTION

Where are memories stored? *(ans. on p. 203)*

CHAPTER 2

BIOLOGY AND BEHAVIOR

Why does memory improve during childhood? *(ans. on p.314)*

CHAPTER 9

HUMAN DEVELOPMENT

Summary

THE NATURE OF MEMORY

▪ **How does information turn into memories?**

Human memory depends on a complex mental system. There are three basic memory processes. *Encoding* transforms stimulus infor-

mation into some type of mental representation. Encoding can be by *acoustic* (sound), *visual* (appearance), or *semantic* (meaning) codes. *Storage* maintains information in the memory system over time. *Retrieval* is the process of gaining access to previously stored information.

Most psychologists agree that there are at least three types of memory. *Episodic memory* contains information about specific events in a person's life. *Semantic memory* contains generalized knowledge about the world. *Procedural memory* contains information about how to do things. Research on memory focuses on *explicit memory,* the processes through which people try to remember something, and *implicit memory,* the unintentional recollection and influence of prior experiences.

Four models of memory have guided most research. The *levels-of-processing model* suggests that the most important determinant of memory is how extensively information is encoded or processed when it is first received. In general, *elaborative rehearsal* is more effective than *maintenance rehearsal* in learning new information, because it represents a deeper level of processing. According to the *transfer-appropriate processing model,* the critical determinant of memory is not how deeply information is encoded but whether the encoding process produces memory codes that are later accessed at the time of retrieval. *Parallel distributed processing (PDP) models* of memory suggest that new experiences not only provide specific information but also become part of, and alter, a whole network of associations. The *information-processing model* suggests that for information to become firmly embedded in memory, it must pass through three stages of processing: sensory memory, short-term memory, and long-term memory.

STORING NEW MEMORIES

What am I most likely to remember?

Sensory memory maintains incoming stimulus information in the *sensory registers* for a very brief time. *Selective attention,* which focuses mental resources on only part of the stimulus field, controls what information in the sensory registers is actually perceived and transferred to short-term memory.

Short-term memory (STM), which is also known as *working memory,* provides a system in which people can store, organize, and integrate facts and thereby solve problems and make decisions. Various memory codes can be used in short-term memory, but acoustic codes seem to be preferred in most verbal tasks. Studies of the *immediate memory span* indicate that the capacity of short-term memory is approximately seven *chunks,* or meaningful groupings of information. Studies using the *Brown-Peterson procedure* show that information in short-term memory is usually forgotten in about eighteen seconds if it is not rehearsed.

Long-term memory (LTM) normally involves semantic coding, which means that people tend to encode the general meaning of information, not specific details, into long-term memory. The capacity of long-term memory to store new information is extremely large, and perhaps unlimited. According to the levels-of-processing model, there is no need to distinguish between short-term and long-term memory. Still, some evidence suggests that these systems may be distinct. For example, although serial-position curves show both a *primacy effect* and a *recency effect,* either effect can be eliminated without affecting the other.

RETRIEVING MEMORIES

How do I retrieve stored memories?

Retrieval cues help people remember things that they would otherwise not be able to recall. The effectiveness of retrieval cues follows the *encoding specificity principle:* Cues help retrieval only if they match some feature of the information that was originally encoded. All else being equal, memory may be better when one attempts to retrieve information in the same environment in which it was learned; this is called *context-dependent memory.* When our internal state can affect retrieval, we have a *state-dependent memory.* Researchers usually study retrieval from semantic memory by examining how long it takes people to answer general-knowledge questions. It appears that ideas are represented as associations in a dense semantic memory network, and that the retrieval of information occurs by a process of *spreading activation.* Each concept in the network is represented as a unique collection of features or attributes. The tip-of-the-tongue phenomenon represents the retrieval of incomplete knowledge.

CONSTRUCTING MEMORIES

How accurate are my memories?

In the process of constructive memory, people use generalized knowledge, or *schemas,* to fill in gaps in the information they encode and retrieve. PDP models provide one explanation of how people make spontaneous generalizations about the world.

Eyewitnesses can remember only what they perceive, and they can perceive only what they attend to. As a result, eyewitness testimony is often much less accurate than witnesses, and jurors, think it is.

FORGETTING

What causes me to forget things?

Through research on long-term memory and forgetting, Ebbinghaus introduced the *method of savings.* He found that most forgetting from long-term memory occurs during the first hour after learning and that savings can be extremely long-lasting. *Decay* and *interference* are two mechanisms of forgetting. There is evidence of both decay and interference in short-term memory; it appears that most forgetting from long-term memory is due to either *retroactive interference* or *proactive interference.*

BIOLOGICAL BASES OF MEMORY

How does my brain change when I store a memory?

Research has shown that memories can result from new synapses forming in the brain and improved communication at existing synapses. Studies of *anterograde amnesia, retrograde amnesia,* and other consequences of brain damage provide information about the brain structures involved in memory. For example, the hippocampus and thalamus are known to play a role in the formation of memories. These structures send nerve impulses to the cerebral cortex, and it is there that memories are probably stored. Memories appear to be both localized and distributed throughout the brain.

IMPROVING YOUR MEMORY

How can I remember more information?

Mnemonics are strategies that are used to remember things better. One of the simplest but most powerful mnemonics is the method of loci. It is useful because it provides a context for organizing material more effectively. The key to remembering textbook material is to read actively rather than passively. One of the most effective ways to do this is to follow the PQ4R method: preview, question, read, reflect, recite, and review. Similarly, to take lecture notes or to study them effectively, organize the points in a meaningful framework, and think about how each main point relates to the others.

Learn by Doing

Put It in Writing

Write a paragraph describing your thoughts on the question of repressed memories of childhood abuse. Be sure to mention what evidence leads you to think as you do about this topic. For example, indicate whether you tend to give more weight to the testimony of clients who say they have recovered traumatic memories or to the results of scientific research on memory and repression. Finally, speculate on why you prefer one kind of evidence over another, and whether the debate over recovered memories will ever be resolved to everyone's satisfaction.

Personal Learning Activity

When you study for your next quiz or exam, try using some of the memory tips contained in this chapter. For example, use one or more mnemonic devices to help you to remember lists of information, and try the PQ4R approach with the next chapter you read. Did these memory-enhancing methods make it easier for you to study and to do well on your next quiz or exam? Why or why not? *For additional projects, see the five Personal Learning Activities in the corresponding chapter of the study guide that accompanies this text.*

Step into Action

Courses

Cognitive Psychology
Social Cognition
Experimental Psychology
Learning and Memory

Movies

The Lazarus Man; Anastasia; Black Out; Lapse of Memory; Regarding Henry (memory loss)
Rashoman; Stagecoach (constructive memory)
On Golden Pond (memory and aging)
Total Recall (futuristic images of constructing memories)

Books

Douglas J. Herrmann, Cathy McEvoy, and Christopher Hertzog (Eds.), *Basic and Applied Memory Research: Theory in Context* (Lawrence Erlbaum Associates, 1996) (overview of memory research)
Steven Pinker, *How the Mind Works* (Norton, 1997) (biology of memory and thought)
William H. Calvin, *The Cerebral Code: Thinking a Thought in the Mosaics of the Mind* (MIT Press, 1996) (brain function and memory)

Akira Miyake and Priti Shah (Eds.), *Models of Working Memory* (Cambridge University Press, 1999) (theories of short-term memory)
Elizabeth Loftus and Katherine Ketcham, *The Myth of Repressed Memory* (St. Martin's Press, 1996) (research casting doubt on the validity of some recovered memories)
E. Sue Blume, *Secret Survivors: Uncovering Incest and Its Aftereffects in Women* (Ballantine, 1998) (presents the position of some therapists who believe in the validity of all reports of recovered memories)

The Web

The World Wide Web is a good source of additional information about the science of psychology, provided you use it carefully and think critically about the information you find. The PsychAbilities web site that accompanies this text offers many resources relevant to this chapter. They include interactive NetLab exercises; Thinking Critically and Evaluating Research exercises; ACE chapter quizzes; recommended web links; and articles on current events, books, and movies. At http://college.hmco.com, select *Psychology* and then this textbook.

Review of Key Terms

Can you define each of the key terms in the chapter? Check your definitions against those on the pages listed in parentheses below or in the Glossary/Index at the end of the text.

acoustic codes *(p. 180)*
anterograde amnesia *(p. 203)*
Brown-Peterson procedure *(p. 186)*
chunks *(p. 185)*

context-dependent memories *(p. 190)*
decay *(p. 198)*
elaborative rehearsal *(p. 182)*
encoding *(p. 180)*

encoding specificity principle *(p. 190)*
episodic memory *(p. 181)*
explicit memory *(p. 181)*
immediate memory span *(p. 185)*

implicit memory *(p. 181)*
information-processing model *(p. 183)*
interference *(p. 198)*
levels-of-processing model *(p. 182)*

long-term memory (LTM) *(p. 186)*

maintenance rehearsal *(p. 182)*

method of savings *(p. 197)*

mnemonics *(p. 205)*

parallel distributed processing (PDP) models *(p. 182)*

primacy effect *(p. 188)*

proactive interference *(p. 198)*

procedural memory *(p. 181)*

recency effect *(p. 189)*

retrieval *(p. 181)*

retrieval cues *(p. 189)*

retroactive interference *(p. 198)*

retrograde amnesia *(p. 204)*

schemas *(p. 194)*

selective attention *(p. 184)*

semantic codes *(p. 180)*

semantic memory *(p. 181)*

sensory memory *(p. 184)*

sensory registers *(p. 184)*

short-term memory (STM) *(p. 184)*

spreading activation *(p. 191)*

state-dependent memory *(p. 190)*

storage *(p. 180)*

transfer-appropriate processing model *(p. 182)*

visual codes *(p. 180)*

working memory *(p. 184)*

Multiple-Choice Self-Test

Select the best answer for each of the questions below. Then check your response against the Answer Key at the end of the text.

1. Riesa was uncomfortable when she found herself alone with her friend's dog. Unconsciously, she was remembering when she was a small child and a similar dog had frightened her. This is an example of _____ memory.

   a. procedural
   b. semantic
   c. implicit
   d. explicit

2. When the police ask you where you were standing when the store you work in was robbed yesterday, they are asking you to use _____ memory.

   a. episodic
   b. procedural
   c. semantic
   d. short-term

3. Matt's ability to effortlessly tie his bow tie is an example of his use of _____ memory.

   a. episodic
   b. procedural
   c. semantic
   d. short-term

4. Raquel was still studying ten minutes before her test. As she entered the classroom, she kept repeating the last sentence she had read: "Henry VIII had six wives." She was using _____ to keep this information in mind.

   a. elaborative rehearsal
   b. maintenance rehearsal
   c. mnemonics
   d. retrieval

5. Larry is thrilled because he just met the girl of his dreams at the mall. She even gave him her phone number before she walked away. If Larry doesn't use any rehearsal methods, he has only about _____ before he will forget the number.

   a. one second
   b. eighteen seconds
   c. one minute
   d. five minutes

6. Reepal is listening to her father describe the party the family is planning. She is also smelling popcorn, hearing her radio, seeing lightning, and feeling warm. Reepal is able to transfer the information about the party to her short-term memory primarily because of

   a. elaborative rehearsal.
   b. implicit memory cues.
   c. selective attention.
   d. transfer-appropriate processing.

7. Remembering your bank account number, 2171982, as your birthday (February 17, 1982) is an example of

   a. chunking.
   b. the Brown-Peterson procedure.
   c. the PQ4R method.
   d. the method of loci.

8. Lisbeth was trying to recall the phrase that her mother always used, but all she could remember was the gist of it, not the exact wording. This phenomenon can be explained because encoding in long-term memory is usually

   a. acoustic.
   b. visual.
   c. semantic.
   d. state dependent.

9. Before Nesta went to the library, she wrote a list of twenty CDs that she wanted to check out. Unfortunately, she lost the list and can now remember only the first few CDs she wrote. This case illustrates the _____ effect.

   a. primacy
   b. recency
   c. fatigue
   d. parallel processing

10. Jerry, a steelworker, experienced a brain injury when a steel beam fell on his head. Jerry cannot remember anything that happened since the accident. Jerry is experiencing _____ amnesia.

   a. retrograde
   b. anterograde
   c. proactive
   d. retroactive

11. Compared with essay questions, multiple-choice questions are easier to answer, because they

    a. cause less interference.
    b. contain more retrieval cues.
    c. require only semantic memory.
    d. require only procedural memory.

12. Because of context dependence, people may remember material better when they

    a. organize it in an outline.
    b. are in the same place as when they learned the material.
    c. are in the same state of mind as when they learned the material.
    d. use mnemonics.

13. Molly knew that she knew the name of her kindergarten teacher, but she could not quite remember it when asked. This tip-of-the-tongue phenomenon is caused by retrieval of incomplete information from her

    a. constructive memory.
    b. sensory memory.
    c. semantic networks.
    d. schemas.

14. When asked if there was a fever thermometer in her doctor's office, Careen says she remembers seeing one, even though it wasn't actually there. This is an example of

    a. the tip-of-the-tongue phenomenon.
    b. forgetting.
    c. constructive memory.
    d. the primacy effect.

15. As a member of the jury, you hear a witness state that he is "absolutely sure" that it was the defendant who drove his car into a bus while ranting about "free public transportation." According to research on the memory of eyewitnesses, you should

    a. be impressed with the witness's confidence and treat his testimony as highly accurate.
    b. recognize that the witness's testimony might not be as accurate as he makes it sound.
    c. give heavy weight to the testimony only if it contains many small details.
    d. be suspicious of the testimony because it came from a male witness.

16. Hermea just finished listening to a wonderful lecture on psychology. If she does nothing to process the information further, forgetting of this material will occur most rapidly over the next

    a. hour.
    b. five hours.
    c. twenty-four hours.
    d. thirty-one days.

17. Robin memorized the names of all of the U.S. presidents when she was ten. Two years later, she had forgotten most of them, but she was pleasantly surprised that she could learn them a second time much more quickly than the first. This is an example of what Ebbinghaus called

    a. mnemonics.
    b. state dependence.
    c. savings.
    d. context dependence.

18. Berean studied French during his first year at college, and then started learning Spanish in his second year. Now he is having difficulty remembering his Spanish vocabulary because the French words keep interfering. This is an example of _____ interference.

    a. retrograde
    b. anterograde
    c. proactive
    d. retroactive

19. Alzheimer's patients experience severe problems with memory. Biologically, this can be explained by

    a. the loss of neurons that use acetylcholine.
    b. the loss of neurons that use dopamine.
    c. damage to the hippocampus.
    d. damage to the thalamus.

20. Loretta was trying to remember the names of famous psychologists. She mentally pictured them all being in her apartment. She imagined Elizabeth Loftus playing video games in the living room, Hermann Ebbinghaus taking a nap in the bathtub, and Sigmund Freud scrubbing the kitchen floor. Loretta is using the memory strategy called

    a. the method of loci.
    b. procedural memorization.
    c. encoding cues.
    d. context dependence.

7

Thought, Language, and Intelligence

"Say what you mean, and mean what you say."

This is good advice, but following it is not always easy, partly because our thoughts don't always come in the form of clear, complete sentences. We have to construct those sentences—using the language we have learned—from the words, images, ideas, and other mental materials that reside in our minds. Often, the complexity of that material makes it difficult to accurately express what we are thinking. We all manage to do it, but with varying degrees of success. In this chapter, we explore what thoughts are, what language is, and how people translate one into the other. We also consider how thinking guides decision making and problem solving and how psychologists measure individual differences in these and other mental abilities that are commonly described as *intelligence*.

Reading this chapter will help you to answer the following questions:

- **What good is thinking, anyway?**
- **What are thoughts made of?**
- **Are people always logical?**
- **What's the best way to solve a problem?**
- **How can I become a better decision maker?**
- **How do babies learn to talk?**
- **How is intelligence measured?**
- **How good are IQ tests?**
- **Is there more than one type of intelligence?**

r. Joyce Wallace, a New York City internist, was having trouble figuring out what was the matter with a forty-three-year-old patient, "Laura McBride." Laura reported pain in her stomach and abdomen, aching muscles, irritability, occasional dizzy spells, and fatigue (Rouéché, 1986). The doctor's initial hypothesis was iron-deficiency anemia, a condition in which there is not enough oxygen-carrying hemoglobin in the blood. There was some evidence to support that hypothesis. A physical examination revealed that Laura's spleen was somewhat enlarged, and blood tests showed low hemoglobin and high production of red blood cells, suggesting that her body was attempting to compensate for the loss of hemoglobin. However, other tests revealed normal iron levels. Perhaps she was losing blood through internal bleeding, but other tests ruled that out. Had Laura been vomiting blood? She said no. Blood in the urine? No. Abnormally heavy menstrual flow? No.

As Dr. Wallace puzzled over the problem, Laura's condition worsened. She reported more intense pain, cramps, shortness of breath, and severe loss of energy. Her blood was

213

FIGURE 7.1

The Circle of Thought

The circle of thought begins as our sensory systems take in information from the world around us. Our perceptual system describes and elaborates this information, which is represented in the brain in ways that allow us to make decisions, formulate plans, and guide our actions. As our actions change our world, we receive new information—and the circle of thought begins again.

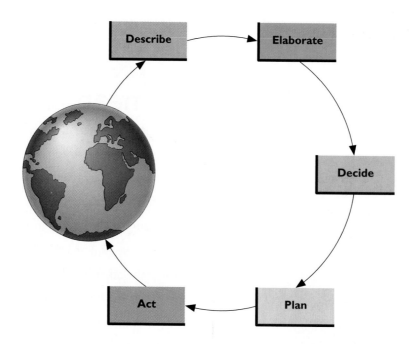

becoming less and less capable of sustaining her; but if it was not being lost, what was happening to it? Finally, the doctor looked at a smear of Laura's blood on a microscope slide. What she saw indicated that a poison was destroying the red blood cells. What could it be? Laura spent most of her time at home, but her teenage daughters, who lived with her, were perfectly healthy. Dr. Wallace asked herself, "What does Laura do that the girls do not?" She repairs and restores paintings. Paint. Lead! She might be suffering from lead poisoning! When the next blood test showed a lead level seven times higher than normal, Dr. Wallace knew she had found the answer at last.

To solve this medical mystery, Dr. Wallace relied on her intelligence, part of which can be seen in her ability to think, solve problems, and make judgments and decisions. She put these vital mental abilities to use in weighing the pros and cons of various hypotheses and in reaching decisions about what tests to order and how to interpret them. In consulting with the patient and other physicians, she relied on another remarkable human mental ability known as *language*. Let's take a look at what psychologists have discovered about these complex mental processes, how to measure them, and how to compare people in terms of intelligence. We begin by examining a general framework for understanding human thinking and then go on to look at some specific cognitive processes.

Basic Functions of Thought

■   **What good is thinking, anyway?**

The main functions, or purposes, of human thinking are to *describe, elaborate, decide,* and *guide action.* You might imagine these functions as forming a circle of thought (see Figure 7.1).

The Circle of Thought

information-processing system   The procedures for receiving information, representing it with symbols, and manipulating those representations so that the brain can interpret and respond.

thinking   The manipulation of mental representations.

Consider how the circle of thought operated in Dr. Wallace's case. It began when she received the information about Laura's symptoms that allowed her to *describe* the problem. Next, Dr. Wallace *elaborated* on this information by using her knowledge, experience, and powers of reasoning to consider what disorders might cause such symptoms. Then she made a *decision* to investigate a possible cause, such as anemia. To implement this decision, she formulated a *plan*—and then *acted* on that plan. But the circle of

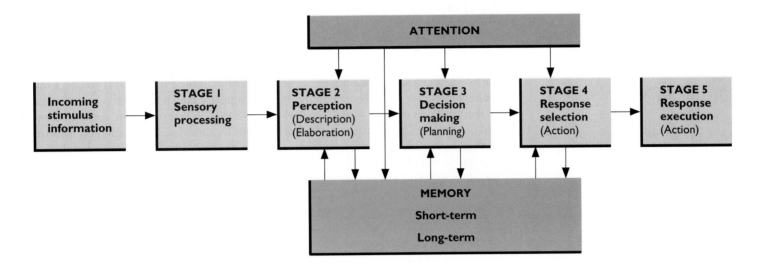

FIGURE 7.2   An Information-Processing Model

Some stages in the information-processing model depend heavily on both short-term and long-term memory and require some attention—that limited supply of mental resources required for information processing to be carried out efficiently.

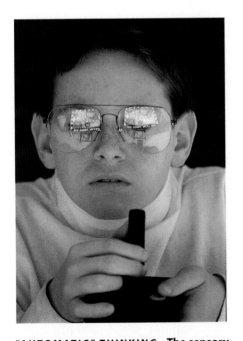

"AUTOMATIC" THINKING The sensory, perceptual, decision-making, and response-planning components of the circle of thought can occur so rapidly that—as when playing a video game— we may only be aware of the incoming information and our quick response to it. In such cases, our thinking processes become so well practiced that they are virtually automatic.

thought did not stop there. Information from the blood test provided new descriptive information, which Dr. Wallace elaborated further to reach another decision, create a new plan, and guide her next action. Each stage in the circle of thought was also influenced by her *intention*—in this case, to find and cure her patient's problem.

Usually, the circle of thought spins so quickly, and its processes are so complex, that slowing it down for careful analysis might seem like trying to nail Jell-O to a tree. Some psychologists approach this task by studying thought processes as if they were part of a computer-like information-processing system. An **information-processing system** receives information, represents the information with symbols, and then manipulates those symbols. According to this model, then, **thinking** is defined as the manipulation of mental representations. Figure 7.2 shows how an information-processing model might view one spin around the circle of thought. Notice that information from the world is somewhat transformed as it passes through each stage of processing (Wickens, Gordon, & Liu, 1998).

In the first stage, information about the world reaches your brain through the senses we discussed in Chapter 3. This stage does not require attention. In the second stage, you must perceive and recognize the information—processes that do require attention. In this stage, you also consciously elaborate information using your short-term, or working, memory, which allows you to think about new information in relation to knowledge stored in your long-term memory. Once the information has been elaborated in this way, you must decide what to do with it. This third stage—decision making—demands attention, too. You may decide to store the information or to take some action. It's in this stage that you plan what action you might take. In the fourth and fifth stages, the action is carried out. This action usually affects the environment, providing new information that is "fed back" to the system for processing in the ongoing circle of thought.

Mental Representations: The Ingredients of Thought

▢ **What are thoughts made of?**

Just as measuring, stirring, and baking are only part of the story of cookie making, describing the *processes* of thinking tells only part of the story behind the circle of thought. Psychologists usually describe the ingredients of thought as *information*. But that is like saying you make cookies with "stuff." What specific forms can information take in our minds? Cognitive psychologists have found that information can be mentally represented in at least five forms: (1) cognitive maps, (2) images, (3) concept schemas and event scripts, (4) propositions, and (5) mental models. Let's explore these ingredients of thought and how people manipulate them as they think.

Cognitive Maps

It is midnight. You are home alone when the power suddenly fails. You can't see a thing, but you know there is a flashlight in the hall closet. Groping in the dark, you find the flashlight with the aid of your cognitive map. A **cognitive map** is a mental representation of familiar parts of your world (J. R. Anderson, 2000). In this case, your cognitive map laid out the floor plan, furniture placements, door locations, and other physical features of your home, allowing you to navigate through the dark. In an unfamiliar dark house you would not have this cognitive map, so you would probably end up stubbing your toes, hitting doors, and bumping into furniture. In other words, experience shapes your cognitive maps.

What kind of experience do you need to create a cognitive map? Looking at your environment is helpful, yet blind people demonstrate that visual experience is not necessary. Barbara Landau (1986) gave a room map with raised features to a young girl who had been blind from birth. The girl had never before touched such a map, but she was immediately able to understand what it was. Also, she could use it as effectively as sighted children her age to plan routes through the actual room and locate toys. Having the general experience of moving through space is enough to allow you to represent information in the form of cognitive maps (Millar, 1994).

Images

Think about how your best friend would look in a clown suit. Did you conjure up a mental picture? Thinking is often based on the manipulation of **images,** which are mental representations of visual information. In much the same way that you might pick up an object to examine it more closely, you can mentally explore images. Manipulations performed on images of objects are very similar to those that would be performed on the objects themselves (Reed, 2000).

Steven Kosslyn (1976) asked people to form a mental image of an object such as a cat. He then asked questions about the image, such as "Does it have a head?" and "Does it have claws?" The smaller the detail in question, the longer people took to answer the question. It was as if they were mentally "zooming in" on the detail necessary to answer the question. The response time was longer for finer details, because those details required closer zooming.

Concept Schemas and Event Scripts

When you think about anything—dogs, happiness, sex, movies, pizza—you are manipulating a basic ingredient of thought called *concepts*. **Concepts** are categories of objects, events, or ideas with common properties. Some concepts, such as "round" and "red," are visual and concrete. Concepts like "truth" and "justice" are more abstract. "To have a concept" is to recognize the properties, relationships, features, or functions that shape, define, and are shared by members of the category in question, and to ignore those that are not. For example, the concept of "bird" includes such properties as having feathers, laying eggs, and being able to fly; the concept of "scissors" includes such properties as having two joined blades and being able to cut through certain materials. Concepts help define the images and other material you conjure up as you think. Concepts allow you to relate each object or event you encounter to a category that is already known. Indeed, concepts make logical thought possible. If you have the concepts "whale" and "bird," you can decide whether a whale is a bird without having either creature in the room with you.

cognitive map   A mental representation of the environment.

images   Mental representations of visual information.

concepts   Categories of objects, events, or ideas that have common properties.

VIOLATING A SCHEMA Schemas, or learned generalizations about objects, events, and people, help to create expectations about the world. People tend to be surprised when schema-based expectations are not met, as in the case of this motorcycle-riding dog. Another example of schema violation occurred in October 1999 when Gordon Elwood, an Oregon man who dressed in rags and collected cans, left over $9 million to charity when he died (McMahon, 2000).

---

formal concept A concept that can be clearly defined by a set of rules or properties.

natural concepts Concepts that have no fixed set of defining features but instead share a set of characteristic features.

prototype A member of a natural concept that possesses all or most of its characteristic features.

schemas Mental representations of what we know and expect about the world.

scripts Mental representations of familiar sequences of activity.

propositions The smallest units of knowledge that can stand as separate assertions.

Types of Concepts A **formal concept** clearly defines objects or events by a set of rules and properties such that each member of the concept has all of the defining properties and no nonmember does. For instance, the concept "square" can be defined as "a shape with four equal sides and four right-angle corners." Any object that does not have all of these features is simply not a square.

Formal concepts are often used to study concept learning in the laboratory, because the members of the concept can be neatly defined (Trabasso & Bower, 1968). But try to define the concepts "home" and "love." These **natural concepts** have no fixed set of *defining* features. Instead, they share a set of *characteristic* features. Members of a natural concept need not have *all* of these characteristic features. The ability to fly may be a characteristic feature of the natural concept "bird," but an ostrich is a bird even though it cannot fly. It is a bird because it possesses enough other characteristic features of "bird" (such as feathers and wings). Having just one bird property is not enough, though. A snake lays eggs and a bat can fly, but neither animal is a bird. A *combination* of properties usually defines a concept. Natural concepts include object categories, such as "bird" or "house." They also include goal-related categories, such as "things to pack in a suitcase," that help us to make plans (Barsalou, 1993).

The boundaries of natural concepts are fuzzy (Rosch, 1975). A robin, a chicken, an ostrich, and a penguin are all birds. But the robin is a better example than the others because it is closer to what most people have learned to think of as a typical bird. A member of a natural concept that possesses all or most of its characteristic features is called a **prototype.** The robin is a prototypical bird. The more prototypical of a concept something is, the more quickly you can decide if it is an example of the concept. This is why people can answer more quickly when asked "Is a robin a bird?" than when asked "Is a penguin a bird?"

Organizing Concepts Concepts tend to be organized as schemas. As described in Chapter 6, **schemas** are generalizations that you develop about categories of objects, events, and people. Let's say you borrow a friend's car. When the time comes to drive it, your "car" schema will give you a good idea of where to put the ignition key, where the gas and brake pedals are, and how to raise and lower the windows. In short, schemas help you understand your world and the elements in it, such as what radios are, when baseball is played, and how police officers usually dress. Schemas also generate *expectations* about objects, events, and people. You expect stereo systems to have speakers, picnics to occur in the summer, and police officers to wear uniforms.

Schemas about familiar sequences of events or activities are called **scripts** (J. R. Anderson, 2000). For instance, your script of the events that typically occur when you enter a classroom tells you what you should and should not do in that situation. You also interpret new information and events according to your scripts. You assume that the person at the front of the class is a teacher, not a mugger. Events that violate scripts may be misinterpreted or even ignored. For instance, in 1993, a heart attack victim lay for nine hours in the hallway of a London apartment building after an ambulance crew smelled alcohol on his breath and assumed he was "sleeping it off." The crew's script for what happens in the poorer sections of big cities told them that someone slumped in a hallway is drunk, not sick. People also recognize and react to expected events more quickly and correctly than to unexpected ones. Scripts are involved in the *top-down processing* that helps you with this recognition. Thus, your script for going to the bank includes waiting in line, depositing a check, withdrawing money, and talking to a teller. If a bank customer pulls a gun and demands money, however, your script would be violated. The fact that you had not expected this event may slow your perception of the situation and interfere with your ability to decide what to do.

Propositions

Schemas and scripts allow us to perform an important aspect of thinking: comparing concepts and mentally representing relationships between them. These mental representations often take the form of **propositions,** which are the smallest units of knowledge that can stand as separate assertions. Propositions can be evaluated as true or false. Some

Ingredients of Thought

Ingredient	Description	How It Is Used
Cognitive maps	Mental representations of familiar locations	Cognitive maps help us describe the world, plan routes, and reach destinations.
Images	Visual mental representations of objects, events, and scenes	Images can be manipulated, expanded, and mentally examined.
Concept schemas and event scripts	Generalizations about concepts formed by experience; mental representations of a typical sequence of activity, usually involving people's behavior	Concept schemas represent a large set of specific examples and create expectations; event scripts may be used to interpret what will happen or is happening in familiar situations—a component of top-down processing.
Propositions	Smallest unit of knowledge that can stand as a separate assertion	Propositions are usually evaluated as to truth or falsity.
Mental models	Mental representations of how things relate to one another in the real world	Mental models guide our interactions with things; they may be correct or incorrect.

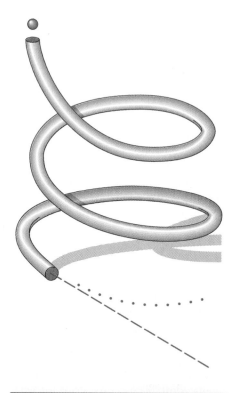

FIGURE 7.3

Applying a Mental Model

LEARN BY DOING   **Try to imagine the path that the marble will follow when it leaves the curved tube. In one study, most people drew the incorrect (curved) path indicated by the dotted line, rather than the correct (straight) path indicated by the dashed line (McCloskey, 1983). Their error was based on the construction of a faulty mental model of the behavior of physical objects.**

propositions, such as "dogs chase cats," describe a relationship between two concepts. Others, such as "birds have wings," describe the relationship between a concept and its properties.

Mental Models

It is also possible to think about the world using **mental models,** which we build from propositions (Johnson-Laird, 1983). For example, suppose someone told you, "My room has four blue walls, a beamed ceiling above the walls, and an oval window across from the door." Hearing this proposition not only conveys mental representations of the room's parts but also allows you to start combining them into three dimensions, much like the scale models or holograms that allow architects to show clients what a house will look like. As more information about the world becomes available, either from existing memories or from new information we hear, see, or read, our mental models become more complete. These models then guide our thinking about things, and our interactions with them (Galotti, 1999). When mental models are incorrect, however, people are likely to make mistakes (Medin & Ross, 1997; see Figure 7.3). ("In Review: Ingredients of Thought" summarizes the ways in which we mentally represent information.)

Thinking Strategies

▪ Are people always logical?

Reasoning, problem solving, and decision making are possible because you can combine, transform, and elaborate mental representations.

PITFALLS IN LOGICAL REASONING "Elderly people cannot be astronauts; this is an elderly man; therefore, he cannot be an astronaut." The logic is correct, but because the first statement is wrong, so is the conclusion. In 1962, a young John Glenn became the first American astronaut to orbit the earth. In 1998, at the age of seventy-seven, he returned to space as a full-fledged member of the crew of the space shuttle *Discovery*.

mental models Sets of propositions that represent people's understanding of how things look and work.

formal reasoning A set of rigorous procedures for reaching valid conclusions.

algorithms Systematic procedures that cannot fail to produce a solution to a problem.

logic Mental procedures that yield a valid conclusion during the reasoning process.

Formal Reasoning

Astronomers say that the temperature at the core of the sun is about 27 million degrees Fahrenheit. How do they know this? It is not possible to place a temperature probe inside the sun, so astronomers base this assertion on inferences from other facts they know about the sun and about physical objects in general, using **formal reasoning**—the process of following a set of rigorous steps for reaching valid, or correct, conclusions. Some of these steps included the application of specific mathematical formulas to existing data in order to generate new data. Such formulas are examples of **algorithms**—systematic methods that always reach a correct result.

The astronomers also followed the rules of **logic,** a set of mental procedures that provide a more general algorithm for drawing valid conclusions about the world. For example, each step in the astronomers' thinking took the form of "if-then" propositions: *If we know how much energy comes from one part of the sun's surface, and if we know how big the whole surface is, then* we can calculate the total energy output. You use the same logical reasoning processes when you conclude, for example, that *if* your friend Jovan is two years older than you are, *then* his twin brother Jermaine will be two years older, too. This kind of reasoning is called *deductive* because it takes a general rule (e.g., twins are the same age) and applies it to deduce conclusions about specific cases (e.g., Jermaine and Jovan).

Most of us try to use logical or deductive reasoning to reach valid conclusions and avoid invalid ones (Rips, 1994). However, even when our logic is perfect, we can make mistakes if we base our reasoning on false assumptions. Likewise, correct assumptions combined with faulty logic can lead to errors. Do you think the following example leads to a valid conclusion?

Assumption 1: *All women want to be mothers.*

Assumption 2: *Jill is a woman.*

Conclusion: *Jill wants to be a mother.*

If you said that the first assumption is not necessarily correct, you're right. Now consider this example:

Assumption 1: *All gun owners are people.*

Assumption 2: *All criminals are people.*

Conclusion: *All gun owners are criminals.*

Here, the assumptions are correct, but the logic is faulty. If "all As are B" and "all Cs are B," it does *not* follow that "all As are C."

Psychologists have discovered that both kinds of pitfalls we just described can lead people to make errors in logical reasoning. This finding is one reason why misleading advertisements or speeches can still attract sales and votes.

Cultural Differences in Formal Reasoning   Most of the time, logic and experience support the same conclusion. If they do not, the ideal option in most Western cultures is to rely on logic. This ideal is not universal, though (Nisbett et al., 2001; Peng & Nisbett, 1999). In some cultures, direct experience is sometimes considered a better guide than logic. Consider the following: *Ivan and Boris always eat together. Boris is eating. Therefore, what is Ivan doing?* Most students in the United States answer, "Eating," but in one study, a majority of Russian students said something like "I don't know. I wasn't there" (Solso, 1987). That answer is not incorrect; it's simply based on a different line of reasoning, in which direct observation is seen as the best way to establish the truth. These differences in reasoning styles do not mean that people in other cultures are illogical or lack intelligence (L. G. Liu, 1985). What they do suggest is that people's thinking in certain situations is shaped by both formal, logic-based schooling and the culture in which that schooling takes place. Because "illogical" answers are sometimes given by smart people in certain cultures (Scribner, 1977), we must be cautious when interpreting non-Westerners' scores on the Western-style intelligence tests described later in this chapter.

Informal Reasoning

Using the rules of formal logic to deduce answers about specific cases is an important kind of reasoning, but it is not the only kind. We also use **informal reasoning** to decide whether a general statement is valid based on the evidence available to support it. Informal reasoning is also known as *inductive reasoning*, because its goal is to induce a general conclusion to appear on the basis of specific facts or examples. Psychologists use informal reasoning when they design experiments and other research methods whose results will provide evidence for (or against) their theories. Jurors, too, use informal reasoning when weighing evidence for the guilt or innocence of a defendant.

Formal reasoning is guided by algorithms, or formulas, but there are no foolproof methods for informal reasoning. For instance, how many white swans would you have to see before concluding that all swans are white? Fifty? A hundred? A million? Formal logic would require that you observe every swan in existence. A more practical approach is to base your conclusion on the number of observations that some mental rule of thumb leads you to *believe* is "enough." In other words, you would take a mental "shortcut" to reach a conclusion that is probably, but not necessarily, correct. Such mental shortcuts are called **heuristics** (pronounced "hyoor-IST-ix").

Heuristics can be helpful, but they can also bias our thinking and cause errors. Suppose your rule of thumb is to vote for all political candidates in a particular party instead of researching the views of each individual. You might end up voting for someone with whom you strongly disagree on some issues. Amos Tversky and Daniel Kahneman described three potentially problematic heuristics that people seem to use intuitively in making judgments (Tversky & Kahneman, 1993).

The Anchoring Heuristic   People use the **anchoring heuristic** when they estimate the probability of an event by adjusting an earlier estimate, not by starting from scratch (Rottenstreich & Tversky, 1997). This strategy sounds reasonable, but the starting value biases the final estimate. Once people have fixed (or anchored to) a starting point, their adjustments of the initial judgment tend to be too small. Suppose you think that the probability of being mugged in New York City is 90 percent, but then you see evidence that the figure is closer to 1 percent. You might reduce your estimate, but only to 80 percent; your new estimate is still way off. The anchoring heuristic presents a challenge for defense attorneys in criminal trials, because the prosecution presents its evidence first. That evidence always suggests that the defendant is guilty, so even if some of it is thrown out by the judge, the initial impression it creates may establish in jurors' minds an unshakable belief in the defendant's guilt (Hogarth & Einhorn, 1992). Similarly, first impressions of people are not easily shifted by later evidence (see Chapter 14, on social psychology).

The Representativeness Heuristic   People use the **representativeness heuristic** when they base conclusions about whether something belongs in a certain class on how similar it is to other items in that class. Suppose you encounter a man who is tidy, short, wears glasses, speaks quietly, and is somewhat shy. If asked whether this person is likely to be a librarian or a farmer, what would you say? In a study by Tversky and Kahneman (1993), most participants chose *librarian*. Chances are that this answer would be wrong. True, the description given is more similar to the prototypical librarian than to the prototypical farmer. However, there are many more farmers in the world than librarians. Therefore, there are probably more farmers than librarians who match this description. In fact, almost *any* set of physical features is more likely to belong to a farmer than to a librarian.

The Availability Heuristic   People use the **availability heuristic** when they judge the likelihood of an event or the correctness of a hypothesis by how easy it is to think of that event or hypothesis (Reed, 2000). In other words, they tend to choose the hypothesis or predict the event that is most mentally "available," much as they might select the quart of milk that happens to be at the front of the supermarket shelf. Although the availability heuristic tends to work well, it, too, can lead to biased judgments—especially when the

informal reasoning   Assessment of a conclusion's validity based on the evidence available to support it.

heuristics   Mental shortcuts or rules of thumb.

anchoring heuristic   A shortcut in the thought process that involves adding new information to existing information to reach a judgment.

representativeness heuristic   A shortcut in the thought process that involves judging the probability that a particular example represents essential features of the larger class.

availability heuristic   A shortcut in the thought process that involves judging the probability of an event by how easily examples of the event can be brought to mind.

mental availability of events and their actual frequency do not match. For example, news reports about airline crashes and classroom shootings lead many people to overestimate how often these memorable, but relatively rare, events actually occur. As a result, people may suffer unjustified worry about flying or going to school.

These three heuristics represent only a few of the many strategies that people use more or less automatically in making judgments, and they describe only some of the biases and limitations evident in human reasoning (Hogarth & Einhorn, 1992). Other biases and limitations will become clear as we consider two important goals of thinking: problem solving and decision making.

Problem Solving

▪ **What's the best way to solve a problem?**

Suppose that you're lost, you don't have a map or navigation system, and there's nobody around to ask for directions. You have a *problem*. The circle of thought suggests that the most efficient approach to solving it would be to first diagnose the problem in the elaboration stage, then formulate a plan for solving it, then execute the plan, and finally evaluate the results to determine whether the problem remains (Bransford & Stein, 1993). However, people's problem-solving skills are not always so systematic. This is one reason why medical tests are sometimes given unnecessarily, diseases are sometimes misdiagnosed, and auto parts are sometimes replaced when there is nothing wrong with them.

Strategies for Problem Solving

Suppose your problem is too complicated to be solved easily. In this case, you can use a strategy called *decomposition* to divide it into smaller, more manageable subproblems. For example, instead of being overwhelmed by the big problem of writing a major term paper, you can begin by writing just an outline. Next, you can select the library and World Wide Web materials most relevant to each section of the outline. Then you can write summaries of those materials, write the first draft of an introduction, and so on.

A second strategy in problem solving is to *work backward*. Many problems are like a tree. The trunk is the information you are given; the solution is a twig on one of the branches. If you work forward by taking the "givens" of the problem and trying to find the solution, it's easy to branch off in the wrong direction. Sometimes the more efficient approach is to start at the end, working backward from your goal (Galotti, 1999). Consider the problem of planning a climb to the summit of Mount Everest. The best strategy is to figure out, first, what equipment and supplies are needed at the highest camp on the night before the attempt to reach the summit, then how many people are needed to stock that camp the day before, then how many people are needed to supply those who must stock the camp, and so on until a plan for the entire expedition is established. People often overlook the working-backward strategy because it runs counter to the way they have learned to think. It is hard for them to imagine that the first step in

Simply knowing about problem-solving strategies, such as decomposition, is not enough. As described in Chapter 8, on motivation and emotion, people must perceive the effort involved as being worth the rewards it is likely to bring.

solving a problem could be to assume that you have already solved it. Sadly, it was partly because of failure to apply this strategy that six climbers died on Mount Everest in 1996 (Krakauer, 1997).

A third problem-solving strategy is to try to find *analogies,* or similarities, between today's problem and others you have encountered before. A supervisor may discover that a seemingly hopeless problem between co-workers can be resolved by the same compromise that worked during a recent family squabble. Of course, to take advantage of analogies, you must first recognize the similarities between current and previous problems. Then you will be in a position to recall the solution that worked before. Most people are surprisingly poor at seeing the similarities between new and old problems (J. R. Anderson, 2000). They tend to concentrate on the surface features that make problems appear different.

Finally, in the case of an especially difficult problem, a helpful strategy is to allow it to "incubate" by laying it aside for a while. A solution that once seemed out of reach may suddenly appear when you engage in unrelated mental activity. The benefits of incubation probably arise from the forgetting of inappropriate ways to solve the problem (J. R. Anderson, 2000).

Problem-Solving Strategies in the Real World

The problem-solving strategies we have described were identified by laboratory studies in which psychologists observed volunteers wrestling with, and perhaps "thinking aloud" about, various types of problems. However, we do not yet know how well the strategies seen in these studies reflect the problem-solving methods that people use in the real world. To explore this question, researchers have reconstructed problem-solving strategies associated with major inventions and scientific discoveries (Klahr & Simon, 1999; Weber, 1992).

■ What was the researcher's question?

On December 17, 1903, Wilbur and Orville Wright successfully flew the first heavier-than-air flying machine. Gary Bradshaw (1993a, 1993b) was interested in identifying the problem-solving strategies that led to this momentous event. He found that forty-nine individuals or teams had worked on the problem of heavier-than-air flight, but only the Wright brothers were successful. In fact, it took them only four years to develop the airplane, whereas others worked for decades without success. Bradshaw asked, How did the Wright brothers solve the problem of creating a heavier-than-air flying machine when so many others had failed?

■ How did the researcher answer the question?

Bradshaw compared the written records left by all the individuals and teams who had worked on an airplane design. Using this "comparative case study" method, he was able to see patterns in the ways they approached the flying machine problem.

■ What did the researcher find?

Bradshaw found several factors that might have contributed to the Wright brothers' success. First, they were bachelors and thus had a lot of spare time to work on their designs. Second, they owned a bicycle shop and thus were familiar with lightweight, but sturdy, structures. Third, they were brothers who had a good working relationship. And finally, as mechanics they were good with their hands. But were any of these features causally related to their successful invention of the airplane?

Perhaps, but Bradshaw's use of comparative case studies revealed that everyone else working on the problem of flight shared one or more of these features with the Wright brothers. For instance, an engineer named Octave Chanute was good with his hands and familiar with lightweight, sturdy structures. And two other pairs of brothers had worked together to try to invent a flying machine.

However, Bradshaw did find one feature unique to the Wright brothers' approach. Of all the inventors working on the problem, only the Wrights spent considerable time and energy testing aircraft *components* before field-testing complete machines. This feature was important because even the best designs of the day flew for only a few seconds—far too briefly to reveal what was working and what was not. As a result, inventors had to guess about what to fix and often ended up with an "improved" model that was worse than the previous one.

■ What do the results mean?

Bradshaw's comparative case study method suggested that the problem-solving strategy of decomposition was the basis for the Wright brothers' success. By testing components, they obtained the information they needed to develop an efficient propeller, improve the shape of the wings for maximum lift, and refine other vital components of their aircraft.

■ What do we still need to know?

Decomposition is a strategy often seen in the laboratory, and as demonstrated by the case of the Wright brothers, it is a potentially important aspect of major inventions and discoveries beyond the laboratory. But is decomposition used in other real-world settings as well? To find out, researchers will need to conduct additional studies of people's mental strategies as they attempt to solve problems ranging from how to connect a new computer to how to efficiently search the World Wide Web.

Obstacles to Problem Solving

The failure of the Wright brothers' competitors to use decomposition is just one example of the obstacles that face problem solvers every day. Difficulties frequently occur at the start, during the diagnosis stage, when a person forms and then tests hypotheses about a problem.

As a case in point, consider the following true story: In September 1998, John Gatiss was in the kitchen of his rented house in Cheltenham, England, when he heard a faint "meowing" sound. Worried that a kitten had become trapped in the walls or under the flooring, he called out the fire brigade to rescue the animal. The sound seemed to be coming from the electric stove, so the rescuers dismantled it, pulling out the power cord in the process. The sound stopped, but everyone assumed that wherever the kitten was, it was now too frightened to meow. The search was reluctantly abandoned, and the stove was reconnected; four days later, however, the meowing began anew. This time, Gatiss and his landlord called the Royal Society for the Prevention of Cruelty to Animals (RSPCA), whose inspectors heard the kitten in distress and asked the fire brigade to come back. They spent the next three days searching for the cat. First, they dismantled parts of the kitchen walls and ripped up the floorboards. Next, they called in plumbing and drainage specialists, who used cables tipped with fiber-optic cameras to search remote cavities where a kitten might hide. Rescuers then brought in a disaster search team, which tried to find the kitten with acoustic and ultrasonic equipment normally used to locate victims trapped under earthquake debris. Not a sound was heard. Increasingly concerned about how much longer the kitten could survive, the fire brigade tried to coax it from hiding with the finest-quality fish, but to no avail. Suddenly, there was a burst of "purring" that, to everyone's surprise (and the landlord's dismay), was traced by the ultrasonic equipment to the clock in the electric stove! Later, the landlord commented that everyone assumed Gatiss's original hypothesis was right—that the "meowing" came from a cat trapped in the kitchen. "I just let them carry on. If there is an animal in there, you have

FIGURE 7.4

The Jar Problem

 The problem is to obtain the number of quarts of liquid shown in the first column by filling jars with the capacities shown in the next three columns. Each line represents a different problem. In dealing with such problems, people often fall prey to mental sets that prevent them from using the most efficient solution (Luchins, 1942).

Quantity	Jar A	Jar B	Jar C
1. 21 quarts	8	35	3
2. 10 quarts	6	18	1
3. 19 quarts	5	32	4
4. 21 quarts	20	57	8
5. 18 quarts	8	40	7
6. 6 quarts	7	17	2
7. 15 quarts	12	33	3

Problem: Measure out the above quantities by using jars with the stated capacities (in quarts).

to do what it takes. The funniest thing was that it seemed to reply when we called out to it" (*London Daily Telegraph*, 1998).

How could fifteen fire-rescue workers, three RSPCA inspectors, four drainage workers, and two acoustics experts waste eight days and cause nearly $2,000 in damage to a house in pursuit of a nonexistent kitten? The answer lies in the fact that they, like the rest of us, were prone to four main obstacles to efficient problem solving, described in the following sections.

Multiple Hypotheses   Often we begin to solve a problem with only a vague notion of which hypotheses to test. Suppose *you* heard a strange sound in your kitchen. It could be caused by several different things, but which hypotheses should you test, and in what order?

People have a difficult time working with more than two or three hypotheses at a time (Mehle, 1982). The limited capacity of working memory may be part of the reason. As discussed in Chapter 6, a person can hold only about seven chunks of information in working memory, and because a single hypothesis, let alone two or three, might include more than seven chunks, it may be difficult or impossible to keep them all in mind at once. As a result, the correct hypothesis is often neglected. The one that is chosen may be influenced by the availability heuristic. In other words, it may be the one that most easily comes to mind, rather than the one that's most likely to be correct (Tversky & Kahneman, 1974). Thus, Gatiss diagnosed the meowing sound he heard as coming from a kitten, not a clock, because such sounds usually come from kittens, not clocks.

Mental Sets   Sometimes people are so blinded by one hypothesis or strategy that they stick with it even when better alternatives should be obvious. This is a clear case of the anchoring heuristic at work. Once Gatiss reported hearing a "trapped kitten," his description created an assumption that everyone else accepted and that no one challenged. Figure 7.4 shows a problem-solving situation in which such errors often appear. In the first problem, the object is to obtain 21 quarts of liquid by using 3 jars that have capacities of 8, 35, and 3 quarts, respectively. Can you figure out how to do it?

The solution is to fill Jar B to its capacity, 35 quarts, and then use its contents to fill Jar A to its capacity of 8 quarts, leaving 27 quarts in Jar B. Then pour from Jar B to fill Jar C twice, leaving 21 quarts in Jar B [27 − (2 × 3) = 21]. Now solve the remaining problems.

If you solved all the problems in Figure 7.4, you found that a similar solution worked each time. But what happened with Problem 7? If you are like most people, you developed a **mental set,** the tendency for old patterns of problem solving to persist (Sweller & Gee, 1978). Your mental set may have caused you to use the same solution formula

FIGURE 7.5

The Nine-Dot Problem

 The problem is to draw no more than four straight lines that run through all nine dots on the page without lifting your pencil from the paper. Figure 7.7 shows two ways of solving this problem that ignore its apparent limitations.

(B − A − 2C) for Problem 7 even though a simpler one (A + C) would have worked. Figures 7.5 and 7.7 show another way in which a mental set can restrict our perception of the possible solutions to a problem.

Another restriction on problem solving may come from experience with objects. Once people become familiar with using an object for one type of function, they may be blinded to other ways of using it. Thus, experience may produce **functional fixedness,** a tendency to use familiar objects in familiar rather than creative ways. Figure 7.6 provides an example. An incubation strategy often helps to break mental sets.

Confirmation Bias   Anyone who has had a series of medical tests knows that diagnosis is not a one-shot decision. Instead, physicians choose an initial hypothesis on the basis of observed symptoms and then order tests or evaluate additional symptoms to confirm or eliminate that hypothesis. This process may be distorted by a **confirmation bias:** Humans have a strong bias to confirm rather than to refute the hypothesis they have chosen, even in the face of strong evidence against the hypothesis. In other words, people are quite willing to perceive and accept data that support their hypothesis, but they tend to ignore information that is inconsistent with it (Groopman, 2000). Confirmation bias may be seen as a form of the anchoring heuristic. Once you've "anchored" to an initial hypothesis, you may be unwilling to abandon it. The would-be rescuers of John Gattis's "trapped kitten" were so intent on their humanitarian efforts to pinpoint its location that they never stopped to question its existence.

Ignoring Negative Evidence   On September 26, 1983, Lt. Col. Stanislav Petrov was in command of a secret facility that analyzed information from Soviet early-warning

FIGURE 7.6   An Example of Functional Fixedness

 Before reading further, ask yourself how you would fasten together two strings that are hanging from the ceiling but are out of reach of each other. Several tools are available, yet most people do not think of attaching, say, the pliers to one string and swinging it like a pendulum until it can be reached while holding the other string. This solution is not obvious, because we tend to fixate on the function of pliers as a tool rather than as a weight. People are more likely to solve this problem if the tools are scattered around the room. When the pliers are in a toolbox, their function as a tool is emphasized, and functional fixedness becomes nearly impossible to break.

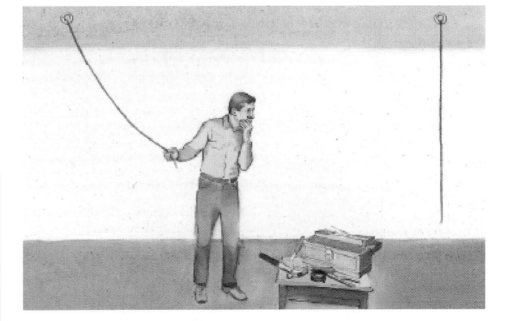

mental set   The tendency for old patterns of problem solving to persist.

functional fixedness   The tendency to think about familiar objects in familiar ways.

confirmation bias   The tendency to pay more attention to evidence in support of one's hypothesis about a problem than to evidence that refutes that hypothesis.

Solving Problems

Steps	Pitfalls	Remedies
Define the problem	Inexperience: the tendency to see each problem as unique	Gain experience and practice in seeing the similarity between present problems and previous problems.
Form hypotheses about solutions	Availability heuristic: the tendency to recall the hypothesis or solution that is most available to memory	Force yourself to write down, and carefully consider, many different hypotheses.
	Anchoring heuristic, or mental set: the tendency to anchor on the first solution or hypothesis and not adjust your beliefs in light of new evidence or failures of the current approach	Break the mental set, stop, and try a fresh approach.
Test hypotheses	The tendency to ignore negative evidence	In evaluating a hypothesis, consider the things you should see (but don't) if the hypothesis were true.
	Confirmation bias: the tendency to seek only evidence that confirms your hypothesis	Look for disconfirming evidence that, if found, would show your hypothesis to be false.

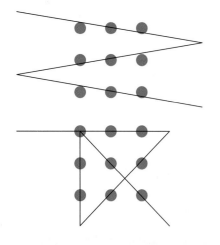

FIGURE 7.7

Two Creative Solutions to the Nine-Dot Problem

Many people find puzzles like this difficult because mental sets create artificial limits on the range of solutions. In this case, the mental sets involve the tendency to draw within the frame of the dots and to draw through the middle of each dot. As shown here, however, there are other possibilities.

satellites. Suddenly, alarms went off as computers found evidence of five U.S. missiles being launched toward the Soviet Union. Tension between the two countries was high at the time, so based on the availability heuristic, Petrov hypothesized that a nuclear attack was under way. He was about to alert his superiors to launch a counterattack on the United States when it occurred to him that if this were a real nuclear attack, there should be evidence of many more than five missiles. Fortunately for everyone, he realized that the "attack" was a false alarm (Hoffman, 1999). As this near-disaster shows, the *absence* of symptoms or events can sometimes provide important evidence for or against a hypothesis. Compared with evidence that is *present*, however, symptoms or events that *do not occur* are less likely to be noticed (R. Hunt & Rouse, 1981). People have a difficult time using the absence of evidence to help eliminate hypotheses from consideration (Ashcraft, 1989). In the "trapped kitten" case, when the "meowing" stopped for several days after the stove was unplugged and reconnected, rescuers assumed that the animal was frightened into silence. They ignored the possibility that their hypothesis was incorrect in the first place. (For a summary of problem solving and its pitfalls, see "In Review: Solving Problems.")

Problem Solving by Computer

Medical and scientific researchers have created artificial limbs, retinas, cochleas, and even hearts to help disabled people move, see, hear, and live more normally. They are developing artificial brains, too, in the form of computer systems that not only see, hear, and manipulate objects but also reason and solve problems. These systems are the product of research in **artificial intelligence (AI),** a field that seeks to develop computers that imitate the processes of human perception and thought. For problems such as those involved in medical diagnosis, computers using relatively simple formulas can already perform just as well as humans, if not better (Gawande, 1998). However, humans and computers seem to work better together than alone. The human's role is to establish the presence and nature of a patient's symptoms. The computer then *combines* this information in a completely unbiased way to identify the most likely diagnosis (Swets, Dawes, & Monahan, 2000). Such teamwork can also help in the diagnosis of psychological problems (Nietzel, Bernstein, & Milich, 1998).

Symbolic Reasoning and Computer Logic   An IBM computer known as Deep Blue has won chess games against the world's best chess masters. This result is not surprising, given that chess is a clearly defined, logical game at which computers can perform effectively. However, it is precisely their reliance on logic and formulas that accounts for the limitations of artificial intelligence systems. For example, these systems are successful in only very narrowly defined fields, not in general problem solving. This limitation stems from the fact that AI systems are based on logical symbolic manipulations that depend on "if-then" rules. Unfortunately, it is difficult to tell a computer how to recognize the "if" condition in the real world (Dreyfus & Dreyfus, 1988). Consider this simple "if-then" rule: "If it is a clock, then set it." Humans recognize all kinds of clocks because they have the natural concept of "clock," but computers are still not very good at forming natural concepts. Doing so requires putting into the same category many examples that have very different physical features, from a bedside digital alarm clock to Big Ben.

Neural Network Models   Recognizing the problems posed by the need to teach computers to form natural concepts, many researchers in AI have moved toward the connectionist, or *neural network*, approach. The neural network approach simulates the information processing taking place at many different, but interconnected, locations in the brain. This approach has contributed to the development of computers that are able to recognize voices, understand speech, read print, guide missiles, forecast solar flares, and perform many other complex tasks. One program, called PAPNET, actually outperforms human technicians at detecting abnormal cells in smears collected during cervical examinations (Kok & Boon, 1996). Unfortunately, however, most computer models of neural networks still fall well short of the capacities of the human perceptual system (Hofstadter, 1995). For example, computers are slow to learn how to classify visual patterns, and they do not show sudden insight when a key common feature is identified. But even though neural networks are far from perfect "thinking machines," they are sure to play an important role in psychologists' efforts to build ever more intelligent systems and to better understand the principles of human problem solving.

Creative Thinking

One of the greatest challenges in the development of artificial intelligence will be to program computers in a way that allows their thinking and problem solving to be as creative as that of humans. Consider the case that opened this chapter. It was Dr. Wallace's knowledge of the chemicals in paint—which has no obvious connection to human body chemistry—that led her to figure out what was causing Laura McBride's illness. Computers are still not nearly as good as humans are at recognizing that information from one area can be used to solve a problem in a seemingly unrelated area.

The ability to blend knowledge from many different domains is only one aspect of the creative thinking that humans display every day. People demonstrate **creativity** by producing original, but useful, solutions to all sorts of challenges (Simonton, 1999). Executives and homemakers, scientists and artists—all may be creative to varying degrees (Klahr & Simon, 1999). How do we know when people are thinking creatively? Psychologists have defined creativity as mental activity that can be inferred from performance on certain tests. To measure creativity, some psychologists have generated tests of **divergent thinking**—the ability to think along many paths to generate multiple solutions to a problem (Guilford & Hoepfner, 1971). The Consequences Test is an example. It contains items such as "Imagine all of the things that might possibly happen if all national and local laws were suddenly abolished" (Guilford, 1959). Divergent thinking tests are

artificial intelligence (AI)   The field that studies how to program computers to imitate the products of human perception, understanding, and thought.

creativity   The capacity to produce original solutions or novel compositions.

divergent thinking   The ability to generate many different solutions to a problem.

scored by counting the *number* of sensible responses that a person can give to each item, and how many of these responses are *different* from those given by most people.

Only sensible responses to creativity tests are counted, because creativity involves divergent thinking that is *appropriate* for a given problem or situation. To be productive rather than weird, a creative person must be firmly anchored in reality, understand society's needs, and learn from the experience and knowledge of others (Sternberg & Lubert, 1992). Theresa Amabile has identified three kinds of cognitive and personality characteristics necessary for creativity (Amabile, 1996; Amabile, Hennessey, & Grossman, 1986):

1. *Expertise in the field of endeavor, which is directly tied to what a person has learned.*   For example, a painter or composer must know the paints, techniques, or instruments available.

2. *A set of creative skills, including persistence at problem solving, capacity for divergent thinking, ability to break out of old problem-solving habits (mental sets), and willingness to take risks.*   Amabile believes that training can influence many of these skills, some of which are closely linked to the strategies for problem solving discussed earlier.

3. *The motivation to pursue creative work for internal reasons, such as satisfaction, rather than for external reasons, such as prize money.*   In fact, Amabile and her colleagues found that external rewards can deter creativity. They asked groups of children and adults to create artistic products such as paintings or stories. Some were simply asked to work on the project. Others were informed that their project would be judged for its creativity and excellence and that rewards would be given or winners announced. Experts, who had no idea which products were created by which group, judged those from the "reward" group to be significantly less creative.

Is creativity inherited? To some extent, perhaps, but evidence suggests that environmental factors also influence creative behavior. Does creativity require high intelligence? Correlations between scores on creativity tests and intelligence tests are almost always positive but relatively small (Simonton, 1999). These results are not surprising, because creativity involves divergent thinking about many solutions to a problem. As you will see later, high scores on most intelligence tests require **convergent thinking,** which uses logic and knowledge to *narrow down* the number of possible solutions to a problem. The low correlation between intelligence test scores and creativity does not mean that the two are completely unrelated; it is just that we don't fully understand the relationship yet (Sternberg & O'Hara, 1999).

Decision Making

■ **How can I become a better decision maker?**

Paper or plastic? Do I go to the concert or study for the test? Should I get out of this relationship? Is it time to start thinking about a nursing home for Mom? Life is full of decisions. Some are easy to make; others are painfully difficult and require considerable time, planning, and mental effort. Even carefully considered decisions can lead to undesirable outcomes, though, because the world is an uncertain place. Decisions made when the outcome is uncertain are called *risky decisions* or *decisions under uncertainty*. Chance aside, psychologists have discovered reasons why human decisions may lead to unsatisfactory outcomes. Let's consider some of these reasons.

Evaluating Options

Suppose that you must choose between (1) an academic major that fascinates you but is unlikely to lead to steady employment or (2) a major that is less interesting but virtually

convergent thinking   The ability to apply the rules of logic and what one knows about the world to narrow down the possible solutions to a problem.

guarantees a high-paying job. The fact that each option has positive and negative features greatly complicates decision making. Deciding which car to buy, which college to attend, or even how to spend the evening are all examples of choices that require you to weigh several options. Such choices are often based on the positive or negative value, or **utility,** that you, personally, place on each feature of each option. Listing the pros and cons of each option is a helpful way of keeping them all in mind as you think about your decisions. You also have to estimate the probabilities and risks associated with the possible outcomes of each choice. For example, you must consider how likely it is that job opportunities in your chosen major will have shrunk by the time you graduate. In studying risky decision making, some psychologists begin with the assumption that the best decision maximizes expected value. The **expected value** of a decision is the total amount of benefit you could expect to receive if the decision were repeated on several occasions.

Biases and Flaws in Decision Making

Most people think of themselves as logical and rational, but they do not always act in ways that maximize expected value (Arkes & Ayton, 1999; Curim & Sarin, 1992; Gilovich, 1997). Why not?

Gains, Losses, and Probabilities   For one thing, people tend to feel worse about losing a certain amount than they feel good about gaining the same amount, a phenomenon known as *loss aversion* (R. Dawes, 1998). Thus, you might go to more trouble trying to collect a $100 debt than trying to win a $100 prize. In addition, the utility of a specific gain depends not on the actual size of the gain but on what the starting point was. Suppose you could have a coupon for a free dinner worth $10, but you have to drive 10 miles to pick it up. Does this gain have the same utility as having an extra $10 added to your paycheck? The dollar amount is the same, but people tend to behave as if the difference between $0 and $10 is greater than the difference between, say, $300 and $310. So the same person who may refuse to drive across town after work to earn a $10 bonus from the boss might gladly make the same trip to pick up a $10 dinner coupon.

People are also biased in how they perceive probability. For example, they tend to overestimate the probability of rare events and to underestimate the probability of frequent ones (Kahneman & Tversky, 1984). This bias helps explain why people gamble in casinos and enter lotteries, even though the odds are against them and the decision to do so has a negative expected value. People overestimate the probability of winning, especially in a casino, so they associate a positive expected value with gambling. The tendency to overestimate rare events is amplified by the availability heuristic: Vivid memories of rare gambling successes and the publicity given to lottery winners encourage people to recall gains rather than losses (Waagenaar, 1989). The same tendency can also be amplified by mood. When people are in a good mood, they tend to overestimate the probability that good things will happen to them. When they are in a bad mood, they tend to exaggerate the likelihood of being mugged, losing a wallet, or other negative events (W. F. Wright & Bower, 1992).

Another bias in estimating probability is called the *gambler's fallacy:* People believe that events in a random process will correct themselves. This belief is false. For example, if you flip a coin and it comes up heads ten times in a row, what is the likelihood of tails on the next flip? Although some people think otherwise, the chance that it will come up tails on the eleventh try is still 50 percent, just as it was for the first ten flips. Yet, many gamblers continue feeding a slot machine that has not paid off much for hours, assuming it is "due."

Poor decision making can also stem from the human tendency to be unrealistically confident in the accuracy of our predictions. Baruch Fischoff and Donald MacGregor (1982) devised a clever way to study this bias. People were asked whether they believed a certain event would occur and then were asked to say how confident they were about their prediction. For example, they were asked whether a particular football team would win an upcoming game. After the events were over, the accuracy of the people's forecasts was compared with their level of confidence. Sure enough, their confidence in their predictions was

utility   In decision making, any subjective measure of value.

expected value   The total benefit to be expected of a decision if it were repeated on several occasions.

A HIGHLY UNLIKELY OUTCOME By focusing public attention on the very few people who win big lottery prizes, state lottery agencies take advantage of the general human tendency to overestimate the probability of rare events. Lottery ads never show any of the millions of people whose tickets turn out to be worthless.

consistently greater than their accuracy. This overconfidence operates even when people make predictions concerning the accuracy of their own memory (Bjork, 1998).

Overconfidence about knowledge and judgments appears in many cultures, and in some more than others. In one study, students in China and the United States were asked to say how confident they were about their answers to general-knowledge questions (G. N. Wright & Phillips, 1980). Both groups were overconfident, but the Chinese were especially so. A study comparing Chinese, Japanese, and North American students found the same result (Yates et al., 1989). Why? Cultural traditions that strongly discourage Chinese students from challenging what they are told by teachers may make them less likely than Americans to question what they tell themselves, and thus more likely to be overconfident. This possibility is supported by the fact that compared with American and Japanese students, Chinese students were able to list the fewest arguments *against* their own judgments (Yates, Lee, & Shinotsuka, 1992). The moral of the story is to be wary when people in any culture express confidence that a forecast or decision is correct. They will be wrong more often than they think.

How Good Are Human Decisions?   Nearly everyone makes decisions they later regret, but these outcomes may not be due entirely to biased thinking about gains, losses, and probabilities. Some decisions are not intended to maximize expected value but rather to satisfy other criteria, such as minimizing expected loss, producing a quick and easy resolution, or preserving a moral principle (Arkes & Ayton, 1999; Zsambok & Klein, 1997). Often, decisions depend not just on how likely we are to gain or lose a particular amount of something but also on what that something is. Accordingly, a decision that could cost or save a human life may be made differently than one that could cost or gain a few dollars, even though the probabilities of each outcome are exactly the same in both cases.

In other words, the "goodness" or "badness" of decisions is often difficult to assess. Many of them depend on personal values (utilities), which can vary from person to person and from culture to culture. People in individualist cultures, for example, may tend to assign high utilities to attributes that promote personal goals, whereas people in collectivist cultures might place greater value on attributes that bring group harmony and the approval of family and friends (Markus, Kitayama, & Heiman, 1996).

A CONTROVERSIAL DECISION Elian Gonzalez's mother and several other Cuban refugees died when their boat sank off the Florida coast in 1999. The boy's Miami relatives took him in and fought all efforts to return him to Cuba. After months of negotiation, Attorney General Janet Reno finally ordered armed agents to take Elian from his relatives' home. Did she make the "right" decision? The fact that many Americans said yes while many others said no highlights the difficulties involved in making, and evaluating, risky decisions.

LINKAGES
Do groups solve problems more effectively than individuals? (a link to Social Psychology)

Problem solving and decision making are often done in groups. The factors that influence an individual's problem solving and decision making continue to operate when the individual is in a group, but group interactions also shape the outcome.

LINKAGES

Group Processes in Problem Solving and Decision Making

Typically, group discussions follow a consistent pattern (Hastie, Penrod, & Pennington, 1984). First, various options are proposed and debated until the group sees that no one has strong objections to one option; that option becomes the minimally acceptable solution. From then on, the group criticizes any other proposal and argues more and more strongly for the first minimally acceptable solution, which is likely to become the group's decision. Thus, the order in which options are considered can determine the outcome (Wittenbaum & Stasser, 1996). (This phenomenon is an example of the anchoring heuristic operating in a group situation.)

Group discussion often results in more extreme decisions than people would make if they were alone. This tendency toward extreme decisions is called **group polarization** (Kaplan, 1987). Two mechanisms appear to underlie group polarization. First, most arguments presented during the discussion favor the majority view, most criticisms are directed at the minority view, and group members seek additional information that supports the majority position (Schulz-Hardt et al., 2000). Thus, it seems rational to those favoring the majority view to adopt an even stronger version of it. Second, once some group members begin to agree that a particular decision is desirable, other members may try to associate themselves with it, perhaps by advocating a more extreme version (Kaplan & Miller, 1987).

Are people better at problem solving and decision making when they work in groups than when on their own? This is one of the questions about human thought studied by researchers in social psychology. In a typical experiment, a group of people is asked to solve a problem like the one in Figure 7.5 or to make a decision about the guilt or innocence of a fictional defendant. Each person is asked to work alone and then to join with the others to try to agree on a decision. Such research indicates that when correct solutions can be made obvious to everyone, groups usually outperform individuals (J. M. Levine & Moreland, 1998). However, when the solution is less clear-cut, groups may do no better than their most talented member (Hackman, 1998). And when people work as

group polarization The tendency for groups to make decisions that are more extreme than the decision any group member might make alone.

part of a group, they are less productive than when working alone (K. D. Williams & Sommer, 1997). In other words, groups can sometimes be more effective than individuals, but they also tend to be less efficient.

Other research (e.g., Stasser, Stewart, & Wittenbaum, 1995) suggests that a critical element in successful group problem solving is the sharing of individual members' unique information and expertise. For example, when asked to diagnose an illness, groups of physicians were much more accurate when they pooled their knowledge (J. R. Larson et al., 1998). However, *brainstorming,* a popular strategy that supposedly encourages group members to generate new and innovative solutions to a problem, may actually produce fewer ideas than those generated by individuals working alone (J. M. Levine & Moreland, 1998), possibly because input by other group members interferes with the creative process in some individuals. Group members who are confident or have high status are most likely to influence a group's deliberations (J. M. Levine & Moreland, 1998), but whether these people will help or hurt the group's efforts depends on whether they express good ideas (Hinsz, 1990). Ironically, there is little evidence that members with the greatest competence (as opposed to status) always contribute more to group deliberations (Hastie, 1986).

As they work to solve a problem, the members of a group experience their own thoughts as words, propositions, images, or other mental representations. How does each member share these private events so as to help the group perform its task? The answer lies in the use of language.

Language

▦ How do babies learn to talk?

Many pet owners would swear that their animals "talk" to them. Maybe Gonzo barks in a particular way when he wants to go outside, or Cleo meows to be fed. But are Gonzo's barks and Cleo's meows really language? Probably not. Although these pets are communicating something to their owners, the noises they make lack many of the components of human language (Rendall, Cheney, & Seyfarth, 2000). So although Gonzo may let out, say, three high-pitched yelps when he wants to go outside, he may bark in exactly the same way when his owner asks him whether he agrees with the local leash laws. For this reason, we wouldn't call his barking "language." Humans, however, can use language to express everything from simple demands to abstract principles. They can create stories that pass on cultural information and traditions from one generation to the next.

A **language** has two basic elements: symbols, such as words, and a set of rules, called **grammar,** for combining those symbols. With their knowledge of approximately 50,000 to 100,000 words (G. A. Miller, 1991), humans can create and understand an infinite number of sentences. Yet all of the sentences ever spoken are created from just a few dozen categories of sounds. The power of language comes from the way these rather unimpressive raw materials are organized according to certain rules. In this section, we describe how people learn to do this.

Learning to Speak: Stages of Language Development

You use the many rules of language naturally and automatically to form correct sentences and make conversation. Yet, like most people, you would probably have a difficult time stating these rules. Children the world over learn language and its rules with impressive speed. Developmental psychologists have carefully studied the steps in this process.

From Babblings to Words **Babblings** are the first sounds infants make that resemble speech. These alternating consonant and vowel sounds ("bababa," "dadada," and "mami-

language　Symbols, and a set of rules for combining them, used as a means of communicating.

grammar　A set of rules for combining the symbols, such as words, used in a given language.

babblings　Repetitions of syllables; the first sounds infants make that resemble speech.

GETTING READY TO TALK   Long before they utter their first words, babies are getting ready to talk. Experiments in Patricia Kuhl's laboratory show that even six-month-olds tend to look longer at faces whose lip movements match the sounds of spoken words. This tendency reflects babies' abilities to focus on, recognize, and discriminate the sounds of speech, especially in their native language. These abilities are crucial to the development of language.

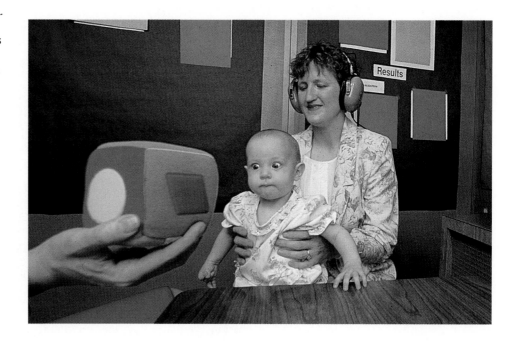

mamima") begin to occur at about four months of age, once the infant has developed the necessary coordination of the tongue and mouth. Though meaningless to the baby, babblings are a delight to parents. Infants of all nationalities initially make the same babbling sounds, but at about nine months of age, they begin to produce only the sounds that occur in the language they hear the most. At about the same time, their babbling becomes more complex and begins to sound like "sentences" in their native language. Infants also begin to shorten some of their vocalizations—for example, to "da," "duh," and "ma." They use these sounds with particular gestures to convey joy, anger, interest, and other messages in specific situations and with obvious purpose (Dore, 1978).

Ten- to twelve-month-old babies can *understand* about a hundred words, which is almost ten times more than they can say (Fenson et al., 1994). Proper names and object words, like *mama, daddy, cookie,* and *doggy,* are among the first words they understand. These are also the first words children are likely to say when, around twelve to eighteen months of age, they begin to talk. Nouns for simple object categories (*dog, flower*) are learned before more general nouns (*animal, plant*) or more specific names (*collie, rose*) (Rosch et al., 1976).

These early words do not sound exactly like adult language. Babies usually reduce them to a shorter, easier form, such as "duh" for *duck* and "mih" for *milk*. They make themselves understood, however, by using gestures, intonations, facial expressions, and endless repetitions. Once they have a word for an object, they may "overextend" it to cover more ground. *Doggy* might include cats, horses, and most animals. And they might use *fly* for all insects and perhaps other small things such as raisins and M&M's (E. V. Clark, 1983). Children make these errors because their vocabulary is limited, not because they fail to notice the difference between dogs and cats or because they want to eat a fly (L. A. Rescorla, 1981). Contact with people who don't understand these overextensions helps encourage children to learn and use more precise words (Markman, 1994).

First Sentences   By eighteen to twenty-four months of age, children usually have a spoken vocabulary of up to 300 words. Then their language undergoes a rapid acceleration. They may learn several new words a day and begin to combine words into sentences (Gleitman & Landau, 1994). Babies' first sentences consist of two-word pairs. These two-word utterances are described as **telegraphic,** because like telegrams, they are brief and to the point. Nonessential words are left out. If a twenty-month-old child wants her mother to give her a book, she might first say, "Give book," then "Mommy give," and if

telegraphic   A term referring to young children's utterances that are brief and to the point and that leave out nonessential words.

LEARNING A SECOND LANGUAGE As these international students are discovering, people who learn a second language after the age of thirteen or fourteen do so more slowly than younger people (J. S. Johnson & Newport, 1989) and virtually never learn to speak it without an accent (Lenneberg, 1967). These age effects support the notion of a critical period for language acquisition.

that doesn't work, "Mommy book." The child also uses rising intonation to indicate a question ("Go out?") and word stress to indicate location ("Play *park*") or new information ("*Big* car").

Three-word sentences come next in the development of language. Although still telegraphic, sentences such as "Mommy give book" are more nearly complete. In this stage, the child begins to use the subject-verb-object form heard in adult sentences. Other words and word endings also begin appearing. In English, these include the suffix -*ing*, the prepositions *in* and *on*, the plural -*s*, and irregular past tenses ("It broke," "I ate") (Dale, 1976). In addition, children learn to use the suffix -*ed* for the past tense ("I walked") and then often apply this rule to irregular verbs they had previously used correctly (Marcus, 1996). "It breaked," "It broked," or "I eated" are examples of such *overgeneralizations*. At the same time, children begin to expand their sentences with adjectives.

Complex Sentences   By age three or so, children begin to use auxiliary verbs ("Adam is going") and to ask questions using *what, where, who,* and *why.* They also begin to put together clauses to form complex sentences ("Here's the ball I was looking for"). Until children are about five years old, however, they describe events in the order in which they occur ("We went to the zoo and had ice cream") and understand sentences better if the sentences follow this sequential ordering (Weist, 1989). By age five, children have acquired most of the grammatical rules of their native language.

How Is Language Acquired?

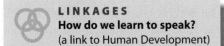

LINKAGES
How do we learn to speak?
(a link to Human Development)

Despite all that has been learned about the steps children follow in learning language, mystery and debate still surround the question of just how they learn it. We do know that children pick up the specific content of language from the speech they hear around them: English children learn English; French children learn French. In fact, it's important that children be exposed to language early in life, because there appears to be a limited window of opportunity, or *critical period*, for language learning (Ridley, 2000). Some unfortunate children have spent their early years in isolation from human contact and the sound of adult language. Even after years of therapy and language training, these individuals were not able to combine ideas into sentences.

Conditioning, Imitation, and Rules   Perhaps children learn grammar because their parents reward them for using it. This idea sounds reasonable, but observations suggest that

ANIMAL LANGUAGE? Several chimpanzees and gorillas have been taught to use American Sign Language (ASL). Here, Koko the gorilla signs "smoke" as Penny Patterson holds Smoky the cat. Are such primates' remarkable accomplishments with ASL the same as human language abilities? Probably not (Rendall, Cheney, & Seyfarth, 2000), but research suggests that with the right tools and training, these animals can master language-like skills (Sevcik & Savage-Rumbaugh, 1994).

positive reinforcement (see Chapter 5) cannot fully explain the learning of grammar. In fact, parents are usually more concerned about what is said than about its grammatical form (Hirsch-Pasek, Treiman, & Schneiderman, 1984). When the little boy with chocolate crumbs on his face says, "I not eat cookie," his mother is more likely to respond, "Yes, you did" than to ask the child to say, "I did not eat the cookie" and then reinforce him for grammatical correctness.

Learning through modeling, or imitation, appears to be more influential. Children learn grammar most rapidly when adults demonstrate the correct form in the course of conversation. For example:

Child: Mommy fix.
Mother: Okay, Mommy will fix the truck.
Child: It breaked.
Mother: Yes, it broke.

But if children learn grammar by imitation, why do children who at one time said "I went" later say "I goed"? Adults do not use this form of speech, so neither imitation nor operant conditioning can account for its sudden appearance. It must be that children analyze for themselves the underlying patterns in the many language examples they hear around them and then learn the rules governing those patterns (Bloom, 1995).

Biological Bases for Language Acquisition The ease with which children everywhere discover these patterns and learn language has led some to argue that they are "prewired," or biologically programmed, to learn language.

Indeed, Noam Chomsky (1965) suggested that human beings are born with a *language acquisition device (LAD)* that allows youngsters to gather ideas about the rules of language without being aware of doing so. They then use these ideas to understand and construct their native language. This hypothesis is supported by the observation that children make up words like *goed,* which shows that they understand language rules (in this case, the rule for forming the past tense). The hypothesis is also supported by the fact that there is some similarity in the grammar of all languages. Furthermore, children who are born deaf and never exposed to language make up gestural systems that have several properties of natural spoken language. These gestural systems place subjects before verbs and include agent-action-object sequences, such as "June saw Bob" (Newport & Meier, 1985).

According to Elizabeth Bates (1993), though, it is not necessary to assume that a LAD exists. She suggests that the development of children's language reflects their development of other cognitive skills (see Chapter 9). Thus, for example, children learn short words before long words because limitations in children's short-term memory and other cognitive abilities lead them to learn easy things before harder ones.

Bilingualism　Does trying to learn two languages at once, even before the critical period for language learning is over, impair the learning of either? Research suggests just the opposite. Like some children in any situation, the early language utterances of children from a bilingual environment may be confused or delayed, but they eventually show good performance in *each* language (de Houwer, 1995). Indeed, there is some evidence that *balanced bilinguals*—those who have roughly equal mastery of two languages—are superior to other children in cognitive flexibility, concept formation, and creativity. It is as if each language offers a slightly different perspective on thinking, and this dual perspective makes the brain more flexible (Hong et al., 2000).

Testing Intelligence

■　**How is intelligence measured?**

People who are good at using and understanding language, and skilled at thinking, solving problems, and making decisions, are likely to be seen as *intelligent*. But intelligence is not limited to these abilities alone. Over the years, psychologists studying people in various cultures around the world have proposed that the concept of "intelligence" is a broad umbrella that can also include attributes such as efficiently storing and retrieving memories; effectively focusing—or dividing—attention; rapidly processing information; quickly learning new things; profiting from experience; adapting well to changing environments; having a good sense of direction; appreciating patterns in nature; being good at music, dance, or athletics; showing eye-hand coordination; understanding oneself and others; and displaying polished social skills (Berry & Bennett, 1992; Eysenck, 1986; H. Gardner, 1998; E. Hunt, 1983; J. D. Meyer & Salovey, 1997; Sternberg, 1996).

So what, exactly, *is* intelligence? Psychologists have never been able to agree on an answer to this question, but many of them accept a working definition proposed by Robert Sternberg (1985). According to Sternberg, **intelligence** can be described in terms of three characteristics: the possession of knowledge, the ability to efficiently use that knowledge to reason about the world, and the ability to use that reasoning adaptively in different environments.

Standard tests of intelligence measure some of these characteristics, but they don't address all of them. Accordingly, some psychologists argue that these tools are not able to capture all that should be tested if we want to get a complete picture of someone's intelligence in its broadest sense. To better understand the controversy, let's take a look at how standard intelligence tests were created, what they are designed to measure, how well they do their job, and some of the alternative intelligence tests that have been proposed by those who find fault with traditional ones.

A Brief History of Intelligence Tests

In 1904 the French government asked psychologist Alfred Binet (pronounced "bih-NAY") to join a committee whose job was to identify, study, and provide special educational programs for children who were not doing well in school. As part of his work, Binet developed a set of intellectual tasks that provided the model for today's intelligence tests. Binet assumed that reasoning, thinking, and problem solving all depend on intelligence, so he chose tasks that would highlight individual differences in children's ability to do these things (Binet & Simon, 1905). Children taking Binet's test were asked to

intelligence　The possession of knowledge, the ability to efficiently use that knowledge to reason about the world, and the ability to use that reasoning adaptively in different environments.

	Age	Task
TABLE 7.1	2	Place geometric shapes into corresponding openings; identify body parts; stack blocks; identify common objects.
The Stanford-Binet	4	Name objects from memory; complete analogies (e.g., fire is hot; ice is _____); identify objects of similar shape; answer simple questions (e.g., "Why do we have schools?").
Here are samples of the type of items included on Lewis Terman's original Stanford-Binet test. As in Binet's test, an age level was assigned to each item.	6	Define simple words: explain differences (e.g., between a fish and a horse); identify missing parts of a picture; count out objects.
	8	Answer questions about a simple story; identify absurdities (e.g., in statements like "John had to walk on crutches because he hurt his arm"); explain similarities and differences among objects; tell how to handle certain situations (e.g., finding a stray puppy).
	10	Define more difficult words; give explanations (e.g., about why people should be quiet in a library); list as many words as possible; repeat 6-digit numbers.
	12	Identify more difficult verbal and pictured absurdities; repeat 5-digit numbers in reverse order; define abstract words (e.g., *sorrow*); fill in a missing word in a sentence.
	14	Solve reasoning problems; identify relationships among points of the compass; find similarities in apparently opposite concepts (e.g., "high" and "low"); predict the number of holes that will appear when folded paper is cut and then opened.
	Adult	Supply several missing words for incomplete sentences; repeat 6-digit numbers in reverse order; create a sentence using several unrelated words (e.g., *forest, businesslike,* and *dismayed*); describe similarities between concepts (e.g., "teaching" and "business").

Source: Nietzel & Bernstein (1987).

unwrap a piece of candy, repeat numbers or sentences from memory, identify familiar objects, and the like (T. B. Rogers, 1995).

Binet also assumed that children's mental abilities increase with age. So after trying out test items on children of various ages, he categorized each item according to how old a child had to be to get the item right. For example, a "six-year-old item" was one that a large majority of six-year-olds could answer correctly. Binet's test was thus a set of *age-graded* items. It measured a child's "mental level," later called *mental age,* by determining the age level of the most advanced items that the child could consistently answer correctly. Children whose mental age equaled their actual age, or *chronological age,* were considered to be of "regular" intelligence (D. P. Schultz & Schultz, 2000).

About a decade after Binet published his test, Lewis Terman at Stanford University developed an English version, known as the **Stanford-Binet** test (Terman, 1916). Table 7.1 gives examples of the kinds of items included on the test. Terman later added items to measure the intelligence of adults and, applying an idea suggested by William Stern, revised the method of scoring. Mental age was divided by chronological age, and the result was multiplied by 100. This figure was called the *intelligence quotient,* or *IQ.* Thus, a child whose mental age and chronological age were equal would have an IQ of 100, which is considered "average" intelligence. A ten-year-old who scored at the mental age of twelve would have an IQ of $12/10 \times 100 = 120$. From this method of scoring came the term **IQ test,** a name now widely used for any test designed to measure intelligence on an objective, standardized scale.

Stanford-Binet A test for determining a person's intelligence quotient, or IQ.

IQ test A test designed to measure intelligence on an objective, standardized scale.

Sample Items from the Performance Section of the Wechsler Intelligence Scale for Children (WISC-III)

Items like these tap aspects of intelligence but require little or no verbal ability.

PICTURE COMPLETION
What part is missing from this picture?

PICTURE ARRANGEMENT
These pictures tell a story, but they are in the wrong order. Put them in the right order so that they tell a story.

BLOCK DESIGN

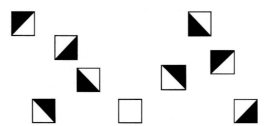

Put the blocks together to make this picture.

Source: Simulated items similar to those in the Wechsler Intelligence Scales for Adults and Children. Copyright © 1949, 1955, 1974, 1981, 1991 by the Psychological Corporation. Reproduced by permission. All rights reserved.

The method used to score the Stanford-Binet allowed testers to rank people based on their IQs. This goal was important to Terman and others who popularized the test in the United States. Terman believed that IQ tests could pinpoint who did and who did not have a suitable "amount" of intelligence. These beliefs led to some unfortunate consequences as enthusiasm for testing outpaced understanding of what was being tested. For example, when the United States entered World War I in 1917, a team of psychologists was asked to develop group-administered tests that could identify the mental ability of army recruits and guide their assignment to appropriate jobs. Soldiers who could speak and read English were tested on mental tasks that required verbal skills, such as defining words, whereas the rest were asked to visualize objects and perform other nonverbal tasks. Unfortunately, the verbal tests contained items that were unfamiliar to many recruits. Further, tests were often given under stressful conditions in crowded rooms where instructions were not always audible or, for non-English speakers, understandable. As a result, almost half of the soldiers tested appeared to have a mental age of thirteen or lower (Yerkes, 1921), leading testers to draw seriously incorrect conclusions about their lack of intelligence—especially in the cases of those who did not speak English (Brigham, 1923). Later tests developed by David Wechsler (1939, 1949) were designed to correct some of the weaknesses of earlier ones.

IQ Tests Today

Modern editions of the Wechsler tests and the Stanford-Binet are the most widely used intelligence tests in schools today. The Wechsler Adult Intelligence Scale includes eleven

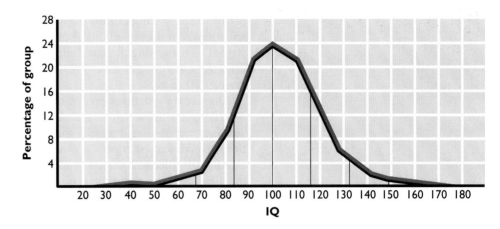

The Distribution of IQ Scores
in the Population

When the IQ scores in the overall population are plotted on a graph, a bell-shaped curve appears. The average IQ score of any given age group is 100. Half of the scores are higher than 100, and half are below 100. Approximately two-thirds of the IQ scores of any age group fall between 84 and 116; about one-sixth fall below 84, and one-sixth fall above 116.

subtests. Six require verbal skills and make up the **verbal scale** of the test. These subtests include such items as remembering a series of digits, solving arithmetic problems, defining vocabulary words, and answering general-knowledge questions. The remaining five subtests have little or no verbal content and make up the **performance scale.** They include tasks that require understanding the relations of objects in space and manipulation of various materials—tasks such as assembling blocks, solving mazes, and completing pictures. Figure 7.8 gives examples of items from one section of the performance scale of the latest version of the Wechsler test for children. With Wechsler tests, an examiner can compute a verbal IQ, a performance IQ, and an overall IQ. Comparisons of the verbal and performance scores can be particularly useful. For example, a high performance score and a low verbal score may mean that a child has a language deficiency that could prevent the verbal scale from accurately measuring the child's mental abilities.

The latest edition of the Stanford-Binet also uses subtests. It provides scores on verbal reasoning (e.g., similarities), quantitative reasoning (e.g., math problems), abstract/visual reasoning (e.g., explaining why we wear coats in cold weather), and working memory (e.g., repeating numbers), along with an overall IQ (R. L. Thorndike, Hagan, & Sattler, 1986).

Calculating IQ

IQ scores are no longer calculated by dividing mental age by chronological age. If you take an IQ test today, the points you earn for each correct subtest or age-level answer are summed. Then your total score is compared with the scores earned by other people. The average score obtained by people at each age level is *assigned* the IQ value of 100. Other scores are assigned IQ values that reflect how much each score differs from the average. If you do better on the test than the average person in your age group, you will receive an IQ score above 100. How far above depends on how much better than average you do. This procedure is based on a well-supported assumption about many characteristics: Most people's scores fall in the middle of the range of possible scores, creating a bell-shaped curve that approximates the *normal distribution* (see Figure 7.9). Half of those tested score below 100, the average for any given age group. The other half score above 100. In short, your **intelligence quotient,** or **IQ score,** reflects your relative standing within a population of your age.

verbal scale   Six subtests in Wechsler tests that measure verbal skills as part of a measure of overall intelligence.

performance scale   Five subtests in Wechsler tests that measure spatial ability and the ability to manipulate materials as part of a measure of overall intelligence.

intelligence quotient (IQ score)   A number that reflects the degree to which a person's score on an intelligence test differs from the average score of others in his or her age group.

Evaluating IQ Tests

■   **How good are IQ tests?**

We have said that no IQ test can accurately measure all aspects of what various people think of as intelligence. So what does your IQ score say about you? Can it predict your performance in school or on the job? Is it a fair summary of your mental abilities? To scientifically answer questions like these, we have to measure the quality of the tests that yield IQ scores, using the same criteria that apply to tests of personality, language skill, driving, or anything else. Let's review these criteria and then see how they are used to evaluate IQ tests.

Any **test** is a systematic procedure for observing behavior in a standard situation and describing it with the help of a numerical scale or system of categories (Cronbach, 1990). Tests are *standardized*, meaning that they present the same tasks, under similar conditions, to each and every person. Standardization helps ensure that test results will not be significantly affected by factors such as who gives and scores the test. To the extent that the biases of those giving a test do not influence the results, the test is said to be *objective*. Testers can use test scores to calculate **norms,** which are descriptions of the frequency of particular scores. Norms tell us, for example, what percentage of high school students obtained each possible score on a college entrance exam. They also tell us whether a particular IQ score or entrance-exam score is above or below the average score.

The two most important measures of a test's value are its reliability and its validity. A test is said to have high **reliability** if its results are repeatable or stable. The test must measure the same thing in the same way every time it is used. Let's suppose you receive a very high score on a test of reasoning. If you immediately take the test again, but now you get a very low score, the test is probably unreliable. The higher the reliability of a test, the less likely it is that scores will be affected by irrelevant environmental factors, such as what day the test is taken or the room in which it is given.

Suppose you stepped on a scale, checked your weight, stepped off, stepped back on, and found that your weight had increased by twenty pounds. You would know that the scale is unreliable, and probably broken. But now imagine that the scale is broken in a different way. It is still reliable, because it shows the same weight every time you step on it, but it says you only weigh thirty pounds! Unless you are a small child, this scale would provide an *invalid* measure of your weight. Tests, like scales, can be reliable and still not be valid. The **validity** of a test is the degree to which it measures what it is supposed to measure (Dooley, 2001).

Researchers evaluate the *reliability* of a test by obtaining two sets of scores on the same test from the same people. They then calculate a correlation coefficient between the two sets of scores (see Chapter 1). When the correlation is high and positive (usually above +.80), the test is considered reliable. Evaluating a test's *validity* usually means calculating a correlation coefficient between test scores and something else. What that "something else" is depends on what the test is designed to measure. Suppose, for example, you wanted to know if a creativity test is valid for identifying creative people. You could do so by computing the correlation between people's scores on the creativity test and experts' judgments about the quality of those same people's artistic creations. If the correlation is high, the test has high validity as a measure of creativity. Notice that a test's validity cannot be said to be high or low until you know how the test is to be used. Measuring how long someone can keep a bare hand in ice water might be a valid test of pain tolerance, but not of intelligence. So a test can be valid for one purpose but not valid for another.

The Reliability and Validity of IQ Tests

The reliability of IQ tests is generally evaluated on the basis of their stability, or consistency. The validity of IQ tests is usually based on their accuracy in making predictions about people.

Reliability   IQ scores obtained before the age of seven typically do not correlate very highly with scores on IQ tests given later. There are two key reasons. First, test items used with very young children are different from those used with older children. Second, cognitive abilities change rapidly in the early years (see Chapter 9). During the school years,

**LINKAGES
How do you know if a personality test, or any other kind of test, is any good?** (a link to Personality)

---

test   A systematic observation of behavior in a standard situation, described by a numerical scale or category.

norms   Descriptions of the frequency of occurrence of particular scores, allowing scores to be compared statistically.

reliability   The degree to which test results or other research evidence occurs repeatedly.

validity   The degree to which evidence from a test or other research method measures what it is supposed to measure.

If only measuring the multifaceted concept of intelligence were this easy!

however, IQ scores tend to remain stable (F. S. Mayer & Sutton, 1996). For teenagers and adults, then, the reliability of IQ tests is high, generally above +.90.

Of course, a person's score may vary from one occasion to another if there are significant changes in testing conditions, motivation, anxiety, health, or other factors. Overall, though, modern IQ tests usually provide exceptionally consistent results, especially compared with most other kinds of mental tests.

Validity If everyone agreed on exactly what intelligence is (having a good memory, for example), we could evaluate the validity of IQ tests simply by correlating people's IQ scores with their performance on various tasks (in this case, memory tasks). IQ tests whose scores correlated most highly with scores on memory tests would be the most valid measures of intelligence. But because psychologists do not fully agree on a single definition of intelligence, they don't have a single standard against which to compare IQ tests. Therefore, they cannot say whether IQ tests are valid measures of intelligence. They can only assess the validity of IQ tests *for specific purposes.*

The results of their research suggest that IQ tests are most valid for assessing aspects of intelligence that are related to schoolwork, such as abstract reasoning and verbal comprehension. Their validity—as measured by correlating IQ scores with high school grades—is reasonably good, about +.50 (Brody & Erlichmann, 1998).

In addition, there is evidence that employees who score high on tests of verbal and mathematical reasoning tend to perform better on the job than those who earn lower scores (Borman, Hanson, & Hedge, 1997; W. R. Johnson & Neal, 1998). A study that kept track of people for sixty years found that those who had high IQ scores as children tended to be well above average in terms of academic and financial success in adulthood (Oden, 1968; Terman & Oden, 1947). IQ scores also appear to be highly correlated with performance on routine tasks such as reading medicine labels and using a telephone book (Barrett & Depinet, 1991).

So, by the standard measures for judging psychological tests, IQ tests have good reliability and reasonably good validity for predicting certain criteria, such as success in school. However, an IQ score is not a perfect measure of how "smart" a person is. Because IQ tests do not measure the full array of mental abilities, a particular test score tells only part of the story, and even that part may be distorted. Many factors other than mental ability, including reactions to the tester, can influence test performance. For example, children who are suspicious of strangers, and adults who fear making mistakes, may become anxious and fail even to try answering some questions, thus artificially lowering their IQ scores (Jones & Appelbaum, 1989; C. M. Steele, 1997).

IQ Scores as a Measure of Innate Ability

Alfred Binet believed that intelligence could be improved with training and practice at mental tasks. Lewis Terman saw it as an inherited characteristic. Both were partly right. Years of research has led psychologists to conclude that hereditary and environmental factors interact to influence intelligence.

To explore the influence of genetics on individual differences in IQ scores, psychologists have compared the correlations in scores between people who share varying degrees of similarity in genetic makeup and environment. For example, they have examined the IQ scores of identical twins (pairs with exactly the same genes) who were separated when very young and reared in different environments. They have also examined the scores of identical twins raised together.

These studies find, first, that genetic factors influence IQ scores. When identical twins who were separated at birth and adopted by different families are tested many years later, the correlation between their scores is usually high and positive, at least +.60 (T. J. Bouchard et al., 1990). If one twin receives a high IQ score, the other probably will, too; if one is low, the other is likely to be low as well. However, studies of IQ correlations also highlight the importance of the environment (Scarr, 1998). Consider any two people—twins, nontwin siblings, or unrelated children—brought up together in a foster home. No matter what the degree of genetic similarity in these pairs, the correlation between

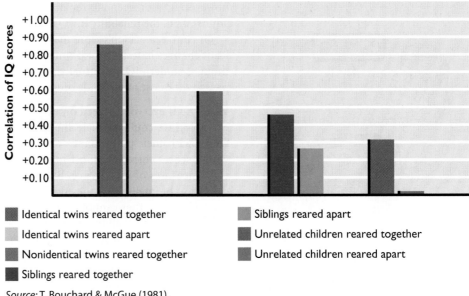

FIGURE 7.10

Correlations of IQ Scores

The correlation in IQ between pairs increases with increasing similarity in heredity *or* environment.

- Identical twins reared together
- Identical twins reared apart
- Nonidentical twins reared together
- Siblings reared together
- Siblings reared apart
- Unrelated children reared together
- Unrelated children reared apart

Source: T. Bouchard & McGue (1981).

their IQ scores will be higher if they share the same home than if they are raised in different homes, as Figure 7.10 shows (Scarr & Carter-Saltzman, 1982).

Environmental influences also show up in studies that compare children's IQ scores before and after environmental changes such as adoption. Children from relatively impoverished backgrounds who were adopted into homes with more enriching intellectual environments—environments with interesting materials and experiences, as well as a supportive, responsive adult—show modest increases in their IQ scores (Weinberg, Scarr, & Waldman, 1992).

A study of French children who were adopted soon after birth demonstrates the importance of both genetic and environmental influences. These children were tested after years of living in their adopted homes. Those whose biological parents were from higher socioeconomic groups (where superior IQs are most common) had higher IQ scores than those whose biological parents came from low socioeconomic groups, regardless of the socioeconomic status of the adopted homes. These findings suggest that a genetic component of the children's mental abilities continued to exert an influence in the adoptive environment. At the same time, the IQ scores of children from low socioeconomic backgrounds who were exposed to academically enriched environments through adoption rose by twelve to fifteen points (Capron & Duyme, 1989). Programs designed to enhance young children's school readiness and academic ability have also been associated with improved scores on tests of intelligence (Neisser et al., 1996; Ripple et al., 1999). These early-intervention programs may be partly responsible for the steady increase in average IQ scores seen throughout the world over the past six decades (Flynn, 1999; Neisser, 1998).

Some researchers have concluded that the influences of genetic and environmental factors on intelligence appear to be about equal. Others see a somewhat larger role for genetic influences (Chorney et al., 1998; Petrill et al., 1998; Plomin, 1994). Still, it must be emphasized that the relative contributions of heredity and environment apply only to groups, not to individuals. It would be inaccurate to say that 50 percent of *your* IQ score is inherited and 50 percent learned. It is more accurate to say that about half of the *variability* in the IQ scores of a group of people can be attributed to genetic influences, and about half can be attributed to environmental influences. (As discussed in the appendix, variability is the degree to which scores spread out around the average score.)

Group Differences in IQ Scores

Much of the controversy over the roles played by genes and the environment in intelligence has been sparked by efforts to explain differences in the average IQ scores earned

FIGURE 7.11

A Representation of Ethnic
Group Differences in IQ Scores

**The average IQ score of Asian Americans
is about four to six points higher than the
average score of European Americans,
who average twelve to fifteen points
higher than African Americans and
Hispanic Americans. Notice, however,
that the variation within these groups is
much greater than the variation between
them.**

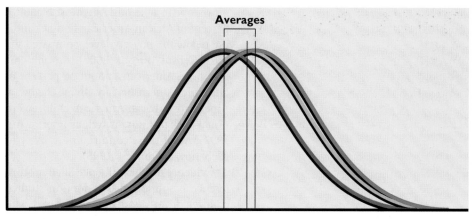

Averages

━━ African Americans and Hispanic Americans
━━ European Americans
━━ Asian Americans

LINKAGES
**How does motivation affect
IQ Scores?** (a link to Motivation
and Emotion)

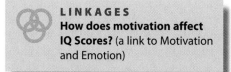

by particular groups of people. For example, the average scores of Asian Americans are
typically the highest among various ethnic groups, followed, in order, by European
Americans, Hispanic Americans, and African Americans (e.g., R. L. Taylor & Richards,
1991). Further, the average IQ scores of people from high-income areas in the United
States and elsewhere are consistently higher than those of people from low-income communities with the same ethnic makeup (Jordan, Huttenlocher, & Levine, 1992; McLoyd,
1998; Rowe, Jacobson, & Van den Oord, 1999).

To understand these differences and where they come from, we have to remember two
things. First, group scores are just that; they do not describe individuals. Although the
mean IQ score of Asian Americans is higher than the mean IQ score of European
Americans, there will still be large numbers of European Americans who score well above
the Asian American mean and large numbers of Asian Americans who score below the
European American mean (see Figure 7.11). Second, inherited characteristics are not
necessarily fixed. A favorable environment can improve a child's intellectual performance, even if the inherited influences on that child's IQ are negative (Flynn, 1999;
Humphreys, 1984; Neisser, 1998).

Socioeconomic Differences   Why is there a relationship between IQ scores and family
income? Four factors seem to account for the correlation. First, parents' jobs and status
depend on characteristics related to their own intelligence. And this intelligence is partly
determined by a genetic component that, in turn, contributes to their children's IQ
scores. Second, parents' income affects their children's environment in ways that can
increase or decrease the children's IQ scores (Bacharach & Baumeister, 1998). Third,
motivational differences may play a role. Upper- and middle-income families tend to
show greater motivation to excel in academic endeavors (Atkinson & Raynor, 1974).
Perhaps these families influence their children to be more highly motivated to succeed
on IQ tests. If so, children from middle- and upper-class families may exert more effort
and therefore obtain higher scores (Bradley-Johnson, Graham, & Johnson, 1986; Zigler
& Seitz, 1982). Fourth, because colleges, universities, and businesses usually select people
with higher scores on IQ tests, those with higher IQs may have greater opportunities to
earn more money (Sternberg & Kaufman, 1998).

Ethnic Differences   Some have argued that the mean differences in IQ among various
ethnic groups in the United States are due mostly to heredity. However, the existence of
hereditary differences among individuals *within* groups does not indicate whether differences *between* groups result from similar genetic causes (Lewontin, 1976). Notice
again in Figure 7.11 that variation *within* ethnic groups is much greater than variation
between those groups (Zuckerman, 1990).

We must also take into account the large differences among the environments in
which the average African American, Hispanic American, and European American child

grows up. To take only the most blatant evidence, the latest figures available show 23.6 percent of African American families and 22.8 percent of Hispanic American families living below the poverty level, compared with 9.8 percent of European American families (U.S. Census Bureau, 2000). Among children under age sixteen, about 15 percent of European Americans, about 36 percent of African Americans, and about 36 percent of Hispanic Americans are living below the poverty line. Compared with European Americans, African American children are more likely to have parents with poor educational backgrounds, as well as inferior nutrition, health care, and schools (W. J. Wilson, 1997). All of these conditions are likely to pull down scores on IQ tests (Brooks-Gunn, Klebanov, & Duncan, 1996).

Evidence for the influence of environmental factors on the average black-white IQ difference is supported by adoption studies. One such study involved African American children from disadvantaged homes who were adopted by middle- to upper-income European American families in the first years of their lives (Scarr & Weinberg, 1976). When measured a few years later, the mean IQ score of these children was 110. Using the scores of nonadopted children from similar backgrounds as a comparison suggests that adoption raised the children's IQ scores at least ten points. A ten-year follow-up study of these youngsters showed that their average IQ scores were still higher than the average scores of African American children raised in disadvantaged homes (Weinberg, Scarr, & Waldman, 1992).

THINKING CRITICALLY

Are IQ Tests Culturally Biased?

If environmental factors such as poverty and inferior educational opportunities are partly responsible for the lower average IQ scores seen in children from disadvantaged groups, is it fair to compare all children on traditional IQ tests? After all, success on these tests depends heavily on knowledge and skills that disadvantaged youngsters may not have had an equal chance to develop.

What am I being asked to believe or accept?

Some critics claim that standard IQ tests are *not* fair. They argue that a disproportionately large number of people from lower socioeconomic backgrounds and disadvantaged minority groups get low scores for reasons that are unrelated to mental ability, job potential, or other criteria that the tests are supposed to predict (Helms, 1992). Thus, they say, using IQ tests to make decisions about people—such as assigning them to particular jobs or special classes—causes members of certain groups to be unfairly deprived of equal opportunities. They worry that this policy perpetuates a social class system in which members of a "cognitive elite" are most likely to succeed in life, while intellectual "have-nots" are more likely drop out of school to face unemployment, poverty, and dependence on welfare to support themselves and their children.

Is there evidence available to support the claim?

There is certainly no doubt that noncognitive factors can influence a person's performance on IQ tests and may put certain groups at a disadvantage. We have seen, for example, that children from some ethnic and socioeconomic groups may be less likely than other children to be motivated to perform well on standardized tests. They may also be less likely to trust adult testers (C. M. Steele, 1997). Consequently, differences in IQ scores may reflect motivational, not intellectual, factors. It is also true that many IQ test items still draw on the vocabulary and experiences of the dominant middle-class culture in the United States. As a result, these tests often measure *achievement* in acquiring knowledge valued by that culture.

Not all cultures value the same things, however (Serpell, 1994). For example, a study of Cree Indians in northern Canada revealed that words and phrases meaning "competent" included *good sense of direction*. At the "incompetent" end of the scale was the

FIGURE 7.12

An Intelligence Test?

 How did you do on this "intelligence test"? If, like most people, you are unfamiliar with the concepts being tested by these rather obscure questions, your score was probably low. Would it be fair to say, then, that you are not very intelligent?

Take a minute to answer each of these questions, and check your answers against the key below.

1. What fictional detective was created by Leslie Charteris?
2. What planet travels around the sun every 248 years?
3. What vegetable yields the most pounds of produce per acre?
4. What was the infamous pseudonym of broadcaster Iva Toguri d'Aquino?
5. What kind of animal is Dr. Dolittle's Pushmi-Pullyu?

Answers: (1) Simon Templar (2) Pluto (3) Cabbage (4) Tokyo Rose (5) A two-headed llama.

phrase *lives like a white person* (Berry & Bennett, 1992). Thus, a European American might not perform well on a Cree intelligence test based on these criteria. Indeed, as illustrated in Figure 7.12, poor performance on a culture-specific test is probably due more to unfamiliarity with culture-based concepts than to lack of mental ability.

Further, a person might interpret IQ test questions in a way that is "intelligent," but that does not produce the answer that the test developer defined as "correct." In one study, when Liberian rice farmers were asked to sort objects, they tended to put a knife in the same group as vegetables. This was the clever way to do it, they said, because the knife is used to cut vegetables. If this task were part of an intelligence test, these farmers' sorting method would have been scored as "incorrect." Yet, when asked to sort the objects as a "stupid" person would, the farmers grouped the cutting tools together, the vegetables together, and so on, as most North Americans would (Ciborowski, cited in Segall et al., 1990). In other words, the fact that you *don't* give the answer that a test designer is looking for does not mean that you *can't*.

Can that evidence be interpreted another way?

The evidence might be interpreted as showing that although traditional IQ tests do not provide a complete and unbiased measure of "intelligence," they *do* provide a fair test of whether a person is likely to succeed in school or on a job. In short, they may be biased, but not in a way that discriminates *unfairly* between groups. Perhaps familiarity with the culture reflected in IQ tests is just as important for success at school or work in that culture as it is for success on the tests themselves. After all, the ranking among various ethnic groups on measures of academic achievement is similar to the ranking for mean IQ scores (S. Sue & Okazaki, 1990). According to this view, it doesn't matter very much if IQ tests measure culture-related achievement, as long as they are useful in predicting whatever criterion is of interest.

What evidence would help to evaluate the alternatives?

Some psychologists have developed "culture-fair" intelligence tests (Bracken & McCallum, 1998), which result in smaller average differences among ethnic groups. Unfortunately, these tests do not predict academic achievement as well as conventional IQ tests do (Aiken, 1994). Other alternative tests are also being explored, including some that assess problem-solving skills and other abilities not measured by most IQ tests (e.g., Sternberg & Kaufman, 1998). If these new tests prove to be less biased than traditional tests but have equal or better predictive validity, many of the issues discussed in this section will have been resolved.

What conclusions are most reasonable?

The American Psychological Association and other organizations set demanding standards for the reliability, validity, fairness, and use of all psychological tests, including IQ

in review

Influences on IQ Scores

Source of Effect	Description	Examples of Evidence for Effect
Genetics	Genes appear to play a significant role in IQ test performance.	The IQ scores of siblings who share no common environment are positively correlated. There is a greater correlation between scores of identical twins than between those of nonidentical twins.
Environment	Environmental conditions interact with genetic inheritance. Nutrition, medical care, sensory and intellectual stimulation, interpersonal relations, and influences on motivation are all significant features of the environment.	IQ scores have risen among children who are adopted into homes that offer a stimulating, enriching environment. Correlations between IQs of twins reared together are higher than for those reared apart.

tests (American Educational Research Association, American Psychological Association, & National Council on Measurement in Education, 1999). "Summarizing" a person through an IQ score runs the risk of oversimplifying reality and making errors, but standard intelligence tests can also *prevent* errors. If boredom makes a child appear mentally slow, even retarded, an IQ test conducted under the right circumstances is likely to reveal the child's potential. And, as Binet had hoped, IQ tests have been enormously helpful in identifying children who need special educational attention. So despite their limitations and potential for bias, IQ tests can minimize the likelihood of assigning children to remedial work they do not need, or to advanced work they cannot yet handle.

Nevertheless, efforts to reduce cultural bias in intelligence tests are well founded, as long as the resulting tests objectively measure the knowledge and skills people need to succeed in the culture where they live and work. The problem of test bias would best be solved, though, by addressing the poverty, inferior schools, poor nutrition, lack of health care, and other conditions that result in lower average IQ scores and reduced economic opportunities for certain groups of people. ("In Review: Influences on IQ Scores" summarizes our discussion of environmental and genetic factors affecting performance on intelligence tests.)

Diversity in Intelligence

Is there more than one type of intelligence?

IQ scores can tell us some things—and predict some things—about people, but we have seen that they don't tell the whole story of intelligence. Let's see how diverse intelligence can be by looking at some nontraditional aspects of intelligence, and some people whose intellectual abilities are unusually high or low.

Multiple Intelligences

Many people with only average scores on IQ tests have exceptional ability in specific areas. Even those with very low IQ scores have been known to show incredible ability in narrowly defined skills (L. K. Miller, 1999). One such child could instantly and correctly state the day of the week for any date between 1880 and 1950 (Scheerer, Rothmann, & Goldstein, 1945). He could also play melodies on the piano by ear and sing Italian operatic pieces he had heard. He could spell—forward or backward—any word spoken to him and could memorize long speeches. However, he was severely retarded and had no understanding of what he was doing.

Cases like this are part of the evidence that led Howard Gardner to propose his theory of *multiple intelligences* (H. Gardner, 1993). Gardner focused on how people learn and use symbol systems like language, mathematics, and music. He asked, Do these systems all require the same abilities and processes—the same "intelligence"? According to Gardner, the answer is no. He believes that everyone possesses a number of intellectual potentials, or "intelligences," each of which involves a somewhat different set of skills. Biology, he says, provides raw capacities for each of these intelligences; cultures provide symbolic systems—such as language—that enable people to use their raw capacities. Although the various intelligences normally interact, they can function with some independence, and individuals may develop certain intelligences further than others.

The specific intelligences that H. Gardner (1998) proposes are (1) *linguistic* intelligence (reflected in good vocabulary and reading comprehension), (2) *logical-mathematical* intelligence (as indicated by skill at arithmetic and certain kinds of reasoning), (3) *spatial* intelligence (seen in understanding relationships between objects), (4) *musical* intelligence (as in abilities involving rhythm, tempo, and sound identification), (5) *body-kinesthetic* intelligence (reflected in skill at dancing, athletics, and eye-hand coordination), (6) *intrapersonal* intelligence (displayed by self-understanding), (7) *interpersonal* intelligence (seen in the ability to understand and interact with others), and (8) *naturalistic* intelligence (the ability to see patterns in nature). Other researchers have suggested that people also possess emotional intelligence, which involves the capacity to perceive emotions and to link them to one's thinking (J. D. Meyer & Salovey, 1997).

Standard IQ tests sample only the first three of these diverse intelligences, mainly because they are the forms of intelligence most valued in school. To measure specific intelligences not tapped by standard IQ tests, Gardner suggests collecting samples of children's writing, assessing their ability to appreciate or produce music, and obtaining teacher reports of their strengths and weaknesses in athletic and social skills.

Gardner's view of intelligence is appealing, partly because it allows virtually everyone to be highly intelligent in at least one way. However, his critics argue that including athletic or musical skill as part of intelligence dilutes the usefulness of the concept, especially as it is applied to school and in many kinds of jobs. Even so, Gardner and his colleagues (Kornhaber, Krechevsky, & Gardner, 1990) are working on new ways of assessing "multiple intelligences." The value of these methods will be decided by further research.

Practical and Creative Intelligence

In contrast to Gardner, Robert Sternberg (1988a, 1999) sees only three types of intelligence: analytic, creative, and practical. *Analytic* intelligence, the kind that is measured by traditional IQ tests, helps you to solve a physics problem; *creative* intelligence is what you would use to compose music; and you would draw on *practical* intelligence to figure out what to do if you were stranded on a lonely road during a storm. (His view is known as the *triarchic theory* of intelligence.)

Sternberg acknowledges the importance of analytic intelligence for success in academics and other areas, but he argues that universities and companies should not select people solely on the basis of tests of this kind of intelligence (Sternberg, 1996; Sternberg & Williams, 1997). Why? Because the tasks posed by tests of analytic intelligence are often of little interest to the people taking them, and these tasks typically have little relationship to their daily experience. In contrast, the practical problems people face every day are generally of personal interest and are related to their actual experiences (Sternberg et al., 1995). It is no wonder, then, that children who do poorly in school and on IQ tests can nevertheless show high degrees of practical intelligence. Some Brazilian street children, for example, are capable of doing the math required for their street business, despite having failed mathematics in school (Carraher, Carraher, & Schliemann, 1985). In other words, their practical intelligence is unrelated to measures of their IQ. There is some evidence that scores on tests of practical and creative intelligence predict success at some jobs at least as well as standard IQ test scores (Leonhardt, 2000; Sternberg et al., 1995; Sternberg & Kaufman, 1998). (See Figure 7.13.)

Unusual Intelligence

Psychologists' understanding of intelligence has been advanced by studying people whose mental abilities are unusual—especially the gifted and the mentally retarded.

Giftedness   Do all people with unusually high IQs become famous and successful in their chosen fields? Do their remarkable intellectual abilities hurt their chances of "fitting in" with the social world? One of the best-known studies of the intellectually gifted was conducted by Louis Terman and his colleagues (Oden, 1968; Sears, 1977: Terman & Oden, 1947, 1959). This study began in 1921 with the identification of more than 1,500 children whose IQ scores were very high—most higher than 135 by age ten. Periodic interviews and tests over the next sixty years revealed that few, if any, became world-famous scientists, inventors, authors, artists, or composers. But only 11 failed to graduate from high school, and more than two-thirds graduated from college. Ninety-seven earned Ph.D.'s; 92, law degrees; and 57, medical degrees. In 1955 their median family income was well above the national average (Terman & Oden, 1959). In general, they were physically and mentally healthier than the nongifted and appeared to have led happier, or at least more fortunate, lives. Thus, high IQ scores tend to predict success in life, but an extremely high IQ does not guarantee special distinction. In fact, research by Veronica Dark and Camilla Benbow (1993) suggests that gifted children are not fundamentally different kinds of people. They just have "more" of the same basic mental abilities seen in all children.

Mental Retardation   People whose IQ is less than about 70 *and* who fail to display the skills at daily living, communication, and other tasks that are expected of those their age have traditionally been described as "mentally retarded." (They are also referred to as "developmentally disabled" or "mentally challenged.") People within this very broad category differ greatly in their mental abilities, and in their ability to function independently in daily life (see Table 7.2).

TABLE 7.2

Categories of Mental Retardation

These categories are approximate. Especially at the upper end of the scale, many retarded persons can be taught to handle tasks well beyond what their IQ scores might suggest. Furthermore, IQ is not the only diagnostic criterion for retardation. Many people with IQs lower than 70 can function adequately in their everyday environment and so would not be classified as mentally retarded.

Level of Retardation	IQ Scores	Characteristics
Mild	50–70	A majority of all the mentally retarded. Usually show no physical symptoms of abnormality. Individuals with higher IQs can marry, maintain a family, and work in unskilled jobs. Abstract reasoning is difficult for those with the lower IQs of this category. Capable of some academic learning to a sixth-grade level.
Moderate	35–49	Often lack physical coordination. Can be trained to take care of themselves and to acquire some reading and writing skills. Abilities of a 4- to 7-year-old. Capable of living outside an institution with their families.
Severe	20–34	Only a few can benefit from any schooling. Can communicate vocally after extensive training. Most require constant supervision.
Profound	Below 20	Mental age less than 3. Very limited communication. Require constant supervision. Can learn to walk, utter a few simple phrases, and feed themselves.

FIGURE 7.13

Testing for Practical and
Creative Intelligence

 Robert Sternberg notes that traditional IQ tests measure mainly analytic intelligence. Here are sample items from tests he developed that test practical and creative intelligence as well. The answers are given at the bottom of the figure. How did you do?

PRACTICAL

1. Think of a problem that you are currently experiencing in real life. Briefly describe the problem, including how long it has been present and who else is involved (if anyone). Then describe three different practical things you could do to try to solve the problem. *(Students are given up to 15 minutes and up to 2 pages.)*

2. Choose the answer that provides the **best** solution, given the specific situation and desired outcome.

    John's family moved to Iowa from Arizona during his junior year in high school. He enrolled as a new student in the local high school two months ago but still has not made friends and feels bored and lonely. One of his favorite activities is writing stories. What is likely to be the most effective solution to this problem?

    A. Volunteer to work on the school newspaper staff.

    B. Spend more time at home writing columns for the school newsletter.

    C. Try to convince his parents to move back to Arizona.

    D. Invite a friend from Arizona to visit during Christmas break.

3. Each question asks you to use information about everyday things. Read each question carefully and choose the best answer.

    Mike wants to buy two seats together and is told there are pairs of seats available only in Rows 8, 12, 49, and 95–100. Which of the following is not one of his choices for the total price of the two tickets?

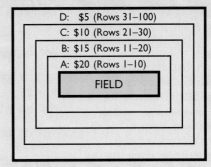

    A. $10.   **B.** $20.   **C.** $30.   **D.** $40.

CREATIVE

1. Suppose you are the student representative to a committee that has the power and the money to reform your school system. Describe your ideal school system, including buildings, teachers, curriculum, and any other aspects you feel are important. *(Students are given up to 15 minutes and up to 2 pages.)*

2. Each question has a "Pretend" statement. You must suppose that this statement is true. Decide which word goes with the third underlined word in the same way that the first two underlined words go together.

    Colors are audible.

    flavor is to *tongue* as *shade* is to

    A. ear.   **B.** light.   **C.** sound.   **D.** hue.

3. First, read how the operation is defined. Then, decide what is the correct answer to the question.

    There is a new mathematical operation called **flix.**
    It is defined as follows:
    $$A \text{ flix } B = A + B, \text{ if } A > B$$
    but $A \text{ flix } B = A \times B, \text{ if } A < B$
    and $A \text{ flix } B = A / B, \text{ if } A = B$
    How much is 4 flix 7?

    A. 28.   **B.** 11.   **C.** 3.   **D.** –11.

Answers: Practical: (2) A. (3) B. Creative: (2) A. (3) A.

Source: Sternberg (1996).

THE EAGLE HAS LANDED　In February 2000, Richard Keebler, twenty-seven, became an Eagle Scout in the Boy Scouts of America. His achievement is notable not only because a mere 4 percent of all Scouts ever reach this rank but also because Keebler has Down syndrome. As the limitations and the potential of individuals who are mentally retarded are better understood, their opportunities and their role in society will continue to expand.

Some cases of mental retardation have a clearly identifiable cause. The best-known example is *Down syndrome,* which is caused by an extra copy of chromosome 21 (Hattori et al., 2000). Children with Down syndrome typically have IQ scores in the range of 40 to 55. Intelligence may also be limited by environmental conditions or traumas such as meningitis or encephalitis contracted during infancy, birth traumas resulting from oxygen deprivation, and drug or alcohol abuse by the mother during pregnancy.

In most cases of mild retardation, however, there is no obvious genetic or environmental cause. This type of impairment is called **familial retardation** for two reasons. First, most people who are mildly mentally retarded come from families of lower socioeconomic status; and second, they are more likely than those suffering from a genetic defect to have a relative who is also retarded (Plomin, 1989). These facts have led psychologists to conclude that familial retardation results from a complex interaction between genetic and environmental influences.

People who are mildly retarded differ from other people in three important ways (Campione, Brown, & Ferrara, 1982):

1. They perform certain mental operations more slowly, such as retrieving information from long-term memory. When asked to repeat something they have learned, they are not as quick as a person of normal intelligence.

2. They simply know fewer facts about the world. It is likely that this deficiency is a consequence of a third problem, listed next.

3. They are not very good at using certain mental strategies that may be important in learning and problem solving. For example, they do not spontaneously rehearse material that must be held in working memory.

Despite such difficulties, the intellectual abilities of people who are mentally retarded can be raised. For example, one program emphasizing positive parent-child communications began when the children were as young as two and a half years old. It helped children with Down syndrome to eventually master reading skills at a second-grade level, providing the foundation for further achievement (Rynders & Horrobin, 1980).

Designing effective programs for children who are retarded is complicated by the fact that learning does not depend on cognitive skills alone. It also depends on social and emotional factors. Much debate has focused on *mainstreaming,* the policy of teaching children with disabilities, including those who are retarded, in regular classrooms along with those without disabilities. Is mainstreaming good for children who are retarded? A number of studies comparing the cognitive and social skills of mainstreamed and separated students show few significant differences overall. However, it does appear that students at higher ability levels may gain more from being mainstreamed than their less mentally able peers (Cole et al., 1991).

familial retardation　Cases of mild retardation for which no environmental or genetic cause can be found.

active review Thought, Language, and Intelligence

Linkages

As noted in Chapter 1, all of psychology's subfields are related to one another. Our discussion of group problem solving illustrates just one way in which the topic of this chapter, thought, language, and intelligence, is linked to the subfield of social psychology (Chapter 14). The Linkages diagram shows ties to two other subfields as well, and there are many more ties throughout the book. Looking for linkages among subfields will help you see how they all fit together and help you better appreciate the big picture that is psychology.

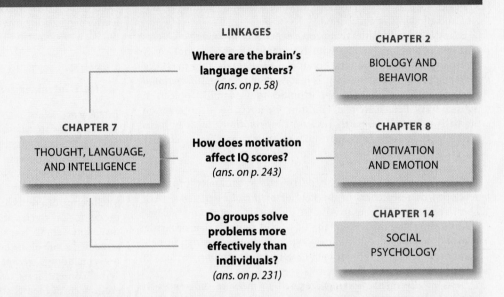

LINKAGES

Where are the brain's language centers?
(ans. on p. 58)

CHAPTER 2
BIOLOGY AND BEHAVIOR

CHAPTER 7
THOUGHT, LANGUAGE, AND INTELLIGENCE

How does motivation affect IQ scores?
(ans. on p. 243)

CHAPTER 8
MOTIVATION AND EMOTION

Do groups solve problems more effectively than individuals?
(ans. on p. 231)

CHAPTER 14
SOCIAL PSYCHOLOGY

Summary

BASIC FUNCTIONS OF THOUGHT

What good is thinking, anyway?

The five core functions of thought are to describe, elaborate, decide, plan, and guide action. Many psychologists think of the components of this circle of thought as constituting an *information-processing system* that receives, represents, transforms, and acts on incoming stimuli. *Thinking,* then, is defined as the manipulation of mental representations by this system.

MENTAL REPRESENTATIONS: THE INGREDIENTS OF THOUGHT

What are thoughts made of?

Mental representations take the form of cognitive maps, images, concept schemas and event scripts, propositions, and mental models. *Cognitive maps* are mental representations of familiar parts of one's world. Mental *images* may also be manipulated when people think.

Concepts are categories of objects, events, or ideas with common properties. They may be formal or natural. *Formal concepts* are precisely defined by the presence or absence of certain features. *Natural concepts* are fuzzy; no fixed set of defining properties determines membership in a natural concept. A member of a natural concept that displays all or most of the concept's characteristic features is called a *prototype. Schemas* serve as generalized mental representations of concepts and also generate expectations about them. *Scripts* are schemas about familiar sequences of events or activities.

The raw material of thought may also take the form of *propositions,* which are assertions that state how different concepts are related or how a concept is related to its properties. Propositions can be true or false. Experience creates accurate or inaccurate *mental models* that help to guide our understanding of, and interaction with, the world.

THINKING STRATEGIES

Are people always logical?

By combining and transforming mental representations, our information-processing system makes it possible for us to reason, solve problems, and make decisions. *Formal reasoning* seeks valid conclusions through the application of rigorous procedures. It is guided by *algorithms,* systematic methods that always reach a correct result. To reach a sound conclusion, people should consider both the truth or falsity of their assumptions and the *logic* of the argument itself. People are prone to logical errors; their belief in a conclusion is often affected by the extent to which the conclusion is consistent with their attitudes, as well as by other factors, including cultural background.

People use *informal reasoning* to assess the validity of a conclusion based on the evidence for it. Errors in informal reasoning often stem from the use of *heuristics,* which are mental shortcuts or rules of thumb. Three important heuristics are the *anchoring heuristic* (estimating the probability of an event by adjusting a starting value), the *representativeness heuristic* (basing conclusions about whether something belongs in a certain class on how similar it is to other items in that class), and the *availability heuristic* (estimating probability by how available an event is in memory).

PROBLEM SOLVING

What's the best way to solve a problem?

Steps in problem solving include diagnosing the problem and then planning, executing, and evaluating a solution. Especially when solutions are not obvious, problem solving can be aided by the use of strategies such as decomposition, working backward, finding analogies, and allowing for incubation.

Many of the difficulties that people experience in solving problems arise when they are dealing with hypotheses. People do not easily entertain multiple hypotheses. Because of *mental sets,* they may stick to one hypothesis even when it is incorrect and, through *functional fixedness,* may tend to miss opportunities to use familiar objects in unusual ways. People are reluctant to revise or change hypotheses on the basis of new data, partly because *confirmation bias* may focus their attention on evidence that supports their hypotheses. They may also fail to use the absence of symptoms or events as evidence in solving problems.

Some specific problems can be solved by computer programs developed by researchers in the field of *artificial intelligence (AI).* There are two approaches to AI. One focuses on programming computers to imitate the logical manipulation of symbols that occurs in human thought; the other (involving connectionist, or neural network, models) attempts to imitate the connections among neurons in the human brain.

Tests of *divergent thinking* are used to measure differences in *creativity.* In contrast, intelligence tests require *convergent thinking.* Although creativity and intelligence are not highly correlated, creative behavior requires a certain amount of intelligence, along with expertise in a creative field, skill at problem solving and divergent thinking, and motivation to pursue a creative endeavor for its own sake.

DECISION MAKING

How can I become a better decision maker?

Decisions are sometimes difficult because there are too many alternatives and too many features of each alternative to consider at one time. Furthermore, decisions often involve comparisons of subjective *utility,* not of objective value. Decision making is also complicated by the fact that the world is unpredictable, which makes decisions risky.

People should act in ways that maximize the *expected value* of their decisions. But they often fail to do so because losses are perceived differently from gains of equal size and because people tend to overestimate the probability of rare events, underestimate the probability of very frequent events, and feel overconfident about the accuracy of their forecasts. The gambler's fallacy leads people to believe that outcomes in a random process are affected by previous outcomes. People also make decisions aimed at goals other than maximizing expected value; these goals may be determined by personal and cultural factors.

Group decisions tend to show *group polarization,* the selection of more extreme outcomes than would have been chosen by the average group member. Group performance at problem solving and decision making tends to be more effective, but less efficient, than that of a person working alone.

LANGUAGE

How do babies learn to talk?

Language consists of *words* or word symbols and rules for their combination—a *grammar.* Children develop grammar according to an orderly pattern. *Babblings* come first, then *telegraphic* two-word sentences. Next come three-word sentences and certain grammatical

forms that appear in a somewhat predictable order. Once children learn certain regular verb forms and plural endings, they may overgeneralize rules. Children acquire most of the syntax of their native language by the time they are five years old.

Both conditioning and imitation play a role in a child's acquisition of language, but neither can provide a complete explanation of how children acquire syntax. Humans may be biologically programmed to learn language. In any event, it appears that language must be learned during a certain critical period if normal language is to occur.

TESTING INTELLIGENCE

How is intelligence measured?

Intelligence refers to the possession of knowledge, the ability to reason, and the capacity to adapt to different environments. Binet's pioneering test of intelligence included questions that required reasoning and problem solving at varying levels of difficulty, graded by age. Terman developed a revision of Binet's test that became known as the *Stanford-Binet;* it included items designed to assess the intelligence of adults as well as that of children, and it became the model for *IQ tests.* Early IQ tests in the United States required not just mental ability but also knowledge of U.S. culture. Wechsler's tests remedied some of the deficiencies of earlier IQ tests. Made up of subtests, including a *verbal scale* but also a *performance scale* with little verbal content, these tests allowed testers to obtain scores for different aspects of mental ability.

In schools, the Stanford-Binet and Wechsler tests are the most popular individually administered intelligence tests. Both include subtests and provide scores for parts of the test, as well as an overall score. Currently, a person's *intelligence quotient,* or *IQ score,* reflects how much the person's performance on the test deviates from the average performance of people in the same age group. An average performance is assigned an IQ of 100.

EVALUATING IQ TESTS

How good are IQ tests?

Tests are standardized, so the performance of different people can be compared; they also produce scores that can be compared with *norms.* A good test must have *reliability,* which means that the results for each person are consistent, or stable. A test is said to have *validity* if it measures what it is supposed to measure.

IQ tests are reasonably reliable and do a good job of predicting academic success. However, IQ tests assess only some of the abilities that might be considered aspects of intelligence, and they may favor people most familiar with middle-class culture. Nonetheless, this familiarity is important for academic and occupational success in that culture.

Both genes and the environment influence IQ scores, and their effects interact. Genetic influences are reflected in the high correlation between IQ scores of identical twins raised in separate households and in the similarity between the IQ scores of children adopted at birth and those of their biological parents. The influence of the environment is revealed by the higher correlation of IQ between siblings who share the same environment than between those who do not and by the effects of environmental changes such as adoption.

Different socioeconomic and ethnic groups have somewhat different mean IQ scores. These differences appear to be due to numerous factors, including differences in motivation, family support, educational opportunity, and other environmental conditions. An enriched environment sometimes raises IQ scores. Despite their limitations, IQ tests can help educators to identify a student's strengths and weaknesses and to offer the curriculum that will best serve that student.

DIVERSITY IN INTELLIGENCE

Is there more than one type of intelligence?

According to Gardner, biology equips us with the capacities for several intelligences that can function with some independence—specifically, linguistic, logical-mathematical, spatial, musical, body-kinesthetic, intrapersonal, interpersonal, and naturalistic intelligences. Sternberg sees three types of intelligence: analytic, practical, and creative. He says that scores on tests of practical intelligence predict job success as well as traditional IQ test scores do.

Knowledge about mental abilities has been expanded by research on giftedness and mental retardation. People with very high IQ scores tend to be successful in life but are not necessarily geniuses. People are considered retarded if their IQ score is below about 70 and if their communication and daily living skills are less than expected of people their age. In cases of *familial retardation,* no genetic or environmental causes are evident. Compared with people of normal intelligence, people who are retarded process information more slowly, know fewer facts, and are deficient at knowing and using mental strategies. Special teaching programs can, to some extent, improve the intellectual abilities of some people who are mentally retarded.

Learn by Doing

Put It in Writing

Try writing your own definition of intelligence. Make a list of at least seven behaviors or characteristics that you feel represent "intelligence," and then decide how they could best be tested in children and adults from your own culture and other cultures. Describe the kinds of difficulties you encountered in making your list and designing your assessment devices.

Personal Learning Activity

Consider a problem that you are facing at the moment, or one that is being faced by someone you know. In accordance with the problem-solving section of this chapter, write down all the alternative solutions you can think of to solve this problem; then list the pros and cons of each option. Which alternative comes out on top? Does the alternative that seems best on paper also strike you as the best solution to try? Why or why not? *For additional projects, see the five Personal Learning Activities in the corresponding chapter of the study guide that accompanies this text.*

Step into Action

Courses

Experimental Psychology
Cognitive Psychology
Psycholinguistics
Engineering Psychology (sometimes called Human Factors)
Tests and Measurement (sometimes called Psychometrics)
Behavioral Genetics

Movies

Nell; Dances with Wolves; Clan of the Cave Bear (language development)
Gorillas in the Mist (animal communication)
Apollo 13; The Negotiator (problem solving)
2001: A Space Odyssey (artificial intelligence)
My Left Foot (assessment of ability)
Forrest Gump; Of Mice and Men; The Other Sister; Charly; Rain Man; Little Man Tate (diversity of intelligence)

Books

Gerd Gigerenzer, Peter M. Todd, and ABC Research Group, *Simple Heuristics That Make Us Smart* (Oxford University Press, 2000) (research on, and ideas for using, mental shortcuts)

Peter Bernstein, *Against the Gods: The Remarkable Story of Risk* (Wiley, 1998) (history of efforts to understand risk and probability in decision making)
Nicholas Lemann, *The Big Test: The Secret History of American Meritocracy* (Farrar, Straus & Giroux, 1999) (history of testing in the United States)
Hans Eysenck, with Darrin Evans, *Test Your IQ* (Penguin, 1995) (self-testing)
Daniel Seligman, *A Question of Intelligence: The IQ Debate in America* (Citadel Press, 1994) (nature, nurture, and IQ)
Howard Gardner, *Intelligence Reframed: Multiple Intelligences for the 21st Century* (Basic Books, 1999) (theory of multiple intelligences)

The Web

The World Wide Web is a good source of additional information about the science of psychology, provided you use it carefully and think critically about the information you find. The PsychAbilities web site that accompanies this text offers many resources relevant to this chapter. These resources include interactive NetLab exercises; Thinking Critically and Evaluating Research exercises; ACE chapter quizzes; recommended web links; and articles on current events, books, and movies. At http://college.hmco.com, select *Psychology* and then this textbook.

Review of Key Terms

Can you define each of the key terms in the chapter? Check your definitions against those on the pages listed in parentheses below or in the Glossary/Index at the end of the text.

algorithms (p. 219)
anchoring heuristic (p. 220)
artificial intelligence (AI) (p. 226)
availability heuristic (p. 220)
babblings (p. 232)
cognitive map (p. 216)
concepts (p. 216)
confirmation bias (p. 225)
convergent thinking (p. 228)
creativity (p. 227)
divergent thinking (p. 227)
expected value (p. 229)

familial retardation (p. 250)
formal concept (p. 217)
formal reasoning (p. 219)
functional fixedness (p. 225)
grammar (p. 232)
group polarization (p. 231)
heuristics (p. 220)
images (p. 216)
informal reasoning (p. 220)
information-processing system (p. 215)
intelligence (p. 236)

intelligence quotient (IQ score) (p. 239)
IQ test (p. 237)
language (p. 232)
logic (p. 219)
mental models (p. 218)
mental set (p. 224)
natural concepts (p. 217)
norms (p. 240)
performance scale (p. 239)
propositions (p. 217)
prototype (p. 217)

reliability (p. 240)
representativeness heuristic (p. 220)
schemas (p. 217)
scripts (p. 217)
Stanford-Binet (p. 237)
telegraphic (p. 233)
test (p. 240)
thinking (p. 215)
utility (p. 229)
validity (p. 240)
verbal scale (p. 239)

Multiple-Choice Self-Test

Select the best answer for each of the questions below. Then check your responses against the Answer Key at the end of the text.

1. *Thinking* is defined as the manipulation of

   a. concepts.
   b. mental models.
   c. heuristics.
   d. mental representations.

2. Jarrod is in his bedroom when the power fails and the lights go off. He can't see a thing, but he is still able to walk confidently through his apartment to get a flashlight. Jarrod used a(n) _____ to find his way.

   a. hypothesis
   b. cognitive map
   c. heuristic
   d. algorithm

3. Clint is frustrated. His uncle has been winning at checkers all night. During the next game he is going to base his strategy on an algorithm, not a heuristic. What problem will this strategy cause?

   a. Clint still may not win the game.
   b. Clint and his uncle may be playing the same game of checkers for a long time.
   c. Clint will be ignoring overall probabilities.
   d. The representativeness heuristic will bias Clint's choice of strategy.

4. Alicia is telling her friend Mona about the new apartment she has rented. As she describes the layout, Mona will construct a _____ of the apartment, probably as a three-dimensional representation.

   a. concept schema
   b. mental model
   c. proposition
   d. script

5. Stephanie has worked for hours on a biochemistry problem without success. She decides to put it aside and work on her psychology homework in the hope that a solution might occur to her while she is thinking about something else. Stephanie is trying the _____ strategy to solve her problem.

   a. decomposition
   b. incubation
   c. working backward
   d. analogies

6. Ebony wanted to leave a note for her husband but couldn't find a pen, so she wrote the note with her lipstick. Ebony was able to overcome the obstacle to problem solving called

   a. absence of information.
   b. multiple hypotheses.
   c. confirmation bias.
   d. functional fixedness.

7. Because Dr. Sand is convinced that Ahmed has appendicitis, he pays more attention to test results that indicate appendicitis than to test results that don't support his original belief. Dr. Sand is displaying

   a. functional fixedness.
   b. a mental model.
   c. confirmation bias.
   d. the availability heuristic.

8. Each time Richard pulls a card from the deck, he has a 1-in-52 chance of selecting the queen of spades (assuming he replaces the selected card and shuffles before drawing again). After drawing the queen of spades twice in a row, he says, "There is no way I will draw the queen of spades next time!" Richard is being influenced by

   a. the gambler's fallacy.
   b. loss aversion.
   c. a disregard of negative evidence.
   d. confirmation bias.

9. The fact that children learning language sometimes make errors, such as saying "I goed" instead of "I went," has been used to suggest that

   a. there is a critical period in language development.
   b. children are born with a knowledge of grammar.
   c. children do not learn language entirely through imitation.
   d. speech is learned mainly through imitation.

10. Children who spend their early years isolated from human contact and the sound of adult language are unable to develop adult language skills despite extensive training efforts later. This phenomenon provides evidence for the notion that

    a. there is a critical period in language development.
    b. children are born with a language acquisition device.
    c. there are no fixed stages in language acquisition.
    d. speech is acquired *only* through imitation.

11. The earliest IQ test was developed to

    a. identify children who needed special educational programs.
    b. help the armed forces make appropriate assignments of recruits.
    c. identify which immigrants were mentally defective and thus should not be allowed into the United States.
    d. help employers decide which employees were most appropriate for the available jobs.

12. "All monsters are ugly. The Creature from the Black Lagoon is a monster. Therefore, the Creature is ugly." Together, these three statements are an example of

    a. a premise.
    b. a proposition.
    c. a natural concept.
    d. formal reasoning.

13. Jonah just took an IQ test. According to the scoring method used today, his IQ score will reflect

    a. his mental age divided by his chronological age, times 100.
    b. how quickly he completed the test.
    c. the degree to which his score differs from the average of other people his age.
    d. his raw score, adjusted for how long he has lived in his present culture.

14. Correlating people's job success with their pre-employment test scores is one way of measuring a test's

    a. reliability.
    b. standardization.
    c. validity.
    d. norms.

15. When Jerrica first took the Handy Dandy Intelligence test, her score was 140. When she took the same test six weeks later, her score was only 102. If other people showed similarly changing score patterns, the Handy Dandy Intelligence test would appear to lack

    a. reliability.
    b. validity.
    c. standardization.
    d. norms.

16. Research shows that today's standardized IQ tests

    a. have good reliability and reasonably good validity for predicting success in school.
    b. do not do a good job of predicting success on the job.
    c. are not correlated with performance on "real-life" tasks.
    d. measure the full array of mental abilities.

17. There are two sets of twins in the Mullis family. Louise and Lanie are identical twins; Andy and Adrian are not. According to research on heredity and IQ, which pair of twins is likely to show the most similarity in IQ scores?

    a. Andy and Adrian, because they are male siblings.
    b. Andy and Adrian, because they are fraternal twins.
    c. Louise and Lanie, because they are female siblings.
    d. Louise and Lanie, because they are identical twins.

18. Rowena is mildly mentally retarded. This means that she

    a. probably has a specific genetic defect.
    b. is quicker than others to remember information, but then forgets it more rapidly.
    c. knows fewer facts about the world than others.
    d. has no potential for employment.

19. Betsy's musical intelligence and body-kinesthetic intelligence are being evaluated by her teacher, who believes that these are important abilities not measured by standard intelligence tests. Her teacher obviously believes in _____.

    a. inherited intelligence
    b. multiple intelligences
    c. environmentally determined intelligence
    d. Wechsler's IQ tests

20. Theresa Amabile identified cognitive and personality characteristics necessary for creativity. Which of the following is *not* one of these characteristics?

    a. A capacity for focusing on the most important element in a problem, which is tied to convergent thinking.
    b. Expertise in the field of endeavor, which is tied to learning.
    c. A set of creative skills, including the capacity for divergent thinking.
    d. The motivation to pursue creative work for internal reasons.

8

Motivation and Emotion

It's five A.M. when your alarm clock goes off.

Do you jump out of bed, eager to face the day, or do you bury your head in the blankets, trying to avoid all that's ahead of you? Once you're out of bed, do you eat a big breakfast, or just have coffee—no matter how hungry you feel? As you leave home, do you notice your attractive neighbor and find yourself wondering if the two of you might someday have a romantic relationship? Or, if you're in a long-term relationship, do you find yourself thinking fond thoughts of your partner? Once you're at your job or on campus, do you try to do your best, or do you work just hard enough to get by? And how do you feel about these experiences and the many others you have in a typical day? In this chapter, we explore the physical, mental, and social factors that motivate human behavior in areas ranging from eating to sexuality to achievement. We also examine what emotions are and how they are expressed.

Reading this chapter will help you to answer the following questions:

- **Where does motivation come from?**
- **What makes me start eating, and stop eating?**
- **How often does the average person have sex?**
- **Why do some people try harder than others to succeed?**
- **Which motives move me most?**
- **How do feelings differ from thoughts?**
- **Is emotion in the heart, in the head, or both?**
- **Which emotional expressions are innate, and which are learned?**

O n July 23, 2000, twenty-four-year-old Tiger Woods won the British Open and became the youngest man to win all four tournaments that make up the Grand Slam in men's professional golf. The same day, Lance Armstrong, a bicyclist who had overcome cancer to win the Tour de France bicycle race in 1999, won it again. Earlier in the month, Venus Williams won the women's singles tennis championship at Wimbledon. On her way to this championship, she won against her sister, Serena Williams. Later, as a pair, they won the women's doubles championship.

Success did not come easily to these athletes; it took years of effort and unwavering determination. Why did they work so hard in the face of daunting challenges and tough competitors to rise to the top of their fields? For that matter, what prompts any person to excel, to perform random acts of kindness, to look for food, to take dancing lessons, to go bungee jumping, to become violent, or to act in any other particular way? What makes

motivation The influences that account for the initiation, direction, intensity, and persistence of behavior.

MOTIVATION AND EMOTION   The link between motivation and emotion can easily be seen in many situations. For example, being motivated to win the U.S. National Spelling Bee creates strong emotions as this contestant struggles with a tough word. And the link works both ways. Often, emotions create motivation, as when anger leads a person to become aggressive toward a child or when love leads a person to provide for that child.

some people go all out to reach a goal, whereas others try only half-heartedly and quit at the first obstacle? These are all questions about **motivation,** the factors that influence the initiation, direction, intensity, and persistence of behavior (Reeve, 1996).

Like the study of *how* people behave and think, the puzzle of *why* they do so has intrigued psychologists for many decades. Part of the motivation for behavior is to feel certain emotions, such as the joy of finishing a race or of becoming a parent. Motivation also affects emotion, as when hunger makes you more likely to become angry if people annoy you. In this chapter we review several aspects of motivation. We also examine the features of emotions and consider their value to humans.

Concepts and Theories of Motivation

Where does motivation come from?

Suppose that a man works two jobs, refuses party invitations, wears old clothes, drives a beat-up car, eats food left behind by others, never gives to charity, and keeps his house at sixty degrees all winter. Why does he do these things? You could propose a separate explanation for each of these behaviors: Perhaps he likes to work hard, hates parties, doesn't care about new clothes and new cars, enjoys other people's leftovers, has no concern for the poor, and likes cold air. Or, you could suggest a **motive,** a reason or purpose that provides a single explanation for this man's diverse behaviors. That unifying motive might be the man's desire to save as much money as possible. This example illustrates the fact that motivation cannot be directly observed. Its presence is inferred from what we *can* observe.

Motivation helps explain why behavior changes over time. For example, many people cannot bring themselves to lose weight, quit smoking, or exercise until they experience a heart attack or other serious health problem. At that point, they may suddenly be motivated to eat a low-fat diet, give up tobacco, and exercise regularly. In other words, depending on motivation, particular stimuli such as ice cream, cigarettes, and health clubs bring different responses from a person at different times.

Sources of Motivation

Human motivation stems from four main sources. First, we can be motivated by *biological factors,* such as the need for food, water, sex, and temperature regulation (Tinbergen, 1989). Second, *emotional factors* can motivate behavior (Izard, 1993). Panic, fear, anger, love, and hatred can underlie behavior ranging from selfless giving to brutal murder. *Cognitive factors* provide a third source of motivation (Weiner, 1993). Your perceptions of the world, your beliefs about what you can do, and your expectation of how others will respond generate certain behaviors. You are more likely to try for a role in the school play, for example, if you have confidence in your acting ability. Fourth, motivation can stem from *social factors,* including reactions to parents, teachers, siblings, friends, television, and other sociocultural forces. For example, have you ever bought a jacket or tried a particular hairstyle, not because you liked it but because it was in fashion? The combined influence of social factors on motivation deeply affects almost all human behavior (Baumeister & Leary, 1995).

No single theory gives a complete explanation of all aspects of motivation. However, each of the four most prominent ones—instinct theory, drive reduction theory, arousal theory, and incentive theory—helps tell part of the story.

Instinct Theory and Its Descendants

Early in this century, many psychologists favored an **instinct theory** of motivation. **Instincts** are automatic, involuntary, and unlearned behavior patterns consistently "released" or triggered by particular stimuli (Tinbergen, 1989). For example, the male stickleback fish attacks when it sees the red underbelly of another male. Such behaviors

motive   A reason or purpose for behavior.

instinct theory   A view that explains human behavior as motivated by automatic, involuntary, and unlearned responses.

instincts   Innate, automatic dispositions to respond in particular ways to specific stimuli.

FIGURE 8.1

Drive Reduction Theory
and Homeostasis

The mechanisms of homeostasis, such
as the regulation of body temperature
or food and water intake, are often
compared to home thermostats. If the
temperature in a house drops below the
thermostat setting, the furnace comes on
and brings the temperature up to that
preset level, achieving homeostasis.
When the temperature reaches the preset
point, the furnace shuts off.

```
┌──────────────┐     ┌──────────────┐     ┌──────────────────┐
│ Unbalanced   │ ──> │ Need         │ ──> │ Drive            │
│ equilibrium  │     │ (biological  │     │ (psychological   │
│              │     │ disturbance) │     │ state that       │
│              │     │              │     │ provides         │
│              │     │              │     │ motivation to    │
│              │     │              │     │ satisfy need)    │
└──────────────┘     └──────────────┘     └──────────────────┘
                                                   │
┌──────────────┐     ┌──────────────┐              │
│ Equilibrium  │ <── │ Behavior that│ <────────────┘
│ restored     │     │ satisfies    │
│              │     │ need and     │
│              │     │ reduces drive│
└──────────────┘     └──────────────┘
```

are called *fixed-action patterns* because they are unlearned, genetically coded responses to specific "releaser" stimuli.

William McDougall (1908) argued that human behavior, too, is motivated by instincts. He began by listing eighteen human instincts, including self-assertion, reproduction, pugnacity (eagerness to fight), and gregariousness (outgoing friendliness). Within a few years, McDougall and other theorists had named more than 10,000 instincts, prompting one critic to suggest that his colleagues had "an instinct to produce instincts" (Bernard, 1924). In other words, instincts had become meaningless labels that described behavior without explaining it. Saying that someone gambles because of a gambling instinct, golfs because of a golfing instinct, or works because of a work instinct explains nothing.

Humans have few, if any, instinctive fixed-action patterns, but some aspects of human behavior are present at birth. For example, sucking, grasping, and other reflexes, as well as certain facial expressions such as smiling, appear to be genetically coded. Babies do not have to learn to be hungry or thirsty. And, as discussed in Chapter 5, humans appear to be biologically prepared to fear snakes and other potential dangers. Psychologists who take an evolutionary approach to behavior suggest that all such behaviors have evolved because they are adaptive; they promote survival of the human species. These theorists argue that many other aspects of human behavior are also motivated by inborn factors—specifically, by the desire to pass on our own genes to the next generation. According to the evolutionary approach, this desire may motivate love, mate selection, and marriage, among other things (Buss, 1999).

Drive Reduction Theory

Drive reduction theory also emphasizes biological factors, but it is based on the concept of homeostasis. **Homeostasis** is the tendency for organisms to keep physiological systems at a steady level, or *equilibrium*, by constantly making adjustments in response to change—much as a thermostat functions to maintain a constant temperature in a home.

According to **drive reduction theory,** any imbalance in homeostasis creates a **need,** which is a biological requirement for well-being. In responding to needs, the brain tries to restore homeostasis by creating a psychological state called **drive**—a feeling that prompts an organism to take action to fulfill the need and thus return to a balanced state. For example, if you have had nothing to drink for some time, the chemical balance of your bodily fluids will be disturbed, creating a biological need for water. One consequence of this need is a drive—thirst—that motivates you to find and drink water. After you drink, the need for water is met, so the drive to drink is reduced. In other words, drives push people to satisfy needs, thus reducing the drives that have been created. This cycle is shown in Figure 8.1.

Proponents of drive reduction theory describe two types of drives. **Primary drives** stem from biological needs, such as the need for food or water. People do not have to learn either these basic biological needs or the primary drives to satisfy them (Hull, 1951). However, we do learn other drives, called *secondary drives*. Once learned, **secondary drives** motivate us to act *as if* we have unmet basic needs. For example, as

homeostasis   The tendency for physiological systems to remain at a stable, steady level by constantly adjusting themselves in response to change.

drive reduction theory   A theory stating that motivation arises from imbalances in homeostasis.

need   A biological requirement for well-being.

drive   A psychological state that arises from an imbalance in homeostasis and prompts action to fulfill a need.

primary drives   Drives that arise from basic biological needs.

secondary drives   Stimuli that take on the motivational properties of primary drives through learning.

Curiosity

This monkey learned to perform a complicated task simply for the opportunity to look at a moving electric train. People's curiosity, too, motivates them to explore anything that is new or unusual, from the latest gossip magazine or talk show to the most exotic and challenging "adventure vacation."

arousal   A general level of activation reflected in several physiological systems.

arousal theory   A theory stating that people are motivated to maintain what is, for them, an optimal level of arousal.

incentive theory   A theory stating that people are pulled toward behaviors offering positive incentives and pushed away from behaviors associated with negative incentives.

people learn to associate money with the ability to buy things to satisfy primary drives for food, shelter, and so on, having money may become a secondary drive. Having too little money thus motivates many behaviors—from hard work to stealing—to obtain more funds. By recognizing secondary and primary drives, drive reduction theory can account for a wider range of behaviors than instinct theory.

Arousal Theory

What about highly motivated behaviors that do not seem to reduce drives? Consider curiosity. People and animals explore and manipulate their surroundings even though these activities do not satisfy a primary drive. Animals will work hard simply to enter a new environment, especially if it is complex and full of novel objects (Loewenstein, 1994). Monkeys are even willing to "pay" for a chance to satisfy their curiosity (Bolles, 1975), as Figure 8.2 shows. People are no less curious. Most cannot resist checking out the new and unusual. They go to the mall, explore the Web, and travel the world just to see what there is to see.

People also go out of their way to ride roller coasters, sky dive, eat chili peppers, and do countless other things that do not reduce any known drive (Zuckerman, 1996). In fact, these behaviors actually *increase* their activation, or arousal. The realization that people sometimes try to reduce arousal and sometimes try to increase it has led theorists to argue that motivation is tied to the regulation of arousal.

Arousal refers to the general level of activation in our physiological systems (Plutchik & Conte, 1997). Thus, a person's level of arousal can be reflected in heart rate, muscle tension, electrical activity in the brain, and many other functions (Deschaumes et al., 1991). Normally, arousal is lowest during deep sleep and highest during panic or great excitement. Many factors increase arousal, including hunger, thirst, intense stimuli, unexpected events, and stimulant drugs.

People perform best, and may feel best, when arousal is moderate (Teigen, 1994). Too much arousal can be harmful to performance, as when anxiety causes a student to forget familiar material on a test. Overarousal can also cause an athlete to "choke," and thus miss an easy catch or a simple shot.

Arousal theory suggests that people are motivated to behave in ways that keep them at their own *optimal level* of arousal (Hebb, 1955). This optimal level is higher for some people than for others (Zuckerman, 1984). People who prefer high levels of arousal are more likely to smoke, drink alcohol, engage in frequent sexual activity, listen to loud music, eat spicy foods, and do things that are novel and risky (Zuckerman, 1993). People with lower levels of optimal arousal tend to behave in ways that bring less intense stimulation; they also take fewer risks. Most of these differences in optimal arousal have a strong biological basis and may help shape broader differences in personality, such as shyness. Generally, however, people try to increase arousal when it is too low and decrease it when it is too high. They seek excitement when they are bored and relaxation when they are overaroused.

Incentive Theory

Instinct, drive reduction, and arousal theories of motivation all focus on the internal processes that prompt behavior. In contrast, **incentive theory** emphasizes the role of external stimuli that motivate behavior. According to this view, people are pulled toward behaviors offering positive incentives and pushed away from behaviors associated with negative incentives. Differences in behavior from one person to another, or from one situation to another, can be traced to the incentives available and the value a person places on them at the time. So if you expect a behavior (such as buying a lottery ticket) to lead to a valued outcome (winning money), you will want to engage in that behavior. The value of an incentive is influenced by biological, as well as cognitive, factors. For example, food is a more motivating incentive when you are hungry than when you are full (Balleine & Dickinson, 1994).

Theories of Motivation	
Theory	**Main Points**
Instinct	Innate biological instincts guide behavior.
Drive reduction	Behavior is guided by biological needs and learned ways of reducing drives arising from those needs.
Arousal	People seek to maintain an optimal level of physiological arousal, which differs from person to person. Maximum performance occurs at optimal arousal levels.
Incentive	Behavior is guided by the lure of rewards and the threat of punishment. Cognitive factors influence expectations of the value of various rewards and the likelihood of attaining them.

"In Review: Theories of Motivation" summarizes the theoretical approaches we have outlined. Each theory emphasizes a different source of motivation, and each has helped to guide research on motivated behaviors such as eating, sex, and work, which we consider in the sections that follow.

Hunger and Eating

▪ What makes me start eating, and stop eating?

Hunger is deceptively simple. You get hungry when you do not eat. Much as a car needs gas, you need fuel from food. Is there a bodily mechanism that, like a car's gas gauge, signals the need for fuel? What causes hunger? What determines which foods you eat, and how do you know when to stop? The answers to these questions involve interactions between the brain and the body, as well as learning and social factors (J. O. Hill & Peters, 1998).

Biological Signals for Hunger and Satiety

A variety of mechanisms underlie **hunger,** the general state of wanting to eat, and **satiety** (pronounced "seh-TYE-eh-tee"), the general state of no longer wanting to eat.

Signals from the Stomach   The stomach would seem to be a logical source of signals for hunger and satiety. You have probably felt "hunger pangs" from an "empty" stomach and felt "stuffed" after overeating. In fact, the stomach does contract during hunger pangs, and increased pressure within the stomach can reduce appetite (W. B. Cannon & Washburn, 1912; Houpt, 1994). But people who have lost their stomachs due to illness still get hungry when they do not eat and still eat normal amounts of food (Janowitz, 1967). And rats eat normally even when their stomachs are temporarily blocked from emptying into the digestive tract (Seeley, Kaplan, & Grill, 1995). So stomach cues can affect eating, but they do not always control it. Indeed, such cues appear to operate mainly when you are very hungry or very full.

Signals from the Blood   More precise signals about the body's fuel level and nutrient needs are sent to the brain from the blood. The brain's ability to "read" blood-borne signals about the body's nutritional needs was discovered when researchers deprived rats of food for a long period and then injected some of the rats with blood from rats that had just eaten. When offered food, the injected rats ate little or nothing (J. D. Davis et al.,

hunger   The general state of wanting to eat.

satiety   The condition of no longer wanting to eat.

ONE FAT MOUSE After surgical destruction of its ventromedial nucleus, this mouse ate enough to triple its body weight. Such animals become picky eaters, choosing only foods that taste good and ignoring all others.

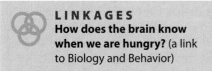

LINKAGES
How does the brain know when we are hungry? (a link to Biology and Behavior)

1969). Something in the injected blood of the well-fed animals apparently signaled the hungry rats' brains that there was no need to eat. What sent that satiety signal? Research has shown that the brain constantly monitors both the level of *food nutrients* absorbed into the bloodstream from the stomach and the level of *hormones* released into the blood in response to those nutrients.

The nutrients that the brain monitors include *glucose* (the main form of sugar used by body cells), *fatty acids* (from fat), and *amino acids* (from protein). When the level of blood glucose drops, eating increases sharply (Mogenson, 1976). When large doses of glucose are injected into the blood of even a food-deprived animal, it refuses to eat.

The brain also monitors hormone levels to regulate hunger and satiety. For example, when glucose levels rise, the pancreas releases *insulin,* a hormone that most body cells need in order to use the glucose they receive. Insulin itself may also provide a satiety signal by acting directly on brain cells (Brüning et al., 2000; M. W. Schwartz et al., 2000).

The hormone *leptin* also appears to provide a satiety signal to the brain, where special receptors for it have been discovered in the hypothalamus (Tartaglia et al., 1996). Leptin appears to be involved mainly in the long-term regulation of body fat rather than in ending a particular meal (Huang & Li, 2000). Cells that store fat normally have genes that produce leptin. As the fat supply increases, leptin is released into the blood, thus helping to reduce food intake. Animals with defects in these genes make no leptin (Zhang et al., 1994) and are obese. Researchers found that injections of leptin cause these animals to rapidly lose weight and body fat, with no effect on muscle or other body tissue. Leptin injections can produce the same changes in normal animals, too (e.g., Campfield et al., 1995; Fox & Olster, 2000). These results initially raised hope that leptin might be a "magic bullet" for treating human obesity. Indeed, it has helped those rare individuals who are obese because their cells make no leptin (Farooqi et al., 1999). However, leptin injections are far less effective for people whose obesity results from a high-fat diet (Gura, 1999; Heymsfield et al., 1999). In these far more common cases of obesity, the brain appears to become less sensitive to leptin's signals (Ahima & Flier, 2000; S. Lin et al., 2000).

Hunger and the Brain

Many parts of the brain contribute to the control of hunger and eating. However, research has focused on three regions of the hypothalamus that may play primary roles in detecting and reacting to the blood's signals about the need to eat. As shown in Figure 8.3, the hypothalamus influences both how much food is taken in and how quickly its energy is used, or metabolized.

Some regions of the hypothalamus detect leptin and insulin; these regions generate signals that either increase hunger and reduce energy expenditure, or reduce hunger and increase energy expenditure. There are at least twenty neurotransmitters that convey these signals to networks in other parts of the hypothalamus and in the rest of the brain (Woods et al., 1998, 2000).

Activity in one part of the network that passes through the *ventromedial nucleus* tells an animal that there is no need to eat. So, if a rat's ventromedial nucleus is electrically or chemically stimulated, the animal will stop eating (Kent et al., 1994). However, if the ventromedial nucleus is destroyed, the animal will eat continuously, increasing its weight up to threefold.

In contrast, the *lateral hypothalamus* contains networks that stimulate eating to begin. When the lateral hypothalamus is electrically or chemically stimulated, rats begin to eat huge quantities, even if they have just had a large meal (Stanley et al., 1993). When the lateral hypothalamus is destroyed, however, rats stop eating almost entirely.

One theory suggests that these two hypothalamic regions interact to maintain a *set point* based on body weight, food intake, or related metabolic signals (Cabanac & Morrissette, 1992). According to this theory, normal animals eat until their set point is reached, then stop eating until desirable intake falls below the set point. Destroying or stimulating the lateral or ventromedial hypothalamus may alter the set point.

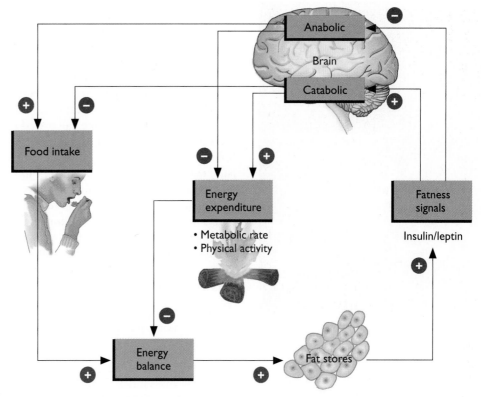

FIGURE 8.3

The Hypothalamus and Hunger

Regions of the hypothalamus generate signals that either increase hunger and reduce energy expenditure, called *anabolic effects*, or reduce hunger and increase energy expenditure, called *catabolic effects*.

Source: Adapted from Schwartz et al. (2000).

Research on other regions of the hypothalamus suggests that the brain's control of eating involves more than just the interaction of "stop-eating" and "start-eating" areas (Winn, 1995). For example, hungers for particular types of food are related to the effects of certain neurotransmitters on certain neurons (Lee, Schiffman, & Pappas, 1994; Woods et al., 1998). One of these neurotransmitters, called *neuropeptide Y,* stimulates carbohydrate eating (Jhanwar et al., 1993), whereas another, serotonin, suppresses it. Similarly, *galanin* motivates the eating of high-fat food (Krykouli et al., 1990), and *enterostatin* reduces it (L. Lin et al., 1998).

In summary, several brain regions help to regulate hunger and eating, and eating is controlled by processes that suggest the existence of a set point. That set point appears variable enough to be overridden by other factors, however.

Flavor, Cultural Learning, and Food Selection

The flavor of food is one factor that can shift a set point. In general, people eat more food during a multi-course meal than when only one food is served. Apparently the flavor of a food becomes less enjoyable as more of it is eaten (Swithers & Hall, 1994). In one study, for example, people rated how much they liked four kinds of food; then they ate one of the foods and rated all four again. The food they had just eaten now got a lower rating, whereas liking increased for all the rest (J. Johnson & Vickers, 1993).

Another factor that can override the blood's signals about satiety is *appetite,* the motivation to seek food's pleasures. The appearance and smell of certain foods come to elicit conditioned physiological responses—such as the secretion of saliva, digestive juices, and insulin—in anticipation of eating those foods. These responses then increase appetite. Thus, merely seeing a pizza on television may suddenly prompt you to order one. And if you see a delicious-looking cookie, you do not have to be hungry to start eating it. In other words, people eat not just to satisfy nutritional needs but also to experience enjoyment.

Social rules and cultural traditions are forms of learning that also influence eating. In North American culture, having lunch at noon, munching popcorn at movies, and

BON APPÉTIT! The definition of *delicacy* differs from culture to culture. At this elegant restaurant in Mexico, diners pay to feast on baby alligators, insects, and other dishes that some people from other cultures would not eat even if the restaurant paid *them*. To appreciate your own food culture, make a list of foods that are traditionally valued by your family or cultural group but that people from other groups do not, or might even be unwilling, to eat.

eating hot dogs at ball games are common examples of how certain social situations can stimulate appetite for particular items at particular times. How much you eat may also depend on what others do. Politeness or custom might prompt you to try foods you would otherwise have avoided. Generally, the mere presence of others, even strangers, tends to increase food consumption. Most people consume 60 to 75 percent more food when they are with others than when eating alone (Clendenen, Herman, & Polivy, 1995).

Celebrations, holidays, vacations, and even daily family interactions often revolve around food and what some call a *food culture* (Rozin, 1996). There are wide cultural variations in food use and selection. For example, chewing coca leaves is popular in the Bolivian highlands but illegal in the United States (Burchard, 1992). And insects called *palm weevils,* a delicacy for people in Papua New Guinea (Paoletti, 1995), are regarded by many Westerners as disgusting (Springer & Belk, 1994). Even within the same general culture, different groups may have sharply contrasting food traditions. Thus, squirrel brains won't be found on most dinner tables in the United States, but some people in the rural South consider them to be a tasty treat. In short, eating serves functions beyond nutrition—functions that help to remind us of who we are and with whom we identify.

Eating Disorders

Problems in the processes regulating hunger and eating may cause an *eating disorder*. The most common and dangerous examples are obesity, anorexia nervosa, and bulimia nervosa.

Obesity   The World Health Organization defines **obesity** as a condition in which a person's body-mass index, or BMI, is greater than 30 (WHO, 1995). BMI is determined by dividing a person's weight (in kilograms) by the square of the person's height (in meters). Thus, someone who is 5 feet 2 inches and weighs 164 pounds would be classified as obese, as would someone 5 feet 10 inches who weighs 207 pounds. (You will find quick BMI calculators at web sites such as www.consumer.gov/weightloss/bmi.htm.) Using this BMI criterion, 27 percent of adults in the United States are obese (USDHHS, 2000). And obesity appears to be on the rise, not only in the United States but also in regions as diverse as Asia, South America, and Africa (Kopelman, 2000; Lewis et al., 2000; Mokdad et al., 2000; Taubes, 1998). Obesity is associated with health problems such as diabetes, high blood pressure, and increased risk of heart attack; nearly 300,000 deaths in the United States alone are attributed to obesity (Allison et al., 1999). Caring for people with obesity-related health problems costs about $51 billion each year (Wolf & Colditz, 1998).

Why do some people become obese? The body maintains a given weight through a combination of food intake and energy output (Keesey & Powley, 1986). Obese people get more energy from food than their body metabolizes, or "burns up." The excess energy, measured in calories, is stored as fat. Obese people tend to eat above-average amounts of high-calorie, tasty foods but below-average amounts of less tasty foods (Kauffman, Herman, & Polivy, 1995). Further, they may be less active than lean people, a pattern that often begins in childhood. Spending long hours in front of the television set is a major cause of the inactivity seen in overweight children (USDHHS, 1996).

In short, inadequate physical activity, combined with overeating—especially of the high-fat foods so prevalent in most Western cultures—has a lot to do with obesity. But not everyone who is inactive and eats a high-fat diet becomes obese, and some obese people are as active as lean people, so other factors must also be involved (Blundell & Cooling, 2000). Some people probably have a genetic predisposition toward obesity (Arner, 2000; J. K. Thompson, 1996b). In addition, being fed an unhealthy diet in childhood may raise the set point for body weight and create larger and more numerous fat cells (Grilo & Pogue-Geile, 1991). Recent brain-imaging studies also suggest that obese people's brains may be slower to "read" satiety signals coming from their blood, thus causing them to continue eating when leaner people would have stopped (Y. Liu et al., 2000). These factors, along with the presence of one or more recently discovered viruses in the body (Dhurandhar et al., 2000), may help explain obese people's tendency to eat more, to accumulate fat, and to feel more hunger than lean people.

obesity   A condition in which a person is severely overweight.

THIN IS IN In Western cultures today, thinness is a much-sought-after ideal, especially among young women who are dissatisfied with their appearance. This ideal is seen in fashion models, as well as in Miss America pageant winners, whose body mass index has decreased from the "normal" range of 20 to 25 in the 1920s to an "undernourished" 18.5 in recent years (Rubinstein & Caballero, 2000). In the United States, 35 percent of normal-weight girls—and 12 percent of under-weight girls!—begin dieting when they are as young as nine or ten. Many of these children try to lose weight in response to criticism by their mothers (Schreiber et al., 1996), and for some, the result is anorexia.

anorexia nervosa An eating disorder characterized by self-starvation and dramatic weight loss.

Losing weight and keeping it off for at least five years is extremely difficult for many people, especially those who are obese (Lewis et al., 2000; McGuire et al., 1999). Part of the problem may be due to metabolic changes that accompany weight loss. When food intake is reduced, the process of homeostasis leads to a drop in metabolic rate, thus saving energy and curbing weight loss (Leibel, Rosenbaum, & Hirsch, 1995). This response makes evolutionary sense: Conserving energy during famine, for example, is adaptive for survival. But when obese people try to lose weight, their metabolic rate drops *below* normal. As a result, they can gain weight even while eating amounts that would maintain constant weight in others.

These facts suggest that attempts to lose a great deal of weight quickly will be offset by changes in one's metabolism (Brownell & Rodin, 1994). Animal studies show that losing and then regaining large amounts of weight, so-called cycling, actually leads to a gradual rise in average weight (Archambault et al., 1989).

Several anti-obesity drugs have been developed, including one that prevents fat in foods from being digested (e.g., Finer et al., 2000; Hauptman et al., 2000). Another was actually being tested as a possible cancer treatment when it was found to interfere with an enzyme that forms fat. This "fatty acid synthase inhibitor" not only caused rapid weight loss in mice but also reduced their hunger (T. M. Loftus et al., 2000). The drug has not yet been tested for safety and effectiveness in humans, but researchers hope that it may someday be possible to give obese people medications that alter brain mechanisms involved in overeating and fat storage (Halford & Blundell, 2000).

Even the best drug treatments are unlikely to solve the problem of obesity on their own. To achieve the kind of gradual weight loss that is most likely to last, obese people are advised to increase regular exercise, because it burns calories without slowing metabolism (A. Tremblay & Bueman, 1995). In fact, regular aerobic exercise *raises* the metabolic rate in the long run (McCarty, 1995). The most effective weight-loss programs thus include components designed to reduce food intake, change eating habits and attitudes toward food, and increase energy expenditure through exercise (Bray & Tartaglia, 2000; Dalton, 1997; National Task Force on the Prevention and Treatment of Obesity, 2000).

Anorexia Nervosa   At the opposite extreme of eating disorders is **anorexia nervosa** (pronounced "ann-or-EX-ee-ah nuhr-VO-suh"). It is characterized by some combination of self-starvation, self-induced vomiting, and laxative use that results in weight loss to below 85 percent of normal (U.S. Surgeon General, 1999). About 95 percent of people who suffer from anorexia are female. Anorexics often feel hungry, and many are obsessed with food and its preparation, yet they refuse to eat. Anorexic self-starvation causes serious, often irreversible, physical damage. Between 4 and 30 percent of anorexics die of starvation, biochemical imbalances, or suicide; their risk of death is twelve times higher than for other young women (Herzog et al., 2000; Sullivan, 1995). Anorexia tends to appear in adolescence, when concern over appearance becomes intense. It affects about 1 percent of young women in the United States and is a growing problem in many other industrialized nations as well (Feingold & Mazzella, 1998; J. K. Thompson, 1996a).

The causes of anorexia are not yet clear, but they probably involve a combination of factors, including genetic predispositions, biochemical imbalances, social influences, and psychological characteristics (Becker et al., 1999; Kaye et al., 2000). Psychological factors that may contribute to the problem include a self-punishing, perfectionistic personality and a culturally reinforced obsession with thinness and attractiveness (Thompson et al., 1999; U.S. Surgeon General, 1999). Anorexics appear to develop a fear of being fat, which they take to dangerous extremes (de Castro & Goldstein, 1995). Many anorexics continue to view themselves as fat or misshapen even as they are wasting away (Feingold & Mazzella, 1998).

Drugs, hospitalization, and psychotherapy are all used to treat anorexia. In most cases, some combination of treatment and the passage of time bring partial or full recovery (Herzog et al., 1999).

Bulimia Nervosa   Like anorexia, bulimia nervosa (pronounced "bu-LEE-mee-uh nuhr-VO-suh") involves intense fear of being fat, but the person may be thin, normal in

in review

Major Factors Controlling Hunger and Eating

	Stimulate Eating	Inhibit Eating
Biological factors	Levels of glucose and insulin in the blood provide signals that stimulate eating; neurotransmitters that affect neurons in different regions of the hypothalamus also stimulate food intake and influence hungers for specific kinds of foods, such as fats and carbohydrates. Stomach contractions are associated with subjective feelings of hunger, but they do not play a substantial role in the stimulation of eating.	Hormones released into the bloodstream produce signals that inhibit eating; hormones such as leptin and insulin affect neurons in the hypothalamus and inhibit eating. The ventromedial nucleus of the hypothalamus appears to monitor these hormones.
Nonbiological factors	Sights and smells of particular foods elicit eating because of prior associations; family customs and social occasions often include norms for eating in particular ways.	Values in contemporary U.S. society encourage thinness, and thus can inhibit eating.

weight, or even overweight (U.S. Surgeon General, 1999). **Bulimia nervosa** involves eating huge amounts of food (say, several boxes of cookies, a half-gallon of ice cream, and a bucket of fried chicken) and then getting rid of the food through self-induced vomiting or strong laxatives. These "binge-purge" episodes may occur as often as twice a day (Weltzin et al., 1995).

Like anorexics, bulimics are usually female, and like anorexia, bulimia usually begins with a desire to be slender. However, bulimia and anorexia are separate disorders (Pryor, 1995). For one thing, most bulimics see their eating habits as problematic, whereas most anorexics do not. In addition, bulimia nervosa is usually not life-threatening (R. C. Hall et al., 1989). There are consequences, however, including dehydration, nutritional problems, and intestinal damage. Many bulimics develop dental problems from the acids associated with vomiting. Frequent vomiting, and the insertion of objects to cause it, can also damage the throat.

Estimates of the prevalence of bulimia in the United States range from 1 to 3 percent of adolescent and college-age women (J. K. Thompson, 1996; U.S. Surgeon General, 1999). It appears to be caused by a combination of factors, including perfectionism, low self-esteem, overconcern with thinness and attractiveness, and depression and other emotional problems, along with as-yet-undetermined biological problems that might include defective satiety mechanisms (Brewerton et al., 1995; Vohs et al., 1999). Treatment for bulimia, which typically includes individual or group psychotherapy and, sometimes, antidepressant drugs, helps the vast majority of bulimic people to eat more normally (Herzog et al., 1999; G. T. Wilson et al., 1999).

For a summary of the processes involved in hunger and eating, see "In Review: Major Factors Controlling Hunger and Eating."

Sexual Behavior

How often does the average person have sex?

bulimia nervosa   An eating disorder that involves eating massive quantities of food and then eliminating the food by self-induced vomiting or laxatives.

Unlike food, sex is not necessary for an individual's survival. A strong desire for reproduction does help ensure the survival of a species, however (Keeling & Roger, 1995). The various factors shaping sexual motivation and behavior differ in strength across species.

They often include a combination of the individual's physiology, learned behavior, and the physical and social environment. For example, one species of desert bird requires adequate sex hormones, a suitable mate, and a particular environment before it engages in sexual behavior. As long as the dry season lasts, it shows no interest in sex, but within ten minutes of the first rainfall, the birds vigorously copulate.

Rainfall is obviously much less influential as a sexual trigger for humans. Indeed, people show an amazing diversity of *sexual scripts,* or patterns of behavior that lead to sex. One survey of college-age men and women identified 122 specific acts and 34 different tactics used for promoting sexual encounters (Greer & Buss, 1994). What happens next? The matter is exceedingly difficult to address scientifically, partly because most people are reluctant to allow researchers to observe their sexual behavior. Many even resist responding to specific questions about their sexual practices (Bancroft, 1997). Yet having valid information about the nature of human sexual behavior is a vital first step for psychologists and other scientists who study such topics as individual differences in sexuality, sources of sexual orientation, types of sexual dysfunctions, and pathways through which AIDS and other sexually transmitted diseases (STDs) reach new victims. This information also has important implications for helping people understand themselves ("Is my sexual behavior common?"), alleviating sexual problems, and curbing the spread of STDs.

FOCUS ON RESEARCH

Tell Me About Your Sex Life

The first extensive studies of sexual behavior in the United States were completed by Alfred Kinsey (Kinsey et al., 1953; Kinsey, Pomeroy, & Martin, 1948) and by William Masters and Virginia Johnson (1966). In the Kinsey studies, volunteers were asked about their sexual practices, whereas Masters and Johnson actually measured physiological response patterns as volunteers received natural or mechanical sexual stimulation in a laboratory. Together, these pioneering studies broke new ground in the exploration of human sexuality. Critics have argued that the people who volunteered for such studies probably did not constitute a representative sample of humankind. Accordingly, the results, and any conclusions drawn from them, might not apply to people in general. Further, the Kinsey data are now so old that they may not reflect sexual practices today. Unfortunately, the results of more recent surveys, such as reader polls in *Cosmopolitan* and other magazines, are flawed by the use of unrepresentative samples.

What was the researchers' question?

Is there a way to gather data on sexual behavior that is more representative and thus more revealing about people in general? The shortcomings of previous work in this area led a team of researchers at the University of Chicago to conduct the "National Health and Social Life Survey," the first extensive survey of sexual behavior in the United States since the Kinsey studies (Laumann et al., 1994).

How did the researchers answer the question?

This survey included important design features that had been neglected in most other surveys of sexual behavior. First, the study did not depend on self-selected volunteers. The researchers sought out a particular sample of 3,432 people, ranging in age from eighteen to fifty-nine. Second, careful construction of the sample made it reflective of the sociocultural diversity of the U.S. population in terms of gender, ethnicity, socioeconomic status, geographical location, and the like. Third, unlike previous surveys, the Chicago study was based on face-to-face interviews. This approach made it easier to ensure that the participants understood each question and allowed them to explain their responses. To encourage honesty, the researchers allowed participants to answer some of the survey's questions anonymously, by placing written responses in a sealed envelope.

■ What did the researchers find?

For one thing, the researchers found that people in the United States have sex less often and with fewer people than many had assumed. For most, sex occurs about once a week, and only with a partner with whom they share a stable relationship. About a third of the participants reported having sex only a few times, or not at all, in the past year. And in contrast to certain celebrities' splashy tales of dozens, even hundreds, of sexual partners per year, the average male survey participant had only six sexual partners in his entire life. The average female respondent reported a lifetime total of two. Further, the survey data suggested that people in committed, one-partner relationships had the most frequent and the most satisfying sex. And although a wide variety of specific sexual practices were reported, the overwhelming majority of heterosexual couples said they tend to engage mainly in penis-vagina intercourse.

■ What do the results mean?

The Chicago survey challenges some of the cultural and media images of sexuality in the United States. In particular, it suggests that people in the United States may be more sexually conservative than one might think on the basis of magazine reader polls and the testimony of guests on daytime talk shows.

■ What do we still need to know?

Many questions remain. The Chicago survey did not ask about some of the more controversial aspects of sexuality, such as the effects of pornography, the nature and prevalence of pedophilia (sexual attraction to children), and the role in sexual activity of sexual fetishes such as shoes or other clothing. Had the researchers asked about such topics, their results might have painted a less conservative picture. Further, because the Chicago survey focused on people in the United States, it told us little or nothing about the sexual practices, traditions, and values of people in the rest of the world. The Chicago team has begun to conduct interviews in other countries, and the results are beginning to fill in the picture about sexual behavior around the world. They have found, for example, that people in the United States tend to engage in a wider variety of sexual behaviors than those in Britain, but that there is less tolerance in the United States of disapproved sexual practices (Michael et al., 1998).

Even the best survey methods—like the best of all other research methods—usually yield results that raise as many questions as they answer. When do people become interested in sex, and why? How do they choose to express these desires, and why? What determines their sexual likes and dislikes? How do learning and sociocultural factors modify the biological forces that seem to provide the raw material of human sexual motivation? These are some of the questions about human sexual behavior that a survey cannot easily or accurately explore.

The Biology of Sex

Some aspects of the sexual behavior observed in Masters and Johnson's laboratory may not have reflected exactly what goes on when people have sex in more typical surroundings. Still, those observations led to important findings about the **sexual response cycle,** the pattern of physiological arousal before, during, and after sexual activity (see Figure 8.4). W. H. Masters and Johnson (1966) found that men show one primary pattern of sexual response and that women display at least three different patterns from time to time. In both men and women, the first, or *excitement,* phase begins with sexually stimulating input from the environment or from one's own thoughts. Further stimulation leads to intensified excitement in the second, or *plateau,* phase. If stimulation continues, the person reaches the third, or *orgasmic,* stage. Although orgasm lasts only a few seconds, it provides an intensely pleasurable release of physical and psychological tension.

sexual response cycle   The pattern of arousal before, during, and after sexual activity.

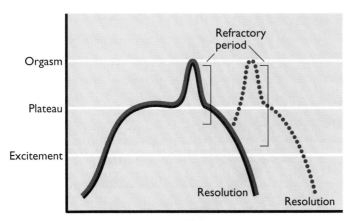

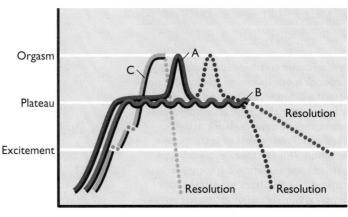

(A) CYCLE IN MEN   **(B) CYCLE IN WOMEN**

Source: Adapted from Masters & Johnson (1966).

FIGURE 8.4

The Sexual Response Cycle

Masters and Johnson (1966) found that men show one primary pattern of sexual response, depicted in Part A, and that women display at least three different patterns from time to time—labeled A, B, and C in Part B. For both men and women, sexual stimulation begins with the excitement phase, which is followed by intensified excitement in the plateau phase, and the pleasurable release of tension in the orgasmic stage. During the resolution phase, both men and women return to a state of relaxation. Following resolution, men (but not women) enter a refractory phase, during which they are unresponsive to sexual stimulation.

sex hormones   Chemicals in the blood that organize and motivate sexual behavior.

estrogens   Feminine hormones that circulate in the bloodstream.

progestins   Feminine hormones that circulate in the bloodstream.

androgens   Masculine hormones that circulate in the bloodstream.

The *resolution* phase follows, during which the person returns to a state of relaxation. At this point, men enter a *refractory period,* during which they are temporarily unable to be aroused. Women are capable of immediately repeating the cycle if stimulation continues.

People's motivation to engage in sexual activity has biological roots in **sex hormones.** The female sex hormones are **estrogens** and **progestins;** the main ones are *estradiol* and *progesterone.* The male hormones are **androgens;** the principal example is *testosterone.* Each sex hormone flows in the blood of both sexes, but males have relatively more androgens, and women have relatively more estrogens and progestins. Figure 8.5 shows how feedback systems control the secretion of these hormones.

Sex hormones have both organizing and activating effects. Their *organizing effects* are permanent changes in the brain that occur around the time of birth and influence it to respond to sex hormones in specific ways. Their *activating* effects are temporary behavioral changes that last only while a sex hormone's level is elevated. As a result of the organizing effects, certain brain areas are sculpted into a "male-like" or "female-like" pattern. For example, a hypothalamic area called BSTc is generally smaller in women than in men. Its possible role in some aspects of human sexuality was suggested by a study of *transsexual* men, genetic males who feel like women and who may request sex-change surgery in order to "be" female. The BSTc in these men was smaller than in other men. In fact, it was about the size usually seen in women (Zhou et al., 1995).

Rising levels of sex hormones during puberty activate increased sexual desire and interest in sexual behavior. Generally, estrogens stimulate females' sexual interest (Burleson, Gregory, & Trevarthen, 1995). Androgens raise males' sexual interest (J. M. Davidson, Camargo, & Smith, 1979), but they may also do so in females (Sherwin & Gelfand, 1987). The ongoing activating effects of hormones are confirmed by the reduced sexual motivation and behavior seen in people whose hormone-secreting ovaries or testes have been removed for medical reasons. Injections of hormones help restore these people's sexual interest and activity (Sherwin, Gelfand, & Brender, 1985).

Generally, hormones affect sexual *desire,* not the physical *ability* to have sex (Wallen & Lovejoy, 1993). This fact may explain why castration (removal of the testes) does not prevent sex crimes in male offenders. Men with low testosterone levels due to medical problems or castration show less sexual desire, but they still have erections in response to erotic stimuli (M. Kwan et al., 1983). Thus a sex offender treated with chemical or physical castration would be less likely to *seek out* sex, but he would still respond as before to his favorite sexual stimuli (Wallen & Lovejoy, 1993).

Social and Cultural Factors in Sexuality

Human sexuality is profoundly shaped by a lifetime of learning and thinking that modifies the biological "raw materials" provided by hormones. For example, children learn some of their sexual attitudes and behaviors as part of the development of *gender roles,*

FIGURE 8.5

The Regulation of Sex Hormones

Sex-hormone secretion is controlled by feedback loops involving the hypothalamus, the pituitary gland, and the ovaries or testes. In males, high levels of testosterone reduce hypothalamic activity, leading to lower levels of testosterone secretion. This feedback system keeps testosterone secretion fairly constant. In females, the feedback loops are more complex. High levels of estrogens increase hypothalamic activity, leading to higher levels of estrogen secretion. At mid-cycle, a hormone surge causes the ovary to release an egg. Androgens fluctuate across the menstrual cycle just as estrogens and progestins do, and their levels peak around ovulation.

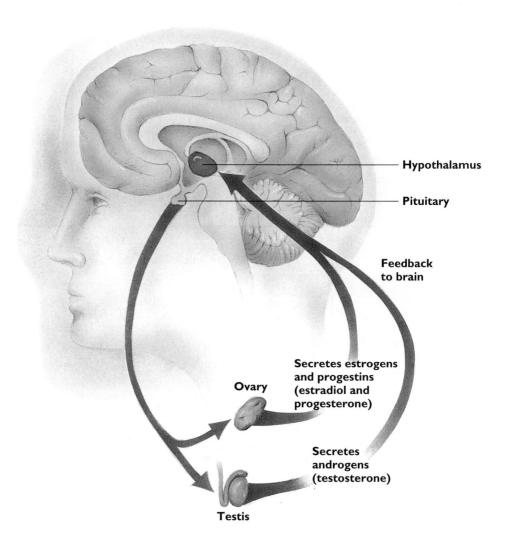

heterosexual   Referring to sexual desire or behavior that is focused on members of the opposite sex.

homosexual   Referring to sexual desire or behavior that is focused on members of a person's own sex.

bisexual   Referring to sexual desire or behavior that is focused on partners of both sexes.

as described in Chapter 9. The specific attitudes and behaviors they learn depend partly on the nature of gender roles in their culture (Baumeister, 2000; Hyde & Durik, 2000).

Sexual behavior is shaped by other sociocultural forces as well. In the United States, concern over sexual transmission of the AIDS virus has prompted mass-media campaigns and school-based educational programs to encourage sexual abstinence prior to marriage or "safe sex" using condoms (e.g., M. V. Smith & DiClemente, 2000). These efforts seem to be altering young people's sexual attitudes and practices. At the beginning of one sex education program, only 36 percent of 1,800 students in grades seven through ten thought premarital sex was a bad idea, and only 35 percent saw many benefits in premarital abstinence from sex. By the end of the semester-long program, these figures had risen to 66 percent and 58 percent, respectively (Eisenman, 1994). Another survey of 1,100 adolescents and young adults in the United States found that prior to 1985, first-time heterosexual intercourse seldom included the use of a condom or other contraceptive. With growing AIDS awareness since 1985, however, condom use has become far more common in first-time heterosexual intercourse and in subsequent sexual activity (Everett et al., 2000; Leigh, Schafer, & Temple, 1995).

Sexual Orientation

Human sexual behavior is most often **heterosexual,** involving opposite sex partners. When sexual desires or behavior are directed toward a member of one's own sex, it is called **homosexual.** People who desire or engage in sexual activities with partners of both sexes are described as **bisexual.** Whether your sexual desires or activities involve members of your own sex, the opposite sex, or both is one aspect of your *sexual orientation* (A. L. Ellis & Mitchell, 2000).

In many cultures, heterosexuality has long been regarded as a moral norm, and homosexuality seen as a disease, a disorder, or even a crime (Hooker, 1993). However, attempts to alter the sexual orientation of homosexuals—using psychotherapy, brain surgery, or electric shock—have usually been ineffective (American Psychiatric Association, 1999; Haldeman, 1994). In 1973 the American Psychiatric Association dropped homosexuality from the *Diagnostic and Statistical Manual of Mental Disorders,* thus ending its official status as a mental disorder.

Nevertheless, many people still view homosexuality as repugnant and immoral. Because homosexuals and bisexuals are often the victims of discrimination and even hate crimes, many are reluctant to let their sexual orientation be known. It is difficult, therefore, to obtain an accurate picture of the mix of heterosexual, homosexual, and bisexual orientations in a population. In the Chicago sex survey mentioned earlier, 1.4 percent of women and 2.8 percent of men identified themselves as exclusively homosexual (Laumann et al., 1994), figures much lower than the 10 percent found earlier in Kinsey's studies. However, the Chicago survey's face-to-face interviews did not allow respondents to give anonymous answers to questions about sexual orientation. Some researchers suggest that if anonymous responses to those questions had been permitted, the prevalence figures for homosexual and bisexual orientations would have been higher (Bullough, 1995). In fact, studies that have allowed anonymous responding estimate that homosexual people make up between 5 and 15 percent of the population in the United States, Canada, and Western Europe (Bagley & Tremblay, 1998; Diamond, 1993; S. M. Rogers & Turner, 1991; Sell, Wells, & Wypij, 1995).

THINKING CRITICALLY

Do Genes Determine Sexual Orientation?

The question of where sexual orientation comes from is a topic of intense debate in scientific circles, on talk shows, and in everyday conversation.

▪ What am I being asked to believe or accept?

One point of view suggests that genes dictate sexual orientation. According to this view, we do not learn a sexual orientation but, rather, are born with it.

▪ Is there evidence available to support the claim?

In 1995, a report by a respected research group suggested that one kind of sexual orientation—namely, homosexuality in males—was associated with a particular gene on the X chromosome (Hu et al., 1995). This particular finding was not supported by later studies (G. Rice et al., 1999), but a growing body of evidence from research in behavioral genetics suggests that genes might indeed influence sexual orientation in humans (Pillard & Bailey, 1998). One study examined pairs of monozygotic male twins (whose genes are identical), nonidentical twin pairs (whose genes are no more alike than those of any brothers), and pairs of adopted brothers (who are genetically unrelated). To participate in this study, at least one brother in each pair had to be homosexual. As it turned out, the other brother was also homosexual or bisexual in 52 percent of the identical-twin pairs, but in only 22 percent of the nonidentical pairs and in just 11 percent of the adoptive pairs (Bailey & Pillard, 1991). Similar findings have been reported for male identical twins raised apart. In such cases, a shared sexual orientation cannot be attributed to the effects of a shared environment (Whitam, Diamond, & Martin, 1993). The few available studies of female sexual orientation have yielded similar results (J. M. Bailey & Benishay, 1993; J. M. Bailey, Dunne, & Nicholas, 2000).

Other evidence for the role of biological factors in sexual orientation comes from research on the impact of sex hormones. In adults, differences in the level of these hormones is not generally associated with differences in sexual orientation. However, hormonal differences during prenatal development might be involved in the shaping of

A COMMITTED RELATIONSHIP, WITH CHILDREN This gay couple is raising two adopted children. Research has shown that the sexual orientation of a child's caregivers has little or no effect on the child's sexual orientation.

sexual orientation (T. J. Williams et al., 2000). For example, one study found that women who had been exposed to high levels of androgens during their fetal development were much more likely to become lesbians than their sisters who were not similarly exposed (B. H. F. L. Meyer et al., 1995). In animals, such hormonal influences alter the structure of the hypothalamus, a brain region known to underlie some aspects of sexual functioning (Swaab & Hofman, 1995). In humans, hormones may likewise be responsible for anatomical differences in the hypothalamus. These differences are seen not only in males versus females but in homosexual versus heterosexual men as well (LeVay, 1991; Swaab et al., 1997). The anterior commissure, an area near the hypothalamus, also appears to differ in people with differing sexual orientations (Allen & Gorski, 1992; Gladue, 1994).

Finally, a biological basis for sexual orientation is suggested by the relatively weak effects of the environment on sexual orientation. For example, the sexual orientation of children's caregivers has little or no effect on those children's own orientation. Several studies have shown that children adopted by homosexual parents are no more or less likely to display a homosexual orientation than are children raised by heterosexual parents (J. M. Bailey et al., 1995; Tasker & Golombok, 1995).

▪ Can that evidence be interpreted another way?

Like all correlational data, correlations between genetics and sexual orientation are open to alternative interpretations. As discussed in Chapter 1, a correlation describes the strength and direction of the relationship between two variables, but it does not guarantee that one variable actually influences the other. Consider again the data showing that the brothers who shared the most genes were also most likely to share a homosexual orientation. It is possible that what they shared was not a gene for homosexuality but, rather, a set of genes that influenced the boys' activity levels, emotionality, aggressiveness, or other general aspects of their temperament or personality. It could have been these characteristics, and other people's reactions to them, that increased the likelihood of a particular sexual orientation. In other words, sexual orientation could arise as a *reaction* to the way people respond to a genetically determined, but nonsexual, aspect of personality. The influence of prenatal hormone levels could also influence sexual orientation by shaping aggressiveness or other nonsexual aspects of behavior.

It is also important to look at behavioral genetics evidence for what it can tell us about the role of *environmental* factors in sexual orientation. When we read a study showing that 52 percent of the time, both members of identical twin pairs have a homosexual or bisexual orientation, it is easy to ignore the fact that the sexual orientation of the twin pair members was *different* in 48 percent of the cases. Viewed in this way, the results suggest that genes do not tell the entire story of sexual orientation. In other words, even if sexual orientation has a biological base, it is probably not determined solely by unlearned, genetic forces. As described in Chapter 2, the bodies we inherit are quite responsive to environmental input. In fact, the behaviors we engage in and the environmental experiences we have often result in physical changes in the brain and elsewhere (Wang et al., 1995). For example, physical changes occur in the brain's synapses as we form new memories. Thus, differences in the brains of people with differing sexual orientations could be the effect, not the cause, of their behavior or experiences.

What evidence would help to evaluate the alternatives?

More research must be done to evaluate the extent to which genetic factors directly determine sexual orientation or shape physical and psychological characteristics that socially encourage particular sexual orientations. In studying this issue, researchers need to learn more about the genetic makeup, mental style, and behavioral characteristics of people with different sexual orientations. Are there personality characteristics associated with particular sexual orientations? If so, do those characteristics have a strong genetic component? To what extent are heterosexuals, bisexuals, and homosexuals similar—and different—in terms of biases, coping skills, developmental histories, and the like?

The more we learn about sexual orientation in general, the easier it will be to interpret data relating to its origins. But even defining *sexual orientation* is not simple. Kinsey and his colleagues (1948) viewed sexual orientation as occurring along a continuum rather than falling into a few discrete categories. Should a man who identifies himself as gay be considered bisexual because he occasionally has heterosexual daydreams? What sexual orientation label would be appropriate for a forty-year-old woman who experienced a few lesbian encounters in her teens but has engaged only in heterosexual sex since then? Progress in understanding the origins of sexual orientation would be enhanced by a generally accepted system for describing and defining what is meant by *sexual orientation* (E. Stein, 1999).

What conclusions are most reasonable?

Given the antagonism and physical danger often faced by people with nonheterosexual orientations (Cramer, 1999; Herek, 1998), it seems unlikely that sexual orientation is entirely a matter of choice. Indeed, much of the evidence reviewed suggests that our sexual orientation chooses us, rather than the other way around. Given this evidence, a reasonable hypothesis is that genetic factors, probably operating via prenatal hormones, create differences in the brains of people with different sexual orientations. Even if this hypothesis is correct, however, the manner in which a person expresses a genetically influenced sexual orientation will be profoundly shaped by what that person learns through social and cultural experiences (Bancroft, 1994). In short, sexual orientation most likely results from the complex interplay of both genetic and nongenetic mechanisms—both nature and nurture. People who characterize sexual orientation as being either "all in the genes" or entirely a matter of choice are probably wrong.

Sexual Dysfunctions

The same biological, social, and psychological factors that shape human sexual behavior can also result in **sexual dysfunctions,** problems in a person's desire for, or ability to have, satisfying sexual activity. Fortunately, most of these problems—which affect 30 to 40 percent of U.S. adults (Laumann, Paik, & Rosen, 1999)—respond to psychotherapy, drugs, or both (de Silva, 1994). For men, a common problem is *erectile disorder* (once called *impotence*), a persistent inability to have or maintain an erection adequate for sex.

sexual dysfunctions Problems with sexual motivation, arousal, or orgasmic response.

Physical causes—such as fatigue, diabetes, hypertension, and alcohol or other drugs—account for some cases. Psychological causes such as anxiety are also common (Everaerd & Laan, 1994). Viagra, a drug that affects blood flow in the penis, is effective in treating many cases of erectile disorder (I. Goldstein et al., 1998; Lue, 2000), and even newer drugs are on the way. As its name implies, *premature ejaculation* is a recurring tendency to ejaculate during sex sooner than the man or his partner desires. Most men experience episodes of at least one of these problems at some point in their lives. These episodes are considered dysfunctions only if they become a distressing obstacle to sexual functioning (American Psychiatric Association, 1994).

For women, the most common sexual dysfunction is *arousal disorder* (once called *frigidity*), which involves a recurring inability to become aroused during sexual activity (N. A. Phillips, 2000; G. T. Wilson et al., 1996). Arousal disorder can stem from inadequate genital stimulation, insufficient vaginal lubrication, or inadequate blood flow to the clitoris (Mansfield, Voda, & Koch, 1995; Wilson et al., 1996). However, it is also often tied to psychological factors such as guilt or self-consciousness, which can affect men as well as women (Davidson & Moore, 1994; Laan et al., 1993).

Achievement Motivation

■ **Why do some people try harder than others to succeed?**

This sentence was written at 6 A.M. on a beautiful Sunday in June. Why would someone get up that early to work on a weekend? Why do people take their work seriously and try to do the best that they can? People work hard partly due to *extrinsic motivation,* a desire for external rewards such as money. But work and other human behaviors also reflect *intrinsic motivation,* a desire to attain internal satisfaction.

The next time you visit someone's home or office, look at the mementos displayed there. You may see framed diplomas and awards, trophies and ribbons, pictures of memorable personal events, and photos of children and grandchildren. These badges of achievement affirm that a person has accomplished tasks that merit approval or establish worth. Much of human behavior is motivated by a desire for approval, admiration, and a sense of achievement—in short, for esteem—from others and from oneself. In this section, we examine two of the most common avenues to esteem: achievement in general and achievement in one's work.

Need for Achievement

Many athletes who hold world records still train intensely; many people who have built multimillion-dollar businesses still work fourteen-hour days. What motivates these people? A possible answer is a motive called **need achievement** (H. A. Murray, 1938). People with a high need for achievement seek to master tasks—such as sports, business ventures, intellectual puzzles, or artistic creations—and feel intense satisfaction from doing so. They work hard at striving for excellence, enjoy themselves in the process, take great pride in achieving at a high level, and often experience success.

Individual Differences   How do people with strong achievement motivation differ from others? To find out, researchers gave children a test to measure their need for achievement and then asked them to play a ring-toss game. Children scoring low on the need-for-achievement test usually stood so close or so far away from the ring-toss target that they either could not fail or could not succeed. In contrast, children scoring high on the need-for-achievement test stood at a moderate distance from the target, making the game challenging but not impossible (McClelland, 1958).

Experiments with adults and children suggest that people with high achievement needs tend to set challenging, but realistic, goals. They actively seek success, take risks as needed, and are intensely satisfied with success. Yet if they feel they have tried their best,

need achievement   A motive influenced by the degree to which a person establishes specific goals, cares about meeting those goals, and experiences feelings of satisfaction by doing so.

Source: H. A. Murray (1971).

FIGURE 8.6

Assessment of
Achievement Motivation

This picture is similar to those included in the Thematic Apperception Test, or TAT (Morgan & Murray, 1935). The strength of people's achievement motivation is inferred from the stories they tell about TAT pictures. A response like "The young woman is hoping that she will be able to make her grandmother proud of her" would be seen as reflecting high achievement motivation.

Children raised in environments that support the development of strong achievement motivation tend not to give up on difficult tasks—even if all the king's horses and all the king's men do!

people with high achievement motivation are not too upset by failure. Those with low achievement motivation also like to succeed, but success tends to bring them not joy but relief at having avoided failure (Winter, 1996).

People with strong achievement motivation tend to be preoccupied with their performance and level of ability (Harackiewicz & Elliot, 1993). They select tasks with clear outcomes, and they prefer feedback from a harsh but competent critic rather than from one who is friendlier but less competent (Klich & Feldman, 1992). They like to struggle with a problem rather than get help. They can wait for delayed rewards, and they make careful plans for the future (F. S. Mayer & Sutton, 1996). In contrast, people who are less motivated to achieve are less likely to seek or enjoy feedback, and they tend to quit in response to failure (Graham & Weiner, 1996). Figure 8.6 shows a picture similar to those included in the Thematic Apperception Test (TAT), which has been used to measure achievement motivation in adults (Morgan & Murray, 1935).

Development of Achievement Motivation   Achievement motivation tends to be learned in early childhood, especially from parents. For example, in one study young boys were given a very hard task, at which they were sure to fail. Fathers whose sons scored low on achievement motivation tests often became annoyed as they watched their boys work on the task, discouraged them from continuing, and interfered or even completed the task themselves (B. C. Rosen & D'Andrade, 1959). A different pattern of behavior emerged among parents of children who scored high on tests of achievement motivation. Those parents tended to (1) encourage the child to try difficult tasks, especially new ones; (2) give praise and other rewards for success; (3) encourage the child to find ways to succeed rather than merely complaining about failure; and (4) prompt the child to go on to the next, more difficult challenge (McClelland, 1985).

Cultural influences also affect achievement motivation. Subtle messages about a culture's view of the importance of achievement often appear in the books children read and the stories they hear. Does the story's main character work hard and overcome obstacles, thus creating expectations of a payoff for persistence? Or does the main character loaf around and then win the lottery, suggesting that rewards come randomly, regardless of effort? And if the main character succeeds, is it the result of personal initiative, as is typical of stories in individualist cultures? Or is success based on ties to a cooperative and supportive group, as is typical of stories in collectivist cultures? Such themes appear to act as blueprints for reaching one's goals. It is not surprising, then, that ideas about achievement motivation differ from culture to culture. In one study, individuals from Saudi Arabia and from the United States were asked to comment on short stories describing people succeeding at various tasks. Saudis tended to see the people in the stories as having succeeded because of the help they got from others, whereas Americans

"Maybe they didn't try hard enough."

tended to attribute success to the internal characteristics of each story's main character (Zahrani & Kaplowitz, 1993).

Achievement motivation can be increased in people whose cultural training did not encourage it in childhood (McClelland, 1985). For example, high school and college students with low achievement motivation were helped to develop fantasies about their own success. They imagined setting goals that were difficult but not impossible. Then they imagined themselves concentrating on breaking a complex problem into small, manageable steps. They fantasized about working hard, failing but not being discouraged, continuing to work, and finally feeling great about achieving success. Afterward, the students' grades and academic success improved, suggesting an increase in their achievement motivation (McClelland, 1985). In short, achievement motivation is strongly influenced by social and cultural learning experiences, and by the beliefs about oneself that these experiences help to create. People who come to believe in their ability to achieve are more likely to do so than those who expect to fail (Butler, 1998; Dweck, 1998; Wigfield & Eccles, 2000).

Achievement and Success in the Workplace

In the workplace, there is usually more concern with employees' motivation to work hard during business hours than with their general level of need achievement. In fact, employers tend to set up jobs in accordance with their ideas about how intrinsic and extrinsic motivation combine to shape employees' performance (Riggio, 1989). Employers who see workers as lazy, untrustworthy, and lacking ambition tend to offer highly structured, heavily supervised jobs. They give the employees little say in deciding what to do or how to do it. These employers assume that workers are motivated mainly by extrinsic rewards—money, in particular. So they are often surprised when their employees are dissatisfied with their jobs and show little motivation to work hard (Amabile et al., 1994; Igalens & Roussel, 2000).

If good pay and benefits alone do not bring job satisfaction and the desire to excel on the job, what does? Research suggests that low worker motivation in Western cultures comes largely from negative thoughts and feelings associated with having little or no control over the work environment (R. Rosen, 1991). Compared with those in highly structured jobs, workers tend to be happier, more satisfied, and more productive if they are (1) encouraged to participate in decisions about how work should be done; (2) given problems to solve, without being told how to solve them; (3) taught more than one skill; (4) given individual responsibility; and (5) given public recognition, not just money, for good performance (C. D. Fisher, 2000; S. M. Friedman et al., 1999; Fuller et al., 1999).

Allowing people to set and achieve clear goals increases both job performance and job satisfaction (Abramis, 1994). Goals that most effectively maintain work motivation have

Applying Psychology

TEAMWORK PAYS OFF A number of U.S. companies are following Japanese examples by redesigning jobs to increase workers' responsibility and flexibility. The goal is to increase productivity and job satisfaction by creating teams in which employees are responsible for solving production problems and making decisions about how best to do their jobs. In such companies, team members are publicly recognized for outstanding work, and part of their pay depends on the quality (not just the number) of their products and on the profitability of the company as a whole.

three features (Katzell & Thompson, 1990). First, they are personally meaningful. When a memo from a high-level administrator tells employees that their goal should be to increase production, they tend to feel unfairly pressured and not particularly motivated to meet the goal. Second, effective goals are specific and concrete. The goal of "doing better" is usually not a strong motivator. A specific target, such as increasing sales by 10 percent, is a far more motivating goal. It is there for all to see, and whether the goal has been reached is easily determined. Finally, goals are most effective if management supports the workers' own goal setting, offers special rewards for reaching goals, and gives encouragement after failure.

To summarize, motivating jobs offer personal challenges, independence, and both intrinsic and extrinsic rewards. They provide enough satisfaction for people to feel excitement and pleasure in working hard. For employers, the rewards are more productivity, less absenteeism, and lower turnover (Ilgen & Pulakos, 1999; S. P. Robbins, 1998).

Achievement and Subjective Well-Being

Some people believe that the more they achieve, and the more money and other material goods they acquire as a result, the happier they will be. Do you agree? As part of a recent focus on *positive psychology* (Seligman & Csikszentmihalyi, 2000), researchers have become increasingly interested in the systematic study of what it actually takes to achieve happiness, or more formally, subjective well-being. **Subjective well-being** is a combination of a cognitive judgment of satisfaction with life, the frequent experiencing of positive moods and emotions, and the relatively infrequent experiencing of unpleasant moods and emotions (Diener, 2000).

Research on subjective well-being indicates that, as you might expect, people living in extreme poverty or in war-torn or politically chaotic countries are less happy than people in better circumstances. And people everywhere react to good or bad events with corresponding changes in mood. As described in Chapter 10, for example, severe or long-lasting stressors—such as the death of a loved one—can lead to psychological and physical problems. But although events do have an impact, the saddening or elevating effects of major changes, such as being promoted or fired, or even being imprisoned or seriously injured, tend not to last as long as we might think they would. In other words, how happy you are may have less to do with what happens to you than you might expect (D. T. Gilbert & Wilson, 1998).

Most event-related changes in mood subside within days or weeks, and most people then return to their previous level of happiness (Suh, Diener, & Fujita, 1996). Even when events create permanent changes in circumstances, most people adapt by changing their expectancies and goals, not by radically and permanently changing their baseline level of happiness. For example, people may be thrilled after getting a big salary increase, but as they get used to having it, the thrill fades, and they may eventually feel just as underpaid as before. In fact, people's level of subjective well-being tends to be remarkably stable throughout their lives. This stable baseline may be related to temperament, or personality, and it has been likened to a set point for body weight (Lykken, 1999). Like many other aspects of temperament, our baseline level of happiness may be influenced by genetics. Twin studies have shown, for example, that individual differences in happiness are more strongly associated with inherited personality characteristics than with environmental factors such as money, popularity, or physical attractiveness (Lykken, 1999; Tellegen et al., 1988).

Beyond inherited tendencies, the things that appear to matter most in generating happiness are close social ties (especially a satisfying marriage or partnership and good friends), religious faith, and having the resources necessary to allow progress toward one's goals (Diener, 2000; D. G. Myers, 2000a). So you don't have to be a rich, physically attractive high-achiever to be happy, and it turns out that most people in Western cultures *are* relatively happy (Diener & Diener, 1995). These results are consistent with the views expressed over many centuries by philosophers, psychologists, and wise people in all cultures. For example, decades ago, Abraham Maslow (1970) noted that when people

subjective well-being A combination of a cognitive judgment of satisfaction with life, the frequent experiencing of positive moods and emotions, and the relatively infrequent experiencing of unpleasant moods and emotions.

in Western cultures *do* experience unhappiness and psychological problems, those problems can often be traced to a *deficiency orientation* (see Chapter 11). That is, these people tend to seek happiness by trying to acquire the goods and status they *don't* have—but think they need—rather than by appreciating life itself and the value of the material and nonmaterial riches they *already* have. Others have amplified this point, suggesting that our efforts to get more of the things we think will bring happiness may actually contribute to unhappiness (Csikszentmihalyi, 1999; D. G. Myers, 2000b).

Relations and Conflicts Among Motives

■ **Which motives move me most?**

It is far too early to tell whether research on subjective well-being will help to channel people's achievement motivation toward a more balanced set of goals, but there is no doubt that people will continue striving to meet whatever needs they perceive to be important. What are those needs?

Maslow's Hierarchy

Maslow (1970) suggested that human behavior is influenced by a hierarchy, or ranking, of five classes of needs, or motives (see Figure 8.7). Needs at the lowest level of the hierarchy must be at least partially satisfied before people can be motivated by higher-level goals. From the bottom to the top of Maslow's hierarchy, these five motives are as follows:

1. *Physiological,* such as food, water, oxygen, activity, and sleep.

2. *Safety,* such as being cared for as a child and having a secure income as an adult.

3. *Belongingness and love,* such as being part of various social groups and participating in affectionate sexual and nonsexual relationships.

4. *Esteem,* or being respected as a useful, honorable individual.

5. *Self-actualization,* which means becoming all that one is capable of. People motivated by this need explore and enhance relationships with others; follow interests for intrinsic pleasure rather than for status or esteem; and are concerned with issues affecting all people, not just themselves.

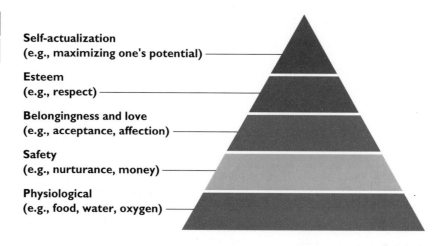

FIGURE 8.7

Maslow's Hierarchy of Motives

 Abraham Maslow saw motives as organized in a hierarchy in which motives at lower levels take precedence over those at higher levels. According to this view, self-actualization is the essence of mental health; but Maslow recognized that only rare individuals, such as Mother Teresa or Martin Luther King, Jr., approach full self-actualization. Take a moment to consider which level of Maslow's hierarchy you are focused on at this point in your life. Which level do you ultimately hope to reach?

Self-actualization (e.g., maximizing one's potential)

Esteem (e.g., respect)

Belongingness and love (e.g., acceptance, affection)

Safety (e.g., nurturance, money)

Physiological (e.g., food, water, oxygen)

In general, research suggests that motives lower in Maslow's hierarchy do take precedence over those higher in the hierarchy (R. F. Baumeister & Leary, 1995). But Maslow's system has been criticized as being too simplistic (Neher, 1991). People do not always act according to his hierarchy: Even when lower-level needs are unmet, some people continue to be motivated by higher-level needs (C. S. Hall, Lindzey, & Campbell, 1998). For example, the motivation of people who starve themselves to draw attention to political and moral causes seems to defy Maslow's hierarchy. Nevertheless, Maslow's classification is useful for thinking about the relationships among human motives.

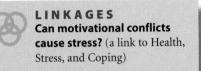

LINKAGES
Can motivational conflicts cause stress? (a link to Health, Stress, and Coping)

LINKAGES

Conflicting Motives and Stress

Maslow's hierarchy suggests that differing motives sometimes conflict. What is the result? Imagine that you are alone and bored on a Saturday night and decide to go to the store for a snack. What are your motives? Hunger might prompt you to go out. So might the prospect of the increased arousal and decreased boredom that a shopping trip will provide. Even sexual motivation might be involved, as you consider the chances of meeting someone exciting in the snack-food aisle. But safety-related motives also concern you. What if you get mugged? Even an esteem motive might come into play, leading you to avoid being seen alone on a weekend night.

These are just a few motives that may shape a trivial decision. When the decision is more important, the number and strength of motivational pushes and pulls are often greater, creating more internal conflict and acting as a source of stress. There are four basic types of motivational conflicts (N. E. Miller, 1959):

1. *Approach-approach conflicts.* When we must choose only one of two desirable activities—say, going to a movie or to a concert—an *approach-approach conflict* exists. As the importance of the choice increases, so does the difficulty of making it.

2. *Avoidance-avoidance conflicts.* An *avoidance-avoidance conflict* arises when we must select one of two undesirable alternatives. Someone forced either to sell the family farm or to declare bankruptcy faces an avoidance-avoidance conflict. Such conflicts are very difficult to resolve and often create intense emotion.

3. *Approach-avoidance conflicts.* If someone you can't stand has tickets to your favorite group's sold-out concert and invites you to come along, what would you do? When a single event or activity has both attractive and unattractive features, an *approach-avoidance conflict* is created. Conflicts of this type are also difficult to resolve and often result in long periods of indecision.

4. *Multiple approach-avoidance conflicts.* Suppose you must choose between two jobs. One offers a high salary with a well-known company, but it requires long hours and relocation to a miserable climate. The other boasts good advancement opportunities, fringe benefits, and a better climate, but it doesn't pay much and requires adjustment to an unpredictable work schedule. This is an example of a *multiple approach-avoidance conflict,* in which two or more alternatives each have both positive and negative features. Such conflicts are difficult to resolve, partly because, as discussed in the decision-making section of Chapter 7, the features of each option are often difficult to compare. For example, how many dollars a year does it take to compensate you for living in a bad climate?

Each of these conflicts may create stress, a topic we explore at length in Chapter 10. Most people in motivational conflict are tense, irritable, and particularly vulnerable to physical and psychological problems. These reactions are especially likely when there is no obvious "right" choice, when varying motives have approximately equal strength, and when a choice can have serious consequences (as in decisions to marry, to divorce, or to approve disconnecting a relative's life-support system). People may devote a lot of time and thought to resolving these conflicts, or they may make the decision quickly and impulsively, if only to end the discomfort of uncertainty. Even after resolving the conflict, people may continue to experience stress responses, such as worry about whether they made the right decision, or self-blame over bad choices. These and other consequences of conflicting motives can even lead to depression or other serious disorders.

The emotions associated with motivational conflicts provide just one example of the close links between human motivation and emotion. Motivation can intensify emotion, as when hunger leads a restaurant customer to angrily complain about slow service. But emotions can also create motivation. Happiness, for example, is an emotion that people want to feel, so they engage in whatever behaviors—studying, artwork, beachcombing—they think will achieve it. Similarly, as an emotion that most people want to avoid, anxiety prompts many behaviors, from leaving the scene of an accident to avoiding poisonous snakes. In the next section of this chapter, we take a closer look at emotions.

The Nature of Emotion

How do feelings differ from thoughts?

Everyone seems to agree that joy, sorrow, anger, fear, love, and hate are emotions. However, it is often hard to identify the shared features that make these experiences emotions rather than, say, thoughts or impulses.

Defining Characteristics

Most psychologists in Western cultures tend to see emotions as organized psychological and physiological reactions to changes in our relationship to the world. These reactions are partly inner, or *subjective*, experiences and partly measurable patterns of behavior and physiological arousal. The subjective experience of emotion has several characteristics:

1. Emotion is usually *temporary*. In other words, it tends to have a relatively clear beginning and end and a relatively short duration. Moods, by contrast, tend to last longer.

2. Emotional experience is either *positive or negative*, pleasant or unpleasant.

3. Emotional experience is triggered partly by a *mental assessment* of how a situation relates to your goals. The same event can bring on very different emotions depending on how you interpret what the event means. An exam score of 75 percent may excite you if your previous score had been 50 percent, but it may upset you if you had never before scored below 90 percent.

4. Emotional experience *alters thought processes*, often by directing attention toward some things and away from others. The anguish of parents whose child is killed by a drunken driver, for example, may alter their perception of the importance of drunk-driving laws.

5. Emotional experience elicits an *action tendency*, a motivation to behave in certain ways. The grieving parents' anger, for example, may motivate them to harm the driver or to work for stronger penalties for drunk driving.

6. Emotional experiences are *passions* that happen to you, usually whether you want them to happen or not. However, you can exert some control over emotions, because they depend partly on how you interpret situations. If you interpret a risky situation as "exciting," for example, you may not feel as fearful as if you interpret it as "dangerous." Still, you cannot simply *decide* what emotions you experience; instead, you "fall in love"

or "explode in anger," or are "overcome by grief." Emotional experiences thus have a different relation to the self than do conscious thoughts.

In other words, the subjective aspects of emotions are experiences that are both *triggered by* the thinking self and felt as *happening* to the self. The extent to which we are "victims" of our passions versus rational controllers of our emotions is a central dilemma of human existence.

The objectively measurable aspects of emotion include learned and innate *expressive displays* and *physiological responses*. Expressive displays—such as a smile or a frown—communicate feelings to others. Physiological responses—changes in heart rate, for example—provide the biological adjustments needed to perform actions generated by the emotional experience. If you throw a temper tantrum, for instance, your heart must deliver additional oxygen and fuel to your muscles.

In summary, an **emotion** is a temporary experience with either positive or negative qualities. It is felt with some intensity as happening to the self, generated in part by a mental assessment of situations, and accompanied by both learned and innate physical responses. Through emotion, people communicate their internal states and intentions to others, but emotion also functions to motivate a person's thoughts and actions.

The Biology of Emotion

Biology plays a major role in emotion. In the *central nervous system,* specific brain areas are involved in the generation of emotions, as well as in our experience of those emotions. The *autonomic nervous system* gives rise to many of the physiological changes associated with emotional arousal.

Brain Mechanisms   Although many questions remain, researchers have described three basic features of the brain's control of emotion. First, it appears that activity in the *limbic system,* especially in the *amygdala,* is central to various aspects of emotion (LeDoux, 1996; see Figure 2.8 on page 53). Disruptions in the amygdala appear to contribute to the emotional problems associated with certain kinds of brain damage (Aggleton, 1993). For example, victims of a disease that destroys only the amygdala cannot judge other people's emotional state by looking at their facial expressions (Adolphs, Tranel, & Damasio, 1998).

A second aspect of the brain's involvement in emotion is seen in its control over emotional and nonemotional facial expressions (Rinn, 1984). Take a moment to look in a mirror, and put on your best fake smile. The voluntary facial movements you just made, like all voluntary movements, are controlled by the *pyramidal motor system,* a brain system that includes the motor cortex. However, a smile that expresses genuine happiness is involuntary. That kind of smile, like the other facial movements associated with emotions, is governed by the *extrapyramidal motor system,* which depends on areas beneath the cortex. Brain damage can disrupt either system (see Figure 8.8). Thus, people with pyramidal motor system damage show normal facial expressions during genuine emotion, but they cannot fake a smile. In contrast, people with damage to the extrapyramidal system can pose facial expressions at will, but they remain straight-faced even when feeling genuine joy or profound sadness (Hopf, Muller, & Hopf, 1992).

A third aspect of the brain's role in emotion is revealed by research on the differing contributions of its two cerebral hemispheres to the perception, experience, and expression of emotion. For example, after suffering damage to the right, but not the left, hemisphere, people no longer laugh at jokes—even though they can still understand the jokes' words, the logic (or illogic) underlying them, and the punch lines (Critchley, 1991). And compared with nondepressed people, depressed people display greater electrical activity in the right frontal cortex (Schaffer, Davidson, & Saron, 1983) and perform more poorly on tasks that depend especially on the right hemisphere (Banich et al., 1992; Heller, Etienne, & Miller, 1995).

There is still some debate about the relationship between hemispheric differences and emotion. However, research has generally shown that the following aspects of emotion depend more on the right hemisphere than on the left: (1) the experiencing of negative

emotion   A transitory experience with positive or negative qualities that is felt as happening to the self.

FIGURE 8.8

Control of Voluntary and
Emotional Facial Movements

**This man has a tumor in his motor cortex
that prevents him from voluntarily moving the muscles on the left side of his
face. In the photograph at the left he is
trying to smile in response to instructions
from the examiner. He cannot smile on
command, but he _can_ smile with happiness, as the photograph at the right
shows, because the movements associated with genuine emotion are controlled
by the extrapyramidal motor system.**

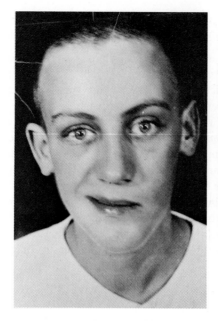
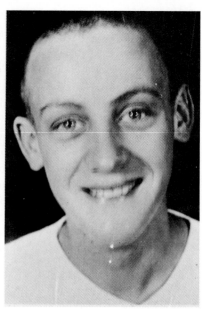

emotion, (2) the perception of any emotion exhibited in faces or other stimuli, and (3)
the facial expression of any emotion (Heller, Nitschke, & Miller, 1998).

If the right hemisphere is relatively dominant in emotion, which side of the face
would you expect to be somewhat more involved in expressing emotion? If you said the
left side you are correct, because as described in Chapter 2, movements of each side of
the body are controlled by the opposite side of the brain.

Mechanisms of the Autonomic Nervous System   The autonomic nervous system (ANS)
triggers many of the physiological changes that accompany emotions (Vernet, Robin, &
Dittmar, 1995; see Figure 8.9). If your hands get cold and clammy when you are nervous,
it is because the ANS has increased perspiration and decreased the blood flow in your
hands.

As described in Chapter 2, the ANS carries information between the brain and most
organs of the body—the heart and blood vessels, the digestive system, and so on. Each
of these organs has its own ongoing activity, but ANS input affects it, too, either by
increasing it or decreasing it. By affecting the activity of organs, the ANS coordinates
their functioning to meet the body's general needs and to prepare the body for change
(Porges, Doussard, & Maita, 1995). If you are aroused to take action, such as running to
catch a bus, you need more glucose to fuel your muscles. The ANS frees needed energy
by stimulating secretion of glucose-generating hormones and promoting blood flow to
the muscles.

Figure 8.9 shows that the autonomic nervous system is organized into two parts: the
sympathetic nervous system and the parasympathetic nervous system. Emotions can
activate either of these divisions, both of which send axon fibers to each organ in the
body. Generally, the sympathetic and parasympathetic fibers have opposite effects on
these *target organs*. Axons from the **parasympathetic nervous system** release the neurotransmitter *acetylcholine* onto target organs, leading to activity related to the protection,
nourishment, and growth of the body. Axons from the **sympathetic nervous system**
release a different neurotransmitter, *norepinephrine*, onto target organs, helping to prepare the body for vigorous activity. It is this system that stimulates the **fight-or-flight
syndrome**, a pattern of increased heart rate and blood pressure, rapid or irregular
breathing, dilated pupils, perspiration, dry mouth, increased blood sugar, "goose
bumps," and other changes that help prepare the body to combat or run from a threat.

The ANS is not directly connected to brain areas involved in consciousness, so information about organ activity reaches the brain at a nonconscious level. Thus, you may
hear your stomach grumble, but you can't actually feel it secrete acids. Similarly, you can-

parasympathetic nervous system
The subsystem of the autonomic nervous
system that typically influences activity
related to the protection, nourishment,
and growth of the body.

sympathetic nervous system   The
subsystem of the autonomic nervous
system that readies the body for action in
the face of crisis.

fight-or-flight syndrome   Physical reactions initiated by the sympathetic nervous
system that prepare the body to fight or
to run from a threatening situation.

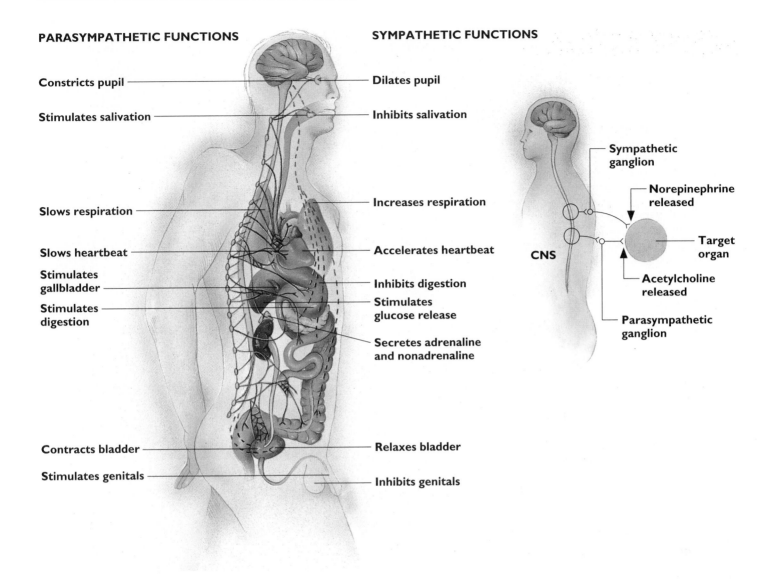

PARASYMPATHETIC FUNCTIONS

- Constricts pupil
- Stimulates salivation
- Slows respiration
- Slows heartbeat
- Stimulates gallbladder
- Stimulates digestion
- Contracts bladder
- Stimulates genitals

SYMPATHETIC FUNCTIONS

- Dilates pupil
- Inhibits salivation
- Increases respiration
- Accelerates heartbeat
- Inhibits digestion
- Stimulates glucose release
- Secretes adrenaline and nonadrenaline
- Relaxes bladder
- Inhibits genitals

Sympathetic ganglion

Norepinephrine released

CNS

Target organ

Acetylcholine released

Parasympathetic ganglion

FIGURE 8.9

The Autonomic Nervous System

 Emotional responses involve activation of the autonomic nervous system, which includes sympathetic and parasympathetic subsystems. Which of the bodily responses depicted do you associate with emotional experiences?

not consciously experience the brain mechanisms that alter the activity of your autonomic nervous system. This is why most people cannot exert direct, conscious control over blood pressure or other aspects of ANS activity. However, you can do things that have indirect effects on the ANS. For example, to create autonomic arousal of your sex organs, you might imagine an erotic situation. To raise your blood pressure, you might hold your breath or strain your muscles. And to lower your blood pressure, you can lie down, relax, and think calming thoughts.

Theories of Emotion

Is emotion in the heart, in the head, or both?

Are the physiological responses associated with emotion sufficient to *produce* an emotional experience? Or are these responses simply the *results* of an emotional experience that is created when we mentally interpret events? Questions about the roles played by physiological and mental activity in the experience of emotion have been the focus of research for over a century—and they have generated several important theories of emotion.

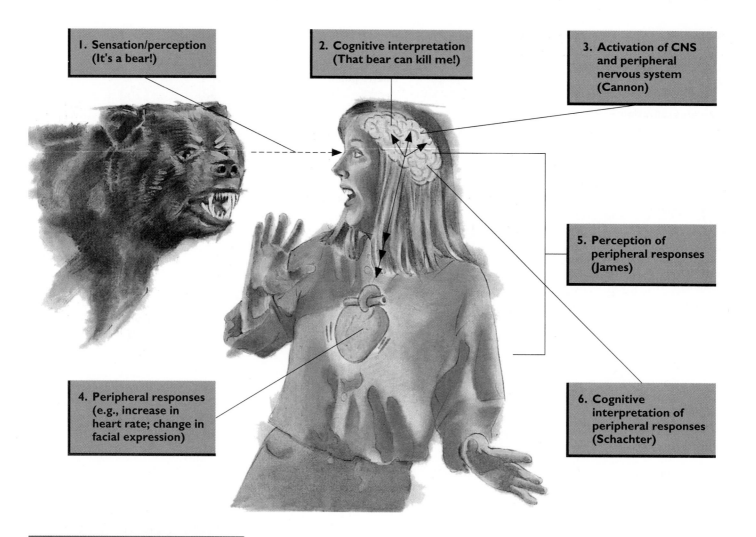

1. Sensation/perception (It's a bear!)

2. Cognitive interpretation (That bear can kill me!)

3. Activation of CNS and peripheral nervous system (Cannon)

5. Perception of peripheral responses (James)

4. Peripheral responses (e.g., increase in heart rate; change in facial expression)

6. Cognitive interpretation of peripheral responses (Schachter)

FIGURE 8.10

Components of Emotion

Emotion is associated with activity in the brain, as well as with responses elsewhere in the body (called "peripheral" responses). Emotion theorists have argued about which of these components are essential for emotion. William James emphasized the perception of peripheral responses, such as changes in heart rate. Stanley Schachter emphasized the cognitive interpretation and labeling of peripheral responses. Walter Cannon asserted that emotion could occur entirely within the brain.

James's Theory

Suppose you are camping in the woods when a huge bear approaches your tent in the middle of the night. Scared to death, you run for dear life. Do you run because you are afraid, or are you afraid because you run? The example and the question come from William James, one of the first psychologists to offer a formal account of how physiological responses relate to emotional experience. He argued that you are afraid *because* you run.

At first glance, James's theory sounds ridiculous. It defies common sense, which says that it would be silly to run from something unless you already feared it. James concluded otherwise after examining his own mental processes. He decided that once all physiological responses are stripped away, nothing remains of the experience of an emotion (James, 1890). Emotion, he reasoned, is simply the result of experiencing a particular set of physiological responses. Without these responses, you would feel no fear, or any other emotion. The idea that emotions depend on experiencing physiological responses was also suggested by Carle Lange, a Danish physician, so James's view is sometimes called the *James-Lange theory* of emotion.

Observing Peripheral Responses   Figure 8.10 outlines the components of emotional experience, including those emphasized by James. First, perception affects the cerebral cortex. The brain interprets a situation and automatically directs a particular set of physiological changes, such as increased heart rate, sinking stomach, perspiration, and certain patterns of blood flow. It is when we become *aware* of these physiological changes, said James, that we experience an emotion. According to this view, each particular emotion is created by a particular pattern of physiological responses.

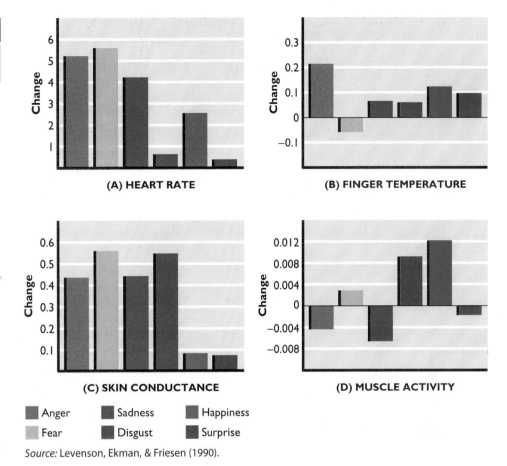

FIGURE 8.11

Patterns of Physiological Change Associated with Different Emotions

In this experiment, movements of the face characteristic of different emotions produced different patterns of change in (A) heart rate; (B) peripheral blood flow, as measured by finger temperature; (C) skin conductance; and (D) muscle activity (Levenson, Ekman, & Friesen, 1990). For example, making an angry face caused heart rate and finger temperature to rise, whereas making a fearful face raised heart rate but lowered finger temperature.

Source: Levenson, Ekman, & Friesen (1990).

Notice that according to James's theory, emotional experience is not generated by the brain alone. There is no special "emotion center" in the brain where the firing of neurons creates a direct experience of emotion. If this theory is accurate, it might account for the difficulty we sometimes have in knowing our true feelings: We must figure out what emotions we feel by perceiving small differences in specific physiological response patterns.

Evaluating James's Theory   Research shows that certain emotional states are indeed associated with particular patterns of autonomic changes (Damasio et al., 2000; Kelter & Buswell, 1996; R. Sinha & Parsons, 1996). For example, blood flow to the hands and feet increases in association with anger and declines in association with fear (Levenson, Ekman, & Friesen, 1990). Thus, fear involves "cold feet"; anger does not. A pattern of activity associated with disgust includes increased muscle activity but no change in heart rate. And when people mentally relive different kinds of emotional experiences, they show different patterns of autonomic activity (Ekman, Levenson, & Friesen, 1983). These emotion-specific patterns of physiological activity have been found in widely different cultures (Levenson et al., 1992).

Furthermore, different patterns of autonomic activity are closely tied to specific emotional facial expressions, and vice versa. When research participants were asked to make various facial movements (Ekman, Levenson, & Friesen, 1983), these movements led to autonomic changes resembling those normally accompanying emotion (see Figure 8.11). In addition, almost all of the participants reported *feeling the emotion* associated with the expression they had created, even though they could not see their own expressions and did not realize that a specific emotion was being portrayed.

To get an idea of how facial expressions can alter, as well as express, emotion, take careful note of another person's facial expression, and try your best to imitate it. Doing this may elicit in you the same feelings and autonomic responses that the other person is experiencing. Research suggests that people do best at describing another person's emotions when their own physiological responses match those of the other person (Levenson

& Ruef, 1992). Edgar Allan Poe noted the relationship between facial expressions and feelings more than a hundred years ago:

> When I wish to find out how wise or how stupid or how good or how wicked is anyone, or what are his thoughts at the moment, I fashion the expression of my face, as accurately as possible, in accordance with the expression of his, and then wait to see what thoughts or sentiments arise in my mind or heart, as if to match or correspond with the expression. (quoted in Levenson, Ekman, & Friesen, 1990)

A variant of James's theory, the *facial feedback hypothesis,* maintains that involuntary facial movements provide enough information about the body to drive emotional experience (Ekman & Davidson, 1993). This hypothesis predicts that feeling yourself smile should make you feel happy. It also helps to explain the results mentioned earlier suggesting that voluntarily posed facial expressions create the emotions normally associated with them. (The next time you want to cheer yourself up, it might help to smile—even though you don't feel like it!)

Lie Detection   James's view that different patterns of physiological activity are associated with different emotions forms the basis for the lie-detection industry. If people experience anxiety or guilt when they lie, specific patterns of physiological activity accompanying these emotions should be detectable on instruments, called *polygraphs,* that record heart rate, breathing rate, perspiration, and other autonomic responses.

To identify the perpetrator of a crime using the *control question test,* a polygraph tester may ask questions specific to the crime, such as "Did you stab someone on January 31, 2001?" Responses to such *relevant questions* are then compared with responses to *control questions,* such as "Have you ever lied to get out of trouble?" Innocent people might have lied at some time in the past and might feel guilty when asked about it, but they should have no reason to feel guilty about what they did on January 31, 2001. Thus, an innocent person should have a stronger emotional response to control questions than to relevant questions (Rosenfeld, 1995). Another approach, called the *directed lie test,* compares a person's physiological reactions when *asked* to lie about something and when telling what is known to be the truth. Finally, the *guilty knowledge test* seeks to determine if a person reacts in a notable way to information about a crime that only the perpetrator would know (Lykken, 1992).

Most people do have emotional responses when they lie, but statistics about the accuracy of polygraphs are difficult to obtain. Estimates vary widely, from those suggesting that polygraphs detect 90 percent of guilty, lying individuals (Honts & Quick, 1995; Kircher, Horowitz, & Raskin, 1988; Raskin, 1986) to those suggesting that polygraphs mislabel as many as 40 percent of truthful, innocent persons as guilty liars (Ben-Shakhar & Furedy, 1990; Saxe & Ben-Shakhar, 1999). Obviously, the results of a polygraph test are not determined entirely by whether a person is telling the truth. What people think about the act of lying, and about the value of the test, can also influence the accuracy of its results. For example, people who consider lying to be acceptable and who do not believe in the power of polygraphs are unlikely to display emotion-linked physiological responses while lying during the test. However, an innocent person who believes in such tests and who thinks that "everything always goes wrong" might show a large fear response when asked about a crime, thus wrongly indicating "guilt."

Polygraphs can catch some liars, but most researchers agree that at least some guilty persons can "fool" a polygraph lie detector, and that some innocent people can be mislabeled as guilty (Lykken, 1998). Accordingly, a large majority of psychologists in the United States have expressed serious reservations about the use of polygraph tests to detect deception (Abeles, 1985; Iacono & Lykken, 1997) and do not support their use as evidence in court.

Schachter's Modification of James's Theory

In the early 1960s, when many psychologists were raising questions about the validity of James's theory of emotion, Stanley Schachter and his colleague, Jerome Singer, argued

that the theory was essentially correct—but required a few modifications (Cornelius, 1996). According to the *Schachter-Singer theory,* emotions result from a *combination* of feedback from the body's responses and our *mental interpretation* of what caused those responses. So cognitive interpretation comes into play twice: first when you perceive the situation that leads to bodily responses and again when you interpret those responses as a particular emotion (see Figure 8.10).

Schachter said that a given pattern of physiological responses can be interpreted in many different ways, and so might give rise to many different emotions. In short, Schachter argued that the core of emotion is the cognitive act of *labeling* a pattern of physiological arousal (S. Schachter & Singer, 1962). Schachter also said that how we label arousal depends on **attribution,** the process of identifying the cause of some event. We attribute our physiological arousal to different emotions depending on the information available about the situation. For example, if you are watching the final seconds of a close ball game, you might attribute your racing heart, rapid breathing, and perspiration to excitement; but you might attribute the same physiological reactions to anxiety if you are waiting for a big exam to begin. So, the emotion you experience upon seeing a bear at your campsite might be fear, excitement, astonishment, or surprise, depending on how you label your bodily reactions.

Evaluating Schachter's Theory Schachter's refinement of James's theory predicts that emotional experience will be less intense if arousal is attributed to a nonemotional cause. If you notice your heart pounding before an exam but say to yourself, "Sure my heart's pounding—I just drank five cups of coffee!" then you should feel "wired" from caffeine rather than afraid or worried. This prediction has received some support (S. Schachter & Singer, 1962; Sinclair et al., 1994).

There is also evidence that physiological arousal from nonemotional sources can intensify emotional experience (Zillman, 1996). For example, people who have been aroused by physical exercise become more angry when provoked, and experience more intense sexual feelings when in the company of an attractive person, than do people who have been less physically active (Allen et al., 1989). When arousal from one experience carries over to an independent situation, it is called **transferred excitation** (Reisenzein, 1983).

Arousal created by one emotion can also transfer to intensify another. For example, arousal from fear, like arousal from exercise, can enhance sexual feelings. One study of

attribution   The process of explaining the causes of people's behavior, including one's own.

transferred excitation   The process by which arousal is carried over from one experience to an independent situation.

this transfer took place in Canada near a deep river gorge. The gorge could be crossed either by a shaky swinging bridge or by a more stable wooden structure. A female researcher asked men who had just crossed each bridge to fill out a questionnaire that included a measure of sexual imagery. The men who met the woman after crossing the more dangerous bridge had much higher sexual imagery scores than the men who had crossed the stable bridge. Furthermore, they were more likely to rate the researcher as attractive (Dutton & Aron, 1974). When the person giving out the questionnaire was a male, however, the type of bridge crossed had no impact on sexual imagery. To test the possibility that the men who crossed the dangerous bridge were simply more adventurous in both bridge crossing and heterosexual encounters, the researcher repeated the study, but with one change. This time, the woman approached the men farther down the trail, long after arousal from the bridge crossing had subsided. Now, the apparently adventurous men were no more likely than others to rate the woman as attractive. So it was probably transfer of excitation, not just adventurousness, that produced the original result.

Cannon's Theory

The theories we have considered so far assume that the experience of emotion depends on facial movements and other bodily responses outside the brain. However, Walter Cannon believed that emotion can result from brain activity alone (W. B. Cannon, 1927/1987). He argued that you feel fear at the sight of a bear even before you run away from it. Emotional experience, he said, begins in the brain. Specifically, it starts in the thalamus, the brain structure that relays information from most sense organs to the cortex.

According to Cannon's theory of emotion (called the *Cannon-Bard theory,* in recognition of Philip Bard's contribution), sensory information about emotional situations first reaches the thalamus. The thalamus then sends signals *simultaneously* to the autonomic nervous system and to the cerebral cortex, where the emotion becomes conscious. So when you see a bear, the brain receives sensory information about it, interprets that information as a bear, and *directly* creates the experience of fear while at the same time sending messages to the heart, lungs, and legs to get you out of the situation. According to Cannon's theory, then, there is a direct, central nervous system experience of emotion, with or without feedback about bodily responses (see Figure 8.10).

Updating Cannon's Theory   Subsequent research indicates that the thalamus is not the "seat" of emotion, as Cannon had suggested. Still, the thalamus does participate in some aspects of emotional processing (Lang, 1995). For example, studies in animals and humans show that the emotion of fear is generated by connections from the thalamus to the amygdala (A. K. Anderson & Phelps, 2000; LeDoux, 1995). The implication is that strong emotions can sometimes bypass the cortex without requiring conscious thought to activate them—thus possibly explaining why people find it so difficult to overcome an intense fear, or phobia, even though they may consciously know the fear is irrational.

An updated version of Cannon's theory suggests that specific brain areas produce the feelings of pleasure or discomfort associated with emotion. This idea arose from studies showing that electrical stimulation of certain parts of the brain is rewarding. Researchers found that rats kept returning to the place in their cage where they received stimulation through electrodes in their brains. When these animals were allowed to control delivery of the stimulation by pressing a lever, they pressed it until they were physically exhausted, ignoring even food and water (Olds & Milner, 1954). The brain areas in which stimulation is experienced as especially pleasurable include the dopamine systems, which, as described in Chapter 4, are activated by cocaine and other psychoactive drugs (Bardo, 1998). In contrast, stimulation of other brain regions is so unpleasant that animals work hard to avoid it.

Presumably, part of the direct central experience of emotion involves areas of the brain whose activity is experienced as either pleasant or aversive. The areas of the brain activated by the kind of events that elicit emotion in humans have widespread connections throughout the brain. Thus, the central nervous system experience of emotion is

in review

Theories of Emotion		
Theory	**Source of Emotions**	**Evidence for Theory**
James-Lange	The central nervous system generates specific physical responses; awareness of the physical responses constitutes emotion.	Different emotions are associated with different physical responses.
Schachter-Singer	The central nervous system generates nonspecific physical responses; interpretation of the physical responses in light of the situation constitutes emotion.	Excitation generated by physical activity can transfer to increase emotional intensity.
Cannon-Bard	Parts of the central nervous system directly generate emotions; experiencing physiological responses is not necessary.	Direct brain stimulation can produce the feelings of pleasure or discomfort associated with emotion.

probably widely distributed, not narrowly localized in any one emotion "center" (Derryberry & Tucker, 1992).

Conclusions

"In Review: Theories of Emotion" summarizes key elements of the three theories we have discussed. It appears that both bodily responses (including facial responses) and the cognitive interpretation of those responses add to emotional experience. In addition, the brain itself can apparently generate emotional experience, independent of physiological arousal. So emotion is probably both in the heart and in the head (including the face). The most basic emotions probably occur directly within the brain, whereas the many shades of emotion probably arise from attributions, including evaluations of physiological responses. No theory has completely resolved the issue of which, if any, component of emotion is primary. However, the theories we have discussed have helped psychologists better understand how these components interact to produce emotional experience.

Communicating Emotion

■ **Which emotional expressions are innate, and which are learned?**

Imagine a woman watching television. You can see her face, but not what she sees on the screen. She might be engaged in complex thought, perhaps comparing her investment decisions with those of the experts on *Wall Street Week*. Or she might be thinking of nothing at all as she loses herself in a rerun of *Seinfeld*. In other words, your observation is not likely to tell you much about what she is thinking. If the television program creates an emotional experience, however, you will be able to make a reasonably accurate guess about which emotion she feels just by looking at the expression on her face. So far, we have described emotion from the inside, as people experience their own emotions. In

WHAT ARE THEY FEELING?
People's emotions are usually
"written on their faces." Jot
down what emotions you think these
people are feeling, and then look at the
footnote on page 292 to see how well you
"read" their emotions.

this section, we examine the social organization of emotion—how people communicate emotions to each other.

Humans communicate emotions partly through tone of voice and body posture or movement, but mainly through facial movements and expressions. The human face can create thousands of different expressions (Zajonc, 1998), and people are good at detecting them. Observers can see even very small facial movements: A twitch of the mouth can carry a lot of information. Are emotional facial expressions innate, or are they learned? And how are they used in communicating emotion?

Innate Expressions of Emotion

Charles Darwin observed that some facial expressions seem to be universal (Darwin, 1872/1965). He proposed that these expressions are genetically determined, passed on biologically from one generation to the next. The facial expressions seen today, said Darwin, are those that have been most effective at telling others something about how a person is feeling. If someone is scowling with teeth clenched, for example, you will probably assume that he or she is angry. And you will be unlikely to choose that particular moment to ask for a loan.

THE UNIVERSAL SMILE The innate
origin of some emotional expressions
is supported by the fact that the facial
movement pattern we call a smile is
related to happiness, pleasure, and other
positive emotions in human cultures
throughout the world.

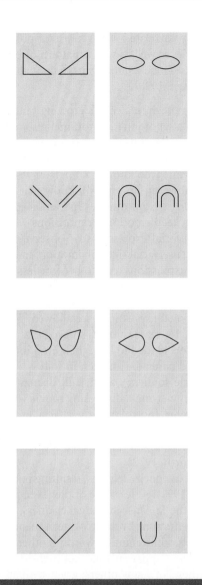

Elements of Ceremonial Facial
Masks That Convey Threat

**Certain geometric patterns are common
to threatening masks in many cultures.
When people in various cultures were
asked which member of each of these
pairs was more threatening, they consistently chose those, shown here on the
left, containing triangular and diagonal
elements. "Scary" Halloween pumpkins
tend to have such elements as well.**

Infants provide one source of evidence for the innateness of some facial expressions. Newborns do not need to be taught to grimace in pain, to smile in pleasure, or to blink when startled (Balaban, 1995). Even blind infants, who cannot imitate adults' expressions, show the same emotional expressions as do sighted infants (Goodenough, 1932).

A second line of evidence for innate facial expressions comes from studies showing that for the most basic emotions, people in all cultures show similar facial responses to similar emotional stimuli (Hejmadi, Davidson, & Rozin, 2000; Zajonc, 1998). Participants in these studies looked at photographs of people's faces and then tried to name the emotion each person was feeling. The pattern of facial movements we call a smile, for example, is universally related to positive emotions. Sadness is almost always accompanied by slackened muscle tone and a "long" face. Likewise, in almost all cultures, people contort their faces in a similar way when shown something they find disgusting. And a furrowed brow is frequently associated with frustration or unpleasantness (Ekman, 1994).

Anger is also linked with a facial expression recognized by almost all cultures. One study examined ceremonial masks of various Western and non-Western cultures (Aronoff, Barclay, & Stevenson, 1988). The angry, threatening masks of all eighteen cultures contained similar elements, such as triangular eyes and diagonal lines on the cheeks. In particular, angular and diagonal elements carry the impression of threat (see Figure 8.12).

Social and Cultural Influences on Emotional Expression

Whereas some basic emotional expressions are innate, many others are neither innate nor universal (Ekman, 1993). Even innate expressions are flexible, changing as necessary in the social situations in which they occur (Fernández-Dols & Ruiz-Belda, 1995). For example, facial expressions become more intense and change more frequently when people are imagining social scenes as opposed to solitary scenes (Fridlund et al., 1990). Similarly, facial expressions in response to odors tend to be more intense when others are watching than when people are alone (Jancke & Kaufmann, 1994).

Further, although a core group of emotional responses is recognized by all cultures (Hejmadi, Davidson, & Rozin, 2000), there is a certain degree of cultural variation in recognizing some emotions (Russell, 1995). In one study, for example, Japanese and North American people agreed about which facial expressions signaled happiness, surprise, and sadness, but they frequently disagreed about which faces showed anger, disgust, and fear (Matsumoto & Ekman, 1989). Members of cultures such as the Fore of New Guinea agree even less with people in Western cultures on the labeling of facial expressions (Russell, 1994). In addition, there are variations in the ways that cultures interpret emotions expressed by tone of voice (Mesquita & Frijda, 1992). An example is provided by a study showing that Taiwanese participants were best at recognizing a sad tone of voice, whereas Dutch participants were best at recognizing happy tones (Van Bezooijen, Otto, & Heenan, 1983).

People learn how to express certain emotions in ways specified by cultural rules. Suppose you say, "I just bought a new car," and all your friends stick their tongues out at you. In North America, this may mean they are envious or resentful. But in some regions of China, such a display expresses surprise.

Even smiles can vary as people learn to use them to communicate certain feelings. Paul Ekman and his colleagues categorized seventeen types of smiles, including "false smiles," which fake enjoyment, and "masking smiles," which hide unhappiness. They called the smile that occurs with real happiness the *Duchenne smile* (pronounced "do-SHEN"), after the French researcher who first noticed a difference between spontaneous, happy smiles and posed smiles. A genuine, Duchenne smile includes contractions of the muscles around the eyes (creating a distinctive wrinkling of the skin in these areas), as well as contractions of the muscles that raise the lips and cheeks. Few people can successfully contract the muscles around the eyes during a posed smile, so this feature can be used to distinguish "lying smiles" from genuine ones (M. G. Frank, Ekman, & Friesen,

1993). In one study, the Duchenne smile was highly correlated with reports of positive emotions experienced while people watched a movie, as well as with a pattern of brain waves known to be associated with positive emotions. These relationships did not appear for other types of smiles (Ekman, Davidson, & Friesen, 1990).

Learning About Emotions   The effects of learning are seen in a child's growing range of emotional expressions. Although infants begin with a set of innate emotional responses, they soon learn to imitate facial expressions and use them to express more and more emotions. In time, these expressions become more precise and personalized so that a particular expression conveys a clear message to anyone who knows that person well.

If facial expressions become too personalized, however, no one will know what the expressions mean, and they will fail to bring responses from others. Operant shaping, described in Chapter 5, on learning, probably helps keep emotional expressions within certain limits. If you could not see other people's facial expressions or observe their responses to yours, you might show fewer, or less intense, facial signs of emotion. Indeed, as congenitally blind people grow older, their facial expressions tend to become less animated (Izard, 1977).

As children grow, they learn an *emotion culture*—rules that govern what emotions are appropriate in what circumstances and what emotional expressions are allowed. These rules can vary from culture to culture. For example, TV news cameras showed that men in the U.S. military leaving for duty in Kosovo in 1999 tended to keep their emotions in check as they said goodbye to wives, girlfriends, and parents. However, in Italy—where mother-son ties are particularly strong—many male soldiers wailed with dismay and wept openly as they left. In a laboratory study, when viewing a distressing movie with a group of peers, Japanese students exhibited much more control over their facial expressions than did North American students. When they watched the film while alone, however, the Japanese students' faces showed the same emotional expressions as those of the North American students (Ekman, Friesen, & Ellsworth, 1972).

Emotion cultures shape how people describe and categorize feelings, resulting in both similarities and differences across cultures (Russell, 1991). At least five of the seven basic emotions listed in an ancient Chinese book called the *Li Chi*—joy, anger, sadness, fear, love, disliking, and liking—are considered primary emotions by most Western theorists. Yet while English has over 500 emotion-related words, some emotion words in other languages have no English meaning. The Czech word *litost* apparently has no English word equivalent: "It designates a feeling that is the synthesis of many others; grief, sympathy, remorse, and an indefinable longing. . . . *Litost* is a state of torment caused by a sudden insight into one's own miserable self" (Russell, 1991). The Japanese word *ijirashii* also has no English equivalent; it describes the feeling of seeing a praiseworthy person overcoming an obstacle (Russell, 1991).

Similarly, other cultures have no equivalent for some English emotion words. Many cultures do not see anger and sadness as different, for example. The Ilongot, a head-hunting group in the Philippines, have only one word, *liget,* for both anger and grief (Russell, 1991). Tahitians have different words for forty-six types of anger, but no word for sadness and, apparently, no concept of it. One westerner described a Tahitian man as being sad over separation from his wife and child. The man himself said that he felt *pe'a pe'a*—a general word for feeling ill, troubled, or fatigued—and did not attribute it to the separation.

Social Referencing   Facial expressions, tone of voice, body postures, and gestures not only communicate information about the emotion someone is experiencing; they can also influence others' behavior, especially the behavior of people who are not sure what to do. An inexperienced chess player, for instance, might reach out to move the queen,

social referencing   A phenomenon in which other people's facial expressions, tone of voice, and bodily gestures serve as guidelines for how to behave in uncertain situations.

The people pictured on page 290 were awaiting word as to whether Chile's former dictator, Augusto Pinochet, would be brought to trial in Britain for torturing their relatives in Chilean prisons. Their emotions at the moment probably included anxiety, worry, dread, uncertainty, excitement, hope, and perhaps anger. Pinochet avoided trial and returned to Chile, but he still faces trial there.

catch sight of a spectator's grimace, and infer that another move would be better. The process of letting another person's emotional state guide our own behavior is called **social referencing** (Campos, 1980). This process begins early; even three-month-old infants will look in the direction in which an adult's eyes have moved (Hood, Willen, & Driver, 1998).

The visual-cliff studies described in Chapter 3 have been used to create an uncertain situation for infants. To reach its mother, an infant in these experiments must cross the visual cliff. If the apparent drop-off is very small or very large, there is no doubt about what to do. One-year-olds crawl across in the first case and stay put in the second case. However, if the apparent drop-off is shallow enough to create uncertainty (say, two feet), the infant relies on its mother's facial expressions to decide what to do. In one study, mothers were asked to make either a fearful or a joyful face. When the mothers made a fearful face, no infant crossed the glass floor. But when they made a joyful face, most infants crossed (Sorce et al., 1981). Here is yet another example of the adaptive value of sending, and receiving, emotional communications.

active review Motivation and Emotion

Linkages

As noted in Chapter 1, all of psychology's subfields are related to one another. Our discussion of motivational conflicts and stress illustrates just one way in which the topic of this chapter, motivation and emotion, is linked to the subfield of health, stress, and coping (Chapter 10). The Linkages diagram shows ties to two other subfields as well, and there are many more ties throughout the book. Looking for linkages among subfields will help you see how they all fit together and help you better appreciate the big picture that is psychology.

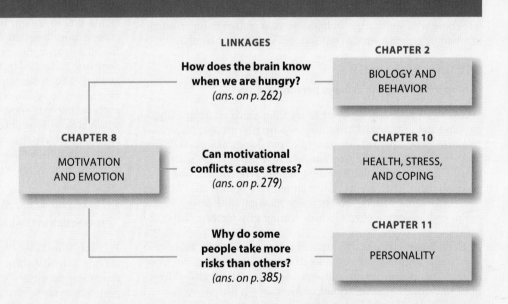

Summary

Motivation refers to factors that influence the initiation, direction, intensity, and persistence of behavior. Emotion and motivation are often linked: Motivation can influence emotion, and people are often motivated to seek certain emotions.

CONCEPTS AND THEORIES OF MOTIVATION

Where does motivation come from?

Focusing on a *motive* often reveals a single theme within apparently diverse behaviors. The many sources of motivation fall into four cate-

gories: biological factors, emotional factors, cognitive factors, and social factors.

An early argument held that motivation follows from *instincts*—automatic, involuntary, and unlearned behavior patterns consistently "released" by particular stimuli. Modern versions of *instinct theory* are seen in evolutionary accounts of helping, aggression, mate selection, and other aspects of social behavior. *Drive reduction theory* is based on *homeostasis*, a tendency to maintain equilibrium in a physical or behavioral process. When disruption of equilibrium creates a *need* of some kind, people are motivated to reduce the resulting *drive* by behaving in some way that satisfies the need and restores balance. *Primary drives* are unlearned; *secondary drives* are learned. According to the *arousal theory* of motivation, people are motivated to behave in ways that maintain a level of *arousal* that is optimal for their functioning. Finally, *incentive theory* highlights behaviors that are motivated by attaining desired stimuli (positive incentives) and avoiding undesirable ones (negative incentives). Each of these theories partially explains where motivation comes from.

HUNGER AND EATING
What makes me start eating, and stop eating?

Hunger and eating are controlled by a complex mix of learning, culture, and biology. The desire to eat *(hunger)* or to stop eating *(satiety)* depends on signals from the stomach and from blood-borne substances such as glucose, fatty acids, insulin, and leptin. Activity in the ventromedial nucleus of the hypothalamus results in satiety, whereas activity in the lateral hypothalamus results in hunger. A variety of neurotransmitters act in various regions of the hypothalamus to create hunger for specific types of foods. These brain regions might be acting in concert to maintain a set point of body weight. Eating may also be influenced by the flavor of food and by appetite for the pleasure of food. Food selection is influenced by many factors, including social contexts and cultural traditions.

Obesity has been linked to overconsumption of certain kinds of foods, low energy metabolism, genetic factors, and even viruses. People suffering from *anorexia nervosa* starve themselves to avoid becoming fat. Those who suffer from *bulimia nervosa* engage in binge eating, followed by purging through self-induced vomiting or laxatives.

SEXUAL BEHAVIOR
How often does the average person have sex?

Sexual motivation and behavior result from a rich interplay of biology and culture. Sexual stimulation generally produces a *sexual response cycle,* a predictable pattern of physiological arousal during and after sexual activity. *Sex hormones,* which include male hormones *(androgens)* and female hormones *(estrogens and progestins),* occur in different relative amounts in both sexes. They can have organizing effects, which create physical differences in the brain, and activating effects, which temporarily increase the desire for sex.

Gender-role learning, educational experiences, media influences, and family dynamics are examples of cultural factors that can bring about variations in sexual attitudes and behaviors. Sexual orientation—*heterosexual, homosexual,* or *bisexual*—is increasingly viewed as a sociocultural variable that affects many other aspects of behavior and mental processes. Although undoubtedly shaped by a lifetime of learning, sexual orientation appears to have strong biological roots.

Common male *sexual dysfunctions* include erectile disorder and premature ejaculation. Females may experience such problems as arousal disorder.

ACHIEVEMENT MOTIVATION
Why do some people try harder than others to succeed?

People gain esteem from achievement in many areas, including the workplace. The motive to succeed is called *need achievement.* Individuals with high achievement motivation strive for excellence, persist despite failures, and set challenging, but realistic, goals.

Workers are most satisfied when they are working toward their own goals and get concrete feedback. Jobs that offer clear and specific goals, a variety of tasks, individual responsibility, and other intrinsic rewards are the most motivating. People tend to have a characteristic level of happiness, or *subjective well-being,* which is not necessarily related to the attainment of money, status, or other material goals.

RELATIONS AND CONFLICTS AMONG MOTIVES
Which motives move me most?

People's behavior reflects many motives, some of which may be in conflict. Maslow proposed a hierarchy of five classes of human motives, from meeting basic biological needs to attaining self-actualization. Motives at the lowest levels, according to Maslow, must be at least partially satisfied before people can be motivated by higher-level goals.

Four basic types of motivational conflict have been identified: approach-approach, avoidance-avoidance, approach-avoidance, and multiple approach-avoidance conflicts. These conflicts act as stressors, and people caught in them often experience physical and psychological problems.

THE NATURE OF EMOTION
How do feelings differ from thoughts?

An *emotion* is a temporary experience with negative or positive qualities that is felt with some intensity as happening to the self, is generated in part by a mental assessment of a situation, and is accompanied by both learned and innate physical responses.

Several brain mechanisms are involved in emotion. The amygdala, in the limbic system, is deeply involved in emotional arousal. The expression of emotion through involuntary facial movement is controlled by the extrapyramidal motor system. Voluntary facial movements are controlled by the pyramidal motor system. The brain's right and left hemispheres play somewhat different roles in emotional expression. In addition to specific brain mechanisms, both the *sympathetic nervous system* and the *parasympathetic nervous system,* which are divisions of the autonomic nervous system, are involved in physiological changes that accompany emotional activation. The *fight-or-flight syndrome,* for example, follows from activation of the sympathetic nervous system.

THEORIES OF EMOTION
Is emotion in the heart, in the head, or both?

William James's theory of emotion holds that physiological responses are the primary source of emotion and that awareness of these responses constitutes emotional experience. James's theory is supported by evidence that, at least for several basic emotions, physiological responses are distinguishable enough for emotions to be generated in this way. Distinct facial expressions are linked to particular patterns of physiological change.

Schachter's refinement of James's theory of emotion suggests that physiological responses are primary sources of emotion but that mental interpretation of these responses in light of the situation is required to label the emotion, a process that depends on *attribution.* Attributing arousal from one situation to stimuli in another situation can produce *transferred excitation,* intensifying the emotion experienced in the second situation.

Cannon's theory of emotion proposes that emotional experience is independent of bodily responses and that there is a direct experience of emotion based on activity of the central nervous system. Updated versions of this theory suggest that various parts of the central nervous system may be involved in different emotions and different aspects of emotional experience. Some pathways in the brain, such as the pathway from the thalamus to the amygdala, allow strong emotions to occur before conscious thought can take place. Specific parts of the brain appear to be responsible for the feelings of pleasure or pain in emotion.

COMMUNICATING EMOTION

Which emotional expressions are innate, and which are learned?

In humans, voice tones, bodily movements, and, mainly, facial movements and expressions are involved in communicating emotions. Darwin suggested that certain facial expressions of emotion are innate and universal, and that these expressions evolved because they effectively communicate one creature's emotional condition to other creatures. Some facial expressions of basic emotions do appear to be innate, and certain facial movements are universally associated with certain emotions.

Other emotional expressions are learned, and even innate expressions are modified by learning and social contexts. As children grow, they learn an emotion culture, the rules of emotional expression appropriate to their culture. Accordingly, the same emotion may be communicated by different facial expressions in different cultures. Especially in ambiguous situations, other people's emotional expressions may serve as a guide about what to do or what not to do, a phenomenon called *social referencing*.

Learn by Doing

Put It in Writing

Write a page or two about what goals you hope to achieve in life, what motivates you to strive for them, and how important it is for you to reach them. In light of our discussion about achievement and subjective well-being, consider the question of whether reaching your goals will make you happy and contented, or leave you always wanting more.

Personal Learning Activity

Videotape a session in which you ask a friend four questions such as: "Who was the best teacher you ever had?" "What's the strangest thing that ever happened to you?" "What is your most surprising talent?" or "Where would you most like to live?" Ask your friend to give truthful answers to two of these questions, but to lie as convincingly as possible while answering the other two. Now play the tape for a group of people, and ask them to say which answers are true and which are lies. How well did your participants do? If they are like most people, they probably were right about half the time on this lie-detection task (DePaulo, 1994). Did those who knew the person on the tape do any better than those who did not? If so, why do you think that happened? *For additional projects, see the five Personal Learning Activities in the corresponding chapter of the study guide that accompanies this text.*

Step into Action

Courses

Health Psychology
Motivation and Emotion
Human Sexuality
Personality
Industrial-Organizational Psychology

Movies

Entrapment; The Edge; Rudy (motivation and motivational conflict)
The Heidi Chronicles (secondary drives)
Wild Reeds (sexual orientation)

Books

David C. Edwards, *Motivation and Emotion: Evolutionary, Physiological, Cognitive, and Social Influences* (AltaMira Press, 1998) (a basic introduction to the field of motivation and emotion)
David Goldstein (Ed.), *The Management of Eating Disorders and Obesity* (Humana Press, 1999) (a summary of research and treatment of eating disorders)
William H. Masters, Virginia E. Johnson, and Robert C. Kolodny, *Heterosexuality* (Grammercy Press, 1998) (an overview of sexuality between males and females)
Jan Clausen and Martin Duberman, *Beyond Gay or Straight: Understanding Sexual Orientation* (Chelsea House, 1996) (an overview of the origins of sexual orientation)
Aldert Vrij, *Detecting Lies and Deceit: The Psychology of Lying and Implications for Professional Practice* (Wiley, 2000) (a summary of various approaches)
David Lykken, *Happiness: The Nature and Nurture of Joy and Contentment* (Griffin, 2000) (a summary of research on the "happiness set point" and other aspects of subjective well-being)

The Web

The World Wide Web is a good source of additional information about the science of psychology, provided you use it carefully and think critically about the information you find. The PsychAbilities web site that accompanies this text offers many resources relevant to this chapter. These resources include interactive NetLab exercises; Thinking Critically and Evaluating Research exercises; ACE chapter quizzes; recommended web links; and articles on current events, books, and movies. At http://college.hmco.com, select *Psychology* and then this textbook.

Review of Key Terms

Can you define each of the key terms in the chapter? Check your definitions against those on the pages listed in parentheses below or in the Glossary/Index at the end of the text.

androgens *(p. 269)*
anorexia nervosa *(p. 265)*
arousal *(p. 260)*
arousal theory *(p. 260)*
attribution *(p. 287)*
bisexual *(p. 270)*
bulimia nervosa *(p. 266)*
drive *(p. 259)*
drive reduction theory *(p. 259)*
emotion *(p. 281)*

estrogens *(p. 269)*
fight-or-flight syndrome *(p. 282)*
heterosexual *(p. 270)*
homeostasis *(p. 259)*
homosexual *(p. 270)*
hunger *(p. 261)*
incentive theory *(p. 260)*
instinct theory *(p. 258)*
instincts *(p. 258)*
motivation *(p. 257)*

motive *(p. 258)*
need *(p. 259)*
need achievement *(p. 274)*
obesity *(p. 264)*
parasympathetic nervous system *(p. 282)*
primary drives *(p. 259)*
progestins *(p. 269)*
satiety *(p. 261)*
secondary drives *(p. 259)*

sex hormones *(p. 269)*
sexual dysfunctions *(p. 273)*
sexual response cycle *(p. 268)*
social referencing *(p. 293)*
subjective well-being *(p. 277)*
sympathetic nervous system *(p. 282)*
transferred excitation *(p. 287)*

Multiple-Choice Self-Test

Select the best answer for each of the questions below. Then check your responses against the Answer Key at the end of the text.

1. Although most researchers do not believe in instinct theories of motivation, psychologists who advocate _____ theory argue that many aspects of human behavior are motivated by a desire to pass on our genes.

   a. drive reduction
   b. evolutionary
   c. arousal
   d. incentive

2. Steve is cold, so he turns up the heat in his house. Soon it gets too warm, so he turns the heat down. This process is similar to the concept of

   a. homeostasis.
   b. secondary drive.
   c. incentive.
   d. arousal.

3. Lisbeth and Harriet work as instructors in an exercise class. After class, Lisbeth prefers to go home and read quietly, whereas Harriet is ready to party. Which theory of motivation best explains this difference?

   a. drive reduction
   b. incentive
   c. evolutionary
   d. arousal

4. Monica wants her daughter to get high grades, so she offers her $10 for each A that she earns and $5 for each B. Monica appears to believe in the _____ theory of motivation.

   a. drive reduction
   b. incentive
   c. evolutionary
   d. arousal

5. Ahmed is desperate to lose weight. To keep from eating, he buys an electrical device that allows him to stimulate the "stop eating" area of his brain. Which brain area should he aim for?

   a. ventromedial nucleus
   b. lateral hypothalamus
   c. paraventricular nucleus
   d. thalamus

6. Ronia is on a diet, again! She is most likely to eat more food if she

   a. eats with a group of friends.
   b. eats by herself.
   c. knows her food culture.
   d. is guided by hunger rather than her appetite.

7. Dr. Stefan is working in the emergency room when a very dehydrated young woman comes in. She is of normal weight, but a medical exam reveals nutritional imbalances and intestinal damage. Which eating disorder is she most likely suffering from?

   a. anorexia nervosa
   b. bulimia nervosa
   c. obesity
   d. ventromedial destruction

8. The University of Chicago's "National Health and Social Life Survey" found that people in the United States

   a. are more sexually active than previously thought.
   b. have sex more often if they are not in a monogamous relationship.
   c. have sex less often and with fewer people than previously thought.
   d. do not enjoy sex very much.

9. Immediately after having orgasms, which of the following will Jim, but not Charlene, be most likely to experience?

   a. another orgasm
   b. a plateau
   c. a refractory period
   d. excitement

10. Edwina wants her son, Egbert, to develop high need achievement and to be successful in life. According to research on need achievement, Edwina should do all of the following *except*

    a. encourage Egbert to try difficult tasks.
    b. encourage Egbert to avoid failure at all costs.
    c. give praise and rewards for success.
    d. read achievement-oriented stories to him.

11. Liang was playing a basketball-shooting game at the school fair. Because there were no prizes, he was allowed to stand anywhere from two to fifteen feet from the basket. The fact that Liang chose to shoot from six feet away suggests that he most likely has

    a. high need achievement.
    b. low need achievement.
    c. high need to avoid success.
    d. high need for affiliation.

12. According to Maslow, which of the following would you most likely do first if you were shipwrecked on a desert island?

    a. look for food and fresh water
    b. look for firewood
    c. establish some form of self-government
    d. build a place to live

13. Jill would like to buy an expensive new stereo, but this would create a financial hardship for her. Jill is faced with a(n) _____ motivational conflict.

    a. approach-approach
    b. avoidance-avoidance
    c. approach-avoidance
    d. multiple approach-avoidance

14. When Debbie received bad news from her fiancé, she experienced the fight-or-flight syndrome. Thus, Debbie's

    a. parasympathetic nervous system was activated.
    b. sympathetic nervous system was activated.
    c. digestion and salivation were stimulated.
    d. respiration and heart rate slowed.

15. When people are afraid to do something, they are said to have "cold feet." The fact that fear *is* indeed associated with decreased blood flow to the feet and hands supports _____ theory of emotion.

    a. James's
    b. Cannon's
    c. Schachter's
    d. Darwin's

16. After she finished a vigorous workout, Lydia saw Thaddeus walk into the gym, and she fell immediately in love. This is an example of _____, which is consistent with _____ theory of emotion.

    a. social referencing; James's
    b. social referencing; Schachter's
    c. transferred excitation; James's
    d. transferred excitation; Schachter's

17. When Yatsira saw someone trying to open her car door while she was stopped at a light, her heart raced, and at the exact same time she felt fear. This is most consistent with _____ theory of emotion.

    a. James's
    b. Cannon's
    c. Schachter's
    d. Darwin's

18. As Jarrod got older, he learned that he could not express his anger by throwing his toys. Jarrod is learning

    a. to use facial feedback.
    b. Darwin's universal rules.
    c. to use social referencing.
    d. an emotion culture.

19. Suppose that Dick, Sally, Harry, and Tommy, the space aliens seen on *Third Rock from the Sun,* first came to earth in your backyard. They tell you they want to learn how to communicate their emotions so that humans will understand them. What should you focus on teaching them?

    a. body postures
    b. facial movements
    c. hand gestures
    d. voice inflections

20. Sam is unsure how to react to a comment from one of his friends, so he glances at his girlfriend, Diane, to see what her reaction is. In doing so, he is using

    a. facial feedback.
    b. social referencing.
    c. attribution.
    d. transferred excitation.

9

Human Development

A colt begins walking within an hour of being born, but it typically takes a human

baby about a year to reach this milestone—a year in which the baby also first smiles, eats solid food, learns to recognize familiar people and objects, and gets ready to talk, to name just a few accomplishments. Four years later, the child is entering school, where learning, development, and change continue. Ten years after that, the adolescent is still changing and developing, becoming more independent and mature with each passing day. In young adulthood, change and development take the form of decisions about jobs, families, and relationships—decisions whose effects echo throughout adulthood. Development occurs in late adulthood, too, as the person adjusts to the joys and challenges of growing older. Developmental psychologists explore how people change, grow, and achieve continuity over the course of the life span.

Reading this chapter will help you to answer the following questions:

▨ **What does "genetic influence" mean?**

▨ **Why should pregnant women stay away from tobacco and alcohol?**

▨ **How do babies think?**

▨ **How do infants become attached to their caregivers?**

▨ **What threatens adolescents' self-esteem?**

▨ **What developmental changes occur in adulthood?**

O ver the last few years, a tragedy was shared by the towns of Springfield, Oregon; Jonesboro, Arkansas; West Paducah, Kentucky; Pearl, Mississippi; Bethel, Alaska; Taber, Alberta; Flint, Michigan; and Littleton, Colorado—the shooting deaths of students and teachers at local schools. With each new incident the cry becomes louder: Why did it happen? In each case, the killers were boys ranging in age from six to eighteen. Had they watched too many violent movies and television shows? Were their actions the fault of a "gun culture" that allows children access to firearms? Had they been victims of abuse and neglect? Were their parents too strict—or not strict enough? Did they come from "broken homes" or witness physical violence within their own families? Did they behave violently because they were going through a difficult "stage," because they had not been taught right from wrong, because they wanted to impress their peers, because males are more aggressive in general, or because their brains were "defective"? Or were they just "bad kids"?

These are the kinds of questions for which developmental psychologists try to find answers. They look into when certain kinds of behavior first appear, how those behaviors change with age, and whether the changes are sudden or gradual. They explore how

A DEADLY CHILD   Andrew Golden was barely out of diapers when he was given camouflage clothing and taught to fire a hunting rifle. In March 1998, at the age of eleven, he and a thirteen-year-old friend, Mitchell Johnson, used their rifles to kill four classmates and a teacher at their elementary school in Jonesboro, Arkansas. Many youngsters learn to hunt; what led these two to commit murder? Researchers in developmental psychology study the genetic and environmental factors that underlie violent aggression and many other patterns of behavior and mental processes.

developmental psychology   The psychological specialty that documents the course of people's social, emotional, moral, and intellectual development over the life span.

maturation   Natural growth or change triggered by biological factors independent of the environment.

development in one area, such as moral reasoning, relates to development in other areas, such as aggressive behavior. Developmental psychologists attempt to discover whether everyone develops at the same rate and, if not, whether slow starters ever catch up to early bloomers. They ask how and why some children develop into well-adjusted, socially competent, caring individuals, whereas others become murderers; or why some adolescents go on to win honors in college and others drop out of high school. They seek to explain how development through infancy, childhood, and adolescence is affected by both genetics and the environment. They analyze the extent to which development is a product of what we arrive with at birth (our inherited, biological *nature*) and the extent to which it is a product of what the world provides (the *nurture* of the environment). And they even pursue the development that occurs over the years of adulthood and try to determine how these changes are related to earlier abilities and the events of life. In short, **developmental psychology** is concerned with the course and causes of developmental changes over a person's entire lifetime.

This chapter focuses on many of these changes, beginning with the physical and biological changes that take place from the moment of conception to the moment of birth.

Exploring Human Development

What does "genetic influence" mean?

Arguments about how nature and nurture affect development can be traced back to philosophers' statements from centuries ago. In essays published in the 1690s, the British empiricist philosopher John Locke argued for the dominance of nurture. He believed that what happens in childhood has a profound and permanent effect on the individual. Empiricists saw the newborn as a blank slate, or *tabula rasa*. Adults write on that slate, said Locke, as they teach children about the world and how to behave in it. About seventy years later, Jean-Jacques Rousseau, a French philosopher, argued just the opposite, claiming that children are capable of discovering how the world operates and how they should behave without instruction from adults. According to Rousseau, children should be allowed to grow as nature commands, with little guidance or pressure from parents.

The first American psychologist to investigate systematically the role of nature in behavior was Arnold Gesell (pronounced "geh-ZELL"). In the early 1900s, Gesell made many observations of children of all ages. He found that motor skills, such as standing and walking, picking up a cube, and throwing a ball, develop in a fixed sequence of stages in all children, as Figure 9.1 illustrates. Gesell argued that the order of the stages and the age at which they appear are determined by nature and relatively unaffected by nurture. Only under extreme conditions, such as famine, war, or poverty, he claimed, are children thrown off their biologically programmed timetable. This type of natural growth or change, which unfolds in a fixed sequence relatively independent of the environment, is called **maturation.** The broader term *development* encompasses not only maturation but also the behavioral and mental processes that are influenced by learning.

John B. Watson disagreed with Gesell's views. He argued that the environment, not nature, molds and shapes development. As described in Chapter 1, Watson founded the behaviorist approach to psychology. In the early 1900s he began conducting experiments with children. From these experiments Watson inferred that children learn *everything*, from skills to fears. In his words, "There is no such thing as an inheritance of capacity, talent, temperament, mental constitution and characteristics. These things . . . depend on training that goes on mainly in the cradle" (J. B. Watson, 1925, pp. 74–75).

The Swiss psychologist Jean Piaget (pronounced "p-ah-ZHAY") first suggested that nature and nurture work together, and that their influences are inseparable and interactive. Through a series of books published from the 1920s until his death in 1980, Piaget's ideas influenced the field of developmental psychology more than those of any other person before or since.

FIGURE 9.1

Motor Development

When did you start walking? The left end of each bar indicates the age at which 25 percent of the infants tested were able to perform the behavior; 50 percent of the babies were performing the behavior at the age indicated by the vertical line in the bars; the right end indicates the age at which 90 percent could do so (Frankenberg & Dodds, 1967). Although different infants, especially in different cultures, achieve milestones of motor development at slightly different ages, all infants—regardless of their ethnicity, social class, or temperament—achieve them in the same order.

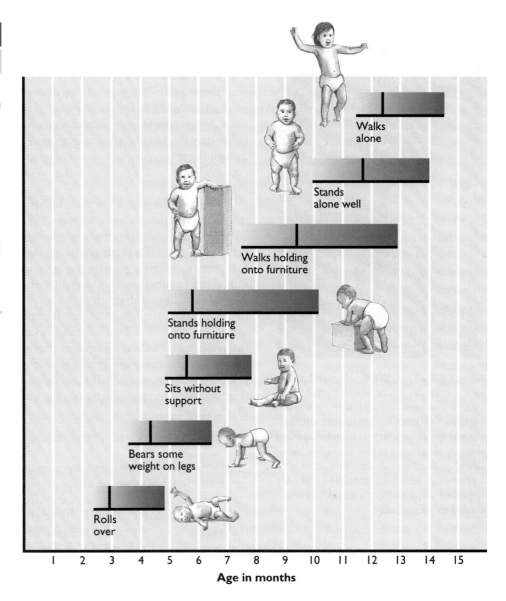

Walks alone

Stands alone well

Walks holding onto furniture

Stands holding onto furniture

Sits without support

Bears some weight on legs

Rolls over

1 2 3 4 5 6 7 8 9 10 11 12 13 14 15

Age in months

Understanding Genetic Influence

Most developmental psychologists now accept Piaget's idea that both nature and nurture contribute to development. Guided by research in **behavioral genetics,** the study of how genes affect behavior, they explore how genes and the environment influence specific aspects of development. Their studies have demonstrated that nature and nurture jointly contribute to development in two ways. First, nature and nurture operate together to make all people *similar* in some respects. For example, nature influences all of us to achieve milestones of motor development in the same order and at roughly the same rate. But supportive nurture, in the form of proper nutrition and exercise, is also necessary to allow normal maturation to unfold. Second, nature and nurture operate together to make each person *unique*. The nature of inherited genes and the nurture of widely different family and cultural environments produce differences among individuals in athletic abilities, intelligence, speech patterns, personality, and many other dimensions (Cross & Markus, 1999; Plomin & Caspi, 1999).

Behavioral geneticists are concerned with these *differences* between individuals or groups of individuals, not with the characteristics of a single individual. Consider height. Whether raised together or apart, identical twins (who have identical genes) are much more similar in height than fraternal twins (who share no more genes than other siblings) or unrelated individuals. This finding suggests that height is more strongly

behavioral genetics   The study of the effect of genes on behavior.

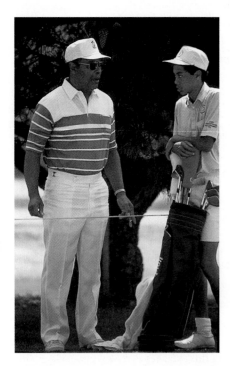

A TIGER IN TRAINING Human behavior develops as a function of both heredity and environment—of both nature and nurture. The joint and inseparable influence of these two factors in development is nicely illustrated in the case of professional golfer Tiger Woods, shown here as a youngster with his father, who not only provided some of Tiger's genes but also served as his golf teacher.

influenced by genes than by the environment. Does this mean that a person who is six feet tall grew four of those feet because of genes and the other two feet because of environment? No. It means that much of the *variability* in height that we see among people can be explained by the genetic differences among them rather than by the environmental differences. In fact, genes do account for about 80 to 95 percent of the variability in height. If a person is, say, shorter than average, genetic reasons are probably the primary cause. We use the term *probably* because determination of a genetic influence on height refers only to the origins of *average* individual differences in the population. So, even though the differences in people's heights are due mainly to genetic factors, a *particular* person's height could be due mainly to an early illness or other growth-stunting environmental factors.

To see how the logic of behavioral genetics applies to conclusions about psychological characteristics, suppose a researcher discovered that a certain personality trait is 50 percent heritable. This finding would mean that approximately half of the *differences between people* on that trait can be explained by genetic factors. It would *not* mean that each person inherits half of the trait and gets the other half from environmental influences. In other words, the results of behavioral genetics research allow us to draw general conclusions about the influence of nature and nurture on certain characteristics, but those conclusions do not necessarily apply to the origins of a *particular* person's characteristics. Keep in mind, too, that the effects of genes on our traits and behaviors are not always simple or inevitable. Complex traits such as intelligence and personality are influenced by many genes, as well as by many environmental factors. So genetic influence means just that: *influence* (Plomin et al., 2000). Genes can affect a trait without completely determining whether that trait will actually appear in a particular individual.

Genes and the Environment

The relative contributions of nature and nurture differ for specific aspects of development, but their influences on *all* human characteristics are forever intertwined. They are also mutually influential. Just as the environment encourages or discourages the expression of an individual's inherited characteristics, those inherited characteristics determine the individual's environment to some extent. In short, heredity creates predispositions that interact with the immediate environment, including family and teachers, books and computers (Plomin & Caspi, 1999). This interaction is what produces developmental outcomes. Let's now consider how it all begins.

Beginnings

■ **Why should pregnant women stay away from tobacco and alcohol?**

Nowhere are the intertwined contributions of heredity and environment clearer than during the eventful nine months before birth, when a single fertilized egg develops into a functioning newborn infant.

Prenatal Development

The process of development begins when sperm from a father-to-be fertilizes the egg of a mother-to-be and forms a brand-new cell. Most human cells contain forty-six **chromosomes** (pronounced "KROH-muh-sohmz"), arranged in twenty-three matching pairs. Each chromosome is made up of thousands of **genes,** the biochemical units of heredity that govern the development of an individual. Genes, in turn, are composed of **deoxyribonucleic acid (DNA).** (*Deoxyribonucleic* is pronounced "dee-OKS-ee-rye-boh-noo-KLAY-ic.") The DNA in genes provides coded messages that serve as blueprints for constructing every aspect of a physical human being, including eye color, height, blood

chromosomes Long, thin structures in every biological cell that contain genetic information in the form of genes.

genes Hereditary units, located on chromosomes, that contain biological instructions inherited from both parents, providing the blueprint for physical development.

deoxyribonucleic acid (DNA) The molecular structure of a gene that provides the genetic code.

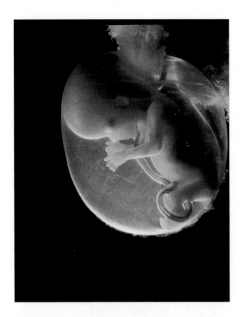

A FETUS AT TWELVE WEEKS At this point in prenatal development, the fetus can kick its legs, curl its toes, make a fist, turn its head, squint, open its mouth, swallow, and take a few "breaths" of amniotic fluid.

type, inherited disorders, and the like. All of this information fits in less space than the period that ends this sentence.

New cells in the body are constantly being produced by the division of existing cells. Most of the body's cells divide through a process called *mitosis* (pronounced "mye-TOH-sis"), in which the cell's chromosomes duplicate themselves so that each new cell contains copies of the twenty-three pairs of chromosomes in the original cell.

A different kind of cell division occurs when a male's sperm cells and a female's egg cells, called *ova,* are formed. This process is called *meiosis* (pronounced "mye-OH-sis"). In meiosis, the chromosome pairs are not copied. Instead, they are randomly split and rearranged, leaving each new sperm and egg cell with just *one* member of each chromosome pair, or twenty-three *single* chromosomes. No two of these special new cells are quite the same, and none contains an exact copy of the person who produced it. So, at conception, when a male's sperm penetrates, or *fertilizes,* the female's ovum, a truly new cell is formed. The fertilized cell, called a *zygote,* carries the usual twenty-three pairs of chromosomes, but half of each pair comes from the mother and half from the father. Thus, the zygote represents a unique heritage—a complete genetic code for a new person that combines randomly selected aspects from both parents. The zygote divides first into copies of itself; then it divides and redivides into the billions of specialized cells that form a complete new human being.

Stages of Prenatal Development   The first two weeks after conception are called the *germinal,* or *zygotic,* stage of development. During this stage, rapidly dividing cells form a *neural tube,* which will become the central nervous system. By the end of the second week of cell division, the zygote has become a cell mass called an **embryo** (pronounced "EM-bree-oh"). During the *embryonic stage* of development, the heart, nervous system, stomach, esophagus, and ovaries or testes form. By two months, when the embryonic stage ends, the embryo looks decidedly human, with eyes, ears, nose, jaw, mouth, and lips. The tiny arms have elbows, hands, and stubby fingers; the legs have knees, ankles, and toes.

The seven-month period remaining until birth is called the *fetal stage* of prenatal development. During this stage, the various organs grow and function more efficiently. By the end of the third month, the **fetus** can kick, make a fist, turn its head, open its mouth, swallow, and frown. In the sixth month, the eyelids, which have been sealed, open. The fetus is now capable of making sucking movements and has a well-developed grasp, taste buds, eyebrows, and eyelashes.

By the end of the seventh month, the organ systems, though immature, are all functional. In the eighth and ninth months, the fetus becomes sensitive to a variety of outside sounds and responds to light and touch. One study showed, for example, that newborns prefer to listen to recordings in the same language—Spanish or English—that they heard from inside the womb as their parents spoke (Moon, Cooper, & Fifer, 1993).

Prenatal Risks   During prenatal development, a spongy organ called the *placenta* sends nutrients from the mother to the developing baby and carries away wastes. It also screens out many potentially harmful substances, including most bacteria. This screening is imperfect, however: Gases, viruses, nicotine, alcohol, and other drugs can pass through. Severe damage can occur if the baby's mother takes certain drugs, is exposed to certain toxic substances, or has certain illnesses while organs are forming in the embryonic stage. A baby whose mother has rubella (German measles) during the third or fourth week after conception has a 50 percent chance of being born blind, deaf, or mentally retarded or of having a heart malformation. If the mother has rubella later in the pregnancy, after the eyes, ears, brain, and heart have formed, the likelihood that the baby will have one of these defects is substantially less.

Harmful substances, such as drugs or radiation, that invade the womb and result in birth defects are called **teratogens** (pronounced "tuh-RAT-uh-jens"). Teratogens are especially damaging in the embryonic stage, because it is a **critical period** in prenatal development, a time during which certain kinds of growth must occur if development is to proceed normally. If the heart, eyes, ears, hands, and feet do not appear during the embryonic stage, they cannot form later on. And if they form incorrectly, the defects will

embryo   The developing individual from two weeks to two months after fertilization.

fetus   The developing individual from the third month after conception until birth.

teratogens   Harmful substances, such as alcohol and other drugs, that can cause birth defects.

critical period   An interval during which certain kinds of growth must occur if development is to proceed normally.

be permanent. Because the embryonic stage begins just two weeks after conception, the organ systems of the embryo can be forming even before the mother is aware of being pregnant. Nevertheless, even accidental exposure to teratogens during the embryonic stage can have devastating effects on the embryo. Later, during the fetal stage, the environment provided by the mother affects the baby's size, behavior, intelligence, and health rather than the formation of organs and limbs.

Critical factors for embryonic and fetal development include the mother's health and age; her nutrition before and during pregnancy; the emotional and physical stresses she experiences; and the nicotine, alcohol, and other drugs she may consume. For example, when a mother-to-be smokes cigarettes, she constricts the flow of blood and oxygen to her baby. The baby's delicate lungs, heart, and circulatory system suffer with each cigarette. Nicotine, a drug contained in tobacco, causes irregular heartbeat and many other harmful effects on the developing baby. No wonder that maternal smoking during pregnancy has been identified as a potential risk factor for low birth weight, respiratory problems, irritability, and attention deficit hyperactivity disorder (Milberger et al., 1997).

Alcohol also threatens normal prenatal development. Babies born to women who abuse alcohol have a 44 percent chance of suffering from **fetal alcohol syndrome,** a pattern of defects that includes mental retardation and malformations of the face. Fetal alcohol syndrome is linked to heavy drinking, but even moderate drinking—a glass or two of wine a day—can harm infants' intellectual functioning (Streissguth et al., 1999). Some research suggests that a woman's eggs can be damaged by alcohol even before she gets pregnant (M. H. Kaufman, 1997).

Of special concern today are the effects of other drugs on infants' development. Pregnant women who use substances such as cocaine create a substantial risk for their fetuses, which do not yet have the enzymes necessary to break down the drug. "Cocaine babies," also called "crack babies," may be born premature, underweight, tense, and fussy (Inciardi, Surratt, & Saum, 1997). They may also suffer delayed physical growth and motor development. Their kidneys, genitals, or other organs may be malformed because the mothers' use of cocaine led to a loss of blood to these developing structures. Research suggests, however, that although "cocaine babies" are more likely to develop behavioral and learning problems, their mental abilities are not all that different from those of any baby born into the impoverished environment typically provided by crack-using mothers (J. M. Johnson et al., 1997). How well they ultimately do in school depends on how supportive their environment turns out to be (Begley, 1997).

The likelihood that harmful conditions and substances will affect a particular infant depends on a combination of (1) the infant's inherited strengths or weaknesses, (2) the stage of prenatal development during which the infant was exposed to a teratogen, and (3) the intensity of the teratogen. Defects are most likely when the negative effects of nature and nurture combine. The worst-case scenario is one in which a genetically vulnerable infant receives a strong dose of a damaging substance during a critical period of prenatal development.

Despite these dangers, mental or physical problems resulting from all harmful factors affect fewer than 10 percent of the babies born in the United States. The vast majority of fetuses are born at the end of their nine-month gestation averaging a healthy seven pounds and ready to continue a normal course of development in the world.

The Newborn

Determining what newborns can see, hear, or do is one of the most fascinating and frustrating challenges of conducting research in developmental psychology. Babies are extremely difficult to study because they sleep about 70 percent of the time. When they are not sleeping, they are drowsy, crying, awake and active, or awake and inactive. It is only when they are in this last state, which is infrequent and lasts only a few minutes, that researchers can assess the infants' abilities.

To do so, psychologists show the infants objects or pictures and record where they look and for how long. They film the infants' eye movements and note changes in heart

fetal alcohol syndrome   A pattern of defects found in babies born to women who drink heavily during pregnancy.

A BABY'S-EYE VIEW OF THE WORLD
The photograph at left simulates what a mother looks like to her infant at three months of age. Although their vision is blurry, infants particularly seem to enjoy looking at faces.

rates, sucking rates, brain waves, bodily movements, and skin conductance (a measure of perspiration associated with emotion) when objects are shown or sounds are made. From studies using these techniques, researchers have pieced together a fair picture of infants' sensory and motor abilities (Kellman & Banks, 1998).

Vision and Other Senses   At birth, infant vision is limited by immaturities in both the eye and the brain. Infants' eyes do not yet have a fovea, which is the retinal area on which images are focused. Their eye movements are slow and jerky. And pathways in the nervous system connecting the eye to the brain remain inefficient, as does the processing of visual information within the brain. Researchers estimate that the newborn has 20:300 eyesight; that is, an object 20 feet away looks the same to a newborn as it would if viewed from 300 feet by an adult with normal vision. Infants thus cannot see small objects across the room, and their vision is blurry. However, they can see large objects up close—the distance at which most interactions with caregivers take place. Infants look longest at what they can see best: large patterns with the most elements, the most movement, the clearest contours, and the greatest amount of contrast.

Newborns actively use their senses to explore the world around them. At first they attend to sights and sounds for only short periods, but gradually their attention span lengthens, and their exploration becomes more systematic. In the first two months, they focus only on the edges of objects, but after two months of age, they scan whole objects (Banks & Salapatek, 1983). Then, when they see an object, they get all the information they can from it before going on to something new (M. A. Hunter & Ames, 1988). Newborns stare at human faces longer than at other figures (Valenza et al., 1996), and their eyes follow moving face-like drawings (M. A. Johnson et al., 1991).

At two or three days of age, newborns can hear soft voices and notice differences between tones about one note apart on the musical scale (Aslin, Jusczyk, & Pisoni, 1998). In addition, they turn their heads toward sounds (Clifton, 1992). But their hearing is not as sharp as that of adults' until well into childhood. This condition is not merely a hearing problem; it also reflects an inability to *listen* selectively to some sounds over others (Bargones & Werner, 1994). As infants grow, they develop sensory capacities *and* the skill to use them.

Infants pay special attention to speech. When they hear someone talking, they open their eyes wider and search for the speaker. Infants also prefer certain kinds of speech. They like rising tones spoken by women or children (J. W. Sullivan & Horowitz, 1983). They also like high-pitched, exaggerated, and expressive speech. In other words, they like to hear the *baby talk* used by most adults in all cultures when talking to babies (Fernald, 1990).

Newborns also like certain smells and tastes better than others. When given something sweet to drink, they suck longer and slower, pause for shorter periods, and smile and lick their lips (Ganchrow, Steiner, & Daher, 1983). Within a few days after birth, breastfed babies prefer the odor of their own mother to that of another mother (Cernoch & Porter, 1985).

Reflexes and Motor Skills   In the first weeks and months after birth, babies show involuntary, unlearned reactions called **reflexes.** These swift, automatic movements occur in

reflexes   Simple, involuntary, unlearned behaviors directed by the spinal cord without instructions from the brain.

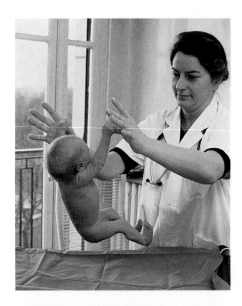

FIGURE 9.2

Reflexes in the Newborn

When a finger is pressed into a newborn's palm, the *grasping reflex* causes the infant to hold on tightly enough to suspend its entire weight. And when a newborn is held upright over a flat surface, the *stepping reflex* leads to walking movements.

response to external stimuli. Figure 9.2 illustrates the *grasping reflex,* one of more than twenty reflexes that have been observed in newborn infants. Another is the *rooting reflex,* whereby the infant turns its mouth toward a finger or nipple that touches its cheek. And the newborn exhibits the *sucking reflex* in response to anything that touches its lips. Many of these reflexive behaviors evolved because they help infants to survive. The absence of reflexes in a newborn signals problems in brain development. So does failure of reflexes to disappear as brain development during the first three or four months allows the infant to control muscles voluntarily.

Voluntary control permits the development of motor skills, allowing the infant to roll over, sit up, crawl, stand, and walk. Until a few years ago, most developmental psychologists accepted Gesell's view that except under extreme environmental conditions, these motor abilities occur spontaneously as the central nervous system and muscles mature. Research demonstrates, however, that maturation does not tell the whole story, even in normal environments (Thelen, 1995).

Psychologists have discovered, for example, that motor development depends on infants' active experimentation. In one study, researchers observed six infants as they learned to crawl on their hands and knees (Freedland & Bertenthal, 1994). Once they had developed sufficient muscle strength to support their abdomens, the infants tried various crawling styles—moving backward, moving one limb at a time, using the arms only, and so on. After a week or two of trial and error, all six infants arrived at the same method: moving the right arm and left leg together, then the left arm and right leg. This pattern turned out to be the most efficient way of getting around quickly without tipping over. Such observations suggest that the brain does not have a "crawling generator" that programs exactly how and when infants crawl. Instead, as maturation increases infants' strength and readiness, they try out various motor patterns and select the ones that work best (C. A. Nelson, 1999).

We know of a mother who tried to teach her infant, Rob, to crawl because he was not learning on his own. First she built a ramp surrounded by pillows for him to inch down. Placing Rob at the top of the gentle slope, she hoped gravity would help him move. No luck. Then she built a padded skateboard and put Rob on it with a safety belt so that his arms dangled to the floor. Did he paddle along and get the mobility idea? No, he threw up on the skateboard. In desperation, his mother asked her pediatrician why Rob did not crawl. The answer: Rob was at the 90th percentile for height and the 95th percentile for weight, so his body was simply too heavy for his immature arm muscles to support. His maturation had increased his readiness, but he didn't have the strength to try out motor patterns for crawling. This was one milestone he (and his mother) would just have to miss. Rob never crawled, but he started walking—and running—on his first birthday!

In short, milestones of motor development result from a combination of maturation and experience, not from the unfolding of a sequence that is genetically etched in the brain. And, as always, nature and nurture influence each other. The brain controls developing behavior, but its own development is affected by experience, including efforts at building motor skills.

Infancy and Childhood: Cognitive Development

■ **How do babies think?**

In a relatively short time, a tiny infant becomes a person who can read a book, write a poem, and argue logically for a new computer game. What leads to the dramatic shifts in thinking, knowing, and remembering that occur between early infancy and later childhood? Researchers studying *cognitive development* try to answer this question.

TABLE 9.1

Piaget's Periods of
Cognitive Development

According to Piaget, a predictable set of features characterizes each period of children's cognitive development. Note that the ages associated with the stages are approximate; Piaget realized that some children move through the stages slightly faster or slower than others.

Period	Activities and Achievements
Sensorimotor Birth–2 years	Infants discover aspects of the world through their sensory impressions, motor activities, and coordination of the two. They learn to differentiate themselves from the external world. They learn that objects exist even when they are not visible and that they are independent of the infant's own actions. Infants gain some appreciation of cause and effect.
Preoperational 2–4 years 4–7 years	Children cannot yet manipulate and transform information in logical ways, but they now can think in images and symbols. They become able to represent something with something else, acquire language, and play games of pretend. Intelligence at this stage is said to be intuitive, because children cannot make general, logical statements.
Concrete operational 7–11 years	Children can understand logical principles that apply to concrete external objects. They can appreciate that certain properties of an object remain the same, despite changes in appearance, and they can sort objects into categories. They can appreciate the perspective of another viewer. They can think about two concepts, such as longer and wider, at the same time.
Formal operational Over 11 years	Only adolescents and adults can think logically about abstractions, can speculate, and can consider what might or what ought to be. They can work in probabilities and possibilities. They can imagine other worlds, especially ideal ones. They can reason about purely verbal or logical statements. They can relate any element or statement to any other, manipulate variables in a scientific experiment, and deal with proportions and analogies. They can reflect on their own activity of thinking.

The Development of Knowledge: Piaget's Theory

Foremost among these researchers was Jean Piaget, who dedicated his life to a search for the origins of intelligence and the factors that lead to changes in knowledge over the life span. Piaget was the first to chart the journey from the simple reflexes of the newborn to the complex understandings of the adolescent. Although his theory turned out to be incomplete, and in some respects incorrect, his ideas about cognitive development are still guiding research (J. H. Flavell, 1996).

Intensive observations of infants (including his own) and extensive interviews with children led Piaget to propose that cognitive development proceeds in a series of distinct stages, or periods. He believed that all children's thinking goes through the same stages, in the same order, without skipping. (Table 9.1 outlines these stages.) Thus, according to Piaget, the thinking of infants is different from the thinking of children, which in turn is different from that of adolescents. He said that children are not just miniature adults, and they are not dumber than adults; they just think in completely different ways at different stages of development. Entering each stage involves a *qualitative* change from whatever preceded it, much as a caterpillar is transformed into a butterfly.

FIGURE 9.3

Accommodation

Because the bars of the playpen are in the way, this child discovers that her schema for grasping and pulling objects toward her will not work. Thus she adjusts, or accommodates, her schema to achieve her goal.

FIGURE 9.3

Accommodation

Because the bars of the playpen are in the way, this child discovers that her schema for grasping and pulling objects toward her will not work. Thus she adjusts, or accommodates, her schema to achieve her goal.

schemas   Mental representations of what we know and expect about the world.

assimilation   The process of taking in new information about objects by using existing schemas on objects that fit those schemas.

accommodation   The process of modifying schemas as an infant tries out familiar schemas on objects that do not fit them.

sensorimotor period   According to Piaget, the first stage of cognitive development, when the infant's mental activity is confined to sensory perception and motor skills.

Building Blocks of Development   To explain how infants and children move to ever higher stages of understanding and knowledge, Piaget introduced the concept of schemas as the basic units of knowledge, the building blocks of intellectual development. As noted in Chapters 3 and 6, **schemas** are the mental images or generalizations that form as people experience the world. Schemas, in other words, organize past experiences and provide a framework for understanding future experiences.

At first, infants form simple schemas. For example, a sucking schema consolidates their experiences of sucking into images of what objects can be sucked on (bottles, fingers, pacifiers) and what kinds of sucking can be done (soft and slow, speedy and vigorous). Later, children form more complex schemas, such as a schema for tying a knot or making a bed. Still later, adolescents form schemas about what it is to be in love.

Two complementary processes guide this development: assimilation and accommodation. In **assimilation,** infants and children take in information about new objects by trying out existing schemas and finding schemas that the new objects will fit. They *assimilate* the new objects into their existing schemas. So a baby boy given a new toy will suck on it and wave it. In doing so, he discovers that this toy, like his familiar rattle, is suckable and waveable. Now suppose a toddler encounters a large dog. How she assimilates this new experience depends on her existing schema of dogs. If she has had positive experiences with the family dog, she will have a positive schema, and expecting the dog to behave like her pet, she will greet it happily. Thus, past experiences affect what and how children think about new ones.

Sometimes, like Cinderella's sisters squeezing their oversized feet into the glass slipper, people distort information about a new object to make it fit an existing schema. When squeezing won't work, though, people are forced to change, or accommodate, their schemas to the new objects. In **accommodation,** the person tries out familiar schemas on a new object, finds that the schemas cannot be made to fit the object, and changes the schemas so that they will fit (see Figure 9.3). So if we now give our little boy a cup, he will again suck on it and wave it. But he soon discovers that he can put only the edge in his mouth, and to wave it, it is best to hold onto the handle. Similarly, the toddler will refine her "doggie" schema if she meets a snarling stray and discovers that her original schema does not extend to all dogs.

Sensorimotor Development   Piaget (1952) called the first stage of cognitive development the **sensorimotor period,** a time when mental activity is confined to schemas about sen-

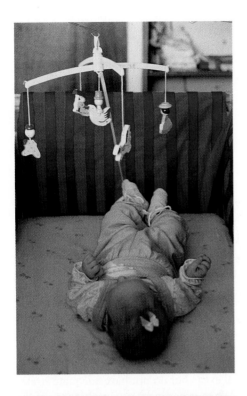

Infant Memory

This infant has learned to move a mobile by kicking her left foot, which is tied to the mobile with a ribbon. Even a month later, the baby will show recognition of this particular mobile by kicking more vigorously when she sees it than when she sees another one.

sory functions, such as seeing and hearing, and to schemas about motor skills, such as grasping and sucking. As motor skills develop and voluntary actions replace reflexes, babies elaborate these simple schemas into complex ones, such as waving and shaking. Later schemas include inserting and building.

Piaget believed that during the sensorimotor stage, infants can form schemas only of objects and actions that are present—things they can see, hear, or touch. They cannot think about absent objects, he said, because they cannot act on them; thinking, for infants, is doing. They do not lie in the crib thinking about Mother or their teddy bear, because they are not yet able to form schemas that are mental representations of objects and actions that are not present.

The sensorimotor period ends when infants *can* form such mental representations. At that point, they can think about objects or actions when the objects are not visible or the actions are not occurring. This milestone, according to Piaget, frees the child from the here-and-now of the sensory environment. It allows for the development of thought. One sign of this milestone is the child's ability to find a hidden object. This behavior reflects the infant's knowledge that an object exists even if it cannot be seen, touched, or sucked. Piaget called this knowledge **object permanence.**

Before they acquire a knowledge of object permanence, infants do not search for objects that are placed out of sight. According to Piaget, out of sight is literally out of mind. The first evidence that object permanence is developing, he said, appears when infants are four to eight months old. At this age, for the first time, they can recognize a familiar object even if part of it is hidden: They know it's their bottle even if they can see only the nipple peeking out from under the blanket. Infants now have some primitive mental representations of objects. If an object is completely hidden, however, they will not search for it.

Several months later, infants will search briefly for a hidden object, but their search is haphazard and ineffective. Not until they are about eighteen to twenty-four months old, said Piaget, do infants appear able to picture and follow events in their minds. They look for the object in places other than where they saw it last, sometimes in completely new places. According to Piaget, their concept of object permanence is now fully developed. They have a mental representation of the object that is completely separate from their immediate perception of it.

New Views on Infant Cognition   In the past forty years, researchers have discovered that infants know a lot more, and know it sooner, than Piaget thought they did. It isn't that infants are smarter now; rather, psychologists have found smarter ways to measure what is going on in infants' minds. Modern advances allow researchers to use infrared photography to record infants' eye movements, time-lapse photography to detect subtle hand movements, and special equipment to measure and analyze infants' sucking rates.

By combining this equipment with advanced computer technology, researchers have found that infants in the sensorimotor period are doing more than just sensing and moving; they are thinking as well. They are not just experiencing isolated sights and sounds but combining these experiences. In one study, for example, infants were shown two different videotapes at the same time, while the soundtrack for only one of them came from a speaker placed between the TV monitors. The infants tended to look at the video that went with the soundtrack—at a toy bouncing in synch with a tapping sound, at Dad's face when his voice was on the audio, or at an angry face when an angry voice was heard (Soken & Pick, 1992). Infants remember, too. Babies as young as two to three months of age can recall a mobile that was hung over their crib a few days before (Rovee-Collier, 1993; see Figure 9.4).

Although Piaget's methods were not sensitive enough to reveal it, young babies even seem to have a sense of object permanence. Piaget had required infants to demonstrate object permanence by making effortful responses, such as removing a cover that had been placed over an object. Today, researchers recognize that finding a hidden object under a cover requires several abilities: mentally representing the hidden object, figuring out where it might be, and pulling off the cover. Piaget's tests did not allow for the

object permanence   The knowledge that an object exists even when it is not in view.

(A)

(B)

(C)

(D)

Source: Baillargeon (1992).

FIGURE 9.5

Events Demonstrating Infants' Knowledge of Physics

Infants look longer at things that interest them—that is, at new things rather than things they have seen before and find boring. In her research on the development of knowledge, Renee Baillargeon (1995) has found that physically impossible events B and C—made possible by an experimenter's reaching through a hidden door to support a moving box—attract the most attention from infants. These results suggest that humans understand some basic laws of physics quite early in life.

possibility that infants *know* a hidden object still exists but do not have adequate strategies for finding it (Ahmed & Ruffman, 1998). When experimenters simply turn off the lights in a room, infants as young as five months of age have reached for now-unseen objects in the dark (Clifton et al., 1991).

Developmental psychologists generally agree that infants develop some mental representations earlier than Piaget suggested. However, they disagree about whether this knowledge is "programmed" in infants (Spelke et al., 1992), develops quickly through interactions with the outside world (Baillargeon, 1995), or is constructed through the recombination of old schemas into new ones (K. W. Fischer & Bidell, 1991).

FOCUS ON RESEARCH

What Do Infants Know About Physics?

Whether you realize it or not, you have quite a storehouse of knowledge about physics. You know about gravity and balance, for example. At what age did you understand that "what goes up must come down" and that an unbalanced tray will tip over?

■ What was the researcher's question?

Renee Baillargeon (1994a, 1994b) used a creative experimental method to explore infants' knowledge about objects, including their understanding of the principles of gravity. She wanted to find out if very young infants possess some of the same fundamental beliefs about objects that adults do. For example, do they know that unsupported objects will fall?

■ How did the researcher answer the question?

In one series of studies, Baillargeon (pronounced "by-er-ZHAN") showed infants a red-gloved hand pushing a box from left to right along the top of a platform. On some trials, they saw physically possible events, as when the hand pushed the box to the edge of the platform or held onto the object as it went beyond the edge of the platform; see events A and D in Figure 9.5. On other trials, they saw physically impossible events, as when the hand pushed the box until only the end of its bottom surface rested on the platform or went beyond the platform; see events B and C in the figure. Baillargeon measured the length of time the infants looked at the objects in each event. Trials continued until the infants had seen at least four pairs of possible and impossible events in alternating order.

What did the researcher find?

Baillargeon found that three-month-old infants looked longest at impossible event C, where the box was entirely off the platform. They were not particularly interested in event D, where the box was held by the gloved hand; in event A, where the box was still on the platform; or even in event B, where only the end of the box rested on the platform. At six-and-a-half months of age, however, infants stared intently at event B.

What do the results mean?

According to Baillargeon (1998), these results suggest that the three-month-olds knew something about physical support. They expected the box to fall if it was entirely off the platform and acted surprised when it did not. But they did not yet know that a box should fall if its center of gravity is unsupported, as in event B. By six-and-a-half months of age, they had apparently developed this understanding.

What do we still need to know?

Baillargeon may have demonstrated that very young infants possess fundamental knowledge about the world that implies an understanding of complex physical principles. But a question remains: Does an infant's tendency to stare longer at a particular sight necessarily indicate "surprise," or could it mean that babies simply recognize that certain images are different from, or more interesting than, things they have seen before (Bogartz, Shinskey, & Speaker, 1997). The answer to this question will require further research using varied visual stimuli that allow researchers to determine whether infants stare longer at physically possible events that are just as novel and vivid as physically impossible events.

Researchers also want to discover *how* babies know about physics (Wynn & Chiang, 1998). Does it develop from their experience with objects, or is the knowledge innate? In an attempt to answer this question, Baillargeon randomly assigned infants, ranging from three to six-and-a-half months old, to receive either normal or extra experience with objects. She then observed the effect on the infants' understanding of gravity. After only a few demonstrations in which unsupported objects fell off platforms, infants in the extra-experience group were surprised when an unsupported object did not fall. Other studies found similar results (Needham & Baillargeon, 1999). It is still too early to say for sure whether Baillargeon's hypothesis about the importance of experience in developing knowledge is correct. However, the next time you see an infant stacking blocks and watching them fall, consider the possibility that you are watching a little scientist testing hypotheses about the workings of the universe.

Preoperational Development According to Piaget, the **preoperational period** follows the sensorimotor stage of development. During the first half of this period, he observed, children begin to understand, create, and use *symbols* that represent things that are not present. They draw, pretend, and talk.

Using and understanding symbols opens up a new world for two- to four-year-olds. At two, for the first time, children are able to play "pretend," perhaps using a finger to stand for a magic sword. They can watch a television show one day and, on the next, imitate what they saw. Before this age, Piaget noted, children imitate what they see at the moment, but not what they saw earlier. At the age of three or four, children can symbolize complex roles and events as they play house, doctor, or superhero. They can

preoperational period According to Piaget, the second stage of cognitive development, during which children begin to understand, create, and use symbols that represent things that are not present.

During the second half of the preoperational period, according to Piaget, children believe that inanimate objects are alive and have intentions, feelings, and consciousness.

"I think the moon likes us. It keeps on followin' us."

appreciate the symbolic value of a miniature model. In one study, for example, three-year-olds shown a scale-model room with a miniature dog hidden behind a miniature sofa could then find an actual stuffed dog in a real room (DeLoache, Miller, & Rosengren, 1997).

During the second half of the preoperational stage, according to Piaget, four- to seven-year-olds begin to make intuitive guesses about the world. However, Piaget observed that they cannot tell the difference between imagination and reality. Thus, in interviews with Piaget, children in this age range claimed that dreams are real and take place outside of themselves as "pictures on the window," "a circus in the room," or "something from the sky." They described inanimate objects as being alive and having intentions, feelings, and consciousness. The clouds go slowly, the children said, because they have no paws or legs. Flowers grow because they want to. Empty cars feel lonely.

Children's thinking at this stage is so dominated by what they can see and touch for themselves that they do not realize something is the same if its appearance is changed. In one study, for example, preoperational children thought that a cat wearing a dog mask was actually a dog, because that's what it looked like (DeVries, 1969). In short, these children do not yet have what Piaget called **conservation,** the ability to recognize that important properties of a substance or a person remain constant despite changes in shape or appearance.

In one test of conservation, Piaget showed children water from each of two equal-sized glasses being poured into either a tall, thin glass or a short, wide one. They were then asked if one glass contained more water than the other. Children at the preoperational stage of development guessed that one glass (usually the taller one) contained more. They were dominated by the evidence of their eyes. If the glass looked bigger, then they thought it contained more.

Children at this stage do not understand the logic of *reversibility*—that if you just poured the water from one container to another, you can pour it back, and it will be the same amount. The concept of *complementarity*—that one glass is taller but narrower, and the other is shorter but wider—also escapes them. They focus on only one dimension at a time—the most obvious or important one—and make their best intuitive guess. In fact, Piaget named this stage *preoperational* because children at this stage do not yet understand logical mental *operations* such as reversibility and complementarity.

conservation   The ability to recognize that the important properties of a substance, such as number, volume, or weight, remain constant despite changes in shape, length, or position.

TESTING FOR CONSERVATION If you know a child who is between the ages of four and seven, get parental permission to test the child for what Piaget called *conservation*. Show the child two identical lumps of clay, and ask which lump is bigger. The child will probably say they are the same. Now roll one lump into a long "rope," and again ask which lump is bigger. If the child says that they are still the same, this is evidence of conservation. If the longer one is seen as bigger, conservation has not yet developed—at least not for this task. The older the child, the more likely it is that conservation will appear, but some children display conservation much earlier than Piaget thought was possible.

Concrete Operational Thought At some time around the age of six or seven, Piaget observed, children do develop the ability to conserve number and amount. When they do so, they enter what he called the stage of **concrete operations.** Now, he said, they can count, measure, add, and subtract. Their thinking is no longer dominated by the appearance of things. They can use simple logic and perform simple mental manipulations and mental operations on things. They can sort objects into classes (such as tools, fruit, and vehicles) or series (such as largest to smallest) by systematic searching and ordering.

Still, concrete operational children can perform their logical operations only on real, concrete objects, such as sticks, glasses, tools, and fruit—not on abstract concepts, such as justice or freedom. They can reason only about what is, not about what is possible. The ability to think logically about abstract ideas comes in the next stage of cognitive development. This *formal operational period* occurs during adolescence, which we discuss later in the chapter.

Modifying Piaget's Theory

Piaget's observations and demonstrations of children's cognitive development are vivid and fascinating. He was right in pointing out that there are significant shifts with age in children's thinking and that thinking becomes more systematic, consistent, and integrated as children get older. His idea that children are active explorers and constructors of knowledge, not passive recipients of input from the environment, influenced our contemporary views of child development. Piaget also inspired other psychologists to test his findings and theory with experiments of their own. The results of these experiments suggest that Piaget's theory needs some modification.

What needs to be modified most is Piaget's notion of developmental stages. Several studies have shown that changes from one stage to the next are less consistent and global than Piaget had described them. For example, three-year-olds *can* sometimes make the distinction between physical and mental phenomena; they know the characteristics of real dogs versus pretend dogs (Woolley, 1997). Children of this age can even succeed at conservation tasks if they are allowed to count the number of objects or have been trained to focus on relevant dimensions such as number, height, and width (Gelman & Baillargeon, 1983).

concrete operations According to Piaget, the third stage of cognitive development, during which children can learn to count, measure, add, and subtract.

Taken together, these studies suggest that children's knowledge and mental strategies develop at different ages in different areas, and in "pockets" rather than at global levels of understanding (Sternberg, 1989). Knowledge in particular areas is demonstrated sooner in children who are given specific experience in those areas or who are faced with very simple questions and tasks. Thus, children's reasoning depends not only on their general level of development but also on (1) how easy the task is, (2) how familiar they are with the objects involved, (3) how well they understand the language being used, and (4) what experiences they have had in similar situations (Siegal, 1997). Research has also shown that the level of a child's thinking varies from day to day and may even shift when the child solves the same problem twice in the same day (Siegler, 1994).

In summary, psychologists are now beginning to think of cognitive development in terms of rising and falling "waves," not fixed stages—that is, in terms of changing frequencies in children's use of different ways of thinking, not sudden, permanent shifts from one way of thinking to another (Siegler, 1995). Psychologists suggest that children systematically try out many different solutions to problems and gradually come to select the best of them.

Information Processing During Childhood

An alternative to Piaget's theory of cognitive development is based on the concept of information processing described in Chapters 6 and 7. The **information-processing** approach to development describes cognitive activities in terms of how people take in information, use it, and remember it. Developmental psychologists taking this approach focus on gradual quantitative changes in children's mental capacities, rather than on qualitative advances or stages in development.

Research by these psychologists demonstrates that as children get older, their information-processing skills gradually get better. Older children have longer attention spans. They take in information and shift their attention from one task to another more rapidly. They are also more efficient in processing information once it is received (L. T. Miller & Vernon, 1997).

Children's memory storage capacity also markedly improves (W. Schneider & Bjorklund, 1998). Preschoolers can keep only two or three pieces of information in mind at the same time; older children can remember more. Children's memory capacities get larger every year, though only up to a point. As noted in Chapter 6, even most adults can hold only about seven pieces of information in short-term memory at any one time.

We don't yet know exactly what causes these increases in children's attention, information processing, and memory capacities. A full explanation will undoubtedly include both nature (specifically, maturation of the brain) and nurture (including increased familiarity with the information to be processed and memorized). Researchers have observed that the cognitive abilities of children improve dramatically when they are dealing with familiar rather than unfamiliar material. In one experiment, Mayan children in Mexico lagged behind their age-mates in the United States on standard memory tests of pictures and nouns. But they did a lot better when researchers gave them a more familiar task, such as recalling miniature objects in a model of a Mayan village (Rogoff & Waddell, 1982).

Better memorization strategies may also help account for the improvement in children's memories. To a great extent, children learn these strategies in school. They learn how to memorize and how to study. They learn to repeat information over and over to help fix it in memory, to place information into categories, and to use other memory aids to help them remember.

After about age seven, schoolchildren are also better at remembering more complex and abstract information. Their memories are more accurate, extensive, and well organized. The knowledge they have accumulated allows them to draw more inferences and to integrate new information into a more complete network of facts. (See "In Review: Milestones of Cognitive Development in Infancy and Childhood").

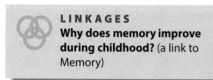

LINKAGES
Why does memory improve during childhood? (a link to Memory)

information processing   The process of taking in, remembering or forgetting, and using information.

in review

Milestones of Cognitive Development in Infancy and Childhood		
Age*	**Achievement**	**Description**
3–4 months	Maturation of senses	Immaturities that limit the newborn's vision and hearing are overcome.
	Voluntary movement	Reflexes disappear, and infants begin to gain voluntary control over their movements.
12–18 months	Mental representation	Infants can form images of objects and actions in their minds.
	Object permanence	Infants understand that objects exist even when out of sight.
18–24 months	Symbolic thought	Young children use symbols to represent things that are not present in their pretend play, drawing, and talk.
4 years	Intuitive thought	Children reason about events, real and imagined, by guessing rather than by engaging in logical analysis.
6–7 years	Concrete operations Conservation	Children can apply simple logical operations to real objects. For example, they recognize that important properties of a substance, such as number or amount, remain constant despite changes in shape or position.
7–8 years	Information processing	Children can remember more information; they begin to learn strategies for memorization.

*These ages are approximate; they indicate the order in which children first reach these milestones of cognitive development rather than the exact ages.

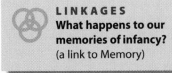

LINKAGES
What happens to our memories of infancy?
(a link to Memory)

LINKAGES

Development and Memory

The ability to remember facts, figures, pictures, and objects improves as we get older and more expert at processing information. But take a minute right now and try to recall anything that happened to you when you were, say, one year old. Most people can accurately recall a few autobiographical memories from age five or six but remember virtually nothing from before the age of three (W. Schneider & Bjorklund, 1998).

Psychologists have not yet found a fully satisfactory explanation for this "infantile amnesia." Some have suggested that young children lack the memory encoding and storage processes described in Chapter 6. Yet children of two or three can clearly recall experiences that happened weeks or even months earlier (Bauer, 1996). Others suggest that infantile amnesia occurs because very young children lack a sense of self. Because they don't even recognize themselves in the mirror, they may not have a framework for organizing memories about what happens to them (Howe, 1995). However, this explanation would hold for only the first two years or so, because after that, children do recognize their own faces, and even their taped voices (Legerstee, Anderson, & Schaffer, 1998).

Another possibility is that early memories, though "present," are implicit rather than explicit. As mentioned in Chapter 6, *implicit memories* form automatically and can affect our emotions and behavior even when we do not consciously recall them. Note, however, that children's implicit memories of their early years, like their explicit memories, are quite limited. For example, Nora Newcombe and Nathan Fox (1994) showed photographs of young children to a group of ten-year-olds. Some of the photos were of preschool classmates whom the participants had not seen since they were five years old. They explicitly recalled 21 percent of their former classmates, and their skin conductance (a measure of emotion) indicated that they had implicit memories of an additional 5 percent. Yet these youngsters had no memory of 74 percent of their preschool pals. Adults, however, can correctly identify 90 percent of photographs of high-school classmates they have not seen for thirty years (Bahrick, Bahrick, & Wittlinger, 1975).

Other explanations of infantile amnesia suggest that our early memories are lost because we do not yet have the language skills to talk about, and thus solidify, those memories (Hudson & Sheffield, 1998). Still others say that early memories are stored, but because the schemas we used in early childhood to mentally represent them have changed, we no longer have the retrieval cues necessary to recall them. A related possibility is that early experiences tend to be fused into *generalized event representations,* such as "going to Grandma's" or "playing at the beach," so that it becomes difficult to remember any specific event. Research on hypotheses such as these is beginning to unravel the mystery of infantile amnesia (Eacott, 1999; Newcombe et al., 2000; Rovee-Collier, 1999).

Culture and Cognitive Development

Whereas Piaget focused on the physical world of objects in explaining development, Russian psychologist Lev Vygotsky (1991) focused on the social world of people. He viewed the human mind as a product of cultural history. The child's mind, said Vygotsky, grows through contact with other minds. It is through interaction with parents, teachers, and other representatives of their culture that children acquire the ideas of that culture.

Researchers in the West have pursued Vygotsky's ideas by studying the effects of the social world on children's development. For example, Katherine Nelson (1986) has studied how participation in social routines affects children's developing knowledge of the world. In North American culture, such routines include shopping, eating at McDonald's, going to birthday parties, and attending religious services. In another culture they might include helping to make pottery, going hunting, and weaving baskets (R. W. Larson & Verma, 1999). Quite early, children develop mental representations, called *scripts,* for these activities (as described in Chapter 7). By the time they are three, children can describe routine activities quite accurately. Scripts, in turn, affect children's knowledge and understanding of cognitive tasks.

Children's cognitive abilities are also influenced by the language of their culture. Korean and Chinese children, for instance, show exceptional ability at adding and subtracting large numbers (K. F. Miller et al., 1995). As third-graders, they do in their heads three-digit problems (such as 702 minus 125) that their peers in the United States labor over or fail to solve. The difference seems traceable in part to the clear and explicit words that Asian languages use for the numbers from eleven to nineteen. In English, the meaning of the words *eleven* and *twelve,* for instance, is not as clear as the Asian *ten-one* and *ten-two.* Moreover, Asians use the abacus and the metric system of measurement, both of which are structured around the number ten. Korean math textbooks emphasize this tens structure by presenting the ones digits in red, the tens in blue, and the hundreds in green. Above all, for children in Asian cultures, educational achievement, especially in

ENCOURAGING ACADEMIC ACHIEVEMENT Asian American children tend to do better in school than European American children, partly because Asian American children's families tend to provide especially strong support for academic achievement.

mathematics, is emphatically encouraged in school (Crystal et al., 1994). Children's cognitive development is thereby affected in ways large and small by the culture in which they live (Tomasello, 2000).

Individual Variations in Cognitive Development

Even within a single culture, some children are mentally advanced while others lag behind their peers. Why? As already suggested, heredity is an important factor, but experience also plays a role. To explore how significant that role is, psychologists have studied the cognitive development of children raised in many different environments.

Cognitive development is profoundly delayed if children are raised in environments where they are deprived of the everyday sights, sounds, and feelings provided by conversation and loving interaction with family members; by pictures and books; and even by television, radio, and the Internet. Children subjected to severe deprivation show significant impairment in intellectual development by the time they are two or three years old (Rymer, 1993). "Genie" was one such child. When discovered at age fourteen, she weighed only fifty-nine pounds and could not hop, skip, or climb. The only things she could say were "stop it" and "no more." Investigators discovered that she had spent her life confined to a small bedroom, harnessed to a potty chair during the day and caged in a crib at night. She had not been permitted to hear or make many sounds. Although scientists and therapists worked intensively with Genie in the years after her discovery, she never learned to speak in complete sentences, and she remains in an adult care facility.

Cognitive development may also be impaired by less extreme conditions of deprivation, including the neglect, malnourishment, noise, and chaos that occur in some homes. An extensive study of children raised in poverty found that they scored nine points lower on IQ tests by the time they were five years old than did children in families whose incomes were twice the poverty level—even after the researchers had controlled for all other family variables, such as family structure and parents' education (Duncan, Brooks-Gunn, & Klebanov, 1994). Such differences continue into the school years (McLoyd, 1998).

In families above the poverty line, too, children's cognitive development is related to their surroundings and experiences. Parents can often make the difference between a child's getting As or getting Cs. To help children achieve those As, adults can expose

PROJECT HEAD START   This teacher is working in Project Head Start, a program funded by the U.S. government to enrich the academic environments of preschoolers from lower-income backgrounds. This program has brought measurable benefits to children's academic and intellectual skills (Barnett, 1998; Lee, Brooks-Gunn, & Schnur, 1988; S. L. Ramey, 1999). Similar programs for infants at risk because of low birth weight, low socioeconomic status, or low parental IQ scores appear to enhance IQ scores by as much as nine points by the age of three. The effects appear to be especially strong for the infants of mothers with a high school education or less (C. T. Ramey et al., 2000).

them, from the early years, to a variety of interesting materials and experiences—though not so many that the child is overwhelmed (Clarke-Stewart, 1988). Children's cognitive development is also promoted when parents read and talk to them, encourage and help them to explore, and actively teach them (Gottfried, 1997)—in short, when they provide both support and challenge for their children's talents (M. M. Wong & Csikszentmihalyi, 1992). Although no substitute for adult attention, electronic games also provide opportunities for school-age children to hone spatial skills that can help improve their performance in math and science (Greenfield et al., 1994).

To improve the cognitive skills of children who do not get these kinds of stimulation, developmental psychologists have provided some children with extra lessons, materials, and educational contact with sensitive adults. In the United States, the most comprehensive effort to provide this kind of help has been through Project Head Start, a preschool program for poor children. Many smaller, more intensive programs have also been carried out. In a variety of such programs, children's cognitive abilities have been enhanced (C. T. Ramey & Ramey, 1998), demonstrating that the environment can directly affect cognitive development.

Infancy and Childhood: Social and Emotional Development

How do infants become attached to their caregivers?

Life for the child is more than learning about objects, doing math problems, and getting good grades. From the first months onward, infants are attracted by people—and most of them are very attractive creatures themselves, with their tiny bodies, large eyes, chubby cheeks, rosebud mouths, and soft gurgles. These qualities exert a powerful pull on people around them, especially parents and other caregivers.

Mutual attraction begins immediately. During the first hour or so after birth, babies are usually awake and, if they are with their mother, they gaze at her face while she gazes back and gives gentle touches (Klaus & Kennell, 1976). This is the first opportunity for

FORMING A BOND Mutual eye contact, exaggerated facial expressions, and shared baby talk are an important part of the early social interactions that promote an enduring bond of attachment between parent and child.

the mother to display her *bond* to her infant—an emotional tie that begins even before the baby is born. Psychologists once believed that this immediate contact was critical—that the mother-infant bond would never be strong if the opportunity for early interaction was missed. Research has revealed, however, that such interaction is a luxury, not a requirement for a close relationship (B. J. Myers, 1987). Mothers and fathers, whether biological or adoptive, gradually form close attachments to their infants by interacting with them day after day.

From an early age, infants are sensitive to the people around them. They gaze at beaming faces and smile at toothy grins (Malatesta & Izard, 1984). In one study, researchers tested the ability of three-month-olds to respond to emotional cues from their mothers (Cohn & Tronick, 1983). Some mothers acted normally, whereas others were asked to act depressed. Babies of the "depressed" mothers spent more time protesting, reacting warily, looking away, or giving only fleeting smiles. By the time they are a year old, children use their mothers' emotional expressions to guide their own behavior when they are uncertain (Saarni, Mummer, & Campos, 1998; R. A. Thompson, 1998). They tend to avoid a stranger, for example, if they see their mother look angry or afraid when the stranger approaches.

Infants also communicate their feelings to their parents, not only by crying and screaming but also more subtly. They signal when they want to interact by looking and smiling; they indicate that they do not want to interact by turning away and sucking their thumbs (Tronick, 1989). If caregivers do not respond to their infants' emotional signals, babies will not learn that their behavior has consequences, and their development will be hindered (M. Lewis & Goldberg, 1969). Children thrive among adults who are attentive and responsive. In families where infants are part of a mutual communication system, where caregivers help infants to achieve their goals, emotional development has a strong foundation.

Individual Temperament

From the moment infants are born, they differ from one another in the emotions they express. Some infants are happy, active, and vigorous; they splash, thrash, and wriggle. Others lie still most of the time. Some infants approach new objects with enthusiasm; others turn away or fuss. Some infants whimper; others kick, scream, and wail. Characteristics like these make up the infant's temperament. **Temperament** refers to the infant's individual style and frequency of expressing needs and emotions; it is constitutional, biological, and genetically based. Although temperament mainly reflects nature's contribution to the beginning of an individual's personality, it can also be affected by the prenatal environment, including—as noted earlier—the mother's smoking and drug use.

In some of the earliest research on infant temperament, Alexander Thomas and Stella Chess (1977) found three main temperament patterns. *Easy babies,* the most common kind, get hungry and sleepy at predictable times, react to new situations cheerfully, and seldom fuss. *Difficult babies* are irregular and irritable. Those in the third group, *slow-to-warm-up babies,* react warily to new situations but eventually come to enjoy them.

Traces of early temperamental characteristics weave their way throughout childhood (Rothbart, Ahadi, & Evans, 2000). Easy infants usually stay easy, and difficult infants often remain difficult (Guerin, Gottfried, & Thomas, 1997). Timid toddlers tend to become shy preschoolers, restrained and inhibited eight-year-olds, and somewhat anxious teenagers (C. Schwartz, Kagan, & Snidman, 1995). However, in temperament, as in cognitive development, nature interacts with nurture. Many events take place between infancy and adulthood to shift the individual's development in one direction or the other.

One influential factor suggested by Thomas and Chess is the match between the infant's temperament and the parents' expectations, desires, and personal styles. When parents believe they are responsible for the infant's behavior, an easy child might reassure them. If parents are looking for signs of assertiveness, a difficult child might be just what they want.

temperament An individual's basic, natural disposition, evident from infancy.

If parent and infant are in tune, chances increase that temperamental qualities will be stable. Consider the temperament patterns of Chinese American and European American children. At birth, Chinese American infants are calmer, less changeable, less excitable, and more easily comforted when upset than European American infants (V. Kagan et al., 1994). This tendency toward self-control is powerfully reinforced by the Chinese culture. Compared with European American parents, Chinese parents are less likely to reward and stimulate babbling and smiling, and more likely to maintain close control of their young children. The children, in turn, are more dependent on their mothers and less likely to play by themselves. They are less vocal, noisy, and active than European American children (S. Smith & Freedman, 1983).

These temperamental differences between children in different ethnic groups illustrate the combined contributions of nature and nurture. Mayan infants, for example, are relatively inactive from birth. The Zinacantecos, a Mayan group in southern Mexico, reinforce this innate predisposition toward restrained motor activity by tightly wrapping their infants and by nursing at the slightest sign of movement (Greenfield & Childs, 1991). This combination of genetic predisposition and cultural reinforcement is adaptive. Quiet infants do not kick off their covers at night, which is important in the cold highlands where they live. Inactive infants are able to spend long periods on their mothers' backs as the mothers work. And infants who do not begin to walk until they can understand some language do not wander into the open fire at the center of the house. This adaptive interplay of innate and cultural factors in the development of temperament operates in all cultures.

The Infant Grows Attached

As infants and caregivers respond to one another in the first year, the infant begins to form an **attachment**—a deep, affectionate, close, and enduring relationship—to these important figures. John Bowlby, a British psychoanalyst, drew attention to the importance of attachment when he observed the dire effects of separation from parents on children who had been orphaned in World War II. These children's depression and other emotional scars led Bowlby to propose a theory about the importance of developing a strong attachment to one's primary caregivers—a tie that normally keeps infants close to those caregivers and, therefore, safe (Bowlby, 1951, 1973). Soon after Bowlby first described his theory, researchers in the United States began to investigate how such attachments are formed and what happens when they fail to form or are broken by loss or separation. The most dramatic of these studies was conducted with monkeys by Harry Harlow.

Motherless Monkeys   Harlow (1959) separated newborn monkeys from their mothers and reared them in cages containing two artificial mothers. One "mother" was made of wire with a rubber nipple from which the infant could get milk (see Figure 9.6). It provided food but no physical comfort. The other artificial mother had no nipple but was made of soft, comfortable terry cloth. If attachments form entirely because caregivers provide food, the infants would be expected to prefer the wire mother. In fact, they spent most of their time with the terry cloth mother. And when they were frightened, the infants immediately ran to their terry cloth mother and clung to it. Harlow concluded that the monkeys were motivated by the need for comfort. The terry cloth mother provided feelings of softness and cuddling, which were things the infants needed when they sensed danger.

Harlow also investigated what happens when attachments do not form. He isolated some monkeys from all social contact from birth. After a year of this isolation, the monkeys showed dramatic disturbances. When visited by normally active, playful monkeys, they withdrew to a corner, huddling or rocking for hours. These monkeys' problems continued into adulthood. The males seldom got further than touching a potential sexual partner; the females quickly ran from any male who made a sexual advance. When some of the females were made pregnant through artificial insemination, their maternal behaviors were woefully inadequate. In most cases, these mothers ignored their infants.

attachment   A deep, affectionate, close, and enduring relationship with a person with whom a baby has shared many experiences.

FIGURE 9.6

Wire and Terry Cloth "Mothers"

Here are the two types of artificial mothers used in Harlow's research. Although baby monkeys received milk from the wire mother, they spent most of their time with the terry cloth version, and they clung to it when frightened.

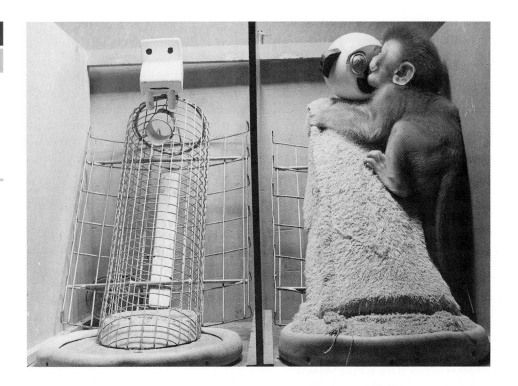

When the infants began to send distress signals, the mothers physically abused and sometimes even killed them.

Tragically, humans who spend their first few years without a consistent caregiver react in a similar manner. In Romanian and Russian orphanages, children who were abandoned by their mothers and neglected by orphanage workers were withdrawn and engaged in constant rocking—just like Harlow's deprived monkeys (Holden, 1996). These effects remained even after the children were adopted. In one study, researchers observed the behavior of four-year-old children who had been in a Romanian orphanage for at least eight months before being adopted and compared them with children who had been adopted before they were four months old (Chisholm, 1997). The late-adopted children were found to have many more serious problems. Depressed or withdrawn, they stared blankly, demanded attention, and could not control their tempers. Although interacting poorly with their adoptive mothers, they were friendly with any and all strangers, usually trying to cuddle and kiss them. Neurologists suggest that the dramatic problems seen in isolated monkeys, as well as humans, are the result of developmental brain dysfunction and damage brought on by a lack of touch and body movement in infancy (Prescott, 1996).

Forming an Attachment Researchers would never raise human babies like Harlow's monkeys, without social contacts as in the studies we just described. However, they have investigated the development of attachment in human babies as it occurs naturally under varying conditions. In most cultures in which the attachment process has been studied, the mother is usually the first person to whom the baby forms an attachment. By the age of six or seven months, infants show signs of preferring the mother to anyone else. They crawl after her, call out to her, hug her, climb into her lap, and protest when she leaves (Ainsworth & Marvin, 1995).

Infants also develop attachments to their fathers, but usually a little later (M. E. Lamb, 1976). Father-infant interaction is also less frequent than mother-infant interaction, and most studies show that it has a somewhat different nature (Parke, 1996). Mothers tend to feed, bathe, dress, cuddle, and talk to their infants, whereas fathers are more likely to play with, jiggle, and toss them, especially sons. In addition, although fathers are usually just as sensitive and responsive as mothers to their infants'

CULTURAL DIFFERENCES IN PARENT-CHILD RELATIONS   Variations in the intimacy of family interactions, including whether infants sleep in their parents' bed, may contribute to cross-cultural differences in attachment patterns.

expressions while things are going well, they may not do as well as mothers when the baby gets bored or distressed.

Variations in Attachment   The amount of closeness and contact the infant seeks with either mother or father depends to some extent on the infant. Those who are ill, tired, or slow to warm up may require more closeness. Closeness also depends to some extent on the parent. An infant whose parent has been absent or unresponsive is likely to need more closeness than one whose parent is accessible and responsive.

Researchers have studied the differences in infants' attachments through a procedure that simulates the natural comings and goings of parents and infants—the so-called Strange Situation Test (Ainsworth et al., 1978). This test occurs in an unfamiliar playroom where the infant interacts with the mother and an unfamiliar woman in brief episodes: The infant plays with the mother and the stranger in the room, the mother and the stranger leave the baby alone in the room, and the mother returns to the room.

Researchers have found that most infants in the United States display a *secure attachment* to the mother in the Strange Situation Test (R. A. Thompson, 1998). Their urge to be close is balanced by their urge to explore the environment. In the unfamiliar room, the infant uses the mother as a home base, leaving her side to explore and play but returning to her periodically for comfort or contact. Securely attached children can tolerate the brief separation from their mother, but they are always happy to see her return, and they are always receptive to her offers of contact. These mother-child pairs, researchers have found, tend to have harmonious interactions from the earliest months. The mothers themselves tend to be sensitive and responsive (Clarke-Stewart, 1988; DeWolff & van IJzendoorn, 1997).

Some infants, however, form an *insecure attachment*. If the relationship is *avoidant,* they avoid or ignore the mother when she approaches or when she returns after the brief separation. If the relationship is *ambivalent,* they are upset when their mother leaves, but when she returns they act angry and reject her efforts at contact, and when picked up they squirm to get down. If the relationship is *disorganized,* their behavior is inconsistent, disturbed, and disturbing; they may begin to cry again after the mother has returned and comforted them, or they may reach out for the mother while looking away from her.

The security of a child's attachment to caregivers has a number of long-term and far-reaching effects. Compared with insecurely attached children, those who are securely attached tend to be more socially and emotionally competent. They are more cooperative, enthusiastic, and persistent; better at solving problems; more compliant and controlled; and more popular and playful (R. A. Thompson, 1998). They also receive more positive reactions from their peers (Fagot, 1997). In fact, first-graders with secure attachments report less loneliness than do those with insecure attachments (Berlin, Cassidy, & Belsky, 1995), and they are less self-centered (Meins et al., 1998).

Patterns of child care and attachment vary widely in different parts of the world. In northern Germany, for example, the proportion of infants who display avoidant behavior in the Strange Situation Test is much higher than in the United States (Spangler, Fremmer-Bombik, & Grossman, 1996). In Japan, mothers are expected to be completely devoted to their children, giving unconditional love and affection, and rarely separating from them (M. White, 1987). Japanese infants, like those in many other cultures, sleep with their parents. Such factors lead to extremely close mother-child attachments. Indeed, it is impossible for many Japanese mothers to leave their infants in the Strange Situation Test, because the infants are so distressed by separation (Miyake, Chen, & Campos, 1985). In Israel, kibbutz babies who sleep in infant houses away from their parents are relatively likely to show insecure attachments (Sagi et al., 1994). Yet another pattern is seen among the Efe, a pygmy people. Efe infants spend almost all their time in contact with other people, but only about half of it is with their mothers (Tronick, Morelli, & Ivey, 1992). As a consequence, their attachments are not as focused on a single maternal figure as are those of infants in other cultures.

With the mothers of half the infants in the United States working outside the home, concern has been expressed about how daily separations from their mothers affect those infants. Some have argued that putting infants in day care, with a baby sitter or in a day-care center, damages the quality of the mother-infant relationship and increases the babies' risk for psychological problems later on (Gallagher, 1998).

Does Day Care Harm the Emotional Development of Infants?

▪ What am I being asked to believe or accept?

The claim is that daily separations created by day care damage the formation of an attachment between the mother and infant and harm the infant's emotional development.

▪ Is there evidence available to support the claim?

There is clear evidence that separation from the mother is painful for young children. If separation lasts a week or more, children who have formed an attachment to their mother tend to protest, then become apathetic and mournful, and finally seem to lose interest in the missing mother (J. Robertson & Robertson, 1971). But day care does not involve such lasting separations. Research has shown that infants who are in day care do form attachments to their mothers. In fact, they prefer their mothers to their daytime caregivers (Clarke-Stewart & Fein, 1983).

Are these attachments as secure as the attachments formed by infants whose mothers do not work outside the home? Researchers have examined this question by comparing how infants react to brief separations from their mother in the Strange Situation Test. A review of about twenty studies done in the 1980s revealed that infants in full-time day care were somewhat more likely to be classified as insecurely attached. About 36 percent of them were classified as insecure; only 29 percent of the infants who were not in full-time day care were counted as insecure (Clarke-Stewart, 1989). These results appear to support the suggestion that day care harms infants' attachments to their mothers.

▪ Can that evidence be interpreted another way?

Perhaps factors other than day care could explain the difference between infants in day care and those at home with their mothers. What could these other factors be?

One factor is the method that was used to assess attachment. Infants in these studies were judged insecure if they were relatively comfortable with a brief separation from their mothers in an unfamiliar room with an unfamiliar woman. Maybe infants who routinely experienced separations from their mothers when they were left in day care felt more comfortable in this situation and therefore sought out less closeness with their mothers. A second factor concerns the possible differences between the infants' mothers. Perhaps mothers who value independence in themselves and in their children are more likely to be working and to place their children in day care, whereas mothers who emphasize closeness with their children are more likely to stay home. This self-selection could have led more infants of working mothers to be classified as insecure.

▪ What evidence would help to evaluate the alternatives?

Finding insecure attachment to be more common among the infants of working mothers does not, by itself, demonstrate that day care is harmful. To judge the effects of day care, we must consider other measures of emotional adjustment as well. If day-care infants showed consistent signs of impaired emotional relations in other situations (at home, say) and with other caregivers (such as the father), this evidence would support the argument that day care harms children's emotional development. Another useful method would be to statistically control for differences in the behavior and attitudes of parents who do and do not put their infants in day care.

In fact, this research design has already been employed. In 1990, the U.S. government funded a study of infant day care in ten sites around the country. The psychological and physical development of more than 1,300 randomly selected infants was tracked from birth through age three. The results available so far show that when factors such as parents' education, income, and attitudes were statistically controlled, infants in day care were no more likely to have emotional problems or to be insecurely attached to their mothers than infants not in day care (NICHD Early Child Care Research Network, 1997, 1998, 1999). However, in cases where infants were placed in *poor-quality* day care, where the caregivers were insensitive and unresponsive, and where the mothers were insensitive to the infants' needs at home, the infants were less likely to develop a secure attachment to their mothers.

▪ What conclusions are most reasonable?

Based on available evidence, the most reasonable conclusion appears to be that day care by itself does not lead to insecure attachment. But if that day care is of poor quality, it can worsen a risky situation at home and increase the likelihood that infants will have problems forming a secure attachment to their mothers. The U.S. government study is still under way, and the children's progress is being followed into elementary school. Time will tell if other problems develop in the future (Azar, 2000).

Relationships with Parents and Peers

Erik Erikson (1968) saw the first year of life as a time when infants develop a feeling of trust (or mistrust) about the world. According to his theory, an infant's first year represents the first of eight stages of lifelong psychosocial development (see Table 9.2). Each stage focuses on a crisis that is especially important at that time of life. Erikson believed that the ways in which people resolve these crises shape their personalities and social relationships. Resolving a crisis in a positive way provides the foundation for characteristics such as trust, autonomy, initiative, or industry. But if the crisis is not resolved positively, according to Erikson, the person will be psychologically troubled and cope less effectively with later crises. In Erikson's theory, trusting caregivers during infancy forms the bedrock for all future social and emotional development.

After children have formed strong emotional attachments to their parents, their next psychological task is to develop a more independent relationship with them. In Erikson's theory, this task is reflected in the second stage (again, see Table 9.2). Children begin to exercise their wills, to develop some independence from their all-powerful parents, and to initiate activities on their own. According to Erikson, children who are not allowed to exercise their wills or initiate their own activities will feel uncertain about doing things for themselves and guilty about seeking independence. The extent to which parents allow or encourage their children's independence is related to their parenting style.

Parenting Styles   Most parents try to channel children's impulses into socially accepted outlets and teach them the skills and rules needed to function in their society. Cultural values strongly shape this **socialization** process. Parents in Hispanic cultures of Mexico, Puerto Rico, and Central America, for example, tend to be influenced by the collectivist tradition discussed in Chapter 1, in which family and community interests are emphasized over individual goals. Children in these cultures are expected to respect and obey their elders, and they are taught to do less of the questioning, negotiating, and arguing that is encouraged—or at least tolerated—in many middle-class European American families (Greenfield, 1995).

socialization   The process by which parents, teachers, and others teach children the skills and social norms necessary to be well-functioning members of society.

TABLE 9.2	Age	Central Psychological Issue or Crisis
Erikson's Stages of Psychosocial Development In each of Erikson's stages of development, a different psychological issue presents a new crisis for the person to resolve. The person focuses attention on the issue and, by the end of the period, has worked through the crisis and resolved it either positively, in the direction of healthy development, or negatively, hindering further psychological development.	First Year	**Trust versus mistrust** Infants learn to trust that their needs will be met by the world, especially by the mother—or they learn to mistrust the world.
	Second year	**Autonomy versus shame and doubt** Children learn to exercise will, to make choices, and to control themselves—or they become uncertain and doubt that they can do things by themselves.
	Third to fifth year	**Initiative versus guilt** Children learn to initiate activities and enjoy their accomplishments, acquiring direction and purpose—or, if they are not allowed initiative, they feel guilty for their attempts at independence.
	Sixth year through puberty	**Industry versus inferiority** Children develop a sense of industry and curiosity and are eager to learn—or they feel inferior and lose interest in the tasks before them.
	Adolescence	**Identity versus role confusion** Adolescents come to see themselves as unique and integrated persons with an ideology—or they become confused about what they want out of life.
	Early adulthood	**Intimacy versus isolation** Young people become able to commit themselves to another person—or they develop a sense of isolation and feel they have no one in the world but themselves.
	Middle age	**Generativity versus stagnation** Adults are willing to have and care for children and to devote themselves to their work and the common good—or they become self-centered and inactive.
	Old age	**Integrity versus despair** Older people enter a period of reflection, becoming assured that their lives have been meaningful and becoming ready to face death with acceptance and dignity—or they are in despair for their unaccomplished goals, failures, and ill-spent lives.

European American parents tend to employ one of three distinct parenting styles, as described by Diana Baumrind (1991). **Authoritarian parents** tend to be strict, punishing, and unsympathetic. They value obedience from children and try to shape their children's behavior to meet a set standard and to curb the children's wills. They do not encourage independence. They are detached and seldom praise their youngsters. In contrast, **permissive parents** give their children complete freedom and provide little discipline. The third group, **authoritative parents,** falls between these two extremes. They reason with their children, encouraging give and take. They allow children increasing responsibility as they get older and better at making decisions. They are firm but understanding. They set limits but also encourage independence. Their demands are reasonable, rational, and consistent.

authoritarian parents   Parents who are firm, punitive, and unsympathetic.

permissive parents   Parents who give their children complete freedom and lax discipline.

authoritative parents   Parents who reason with their children and are firm but understanding.

In her research with middle-class parents in Berkeley, California, Baumrind found these three parenting styles to be consistently related to young children's social and emotional development. Authoritarian parents had children who were unfriendly, distrustful, and withdrawn. The children of permissive parents were immature, dependent, and unhappy; they were likely to have tantrums or to ask for help when they encountered even slight difficulties. Children raised by authoritative parents were friendly, cooperative, self-reliant, and socially responsible. A follow-up study of the same children at age nine showed that the advantages of authoritative discipline were still present (Baumrind, 1986).

Other researchers following Baumrind's lead found that authoritative parenting styles were associated with additional positive outcomes, including better school achievement and better psychological adjustment to parental divorce (Hetherington & Clingempeel, 1992; Steinberg et al., 1994). Parenting styles may also help mold children's moral behavior. Children who are given orders, threats, and punishments are more likely than others to cheat and less likely to experience guilt or to accept blame after doing something wrong (Eisenberg & Fabes, 1998).

The results of these parenting studies are interesting, but they are limited in several ways. First, they are based on *correlations,* which, as discussed in Chapter 1, do not prove causation. Finding consistent correlations between parents' and children's behavior does not establish that the parents are *creating* the differences seen in their children. Even evidence that differences between the children of authoritative and nonauthoritative parents tend to increase over time can only *suggest* that parents' socialization styles have a direct influence on children's behavior (Steinberg et al., 1994). In fact, parents' behavior may be shaped to some extent by the children themselves, especially by their temperaments (Bugental & Goodnow, 1998).

Second, some developmental psychologists suggest that it is not the parents' socialization practices that influence children but, rather, how the children *perceive* the discipline they receive—as stricter or more lenient than what an older sibling received, for example (J. F. Dunn & Plomin, 1990). A third limitation of parenting studies is that the correlations between parenting styles and children's behavior, though statistically significant, are not terribly strong. Expected outcomes do not always appear. For example, Baumrind (1971) found a small group of families in which discipline was never observed, yet the children were thriving.

Finally, most parenting research has been done with European American families in the United States. Therefore, the findings do not necessarily represent universal principles. As psychologists study families in many different cultures and subcultures, they are discovering that the authoritative discipline so consistently linked with positive outcomes in European American families may not be the ideal parenting style for everyone. It was not, for example, related to better school performance among African American or Asian American youngsters (Steinberg, Dornbusch, & Brown, 1992). One reason for this lack of relationship could be that different disciplinary styles have different meanings in different cultures. When Chinese American parents use authoritarian discipline—which they do to a greater extent than European American parents—their goal is usually to "train" *(chiao shun)* and "govern" *(guan)* children so that they will know what is expected of them (Chao, 1994). By contrast, European American parents who use authoritarian discipline are more likely to do so to "break the child's will." In short, each parenting style and its outcomes must be evaluated in its cultural context.

Some people have suggested that parenting styles are a less significant influence on children's social development than are the influences they encounter outside the home—especially by interacting with peers (J. R. Harris, 1995, 1998). Research evidence does not justify dismissing the impact of parenting styles, but there is no denying the impact of peer influences, either (W. A. Collins et al., 2000; Leventhal & Brooks-Gunn, 2000).

Relationships with Peers   Social development over the years of childhood spans an ever-enlarging social world that broadens to include brothers and sisters, playmates and classmates. Psychologists have observed that from a remarkably early age—as young as one

CHILDREN'S FRIENDSHIPS Although relationships with peers may not always be cordial, they are often among the closest and most positive in a child's life. Friends are more interactive than nonfriends; they smile and laugh together more, pay closer attention to equality in their conversations, and talk about mutual goals.

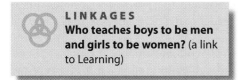

LINKAGES
Who teaches boys to be men and girls to be women? (a link to Learning)

gender roles   Patterns of work, appearance, and behavior that society associates with being male or female.

year—children are interested in the behavior of other children (usually their siblings), and by the time they are a year and a half old, they know how to hurt or comfort other children (K. H. Rubin, Bukowski, & Parker, 1998).

It takes time for children to learn how to interact with other children. Two-year-olds in Western cultures are only able to exchange or fight over toys. By the time they are three, they can use toys to get a response from peers. At age four, children converse about the toys they are playing with, and at the end of the preschool period, they are able to share toys and tasks cooperatively.

In the school years, peer interaction becomes more complex and structured as children play games with rules, play on teams, tutor each other, and cooperate or compete in achieving goals. The school years are also the time when friends become important and friendships become long-lasting (Hartup & Stevens, 1997). In interviews with researchers, schoolchildren reveal that they now realize that feelings, not things, keep friends together (Selman, 1981). In North American cultures, children's friendships are almost always with children of the same sex. The reasons, presumably, are that children share the same play interests with those of the same sex, are attracted to others who are like themselves, and want to avoid those who are different. Children without friends usually experience problems in later life (Bagwell, Newcomb, & Bukowski, 1998).

Social Skills

The changes in peer interactions and relationships over the years of childhood reflect children's increasing social competence and understanding. *Social skills*, like cognitive skills, must be learned. Very young children do not have the social skills necessary to sustain responsive interactions with other children, but parents can help their children develop these skills (Parke & O'Neil, 2000). Specifically, they can initiate lots of pretend play and other positive social behaviors with their children (Kahen, Katz, & Gottman, 1994), and can help them to constructively express and deal with their emotions (Eisenberg, 1998).

Parents and other adults can also help children detect and interpret emotional signals from others. Three- or four-year-old children can name typical facial expressions of happiness, sadness, anger, and fear; girls can do this at younger ages than boys (Dunn et al., 1991). As children get older, they learn to recognize a wider range of emotions and to predict how a person will feel in emotion-provoking situations (J. R. Brown & Dunn, 1996). These abilities are important: Much as children's school performance depends on processing academic information, their social performance depends on processing information about other people (Slomkowski & Dunn, 1996). Children whose social skills allow them to understand another person's perspective, appreciate how that person might be feeling, and offer sympathy, cooperation, and help tend to be the most popular members of a peer group (K. H. Rubin, Bukowski, & Parker, 1998). Children without these skills tend to be rejected or neglected; they may become bullies or the victims of bullies.

Gender Roles

An important aspect of understanding other people is knowing about social roles, including those linked to being male or female. All cultures establish expectations about **gender roles,** the general patterns of work, appearance, and behavior associated with being a man or a woman. In North America, some roles—such as homemaker and firefighter—have traditionally been tied to gender, although these traditions are weakening. Research by Deborah Best suggests that children learn gender-role expectations earliest in Muslim countries (where the roles are perhaps most extreme), but children in all twenty-five countries she studied eventually developed them (D. Best, 1992; J. E. Williams & Best, 1990).

Gender roles persist because they are deeply rooted in both nature and nurture. Small physical and behavioral differences between the sexes appear early on and tend to increase over the years (Eagly, 1996). For example, girls suffer less often than boys from speech, learning, and behavior disorders; mental retardation; emotional problems; and

LEARNING GENDER ROLES **Parents often encourage gender-stereotypic behaviors by providing the toys, clothes, and experiences traditionally associated with "appropriate" roles for boys versus girls.**

sleep disorders. They tend to speak and write earlier and to be better at grammar and spelling (Halpern, 1997). They nurture others more than boys do and show more emotional empathy. Their play tends to be more orderly. At the same time, boys tend to be more skilled than girls at manipulating objects, constructing three-dimensional forms, and mentally manipulating complex figures and pictures. They are more physically active and aggressive and more inclined to hit obstacles or people. They play in larger groups and spaces and enjoy noisier, more strenuous physical games (Eisenberg & Fabes, 1998).

A biological contribution to these male-female differences is supported by studies of differences in anatomy, hormones, and brain organization and functioning (Geary, 1999; Ruble & Martin, 1998). A biological basis for male-female differences is also supported by cross-cultural research showing consistency in gender patterns despite differing socialization (Simpson & Kenrick, 1997). In virtually every culture, for example, males are more violent than females. In one survey, there was not a single culture in which the number of women who killed women was even one-tenth as great as the number of men who killed men. On average, men's homicides outnumbered women's by more than 30 to 1 (M. Daly & Wilson, 1988; Federal Bureau of Investigation, 1999).

As always, however, it is difficult, if not impossible, to untangle biologically based gender differences from socially created ones. From the moment they are born, boys and girls are treated differently. Adults usually play more gently with, and talk more to, infants they believe to be girls than infants they believe to be boys (Culp, Cook, & Housley, 1983). They often shower their daughters with dolls and tea sets, their sons with trucks and tools (Rheingold & Cook, 1975). They tend to encourage boys to achieve, compete, and explore; to control their feelings; to be independent; and to assume personal responsibility. They more often encourage girls to be expressive, nurturant, reflective, dependent, domestic, obedient, and unselfish (Ruble & Martin, 1998). Thus parents, teachers, and television role models consciously or inadvertently pass on their ideas about "appropriate" behaviors for boys and girls (Witt, 1997).

Children also pick up ideas about gender-appropriate behavior from their peers. Peer pressure exaggerates whatever differences may already exist. For example, boys tend to be better than girls at computer or video games (Greenfield, 1994). However, this difference stems partly from the fact that boys encourage and reward each other for skilled performance at these games more than girls do (Law, Pellegrino, & Hunt, 1993). Children are also more likely to play with children of the same sex, and in gender-typical ways, on the playground than they are in private, at home, or in the classroom (Luria, 1992). An analysis of 143 studies of sex differences in aggression showed that boys acted significantly and consistently more aggressively than girls, but especially so when they knew they were being watched (Hyde, 1986). Among girls, aggression is less obvious; it is usually "relational aggression" that shows up in nasty words, not punching (N. R. Crick, Casas, & Mosher, 1997; N. R. Crick et al., 1999).

Gender roles appear in every culture, but they are more pronounced in some cultures than others. One recent analysis revealed, for example, that where social status differences between men and women were smaller, gender role differences were smaller as well (Eagly & Wood, 1999).

In short, social and cultural training tends to support and amplify any biological predispositions that distinguish boys and girls. Gender roles thus reflect a mix of nature and nurture. (This and other elements of early development are summarized in "In Review: Social and Emotional Development During Infancy and Childhood.")

The efforts of some parents to de-emphasize gender roles in their children's upbringing may be helping to reduce the magnitude of gender differences in areas such as verbal and quantitative skills (Hyde, 1994). However, the evolutionary approach to psychology suggests that other gender differences are unlikely to change much. These differences include males' greater ability to visualize the rotation of objects in space and females' greater ability to read facial expressions. Evolutionary psychologists see these differences as deeply rooted reflections of gender-related hunting versus child-rearing duties that were adaptive eons ago for the survival of both sexes (D. M. Buss, 1999). This view is

in review

	Social and Emotional Development During Infancy and Childhood		
Age	**Relationships with Parents**	**Relationships with Other Children**	**Social Understanding**
Birth–2 years	Infants form an attachment to the primary caregiver.	Play focuses on toys, not on other children.	Infants respond to emotional expressions of others.
2–4 years	Children become more independent and no longer need their parents' constant attention.	Toys are a way of eliciting responses from other children.	Young children can recognize emotions of others.
4–10 years	Parents actively socialize their children.	Children begin to cooperate, compete, play games, and form friendships with peers.	Children learn social rules, like politeness, and roles, like being a male or female.

being challenged by psychologists who see such differences as reflecting social inequality, not just biological destiny (Eagly & Wood, 1999).

Adolescence

▪ What threatens adolescents' self-esteem?

The years of middle childhood usually pass smoothly, as children busy themselves with schoolwork, hobbies, friends, and clubs. But in adolescence, things change dramatically. All adolescents undergo significant changes in size, shape, and physical capacities. In Western cultures, many adolescents also experience huge changes in their social life, reasoning abilities, and views of themselves.

The Challenges of Change

A sudden spurt in physical growth is a visible signal that adolescence has begun. This growth spurt peaks at about age twelve for girls and at about age fourteen for boys (Tanner, 1978; see Figure 9.7). Suddenly, adolescents find themselves in new bodies. At the end of the growth spurt, menstruation begins in females, and live sperm are produced in males. This condition of being able for the first time to reproduce is called **puberty.**

In Western cultures, *early adolescence* (the period from age eleven to fourteen or so) is filled with challenges. Sexual interest stirs, and there are opportunities to smoke, drink alcohol, and take other drugs. All of this can be very disorienting. Indeed, adolescents may experience bouts of depression and are vulnerable to other psychological difficulties as well (Kashani et al., 1989).

Some of these problems appear as adolescents begin to face challenges to their *self-esteem,* their sense of being worthy, capable, and deserving of respect—especially if other stressors occur at the same time (Kling et al., 1999). Researchers have found that youths who experience more or stronger stressors, such as inadequate study space at home or parental divorce or unemployment, have more difficulty adapting to adolescence (DuBois et al., 1992). The switch from elementary school to middle school is particularly challenging for young adolescents. Declining grades are especially likely among students who were already having trouble in school or who don't have confidence in their own abilities.

puberty The condition of being able, for the first time, to reproduce.

FIGURE 9.7 Physical Changes in Adolescence

At about ten and a half years of age, girls begin their growth spurt, and by age twelve, they are taller than their male peers. When boys, at about twelve and a half years of age, begin their growth spurt, they usually grow faster and for a longer period of time than girls. Adolescents may grow as much as five inches a year. The development of sexual characteristics accompanies these changes in height. The ages at which these changes occur vary considerably across individuals, but their sequence is the same.

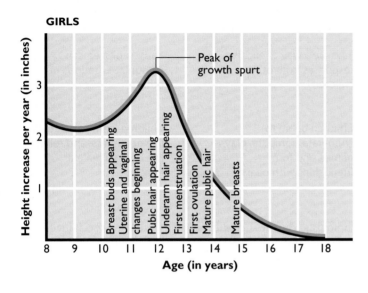
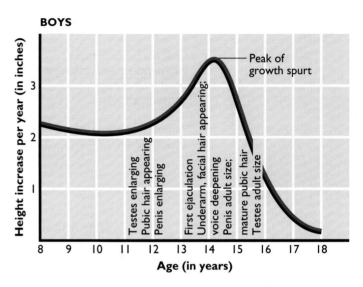

Self-esteem is also related to physical maturity. In Western cultures, boys who go through puberty early tend to have higher status; to become leaders; and to be happy, poised, and relaxed. Those who reach puberty late are more likely to feel rejected, dependent, and dominated by others (A. C. Peterson, 1987). For girls, maturing early is likely to lead to embarrassment, sexual activity, and strained relations with their parents (Brooks-Gunn, 1988). Differences between early and late maturers may persist into adulthood.

The changes and pressures of adolescence are often played out at home. Many teenagers become discontented with their parents' rules and values, leading to arguments over everything from taking out the garbage to who left the gallon of milk on top of the refrigerator. Serious conflicts may lead to serious problems, including running away, pregnancy, stealing, drug taking, or even suicide—especially among teens who do not feel close to their parents (Resnick, 1997). In most families, however, the level of conflict is moderate (Steinberg, 1990). Especially in European American families, adolescents whose parents retain an authoritative disciplinary style and maintain a balance between being too strict (authoritarian) and too lax (permissive) tend to remain well adjusted (Baumrind, 1991; Bronstein et al., 1998).

In fact, research suggests that in Western cultures, more than half of today's teens find early adolescence relatively trouble-free (Arnett, 1999). Only about 15 percent of the adolescents studied experience serious turmoil (Steinberg, 1990). Of those who do, sexuality is often involved. Surveys suggest that about half of North America's youth have had sexual intercourse by age sixteen (National Center for Health Statistics, 1997). Fifty years ago, the comparable figure was less than 10 percent (Resnick, 1997). The most dramatic increase has occurred among fifteen-year-old girls, of whom 38 percent are now sexually active (National Center for Health Statistics, 1997). Teens who have sex differ from those who do not in a number of ways. They hold less conventional attitudes and values, and they are more likely to smoke, drink alcohol, and use other drugs. Their parents tend to be less educated, less likely to exert control over them, and less likely to talk openly with them. Sexual activity in adolescence is also related to ethnicity. For instance, teens from Asian American families are less likely to be sexually active than those from European American families (McLaughlin et al., 1997).

Too often, sexual activity leads to declining school achievement and interest, sexually transmitted diseases, and unplanned and unwanted pregnancies. Teenagers have the highest rates of sexually transmitted diseases (such as gonorrhea, chlamydia, and pelvic inflammatory disease) of any age group (Grady, 1998). One-fifth of all AIDS cases start in adolescence (J. E. Brody, 1998), and although teenage pregnancy rates have been declining of late, nearly 10 percent of all teenage girls in the United States get pregnant before they reach age nineteen (National Center for Health Statistics, 2000). More than half of U.S. adolescents who become pregnant elect to keep their babies and become single mothers. A teenage pregnancy can wreak havoc for the baby, as well as for the parents. Teenage parents tend to be less positive and stimulating with their children than older parents (Garcia-Coll, Oh, & Hoffman, 1987); they are also more likely to abuse them (Coley & Chase-Lansdale, 1998). The children of teenage parents, in turn, are more likely to develop behavior problems and to do poorly in school than those whose parents are older (Furstenberg, Brooks-Gunn, & Chase-Lansdale, 1989).

Identity and Development of the Self

In many cultures of less developed nations today, and in the United States during earlier times, the end of early adolescence (around the age of fourteen) marks the onset of adulthood—a time when work, parenting, and grown-up responsibilities begin. In modern North America, the transition from childhood to adulthood often lasts well into the twenties. Adolescents spend a lot of time being students or trainees. This lengthened adolescence has created special problems—among them, the matter of finding or forming an identity.

Forming a Personal and Ethnic Identity Preschool children asked to describe themselves often mention a favorite or habitual activity: "I watch TV" or "I do the dishes." At eight or nine, children identify themselves by giving facts such as their sex, age, name, physical appearance, and likes and dislikes. They may still describe themselves in terms of what they do, but they now include how well they do it compared with other children. Then, at about age eleven, children begin to describe themselves in terms of social relationships, personality traits, and other general, stable psychological characteristics such as "smart" or "friendly" (Shaffer, 1999). These changes in the way children and adolescents describe themselves suggest changes in the way they think about themselves. As they become more self-conscious, they gradually develop a personal identity as unique individuals.

Adolescents may also describe themselves in terms of their ethnic or national identity. In the multicultural United States, some members of ethnic minorities may identify with their ethnic group—Chinese, Mexican, or Italian, for example—even more than with being Americans. Children are aware of ethnic cues such as skin color before they reach the age of three. Minority-group children notice these cues earlier than other children and prefer to play with children from their own group (D. Milner, 1983). In high school, most students hang out with members of their own ethnic group. They tend not to know classmates in other ethnic groups well, seeing them more as members of those groups than as individuals (Steinberg, Dornbusch, & Brown, 1992). These social processes may solidify *ethnic identity*. A positive ethnic identity contributes to self-esteem, partly because seeing their own group as superior makes people feel good about themselves (J. C. Turner, 1987). *Bicultural people*, who affirm both their ethnic and their national identities, also typically have a positive self-concept (Phinney, 1990). However, as described in Chapter 14, the same processes that foster ethnic identity can also sow the seeds of ethnic prejudice.

Facing the Identity Crisis Identity formation is the central task of adolescence in Erik Erikson's theory of psychosocial development. According to Erikson (1968), events of late adolescence—graduating from high school, going to college, and forging new relationships—challenge the adolescent's self-concept, precipitating an **identity crisis** (see Table 9.2). In this crisis, the adolescent must develop an integrated self-image as a unique person by pulling together self-knowledge acquired during childhood. If infancy and

identity crisis A phase during which an adolescent attempts to develop an integrated self-image as a unique person by pulling together self-knowledge acquired during childhood.

ETHNIC IDENTITY　Ethnic identity is that part of our personal identity that reflects the racial, religious, or cultural group to which we belong. Ethnic identity often leads people to interact mainly with others who share that same identity.

childhood brought trust, autonomy, and initiative, according to Erikson, the adolescent will resolve the identity crisis positively, feeling self-confident and competent. If infancy and childhood resulted in feelings of mistrust, shame, guilt, and inferiority, the adolescent will be confused about his or her identity and goals.

Some limited empirical support exists for Erikson's ideas about the identity crisis in Western cultures. In late adolescence, young people do consider alternative identities (Waterman, 1982). They "try out" being rebellious, studious, or detached as they attempt to resolve questions about sexuality, self-worth, industriousness, and independence. By the time they are twenty-one, about half of the adolescents studied have resolved the identity crisis in a way that is consistent with their self-image and the historical era in which they are living. They enter young adulthood with self-confidence. Basically the same people who entered adolescence, they now have more mature attitudes and behavior, more consistent goals and values, and a clearer idea of who they are (Savin-Williams & Demo, 1984). For those who fail to resolve identity issues—either because they avoided the identity crisis by accepting whatever identity their parents set for them or because they postponed dealing with the crisis and remain uncommitted and lacking in direction—there are often problems ahead (Hart & Yates, 1997).

Abstract Thought and Moral Reasoning

Adolescents are able to develop a conscious identity partly because, for the first time, they can think and reason about abstract concepts. For many young people in Western cultures, adolescence begins a stage of cognitive development that Piaget called the **formal operational period,** a stage marked by the ability to engage in hypothetical thinking, including the imagining of logical consequences. For instance, adolescents who have reached the level of formal operations can consider various strategies for finding a part-time job and recognize that some methods are more likely to be successful than others. They can form general concepts and understand the impact of the past on the present and the present on the future. They can question social institutions; think about the world as it might be and ought to be; and consider the consequences of love, morality, work, politics, philosophy, and religion. They can think logically and systematically about symbols and propositions, regardless of whether the propositions are true.

Piaget explored adolescents' formal operational abilities by asking them to perform science experiments that involved formulating and systematically investigating hypotheses. Research indicates that only about half the people in Western cultures ever reach the

formal operational period　According to Piaget, the fourth stage of cognitive development, characterized by the ability to engage in hypothetical thinking.

formal operational level necessary to succeed in Piaget's experiments. Those without high school science and math are less likely to succeed (Keating, 1990). In other cultures, too, people who have not gone to school are less likely to exhibit formal operations. Consider the following conversation, in which a researcher tests the formal operations of an illiterate Kpelle farmer in a Liberian village (Scribner, 1977):

> *Researcher:* All Kpelle men are rice farmers. Mr. Smith is not a rice farmer. Is he a Kpelle man?
> *Kpelle Farmer:* I don't know the man. I have not laid eyes on the man myself.

Kpelle villagers who had had formal schooling answered the question logically: "No, Mr. Smith is not a Kpelle man."

Even people who have been to school do not use a single mode of thinking in all situations. In adulthood, people are more likely to use formal operations for problems based on their own occupations. This is one reason why people whose logic is impeccable at work may still become victims of a home-repair or investment scam (Cialdini, 1993).

Kohlberg's Stages of Moral Reasoning   Adolescents often find themselves applying their advanced cognitive skills to questions of morality. To examine how people think about morality, psychologists have asked them how they would resolve moral dilemmas, and why. Perhaps the most famous of these is the "Heinz dilemma," in which people must decide whether a man named Heinz should steal a rare and unaffordably expensive drug in order to save his wife from cancer.

Posing moral dilemmas like this one to males between the ages of ten and twenty-six, Lawrence Kohlberg found that the reasons given for moral choices change systematically and consistently with age (Kohlberg & Gilligan, 1971). Young children make moral judgments that differ from those of older children, adolescents, or adults. Kohlberg proposed that moral reasoning develops in six stages, which are summarized in Table 9.3. These stages, he said, are not tightly linked to a person's chronological age. Instead, there is a range of ages for reaching each stage, and not everyone reaches the highest level.

Stage 1 and Stage 2 moral judgments, which are most typical of children under the age of nine, tend to be selfish in nature. Kohlberg called this level of moral reasoning **preconventional** because it is not based on the conventions or rules that guide social interactions in society. People at this level of moral development are concerned with avoiding punishment or following rules when it is to their own advantage. At the **conventional** level of moral reasoning, Stages 3 and 4, people care about other people. They think that morality consists of following rules and conventions such as duty to the family, to marriage vows, to the country. The moral reasoning of children from nine to nineteen is most often at this level. Stages 5 and 6 represent the highest level of moral reasoning, which Kohlberg called **postconventional** because it occurs after conventional reasoning. Moral judgments at this level are based on personal standards or universal principles of justice, equality, and respect for human life, not on the dictates of authority figures or society. People who have reached this level view rules and laws as arbitrary but respect them because they protect human welfare. They believe that individual rights can sometimes justify violating these laws if the laws become destructive. People do not usually reach this level until sometime after the end of adolescence. Stage 6 is seen only rarely, in extraordinary individuals. Studies of Kohlberg's stages (e.g., L. J. Walker, 1989) have generally supported the sequence he proposed.

Limitations of Kohlberg's Stages   Have Kohlberg's findings been replicated across cultures? Forty-five studies in twenty-seven cultures from Alaska to Zambia showed that people do tend to make upward progress through Kohlberg's stages, without reversals (Snarey, 1987). Further, although Stages 5 and 6 did not always appear, Stages 1 through 4 did and thus appear universal. The reason may be that these lower levels of reasoning are more closely linked to cognitive development than is the highest level.

However, there are moral judgments made in some cultures that do not fit into Kohlberg's stages. Some people in collectivist cultures such as Papua New Guinea,

preconventional   Referring to moral reasoning that is not based on the conventions or rules that guide social interactions in a society.

conventional   Referring to moral reasoning that reflects a concern about other people, as well as the belief that morality consists of following rules and conventions.

postconventional   Referring to moral reasoning that reflects moral judgments based on personal standards or universal principles of justice, equality, and respect for human life.

TABLE 9.3	Stage	What Is Right?	Should Heinz Steal the Drug?
Kohlberg's Stages of Moral Development	**Preconventional**		
	1	Obeying and avoiding punishment from a superior authority	"Heinz should not steal the drug, because he will be jailed."
	2	Making a fair exchange, a good deal	"Heinz should steal the drug, because his wife will repay him later."
	Conventional		
	3	Pleasing others and getting their approval	"Heinz should steal the drug, because he loves his wife and because she and the rest of the family will approve."
	4	Doing your duty, following rules and social order	"Heinz should steal the drug for his wife, because he has a duty to care for her, or he should not steal the drug, because stealing is illegal.
	Postconventional		
	5	Respecting rules and laws, but recognizing that they may have limits	"Heinz should steal the drug, because life is more important than property."
	6	Following universal ethical principles, such as justice, reciprocity, equality, and respect for human life and rights	"Heinz should steal the drug because of the principle of preserving and respecting life."

Kohlberg's stages of moral reasoning describe differences in how people think about moral issues. Here are some examples of answers that people at different stages of development might give to the "Heinz dilemma" described in the text. This dilemma is more unrealistic than you might think. In 1994, a man was arrested for robbing a bank after being turned down for a loan to pay for his wife's cancer treatments.

Taiwan, and Israeli kibbutzim, for example, explained their answers to moral dilemmas by pointing to the importance of the community. And people in India included in their moral reasoning the importance of acting in accordance with one's gender and caste and with maintaining personal purity (Shweder et al., 1994). In shaping moral judgments, as in other areas, culture plays a significant role.

Does gender play a role, too? Carol Gilligan (1982, 1993) has suggested that Kohlberg's research documented mainly the abstract, impersonal concept of justice typically seen in males. When Gilligan asked people about moral conflicts, the majority of men focused on justice, but only half of the women did. The other half focused on caring. This finding supports Gilligan's belief that for North American females, the moral ideal is to protect enduring relationships and fulfill human needs. This difference between men and women has not been found consistently, however. In fact, a recent reanalysis of 180 studies found that the tendency for females to focus on caring more than males and for males to focus on justice more than females may not be as strong as Gilligan suggested (Jaffee & Hyde, 2000). Indeed, it appears that males and females are capable of using either approach to moral reasoning, depending on the issues involved and other factors (Johnston, 1998).

Taken together, the results of research in different countries and with both genders suggest that moral ideals are not absolute and universal. Moral development is apparently an adaptation to the moral world—and the specific situations in which one finds oneself (Bersoff, 1999). Formal operational reasoning may be necessary for people to reach the highest level of moral reasoning, but this kind of reasoning alone is not sufficient. To some extent, at the highest levels, moral reasoning is a product of culture and history.

Adulthood

■ What developmental changes occur in adulthood?

Development does not end with adolescence. Adults, too, go through transitions and experience physical, cognitive, and social changes. It has been suggested that adulthood emerges as early as eighteen (Arnett, 2000), but, for our purposes, adulthood can be divided into three periods: *early adulthood* (ages twenty to forty), *middle adulthood* (ages forty to sixty-five), and *late adulthood* (age sixty-five on).

Physical Changes

In early adulthood, physical growth continues. Shoulder width, height, and chest size increase, and people continue to develop their athletic abilities. By their mid-thirties nearly everyone shows some hearing impairment, but for most people, the years of early adulthood are the prime of life.

In middle adulthood, other physical changes slowly emerge. The most common of these involve the further loss of sensory sharpness (Fozard et al., 1977). People become less sensitive to light, less accurate at perceiving differences in distance, and slower and less acute at seeing details. At about age forty, increased farsightedness is common, and glasses may be necessary to correct for it. In their late forties or early fifties, women generally experience *menopause,* the shutdown of reproductive capability. Estrogen and progesterone levels drop, and the menstrual cycle eventually ceases.

Most people are well into late adulthood before their bodily functions show noticeable impairment. However, inside the body, bone mass is dwindling, and the risk of heart disease is increasing. Men shrink about an inch in height, and women about two inches, as their posture changes and cartilage disks between the spinal vertebrae become thinner. Hardening of the arteries and a buildup of fat deposits on the artery walls may lead to heart disease. The digestive system slows down and becomes less efficient. Both digestive disorders and heart disease sometimes result from problems of diet—too little fluid, too little fiber, too much fat—and inactivity. In addition, the brain shrinks during late adulthood. The few reflexes that remained after infancy, such as the knee-jerk reflex, weaken or disappear. The flow of blood to the brain slows. As in earlier years, many of these changes can be delayed or diminished by healthy diets and exercise.

Cognitive Changes

Despite the aging of the brain, cognition undergoes little change for the worse until late adulthood. Before that time, alert older people can think just as quickly as alert younger people. In fact, older adults may function as well as or better than younger adults in situations that tap their memories and learning skills. The experienced teacher may deal with an unruly child more skillfully than the novice, and the senior lawyer may understand the implications of a new law more quickly than the recent graduate. Their years of accumulating and organizing information can make older adults practiced, skillful, and wise.

Early and Middle Adulthood Until age sixty at least, important cognitive abilities improve. During this period, adults do better on tests of vocabulary, comprehension, and general knowledge—especially if they use these abilities in their daily lives or engage in enriching activities such as travel or reading (Eichorn et al., 1981). Young and middle-aged adults learn new information and new skills; they remember old information and hone old skills. Indeed, it is in their forties through their early sixties that people tend to

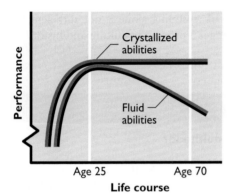

Source: Adapted from Baltes (1994).

FIGURE 9.8

Mental Abilities over the Life Span

Mental abilities collectively known as "fluid" intelligence—speed of information processing, accuracy, and basic memory, for example—begin to decline quite early in adult life. Changes in these biologically based aspects of thinking are usually not noticeable until late adulthood, however. "Crystallized" abilities learned over a lifetime—such as reading, writing, comprehension of language, and professional skills—do not diminish until old age (S. L. Willis & Schaie, 1999).

put in the best performance of their lives on complex mental tasks such as reasoning, verbal memory, and vocabulary (S. L. Willis & Schaie, 1999).

The *nature* of thought may also change during adulthood. Adult thought is often more complex and adaptive than adolescent thought (Labouvie-Vief, 1992). Unlike adolescents, adults understand the contradictions inherent in thinking. They see both the possibilities and the problems in every course of action—in deciding whether to start a new business, back a political candidate, move to a new place, or change jobs. Middle-aged adults are more expert than adolescents or young adults at making rational decisions and at relating logic and abstractions to actions, emotions, social issues, and personal relationships (A. Tversky & Kahneman, 1981). As they appreciate these relationships, their thought becomes more global, more concerned with broad moral and practical issues (Labouvie-Vief, 1982). It has been suggested that the achievement of these new kinds of thinking reflects a stage of cognitive development that goes beyond Piaget's formal operational period (Lutz & Sternberg, 1999). In this stage, people's thinking becomes *dialectical,* which means they understand that knowledge is relative, not absolute—such that what is seen as wise today may have been thought foolish in times past. They see life's contradictions as an inevitable part of reality, and they tend to weigh various solutions to problems rather than just accepting the first one that springs to mind.

Late Adulthood   It is not until late in adulthood, after the age of sixty-five or so, that some intellectual abilities decline in some people. Generally, these are abilities that require rapid and flexible manipulation of ideas and symbols, active thinking and reasoning, and sheer mental effort (Baltes, 1994; Craik, 1994; see Figure 9.8). Older adults do just as well as younger ones at tasks they know well, like naming familiar objects (Radvansky, 1999). However, when asked to perform an unfamiliar task or to solve a complex problem they have not seen before, older adults are generally slower and less effective than younger ones (Craik & Rabinowitz, 1984). When faced with complex problems, older people apparently suffer from having too much information to sift through. They have trouble considering, choosing, and executing solutions (Arenberg, 1982). As people age, they grow less efficient at organizing the elements of a problem and at holding and mentally manipulating more than one idea at a time. They have difficulty doing tasks that require them to divide their attention between two activities and are slower at shifting their attention back and forth between those activities (Korteling, 1991). If older adults have enough time, though, and can separate the two activities, they can perform just as well as younger adults (H. L. Hawkins, Kramer, & Capaldi, 1993).

Usually, the loss of intellectual abilities is slow and need not cause severe problems. A study of Swedish older adults (Nilsson, 1996) showed, for example, that their memory problems were largely confined to *episodic memory* (e.g., remembering what they had for lunch yesterday) rather than *semantic memory* (e.g., remembering general information, such as the capital of France).

In short, everyday competencies that involve verbal processes are likely to remain intact into advanced old age (Willis & Schaie, 1999). Further, the risk of cognitive decline is significantly lower for people who are healthy and psychologically flexible; who have a high level of education, income, and occupation; and who live in an intellectually stimulating environment with mentally able spouses or companions (Albert et al., 1995; Shimamura et al., 1995). Continued mental exercise—such as doing puzzles, painting, and having intellectually stimulating conversations with friends—can help older adults think and remember effectively and creatively.

Research on people tested repeatedly since 1956 shows that scores on mental ability tests decline less rapidly in old age now than they did before 1970 (Schaie, 1993). Even at age eighty-one, fewer than half of the participants exhibited losses in mental abilities over the preceding seven years. This finding is probably due to the improved physical health and longer involvement in work and other mental activities seen in older adults over the last fifty years. Other research demonstrates that it is never too late to work at preserving mental ability. Practice at memory and other information-processing tasks, for example, leads to some improvement in skills impaired by old age and disuse (Baltes, 1993).

The greatest threat to cognitive abilities in late adulthood is Alzheimer's disease, which strikes 3 percent of the world's population by age seventy-five. As the disease progresses, it leaves even the brightest minds incapable. The victim becomes emotionally flat, then disoriented, then incontinent, then mentally vacant; finally, the person dies. The average course of the disease, from onset to death, is seven years, but it can vary. In men, it averages only five years, and in women, eight (Molsa, Marttila, & Rinne, 1995). Alzheimer's also progresses more rapidly, and is more severe, the earlier it starts (Jagger, Clarke, & Stone, 1995). The disease also tends to appear later in more educated people (Y. Stern et al., 1995).

Social Changes

Adulthood is a time when changes occur in social relationships and positions. These changes do not come in neat, predictable stages but instead follow various paths, depending on individual experiences—such as being abandoned by a spouse, getting fired from a job, going back to school, remarrying, or suffering the death of a spouse (Caspi, 1998).

Early Adulthood   Men and women in Western cultures usually enter the adult world in their twenties. They decide on an occupation, or at least take a job, and often become preoccupied with their careers. They also become more concerned with issues of love (Whitbourne et al., 1992). Recall the sixth of Erikson's stages of psychosocial development noted in Table 9.2: intimacy versus isolation. This intimacy may include sexual intimacy, friendship, or mutual intellectual stimulation. It may lead to marriage or some other form of committed relationship. All this comes at a time when, having separated from their parents, young adults may also be experiencing isolation and loneliness. They may view the future with a mixture of anticipation, fear, and insecurity.

Just how willing and able people are to make intimate commitments may depend on their earlier attachment relationships. Researchers have discovered that young adults' views of intimate relationships parallel the patterns of infant attachment that we described earlier (Horowitz, Rosenberg, & Bartholomew, 1993). If their view reflects a secure attachment, they tend to feel valued and worthy of support and affection; develop closeness easily; and have relationships characterized by joy, trust, and commitment. If their view reflects an insecure attachment, however, they tend to be preoccupied with relationships and may feel misunderstood, underappreciated, and worried about being abandoned; their relationships are often negative, obsessive, and jealous. Alternatively, they may be aloof and unable to commit or trust. Researchers have videotaped young adult dating partners in situations producing slight anxiety that somewhat resemble the Strange Situation Test used with infants (Simpson, Rholes, & Nelligan, 1992). The tapes reveal that as anxiety increases, people with a secure attachment style increase their requests for support from their partners, whereas those with an insecure style decrease support-seeking behaviors. In another study, insecurely attached individuals were found to engage in more one-night stands and less cuddling than did those whose attachment style was secure (Tidwell, Reis, & Shaver, 1996).

During young adulthood, the experience of becoming parents represents entry into a major new developmental phase accompanied by personal, social, and often occupational changes. For many couples, marital satisfaction declines (Belsky & Kelly, 1994), and about half of all marriages crack under the strain. Young mothers experience particular dissatisfaction—especially if they resent the constraints an infant brings, if they see their career as important, if the infant is temperamentally difficult, and if their partner is not supportive. When the father does not do his share of caring for the baby, both mothers and fathers are dissatisfied (Levy-Shiff, 1994).

Relationship difficulties uncovered during the transition to parenthood not only threaten marriages but also can interfere with child care (Erel & Burman, 1995). The quality of that care is also related to young parents' own attachment histories. New mothers whose attachment to their own mother is secure tend to be more responsive to their infants, and the infants, in turn, are more likely to develop secure attachments to them (van IJzendoorn, 1995).

STAYING ACTIVE   A lifetime of fitness through skiing or other forms of aerobic exercise has been associated with better maintenance of skills on a variety of mental tasks, including reaction time, reasoning, and divided attention (e.g., H. L. Hawkins, Kramer, & Capaldi, 1993).

BUILDING MONUMENTS   Middle adult-hood tends to be a time during which people become deeply committed to building personal monuments, either by raising children or through achievements outside the home. This parent seems to have accomplished both goals.

Middle Adulthood   By their forties, people become concerned with producing some-thing that will outlast them, usually through parenthood or job achievements. Erikson called this concern the crisis of **generativity,** because people are focused on producing or generating something. If people do not resolve this crisis, he suggested, they stagnate.

For many North American adults, however, the greatest tension occurs between two types of generativity: parenthood versus achievement. The demands of children and career often pull in opposite directions. Devotion to a job may lead to guilt about depriv-ing children of attention; too much emphasis on home life may impair productivity at work. This stressful balancing act can lead to anxiety, frustration, and conflicts at home and on the job.

Sometime around age forty, people go through a **midlife transition.** They may reap-praise and modify their lives and relationships. They may feel invigorated and liberated, or they may feel upset and have a "midlife crisis" (M. Beck, 1992). No one knows how many people experience a crisis during the midlife transition, but researchers suspect that these people are in the minority (M. Beck, 1992). The contrast between youth and middle age may be especially upsetting for men who matured early in adolescence and were sociable and athletic rather than intellectual (J. A. Block, 1971). Some women who chose a career over a family may feel conflict and distress as their last childbearing years pass. Women who have had children, however, often become more independent, confi-dent, and oriented toward achievement and events outside the family (Helson & Moane, 1987). For both men and women who are parents, the emerging sexuality of their teenage children, the emptiness of the nest as children leave home, or the declining health of a parent may precipitate a crisis. The transition is easier for those who can accept the idea that life may not turn out as planned—or whose lives *have* turned out as planned.

Preliminary results from a study of more than 7,000 adults suggest that the happiness and healthiness of people in midlife depend on how much control they feel they have over their job, finances, marriage, children, and sex life; the level of education they have attained; and the type of work they are doing (Azar, 1996). However, once the midlife transition is past, the middle years of adulthood are usually a time of satisfaction and happiness (Diener & Diener, 1995; MacArthur Foundation, 1999).

Late Adulthood   Most people between sixty-five and seventy-five years of age think of themselves as middle-aged, not old (Neugarten, 1977). They are active and influential politically and socially; they often are physically vigorous. Ratings of life satisfaction and self-esteem are, on average, as high in old age as during any other period of adulthood

generativity   The concern of adults in their forties with producing or generating something enduring.

midlife transition   A point at around age forty when adults take stock of their lives.

terminal drop   A sharp decline in mental functioning that tends to occur in late adulthood, a few months or years before death.

THE "SANDWICH" GENERATION
People in the midlife transition may feel "sandwiched" between generations, pressured by the demands of their children on one side and the needs of their aging parents on the other.

STILL ON A ROLL   Actor Paul Newman, seventy-six, is a famous example of the thousands of people whose late adulthood is healthy and vigorous. In January 2000, Newman received bruised ribs in a minor accident while preparing to drive his race car in the 24 Hours of Daytona. He was racing again the following month.

(Mroczek & Kolarz, 1998; J. Volz, 2000). Men and women who have been employed usually retire from their jobs during this period. They adjust most easily to retirement if they view it as a choice (Swan, 1996).

Today, more people than ever are reaching old age. In fact, those over 75 make up the fastest-growing segment of the population, a group that is 25 times larger than it was a century ago. Today, 77,000 people in the United States are over 100, and the Census Bureau predicts that number will rise to 834,000 by 2050 (J. Volz, 2000). Old age is not necessarily a time of loneliness and desolation, but it is a time when people generally become more inward looking, cautious, and conforming (Reedy, 1983). It is a time when people develop coping strategies that increasingly take into account the limits of their control—accepting what they cannot change, such as chronic health problems (Brandtstadter & Renner, 1990). Although they interact with others less frequently, older adults enjoy these interactions more (Carstensen, 1997). They find relationships more satisfying, supportive, and fulfilling than earlier in life. As they sense that time is running out, they value positive interactions and become selective about their social partners. As long as they have a network of at least three close relatives or friends, they are usually content.

The many changes associated with adolescence and adulthood are summarized in "In Review: Milestones of Adolescence and Adulthood."

Death and Dying

With the onset of old age, people become aware that death is approaching. They watch as their friends disappear. They feel their health deteriorating, their strength waning, and their intellectual capabilities declining. A few years or a few months before death, some people experience a sharp decline in mental functioning known as **terminal drop** (B. J. Small & Bäckman, 1999).

The awareness of impending death brings about the last psychological crisis, according to Erikson's theory. During this stage, people evaluate their lives and accomplishments and affirm them as meaningful (leading to a feeling of integrity) or meaningless (leading to a feeling of despair). They tend to become more philosophical and reflective. They attempt to put their lives into perspective. They reminisce, resolve past conflicts, and integrate past events. They may also become more interested in the religious and spiritual side of life. This "life review" may trigger anxiety, regret, guilt, and despair, or it may allow people to face their own death and the deaths of friends and relatives with a feeling of peace and acceptance (Erikson, 1968; M. A. Lieberman & Tobin, 1983).

Even the actual confrontation with death does not have to bring despair and depression. When death finally is imminent, old people strive for a death with dignity, love,

Milestones of Adolescence and Adulthood

Age	Physical Changes	Cognitive Changes	Social Events and Psychological Changes
Early adolescence (11–15 years)	Puberty brings reproductive capacity and marked bodily changes.	Formal operations and principled moral reasoning become possible for the first time. (This occurs only for some people.)	Social and emotional changes result from growing sexual awareness; adolescents experience mood swings, physical changes, and conflicts with parents.
Late adolescence (16–19 years)	Physical growth continues.	Formal operations and principled moral reasoning become more likely.	An identity crisis accompanies graduation from high school.
Early adulthood (20–39 years)	Physical growth continues.	Increases continue in knowledge, problem-solving ability, and moral reasoning.	People choose a job and often a mate; they may become parents.
Middle adulthood (40–65 years)	Size and muscle mass decrease; fat increases; eyesight declines; reproductive capacity in women ends.	Thought becomes more complex, adaptive, and global.	Midlife transition may lead to change; for most, the middle years are satisfying.
Late adulthood (over 65 years)	Size decreases; organs become less efficient.	Reasoning, mathematical ability, comprehension, novel problem solving, and memory may decline.	Retirement requires adjustments; people look inward; awareness of death precipitates life review.

affection, physical contact, and no pain (Schulz, 1978). As they think about death, they are comforted by their religious faith, their achievements, and the love of their friends and family (Kastenbaum, Kastenbaum, & Morris, 1989).

Longevity Facing death with dignity and openness helps people to complete the life cycle with a sense of life's meaningfulness, but most of us want to live as long as possible. How can we do so? Research suggests that people live longer if they do not have a history of heavy drinking and if they live independently in old age rather than in nursing homes. Longevity is *not* related to higher levels of education, income, or occupation—you can't buy long life (Jagger, Clarke, & Stone, 1995). However, certain personality characteristics are associated with longer lives. These include being curious, being conscientious, and not overemphasizing the importance of negative events in life (H. S. Friedman et al., 1995a; C. Peterson et al., 1998; Swan & Carmelli, 1996). Older adults also tend to live longer if they eat a low-calorie diet, get regular physical and mental exercise, and retain a sense of control over their lives (Hayflick, 1994).

So eat your veggies, keep fit, and continue to think actively. You will live better now, and you may also live longer.

active review Human Development

Linkages

As noted in Chapter 1, all of psychology's subfields are related to one another. Our discussion of infantile amnesia illustrates just one way in which the topic of this chapter, human development, is linked to the subfield of memory (Chapter 6). The Linkages diagram shows ties to two other subfields as well, and there are many more ties throughout the book. Looking for linkages among subfields will help you see how they all fit together and better appreciate the big picture that is psychology.

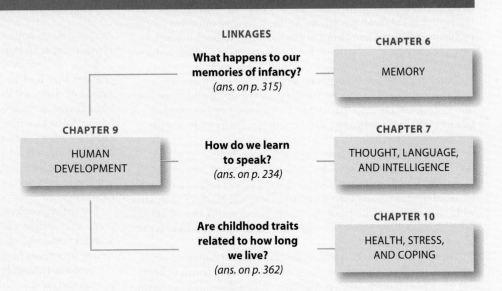

LINKAGES

CHAPTER 9
HUMAN DEVELOPMENT

What happens to our memories of infancy?
(ans. on p. 315)

CHAPTER 6
MEMORY

How do we learn to speak?
(ans. on p. 234)

CHAPTER 7
THOUGHT, LANGUAGE, AND INTELLIGENCE

Are childhood traits related to how long we live?
(ans. on p. 362)

CHAPTER 10
HEALTH, STRESS, AND COPING

Summary

Developmental psychology is the study of the course and causes of systematic, sequential, age-related changes in mental abilities, social relationships, emotions, and moral understanding over the life span.

EXPLORING HUMAN DEVELOPMENT

What does "genetic influence" mean?

A central question in developmental psychology concerns the relative influences of nature and nurture. Gesell stressed nature in his theory of development, proposing that development is *maturation*—the natural unfolding of abilities with age. Watson took the opposite view, claiming that development is learning, as shaped by the external environment. In his theory of cognitive development, Piaget described how nature and nurture work together. Today we accept as given the notion that both nature and nurture affect development and ask not whether, but how and to what extent, each contributes. Research in *behavioral genetics* shows that complex traits, such as intelligence and personality, are influenced by many genes, as well as by many environmental factors.

BEGINNINGS

Why should pregnant women stay away from tobacco and alcohol?

Development begins with the union of an ovum and a sperm to form a zygote, which develops into an *embryo. Genes,* which are

made up of *deoxyribonucleic acid (DNA),* make up the *chromosomes* that are in each body cell. The embryonic stage is a *critical period* for development, a time when certain organs must develop properly or they never will. The development of organs at this stage is permanently affected by harmful *teratogens* such as radiation, drugs, or alcohol. After the embryo develops into a *fetus,* adverse conditions may harm the infant's size, behavior, intelligence, or health. Babies born to women who drink heavily are at risk for *fetal alcohol syndrome.*

Newborns have limited but effective senses of vision, hearing, taste, and smell. They exhibit many *reflexes:* swift, automatic responses to external stimuli. Motor development proceeds as the nervous system matures, muscles grow, and the infant experiments with and selects the most efficient movement patterns.

INFANCY AND CHILDHOOD: COGNITIVE DEVELOPMENT

How do babies think?

Cognitive development refers to the development of thinking, knowing, and remembering. According to Piaget, *schemas* are modified through the complementary processes of *assimilation* (fitting new objects or events into existing schemas) and *accommodation* (changing schemas when new objects will not fit existing schemas). During the *sensorimotor period,* infants progress from using only simple senses and reflexes to forming mental representations of objects and actions. Thus, the child becomes capable of thinking about objects that are not present. The ability to recognize that objects continue to exist even when they are hidden from view is what Piaget called *object permanence.* During the *preoperational period,* children can use symbols, but they do not have the ability to think logically and rationally. Their understanding of the world is intuitive. When children develop the ability to think logically about concrete objects, they enter the period of *concrete operations.* At this time they can solve simple problems and have a knowledge of *conservation,* recognizing that, for example, the amount of a substance is not altered even when its shape changes.

Developmental psychologists now believe that new levels of cognition are reached not in sharply marked stages of global understanding but more gradually, and that children's reasoning can be affected by factors such as task difficulty and degree of familiarity with the objects and language involved.

Psychologists who explain cognitive development in terms of *information processing* have documented age-related improvements in children's attention, their abilities to explore and focus on features of the environment, and their memories. "Infantile amnesia" leaves us with virtually no memory of events from before the age of three. Several explanations have been suggested, but this phenomenon is not yet fully understood.

The specific content of cognitive development, including the development of scripts, depends on the cultural context in which children live. How fast children develop cognitive abilities depends to a certain extent on how stimulating and supportive their environments are. Children growing up in poverty are likely to have delayed or impaired cognitive abilities.

INFANCY AND CHILDHOOD: SOCIAL AND EMOTIONAL DEVELOPMENT

How do infants become attached to their caregivers?

Infants and their caregivers, from the early months, respond to each other's emotional expressions. Most infants can be classified as having easy, difficult, or slow-to-warm-up *temperaments.* Whether they retain these temperamental styles depends to some extent on their parents' expectations and demands. Over the first year of life, infants form a deep, long-lasting emotional *attachment* to their mother or other primary caregiver. This attachment may be secure or insecure, depending largely on whether the caregiver is responsive and loving, or rejecting. The process of *socialization* begins as parents teach their children the skills and rules needed in their culture, using parenting styles described as *authoritarian, permissive,* or *authoritative.* Among European American parents, those with an authoritative style tend to have more competent and cooperative children. Patterns of socialization depend upon the culture and conditions in which parents find themselves.

Over the childhood years, interactions with peers are increasingly characterized by cooperation and competition. Children come to base their friendships on feelings, not things. Changes in children's relationships are in part related to their growing social competence. Children become increasingly able to interpret and understand social situations and emotional signals. They also learn social rules and roles,

including those related to gender. *Gender roles* are based both on biological differences between the sexes and on implicit and explicit socialization by parents, teachers, and peers.

ADOLESCENCE

What threatens adolescents' self-esteem?

Adolescents undergo significant changes not only in size, shape, and physical capacity but also, typically, in their social lives, reasoning abilities, and views of themselves. *Puberty* brings about physical changes that lead to psychological changes. Early adolescence is a period of shaky self-esteem. It is also a time when conflict with parents, as well as closeness and conformity to friends, is likely to arise. Later adolescence focuses on finding an answer to the question, Who am I? Events such as graduating from high school and going to college challenge the adolescent's self-concept, precipitating an *identity crisis.* To resolve this crisis, the adolescent must develop an integrated self-image as a unique person, an image that often includes ethnic identity.

For many people, adolescence begins a stage of cognitive development that Piaget called the *formal operational period.* Formal abstract reasoning now becomes more sophisticated, and moral reasoning progresses from *preconventional* to *conventional* and, possibly, *postconventional* stages. Principled moral judgment—shaped by gender and culture—becomes possible for the first time.

ADULTHOOD

What developmental changes occur in adulthood?

Physical, cognitive, and social changes occur throughout adulthood. Middle adulthood sees changes that include decreased acuity of the senses, increased risk of heart disease, and declining fertility. Nevertheless, most people do not experience major health problems until late adulthood.

The cognitive changes that occur in early and middle adulthood are generally positive, including improvements in reasoning and problem-solving ability. In late adulthood, some intellectual abilities decline—especially those involved in tasks that are unfamiliar, complex, or difficult. Other abilities, such as recalling facts or making wise decisions, tend not to decline.

In their twenties, young adults make occupational choices and form intimate commitments. By the end of their thirties, they settle down and decide what is important. They become concerned with *generativity*—with producing something that will outlast them. Sometime around age forty, adults experience a *midlife transition,* which may or may not be a crisis. The forties and fifties are often a time of satisfaction. In their sixties, people contend with the issue of retirement. They generally become more inward looking, cautious, and conforming. In their seventies, eighties, and beyond, people confront their own mortality. They may become more philosophical and reflective as they review their lives. A few years or months before death, many experience a sharp decline in mental functioning known as *terminal drop.* Still, they strive for a death with dignity, love, and no pain.

Learn by Doing

Put It in Writing

Write a short paper describing some of the ways in which you have developed over the last five years. Include comments on physical changes, as well as changes in your thoughts, feelings, and behavior. Imagine yourself in another five years, and describe what further changes you expect in your physical condition, lifestyle, relationships, ideas, emotional state, and behaviors. Compare the changes that have taken place in your life with those we have described in this chapter for the average person of your age.

Personal Learning Activity

Ask several of your friends about the way their parents raised them, and especially about how strict or lenient they were in providing discipline. Take notes on these interviews, and then try to categorize your friends' parents as either authoritarian, permissive, or authoritative. (You might try categorizing your own parents, as well.) Was it easy to decide which category to use in each case, or do you think that additional categories are necessary to describe parenting styles? Do you think that your friends' personalities reflect the effects of the parenting styles described in this chapter? *For additional projects, see the five Personal Learning Activities in the corresponding chapter of the study guide that accompanies this text.*

Step into Action

Courses

Infancy
Child Development
Adolescence
Life-Span Development
Social Development
Cognitive Development
Death and Dying

Movies

Lord of the Flies (nature-nurture)
Stand by Me (childhood)
Parenthood (child rearing)
Little Man Tate; Searching for Bobby Fisher; What's Eating Gilbert Grape? (raising special children)
Revenge of the Nerds; Ferris Beuller's Day Off; The Breakfast Club; My Life in Pink; Rushmore (adolescence)
St. Elmo's Fire; Good Will Hunting; Reality Bites; Clerks; Chasing Amy (young adulthood)
The Big Chill; American Beauty; Same Time Next Year (adulthood)
City Slickers (midlife transition)
On Golden Pond; Cocoon; Space Cowboys (aging)
Do the Right Thing (moral reasoning and moral action)
The Color Purple (development of self-esteem)

Books

Jeffrey W. Trawick-Smith, *Early Childhood Development: A Multicultural Perspective* (Prentice-Hall, 1999) (introduction to cultural influences on development)

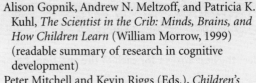

Alison Gopnik, Andrew N. Meltzoff, and Patricia K. Kuhl, *The Scientist in the Crib: Minds, Brains, and How Children Learn* (William Morrow, 1999) (readable summary of research in cognitive development)

Peter Mitchell and Kevin Riggs (Eds.), *Children's Reasoning and the Mind* (Psychology Press, 1999) (cognitive development in childhood)

John Janeway Conger and Nancy L. Galambos, *Adolescence and Youth: Psychological Development in a Changing World* (Addison-Wesley, 1996) (adolescent development)

Richard Shulz and Timothy A. Salthouse, *Adult Development and Aging: Myths and Emerging Realities* (Prentice-Hall, 1998) (the title says it all)

The Web

The World Wide Web is a good source of additional information about the science of psychology, provided you use it carefully and think critically about the information you find. The PsychAbilities web site that accompanies this text offers many resources relevant to this chapter. These resources include interactive NetLab exercises; Thinking Critically and Evaluating Research exercises; ACE chapter quizzes; recommended web links; and articles on current events, books, and movies. At http://college.hmco.com, select *Psychology* and then this textbook.

Review of Key Terms

Can you define each of the key terms in the chapter? Check your definitions against those on the pages listed in parentheses below or in the Glossary/Index at the end of the text.

accommodation *(p. 308)*

assimilation *(p. 308)*

attachment *(p. 320)*

authoritarian parents *(p. 325)*

authoritative parents *(p. 325)*

behavioral genetics *(p. 301)*

chromosomes *(p. 302)*

concrete operations *(p. 313)*

conservation *(p. 312)*

conventional (moral reasoning) *(p. 333)*

critical period *(p. 303)*

deoxyribonucleic acid (DNA) *(p. 302)*

developmental psychology *(p. 300)*

embryo *(p. 303)*

fetal alcohol syndrome *(p. 304)*

fetus *(p. 303)*

formal operational period *(p. 332)*

gender roles *(p. 327)*

generativity *(p. 338)*

genes *(p. 302)*

identity crisis *(p. 331)*

information processing *(p. 314)*

maturation *(p. 300)*

midlife transition *(p. 338)*

object permanence *(p. 309)*

permissive parents *(p. 325)*

postconventional (moral reasoning) *(p. 333)*

preconventional (moral reasoning) *(p. 333)*

preoperational period *(p. 311)*

puberty *(p. 329)*

reflexes *(p. 305)*

schemas *(p. 308)*

sensorimotor period *(p. 308)*

socialization *(p. 324)*

temperament *(p. 319)*

teratogens *(p. 303)*

terminal drop *(p. 339)*

Multiple-Choice Self-Test

Select the best answer for each of the questions below. Then check your response against the Answer Key at the end of the text.

1. Which of the following is *not* true? Research in behavioral genetics

   a. explores how nature and nurture contribute to make all people alike as human beings.
   b. explores how nature and nurture operate together to make people unique.
   c. is concerned with differences between individuals or groups, not with the characteristics of a single individual.
   d. can determine what percentage of your intelligence is due to heredity.

2. When she became pregnant, Alyse was advised to avoid teratogens. These include all of the following *except*

   a. alcohol.
   b. drugs.
   c. smoking.
   d. exercise.

3. Lisa is pregnant and has been smoking a pack of cigarettes a day. We would expect that her baby will be at risk for being born

   a. addicted to nicotine.
   b. with a low birth weight and respiratory problems.
   c. mentally retarded and with malformations of the face.
   d. with malformed kidneys and/or genitals.

4. Keshawn is one month old. He is most likely to look longest at

   a. small figures on the wallpaper.
   b. a ribbon hanging above his crib.
   c. colorful figures.
   d. a human face.

5. At six months of age, Jacob still demonstrates the grasping and rooting reflexes. This could signal that Jacob

   a. has advanced motor skills.
   b. has muscles that cannot support his body.
   c. has a problem with brain development.
   d. needs less environmental stimulation than the average baby.

6. Two-year old Jessie sees a scuba diver emerge on the beach. "Big fish!" says Jessie. According to Piaget, Jessie has just used _____ to try to understand the new stimulus of a scuba diver.

   a. assimilation
   b. accommodation
   c. object permanence
   d. conservation

7. Adriana is crying because her teddy bear, Boyd, has fallen off the table and landed on his face. She insists that her mother put a bandage on Boyd's nose. According to Piaget's theory, Adriana is most likely in the _____ stage of cognitive development.

   a. sensorimotor
   b. preoperational
   c. concrete operational
   d. formal operational

8. Renee Baillargeon's research focused on infants' understanding about objects and gravity. Baillargeon found that infants

   a. looked longer at "possible" events that they had experienced many times.
   b. looked longer at "impossible" events that defied physical principles.
   c. have no knowledge of physical principles until they have actual experience with such principles.
   d. do not improve their understanding of physical principles between the age of three months and one year.

9. You try to recall what occurred on your first birthday. According to research on information processing and memory, you are likely to

   a. recall a general schema of "birthday," as well as details about your first one.
   b. be unable to recall anything about your first birthday due to infantile amnesia.
   c. recall information about your first birthday if you are shown pictures of yourself taken that day.
   d. recall information about the birthday if you hear a tape recorded at your party.

10. Tara is an infant who goes to sleep at fairly predictable times and cries only when she is hungry or uncomfortable. She is generally cheerful and is happy when taken new places. According to research on temperament, Tara would be described as a(n) _____ infant.

    a. easy
    b. slow-to-warm-up
    c. difficult
    d. independent

11. Harlow's research with infant monkeys and artificial mothers demonstrated that

    a. infant monkeys are attached to the "mothers" that feed them.
    b. infant monkeys are attached to the "mothers" that provide contact comfort.
    c. attachment is entirely innate, with no learned component.
    d. "mothering" is instinctive, with no learned component.

12. When Habib's mother drops him off at the day care center, he always cries when she leaves. When his mother returns and picks him up, Habib tries to squirm away and refuses to be held by her. Habib is demonstrating a(n) _____ attachment to his mother.

    a. secure
    b. anxious insecure
    c. avoidant insecure
    d. ambivalent insecure

13. Sam and Alex are sixteen and want to drive to a rock concert in a big city, five hours from their home. Sam's parents explain that it is too dangerous for him to drive that distance and be in a major city without an adult. They offer to drive him and Alex to the concert. Alex's parents tell him that it is no problem if he wants to drive their car and stay in the city overnight. According to Baumrind's research, Sam's parents are displaying a(n) _____ style of parenting, whereas Alex's parents are displaying a(n) _____ style.

    a. authoritative; authoritarian
    b. authoritarian; authoritative
    c. authoritative; permissive
    d. authoritarian; permissive

14. Pat is seven years old. Pat's parents encourage Pat to achieve, be independent, explore the environment, and assume personal responsibility. From this information we can conclude that Pat is most likely

    a. female.
    b. male.
    c. Chinese.
    d. androgenous.

15. Ludmilla recently graduated from high school but can't decide whether to attend a local community college or work full-time. She doesn't know what career she would like to pursue, and she is also uncertain if she should stay with her current boyfriend. According to Erikson, Ludmilla is most likely experiencing the psychosocial crisis characterized by _____.

    a. trust versus mistrust
    b. initiative versus guilt
    c. identity versus role confusion
    d. integrity versus despair

16. According to research on adolescence, which of the following is *not* true of teens who engage in sexual activity? They are _____.

    a. more likely to hold unconventional attitudes and values.
    b. more likely to smoke and drink.
    c. more likely to be Asian American.
    d. less likely to have highly educated parents.

17. Jeanine and Helen are in a drugstore when Jeanine suggests that they steal some candy. Helen argues that they should not steal the candy because they might get caught and be put into jail. According to Kohlberg's theory, Helen is at the _____ stage of moral reasoning.

    a. preconventional
    b. conventional
    c. postconventional
    d. universal

18. In the past ten years, Vernon has gained weight, especially around the middle. He also now needs glasses. If he is typical of most people his age, Vernon has most likely reached

    a. adolescence.
    b. early adulthood.
    c. middle adulthood.
    d. old age.

19. Verna is sixty-five years old. Based on developmental research, we would assume that Verna

    a. is slower at solving complex new problems than younger people.
    b. has better mathematical skills than younger people.
    c. finds her mental abilities improving every day.
    d. will do better at mental tasks if her mind has "rested" as a result of being retired and inactive for many years.

20. Patrice is eighty years old and has recently been unable to read her books and comprehend what they say. She can't make sense of her checkbook, even though she was once an expert accountant. Her health is deteriorating, and her strength waning. Patrice is most likely experiencing

    a. cognitive dissonance.
    b. terminal drop.
    c. the crisis of initiative versus guilt.
    d. androgyny.

10

Health, Stress, and Coping

Have you ever gotten a terrible cold

"at the worst possible time"—at the end of the semester, say, or during the holidays, when there's just too much to do and everybody seems to be making demands on you? Most people would answer yes, but a more important question is whether there's anything you can do to avoid getting sick at these times. This is a question of concern to health psychologists. They explore the ways in which health relates to psychological, social, and behavioral factors, and they apply their research to preventing illness and promoting health. They develop programs to help people make lifestyle changes that can lower their risk of illness and premature death. And they study how stress affects people's mental and physical health. Of particular importance is the immune system's response to stress. In this chapter, you will learn about several kinds of stressors, how people respond to them, and the relationship between stress reactions and illness. You will also discover what you can do to protect your own health and change risky behaviors that may affect it.

Reading this chapter will help you to answer the following questions:

- **What do health psychologists do?**
- **How do psychological stressors affect physical health?**
- **How does stress affect your immune system?**
- **Who is most likely to adopt a healthy lifestyle?**

I
n Bangor, Maine, where snow and ice have paralyzed the community, Angie's headache gets worse as her four-year-old daughter and six-year-old son start bickering again. The day-care center and elementary school are closed, so Angie must stay home from her job at the grocery store. She probably couldn't have gotten there anyway, because the buses have stopped running. During the latest storm the power went out, and the house is now almost unbearably cold; the can of spaghetti Angie opens is nearly frozen. Worry begins to creep into her head: "If I can't work, how will I pay for rent and day care?" Her parents have money problems, too, so they can't offer financial help, and her ex-husband rarely makes his child-support payments. On top of everything else, Angie is coming down with the flu.

How do people manage such adversity, and what are its consequences for the individual? Psychologists who study questions like these have established a specialty known as **health psychology,** "a field within psychology devoted to understanding psychological influence on how people stay healthy, why they become ill, and how they respond when they do get ill" (S. E. Taylor, 1998a, p. 4).

health psychology   A field in which psychologists conduct and apply psychological research to promote human health and prevent illness.

Health Psychology

■ What do health psychologists do?

The themes underlying health psychology date back to ancient times. For thousands of years, in many cultures around the world, people have believed that their mental state, their behavior, and their health are linked. Today, there is scientific evidence to support this belief (S. E. Taylor, 1998a). We now know that the stresses of life influence health through their impact on psychological and physical processes. Anger, hostility, pessimism, depression, and hopelessness can affect the onset, duration, and outcome of physical illnesses. Similarly, poor health has been linked to behavioral factors such as lack of exercise, inadequate diet, smoking, and use of alcohol and other drugs.

Health psychology has become a prominent field, in part because of changing patterns of illness. Until the middle of the twentieth century, acute infectious diseases such as influenza, tuberculosis, and pneumonia were the major causes of illness and death in the Western world. With these deadly diseases now tamed, chronic illnesses—such as coronary heart disease, cancer, and diabetes—have become the leading causes of disability and death. Compared with acute diseases, these chronic diseases develop more slowly and are more strongly associated with people's psychological makeup, lifestyle, and environment (Lichtenstein et al., 2000; S. E. Taylor, Repetti, & Seeman, 1997; see Table 10.1). The psychological and behavioral factors that contribute to these illnesses can be changed by psychological methods, such as programs that promote nonsmoking and a low-fat diet. Indeed, about half the deaths in the United States are due to potentially preventable health-risky behaviors (National Cancer Institute, 1994).

One goal of health psychology is to help people understand the role they can play in controlling their own health and life expectancy. For example, health psychologists have promoted early detection of disease by educating people about the warning signs of cancer, heart disease, and other serious illnesses and encouraging them to seek medical attention while life-saving treatment is still possible. Encouraging women to perform breast self-examinations and men to do testicular exams are just two examples of health psychology programs that save thousands of lives each year (S. E. Taylor, 1998a). In addition, health psychologists have tried to understand why some people fail to follow prescribed treatment programs for controlling diseases such as diabetes, heart disease, and high blood pressure. Discovering what causes noncompliance with medical advice and creating procedures that encourage greater compliance can speed recovery, prevent unnecessary suffering, and save lives. Health psychologists also study, and help people to understand, the role played by stress in physical health and illness.

TABLE 10.1					
Lifestyle Behaviors That Affect the Leading Causes of Death in the United States					
This table shows five of the leading causes of death in the United States today, along with behavioral factors that contribute to their development.					

Cause of Death	Alcohol	Smoking	Diet	Exercise	Stress
Heart diease	x	x	x	x	x
Cancer	x	x	x		?
Stroke	x	x	x	?	?
Lung disease		x			
Accidents and Injury	x	x			x

Source: Data from USDHHS (1990); Centers for Disease Control and Prevention (1999a).

Understanding Stress

▪ **How do psychological stressors affect physical health?**

You have probably heard that death and taxes are the only two things guaranteed in life. If there is a third, it surely must be stress. Stress is woven into the fabric of life. No matter how wealthy, powerful, attractive, or happy you might be, stress happens. It comes in many forms, from a difficult exam to an automobile accident, to standing in a long line, to a day when everything goes wrong. Mild stress, like waiting to be with that special person, can be stimulating, motivating, and even desirable, but as stress becomes more severe, it can bring on physical, psychological, and behavioral problems.

Stress is the emotional and physiological process that occurs as individuals try to adjust to or deal with environmental circumstances that disrupt, or threaten to disrupt, their daily functioning (S. E. Taylor, 1998a). Stress thus involves a transaction between people and their environments. The environmental circumstances (such as exams or accidents) that cause people to make adjustments are called **stressors. Stress reactions** are the physical, psychological, and behavioral responses (such as nervousness, nausea, and fatigue) displayed in the face of stressors.

Why are some people more strongly affected by stressors than other people, or more affected on one occasion than another? The answer appears to lie in *mediating factors* that influence the relationship between people and their environments. Mediating factors include (1) the extent to which people can *predict* and *control* their stressors, (2) how they *interpret* the threat involved, (3) the *social support* they get, and (4) their *stress-coping skills*. These mediating factors dampen or magnify a stressor's impact. Thus, as shown in Figure 10.1, stress is not a specific event but a *process* in which the nature and intensity of stress responses depend on how stressors are mediated by factors such as the way people think about them and the skills and resources they have to cope with them.

Stressors

Most of the stressors people face have both physical and psychological components. Students, for example, are challenged by psychological demands to do well in their courses, as well as by the physical fatigue resulting from the pressures of academics. Here, we focus on psychological stressors.

stress   The process of adjusting to circumstances that disrupt, or threaten to disrupt, a person's daily functioning.

stressors   Events or situations to which people must adjust.

stress reactions   Physical, psychological, and behavioral responses to stressors.

FIGURE 10.1	The Process of Stress

Stressful events, people's reactions to those events, and interactions between people and the situations they face are all important components of stress. Notice the two-way relationships in the stress process. For example, if a person has effective coping skills, stress responses will be less severe. Having milder stress responses will act as a "reward" that will strengthen those skills. Further, as coping skills (such as refusing unreasonable demands) improve, certain stressors (such as a boss's unreasonable demands) may become less frequent.

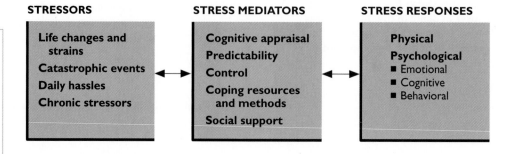

Applying Psychology

ANOTHER CATASTROPHE
Catastrophic events such as explosions, hurricanes, plane crashes, school shootings, and other traumas are stressors that can be psychologically devastating for victims, their families, and rescue workers. As was the case in the wake of this train wreck, health psychologists and other professionals provide on-the-spot counseling and follow-up sessions to help people deal with the consequences of trauma.

Psychological Stressors Any event that forces a person to change or adapt can be a psychological stressor. Even pleasant events can qualify as stressful. For example, a vacation is supposed to be relaxing, but it can be exhausting as well. And though the higher pay of a new job may be desirable, the change may also bring new pressures. Still, it is usually unpleasant circumstances that produce the most adverse psychological and physical effects (Kessler, 1997). These circumstances include catastrophic events, life changes and strains, chronic stressors, and daily hassles (Baum, Gatchel, & Krantz, 1997).

Sudden, unexpected, potentially life threatening experiences or traumas qualify as *catastrophic events.* Physical or sexual assault, military combat, natural disasters, explosions, plane crashes, and accidents fall into this category. *Life changes and strains* include divorce, illness in the family, difficulties at work, moving to a new place, and other circumstances that create demands to which people must adjust (Price, 1992; see Table 10.2). *Chronic stressors*—stressors that continue over a long period of time—

TABLE 10.2
The Undergraduate Stress Questionnaire

Here are some items from the Undergraduate Stress Questionnaire, which asks students to indicate whether various stressors have occurred during the previous week.

Has this stressful event happened to you at any time during the last week? If it has, please check the space next to it. If it has not, please leave it blank.

_____ 1. Assignments in all classes due the same day

_____ 2. Having roommate conflicts

_____ 3. Lack of money

_____ 4. Trying to decide on major

_____ 5. Can't understand your professor

_____ 6. Stayed up late writing a paper

_____ 7. Sat through a boring class

_____ 8. Went into a test unprepared

_____ 9. Parent getting divorced

_____ 10. Incompetence at the registrar's office

Source: Crandall, Preisler, & Aussprung (1992).

include such circumstances as living near a noisy airport, being unable to earn a decent living, residing in a high-crime neighborhood, being the victim of discrimination, and even enduring years of academic pressure (G. W. Evans, Hygge, & Bullinger, 1995). Finally, *daily hassles* involve irritations, pressures, and annoyances that may not be major stressors by themselves but whose effects add up to become significant. The frustrations of daily commuting in heavy traffic, for example, can become so intense for some drivers that they display a pattern of aggression called "road rage" (Levy et al., 1997).

Measuring Stressors   Which stressors do the most harm? To study stress more precisely, psychologists have tried to measure the impact of particular stressors. In 1967, Thomas Holmes and Richard Rahe (pronounced "ray") pioneered the effort to find a standard way of measuring the stress in a person's life. Working on the assumption that all change, positive or negative, produces stress, they asked a large number of people to rate—in terms of *life-change units,* or *LCUs*—the amount of change and demand for adjustment represented by a list of events such as divorcing, being fired, retiring, losing a loved one, or becoming pregnant. (Getting married, the event against which raters were to compare all other stressors, was judged to be slightly more stressful than losing one's job.) On the basis of these ratings, Holmes and Rahe created the Social Readjustment Rating Scale, or SRRS. People taking the SRRS receive a stress score equal to the sum of the LCUs for all the stressful events they have recently experienced.

Numerous studies show that people scoring high on the SRRS and other life-change scales are more likely to suffer physical illness, mental disorder, or other problems than those with lower scores (e.g., Monroe, Thase, & Simons, 1992). However, questions have been raised about whether measuring life changes alone tells the whole stress story (Birnbaum & Sotoodeh, 1991). Accordingly, investigators have developed scales such as the *Life Experiences Survey,* or *LES* (I. G. Sarason, Johnson, & Siegal, 1978), which go beyond the SRRS to measure not just life events but also the respondents' *perception* of how intensely positive or negative the events were. As you might expect, scales like the LES generally show that negative events have a stronger negative impact on health than do positive events (De Benedittis, Lornenzetti, & Pieri, 1990).

The LES gives respondents the opportunity to write in and rate any stressors they have experienced that are not on the printed list. This individualized approach can capture the differing impact and meaning that experiences may have for men compared with women and for members of various cultural or subcultural groups. Divorce, for example, may have different meanings to people of different religious and cultural backgrounds. And members of some ethnic groups may experience prejudice and discrimination that is not felt by other groups (Contrada et al., 2000).

Stress Responses

Physical, psychological, and behavioral stress reactions often occur together, especially as stressors become more intense. Furthermore, one type of stress response can set off a stress response in another dimension. For example, a physical stress reaction such as mild chest pains may trigger the psychological stress response of worrying about a heart attack. Still, it is useful to analyze separately each category of stress responses.

Physical Stress Responses: The GAS   If you have experienced a near accident or some other sudden, frightening event, you know that the physical responses to stressors include rapid breathing, increased heartbeat, sweating, and a little later, shakiness. These reactions make up a general pattern known as the *fight-or-flight syndrome.* As described in Chapters 2 and 8, this vital syndrome prepares the body to face or to flee an immediate threat. When the danger passes, fight-or-flight responses subside. However, when stressors last a long time, these responses are only the beginning of a sequence of reactions.

Careful observation of animals and humans led Hans Selye (pronounced "SELL-yay") to suggest that the sequence of physical responses to stress occurs in a consistent pattern that is triggered by the effort to adapt to any stressor. Selye called this sequence the

FIGURE 10.2

The General Adaptation Syndrome

Hans Selye's research showed that physical reactions to stressors include an initial alarm reaction, followed by resistance and then exhaustion. During the alarm reaction, the body's resistance to stress temporarily drops below normal as it absorbs a stressor's initial impact. Resistance increases and then levels off in the resistance stage, but it ultimately declines if the exhaustion stage is reached.

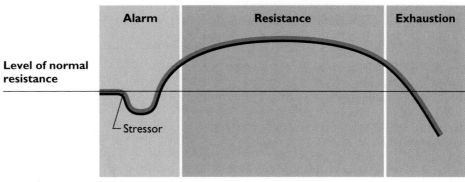

Source: Adapted from Selye (1974).

general adaptation syndrome, or **GAS** (Selye, 1956, 1976). The GAS has three stages, as shown in Figure 10.2.

The first stage, the *alarm reaction,* involves some version of the fight-or-flight syndrome. The reaction to a mild stressor, such as a hot room, may simply involve changes in heart rate, respiration, and perspiration that help the body regulate its temperature. More severe stressors prompt more dramatic alarm reactions, rapidly mobilizing the body's adaptive energy, much as a burglar alarm alerts police to take action (Kiecolt-Glaser et al., 1998).

Alarm reactions are controlled by the sympathetic nervous system through organs and glands that make up the *sympatho-adreno-medullary (SAM)* system. As shown on the right side of Figure 10.3, stressors trigger a process that begins when the brain's hypothalamus activates the sympathetic branch of the autonomic nervous system (ANS), which stimulates the medulla (inner part) of the adrenal glands. The adrenal glands, in turn, secrete catecholamines (pronounced "kat-uh-KOH-luh-meens")—especially adrenaline and noradrenaline—which circulate in the bloodstream, activating the liver, kidneys, heart, lungs, and other organs. The result is increased blood pressure, muscle tension, and blood sugar, along with other physical changes needed to cope with stressors. Even brief exposure to a stressor can produce major changes in these coordinated regulatory body systems (Cacioppo et al., 1995).

As shown on the left side of Figure 10.3, stressors also activate the *hypothalamic-pituitary-adrenocortical (HPA)* system, in which the hypothalamus stimulates the pituitary gland in the brain. The pituitary, in turn, secretes hormones such as adrenocorticotropic hormone (ACTH). Among other things, ACTH stimulates the cortex (outer surface) of the adrenal glands to secrete *corticosteroids;* these hormones release the body's energy supplies and fight inflammation. The pituitary gland also triggers the release of *endorphins,* the body's natural painkillers.

The overall effect of these stress systems is to generate emergency energy. The more stressors there are and the longer they last, the more resources the body must expend in an effort to resist them. If the stressors persist, the *resistance stage* of the GAS begins. Here, the initial obvious signs of the alarm reaction fade as the body settles in to resist the stressor on a long-term basis. The drain on adaptive energy is less during the resistance stage compared with the alarm stage, but the body is still working hard to cope with stress.

This continued biochemical resistance is costly. It slowly but surely uses up the body's reserves of adaptive energy until the capacity to resist is gone. The body then enters the third GAS stage, known as *exhaustion.* In extreme cases, such as prolonged exposure to freezing temperatures, the result is death. More commonly, the exhaustion stage brings signs of physical wear and tear. Especially hard-hit are the organ systems that were weak to begin with or were heavily involved in the resistance process. For example, if adrenaline and cortisol (which help fight stressors during the resistance stage) remain elevated for an extended time, the result can be damage to the heart and blood vessels; suppression of the body's disease-fighting immune system; and vulnerability to illnesses

general adaptation syndrome (GAS)
A pattern of responses triggered by the effort to adapt to stressors. The GAS consists of three stages: the alarm reaction, resistance, and exhaustion.

FIGURE 10.3

Organ Systems Involved in the GAS

Stressors produce a variety of physiological responses that begin in the brain and spread to organs throughout the body. For example, the pituitary gland triggers the release of endorphins, the body's natural painkillers. It also stimulates the release of corticosteroids, which help resist stress but, as described later, also tend to suppress the immune system. As described later, some of these substances may interact with sex hormones to create different physical stress responses and coping methods in men and women (S. E. Taylor et al., 2000b).

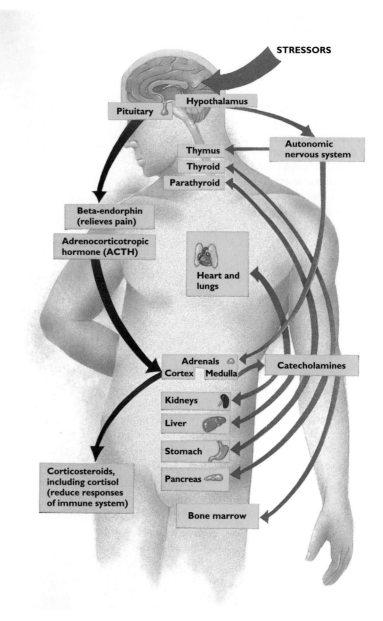

such as heart disease, high blood pressure, arthritis, colds, and flu (e.g., McEwen, 1998). Selye referred to illnesses caused or worsened by stressors as **diseases of adaptation.**

Although quite influential, Selye's description of the stress process has been criticized for underestimating the role of psychological factors in stress. For example, a person's emotional state or the way the person thinks about stressors can affect responses to those stressors. These criticisms led to the development of *psychobiological models,* which emphasize the importance of psychological, as well as biological, variables in producing and regulating stress responses (R. S. Lazarus & Folkman, 1984; Wickramasekera, Davies, & Davies, 1996). These psychological responses can involve changes in emotion and/or cognition (thinking).

Emotional Stress Responses   The physical stress responses we have described are usually accompanied by emotional stress responses. If someone shows a gun and demands your money, you will most likely experience the GAS alarm reaction. You will also feel some strong emotion—probably fear, maybe anger. In describing stress, people tend to say, "I was angry and frustrated!" rather than "My heart rate increased, and my blood pressure went up." In other words, they tend to mention changes in how they *feel.*

diseases of adaptation   Illnesses caused or worsened by stressors.

High-pressure salespeople know that stress can impair decision making. They take advantage of this stress response by creating time-limited offers or by telling customers that others are waiting to buy the item they are considering (Cialdini, 1995).

In most cases, emotional stress reactions diminish soon after the stressors are gone. Even severe emotional stress responses ease eventually. However, if stressors continue for a long time or if many occur in a short time, emotional stress reactions may persist. When people don't have a chance to recover their emotional equilibrium, they feel tense, irritable, short-tempered, or anxious, and they may experience increasingly intense feelings of fatigue, depression, and hopelessness. These reactions can become severe enough to be diagnosed as major depressive disorder, generalized anxiety disorder, or any of the other stress-related mental disorders discussed in Chapter 12.

Cognitive Stress Responses   In 1995, in the busy, noisy intensive care unit of a London hospital, a doctor misplaced a decimal point while calculating the amount of morphine a one-day-old premature baby should receive. The child died of a massive overdose (C. Davies, 1999). Reductions in the ability to concentrate, to think clearly, or to remember accurately are typical cognitive stress reactions. These problems appear partly because of *ruminative thinking,* the recurring intrusion of thoughts about stressful events (Lyubomirsky & Nolen-Hoeksema, 1995). Ruminative thoughts about relationship problems, for example, can seriously interfere with studying for a test. A related phenomenon is *catastrophizing,* which means dwelling on and overemphasizing the possible negative consequences of events (I. G. Sarason et al., 1986). Thus, during exams, test-anxious college students are likely to say to themselves, "I'm falling behind" or "Everyone is doing better than I am." As catastrophizing or ruminative thinking impairs cognitive functioning, resulting feelings of anxiety and other emotional arousal add to the total stress response, further hampering performance (Mendl, 1999).

Overarousal created by stressors also tends to narrow the scope of attention, making it harder to scan the full range of possible solutions to complex problems (Keinan, Friedland, & Ben-Porath, 1987). In addition, stress-narrowed attention may increase the problem-solving errors described in Chapter 7, on thought, language, and intelligence. People under stress are more likely to cling to *mental sets,* which are well-learned, but not always efficient, approaches to problems. Stress may also intensify *functional fixedness,* the tendency to use objects for only one purpose. Victims of hotel fires, for example, sometimes die trapped in their rooms because, in the stress of the moment, it did not occur to them to use the telephone or a piece of furniture to break a window. Stressors may also impair decision making. Under stress, people who normally consider all aspects of a situation before making a decision may act impulsively and sometimes foolishly (Keinan, Friedland, & Ben-Porath, 1987).

Behavioral Stress Responses   Clues about people's physical and emotional stress reactions come from changes in how they look, act, or talk. Strained facial expressions, a shaky voice, tremors, and jumpiness are common behavioral stress responses. Posture can also convey information about stress, a fact well known to skilled interviewers.

Even more obvious behavioral stress responses appear as people attempt to escape or avoid stressors. Some people quit their jobs, drop out of school, turn to alcohol, or even attempt suicide. Unfortunately, as discussed in Chapter 5, on learning, escape and avoidance tactics deprive people of the opportunity to learn more adaptive ways of coping with stressful environments, including college (M. L. Cooper et al., 1992). Aggression is another common behavioral response to stressors. All too often, this response is directed at members of one's own family (Polusny & Follette, 1995). For instance, in the wake of hurricanes and other natural disasters, it is not uncommon to see dramatic increases in the rate of domestic-violence reports in the devastated area (Rotton, 1990).

LINKAGES

When do stress responses become mental disorders? (a link to Psychological Disorders)

LINKAGES

Stress and Psychological Disorders

Physical, psychological, and behavioral stress responses sometimes appear together in patterns known as *burnout* and *posttraumatic stress disorder*. **Burnout** is an increasingly intense pattern of physical, psychological, and behavioral dysfunction in response to a continuous flow of stressors or to chronic stress (Maslach & Goldberg, 1998). As burnout nears, previously reliable workers or once-attentive spouses become indifferent, disengaged, impulsive, or accident-prone. They miss work frequently; oversleep; perform their jobs poorly; abuse alcohol or other drugs; and become irritable, suspicious, withdrawn, and depressed (S. E. Taylor, 1998a). Burnout is particularly common among those who do "people work," such as teachers and nurses (D. P. Schultz & Schultz, 1998).

A different pattern of severe stress reactions is illustrated by the case of Mary, a thirty-three-year-old nurse who was raped at knife point by an intruder in her apartment. In the weeks following this trauma, she became afraid of being alone and was preoccupied with the attack and with the fear that it might happen again. She installed additional locks on her doors and windows but experienced difficulty concentrating and could not immediately return to work. The thought of sex repelled her.

Mary suffered from **posttraumatic stress disorder (PTSD),** a pattern of severe negative reactions following a traumatic event (R. L. Spitzer et al., 1983). Among the characteristic reactions are anxiety, irritability, jumpiness, inability to concentrate or work productively, sexual dysfunction, and difficulty in getting along with others. PTSD sufferers also experience sleep disturbances and intense startle responses to noise or other sudden stimuli (Shalev et al., 2000). The most common feature of posttraumatic stress disorder is experiencing the trauma through nightmares or vivid memories. In rare cases, *flashbacks* occur in which the person behaves for minutes, hours, or days as if the trauma were occurring again.

Posttraumatic stress disorder is most commonly associated with events such as war, assault, or rape (e.g., Schnurr et al., 2000), but researchers now believe that some PTSD symptoms can be triggered by any major stressor (Ironson et al., 1997). PTSD may appear immediately following a trauma, or it may not occur until weeks, months, or even years later (Heim et al., 2000). The majority of those affected require professional help, although some seem to recover without it. For most, improvement takes time; for nearly all, the support of family and friends is vital to recovery (Foa et al., 1999; LaGreca et al., 1996).

As described in Chapter 12, stress has been implicated in the development of a number of other psychological disorders, including depression and schizophrenia. The *diathesis-stress* approach suggests that certain people are predisposed to these disorders, which they may or may not display depending on the frequency, nature, and intensity of the stressors they encounter.

burnout   A pattern of physical, psychological, and behavioral dysfunctions in response to continuous stressors.

posttraumatic stress disorder (PTSD) A pattern of adverse reactions following a traumatic event, commonly involving re-experiencing the event through nightmares or vivid memories.

Stress Mediators

The interaction of particular people with particular stressors can be important in other ways, too. For example, in Kosovo in 1999, at least one UN air strike was known to have

killed some of the ethnic Albanians whom the bombing was designed to protect. This "friendly fire" incident occurred because the pilots mistakenly identified the Albanians' trucks as Serbian army vehicles. The stress of combat is partly responsible for similarly tragic decision errors in almost every military operation (Adler, 1993). But why does stress disrupt the performance of some individuals and not others? And why does one individual survive, and even thrive, under the same circumstances that lead another to break down, give up, and burn out? A number of the mediating factors listed in Figure 10.1 help determine how much impact a given stressor will have (McEwen & Seeman, 1999).

Perceiving Stressors   Just as our perceptions of the world depend on which stimuli we attend to and how we interpret, or appraise, them (see Chapter 3, on sensation and perception), our emotional reactions to events depend somewhat on how we think about them. Any potential stressor usually has more negative impact on those who perceive it as a threat than on those who see it as a challenge (Rhodewalt & Zone, 1989). This holds true whether the stressor is a long waiting line or a deskful of work.

A classic experiment by Richard Lazarus demonstrated the effects of people's thoughts on their stress responses. He gave differing instructions to three groups of students who were about to watch a film showing bloody industrial accidents (R. S. Lazarus et al., 1965). One group (the "intellectualizers") was instructed to remain mentally detached from the bloody scenes; a second group (the "denial" group) was instructed to think of the bloody scenes as unreal; and a third group (the "unprepared" group) was not told anything about the film. As Figure 10.4 shows, the intensity of physiological arousal during the film, as measured by sweat-gland activity, depended on how the viewers were instructed to think about the film. The unprepared students were more upset than either of the other two groups. Similarly, physical and psychological symptoms associated with the stress of airport noise or learning about toxins in local soil are more common in people who engage in more catastrophic thinking about these problems (Kjellberg et al., 1996; Matthies, Hoeger, & Guski, 2000).

The influence of cognitive factors weakens somewhat as stressors become more extreme. For example, chronic-pain patients tend to engage in more physical activity if they feel a sense of control over their pain, but this effect does not hold for those whose pain is severe

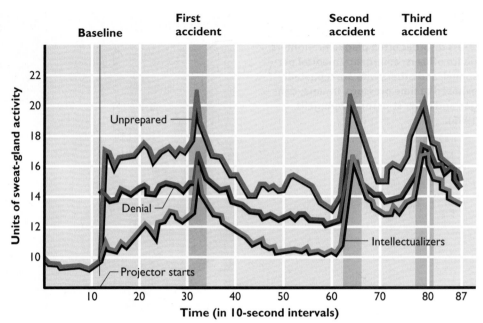

Source: Adapted from R. S. Lazarus et al. (1965).

FIGURE 10.4

Cognitive Influences on Stress Responses

Richard Lazarus and his colleagues found that students' physiological stress reaction to a film showing bloody industrial accidents was affected by they way they *thought about* what they saw. Those who had been instructed to remain detached from the film (the "intellectualizers") or to think of it as unreal (the "denial" group) were less upset—as measured by sweat-gland activity—than those in an "unprepared" group. These results were among the first to show that people's cognitive appraisal of stressors can affect their responses to those stressors.

(M. Jensen & Karoly, 1991). Still, even the impact of major stressors such as natural disasters or divorce may be less severe for those who think of them as challenges to be overcome. In other words, many stressful events are not inherently stressful; their impact depends partly on how people perceive them (Wiedenfeld et al., 1990). An important part of this appraisal is the degree to which the stressors are perceived to be predictable or controllable.

Predictability and Control   Uncertainty about when and if a particular stressor might occur tends to increase the stressor's impact (Boss, 1999; Sorrentino & Roney, 2000). For example, wives of American men missing in action during the Vietnam War showed poorer physical and emotional health than those who knew that their spouses had been killed in action or were being held prisoner (E. J. Hunter, 1979).

In short, predictable stressors tend to have less impact than those that are unpredictable (R. S. Lazarus & Folkman, 1984)—especially when the stressors are intense and occur for relatively short periods. For example, rats given a reliable warning signal every time they are to receive a shock show less severe physiological responses than animals given no warning (J. Weinberg & Levine, 1980). Among humans, men and women whose spouses died suddenly tend to display more immediate disbelief, anxiety, and depression than those who had weeks or months to prepare for the loss (Parkes & Weiss, 1983). However, predictability does not provide total protection against stressors. Research with animals shows that predictable stressors can be more damaging than unpredictable ones if they occur over long periods of time (Abbott, Schoen, & Badia, 1984).

The perception of control also mediates the effects of stressors. Stressors over which people believe they exert some control usually have less impact (Christensen, Stephens, & Townsend, 1998). For example, studies of several thousand employees in the United States, Sweden, and the United Kingdom have found that those who had little or no control over their work environment were more likely to suffer heart disease and other health problems than workers with a high degree of control over their work environment (Bosma et al., 1997; Cheng et al., 2000; Hancock, 1996). And at many hospitals, it is now standard practice to help patients to manage or control the stress of emergency treatment or the side effects of surgery, because doing so helps them heal faster and go home sooner (Chamberlin, 2000; Kiecolt-Glaser et al., 1998).

Simply *believing* that a stressor is controllable, even if it isn't, can also reduce its impact (S. C. Thompson et al., 1993). This effect was demonstrated in a study in which participants with panic disorder inhaled a mixture of oxygen and carbon dioxide that

Coping Skills	Example
Problem-focused coping	
Confronting	"I stood my ground and fought for what I wanted."
Seeking social support	"I talked to someone to find out more about the situation."
Planful problem solving	"I made a plan of action, and I followed it."
Emotion-focused coping	
Self-controlling	"I tried to keep my feelings to myself."
Distancing	"I didn't let it get to me; I tried not to think about it too much."
Positive reappraisal	"I changed my mind about myself."
Accepting responsibility	"I realized I brought the problem on myself."
Escape/avoidance (wishful thinking)	"I wished that the situation would go away or somehow be over with."

Source: Adapted from Folkman et al. (1986a); S. E. Taylor (1995).

TABLE 10.3

Ways of Coping

Coping is defined as one's cognitive and behavioral efforts to manage specific demands that are appraised as taxing one's resources (Folkman et al., 1986). This table illustrates two major approaches to coping. Ask yourself which approach you usually take when faced with stressors. Now rank-order the coping skills under each major approach in terms of how often you tend to use each. Do you rely on just one or two, or do you adjust your coping strategies to fit different kinds of stressors?

typically causes a panic attack (Sanderson, Rapee, & Barlow, 1989). Half the participants were led to believe (falsely) that they could control the concentration of the mixture. Compared with those who believed they had no control, significantly fewer of the "in-control" participants experienced full-blown panic attacks during the session, and their panic symptoms were fewer and less severe.

People who feel they have *no* control over negative events appear especially prone to physical and psychological problems. They often experience feelings of helplessness and hopelessness that, in turn, may promote depression or other mental disorders (S. E. Taylor & Aspinwall, 1996).

Coping Resources and Coping Methods   People usually suffer less from a stressor if they have adequate coping resources and effective coping methods. *Coping resources* include, among other things, the money and time to deal with stressful events. Thus, the physical and psychological responses to your car breaking down tend to be more negative if you are broke and pressed for time than if you have the money for repairs and the freedom to take a day off from work.

The impact of stressors can also be reduced by effective *coping methods* (Benight et al., 1999). Most of these methods can be classified as either problem-focused or emotion-focused. *Problem-focused* methods involve efforts to alter or eliminate a source of stress, whereas *emotion-focused* techniques attempt to regulate the negative emotional consequences of stressors (Folkman et al., 1986). These two forms of coping sometimes work together. For example, you might deal with the problem of noise from a nearby airport by forming a community action group to push for tougher noise-reduction laws and, at the same time, calm your anger when noise occurs by mentally focusing on the group's efforts to improve the situation (Folkman & Moskowitz, 2000). Susan Folkman and Richard Lazarus (1988) have devised a scale to assess the specific ways that people cope with stressors; Table 10.3 shows some examples from their scale.

Particularly when a stressor is difficult to control, it is sometimes helpful to fully express and think about the emotions one is experiencing in relation to the stressful event (J. E. Bower et al., 1999; Pennebaker, 1993). The benefits of this coping strategy have been observed among many individuals whose religious beliefs allow them to bring meaning to the death of a loved one or the devastation of natural disasters that might otherwise seem senseless tragedies (Paloutzian & Kirkpatrick, 1995; B. W. Smith et al., 2000). Some individuals who use humor to help them cope also show better adjustment and lower physiological reactivity to stressful events (Lefcourt et al., 1997).

Applying Psychology

YOU'VE GOT A FRIEND **Even when social support cannot eliminate stressors, it can help people, such as these breast cancer survivors, to feel less anxious, more optimistic, more capable of control, and more willing to try new ways of dealing with stressors.**

Social Support   Has a good friend ever given you comfort and reassurance during troubled times? If so, you have experienced the value of social support in tempering the impact of stressful events. Social support consists of resources provided by other people; the friends and social contacts on whom you can depend for support make up your **social support network** (B. R. Burleson, Albrecht, & Sarason, 1994). The support can take many forms, from eliminating a stressor (as when a friend helps you fix your car) to lessening a stressor's impact by providing companionship, ideas for coping, or reassurance that you are cared about and valued and that everything will be all right (Sarason, Sarason, & Gurung, 1997).

The stress-reducing effects of social support have been documented for a wide range of stressors, including cancer, military combat, loss of loved ones, natural disasters, arthritis, AIDS, and even ethnic discrimination (e.g., Foster, 2000; Holahan et al., 1997; Penner, Dovidio, & Albrecht, 2001; Savelkoul et al., 2000). These effects were well illustrated in two studies of undergraduate and graduate students (Goplerud, 1980; Lepore, 1995a). Some of the students were part of a supportive network; others were not. Those with the least adequate social support tended to suffer the most emotional distress and were more vulnerable to upper respiratory infections during times of high academic stress. Indeed, one team of researchers concluded that having inadequate social support is as dangerous as smoking cigarettes, because it nearly doubles a person's risk of dying from disease, suicide, or other causes (House, Umberson, & Landis, 1988).

Having strong social support can reduce the likelihood of illness, improve recovery from existing illness, and promote healthier behaviors (Grassi et al., 2000; Uchino, Uno, & Holt-Lunstad, 1999). However, the relationship between social support and the impact of stressors is not a simple one. First, just as the quality of social support can influence your ability to cope with stress, the reverse may also be true: Your ability to cope may determine the quality of the social support you receive (McLeod, Kessler, & Landis, 1992). For example, people who complain endlessly about stressors but never do anything about them may discourage social support, whereas those with an optimistic, action-oriented approach may attract support.

Second, *social support* refers not only to your relationships with others but also to the recognition that others care and will help (Pierce, Sarason, & Sarason, 1995). Some relationships in a seemingly strong social network can be stormy, fragile, or shallow, resulting in interpersonal conflicts that can have an adverse effect on health (Malarkey et al., 1994).

Finally, having too much support or the wrong kind of support can be as bad as not having enough. People whose friends and family overprotect them may actually put less

social support network   The friends and social contacts on whom one can depend for help and support.

energy into coping efforts or have less opportunity to learn effective coping strategies. Further, if the efforts of people in our social support network become annoying, disruptive, or interfering, they can increase stress and intensify psychological problems (Newsome, 1999; Newsome & Schulz, 1998).

Stress, Personality, and Gender   The impact of stress on health appears to depend not only on how people think about particular stressors, but to some extent on how they think about and react to the world in general (Prior, 1999). For instance, stress-related health problems tend to be especially common among people whose "disease-prone" personalities lead them to (1) try to ignore stressors when possible; (2) perceive stressors as long-term, catastrophic threats that they brought on themselves; and (3) be pessimistic about their ability to overcome stressors or other negative situations (e.g., Jorgensen et al., 1996; C. Peterson et al., 1998; Segerstrom et al., 1998).

Other cognitive styles appear to help insulate people from stressors. People who tend to think of stressors as temporary and who do not constantly blame themselves for bringing them about appear to be harmed less by them. This cognitive habit can be especially adaptive when combined with a tendency to see stressors as challenges. Its benefits can also be seen in many devout people whose religious beliefs lead them to think of poverty and other stressors as temporary conditions to be endured until their suffering is ultimately rewarded in an afterlife (McIntosh, Silver, & Wortman, 1993). Whatever the specifics, one important component of the "stress-hardy" or "disease-resistant" personality seems to be *dispositional optimism,* the belief or expectation that things will work out positively (Scheier, Carver, & Bridges, 1994; S. E. Taylor et al., 2000a). For example, optimistic students experience fewer physical symptoms at the end of the academic term (Aspinwall & Taylor, 1992). Optimistic coronary bypass surgery patients heal faster than pessimists (Scheier et al., 1989) and perceive their quality of life following coronary surgery to be higher than do patients with less optimistic outlooks (Fitzgerald et al., 1993). And among HIV-positive men, dispositional optimism has been associated with lower psychological distress, fewer worries, and lower perceived risk of acquiring full-blown AIDS (S. E. Taylor & Armor, 1996). These effects appear due in part to optimists' tendency to use challenge-oriented, problem-focused coping strategies that attack stressors directly, in contrast to pessimists' tendency to use emotion-focused coping such as denial and avoidance (S. E. Taylor, 1998a).

Recent research suggests that gender may also play a role in responses to stress. In a review of 200 studies of stress responses and coping methods, Shelley Taylor and her colleagues found that males under stress tended to get angry, avoid stressors, or both, whereas females were more likely to help others and to make use of their social support network (S. E. Taylor et al., 2000b). This was not true in every case, of course, but why should a significant difference show up at all? The gender-role learning discussed in Chapter 9 surely plays a part (Eagly & Wood, 1999). But Taylor also proposes that women's "tend and befriend" style differs from the "fight-or-flight" pattern so often seen in men because of gender differences in how hormones combine under stress. For example, oxytocin, a hormone released in both sexes as part of the general adaptation syndrome, interacts differently with male and female sex hormones—amplifying men's physical stress responses and reducing women's. This difference could lead to the more intense emotional and behavioral stress responses typical of men, and it might be partly responsible for their greater vulnerability to heart disease and other stress-related illnesses. If that is the case, gender differences in stress responses may help to explain why women live an average of 7.5 years longer than men.

FOCUS ON RESEARCH

Personality and Health

The way people think and act in the face of stressors, the ease with which they attract social support, and their tendency to be optimists or pessimists are but a few aspects of personality (see Chapter 11).

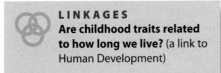

LINKAGES
Are childhood traits related to how long we live? (a link to Human Development)

■ What was the researchers' question?

Are there other personality characteristics that play a role in people's stress responses? One research team has focused on a more specific version of this question: Are there personality characteristics that help people to live longer in the face of life's inevitable stressors?

■ How did the researchers answer the question?

Howard Friedman and his colleagues sought the answer to this question by reanalyzing some data from a major longitudinal research project described in Chapter 7 (H. S. Friedman et al., 1995a, 1995b). That project was called the Terman Life Cycle Study because it was begun by Lewis Terman (author of the Stanford-Binet intelligence test). Terman wanted to document the long-term development of 1,528 exceptionally intelligent boys and girls, who came to be nicknamed the "Termites" (Terman & Oden, 1947).

Starting in 1921, and every five to ten years thereafter, Terman's research team had gathered information about the Termites' personality traits, social relationships, stressors, health habits, and many other variables. The data were collected through questionnaires and interviews with the Termites themselves, as well as with their teachers, parents, and other family members. By the early 1990s, about half of the Termites had died. It was then that Friedman realized that the Terman Life Cycle Study could shed some light on the relationship between personality and health, because the various personality traits identified in these people could be related to how long they lived. Accordingly, Friedman gathered the death certificates of the Termites, noted the dates and causes of death, and then looked for associations between their personalities and how long they lived.

■ What did the researchers find?

Friedman and his colleagues found that one of the most important predictors of long life was a basic dimension of personality known as *conscientiousness,* or *social dependability* (described in Chapter 11). Termites who, in childhood, had been seen as truthful, prudent, reliable, hardworking, and humble tended to live longer than those whose parents and teachers had identified them as impulsive and lacking in self-control.

Friedman also examined the Terman Life Cycle Study for what it suggested about the relationship between health and social support. In particular, he compared Termites whose parents had divorced or Termites who had been in unstable marriages with those who grew up in stable homes and who had stable marriages. He discovered that people who had experienced parental divorce during childhood, or who themselves had unstable marriages, died an average of four years earlier than those whose close social relationships had been less stressful.

■ What do the results mean?

You may be wondering whether differences in personality traits and social support actually *caused* some Termites to live longer than others. As Friedman's research is based mainly on correlational analyses, it is difficult to draw conclusions about what might have caused the relationships observed. Still, Friedman and his colleagues searched the Terman data for clues to mechanisms through which personality and other factors *might* have exerted a causal influence on how long the Termites lived (C. Peterson et al., 1998). For example, they evaluated the hypothesis that conscientious, dependable Termites who lived socially stable lives might have followed healthier lifestyles than impulsive, socially stressed Termites. Indeed, people in the latter group did tend to eat less healthy diets and were more likely to smoke, drink to excess, or use drugs. But health behaviors alone did not fully account for their shorter average life spans. Another possible explanation is that conscientiousness and stability in social relationships reflect a general attitude of caution that goes beyond eating right and avoiding substance abuse. Friedman found some support for this idea in the Terman data. Termites who were impulsive or nonconscientious were somewhat more likely to die from accidents or violence than those who were less impulsive.

in review

Stress Responses and Stress Mediators

Category	Examples
Responses	
Physical	Fight-or-flight syndrome (increased heart rate, respiration, and muscle tension; sweating; pupillary dilation; SAM and HPA activation (involving release of catecholamines and corticosteroids); eventual breakdown of organ systems involved in prolonged resistance to stressors.
Psychological	*Emotional:* anger, anxiety, depression, and other emotional states. *Cognitive:* inability to concentrate or think logically, ruminative thinking, catastrophizing. *Behavioral:* aggression and escape/avoidance tactics (including suicide attempts).
Mediators	
Appraisal	Thinking of a difficult new job as a challenge will create less discomfort than focusing on the threat of failure.
Predictability	A tornado that strikes without warning may have a more devastating emotional impact than a long-predicted hurricane.
Control	Repairing a disabled spacecraft may be less stressful for the astronauts doing the work than for their loved ones on earth, who can do nothing to help.
Coping resources and methods	Having no effective way to relax after a hard day may prolong tension and other stress responses.
Social support	Having no one to talk to about a rape or other trauma may amplify the negative impact of the experience.

What do we still need to know?

The Terman Life Cycle Study does not provide final answers about the relationship between personality and health. However, it has generated some important clues and a number of intriguing hypotheses to be evaluated in future research with more representative samples of participants. It also stands as an excellent example of how a creative researcher can pursue answers to complex questions that are difficult or impossible to study with controlled experiments.

Our discussion of personality and other factors that can alter the impact of stressors should make it obvious that what is stressful for a given individual is not determined fully and simply by predispositions, coping styles, or situations. (See "In Review: Stress Responses and Stress Mediators.") Even more important are interactions between the person and the situation, the mixture of each individual's coping resources with the specific characteristics of the situation encountered (J. Smith, 1993).

The Physiology and Psychology of Health and Illness

How does stress affect your immune system?

Several studies mentioned so far have suggested that stress shapes the development of physical illness by affecting our thoughts, our organ systems, and our behavior. In this section, we focus more specifically on the ways in which stress can directly or indirectly lead to physical illness. One of the most important connections between stress and illness occurs through the immune system.

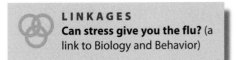

LINKAGES
Can stress give you the flu? (a link to Biology and Behavior)

Stress, the Immune System, and Illness

On March 19, 1878, at a seminar before the Académie de Médecine de Paris, Louis Pasteur showed his distinguished audience three chickens. One bird had been raised normally and was healthy. A second bird had been intentionally infected with bacteria but given no other treatment; it was also healthy. The third chicken that Pasteur presented was dead. It had been infected with the same bacteria as the second bird, but it had also been physically stressed by being exposed to cold temperatures; as a result, the bacteria killed it (Kelley, 1985).

Research conducted since Pasteur's time has greatly expanded knowledge about how stressors affect the body's reaction to disease. **Psychoneuroimmunology** is the field that examines the interaction of psychological and physiological processes that alter the body's ability to defend itself against disease.

The Immune System and Illness   The body's first line of defense against invading substances and microorganisms is the **immune system.** The immune system is perhaps as complex as the nervous system, and it contains as many cells as the brain (Guyton, 1991). Some of these cells are in organs such as the thymus and spleen, whereas others circulate in the bloodstream, entering tissues throughout the body. Components of the immune system kill or inactivate foreign or harmful substances in the body such as viruses and bacteria (Simpson, Hurtley, & Marx, 2000). If the immune system is impaired—by stressors, for example—a person is left more vulnerable to colds, mononucleosis, and many other infectious diseases (Potter & Zautra, 1997). It is by disabling the immune system that the human immunodeficiency virus (HIV) leads to AIDS and leaves the HIV-infected person defenseless against other infections or cancers. The immune system can also become overactive, with devastating results. Many chronic, progressive diseases—including arthritis, diabetes, and lupus erythematosus—are now recognized as *autoimmune* disorders. In these cases, cells of the immune system begin to attack and destroy normal body cells (Oldenberg et al., 2000).

One important facet of the human immune system is the action of the white blood cells, called *leukocytes* (pronounced "LU-koh-sites"), which are formed in the bone marrow and serve as the body's mobile defense units. Leukocytes are called to action when foreign substances are detected. Among the varied types of leukocytes are *B-cells,* which produce *antibodies* to fight foreign toxins; *T-cells,* which kill other cells; and *natural killer cells,* which destroy a variety of foreign organisms and have particularly important antiviral and antitumor functions. The brain can influence the immune system indirectly by altering the secretion of adrenal hormones, such as cortisol, that modify the circulation of T-cells and B-cells. The brain can also influence the immune system directly by making connections with the immune organs, such as the thymus, where T-cells and B-cells are stored (Felten et al., 1991; Maier & Watkins, 2000).

The Immune System and Stress   Researchers have convincingly demonstrated that people under stress are more likely to develop infectious diseases than their less stressed counterparts and to experience flare-ups of the latent viruses responsible for oral herpes (cold sores) or genital herpes (S. Cohen & Herbert, 1996).

These findings are supported by other studies showing more directly that a variety of stressors lead to suppression of the immune system. For example, a study of first-year law students found that as these students participated in class, took exams, and experienced other stressful aspects of law school, they showed a decline in several measures of immune functioning (Segerstrom et al., 1998). Similarly, decreases in natural killer cell activity have been observed in both men and women following the death of their spouses (Irwin et al., 1987), and a variety of immune system impairments have been found in people suffering the effects of divorce or of extended periods of caring for elderly relatives (Cacioppo et al., 1998; Wu et al., 1999).

The relationship between stress and the immune system can be critical to people who are HIV-positive but do not yet have AIDS. Because their immune system is already fragile, further stress-related impairments could be life threatening. Research indicates that psycho-

psychoneuroimmunology   The field that examines the interaction of psychological and physiological processes affecting the body's ability to defend itself against disease.

immune system   The body's first line of defense against invading substances and microorganisms.

YOU CAN'T FIRE ME—I QUIT! Researchers originally thought that anyone who fit the "Type A" behavior pattern was at special risk for heart disease. More recent research shows, however, that the danger lies mainly in cynical hostility, a characteristic seen in some, but not all, Type A people.

logical stressors are associated with the progression of HIV-related illnesses (e.g., Antoni et al., 2000; Kemeny & Dean, 1995). Unfortunately, people with HIV (and AIDS) face a particularly heavy load of immune-suppressing psychological stressors, including grief, unemployment, uncertainty about the future, and daily reminders of serious illness. A lack of perceived control and resulting depression can further magnify their stress responses.

Moderators of Immune Functioning Just as stressors can suppress the immune system, social support and other stress-mediating factors can help to sustain it. For example, students who get emotional support from friends during stressful periods appear to have better immune system functioning than those with less adequate social support (Cohen & Herbert, 1996).

James Pennebaker (1995) has suggested that social support may help prevent illness by providing the person under stress with an opportunity to express pent-up thoughts and emotions. Keeping important things to oneself, says Pennebaker, is itself a stressor (Gross & Levenson, 1997, Pennebaker, Colder, & Sharpe, 1990). In a laboratory experiment, for example, participants who were asked to deceive an experimenter showed elevated physiological arousal (Pennebaker & Chew, 1985). Further, the spouses of suicide or accidental-death victims who do not or cannot confide their feelings to others are especially likely to develop physical illness during the year following the death (Pennebaker & O'Heeron, 1984). Disclosing, even anonymously, the stresses and traumas one has experienced is associated with enhanced immune functioning, reduced physical symptoms, and decreased use of health services (Petrie et al., 1995; J. M. Richards et al., 2000; Smyth et al., 1999). This may explain why support groups for problems ranging from bereavement to overeating to alcohol and drug abuse tend to promote participants' physical health. Future research in psychoneuroimmunology promises to reveal vital links in the complex chain of mental and physical events that determine whether people become ill or stay healthy.

Heart Disease and Behavior Patterns

A number of stress responses, especially anger and hostility, have been linked to coronary heart disease, particularly in men (M. Friedman & Rosenman, 1959, 1974). For a time, researchers believed that anyone who displayed the pattern of aggressiveness, competitiveness, and nonstop work known as "Type A" behavior was at elevated risk for heart disease. More recent research suggests, however, that the danger lies not in these characteristics alone but in cynical hostility—a pattern characterized by suspiciousness, resentment, frequent anger, antagonism, and distrust of others (Helmers & Krantz, 1996).

The identification of cynical hostility as a risk factor for coronary heart disease and heart attack may be an important breakthrough in understanding these illnesses, which remain chief causes of death in the United States and most other Western nations.

THINKING CRITICALLY

Does Cynical Hostility Increase the Risk of Heart Disease?

Further, the fact that cynical hostility often develops in childhood (Woodall & Matthews, 1993) suggests a need for intervention programs capable of altering this interpersonal style in time to prevent its negative consequences for health. But is cynical hostility as dangerous as health psychologists suspect?

What am I being asked to believe or accept?

Many researchers claim that individuals displaying cynical hostility increase their risk for coronary heart disease and heart attack. This risk, they say, is independent of other risk factors such as heredity, diet, smoking, and drinking.

Is there evidence available to support the claim?

There is evidence that hostility and heart disease are related, but the exact mechanism underlying the relationship is not clear. There are several possibilities (Helmers et al., 1995). The risk of coronary heart disease and heart attack may be elevated in cynically hostile people because these people tend to be unusually reactive to stressors, especially when challenged (Suls & Wan, 1993). There is evidence, for example, that during interpersonal conflicts, people predisposed to hostile behavior display not only overt hostility but also unusually large increases in blood pressure, heart rate, and autonomic reactivity. More important, it takes hostile individuals longer than normal to get back to their resting levels of functioning. Like a driver who damages a car by flooring the accelerator and applying the brakes at the same time, these "hot reactors" may create excessive wear and tear on the arteries of the heart as their increased heart rate forces blood through constricted vessels. Increased sympathetic nervous system activation not only puts stress on the coronary arteries but also leads to surges of stress-related hormones from the adrenal glands (Suarez et al., 1991). High levels of these hormones are associated with increases in fatty substances, such as blood cholesterol, that contribute to "hardening" of the arteries and coronary heart disease. Cholesterol levels do appear to be elevated in the blood of hostile people (Dujovne & Houston, 1991).

Hostility may affect heart disease risk less directly as well, through its impact on social support. Some evidence suggests that hostile people get fewer benefits from their social support network (Lepore, 1995b). Failure to use this support—and possibly offending potential supporters in the process—may intensify the impact of stressful events on hostile people. The result may be increased anger, antagonism, and ultimately, additional stress on the cardiovascular system (T. W. Smith, 1992; Suls & Wan, 1993).

Can that evidence be interpreted another way?

The studies cited in support of the relationship between hostility and coronary heart disease are not true experiments. Researchers cannot manipulate the independent variable by creating hostility in people; nor can they create experimental conditions in which groups of individuals who differ *only* in terms of hostility are compared on heart disease, the dependent variable. Accordingly, it is difficult to reach firm conclusions about cause-effect relationships in this and many other areas of health psychology.

Some researchers suggest that higher rates of heart problems among hostile people are due not to the impact of hostility on autonomic reactivity and hormone surges but to a third variable that causes the other two. Specifically, it may be that genetically determined autonomic reactivity increases the likelihood of both hostility *and* heart disease (Krantz et al., 1988). There is indeed evidence to suggest a genetic contribution to the development of hostility (Cacioppo et al., 1998). It is at least plausible, then, that some individuals are biologically predisposed to exaggerated autonomic reactivity and to hostility, each of which is independent of the other.

What evidence would help to evaluate the alternatives?

Several lines of evidence could assist in evaluating hypotheses about the relationship between hostility and heart problems. One approach would examine the relationships among hostility, coronary heart disease, and social and cultural factors (Thoresen & Powell, 1992). If the strength of the relationship between hostility and heart disease varied across social or cultural groups, then the theory of biological predisposition would be less defensible.

One way to test whether hostile people's higher rates of heart disease are related to their hostility or to a more general tendency toward intense physiological arousal is to examine how these individuals react to stress when they are not angry. Some researchers have done this by observing the physiological reactions of hostile people during the stress of surgery. One study found that even under general anesthesia, such people show unusually strong autonomic reactivity (Krantz & Durel, 1983). Because these patients were not conscious, it appears that oversensitivity to stressors, not hostile thinking, caused their exaggerated stress responses.

■ What conclusions are most reasonable?

Most studies continue to find that hostile individuals stand a greater risk of heart disease and heart attacks than their nonhostile counterparts (S. E. Taylor, 1998a). But the causal relationships between hostility and heart disease are probably more complex than any current theory suggests; it appears that many factors underlie these relationships.

A more elaborate psychobiological model may be required—one that takes into account that (1) some individuals may be biologically predisposed to react to stress with hostility *and* increased cardiovascular activity, which in turn can contribute to heart disease; (2) hostile people help to create and maintain stressors through aggressive thoughts and actions, which can provoke others to be aggressive; and (3) hostile people are more likely than others to smoke, drink to excess, overeat, fail to exercise, and engage in other heart-damaging behaviors.

We must also keep in mind that the relationship between heart problems and hostility may not be universal. Some evidence suggests that this relationship may hold for women as well as men, and for individuals in various ethnic groups (e.g., Davidson, Hall, & MacGregor, 1996; Powch & Houston, 1996). Final conclusions, however, must await further research that examines the relationship between hostility and heart disease in other cultures.

Risking Your Life: Health-Endangering Behaviors

As we have seen, many major health problems are caused or aggravated by preventable behaviors such as those listed in Table 10.1.

Smoking   Smoking is the most significant preventable risk factor for fatal illnesses in the United States (Centers for Disease Control and Prevention, 1999a). Even nonsmokers who inhale "secondhand" smoke face an elevated risk for lung cancer and other respiratory diseases (G. Collins, 1997). The American Cancer Society has estimated that if people did not smoke cigarettes, 400,000 fewer U.S. citizens would die in the next twelve months, and 25 percent of all cancer deaths and thousands of heart attacks would never occur. Cigarette smoking accounts for 430,000 deaths each year—which is 20 percent of all U.S. deaths, and more than those caused by all other drugs, car accidents, suicides, homicides, and fires *combined* (Centers for Disease Control and Prevention, 1999a).

Although smoking is on the decline in the United States overall—only about 26 percent of adults now smoke—the habit is actually increasing in some groups, especially Latinos and young African American men (Centers for Disease Control and Prevention, 1999a). Poorer, less educated people are particularly likely to smoke. Conversely, some American Indian tribes in the Southwest and most Asian groups are less likely than other groups to smoke. In many other countries, especially less developed countries, smoking is still the rule rather than the exception.

Breaking the smoking habit is difficult. Only about 10 to 40 percent of people participating in the stop-smoking programs available today show long-term success (Irvin et al., 1999; Klesges et al., 1999; USDHHS, 2000).

Alcohol   Like tobacco, alcohol is a potentially addicting substance that can lead to major health problems. Alcohol abuse is associated with most leading causes of death, including heart disease, stroke, cancer, and liver disease (Centers for Disease Control and Prevention, 1999a). It also contributes to irreversible damage to brain tissue, to gastrointestinal illnesses, and to many other conditions. Both male and female abusers may experience disruption of their reproductive functions, such as early menopause in women and erectile disorder in men. And, as noted in Chapter 9, on human development, alcohol consumption by pregnant women is the most preventable cause of birth defects.

A DEADLY HABIT   Today, about 26 percent of U.S. adults are smokers. Health authorities estimate that unless they quit, 25 million of these smokers will die of smoking-related illnesses (Centers for Disease Control and Prevention, 1999a).

PREVENTING AIDS Health psychologists are helping to create adolescent-oriented AIDS prevention programs. These efforts focus on safe-sex media campaigns and studies of the cognitive and emotional factors that can enhance their effectiveness.

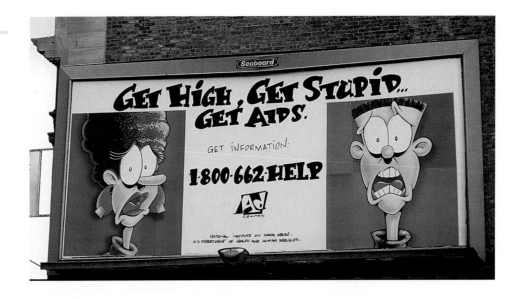

More than 100,000 deaths occur each year in the United States as a result of excessive alcohol consumption (U.S. Surgeon General, 1999).

Unsafe Sex According to the World Health Organization, about 47 million people worldwide are HIV-positive (WHO, 1998). In the United States, more than 600,000 people have been diagnosed as having AIDS, and as many as 900,000 more have been infected with HIV (Centers for Disease Control and Prevention, 1999b). With growing public awareness of how to prevent HIV infection, the rate of new AIDS cases is now falling in the United States, but not everyone is getting the message.

Unsafe sex—especially sexual relations without the use of a condom—greatly increases the risk of contracting HIV. Yet many adolescents and adults continue this dangerous practice (Centers for Disease Control and Prevention, 1999c; Dodds et al., 2000). Like smoking and many other health-threatening behaviors, unprotected sex is more common among low-income individuals, many of whom belong to ethnic minority groups (St. Lawrence, 1993). Among African American men, the risk of contracting AIDS is three times greater than for European American men. The risk for African American women is fifteen times higher than for European American women (Centers for Disease Control, 1998).

Promoting Healthy Behavior

Who is most likely to adopt a healthy lifestyle?

Health psychologists are deeply involved in the development of smoking cessation programs, in campaigns to prevent young people from taking up smoking, in alcohol-education efforts, and in the fight against the spread of HIV and AIDS (Kalichman, Cherry, & Browne-Sperling, 1999; S. E. Taylor, 1998a). For example, they are working on methods for lowering the risk of AIDS among adolescents (St. Lawrence et al., 1995)—an important target group because many sexually active adolescents hold health beliefs that lead them to greatly underestimate the risk of contracting the disease through unprotected sex.

Efforts to reduce, eliminate, or prevent behaviors that pose health risks and to encourage healthy behaviors are called **health promotion** (Taylor, 1998). The aim of health psychologists working in this area is to understand the thought processes that lead people to engage in health-endangering behaviors and, then, to create intervention programs that can alter those thought processes, or at least take them into account (Klepp, Kelder, & Perry, 1995).

health promotion The process of altering or eliminating behaviors that pose risks to health and, at the same time, fostering healthier behavior patterns.

Health Beliefs and Health Behaviors

This cognitive approach to health psychology appears in various *health-belief models.* Irwin Rosenstock (1974) developed the most influential and extensively tested of these models (e.g., Aspinwall & Duran, 1999). Rosenstock based his model on the assumption that people's decisions about health-related behaviors (such as smoking) are guided by four main factors:

1. A perception of *personal* threat or susceptibility to contracting a specific illness. (Do you believe that *you* will get lung cancer from smoking?)

2. A perception of the seriousness of the illness and the severity of the consequences of having it. (How serious do *you* think lung cancer is? What will happen to *you* if you get it?)

3. The belief that a particular practice will reduce the threat. (Will *your* stopping smoking prevent *you* from getting lung cancer?)

4. The balance between the perceived costs of starting a health practice and the benefits expected from this practice. (Will the reduced chance of getting cancer in the future be worth the discomfort and loss of pleasure from not smoking?)

On the basis of this health-belief model, one would expect that the people most likely to quit smoking would be those who believe that they are susceptible to getting cancer from smoking, that cancer is serious and life-threatening, and that the benefits of preventing cancer clearly outweigh the difficulties associated with quitting.

Other belief factors not included in Rosenstock's model may also be important (Gerrard, Gibbons, & Bushman, 1996). For example, people generally do not try to quit smoking unless they believe they can succeed. Thus, *self-efficacy,* the belief that one is able to perform some behavior, is an additional determinant of decisions about health behaviors (Bandura, 1992; Dijkstra, DeVries, & Bakker, 1996). A related factor is the *intention* to engage in a healthy behavior (Maddux & DuCharme, 1997).

Health-belief models help predict a variety of health behaviors, including exercise (McAuley, 1992), safe-sex practices among gay men at risk for AIDS (W. A. Fisher, Fisher, & Rye, 1995), adherence to doctors' orders among diabetic adolescents (Bond, Aiken, & Somerville, 1992), and the decision to undergo mammogram screening for breast cancer (Champion & Huster, 1995).

Changing Health Behaviors: Stages of Readiness

Knowing *who* is most likely to practice healthy behaviors is important, but health psychologists have also tried to understand *how* people change their health habits. According to James Prochaska and his colleagues, successful change involves five stages (Prochaska, DiClemente, & Norcross, 1992):

1. *Precontemplation.*   The person does not perceive a health-related problem and has no intention of changing in the foreseeable future.

2. *Contemplation.*   The person is aware of a problem behavior and is seriously thinking about changing it.

3. *Preparation.*   The person has a strong intention to change and has made specific plans to do so.

4. *Action.*   The person at this stage is engaging successfully in behavior change.

5. *Maintenance.*   The healthy behavior has continued for at least six months, and the person is using newly learned skills to prevent relapse.

The path from precontemplation through maintenance can be a rough one (Prochaska, 1994). Usually, people relapse and go through the stages repeatedly until they finally achieve stability in the healthy behavior they desire. Smokers, for example, typically require three to four cycles through the stages and up to seven years before they finally reach the maintenance stage.

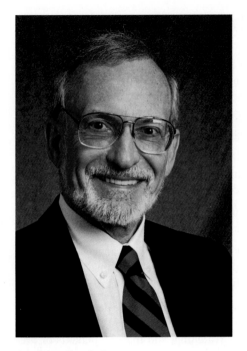

Applying Psychology

TAKING TIME OUT Nearly half of all Americans say the workplace is their number one source of stress (NIOSH, 1999). On January 1, 2000, Raymond Fowler, chief executive officer of the American Psychological Association, joined the ranks of those whose elevated blood pressure, heart arrhythmias, and other physical stress responses required a temporary leave of absence from highly stressful jobs (Fowler, 2000). The National Institute for Occupational Safety and Health (1999) suggests a wide range of other behavioral coping options for stressed employees who cannot take time off.

LINKAGES
How can people manage stress? (a link to Treatment of Psychological Disorders)

Programs for Coping with Stress

An important aspect of health psychologists' health promotion activities has been to improve people's stress-coping skills. Let's consider a few specific procedures and programs associated with this effort.

Planning to Cope   Just as people with extra money in the bank have a better chance of weathering a financial crisis, people with effective coping skills have a better chance of escaping some of the more harmful effects of intense stress. Like family money, the ability to handle stress appears to come naturally to some people, but coping strategies can also be learned. Programs that teach such strategies move through several stages, which are summarized in Table 10.4.

Bear in mind, however, that no single method of coping with stressors is universally successful. For example, denying the existence of an uncontrollable stressor may be fine in the short run but may lead to problems if no other coping method is used (Suls & Fletcher, 1985). Similarly, people who rely exclusively on an active, problem-focused approach to coping may handle controllable stressors well but find themselves nearly helpless in the face of uncontrollable ones (J. A. Murray & Terry, 1999). Individuals who are most successful at stress management may be those who are best able to adjust their coping methods to the demands of changing situations and differing stressors (S. E. Taylor, 1998a).

Developing Coping Strategies   Strategies for coping with stress can be cognitive, emotional, behavioral, or physical. *Cognitive coping strategies* change how people interpret stimuli and events. They help people think more calmly, rationally, and constructively in the face of stress and may generate a more hopeful emotional state. For example, students with heavy course loads may experience anxiety, confusion, discouragement, lack of motivation, and the desire to run away from it all. Frightening, catastrophizing thoughts (such as "What if I fail?") magnify stress responses. Cognitive coping strategies replace catastrophic thinking with thoughts in which stressors are viewed as challenges rather than threats. This substitution process is called **cognitive restructuring** (Meichenbaum, 1977). It involves first identifying upsetting thoughts (such as "I'll never figure this out!") and then developing and practicing more constructive thoughts (such as "All I can do is the best I can") when under stress. Cognitive coping does not eliminate

TABLE 10.4	Stages in Coping with Stress

Many successful programs for systematically coping with stress guide people through several stages and are aimed at removing stressors that can be changed and at reducing responses to stressors that cannot be changed (R. L. Silver & Wortman, 1980).

Stage	Task
1. Assessment	Identify the sources and effects of stress.
2. Goal setting	List the stressors and stress responses to be addressed. Designate which stressors are and are not changeable.
3. Planning	List the specific steps to be taken to cope with stress.
4. Action	Implement coping plans.
5. Evaluation	Determine the changes in stressors and stress responses that have occurred as a result of coping methods.
6. Adjustment	Alter coping methods to improve results, if necessary.

Methods for Coping with Stress	
Type of Coping Method	**Examples**
Cognitive	Thinking of stressors as challenges rather than as threats; avoiding perfectionism.
Emotional	Seeking and obtaining social support; getting advice and feedback.
Behavioral	Implementing a time-management plan; where possible, making life changes to eliminate stressors.
Physical	Progressive relaxation training and exercise.

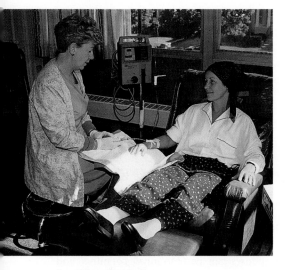

Applying Psychology

DEALING WITH CHEMOTHERAPY
Progressive relaxation training can be used to ease a variety of health-related problems. For example, one study found that this training resulted in significant reductions in anxiety, physiological arousal, and nausea following cancer chemotherapy (Burish & Jenkins, 1992).

cognitive restructuring   A technique for coping with stress that involves replacing stress-provoking thoughts with more constructive thoughts in order to make stressors less threatening and disruptive.

progressive relaxation training   A method for coping with stress that involves tensing a group of muscles, then releasing the tension and focusing on the resulting feelings of relaxation.

stressors, but it can help people perceive them as less threatening and therefore make them less disruptive (Antoni et al., 2000).

Seeking and obtaining social support from others are effective *emotional coping strategies.* The perception that one has emotional support and is cared for and valued by others tends to be an effective buffer against the ill effects of many stressors (S. E. Taylor, 1998a). Having enhanced emotional resources is associated with increased survival time in cancer patients (B. L. Anderson, 1992), improved immune functioning (Kiecolt-Glaser & Glaser, 1992), and more rapid recovery from illness (S. E. Taylor, 1998a).

Behavioral coping strategies involve changing behavior to minimize the impact of stressors. Time management is one example. You might keep track of your time for a week and start a time-management plan. The first step is to set out a schedule that shows how your time is typically spent; then decide how to allocate your time in the future. A time-management plan can help control catastrophizing thoughts by providing reassurance that there is enough time for everything and a plan for handling it all.

Physical coping strategies can be used to alter one's physical responses before, during, or after stressors occur. Unfortunately, the most common physical coping strategy is some form of drug use. Prescription medications are sometimes an appropriate coping aid, especially when stressors are severe and acute, such as the sudden death of one's child. However, people who depend on prescriptions or other drugs, including alcohol, to help them face stressors often attribute any success to the drug, not to their own skill. Furthermore, the drug effects that blunt stress responses may also interfere with the ability to apply coping strategies. The resulting loss of perceived control over stressors may make those stressors even more threatening and disruptive.

Physical exercise is a popular and well-known nonchemical method of reducing physical stress reactions. Another is **progressive relaxation training,** which is learned by tensing a group of muscles (such as the hand and arm) for a few seconds, then releasing the tension and focusing on the resulting feelings of relaxation. This procedure is repeated for each of sixteen muscle groups throughout the body (D. A. Bernstein, Borkovec, & Hazlette-Stevens, 2000). Once people become skilled at progressive relaxation, they can use it to calm down anywhere and anytime. "In Review: Methods for Coping with Stress" summarizes our discussion of stress-coping methods.

active review   Health, Stress, and Coping

Linkages

As noted in Chapter 1, all of psychology's subfields are related to one another. Our discussion of how stressors can lead to the development of mental disorders illustrates just one way in which the topic of this chapter, health, stress, and coping, is linked to the subfield of psychological disorder (Chapter 12). The Linkages diagram shows ties to two other subfields as well, and there are many more ties throughout the book. Looking for linkages among subfields will help you see how they all fit together and better appreciate the big picture that is psychology.

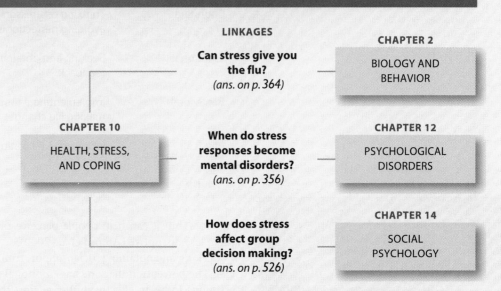

LINKAGES

CHAPTER 10
HEALTH, STRESS, AND COPING

Can stress give you the flu?
(ans. on p. 364)

CHAPTER 2
BIOLOGY AND BEHAVIOR

When do stress responses become mental disorders?
(ans. on p. 356)

CHAPTER 12
PSYCHOLOGICAL DISORDERS

How does stress affect group decision making?
(ans. on p. 526)

CHAPTER 14
SOCIAL PSYCHOLOGY

Summary

HEALTH PSYCHOLOGY

What do health psychologists do?

The development of *health psychology* was prompted by recognition of the link between stress and illness, and of the role of behaviors such as smoking, in elevating the risk of illness. Health psychologists seek to understand how psychological factors are related to physical disease and to help people behave in ways that prevent or minimize disease and promote health.

UNDERSTANDING STRESS

How do psychological stressors affect physical health?

The term *stress* refers in part to *stressors,* which are physical or psychological events and situations to which people must adjust. The term is also used to refer to *stress reactions.* Most generally, however, stress is viewed as an ongoing, interactive process that takes place as people adjust to, and cope with, their environment. Psychological stressors include catastrophic events, life changes and strains, chronic stressors, and daily hassles. Stressors can be measured by tests like the Social Readjustment Rating Scale (SRRS) and the Life Experiences Survey (LES), but scores on such tests provide only a partial picture of the stress in a person's life.

Responses to stressors can be physical and psychological. These stress responses can occur alone or in combination, and the appearance of one can often stimulate others.

Physical stress responses include changes in heart rate, respiration, and many other processes that are part of a pattern known as the *general adaptation syndrome,* or *GAS.* The GAS has three stages:

alarm reaction, resistance, and exhaustion. The GAS helps people resist stress but, if present too long, can lead to depletion of immune system functions, as well as to physical illnesses, which Selye called *diseases of adaptation.*

Psychological stress responses can be emotional, cognitive, and behavioral. Anxiety, anger, and depression are among the most common emotional stress reactions. Cognitive stress reactions include ruminative thinking; catastrophizing; and disruptions in the ability to think clearly, remember accurately, and solve problems efficiently.

Behavioral stress responses include changes in posture, as well as facial expressions, tremors, or jumpiness, that reflect physical tension or emotional stress reactions. More global behavioral stress responses include irritability, absenteeism, and even suicide attempts. Patterns of response to severe or long-lasting stressors can lead to *burnout* or to psychological disorders such as *posttraumatic stress disorder (PTSD).*

The key to understanding stress appears to lie in observing the interaction of specific stressors with particular people. Stressors are likely to have greater impact if they are appraised as threats, or if they are unpredictable or uncontrollable. The people most likely to react strongly to a stressor are those whose coping resources, coping methods, and *social support networks* are inadequate.

THE PHYSIOLOGY AND PSYCHOLOGY OF HEALTH AND ILLNESS

How does stress affect your immune system?

Psychoneuroimmunology is the field that examines the interaction of psychological and physiological processes that affect the body's ability to defend itself against disease. When a person is under stress, some of the hormones released from the adrenal glands, such as cortisol, reduce the effectiveness of the cells of the *immune system* (T-cells, B-cells, natural killer cells) in combating foreign invaders, such as viruses, and cancer cells.

People who are cynically hostile appear at greater risk for heart disease than other people. The heightened reactivity to stressors that these people experience may damage their cardiovascular system.

Most of the major health problems in Western cultures are related to preventable behaviors such as smoking and drinking alcohol. Having unsafe sex is a major risk factor for contracting HIV.

PROMOTING HEALTHY BEHAVIOR

Who is most likely to adopt a healthy lifestyle?

The process of altering or eliminating health-risky behaviors and fostering healthy behavior patterns is called *health promotion.* People's

health-related behaviors are partly guided by their beliefs about health risks and what they can do about them.

The process of changing health-related behaviors appears to involve several stages, including precontemplation, contemplation, preparation, action, and maintenance. Understanding which stage people are in, and helping them move through these stages, is an important task in health psychology.

To cope with stress, people must recognize the stressors affecting them and develop a plan for coping with these stressors. Important coping skills include *cognitive restructuring,* acting to minimize the number or intensity of stressors, and using *progressive relaxation training* and other techniques for reducing physical stress reactions.

Learn by Doing

Put It in Writing

What is stress like for you? To help you understand the role of stress in your life, write a page or two describing a stressful incident that you had to face in the recent past. Identify what the stressors were, and classify each of them as physical or psychological. List your physical, emotional, cognitive, and behavioral responses to these stressors, and how long the responses lasted. Also include a brief summary of how you coped with these stressors and how successful your coping efforts were. Some research suggests that writing about stressful experiences can help people to deal with those experiences. Did this writing project have any such benefits for you?

Personal Learning Activity

To get an idea of how much people differ in their approach to coping with stressors, create a one-paragraph story of a stressful situation (e.g., losing a job, having one's home destroyed by fire, working with an obnoxious boss, or being overburdened by schoolwork). Now show this description to ten people, and ask each of them to tell you how they would cope with the situation if it happened to them. Classify their responses in terms of whether they were problem-focused or emotion-focused coping methods. Did you notice any relationships between the kind of coping responses these people chose and characteristics such as age, gender, ethnicity, or experience with stress? If so, why do you think those relationships appeared? *For additional projects, see the five Personal Learning Activities in the corresponding chapter of the study guide that accompanies this text.*

Step into Action

Courses

Biological Psychology
Health Psychology
Stress Management
Stress and Coping

Movies

Courage Under Fire (general adaptation syndrome)
Falling Down (behavioral stress responses)
The Deer Hunter (posttraumatic stress responses)
Do the Right Thing (social support networks)
Women on the Verge of a Nervous Breakdown (impact of sudden stressor)
Glengarry Glen Ross (effects of stress in the workplace)
Angela's Ashes (impact of stress on development)
Saving Private Ryan (individual differences in responses to traumatic stress)

Books

Richard Sorrentino and Christopher Roney, *The Uncertain Mind: Individual Differences in Facing the Unknown* (Psychology Press, 2000) (discusses the impact of uncertainty on physical and mental health)

Tony Cassidy, *Stress, Cognition, and Health* (Routledge, 1999) (summarizes research on the effects of stress on thinking and physical well-being)

Jerrold Greenberg, *Comprehensive Stress Management* (McGraw-Hill, 1999) (ideas for stress management)

James W. Pennebaker, *Opening Up: The Healing Power of Expressing Emotions* (Guilford, 1997) (describes research on the benefits of self-disclosure).

The Web

The World Wide Web is a good source of additional information about the science of psychology, provided you use it carefully and think critically about the information you find. The PsychAbilities web site that accompanies this text offers many resources relevant to this chapter. These resources include interactive NetLab exercises; Thinking Critically and Evaluating Research exercises; ACE chapter quizzes; recommended web links; and articles on current events, books, and movies. At http://college.hmco.com, select *Psychology* and then this textbook.

Review of Key Terms

Can you define each of the key terms in the chapter? Check your definitions against those on the pages listed in parentheses below or in the Glossary/Index at the end of the text.

burnout *(p. 356)*

cognitive restructuring *(p. 370)*

diseases of adaptation *(p. 354)*

general adaptation syndrome (GAS) *(p. 353)*

health promotion *(p. 368)*

health psychology *(p. 348)*

immune system *(p. 364)*

posttraumatic stress disorder (PTSD) *(p. 356)*

progressive relaxation training *(p. 371)*

psychoneuroimmunology *(p. 364)*

social support network *(p. 360)*

stress *(p. 350)*

stress reactions *(p. 350)*

stressors *(p. 350)*

Multiple-Choice Self-Test

Select the best answer for each of the questions below. Then check your response against the Answer Key at the end of the text.

1. According to health psychology research,

   a. acute diseases cause more U.S. deaths than chronic ones.
   b. psychological methods cannot change behaviors that contribute to illness.
   c. teaching people to take an active role in protecting their own health has not had a major impact on the death rate.
   d. the stresses of life influence health through their impact on psychological and physical processes.

2. Lila got married, moved to a new city, and took a new job, all in the same month. We would expect Lila to

   a. display physical or psychological stress responses, or both.
   b. experience little stress, because these are all desirable changes.
   c. experience little stress, because these are not chronic stressors.
   d. experience physical stress responses only.

3. Psychological stressors

   a. always stem from a lack of social support.
   b. are by definition long term, or chronic.
   c. result mainly from catastrophic events.
   d. include anything that forces a person to change or adapt.

4. It is 2:00 A.M., and Aaron is lost in a big city with no money. His sympathetic nervous system has initiated the fight-or-flight syndrome. Which stage of the general adaptation syndrome (GAS) is he experiencing?

   a. alarm   b. resistance
   c. exhaustion   d. precontemplative

5. According to Hans Selye, diseases of adaptation occur when the body enters the _____ stage of the GAS.

   a. alarm
   b. resistance
   c. exhaustion
   d. precontemplative

6. While watching TV, taking a shower, or even having dinner with his girlfriend, Enrico finds that he can't stop thinking about all the stressful things happening in his life. Enrico is experiencing _____.

   a. catastrophizing
   b. ruminative thinking
   c. functional fixedness
   d. cognitive restructuring

7. Caitlin just failed her high school math test. She says to herself, "Mom is going to be furious with me! She will probably ground me, which means I won't be able to go to the prom. If I don't go to the prom, I will be a social outcast, and no one will talk to me. I'll never have any friends or find a partner, and no one will ever love me!" This is an example of

   a. cognitive restructuring.
   b. catastrophizing.
   c. posttraumatic stress disorder.
   d. the fight-or-flight syndrome.

8. Dr. Angelica's teenage patient, Juan, is under a lot of stress. If the doctor is most worried about Juan's behavioral stress responses, she would focus mainly on his

   a. depression.
   b. catastrophic thoughts.
   c. blood pressure.
   d. aggressiveness.

9. Shane, a veteran, occasionally experiences flashbacks involving vivid recollections of his wartime experiences. Flashbacks are associated with

   a. generalized anxiety disorder.
   b. posttraumatic stress disorder.
   c. the general adaptation syndrome.
   d. the fight-or-flight syndrome.

10. Robin, Sarah, and Travis all work in the same office complex, which is plagued by temperature-regulation problems. Based on research on stress mediators, which of the three workers will display the most stress responses?

    a. Robin, whose office is always too warm.
    b. Sarah, whose office is always too cold.
    c. Travis, whose office changes from hot to cold without warning.
    d. There is no way to predict who will be most stressed.

11. When postsurgery patients are allowed to adjust their own level of painkillers, they tend to self-administer less pain medication than patients who must ask for it. This phenomenon is consistent with research showing that

    a. people's social support can mediate stress.
    b. predictable stressors are easier to manage.
    c. the perception of control reduces the impact of stressors.
    d. thinking of stressors as threats amplifies their effects.

12. Laton, the head of personnel at his company, knows that the employees have very stressful jobs. Thus, he schedules group picnics and lunches so that employees who don't know each other can get acquainted. Laton is trying to ease the employees' stressors by

    a. promoting cognitive restructuring.
    b. improving social support networks.
    c. increasing employees' sense of control.
    d. helping employees think of their stressors as challenges rather than threats.

13. In the Focus on Research section of this chapter, on the relationship between personality and life expectancy, the researchers found

    a. no relationship between the two.
    b. that conscientiousness was associated with longer life.
    c. that social relationships had no impact on longevity.
    d. that impulsiveness was associated with longer life.

14. Dr. Porter studies immune system cells that have antiviral properties and help prevent tumors. What type of cells does he study?

    a. B-cells   b. T-cells
    c. natural killer cells   d. macrophages

15. Fred is at high risk for coronary heart disease. As his friend, you tell him that current research suggests that he could lower his risk if he

    a. takes up fishing as a hobby.
    b. works at being less cynical and hostile.
    c. reduces his workload.
    d. restructures his thinking about stress.

16. The most significant preventable risk factor for fatal illness in the United States is

    a. smoking.   b. consumption of alcohol.
    c. illegal drug use.   d. unsafe sex.

17. According to Rosenstock's health-belief model, which of the following would most help Bridgit decide to quit smoking?

    a. perceiving a personal threat of getting cancer from her smoking
    b. knowing that smoking causes cancer
    c. knowing that quitting can lower people's risk of cancer
    d. carefully reading the statistics of smoking and health in general

18. Amanda is severely overweight. She knows that for her health's sake, she needs to limit her caloric intake, but she loves to eat and has made no specific plans to go on a diet. Amanda is at the _____ stage of readiness to change a health-risky behavior.

    a. precontemplation   b. contemplation
    c. preparation   d. maintenance

19. Sayumi is trying to control her stress. In response to a hurtful comment from a friend, Sayumi thinks to herself, "Don't jump to conclusions; he probably didn't mean it the way it sounded," instead of "That jerk! Who does he think he is?" Sayumi is using the coping strategy of

    a. cognitive restructuring.   b. emotional restructuring.
    c. catastrophizing.   d. contemplation.

20. Loretta, a marriage counselor, finds her job very stressful. She has found that physical coping strategies help her the most. Loretta most likely engages in

    a. cognitive restructuring.
    b. emotional restructuring.
    c. progressive relaxation training.
    d. problem-focused coping.

11

Personality

"Who are you?" When we posed this question in the first chapter,

you probably answered it in terms of your personality. Indeed, your personality represents the sum of all the psychological, behavioral, and biological processes we have discussed in this book. It reflects the consistent patterns of thinking, feeling, and behaving that make you different from, and in some ways similar to, others. In this chapter, we examine four views of personality and review some of the personality tests that psychologists have developed to measure and compare people's personalities. These instruments are widely used in research on personality, and in other areas as well. We will also examine some of the ways in which personality theory and research are being applied.

Reading this chapter will help you to answer the following questions:

- **How did paralyzed patients lead Freud to psychoanalysis?**
- **How many personality traits are there?**
- **Do we learn our personality?**
- **Is everyone basically good?**
- **How do psychologists measure personality?**

Take out your wallet, look through it, and select the four most important things you carry with you. One person we know picked a driver's license, a credit card, the phone number of a friend, and a witty prediction from a fortune cookie. The driver's license describes his physical traits. The credit card represents information about his buying history and responsibility in paying debts. His friends provide support, affection, and intimacy. And the fortune cookie prediction says something about his wishes, beliefs, or hopes. In other words, the selected items form a crude personality sketch.

There is no universally accepted definition, but psychologists generally view **personality** as the unique pattern of enduring psychological and behavioral characteristics by which each person can be compared and contrasted with other people. Personality research, in turn, focuses on understanding the consistent patterns of cognition, emotion, and behavior that make people both different from and similar to one another.

To gain a full understanding of just one individual's personality, a researcher would have to learn about many things, including the person's developmental experiences and cultural influences, genetic and other biological characteristics, perceptual and other information-processing habits and biases, typical patterns of emotional expression, and social skills. Psychologists also want to know about personality in general, such as how it develops and changes across the life span. They ask why some people are usually optimistic, whereas others are usually pessimistic, and whether people respond consistently or inconsistently from one situation to the next.

personality The pattern of psychological and behavioral characteristics by which each person can be compared and contrasted with other people.

377

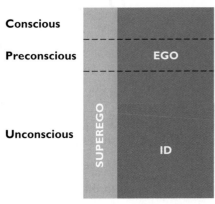

Conscious

Preconscious EGO

SUPEREGO

Unconscious ID

Source: Adapted from R. M. Liebert & Spiegler (1994).

FIGURE 11.1

Freud's Conception of the Personality Structure

According to Freud, some parts of the personality are conscious, whereas others are unconscious. Between these levels, Freud saw the preconscious as the location of memories and other material not usually in awareness but that can be brought into consciousness with little or no effort.

psychodynamic approach A view developed by Freud emphasizing unconscious mental processes in explaining human thoughts, feelings, and behavior.

id According to Freud, a personality component containing basic instincts, desires, and impulses with which all people are born.

pleasure principle The operating principle of the id, which guides people toward whatever feels good.

ego According to Freud, the part of the personality that makes compromises and mediates conflicts between and among the demands of the id, the superego, and the real world.

reality principle The operating principle of the ego, which takes into account the constraints of the social world.

superego According to Freud, the component of personality that tells people what they should and should not do.

The specific questions psychologists ask and the methods they use to investigate personality often depend on which of the four main approaches to personality they take. These four are known as the psychodynamic, trait, social-cognitive, and phenomenological approaches.

The Psychodynamic Approach

■ **How did paralyzed patients lead Freud to psychoanalysis?**

People often think they can understand personality by simply watching others behave. A person with an "obnoxious personality" shows it by acting obnoxiously. But is that all there is to personality? Not according to Sigmund Freud, who compared personality to an iceberg, whose tip is clearly visible but whose bulk is hidden underwater.

As a physician in Vienna during the 1890s, Freud specialized in treating "neurotic" disorders such as blindness or paralysis for which there was no physical cause and that hypnosis could often remove. One patient sleepwalked on legs that were paralyzed during the day. These cases led Freud to believe in *psychic determinism,* the idea that personality and behavior are determined more by psychological factors than by biological conditions or current events. He proposed that people may not know why they feel, think, or act the way they do, because they are partly controlled by the *unconscious* portion of the personality—the part of which people are normally unaware. From these ideas Freud created *psychoanalysis,* a theory of personality and a way of treating mental disorders. Freud's theory became the basis of the **psychodynamic approach** to personality, which holds that various unconscious psychological processes interact to determine our thoughts, feelings, and behavior.

Structure of Personality

Freud believed that people are born with basic instincts or needs—not only for food, water, and air but also for sex and aggression. He believed that needs for love, knowledge, security, and the like arise from these more fundamental desires. Each person faces the task of figuring out how to meet his or her needs in a world that often frustrates these efforts. According to Freud, personality develops out of each person's struggle with this task and is reflected in the ways he or she goes about satisfying a range of needs.

Id, Ego, and Superego Freud described the personality as having three major components: the id, the ego, and the superego (C. S. Hall, Lindzey, & Campbell, 1998; see Figure 11.1). The **id** represents the inborn, unconscious portion of the personality where life and death instincts reside. The life instincts promote positive, constructive behavior; the death instincts are responsible for human aggression and destructiveness. The id operates on the **pleasure principle,** seeking immediate satisfaction of both kinds of instincts, regardless of society's rules or the rights and feelings of others. The hungry person who steals french fries from someone's table at McDonald's would be satisfying an id-driven impulse, as would the angry child who impulsively grabs another child's toy.

As parents, teachers, and others place greater restrictions on the expression of id impulses, a second part of the personality, called the ego (or "self"), evolves from the id. The **ego** is responsible for organizing ways to get what a person wants in the real world, as opposed to the fantasy world of the id. Operating on the **reality principle,** the ego makes compromises between the id's unreasoning demands for immediate satisfaction and the restrictions of the social world. Thus, the hungry person buys some french fries, and the angry child avoids a fight, perhaps by distracting the other child and then hiding the toy away for later.

As people gain experience with the rules and values of society, they tend to adopt them. This process of *internalizing* parental and societal values creates the third component of personality, the **superego,** which tells us what we should and should not do. The

TABLE 11.1

Ego Defense Mechanisms

 According to Freud, defense mechanisms deflect anxiety or guilt in the short run, but they sap energy. Further, using them to avoid dealing with the source of one's problems can make those problems worse in the long run. Try listing some incidents in which you or someone you know might have used each of the defenses described here. What questions would a critical thinker ask to determine whether these behaviors were unconscious defense mechanisms or actions motivated by conscious intentions?

Defense Mechanism	Description
Repression	Unconsciously pushing threatening memories, urges, or ideas from conscious awareness: A person may experience loss of memory for unpleasant events.
Rationalization	Attempting to make actions or mistakes seem reasonable: The reasons or excuses given (e.g., "I spank my children because it is good for them") sound rational, but they are not the real reasons for the behavior.
Projection	Unconsciously attributing one's own unacceptable thoughts or impulses to another person: Instead of recognizing that "I hate him," a person may feel that "He hates me."
Reaction formation	Defending against unacceptable impulses by acting opposite to them: Sexual interest in a married friend might appear as strong dislike instead.
Sublimation	Converting unacceptable impulses into socially acceptable actions, and perhaps symbolically expressing them: Sexual or aggressive desires may appear as artistic creativity or devotion to athletic excellence.
Displacement	Deflecting an impulse from its original target to a less threatening one: Anger at one's boss may be expressed through hostility toward a clerk, a family member, or even the dog.
Denial	Simply discounting the existence of threatening impulses: A person may vehemently deny ever having had even the slightest degree of physical attraction to a person of the same sex.
Compensation	Striving to make up for unconscious impulses or fears: A business executive's extreme competitiveness might be aimed at compensating for unconscious feelings of inferiority.

superego represents our sense of morality and is just as relentless and unreasonable as the id in its demands to be obeyed. It would make the hungry person feel guilty for stealing the french fries, and it would tell the angry child not to hide that toy.

Conflicts and Defenses Freud described the inner turmoil among id, ego, and superego as *intrapsychic,* or *psychodynamic, conflict* and believed that each individual's personality is shaped by the number, nature, and outcome of these conflicts. Freud said that the ego works to prevent the anxiety or guilt that would arise if we became conscious of socially unacceptable id impulses, especially those that would violate the superego's rules (Carver & Scheier, 2000). These efforts may appear in the form of **defense mechanisms,** which are unconscious tactics that either prevent threatening material from surfacing or disguise it when it does (see Table 11.1).

Stages of Personality Development

Freud proposed that personality develops during childhood through a series of **psychosexual stages.** Failure to resolve the conflicts that arise at any stage can leave a person *fixated*—that is, unconsciously preoccupied with the area of pleasure associated with that stage. Freud believed that the stage at which a person became fixated in childhood can be seen in the person's adult personality characteristics.

defense mechanisms Unconscious tactics that either prevent threatening material from surfacing or disguise it when it does.

psychosexual stages In Freud's psychodynamic theory, periods of personality development in which internal and external conflicts focus on particular issues.

THE ORAL STAGE   According to Freudian theory, personality develops over time through a series of psychosexual stages. At each stage, a different part of the body becomes the primary focus of pleasure. This baby would appear to be in the oral stage.

oral stage   The first of Freud's psychosexual stages, occurring during the first year of life, in which the mouth is the center of pleasure.

anal stage   The second of Freud's psychosexual stages, occurring during the second year of life, in which the focus of pleasure shifts from the mouth to the anus.

phallic stage   The third of Freud's psychosexual stages, lasting from approximately ages three to five, in which the focus of pleasure shifts to the genital area.

Oedipus complex   The Freudian notion that young boys' impulses involve sexual feelings for the mother and the desire to eliminate the father.

Electra complex   The Freudian notion that young girls develop an attachment to the father and compete with the mother for the father's attention.

The Oral Stage   In Freud's theory, a child's first year or so is called the **oral stage** because the mouth—which infants use to eat and to explore everything from toys to their own hands and feet—is the center of pleasure associated with this period. Personality problems arise, said Freud, when oral needs are either neglected or overindulged. For example, early or late weaning from breastfeeding or bottle feeding may leave a child fixated at the oral stage, resulting in adult characteristics such as talking too much, overeating, smoking, excessive drinking, or using "biting" sarcasm. Childlike dependence on others is another possible sign of oral fixation.

The Anal Stage   The **anal stage** occurs during the second year, when—in most Western cultures—toilet training clashes with the child's instinctual pleasure in having bowel movements at will. According to Freud, it is at this stage that the child's ego develops to cope with parental demands for socially appropriate behavior. However, toilet training that is too harsh or starts too early or too late can lead to anal fixation. Adults fixated at this stage may be stingy; extremely organized; stubborn; and perhaps excessively concerned with control, cleanliness, orderliness, or details (thus symbolically withholding feces). Or they might be sloppy, disorganized, or impulsive (symbolically expelling feces).

The Phallic Stage   Between the ages of three and five, according to Freud, the focus of pleasure shifts to the genital area. Because he emphasized the psychosexual development of boys, Freud called this period the **phallic stage** (*phallus* is another word for *penis*). It is then, he claimed, that the boy experiences sexual feelings for his mother and a desire to eliminate, or even kill, his father, with whom the boy competes for the mother's affection. Freud called this set of impulses the **Oedipus complex,** because it reminded him of the Greek tragedy *Oedipus Rex*. (In this play, Oedipus unknowingly kills his father and marries his mother.) The boy's fantasies create so much fear, however, that the ego represses his incestuous desires, and he seeks to "identify" with his father and be like him. In the process, the child's superego begins to develop.

According to Freud, the female child begins the phallic stage with a strong attachment to her mother; but when she realizes that boys have penises and girls do not, she supposedly develops *penis envy* and transfers her love to the father—a phenomenon Freud termed the **Electra complex** because it reflected the plot of another Greek tragedy. To avoid her mother's disapproval, the girl identifies with and imitates her, thus forming the basis for her own superego.

Freud believed that fixation at the phallic stage can lead to problems in adulthood that reflect unresolved conflicts with a person's same-sex parent. Such problems include fear, aggression, difficulties with authority figures, uncertainty about one's identity as a male or female, problems in maintaining a stable love relationship, and socially disapproved sexual behavior.

The Latency Period   As the phallic stage draws to a close and its conflicts are quieted by the ego, an interval of psychological peace ensues. During this **latency period,** which lasts through childhood, sexual impulses stay in the background as the youngster focuses on education, same-sex peer play, and the development of social skills.

The Genital Stage   During adolescence, when sexual impulses reappear at the conscious level, the genitals again become the focus of pleasure. Thus begins what Freud called the **genital stage,** which spans the remainder of the person's life. The quality of relationships and the degree of fulfillment experienced during this stage, he claimed, are directly affected by how intrapsychic conflicts were resolved during the earlier stages.

Variations on Freud's Personality Theory

Freud's ideas—especially those concerning infantile sexuality and the Oedipus and Electra complexes—created instant controversy in the media of the day and in professional circles as well. Even many of Freud's followers disagreed with him. Some of these dissenters have been called *neo-Freudian* theorists, because they maintained many of the basic ideas in Freud's theory but developed their own approaches. Others are known as

FOUNDER OF THE PSYCHODYNAMIC APPROACH Here is Sigmund Freud, on a stroll with his daughter, Anna, who became a psychoanalyst herself and eventually developed a revised version of her father's theories.

ego-psychologists, because their theories focus more on the ego than on the id (C. S. Hall, Lindzey, & Campbell, 1998).

Jung's Analytic Psychology   Carl Jung (pronounced "yoong") was the most prominent dissenter among Freud's early followers. Jung (1916) argued that people are born with a general life force that includes a drive for creativity, for growth-oriented resolution of conflicts, and for the productive blending of basic impulses with real-world demands. Jung did not identify specific stages in personality development. He suggested instead that people gradually develop differing degrees of *introversion* (a tendency to reflect on one's own experiences) or *extraversion* (a tendency to focus on the social world), along with differing tendencies to rely on specific psychological functions, such as thinking versus feeling. The combination of these tendencies and functions, said Jung (1933), creates personalities that show distinctive and predictable patterns of behavior.

Other Neo-Freudian Theorists   Alfred Adler, one of Freud's first followers, also questioned his theories. Adler came to believe that the most important innate factor driving the development of personality was not id impulses but a desire to overcome infantile feelings of helplessness and gain some control over the environment. Other prominent neo-Freudians emphasized social relationships in the development of personality. Some, including Erik Erikson, Erich Fromm, and Harry Stack Sullivan, argued that once biological needs are met, the attempt to meet social needs (to feel protected, secure, and accepted, for example) is the main shaper of personality. According to these theories, the strategies that people use to meet social needs, such as dominating other people or being dependent on them, become core features of their personalities.

The first feminist personality theorist, Karen Horney (pronounced "horn-eye"), challenged Freud's view that women's lack of a penis causes them to envy men and feel inferior to them. Horney (1937) argued that it is men who envy women. Realizing that they cannot bear children, males see their lives as having less meaning and substance than women's. Horney called this condition *womb envy*. She believed that when women feel inferior, it is because of cultural factors—such as the personal and political restrictions that men have placed upon them—not because of penis envy (Feist & Feist, 1998).

Contemporary Psychodynamic Theories

Today, some of the most influential psychodynamic approaches to personality focus on *object relations*—that is, on how people's perceptions of themselves and others influence their view of, and reactions to, the world (C. S. Hall, Lindzey, & Campbell, 1998; Westen, 1998). According to object relations theorists, early relationships between infants and their love objects (usually the mother and other primary caregivers) are critically important in the development of personality (Kernberg, 1976; M. Klein, 1975; Kohut, 1984). These relationships, they say, shape our thoughts and feelings about social relationships in later life.

As described in Chapter 9, children ideally form a secure early bond to the mother or other caregiver, gradually tolerate separation from this "object" of attachment, and finally develop the ability to relate to others as independent, secure individuals (Ainsworth, 1989). Object relations theorists study how an infant's experience of a primary caregiver's protection, acceptance, and recognition influences development of the child's self-image, identity, security, social relationships, and other aspects of personality (Mikulincer, 1995; van IJzendoorn, 1995). In one study, for example, people with secure and stable attachments to others were found to be less likely to abuse alcohol or other drugs (Mikelson, Kessler, & Shaver, 1997). In another study, students whose attachments were insecure tended to have shorter and less satisfying romances (Shaver & Clark, 1996). From an object relations standpoint, child abuse may reflect the abusive parents' perceptions of how their own parents treated them (van IJzendoorn, 1995). Children who, because of abuse, neglect, or rejection, miss the opportunity to attach to a love object (their mother) in a healthy fashion may suffer severe disturbances in their later relationships.

latency period   The fourth of Freud's psychosexual stages, usually beginning during the fifth year of life, in which sexual impulses become dormant and the child focuses on education and other matters.

genital stage   The fifth and last of Freud's psychosexual stages, which begins during adolescence, when sexual impulses begin to appear at the conscious level.

Evaluating the Psychodynamic Approach

Freud developed the most comprehensive and influential personality theory ever proposed. His ideas have been applied in psychodynamic therapies aimed at helping people become aware of the unconscious aspects of personality so that they can resolve old conflicts (see Chapter 13). Freud also stimulated the development of personality assessment techniques, including the projective tests described later in this chapter. Some of Freud's ideas have found support in research on cognitive processes, especially social cognition (Andersen & Berk, 1998). There is evidence, for example, that events and experiences that people are unable to recall can influence their thoughts and actions (Westen, 1998). And researchers who take an evolutionary approach to personality (e.g., A. H. Buss, 1997) argue that personality is determined at least in part by innate human tendencies that are similar to instincts.

However, there are several problems and weaknesses in Freud's psychodynamic theory (Crews, 1996). For one thing, his theories are based almost entirely on case studies of a few individuals. As discussed in Chapter 1, conclusions drawn from case studies may not apply to people in general. Nor was Freud's sample of cases representative of people in general. Most of his patients were upper-class Viennese women who not only had mental problems but were raised in a social climate in which the discussion of sex was considered uncivilized. Second, Freud's theory reflected Western European and North American cultural values, which may or may not be helpful in understanding people in other cultures (Landrine & Klonoff, 1992). For example, the concepts of ego and self that are so central to Freud's personality theory are based on the self-oriented values of individualist cultures and thus may be less descriptive of personality development in collectivist cultures, such as those of Asia and Africa (Triandis, 1997).

Freud's conclusions may have been distorted by other biases as well. For example, some Freud scholars believe he might have (perhaps unconsciously) modified reports of what happened during therapy to better fit his theory (Esterson, 1993). He may also have asked leading questions that influenced patients to "recall" events from their childhood that never happened (Bowers & Farvolden, 1996). Today, there are similar concerns that some patients who recover allegedly repressed memories about childhood sexual abuse may actually be reporting false memories implanted by their therapists (E. F. Loftus, 1998; see Chapter 6).

Freud's belief that women envy male anatomy and his focus on male psychosexual development have also been attacked. In the tradition of Horney, some contemporary neo-Freudians have proposed theories that focus specifically on the psychosexual development of women (Sayers, 1991).

Finally, as judged by current standards, Freud's theory is not very scientific. His definitions of *id, ego, unconscious conflict,* and other concepts lack the precision required for scientific measurement and testing (Feist & Feist, 1998). Further, his belief that unconscious instinctual desires drive most human behavior ignores evidence showing that much of that behavior goes beyond instinct gratification. For example, the conscious drive to attain personal, social, and spiritual goals is an important determinant of behavior, as is learning from others. Taken together, these shortcomings have made the psychodynamic approach to personality less popular today than it was in past decades (Mischel, 1999; R. W. Robins, Gosling, & Craik, 1999).

The Trait Approach

How many personality traits are there?

If you were to describe the personality of someone you know, you would probably make a small number of descriptive statements. For example, you might say,

Applying Psychology

SELECTING A JURY   Some psychologists employ trait theories of personality in advising prosecution or defense attorneys about which potential jurors are most likely to be sympathetic to their side of a court case.

She's a really caring person, and very outgoing. She's generous with her time, and she works very hard at everything she does. Yet, sometimes I think she also lacks self-confidence. She always gives in to other people's demands because she wants to be accepted by them.

Indeed, most people describe others by referring to the kind of people they are ("outgoing"); to the thoughts, feelings, and actions that are most typical of them ("caring," "lacks self-confidence"); or to their needs ("wants to be accepted"). Together, these statements describe personality *traits*—the tendencies that help direct how a person usually thinks and behaves (Pervin & John, 1997).

The trait approach to personality makes three main assumptions:

1. Personality traits remain relatively stable, and therefore predictable, over time. Thus, a gentle person tends to stay that way day after day, year after year (Costa & McCrae, 1997).

2. Personality traits remain relatively stable across situations, and they can explain why people act in predictable ways in many different settings. A person who is fiercely competitive at work will probably also be competitive on the tennis court or at a party.

3. People differ with regard to how much of a particular personality trait they possess; no two people are exactly alike on all traits. The result is an endless variety of unique personalities.

In short, the **trait approach** views personality as the combination of stable internal characteristics that people display consistently over time and across situations (Carver & Scheier, 2000).

Prominent Trait Theories

Trait theorists measure the relative strength of many personality characteristics appearing in each individual (see Figure 11.2).

Allport's Trait Theory   Gordon Allport (1961) spent thirty years searching for the traits that combine to form the normal personality. When he listed the nearly 18,000 dictionary terms used to describe human behavior (Allport & Odbert, 1936; Hergenhahn &

trait approach   A perspective on personality that views it as the combination of stable characteristics that people display over time and across situations.

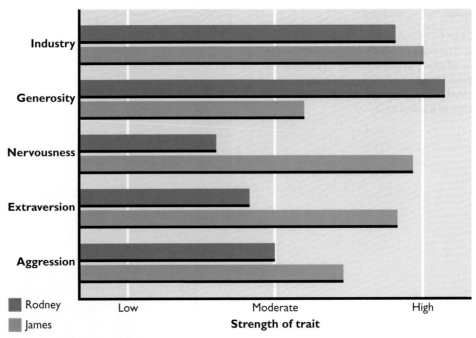

FIGURE 11.2

Two Personality Profiles

 Trait theory describes personality in terms of the strength of particular dimensions, or traits. Here are trait profiles for Rodney, an inner-city social worker, and James, a sales clerk in a department store. Compared with James, Rodney is about equally industrious; more generous; and less nervous, extraverted, and aggressive. Just for fun, mark this figure to indicate how strong you think you are on each of the listed traits. Trait theorists suggest that this should be easy for you to do because, they say, virtually everyone displays a certain amount of almost any personality characteristic.

■ Rodney
■ James

Source: Costa & McCrae (1992).

Olson, 1999), he noticed that many of these terms referred to the same thing. For example, *hostile, nasty,* and *mean* all convey a similar meaning. To better understand this clustering, think of a close relative and jot down all the personality traits that describe him or her. If you are like most people, you were able to capture your relative's personality using only a few trait labels. Allport believed that the set of labels chosen to describe a particular person reflects that person's *central traits,* those that organize and control behavior in many different situations and are usually apparent to others. Central traits are roughly equivalent to the descriptive terms used in letters of recommendation (*reliable* or *distractible,* for example) that are meant to tell what can be expected from a person most of the time (Schultz & Schultz, 2001). Allport also believed that people possess *secondary traits,* those that are more specific to certain situations and control far less behavior. "Dislikes crowds" is an example of a secondary trait.

Allport's research helped to lay the foundation for modern research on personality traits. However, his focus on the uniqueness of each individual personality makes it difficult to draw general conclusions about the structure of human personality.

Eysenck's Biological Trait Theory   British psychologist Hans Eysenck (pronounced "eye-sink") used a technique called *factor analysis* to study the structure of both normal and disordered personalities. Factor analysis helps researchers to discover which personality traits are correlated with one another. For example, it can reveal whether people who are anxious are also moody, and whether optimistic people are usually also friendly. From his research, Eysenck concluded that our personality can be described in terms of three main factors or dimensions (Eysenck, 1990a, 1994):

1. *Introversion-extraversion.*   Extraverts are sociable and outgoing, enjoy parties and other social activities, take risks, and love excitement and change. Introverts tend to be quiet, thoughtful, and reserved, enjoying solitary pursuits and avoiding excitement and social involvement.

2. *Emotionality-stability.*   At one extreme of this dimension are people who exhibit such characteristics as moodiness, restlessness, worry, anxiety, and other negative emotions. People at the opposite end are calm, even-tempered, relaxed, and emotionally stable. (This dimension is also often called *neuroticism.*)

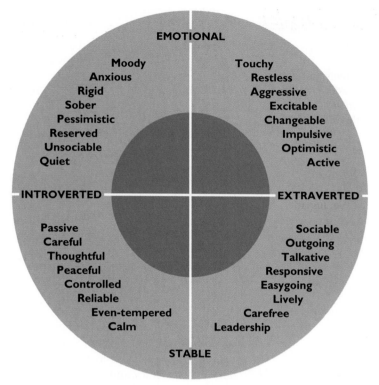

Source: Eysenck & Rachman (1965).

FIGURE 11.3

Eysenck's Major
Personality Dimensions

Eysenck found that varying degrees of emotionality-stability and introversion-extraversion combine to produce predictable trait patterns. Which section of the figure do you think best describes your personality?

3. *Psychoticism.* People high on psychoticism (pronounced "si-KOT-eh-siz-em") show characteristics such as cruelty, hostility, coldness, oddness, and rejection of social customs.

According to Eysenck, personality can be described in terms of where a person falls along these three dimensions, especially emotionality-stability and introversion-extraversion. For example, an introverted but stable person is likely to be controlled and reliable. An introverted but emotional person is likely to be rigid and anxious (see Figure 11.3). Eysenck presented data to show that scores on tests measuring these dimensions—such as the Eysenck Personality Inventory—can predict people's key characteristics, including specific behavior disorders. Criminals, for example, are likely to display restless, aggressive, and impulsive behavior.

Eysenck argued that variations in personality characteristics can be traced to inherited differences in the brain. These biological differences, he said, explain why some people are more physiologically aroused than others. For example, people who inherit a nervous system with a consistently low level of arousal will be relatively insensitive to the effects of rewards and punishments, and therefore will not readily develop conditioned responses, including conditioned fears. Without such conditioned responses, said Eysenck, they will not easily learn to play by society's rules. Further, having a low arousal level may lead such people to look constantly for excitement and change in order to increase their arousal; in short, they will be extraverted. In contrast, Eysenck's theory predicts that people with more sensitive, "overaroused" nervous systems are likely to be strongly affected by rewards and punishments, to readily develop conditioned fear responses, and to avoid excessive stimulation—in other words, to be introverted.

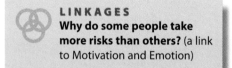

LINKAGES
Why do some people take more risks than others? (a link to Motivation and Emotion)

The Big-Five Model of Personality

Other factor analysis research, especially by Paul Costa and Robert McCrae (1992), has led many trait theorists today to conclude that personality is actually organized around five basic factors, not just three (Wiggins & Trapnell, 1997). The components of this so-called **big-five model,** or **five-factor model,** of personality are openness, conscientiousness,

big-five model   A view based on factor-analytic studies suggesting the existence of five basic components of human personality: openness, conscientiousness, extraversion, agreeableness, and neuroticism. Also called *five-factor model.*

five-factor model   See *big-five model.*

TABLE 11.2

The Big-Five Personality Dimensions

Here is a list of the adjectives that define the big-five personality factors. You can more easily remember the names of these factors by noting that their first letters spell the word *ocean*.

Dimension	Defining Descriptors
Openness	Artistic, curious, imaginative, insightful, original, wide interests, unusual thought processes, intellectual interests
Conscientiousness	Efficient, organized, planful, reliable, thorough, dependable, ethical, productive
Extraversion	Active, assertive, energetic, outgoing, talkative, gesturally expressive, gregarious
Agreeableness	Appreciative, forgiving, generous, kind, trusting, noncritical, warm, compassionate, considerate, straightforward
Neuroticism	Anxious, self-pitying, tense, emotionally unstable, impulsive, vulnerable, touchy, worrying

Source: Adapted from McCrae & John (1992).

extraversion, agreeableness, and neuroticism (see Table 11.2). Several different investigators have found these factors (or a set very similar to them) when they factor-analyzed data from numerous sources, including personality inventories, peer ratings of personality characteristics, and checklists of descriptive adjectives (Costa & McCrae, 1995; L. R. Goldberg, 1995). The fact that some version of the big-five factors reliably appear in many countries and cultures—including Canada, China, Germany, Finland, India, Japan, Korea, the Philippines, and Poland (McCrae & Costa, 1997)—provides further evidence that these factors may represent basic components of human personality.

The emergence of the big-five model is considered by many trait theorists to be a major breakthrough in personality research (Carver & Scheier, 2000). Identification of the big-five traits provides a standard way of examining the personalities of all people, regardless of where they live or the nature of their economic, social, and cultural backgrounds. The big-five model also allows researchers to precisely describe the similarities and differences in people's personalities and, most recently, to relate personality characteristics to happiness, or subjective well-being (e.g., Diener, 2000; DeNeve, 1999).

ANIMAL PERSONALITIES   The idea that personality can be described on five main dimensions seems to hold for some animals as well as humans. The five animal dimensions differ from, but are still related to, human traits. For example, an observational study found that hyenas differ from one another in terms of dominance, excitability, agreeableness (toward people), sociability (toward each other), and curiosity. Some of these same traits have been observed in chimpanzees and other primates (Gosling & John, 1999), and dog and cat lovers often report such traits in their pets.

Where do the big-five factors or other personality traits come from? Do they arise, as some researchers suggest, from our genes? One study described a pair of male twins who had been separated at five weeks of age and did not meet again for thirty-nine years. Both men drove Chevrolets, chain-smoked the same brand of cigarettes, had divorced a woman named Linda, were remarried to a woman named Betty, had sons named James Allan, had dogs named Toy, enjoyed similar hobbies, and had served as sheriff's deputies (Tellegen et al., 1988).

What am I being asked to believe or accept?

Cases like this have helped focus the attention of behavioral geneticists on the possibility that some core aspects of personality might be partly inherited (Rowe, 1997).

Is there evidence available to support the claim?

The evidence and the arguments regarding this assertion are much like those presented in Chapter 7, where we discuss the origins of differences in mental abilities. Anecdotes about children who seem to "have" their parents' or grandparents' bad temper, generosity, or shyness are often presented to support the idea that personality is inherited. Indeed, resemblances in personality among family members do provide one important source of evidence. Several studies have found moderate but significant correlations between children's personality test scores and those of their parents and siblings (M. H. Davis, Luce, & Kraus, 1994; Loehlin, 1992).

Stronger evidence comes from studies conducted around the world comparing identical twins raised together, identical twins raised apart, nonidentical twins raised together, and nonidentical twins raised apart (e.g., Saudino, 1998; Waller & Shaver, 1994). Identical twins (who have exactly the same genes) tend to be more alike in personality than nonidentical twins (whose genes are no more similar than those of other siblings)—regardless of whether they are raised apart or together. Further, research consistently shows that identical twins are more alike than nonidentical twins in general temperament, such as how active, sociable, anxious, and emotional they are (D. M. Buss, 1995; Rowe, 1997). On the basis of such twin studies, behavioral geneticists have concluded that at least 30 percent, and perhaps as much as 60 percent, of the variability in adult personality traits is due to genetic factors (N. Brody & Ehrlichman, 1998).

Can that evidence be interpreted another way?

Family resemblances in personality could reflect inheritance or social influence. Thus, an alternative interpretation of this evidence might be that family similarities come not from common genes but from a common environment. Children learn many rules, skills, and behaviors by watching parents, siblings, and others around them; perhaps they learn their personalities as well. And the fact that nontwin siblings are less alike than twins may well result from what is called *nonshared environments* (Plomin, 1994). A child's place in the family birth order, differences in the way parents treat each of their children, and accidents and illnesses that alter a particular child's life or health are examples of nonshared factors (Paulhus, Trapnell, & Chen, 1999). Each nonshared factor can have a different impact on each individual. Compared with twins, nontwins tend to be affected by more nonshared environmental factors.

What evidence would help to evaluate the alternatives?

One way to evaluate the degree to which personality is inherited would be to study people in infancy, before the environment has had a chance to exert its influence. If the environment were entirely responsible for personality, newborn infants should be essentially alike.

However, as discussed in Chapter 9, newborns do show differences in activity level, sensitivity to the environment, the tendency to cry, and interest in new stimuli (D. M. Buss, 1995). These temperamental differences suggest biological, and perhaps genetic, influences.

To evaluate the relative contributions of nature and nurture beyond infancy, psychologists have examined characteristics of adopted children. If adopted children are more like their biological than their adoptive parents, this suggests the influence of heredity in personality. If they are more like their adoptive family, a strong role for environmental factors in personality is suggested. In actuality, adopted children's personalities tend to resemble the personalities of their biological parents and siblings more than those of the families in which they are raised (Carey & DiLalla, 1994; Loehlin, 1992).

Further research will determine more clearly what aspects of the environment are most important in shaping personality (Turkheimer & Waldron, 2000). Thus far, most investigators conclude that elements of the shared environment that equally affect all children in the same family, such as socioeconomic status, appear to have little influence on personality variation. However, nonshared environmental influences, at home and elsewhere, appear to be very important in personality development (Halverson & Wampler, 1997; Harris, 2000). We need to know more about the exact impact on personality development of nonshared environmental factors that may be different for twins and nontwin siblings.

◾ What conclusions are most reasonable?

Even those researchers, such as Robert Plomin, who support genetic theories of personality caution that we should not replace "simple-minded environmentalism" with the equally incorrect view that personality is almost completely biologically determined (Plomin, Chipuer, & Loehlin, 1990). Indeed, it is pointless to talk about heredity *versus* environment as causes of personality, because nature and nurture always intertwine to exert joint and simultaneous influences. With this caution in mind, we would be well advised to draw rather tentative conclusions about the sources of personality.

The evidence available so far suggests that genetic influences do appear to contribute significantly to the differences between people in many personality traits. However, there is no evidence of a specific gene for any specific personality trait. The genetic contribution to personality most likely comes in the form of physical characteristics and temperament, as measured by levels of activity, emotionality, and sociability (A. H. Buss, 1995; Kagan & Snidman, 1991). These physical characteristics and temperaments then interact with environmental factors, such as family experiences, to produce specific features of personality. For example, children who inherit a frail body and/or high emotionality might play less with other children, withdraw from social interactions, and thus tend to fail to learn important social skills (Eisenberg, Fabes, & Murphy, 1995). These experiences and tendencies, in turn, might foster the self-consciousness and shyness seen in introverted personalities.

Note, however, that genetic predispositions toward particular personality characteristics may or may not appear in behavior, depending on whether the environment supports or suppresses them. Changes in genetically predisposed traits are not only possible but may actually be quite common as children develop (Kagan & Snidman, 1991). Even the personalities of identical twins become less similar over time as they encounter different environmental experiences (McCartney, Harris, & Bernieri, 1990). Rather than inheriting specific traits, people appear to inherit raw materials that are then shaped by the world into individual personalities.

Evaluating the Trait Approach

The trait approach, especially the big-five model, tends to dominate contemporary research in personality. Yet there are several problems and weaknesses associated with this approach.

For one thing, trait theories are better at describing people than at explaining them. They say a lot about how people behave, but they don't always explain *why* (Funder, 1993; Pervin, 1996). In addition, trait theories tell little about how traits relate to the thoughts and feelings that precede, accompany, and follow behavior. Do introverts and extraverts *decide* to act as they do? Can they behave otherwise? And how do they feel about their actions and experiences (Mischel, 1999)? Some personality psychologists are trying to link their research with that of cognitive psychologists in an effort to better understand how thoughts and emotions influence, and are influenced by, personality traits (M. Snyder & Cantor, 1998).

The trait approach has also been criticized for offering a superficial description of personality that fails to capture how traits combine to form a complex and dynamic individual (J. A. Block, 1995; McAdams, 1997). Even if the big-five model of personality proves to be correct and universal, its factors are not all-powerful; situations, too, affect behavior. Thus, for example, people high in extraversion are not always socially outgoing: Whether they behave sociably depends, in part, on where they are and who else may be present. The importance of these person-situation interactions is emphasized by the social-cognitive approach to personality, which we describe next.

The Social-Cognitive Approach

Do we learn our personality?

According to the psychodynamic and trait approaches, personality consists of inner dynamics or traits that guide thinking and behavior. In contrast, researchers who take a **social-cognitive approach** view personality as a set of behaviors that people acquire through learning and then display in particular situations. Some aspects of this approach reflect a traditional behavioral assumption—namely, that all behavior is learned through classical and operant conditioning (see Chapter 5). However, as we shall see, the social-cognitive approach expands on that assumption by emphasizing (1) the role of *learned patterns of thought* in guiding our actions and (2) the fact that much of personality is learned in *social situations* through interaction with, and observation of, other people, including family members (Kimble, 1999; Mischel & Shoda, 1998; Rotter, 1990). For this reason, the social-cognitive approach is sometimes called the *social-learning approach;* it defines personality as the sum total of the behaviors and cognitive habits that develop as people learn through experience in the social world. Accordingly, researchers in this area are especially concerned with understanding how learned patterns of thought contribute to behavior and how behavior and its consequences alter cognitive activity, as well as future actions.

Prominent Social-Cognitive Theories

Julian Rotter, Albert Bandura, and Walter Mischel rank among the most influential social-cognitive or social-learning theorists.

Rotter's Expectancy Theory   Julian Rotter (1982) argued that learning creates cognitive expectancies that guide behavior. In particular, he suggested that a person's decision to engage in a behavior is determined by (1) what the person expects to happen following the behavior and (2) the value the person places on the outcome. For example, people spend a lot of money on clothes to be worn at job interviews because past learning leads them to expect that doing so will help get them the job, and they place a high value on having the job. To Rotter, then, behavior is determined by rewarding consequences and by a cognitive *expectation* that a particular behavior will be rewarded (Mischel, 1999).

Rotter also suggested that people learn general ways of thinking about the world, especially about how life's rewards and punishments are controlled. Some people *(internals)* expect events to be controlled mainly by their own efforts. That is, what they

social-cognitive approach   An approach to personality that views personality as a label summarizing the unique patterns of thinking and behavior that a person learns.

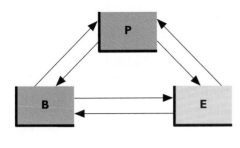

B = Behavior

E = The external environment

P = Personal factors, such as
thoughts, feelings, and
biological events

Source: Bandura (1999).

FIGURE 11.4

Reciprocal Determinism

As shown here, Bandura's notion of reciprocal determinism suggests that thoughts, behavior, and the environment are constantly affecting each other. A person's hostile thoughts, for example, may lead to hostile behavior, which creates even more hostile thoughts. At the same time, the hostile behavior offends other people, which creates an angry environment that causes the person to think and act in even more negative ways. As increasingly negative thoughts alter the person's perceptions of the environment, it seems to be more threatening than ever.

self-efficacy   According to Bandura, the learned expectation of success in given situations.

achieve and the reinforcements they get result from efforts they make themselves. Others *(externals)* tend to expect external forces, over which they have no control, to determine events. When externals succeed, they tend to believe that their success occurred due to chance or luck.

Differences in generalized expectancies tend to correlate with differences in behavior (Rotter, 1990). For example, internals tend to get better grades and to score higher on standardized academic tests than externals (Schultz & Schultz, 2001). Internals are also more likely than externals to work at staying healthy; they are less likely to smoke, and more likely to exercise and to wear seat belts (Maddux, 1993). If they are hospitalized, internals are more cooperative patients than externals, and they are released sooner (Phares, 1991).

Bandura and Reciprocal Determinism   Whether people learn through direct experience with reward and punishment or through observational learning processes, their behavior tends to affect their environment. Observing this effect on their environment may, in turn, affect their cognitions, which affects their behavior, and so on. According to Albert Bandura (1997), this *reciprocal determinism* shapes personality through the complex and constant interaction among thoughts, the environment, and behavior (see Figure 11.4).

One especially important cognitive element in this mutual-influence system is **self-efficacy,** the learned expectation of success. People with a sense of self-efficacy believe that they can successfully perform a behavior regardless of past failures or current obstacles. Bandura (1997, 2000) suggests that this expectation controls overt behavior. The higher your self-efficacy regarding a particular situation, the greater will be your actual accomplishments in that situation. Thus, going to a job interview with the belief that you have the skills for the job may help you to get the job or, at least, blunt the impact of rejection if you do not. (Perhaps you recall the classic children's story *The Little Engine That Could.* Trying to get up a steep hill, the scared little engine starts by saying "I think I can, I think I can" and ends up saying "I know I can, I know I can." And it did.)

According to Bandura, self-efficacy interacts with expectancies about the outcome of behavior in general, and the result of this interplay helps to shape a person's psychological well-being (Bandura, 1997). For example, if a person has low self-efficacy and also expects that nothing anyone does has much effect on the world, apathy may result. But if a person with low self-efficacy believes that other people enjoy the benefits of their efforts, the result may be self-disparagement and depression.

Mischel's Person-Situation Theory   Social-cognitive theorists believe that learned expectations characterize each individual and make that individual different from others. Walter Mischel calls these cognitive characteristics *person variables.* He believes that they outline the dimensions along which individuals differ (Mischel & Shoda, 1995). The most important person variables, according to Mischel, are (1) *competencies* (the thoughts and actions the person can perform), (2) *perceptions* (how the person perceives the environment), (3) *expectations* (what the person expects to follow from various behaviors and what the person believes he or she is capable of doing—again, a matter of self-efficacy), (4) *subjective values* (the person's ideals and goals), and (5) *self-regulation and plans* (the person's standards for self-reward and plans for reaching goals).

Mischel distinguishes between person variables and personality traits, noting that traits may not be helpful in predicting behavior, because people often behave differently in different situations. To predict how a person might behave, he says, we also need to know about the situation in which the behavior will occur. Mischel's views sparked a "person-situation" debate between social-cognitive and trait theorists about whether personality traits or situational factors are more influential in guiding behavior. This debate produced no clear winners, and theorists on both sides now tend to focus on the similarities, not the differences, in their points of view (Mischel & Shoda, 1998; Wiggins, 1997). This new focus has helped to clarify the relationships between person variables and situation variables and how they affect behavior under various conditions. Many of the conclusions that emerged are consistent with Bandura's concept of reciprocal determinism:

"You know, we're just not reaching that guy."

As noted in Chapter 10, being "internal" and optimistic are aspects of the so-called stress-hardy personality.

1. Traits influence behavior only in relevant situations. The trait of anxiousness, for example, may predict that a person will experience anxiety, but only in situations where the person feels threatened.

2. Traits can lead to behaviors that alter situations that, in turn, promote other behaviors. Thus, a hostile child can provoke aggression in others and thus start a fight.

3. People choose to be in situations that are in accord with their traits. Introverts, for example, are more likely to choose quiet environments, and extraverts tend to seek out livelier, more social circumstances.

4. Traits are more important in some situations than in others. In situations where a wide range of behaviors is appropriate—a picnic, for example—people's behavior may be predicted from their personality traits (extraverts will probably socialize and play games while introverts watch). However, in situations that allow fewer social options, such as a funeral, personality traits will not distinguish one person from another; all are likely to be quiet and somber.

Today, social-cognitive and social-learning theorists attempt to discover how person variables develop, how they relate to stress and health, and how they interact with situational variables to affect behavior.

Evaluating the Social-Cognitive Approach

The social-cognitive approach to personality has expanded the applications of classical and operant learning principles to include socially important areas such as aggression, the effects of mass media on children, and the development of techniques that enhance personal control over behavior. Social-cognitive principles have also been translated into cognitive-behavioral treatment procedures for many types of psychological disorders (D. M. Clark & Fairburn, 1997; see Chapter 13).

The social-cognitive approach has not escaped criticism, however. One concern is that theories emphasizing the role of learning reduce human beings to a set of learned responses based solely on relationships with the environment. This view is also said to minimize the importance of subjective experience; to fail to consider unconscious processes; to neglect the contribution of emotion to personality; and to exclude genetic,

THE IMPACT OF SITUATIONS Like the rest of us, professional wrestler Jesse Ventura tends to behave differently in different situations, such as in the ring and in the office where he serves as governor of Minnesota. Mischel's theory of personality underscores the importance of such person-situation interactions in determining behavior.

physiological, and other influences that are not based on learning. Social-cognitive theories have addressed some of these objections through their emphasis on expectancies, self-efficacy, and person variables, but they are criticized by some for not going far enough in that direction (Carver & Scheier, 1996). For many, a preferable alternative is the phenomenological approach to personality.

The Phenomenological Approach

Is everyone basically good?

Suppose you and a friend meet someone new at a party. Comparing notes later, you discover a major difference in your reactions. You thought the new person was entertaining, warm, and showed a genuine interest in others. Your friend saw the same person as a "phony" who merely pretended to be interested. How can two people draw such opposite conclusions from the same conversation? Just as each person sees something different in a cloud formation, each of you perceived a different reality, a different conversation, and a different person.

This interpretation reflects an approach to personality that assumes that the way people perceive and interpret the world forms their personalities and guides their behavior. Proponents of this **phenomenological approach** emphasize that each individual perceives reality somewhat differently (as noted in Chapter 3, on sensation and perception) and that these differences, rather than traits, instincts, or learning experiences, are central to creating personality differences. From this standpoint, no one can understand another person without somehow perceiving the world through that person's eyes. All behavior, even if it looks "weird," is meaningful to the person displaying it. Because the phenomenological approach focuses on uniquely human mental qualities—including self-awareness, creativity, planning, decision making, and responsibility—it is also sometimes called the *humanistic* view of personality.

According to the phenomenological approach, the primary human motivator is an innate drive toward personal growth that prompts people to fulfill their unique and natural potential. Like the planted seed that naturally becomes a flower, people are inclined toward goodness, creativity, love, and joy.

Major Phenomenological Theories

The most prominent phenomenological theories are those of Carl Rogers and Abraham Maslow.

Rogers' Self Theory   The name Carl Rogers is almost synonymous with the phenomenological approach (C. R. Rogers, 1942, 1951, 1961, 1970, 1980). Rogers believed that each person responds as an organized whole to reality as he or she perceives it. He emphasized **self-actualization,** which he described as an innate tendency toward growth that motivates all human behavior. To Rogers, personality is the expression of each individual's self-actualizing tendency as it unfolds in that individual's uniquely perceived reality.

Central to Rogers's theory is the *self,* the part of experience that a person identifies as "I" or "me." According to Rogers, those who accurately experience the self—with all its preferences, abilities, fantasies, shortcomings, and desires—are on the road to self-actualization. The progress of those whose experiences of the self become distorted, however, is likely to be slowed or stopped.

Very early in life, children learn to need the approval, or *positive regard*, of others. As a result, evaluations by parents, teachers, and others begin to affect children's self-evaluations. When evaluations by others agree with a child's own evaluation, the child's genuine reaction matches, or is *congruent* with, self-experience. The child not only feels the others' positive regard but also evaluates the self as "good" for having earned

phenomenological approach   A view based on the assumption that personality is created out of each person's unique way of perceiving and interpreting the world.

self-actualization   According to Rogers, an innate tendency toward growth that motivates all people to seek the full realization of their highest potential.

SEEKING SELF-ACTUALIZATION
According to Rogers, conditions of worth can make it harder for children to become aware of and accept aspects of themselves that conflict with their parents' values. Progress toward self-actualization may be enhanced by associating with those whose positive regard is not conditional on displaying any particular pattern of behavior. Has your own behavior ever brought you in conflict with your parents' values, and if so, how did you handle the situation?

approval. The result is a clearly identified and positively evaluated experience of the self. This self-experience becomes part of the **self-concept,** which is the way one thinks of oneself. Unfortunately, things may not always go so smoothly. If a pleasurable self-experience is evaluated negatively by others, the child must either do without their positive regard or reevaluate the experience. Thus, a little boy who is teased by his parents because he enjoys playing with dolls might adopt a distorted self-experience ("I don't like dolls" or "Feeling good is bad").

In other words, said Rogers, personality is shaped partly by self-actualizing tendencies and partly by others' evaluations. In this way, people come to like what they are "supposed" to like and to behave as they are "supposed" to behave. Although this socialization process helps people to get along in society, it often requires that they stifle their self-actualizing tendency and distort their experience. Rogers argued that psychological discomfort, anxiety, or mental disorder can result when the feelings people experience or express are *incongruent* with their true feelings.

Incongruence is likely, Rogers said, when parents and teachers lead children to believe that their worth as a person depends on displaying the "right" attitudes, behaviors, and values. These **conditions of worth** are created whenever people are evaluated instead of their behavior. For example, parents who find their child drawing on the wall with crayons are unlikely to say, "I love you, but I don't approve of this behavior." They are more likely to shout, "Bad boy!" or "Bad girl!" thus suggesting that the child is lovable and worthwhile only when well-behaved. As a result, the child's self-experience is not "I like drawing on the wall, but Mom and Dad don't approve," but instead, "Drawing on the wall is bad, and I am bad if I like it, so I don't like it." The child may eventually show overly neat and tidy behaviors that do not reflect the real self but, rather, are part of an ideal self dictated by the parents. Conditions of worth, said Rogers, make it harder for children to become aware of and accept aspects of themselves that conflict with their parents' values.

Like Freud's concept of superego, conditions of worth are initially set up by external pressure but eventually become part of the person's belief system. Thus, to Rogers, rewards and punishments are important in personality development not just because they shape behavior but also because they so easily create distorted self-perceptions and

self-concept The way one thinks of oneself.

conditions of worth According to Rogers, the feelings an individual experiences when others provide positive regard only if certain behaviors or attitudes are displayed.

incongruence. He believed that a person can resume progress toward self-actualization by interacting with those whose positive regard is not conditional on any particular pattern of behavior.

Maslow's Humanistic Psychology   Like Rogers, Abraham Maslow (1954, 1962, 1971) viewed personality as the expression of a basic human tendency toward growth and self-actualization. However, Maslow believed that self-actualization is not just a human capacity but a human *need;* as noted in Chapter 8, he described self-actualization as the highest in a hierarchy of needs. Yet, said Maslow, people are often distracted from seeking self-actualization because they focus exclusively on needs that are lower on the hierarchy.

Maslow saw most people as controlled by a *deficiency orientation,* a preoccupation with perceived needs for material things. Ultimately, he said, deficiency-oriented people come to see life as a meaningless exercise in disappointment and boredom, and they may begin to behave in problematic ways. For example, in an attempt to satisfy the need for love, many people focus on what love can give them (security), not on what they can give to another. This deficiency orientation may lead to jealousy and a tendency to focus on what is missing; as a result, such people never truly experience either love or security.

In contrast, people with a *growth orientation* do not focus on what is missing but draw satisfaction from what they have, what they are, and what they can do. This orientation opens the door to what Maslow called *peak experiences,* in which people feel joy, and even ecstasy, in the mere fact of being alive, being human, and knowing that they are utilizing their fullest potential.

Evaluating the Phenomenological Approach

The phenomenological approach to personality is consistent with the way many people view themselves. It gives a central role to immediate experience and emphasizes each person's uniqueness. The best-known application of the phenomenological approach is the client-centered therapy of Carl Rogers, which is discussed in Chapter 13. The phenomenological approach has also inspired short-term group experiences, such as sensitivity training and encounter groups, designed to help people become more aware of themselves and the way they relate to others. This approach has also influenced the development of techniques to teach parents how to avoid creating conditions of worth while maximizing their children's potential.

Yet to its critics, the phenomenological approach is naive, romantic, and unrealistic. They question whether all people are as inherently good and "growth oriented" as this approach suggests. They also fault phenomenologists for paying too little attention to the role of inherited characteristics, learning, situational influences, and unconscious motivation in shaping personality. In addition, these critics argue, the idea that personality development is directed only by an innate growth potential is an oversimplification. So, too, is the phenomenological assumption that all human problems stem from blocked self-actualization. Like the trait approach, phenomenological theories seem to do a better job of describing personality than explaining it. And phenomenological concepts seem too vague to be tested empirically. Accordingly, most people who conduct empirical research to learn about personality do not favor the phenomenological approach.

Finally, the phenomenologists' tendency to define healthy people as independent and autonomous individuals reflects culture-specific ideals about mental health that may not apply outside of North American and other Western cultures (Triandis, 1997). As discussed in the Linkages section of this chapter, the foundations of phenomenological self theories may be in direct conflict with the values of non-Western, collectivist cultures. ("In Review: Major Approaches to Personality" summarizes key features of the phenomenological approach, along with those of the other approaches we have described.)

Major Approaches to Personality

Approach	Basic Assumptions About Behavior	Typical Research Methods
Psychodynamic	Determined by largely unconscious intrapsychic conflicts	Case studies
Trait	Determined by traits or needs	Analysis of tests for basic personality dimensions
Social-cognitive	Determined by learning cognitive factors, and specific situations	Analysis of interactions between people and situations
Phenomenological	Determined by unique perception of reality	Studies of relationships between perceptions and behavior

LINKAGES
Does culture determine personality? (a link to Human Development)

LINKAGES

Personality, Culture, and Human Development

In many Western cultures, people encourage others to "stand up for yourself" or to "blow your own horn" in order to "get what you have coming to you." In middle-class North America, the values of achievement and personal distinction are taught to children, particularly male children, very early in life (Markus & Kitayama, 1997). North American children are encouraged to feel special, to want self-esteem, and to feel good about themselves. Those who learn and show these values tend to receive praise for doing so.

As a result of this cultural training, many people in North America develop personalities largely based on a sense of high self-worth. In a study by Hazel Markus and Shinobu Kitayama (1991), for example, 70 percent of a sample of U.S. students believed they were superior to their peers. In addition, 60 percent believed they were in the top 10 percent on a wide variety of personal attributes! This tendency toward self-enhancement is evident as early as age four.

It is no wonder that many Western personality theorists see a sense of independence, uniqueness, and self-esteem as fundamental to mental health. As noted in Chapter 9, for example, Erik Erikson included the appearance of personal identity and self-esteem as part of normal psychosocial development. Middle-class North Americans who fail to value and strive for independence, self-promotion, and unique personal achievement may be seen as having a personality disorder, some form of depression, or other psychological problems.

Do these ideas reflect universal truths about personality development or, rather, the influence of the cultures that generated them? It is certainly clear that people in many non-Western cultures develop personal orientations that are very different from those of North Americans and Europeans. In China and Japan, for example, an independent, unique self is not emphasized (Ho & Chiu, 1998). In fact, children there are encouraged to develop and maintain pleasant, respectful relations with others and not to stand out from the crowd, lest they diminish someone else. So in the United States, one often hears that "the squeaky wheel gets the grease" (meaning that you don't get what you want

INDIVIDUAL ACHIEVEMENT In individualist cultures, personal distinction is valued by parents and teachers early in life. These cultural values help to shape personality. Make a list of the values you have learned from your family, religious leaders, teachers, and friends. Which of them are typical of individualist cultures, which are typical of collectivist cultures, and which reflect a combination of both?

unless you make your needs known); in Japan you are more likely to hear that "the nail that stands up gets pounded down" (meaning that it is not a good idea to make yourself stand out from the crowd). In Japanese, the word for "different" *(tigau)* also means "wrong" (Kitayama & Markus, 1992). Japanese children are taught to be modest and to play down the value of personal contributions. At an age as young as two-and-a-half, these children learn about the joy and value of group work (Kitayama & Markus, 1992).

In contrast to the *independent* self-system common in individualist cultures such as Great Britain, Switzerland, and the United States, cultures with a more collectivist orientation (such as Brazil, China, Japan, and Nigeria) promote an *interdependent* self-system through which people see themselves as a fraction of the social whole. Each person has little or no meaningful definition without reference to the group. These different kinds of self-systems produce differences in what gives people a sense of well-being and a feeling of satisfaction with their lives. For example, in the United States, a sense of well-being is usually associated with *having positive attributes,* such as intelligence, creativity, competitiveness, persistence, and so on. In Japan, feelings of well-being are more likely to be associated with *having no negative attributes* (A. P. Fiske et al., 1998; Kitayama et al., 1997). Accordingly, studies of thousands of people all over the world indicate that in collectivist cultures, those who are most satisfied with their lives are those whose behavior brings social approval and harmonious relations with others. In individualist cultures, life satisfaction is highest among those who experience high self-esteem and who feel good about their personal accomplishments (V. S. Y. Kwan, Bond, & Singelis, 1997; Suh et al., 1998).

Because cultural factors shape ideas about how the ideal personality develops, all approaches to personality must be evaluated in terms of how well they apply to cultures other than the one in which they were developed (Enns, 1994). Their applicability to males and females must be considered as well. Even within North American cultures, for example, gender differences exist in the development of self-esteem. Females tend to show an interdependent self-system, achieving their sense of self and self-esteem from attachments to others. By contrast, males' self-esteem tends to develop in relation to personal achievement, in a manner more in keeping with an independent self-system (Cross & Madson, 1997). Cross-gender and cross-cultural differences in the nature and determinants of a sense of self underscore the widespread effects of gender and culture on the development of many aspects of human personality.

Personality Development over Time

Psychologists have long been interested in *how* people differ in personality traits and behavior, but they also want to know *why* those differences appear. Some began their search for the source of personality differences by looking at infants' differing temperaments. As noted in Chapter 9, temperament is reflected in the unlearned, generalized patterns of emotional expression and other behavior that humans display from birth (A. H. Buss, 1997).

■ What was the researchers' question?

Can young children's temperaments predict their personality characteristics and behaviors as adults?

■ How did the researchers answer the question?

To answer this question, Avasholom Caspi and his colleagues conducted a longitudinal study in which the same people were assessed at several different times in their lives (Caspi et al., 1997; Caspi et al., 1995; Caspi & Silva, 1995). Their research sample included all the children born in Dunedin, New Zealand, between April 1972 and March 1973, a total of about 1,000 people. When these children were three, research assistants observed them in a standard situation and rated them on a number of dimensions, including the degree to which they showed explosive or uncontrolled behavior, interacted easily with others, and acted withdrawn and unresponsive. These observations were used to place each child into one of five temperament categories: *undercontrolled* (irritable, impatient, emotional), *inhibited* (shy, fearful, easily distracted), *confident* (eager to perform, responsive to questions), *reserved* (withdrawn, uncomfortable), and *well adjusted* (confident, friendly, well controlled). The children were observed and categorized again when they were five, seven, and nine years old. If it occurs to you that seeing a child at one point in life might bias an observer's ratings of that child later on, you are right. To ensure that ratings would not be influenced by this kind of observer bias, the researchers arranged for different people to make the ratings at each point in time. These ratings indicated that the children's temperaments stayed about the same over the years from age three to age nine.

Nine years later, when the research participants were eighteen years old, they filled out a standard personality test; and when they were twenty-one, they were interviewed about their involvement in risky and unhealthy behaviors, such as excessive drinking, violent criminal activities, unprotected sex, and unsafe driving habits. To avoid bias, the interviewers were given no information about the participants' temperament when they were children or about their scores on the personality test.

■ What did the researchers find?

Several significant differences were found in the personality test results of the five original temperament groups. For example, the average test scores of eighteen-year-olds who had been classified as "undercontrolled" in childhood showed that they were much more aggressive, alienated, negative, and hostile than any other temperament group. Further, people who had been classified as "confident" or "well adjusted" as children were more forceful, decisive, and effective at age eighteen than people who had been classified as "inhibited" or "reserved." These findings held true for males and females alike.

There were also small but significant correlations between childhood temperament and risky behavior in young adulthood. For example, "undercontrolled" children were about twice as likely as others to develop personalities that are associated with violence, excessive drinking, and other health-risky behaviors.

■ What do the results mean?

The results of this research indicate that we can make relatively accurate predictions about people's personality and behavior as adults if we know about their temperament as children. But as critical thinkers, we must be careful not to overstate the strength of these results. Although the correlations between temperament and personality, and between temperament and health-risky behaviors, were statistically significant, they were also relatively small. In other words, not all children classified as "undercontrolled" at age three turned out to be aggressive or violent at eighteen. So it is more accurate to say that personality may be influenced and shaped by temperament, but not completely determined by it.

▓ What do we still need to know?

Valuable as it is, this study leaves unanswered a number of questions about the relationship between temperament and personality (Roberts & DelVecchio, 2000). For example, *why* is there continuity between temperament as a child and personality as an adult? The link is probably a complex one, involving both nature and nurture. Caspi and his colleagues (1989) offered one explanation that draws heavily on Bandura's concept of *reciprocal determinism*. They proposed that long-term consistencies in behavior result from the mutual influence that temperament and environmental events have on one another. For example, undercontrolled people might choose to spend time with people who accept, and even encourage, rude or impolite behavior. When such behavior brings negative reactions, the world seems that much more hostile, and the undercontrolled people become even more aggressive and negative. Caspi and his colleagues see the results of their studies as evidence that this process of mutual influence between personality and situations can continue over a lifetime.

Assessing Personality

▓ How do psychologists measure personality?

Suppose you are an industrial-organizational psychologist whose job is to ensure that your company hires only honest, cooperative, and hard-working employees. How would you know which candidates had these characteristics? There are three basic methods of assessing and describing personality: observations, interviews, and tests (Nietzel, Bernstein, & Milich, 1998). Data gathered through these methods assist in personnel selection, in the diagnosis of psychological disorders, in making predictions about a convict's or mental patient's dangerousness, and in other risky decision situations (Groth-Marnat, 1997).

Observational methods allow direct assessment of many aspects of behavior, including how often, how effectively, and how consistently various actions occur. *Interviews* provide a way to gather information about personality from the person's own point of view. They can be *open-ended* and tailored to the intellectual level, emotional state, and special needs of the person being assessed. Interviews can also be *structured,* which means they ask about certain specific topics without spending much time on other matters. Structured interviews are routinely used in personality research because they elicit the same information from each person.

Personality tests offer a way to gather information that is more standardized and economical than either observations or interviews. To be useful, however, a personality test must be reliable and valid. As described in Chapter 7, *reliability* refers to how stable or consistent the results of a test are, and *validity* reflects the degree to which a test measures what it is intended to measure. The many personality tests available today are traditionally classified as either *objective* or *projective*.

Objective Tests

Objective tests ask clear and direct questions about a person's thoughts, feelings, or behavior (e.g., "Have you ever worried about your family without good reason?"). The

objective test A form listing clear, specific questions, statements, or concepts to which people are asked to respond.

FIGURE 11.5

The MMPI: Clinical Scales and Sample Profiles

A score of 50 on the clinical scales is average. Scores at or above 65 mean that the person's responses on that scale are more extreme than at least 95 percent of the normal population. The red line represents the profile of Kenneth Bianchi, the infamous "Hillside Strangler," who murdered thirteen women in the late 1970s. His profile would be interpreted as characteristic of a shallow person with poor self-control and little personal insight who is sexually preoccupied and unable to reveal himself to others. The profile in green comes from a more normal man, but it is characteristic of someone who is self-centered, passive, unwilling to accept personal responsibility for his behavior, and, when under stress, complains of numerous vague physical symptoms.

The clinical scales abbreviated in the figure are as follows:

1. **Hypochondriasis (Hs)** (concern with bodily functions and symptoms)

2. **Depression (D)** (pessimism, hopelessness, slowed thinking)

3. **Hysteria (Hy)** (use of physical or mental symptoms to avoid problems)

4. **Psychopathic deviate (Pd)** (disregard for social customs, emotional shallowness)

5. **Masculinity/femininity (Mf)** (interests associated with a particular gender)

6. **Paranoia (Pa)** (delusions, suspiciousness)

7. **Psychasthenia (Pt)** (worry, guilt, anxiety)

8. **Schizophrenia (Sc)** (bizarre thoughts and perceptions)

9. **Hypomania (Ma)** (overactivity, excitement, impulsiveness)

10. **Social introversion (Si)** (shy, insecure)

LINKAGES

Can personality tests be used to diagnose mental disorders? (a link to Psychological Disorders)

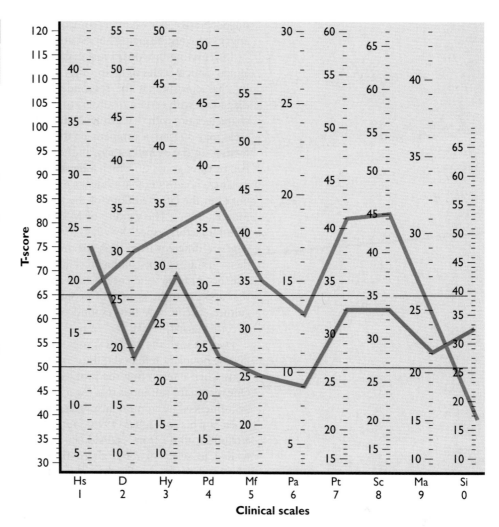

Clinical scales

answers are used to draw conclusions about the individual's personality. These *self-report* tests are usually set up in a multiple-choice or true-false format that allows them to be given individually or to many people at once, much like the academic tests taken by many college students. And as in the classroom, objective personality tests can be scored by hand or by machine and then compared mathematically. For example, before interpreting your apparently high score on an objective test of anxiety, a psychologist would compare your score with *norms*, or average scores from others of your age and gender. Only if you were well above these averages would you be considered unusually anxious.

Some objective tests focus on one personality trait, such as optimism (Scheier et al., 1989). Others measure a small group of related traits, such as empathy and social responsibility (Penner et al., 1995). Still other objective tests measure the strength of a wider variety of traits to reveal general psychological functioning or signs of psychological disorder.

The most commonly used objective test for diagnosing psychological disorders is the *Minnesota Multiphasic Personality Inventory,* better known as the *MMPI* (Dahlstrom, 1992). This 556-item true-false test was originally developed during the 1930s at the University of Minnesota by Starke Hathaway and J. C. McKinley. It has subsequently been revised and updated in the MMPI-2 (National Computer Systems, 1992).

The MMPI is organized into ten groups of items called *clinical scales*. Characteristic patterns of responses to the items on these scales have been associated with people who display particular psychological disorders or personality characteristics (see Figure 11.5). The MMPI and MMPI-2 also contain four *validity scales*. Responses to these scales detect whether respondents are distorting their answers, misunderstanding the items, or being uncooperative. For example, someone who responds "true" to items such as "I never get angry" may not be giving honest answers to the test as a whole.

Interpreting the MMPI is a matter of comparing a respondent's profile of scores on all ten clinical scales to the profiles of persons already known to show certain personality characteristics. If the respondent's profile resembles those obtained from people diagnosed with certain disorders or characteristics, the respondent is presumed to share characteristics with that group. Note, however, that although a high score on one clinical scale may suggest a problem in that dimension, interpretation of the MMPI usually focuses on the overall *pattern* in the clinical scales—particularly on the combination of two or three scales on which a person's scores are unusually high.

There is considerable evidence for the reliability and validity of MMPI clinical scales, but even the latest editions of the test are far from perfect measurement tools (Groth-Marnat, 1997). The validity of MMPI interpretations may be particularly impaired by cultural factors, especially when the perceptions, values, and experiences of the respondent are different from those of the test developer or the people to whom the respondent's results will be compared. Thus a test constructed and standardized in one culture may not provide valid conclusions about people from another culture. Indeed, a profile that appears to be typical of people with a certain disorder might actually reflect the culture-specific way the respondent interpreted the test items, not a mental problem (Groth-Marnat, 1997).

Even though the MMPI-2 uses comparison norms that represent a more culturally diverse population than did those of the original MMPI, psychologists must still be cautious when interpreting the profiles of people who identify with minority subcultures. One reason for caution is that the responses people give on objective personality tests can be influenced by cultural factors, as well as by individual personality traits. For example, Chen and his colleagues (1995) found that when people were asked to rate their personal attributes, those from individualist countries such as Canada and the United States tended to select extreme alternatives ("very important" or "much below average"), whereas those from collectivist countries, such as China and Japan, tended to select more moderate alternatives ("somewhat important" or "average").

A number of other objective tests are designed to measure personality variables in normal populations, especially the big-five personality traits described earlier. One of these tests includes both a self-assessment and an assessment made by someone who knows the person taking the test (Costa & McCrae, 1992). The personality descriptions based on these two perspectives are often quite similar, but discrepancies may indicate problems. For example, if a person's self-assessment is quite different from what a spouse says about the person, marital difficulties may be indicated; in addition, the nature of the discrepancies could suggest a focus for marital therapy.

Projective Tests

Unlike the clearly stated items found in objective tests, the stimuli in **projective tests** are ambiguous, meaning that they can be perceived in more than one way. Proponents of projective tests tend to take a psychodynamic approach to personality. They believe that unconscious needs, motives, fantasies, conflicts, and thoughts guide people's responses to projective test stimuli. Some of these tests ask people to draw items such as a house, a person, or a tree; to fill in the missing parts of incomplete pictures or sentences; or to say what they associate with particular words.

One projective test, called the *Thematic Apperception Test,* or *TAT,* is described in Chapter 8 as a measure of need for achievement. Henry Murray and Christina Morgan developed this test to assess the needs they saw as the basis of personality. Another well-known projective test, the *Rorschach Inkblot Test,* features a series of ten inkblots like the one in Figure 11.6. The respondent is asked to tell what the blot might be and then to explain why. Most scoring methods pay attention to (1) what part of the blot the person responds to; (2) what features, such as details or color, appear to determine each response; (3) the content of the responses; and (4) how unusual the responses are.

projective tests Personality tests made up of relatively unstructured stimuli in which responses are seen as reflecting the individual's unconscious needs, fantasies, conflicts, thought patterns, and other aspects of personality.

Problems with the validity of word association tests and other projective measures of personality have made them the target of humorists and have generated considerable controversy over their use (Garb, Florio, & Grove, 1999).

"I'll say a normal word, then you say the first sick thing that pops into your head."

In comparison to objective test results, responses to projective tests are much more difficult to translate into numerical scores. However, projective tests are designed to keep respondents from knowing what is being measured and what the "best" answers might be. Those who favor projective tests argue, therefore, that these tests can measure aggressiveness, sexual impulses, and other personality features that the respondent might be able to hide on an objective test. They also point to specific instances, as in studies assessing achievement motivation with the TAT, in which projective tests show acceptable reliability and validity (W. Spangler, 1992). Accordingly, projective tests continue to be used by many clinical psychologists (Rossini & Morretti, 1997).

Overall, however, projective personality tests are less reliable and valid than objective tests (Garb, Florio, & Grove, 1998, 1999; Hunsley & Bailey, 1999; Lilienfeld, Wood, & Garb, 2001). Indeed, because of their generally poor ability to predict behavior, they often add little beyond what might be inferred from other information. One study showed, for example, that even untrained observers can make relatively accurate judgments about people's personality characteristics simply by watching a sample of their behavior on videotape (Funder & Colvin, 1997). "In Review: Personality Tests"

FIGURE 11.6

The Rorschach Inkblot Test

People taking the Rorschach test are shown ten patterns similar to this one and asked to tell what the blot looks like—and why. What do you see?

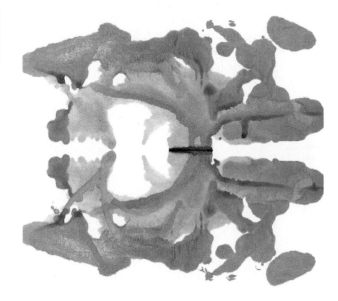

Personality Tests			
Type of Test	**Characteristics**	**Advantages**	**Disadvantages**
Objective	Paper-and-pencil format; quantitatively scored	Efficiency, standardization	Subject to deliberate distortion
Projective	Ambiguous stimuli create maximum freedom of response; scoring is relatively subjective	"Correct" answers not obvious; designed to tap unconscious impulses; flexible use	Reliability and validity lower than those of objective tests

summarizes the characteristics of objective and projective tests, along with some of their advantages and disadvantages.

Personality Tests and Employee Selection

How good are objective personality tests at selecting people for jobs? Most industrial-organizational psychologists believe that they are valuable tools for the selection of good employees. Tests such as the MMPI (and even some projective tests) are sometimes used to help guide hiring decisions, but large organizations usually choose objective tests that are designed to measure the big-five personality dimensions or related characteristics (Borman, Hanson, & Hedge, 1997). Several researchers have found significant relationships between scores on the big-five dimensions and overall job performance (Barrick & Mount, 1991; Ones, Viswesvaran, & Schmidt, 1993). A review of studies involving over 300,000 people showed that objective personality tests can help businesses reduce thefts and other disruptive employee behaviors (Ones et al., 1993).

Still, personality tests are not perfect predictors of behavior. Sometimes situational factors rather than personality variables are responsible for people's actions (Motowidlo, Borman, & Schmidt, 1997). Further, some employees see personality tests as an invasion of their privacy. They worry also that test results in their personnel files might later be misinterpreted and hurt their chances for promotion or for employment by other companies. Lawsuits have resulted in a ban on the use of personality tests in the selection of U.S. federal employees. Concerns about privacy and other issues surrounding personality testing have also led the American Psychological Association and related organizations to publish ethical standards relating to procedures for the development, distribution, and use of all psychological tests (American Educational Research Association, American Psychological Association, and National Council on Measurement in Education, 1999; American Psychological Association, 1992). The goal is not only to improve the reliability and validity of tests but also to ensure that their results are properly used and do not infringe on individuals' rights.

active review Personality

Linkages

As noted in Chapter 1, all of psychology's subfields are related to one another. Our discussion of cultural factors and personality illustrates just one way in which the topic of this chapter, personality, is linked to the subfield of developmental psychology (Chapter 9). The Linkages diagram shows ties to two other subfields as well, and there are many more ties throughout the book. Looking for linkages among subfields will help you see how they all fit together and better appreciate the big picture that is psychology.

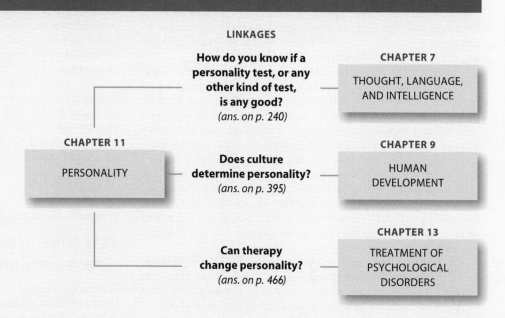

LINKAGES

CHAPTER 11

PERSONALITY

How do you know if a personality test, or any other kind of test, is any good?
(ans. on p. 240)

CHAPTER 7

THOUGHT, LANGUAGE, AND INTELLIGENCE

Does culture determine personality?
(ans. on p. 395)

CHAPTER 9

HUMAN DEVELOPMENT

Can therapy change personality?
(ans. on p. 466)

CHAPTER 13

TREATMENT OF PSYCHOLOGICAL DISORDERS

Summary

Personality refers to the unique pattern of psychological and behavioral characteristics by which each person can be compared and contrasted with other people. The four main theoretical approaches to personality are the psychodynamic, trait, social-cognitive, and phenomenological approaches.

THE PSYCHODYNAMIC APPROACH

How did paralyzed patients lead Freud to psychoanalysis?

The *psychodynamic approach,* first proposed by Freud, assumes that personality arises out of unconscious psychological processes that interact to determine our thoughts, feelings, and behavior. Freud believed that personality has three components—the *id,* which operates according to the *pleasure principle;* the *ego,* which operates according to the *reality principle;* and the *superego,* which internalizes society's rules and values. The ego uses *defense mechanisms* to prevent unconscious conflicts among these components from becoming conscious and causing anxiety or guilt.

Freud proposed that the focus of conflict changes as the child passes through *psychosexual stages* of development. These include the *oral stage,* the *anal stage,* the *phallic stage* (during which the *Oedipus* or *Electra complex* occurs), the *latency period,* and the *genital stage.*

Many of Freud's followers developed new theories that differed from his. Among these theorists were Jung, Adler, and Horney. They tended to downplay the role of instincts and the unconscious, emphasizing instead the importance of conscious processes, ego functions, and social and cultural factors. Horney also challenged the male-oriented nature of Freud's original theory.

Current psychodynamic theories reflect the neo-Freudians' emphasis on family and social relationships. According to object relations theorists, personality development depends mainly on the nature of early interactions between individuals and their caregivers.

The psychodynamic approach is reflected in many forms of psychotherapy, but critics fault the approach for its lack of a scientific base and for its view of human behavior as driven by unmeasurable forces.

THE TRAIT APPROACH

How many personality traits are there?

The *trait approach* assumes that personality is created by a small set of central traits in each individual. Allport studied unique patterns of traits, whereas Eysenck used factor analysis to identify common traits or core dimensions of personality. Eysenck believed that biological factors are responsible for these core dimensions. Recently, researchers have used factor analysis to identify five basic dimensions of personality, collectively referred to as the *big-five model* or *five-factor model.* These dimensions, which have been found in many different cultures, may arise partly from inherited differences in temperament that provide the raw materials out of which experience molds each personality.

The trait approach has been criticized for being better at describing personality than at explaining it, for failing to consider mechanisms that motivate behavior, and for underemphasizing the role of situational factors. Nevertheless, the trait approach—particularly the big-five model—currently dominates the field.

THE SOCIAL-COGNITIVE APPROACH

Do we learn our personality?

The *social-cognitive approach* assumes that personality is a set of unique patterns of thinking and behavior that a person acquires through learning and then displays in particular situations. With roots in research on classical and operant conditioning, the social-cognitive approach has expanded on traditional behavioral approaches by emphasizing the role of cognitive factors, such as observational learning, in personality development.

Rotter's theory focuses on expectancies that guide behavior, especially general beliefs about whether rewards occur because of personal efforts (internal control) or chance (external control). Bandura believes that personality develops largely through cognitively mediated learning, including observational learning. He sees personality as reciprocally determined by interactions among cognition, environmental stimuli, and behavior. *Self-efficacy*—the belief in one's ability to accomplish a given task—is an important determinant of behavior. Mischel emphasizes the importance of situations—and their interactions with person variables—in determining behavior. According to Mischel, we must look at both person and situational variables in order to understand human consistencies and inconsistencies.

The social-cognitive approach has led to new forms of psychological treatment and many other applications. Critics of this approach, however, consider even its latest versions to be too mechanistic and incapable of capturing all the unlearned factors that many psychologists see as important in personality.

THE PHENOMENOLOGICAL APPROACH

Is everyone basically good?

The *phenomenological approach,* also called the humanistic approach, is based on the assumption that personality is determined by the unique ways in which each individual views the world. These perceptions form a personal version of reality and guide behavior as the individual strives to reach his or her fullest potential.

Rogers believed that personality development is driven by an innate tendency toward *self-actualization,* but also that one's *self-concept* is shaped by social evaluations. He proposed that when peo-

ple are free from the effects of *conditions of worth,* they will be psychologically healthy. Maslow saw self-actualization as the highest in a hierarchy of needs. Personality development is healthiest, he said, when people have a growth orientation rather than a deficiency orientation.

Applications of the phenomenological approach include certain forms of psychotherapy and group experiences designed to enhance personal growth. Although it has a large following, the phenomenological approach is faulted for being too idealistic, for failing to explain personality development, for being vague and unscientific, and for underplaying cultural differences in "ideal" personalities.

Many people in the individualist cultures of North America and Europe are taught to believe in the importance of self-worth and personal distinction. This independent self-system contrasts with the interdependent self-system often fostered in collectivist cultures, where the self is defined mainly in relation to family or other groups. Contrasting definitions of the self in different cultures, and among males versus females, tend to exert differing influences on the development of personality.

Research suggests that temperament in childhood may influence personality development into adulthood.

ASSESSING PERSONALITY

How do psychologists measure personality?

Personality is usually assessed through some combination of observations, interviews, and tests. To be useful, personality assessments must be both reliable and valid.

Objective tests usually present clearly written items; their scores can be compared with group norms. The MMPI is an example of an objective test.

Based on psychodynamic theories, *projective tests* present ambiguous stimuli in an attempt to tap unconscious personality characteristics. Two popular projective tests are the TAT and the Rorschach. In general, projective personality tests are less reliable and valid than objective personality tests.

Objective personality tests are often used to identify the people best suited for certain occupations. Although such tests can be helpful in this regard, those who use them must be aware of the tests' limitations and take care not to violate the rights of test respondents.

Learn by Doing

Put It in Writing

Choose a well-known person who interests you. It could be a rock star; an actor; a television personality; a leading political, religious, or business figure; or even a famous criminal. Write a one-paragraph description of this individual's personality traits as they seem to you. Now continue by writing a page or two to discuss how you think the development of these traits would be explained by the psychodynamic, social-cognitive, and phenomenological personality theories.

Personal Learning Activity

To get an idea of the problems involved in scoring projective personality tests, try creating your own projective test that contains vague

pictures, drawings, or other stimuli that can be interpreted in many different ways. Administer your test to some friends, and record their responses to each stimulus (in writing or on tape). How will you decide what your friends' responses tell you about their personalities? Do you think your conclusions about their personalities were affected mainly by their test responses or by what you already knew about them? Now give your test to someone you don't know. Was it easier or harder to draw conclusions about this person's personality? How will you know if your conclusions about this new person are correct, or valid? *For additional projects, see the five Personal Learning Activities in the corresponding chapter of the study guide that accompanies this text.*

Step into Action

Courses

Personality Psychology
Personality Research Methods
Personality Theories
History and Systems of Psychology

Movies

Good Will Hunting; Unforgiven; The Cider House Rules (personality development)
Hoop Dreams (self-efficacy)
Freud (development of psychoanalytic theory)
Girl, Interrupted (conditions of worth and self-concept)
Gandhi (self-actualization)

Books

Frank J. Sulloway, *Born to Rebel: Birth Order, Family Dynamics and Creative Lives* (Vintage Books, 1997) (psychodynamics in personality development)
John F. Clarkin, *Major Theories of Personality Disorder* (Guilford Press, 1996) (personality disorders)

Duane P. Schultz and Sydney E. Schultz, *Theories of Personality* (Brooks-Cole, 2001) (summary of personality theories)
Stella Chess and M. D. Alexander, *Temperament: Theory and Practice* (Brunner/Mazel, 1996) (differences in temperament)

The Web

The World Wide Web is a good source of additional information about the science of psychology, provided you use it carefully and think critically about the information you find. The PsychAbilities web site that accompanies this text offers many resources relevant to this chapter. These resources include interactive NetLab exercises; Thinking Critically and Evaluating Research exercises; ACE chapter quizzes; recommended web links; and articles on current events, books, and movies. At http://college.hmco.com, select *Psychology* and then this textbook.

Review of Key Terms

Can you define each of the key terms in the chapter? Check your definitions against those on the pages listed in parentheses below or in the Glossary/Index at the end of the text.

anal stage *(p. 380)*
big-five model *(p. 385)*
conditions of worth *(p. 393)*
defense mechanisms *(p. 379)*
ego *(p. 378)*
Electra complex *(p. 380)*
five-factor model *(p. 385)*

genital stage *(p. 380)*
id *(p. 378)*
latency period *(p. 380)*
objective tests *(p. 398)*
Oedipus complex *(p. 380)*
oral stage *(p. 380)*
personality *(p. 377)*

phallic stage *(p. 380)*
phenomenological approach *(p. 392)*
pleasure principle *(p. 378)*
projective tests *(p. 400)*
psychodynamic approach *(p. 378)*
psychosexual stages *(p. 379)*
reality principle *(p. 378)*

self-actualization *(p. 392)*
self-concept *(p. 393)*
self-efficacy *(p. 390)*
social-cognitive approach *(p. 389)*
superego *(p. 378)*
trait approach *(p. 383)*

Multiple-Choice Self-Test

Select the best answer for each of the questions below. Then check your responses against the Answer Key at the end of the text.

1. When psychologists talk about the unique pattern of enduring psychological and behavioral characteristics by which each person can be compared and contrasted with other people, they are referring to

   a. motivation.
   b. personality.
   c. reciprocal determinism.
   d. conditions of worth.

2. As Jared is jostled by a passerby he thinks, "I'd like to hit that guy!" Freud would say that this impulse comes from Jared's _____, which operates on the _____ principle.

   a. id; pleasure
   b. id; reality
   c. ego; pleasure
   d. ego; reality

3. Nine-year-old Jeffrey has just bounded into the room with his latest artistic creation. He chatters about his friends at school and how much he likes reading and working math problems. According to Freud, Jeffrey is most likely in the _____ stage of psychosexual development.

    a. oral
    b. anal
    c. phallic
    d. latency

4. Elizabeth's boss yells at her for something that wasn't her fault, but Elizabeth is unable to yell back at him. When Elizabeth gets home, her husband asks, "What's for dinner?" and Elizabeth yells about how insensitive he is. Her response illustrates which ego defense mechanism?

    a. rationalization
    b. displacement
    c. reaction-formation
    d. projection

5. Oscar never cleans up after himself. He is disorganized and impulsive. Freud would say that Oscar is fixated at the anal stage, which means that

    a. his parents did not toilet train him appropriately.
    b. his parents did not wean him appropriately.
    c. he uses defense mechanisms to relieve anxiety.
    d. his progress toward self-actualization is blocked.

6. Which of the following is *not* a common criticism of Freud's psychodynamic approach to personality?

    a. His sample was small and unrepresentative of the general population.
    b. The theory reflects Western European and North American cultural values.
    c. The theory was not developed scientifically and thus is subject to bias.
    d. The theory was not comprehensive and has had little influence on psychology.

7. Dr. Rajeem believes that each person is unique because we each possess differing combinations of internal characteristics that don't change much as we age. Dr. Rajeem believes in the _____ approach to personality.

    a. psychodynamic
    b. trait
    c. social-cognitive
    d. phenomenological

8. A politician is described by her critics as dishonest, intelligent, industrious, extraverted, aggressive, generous, and charming. This method of describing personality most closely matches _____ model of personality.

    a. Eysenck's biological
    b. Rotter's expectancy
    c. Allport's trait
    d. the big-five

9. Tamerika has been described as high on openness (very curious and imaginative), low in conscientiousness (disorganized and unproductive), high in extraversion (very active, talkative, and energetic), high in agreeableness (generous, kind, and trusting), and high in neuroticism (impulsive, touchy, and vulnerable). This description reflects _____ model of personality

    a. Eysenck's biological
    b. Rotter's expectancy
    c. Allport's trait
    d. the big-five

10. One criticism of trait theories of personality is that they

    a. put too much emphasis on unconscious wishes.
    b. put too much emphasis on the influence of situations.
    c. are better at describing personality than at explaining it.
    d. have no scientific basis.

11. According to the Thinking Critically section of this chapter, research on the question of whether or not personality is inherited concludes that

    a. there are specific genes for specific personality traits.
    b. there are genetic predispositions toward particular personality characteristics.
    c. the environment is the strongest influence on personality development.
    d. personality is essentially determined by the age of six months.

12. Sandy believes that if she works hard, she will be rewarded. So when she gets a D on her psychology test, she decides that she didn't study hard enough. When she wins the "Outstanding Senior of the Month" award, she believes that she earned it. Rotter's theory suggests that Sandy is

    a. internal.
    b. external.
    c. deficiency oriented.
    d. growth oriented.

13. Darma was standing in line at a movie theater, thinking about how her boyfriend dumped her, when she was accidentally shoved from behind. She shouted "Hey! Back off, you jerks!" This prompted angry comments from the people behind her, which made Darma even angrier, so she refused to move forward in line. This case is an example of

    a. conditions of worth.
    b. growth orientation.
    c. reciprocal determinism.
    d. internal locus of control.

14. At college basketball games, Melinda jumps up and down and yells and screams continuously. Otherwise, however, she is a quiet person who chooses peaceful environments without much social stimulation. She finds that when she is around other people, they often become quiet, too. Melinda's personality can best be explained by _____ theory.

    a. psychodynamic
    b. Allport's trait
    c. Rotter's expectancy
    d. Mischel's person-situation

15. Rolf believes that his children's personalities are shaped by the way he rewards and punishes them. He thinks that most of each child's personality is learned in social situations where the child interacts with others and observes others' behavior. Rolf's beliefs most closely match the _____ approach to personality.

    a. psychodynamic
    b. trait
    c. social-cognitive
    d. phenomenological

16. When Lizzie finger paints on the wall, her mother gets angry and shouts, "You are a very bad girl!" Rogers would say that Lizzie's mother is creating

    a. a growth orientation.
    b. a deficiency orientation.
    c. conditions of worth.
    d. a psychodynamic conflict.

17. Ruben is constantly thinking about all that he does not have. He has a good job, but he would really like to be president of his own company. He has a great wife, but he wishes she were more attractive. He gets a new car every year because he wants "the best." Maslow would say that Ruben is controlled by

    a. growth orientation.
    b. deficiency orientation.
    c. conditions of worth.
    d. self-actualization.

18. Which of the following would a psychodynamic psychologist use most frequently to assess personality?

    a. behavioral observations
    b. objective tests
    c. assessments of physiological activity
    d. projective tests

19. Paul is an undercontrolled boy who regularly has tantrums. Based on the longitudinal study described in the chapter, which of these outcomes would you say is most likely? Paul will

    a. reach a high rank if he joins the military.
    b. have outgrown his lack of control by adulthood.
    c. be aggressive as an adult.
    d. keep jobs longer than most reserved men.

20. In an effort to summarize her clients' personality traits, Peggy administers tests that present a long series of true-false items. She is using a(n) _____ personality test.

    a. multifaceted
    b. objective
    c. projective
    d. social-cognitive

Psychological Disorders

When does oddness become abnormality? When does sadness

become depression? What are psychological disorders? In this chapter, we describe major categories of psychological disorders, discuss some of their possible causes, consider how they have been explained over the centuries, and examine their role in the insanity defense.

Reading this chapter will help you to answer the following questions:

- **How do psychologists define abnormal behavior?**
- **What causes abnormality?**
- **How many psychological disorders have been identified?**
- **What is a phobia?**
- **Can mental disorder cause blindness?**
- **What disorders create sudden memory loss?**
- **How common is depression?**
- **Is schizophrenia the same as "split personality"?**
- **Which personality disorder often leads to crime?**
- **How do children's disorders differ from adults' disorders?**
- **Can insanity protect criminals from punishment?**

José is a fifty-five-year-old electronics technician. A healthy and vigorous father of two adult children, he was recently forced to take medical leave because of a series of sudden, uncontrollable panic attacks in which dizziness, heart palpitations, sweating, and other terrifying symptoms made him fear that he was about to die. José's case provides an example of someone who suffers from a psychological disorder, also called a *mental disorder* or *psychopathology*. **Psychopathology** involves patterns of thought, emotion, and behavior that are maladaptive, disruptive, or uncomfortable either for the person affected or for others.

The number of people who exhibit some form of psychological disorder is staggering. Surveys reveal that in any given year in the United States alone, about 57 million people, or about 30 percent of the adult population, have displayed some form of mental disorder, and that as many as 48 percent have experienced a disorder at some point in their lives (Kessler et al., 1996; Regier, Farmer, et al., 1993; Regier, Narrow, et al., 1993; L. N. Robins & Regier, 1991; U.S. Surgeon General, 1999; see Figure 12.1). In addition, about 20 percent of U.S. children display significant mental disorder in any given year (Costello et al., 1988; U.S. Surgeon General, 1999). These overall rates of mental disorder are found, with only minor variations, in all segments of U.S. society, including males and females in all ethnic groups (A. Peterson et al., 1993). Psychological disorders are enormously costly in terms of human suffering, wasted potential, economic burden, and lost resources (Druss, Rosenheck, & Sledge, 2000).

psychopathology Patterns of thinking and behaving that are maladaptive, disruptive, or uncomfortable for the affected person or for others.

409

FIGURE 12.1

Incidence of Specific
Psychological Disorders

**Several large-scale surveys of adults
throughout the United States revealed
that about 30 percent of them experience
some form of mental disorder in any
given year, and that almost half of them
have displayed a disorder at some time in
life. The data shown here summarize
these findings by category of disorder.**

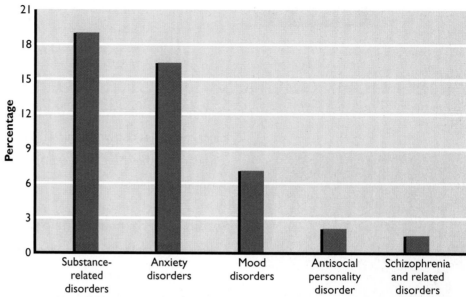

Source: Data from Regier, Farmer, et al. (1993); Regier, Narrow, et al. (1993); L. N. Robins & Regier (1991); U.S. Surgeon General (1999).

Defining Psychological Disorders

How do psychologists define abnormal behavior?

A woman's husband dies. In her grief, she stays in bed all day, weeping, refusing to eat, at times holding "conversations" with him. In India, a Hindu holy man on a pilgrimage rolls along the ground for more than 1,000 miles of deserts and mountains, in all kinds of weather, until he reaches the sacred place he seeks. Eight percent of U.S. adults surveyed say they have seen a UFO (CNN/Time, 1997), and hundreds claim to have been abducted by space aliens (Appelle et al., 2000). These examples and countless others raise the question of where to draw the line between normality and abnormality, between eccentricity and mental disorder (Kanner, 1995).

What Is Abnormal?

There are several criteria for judging the abnormality of a person's thinking, emotions, or behavior. Each criterion has value, but also some flaws.

If we define *normality* as what most people do, then the criterion for abnormality becomes *statistical infrequency,* or that which is unusual or rare. By this criterion, the few people who believe that space aliens steal their thoughts would be judged as abnormal; the many people who worry about becoming victims of crime would not. But statistical infrequency alone is a poor criterion for abnormality, because *any* rare quality or characteristic, such as creative genius or world-class athletic ability, would be considered abnormal. Further, because this definition implies that conformity with the majority is normal, equating rarity with abnormality may result in the oppression of nonconformists who express unusual or unpopular views or ideas.

Another possible criterion for abnormality is violation of social norms—the cultural rules that tell us how we should and should not behave in various situations, especially in relation to others. According to this *norm violation* criterion, when people behave in ways that are unusual or disturbing enough to violate social norms, they may be described as abnormal. However, norm violation alone is an inadequate measure of abnormality. For one thing, some norm violations are better characterized as eccentric or illegal than as abnormal (Weeks & Weeks, 1995). People who bathe infrequently or who stand too close during conversation violate social norms, but are they abnormal or

IS THIS PERSON ABNORMAL?
**Whether unusual individuals are labeled
"abnormal" and perhaps given treatment
for psychological disorder depends on a
number of factors, including how abnormality is defined by the culture in which
they live, who is most directly affected by
their behavior, and how much distress
they suffer or cause.**

SITUATIONAL FACTORS IN DEFINING *ABNORMALITY* **When this University of California-Berkeley student attended classes virtually nude to protest "social repression," complaints from other students led to his dismissal. Yet if he lived in a nudist colony, he might be seen as "overdressed." Make a list of the reasons you would give in support of, or in opposition to, his having been labeled as abnormal. Which criteria for abnormality did you use in making your list?**

merely annoying? Further, whose norms are we talking about? Social norms vary across cultures, subcultures, and historical eras, so the behaviors that qualify as abnormal in one part of the world might be perfectly acceptable elsewhere.

Abnormality can also be described in terms of *personal suffering*. The experience of distress often motivates people to decide that their psychological problems are severe enough to require treatment. But personal suffering alone is an inadequate criterion for abnormality. For one thing, it does not take into account the fact that people are sometimes distressed about behaviors (e.g., homosexuality) that are not mental disorders. Second, some disorders result in behavior, such as the sexual abuse of children, that cause intense distress in others, but little discomfort in the perpetrator.

Behavior in Context: A Practical Approach

Obviously, no single criterion fully defines abnormality. Accordingly, mental health practitioners and researchers tend to adopt a *practical approach* that combines aspects of all the criteria we've discussed. They consider the *content* of behavior (that is, what the person does), the sociocultural *context* in which the person's behavior occurs, and the *consequences* of the behavior for that person and for others. This practical approach pays special attention to whether a person's thoughts, behavior, or emotions cause **impaired functioning**—that is, difficulty in fulfilling appropriate and expected social roles (U.S. Surgeon General, 1999; Wakefield, 1999).

What is "appropriate" and "expected" depends on age, gender, culture, and the particular situation and historical era in which the individual lives. The very short attention span considered normal in a two-year-old, for instance, would be described as inappropriate and problematic in an adult. There are gender-specific norms, too. In the United States, many people consider it more appropriate for women than for men to display emotion. Accordingly, kisses, tears, and long embraces are common when women greet each other after a long absence; men tend to simply shake hands or hug briefly. Given cultural differences, hearing a dead relative's voice calling from the afterlife would be considered more acceptable in certain American Indian tribes than among, say, the families of suburban Toronto. Situational factors are important as well. Falling to the floor and "speaking in tongues" is considered appropriate, even desirable, during the worship services of some religious groups; but the same behavior would be considered inappropriate, and possibly a sign of disorder, in a college classroom. Finally, judgments about behavior are shaped by changes in social trends and cultural values. For example, the American Psychiatric Association once listed homosexuality as a mental disorder but dropped this category from its *Diagnostic and Statistical Manual of Mental Disorders (DSM)* in 1973. In taking this step, it was responding to changing views of homosexuality prompted in part by the political and educational efforts of gay and lesbian rights groups.

In summary, it is difficult, and probably impossible, to define a specific set of behaviors that everyone, everywhere, will agree constitutes abnormality (Lilienfeld & Marino, 1999; Wakefield, 1999). Instead, the practical approach sees abnormality as including those patterns of thought, behavior, and emotional reaction that impair functioning, cause discomfort, and/or disrupt the lives of others.

Explaining Psychological Disorders

What causes abnormality?

Since the dawn of civilization, people have tried to understand the causes of psychological disorder. Centuries ago, explanations of abnormal behavior focused on gods or demons. Disordered people were seen either as innocent victims of evil spirits or as social or moral deviants suffering supernatural punishment. In Europe during the late Middle

impaired functioning Difficulty in fulfilling appropriate and expected social roles.

AN EXORCISM   Although no longer dominant in Western cultures, supernatural explanations of mental disorder and supernaturally oriented cures—such as the exorcism being performed by this Buddhist monk in Thailand—remain influential in many other cultures and subcultures.

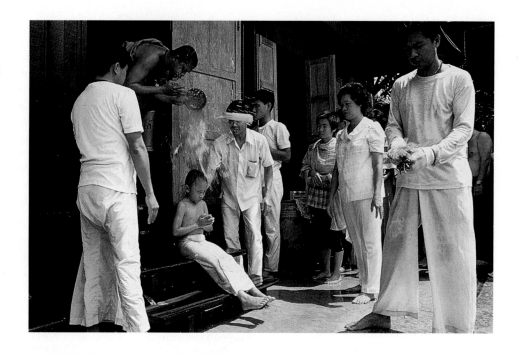

Ages, for example, people who engaged in threatening or unusual behavior were seen as controlled by the devil or other evil beings. Hundreds of "witches"—mostly women— were burned at the stake, and exorcisms were performed to rid people of controlling demons. Supernatural explanations of psychological disorders are still invoked today in many cultures around the world—including certain ethnic and religious subcultures in North America (Nickell, 2001; Tagliabue, 1999).

The Biopsychosocial Model

More generally, however, mental health researchers in Western cultures attribute the appearance of psychopathology to three other causes: biological factors, psychological processes, and sociocultural contexts. For many decades, there was controversy over which of these three causes was most important, but most researchers now agree that they can *all* be important. They have adopted a **biopsychosocial model** in which mental disorders are seen as caused by the *combination* and *interaction* of biological, psychological, and sociocultural factors, each of which contributes in varying degrees to particular problems in particular people (U.S. Surgeon General, 1999).

Biological Factors   The biological factors thought to be involved in causing mental disorders include physical illnesses and disruptions of bodily processes. This *medical model* of psychological disorder has a long history. For example, Hippocrates, a physician in ancient Greece, said that psychological disorders result from imbalances among four *humors,* or bodily fluids (blood, phlegm, black bile, and yellow bile). In ancient Chinese cultures, psychological disorders were seen as arising from an imbalance of *yin* and *yang,* the dual forces of the universe flowing in the physical body.

As the medical model gained prominence in Western cultures after the Middle Ages, specialized hospitals for the insane were established throughout Europe. Treatment in these early asylums consisted mainly of physical restraints, laxative purges, bleeding of "excess" blood, and induced vomiting. Cold baths, fasts, and other physical discomforts were also used in efforts to "shock" patients back to normality. In the 1700s, most of these asylums were little more than prisons where the public could buy tickets to look at patients, much as people go to the zoo today.

The medical model gave rise to the concept of abnormality as *mental illness*—and indeed, most people in Western cultures today still tend to seek medical doctors and hospitals for the diagnosis and treatment of psychological disorders. The medical model is

biopsychosocial model   Explaining mental disorders as the combined result of biological, psychological, and sociocultural factors.

neurobiological model   A view of mental disorder as caused by physical illness or an imbalance in bodily processes, including disturbances in the anatomy and chemistry of the brain.

psychological model   An approach that views mental disorder as arising from inner turmoil or other psychological processes.

VISITING BEDLAM **Here is the artist William Hogarth's portrayal of "Bedlam" (the local name for Saint Mary's of Bethlehem, a London hospital), which was an eighteenth-century "insane asylum." Notice the well-dressed visitors who paid to tour the cells and gawk at the patients.**

now more properly called the **neurobiological model,** because it explains psychological disorders in terms of particular disturbances in the anatomy and chemistry of the brain and in other biological processes. Neuroscientists and others who adopt a neurobiological approach investigate these disorders as they would investigate any physical illness, seeing problematic symptoms stemming primarily from an underlying illness that can be diagnosed, treated, and cured.

Psychological Processes   If biological factors provide the "hardware" of mental disorders, the "software" includes psychological processes, such as our wants, needs, and emotions; our learning experiences; and our way of looking at the world. The roots of this **psychological model** of disorder can be found in ancient Greek literature and drama dealing with *psyche,* or mind—and especially with the problems people experience as they struggle to resolve inner conflicts or to overcome the effects of stressful events.

These ideas took center stage in the late 1800s when Sigmund Freud, a Viennese physician, formally challenged the assumption that psychological disorders had *only* physical causes. Freud viewed psychological disorders as resulting mainly from the effects of unresolved, mostly unconscious clashes between people's instinctual impulses and the limits placed on those impulses in the real world. These conflicts, he said, begin early in childhood. As described in Chapter 11, contemporary versions of this *psychodynamic* model focus less on instinctual urges and more on the role of attachment and other early interpersonal relationships (Schultz & Schultz, 2001).

The other theories of personality discussed in Chapter 11 suggest other psychological processes that can contribute to the appearance of mental disorders. For example, *social-cognitive* theorists, also known as social-learning theorists, see most psychological disorders as the result of past learning and current situations. Just as people learn to avoid hot grills after being burned, say these theorists, bad experiences in school or a dental office can "teach" people to fear such places. Social-cognitive theorists also emphasize the effects of expectancies and other mental processes. They see depression, for example, as stemming from negative events, such as losing a job, and from learned patterns of thoughts about these events, such as "I never do anything right."

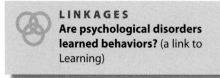

LINKAGES
Are psychological disorders learned behaviors? (a link to Learning)

According to the humanistic, or *phenomenological,* approach to personality, behavior disorders appear when self-actualization is blocked, usually by a failure to be aware of and to express true feelings. When this happens, one's perceptions of reality become distorted. The greater the distortion, the more serious the psychological disorder. Phenomenologists assume that abnormal behavior, no matter how unusual or seemingly irrational, is a reasonable reaction to the world as the person perceives it.

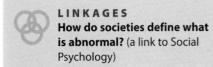

LINKAGES
How do societies define what is abnormal? (a link to Social Psychology)

Sociocultural Context   Together, neurobiological and psychological factors can go a long way toward explaining many forms of mental disorder. Still, they focus mainly on causes residing *within* the individual. The **sociocultural model** of disorder suggests that we cannot fully explain *all* forms of psychopathology without also looking *outside* the individual—at the social and cultural factors that form the context, or background, of abnormal behavior. Looking for causes of disorders in this *sociocultural context* means paying attention to factors such as gender, age and marital status; the physical, social, and economic situations in which people live; and the cultural values, traditions, and expectations in which they are immersed (G. W. Evans et al., 2000; J. G. Johnson et al., 1999; Whisman, 1999). Sociocultural context influences not only what is and is not labeled "abnormal" but also who displays what kind of disorder.

Consider gender, for instance. The greater tolerance in many cultures for open expression of emotional distress among women, but not men, may contribute to the higher rates of depression reported by women compared with men (Nolen-Hoeksema, Larson, & Grayson, 1999). Similarly, the view held in many cultures that excessive alcohol consumption is less appropriate for women than for men is a sociocultural factor that may set the stage for higher rates of alcohol abuse in men (Helzer et al., 1990).

Sociocultural factors also influence the *form* that abnormality takes. For example, *culture-general* disorders such as depression appear virtually everywhere in the world. However, their specific symptoms tend to differ depending on a person's cultural background. In Western cultures, where emotional and physical components of disorder are generally viewed separately, symptoms of depression tend to revolve around despair and other signs of emotional distress (Kleinman, 1991). But in China and certain other Asian cultures where emotional and physical experiences tend to be viewed as one, depressed people are as likely to report stomach or back pain as to complain of sadness (Brislin, 1993).

There are also *culture-specific* forms of disorder. For instance, Puerto Rican and Dominican Hispanic women sometimes experience *ataques de nervios,* a unique way of reacting to stress that includes heart palpitations, shaking, shouting, nervousness, depression, and on occasion, fainting or seizure-like episodes (D. Spiegel, 1994). Another example can be found in Southeast Asia, southern China, and Malaysia, where one encounters a condition called *koro.* Male victims of this condition fear that their penis will shrivel, retract into the body, and cause death. In females, the fear relates to shriveling of the breasts. *Koro* appears only in cultures holding the specific supernatural beliefs that explain it (Tseng et al., 1992).

In short, sociocultural factors create differing social roles, stressors, opportunities, and experiences for people who differ in age, gender, and cultural traditions. They also help shape the disorders and symptoms to which certain categories of people are prone. Any attempt to fully explain psychological disorders must take these sociocultural factors into account.

Diathesis-Stress as an Integrative Approach

The biopsychosocial model is currently the most comprehensive and influential approach to explaining psychological disorders. It is prominent partly because it encompasses so many important causal factors, including biological imbalances, genetically inherited characteristics, brain damage, enduring psychological traits, socioculturally influenced learning experiences, stressful life events, and many more.

sociocultural model   An approach to explaining mental disorder that emphasizes the role of factors such as gender and age, physical situations, cultural values and expectations, and historical era.

TABLE 12.1	Possible Causes	Specific Problem
The Biopsychosocial Model of Psychopathology	Neurobiological	José may have organic disorders (e.g., genetic tendency toward anxiety; brain tumor, endocrine dysfunction; neurotransmitter imbalance).
Here are the factors that would be highlighted by the biopsychosocial model and the diathesis-stress approach in the case of José, the man described at the beginning of this chapter.	Psychological: psychodynamic	José has unconscious conflicts and desires. Instinctual impulses are breaking through ego defenses into consciousness, causing panic.
	Psychological: social-cognitive	Physical stress symptoms are interpreted as signs of serious illness or impending death. Panic is rewarded by avoidance of work stress and the opportunity to stay home.
	Psychological: phenomenological	José fails to recognize his genuine feelings about work and his place in life, and he fears expressing himself.
	Sociocultural	A culturally based belief that "a man should not show weakness" amplifies the intensity of stress reactions and delays José's decision to seek help.
	Diathesis-stress	José has a biological (possibly genetic) predisposition to be overly responsive to stressors. The stress of work and extra activity exceeds his capacity to cope and triggers panic as a stress response.

But how do all these factors interact to create disorder? Most researchers who study psychopathology believe that inherited characteristics, biological processes, learning experiences, and sociocultural forces combine to create a predisposition (or *diathesis* [pronounced "dye-A-thuh-sis"]) for psychological disorders. However, whether or not a person actually develops symptoms of disorder depends on the nature and amount of *stress* the person encounters (National Advisory Mental Health Council, 1996; Zuckerman, 1999). For example, a person may have inherited a biological tendency toward depression or may have learned depressing patterns of thinking, but these predispositions may be expressed as a depressive disorder only after the person is faced with a financial crisis or suffers the loss of a loved one. If such circumstances do not occur, or if the person has adequate skills for coping with stress, depressive symptoms may never appear, or they may be quite mild.

So the **diathesis-stress approach** to psychological disorder assumes that biological, psychological, and sociocultural factors can predispose us toward disorder, but that it takes a certain amount of stress to actually trigger it. For those with a strong diathesis, relatively mild stress might be sufficient to create a problem. Those whose predisposition is weaker might not show signs of disorder until stress becomes extreme or prolonged. Another way to think about the notion of diathesis-stress is in terms of risk: The more risk factors for a disorder a person has—whether they take the form of genetic tendencies, personality traits, cultural traditions, or stressful life events—the more likely it is that the person will display a form of psychological disorder associated with those risk factors.

Table 12.1 provides an example of how the diasthesis-stress approach and the factors contained in the biopsychosocial model of disorder might explain a particular case of psychopathology. Later in this chapter, you will see how the biopsychosocial model and the diathesis-stress approach are applied to understanding the causes of a number of other psychological disorders.

diathesis-stress approach An approach that recognizes the roles of both predispositions and situational factors in the appearance of psychological disorders.

Classifying Psychological Disorders

■ **How many psychological disorders have been identified?**

Although definitions of abnormality differ within and across cultures, there does seem to be a set of behavior patterns that roughly defines the range of most abnormality in most cultures. It has long been the goal of those who study abnormal behavior to establish a system of classifying such patterns in order to understand and deal with them.

In 1952 the American Psychiatric Association published the first edition of what has become the "official" North American diagnostic classification system, the *Diagnostic and Statistical Manual of Mental Disorders (DSM)*. Each edition of the *DSM* has included more categories. The latest edition, *DSM-IV*, contains more than 300 specific diagnostic labels (American Psychiatric Association, 1994, 2000). Mental health professionals outside North America diagnose mental disorders using the World Health Organization's *International Classification of Diseases*, now in its tenth edition (*ICD-10*). The *DSM-IV* was designed to be compatible with the *ICD-10*, but some inconsistencies still exist between the two systems (Frances, Pincus, & Widiger, 1996).

A Classification System: *DSM-IV*

DSM-IV describes the abnormal patterns of thinking, emotion, and behavior that define various mental disorders. For each disorder, *DSM-IV* provides specific criteria outlining the conditions that must be present before a person is given that diagnostic label. In keeping with the biopsychosocial model, diagnosticians using *DSM-IV* can evaluate troubled people on five dimensions, or *axes*. Together, these axes provide a broad picture of each person's biological and psychological problems, as well as of the sociocultural context in which they appear. As shown in Table 12.2, mental disorders such as schizophrenia or major depressive disorder would be recorded on Axis I, whereas personality disorders and mental retardation would be noted on Axis II. Any medical conditions that might be important in understanding the person's mental or behavioral problems would be listed on Axis III. On Axis IV, the diagnostician would note any difficulties (such as the loss of a loved one, physical or sexual abuse, discrimination, unemployment, poverty, homelessness, inadequate health care, or conflict with religious or cultural traditions) that are important for understanding the social, environmental, and cultural context in which the person's psychological problems appear. Finally, a rating (from 1 to 100) of the person's current level of psychological, social, and occupational functioning would appear on Axis V. Here is a sample of a complete *DSM-IV* diagnosis:

Axis I. Major depressive disorder, single episode; alcohol abuse.

Axis II. Dependent personality disorder.

Axis III. Alcoholic cirrhosis of the liver.

Axis IV. Problems with primary support group (death of spouse).

Axis V. Global assessment of functioning = 50.

The terms *neurosis* and *psychosis* are no longer major categories in the *DSM* because they are not specific enough; however, some mental health professionals still sometimes use them as shorthand descriptions. Neurosis refers to conditions in which some form of anxiety is the major characteristic. Psychosis refers to conditions involving more extreme problems that leave people "out of touch with reality" or unable to function on a daily basis. The disorders once gathered under these headings now appear in various Axis I categories in the *DSM-IV*.

Purposes and Problems of Diagnosis

The purpose of diagnosis is to determine the nature of clients' problems. Once the characteristics of these problems are understood, their probable course can be predicted, and the most appropriate method of treatment can be administered.

TABLE 12.2	The *Diagnostic and Statistical Manual (DSM)* of the American Psychiatric Association

Axis I of the fourth edition *(DSM-IV)* lists the major categories of mental disorders. Personality disorders and mental retardation are listed on Axis II.

Axis I (Clinical Syndromes)

1. *Disorders usually first diagnosed in infancy, childhood, or adolescence.* Problems such as hyperactivity, childhood fears, conduct disorders, frequent bedwetting or soiling, and other problems in normal social and behavioral development. Autistic disorder (severe impairment in social, behavioral, and language development), as well as learning disorders.

2. *Delirium, dementia, and amnestic and other cognitive disorders.* Problems caused by physical deterioration of the brain due to aging, disease, drugs or other chemicals, or other possible unknown causes. These problems can appear as an inability to "think straight" (delirium) or as loss of memory and other intellectual functions (dementia).

3. *Substance-related disorders.* Psychological, behavioral, physical, social, or legal problems caused by dependence on, or abuse of, a variety of chemical substances, including alcohol, heroin, cocaine, amphetamines, hallucinogens, marijuana, and tobacco.

4. *Schizophrenia and other psychotic disorders.* Severe conditions characterized by abnormalities in thinking, perception, emotion, movement, and motivation that greatly interfere with daily functioning. Problems involving false beliefs (delusions).

5. *Mood disorders* (also called *affective disorders*). Severe disturbances of mood, especially depression, overexcitement (mania), or alternating episodes of each extreme (as in bipolar disorder).

6. *Anxiety disorders.* Specific fears (phobias); panic attacks; generalized feelings of dread; rituals of thought and action (obsessive-compulsive disorder) aimed at controlling anxiety; and problems caused by traumatic events, such as rape or military combat (see Chapter 10 for more on posttraumatic stress disorder).

7. *Somatoform disorders.* Physical symptoms, such as paralysis and blindness, that have no physical cause. Unusual preoccupation with physical health or with nonexistent physical problems (hypochondriasis, somatization disorder, pain disorder).

8. *Factitious disorders.* False mental disorders, which are intentionally produced to satisfy some psychological need.

9. *Dissociative disorders.* Psychologically caused problems of consciousness and self-identification, e.g., loss of memory (amnesia) or the development of more than one identity (multiple personality).

10. *Sexual and gender identity disorders.* Problems of (a) finding sexual arousal through unusual objects or situations (like shoes or exposing oneself), (b) unsatisfactory sexual activity (sexual dysfunction; see Chapter 8), or (c) identifying with the opposite gender.

11. *Eating disorders.* Problems associated with eating too little (anorexia nervosa) or binge eating followed by self-induced vomiting (bulimia nervosa). (See Chapter 8).

12. *Sleep disorders.* Severe problems involving the sleep-wake cycle especially an inability to sleep well at night or to stay awake during the day. (See Chapter 4.)

13. *Impulse control disorders.* Compulsive gambling, stealing or fire setting.

14. *Adjustment disorders.* Failure to adjust to, or deal well with, such stressors as divorce, financial problems, family discord, or other unhappy life events.

Axis II (Personality Disorders and Mental Retardation)

1. *Personality disorders.* Diagnostic labels given to individuals who may or may not receive an Axis I diagnosis but who show lifelong behavior patterns that are unsatisfactory to them or that disturb other people. These patterns may involve unusual suspiciousness, unusual ways of thinking, self-centeredness, shyness, overdependency, excessive concern with neatness and detail, or overemotionality, among others.

2. *Mental retardation.* As described in Chapter 7, the label of mental retardation is applied to individuals whose measured IQ is less than about 70 and who fail to display the skills at daily living, communication, and other tasks expected of those their age.

How good is the diagnostic system now in use? One way to assess the *DSM-IV* is to consider *interrater reliability,* the degree to which different mental health professionals give the same person the same diagnostic label. Some studies indicate that interrater agreement is as high as 83 percent for schizophrenia and mood disorders; agreement on many other Axis I categories is also high (e.g., Foa & Kozak, 1995; Lahey et al., 1994). Still other categories, such as Axis II personality disorders, remain more difficult to diagnose reliably.

Do diagnostic labels give accurate information about people? This *validity* question is difficult to answer, because it is hard to find a fully acceptable standard for accuracy. Still, evidence does support the validity of some *DSM* criteria (L. A. Clark, Watson, & Reynolds, 1995). And validity is likely to improve even more as diagnostic labels are refined in future *DSM* editions to reflect what researchers are learning about the characteristics, causes, courses, and cultural factors involved in various disorders.

The diagnostic system is far from perfect, however. First, people's problems often do not fit neatly into a single category. Second, the same symptoms sometimes appear as part of more than one disorder. And third, because diagnostic judgments are to some extent subjective, personal bias can creep into the labeling system. All of these factors may lead to misdiagnosis in some cases. Psychiatrist Thomas Szasz (pronounced "zaws") and other critics also argue that labeling *people* instead of describing problems is dehumanizing, because it ignores features that make each person's case unique (Kutchins & Kirk, 1997; Szasz, 1987). Calling people "schizophrenics" or "alcoholics," he says, actually encourages the behaviors associated with these labels and undermines the confidence of clients and therapists about the chances of improvement. Indeed, no shorthand label can specify each person's problems or predict exactly how that person will behave in the future. All that can be reasonably expected of a diagnostic system is that it allows informative, general descriptions of the types of problems displayed by people who have been placed in different categories.

Is Psychological Diagnosis Biased?

Some researchers and clinicians worry that problems with the reliability and validity of the diagnostic system are due partly to bias in its construction and use. They point out, for example, that if the research underlying the diagnostic criteria for a certain disorder focuses mainly on one gender, one ethnic group, or one age group, those criteria might not apply widely enough. Moreover, because diagnosticians, like other people, hold expectations and make assumptions about males versus females, and about individuals from differing cultures or ethnic groups, these cognitive biases could color their judgments, leading them to apply diagnostic criteria in ways that are subtly, but significantly, different from one case to the next (Garb, 1997; Hartung & Widiger, 1998).

■ What am I being asked to believe or accept?

Here, we focus on ethnicity as a possible source of bias in diagnosing psychopathology. It is of special interest because there is evidence that, like social class and gender, ethnicity is an important sociocultural factor in the development of mental disorder. Thus the assertion to be considered is that clinicians in the United States base their diagnoses partly on the ethnic group to which their clients belong and, more specifically, that there is bias in diagnosing African Americans.

■ What evidence is available to support the claim?

Several facts suggest the possibility of ethnic bias in psychological diagnosis. For example, African Americans receive the diagnosis of schizophrenia more frequently than European Americans do (Manderscheid & Barrett, 1987). Further, relative to their presence in the general population, African Americans are overrepresented in public mental hospitals, where the most serious forms of disorder are seen, and they are underrepresented in private hospitals and outpatient clinics, where less severe problems are treated (Lindsey & Paul, 1989; Snowden & Cheung, 1990; U.S. Surgeon General, 1999).

Can that evidence be interpreted in another way?

Differences among ethnic groups in diagnosis or treatment do not automatically indicate bias based on ethnicity. Perhaps real differences in psychological functioning are associated with different ethnic groups. For example, if, relative to other groups, African Americans are exposed to more risk factors for disorder, including poverty, violence, and other major stressors, they could be especially vulnerable to more serious forms of mental disorder. And poverty, not diagnostic bias, could be responsible for the fact that African Americans more often seek help at less expensive public hospitals than at more expensive private ones.

What evidence would help to evaluate the alternatives?

Do African Americans actually display more signs of mental disorder, or do diagnosticians just perceive them as more disordered? One way of approaching this question is to conduct experiments in which diagnosticians assign labels to clients on the basis of case histories, test scores, and the like. In some studies, the cases are selected so that pairs of clients show about the same objective amount of disorder, but one member of the pair is identified as European American and the other, as African American. In other studies, the same case materials, identified as representing either African American or European American patients, are presented to different diagnosticians. Bias in diagnosis would be suggested if, for example, patients identified as African American were seen as more seriously disordered than others. Most studies of this type have actually found little or no ethnic bias (e.g., Littlewood, 1992). These results are difficult to interpret, however, because the diagnosticians participating in such studies may be aware of the purpose of the study, and thus may go out of their way to be unbiased (Abreu, 1999). Indeed, researchers *have* found evidence of some diagnostic bias against African Americans when clinicians were unaware of the purpose of the research (e.g., Baskin, Bluestone, & Nelson, 1981; J. E. Jones, 1982).

Bias has also appeared in studies aimed at identifying the factors influencing clinicians' diagnostic judgments following extensive interviews with patients. For example, one study conducted in a hospital setting found that, in arriving at their diagnoses, psychiatrists were more likely to attribute hallucinations and paranoid thinking to African American patients than to non–African American patients. Symptoms of mood disorders were more likely to be attributed to non–African Americans (Trierweiler et al., 2000). As noted earlier, these differences could reflect ethnic differences in the rate of disorder in the population, but when people were interviewed in their own homes as part of large-scale mental health surveys, the diagnosis of schizophrenia was given only slightly more often to African Americans than to European Americans (L. N. Robins & Regier, 1991; Snowden & Cheung, 1990). Thus, the presence of ethnic bias is suggested, at least for some diagnoses, for patients who are evaluated in mental hospitals (Trierweiler et al., 2000).

What conclusions are most reasonable?

Just as *DSM-IV* is imperfect, so are the people who use it. Cognitive biases and stereotypes shape human thought in matters large and small (see Chapter 7), so it should not be surprising that they operate in diagnosis as well. Diagnostic bias does not necessarily reflect deliberate discrimination, however. At least one study has shown, for example, that like the processes of prejudice discussed in Chapter 14, diagnostic bias based on ethnicity can operate unconsciously, without the diagnostician being aware of it (Abreu, 1999). So no matter how precisely researchers specify the criteria for assigning diagnostic labels, biases and stereotypes are likely to threaten the objectivity of the diagnostic process (Funtowicz & Widiger, 1999; Trierweiler et al., 2000).

Minimizing diagnostic bias requires a better understanding of it. Hope Landrine (1991) suggests that diagnosticians need to focus more intently than ever on the fact that their concepts of "normality" and "abnormality" are affected by sociocultural values that they may or may not share with a given client. And Steven Lopez (1989) argues that mental health professionals must become more aware that the same cognitive biases that affect everyone else's thinking and decision making can impair their own clinical judgments. Indeed, research on memory, problem solving, decision making, social attributions, and other aspects of culture and cognition may turn out to be key ingredients in reducing bias in the diagnosis of psychological disorders. Meanwhile, perhaps the best way to counteract clinicians' cognitive shortcomings is to teach them to base their diagnoses solely on standard diagnostic criteria and decision rules rather than relying on their (potentially biased) clinical impressions (Garb, 1997).

We do not have the space to cover all the *DSM-IV* categories, so we will sample several of the most prevalent, socially significant, or unusual examples. As you read, try not to catch "medical student's disease." Just as medical students often think they have the symptoms of every illness they read about, some psychology students worry that their behavior (or that of a relative or friend) signals a mental disorder. Remember that everyone has problems sometimes. Before deciding that you or someone you know needs psychological help, consider whether the *content, context,* and *functional impairment* associated with the behavior would qualify it as abnormal according to the criteria of the practical approach.

Anxiety Disorders

■ **What is a phobia?**

If you have ever been tense before an exam, a date, or a job interview, you have a good idea of what anxiety feels like. Common components of anxiety include increased heart rate, sweating, rapid breathing, dry mouth, and a sense of dread. Brief episodes of moderate anxiety are a normal part of life for most people. For others, anxiety is so intense and long-standing that it disrupts a person's daily functioning; in such cases it is called an **anxiety disorder**.

Types of Anxiety Disorders

Here, we discuss four types of anxiety disorders: phobia, generalized anxiety disorder, panic disorder, and obsessive-compulsive disorder. Another type, called *posttraumatic stress disorder,* is described in Chapter 10, on health, stress, and coping. Together, these are the most common psychological disorders in North America.

Phobia　An intense, irrational fear of an object or situation that is not likely to be dangerous is called a **phobia.** The phobic person usually realizes that the fear makes no sense. However, the discomfort and avoidance of the object or event greatly interfere with daily life. Thousands of phobias have been described; some of them are listed in Table 12.3.

DSM-IV classifies phobias into specific phobia, social phobia, and agoraphobia subtypes. **Specific phobias** involve fear and avoidance of heights, blood, animals, automobile or air travel, and other specific stimuli and situations. They are the most prevalent of the anxiety disorders, affecting 7 to 10 percent of U.S. adults and children (Kessler et al., 1994; L. N. Robins et al., 1984; U.S. Surgeon General, 1999). Here is an example:

TABLE 12.3

Some Phobias

***Phobia* is the Greek word for "morbid fear," after the lesser Greek god Phobos. Phobias are usually named using the Greek word for the feared object or situation, followed by the suffix *phobia*.**

Name	Feared Stimulus
Acrophobia	Heights
Aerophobia	Flying
Claustrophobia	Enclosed places
Cynophobia	Dogs
Entomophobia	Insects
Gamophobia	Marriage
Gephyrophobia	Crossing a bridge
Hematophobia	Blood
Kenophobia	Empty rooms
Melissophobia	Bees
Ophdophobia	Snakes
Xenophobia	Strangers

Mr. L. was a fifty-year-old office worker who became terrified whenever he had to drive over a bridge. For years, he avoided bridges by taking roundabout ways to and from work, and he refused to be a passenger in anyone else's car, in case they used a bridge. Even these inconvenient strategies failed when Mr. L. was transferred to a job requiring frequent automobile trips, many of which were over bridges. He refused the transfer and was fired as a result.

Social phobias involve anxiety about being negatively evaluated by others or acting in a way that is embarrassing or humiliating. The anxiety is so intense and persistent that it impairs the person's normal functioning. In the United States, social phobia affects about 2 percent of the adult population (U.S. Surgeon General, 1999). Common social phobias include fear of public speaking or performance ("stage fright"), fear of eating in front of others, and fear of using public restrooms (Kleinknecht, 2000). *Generalized social phobia* is a more severe form of social phobia in which fear occurs in virtually all social situations (Mannuzza et al., 1995). Sociocultural factors can alter the form of social phobias. For example, in Japan, where cultural training emphasizes group-oriented values and goals, a common social phobia is *tai-jin kyofu sho,* fear of embarrassing those around you (Kleinknecht et al., 1994).

Agoraphobia is a strong fear of being separated from a safe place or from a safe person, or of being trapped in a place from which escape might be difficult or where help may be unavailable. Attempts to leave home lead to intense anxiety. In Western cultures, agoraphobia is more often reported by women, many of whom are totally homebound by the time they seek help. However, in other cultures, such as India, where homebound women are considered less unusual than in the United States, those diagnosed as agoraphobic tend to be male (Raguram & Bhide, 1985). Agoraphobia occurs less frequently than specific phobias (affecting about 5 percent of the U.S. population), but it is the phobia that most often leads people to seek treatment—mainly because it so severely disrupts everyday life (U.S. Surgeon General, 1999).

Generalized Anxiety Disorder   Excessive and long-lasting anxiety that is not focused on any particular object or situation marks **generalized anxiety disorder.** Because the problem occurs in virtually all situations and because the person cannot pinpoint its source, this type of anxiety is sometimes called *free-floating anxiety.* For weeks at a time, the person feels anxious and worried, sure that some disaster is imminent. The person becomes jumpy and irritable, and cannot sleep soundly. Fatigue, inability to concentrate, and physiological signs of anxiety are also common. Generalized anxiety disorder affects about 3.4 percent of the U.S. population in any given year, and about 5 percent of the population at some point in their lives (Kessler et al., 1994; U.S. Surgeon General, 1999). It is more common in women, often accompanying other problems such as depression or substance abuse (Wittchen et al., 1994).

Panic Disorder   For some people, anxiety takes the form of **panic disorder.** Like José, whom we met at the beginning of the chapter, people suffering from panic disorder experience recurrent, terrifying *panic attacks* that seem to come without warning or obvious cause and are marked by intense heart palpitations, pressure or pain in the chest, dizziness, and sweating. Often, victims believe they are having a heart attack. They may worry constantly about suffering future panic episodes and limit activities to avoid possible embarrassment. In fact, it is the fear of experiencing panic attacks that may lead to agoraphobia as the person begins to fear and avoid places where help won't be available should panic recur (Carter & Barlow, 1995). Panic disorder may last for many years, with periods of improvement followed by recurrence (Ehlers, 1995). Panic disorder is seen in only about 1.6 percent of the U.S. population in any given year (U.S. Surgeon General, 1999), though as many as 30 percent of the U.S. population have experienced at least one panic attack within the past year (Ehlers, 1995). In most cases, panic attacks do not lead to full-blown panic disorder; here is one that did:

anxiety disorder   A condition in which intense feelings of fear and dread are long-standing or disruptive.

phobia   An anxiety disorder that involves strong, irrational fear of an object or situation that does not objectively justify such a reaction.

specific phobias   Phobias that involve fear and avoidance of heights, blood, animals, and other specific stimuli and situations.

social phobias   Strong, irrational fears relating to social situations.

agoraphobia   A strong fear of being alone or away from the safety of home.

generalized anxiety disorder   A condition that involves long-lasting anxiety that is not focused on any particular object or situation.

panic disorder   Anxiety in the form of severe panic attacks that come without warning or obvious cause.

Geri, a thirty-two-year-old nurse, had her first panic attack while driving on a freeway. Afterward, she would not drive on freeways. Her next attack occurred while with a patient and a doctor in a small examining room. A sense of impending doom flooded over her, and she burst out of the office and into the parking lot, where she felt immediate relief. From then on, fear of another attack made it impossible for her to tolerate any close quarters, including crowded shopping malls. She eventually quit her job because of terror of the examining rooms.

Obsessive-Compulsive Disorder   Anxiety is also at the root of **obsessive-compulsive disorder (OCD),** which affects about 2.4 percent of the U.S. population in any given year (U.S. Surgeon General, 1999). People diagnosed with this disorder are plagued by persistent, upsetting, and unwanted thoughts—called *obsessions*—that often revolve around the possibility of infection, contamination, or doing harm to themselves or others. These obsessive thoughts may then motivate repetitive behaviors—called *compulsions*—that the person believes will prevent infection, aggressive acts, or other events associated with the obsessions (Foa & Kozak, 1995). Common compulsions include rituals such as checking locks; repeating words, images, or numbers; counting things; or arranging objects "just so." Obsessions and compulsions are much more intense than the familiar experience of having a repetitive thought or tune "in the back of your mind" or rechecking a door to see that it is locked. In OCD, the obsessions and compulsions are disturbing, often bizarre intrusions that can severely impair daily activities. (*DSM-IV* defines *compulsions* as taking up more than one hour a day.) Many of those who display OCD recognize the irrationality of their thoughts and actions, but they still experience severe anxiety if they try to interrupt their obsessions or give up their compulsive behaviors.

Causes of Anxiety Disorders

As with all the forms of psychopathology we will consider, the exact causes of anxiety disorders are a matter of debate. However, there is good evidence that biological, psychological, and social factors all contribute. Biological predispositions, distortions in thinking, and learning experiences appear to be particularly important (U.S. Surgeon General, 1999).

Biological Factors   Some people may be genetically predisposed to anxiety disorders. Research shows that if one identical twin has an anxiety disorder, the other is more likely also to have an anxiety disorder than is the case in nonidentical twin pairs (Kendler et al., 1992). Indeed, most anxiety disorders appear to run in families (e.g., Kendler et al., 1995). They might develop out of a physiological predisposition to react with anxiety to a wide range of situations, and this predisposition, in turn, might result partly from inheriting an autonomic nervous system that is oversensitive to stress (e.g., Zinbarg & Barlow, 1996).

Unlike other people, many panic-disorder patients have a panic episode after receiving an injection of lactate or caffeine or after inhaling carbon dioxide (Papp et al., 1993). Because these substances all stimulate brainstem areas that control the autonomic nervous system, one hypothesis is that people suffering from panic disorder have hypersensitive brainstem mechanisms and are therefore especially prone to fear responses (Gorman et al., 1989).

Cognitive Factors   Although biological predispositions may set the stage for anxiety disorders, most researchers agree that environmental stressors and psychological factors, including cognitive processes and learning, are also involved in bringing about most anxiety disorders (Ley, 1994; Schmidt, Lerew, & Jackson, 1997; Schmidt et al., 2000). In particular, persons displaying an anxiety disorder may exaggerate dangers in their environment, thereby creating an unrealistic expectation that bad things are going to happen (Foa et al., 1996). In addition, they tend to underestimate their own capacity for dealing with threatening events, experiencing anxiety and desperation when feared events do occur (A. T. Beck & Emery, 1985).

obsessive-compulsive disorder (OCD)
An anxiety disorder in which a person becomes obsessed with certain thoughts or feels a compulsion to do certain things.

As an example, consider the development of a panic attack. Whereas the appearance of unexplained symptoms of physical arousal may set the stage for a panic attack, it is the person's sensitivity to, and cognitive interpretation of, those symptoms that can determine whether or not the attack actually develops (D. M. Clark et al., 1997; Schmidt, Lerew, & Jackson, 1999). In one study, panic-disorder patients breathed air rich in carbon dioxide. Some were told that they could control the amount of carbon dioxide they were inhaling by turning a dial on a control panel. Others were told they could not control it. In fact, the dial had no effect for either group, but the patients who believed they had control were far less likely to have a full-blown panic attack (Rapee et al., 1992). In another study, panic-disorder patients who inhaled carbon dioxide in the presence of a person they associated with safety were significantly less fearful than patients whose "safe person" was not present (Carter et al., 1995). Results like these suggest that cognitive factors play a role in panic disorder.

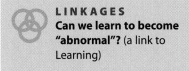

LINKAGES
Can we learn to become "abnormal"? (a link to Learning)

LINKAGES

Anxiety Disorders and Learning

Problems in life such as money troubles, illness, final exams, or unhappy relationships often create upsetting thoughts and worry. And upsetting thoughts create anxiety. These thoughts become particularly difficult to dismiss when you are under stress or feel incapable of dealing effectively with the problems you are worried about. As the thoughts become more persistent, anxiety increases. If an action such as cleaning temporarily relieves the anxiety, that action may be strengthened through the process of negative reinforcement (see Chapter 5, on learning). But such actions do nothing to eliminate the obsessive thoughts, so they become compulsive, endlessly repeated rituals that keep the person trapped in a vicious circle of anxiety (Barlow, 1988). Thus, social-learning theorists see obsessive-compulsive disorder as a learned pattern sparked by distressing thoughts and maintained by operant conditioning.

Phobias may also be explained in part by the principles of classical conditioning. The object of the phobia becomes a conditioned aversive stimulus through association with a traumatic event that acts as an unconditioned stimulus (Öst, 1992). Fear of dogs, for example, may result from a dog attack. Observing or hearing about other people's bad experiences can produce the same result: Most people who fear flying have never been in a plane crash, and many phobias, including those of needles, blood, and medically related situations, are acquired secondhand. Fears developed through observational learning can be as strong as fears developed through direct experience (Kleinknecht, 1991, 1994), though direct conditioning is the most common pathway to a phobia (Öst, 1992). Once the fear is learned, avoidance of the feared object prevents the person from finding out that there is no need to be afraid. This cycle of avoidance helps explain why many fears do not simply disappear on their own.

Why are phobias involving snakes and spiders so common, even though people are seldom harmed by them? And why are there so few cases of electrical-outlet phobia, when people are frequently shocked by outlets? The answer may be that people are biologically prepared to learn to fear and avoid stimuli that had the potential to harm their evolutionary ancestors (Seligman, 1971; Staddon & Ettinger, 1989). Laboratory research does support the idea that people are biologically prepared to learn certain phobias (Hamm, Vaitl, & Lang, 1989). In one study, a group of Swedish psychologists created conditioned fear reactions to certain stimuli by associating photographs of those stimuli with electric shocks (Öhman, Dimberg, & Öst, 1985). Their volunteer participants developed approximately equal conditioned anxiety reactions to photos of houses, human faces, and snakes. Later, however, when the participants were shown the photos alone, their conditioned fear reaction to snakes remained long after the houses and faces had failed to elicit a response. These results suggest that anxiety disorders probably arise through the combined effects of genetic predispositions and learning.

BIOLOGICAL PREPARED-NESS Having a predisposition to learn to fear snakes and other potentially dangerous stimuli makes evolutionary sense. Animals (and humans) who rapidly learn a fear response to objects or situations that they see frightening their parents or peers are more likely to survive to pass on their genes to the next generation. Make a list of the things that you might be especially afraid of. How many of your fears appear to have "survival value"?

Somatoform Disorders

▪ Can mental disorder cause blindness?

Sometimes people show symptoms of a *somatic,* or bodily, disorder even though there is no physical cause. Because these are psychological problems that take somatic form, they are called **somatoform disorders.** The classic example is **conversion disorder,** a condition in which a person appears to be, but is not, blind, deaf, paralyzed, or insensitive to pain in various parts of the body. (An earlier term for this disorder was *hysteria.*) Conversion disorders are rare, accounting for only about 2 percent of diagnoses (American Psychiatric Association, 1994, 2000). Although they can occur at any point in life, they usually appear in adolescence or early adulthood.

Conversion disorders differ from true physical disabilities in several ways. First, they tend to appear when a person is under severe stress. Second, they often help reduce that stress by enabling the person to avoid unpleasant situations. Third, the symptoms may be organically impossible or improbable, as Figure 12.2 illustrates. Finally, the person may show remarkably little concern about what most people would think was a rather serious problem. One college student, for example, experienced visual impairment that began each Sunday evening and became total blindness by Monday morning. Her vision would begin to return on Friday evenings and was fully restored in time for weekend football games and other social activities. She expressed no undue concern over her condition (Holmes, 1991). In such cases, the visual system remains intact, but the person appears to be unaware of the sensory information that the brain is still processing (Blake, 1998).

Another type of somatoform disorder is **hypochondriasis** (pronounced "hye-poh-kon-DRY-a-sis"), a strong, unjustified fear that one has, or might get, cancer, heart disease, AIDS, or some other serious physical problem. The fear prompts frequent visits to doctors and reports of numerous symptoms. Their preoccupation with illness often leads hypochondriacs to become "experts" on their most feared diseases. In a related condition called **somatization disorder,** individuals make dramatic, but vague, reports about a multitude of physical problems rather than any specific illness. **Pain disorder** is marked by complaints of severe, often constant pain (typically in the neck, chest, or back) with no physical cause.

somatoform disorders Psychological problems in which a person shows the symptoms of some physical (somatic) disorder for which there is no physical cause.

conversion disorder A somatoform disorder in which a person appears to be, but actually is not, blind, deaf, paralyzed, or insensitive to pain in various parts of the body.

hypochondriasis A strong, unjustified fear of physical illness.

somatization disorder A psychological problem in which a person has numerous physical complaints without verifiable physical illness.

pain disorder A somatoform disorder marked by complaints of severe, often constant pain with no physical cause.

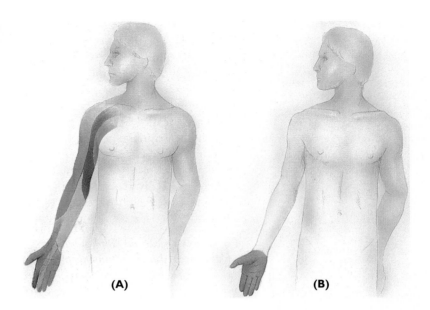

FIGURE 12.2

Glove Anesthesia

In this form of conversion disorder, lack of feeling stops abruptly at the wrist (Part B). But as shown in Part A, the nerves of the hand and arm blend, so if they were actually impaired, part of the arm would also lose sensitivity. Other neurologically impossible symptoms of conversion disorder include sleepwalking at night on legs that are "paralyzed" during the day.

(A)   (B)

Traditional explanations of somatoform disorders focus on the origins of conversion disorder. Freud believed that conversion disorder results when anxiety related to unconscious conflict is converted into physical symptoms. (This belief is the source of the term *conversion*.) This is no longer a prevalent view, but social-learning, as well as psychodynamic, theorists agree that somatoform disorders can produce benefits by relieving sufferers of unpleasant responsibilities. And some youngsters who endured stressful childhoods may have learned that illness is associated with nurturance (e.g., Barsky et al., 1994). Based on this line of reasoning, many researchers have adopted a diathesis-stress approach to explaining somatoform disorders. The results of their work suggest that certain people may have biological and psychological traits that make them especially vulnerable to somatoform disorders, particularly when combined with a history of physical illness. Among these traits are oversensitivity to physical sensations and self-consciousness. If such people experience a number of long-lasting stressors, intense emotional conflicts, or severe traumas, they are more likely than others to display physical symptoms in association with emotional arousal (Nietzel et al., 1998).

Sociocultural factors may also shape somatoform disorders. In many Asian, Latin American, and African cultures, people commonly channel psychological or interpersonal conflicts into headaches and other physical symptoms, whereas in North America such conflicts are more likely to result in anxiety or depression (Brislin, 1993). Genetic factors do not seem to be important in somatoform disorders.

Dissociative Disorders

What disorders create sudden memory loss?

A sudden and usually temporary disruption in a person's memory, consciousness, or identity characterizes **dissociative disorders.** Most people experience mild dissociative states when, for example, after many hours of highway driving they suddenly realize they have little or no recollection of what happened during the last half-hour. Dissociative disorders are more intense and long-lasting, as in the case of John, a thirty-year-old computer executive. When his wife suddenly announced that she was leaving him to live with his younger brother, John did not go to work the next day. In fact, nothing was heard from him for two weeks. Then he was arrested for public drunkenness and assault in a city more than three hundred miles from his home. Upon interviewing him, the police

dissociative disorders   Conditions involving sudden and usually temporary disruptions in a person's memory, consciousness, or identity.

A FAMOUS CASE OF DISSOCIATIVE IDENTITY DISORDER In this scene from the film *Sybil,* Sally Field portrays a woman diagnosed with dissociative identity disorder—previously known as *multiple personality disorder*—whose behavior created the appearance of as many as seventeen distinct personalities. The causes of such dramatic cases, and the reasons behind their increasing incidence in recent years, are matters of intense debate.

dissociative fugue A psychological disorder involving sudden loss of memory and the assumption of a new identity in a new locale.

dissociative amnesia A psychological disorder marked by a sudden loss of memory for one's own name, occupation, or other identifying information.

dissociative identity disorder (DID) A dissociative disorder in which a person appears to have more than one identity, each of which speaks and acts in a different way.

discovered that John had taken on a new name, did not know his real name or home address, and could not explain how he reached his present location.

John's case illustrates a disorder known as **dissociative fugue,** a sudden loss of personal memory and the adoption of a new identity in a new locale. Another dissociative disorder, **dissociative amnesia,** also involves sudden memory loss. As in fugue, all personal identifying information may be forgotten, but the person does not leave home or create a new identity. These rare conditions usually last only hours or days, but they tend to attract intense publicity because they are so dramatic.

The most famous dissociative disorder is **dissociative identity disorder (DID),** formerly known as—and still commonly called—*multiple personality disorder (MPD).* A person with DID displays more than one identity, each of which speaks and acts in a different way. Each personality seems to have its own memories, wishes, and (often conflicting) impulses. Here is a case example:

A forty-two-year-old woman was brought to a psychiatrist by her husband, who complained that during arguments about money or other matters, she would suddenly either change into uncharacteristically flamboyant clothes and go to a nearby bar to flirt with strangers, or curl up on the floor and talk as if she were a young child. An interview conducted under hypnosis revealed that during these times she experienced being "Frieda," the girlfriend of a Russian soldier who had been sexually molested in her native Poland after World War II. Once hypnosis was terminated, she had no memory of "Frieda." (Spitzer et al., 1983)

How do dissociative disorders develop? Psychodynamic theorists see massive repression of unwanted impulses or memories as the basis for creating a "new person" who acts out otherwise unacceptable impulses or recalls otherwise unbearable memories (e.g., C. A. Ross, 1997). Social-learning theorists focus on the fact that everyone is capable of behaving in different ways depending on circumstances (e.g., rowdy in a bar, quiet in a museum) and that, in rare cases, this variation can become so extreme that a person feels, and is perceived by others as, a "different person." Further, sudden memory loss or unusual behavior may be rewarded by providing escape from unpleasant situations, responsibilities, or punishment for misbehavior (Lilienfeld et al., 1999).

Evaluating these hypotheses has been difficult, in part because of the rarity of dissociative disorders. Recently, however, DID has been diagnosed more frequently, either because clinicians are looking for it more carefully or because the conditions leading to it are more widespread. Research available so far suggests three conclusions. First, many people displaying DID have experienced events they would like to forget or avoid. The majority (some clinicians believe all) have suffered severe, unavoidable, persistent abuse in childhood (C. A. Ross et al., 1991). Second, most of these people appear to be skilled at self-hypnosis, through which they can induce a trance-like state. Third, most found that they could escape the trauma of abuse, at least temporarily, by creating "new personalities" to deal with stress (D. Spiegel, 1994). However, not all abused children display DID, and it has been suggested that some cases of DID may be triggered by media stories or by suggestions made to clients by their therapists (Spanos, 1996). From this sociocultural perspective, the increased incidence of DID may reflect its status as a socially approved method of expressing distress (Acocella, 1998; Hacking, 1995).

In fact, it was observations such as these that prompted the change in designation from *multiple personality disorder* to *dissociative identity disorder.* The authors of *DSM-IV* made this change partly to avoid perpetuating the notion that people harbor multiple personalities that can easily be "contacted" through hypnosis or related techniques. The new name was chosen to suggest, instead, that dissociation, or separation, between one's memories and other aspects of identity can be so dramatic that people experiencing it may come to *believe* that they have more than one personality (D. Spiegel, 1994). Research on the existence and effects of repressed memories (discussed in Chapter 6) is sure to have an impact on our understanding of, and the controversy over, the causes of dissociative identity disorder. ("In Review: Anxiety, Somatoform, and Dissociative Disorders" presents a summary of our discussion of these topics.)

Anxiety, Somatoform, and Dissociative Disorders

Disorder	Subtypes	Major Symptoms
Anxiety disorders	Phobias	Intense, irrational fear of objectively nondangerous situations or things, leading to disruptions of behavior.
	Generalized anxiety disorder	Excessive anxiety not focused on a specific situation or object; free-floating anxiety.
	Panic disorder	Repeated attacks of intense fear involving physical symptoms such as faintness, dizziness, and nausea.
	Obsessive-compulsive disorder	Persistent ideas or worries accompanied by ritualistic behaviors performed to neutralize the anxiety-driven thoughts.
Somatoform disorders	Conversion disorder	A loss of physical ability (e.g., sight, hearing) that is related to psychological factors.
	Hypochondriasis	Preoccupation with, or belief that one has, serious illness in the absence of any physical evidence.
	Somatization disorder	Wide variety of somatic complaints that occur over several years and are not the result of a known physical disorder.
	Pain disorder	Preoccupation with pain in the absence of physical reasons for the pain.
Dissociative disorders	Amnesia/fugue	Sudden, unexpected loss of memory, which may result in relocation and the assumption of a new identity.
	Dissociative identity disorder (multiple personality disorder)	Appearance within the same person of two or more distinct identities, each with a unique way of thinking and behaving.

Mood Disorders

■ How common is depression?

Everyone's mood, or *affect,* tends to rise and fall from time to time. However, when people experience long periods of extreme moods such as wild elation or deep depression, when they shift from one extreme to another, and especially when their moods are not consistent with the events around them, they are said to show a **mood disorder,** also known as *affective disorder.* We will describe two main types: depressive disorders and bipolar disorder.

Depressive Disorders

Depression can range from occasional, normal "down" periods to episodes severe enough to require hospitalization. A person suffering **major depressive disorder** feels sad and overwhelmed for weeks or months, typically losing interest in activities and relationships and taking pleasure in nothing (Coryell et al., 1993). Exaggerated feelings of inadequacy, worthlessness, hopelessness, or guilt are common. Despite one's best efforts, anything from conversation to bathing can become an unbearable, exhausting task (A. Solomon, 1998). Changes in eating and sleeping habits resulting in weight loss or, sometimes, weight gain often accompany major depressive disorder. Problems in working, concentrating, making decisions, and thinking clearly are also typical. In extreme cases, depressed people may express false beliefs, or **delusions**—worrying, for example, that the government is planning to punish them. Major depressive disorder may come on

mood disorder   A condition in which a person experiences extremes of mood for long periods, shifts from one extreme mood to another, and experiences moods that are inconsistent with events.

major depressive disorder   A condition in which a person feels sad and hopeless for weeks or months, often losing interest in all activities and taking pleasure in nothing.

delusions   False beliefs, such as those experienced by people suffering from schizophrenia or severe depression.

suddenly or gradually. It may consist of a single episode or, more commonly, repeated depressive periods. Here is a case example:

> *Mr. J. was a fifty-one-year-old industrial engineer. . . . Since the death of his wife five years earlier, he had been suffering from continuing episodes of depression marked by extreme social withdrawal and occasional thoughts of suicide. . . . He drank, and when thoroughly intoxicated would plead to his deceased wife for forgiveness. He lost all capacity for joy. . . . Once a gourmet, he now had no interest in food and good wine . . . and could barely manage to engage in small talk. As might be expected, his work record deteriorated markedly. Appointments were missed and projects haphazardly started and left unfinished.* (Davison & Neale, 1990, p. 221)

Depression is not always so extreme. In a less severe pattern of depression, called **dysthymic disorder,** the person shows the sad mood, lack of interest, and loss of pleasure associated with major depression, but less intensely and for a longer period. (The duration must be at least two years to qualify as dysthymic disorder.) Mental and behavioral disruptions are also less severe. Most people exhibiting dysthymic disorder do not require hospitalization.

Major depressive disorder occurs sometime in the lives of up to 17 percent of the North American or European population; at any given time, about 6.5 percent of these people are affected (Blazer et al., 1994; Kessler et al., 1994; U.S. Surgeon General, 1999). Anyone can become depressed, but major depressive disorder is most likely to appear during the late teenage and early adult years (Burke et al., 1990). There is also evidence of increasing rates of depression among young people (Cross-National Collaborative Group, 1992; Fassler & Dumas, 1997). In the United States and other Western countries, women are two to three times more likely than men to experience depression (Weissman et al., 1993). However, there are no reported gender differences in depression in some less economically developed countries in the Middle East, Africa, and Asia (Culbertson, 1997).

Suicide and Depression   Suicide is associated with a variety of psychological disorders, but it is most closely tied to depression: Some form of depression has been implicated in 40 to 60 percent of all suicides (Angst, Angst, & Stassen, 1999; D. C. Clark & Fawcett, 1992). Indeed, suicidal thoughts are a symptom of depressive disorders. Hopelessness about the future—another depressive symptom—and a desire to seek instant escape from problems are also related to suicide attempts (A. T. Beck et al., 1990; G. K. Brown et al., 2000).

About 31,000 people in the United States and Canada commit suicide each year, and 10 to 20 times that many people attempt it (Statistics Canada, 1998; U.S. Surgeon General, 1999). Worldwide, the annual death toll from suicide is 120,000. Suicide rates differ considerably depending on sociocultural variables such as age, gender, and ethnicity. The rate is as high as 25 per 100,000 individuals in some northern European countries and Japan (Lamar, 2000), and as low as 6 per 100,000 in countries with stronger religious prohibitions against suicide, such as Greece, Italy, Ireland, and the nations of the Middle East.

In the United States, where the overall rate is 11.4 per 100,000, suicides are most common among people sixty-five and older (Centers for Disease Control and Prevention, 1998; Hoyert, Kochanek, & Murphy, 1999; U.S. Surgeon General, 1999). However, since 1950, suicide among adolescents—especially fifteen- to nineteen-year-olds—has tripled. It is now the third leading cause of death among adolescents (Centers for Disease Control and Prevention, 1998). Suicide is the second leading cause of death among college students; about 10,000 try to kill themselves each year, and about 1,000 succeed. These figures are much higher than for eighteen- to twenty-four-year-olds in general, but much lower than for the elderly (U.S. Surgeon General, 1999). Women attempt suicide 3 times as often as men, but men are 4 times as likely to actually kill themselves (Centers for Disease Control and Prevention, 1998). Suicide rates also differ across ethnic groups in the United States (see Figure 12.3). The suicide rate among adolescent European American males has stabilized since 1986, but it has continued to increase among African

dysthymic disorder   A pattern of depression in which the person shows the sad mood, lack of interest, and loss of pleasure associated with major depressive disorder, but to a lesser degree and for a longer period.

Suicide Rates Among Various
Ethnic Groups

The suicide rates of ethnic groups in the
United States vary widely. For example,
the rate among American Indians is more
than twice that of African Americans. In
1997, more teenagers and young adults
died from suicide than from cancer, heart
disease, AIDS, birth defects, stroke, pneumonia and influenza, and chronic lung
disease *combined* (Centers for Disease
Control and Prevention, 1998).

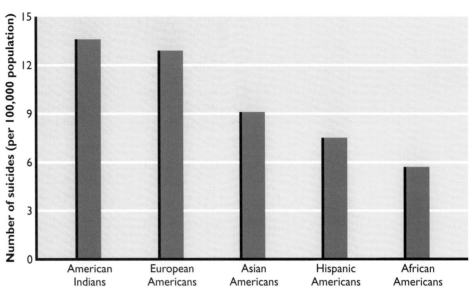

Source: Data from Garland & Zigler (1993); Howard-Pitney et al. (1992); J. L. McIntosh (1992).

American male teens (Centers for Disease Control and Prevention, 1998; Hoyert, Kochanek, & Murphy, 1999).

Predicting exactly who will commit suicide is difficult. For one thing, suicidal thoughts are not uncommon; in surveys, 5.6 percent of all adults and as many as 10 percent of college students report having had such thoughts in the previous year (Brener, Hassan, & Barrios, 1999; Crosby, Cheltenham, & Sacks, 1999). Still, the results of hundreds of research studies provide some predictive guidelines. In the United States, at least, suicide is most likely among European American males, especially those older than forty-five, single or divorced, and living alone. The risk of suicide is also heightened among people who have made a specific plan and given away possessions. Among the elderly, suicide is most common among males who suffer depression over health problems (U.S. Surgeon General, 1999). A previous suicide attempt may not always be a good predictor of eventual suicide, because such attempts may have been help-seeking gestures, not failed efforts to die. In fact, although about 10 percent of unsuccessful attempters try again and succeed, most people who commit suicide had made no prior attempts (D. C. Clark & Fawcett, 1992).

One myth about suicide is that people who talk about it will never try it. On the contrary, those who say they are thinking of suicide are much more likely to try suicide than people from the general population. In fact, according to Edwin Shneidman (1987), 80 percent of suicides are preceded by some kind of warning, whether direct ("I think I'm going to kill myself") or vague ("Sometimes I wonder if life is worth living"). Although not everyone who threatens suicide follows through, if you suspect that someone you know is thinking about suicide, encourage the person to contact a mental health professional or a crisis hotline. If the danger is imminent, make the contact yourself, and ask for advice about how to respond. For more information, visit suicide-related web sites, such as that of the American Association of Suicidology (www.suicidology.org).

Bipolar Disorder

The alternating appearance of two emotional extremes, or poles, characterizes **bipolar disorder.** We have already described one emotional pole: depression. The other is **mania,** which is a very agitated, usually elated, emotional state. During periods of mania, people tend to be utterly optimistic, boundlessly energetic, certain of having extraordinary powers and abilities, and bursting with all sorts of ideas. They become irritated with anyone who tries to reason with them or "slow them down," and they may make impulsive and unwise decisions, including spending their life savings on foolish schemes.

bipolar disorder A condition in which a person alternates between the two emotional extremes of depression and mania.

mania An elated, very active emotional state.

in review

Mood Disorders		
Type	**Typical Symptoms**	**Related Features**
Major depressive disorder	Deep sadness, feelings of worthlessness, changes in eating and sleeping habits, loss of interest and pleasure	Lasts weeks or months; may occur in repeating episodes; severe cases may include delusions; danger of suicide
Dysthymic disorder	Similar to major depressive disorder, but less severe and longer lasting	Hospitalization usually not necessary
Bipolar disorder	Alternating extremes of mood, from deep depression to mania, and back	Manic episodes include impulsivity, unrealistic optimism, high energy, severe agitation
Cyclothymic disorder	Similar to bipolar disorder, but less severe	Hospitalization usually not necessary

In bipolar disorder, episodes of mania may alternate with periods of deep depression. (Sometimes, periods of relatively normal mood separate these extremes.) This pattern has also been called *manic depression*. Compared with major depressive disorder, bipolar disorder is rare. It occurs in only about 1 percent of adults, and it affects men and women about equally. Slightly more common is a pattern of less extreme mood swings known as **cyclothymic disorder,** the bipolar equivalent of dysthymia. Like major depressive disorder, bipolar disorder is extremely disruptive to a person's ability to work or maintain social relationships (J. F. Goldberg, Harrow, & Grossman, 1995). "In Review: Mood Disorders" summarizes the main types of mood disorders.

Causes of Mood Disorders

Research on the causes of mood disorders has focused on biological, psychological, and sociocultural risk factors.

Biological Factors   The role in mood disorders of one biological factor, genetics, is suggested by twin studies and family studies showing that mood disorders, especially bipolar disorder, tend to run in families. For example, if one twin displays bipolar disorder, the likelihood that the other one will, too, is much higher in genetically identical, rather than nonidentical, pairs (Bowman & Nurnberger, 1993; NIMH, 1998a). Family studies also show that those who are closely related to people with bipolar disorder are more likely than others to develop the disorder themselves (Winokur et al., 1995). Further, major depressive disorder is more likely to occur in both members of identical, compared with nonidentical, twins (Kendler et al., 1995; Nurnberger, 1993). This genetic influence is especially strong in female twins (Bierut et al., 1999). Researchers continue to look for the specific genes that might be involved in the transmission of elevated risk for mood disorders (M. Baron, 1997; U.S. Surgeon General, 1999).

Other potential biological causes of mood disorders include imbalances in the brain's neurotransmitters, malfunctioning of the endocrine system, and disruption of biological rhythms. Neurotransmitters such as norepinephrine, serotonin, and dopamine were implicated decades ago when scientists discovered that drugs capable of altering these substances also relieved mood disorders. However, the precise nature of this relationship is still not fully understood (Schloss & Williams, 1998; U.S. Surgeon General, 1999).

Mood disorders have also been related to malfunctions of the endocrine system, especially the subsystem involved in the body's responses to stress (see Chapter 10). For

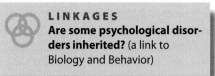

LINKAGES
Are some psychological disorders inherited? (a link to Biology and Behavior)

cyclothymic disorder   A mood disorder characterized by an alternating pattern of mood swings that are less extreme than those seen in bipolar disorder.

TREATING SAD Seasonal affective disorder (SAD) can often be relieved by exposure to full-spectrum light for as little as a couple of hours a day (S. S. Campbell & Murphy, 1998; Sato, 1997).

example, research shows that as many as 70 percent of depressed people secrete abnormally high levels of the stress hormone cortisol (Nemeroff, 1998; Posener et al., 2000).

The cyclical pattern seen in bipolar disorder and in recurring episodes of major depressive disorder suggests that mood disorders may be related to stressful triggering events (Miklowitz & Alloy, 1999) and perhaps to disturbances in the body's biological clock, which is described in Chapter 2 (Goodwin & Jamison, 1990). This second possibility seems especially likely to apply to the 15 percent of depressed people who experience a pattern known as *seasonal affective disorder (SAD)*. During months of shorter daylight, these people slip into severe depression, accompanied by irritability and excessive sleeping (Blehar & Rosenthal, 1989). Their depression tends to lift as daylight hours increase (Faedda et al., 1993). Evidence for disrupted biological rhythms in mood disorders indirectly supports neurotransmitter theories of causation inasmuch as the disruptions may be traceable to abnormalities in norepinephrine, serotonin, dopamine, and other neurotransmitters that regulate the body's internal clock (Wehr et al., 1983).

Psychological and Social Factors   Researchers have come to recognize that whatever biological causes are involved in mood disorders, their effects are always combined with those of psychological and social causes (U.S. Surgeon General, 1999). As mentioned earlier, the very nature of depressive symptoms can depend on the culture in which a person lives. Biopsychosocial explanations of mood disorders also emphasize the impact of anxiety, negative thinking, and the other psychological and emotional responses triggered by trauma, losses, and other stressful events (Monroe et al., 1999). For example, the higher prevalence of depression among females—and especially among poor, ethnic minority, single mothers—has been attributed to their greater exposure to stressors of all kinds (G. W. Brown & Moran, 1997; Miranda & Green, 1999). Environmental stressors affect men, too (Bierut et al., 1999), which may be one reason why gender differences are smaller in countries where men and women face equally stressful lives.

Social-cognitive theories suggest that the way people *think* about their stressors can increase or decrease the likelihood of mood disorders. One of these theories is based on the *learned helplessness* research described in Chapter 5. Just as animals become inactive and appear depressed when they have no control over negative events, humans may experience depression as a result of feeling incapable of controlling their lives, especially the stressors confronting them (D. C. Klein & Seligman, 1976; Seligman, 1991). But most of us have limited control; why aren't we all depressed? The ways in which people learn to *think* about events in their lives may hold the cognitive key. For example, Aaron Beck's (1967, 1976) cognitive theory of depression suggests that depressed people develop mental habits of (1) blaming themselves when things go wrong, (2) focusing on and exaggerating the dark side of events, and (3) jumping to overly generalized, pessimistic conclusions. Such cognitive habits, says Beck, are errors that lead to depressing thoughts and other symptoms of depression (J. S. Beck & Beck, 1995).

Some researchers have found that severe, long-lasting depression is especially likely among people who attribute lack of control or other problems they experience to a permanent, generalized lack of personal competence rather than to a temporary lapse or some external cause (Seligman et al., 1988). Thus, *attributional style* may be another important cognitive factor in depression (Alloy, Abramson, & Francis, 1999; Ingram, Miranda, & Segal, 1998).

Depressed people do hold more negative beliefs about themselves and their lives than other people, but the exact significance of these beliefs is not yet clear (Gara et al., 1993). For one thing, pessimistic beliefs may be a symptom of depression rather than its cause. In any case, the social-cognitive perspective suggests that whether depression continues or worsens depends in part on how people respond once they start to feel depressed. Those who continuously think about negative events, about why they occur, and even about being depressed are likely to feel more and more depressed (Just & Alloy, 1997). According to Susan Nolen-Hoeksema (1990), this *ruminative style* is especially characteristic of women and may help explain gender differences in the frequency of depression. When men start to feel sad, she says, they tend to use a *distracting style*. That is, they engage in activity that focuses attention away from what is bothering them, thus helping to relieve their depressed mood (Just & Alloy, 1997; Nolen-Hoeksema, Morrow, & Fredrickson, 1993).

Notice that social-cognitive explanations of depression are consistent with the diathesis-stress approach to disorder. These explanations suggest that certain cognitive styles constitute a predisposition (or diathesis) that makes a person vulnerable to depression, the occurrence of which is made more likely by stressors. As suggested in Chapter 10, the depressing effects of these stressors are likely to be magnified by lack of social support, inadequate coping skills, and the presence of other stressful conditions, such as poverty.

Given the number and complexity of biological, psychological, social, and situational factors potentially involved in causing mood disorders, the diathesis-stress approach appears to be an especially appropriate guide to future research. One study based on this approach looked at the role of genetics and stressful events in shaping mood disorders in a large group of female twin pairs. Both factors were associated with major depression; the women at highest genetic risk were the most likely to become depressed following a significant stressor (Kendler et al., 1995; Kendler, Thorton, & Gardner, 2000). In the final analysis, it may turn out that each subtype of mood disorder is caused by a unique combination of factors. The challenge for researchers is to identify these subtypes and map out their causal ingredients.

Schizophrenia

▣ **Is schizophrenia the same as "split personality"?**

Here is part of a letter that arrived in the mail a few years ago:

Dear Sirs:

Pertaining to our continuing failure to prosecute violations of minor's rights to sovereign equality which are occurring in gestations being compromised by the ingestation of controlled substances, . . . the skewing of androgyny which continues in female juveniles even after separation from their mother's has occurred, and as a means of promulflagi-tating my paying Governor Hickel of Alaska for my employees to have personal services endorsements and controlled substance endorsements, . . . the Iraqi oil being released by the United Nations being identified as Kurdistanian oil, and the July, 1991 issue of the Siberian Review spells President Eltsin's name without a letter y.

The disorganization and bizarre content of this letter suggest that its writer might be displaying **schizophrenia** (pronounced "skit-so-FREE-nee-uh"), a pattern of severely disturbed thinking, emotion, perception, and behavior that seriously impairs the ability to communicate and relate to others and disrupts most other aspects of daily functioning. Schizophrenia is one of the most severe and disabling of all mental disorders. Its core symptoms are seen virtually everywhere in the world, occurring in about 1 to 2 percent of the population (American Psychiatric Association, 1994, 2000). In the United States, it appears about equally in various ethnic groups, but like most disorders, it tends to be diagnosed more frequently in economically disadvantaged populations. Schizophrenia is seen about equally in men and women, although some studies have suggested that in women, it may appear later in life, be less severe, and respond better to treatment (American Psychiatric Association, 2000; U.S. Surgeon General, 1999).

Schizophrenia tends to develop in adolescence or early adulthood. The onset is gradual in some people and more rapid in others. About 40 percent of schizophrenics improve with treatment and are able to function reasonably well; the rest show continuous or intermittent symptoms that permanently impair their functioning (Hegarty et al., 1994). It has been estimated that 10 to 13 percent of homeless individuals suffer from schizophrenia (P. J. Fischer & Breakey, 1991).

One of the best predictors of the course of schizophrenia is *premorbid adjustment,* the level of functioning a person had achieved before schizophrenic symptoms first appeared. Improvement is more likely in those who had attained higher levels of education and occupation, and who had established supportive relationships with family and friends (Watt & Saiz, 1991).

Symptoms of Schizophrenia

Schizophrenics display problems in both how they think and what they think. In fact, the nineteenth-century psychiatrist Eugen Bleuler coined the word *schizophrenia,* or "split mind," to refer to the peculiarities of schizophrenic thinking. Contrary to popular belief, schizophrenia does not mean "split personality," as in dissociative identity disorder (multiple personality disorder), but refers instead to a splitting of normally integrated mental processes such as thoughts and feelings.

Schizophrenic thought and language are often disorganized. *Neologisms* ("new words" that have meaning only to the person speaking them) are common; "promulflagitating" in the letter above is one example. That letter also illustrates *loose associations,* the tendency for one thought to be logically unconnected or only superficially related to the next. In the most severe cases, thought becomes just a jumble known as *word salad.* For example, one patient was heard to say, "Upon the advisability of held keeping, environment of the seabeach gathering, to the forest stream, reinstatement to be placed, poling the paddleboat, of the swamp morass, to the forest compensation of the dunce" (Lehman, 1967, p. 627).

The *content* of schizophrenic thinking is also disturbed. Often it includes a bewildering assortment of delusions, especially delusions of persecution. Some patients believe that space aliens are trying to steal their internal organs, and they may interpret everything from TV commercials to casual hand gestures as part of the plot. Delusions that common events are somehow related to oneself are called *ideas of reference.* Delusions of grandeur may also be present; one young man was convinced that the president of the United States was trying to contact him for advice. Other types of delusions include (1) *thought broadcasting,* in which patients believe that their thoughts can be heard by others; (2) *thought blocking* or *thought withdrawal,* the belief that someone is either preventing thoughts or "stealing" them as they appear; and (3) *thought insertion,* the belief that other people's thoughts are appearing in one's own mind. Some schizophrenics believe that like puppets, their behavior is controlled by others.

Schizophrenics often report that they cannot focus their attention, and they may feel overwhelmed as they try to attend to everything at once. Various perceptual disorders

schizophrenia   A pattern of severely disturbed thinking, emotion, perception, and behavior that constitutes one of the most serious and disabling of all mental disorders.

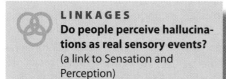

LINKAGES
Do people perceive hallucinations as real sensory events?
(a link to Sensation and Perception)

may also appear. The person may feel detached from the world and see other people as flat cutouts. The body may feel like a machine, or parts of it may seem to be dead or rotting. **Hallucinations,** or false perceptions, are common, often emerging as voices. These voices may sound like an overheard conversation, or they may urge the person to do or not to do things; sometimes they comment on, narrate, or criticize the person's actions. Hallucinations can also involve the experience of nonexistent sights, smells, tastes, and touches. Emotional expression is often muted—a pattern called *flat affect*. But when schizophrenics do display emotion, it is often exaggerated or inappropriate. For example, they may cry for no apparent reason or fly into a rage in response to a simple question.

Some schizophrenics are quite agitated, constantly fidgeting, grimacing, or pacing the floor in ritualized patterns. Others become so withdrawn that they move very little. Lack of motivation and poor social skills, deteriorating personal hygiene, and an inability to function day to day are other common characteristics of schizophrenia.

Categorizing Schizophrenia

The *DSM-IV* lists five major subtypes of schizophrenia: paranoid, disorganized, catatonic, undifferentiated, and residual. These subtypes are summarized in Table 12.4.

Researchers have also made other useful distinctions among various forms of schizophrenia. One of these distinctions involves the positive-negative symptom dimension. Disorganized thoughts, delusions, and hallucinations are sometimes called *positive symptoms* of schizophrenia, because they appear as undesirable *additions* to a person's mental life (Andreasen et al., 1995). Conversely, the absence of pleasure and motivation, lack of emotional reactivity, social withdrawal, reduced speech, and other deficits seen in schizophrenia are sometimes called *negative symptoms,* because they appear to *subtract* elements from normal mental life (I. R. Nicholson & Neufeld, 1993). Many patients exhibit both positive and negative symptoms, but when the negative symptoms are stronger, schizophrenia generally has a more severe course, including long-term disability and relative lack of response to treatment (e.g., Fenton & McGlashan, 1994). Some researchers believe that forms of schizophrenia dominated by positive versus negative symptoms may stem from different causes.

Causes of Schizophrenia

The search for causes of schizophrenia has been more intense than for any other psychological disorder. The findings so far confirm one thing for certain: No single cause can adequately account for all forms of schizophrenia.

Biological Factors   Certain biological factors have been uncovered. Research in behavioral genetics, for example, shows that schizophrenia runs in families (Gottesman, 1991). One family study found that 16 percent of the children of schizophrenic mothers—compared with 2 percent of those of nonschizophrenic mothers—developed schizophrenia themselves over a twenty-five-year period (Parnas et al., 1993). Even if they are adopted by nonschizophrenic families, the children of schizophrenic parents are ten times more likely to develop schizophrenia than adopted children whose biological parents are not schizophrenic (Kety et al., 1994). Still, it is unlikely that a single gene transmits schizophrenia (Kendler & Diehl, 1993). Among identical-twin pairs in which one of the members displays schizophrenia, 40 percent of the other members display it, too; but 60 percent of them do not (McGue, 1992). It is more likely that some people inherit a *genetic predisposition,* or diathesis, for schizophrenia (Moldin & Gottesman, 1997).

Researchers are also investigating the possibility that abnormalities in brain chemistry—especially in neurotransmitter systems that use dopamine (see Chapter 2)—play a role in causing or intensifying schizophrenic symptoms. Because drugs that block the brain's dopamine receptors often reduce schizophrenics' hallucinations, disordered thinking, and other positive symptoms, some investigators speculate that schizophrenia results from excess dopamine. However, the relationship between dopamine and

CATATONIC STUPOR   The symptoms of schizophrenia often occur in characteristic patterns. This woman displays the inactivity and odd posturing associated with catatonic schizophrenia.

TABLE 12.4

Subtypes of Schizophrenia

These traditional categories of schizophrenia convey some useful information. For example, the prognosis for paranoid schizophrenia is somewhat better than for the other subtypes (Fenton & McGlashan, 1991). However, some symptoms of schizophrenia appear in more than one subtype, and people first placed in one subtype might later display characteristics of another. These concerns, plus the fact that the *DSM-IV* subtypes may not be linked to different causal factors, have led researchers to develop additional ways of categorizing schizophrenia.

Type	Frequency	Prominent Features
Paranoid schizophrenia	40 percent of schizophrenics; appears late in life (after age 25–30)	Delusions of grandeur or persecution; anger; anxiety; argumentativeness; extreme jealousy; onset often sudden; signs of impairment may be subtle
Disorganized schizophrenia	5 percent of all schizophrenics; high prevalence in homeless population	Delusions; hallucinations; incoherent speech; facial grimaces; inappropriate laughter/giggling; neglected personal hygiene; loss of bladder/bowel control
Catatonic schizophrenia	8 percent of all schizophrenics	Disordered movement, alternating between total immobility (stupor) and wild excitement. In stupor, the person does not speak or attend to communication; also, the body is rigid or can be posed in virtually any posture (a condition called "waxy flexibility").
Undifferentiated schizophrenia	40 percent of all schizophrenics	Patterns of disordered behavior, thought, and emotion that do not fall easily into any other subtype
Residual schizophrenia	Varies	Applies to people who have had prior episodes of schizophrenia but are not currently displaying symptoms

schizophrenia is a complex one (Healy et al., 1998). Some research suggests, for example, that *excessive* activity in dopamine systems may be related to the appearance of hallucinations, delusions, and other positive symptoms of schizophrenia. Abnormally *low* dopamine system activity, especially in prefrontal brain areas, has been associated with negative symptoms such as withdrawal (e.g., J. Cohen & Servan-Schreiber, 1992).

Some researchers are integrating genetic and environmental explanations of schizophrenia by looking for *neurodevelopmental* abnormalities (T. D. Cannon, 1998; Gur et al., 2000; McGlashan & Hoffman, 2000). Perhaps, they say, some forms of schizophrenia arise from disruptions in brain development from before birth through childhood, when the brain is growing and its various functions are maturing. Studies have shown, for instance, that prenatal exposure to viral infections or other physical traumas are associated with increased risk for developing schizophrenia (Takei et al., 1994). It may be that the expression of a genetically transmitted predisposition for brain abnormality is enhanced by environmental stressors such as maternal drug use during pregnancy, complications during birth, and childhood malnutrition. Neurodevelopmental factors may help explain why children of schizophrenic parents tend to show

hallucinations   False or distorted perceptions of objects or events, often associated with mental disorder.

Schizophrenia	
Aspect	**Key Features**
Common Symptoms	
Disorders of thought	Disturbed *content*, including delusions; disorganization, including loose associations, neologisms, and word salad
Disorders of perception	Hallucinations or false perceptions; poorly focused attention
Disorders of emotion	Flat affect; inappropriate tears, laughter, or anger
Possible Causes	
Biological	Genetics; abnormalities in brain structure; abnormalities in dopamine systems; neurodevelopmental problems
Psychological	Learned maladaptive behavior; disturbed patterns of family communication

cognitive and intellectual problems associated with brain abnormalities (T. D. Cannon et al., 1994; McGlashan & Hoffman, 2000; Neumann et al., 1995).

Psychological Factors   Psychological factors are no longer considered as primary causes of schizophrenia, but there is evidence that psychological processes and social influences, including maladaptive learning experiences and stressful family communication patterns, can contribute to the appearance of schizophrenia and influence its course. For example, schizophrenic individuals who live with relatives who are critical, unsupportive, or emotionally overinvolved are especially likely to relapse following improvement (Kavanagh, 1992; Wearden et al., 2000). Family members' negative attitudes may be a source of stress that actually increases the chances that disruptive or odd behaviors will persist or worsen (Rosenfarb et al., 1995). In contrast, helping schizophrenia patients to develop cognitive stress-coping skills can improve their long-term adjustment (Velligan et al., 2000).

Vulnerability Theory   The causal theories of schizophrenia we have outlined are consistent with the diathesis-stress approach, which assumes that stress may activate a person's predisposition for disorder (Fowles, 1992). This approach forms the basis of the *vulnerability theory* of schizophrenia (Cornblatt & Erlenmeyer-Kimling, 1985; Zubin & Spring, 1977). This theory suggests that (1) vulnerability to schizophrenia is mainly biological; (2) different people have differing degrees of vulnerability; (3) vulnerability is influenced partly by genetic influences on development and partly by abnormalities that arise from environmental risk factors; and (4) psychological components, such as exposure to poor parenting, a high-stress environment, or inadequate coping skills, may help determine whether schizophrenia actually appears, and also influence the course of the disorder (E. F. Walker & Diforio, 1998; Wearden et al., 2000).

Many different blendings of vulnerability and stress can lead to schizophrenia. People whose genetic characteristics or prenatal experiences leave them vulnerable to develop schizophrenia may be especially likely to do so if they are later exposed to learning experiences, family conflicts, or other stressors that elicit and maintain schizophrenic patterns of thought and action. Those same experiences and stressors would not be expected to lead to schizophrenia in people who are less vulnerable to developing the disorder. Clearly, then, schizophrenia is a highly complex disorder—probably more than one disorder (Tsuang, Stone, & Faraone, 2000)—whose origins appear to lie in numerous biological and psychological domains, some of which are yet to be discovered (Durand & Barlow, 1997). "In Review: Schizophrenia" summarizes what we know about this disorder.

Personality Disorders

■ **Which personality disorder often leads to crime?**

Personality disorders are long-standing, inflexible ways of behaving that are not so much severe mental disorders as dysfunctional styles of living. These disorders affect all areas of functioning and, from childhood or adolescence on, create problems for those who display them and for others (Millon & Davis, 1996). Some psychologists view personality disorders as interpersonal strategies (D. J. Kiesler, 1996) or as the expression of extreme, rigid, and maladaptive personality traits (Widiger, 1997).

The ten personality disorders found on Axis II of *DSM-IV*, and listed in Table 12.5, are grouped into three clusters that share certain features. The *odd-eccentric* cluster includes paranoid, schizoid, and schizotypal personality disorders. People diagnosed as having schizotypal personality disorder, for example, display some of the peculiarities seen in schizophrenia but are not disturbed enough to be labeled as schizophrenic. The *anxious-fearful* cluster includes dependent, obsessive-compulsive, and avoidant personality disorders. The avoidant personality disorder, for example, is akin to social phobia in the sense that persons labeled with this disorder tend to be "loners" with a long-standing pattern of avoiding social situations and of being particularly sensitive to criticism or rejection. Finally, the *dramatic-erratic* cluster includes the histrionic, narcissistic, borderline, and antisocial personality disorders. The main characteristics of narcissistic personality disorder, for example, are an exaggerated sense of self-importance, extreme sensitivity to criticism, a constant need for attention, and a tendency to arrogantly overestimate personal abilities and achievements.

TABLE 12.5

Personality Disorders

Here are brief descriptions of the ten personality disorders listed on Axis II of *DSM-IV*.

Type	Typical Features
Paranoid	Suspiciousness and distrust of others, all of whom are assumed to be hostile
Schizoid	Detachment from social relationships; restricted range of emotion
Schizotypal	Detachment from, and great discomfort in, social relationships; odd perceptions, thoughts, beliefs, and behaviors
Dependent	Helplessness; excessive need to be taken care of; submissive and clinging behavior; difficulty in making decisions
Obsessive-compulsive	Preoccupation with orderliness, perfection, and control
Avoidant	Inhibition in social situations; feelings of inadequacy; oversensitivity to criticism
Histrionic	Excessive emotionality and preoccupation with being the center of attention; emotional shallowness; overly dramatic behavior
Narcissistic	Exaggerated ideas of self-importance and achievements; preoccupation with fantasies of success; arrogance
Borderline	Lack of stability in interpersonal relationships, self-image, and emotion; impulsivity; angry outbursts; intense fear of abandonment; recurring suicidal gestures
Antisocial	Shameless disregard for, and violation of, other people's rights

personality disorders Long-standing, inflexible ways of behaving that become styles of life that create problems, usually for others.

A DANGEROUS CASE OF ANTISOCIAL PERSONALITY DISORDER Andrew Phillip Cunanan murdered fashion designer Gianni Versace and several other men across the United States in 1997. His violent crime spree—which ended with his suicide in July of that year—represents antisocial personality disorder at its worst.

From the perspective of public welfare and safety, the most serious personality disorder is **antisocial personality disorder.** It is marked by a long-term pattern of irresponsible, impulsive, unscrupulous, and sometimes criminal behavior, beginning in childhood or early adolescence. In the nineteenth century, the pattern was called *moral insanity* because such persons appear to have no morals or common decency. Later, people in this category were called *psychopaths* or *sociopaths.* The current "antisocial personality" label more accurately portrays them as troublesome, but not "insane" by the legal standards we discuss later. About 3 percent of men and about 1 percent of women in the United States fall into this diagnostic category (American Psychiatric Association, 1994, 2000).

At their least troublesome, these people are a nuisance. They are often charming, intelligent, "fast talkers" who borrow money and fail to return it; they are arrogant, selfish manipulators who "con" people into doing things for them, usually by lying and taking advantage of the decency and trust of others. A hallmark of those displaying antisocial personality is a lack of anxiety, remorse, or guilt, whether they have wrecked a borrowed car or killed an innocent person (Hare, 1993). No method has yet been found for permanently altering the behavior of these people (M. E. Rice, 1997). Research suggests that the best hope for dealing with this disorder is to identify antisocial personalities early, before the most treatment-resistant traits are fully developed (Lynam, 1996; Stoff, Breiling, & Maser, 1997).

There are numerous theories about the causes of antisocial personality. Some research suggests a genetic predisposition, possibly in the form of abnormal brain development or chronic underarousal of both the autonomic and central nervous systems (Patrick, Cuthbert, & Lang, 1994; Raine et al., 2000; Raine, Venables, & Williams, 1990). This underarousal may render people less sensitive to punishment, and more likely to seek excitement, than is normally the case (Stoff, Breiling, & Maser, 1997). Broken homes, rejection by parents, poor discipline, lack of good parental models, lack of attachment to early caregivers, impulsivity, conflict-filled childhoods, and poverty have all been suggested as psychological and social factors contributing to the development of antisocial personality disorder (Lahey et al., 1995; Raine, Brennan, & Mednick, 1994; R. E. Tremblay et al., 1994). The biopsychosocial model suggests that antisocial personality disorder results when these psychosocial and environmental conditions combine with genetic predispositions to low arousal and the sensation seeking and impulsivity associated with it (Rutter, 1997).

antisocial personality disorder A personality disorder involving a long-term, persistent pattern of impulsive, selfish, unscrupulous, even criminal behavior.

FOCUS ON RESEARCH

Exploring Links Between Child Abuse and Antisocial Personality Disorder

One of the most prominent environmental factors associated with the more violent forms of antisocial personality disorder is the experience of abuse in childhood. However, most of the studies that have found a relationship between childhood abuse and antisocial personality disorder were based on potentially biased reports (Monane, Leichter, & Lewis, 1984; Rosenbaum & Bennett, 1986). People with antisocial personalities—especially those with criminal records—are likely to make up stories of abuse in order to shift blame for their behavior onto others. Even if their reports were accurate, however, most of these studies lacked a control group of non-antisocial people from similar backgrounds. Because of this research design flaw, it is virtually impossible to separate the effects of reported child abuse from the effects of poverty or other factors that might also have contributed to the development of antisocial personality disorder.

■ **What was the researcher's question?**

Can childhood abuse cause antisocial personality disorder? To help answer this question and to correct some of the flaws in earlier studies, Cathy Widom (1989a) used a prospective quasi-experimental design, first finding cases of childhood abuse and then looking for the effects of that abuse on adult behavior.

▨ How did the researcher answer the question?

Widom began by identifying 416 adults whose backgrounds included official records of their having been physically or sexually abused before the age of eleven. She then explored the stories of these people's lives, as told in police and school records, as well as in a two-hour diagnostic interview. To reduce experimenter bias and distorted reporting, Widom ensured that the interviewers remained "blind" to the purpose of the study and that the respondents were told only that the study's purpose was to talk to people who had grown up in a midwestern metropolitan area of the United States in the late 1960s and early 1970s. Widom also selected a comparison group of 283 people who had no history of abuse, but who were similar to the abused sample in terms of age, gender, ethnicity, hospital of birth, schools attended, and area of residence. Her goal was to obtain a nonabused control group that had been exposed to approximately the same environmental risk factors and socioeconomic conditions as the abused children.

▨ What did the researcher find?

First, Widom (1989a) tested the hypothesis that exposure to abuse in childhood is associated with criminality and/or violence in later life. She found that 26 percent of the abused youngsters went on to commit juvenile crimes, 29 percent were arrested as adults, and 11 percent committed violent crimes. These percentages were significantly higher than the figures for the nonabused group. The correlations between criminality and abuse were higher for males than for females, and higher for African Americans than for European Americans. And overall, victims of physical abuse were more likely to commit violent crimes as adults than were victims of sexual abuse.

Next, Widom tested the hypothesis that childhood abuse is associated with the development of antisocial personality disorder (Luntz & Widom, 1994). Indeed, the abused group exhibited a significantly higher rate of antisocial personality disorder (13.5 percent) than did the comparison group (7.1 percent). The apparent role of abuse in antisocial personality disorder was particularly pronounced in men, and it remained strong even when other factors—such as age, ethnicity, and socioeconomic status—were accounted for in the statistical analyses. Interestingly, one other factor—failure to graduate from high school—was also strongly associated with the appearance of antisocial personality, whether or not childhood abuse had occurred.

▨ What do the results mean?

Widom's research supported earlier studies in finding an *association* between childhood abuse and criminality, violence, and antisocial personality disorder. Further, although her study did not permit a firm conclusion that abuse alone *causes* antisocial personality disorder, the data from its prospective design added strength to the argument that abuse may be an important causal factor (Widom, 2000). The results suggest that there are probably other causes as well. For one thing, abuse is often part of a larger pool of experiences such as exposure to deviant models, social rejection, poor supervision, and the like.

Finally, Widom's work offers yet another reason—as if more reasons were needed—why it is so important to prevent the physical and sexual abuse of children. The long-term consequences of such abuse can be tragic not only for its immediate victims but also for those victimized by the violence, criminal actions, and antisocial behavior perpetrated by some abused children as they grow up (Weiler & Widom, 1996).

▨ What do we still need to know?

Further research is needed to discover whether antisocial personality disorder stems from abuse itself, from one of the factors accompanying it, or from some other specific combination of known and still-unknown risk factors. For example, Widom's study suggests that one or more of the factors leading teenagers to drop out (or be thrown out) of high school might be an independent cause of antisocial personality disorder.

In addition, because Widom's study found that violence, criminal behavior, and antisocial personality disorder are seen in only a minority of abused children, her results raise the question of whether certain genetic characteristics or environmental experiences serve to protect children from at least some of the devastating effects of abuse. An understanding of what these protective elements are might go a long way toward the development of programs for the prevention of antisocial personality disorder.

A Sampling of Other Psychological Disorders

▪ **How do children's disorders differ from adults' disorders?**

The disorders described so far represent some of the most prevalent and socially disruptive psychological problems encountered in cultures around the world. Several others are mentioned in other chapters. In Chapter 4, for example, we discuss insomnia, night terrors, and other sleep disorders; mental retardation is covered in Chapter 7; sexual dysfunctions are mentioned in Chapter 8; and posttraumatic stress disorder is described in Chapter 10. Here we consider two other significant psychological problems: disorders of childhood and substance-related disorders.

Psychological Disorders of Childhood

The physical, cognitive, emotional, and social changes seen in childhood—and the stress associated with them—can create or worsen psychological disorders in children. Stress can do the same in adults, but childhood disorders are not just miniature versions of adult psychopathology. Because children's development is still incomplete, and because their capacity to cope with stress is limited in important ways, children are often vulnerable to special types of disorders. The majority of childhood behavior problems can be placed in two broad categories: externalizing disorders and internalizing disorders (Achenbach, 1997; Nigg, 2000).

The *externalizing,* or *undercontrolled,* category includes behaviors that disturb people in the child's environment. Lack of control shows up as *conduct disorders* in 4 to 10 percent of children, mostly boys (American Psychiatric Association, 1994; B. Martin & Hoffman, 1990). Conduct disorders are characterized by a relatively stable pattern of aggression, disobedience, destructiveness, and other obnoxious behaviors (Lahey et al., 1995). Often these behaviors involve criminal activity, and they may signal the development of antisocial personality disorder (Loeber & Stouthamer-Loeber, 1998). Environmental and parenting factors, possibly combined with genetic predisposition, appear to shape these children's antisocial behavior (Lahey et al., 1995; U.S. Surgeon General, 1999).

Another kind of externalizing problem, also seen primarily in boys, is *attention deficit hyperactivity disorder (ADHD).* This label is given to children who are impulsive and unable to concentrate on an activity as well as other children their age can (Schachar & Logan, 1990). Many of these children also have great difficulty sitting still or otherwise controlling their physical activity. Their impulsiveness and lack of self-control annoy and exhaust those around them and create numerous problems, especially at school (Henker & Whalen, 1989). Genetic predisposition, brain damage, dietary problems, poisoning from lead or other household substances, and ineffective parenting have all been proposed as possible causes of ADHD, but the role played by each of these factors is still uncertain (G. Daly et al., 1999; U.S. Surgeon General, 1999). Also uncertain is exactly what constitutes hyperactivity. Cultural standards about acceptable activity levels in children vary, so a "hyperactive" child in one culture might be considered merely "active" in another. Indeed, when mental health professionals from four cultures used the same

LEARN BY DOING

ACTIVE OR HYPERACTIVE? Normal behavior for children in one culture might be considered hyperactive in other cultures. Do people in the same culture disagree on this point? To find out, ask two or three friends to join you in observing a group of children at a playground, a schoolyard, a park, or some other public place. Ask your friends to privately identify which children they would label as "hyperactive," and then count how many of their choices agree with yours and with each other's.

rating scale to judge the presence and severity of hyperactivity in a videotaped sample of children's behavior, the Chinese and Indonesians rated the children as significantly more hyperactive than did their U.S. and Japanese colleagues (Mann et al., 1992). Such findings remind us that sociocultural factors can be important determinants of what is acceptable, and hence what is abnormal, in various parts of the world.

The second broad category of child behavior problems involves *internalizing,* or *overcontrol.* Children in this category experience significant distress, especially depression and anxiety, and may be socially withdrawn. Those displaying *separation anxiety disorder,* for example, constantly worry that they will be lost, kidnapped, or injured or that some harm may come to a parent (usually the mother). The child clings desperately to the parent and becomes upset or sick at the prospect of any separation. Refusal to go to school (sometimes called "school phobia") is often the result.

A few childhood disorders, such as *pervasive developmental disorders,* do not fall into either the externalizing or internalizing category. Children diagnosed with these disorders show severe deficits in communication, impaired social relationships, and, often, repetitive, stereotyped behaviors and unusual preoccupations and interests (American Psychiatric Association, 2000; Filipek et al., 1999). The disorders in this group, also known as *autistic spectrum disorders* (Filipek et al., 1999; Rutter & Schopler, 1992; USD-HHS, 1999), share many of these core symptoms, although the severity of the symptoms may vary. Autistic spectrum disorders occur in ten to twenty children per 10,000 births (Bryson & Smith, 1998; Filipek et al., 1999). About half of these children suffer *autistic disorder,* which can be the most severe disorder of the group. The earliest signs of autistic disorder usually occur within the first thirty months after birth, as these babies show little or no evidence of forming an attachment to their caregivers. Language development is seriously disrupted in most of these children; half of them never learn to speak at all. However, those who display "high functioning autism," or a less severe autistic spectrum disorder called *Asperger's disorder,* are able to function adaptively and, in some cases, independently as adults (e.g., Grandin, 1996).

Possible biological roots of autistic disorder include genetic factors (A. J. Bailey, 1993; Burac, 2001; Szatmari et al., 1998) or neurodevelopmental abnormalities affecting language and communication (Minshew, Payton, & Sclabassi, 1986; Ornitz, 1989; U.S. Surgeon General, 1999). The specific causes of autistic disorder remain unknown but it is likely that genetic influences, along with prenatal damage leading to structural brain abnormalities, are involved (Rodier, 2000; Szatmari et al., 1998; U.S. Surgeon General, 1999). Researchers today have rejected the once-popular hypothesis that its profound problems are caused by cold and unresponsive parents.

Disorders of childhood differ from adult disorders not only because the patterns of behavior are distinct but also because their early onset disrupts development. To take one example, children who attend school irregularly not only may fall behind academically but also may fail to form the relationships with other children that promote normal social development. Some children never make up for this deficit. They may drop out of school and risk a life of poverty, crime, and violence. Moreover, children depend on others to get help for their psychological problems, but all too often those problems may go unrecognized or untreated. For some, the long-term result may be adult forms of mental disorder.

Substance-Related Disorders

Childhood disorders, especially externalizing disorders, often lead to substance-related disorders in adolescence and adulthood. *DSM-IV* defines **substance-related disorders** as the use of psychoactive drugs for months or years in ways that harm oneself or others. These disorders create major political, economic, social, and health problems worldwide. The substances involved most often are alcohol and other depressants (such as barbiturates), opiates (such as heroin), stimulants (such as cocaine or amphetamines), and hallucinogens (such as LSD).

One effect of using some substances (including alcohol, heroin, and amphetamines) is **addiction,** a physical need for the substance. *DSM-IV* calls addiction *physiological*

substance-related disorders Problems involving the use of psychoactive drugs for months or years in ways that harm the user or others.

addiction The development of a physical need for a psychoactive drug.

dependence. Even when the use of a drug does not create physical addiction, some people may overuse, or *abuse,* it because it gives them temporary self-confidence, enjoyment, or relief from tension. *DSM-IV* defines *substance abuse* as a pattern of use that causes serious social, legal, or interpersonal problems. Thus, people can become *psychologically dependent* on psychoactive drugs without becoming physiologically addicted to them. People who are psychologically dependent on a drug often display problems that are at least as serious as, and sometimes more difficult to treat than, those exhibited by people who are addicted. In Chapter 4, we describe several psychoactive drugs and their impact on consciousness. Here, we focus on some of the causes and broader consequences of their use and abuse.

Alcohol Use Disorders   About 7.4 percent of U.S. adults—about 14 million people—display *alcohol dependence* or *abuse,* a pattern of continuous or off-and-on drinking that may lead to addiction and almost always causes severe social, physical, and other problems (NIAAA, 2000). Sadly, this figure is expected to increase in the twenty-first century. Males exceed females in this category by a ratio of about 3 to 1, although the problem is on the rise among women and among teenagers of both genders (Blum, Nielsen, & Riggs, 1998; USDHHS, 1997). Prolonged overuse of alcohol can result in life-threatening liver damage, reduced cognitive abilities, vitamin deficiencies that can lead to severe and permanent memory loss, and a host of other physical ailments. Alcohol dependence or abuse, commonly referred to as **alcoholism,** has been implicated in half of all the traffic fatalities, homicides, and suicides that occur each year (NIAAA, 1998). Alcoholism also figures prominently in rape and child abuse, as well as in elevated rates of hospitalization and absenteeism from work, resulting in total costs to society of over $180 *billion* each year (H. Harwood, Fountain, & Livermore, 1998; NIAAA, 2000; U.S. Department of Justice, 1998). It is estimated that about half of U.S. adults have a close relative who is or was an alcoholic, and that about 25 percent of children are exposed to adults who display alcohol abuse or dependence (NIAAA, 2000). Children growing up in families in which one or both parents abuse alcohol are at increased risk for developing a host of mental disorders, including substance-abuse disorders (Sher et al., 1991). And as described in Chapter 9, children of mothers who abused alcohol during pregnancy may be born with fetal alcohol syndrome.

The biopsychosocial model suggests that alcohol abuse stems from a combination of genetic characteristics (including inherited aspects of temperament such as impulsivity and emotionality) and what people learn in their social and cultural environment. For example, youngsters typically learn to drink by watching others (especially their friends), and by developing expectations that alcohol will make them feel good and help them cope with stressors (Koopmans & Boomsma, 1996). But alcohol use can become abuse, and often addiction, if drinking is a person's main coping strategy (NIAAA, 2000; see Table 12.6). The importance of learning is supported by evidence that alcoholism is more common among ethnic and cultural groups (such as the Irish and English) in which frequent drinking tends to be socially reinforced than among groups (such as Jews, Italians, and Chinese) in which all but moderate drinking tends to be discouraged (G. T. Wilson et al., 1996). Moreover, different forms of social support for drinking can result in different consumption patterns within a cultural group. For example, one study found significantly more drinking among Japanese men living in Japan (where social norms for males' drinking are most permissive) compared with Japanese men living in Hawaii or California, where excessive drinking is less strongly supported (Kitano et al., 1992).

Learning, then, appears to be implicated in excessive drinking, but heredity also plays a role. For example, the children of alcoholics are more likely than others to become alcoholics themselves; and if the children are identical twins, both are at increased risk for alcoholism, even when raised apart (Kendler et al., 1992; McGue, 1999; Slutske et al., 1998). The role of genetics appears to be greatest among people who begin their alcoholic drinking pattern at an early age and display other conduct problems as teenagers (McGue, Pickens, & Svikis, 1992; Slutske et al., 1998). It is still unclear just what might be inherited or which genes are involved. One possibility involves inherited abnormalities in the brain's neurotransmitter systems or in the body's metabolism of alcohol (Devor, 1994; Kranzler & Anton, 1994). Alcoholics do tend to be less sensitive than other

alcoholism A pattern of continuous or intermittent drinking that may lead to addiction and almost always causes severe social, physical, and other problems.

TABLE 12.6

Social Drinking Versus Alcoholism

Social drinking differs markedly from alcoholism, but it is all too easy for people to drift from social to alcoholic drinking patterns. Alcoholism can include heavy drinking on a daily basis, on weekends only, or in isolated binges lasting weeks or months (NIAAA, 2000).

Social Drinkers	Alcoholics
Sip drinks.	Gulp drinks.
Usually drink in moderation and can control the amount consumed.	Drink increasing quantities (develop tolerance). Sometimes drink until blacking out. May not recall events that occur while drinking.
Usually drink to enhance the pleasure of social situations.	Drink for the chemical effect, often to relieve tension or face problems. Often drink alone, including in the morning to reduce hangover or to face the day.
Do not usually think about or talk about drinking in nondrinking situations.	Become preoccupied with getting the next drink, often sneaking drinks during working hours or at home.
Do not experience physical, social, or occupational problems caused by drinking.	Suffer physical disorders, damaged social relationships, and impaired capacity to work because of drinking.

people to the effects of alcohol—a factor that may contribute to greater consumption (V. Pollack, 1992; Schuckit, 1998). Recent progress in decoding the human genome has guided researchers to focus on a few specific chromosomes as the possible location of genes that predispose people to—or protect them from—the development of alcoholism (Long et al., 1998; NIAAA, 2000; Reich et al., 1998).

Heroin and Cocaine Dependence Like alcoholics, heroin and cocaine addicts suffer many serious health problems, as a result of both the drugs themselves and the poor eating and health habits related to use of those drugs. The risk of death from overdose, contaminated drugs, or AIDS (contracted through blood in shared needles), as well as from suicide, is also always present. Drug dependence tends to be more prevalent among males, especially young males (Warner et al., 1995).

Addiction to substances like heroin and cocaine is largely seen as a biological process brought about by the physical effects of the drugs, but explaining why people first use them is more complicated. The causes of initial drug use are even less well established than the reasons for alcohol abuse. One line of theorizing suggests that there might be a genetic tendency toward behavioral compulsions that predisposes some people to abuse many kinds of drugs, including alcohol (NIAAA, 2000). One study supporting this idea found a link between alcoholism in biological parents and drug abuse in the sons they had given up for adoption (Cadoret et al., 1995). The same study also found a link between antisocial personality traits in biological parents and antisocial acts—including drug abuse—in the sons they had put up for adoption.

Psychological factors, such as the need to reduce stress, peer pressure, thrill seeking, and poor social adjustment, have all been proposed as triggers for starting to use drugs. Research has not yet established why continued drug use occurs in some people and not in others, but again, it is likely that a biological predisposition sets the stage on which specific psychological processes and stressors play out their roles.

Mental Illness and the Law

■ Can insanity protect criminals from punishment?

Have you wondered why the word *insanity* did not appear in our definition of *mental disorder*, or in the *DSM-IV* categories we have described? The reason is that *insanity* is a

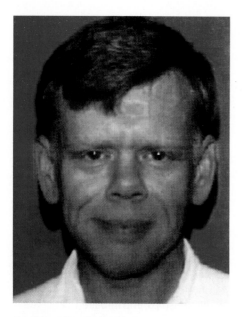

Applying Psychology

ASSESSMENT OF MENTAL INCOMPE-TENCE   Russell Eugene Weston, Jr., killed two police officers during an armed rampage at the U.S. Capitol Building in July 1998. Weston had been diagnosed two years earlier as suffering from paranoid schizophrenia, and after being examined by a psychiatrist, he was declared mentally incompetent to stand trial for the killings. He remains confined in a mental hospital. Protection from trial on criminal charges is one of several legal rights accorded to persons who display severe mental disorders.

legal term, not a psychiatric diagnosis (Cassel & Bernstein, 2001). For example, in 1984 John Hinckley, Jr., was found "not guilty by reason of insanity" for his attempted assassination of President Ronald Reagan. This verdict reflected U.S. laws and rules that protect people with severe psychological disorders when they are accused of crimes.

This protection takes two forms. First, under certain conditions, people designated as mentally ill may be protected from prosecution. If, at the time of their trial, individuals accused of a crime are unable to understand the proceedings and charges against them or to help in their own defense, they are declared *mentally incompetent* to stand trial. Second, the mentally ill may be protected from punishment. In most U.S. states, defendants may be judged *not guilty by reason of insanity* if, at the time of the crime, mental illness prevented them from (1) understanding what they were doing, (2) knowing that what they were doing was wrong, and (3) resisting the impulse to do wrong. The first two of these criteria, which relate to a person's ability to think clearly, are known as the *M'Naughton rule*. The third criterion, which relates to one's emotional state, is known as the *irresistible impulse test*. All three were combined in a rule proposed by the American Law Institute in 1962—a rule that is now followed in many U.S. states.

After the Hinckley verdict, the U.S. Congress passed the Insanity Defense Reform Act, which eliminated the irresistible impulse criterion from the definition of insanity in federal cases. In both federal and state courts, however, the responsibility falls on judges and juries to weigh evidence and testimony and decide whether or not a defendant should be held responsible for criminal acts. Defendants who are judged not guilty by reason of insanity and who still display a psychological disorder are usually required to receive treatment, typically through commitment to a hospital, until judged to be cured or no longer dangerous. Twelve U.S. states have laws allowing jurors to find defendants "guilty but mentally ill." These defendants are to receive treatment while in prison, though they seldom do (Cassel & Bernstein, 2001).

Critics of insanity rules complain that these rules allow criminals to "get away with murder." Actually, such outcomes are rare. Insanity pleas occur in only 1 out of every 200 criminal felony cases in the United States, and they are successful in only 2 of every 1,000 attempts (E. Silver, Cirincione, & Steadman, 1994). Even the few defendants found not guilty by reason of insanity are usually hospitalized for two to nine times as long as they would have spent in prison had they been convicted (E. Silver, 1995; Steadman, 1993). John Hinckley, Jr., has been in Saint Elizabeth's hospital in Washington, D.C., since 1982, and in spite of his annual efforts to be released, he is unlikely to get out any time soon (B. Miller, 1998).

Society is constantly seeking the proper balance between protecting the rights of defendants and protecting society from dangerous criminals. In doing so, the sociocultural values that shape our views about what is abnormal also influence judgments about the extent to which abnormality should relieve people of responsibility for criminal behavior.

active review   Psychological Disorders

Linkages

As noted in Chapter 1, all of psychology's subfields are related to one another. Our discussion of how mental disorders might be learned illustrates just one way in which the topic of this chapter, psychological disorders, is linked to the subfield of learning (Chapter 5). The Linkages diagram shows ties to two other subfields as well, and there are many more ties throughout the book. Looking for linkages among subfields will help you see how they all fit together and help you better appreciate the big picture that is psychology.

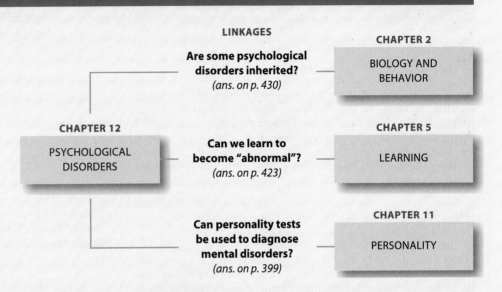

LINKAGES

CHAPTER 12
PSYCHOLOGICAL DISORDERS

Are some psychological disorders inherited?
(ans. on p. 430)

CHAPTER 2
BIOLOGY AND BEHAVIOR

Can we learn to become "abnormal"?
(ans. on p. 423)

CHAPTER 5
LEARNING

Can personality tests be used to diagnose mental disorders?
(ans. on p. 399)

CHAPTER 11
PERSONALITY

Summary

Psychopathology involves patterns of thinking, feeling, and behaving that are maladaptive, disruptive, or distressing—either for the person affected or for others.

DEFINING PSYCHOLOGICAL DISORDERS

How do psychologists define abnormal behavior?

The definition of abnormality is largely determined by social and cultural factors. The criteria for judging abnormality include statistical infrequency (a comparison with what most people do), norm violations, and personal suffering. Each of these criteria is flawed to some extent. The practical approach, which considers the content, context, and consequences of behavior, emphasizes the question of whether people show *impaired functioning* in fulfilling the roles appropriate for particular people in particular settings, cultures, and historical eras.

EXPLAINING PSYCHOLOGICAL DISORDERS

What causes abnormality?

At various times and places, abnormal behavior has been attributed to the action of gods or the devil. Mental health professionals in Western cultures rely on a *biopsychosocial model,* which attributes mental disorders to a combination of biological, psychological, and sociocultural factors. Biological factors, such as brain chemistry, are emphasized in the medical or *neurobiological model* of disorder. The *psychological model* focuses on processes such as inner turmoil, maladaptive learning experiences, or blocked self-actualization. The *sociocultural model* helps to explain disorder by highlighting gender, ethnicity, and other social and cultural factors that form the context of abnormality.

The *diathesis-stress approach* suggests that biological, psychological, and sociocultural characteristics create predispositions for disorder that are translated into symptoms in the face of sufficient amounts of stress.

CLASSIFYING PSYCHOLOGICAL DISORDERS

How many psychological disorders have been identified?

The dominant system for classifying abnormal behavior in North America is the fourth edition of the *Diagnostic and Statistical Manual of Mental Disorders (DSM-IV)* of the American Psychiatric Association. It includes more than 300 specific categories of mental disorder that can be described using five dimensions, or axes. Diagnosis helps to identify the features, causes, and most effective methods of treating various psychological disorders. Research on the reliability and validity of the *DSM-IV* shows that it is a useful, but not perfect, classification system.

ANXIETY DISORDERS

What is a phobia?

Long-standing and disruptive patterns of anxiety characterize *anxiety disorders.* The most prevalent type of anxiety disorder is *phobia,* a category that includes *specific phobias, social phobias,* and *agoraphobia.* Other anxiety disorders are *generalized anxiety disorder,* which involves nonspecific anxiety; *panic disorder,* which brings unpredictable attacks of intense anxiety; and *obsessive-compulsive disorder (OCD),* which is characterized by uncontrollable repetitive thoughts and ritualistic actions.

The most influential explanations of anxiety disorders suggest that they may develop as a result of a combination of a biological predisposition for strong anxiety reactions and the impact of fear-enhancing thought patterns and learned anxiety responses. Many anxiety disorders appear to develop in accordance with the principles of classical and operant conditioning, as well as with those of observational learning. People may be biologically prepared to learn fear of certain objects and situations.

SOMATOFORM DISORDERS

Can mental disorder cause blindness?

Somatoform disorders include *conversion disorder,* which involves physical problems, such as blindness, deafness, and paralysis, that have no apparent physical cause; *hypochondriasis,* an unjustified concern over being or becoming ill; *somatization disorder,* in which the person complains of numerous unconfirmed physical complaints; and *pain disorder,* in which pain is felt in the absence of a physical cause.

DISSOCIATIVE DISORDERS

What disorders create sudden memory loss?

Dissociative disorders involve such rare conditions as *dissociative fugue* and *dissociative amnesia,* both of which involve sudden and severe memory loss, and *dissociative identity disorder (DID),* or multiple personality disorder, in which a person appears to develop two or more identities. There has been considerable controversy recently about the origins of dissociative identity disorder.

MOOD DISORDERS

How common is depression?

Mood disorders, also known as affective disorders, are quite common and involve extreme moods that may be inconsistent with events. *Major depressive disorder* is marked by feelings of inadequacy, worthlessness, and guilt; in extreme cases, *delusions* may also occur. Also seen is *dysthymic disorder,* which includes similar but less severe symptoms persisting for a long period. Suicide is often related to these disorders. Alternating periods of depression and *mania* characterize *bipolar disorder,* which is also known as manic depression. *Cyclothymic disorder,* an alternating pattern of less extreme mood swings, is more common.

Mood disorders have been attributed to biological causes such as genetic inheritance, disruptions in neurotransmitter and endocrine systems, and irregularities in biological rhythms. Significant stressors, and maladaptive patterns of thinking about them, are among the psychological causes proposed. A predisposition toward some of these disorders may be inherited, although their appearance is probably determined by a diathesis-stress process.

SCHIZOPHRENIA

Is schizophrenia the same as "split personality"?

Schizophrenia is perhaps the most severe and puzzling disorder of all. Among its symptoms are problems in thinking, perception (often including *hallucinations*), attention, emotion, movement, motivation, and daily functioning. Positive symptoms of schizophrenia include the presence of such features as hallucinations or disordered speech; negative symptoms can include withdrawal, immobility, and the absence of affect.

Genetic factors, neurotransmitter problems, abnormalities in brain structure and functioning, and neurodevelopmental abnormalities are biological factors implicated in schizophrenia. Psychological explanations have pointed to maladaptive learning experiences and disturbed family interactions. The diathesis-stress approach, often described in terms of vulnerability theory, remains a promising framework for research into the multiple causes of schizophrenia.

PERSONALITY DISORDERS

Which personality disorder often leads to crime?

Personality disorders are long-term patterns of maladaptive behavior that, although not always associated with personal discomfort, may be disturbing to others. These include odd-eccentric types (paranoid, schizoid, and schizotypal personality disorders), anxious-fearful types (dependent, obsessive-compulsive, and avoidant personality disorders), and dramatic-erratic types (histrionic, narcissistic, borderline, and antisocial personality disorders). *Antisocial personality disorder* is marked by impulsive, irresponsible, unscrupulous behavior patterns that often begin in childhood. Childhood abuse appears to be related to the appearance of this potentially dangerous personality disorder.

A SAMPLING OF OTHER PSYCHOLOGICAL DISORDERS

How do children's disorders differ from adults' disorders?

Childhood psychological disorders can be categorized as externalizing conditions (such as conduct disorders or attention deficit hyperactivity disorder) and as internalizing disorders, in which children show overcontrol, experiencing internal distress (as in separation anxiety disorder). The most severe childhood psychological disorder is autistic disorder, in which the child may show no interest in, or attachment to, others.

Substance-related disorders involving alcohol and other drugs affect millions of people. *Addiction* to, and psychological dependence on, these substances contributes to disastrous personal and social problems, including physical illnesses, accidents, and crime. Genetic factors probably create a predisposition for *alcoholism,* but learning, cultural traditions, and other nonbiological processes are also important. Stress reduction, imitation, thrill seeking, and social maladjustment have been proposed as important factors in drug addiction, along with genetic predisposition; but the exact causes of initial use of these drugs are unknown.

MENTAL ILLNESS AND THE LAW

Can insanity protect criminals from punishment?

"Insanity" is a legal term, not a psychiatric diagnosis. Current rules protect people accused of crimes from prosecution or punishment if they are declared "mentally incompetent" at the time of their trial or if they were legally insane at the time of their crime. Defendants judged "not guilty by reason of insanity" and who still display a psychological disorder are usually required to receive treatment until judged to be cured or no longer dangerous. Those found "guilty but mentally ill" are to receive treatment in prison.

Learn by Doing

Put It in Writing

Think about something you have seen someone do recently that you considered truly abnormal. Now write a page describing what happened, and the specific rules or criteria—such as statistical infrequency, norm violation, personal suffering, or impaired functioning—that you used in deciding that this person's behavior qualifies as abnormal. Include a statement about whether you think this person should be treated for his or her behavior problem. Mention also why you think this behavior would be considered abnormal by other people in your culture, and whether you think people in other cultures would agree.

Personal Learning Activity

To what extent do people agree on what is abnormal? To find out, ask at least twenty friends, family members, teachers, classmates in other courses, casual acquaintances, and maybe even some strangers to read your description of the behavior you diagnosed as abnormal in the Put It in Writing exercise. (Show them only the description, not your comments.) Ask these people to tell you if they think the behavior is normal, merely odd, or seriously abnormal, and if they think the person is in need of treatment. Analyze the results in terms of how many of these people agreed with your diagnosis, and with one another. Did you notice any trends in their responses based on age, gender, educational status, or cultural background? What do your results say about how easy or difficult it is to precisely define abnormality? *For additional projects, see the five Personal Learning Activities in the corresponding chapter of the study guide that accompanies this text.*

Step into Action

Courses

Abnormal Psychology
Child Psychopathology
Psychology and the Law

Movies

One Flew over the Cuckoo's Nest (life in a state mental hospital of the 1960s)
Three Faces of Eve; Sybil (dissociative identity disorder)
Vertigo (anxiety disorders)
As Good as it Gets (obsessive-compulsive disorder)
The Days of Wine and Roses; Leaving Las Vegas (alcoholism)
Trainspotting (heroin addiction)
In Cold Blood; Natural Born Killers (antisocial personality disorder)
Man on the Moon (defining abnormality)
Anatomy of a Murder (use of the insanity defense in a murder case)

Books

Karlene K. Hale, *Being There: Profiles of Mental Illness* (Diligaf, 1997) (case studies of mental disorder)
Clark R. Clipson and Jocelyn M. Steer, *Case Studies in Abnormal Psychology* (Houghton Mifflin, 1998) (more case studies)
Charles D. Mellon, *The Genetic Basis of Abnormal Human Behavior* (Genetics Heritage Publishing, 1997) (a summary of research on the genetics of abnormality)
Joan Acocella, *Creating Hysteria: Women and Multiple Personality Disorder* (Jossey-Bass, 1999) (a description of the influence of culture and other social forces in shaping dissociative identity disorder)
Robert Spitzer, Miriam Gibson, Andrew Skodol, Janet Williams, and Michael First, *DSM-IV Casebook: A Learning Companion to the Diagnostic and Statistical Manual of Mental Disorders* (American Psychiatric Press, 1994) (a casebook illustrating the disorders listed in the *DSM-IV*)
Meyer Glantz and Christine Hartel (Eds.), *Drug Abuse: Origins and Interventions* (American Psychological Association, 2000) (information that challenges various myths about drug abuse)

The Web

The World Wide Web is a good source of additional information about the science of psychology, provided you use it carefully and think critically about the information you find. The PsychAbilities web site that accompanies this text offers many resources relevant to this chapter. These resources include interactive NetLab exercises; Thinking Critically and Evaluating Research exercises; ACE chapter quizzes; recommended web links; and articles on current events, books, and movies. At http://college.hmco.com, select *Psychology* and then this textbook.

Review of Key Terms

Can you define each of the key terms in the chapter? Check your definitions against those on the pages listed in parentheses below or in the Glossary/Index at the end of the text.

addiction *(p. 441)*

agoraphobia *(p. 421)*

alcoholism *(p. 442)*

antisocial personality disorder *(p. 438)*

anxiety disorder *(p. 420)*

biopsychosocial model *(p. 412)*

bipolar disorder *(p. 429)*

conversion disorder *(p. 424)*

cyclothymic disorder *(p. 430)*

delusions *(p. 427)*

diathesis-stress approach *(p. 415)*

dissociative amnesia *(p. 426)*

dissociative disorders *(p. 425)*

dissociative fugue *(p. 426)*

dissociative identity disorder (DID) *(p. 426)*

dysthymic disorder *(p. 428)*

generalized anxiety disorder *(p. 421)*

hallucinations *(p. 434)*

hypochondriasis *(p. 424)*

impaired functioning *(p. 411)*

major depressive disorder *(p. 427)*

mania *(p. 429)*

mood disorder *(p. 427)*

neurobiological model *(p. 413)*

obsessive-compulsive disorder (OCD) *(p. 422)*

pain disorder *(p. 424)*

panic disorder *(p. 421)*

personality disorders *(p. 437)*

phobia *(p. 420)*

psychological model *(p. 413)*

psychopathology *(p. 409)*

schizophrenia *(p. 433)*

social phobias *(p. 421)*

sociocultural model *(p. 414)*

somatization disorder *(p. 424)*

somatoform disorders *(p. 424)*

specific phobias *(p. 420)*

substance-related disorders *(p. 441)*

Multiple-Choice Self-Test

Select the best answer for each of the questions below. Then check your response against the Answer Key at the end of the text.

1. According to the statistics on psychopathology, in the United States ———— of the population experience a mental disorder in their lifetime.

   a. less than 5%
   b. approximately 25%
   c. almost 50%
   d. over 75%

2. Babette, a successful opera singer, believes that aliens could snatch her at any time if she isn't wearing her lucky charm. She is constantly worried and insists that the stage be rimmed with foil to ward off evil spirits. According to which criterion of abnormality would Babette *not* be considered abnormal?

   a. statistical
   b. norm violation
   c. practical approach
   d. personal suffering

3. In Western cultures after the Middle Ages, there was a large growth in institutions for the insane. This phenomenon was the result of the ———— model of explaining psychological disorders.

   a. sociocultural
   b. medical
   c. supernatural
   d. psychological

4. Roberta and Rhonda are identical twins who inherited identical predispositions for depression. Roberta has lived an easy life and has not developed any depressive symptoms. Rhonda, who has been divorced and lost several jobs over the years, has been diagnosed with major depressive disorder. The difference between these twins is most consistent with the ———— approach to abnormality.

   a. neurobiological
   b. psychological
   c. sociocultural
   d. diathesis-stress

5. Dr. Kramer is evaluating a patient brought in for psychiatric treatment. In his report he indicates that his global assessment of the patient's functioning is about 30 on a 100-point scale. Dr. Kramer is using ———— to evaluate the patient.

   a. the M'Naughton rule
   b. norm violation criteria
   c. insanity criteria
   d. *DSM-IV*

6. Kat dropped out of school because the thought of leaving her apartment makes her feeling nauseated, anxious, and faint. She can't even go out to the mailbox without suffering anxiety. Kat most likely would be diagnosed with

   a. agoraphobia.
   b. simple phobia.
   c. generalized anxiety disorder.
   d. social phobia.

7. Terraba had a difficult time driving to work. Every time she went over a bump she had to drive back around to make sure that she had not run over anything. This occurred ten or twelve times each day, so Terraba was always late for everything. Terraba appears to be suffering from

   a. specific phobia.
   b. panic attacks.
   c. OCD.
   d. generalized anxiety disorder.

8. Conversion disorder is characterized by

   a. impairment of movement or sensory ability with no apparent physical cause.
   b. severe pain with no apparent physical cause.
   c. fear of becoming seriously ill.
   d. frequent, vague complaints of physical symptoms.

9. Tomas has been suffering severe back pain for several weeks, but extensive medical tests reveal no physical problem. Tomas appears to be displaying

   a. pain disorder.
   b. hypochondriasis.
   c. paranoid schizophrenia.
   d. somatization disorder.

10. Einer displays many different personalities. One is a young girl named Lili. Another is a five-year old boy. Each personality is unaware of the others. Einer is displaying symptoms of

    a. dissociative fugue.
    b. dissociative identity disorder.
    c. obsessive-compulsive disorder.
    d. schizophrenia.

11. Over the past three months, Barb has been feeling very sad; she has been sleeping as much as fifteen hours a day and has gained 30 pounds. Debbie, too, feels very low, but she can barely sleep and has lost both her appetite and 15 pounds. Both Barb and Debbie have symptoms of

    a. obsessive-compulsive disorder.
    b. major depressive disorder.
    c. bipolar disorder.
    d. hypochondriasis.

12. Suicide is closely tied to depression. Studies of suicide in the United States have found that

    a. people who talk about suicide typically do not commit suicide.
    b. males over the age of forty-five who are living alone are the most likely to commit suicide.
    c. suicide rates do not vary across ethnic groups or between men and women.
    d. depressed women almost never commit suicide.

13. Carlisle has been very depressed. He can't face his responsibilities and often spends days at a time in bed. A psychologist who adopts the social-cognitive approach would be most likely to see this depression as caused by

    a. Carlisle's attributional style.
    b. brain chemicals.
    c. unconscious conflicts.
    d. blocked self-actualization.

14. As you sit down next to a disheveled person on a bus, the person says, "Ohms vibrate orange and dishwrings obvious dictionary." The person continues to talk in this manner, so based on your reading of this chapter, you decide that this person is displaying symptoms of

    a. anxiety disorder.
    b. dissociative identity disorder.
    c. schizophrenia.
    d. somatoform disorder.

15. Juan has been diagnosed with schizophrenia. He says he is certain that all the students sitting around him during a test are cheating by reading his thoughts. Juan is displaying a symptom known as thought _____.

    a. blocking
    b. insertion
    c. withdrawal
    d. broadcasting

16. Forty-year-old Richard believes that he was ordered by God to save the world. He is suspicious of other people because he thinks they want to prevent him from fulfilling his mission. He is unable to keep a job because he is angry and argumentative most of the time. Richard would most likely be diagnosed as displaying

    a. mood disorder.
    b. dissociative identity disorder.
    c. paranoid schizophrenia.
    d. catatonic schizophrenia.

17. Al is charming and intelligent, but he has always been irresponsible, impulsive, and unscrupulous. None of his girlfriends knows he is dating other women. He borrows money from friends and doesn't pay it back. He doesn't care about anyone else, including his family. Al would probably be diagnosed as displaying _____ personality disorder.

    a. antisocial
    b. narcissistic
    c. passive-aggressive
    d. inadequate

18. Cathy Widom's research study, discussed in the Focus on Research section, found that there was a relationship between antisocial personality disorder and

    a. narcissistic personality disorder.
    b. schizophrenia.
    c. high intelligence.
    d. being abused as a child.

19. Angelo drinks alcohol until he passes out. He is unable to hold a job or take care of himself. Angelo would most likely be diagnosed with

    a. a substance-related disorder.
    b. undercontrolled disorder.
    c. schizophrenia.
    d. a personality disorder.

20. Aaron is an infant who shows no signs of attachment to his parents. He dislikes being held and doesn't smile or laugh. Aaron's symptoms are most consistent with

    a. infantile schizophrenia.
    b. autistic disorder.
    c. antisocial personality disorder.
    d. an externalizing disorder of childhood.

13

Treatment of Psychological Disorders

Have you ever sought help for a psychological problem? Do you know someone who has?

Being treated for psychological problems was once considered a shameful admission of failure or even a sign of "insanity." Today, however, the decision to get professional help for anxiety, depression, relationship difficulties, or many other troublesome personal situations is widely viewed as proper and sensible. Even if you have no personal experience with psychotherapy, you probably know something about it from magazines and newspapers, and you have probably seen psychotherapy sessions in movies such as *Good Will Hunting* and on television shows such as *The Sopranos*. Unfortunately, these brief portrayals do not convey what psychotherapy is really like, and even the best of them tell only part of the story of how psychological disorders can be treated. In this chapter we describe a wide range of treatment options, including methods based on psychodynamic, phenomenological, behavioral, and biological theories of psychological disorders. We also consider research on the effectiveness of treatment and methods for preventing disorders.

Reading this chapter will help you to answer the following questions:

- **What features do all treatment techniques have in common?**
- **How did Freud get started as a therapist?**
- **Why won't some therapists give advice?**
- **Can we learn to conquer fears?**
- **How does group therapy differ from individual therapy?**
- **How effective is psychotherapy?**
- **Is electric shock still used to treat disorders?**
- **How can we prevent psychological disorders?**

In Chapter 12, we described José, a fifty-five-year-old electronics technician who had to take medical leave from his job after experiencing panic attacks. After four months of diagnostic testing turned up no physical problems, José's physician suggested that he see a psychologist. José resisted at first, insisting that his condition was not "just in his head," but he eventually began psychological treatment. Within a few months, his panic attacks had ceased, and José had returned to all his old activities. After the psychologist helped him to reconsider his workload, José decided to retire from his job in order to pursue more satisfying work at his home-based computer business.

José's case is by no means unique. During any given year in the United States alone, about 15 percent of adults and about 21 percent of children and adolescents are receiving some form of treatment for a psychological disorder, including substance abuse problems (U.S. Surgeon General, 1999). The economic impact of mental disorders—in treatment costs, disability payments, and lost productivity—is staggering, reaching $150 billion per year in the United States alone. Fortunately, the treatments that are available today for various disorders can pay for themselves. The savings realized from treatment are actually greater than its costs (Clay, 2000a; National Institute of Mental Health, 1998b).

In this chapter, we describe a variety of treatment methods, most of which are based on the theories of stress and coping, personality, and psychological disorders reviewed in Chapters 10, 11, and 12. First, we examine the basic features common to all forms of treatment. Then we discuss approaches that rely on **psychotherapy,** the treatment of psychological disorders through psychological methods, such as talking about problems and exploring new ways of thinking and acting. Next, we consider biological approaches to treatment, which depend mainly on drugs and other physical therapies. (Many clients receive psychoactive drugs in addition to therapy during the course of psychological treatment.)

Basic Features of Treatment

■ What features do all treatment techniques have in common?

All treatments for psychological disorders share certain basic features—not only with one another but also with efforts to help the physically ill (J. S. Frank, 1978). These common features include a *client* or *patient,* a *therapist* or helper who is accepted as capable of helping the client, and a special relationship between the client and therapist. In addition, all forms of treatment are based on some *theory* about the causes of the client's problems (Corsini & Wedding, 1995; Dumont & Corsini, 2000). The presumed causes can range from magic spells to infections and everything in between (J. D. Frank & Frank, 1991). From causal theories come *procedures* for dealing with the client's problems. Thus, traditional healers combat supernatural forces with ceremonies and prayers, medical doctors treat chemical imbalances with drugs, and psychologists focus on altering psychological processes through psychotherapy.

People receiving treatment can be classified into two general categories: inpatients and outpatients. *Inpatients* are treated in a hospital or other residential institution. They are hospitalized because their impairments are severe enough to create a threat to their own well-being or that of others. Depending on their level of functioning, inpatients' stays in the hospital can range from a few days to several years. Their treatment almost always includes psychoactive drugs. *Outpatients* receive psychotherapy and/or psychoactive drugs while living in the community.

Those who provide psychological treatment are a diverse group. **Psychiatrists** are medical doctors who complete specialty training in the treatment of mental disorders. Like other physicians, they are authorized to prescribe drugs for the relief of psychological problems. **Psychologists** who offer psychotherapy have usually completed a doctoral degree in clinical or counseling psychology, often followed by additional specialized training. Psychologists are not authorized to prescribe drugs, although a controversial proposal to allow specially trained clinical psychologists to do so is currently being debated (Kilbey, 1999; P. A. McGuire, 1998; Rabasca, 1999a). *Clinical social workers, marriage and family therapists,* and *licensed professional counselors* typically hold a master's degree from a graduate program in their respective fields. They provide treatment in many settings, including hospitals, clinics, and private practice. *Psychiatric nurses, substance abuse counselors,* members of the clergy who become *pastoral counselors,* and a host of *paraprofessionals* also provide therapy services, often as part of a hospital or outpatient treatment team (U.S. Surgeon General, 1999). Recent surveys suggest that

psychotherapy   The treatment of psychological disorders through psychological methods, such as analyzing problems, talking about possible solutions, and encouraging more adaptive ways of thinking and acting.

psychiatrists   Medical doctors who have completed special training in the treatment of mental disorders and are authorized to prescribe drugs.

psychologists   In the area of treatment, therapists with advanced training in clinical or counseling psychology.

MEDIEVAL TREATMENT METHODS
Methods used to treat psychological disorders have always been related to the presumed cause of those disorders. In medieval times, when demons were widely blamed for abnormal behavior, physician-priests tried to make the victim's body inhospitable to evil spirits. Here, we see a depiction of such spirits leaving an afflicted person's head as it is placed in an oven.

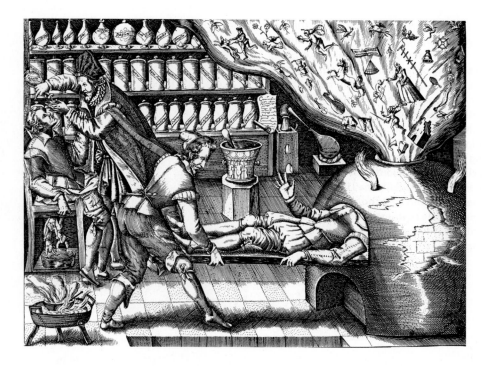

troubled people are increasingly likely to seek help from psychologists and other non-medical helpers (Swindle et al., 2000).

The general goal of treatment providers is to help troubled people change their thinking, feelings, and behavior in ways that relieve discomfort; promote happiness; and improve functioning as parents, students, workers, and the like. The particular methods used in each case—whether some form of psychotherapy, a drug treatment, or both—depend on the problems, preferences, and financial circumstances of the client; the time available for treatment; and the therapist's theoretical leanings, methodological preferences, and professional qualifications. Later, we will discuss drugs and other biological treatments; for now, however, let's consider several forms of psychotherapy, each of which is based on psychodynamic, phenomenological, or behavioral explanations of mental disorder.

Although we describe different approaches in separate sections, keep in mind that the majority of mental health professionals see themselves as *eclectic therapists*. As eclectics, they might lean toward one treatment approach, but in working with particular clients or particular problems, they borrow methods from other types of therapy as well (Jensen, Bergin, & Greaves, 1990; Northcut & Heller, 1999).

Psychodynamic Psychotherapy

How did Freud get started as a therapist?

The field of formal psychotherapy began in the late nineteenth century when Sigmund Freud established the psychodynamic approach to personality and mental disorder (see Chapter 11). Freud's method of treatment, **psychoanalysis,** is aimed at understanding unconscious conflicts and how they affect clients. Almost all forms of psychotherapy reflect some of Freud's ideas, including (1) his one-to-one method of treating people, (2) his systematic search for relationships between an individual's life history and current problems, (3) his emphasis on thoughts and emotions in treatment, and (4) his focus on the client-therapist relationship. We will describe Freud's original methods first and then consider some more recent treatments that are rooted in his psychodynamic approach.

psychoanalysis A method of psychotherapy that seeks to help clients gain insight into, and work through, unconscious thoughts and emotions presumed to cause psychological problems.

FREUD'S CONSULTING ROOM During psychoanalytic sessions, Freud's patients lay on this couch, free-associating or describing dreams and events in their lives, while he sat in the chair behind them. According to Freud, even apparently trivial or accidental behavior may hold important messages from the unconscious. Thus, forgetting a dream or missing a therapy appointment might reflect a client's unconscious resistance to treatment. Even accidents may be meaningful. The waiter who spills hot soup on an elderly male customer might be seen as acting out unconscious aggressive impulses against a father figure.

Classical Psychoanalysis

Classical psychoanalysis developed mainly out of Freud's medical practice. He was puzzled by patients who suffered from "hysterical" ailments—blindness, paralysis, or other symptoms that had no physical cause. (As noted in Chapter 12, these are now called *conversion disorders*.) Freud tried to cure these patients with hypnotic suggestions, but he found this method to be only partially and temporarily successful. Later, he asked hypnotized patients to recall events that might have caused their symptoms. Eventually, however, he stopped using hypnosis and merely had patients lie on a couch and report whatever thoughts, memories, or images came to mind. Freud called this process *free association*.

Freud's "talking cure" produced surprising results. He was struck by how many patients reported childhood memories of sexual abuse, usually by a parent or other close relative. Either child abuse was rampant in Vienna or his patients' reports were distorted by psychological factors. Freud ultimately concluded that his patients' memories of childhood seduction probably reflected fantasies—a conclusion that triggered a controversy that has lasted for over a hundred years (see Chapter 11). Accordingly, psychoanalysis came to focus on exploring unconscious impulses and fantasies. His patients' hysterical symptoms, Freud concluded, developed out of conflicts about those impulses and fantasies.

Classical psychoanalytic treatment involves the use of free association, dream analysis, and analysis of the way the client reacts to the therapist (called *transference*) to help the client gain insight into problems. The client is encouraged to recognize unconscious thoughts and emotions, and then to discover, or *work through,* the many ways in which those unconscious elements affect everyday life. The treatment may require as many as three to five sessions per week, usually over several years. Generally, the psychoanalyst remains compassionate but neutral during treatment, as the client slowly develops insight into how past conflicts have shaped current problems.

Contemporary Variations on Psychoanalysis

Though classical psychoanalysis is still practiced, it is not as prevalent as it was several decades ago (Horgan, 1996). The decline is due in part to the availability of many alternative forms of treatment, including variations on classical psychoanalysis. Many of these variations were developed by neo-Freudian theorists. As noted in Chapter 11, these theorists placed less emphasis than Freud did on biologically based drives coming from the id and the unconscious. They focused on the role played by social relationships in clients' problems and how the power of the ego can be harnessed to solve them.

Applying Psychology

A PLAY THERAPY SESSION
Modern versions of psychoanalytic treatment include fantasy play and other techniques that make the approach more useful with children. A child's behavior and comments while playing with puppets representing family members, for example, allow a form of free association that the therapist hopes will reveal important unconscious material, such as fear of abandonment (Booth & Lindaman, 2000).

Psychotherapists who adopt various neo-Freudian treatment methods tend to take a much more active role than classical analysts do—in particular, by directing the client's attention to evidence of certain conflicts in social relationships.

Many of these methods have come to be known as *short-term dynamic psychotherapy* because they aim to provide benefits in far less time than is required in classical psychoanalysis (Davanloo, 1999). In one short-term psychodynamic treatment called *supportive-expressive therapy,* the therapist helps the client recognize a "core conflict" that appears repeatedly across a variety of relationships, including the therapy relationship (Luborsky, 1997). In another particularly popular contemporary psychodynamic approach, called *object relations therapy* (Scharff & Scharff, 1998; St. Clair, 1999), the powerful need for human contact and support takes center stage. Object relations therapists believe that most of the problems that bring clients to treatment ultimately stem from their relationships with others, especially their earliest caregivers. (The term *object* usually refers to a person who has emotional significance for the client.) Object relations therapists work to develop a nurturing relationship with their clients, providing a "second chance" for these clients to receive the support that might have been absent in infancy and to counteract some of the consequences of maladaptive early attachment patterns (A. Lieberman & Pawl, 1988). For example, the therapist takes pains to demonstrate that he or she will not abandon the client.

With their focus on interpersonal relationships rather than instincts, their emphasis on clients' potential for self-directed problem solving, and their reassurance and emotional supportiveness, contemporary variants on classical psychoanalysis have helped the psychodynamic approach to retain its influence among mental health professionals (Westen & Gabbard, 1999).

Phenomenological Psychotherapy

■ **Why won't some therapists give advice?**

Whereas some therapists revised Freud's ideas, others developed radical new therapies based on a phenomenological approach to personality (see Chapter 11). *Phenomenologists,* also sometimes called *humanistic psychologists,* emphasize the ways in which people interpret the events in their lives. They view people as capable of consciously controlling their own actions and taking responsibility for their decisions. Many phenomenological therapists believe that human behavior is motivated not by sexual or aggressive instincts but by an innate drive toward growth that is guided from moment to moment by the way people interpret the world. Disordered behavior, they say, reflects a blockage in natural growth brought on by distorted perceptions or lack of awareness about feelings. Accordingly, phenomenological therapists operate on the following assumptions:

1. Treatment is a human encounter between equals, not a "cure" given by an expert. It is a way to help clients restart their natural growth and to feel and behave in a more genuine way.

2. Clients will improve on their own, given the right conditions. These ideal conditions promote clients' awareness, acceptance, and expression of their feelings and perceptions.

3. Ideal conditions in therapy can best be established through a therapeutic relationship in which clients are made to feel accepted and supported as human beings, no matter how problematic or undesirable their behavior may be. It is the client's experience of this relationship that brings beneficial changes.

4. Clients must remain responsible for choosing how they will think and behave.

Of the many phenomenological treatments in use today, the most influential are client-centered therapy, developed by Carl Rogers, and Gestalt therapy, developed by Frederick and Laura Perls.

Client-Centered Therapy

Carl Rogers was trained to use psychodynamic therapy methods during the 1930s, but he soon began to question their value. He especially disliked being a detached expert who "figured out" the client. Eventually convinced that a less formal approach would be more effective, Rogers allowed his clients to decide what to talk about and when, without direction, judgment, or interpretation by the therapist. This approach, now called **client-centered**—or **person-centered—therapy,** relies on the creation of a relationship that reflects three intertwined therapist attitudes: unconditional positive regard, empathy, and congruence.

Unconditional Positive Regard   The attitude Rogers called **unconditional positive regard** consists of nothing more or less than treating the client as a valued person, no matter what. This attitude is communicated through the therapist's willingness to listen, without interrupting, and to accept what is said without evaluating it. The therapist need not *approve* of everything the client says, just *accept* it as reflecting a part of the person who said it. Because Rogerian therapists trust clients to solve their own problems, they rarely give advice. Doing so, said Rogers, would send clients an unspoken message that they are incompetent, making them less confident and more dependent on help.

Empathy   In addition, the client-centered therapist tries not to look at clients from the outside, as a stranger might, but rather tries to see the world as the client sees it. In other words, the therapist tries to develop **empathy,** an emotional understanding of what the client might be thinking and feeling. Client-centered therapists convey empathy by showing that they are *actively listening* to the client. Like other skillful interviewers, they make eye contact with the patient, nod in recognition as the client speaks, and give other signs of careful attention. They also use **reflection,** a paraphrased summary of the client's words and especially the feelings and meanings that appear to go along with them. Reflection is a good way to confirm what the client has said while also expressing the therapist's interest and helping the client to be aware of the thoughts and feelings expressed. Here is an example:

client-centered therapy   A type of therapy in which the client decides what to talk about and when, without direction, judgment, or interpretation from the therapist. Also called *person-centered therapy.*

person-centered therapy   See *client-centered therapy.*

unconditional positive regard   In client-centered therapy, the therapist's attitude that expresses caring for, and acceptance of, the client as a valued person.

empathy   In client-centered therapy, the therapist's attempt to appreciate how the world looks from the client's point of view.

reflection   Restating or paraphrasing what the client has said.

A CLIENT-CENTERED THERAPY GROUP Carl Rogers (shown here in shirtsleeves) believed that as successful client-centered therapy progresses, clients become more self-confident, more aware of their feelings, more accepting of themselves, more comfortable and genuine with other people, more reliant on self-evaluation than on the judgments of others, and more effective and relaxed.

Client: This has been such a bad day. I've felt ready to cry any minute, and I'm not even sure what's wrong!

Therapist: You really do feel so bad. The tears just seem to well up inside, and I wonder if it is a little scary to not even know why you feel this way.

Notice that by rephrasing the client's statements, the therapist reflected back not only the obvious feelings of sadness but also the fear in the client's voice. Most clients respond to empathic reflection by giving more details about their feelings. In this example, the client went on to say, "It *is* scary, because I don't like to feel in the dark about myself. I have always prided myself on being in control."

Empathic listening tends to be so effective in promoting self-understanding and awareness that it is used across a wide range of therapies (Corsini & Wedding, 1995). Even outside of therapy, people who are thought of as easy to talk to often tend to be "good listeners" who reflect back the important messages they hear from others.

Congruence   Rogerian therapists also try to convey **congruence** (sometimes called *genuineness*) by acting in ways that are consistent with their feelings during therapy. For example, if confused by what a client has said, they would say so rather than trying to pretend that they always understand everything. When the therapist's unconditional positive regard and empathy are genuine, the client is able to see that relationships can be built on openness and honesty. Ideally, this experience will help the client become more congruent in other relationships.

Gestalt Therapy

Another form of phenomenological treatment was developed by Frederick S. (Fritz) Perls, along with his wife, Laura. A European psychoanalyst, Frederick Perls was greatly influenced by Gestalt psychology. (As noted in Chapter 3, on sensation and perception, Gestalt psychologists emphasized the idea that people actively organize their perceptions of the world.) As a result, he believed that (1) people create their own versions of reality, and (2) people's natural psychological growth continues only as long as they perceive, remain aware of, and act on their true feelings. Growth stops and symptoms of mental disorder appear, said Perls, when people are not aware of all aspects of themselves (Perls, 1969; Perls, Hefferline, & Goodman, 1951).

Like client-centered therapy, **Gestalt therapy** seeks to create conditions in which clients can become more unified, self-aware, and self-accepting, and thus ready to grow again. However, Gestalt therapists use more direct and dramatic methods than do

congruence In client-centered therapy, a consistency between the way therapists feel and the way they act toward the client.

Gestalt therapy A form of treatment that seeks to create conditions in which clients can become more unified, more self-aware, and more self-accepting.

Rogerians. Often working in group settings, Gestalt therapists prod clients to become aware of feelings and impulses that they have disowned and to discard feelings, ideas, and values that are not really their own. For example, the therapist or other group members might point out inconsistencies between what clients say and how they behave. (Gestalt therapists pay particular attention to clients' "body language," especially when it conflicts with what they are saying.) The therapist may also ask clients to engage in imaginary dialogues with other people, with parts of their own personalities, and even with objects. Like a shy person who can be socially outgoing only while at a costume party, clients often find that these dialogues help to get them in touch with, and express, their feelings (Paivio & Greenberg, 1995).

Behavior Therapy

▧ Can we learn to conquer fears?

Behavior therapists emphasize a different kind of self-awareness: They try to help clients view psychological problems as *learned behaviors* that can be changed without first searching for hidden meanings or unconscious causes. For example, suppose you have a panic attack every time you leave home and find relief only when you return. Making excuses when friends invite you out temporarily eases your anxiety but does nothing to solve the problem. Could you reduce your fear without looking for its "meaning"? Behavior therapy would offer just such an alternative by first helping you to understand the learning principles that maintain your fear and then helping you to learn new responses in feared situations.

This approach is the logical outcome of the assumptions of the behavioral approach to psychology in general and the social-learning approach to personality in particular. As described in Chapter 11, social-learning theorists see learning as the basis of normal personality, and of most behavior disorders. According to this perspective, disordered behavior and thinking are examples of the maladaptive thoughts and actions that the client has learned. Thus, fear of leaving home (agoraphobia) would be seen as stemming from classically conditioned associations between having panic attacks and being away from home. The problem is then maintained through operant conditioning: Staying home, and making excuses for doing so, is rewarded by reduced anxiety. Therapists who adopt a behavioral approach argue that if past learning experiences can produce problems, systematic new learning experiences can help alleviate them. Even if the learning that led to phobias and other problems began in childhood, behaviorists focus on solving today's problems through new experiences based on the principles of learning discussed in Chapter 5.

Behavioral approaches to treatment have their roots in the work of John B. Watson, Ivan Pavlov, and others who studied the learned nature of fear in the 1920s, as well as in B. F. Skinner's research on the impact of reward and punishment on behavior. In the late 1950s and early 1960s, researchers began using classical and operant conditioning principles to alter disordered human behavior (Thorpe & Olson, 1997). By 1970, behavioral treatment had become a popular alternative to psychodynamic and phenomenological methods. The most notable features of behavioral treatment include the following:

1. Developing a good therapist-client relationship. As in other therapies, this relationship enhances clients' confidence that change is possible and makes it easier for them to speak freely and to cooperate in, and benefit from, treatment (Wilson, 1995).

2. Careful listing of the behaviors and thoughts to be changed. This assessment and the establishment of specific goals sometimes replace the formal diagnosis used in some other approaches. Thus, instead of treating "depression" or "schizophrenia," behavior therapists work to change the specific thoughts, behaviors, and emotional reactions that cause people to receive these labels.

TABLE 13.1

A Desensitization Hierarchy

Desensitization hierarchies are lists of increasingly fear-provoking situations that clients visualize while using relaxation methods to remain calm. Here are a few items from the beginning and the end of a hierarchy that was used to help a client overcome fear of flying.

1. You are reading a newspaper and notice an ad for an airline.
2. You are watching a television program that shows a group of people boarding a plane.
3. Your boss tells you that you need to take a business trip by air.
4. You are in your bedroom packing your suitcase for your trip.
.
.
.
12. Your plane begins to move as you hear the flight attendant say, "Be sure your seat belt is securely fastened."
13. You look at the runway as the plane is readied for takeoff.
14. You look out the window as the plane rolls down the runway.
15. You look out the window as the plane leaves the ground.

3. A therapist who acts as a kind of teacher/assistant by providing learning-based treatments, giving "homework" assignments, and helping the client make specific plans for dealing with problems.

4. Continuous monitoring and evaluation of treatment, along with constant adjustments to any procedures that do not seem to be effective.

Behavioral treatment can take many forms. By tradition, those that rely mainly on classical conditioning principles are referred to as **behavior therapy.** Those that focus on operant conditioning methods are usually called **behavior modification.** And behavioral treatment that focuses on changing thoughts as well as overt behaviors is called **cognitive-behavior therapy.**

Techniques for Modifying Behavior

Some of the most important and commonly used behavioral treatment techniques are systematic desensitization, modeling, positive reinforcement, extinction, aversive conditioning, and punishment.

Systematic Desensitization   Joseph Wolpe (1958) developed one of the first behavioral methods for helping clients overcome phobias and other forms of anxiety. Called **systematic desensitization,** it is a treatment in which the client visualizes a series of anxiety-provoking stimuli while maintaining a state of relaxation. Wolpe believed that this process gradually weakens the learned association between anxiety and the feared object until the fear disappears.

Wolpe first helped his clients learn to relax, often using *progressive relaxation training* (described in Chapter 10) to prevent anxiety. Then, while relaxing, the client would be asked to imagine an item from a *desensitization hierarchy,* a list of increasingly fear-provoking situations (see Table 13.1). The client would imagine each item in the hierarchy, one at a time, moving to a more difficult item only after learning to imagine the previous one without distress. Wolpe found that once clients can calmly *imagine* being in feared situations, they are better able to deal with them in reality later on. Desensitization appears especially effective if it slowly and carefully presents clients with real rather than imagined hierarchy items (Chambless, 1990; McGlynn et al., 1999). This *in vivo,* or "real life," desensitization was once difficult to arrange or control, especially in cases involving fear of flying, heights, or highway driving, for example.

LINKAGES
Can people learn their way out of a disorder? (a link to Learning)

behavior therapy   Treatments that use classical conditioning principles to change behavior.

behavior modification   Treatments that use operant conditioning methods to change behavior.

cognitive-behavior therapy   Treatment methods that help clients change the way they think as well as the way they behave.

systematic desensitization   A behavioral method for treating anxiety in which clients visualize a graduated series of anxiety-provoking stimuli while maintaining a state of relaxation.

VIRTUAL DESENSITIZATION A client who fears heights wears a virtual reality display that allows him to "experience" what he would see as a glass elevator gradually rises higher and higher. After learning to tolerate these realistic images without anxiety, clients are better able to fearlessly face the situations they once avoided.

Recently, however, a technique known as *virtual reality graded exposure* has made it possible for clients to "experience" vivid and precisely graduated versions of feared situations without actually being exposed to them. In one study, clients who feared heights wore a head-mounted virtual reality display that gave them the impression of standing on bridges of gradually increasing heights, on outdoor balconies at higher and higher floors, and in a glass elevator as it slowly rose forty-nine stories (Rothbaum et al., 1995). The same technology has been used successfully in the treatment of many other anxiety disorders, ranging from fear of spiders and flying to posttraumatic stress disorder (R. A. Klein, 1999; J. Robbins, 2000; Rothbaum et al., 1999; Rothbaum & Hodges, 1999).

Modeling   Therapists often teach clients desirable behaviors by demonstrating those behaviors. In **modeling** treatments, the client watches other people perform desired behaviors, thus learning important skills. For example, modeling can teach fearful clients how to respond fearlessly and confidently. In one case, a therapist first showed a spider-phobic client how to calmly kill spiders with a fly swatter and then assigned her to practice this skill at home with rubber spiders (M. MacDonald & Bernstein, 1974). The combination of fearless demonstrations and then first-hand practice is called *participant modeling*; it is one of the most powerful treatments for fear (e.g., Bandura, Blanchard, & Ritter, 1969; Faust, Olson, & Rodriguez, 1991).

Modeling is also a major part of assertiveness training and social skills training, which teach clients how to deal with people more comfortably and effectively. The goals of social skills training range from helping college students with social phobias make conversation on dates to rebuilding mental patients' ability to interact normally with people outside the hospital (Fairweather & Fergus, 1993; Trower, 1995; S. E. Wong et al., 1993). In **assertiveness training,** the therapist helps clients learn to express their feelings and stand up for their rights in social situations (Alberti & Emmons, 1986; Ballou, 1995). Assertiveness training is often done in groups and involves both modeling and role playing of specific situations. For example, group assertiveness training helped wheelchair-bound adults and learning-disabled students more comfortably handle the socially awkward situations in which they sometimes find themselves (Gleuckauf & Quittner, 1992; Weston & Went, 1999).

Positive Reinforcement   Behavior therapists also use **positive reinforcement** to alter problematic behaviors and to teach new skills in cases ranging from childhood tantrums and juvenile delinquency to schizophrenia and self-starvation. Employing operant conditioning principles, they set up *contingencies,* or rules, that specify the behaviors to be strengthened through reinforcement. In one study, autistic children, who typically speak very little, were given grapes, popcorn, or other items they liked in return for saying "please," "thank you," and "you're welcome" while exchanging crayons and blocks with a therapist. After the therapist modeled the desired behavior by saying the appropriate words at the appropriate times, the children began to say these words on their own. Their use of language also began to appear in other situations, and as shown in Figure 13.1, the new skills were still evident six months later (Matson et al., 1990).

For severely retarded or disturbed clients in institutions, behavior therapists sometimes establish a **token economy,** a system for reinforcing desirable behaviors with poker chips or other tokens that can be exchanged later for snacks, access to television, or other desired rewards (Ayllon, 1999; Ayllon & Azrin, 1968; Paul & Lentz, 1977). The goal is to shape behavior patterns that will persist outside the institution (Paul, 2000; Paul, Stuve, & Cross, 1997).

Extinction   Just as reinforcing desirable behaviors can make them more likely to occur, failing to reinforce undesirable behaviors can make them less likely to occur, a process known as **extinction.** Treatment methods designed to produce extinction change behavior rather slowly, but they provide a gentle way of reducing inappropriate behavior in children and in retarded or seriously disturbed adults. For example, a client who gets attention by disrupting a classroom, damaging property, or violating hospital rules might be placed in a quiet, boring "time out" room for a few minutes to eliminate reinforcement for misbehavior (e.g., Kee, Hill, & Weist, 1999; Reitman & Drabman, 1999).

modeling   A method of therapy in which desirable behaviors are demonstrated as a way of teaching them to clients.

assertiveness training   A set of methods for teaching clients who are anxious or unproductive in social situations how to interact with others more comfortably and effectively.

positive reinforcement   Presenting a positive reinforcer (reward) after a desired response.

token economy   A system for improving the behavior of severely disturbed or mentally retarded clients in institutions by rewarding desirable behaviors with tokens that can be exchanged for snacks, access to television, or other privileges.

extinction   The gradual disappearance of a conditioned response.

FIGURE 13.1

Positive Reinforcement for an Autistic Child

Before the positive reinforcement treatment program began, an autistic child rarely said "please," "thank you," or "you're welcome," but these statements began to occur spontaneously once they were reinforced. Did modeling and reinforcement actually cause the change? Probably, because each type of response did not start to increase until the therapist began demonstrating and reinforcing it.

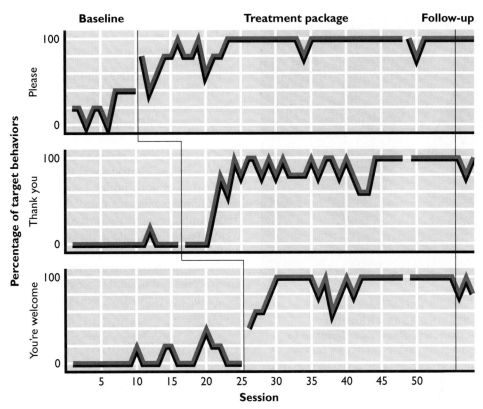

Source: Matson et al. (1990).

Extinction is also the basis of a fear-reduction treatment called **flooding,** which puts clients into the very situation they fear the most. The client is flooded with fear at first, but after an extended period of exposure to the conditioned fear stimulus (a frog, say) without experiencing pain, injury, or any other dreaded result, the association between the feared stimulus and the fear response gradually weakens, and the conditioned fear response is extinguished (Barlow, 1988; C. V. Harris & Goetsch, 1990). In one study, twenty clients who feared needles were exposed for two hours to the sight and feel of needles, including mild finger pricks, harmless injections, and blood samplings (Öst, Hellström, & Kåver, 1992). Afterward, all but one client was able to have a blood sample drawn without experiencing significant anxiety. These effects were maintained at a one-year follow-up assessment.

Aversive Conditioning Some unwanted behaviors, such as eating junk food, can become so habitual and rewarding that they must be made less attractive if a client is to have any chance of giving them up in favor of a more desirable alternative. Methods for lessening the appeal of certain stimuli are known as **aversive conditioning,** because they employ classical conditioning principles to associate physical or psychological discomfort with stimuli or actions the client wishes to avoid (e.g., Clapham & Abramson, 1985).

One form of aversive conditioning, called *covert sensitization,* operates in a way that is the reverse of systematic desensitization. The client first visualizes the stimulus or situation that is to be made less attractive and is then exposed to frightening or disgusting stimuli. For example, a man who had been repeatedly arrested for making obscene phone calls was asked to imagine making such a call. As he did so, the therapist presented vivid descriptions of things the client feared the most: snakes, vomiting, and choking. He was also instructed to imagine his mother walking in on him during an obscene call. After a month of covert sensitization, the thought of making obscene calls no longer created sexual arousal, and even two years later, the client still had not made any (Moergen, Merkel, & Brown, 1990).

flooding A procedure for reducing anxiety that involves keeping a person in a feared, but harmless, situation.

aversive conditioning A method for reducing unwanted behaviors by using classical conditioning principles to create a negative response to some stimulus.

Applying Psychology

**TREATING FEAR THROUGH
FLOODING   Flooding** is designed to
extinguish severe anxiety by continuously presenting strong conditioned fear
stimuli, but without the harmful consequences the person had dreaded.
Although often highly effective, flooding
is equivalent to immediately exposing a
fearful client to the most distressing item
on a desensitization hierarchy. Accordingly, some therapists and clients prefer
more gradual exposure methods similar
to those of *in vivo* desensitization, which
start with the least distressing item on
the hierarchy (Al-Kubaisy et al., 1992;
Fritzler, Hecker, & Losee, 1997).

punishment   The presentation of an
aversive stimulus or the removal of a
pleasant one following some behavior.

**rational-emotive behavior therapy
(REBT)**   A treatment that involves
identifying self-defeating, problem-
causing thoughts that clients have
learned and using modeling, encouragement, and logic to help the client replace
these maladaptive thought patterns with
more realistic and beneficial ones.

Because aversive conditioning is unpleasant and uncomfortable, and because its effects are often temporary, most behavior therapists avoid this method or use it only long enough to allow the client to learn alternative behaviors.

Punishment   Sometimes the only way to eliminate a dangerous or disruptive behavior is to punish it with an unpleasant, but harmless, stimulus, such as a shouted "No!" or a mild electric shock. Unlike aversive conditioning, in which the unpleasant stimulus occurs along with the behavior that is to be eliminated (a classical conditioning approach), **punishment** is an operant conditioning technique; it presents the unpleasant stimulus *after* the undesirable response occurs.

Before using electric shock or other forms of punishment, behavior therapists are required by ethical and legal guidelines to ask themselves several important questions: Have all other methods failed? Would the client's life be in danger without treatment? Has an ethics committee reviewed and approved the procedures? Has the adult client or a close relative of a child client agreed to the treatment? (Kazdin, 1994). When the answer to these questions is yes, punishment can be an effective, sometimes life-saving, treat-ment—as in the case illustrated in Figure 5.12 on page 161. Like extinction, punish-ment works best when it is used just long enough to eliminate undesirable behavior and is combined with other behavioral methods designed to reward more appropriate behavior.

Cognitive-Behavior Therapy

Like psychodynamic and phenomenological therapists, behavior therapists recognize that depression, anxiety, and many other behavior disorders can stem from how clients think about themselves and the world. And like other therapists, behavior therapists also try to change their clients' troublesome ways of thinking. However, the methods used by behavior therapists—known collectively as *cognitive-behavior therapy*—rely on *learning principles* to help clients change the way they think, as well as how they behave (Goldfried et al., 1997; McMullin, 2000; L. Sperry, 1999). For example, some clients already know *how* to stand up for themselves in social situations, but they have not learned to recog-nize the habitual thoughts (such as "I shouldn't make a fuss") that keep them from doing so. Cognitive-behavioral therapists help clients learn to identify these cognitive obstacles, and then encourage them to try new ways of thinking that promote more desirable behavior (Meichenbaum, 1995).

Rational-Emotive Behavior Therapy   One prominent form of cognitive-behavior therapy is **rational-emotive behavior therapy (REBT),** which was developed by Albert Ellis (1962, 1993, 1995). REBT aims first at identifying self-defeating thoughts, such as "I must be loved or approved by everyone" or "I must be competent, adequate, and achieving to be worthwhile." After the client learns to recognize thoughts like these and to see how they cause problems, the therapist uses suggestions, encouragement, and logic to help the client replace such thoughts with more realistic and beneficial ones. The client is then given "homework" assignments to try out these new ways of thinking in everyday situa-tions. Here is part of an REBT session with a woman who suffered from panic attacks. She has just said that it would be "terrible" if she had an attack in a restaurant and that people "should be able to handle themselves!"

Therapist: *. . . The reality is that . . . "shoulds" and "musts" are the rules that other peo-ple hand down to us, and we grow up accepting them as if they are the abso-lute truth, which they most assuredly aren't.*

Client: *You mean it is perfectly okay to, you know, pass out in a restaurant?*

Therapist: *Sure!*

Client: *But . . . I know I wouldn't like it to happen.*

Therapist: *I can certainly understand that. It would be unpleasant, awkward, inconve-nient. But it is illogical to think that it would be terrible, or . . . that it some-how bears on your worth as a person.*

Client: *What do you mean?*

Therapist: *Well, suppose one of your friends calls you up and invites you back to that restaurant. If you start telling yourself, "I might panic and pass out and people might make fun of me and that would be terrible," . . . you might find you are dreading going to the restaurant, and you probably won't enjoy the meal very much.*

Client: *Well, that is what usually happens.*

Therapist: *But it doesn't have to be that way. . . . The way you feel, your reaction . . . depends on what you choose to believe or think, or say to yourself. (J. C. Masters et al., 1987)*

Cognitive-behavior therapists use many techniques related to REBT to help clients learn to think in more adaptive ways. Techniques aimed at replacing upsetting thoughts with alternative thinking patterns were originally described by behaviorists as *cognitive restructuring* (A. A. Lazarus, 1971). They help clients plan calming thoughts to use during exams, tense discussions, and other anxiety-provoking situations. Such thoughts may take the form of "OK, stay calm, you can handle this if you just focus on the task and don't worry about being perfect." Sometimes, these techniques are expanded to include *stress inoculation training,* in which clients imagine being in a stressful situation and then practice newly learned cognitive skills to remain calm (Meichenbaum, 1995).

Beck's Cognitive Therapy   Many behavior therapists seek a different kind of cognitive restructuring using Aaron Beck's **cognitive therapy** (A. T. Beck, 1976, 1995; J. S. Beck & Beck, 1995). Beck's treatment approach is based on the idea that certain mental disorders—especially those involving depression and anxiety—can often be traced to errors in logic (e.g., "If I fail my driver's test the first time, I will never pass it") and false beliefs (e.g., "Everyone ignores me"). Beck says that over time, these learned *cognitive distortions* occur so quickly and automatically that the client never stops to consider that they might not be true.

Cognitive therapy is an organized problem-solving approach in which the therapist first helps clients learn to identify the logical errors, false beliefs, and other cognitive distortions that precede anxiety, depression, and other psychological problems (see Table 13.2). Then, much as in the five-step critical thinking system illustrated throughout this book, these thoughts and beliefs are considered as hypotheses to be tested, not as "facts"

ALBERT ELLIS   Rational-emotive behavior therapy (REBT) focuses on altering the self-defeating thoughts that Ellis believes underlie people's behavior disorders. Ellis argues, for example, that students do not get upset because they fail a test but because they have learned to believe that failure is a disaster that indicates they are worthless. Many of Ellis's ideas have been incorporated into various forms of cognitive-behavior therapy, and they have helped Ellis himself to deal rationally with the health problems he encountered when he reached his eighties (A. Ellis, 1997).

cognitive therapy   An organized problem-solving approach in which the therapist actively collaborates with clients to help them notice how certain negative thoughts precede anxiety and depression.

TABLE 13.2	Some Examples of Negative Thinking

LEARN BY DOING   Here are just a few examples of the kinds of thoughts that cognitive-behavior therapists see as underlying anxiety, depression, and other distressing behavior problems. After reading this list, try writing an alternative thought that clients could use to replace each of these ingrained cognitive habits. Then jot down a "homework assignment" that you would recommend to help clients challenge each maladaptive statement, and thus develop new ways of thinking about themselves.

"I shouldn't draw attention to myself."

"I will never be any good at this."

"It would be so awful if I don't know the answer."

"Everyone is smarter than I am."

"Nobody likes me."

"I should be able to do this job perfectly."

"What if I panic?"

"I'll never be happy."

"I should have accomplished more by this point in my life."

to be uncritically accepted. In other words, the therapist and client become a team of "investigators" as they plan ways to test beliefs such as "I'm no good around the house." For example, they might agree on tasks that the client will attempt as "homework"—such as cleaning out the basement, getting advice on hanging a picture, or just cutting the grass. Success at accomplishing even one of these tasks provides concrete evidence to challenge a false belief that has supported depression, thus helping to reduce it (A. T. Beck et al., 1992).

As described in Chapter 12, however, depression and anxiety may not be due entirely to specific thoughts or beliefs about certain situations. Sometimes they stem from a more general cognitive style that leads people to expect that the worst will always happen to them and to assume that negative events occur because they are completely and permanently incompetent and worthless (Peterson & Seligman, 1984). Accordingly, cognitive-behavior therapists also help depressed clients to develop more optimistic ways of thinking and to reduce their tendency to blame themselves for negative outcomes (N. S. Jacobson & Hollon, 1996). In some cases, cognitive restructuring is combined with practice at using logical thinking, anxiety management techniques, and skill training—all designed to help clients experience success and develop confidence in situations where they had previously expected to fail (J. S. Beck & Beck, 1995; W. A. Bowers, 1989).

Group, Family, and Couples Therapy

■ How does group therapy differ from individual therapy?

Psychodynamic, phenomenological, and behavioral methods of psychotherapy can be used not just with individuals but also with groups of clients or with family units.

Group Therapy

Group therapy refers to the treatment of several clients under the guidance of a therapist who encourages helpful interactions among group members. Many groups are organized around one type of problem (such as alcoholism) or one type of client (such as adolescents). In most cases, six to twelve clients meet with their therapist at least once a week for about two hours. All group members agree to hold confidential everything that occurs within group sessions.

Group therapy offers features not found in individual treatment (Yalom, 1995). First, group therapy allows the therapist to observe clients interacting with one another. Second, clients often feel less alone as they listen to others and realize that many people struggle with difficulties as least as severe as their own. This realization tends to raise each client's expectations for improvement, a factor important in all forms of treatment. Third, group members can boost one another's self-confidence and self-acceptance as they come to trust and value one another. Fourth, clients learn from one another. They share ideas for solving problems and give one another honest feedback about their attitudes and behavior. Fifth, perhaps through mutual modeling, the group experience makes clients more willing to share their feelings and more sensitive to other people's needs, motives, and messages. Finally, group therapy allows clients to try out new skills in a supportive environment.

Family Therapy

As its name implies, **family therapy** involves treatment of two or more individuals from the same family. One of these, often a troubled adolescent or child, is the initially identified client. However, family therapists believe that the problems displayed by one family member often reflect problems in the functioning of the entire *family system* (Clarkin & Carpenter, 1995; Shlomo, 1999). Ultimately, then, the family becomes the client, and

group therapy Psychotherapy involving six to twelve individuals.

family therapy A type of treatment involving two or more clients from the same family.

in review

Approaches to Psychological Treatment

Dimension	Classical Psychoanalytic	Contemporary Psychodynamic	Phenomenological	Behavioral/ Cognitive-Behavioral
Nature of the human being	Driven by sexual and aggressive urges	Driven by the need for human relationships	Has free will, choice, and capacity for self-actualization	Is a product of social learning and conditioning; behaves on the basis of past experience
Therapist's role	Neutral; helps client explore meaning of free associations and other material from the unconscious	Active; develops relationship with client as a model for other relationships	Facilitates client's growth; some therapists are active, some are nondirective	Teacher/trainer who helps client replace undesirable thoughts and behaviors; active, action oriented
Focus	Emphasizes unresolved unconscious conflicts from the distant past	Understanding the past, but focusing on current relationships	Here and now; focus on immediate experience	Current behavior and thoughts; may not need to know original causes to create change
Goals	Psychosexual maturity through insight; strengthening of ego functions	Correction of effects of failures of early attachment; development of satisfying intimate relationships	Expanded awareness; fulfillment of potential; self-acceptance	Changes in thinking and behaving in particular classes of situations; better self-management
Typical methods	Free association; dream analysis, analysis of transference	Analysis of interpersonal relationships, including the client-therapist relationship	Reflection-oriented interviews designed to convey unconditional positive regard, empathy, and congruence; exercises to promote self-awareness	Systematic desensitization, modeling, assertiveness and social skills training, positive reinforcement, extinction, aversive conditioning, punishment, cognitive restructuring

treatment involves as many members as possible. Indeed, the goal of family therapy is not just to ease the identified client's problems but also to create harmony and balance within the family by helping each member understand family interaction patterns and the problems they create. As with group therapy, the family therapy format gives the therapist an excellent view of how the initially identified client interacts with others, thus providing a basis for discussion of topics important to each family member.

Couples Therapy

In **couples therapy,** improving communication between partners is one of the most important targets of treatment. Discussion in couples therapy sessions typically focuses on identifying and improving the miscommunication or lack of communication that is interfering with the couples' happiness and intimacy. Often, the sessions revolve around learning to abide by certain "rules for talking," such as those listed in Table 13.3. Some therapists also focus on helping couples to accept one another as a way of becoming closer; they even offer preventive treatment to couples who are at risk for relationship problems (Berger & Hannah, 1999; N. S. Jacobson et al., 2000). ("In Review: Approaches to Psychological Treatment" summarizes key features of the main approaches to treatment that we have discussed.)

couples therapy   A form of therapy that focuses on improving communication between partners.

TABLE 13.3

Some "Rules for Talking" in Couples Therapy

 Many forms of couples therapy help partners improve communication through establishing rules such as these. Think about your own experience in relationships or your observations of couples as they interact, and then write down some rules you would add to this list. Why do you think it would be important for couples to follow the rules on your list?

1. Always begin with something positive when stating a problem.
2. Use specific behaviors rather than derogatory labels or overgeneralizations to describe what is bothersome about the other person.
3. Make connections between those specific behaviors and feelings that arise in response to them (e.g., "It makes me sad when you . . .").
4. Admit your own role in the development of the problem.
5. Be brief, don't lecture or harangue.
6. Maintain a focus on the present or the future; don't review all previous examples of the problem or ask "why" questions such as "Why do you always . . . ?"
7. Talk about observable events; don't make inferences about them (e.g., say "I get angry when you interrupt me" rather than "Stop trying to make me feel stupid").
8. Paraphrase what your partner has said; and check out your own perceptions of what was said before responding. (Note that this suggestion is based on the same principle as Rogers' empathic listening.)

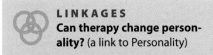 **LINKAGES**
Can therapy change personality? (a link to Personality)

Evaluating Psychotherapy

■ **How effective is psychotherapy?**

Psychotherapy has been available for over a hundred years, and people are still asking if it works. The question persists because although most psychotherapists and their clients find psychotherapy effective (*Consumer Reports,* 1995), confirming that effectiveness through experimental research has proven to be challenging and controversial (Bickman, 1999; T. C. Brock, Green, & Reich, 1998; R. M. Dawes, 1994; Seligman, 1995).

The value of psychotherapy was first widely questioned in 1952, when British psychologist Hans Eysenck reviewed studies in which thousands of clients had received either traditional psychodynamic therapy, various other therapies, or no treatment. To the surprise and dismay of many therapists, Eysenck (1952) found that the percentage of clients who improved following any kind of psychotherapy was actually lower than among people who received no treatment. Eysenck (1961, 1966) later supported his conclusions with additional evidence.

Critics argued that Eysenck was wrong (e.g., Bergin, 1971; Luborsky, 1972). They claimed that he ignored studies supporting the value of psychotherapy and misinterpreted his data. They pointed out, for example, that untreated clients may have been less disturbed than those in treatment, that so-called untreated clients may have received informal treatment from their medical doctors, and that physicians who judged untreated clients' progress might have used less demanding criteria than the psychotherapists who rated their own clients. Indeed, when some of these critics reviewed treatment successes and failures themselves, they concluded that psychotherapy tends to be *more* helpful than no treatment (e.g., Bergin, 1971).

Debate over Eysenck's findings—and the contradictory reports that followed them—highlighted several reasons why it is so difficult to answer the apparently simple question, Does psychotherapy work? For one thing, there is the problem of how to measure improvement in psychotherapy. Should such assessment depend on psychological tests, behavioral observations, interviews, or a combination of all three? For that matter, what *kinds* of tests should be used; where should clients be observed (and by whom); and should equal weight be given to interviews with clients, friends, relatives, therapists, and teachers? The question of effectiveness is further complicated by the broad range of clients, therapists, and treatments involved in the psychotherapy enterprise. Clients differ not only in terms of their problems but also in terms of their motivation to solve them. Therapists differ in skill, experience, and personality—and as we have seen, their treatment procedures can vary widely. To the extent that a client's improvement is influenced by all these factors, results from any particular treatment evaluation study might not tell us much about how well different therapists, using different methods, would do with other kinds of clients and problems (Kazdin, 1994).

LINKAGES

Does psychotherapy work? (a link to Introduction to the Science of Psychology)

Are All Forms of Psychotherapy Equally Effective?

In short, the question of whether psychotherapy "works" is difficult or impossible to answer scientifically in a way that applies across the board. However, several research reviews (E. M. Anderson & Lambert, 1995; Galatzer-Levy et al., 2000; Shadish et al., 2000; M. L. Smith, Glass, & Miller, 1980; Weisz & Jensen, 1999) and personal experience leave psychotherapists convinced that it *does* work (see Figure 13.2). Further, most of them believe that the theoretical approach and treatment methods *they* use are superior to those of other therapists (e.g., Giles, 1990). They can't all be right, of course, so what is going on?

■ What am I being asked to believe or accept?

Some researchers argue that theories of behavior disorder and the specific treatment methods based on them don't have much to do with the success of psychotherapy. All approaches, they say, are equally effective. This has been called the "Dodo Bird Verdict," after the *Alice in Wonderland* creature who, when called upon to judge who had won a race, answered, "Everybody has won and all must have prizes" (Luborsky, Singer, & Luborsky, 1975).

■ Is there evidence available to support the claim?

Some evidence does suggest that there are no significant differences in the overall effectiveness of the psychodynamic, phenomenological, and behavioral approaches to therapy. Statistical analyses that combine the results of a large number of therapy studies show that the three approaches are associated with about the same degree of success (M. J. Lambert & Bergin, 1994; M. L. Smith, Glass, & Miller, 1980).

■ Can that evidence be interpreted another way?

It is possible, however, that the evidence for the Dodo Bird Verdict is based on methods that cannot detect genuine differences among treatments. For example, a statistical analysis that

FIGURE 13.2

An Analysis of Psychotherapy's Effects

These curves show the results of one large-scale analysis of the effects of psychotherapy. Notice that on average, people who received therapy were better off than 80 percent of those who did not. The overall effectiveness of psychotherapy has also been confirmed in a more recent analysis of ninety treatment outcome studies (Shadish et al., 2000).

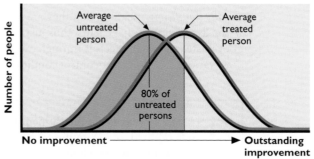

Source: Data from M. L. Smith, Glass, & Miller (1980).

averages the results of many different studies might not reveal important differences in the impact of particular treatments for particular problems (Eysenck, 1978; G. T. Wilson, 1985). It may also be that some specific techniques are more successful than others, but because the therapies have been grouped by theoretical approach (psychodynamic, phenomenological, or behavioral) rather than by specific procedures, the impact of those procedures might not be noticed (Giles, 1990; Mahrer & Nadler, 1986; Marmar, 1990).

Further, differences among the effects of specific procedures might be overshadowed by the beneficial features shared by almost all forms of therapy—such as the support of the therapist, the hope and expectancy for improvement that therapy creates, and the trust that develops between client and therapist (Grencavage & Norcross, 1991). Thus, a therapist whose personal characteristics motivate a client to change might promote that change regardless of the therapeutic methods being used (Elkin, 1999; Hubble, Duncan, & Miller, 1999).

■ What evidence would help to evaluate the alternatives?

The debate about whether all forms of psychotherapy are about equally effective on the average is likely to continue, but many researchers believe that it focuses on the wrong question. They believe that it is pointless to compare the effects of psychodynamic, phenomenological, and behavioral methods in general. It is more important, they say, to address what Gordon Paul called the "ultimate question" about psychotherapy: "What treatment, by whom, is most effective for this individual with that specific problem, under what set of circumstances?" (Paul, 1969, p. 44).

■ What conclusions are most reasonable?

Statistical analyses show that various treatment *approaches* appear about equally effective overall. But this does not mean that every psychotherapy *experience* will be equally helpful. Potential clients must realize that the success of *their* treatment can still be affected by how severe their problems are, by the quality of the relationship they form with a therapist, and by the appropriateness of the therapy methods chosen for their problems.

Like those seeking treatment, many clinical psychologists, too, are eager for more specific scientific evidence about the effectiveness of particular therapies for particular kinds of clients and disorders. These empirically oriented clinicians are concerned that all too often, therapists' choice of therapy methods depends too much on personal preferences or current trends and not enough on scientific evidence of effectiveness (Davison, 1998). They believe that advocates of any treatment—whether it is object relations therapy or systematic desensitization—must demonstrate that its benefits are the result of the treatment itself and not just of the passage of time, the effects of repeated assessment, the client's motivation and personal characteristics, or other confounding factors (Chambless & Hollon, 1998). They also want to see evidence that the benefits of treatment are *clinically significant,* meaning that they are large enough to make an important difference in the lives of individual clients, thus justifying their cost (Kendall, 1999). The ideal way to evaluate treatment effects is through experiments in which clients are randomly assigned to various treatments or control conditions and their progress is objectively measured.

FOCUS ON RESEARCH

Which Therapies Work Best for Which Problems?

To help clinicians select treatment methods on the basis of empirical evidence, the American Psychological Association's Division of Clinical Psychology created a task force on effective psychotherapies (Task Force on Promotion and Dissemination of Psychological Procedures, 1995).

▪ What was the researchers' question?

The question addressed by this task force was "What therapies have proven themselves most effective in treating various kinds of psychological disorders?"

▪ How did the researchers answer the question?

Working with other empirically oriented clinical psychologists, members of this task force examined the outcomes of thousands of experiments that evaluated psychotherapy methods used to treat mental disorder, marital distress, and health-related behavior problems in adults, children, and adolescents (Baucom et al., 1998; Compas et al., 1998; DeRubeis & Crits-Christoph, 1998; Kazdin & Weisz, 1998; Kendall & Chambless, 1998).

▪ What did the researchers find?

The task force found that a number of treatments—known as **empirically supported therapies,** or **ESTs**—have been validated by controlled experimental research (DeRubeis & Crits-Christoph, 1998; Kendall & Chambless, 1998). As shown in Table 13.4, the therapies identified as effective for particular problems in adult clients are mainly behavioral, cognitive, and cognitive-behavioral methods, along with interpersonal therapy, a contemporary psychodynamic approach initially developed to treat depression (Klerman & Weissman, 1993; Markowitz & Swartz, 1997).

▪ What do the results mean?

The authors of the report on empirically supported therapies, and those who support their efforts, claim that relying on analysis of experimental research has allowed a scientific evaluation of various treatments and generated a list of methods from which clinicians and consumers can choose with confidence when facing specific disorders (e.g., Hunsley & Rumstein-McKean, 1999; Kendall & Chambless, 1998). Therapists are even being urged to follow *treatment manuals* stemming from this research to help them deliver empirically supported therapies exactly as they were intended (Addis, 1997; W. A. Wade, Treat, & Stuart, 1998).

Not everyone agrees with this interpretation or this recommendation. Critics argue that the list of empirically supported therapies is based on research that may not be relevant to clinicians practicing in the real world. They point out, for example, that experimental studies of psychotherapy have focused mainly on the therapeutic procedures used rather than on the characteristics and interactions of therapists and clients (Garfield, 1998; Hilliard, Henry, & Strupp, 2000). This emphasis on procedure is a problem, they say, because the outcome of therapy in these experiments might have been affected by whether the random assignment of clients to therapists resulted in a match or a mismatch on certain personal characteristics. These critics say that in real clinical situations, clients and therapists are not paired up at random (Persons & Silberschatz, 1998; Seligman, 1995). Finally, because therapists participating in experimental research were required to follow standard treatment manuals, they were not free to adapt treatment methods, as they normally would, to the needs of particular clients (Garfield, 1998). Perhaps, say these critics, when there is less experimental control over the treatment situation, all therapies are about equally effective, as suggested by the statistical analyses of outcome research we mentioned earlier (Shadish et al., 2000; Smith, Glass, & Miller, 1980).

In short, critics reject the empirically supported therapies list as a useful guide. In fact, some see it as an incomplete, irrelevant, and ultimately misleading document. They worry that it is based on research designed to evaluate treatment effects without adequately taking into account either the personal qualities and theoretical biases of those who offer therapy, or how those factors might interact with the characteristics of the clients who receive therapy (e.g., Henry, 1998). There is worry, too, that widespread use of treatment manuals would make psychotherapy too mechanical and less effective, and that it might suppress therapists' creativity in developing new treatment methods (Addis & Krasnow, 2000; Beutler, 2000; Garfield, 1998).

empirically supported therapies (ESTs) Treatments for psychological disorders whose effectiveness has been validated by controlled experimental research.

■ **What do we still need to know?**

The efforts of the APA task force represent an important step in responding to Paul's (1969) "ultimate question" about psychotherapy: "What treatment, by whom, is most effective for this individual with that specific problem, under what set of circumstances?" We still have a long way to go, but empirically oriented clinical psychologists are determined to find scientific answers to this challenging question.

What we know so far is that when differences do show up in comparative studies of adult psychotherapy, they tend to reveal a small to moderate advantage for behavioral and cognitive-behavioral methods, especially in the treatment of phobias and certain other anxiety disorders (DeRubeis & Crits-Christoph, 1998; M. J. Lambert & Bergin,

TABLE 13.4	Some Empirically Supported Therapies

Treatments are listed as "efficacious" (pronounced "eff-eh-KAY-shus"), or capable of helping clients, if they were superior to no treatment in at least two experiments by different research teams. Those listed as "efficacious and specific" were shown to produce clinically significant benefits that were superior to another form of therapy or a placebo control group. "Possibly efficacious" treatments have been found effective in only a single study or by a single research team (DeRubeis & Crits-Christoph, 1998).

Problem	Efficacious and Specific	Efficacious	Possibly Efficacious
Major depressive disorder	Cognitive therapy	Behavior therapy; interpersonal therapy	Problem solving therapy for depression
Generalized anxiety disorder	Cognitive therapy	Applied relaxation (a form of desensitization)	
Social phobia	Exposure therapy, exposure plus cognitive restructuring		
Obsessive compulsive disorder	Exposure and response prevention		Cognitive therapy
Agoraphobia	Exposure therapy		
Panic disorder	Panic control therapy; cognitive therapy	Exposure therapy, applied relaxation	
Posttraumatic stress disorder	Exposure therapy		Stress inoculation training; eye movement desensitization and reprocessing (see Chapter 1)
Schizophrenia			Social skills training
Alcohol abuse and dependence			Social skills training; exposure to drinking cues; cue exposure plus coping skills training
Substance dependence (Opiates) (Cocaine)			Supportive-expressive therapy; cognitive therapy; behavior therapy (reinforcement) Relapse prevention therapy

1994; Weisz et al., 1995), as well as bulimia nervosa, an eating disorder (G. T. Wilson, 1997). The same tends to be true for child and adolescent clients (Epstein et al., 1994; B. Weiss & Weisz, 1995; Weisz et al., 1995).

Further, the client-therapist relationship seems to play a consistent role in the success of many forms of treatment (Beutler, 2000; P. D. Brown & O'Leary, 2000; Elkin et al, 1999; D. J. Martin, Garske, & Davis, 2000). Certain people seem to be particularly effective in forming productive human relationships. Even without formal training, these people can sometimes be as helpful as professional therapists because of personal qualities that are inspiring, healing, and soothing to others (D. M. Stein & Lambert, 1995). These qualities may help account for the success of many kinds of therapy. (It would be ideal if we could learn more about these people's qualities and, if possible, train others to develop them, too.)

Before choosing a therapist and treatment approach, then, a potential client must carefully consider (1) what treatment approach, methods, and goals the person finds comfortable and appealing; (2) information about the potential therapist's "track record" with a particular method for treating problems similar to those the person faces; and (3) the likelihood of forming a productive relationship with the therapist. This last consideration assumes special importance when client and therapist do not share similar cultural backgrounds.

Cultural Factors in Therapy

If cultural differences, including religious differences, create miscommunication or a lack of trust, the potential for a good client-therapist relationship can be threatened. Accordingly, major efforts are under way to ensure that such differences do not impede the delivery of treatment to anyone who wants or needs it (P. S. Richards & Bergin, 2000; D. W. Sue et al., 1999). Virtually every mental health training program in North America is seeking to recruit more students from traditionally underserved minority groups to eventually make it easier to match clients with therapists from similar cultural backgrounds (e.g., Hammond & Yung, 1993; Sleek, 1999). In the meantime, many minority clients are likely to encounter a therapist from a differing background, so researchers are also examining the value of matching therapeutic techniques with

MAKING A CONNECTION The formation of a productive therapeutic relationship can be easier when clients and therapists share similar sociocultural backgrounds (S. Sue, 1998).

clients' culturally based expectations and preferences (Hays, 1995; Preciado, 1994; Tanaka-Matsumi & Higginbotham, 1994).

Today, psychotherapists are more sensitive than ever to the cultural values of particular groups and the difficulties that can impair intercultural communication (LaFromboise, Foster, & James, 1996; Mishina, 1999; Shlomo, 1999). Some U.S. states now require psychologists to complete courses on the role of cultural factors in therapy before being licensed. This training helps clinicians appreciate, for example, that it is considered impolite in some cultures to make eye contact with a stranger and, hence, that clients from those cultures are not necessarily depressed, lacking in self-esteem, or inappropriately submissive just because they look at the floor during an interview. Graduate students are getting similar training and practical experience as part of their coursework in clinical or counseling psychology (Neville et al., 1996). Research with these students suggests that the training increases their sensitivity to cultural factors in treatment but does not necessarily increase their competence in actually working with members of ethnic minorities (Pope-Davis et al., 1995; Quintana & Bernal, 1995). Nevertheless, by providing a cultural extension of Carl Rogers's concept of empathy, cultural sensitivity training helps therapists to appreciate the client's view of the world and thus to set goals that are in harmony with that view (S. Sue, 1998; Yutrzenka, 1995).

Rules and Rights in the Therapeutic Relationship

Treatment can be an intensely emotional experience, and the relationship established with a therapist can profoundly affect a client's life. Professional ethics and common sense require the therapist to ensure that this relationship does not harm the client. For example, the American Psychological Association's *Ethical Principles of Psychologists and Code of Conduct* forbids a sexual relationship between therapist and client—during treatment and for at least two years afterward—because of the severe harm it can cause the client (American Psychological Association, 1992b; S. Martin, 1999; Samuel & Gorton, 1998). These standards also require therapists to keep everything a client says in therapy strictly confidential.

Indeed, confidentiality is one of the most important features of a successful therapeutic relationship. It allows the client to reveal unpleasant or embarrassing impulses, behaviors, or events without fear that this information will be repeated to anyone else. Professionals do sometimes consult with one another about a client, but each is required not to reveal information to outsiders (including members of the client's family) without the client's consent. The next edition of the APA's code of ethics is sure to include new standards for protecting confidentiality for the growing number of clients who seek psychological services via *telehealth* channels, which include telephone, videophone, e-mail, or other Internet links (American Psychological Association, 1996; Foxhall, 2000; Kulynych & Stromberg, 1998; Winzelberg et al., 2000). Among other things, these standards will probably require therapists to inform clients that others might be able to gain access to their e-mail messages (D. E. Shapiro & Schulman, 1996).

Professional rules about confidentiality are backed up in most U.S. states by laws recognizing that information revealed in therapy (like information given to a priest, a lawyer, or a physician) is privileged communication. This means that a therapist can refuse, even in court, to answer questions about a client or to provide personal notes or tape recordings from therapy sessions. Only under special circumstances can therapists be legally required to violate confidentiality. These circumstances include those in which (1) a client is so severely disturbed or suicidal that hospitalization is needed, (2) a client uses his or her mental condition and history of therapy as part of his or her defense in a civil or criminal trial, (3) the therapist must defend against a client's charge of malpractice, (4) a client reveals information about sexual or physical abuse of a child, and (5) the therapist believes a client may commit a violent act against a specific person.

ELECTROCONVULSIVE THERAPY
Some theorists believe that ECT alters mood by improving neurotransmitter function (Julien, 1995; S. Kapur & Mann, 1993). Others suggest that the neurotransmitters that help the brain recover from convulsions also reduce activity in areas of the brain associated with depression, thus relieving it (Sackeim, 1985). The truth is that no one knows for sure how ECT works (R. Abrams, 1997).

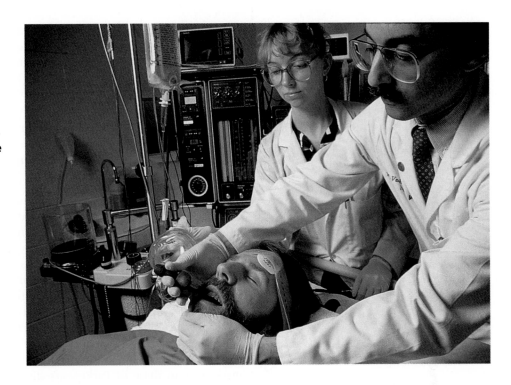

Biological Treatments

■ Is electric shock still used to treat disorders?

So far, we have described psychological approaches to the treatment of mental disorders. But biological treatments are also available—primarily through psychiatrists and other medical doctors, who often work in cooperation with psychologists. Today, biological treatments for psychological problems mainly involve the prescribing of psychoactive drugs. Earlier in this century, however, the most common biological treatment was inducement of seizures using electric shock.

Electroconvulsive Therapy

In the 1930s, a Hungarian physician named Ladislaus Von Meduna used a drug to induce convulsions in schizophrenics. He believed—incorrectly—that because schizophrenia and epilepsy rarely occur in the same person, epileptic-like seizures might combat schizophrenia. In 1938, Italian physicians Ugo Cerletti and Lucio Bini created seizures by passing an electric current through schizophrenics' brains. During the next twenty years or so, this procedure, called **electroconvulsive therapy (ECT)**, became a routine treatment for schizophrenia, depression, and sometimes mania. Although many patients improved, they often relapsed. The benefits of ECT also had to be weighed against such side effects as memory loss, confusion, speech disorders, and in some cases, death due to cardiac arrest (Lickey & Gordon, 1991).

To make ECT safer, patients are now given an anesthetic so that they are unconscious before the shock is delivered, along with a muscle relaxant to prevent bone fractures during convulsions. Also, the shock now lasts only about half a second and is usually delivered to only one side of the brain (R. Abrams, 1997). Finally, in contrast to the dozens of treatments administered decades ago, patients now receive only about six to twelve shocks, one approximately every two days (Fink, 1999). Today, ECT is used mainly for patients with severe depression (and occasionally with manic patients) who do not respond to less drastic treatments (American Psychiatric Association, 1993).

electroconvulsive therapy (ECT) A brief electric shock administered to the brain, usually to reduce severe depression that does not respond to drug treatments.

Because of its dramatic and potentially dangerous nature, ECT remains a controversial method of treatment. Critics want it outlawed, but proponents of ECT perceive its benefits to certain patients as outweighing its potential costs (Breggin, 1997; Fink, 1999).

Psychoactive Drugs

The use of ECT declined after the 1950s, in part because psychoactive drugs had begun to emerge as more convenient and effective treatment alternatives. In Chapters 2 and 4 we discuss how psychoactive drugs affect neurotransmitter systems and consciousness. Here, we describe their role in combating anxiety, depression, mania, and schizophrenia.

Neuroleptics   One group of drugs, called **neuroleptics** or **antipsychotics,** dramatically reduces the intensity of psychotic symptoms such as hallucinations, delusions, paranoid suspiciousness, disordered thinking, and confused speech in many mental patients, especially schizophrenics. The most widely used antipsychotic drugs are the *phenothiazines* (pronounced "fee-noh-THIGH-uh-zeens"), of which the first, chlorpromazine (Thorazine), has been especially popular. Another neuroleptic called haloperidol (Haldol) is about as effective as the phenothiazines, but it creates less sedation (Julien, 1997). Patients who do not respond to one type of neuroleptic may respond to the other. Between 60 and 70 percent of patients receiving these drugs show improvement, though fewer than 30 percent respond well enough to live entirely on their own.

These neuroleptics have side effects ranging from dry mouth and dizziness to symptoms similar to those of Parkinson's disease, including muscle rigidity, restlessness, tremors, and slowed movement. Some of these side effects can be treated with medication, but at least 25 percent of patients who take chlorpromazine or haloperidol for several years develop an irreversible disorder of the motor system. This disorder, called *tardive dyskinesia (TD),* causes uncontrollable, repetitive movements of the body, often including twitching of the face and body and thrusting of the tongue.

Clozapine (Clozaril) has effects like those of the phenothiazines, but it is much less likely to cause movement disorders. Although no more effective overall than the phenothiazines, clozapine has helped many patients who did not respond to the phenothiazines or haloperidol (A. I. Green & Patel, 1996). Unfortunately, taking clozapine carries the risk of developing a fatal blood disease called *agranulocytosis* (Lickey & Gordon, 1991).

Several antipsychotics similar to clozapine have been introduced recently, including risperidone (Risperdal), olanzapine (Zyprexa) and quetiapine (Seroquel). These newer medications are expensive, but they have even fewer side effects than clozapine, and they do not cause agranulocytosis. They also appear to reduce the "negative" symptoms of schizophrenia, such as lack of emotion, social withdrawal, and reduced speech (National Institute on Mental Health, 1995).

Antidepressants   Soon after antipsychotic drugs appeared, they were joined by **antidepressants,** which relieve symptoms of depression. About 50 to 60 percent of depressed patients who take these drugs show improved mood, greater physical activity, increased appetite, and better sleep. This improvement is seen in only 10 to 20 percent of the most severe cases of psychotic depression (Agency for Healthcare Research and Quality, 1999; U.S. Surgeon General, 1999).

There are several classes of antidepressant drugs. The *monoamine oxidase inhibitors (MAO-I)* are effective in many cases of depression, especially for clients who also experience anxiety and panic (Julien, 1997). The *tricyclic antidepressants (TCAs)* are another popular class of antidepressants. The TCAs have been prescribed more frequently than MAO-I drugs because they seem to work somewhat better and have fewer side effects. However, taking TCAs and drinking alcohol can increase the effects of both, with potentially fatal results.

The most prominent of several newer antidepressants is fluoxetine (Prozac). Introduced in 1986, fluoxetine quickly became the most widely used antidepressant in the United States. Its popularity is due to the fact that it is about as effective as older drugs and, in most cases, has milder side effects (Cookson & Duffett, 1998; Harvard Mental Health

---

neuroleptics   Drugs that alleviate the symptoms of schizophrenia or other severe forms of psychological disorder. Also called *antipsychotics.*

antipsychotics   See *neuroleptics.*

antidepressants   Drugs that reduce depression.

Letter, 1998a, 1998b; Stokes, 1998). An improved version of Prozac, containing a purer active ingredient called R-fluoxetine, is currently being developed. Other, even newer antidepressants, including venlafaxine (Effexor), nefazodone (Serzone), and bupropion (Wellbutrin), show similar promise (Appleton, 2000; Croft et al., 1999; Quitkin et al., 2000).

Another recent development in the pharmacological treatment of depression is the use of an herbal remedy from a plant called St. John's wort *(Hypericum).* In Germany, where this treatment is covered by health insurance, it is more popular than Prozac. One of the active ingredients in St. John's wort is *hypericin,* a substance that, like Prozac, is thought to affect the neurotransmitter serotonin. A number of double-blind, placebo-controlled studies have shown St. John's wort to be as effective as Prozac and other antidepressants, especially in milder forms of depression (e.g., Brenner et al., 2000; Gaster & Holroyd, 2000; H. P. Volz & Laux, 2000; Woelk, 2000). Final conclusions about its safety and effectiveness for more severe depression must await the results of further research (Ernst, 2000; Nathan, 1999; U.S. Surgeon General, 1999).

The mineral salt *lithium carbonate,* when taken regularly, prevents both the depression and the mania associated with bipolar disorder in some, but not all, patients (Baldessarini & Tondo, 2000; Manji, Bowden, & Belmaker, 2000). Without lithium, the typical bipolar patient has a manic episode about every fourteen months and a depressive episode about every seventeen months; with lithium, attacks of mania occur as rarely as every nine years (Bowden, 2000; Lickey & Gordon, 1991). The lithium dosage must be exact and carefully controlled, however, because taking too much can cause vomiting, nausea, tremor, fatigue, slurred speech, and with severe overdoses, coma or death. In recent years, anti-convulsant drugs such as divalproex (Epival) have been used as an alternative to lithium in treating mania. These drugs appear to cause fewer side effects, are less dangerous at higher doses, and are easier to regulate (Bowden et al., 2000; Hirschfeld et al., 1999).

Anxiolytics   During the 1950s, a new class of drugs called *tranquilizers* was shown to reduce mental and physical tension and the symptoms of anxiety. The first of these drugs, called meprobamate (Miltown or Equanil), acts somewhat like barbiturate sleeping pills, meaning that overdoses can cause sleep and even death. Because they do not pose this danger, the *benzodiazepines*—particularly chlordiazepoxide (Librium) and diazepam (Valium)—became the favored drug treatment for anxiety (Blackwell, 1973). Today, these and other anti-anxiety drugs, now called **anxiolytics** (pronounced "ang-zee-oh-LIT-ix), continue to be the most widely prescribed and used of all legal drugs. They have an immediate calming effect and are quite useful in treating the symptoms of generalized anxiety and posttraumatic stress disorder. One of the newest of the benzodiazepines, alprazolam (Xanax), has become especially popular for the treatment of panic disorder and agoraphobia (Greenblatt, Harmatz, & Shader, 1993). Another benzodiazepine, clonazepam (Klonopin), is also being used, alone or in combination with other anxiolytics, in the treatment of anxiety ranging from phobia to panic disorder (Worthington et al., 1998). A number of antidepressant drugs, including fluoxetine (Prozac), paroxetine (Paxil), clomipramine (Anafranil), and fluvoxamine (Luvox), are also effective in treating panic disorder and/or obsessive-compulsive disorder (Lydiard et al., 1998; Todorov, Freeston, & Borgeat, 2000).

Benzodiazepines can have bothersome side effects, such as sleepiness, lightheadedness, and impaired thinking. Combining these drugs with alcohol can be fatal, and continued use of anxiolytics can lead to tolerance and physical dependence. After heavy or long-term use, attempts to stop taking these drugs can result in severe withdrawal symptoms, including seizures and anxiety attacks (Rickels et al., 1993). An anxiolytic called buspirone (BuSpar) provides an alternative anxiety treatment that eliminates some of these problems, but its effects do not occur for days or weeks after treatment begins (Lickey & Gordon, 1991). Yet buspirone can ultimately equal diazepam in reducing generalized anxiety (Schnabel, 1987). Further, it does not seem to promote dependence, it causes less interference with thinking, and it does not interact dangerously with alcohol. Table 13.5 lists the effects and side effects of some of the psychoactive drugs we have described.

anxiolytics   Drugs that reduce tension and symptoms of anxiety.

A Sampling of Psychoactive Drugs Used for Treating Psychological Disorders

Psychoactive drugs have been successful in helping clients by dramatically reducing the symptoms of many psychological disorders. Critics point out that drugs can have troublesome side effects, however, and they may create dependence, especially after years of use (e.g., Breggin, 1997). They note, too, that drugs do not "cure" mental disorders (NIH, 1995), and that symptom relief may make some patients less likely to seek a permanent solution to their anxiety, depression, or other psychological problems.

For Schizophrenia: Neuroleptics (Antipsychotics)

Chemical Name	Trade Name	Effects and Side Effects
Chlorpromazine	Thorazine	Reduce hallucinations, delusions, incoherence, jumbled thought processes; cause movement-disorder side effects, including tardive dyskinesia
Haloperidol	Haldol	
Clozapine	Clozaril	Reduces psychotic symptoms; causes no movement disorders, but raises risk of serious blood disease
Risperidone	Risperdal	Reduces positive and negative psychotic symptoms without risk of blood disease

For Mood Disorders: Antidepressants and Mood Elevators

Tricyclics

Imipramine	Tofranil	Act as antidepressants, but also have anti-panic action; cause sleepiness and other moderate side effects; potentially dangerous if taken with alcohol
Amitriptyline	Elavil, Amitid	

Other Antidepressants

Fluoxetine	Prozac	Have antidepressant, anti-panic, and anti-obsessive action
Clomipramine	Anafranil	
Fluvoxamine	Luvox	
Sertraline	Zoloft	

Other Drugs

Lithium carbonate	Carbolith, Lithizine	Calms mania; reduces mood swings of bipolar disorder; overdose harmful, potentially deadly
Divalproex	Depakote	Is effective against mania, with fewer side effects

For Anxiety Disorders: Anxiolytics

Benzodiazepines

Chlordiazepoxide	Librium	Act as potent anxiolytics for generalized anxiety, panic stress; extended use may cause physical dependence and withdrawal syndrome if abruptly discontinued
Diazepam	Valium	
Alprazolam	Xanax	Also has antidepressant effects; often used in agoraphobia (has high dependence potential)
Clonazepam	Klonopin	Is often used in combination with other anxiolytics for panic disorder

Other Anti-Anxiety Agents

Buspirone	BuSpar	Has slow-acting anti-anxiety action; no known dependence problems

There is widespread concern that psychiatrists, and especially general practitioners, rely too heavily on drugs to deal with psychological problems (Beardsley et al., 1988; Glenmullen, 2000). In one case, dramatically increased medication failed to stop a paranoid schizophrenia patient from repeatedly running away from a mental hospital. But allowing him to use a telephone at a nearby shopping mall eliminated the problem. A psychologist discovered that the man had been afraid to use "bugged" hospital phones and kept escaping to call his mother (Rabasca, 1999b).

"I medicate first and ask questions later."

Drugs and Psychotherapy

We have seen that drugs and psychotherapy can be effective in treating psychological disorders. Which is better? Although one approach may be more effective than the other in some cases, neither form of therapy is clearly superior overall for treating problems such as anxiety disorders and major depressive disorder (Antonuccio, Danton, & DeNelsky, 1995). For example, several large-scale studies of treatment for severe depression found that two forms of psychotherapy (cognitive-behavior therapy and interpersonal therapy) were as effective as an antidepressant drug (DeRubeis et al., 1999; Elkin et al., 1989). Cognitive-behavior therapy has also equaled drug effects in the initial treatment of phobia (Thom, Sartory, & Jöhren, 2000), panic disorder (Klosko et al., 1990), generalized anxiety disorder (Gould et al., 1997), and obsessive-compulsive disorder (Abramowitz, 1997). Further, the benefits of many kinds of psychotherapy may last longer than those of drug therapies (e.g., Bovasso, Eaton, & Armenian, 1999; Z. V. Segal, Gemar, & Williams, 2000; Thom, Sartory, & Jöhren, 2000).

What about combining drugs and psychotherapy? One research team compared the effects of gradual exposure treatment and an anti-anxiety drug (Xanax) in the treatment of agoraphobia. Clients receiving gradual exposure alone showed better short- and long-term benefits than those getting either the drug alone or a combination of the drug and gradual exposure (Echeburua et al., 1993). Other studies, too, have found that combining drugs and psychotherapy may produce surprisingly little advantage (e.g., Elkin, 1994; D. A. Spiegel & Bruce, 1997). However, the combination of drugs and psychotherapy has been shown to be more effective than either method alone in treating certain disorders, including attention deficit hyperactivity disorder, obsessive-compulsive disorder, alcoholism, stammering, compulsive sexual behavior, and chronic depression (e.g., deBeurs et al., 1995; Engeland, 1993; Keller et al., 2000; Reynolds et al., 1999). This combined approach may be especially helpful for clients who are initially too distressed to cooperate in psychotherapy (Kahn, 1995). Another approach, already found successful with clients who have been taking drugs for panic disorder, is to use psychotherapy to prevent relapse and make further progress as drug treatment is discontinued (e.g., T. J. Bruce, Spiegel, & Hegel, 1999).

Perhaps the most conservative strategy for treating most cases of anxiety and depression is to begin with cognitive or interpersonal psychotherapy (which have no major negative side effects) and then to add or switch to drug treatment if psychotherapy alone is ineffective.

LINKAGES
How do psychoactive drugs work? (a link to Biology and Behavior)

LINKAGES

Biology, Behavior, and the Treatment of Psychological Disorders

We noted in Chapter 2 that human thoughts and actions, whether normal or abnormal, are ultimately the result of biological processes, especially those involving neurotransmitters and their receptors in the brain. Because different neurotransmitters are especially prominent in particular brain regions or circuits, altering the functioning of particular neurotransmitter systems will have relatively specific psychological and behavioral effects.

Let's consider some of the ways in which therapeutic psychoactive drugs affect neurotransmitters and their receptors. Some therapeutic drugs act to cause neurons to fire, whereas others inhibit neuron firing. For example, the benzodiazepines (e.g., Valium and Xanax) exert their anti-anxiety effects by helping the inhibitory neurotransmitter GABA bind to receptors and thus suppress neuron firing. This enhanced inhibitory effect acts as a sort of braking system that slows the activity of GABA-sensitive neurons involved in the experience of anxiety. However, benzodiazepines also slow the action of all neural systems that use GABA, including those associated with motor activity and mental processing, which are spread throughout the brain. The result is the decreased motor coordination and clouded thinking that appear as benzodiazepine side effects. Recent research suggests that it might be possible to develop benzodiazepines that will bind only to certain kinds of GABA receptors and thus greatly reduce these side effects (Löw et al., 2000).

Other therapeutic drugs serve as receptor antagonists (see Figure 4.8 on page 132), acting to block the receptor site normally used by a particular neurotransmitter. The phenothiazines and haloperidol, for example, exert their antipsychotic effects by blocking receptors for dopamine, a neurotransmitter that, as described in Chapter 2, is important for movement. Dopamine blockage seems to normalize the jumbled thinking of many schizophrenics, but it can create severe disorders—including tardive dyskinesia—in the movement systems that are also controlled by dopamine.

Some psychoactive drugs exert their therapeutic influence by increasing the amount of a neurotransmitter available to act on receptors. This effect usually occurs because the drug slows a process called *reuptake,* by which the neurotransmitter would normally return to the tiny sacs, or vesicles, from which it was released. The tricyclic antidepressants, for example, operate by slowing the reuptake of norepinephrine. Prozac, Anafranil, and some other antidepressants are called *selective serotonin reuptake inhibitors (SSRIs)* because they slow the reuptake of serotonin. Others, such as Effexor, slow the reuptake of both serotonin and norepinephrine.

LINKAGES
How do drugs help people who suffer from schizophrenia? (a link to Biology and Behavior)

Community Psychology

■ How can we prevent psychological disorders?

community psychology   A mental health approach whose goal is to minimize or prevent psychological disorders by promoting social change and making treatment methods more accessible to the poor and others who normally have little or no access to psychological services.

It has long been argued that even if psychologists and psychiatrists knew exactly how to treat every psychological problem, there would never be enough mental health professionals to help everyone who needs it (Albee, 1968). This view fostered the rise of **community psychology,** an approach whose goals are to treat people in their home communities and to work for social changes that can prevent psychological disorders.

COMMUNITY MENTAL HEALTH EFFORTS Professional and nonprofessional staff of community mental health centers provide therapy and mental health education, as well as walk-in facilities and "hotlines" for people in crisis. They also offer day treatment to former mental patients, many of whom are homeless.

One aspect of community psychology, the *community mental health movement,* arose during the 1960s as an attempt to make treatment available to people in their own communities. As antipsychotic drugs became available, and as concern grew that patients were not improving—and might be getting worse—after years of confinement in mental hospitals, thousands of these patients were released. The plan was for them to receive drugs and other mental health services in newly funded community mental health centers. This *deinstitutionalization* process did spare patients the boredom and isolation of the hospital environment, but the mental health services available in the community never matched the need for them. Some former hospital patients and many people whose disorders might once have sent them to mental hospitals are now living in halfway houses and other community-based facilities where they receive *psychosocial rehabilitation.* These community support services are designed not to "cure" them but to help them cope with their problems and develop the social and occupational skills necessary for semi-independent living (R. H. Hunter, 1995; Liberman et al., 1998). All too many others with severe psychological disorders are to be found enduring the dangers of homelessness on city streets or of confinement in jails and prisons (Ditton, 1999; McBride et al., 1998).

Community psychology attempts to prevent psychopathology by addressing unemployment, poverty, overcrowded substandard housing, and other stressful social problems that may underlie some disorders (Albee, 1985; J. D. Hawkins et al., 1999). Less ambitious, but perhaps even more significant, are efforts to detect psychological problems in their earliest stages and keep them from becoming worse (e.g., Dadds et al., 1997; Sanders et al., 2000). Examples include suicide prevention (Garland & Zigler, 1993); programs, including Project Head Start, that help preschoolers whose backgrounds hurt their chances of doing well in school and put them at risk for delinquency (R. E. Tremblay et al., 1995; Zigler, Taussig, & Black, 1992); identification of children who are at risk for disorder because of being rejected or victimized at school (e.g., Greenberg et al., 1999); and interventions to head off anxiety disorders in children (Dadds et al., 1999).

Community psychology also supports the notion that nonprofessionals—including the relatives and friends of troubled clients—can be enlisted in efforts to combat psychological disorders (e.g., Bright, Baker, & Neimeyer, 1999). This idea is compatible with, and has encouraged the development of, *self-help* or *mutual-help* organizations. Self-help groups, such as Alcoholics Anonymous (AA), are made up of people who share some problem and want to help one another (Nowinski, 1999; Zimmerman et al., 1991). Millions of people take part each year in self-help groups for alcohol and drug addiction, childhood sexual abuse, cancer, overeating, compulsive gambling, schizophrenia, and many other problems (Kurtz, 1997; O'Conner & Kratochwill, 1999). The services provided by these nonprofessional groups make up about 20 percent of the total mental health and anti-addiction services offered in the United States (Borkman, 1997; Regier, Narrow, et al., 1993; Swindle et al., 2000).

Lack of reliable data makes it difficult to assess the value of many self-help groups, but available information suggests that active members may obtain some moderate improvement in their lives (Morganstern et al., 1997; Ouimette, Finney, & Moos, 1997). Some professional therapists view these groups with suspicion (Salzer, Rappaport, & Segre, 1999); others encourage clients to participate in them as part of their treatment or as a first step that might lead to more formal treatment (Haaga, 2000). This is especially true for clients with problems such as eating disorders, alcoholism, and other substance-related disorders (Dunne & Fitzpatrick, 1999).

active review   Treatment of Psychological Disorders

Linkages

As noted in Chapter 1, all of psychology's subfields are related to one another. Our discussion of the psychopharmacology of drug treatment illustrates just one way in which the topic of this chapter, treatment of psychological disorders, is linked to the subfield of biological psychology (Chapter 2). The Linkages diagram shows ties to two other subfields as well, and there are many more ties throughout the book. Looking for linkages among subfields will help you see how they all fit together and help you better appreciate the big picture that is psychology.

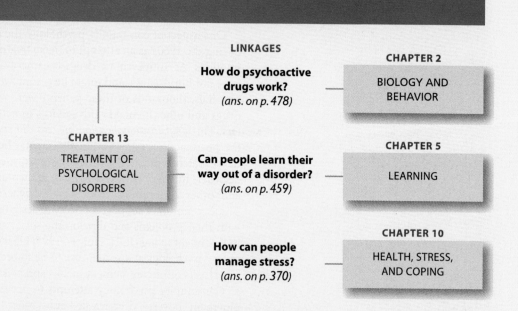

LINKAGES

How do psychoactive drugs work?
(ans. on p. 478)

CHAPTER 13
TREATMENT OF PSYCHOLOGICAL DISORDERS

Can people learn their way out of a disorder?
(ans. on p. 459)

How can people manage stress?
(ans. on p. 370)

CHAPTER 2
BIOLOGY AND BEHAVIOR

CHAPTER 5
LEARNING

CHAPTER 10
HEALTH, STRESS, AND COPING

Summary

BASIC FEATURES OF TREATMENT

What features do all treatment techniques have in common?

Psychotherapy for psychological disorders is usually based on psychodynamic, phenomenological, or behavioral theories of personality and behavior disorder. Many therapists employ elements of more than one approach. The biological approach is reflected in the use of drugs and other physical treatment methods.

All forms of treatment include a client, a therapist, a theory of behavior disorder, a set of treatment procedures suggested by the theory, and a special relationship between the client and therapist. Therapy may be offered to inpatients and outpatients in many different settings by *psychologists, psychiatrists,* and other helpers. The

goal of treatment is to help people change their thinking, feelings, and behavior so that they will be happier and function better.

PSYCHODYNAMIC PSYCHOTHERAPY

How did Freud get started as a therapist?

Psychodynamic psychotherapy began with Freud's *psychoanalysis,* which seeks to help clients gain insight into unconscious conflicts and impulses and then to explore how those factors have created disorders. Exploration of the unconscious is aided by the use of free association, dream interpretation, and related methods. Some variations on psychoanalysis retain most of Freud's principles but use a more flexible format. Others, such as object relations therapy, focus less on the id and the unconscious and more on helping clients to understand the role of early relationships with caregivers in current relationship problems.

PHENOMENOLOGICAL PSYCHOTHERAPY

Why won't some therapists give advice?

Phenomenological psychotherapy helps clients to become more aware of discrepancies between their feelings and their behavior. According to the phenomenological approach, these discrepancies are at the root of behavior disorders and can be resolved by the client once they are brought to light in the context of a genuine, trusting relationship with the therapist.

Therapists using Rogers's *client-centered therapy,* also known as *person-centered therapy,* help mainly by adopting attitudes toward the client that express *unconditional positive regard, empathy,* and *congruence.* These attitudes create a nonjudgmental atmosphere that facilitates clients' honesty with the therapist, with themselves, and with others. One way of creating this atmosphere is through *reflection.* Therapists employing the *Gestalt therapy* of Fritz and Laura Perls use more active techniques than Rogerian therapists, often pointing out inconsistencies between what clients say and how they behave.

BEHAVIOR THERAPY

Can we learn to conquer fears?

Behavior therapy and *behavior modification* apply learning principles to eliminate undesirable behavior patterns and to strengthen more desirable alternatives. The methods they employ include *systematic desensitization, modeling, assertiveness training* and social skills training, *positive reinforcement* (sometimes within a *token economy*), *extinction* techniques (such as *flooding*), *aversive conditioning,* and *punishment.*

Many behavior therapists also employ *cognitive-behavior therapy* to help clients alter the way they think, as well as the way they behave. Among the specific cognitive-behavioral methods are *rational-emotive behavior therapy (REBT),* cognitive restructuring, stress inoculation training, and *cognitive therapy.*

GROUP, FAMILY, AND COUPLES THERAPY

How does group therapy differ from individual therapy?

Therapists of all theoretical persuasions offer *group therapy, family therapy,* and *couples therapy.* These forms of treatment take advantage of relationships in the group, family, or couple to enhance the effects of treatment.

EVALUATING PSYCHOTHERAPY

How effective is psychotherapy?

Research has found that clients who receive psychotherapy are better off than most clients who receive no treatment, but that no single approach is uniformly better than all others for all clients and problems. Cognitive-behavior and interpersonal therapies have been designated as *empirically supported therapies (ESTs)* for certain kinds of problems. Further research is needed to discover all the combinations of therapists, clients, and treatments ideally suited to treating particular psychological problems. Several factors, including personal preferences, must be considered when choosing a form of treatment and a therapist. The effects of cultural differences in the values and goals of therapist and client have also attracted increasing attention. Whatever the specific form of treatment, the client's rights include the right to confidentiality.

BIOLOGICAL TREATMENTS

Is electric shock still used to treat disorders?

Biological treatment methods seek to relieve psychological disorders by physical rather than psychological means. *Electroconvulsive therapy (ECT)* involves passing an electric current through the patient's brain, usually in an effort to relieve severe depression. Today, the most prominent form of biological treatment involves psychoactive drugs, including those with *antipsychotic (neuroleptic), antidepressant,* or tranquilizing *(anxiolytic)* effects. Psychoactive drugs have proven to be impressively effective in many cases, but critics point out a number of undesirable side effects associated with these drugs. Drugs may be no more effective than some forms of psychotherapy for many people. Combining drugs and psychotherapy may help in some cases, but their joint effect may be no greater than either one alone.

COMMUNITY PSYCHOLOGY

How can we prevent psychological disorders?

The realization that there will never be enough therapists to treat all who need help prompted the development of *community psychology.* Community mental health programs and efforts to prevent mental disorders are the two main elements of community psychology. The growth of self-help or mutual-help organizations is compatible with the goals of community psychology.

Learn by Doing

Put It in Writing

Imagine that you have decided to get help for depression, anxiety, or some other psychological problem. Using what you have learned in this chapter, write a page describing what approach to treatment you would prefer, and why. Tell whether you would choose that approach for all kinds of problems, or whether your choice would depend on the nature of the problem. Finally, list the characteristics of your ideal therapist, and say why you think those characteristics might lead to successful treatment.

Personal Learning Activity

To get a better idea of how practicing therapists choose their treatment methods, ask a local psychologist, psychiatrist, or counselor (at the student counseling center on campus, perhaps) to meet with you for a short research interview. Ask this person what treatment approach and methods he or she prefers, how this preference developed, and what convinces him or her to continue using these methods. Write a summary of what you learned in this interview, and don't forget to include your impressions of whether this therapist's choice of treatment methods depends mainly on personal experience, empirical research evidence, or a combination of both. *For additional projects, see the five Personal Learning Activities in the corresponding chapter of the study guide that accompanies this text.*

Step into Action

Courses

Clinical Psychology
Methods of Psychotherapy
Psychopharmacology
Behavior Modification
Community Psychology

Movies

Good Will Hunting; Analyze This!; Vertigo (Hollywood portrayals of psychotherapy)
One Flew over the Cuckoo's Nest; Girl, Interrupted (institutional treatment)

Books

Raymond J. Corsini and Danny Wedding, *Current Psychotherapies* (5th ed.) (Peacock, 1995) (a comparison of eleven major approaches to psychotherapy)
Frank Dumont and Raymond J. Corsini (Eds.), *Six Therapists and One Client* (Springer, 2000) (therapists representing six different treatment methods describe how they would help the same client)

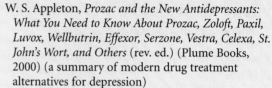

W. S. Appleton, *Prozac and the New Antidepressants: What You Need to Know About Prozac, Zoloft, Paxil, Luvox, Wellbutrin, Effexor, Serzone, Vestra, Celexa, St. John's Wort, and Others* (rev. ed.) (Plume Books, 2000) (a summary of modern drug treatment alternatives for depression)
T. M. Luhrmann, *Of Two Minds: The Growing Disorder in American Psychiatry* (Knopf, 2000) (summary of the conflict between biological and psychological approaches to treatment)

The Web

The World Wide Web is a good source of additional information about the science of psychology, provided you use it carefully and think critically about the information you find. The PsychAbilities web site that accompanies this text offers many resources relevant to this chapter. These resources include interactive NetLab exercises; Thinking Critically and Evaluating Research exercises; ACE chapter quizzes; recommended web links; and articles on current events, books, and movies. At http://college.hmco.com, select *Psychology* and then this textbook.

Review of Key Terms

Can you define each of the key terms in the chapter? Check your definitions against those on the pages listed in parentheses below or in the Glossary/Index at the end of the text.

antidepressants *(p. 474)*

antipsychotics *(p. 474)*

anxiolytics *(p. 475)*

assertiveness training *(p. 460)*

aversive conditioning *(p. 461)*

behavior modification *(p. 459)*

behavior therapy *(p. 459)*

client-centered therapy *(p. 456)*

cognitive-behavior therapy *(p. 459)*

cognitive therapy *(p. 463)*

community psychology *(p. 478)*

congruence *(p. 457)*

couples therapy *(p. 465)*

electroconvulsive therapy (ECT) *(p. 473)*

empathy *(p. 456)*

empirically supported therapies (ESTs) *(p. 469)*

extinction *(p. 460)*

family therapy *(p. 464)*

flooding *(p. 461)*

Gestalt therapy *(p. 457)*

group therapy *(p. 464)*

modeling *(p. 460)*

neuroleptics *(p. 474)*

person-centered therapy *(p. 456)*

positive reinforcement *(p. 460)*

psychiatrists *(p. 452)*

psychoanalysis *(p. 453)*

psychologists *(p. 452)*

psychotherapy *(p. 452)*

punishment *(p. 462)*

rational-emotive behavior therapy (REBT) *(p. 462)*

reflection *(p. 456)*

systematic desensitization *(p. 459)*

token economy *(p. 460)*

unconditional positive regard *(p. 456)*

Multiple-Choice Self-Test

Select the best answer for each of the questions below. Then check your response against the Answer Key at the end of the text.

1. Claudia's therapist asks her to talk about whatever thoughts, memories, or ideas come into her mind. He asks her not to "edit" any of her thoughts. This technique is called _____ and is part of _____ therapy.

   a. reflection; psychodynamic
   b. reflection; phenomenological
   c. free association; psychodynamic
   d. free association; phenomenological

2. Vernon tells his therapist about a dream in which a fish got stuck between his toes. The therapist says to Vernon, "Be the fish. What is that fish saying?" Vernon's therapist is using _____ therapy methods.

   a. Gestalt
   b. psychodynamic
   c. behavior
   d. cognitive

3. Melinda is a licensed clinical psychologist, which means she probably has

   a. a doctoral degree in psychology.
   b. a psychodynamic approach to therapy.
   c. the right to prescribe drugs.
   d. a medical degree.

4. A main aim of classical psychoanalysis is to

   a. help clients get in touch with their current feelings.
   b. help clients gain insight into their unconscious conflicts.
   c. replace clients' problematic behaviors with more desirable behaviors.
   d. teach clients new ways of thinking.

5. Client-centered therapists convey empathy by

   a. trying to see the world from the client's point of view.
   b. being self-actualized.
   c. exhibiting unconditional positive regard.
   d. being congruent.

6. Carl Rogers developed

   a. client-centered therapy.
   b. rational-emotive behavior therapy.
   c. cognitive-behavior therapy.
   d. object relations therapy.

7. Shanobi is tearfully telling a friend that she is depressed and does not know why. Her friend says, "You seem so unhappy, and maybe a bit scared, too." The friend's response is most like which method used in client-centered therapy?

   a. sympathy
   b. empathy
   c. reflection
   d. self-actualization

8. In psychoanalysis, insight begins when

   a. unconscious thoughts become conscious.
   b. clients shift feelings about a significant person onto the therapist.
   c. the manifest content of a dream is translated into latent content.
   d. free association reveals conscious processes.

9. Brandon complains that he has an intense need to repeatedly touch all four walls of any room he enters for the first time. His therapist suggests that Brandon might have learned this compulsive behavior because it helped him avoid anxiety. The therapist appears to be an adherent of the _____ approach to treatment.

   a. psychodynamic
   b. phenomenological
   c. behavioral
   d. neurobiological

10. Compared with classical psychoanalysis, contemporary variations on psychoanalysis _____.

    a. use group rather than individual treatment
    b. emphasize behaviors, not feelings
    c. focus on interpersonal relationships rather than instincts
    d. focus less on the client-patient relationship

11. According to the American Psychological Association's *Ethical Principles of Psychologists and Code of Conduct*, a therapist may reveal information learned about a client during therapy if

    a. the client is applying for a job and the employer requests this information.
    b. the client terminates the therapy.
    c. the client is suicidal and needs immediate hospitalization.
    d. he or she feels it will do no harm.

12. Juanita is trying to influence lawmakers to pass laws that will help prevent psychological problems caused by malnutrition, overcrowding, and homelessness. She is most likely a _____ psychologist.

    a. behavioral
    b. community
    c. phenomenological
    d. psychodynamic

13. Rafer's intense fear of spiders greatly interferes with his job as a forest ranger. His therapist suggests that he stay in a room full of harmless spiders until he feels no further anxiety. This therapy technique is known as

    a. flooding.
    b. punishment.
    c. systematic desensitization.
    d. aversive conditioning.

14. Sally constantly tells herself that she is "worthless" and will "never succeed at anything." Her therapist helps her practice new thoughts such as "I'm as good as the next person" and "I am going to try my best." Her therapist is using the technique of _____, which is part of _____ therapy.

    a. free association; psychodynamic
    b. reflection; phenomenological
    c. stress inoculation; behavioral
    d. cognitive restructuring; cognitive-behavior

15. Lucinda is experiencing severe depression that leaves her unable to enjoy life. She has not responded to psychotherapies or medication. Lucinda would be a candidate for

    a. neuroleptics.
    b. ECT.
    c. aversive conditioning.
    d. cognitive restructuring.

16. The "Dodo Bird Verdict" about psychotherapy is that

    a. all treatments are equally effective.
    b. some treatments are better for some disorders.
    c. people receiving treatment get better at the same rate as people not receiving treatment.
    d. bartenders and hair stylists are as effective as therapists.

17. An important element in the success of many forms of psychotherapy is

    a. the client-therapist relationship.
    b. randomly assigning therapists to clients.
    c. having a therapist trained in a variety of therapeutic methods.
    d. having appropriate assessment methods to measure outcomes.

18. When prescribing neuroleptics for schizophrenics, psychiatrists must consider that patients may

    a. become addicted to them.
    b. become insensitive to them after an extended period of time.
    c. develop problematic side effects such as tardive dyskinesia.
    d. experience hallucinations after extensive use.

19. Jon's therapist has prescribed anxiolytics for him. Jon is probably being treated for

    a. depression.
    b. an anxiety disorder.
    c. schizophrenia.
    d. somatoform disorder.

20. Which of the following is *not* an advantage of group therapy?

    a. It allows the therapist to observe clients interacting with each other.
    b. Clients learn from one another.
    c. Clients improve more quickly.
    d. Clients feel less alone.

14

Social Psychology

We all live with and among other people, and how we manage to do that

is the realm of social psychology. This chapter looks at how our thoughts and behaviors affect other people and how, in turn, the thoughts and behaviors of others affect us. It explores how perception, learning, memory, thinking, and emotion occur in relation to other people; how people think about themselves and others; why we may like one person but dislike another; how people form and change attitudes; and why and how we judge other people, sometimes in biased ways. Social pressure, ranging from unspoken social rules to commands for obedience, is another concern of social psychologists. The chapter also reviews some of the helpful, cooperative, competitive, and aggressive ways in which people behave toward one another in the workplace and in other social situations. Finally, it considers the impact of social influence on group decision making and group processes.

Reading this chapter will help you to answer the following questions:

- **How do we compare ourselves to others?**
- **Do we perceive people and objects in similar ways?**
- **Do attitudes always determine behavior?**
- **How does prejudice develop?**
- **What factors affect who likes whom?**
- **What social rules shape our behavior?**
- **How far will people go to obey authority?**
- **Are people born aggressive?**
- **What motivates people to help one another?**
- **What makes a good leader?**

n the mid-1990s, during a bloody civil war between two ethnic groups in the African nation of Rwanda, Tutsi residents of a small village learned that they were about to be attacked by Hutu soldiers. They asked a local minister to hide them in his church. The minister, himself a Hutu, agreed to help, but when the soldiers arrived, he revealed the Tutsi's hiding place. Under orders from their leaders, the soldiers killed all 400 people they found in the church (Gourevitch, 1999). In March 2000, in the neighboring country of Uganda, another 400 people died when fire swept through the church where they had been summoned by leaders of a religious sect called the Movement for the Restoration of the Ten Commandments of God. Their leaders set the fire after telling their followers that the end of the world had come. How could soldiers murder unarmed civilians in cold blood? Why would religious leaders betray or murder those who trusted them? We may never fully understand why human beings do such terrible things to one another, or why similar tragedies continue to occur in virtually every country on earth. Parts of the answer surely lie in understanding how people are influenced to think about those who are different from themselves, as well as how leaders create blind obedience in their followers.

The study of how people influence and are influenced by other people is the domain of **social psychology.** In this chapter, we focus on several topics in social psychology, including **social cognition** (the mental processes associated with how people perceive and react to other individuals and groups) and group and interpersonal behaviors such as conformity, aggression, and cooperation. One important aspect of social cognition is how it affects the way we see ourselves (E. Smith & Mackie, 2000).

Social Influences on the Self

■ **How do we compare ourselves to others?**

Each of us lives in both a personal and a social world. This means that although you experience your thoughts and feelings as your own, they have been strongly influenced by other people.

The thoughts, feelings, and beliefs about what characteristics you have and who you are make up your **self-concept.** Although your self-concept is unique to you, it is a product of your social and cultural environment. In the chapters on human development and personality, we described how each individual develops within a cultural context, and how collectivist and individualist cultures emphasize different core values and encourage contrasting definitions of the self. As you will see in this chapter, culture also provides the context for **self-esteem,** the evaluations you make of your worth as a human being. Let's look at how self-esteem develops.

Social Comparison

People spend a lot of time thinking about themselves, trying to evaluate their own perceptions, opinions, values, abilities, and so on. Decades ago, Leon Festinger (1954) noted that self-evaluation involves two distinct types of questions: those that can be answered by taking objective measurements and those that cannot. You can determine your height or weight by measuring it, but for other types of questions—about your creativity or attractiveness, for example—there are no objective criteria. In these cases, according to Festinger's theory of **social comparison,** people evaluate themselves in relation to others. When you wonder how creative, interesting, or attractive you are, you use social rather than objective criteria (Lyubomirsky & Ross, 1997).

To whom do you compare yourself? Festinger said that people usually look to others who are similar to themselves. For example, if you are curious about how good at science you are, you most likely compare yourself to fellow students at your own level of experience and ability, not to Albert Einstein or Marie Curie (Major, Sciacchtinano, & Crocker, 1993). The categories of people you feel you belong to, and usually compare yourself to, are called your **reference groups.**

The performance of individuals in your reference groups can affect your self-esteem (Baumeister, 1998). For example, if being good at science is important to you, knowing that someone in your reference group always scores much higher than you on science tests can lower your self-esteem. To protect their self-esteem, people sometimes compare themselves to those who are not as good, a strategy called *downward social comparison* (Wills, 1991). Alternatively, they might tell themselves that the superior performer is not really similar enough to be in their reference group, or even that the ability in question is not that important to them (Baumeister, 1995).

social psychology The subfield of psychology that explores the effects of the social world on the behavior and mental processes of individuals and groups.

social cognition Mental processes associated with people's perceptions of, and reactions to, other people.

self-concept The way one thinks of oneself.

self-esteem The evaluations people make about their worth as human beings.

social comparison Using other people as a basis of comparison for evaluating oneself.

reference groups Categories of people to whom individuals compare themselves.

FIGURE 14.1

A Schema-Plus-Correction

People who see a drawing like this tend to use a pre-existing mental representation (their schema of a square) and then correct or modify it in some way (here, with a notch).

An unfavorable comparison of your own status with that of others often produces **relative deprivation**—the belief that whatever you are getting, it is less than what you deserve (M. B. Brewer & Brown, 1998). If a person with an average income constantly identifies very wealthy people as a reference group, the resulting relative deprivation can create depression and anxiety (S. E. Taylor & Lobel, 1989). And if a large group experiences relative deprivation, political unrest may follow. The turmoil leading to great political upheavals, from the American Revolution to the overthrow of European communism, usually starts after the members of an oppressed group experience some improvement in their lives and begin to compare their circumstances with those in other groups (M. B. Brewer & Brown, 1998). This improvement brings higher expectations about what they deserve.

Social Identity Theory

Stop reading for a moment, and complete the following sentence: I am a(n) ————. Some people fill in the blank using characteristics such as "hard worker," "good sport," or some other aspect of their personal identity. However, many others identify themselves using a word or phrase that refers to their nationality, gender, or religion. These responses reflect **social identity,** our beliefs about the groups to which we belong. Our social identity is therefore a part of our self-concept (Walsh & Banaji, 1997).

Our social or group identity permits us to feel part of a larger whole (E. Smith & Mackie, 2000). Its importance is seen in the pride that people feel when a member of their family graduates from college or when a local team wins a big game (Burris, Branscombe, & Klar, 1997). In wars between national, ethnic, or religious groups, individuals sacrifice and sometimes die for the sake of their group identity. A group identity is also one reason people donate money to those in need, support friends in a crisis, and display other helping behaviors. As we shall see later, however, defining ourselves in terms of a group identity can foster an "us versus them" mentality that sets the stage for prejudice, discrimination, and intergroup conflict (Brewer & Brown, 1998).

Social Perception

■ Do we perceive people and objects in similar ways?

There is a story about a company president who was having lunch with a man being considered for an executive position. When the man salted his food without first tasting it, the president decided not to hire him. The reason, she explained, was that the company had no room for a person who acted before collecting all relevant information. The candidate lost his chance because of the president's **social perception,** the processes through which people interpret information about others, form impressions of them, and draw conclusions about the reasons for their behavior. In this section we will examine how and why social perception influences our thoughts, feelings, and actions.

The Role of Schemas

The perception of people follows many of the same laws that govern the perception of objects, including the Gestalt principles discussed in Chapter 3. Consider Figure 14.1. Consistent with Gestalt principles, most people would describe it as "a square with a notch in one side," not as eight straight lines (Woodworth & Schlosberg, 1954). The reason is that they interpret new information using the mental representations, or **schemas,** that they already have about squares. In short, they interpret this diagram as a square with a slight modification.

Schemas about people, too, can affect our perception of them. For one thing, schemas influence what we pay attention to and what we ignore. We tend to process information about the other person more quickly if it confirms our beliefs about that person's gender or ethnic group, for example, than if it violates those beliefs (S. T. Fiske, 1998). Second,

relative deprivation   The sense that a person is not doing as well as those in the person's reference group.

social identity   The beliefs we hold about the groups to which we belong.

social perception   The processes through which people interpret information about others, draw inferences about them, and develop mental representations of them.

schemas   Mental representations of what we know and expect about the world.

MAY I HELP YOU? Schemas help us to quickly categorize people and respond appropriately to them, but they can also create narrow-mindedness and, as we shall see later, prejudice. If this woman does not fulfill your schema—your mental representation—of how carpenters are supposed to look, you might be less likely to ask her advice on your home improvement project. Indeed, one expert carpenter who manages the hardware department of a large home improvement store told us that most customers walk right past her in order to ask the advice of one of her less-experienced male clerks.

LINKAGES
Do we sometimes perceive people the same way we perceive objects? (a link to Sensation and Perception)

schemas influence what we remember about others. In one study, if people thought a woman they saw in a videotape was a waitress, they recalled that she had a beer with dinner and owned a TV set. Those who thought she was a librarian remembered that she was wearing glasses and liked classical music (C. E. Cohen, 1981). Finally, schemas affect our judgment about the behavior of others (S. T. Fiske, 1995). Thomas Hill and his colleagues (1989) found that participants' ratings of male and female friends' sadness were influenced not only by the friends' actual behavior but also by the participants' general schemas about how much sadness men versus women experience.

In other words, through top-down processing (see Chapter 3), our schemas about people influence our perceptions of them. And just as schemas help us read sentences whose words have missing letters, they also allow us to efficiently "fill in the blanks" about people. Our schemas tell us, for example, that someone wearing a store uniform or name tag is likely to know where merchandise is located, so we usually approach that person for help. Accurate schemas help us to categorize people quickly and respond appropriately in social situations, but if schemas are incorrect they can create false expectations and errors in judgment about people that can lead to narrow-mindedness and even prejudice.

First Impressions

Our schemas about people shape our first impression of them. That impression, in turn, influences both our later perceptions of their behavior and our reactions to it. First impressions are formed quickly, usually change slowly, and typically have a long-lasting influence. No wonder they are so important in the development of social relations (D. T. Gilbert, 1998). How do people form impressions of other people? And why are these impressions so resistant to change?

Forming Impressions   Think about your first impression of a close friend. It probably formed rapidly, because existing schemas create a tendency to automatically infer a great deal about a person on the basis of limited information (E. Smith, 1998). An ethnic name, for example, might have caused you to draw inferences about your friend's religion, food preferences, or temperament. Clothing or hairstyle might have led you to make assumptions about her political views or taste in music. These inferences and assumptions may or may not be accurate. How many turned out to be true in your friend's case?

Noticeable features or actions help shape our impressions of others, which may or may not be correct.

DILBERT reprinted by permission of United Feature Syndicate, Inc.

One type of schema has a particularly strong influence on first impressions: We tend to assume that the people we meet hold attitudes and values similar to our own (Hoyle, 1993). So, all else being equal, we are predisposed to like other people. However, it takes very little negative information to change our minds. Why? Others can behave positively toward us because they are nice, because they like us, because they want to sell us insurance, or for many other reasons. People's negative acts, however, suggest only that they are unfriendly or have other undesirable traits (Coovert & Reeder, 1990). Accordingly, negative information attracts more attention and carries more weight than positive information in shaping first impressions (J. D. Klein, 1991).

Lasting Impressions   Does your friend seem the same today as when you first met? First impressions can change, but the process is usually very slow. One reason is that humans tend to be "cognitive misers" (S. T. Fiske, 1995). We like to maintain our existing beliefs about the world, often using our schemas to preserve a reality that fits our expectations. Holding on to existing impressions appears to be part of this effort. Thus, if your friend recently violated your expectations by being impatient, your view of her probably did not change much, if at all. In fact, you may have acted to preserve your impression of her by thinking something like, "She is not herself today." In other words, impressions change slowly because the meaning we give to new information about people is shaped by what we already know or believe about them (Ditto & Lopez, 1992).

Self-Fulfilling Prophecies   Another reason first impressions tend to be stable is that we often do things that cause others to confirm our impressions (Kenrick, Neuberg, & Cialdini, 1999). For example, counselors can draw extraverted behavior from clients whom they *believe* to be extraverted, whether or not the clients actually are extraverted (Copeland & Snyder, 1995). When, without our awareness, schemas cause us to subtly lead people to behave in line with our expectations, a **self-fulfilling prophecy** is at work.

Self-fulfilling prophecies also help maintain judgments about groups. If you assume that members of a certain ethnic group are pushy or aggressive, for example, you might display defensiveness or even hostility toward them. Faced with this behavior, members of the group might become frustrated and angry. Their reactions fulfill your prophecy and strengthen the impressions that created it (S. I. Ross & Jackson, 1991).

Explaining Behavior: Attribution

So far, we have examined how people form impressions about other people's characteristics. But perceptions of others also include explanations of their behavior. People tend to form ideas about why people (including themselves) behave as they do and about what behavior to expect in the future (D. T. Gilbert, 1998). Psychologists use the term **attribution** to describe the process we go through to explain the causes of behavior (including our own).

Suppose a classmate fails to return borrowed notes on time. You could attribute the behavior to many causes, from an emergency situation to selfishness. Which of these explanations you choose is important, because it will help you *understand* your class-

self-fulfilling prophecy   A process in which an initial impression causes us to bring out behavior in another that confirms the impression.

attribution   The process of explaining the causes of people's behavior, including our own.

mate's behavior, *predict* what will happen if this person asks to borrow something in the future, and decide how to *control* the situation should it arise again. Similarly, attributing your partner's nagging to irritability caused by stress or to lack of love can influence whether you will work on the relationship or seek to dissolve it.

People usually attribute behavior in a particular situation to either internal causes (characteristics of the person) or external causes (aspects of the situation). For example, if you thought your classmate's failure to return your notes was due mainly to lack of consideration or laziness, you would be making an *internal attribution*. If you thought that the oversight was due mainly to time pressure caused by an upcoming exam or a family crisis, you would be making an *external attribution*. Similarly, if you were to fail a test, you could explain it by concluding that you're not very smart (internal attribution) or that your work schedule left you too little time to study (external attribution). The attribution that you make, in turn, might determine how much you study for the next exam or even whether you decide to stay in school.

Biases in Attribution

Most people are usually logical in their attempts to explain behavior (Trope, Cohen, & Alfieri, 1991). However, they are also prone to *attributional biases,* or errors, that can distort their view of behavior (D. T. Gilbert, 1998).

North American psychologists have paid special attention to the **fundamental attribution error,** a tendency to overattribute the behavior of others to internal factors (D. T. Gilbert & Malone, 1995). Imagine that you hear a student give an incorrect answer in class. You will probably attribute this behavior to an internal cause and infer that the person is not very smart. In doing so, however, you might not be taking into account possible external factors (such as lack of study time).

The fundamental attribution error has some important consequences. For one thing, it can make us too confident about our impressions of other people's personalities. And because it leads us to underestimate the extent to which another person's behavior is due to external causes, we may also underestimate how much that person's behavior might vary across situations (D. T. Gilbert & Malone, 1995). No wonder we are so surprised to see that "quiet" person in our psychology class screaming wildly at a football game or doing a standup routine at a comedy club.

A related form of attributional bias is called the *ultimate attribution error.* Through this error, the positive actions of people from a different ethnic or social group are attributed to external causes, such as luck, whereas their negative actions are attributed to internal causes, such as dishonesty (Pettigrew, 1979). The ultimate attribution error causes people to see good deeds done by those in their own group as being due to internal factors and bad deeds as stemming from external causes. Thus, the ultimate attribution error fosters and maintains negative views of other groups and positive views of one's own group (S. T. Fiske, 1998).

Like other aspects of social cognition, these attributional biases are not universal (Choi, Nisbett, & Norenzayan, 1999). Research suggests that people in collectivist cultures such as India, China, Japan, and Korea are less likely than those in the individualist cultures of North America and Europe to commit the fundamental attribution error or the ultimate attribution error (A. P. Fiske et al., 1998; M. W. Morris & Peng, 1994). And even within cultures, there are individual differences in people's vulnerability to these errors (L. Ross & Nisbett, 1991). According to one study, for example, people raised in the southern United States were more inclined than northerners to make external attributions (Sims & Baumann, 1972).

The inclination toward internal attributions is much less pronounced when people explain their own behavior. In fact, there tends to be an **actor-observer bias:** Whereas people often attribute *other* people's behavior to internal causes, they tend to attribute *their own* behavior to external factors, especially when that behavior is inappropriate or inadequate (Baumeister, 1998). For example, when *you* drive slowly, it is because you are looking for an address, not because you are a big loser like that jerk who crawled along in front of you yesterday.

fundamental attribution error A bias toward overattributing the behavior of others to internal factors.

actor-observer bias The tendency to attribute other people's behavior to internal causes while attributing one's own behavior to external causes.

WHY ARE THEY HELPING? Attributional biases are more common in some cultures than others (Norenzayan & Nisbett, 2000). In one study, students in an individualist culture were more likely than those in a collectivist culture to explain spontaneous acts of helping as being due to internal causes such as kindness or enjoyment of helping (J. G. Miller & Bersoff, 1995).

The actor-observer bias occurs mainly because people have different kinds of information about their own behavior and the behavior of others (Krueger, Ham, & Linford, 1996). When *you* are behaving in some situation—giving a speech, perhaps—the information most available to you is likely to be external and situational, such as the temperature of the room and the size of the audience. You also have a lot of information about other external factors, such as the amount of time you had to prepare your talk or the upsetting conversation that occurred this morning. Whatever the outcome of your efforts, you can easily attribute it to one or all of these external causes. But when you observe someone else, the most obvious information in the situation is *that person*. You do not know what happened to the person last night or this morning, so you are likely to attribute whatever he or she does to stable, internal characteristics (D. T. Gilbert, 1998).

Of course, people do not always attribute their own behavior to external forces. In fact, whether they do so often depends on whether the outcome is positive or negative. One group of researchers assigned pairs of students to work together on a task and then, no matter how well the teams actually did, told them that they had either succeeded or failed on the task. If told the team was successful, the students took personal credit for the success; but if they failed, they blamed their partner (Sedikides et al., 1998). These students showed a **self-serving bias,** the tendency to take personal credit for success but to blame external causes for failure.

The self-serving bias occurs, in part, because people are motivated to maintain their self-esteem—and ignoring negative information is one way to do so. If you just failed an exam, it is painful to admit that it was fair. In short, people think about their failures and shortcomings in ways that protect their self-esteem (Aronson, Wilson, & Akert, 1999).

Self-protective cognitive biases help us temporarily escape from painful situations, but they also set the stage for a distorted view of reality and create problems in the long run (Kruger & Dunning, 1999). One such problem is *unrealistic optimism*, the tendency to believe that good things (e.g., financial success) are likely to happen to you, but that negative things (e.g., accidents or illness) are not (Krueger, 1998). Unrealistic optimism tends to persist even when there is strong evidence against it, and it can lead to potentially harmful behaviors. For example, people who are unrealistically optimistic about their health may exercise infrequently and may not pay much attention to information about how to prevent heart disease (K. Davidson & Prkachin, 1997). ("In Review: Some Biases in Social Perception" summarizes the common cognitive biases discussed here.)

self-serving bias   The cognitive tendency to attribute one's successes to internal characteristics while blaming one's failures on external causes.

in review

Some Biases in Social Perception

Bias	Description
Importance of first impression	Ambiguous information is interpreted in line with a first impression, and the initial schema is recalled better and more vividly than any later correction to it. Actions based on this impression may elicit behavior that confirms it.
Fundamental attribution error	The tendency to overattribute the behavior of others to internal factors.
Actor-observer bias	The tendency for actors to attribute their own behavior to external causes and for observers to attribute the behavior of others to internal factors.
Self-serving bias	The tendency to attribute one's successes to internal factors and one's failures to external factors.
Unrealistic optimism	The tendency of people to believe that good things will happen to them but that bad things will not.

Attitudes

■ **Do attitudes always determine behavior?**

Our views about health, safety, or any other topic reflect our attitudes. Social psychologists have studied this aspect of social cognition longer and more intensely than any other. An **attitude** is the tendency to think, feel, or act positively or negatively toward objects in our environment (Eagly & Chaiken, 1998). Attitudes play an important role in guiding how we react to other people, what causes and politicians we support, which products we buy, and countless other daily decisions.

The Structure of Attitudes

Social psychologists have long viewed attitudes as having three components (Haddock & Zanna, 1998a). The *cognitive* component is a set of beliefs about the attitude object. The emotional, or *affective,* component includes feelings about the object. And the *behavioral* component pertains to the way people act toward the object. Ideally, these components would be in harmony, allowing us to predict people's behavior toward the homeless, for example, on the basis of the thoughts or feelings they express, and vice versa. This is often not the case, however (Kraus, 1995). Many people's charitable thoughts and sympathetic emotions regarding the homeless are never translated into actions aimed at helping them.

What determines whether people's behavior will be consistent with the cognitive and affective components of their attitudes? Several factors are important. For one thing, consistency is most likely when the person's thoughts and feelings agree with one another (Lord, 1997). Second, consistency is more likely when the behavioral component of the attitude is in line with a *subjective norm,* our view of how important people in our lives want us to act. If there is a conflict between what we want to do and what subjective norms tell us we should do, we may end up behaving in ways that are inconsistent with our attitudes (Eagly & Chaiken, 1998). Thus, someone who believes that the rights of gay men and lesbians should be protected might not go out and campaign for this cause, because doing so would upset family members or co-workers who are strongly against it. Third, attitude-consistent behavior is more likely when people have *perceived control,* a

attitude A tendency toward a particular cognitive, emotional, or behavioral reaction to objects in one's environment.

belief that they can actually perform such behavior (Madden, Ellen, & Ajzen, 1992). You may hold a positive attitude about becoming an opera star, but if you don't believe it is possible, you are not likely to even try. Finally, *direct experience* with the object of an attitude increases the likelihood of attitude-consistent behavior (Lord, 1997). If your positive attitude toward caviar, say, is based on having actually tasted it, you are more likely to buy it than if your attitude stems solely from caviar's image as fancy food.

Forming Attitudes

People are not born with specific attitudes toward specific objects, but their attitudes about new objects begin to appear in early childhood and continue to emerge throughout life. How do attitudes form?

Inherited predispositions toward the temperaments described in Chapters 9 and 11 may have some indirect effects on attitudes (Tesser, 1993), but the formation of new attitudes is influenced mainly by the learning principles discussed in Chapter 5. In childhood, modeling and other forms of social learning play a major role. Children learn not only the names of objects but also what they should believe and feel about them and how they should act toward them. For example, a parent's words may teach a child not only that snakes are reptiles but also that they should be feared and avoided. So as children learn concepts such as "reptile" or "work," they learn attitudes about those concepts, too (J. M. Olson & Zanna, 1993).

Classical and operant conditioning can also shape positive or negative attitudes (Krosnick et al., 1992). Advertisers associate enjoyable music or soothing colors with the products they try to sell (Pratkanis & Aronson, 1991), and parents, teachers, and peers reward children for stating particular views. The *mere-exposure effect* described in Chapter 4 is influential as well. All else being equal, attitudes toward an object will become more positive the more frequently people are exposed to the object (Seamon et al., 1997). One study even found that newborns preferred to listen to stories that had been read aloud while they were still in the womb (Cacioppo, Berntson, & Petty, 1997). This exposure effect helps explain why we sometimes come to like a song only after hearing it several times—and why commercials and political ads are aired over and over.

Changing Attitudes

The nearly $100 billion a year spent on advertising in the United States alone provides but one example of how people constantly try to change our attitudes. Stop for a moment and make a list of other examples, starting, perhaps, with the persuasive messages of groups concerned with abortion or gun control or recycling—and don't forget your friends who want you to do something that you think is a waste of time.

A Model of Attitude Change   Whether a persuasive message succeeds in changing attitudes depends mainly on three factors: (1) the person communicating the message, (2) the content of the message, and (3) the audience who receives it (Petty & Wegener, 1998). The **elaboration likelihood model** of attitude change—illustrated in Figure 14.2—provides a framework for understanding when and how these factors affect attitude change. The model is based on the idea that persuasive messages can change people's attitudes through one of two main routes. The first is called the *peripheral route* because when it is activated, we devote little attention to the central content of the persuasive message and tend to be affected instead by peripheral persuasion cues, such as the confidence, attractiveness, or other characteristics of the person who delivers the message. These persuasion cues influence attitude change even though they may be irrelevant to the logic or validity of the message itself. Commercials in which movie stars or other attractive nonexperts endorse pain relievers are designed to encourage the peripheral route to attitude change. By contrast, when the *central route* to attitude change is activated, the content of the message becomes more important in determining attitude change than the characteristics of the communicator. A person following the central route uses logical steps—like those outlined in the Thinking Critically sections of this book—to analyze the

A REMINDER ABOUT POVERTY Photographs like this one are used by fundraising organizations to remind people of the kind thoughts and charitable feelings they have toward needy people and other social causes. As a result, people may be more likely to behave in accordance with the cognitive and affective components of their attitudes and make a donation to these good causes. Browse through several popular magazines, and calculate the percentage of such photos you find in ads for charitable organizations. While you are at it, make a note of other stimuli in these organizations' appeals that remind us of our concern for the less fortunate.

elaboration likelihood model   A model of attitude change suggesting that people can change their attitudes through a central route, by considering an argument's content, or through a peripheral route in which they rely on irrelevant persuasion cues.

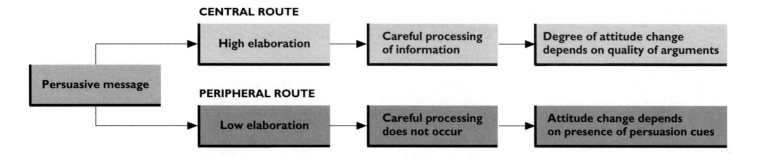

FIGURE 14.2

The Elaboration Likelihood
Model of Attitude Change

The central route to attitude change begins with high elaboration, which includes careful processing and evaluation of a message's content. The peripheral route involves low elaboration and reliance on persuasion cues such as the attractiveness of the person making the argument (Cacioppo, Petty, & Crites, 1993).

content of the persuasive message, including the validity of its claims, whether it leaves out pertinent information, alternative interpretations of evidence, and so on.

What determines which route people will follow? Personal involvement with message content is an important factor. The elaboration likelihood model predicts that the more personally involving a topic is, the more likely it is that the central route will be activated (Petty & Wegener, 1998). Suppose, for example, that you hear someone advocating the cancellation of student loans in Chile. This message might persuade you via the peripheral route if it comes from someone who looks attractive and sounds intelligent. However, you are more likely to follow the central route if the message proposes terminating student loans at *your* school. You might be persuaded, but only if the logic of the message is clear and convincing. This is why celebrity endorsements tend to be more effective when the products being advertised are relatively unimportant to the audience.

Persuasive messages are not the only means of changing attitudes. Another approach is to get people to act in ways that are inconsistent with their current attitudes, in the hope that they will adjust those attitudes to match their behavior. Often, such adjustments do occur. Cognitive dissonance theory attempts to explain why.

Cognitive Dissonance Theory Leon Festinger's (1957) classic **cognitive dissonance theory** holds that people want their thoughts, beliefs, and attitudes to be in harmony with one another and with their behavior. When these various elements are inconsistent, or *dissonant,* people become anxious and motivated to make them more consistent (Harmon-Jones et al., 1996). For example, someone who believes that "smoking is bad" but who must also acknowledge that "I smoke" would be motivated to reduce the resulting dissonance. But it is often difficult to change behavior, so people usually reduce cognitive dissonance by changing attitudes that are inconsistent with the behavior. So rather than quit smoking, the smoker might decide that smoking is not so bad.

In one of the first studies of cognitive dissonance, Festinger and his colleague Merrill Carlsmith (1959) asked people to turn pegs in a board, a very dull task. Later, some of these people were asked to persuade a person waiting to participate in the study that the task was "exciting and fun." Some were told that they would be paid $1 to tell this lie. Others were promised $20. After they had talked to the waiting person, their attitudes toward the dull task were measured. Figure 14.3 shows and explains the surprising results. The people who were paid just $1 to lie liked the dull task more than those who were paid $20 (Festinger & Carlsmith, 1959).

Hundreds of other experiments support the conclusion that people often reduce dissonance by changing their attitudes (Aronson et al., 1999; McGregor, Newby-Clark, & Zanna, 1999). These experiments have found that attitude-behavior inconsistency is most likely to change attitudes when (1) the inconsistency causes the person to feel psychologically uncomfortable and (2) changing attitudes will reduce that discomfort. But why should attitude-behavior inconsistency cause discomfort in the first place? There is considerable debate among attitude researchers about this question (Petty & Wegener, 1998).

One of the most popular of several proposed answers is that the discomfort is caused when people's positive self-concept (e.g., "I am honest") is threatened by the fact that they have, say, encouraged others to do something that they don't actually believe in or wouldn't do themselves. When their behavior is inconsistent with their self-concept, most people feel dishonest or hypocritical, so they change their attitudes to reduce or

cognitive dissonance theory   A theory stating that uneasiness results when people's thoughts, beliefs, and attitudes are inconsistent with one another and with their behavior, and that such uneasiness motivates people to try to restore consistency.

in review

Forming and Changing Attitudes

Type of Influence	Description
Modeling and conditioning	Attitudes are usually formed through observation of how others behave and speak about an attitude object, as well as through classical and operant conditioning.
Elaboration likelihood model	People change attitudes through either a central or peripheral route, depending on factors such as personal involvement.
Cognitive dissonance	Holding inconsistent cognitions can motivate attitude change.

eliminate such feelings (Stone et al., 1997). In other words, if people can persuade *themselves* that they really believe in what they have said or done, the inconsistency disappears, their positive self-concept is restored, and they can feel good about themselves again.

The power of cognitive dissonance to change attitudes may be greater in the individualist cultures of Europe and North America than in the collectivist cultures of Asia, for example. One study showed that Canadian students were much more likely to experience cognitive dissonance than their counterparts in Japan (Heine & Lehman, 1997). What is behind these cultural differences? Where group rather than individual values and goals are emphasized, behaving at odds with one's personal beliefs may create less discomfort—and less motivation for attitude change—because holding to those beliefs tends to be less important for self-esteem. ("In Review: Forming and Changing Attitudes" summarizes some of the main processes through which attitudes are formed and changed.)

Prejudice and Stereotypes

How does prejudice develop?

All of the principles underlying impression formation, attribution, and attitudes come together in prejudice and stereotypes. **Stereotypes** are the perceptions, beliefs, and expectations a person has about members of some group. They are schemas about entire groups of people (S. T. Fiske, 1998). Typically, they involve the false assumption that all members of a group share the same characteristics. The characteristics that make up the stereotype may be positive, but more often they are negative. The most prevalent and powerful stereotypes focus on observable personal attributes, particularly ethnicity, gender, and age (Eberhardt & Fiske, 1998).

The stereotypes people hold can be so ingrained that their effects on behavior are automatic and unconscious (Abreu, 1999). In one study, for example, white participants were shown pictures of black individuals (M. Chen & Bargh, 1997). The pictures were flashed so quickly, though, that the images were *subliminal*, meaning that the participants were not aware of seeing them (see Chapter 4). The images did have an effect, however. When these participants interacted with an African American man soon afterward, they behaved more negatively toward him and saw him as more hostile than did participants who had not been exposed to the pictures. The subliminally presented pictures had apparently activated the participants' negative stereotypes about blacks, thus altering their perceptions and behavior—all without their being aware of it.

Stereotyping often leads to **prejudice,** which is a positive or negative attitude toward an individual based simply on his or her membership in some group (Worchel et al.,

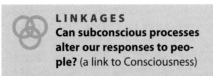

LINKAGES
Can subconscious processes alter our responses to people? (a link to Consciousness)

stereotypes Impressions or schemas of an entire group of people that involve the false assumption that all members of the group share the same characteristics.

prejudice A positive or negative attitude toward people in certain groups.

discrimination Differential treatment of people in certain groups; the behavioral component of prejudice.

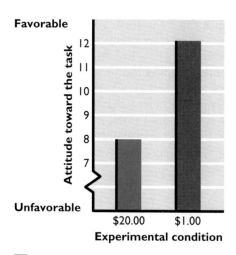

FIGURE 14.3

Cognitive Dissonance
and Attitude Change

According to cognitive dissonance theory, people given $20 to say a boring task was enjoyable had clear justification for lying and should experience little dissonance between what they said and what they felt about the task. Indeed, their attitude toward the task did not change much. However, people who received only $1 had little financial justification to lie and reduced their dissonance mainly by displaying a more positive attitude toward the task.

2000). *Prejudice* means literally "to prejudge." Many theorists believe that prejudice, like other attitudes, has cognitive, affective, and behavioral components. Stereotyped thinking is the cognitive component of prejudicial attitudes. The hatred, admiration, anger, and other feelings people have about stereotyped groups constitute the affective component. The behavioral component of prejudice involves **discrimination,** which is differential treatment of individuals who belong to different groups.

Theories of Prejudice and Stereotyping

Not all prejudice and stereotyping occur for the same reason. Three theories, each with supporting research, help to explain many instances of stereotyping and prejudice.

Motivational Theories   For some people, prejudice serves to meet certain needs and increases their sense of security. This idea was first proposed by T. W. Adorno and his associates fifty years ago (Adorno et al., 1950) and elaborated more recently by Robert Altemeyer (1988, 1994). These researchers suggest that prejudice is especially likely among people who display a personality trait called *authoritarianism*. According to Altemeyer, authoritarianism is composed of three main elements: (1) acceptance of very conventional or traditional values, (2) willingness to unquestioningly follow the orders of authority figures, and (3) an inclination to act aggressively toward individuals or groups identified by these authority figures as threats to the person's values or wellbeing. Indeed, people with an authoritarian orientation tend to view the world as a threatening place (Winter, 1996). One way to protect themselves from the threats they perceive all around them is to strongly identify with people like themselves—their *in-group*—and to reject, dislike, and perhaps even punish people from groups that are different from their own. Looking down on and discriminating against members of these *out-groups*—such as people from other religious or ethnic groups, gay men and lesbians, the elderly, or people with physical disabilities—may help authoritarian people feel safer and better about themselves (Haddock & Zanna, 1998b).

Another motivational explanation of prejudice involves the concept of social identity discussed earlier. Recall that whether or not they display authoritarianism, most people are motivated to identify with their in-group and tend to see it as better than other groups (M. B. Brewer & Brown, 1998). As a result, members of an in-group often see all members of out-groups as less attractive and less socially appropriate than members of the in-group and may thus treat them badly (Dovidio, Gaertner, & Validzic, 1998). In short, prejudice may result when people's motivation to enhance their self-esteem causes them to belittle other people.

Cognitive Theories   Stereotyping and prejudice may also result from the social-cognitive processes that people use in dealing with the world. There are so many other people, so many situations in which one meets them, and so many behaviors that others might display that one cannot possibly attend to and remember them all. Therefore, people must use schemas and other cognitive shortcuts to organize and make sense of their social world (Fiske, 1998). Often these cognitive processes provide accurate and useful summaries of other people, but sometimes they lead to inaccurate stereotypes. Instead of remembering every single detail about every person we meet, we often group people into social categories such as doctor, senior citizen, Republican, student, Italian, and the like (Rothbart & Lewis, 1994). To further simplify perception of these categories, we tend to see group members as being quite similar to one another. Thus, members of an ethnic group may find it harder to distinguish among specific faces in other ethnic groups than in their own (Anthony, Cooper, & Mullen, 1992). People also tend to assume that all members of a different group hold the same beliefs and values, and that those beliefs and values differ from their own (Dovidio, Gaertner, & Validzic, 1998). Finally, because particularly noticeable stimuli tend to draw a lot of attention, noticeably rude behavior by even a few members of an easily identified ethnic group may lead people to see an *illusory correlation* between rudeness and ethnicity (D. L. Hamilton & Sherman, 1994). As a result, they may incorrectly believe that all or most members of that group are rude.

Learning Theories   Like other attitudes, prejudice can be learned. Some prejudice is learned as a result of conflicts between members of different groups, but people also develop negative attitudes toward groups with whom they have had little or no contact. Learning theories suggest that children can acquire prejudices just by watching and listening to the words and deeds of parents, peers, and others (Rohan & Zanna, 1996). Movies and television also portray ethnic or other groups in ways that teach stereotypes and prejudice (Liebert & Sprafkin, 1988). And as mentioned earlier, children may be directly reinforced for expressing prejudice. In fact, small children often know about the supposed negative characteristics of many groups long before they ever meet people in those groups (Quintana, 1998).

Reducing Prejudice

One clear implication of the cognitive and learning theories of prejudice and stereotyping is that members of one group are often ignorant or misinformed about the characteristics of people in other groups. Before 1954, for example, most black and white schoolchildren in the United States knew very little about one another because they went to separate schools. Then the Supreme Court declared that segregated public schools should be prohibited. In doing so, the court provided a real-life test of the **contact hypothesis,** which states that stereotypes and prejudice toward a group will diminish as contact with the group increases (Pettigrew, 1997).

Did the school desegregation process of the 1960s and 1970s confirm the contact hypothesis? In a few schools, integration was followed by a decrease in prejudice, but in most places either no change occurred or prejudice actually increased (Oskamp & Schultz, 1998). However, these results did not necessarily disprove the contact hypothesis. In-depth studies of schools with successful desegregation suggested that contact alone was not enough—indeed, that integration reduced prejudice only when certain social conditions were created (M. B. Brewer & Brown, 1998). First, members of the two groups had to be of roughly equal social and economic status. Second, school authorities had to promote cooperation and interdependence between ethnic groups by having members of the two groups working together on projects that required reliance on one another to achieve success. Third, the contact between group members had to occur on a one-to-one basis. It was only when *individuals* got to know each other that the errors contained in stereotypes became apparent. Finally, the members of each group had to be seen as typical and not unusual in any significant way. When these four conditions were met, the children's attitudes toward one another became more positive.

Elliot Aronson (1995) describes a teaching strategy, called the *jigsaw technique,* that helps create these conditions. Children from several ethnic groups must work together on a team to complete a task such as writing a report about a famous person in history. Each child learns, and provides the team with, a separate piece of information about this person, such as place of birth or greatest achievement (Aronson, 1990). Studies show that children from various ethnic groups who take part in the jigsaw technique and other cooperative learning experiences show substantial reductions in prejudice toward other groups (e.g., Aronson, Wilson, & Akert, 1999). The success reported in these studies has greatly increased the popularity of cooperative learning exercises in U.S. classrooms. Such exercises may not eliminate all aspects of ethnic prejudice in children, but they seem to be a step in the right direction.

Can friendly, cooperative, interdependent contact reduce the more entrenched forms of prejudice seen in adults? It may. When equal-status adults from different ethnic groups work jointly toward a common goal, bias and distrust can be reduced. This is especially true if they come to see themselves as members of the same group rather than belonging to opposing groups (Dovidio & Gaertner, 1999; Gaertner, Dovidio, & Bachman, 1997). The challenge to be met in creating such cooperative experiences in the real world is that the participants must be of equal status—a challenge made more difficult in many countries by the sizable status differences that still exist between ethnic groups (Dovidio, Gaertner, & Validzic, 1998).

contact hypothesis   The idea that stereotypes and prejudice toward a group will diminish as contact with the group increases.

FIGHTING ETHNIC PREJUDICE
Negative attitudes about members of ethnic groups are often based on negative personal experiences or the negative experiences and attitudes people hear about from others. Cooperative contact between equals can help promote mutual respect and reduce ethnic prejudice.

In the final analysis, contact can provide only part of the solution to the problems of stereotyping, prejudice, and discrimination. To reduce ethnic prejudice, we must develop additional techniques to address the social cognitions and perceptions that lie at the core of bigotry and hatred toward people who are different from us (Monteith, Zuwerink, & Devine, 1994). Altering these mental processes will be difficult because, as we saw earlier, they can operate both consciously and unconsciously, causing even those who do not see themselves as prejudiced to discriminate against individuals who are different (Blair & Banaji, 1996; McPhail & Penner, 1995; Phelps et al., 2000).

Interpersonal Attraction

■ **What factors affect who likes whom?**

Research on prejudice suggests some of the reasons for which people, from childhood on, may come to dislike or even hate other people. An equally fascinating aspect of social cognition is why people like each other. Folklore tells us that "opposites attract," but also that "birds of a feather flock together." Although valid to some degree, each of these statements needs to be qualified. We begin our coverage of interpersonal attraction by discussing the factors that lead to initial attraction; we then examine how liking sometimes develops into more intimate relationships.

Keys to Attraction

Whether you like someone or not depends partly on situational factors and partly on personal characteristics.

The Environment   One of the most important determinants of attraction is simple physical proximity (Berscheid & Reis, 1998). As long as you do not initially dislike the person, your liking for him or her will increase with additional contact. This phenomenon— another example of the mere-exposure effect mentioned earlier (Seamon et al., 1997)— helps account for why next-door neighbors are usually more likely to become friends

LIKING AND PROXIMITY
Make a list of your closest friends; then jot down a sentence or two about how you met each of them. Research on environmental factors in attraction suggests that barring bad first impressions, we tend to like people we see often—our neighbors, co-workers, roommates, or classmates. Is this true in your case? If there are exceptions to this rule for you, what do you think interfered with the formation of friendship?

than people who live farther from one another. Chances are, most of your friends are people you met as neighbors, co-workers, or classmates.

The circumstances under which people first meet also influence attraction. You are much more likely to be attracted to a stranger you meet in comfortable, as opposed to uncomfortable, physical conditions. Similarly, if you receive a reward in the presence of a stranger, the chances that you will like that stranger are increased, even if the stranger is not the one giving the reward (M. S. Clark & Pataki, 1995). In one study, for example, an experimenter judged one person's creativity while another person watched. Compared with those who received a negative evaluation, participants who were evaluated positively tended to like the observer more (Griffitt & Guay, 1969). At least among strangers, then, liking can occur through associating someone with something pleasant.

Similarity People also tend to like those they perceive as similar to themselves on variables such as age, religion, smoking or drinking habits, or being a "morning" or "evening" person. Similarity in attitudes is another important influence on attraction (Lord, 1997).

An especially good predictor of liking is similarity in attitudes about mutual acquaintances, because in general, people prefer relationships that are *balanced*. Thus, as illustrated in Figure 14.4, if Meagan likes Abigail, the relationship is balanced as long as they agree on their evaluation of a third person, regardless of whether they like or dislike that third person. However, the relationship will be imbalanced if Meagan and Abigail disagree on their evaluation of a third person.

One reason for the correlation between attitude similarity and liking is that people who share attitudes tend to confirm one another's view of the world (Swann, Stein-Seroussi, & Giesler, 1992). It's hard to say, though, whether attraction is a cause or an effect of similarity (Berscheid & Reis, 1998). For example, you might like someone because his attitudes are similar to yours, but it is also possible that as a result of liking him, your attitudes will become more similar to his. Some people even change their perceptions of a liked person's attitudes so that the other person's attitudes seem more similar to their own (Brehm, 1992).

Physical Attractiveness Physical characteristics are another important factor in attraction, particularly in the early stages of a relationship (Berscheid & Reis, 1998). From preschool through adulthood, physical attractiveness is a key to popularity with members of both sexes (Dion, 1992; Langlois et al., 2000). Consistent with the **matching hypothesis** of interpersonal attraction, however, people tend to date, marry, or form other committed relationships with those who are similar in physical attractiveness (Berscheid & Reis, 1998). One possible reason for this outcome is that although people tend to be most attracted to those with the greatest physical appeal, they also want to avoid being rejected by such individuals. In short, it may be compromise, not preference,

FIGURE 14.4

Balanced and Imbalanced Relationships

Shown here are some common examples of balanced and imbalanced patterns of relationships among three people. The plus and minus signs refer to liking and disliking, respectively. Balanced relationships are comfortable and harmonious; imbalanced ones often bring conflict.

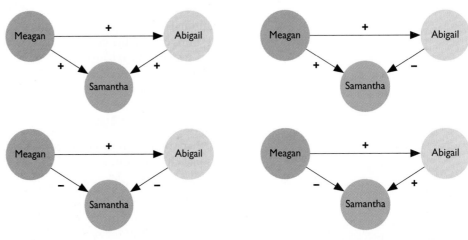

(A) BALANCED RELATIONSHIPS   **(B) IMBALANCED RELATIONSHIPS**

FIGURE 14.5

Sex Differences in Date and Mate Preferences

According to evolutionary psychologists, men and women have developed different strategies for selecting sexual partners. Specifically, they say that women became more selective than men because they can have relatively few children and want a partner who has the ability to help care for them. Here are some data that support this idea. When asked about the intelligence of people they would choose for one-night stands, dating, and sexual relationships, women preferred much smarter partners than men did. Only when the choices concerned steady dating and marriage did the men's preference for bright partners equal that of the women. Critics of the evolutionary approach explain such sex differences as reflecting social norms and people's expectations of the way men and women should behave (Eagly & Wood, 1999).

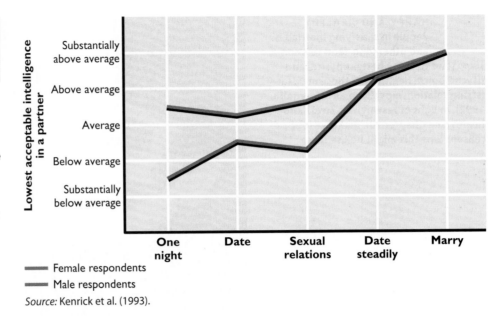

Source: Kenrick et al. (1993).

that leads people to pair off with those who are roughly equivalent to themselves in physical attractiveness (Carli, Ganley, & Pierce-Otay, 1991).

Intimate Relationships and Love

There is much about intimate relationships that psychologists do not, and may never, understand. However, they do know something about the characteristics that affect people's reactions to other people. For example, the physical appearance of a partner tends to be more important to men than women, whereas the partner's intelligence tends to be more important to women than men (D. M. Buss, 1999; see Figure 14.5).

Intimate Relationships Eventually, people who are attracted to each other usually become *interdependent,* which means that the thoughts, emotions, and behaviors of one person affect the thoughts, emotions, and behaviors of the other (M. S. Clark & Pataki, 1995). Interdependence occurs in large measure as the thoughts and values of one person become part of the self-concept of the other (Agnew et al., 1998). It is thus one of the defining characteristics of intimate relationships.

Another key component of successful intimate relationships is *commitment,* which is the extent to which each person is psychologically attached to, and wants to remain in, the relationship (Rusbult & Van Lange, 1996). People feel committed to a relationship when they are satisfied with the rewards they receive from it, have invested considerable resources (both tangible and intangible) in it, and have few attractive alternative relationships available to them (Bui, Peplau, & Hill, 1996).

Analyzing Love Affection, emotional expressiveness, social support, cohesiveness, sexuality—these characteristics of intimate relationships bring something else to mind: love. Yet *intimacy* and *love* are not synonymous. Most theorists agree that there are several different types of love (Brehm, 1992). One widely accepted view distinguishes between passionate love and companionate love (Hatfield & Rapson, 1996). *Passionate love* is intense, arousing, and marked by both strong physical attraction and deep emotional attachment. Sexual feelings are very strong, and thoughts of the other intrude on each person's awareness frequently. *Companionate love* is less arousing but psychologically more intimate. It is marked by mutual concern for the welfare of the other (Hendrick & Hendrick, 1986).

Robert Sternberg (1988b) has offered a more detailed analysis of love. According to his *triangular theory,* the three basic components of love are passion, intimacy, and commitment. Various combinations of these components result in various types of love. For

matching hypothesis A proposition stating that people are most likely to date, marry, or form committed relationships with others who are similar to themselves in physical attractiveness.

HAPPY AND HEALTHY
People in satisfying marriages and other long-term relationships tend to enjoy better physical and psychological health than those in unsatisfying relationships (Burman & Margolin, 1992). In light of research on stress and health (see Chapter 10), make a list of reasons why this might be the case.

example, Sternberg suggests that *romantic love* involves a high degree of passion and intimacy, yet lacks substantial commitment to the other person. *Companionate love* is marked by a great deal of intimacy and commitment but little passion. *Consummate love* is the most complete and satisfying. It is the most complete because it includes a high level of all three components. It is the most satisfying because the relationship is likely to fulfill many of the needs of each partner.

Cultural factors have a strong influence on the value that people place on love. In the United States and the United Kingdom, for example, the vast majority of people believe that they must love the person they marry. In India and Pakistan, about half the people interviewed in one survey said they would marry someone they did not love if that person had other qualities that they desired (R. Levine et al., 1995). Research in the former Soviet Union found only 40 percent of people saying that they married for love; rather, most married because of loneliness, shared interests, or an unplanned pregnancy (R. A. Baron & Byrne, 1994).

Strong and Weak Marriages   Long-term studies of successful and unsuccessful marriages suggest that premarital attitudes and feelings are predictive of marital success. In one such study, couples who had a close, intimate relationship and similar attitudes when they where dating were more likely to still be married fifteen years later (C. T. Hill & Peplau, 1998).

Among married couples, women—but not men—generally tend to be more satisfied with their marriage when the partners talk a lot about the relationship (Acitelli, 1992). The perception that the relationship is fair or equitable also enhances marital satisfaction (M. Clark, 1994). After the birth of a first child, for example, many wives find that they have much more work than they had anticipated. If their husbands do not share this work to the degree they expected, wives' marital satisfaction tends to decrease (Hackel & Ruble, 1992).

A related factor in long-term marital satisfaction is how the couple deals with the conflict and anger that occur in virtually all marriages. In unhappy marriages and marriages that end in divorce, husbands and wives trade increasingly nasty and hurtful remarks until communication breaks down (Gottman et al., 1998). In happy marriages, the cycle of hostile reactions is ultimately broken, allowing the couple to deal with the problem at hand during moments of calm (Rusbult et al., 1991). Husbands and wives in long-term, happy marriages are also able to generally agree on how they should deal with important issues in their marriage (Gottman et al., 1998; Rogge & Bradbury, 1999).

Social Influence

▪ What social rules shape our behavior?

So far, we have considered social cognition, the mental processes associated with people's perceptions of, and reactions to, other people. Let's now explore *social influence,* the process through which individuals and groups directly and indirectly influence a person's thoughts, feelings, and behavior. Research has shown, for example, that suicide rates increase following well-publicized suicides and that murder rates increase after well-publicized homicides (D. P. Phillips, 1983; D. P. Phillips & Cartensen, 1986). Do these correlations mean that media coverage of violence triggers similar violence? As described in Chapter 5, televised violence can play a causal role in aggressive behavior, but there's more to the story than that. For one thing, many of the people murdered soon after a sensational homicide are similar in some way to the victim (Cialdini, 1993). This phenomenon—known as "copycat" violence—illustrates the effects of social influence.

Social Norms

The most pervasive, yet subtle, form of social influence is communicated through social norms. **Norms** are learned, socially based rules that prescribe what people should or should not do in various situations (Cialdini & Trost, 1998). Parents, teachers, clergy, peers, and other "agents of culture" transmit norms. Because of the power of norms, people often follow them automatically. In North America and Britain, for example, norms tell us that we should get in line to buy a movie ticket rather than crowd around the box office window. They also lead us to expect that others will do the same. By providing information to people about what is expected of them and others, norms make social situations clearer, more predictable, and thus more comfortable.

One particularly powerful norm is *reciprocity,* the tendency to respond to others as they have acted toward you (Cialdini & Trost, 1998). To explore the nature of reciprocity, a researcher sent Christmas cards to strangers, most of whom responded with a card of their own. Some even added a personal note of good cheer (Kunz & Woolcott, 1976). But this norm and others are neither universal nor unchanging (Triandis, 1997). For instance, people around the world differ greatly in terms of the physical distance they keep between themselves and others while talking. Thus, people from South America usually stand much closer to each other than do people from North America. Thus, as suggested in Chapter 12, on psychological disorders, behavior considered normal and friendly in one culture may be seen as offensive, or even abnormal, in another.

The social influence exerted by norms creates orderly social behavior. But social influence can also lead to a breakdown in order. For example, **deindividuation** is a psychological state in which a person becomes "submerged in the group" and loses the sense of individuality (Lord, 1997). When people experience deindividuation, they become emotionally aroused and feel intense closeness with the group. In fact, they appear to become part of the "herd," and they may perform acts that they would not do otherwise. Deindividuation appears to occur when two factors are present (Prentice-Dunn & Rogers, 1989). The first is believing that one cannot be held personally accountable for one's actions. The second is a shifting of attention away from internal thoughts and standards and toward stimuli in the immediate environment. Having members of a group sing in unison or wear unusual uniforms (such as Ku Klux Klan robes) helps create this shift in attention.

Deindividuation usually results in antisocial acts, and the emotional arousal associated with it makes these acts difficult to stop (E. Smith & Mackie, 2000). Fans at rock concerts and athletic events have trampled one another to death in their frenzy to get the best seats; normally mild-mannered adults have thrown rocks or fire bombs at police during political protests. Such behavior becomes more extreme as people feel less identifiable. It is not surprising, then, that an analysis of old newspaper accounts of lynchings in the United States showed that larger lynch mobs were more savage and vicious than

norms Learned, socially based rules that prescribe what people should or should not do in various situations.

deindividuation A psychological state occurring in group members that results in loss of individuality and a tendency to do things not normally done when alone.

smaller ones (Mullen, 1986). Deindividuation provides an example of how, given the right circumstances, quite normal people can engage in destructive, even violent, behavior.

LINKAGES
Do people perform better or worse when others are watching? (a link to Motivation and Emotion)

LINKAGES

Motivation and the Presence of Others

In Chapter 8 we noted that social factors such as parental attitudes toward achievement often affect motivation. But a person's current motivational state is also affected by the mere presence of other people. To illustrate, consider what was probably the first experiment in social psychology, conducted by Norman Triplett in 1897.

Triplett noticed that bicyclists tended to race faster when a competitor was near than when all competitors were out of sight. Did seeing one another remind the riders of the need to go faster to win? To test this possibility, Triplett arranged for bicyclists to complete a twenty-five-mile course under three conditions: riding alone in a race against the clock; riding with another cyclist, but not in competition; or competing directly with another rider. The cyclists went much faster when another rider was present than when they were simply racing against time. This was true even when they were not competing against the other person. Something about the presence of the other person, rather than competition, produced increased speed.

The term **social facilitation** describes circumstances in which the presence of other people can improve performance. This improvement does not always occur, however. Sometimes, having other people present hurts performance, a process known as **social impairment.** For decades, these results seemed contradictory; then Robert Zajonc (pronounced "ZYE-onze") suggested that both effects could be explained by one process: arousal.

The presence of other people, said Zajonc, increases a person's general level of arousal or motivation (Zajonc, 1965). Arousal increases the tendency to perform those behaviors that are most *dominant*—the ones you know best. This tendency may either help or hinder performance. When you are performing an easy, familiar task such as riding a bike, increased arousal due to the presence of others should allow you to ride even faster than normal. But when a task is hard or unfamiliar—such as trying to perform a complex new dance routine in front of an audience—the most dominant responses may be incorrect and cause performance to suffer. Thus, the impact of other people on performance depends on whether the task is easy or difficult.

Why does the presence of others increase arousal? One reason is that being watched increases our sense of being evaluated, producing apprehension that in turn increases emotional arousal (Penner & Craiger, 1992). The presence of others may also distract us from the task at hand, or cause us to focus on only one part of it, thus impairing performance (R. S. Baron, Kerr, & Miller, 1992).

What if a person is not merely with others but is working with them on some task? It appears that the impact of others changes slightly (Sanna, 1992). When a group performs a task, it is not always possible to identify each individual's contributions. In these situations, people often exert less effort than when performing alone, a phenomenon called **social loafing** (Karau & Williams, 1997). Whether the task is pulling on a rope, clapping as loudly as possible, or trying to solve mental puzzles, people tend to work harder when alone than with others (R. S. Baron, Kerr, & Miller, 1992; M. Green, 1991). Steven Karau and Kipling Williams (1993) have proposed that social loafing occurs for two reasons: first, because rewards may come to a group whether or not every member works as hard as possible, and second, because rewards are usually divided equally among the group members. A review of experiments on social loafing shows that it occurs more often among men than women in Western cultures, and that it is much less likely among people of either gender in cultures such as China and Japan (P. B. Smith & Bond, 1999). These differences probably reflect the collectivist orientation, which tends to be

social facilitation   A phenomenon in which the mere presence of other people improves a person's performance on a given task.

social impairment   A reduction in performance due to the presence of other people.

social loafing   Exerting less effort when performing a group task because one's contribution cannot be identified.

SOCIAL FACILITATION OR SOCIAL IMPAIRMENT? When ballplayers such as Sammy Sosa try for a new home run record, they are able to perform at their best even when thousands watch. In fact, big crowds probably *help* them hit well. The presence of others tends to increase arousal, which facilitates performance of familiar skills such as a well-practiced batting swing. But increased arousal impairs the performance of unfamiliar behavior. So the same athletes who show flawless grace in a jammed stadium are likely to freeze up or blow their lines in front of a small production crew the first time they try to tape a TV ad or a public service announcement.

associated not only with women but also with people from Eastern cultures. This orientation emphasizes the importance of group performance and discourages social loafing.

In Western countries, social loafing can be seen in groups of all sorts, from volunteer committees to search parties. Because social loafing can hurt productivity in business situations, it is important for managers to develop ways of evaluating the efforts of every individual in a work group, not just the overall output of a team (T. L. Robbins, 1995).

Conformity and Compliance

Suppose you are with three friends. One says that Franklin Roosevelt was the greatest president in the history of the United States. You think that the greatest president was Abraham Lincoln, but before you can say anything, another friend agrees that it was Roosevelt, and then the other one does, too. What would you do? Disagree with all three? Maintain your opinion but keep quiet? Change your mind?

When people change their behavior or beliefs to match those of other members of a group, they are said to conform. **Conformity** occurs as a result of *unspoken* group pressure, real or imagined (Cialdini & Trost, 1998). You probably have experienced group pressure when everyone around you stands to applaud a performance you thought was not that great. You may conform by standing as well, though no one told you to do so; the group's behavior creates a silent, but influential, pressure to follow suit.

Compliance, in contrast, occurs when people adjust their behavior because of a request, such as "Please pass the salt." When the last holdouts for conviction on a jury give in to other jurors' browbeating, they have complied with overt social pressure.

Conformity and compliance are usually generated by a group's spoken or unspoken norms. In a classic experiment, Muzafer Sherif (1937) charted the formation of a group norm by taking advantage of the perceptual illusion whereby a stationary point of light in a completely dark room appears to move. Estimates of how far the light seems to move tend to stay the same over time if the observer is alone in the room. But when Sherif tested several people at once, asking each person to say aloud how far the light moved on repeated trials, their estimates tended to converge; they had established a group norm. Even more important, when individuals who had been in the group were later tested alone, they continued to be influenced by this norm.

conformity The changing of one's behavior or beliefs to match those of others, generally as a result of real or imagined, though unspoken, group pressure.

compliance The adjustment of one's behavior because of a direct request.

(A) STANDARD LINE

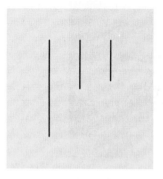

(B) TEST LINES

FIGURE 14.6

Types of Stimulus Lines Used
in Experiments by Asch

 **Participants in Asch's
experiments saw a new set of
lines like these on each trial.**
The middle line in Part B matches the one
in Part A, but when several of Asch's
(1955) assistants chose an incorrect line,
so did many of the participants. Try re-
creating this experiment with four friends.
Privately ask three of them to choose the
line on the left when you show this
drawing to all four, and then see if the
fourth person conforms to the group
norm. If not, do you think it was
something about the person, the length
of the incorrect line chosen, or both that
led to noncomformity? Would conformity
be more likely if the first three people
were to choose the line on the right?
(Read on for more on this possibility.)

In another classic experiment, Solomon Asch (1956) explored what people do when
faced with a norm that is obviously wrong. The participants in this experiment saw a
standard line like the one in Figure 14.6(A); then they saw a display like that in Figure
14.6(B). Their task was to pick out the line in the display that was the same length as the
one they had first been shown.

Each participant performed this task in a small group of people who appeared to be
fellow participants, but who were actually working for the experimenter. There were two
conditions. In the control condition, the real participant responded first. In the experimental condition, the participant did not respond until after the other people did. The
experimenter's assistants chose the correct response on six trials, but on the other twelve
trials they all gave the same, obviously incorrect, response. So, on twelve trials, each participant was confronted with a "social reality" created by a group norm that conflicted
with the physical reality created by what the person could clearly see. Only 5 percent of
the participants in the control condition ever made a mistake on this easy perceptual
task. However, among participants who heard the others' responses before giving their
own, about 70 percent made at least one error by conforming to the group norm. A
recent analysis of 133 studies conducted in 17 countries reveals that conformity in Asch-
type situations has declined somewhat in the United States since the 1950s, but that it
still occurs. It is especially likely in collectivist cultures, where conformity to group
norms is emphasized (P. B. Smith & Bond, 1999).

Why Do People Conform?   Why did so many people in Asch's experiment give incorrect
responses when they were capable of near-perfect performance? One possibility, called
public conformity, is that they gave an answer they did not believe in simply because it was
the socially desirable thing to do. Another possibility is called *private acceptance,* meaning that the participants used the other people's responses as legitimate evidence about
reality, were convinced that their own perceptions were wrong, and actually changed
their minds. Morton Deutsch and Harold Gerard (1955) reasoned that if conformity disappeared when people gave their responses without identifying themselves, then Asch's
findings must reflect public conformity, not private acceptance. In fact, conformity does
decrease when people respond privately instead of publicly, but it is not eliminated
(Deutsch & Gerard, 1955). People sometimes publicly produce responses that they do
not believe in, but hearing other people's responses also influences their private beliefs
(Moscovici, 1985).

Why are group norms so powerful? Research suggests three influential factors
(Cialdini & Trost, 1998). First, people are motivated to be correct, and norms provide
information about what is right and wrong. This factor may help explain why some
extremely disturbed or distressed people consider stories about suicide to be "social
proof" that self-destruction is a reasonable way out of their problems (Cialdini, 1993).
Second, people want to be liked by other group members. Finally, norms guide the distribution of social reward and punishment (Cialdini, 1995). From childhood on, people
in many cultures learn that going along with group norms is good and earns rewards.
These positive outcomes presumably help compensate for not always saying or doing
exactly what we please. People also learn that breaking a norm may bring punishments
ranging from scoldings for small transgressions to imprisonment for violation of norms
that have been translated into laws.

When Do People Conform?   People do not always conform to group influence. In the
Asch studies, for example, nearly 30 percent of the participants did not go along with the
assistants' obviously wrong judgments. Countless experiments have probed the question
of what combinations of people and circumstances do and do not lead to conformity.

Ambiguity, for example, is important in determining how much conformity will
occur. As the physical reality of a situation becomes less certain, people rely more and
more on others' opinions, and conformity to a group norm becomes increasingly likely
(Aronson, Wilson, & Akert, 1999). You can demonstrate this aspect of conformity on any
street corner. First, create an ambiguous situation by having several people look at the sky
or the top of a building. When passersby ask what is going on, be sure everyone excitedly

SIGN HERE, PLEASE Have you ever been asked to sign a petition in favor of a political, social, or economic cause? Supporters of such causes know that those who comply with this small request are the best people to contact later with requests to do more. Complying with larger requests is made more likely because it is consistent with the signer's initial commitment to the cause. If you were contacted after signing a petition, did you agree to donate money or become a volunteer?

reports seeing something interesting but fleeting—perhaps a faint light or a tiny, shiny object. If you are especially successful, conforming newcomers will begin persuading other passersby that there is something fascinating to be seen.

If ambiguity contributes so much to conformity, though, why did so many of Asch's participants conform to a judgment that was clearly wrong? The answer has to do with the *unanimity* of the group's judgment and the *size of the majority* expressing it. Specifically, people experience intense pressure to conform as long as the majority is unanimous. If even one other person in the group disagrees with the majority view, conformity drops greatly. For example, when Asch (1951) arranged for just one assistant to disagree with the others, fewer than 10 percent of the real participants conformed. Once unanimity is broken, it becomes much easier to disagree with the majority, even if the other nonconformist does not agree with the person's own view (J. C. Turner, 1991). Conformity also depends on the size of the majority. Asch (1955) demonstrated this phenomenon by varying the number of assistants in the group from one to fifteen. Conformity to incorrect norms grew as the number of people in the group increased. However, most of the growth in conformity occurred as the size of the majority rose from one to about three or four members. Psychologists believe that this effect occurs because pressure to conform has already reached a peak after someone has heard three or four people agree. Hearing more people confirm the majority view thus has little additional social impact (Latané, 1981).

Gender has also been studied as a factor influencing conformity. Early research on conformity suggested that women conform more than men, but this difference stemmed mainly from the fact that the tasks used in those experiments were often more familiar to men than to women. Indeed, people are especially likely to conform when they are faced with an unfamiliar situation (Cialdini & Trost, 1998). However, no male-female differences in conformity have been found in subsequent research using materials that are equally familiar to both genders (Maupin & Fisher, 1989).

Inducing Compliance   In the experiments just described, the participants experienced psychological pressure to conform to the views or actions of others, even though no one specifically asked them to do so. In contrast, *compliance* involves changing what you say or do because of a direct request. How is compliance brought about? Many people believe that the direct approach is always best: If you want something, ask for it. But salespeople, political strategists, social psychologists, and other experts have learned that often the best way to get something is to ask for something else. Three examples of this strategy are the foot-in-the-door technique, the door-in-the-face procedure, and the low-ball approach.

The *foot-in-the-door technique* consists of getting a person to agree to small requests and then working up to larger ones. In the original experiment on this strategy, homeowners were asked to do one of two things. Some were asked to allow placement of a large, unattractive "Drive Carefully" sign on their front lawn. Approximately 17 percent of the people approached in this way complied with the request. In the foot-in-the-door condition, however, homeowners were first asked only to sign a petition supporting laws aimed at reducing traffic accidents. Several weeks later, when a different person asked these same homeowners to put the "Drive Carefully" sign on their lawns, 55 percent of them complied (Freedman & Fraser, 1966).

Why should the granting of small favors lead to granting larger ones? First, people are usually far more likely to comply with a request that costs little in time, money, effort, or inconvenience. Second, complying with a small request makes people think of themselves as being committed to the cause or issue involved (Cialdini, 1995). In the study just described, participants who signed the petition might have thought, "I must care enough about traffic safety to do something about it." Compliance with the higher-cost request (displaying the sign) increased because it was consistent with these people's self-perceptions and past actions (Eisenberg et al., 1987).

The foot-in-the-door technique can be very effective. Steven Sherman (1980) created a 700 percent increase in the rate at which people volunteered to work for a charity simply by first getting them to say that in a hypothetical situation, they would volunteer if asked. For some businesses, the foot in the door is a request that potential customers merely answer a few questions; the request to buy something comes later. Others offer a small gift, or "door opener," as salespeople call it. Acceptance of the gift not only gives the salesperson a foot in the door but may also invoke the reciprocity norm: Many people who get something free feel obligated to reciprocate by buying something (Cialdini, 1993).

The second approach, known as the *door-in-the-face procedure,* also effectively obtains compliance (Cialdini, 1995). This strategy begins with a request for a favor that is likely to be denied. The person making the request then concedes that the initial favor was excessive and substitutes a lesser alternative—which is what he or she really wanted in the first place! Because the person appears willing to compromise, and because the new request seems small in comparison with the first one, it is more likely to be granted than if it had been made at the outset. The door-in-the-face strategy is at the heart of bargaining among political groups and between labor and management.

The third technique, called the *low-ball approach,* is commonly used by car dealers and other businesses (Cialdini & Trost, 1998). The first step in this strategy is to get a person's oral commitment to do something, such as to purchase a car. Once this commitment is made, the cost of fulfilling it is increased, often because of an "error" in computing the car's price. Why do buyers end up paying much more than originally planned for "low-balled" items? Apparently, once people commit themselves to do something, they feel obligated to follow through, especially when the person who obtains the initial commitment also makes the higher-cost request (Burger & Petty, 1981).

Obedience

▪ How far will people go to obey authority?

Compliance involves a change in behavior in response to an explicit request. In the case of **obedience,** the behavior change comes in response to a demand from an authority figure (Lutsky, 1995). In the 1960s, Stanley Milgram developed a laboratory procedure to study obedience. In his first experiment he used newspaper ads to recruit forty male volunteers between the ages of twenty and fifty from the local community. Among the participants were professionals, white-collar businessmen, and unskilled workers (Milgram, 1963).

Imagine you are one of the people who answered the ad. When you arrive for the experiment, you join a fifty-year-old gentleman who has also volunteered and has been scheduled for the same session. The experimenter explains that the purpose of the experiment is to examine the effects of punishment on learning. One of you—the "teacher"—will help the learner remember a list of words by administering electric shock whenever the learner makes a mistake. Then the experimenter turns to you and asks you to draw one of two cards out of a hat. Your card says, "TEACHER." You think to yourself that this must be your lucky day.

Now the learner is taken into another room and strapped into a chair, as illustrated in Figure 14.7. Electrodes are attached to his arm. You are shown a shock generator with thirty switches. The experimenter explains that the switch on the far left administers a mild, 15-volt shock and that each succeeding switch increases the shock by 15 volts. The one on the far right delivers 450 volts. The far left section of the shock generator is labeled "Slight shock." Looking across the panel, you see "Moderate shock," "Very strong shock," and at the far right, "Danger—severe shock." The last two switches are ominously labeled "XXX." The experimenter explains that you, the teacher, will begin by reading a list of word pairs to the learner. Then you will go through the list again, presenting just one word of each pair. The learner will have to say which word went with it. After the first mistake, you are to throw the switch to deliver 15 volts of shock. Each time the learner makes another mistake, you are to increase the shock by 15 volts.

obedience A form of compliance in which people comply with a demand from an authority figure.

You begin, following the experimenter's instructions. But after the learner makes his fifth mistake and you throw the switch to give him 75 volts, you hear a loud moan. At 90 volts, the learner cries out in pain. At 150 volts, he screams and asks to be let out of the experiment. You look to the experimenter, who says, "Proceed with the next word."

No shock was actually delivered in Milgram's experiments. The "learner" was always an employee of the experimenter, and the moans and other sounds of pain came from a prerecorded tape. But you do not know that. What would you do in this situation? Suppose you continue and eventually deliver 180 volts. The learner screams that he cannot stand the pain any longer and starts banging on the wall. The experimenter says, "You have no other choice; you must go on." Would you continue? Would you keep going even when the learner begged to be let out of the experiment and then fell silent? Would you administer 450 volts of potentially deadly shock to an innocent stranger just because an experimenter demands that you do so?

Figure 14.8 shows that only 5 participants in Milgram's experiment stopped before 300 volts, and 26 out of 40 (65 percent) went all the way to the 450-volt level. The decision to continue was difficult and stressful for the participants. Many protested repeatedly. But each time the experimenter told them to continue, they did so. Here is a partial transcript of what a typical participant said:

> *[After throwing the 180-volt switch]: He can't stand it. I'm not going to kill that man in there. Do you hear him hollering? He's hollering. He can't stand it. What if something happens to him? I'm not going to get that man sick in there. He's hollering in there. Do you know what I mean? I mean, I refuse to take responsibility. He's getting hurt in there. . . . Too many left here. Geez, if he gets them wrong. There are too many of them left. I mean, who is going to take responsibility if anything happens to that gentleman?*
>
> *[After the experimenter accepts responsibility]: All right. . . .*
>
> *[After administering 240 volts]: Oh, no, you mean I've got to keep going up the scale? No sir, I'm not going to kill that man. I'm not going to give him 450 volts.*
>
> *[After the experimenter says, "The experiment requires that you go on"]: I know it does, but that man is hollering in there, sir.*

This participant administered shock up to 450 volts (Milgram, 1974).

Factors Affecting Obedience

Milgram had not expected so many people to deliver such apparently intense shocks. Was there something about his procedure that produced such a high level of obedience? To

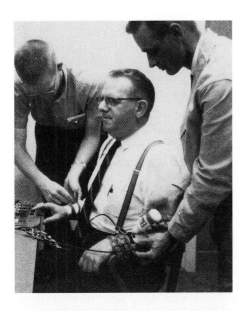

FIGURE 14.7

Studying Obedience in the Laboratory

In this photograph from Milgram's original experiment, a man is being strapped into a chair with electrodes on his arm. Although participants in the experiment do not know it, the man is actually an employee of the experimenter and receives no shock.

FIGURE 14.8

Results of Milgram's Obedience Experiment

When Milgram asked a group of undergraduates and a group of psychiatrists to predict how participants in his experiment would respond, they estimated that fewer than 2 percent would go all the way to 450 volts. In fact, 65 percent of the participants did so. What do you think you would have done in this situation?

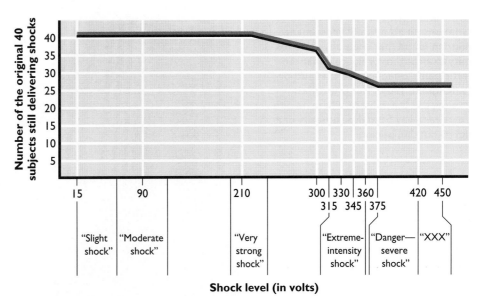

Source: Milgram (1963).

find out, Milgram and other researchers varied the original procedure in numerous ways. The overall level of obedience to an authority figure was usually quite high, but the degree of obedience was affected by several characteristics of the situation and procedure.

Prestige   One possibility is that the experimenter's status as a Yale University professor helped produce high levels of obedience in Milgram's original experiment. To test the effects of status and prestige, Milgram rented an office in a run-down building in Bridgeport, Connecticut. He then placed a newspaper ad for research sponsored by a private firm. There was no mention of Yale. In all other ways, the experimental procedure was identical to the original.

Under these less prestigious circumstances, the level of obedience dropped, but not as much as Milgram expected: 48 percent of the participants continued to the maximum level of shock, compared with 65 percent in the original study. Milgram concluded that people are willing to obey orders to do great harm to another even when the authority making the demand is not a particularly reputable or distinguished person.

Presence of Others Who Disobey   To assess how the presence of other people might affect obedience, Milgram (1965) created a situation in which there were three teachers. Teacher 1 (an employee of the experimenter) read the words to the learner. Teacher 2 (also an employee) stated whether or not the learner's response was correct. Teacher 3 (the actual participant) delivered the shock when the learner made mistakes. At 150 volts, when the learner began to complain that the shock was too painful, Teacher 1 refused to participate any longer and left the room. The experimenter asked him to come back, but he refused. The experimenter then instructed Teachers 2 and 3 to continue by themselves. The experiment continued for several more trials. However, at 210 volts, Teacher 2 said that the learner was suffering too much and also refused to participate further. The experimenter then told Teacher 3 (the actual participant) to continue the procedure. In this case, only 10 percent of the participants (compared with 65 percent in the original study) continued to deliver shock all the way up to 450 volts. In line with research on conformity, the presence of others who disobey appears to be the most powerful factor reducing obedience.

Personality Characteristics   Were the participants in Milgram's original experiment heartless creatures who would have given strong shocks even if there had been no pressure on them to do so? Quite the opposite; most of them were nice people who were

PROXIMITY AND OBEDIENCE In variations on his original experiment, Milgram found that close physical proximity to an authority figure enhanced participants' obedience to that authority (Milgram, 1965). This principle is employed in the military, where no one is ever far away from the authority of a higher-ranking person.

in review

Types of Social Influence

Type	Definition	Key Findings
Conformity	A change in behavior or beliefs to match those of others	In cases of ambiguity, people develop a group norm and then adhere to it. Conformity occurs because people want to be right, because they want to be liked by others, and because conformity to group norms is usually reinforced. Conformity usually increases with the ambiguity of the situation, as well as with the unanimity and size of the majority.
Compliance	A change in behavior or beliefs because of a request	Compliance increases with the foot-in-the-door technique, which begins with a small request and works up to a larger one. The door-in-the-face procedure can also be used. After making a large request that is denied, the person substitutes a less extreme alternative that was desired all along. The low-ball approach also elicits compliance. An oral commitment for something is first obtained; then the person claims that only a higher-cost version of the original request will suffice.
Obedience	A change in behavior in response to an explicit demand, typically from an acknowledged authority figure	People may inflict great harm on others when an authority demands that they do so. Even when people obey orders to harm another person, they often agonize over the decision. People are most likely to disobey orders to harm someone else when they see another person disobey.

influenced by experimental situations to behave in apparently antisocial ways. In a later demonstration of the same phenomenon, college students playing the role of prison guards behaved with aggressive heartlessness toward other students who were playing the role of prisoners (Zimbardo, 1973).

Still, not everyone is equally obedient to authority. For example, people who display what we described earlier as authoritarianism are more likely than others to comply with an experimenter's request to shock the learner. The same tends to be true of people who are *"externals"* (T. Blass, 2000). As described in Chapter 11, such people believe that what happens to them is controlled by factors outside themselves. (For a summary of Milgram's results, plus those of studies on conformity and compliance, see "In Review: Types of Social Influence.")

Evaluating Obedience Research

Milgram's obedience studies were conducted more than thirty-five years ago. How relevant are they today? Consider this fact: The U.S. Federal Aviation Authority attributes many commercial airplane accidents to "Captainitis." This phenomenon occurs when the captain of an airliner makes an obvious error, but none of the other crew members are willing to challenge the captain's authority by pointing out the error. As a result, planes have crashed and many people have died (Kanki & Foushee, 1990). Obedience to authority may also explain why a few years ago, many travelers at the airport in Frankfurt, Germany, followed an airport official's incorrect instructions to move *toward* a fire that had broken out rather than *away* from it. Several of those travelers died in the fire. These tragic events suggest that Milgram's findings are still relevant and important (Saks, 1992). Indeed, the results of his experiments have been confirmed in recent years in several Western countries, with female as well as male participants (T. Blass, 2000; P. B. Smith & Bond, 1999). Nevertheless, debate continues over the ethics and meaning of Milgram's work.

Questions About Ethics   Although the "learners" in Milgram's experiment suffered no discomfort, the participants did. Milgram (1963) observed participants "sweat, stutter, tremble, groan, bite their lips, and dig their fingernails into their flesh" (p. 375). Against the potential harm inflicted by Milgram's experiments stand the potential gains. For example, people who learn about Milgram's work often take his findings into account when deciding how to act in social situations (S. J. Sherman, 1980). But even if social value has come from Milgram's studies, a question remains: Was it ethical for Milgram to treat his participants as he did?

In the years before his death in 1984, Milgram defended his experiments (e.g., Milgram, 1977). He argued that the way he dealt with his participants after the experiment prevented any lasting harm. For example, he explained to them that the learner did not experience any shock, and the learner came in and chatted with each participant. And on a later questionnaire, 84 percent of the participants said that they had learned something important about themselves and that the experience had been worthwhile. Thus, Milgram argued, the experience was actually a positive one. Still, the committees charged with protecting human participants in research today would be unlikely to approve Milgram's experiments, and less controversial ways to study obedience have now been developed (Meeus & Raaijmakers, 1995).

Questions About Meaning   Do Milgram's dramatic results mean that most people are putty in the hands of authority figures and that most of us would blindly follow inhumane orders from our leaders? Some critics have argued that Milgram's results cannot be interpreted in this way because his participants knew they were in an experiment and may simply have been playing a cooperative role. If so, the specific social influence processes identified in his studies may not explain obedience in the real world today (Lutsky, 1995). Most psychologists believe, however, that Milgram did demonstrate a basic truth about human behavior—namely, that under certain circumstances people are capable of unspeakable acts of brutality toward other people. Sadly, examples abound. One of the most horrifying aspects of Nazi atrocities against the Jews—and of more recent attempts at genocide against ethnic groups in Eastern Europe and Africa—is that the perpetrators are not necessarily demented, sadistic fiends. Most of them are normal people who, because of the situations they face, are influenced to behave in a demented and fiendish manner.

Worse, inhumanity can occur even without pressure to obey. For example, a good deal of people's aggressiveness toward other people appears to come from within. In the next section, we consider human aggressiveness and some of the circumstances that influence its expression.

LINKAGES
Is it ethical to deceive people to learn about their social behavior? (a link to Introduction to the Science of Psychology)

Aggression

▮ Are people born aggressive?

Aggression is an action intended to harm another person. It is all too common. Overall, more than 1.5 million violent crimes are committed each year in the United States, including nearly 90,000 rapes and 15,500 murders (Federal Bureau of Investigation, 2000). In the United States, homicide is the second leading cause of death for people between fifteen and twenty-four years of age (Hoyert, Kochanek, & Murphy, 1999). Surprisingly, over 50 percent of all murder victims knew their assailants—as family members, friends, or acquaintances (Federal Bureau of Investigation, 2000). Indeed, one study found that almost half of the dating couples interviewed reported that one partner

aggression   An act that is intended to cause harm to another person.

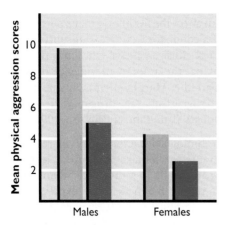

FIGURE 14.9

Testosterone and Aggression

In the study illustrated here, the children of women who had taken testosterone during pregnancy to prevent miscarriage became more aggressive than the mothers' other children of the same sex who had not been exposed to testosterone during prenatal development. This outcome appeared in both males and females.

had been physically aggressive toward the other (O'Leary, Malone, & Tyree, 1994). Other studies reveal that up to about one-third of married and unmarried partners in the United States have displayed aggression toward each other ranging from pushing, shoving, and slapping to beatings and the threatened or actual use of weapons (Archer, 2000; Heyman & Neidig, 1999; Pan, Neidig, & O'Leary, 1994).

Why Are People Aggressive?

Sigmund Freud suggested that people have death instincts that account for aggression. Evolutionary psychologists believe that aggression helped prehistoric people compete for mates, thus ensuring the survival of their genes in the next generation. Through natural selection, they say, aggressive tendencies are passed on through successive generations.

Freudian and evolutionary theories seem too simplistic to fully account for human aggressiveness, however. For one thing, there are large differences in aggression from culture to culture. The murder rate in the Philippines, for example, is forty-six times higher than in China or Finland, and almost nine times higher in the United States than in those latter two countries (Geen 1998b; Triandis, 1994). These data suggest that even if aggressive *impulses* are universal, the appearance of aggressive *behavior* reflects an interplay of nature and nurture (Geen, 1998b). No equation can predict when people will be aggressive, but years of research have revealed a number of important biological, learning, emotional, and environmental factors that combine in various ways to produce aggression in various situations.

Genetic and Biological Mechanisms   The evidence for hereditary influences on aggression is strong, especially in animals (Cairns, Gariepy, & Hood, 1990). In one study, the most aggressive members of a large group of mice were interbred; then the most aggressive of their offspring were also interbred. After this procedure was followed for twenty-five generations, the resulting animals would immediately attack any mouse put in their cage. Continuous inbreeding of the least aggressive members of the original group produced animals that were so nonaggressive that they would refuse to fight even when attacked (Lagerspetz & Lagerspetz, 1983). Research on human twins reared together or apart suggests that there is a genetic component to aggression in people as well (Tellegen et al., 1988). However, other research suggests that people do not necessarily inherit the tendency to be aggressive. Instead, they may inherit certain temperaments, such as impulsiveness, that in turn make aggression more likely (R. A. Baron & Richardson, 1994; Rowe, Almeida, & Jacobson, 1999).

Several parts of the brain influence aggression (C. A. Anderson & Anderson, 1998). One of these is the limbic system, which includes the amygdala, the hypothalamus, and related areas. Damage to these structures may produce defensive aggression, which includes heightened aggressiveness to stimuli that are not usually threatening or a decrease in the responses that normally inhibit aggression (Coccaro, 1989; Eichelman, 1983). The prefrontal cortex may also be involved in aggression (Raine et al., 2000).

Hormones, too, play an important role in aggression. One possibility is that aggression is related to a person's level of *testosterone,* the masculine hormone that is present in both sexes (Bernhardt, 1997). Experiments have shown that aggressive behavior increases or decreases dramatically with the amount of testosterone in an animal's body (L. G. Frank, Glickman, & Licht, 1991). Violent criminals appear to have higher levels of testosterone than nonviolent ones (Dabbs et al., 1995). And among normal men, variations in testosterone show a small, but statistically significant, correlation with aggressiveness (Dabbs & Morris, 1990).

Testosterone may have its most significant and durable influence through its impact on early brain development. One natural test of this hypothesis occurred when pregnant women were given testosterone in an attempt to prevent miscarriage. Accordingly, their children were exposed to high doses of testosterone during prenatal development. Figure 14.9 shows that these children grew up to be more aggressive than their same-sex siblings who were not exposed to testosterone during prenatal development (Reinisch, Ziemba-Davis, & Sanders, 1991).

FOLLOWING ADULT EXAMPLES
Learning to express aggression is especially easy for children in Kosovo and other places where aggressive acts are modeled daily.

Drugs that affect the central nervous system also affect the likelihood that a person will act aggressively. Even relatively small amounts of alcohol, for example, can substantially increase some people's aggressiveness (S. P. Taylor & Hulsizer, 1998). One study demonstrated that when male alcoholics stopped drinking, the amount of violence directed toward their spouses decreased significantly (O'Farrell & Murphy, 1995). No one knows exactly why alcohol affects aggression, but research suggests that the drug may affect areas of the brain that normally inhibit aggressive responses (Lau, Pihl, & Peterson, 1995).

Learning and Cultural Mechanisms Although biological factors may increase or decrease the likelihood of aggression, cross-cultural research makes it clear that learning also plays a role. Aggressive behavior is much more common in individualist than in collectivist cultures, for example (Oatley, 1993). Cultural differences in the expression of aggression appear to stem in part from differing cultural values (D. Cohen et al., 1996). For example, the Utku (an Inuit culture) view aggression in any form as a sign of social incompetence. In fact, the Utku word for "aggressive" also means "childish" (Oatley, 1993). The effects of culture on aggression can likewise be seen in the fact that the amount of aggression in a given culture changes over time as cultural values change (Baron & Richardson, 1994).

In addition, people learn many aggressive responses by watching others (S. L. Smith & Donnerstein, 1998). The most obvious illustrations appear as "copycat" crimes. More generally, children learn and perform many novel aggressive responses that they see modeled by others. Bandura's "Bobo" doll experiments, which are described in Chapter 5, on learning, provide impressive demonstrations of the power of observational learning. The significance of observational learning is underscored by studies of the effects of televised violence, also discussed in Chapter 5. For example, the amount of violent content watched on television by eight-year-olds predicts aggressiveness in these children even fifteen years later (Huesmann et al., 1997). Fortunately, not everyone who sees aggression becomes aggressive; individual differences in temperament, the modeling of nonaggressive behavior by parents, and other factors can temper the effects of violent television. Nevertheless, observational learning does play a significant role in the development and display of aggressive behavior (C. A. Anderson, 1997).

Immediate reward or punishment can also alter the frequency of aggressive acts. People become more aggressive when rewarded for aggressiveness and less aggressive when punished for aggression (Geen, 1998b). In short, a person's accumulated experiences, including culturally transmitted teachings, combine with daily rewards and punishments to influence whether, when, and how aggressive acts occur (R. A. Baron & Richardson, 1994).

When Are People Aggressive?

In general, people are more likely to be aggressive when they are both physiologically aroused and experiencing a strong emotion such as anger (Geen, 1998a). People tend either to lash out at those who make them angry or to displace their anger onto children, pets, or other defenseless targets. However, aggression can also be made more likely by other forms of emotional arousal, especially *frustration,* which is a condition that occurs when obstacles block the fulfillment of goals.

Frustration and Aggression Suppose that a friend interrupts your studying for an exam by asking to borrow a book. If things have been going well that day and you are feeling confident about the exam, you are likely to be friendly and accommodating. But what if you are feeling frustrated because your friend's visit represents the fifth interruption in the last hour? Under these emotional circumstances, you may react aggressively, perhaps yelling at your startled visitor for bothering you.

Your aggressiveness in this situation would be predicted by the **frustration-aggression hypothesis**, which suggests that frustration leads to aggression (Dollard et al., 1939). Research on this hypothesis has shown that it is too simple and too general, however. For one thing, frustration sometimes produces depression and withdrawal, not

frustration-aggression hypothesis A proposition stating that the existence of frustration always leads to some form of aggressive behavior.

aggression (Berkowitz, 1998). In addition, not all aggression is preceded by frustration (Berkowitz, 1994).

In recent years Leonard Berkowitz has modified the frustration-aggression hypothesis in two ways. First, he proposes that stress in general, not just frustration, is involved in aggression. Stress, he says, produces a *readiness* for aggression that may or may not be translated into aggressive behavior (Berkowitz, 1998). Once this readiness exists, however, aggression can be more easily triggered by stimuli in the environment. The triggering stimuli might be guns or knives, televised scenes of people arguing, or other cues associated with aggression (C. A. Anderson, Benjamin, & Bartholow, 1998). In other words, neither stress alone nor environmental cues alone are sufficient to set off aggression. When combined, however, they often do. Support for this revision of the frustration-aggression hypothesis has been quite strong (Carlson, Marcus-Newhall, & Miller, 1990).

In the second modification of that hypothesis, frustration and other stressors are seen as important in aggression mainly because they create negative feelings, or *negative affect* (Berkowitz, 1998). Research suggests that the more negative affect people experience, regardless of what caused it, the stronger is their readiness to be aggressive. Participants in one study experienced negative affect caused by the pain of immersing their hands in ice water. They became more aggressive than participants in a control group whose hands were in water of room temperature (Berkowitz, 1998).

Generalized Arousal   Imagine that you've just jogged three miles. You are hot, sweaty, and out of breath, but you are not angry. Still, the physiological arousal caused by jogging may increase the probability that you will become aggressive if, say, a passerby shouts an insult (Zillmann, 1988). Why? The answer lies in a phenomenon described in Chapter 8, on motivation and emotion: Arousal from one experience may carry over to a new situation, producing what is called *transferred excitation*. Thus, the physiological arousal caused by jogging may intensify your reaction to an insult (Geen, 1998a).

By itself, however, arousal does not lead to aggression. It is most likely to produce aggression when the situation presents some reason, opportunity, or target for aggression (Zillmann, 1988). In one study, for example, people engaged in two minutes of vigorous exercise. Then they had the opportunity to deliver electric shock to another person. The exercise caused them to increase the amount of shock delivered only if the participants had first been insulted (Zillmann, Katcher, & Milavsky, 1972). Apparently, the arousal resulting from the exercise made aggression more likely; the insult "released" it. These findings are in keeping with the notion suggested by learning theorists (and by Berkowitz's revisions of the frustration-aggression hypothesis) that aggression is caused not by internal impulses alone *or* by particular situations alone but by the interaction of the two.

Does Pornography Cause Aggression?

In both men and women, sexual stimulation produces strong, generalized physiological arousal, especially in the sympathetic nervous system. If arousal in general can make a person more likely to be aggressive (given a reason, opportunity, and target), could stimuli that create sexual excitement be dangerous? In particular, does viewing pornographic material make people more likely to be aggressive? Prior to the mid-1980s, numerous scholars had concluded that there is no evidence for an overall relationship between any type of antisocial behavior and mere exposure to pornographic material (Donnerstein, 1984b). However, in 1986 the U.S. Attorney General's Commission on Pornography reexamined the question and concluded that pornography is dangerous.

■ What am I being asked to believe or accept?

Specifically, the commission proposed that there is a cause-effect link between viewing erotic material and several forms of antisocial behavior, including sexually related crimes.

Is there evidence available to support the claim?

The commission cited several types of evidence in support of its conclusion. First, there was the testimony of men convicted of sex crimes. Rapists, for example, are unusually heavy consumers of pornography, and they often say that they were aroused by erotic material immediately before committing a rape (Silbert & Pines, 1984). Similarly, child molesters often view child pornography immediately before committing their crimes (Marshall, 1989).

In addition, the commission cited experimental evidence that men who are most aroused by aggressive themes in pornography are also the most potentially sexually aggressive. One study, for example, showed that men who said they could commit a rape became sexually aroused by scenes of rape and less aroused by scenes of mutually consenting sex; this was not true for men who said they could never commit a rape (Malamuth & Check, 1983).

Perhaps the strongest evidence cited by the commission, however, came from transferred excitation studies. In a typical experiment of this type, people are told that a person in a separate room (actually an employee of the experimenter) will be performing a learning task and that they are to administer an electric shock every time the person makes a mistake. The intensity of shock can be varied (as in the Milgram studies, no shock actually reaches the employee), but participants are told that changing the intensity will not affect the speed of learning. So the shock intensity (and presumed pain) that they choose to administer is taken as a measure of aggressive behavior. Some participants watch a sexually explicit film before the learning trials begin, and the arousal created by the film appears to make them more aggressive than participants who don't see such films (Donnerstein, 1984b).

Can that evidence be interpreted another way?

The commission's interpretation of the evidence was faulted on several counts. First, critics argued that some of the evidence should be given little weight. In particular, how believable is the testimony of convicted sex offenders? It may reflect self-serving attempts to lay the blame for their crimes on pornography. These reports cannot establish that exposure to pornography causes aggression. Indeed, it may be that pornography partially *satisfies* sex offenders' aggressive impulses rather than creating them (Aronson, Wilson, & Akert, 1999). Similarly, the fact that potential rapists are most aroused by rape-oriented material may show only that they prefer violence-oriented pornography, not that such materials created their impulse to rape.

What about the evidence from transferred excitation studies? To interpret these studies, you need to know that the pornography that led to increased aggression contained violence as well as sex. The sexual activity depicted was painful for, or unwanted by, the woman. So the higher levels of aggression that followed viewing these films could have been due to the transfer of sexual arousal, the effects of observing violent behavior, or the effects of seeing sex combined with violence (Donnerstein, Slaby, & Eron, 1995).

In fact, several careful experiments have found that highly arousing sexual themes, in and of themselves, do not produce aggression. When men in transferred excitation studies experience pleasant arousal by viewing a film depicting nudity or mutually consenting sexual activity, their subsequent aggression is actually less than when they viewed no film or a neutral film (Lord, 1997). In short, transferred excitation studies might be interpreted as demonstrating that portrayals of sexual *violence* influence aggressiveness.

What evidence would help to evaluate the alternatives?

Two types of evidence are needed to better understand the effects of pornography on aggression. First, because pornography can include sexual acts, aggressive acts, or both, the effects of each of these components must be more carefully examined (G. C. V. Hall & Hirschman, 1991). Second, factors affecting males' reactions to pornography, particularly pornography that involves violence, must be more clearly understood (Malamuth et al., 1991). Work has already begun on each of these fronts.

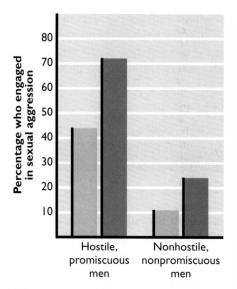

FIGURE 14.10

Pornography and Sexual Aggression

Extensive exposure to pornography does not make most men more sexually aggressive. Sexual aggressiveness is much more likely, however, among men who not only watch a lot of pornography but are also hostile toward women and sexually promiscuous.

environmental psychology   The study of the effects of the physical environment on people's behavior and mental processes.

Whether specifically paired with sexual activity or not, aggressive themes do appear to increase subsequent aggression (Malamuth, Heavy, & Linz, 1993). Research has focused on *aggressive pornography,* which contains sexual themes but also scenes of violence against women (Worchel et al., 2000). In laboratory experiments, males often administer larger amounts of shock to females after viewing aggressive pornographic films as compared with neutral films. Yet there is no parallel increase in aggression against other males, indicating that the films create not a generalized increase in aggression but an increase in aggressiveness directed toward women (Malamuth, 1998). Similarly, viewing aggressive pornography in which the victim appears aroused by the aggression usually leads males to become less sympathetic toward the rape victim and more tolerant of aggressive acts toward women (Donnerstein & Linz, 1995). Sexually explicit films that do not contain violence have no effects on attitudes toward rape (Linz, Donnerstein, & Penrod, 1987).

Are all men who are exposed to aggressive pornography equally likely to become rapists? The evidence available so far suggests that the answer is no. Whether aggressive pornography alters men's behavior and attitudes toward women depends to some extent on the men. For example, a study of over 2,700 men across the United States showed that three factors—a history of sexual promiscuity (casual sex with many partners), feelings of hostility toward women, and the consumption of pornography—interact to affect sexual aggression against women (Malamuth, 1998). Among men *low* in promiscuity and hostility, viewing pornography had little, if any, impact on sexual aggression; but among men who were *high* in promiscuity and hostility, pornography dramatically increased the chances that these men would engage in sexual aggression. In fact, 72 percent of the men who were high on all three factors had done so (see Figure 14.10).

What conclusions are most reasonable?

The attorney general's commission appeared to ignore numerous studies showing that the relationship between sexual arousal and aggression is neither consistent nor simple (Malamuth, 1998). Analysis of this relationship reveals the importance of distinguishing between pornography in general and aggressive pornography in particular. Overall, there is no reason to assume that sexual arousal created by nonaggressive pornography is associated with aggressive behavior. Indeed, for most people, sexual arousal and aggression remain quite separate.

However, *aggressive* pornography can lead to violence against women, especially in men who are already inclined to abuse and exploit women. Thus, there is reason for concern over the impact of sexual violence commonly seen on television and in movies—especially in "slasher" films. Remarkably, such films are sometimes given less-restrictive ratings ("R" or even "PG-13") than films that are nonviolent but erotic.

In short, pornography *per se* is probably not a cause of violence against women. In combination with other factors, however, certain kinds of pornography can play a role in sexual aggression.

Environmental Influences on Aggression   The link between physiological arousal and the likelihood of aggressive behavior suggests that stressful environmental conditions can create enough arousal to make aggressive behavior more likely (C. A. Anderson & Anderson, 1998). This possibility is one of the research topics in **environmental psychology,** the study of the relationship between people's physical environment and their behavior (Sommer, 1999). One aspect of the environment that clearly affects social behavior is the weather, especially temperature. High temperatures are a source of stress; as Figure 14.11 indicates, murder and other violent crimes are most likely to occur during the hottest months of the year (C. A. Anderson & Anderson, 1998).

Living arrangements also influence aggressiveness. Compared with the tenants of crowded apartment buildings, those in buildings with relatively few residents are less

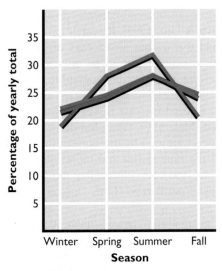

Source: C. A. Anderson & Anderson (1998).

FIGURE 14.11

Temperature and Aggression

Studies from around the world indicate that aggressive behaviors are most likely to occur during the hottest months of the year. These studies support the hypothesis that environmental factors can affect aggression.

---

likely to behave aggressively (P. A. Bell et al., 1996). This difference appears to be due in part to how people feel when they are crowded. Crowding tends to create physiological arousal and to make people tense, uncomfortable, and more likely to report negative feelings (Oskamp & Schultz, 1998). This arousal and tension can influence people to like one another less and to be more aggressive.

Altruism and Helping Behavior

▪ What motivates people to help one another?

At the beginning of this chapter we told of soldiers in Rwanda who massacred 400 unarmed civilians who had sought refuge in a church. Incidents such as this illustrate the worst of human behavior—aggression and violence. But in almost every tragic episode of senseless mayhem, one can also find the best of human behavior as well—selflessness and heroism. When two young boys opened fire in an Arkansas schoolyard in 1998, for example, Shannon Wright, a teacher, placed herself between the shooters and her students. She died because she chose to protect her students rather than herself. Consider also the people who saved the life of Reginald Denny. He had the misfortune to be driving his truck through the center of the riots that broke out in Los Angeles, California, in 1992. As his path was blocked by crowds, four men pulled him out of the truck and beat him mercilessly as a local TV helicopter beamed live pictures of the scene. Among the thousands watching the broadcast were two men and two women living in the riot area who left the safety of their homes to try to help Denny. Although threatened by Denny's attackers and the crowd, these four people got the severely injured man into his truck and drove him to the hospital. Doctors there said that had he arrived at the hospital five minutes later, Denny would have died (Schroeder et al., 1995).

The actions of these individuals provide dramatic examples of a social behavior that may be more common than aggression: people helping one another. **Helping behavior** is defined as any act that is intended to benefit another person. Helping can range from picking up dropped packages to donating a kidney. Closely related to helping is **altruism,** an unselfish concern for another's welfare (Dovidio & Penner, 2001). In the following sections we examine some of the reasons for helping and altruism, along with some of the conditions under which people are most likely to help others.

Why Do People Help?

The tendency to help others begins early, although at first it is not spontaneous; children have to learn to be helpful (Eisenberg & Fabes, 1998). In most cultures, very young children usually help others only when they are asked to do so or are offered a reward (Grusec, 1991). Still, Carolyn Zahn-Waxler and her associates (1992) found that almost half of the two-year-olds they observed acted helpfully toward a friend or family member. Even before their second birthday, some children offer help to those who are hurt or crying by snuggling, patting, or offering food or even their own teddy bears. As they grow older, children use helping behavior to gain social approval, and their efforts at helping become more elaborate. The role of social influence in the development of helping is seen as children follow examples set by people around them. Their helping behaviors are shaped by the norms established by their families and the broader culture (Grusec & Goodnow, 1994). In addition, children are usually praised and given other rewards for helpfulness, but scolded for selfishness. Eventually most children come to believe that being helpful is good and that they are good when they are helpful. By the late teens, people often help others even when no one is watching and no one will know that they did so (Cialdini, Baumann, & Kenrick, 1981). There are three major theories about why people help even when they cannot expect any external rewards for doing so.

---

helping behavior   Any act that is intended to benefit another person.

altruism   An unselfish concern for another's welfare.

A YOUNG HELPER **Even before their second birthday, some children offer help and comfort to those who are hurt or crying.**

Arousal:Cost-Reward Theory   One approach to explaining why people help is called the **arousal:cost-reward theory** (Piliavin et al., 1981). This theory proposes that people find the sight of a victim distressing and anxiety-provoking and that this experience motivates them to do something to reduce the unpleasant arousal. Before rushing to a victim's aid, however, the bystander will first evaluate two aspects of the situation: the costs associated with helping and the costs (to the bystander and the other person) of not helping. Whether or not the bystander actually helps depends on the outcome of this evaluation (Dovidio et al., 1991). If the costs of helping are low (as when helping someone pick up a dropped grocery bag) and the costs of not helping are high (as when the other person is physically unable to do this alone), the bystander will almost certainly help. However, if the costs of helping are high (as when helping someone lift a heavy box into a car) and the costs of not helping are low (as when the other person is obviously strong enough to do the job alone), the bystander is unlikely to offer help (Fritzsche, Finkelstein, & Penner, 2000). One of the strengths of the arousal:cost-reward theory is that it is comprehensive enough to explain several factors that affect helping. Let's consider some of these factors now.

In March 2000, a sixty-two-year-old woman in Darby, Pennsylvania, was walking to the grocery store when she was pushed from behind by an attacker. She fended him off and then did her shopping as usual. It was only when she got home and her daughter saw the handle of a knife protruding from her back that she realized that the assailant had stabbed her! No one in the grocery store said anything to her about the knife, let alone offered to help. Why? Mainly because the woman did nothing to suggest that help was necessary. This bizarre case illustrates that the first major factor affecting whether people offer help is the *clarity* of the need for help (Dovidio et al., 1991). In one study, undergraduate students waiting alone in a campus building observed what appeared to be an accident involving a window washer. The man screamed as he and his ladder fell to the ground; then he clutched his ankle and groaned in pain. All of the students looked out of the window to see what had happened, but only 29 percent of them did anything to help. Other students witnessed the same "accident," but with one important added element: The man *said* he was hurt and needed help. In this case, more than 80 percent of the participants came to his aid (Yakimovich & Saltz, 1971). Why so many? Apparently, this one additional cue eliminated any uncertainty in the students' minds that the person needed help. The man's more obvious need for help served to raise the perceived costs of not helping him, thus making helping more likely.

The *presence of others* also has a strong influence on the tendency to help. Somewhat surprisingly, however, their presence tends to *inhibit* helping behavior. One of the most highly publicized examples of this phenomenon was the Kitty Genovese incident, which occurred on a New York City street in 1964. During a thirty-minute struggle, a man stabbed Genovese repeatedly, but none of the dozens of neighbors who witnessed the attack intervened or even called the police until it was too late to save her life. Public dismay and disbelief followed. Psychologists wondered whether something about the situation that night had prevented people from helping.

The numerous studies of helping behavior stimulated by this tragedy revealed a social phenomenon that may explain why Genovese's neighbors did nothing to help her. This phenomenon, called the **bystander effect,** can be described as follows: The chance that someone will help in an emergency usually decreases as the number of people present increases (Dovidio & Penner, 2001). Why does the bystander effect occur? One explanation is that each witness assumes someone else will take responsibility for helping the victim. This *diffusion of responsibility* among all the witnesses leaves each witness feeling less obligated to help and thus lowers the perceived cost of not helping (Schroeder et al., 1995). The bystander effect is strongest when the cost of helping is high, as when a helper would have to exert physical effort or risk personal injury.

The degree to which the presence of other people will inhibit helping may depend on who those other people are. When they are strangers, perhaps poor communication inhibits helping. Many people have difficulty speaking to strangers, particularly in an emergency; and without speaking, they have difficulty knowing what the others intend to

arousal:cost-reward theory   A theory that attributes helping behavior to people's efforts to reduce the unpleasant arousal they feel when confronted with a suffering victim, while also considering the costs involved.

bystander effect   A phenomenon in which the chance that someone will help in an emergency usually decreases as the number of people present increases.

DIFFUSION OF RESPONSIBILITY
Does the man lying on the sidewalk need help? The people walking by him were probably not sure, and they might have assumed that if he did need help, someone else would assist him. Research on social factors affecting helping suggests that if you are ever in need of help, especially in a crowd, it is important not only to clearly ask for help but also to tell a specific onlooker to take specific action (for example, "You, in the yellow shirt, please call an ambulance!").

do. According to such logic, if people are with friends rather than strangers, they should be less embarrassed, more willing to discuss the problem, and thus more likely to help.

In one experiment designed to test this idea, a female experimenter left a research participant in a waiting room, either alone, with a friend, with a stranger, or with a stranger who was actually an assistant to the experimenter (Latané & Rodin, 1969). The experimenter then stepped behind a curtain into an office. For nearly five minutes, she could be heard opening and closing the drawers of her desk, shuffling papers, and so on. Then there was a loud crash, and she screamed, "Oh, my god—my foot, I—I can't move it. Oh, my ankle—I can't get this—thing off me." Then the participant heard her groan and cry.

Would the participant go behind the curtain to help? Once again, people were most likely to help if they were alone. When one other person was present, participants were more likely both to communicate with one another and to offer help if they were friends than if they were strangers. When the stranger was the experimenter's assistant—who had been instructed not to help—very few participants offered to help. Other studies have confirmed that bystanders' tendency to help increases when they know one another (Rutkowski, Gruder, & Romer, 1983).

Valuable as it is, the arousal:cost-reward theory does not account for all of the factors that affect helping. For instance, it cannot easily explain why helping differs in different environments. Research conducted in several countries has shown that people in urban areas are generally less helpful than those in rural areas (Aronson et al., 1999). Why? It is probably not the simple fact of living in a city but rather the stressors one finds there that tend to make some urban people less helpful than those in rural settings. One study of thirty-six U.S. cities found that *population density* (the number of people per square mile) in a community was much more strongly related to helping than was the size of the city in which people lived (R. V. Levine et al., 1994). The higher the density, the less likely people were to help others. Why should stress make people less helpful? Two explanations have been suggested. The first is that stressful environments create bad moods—and generally speaking, people in a bad mood are less likely to help (Salovey, Mayer, & Rosenhan, 1991). A second possibility is that noise, crowding, and other urban stressors create too much stimulation. To reduce this excessive stimulation, people may pay less attention to their surroundings, including less attention to individuals who need help.

The arousal:cost-reward theory also fails to address *personality factors* that might affect helping. Research shows that some people are simply more likely to help than others. Consider, for example, the Christians who risked their lives to save Jews from the

Nazi Holocaust. Samuel and Pearl Oliner (1988) interviewed over 200 of these rescuers and compared their personalities with those of people who had had a chance to save Jews but did not do so. The rescuers were found to have more *empathy* (the ability to understand or experience another's emotional state), more concern about others, a greater sense of responsibility for their own actions, and greater confidence that their efforts would succeed. Louis Penner and his associates (Penner et al., 1995; Penner & Finkelstein, 1998) found that these same personality traits predict a broad range of helping behaviors, ranging from how quickly bystanders intervene in an emergency to how much time volunteers spend helping AIDS patients.

Empathy-Altruism Theory   The second major approach to explaining helping is embodied in the **empathy-altruism theory,** which asserts that people are more likely to engage in altruistic, or unselfish, helping—even at a high cost—if they feel empathy toward the person in need (Batson, 1998). In one experiment illustrating this phenomenon, students listened to a tape-recorded interview in which a young woman told how her parents had died in an automobile accident, leaving no life insurance (Batson et al., 1997). She said that she was trying to take care of her younger brother and sister while going to college, but that time and money were so tight that she might have to quit school or give up her siblings for adoption. Actually, the woman was an actress telling a story written by the researchers, but the participants thought it was real. Before hearing the tape, half the participants were given information about the woman that would increase their empathy for her; the other half were not. After listening to the tape, all participants were asked to help the woman raise money for herself and her siblings. Consistent with empathy-altruism theory, more participants in the empathy group offered to help than did those in the control group.

Were the students who offered help in this experiment being utterly unselfish, or could there have been other reasons for their apparent altruism? This is a hotly debated question. Some researchers dispute the concept of truly altruistic helping and suggest that people help in such situations for more selfish reasons. For example, helping may serve to relieve the distress people feel when hearing of other people's problems (Cialdini et al., 1997). Although the final verdict on this question is not yet in, the evidence appears to support the contention that empathizing with another person can sometimes lead to unselfish helping (Dovidio, Allen, & Schroeder, 1990).

Evolutionary Theory   The evolutionary approach to social psychology sees many human behaviors as echoes of actions that contributed to the survival of our prehistoric ancestors (D. M. Buss, 1999). At first glance, it might not seem reasonable to apply evolutionary theory to helping and altruism, because helping others at the risk of our own well-being does not appear adaptive. If we die while trying to save others, it will be their genes, not ours, that will survive. Indeed, according to Darwin's concept of the "survival of the fittest," helpers—and their genes—should have disappeared long ago. Contemporary evolutionary theorists suggest, however, that Darwin's thinking about natural selection focused too much on the survival of the fittest *individuals* and not enough on the survival of their genes *in others*. Thus, survival of the fittest has been replaced by the concept of *inclusive fitness,* the survival of one's genes in future generations (W. D. Hamilton, 1964). Because we share genes with our relatives, helping—or even dying for—a cousin, a sibling, or above all, our own child potentially increases the likelihood that at least some of our genetic characteristics will be passed on to the next generation through the beneficiary's future reproduction (D. M. Buss, 1999). Thus, *kin selection,* or helping a relative to survive, may produce genetic benefits for the helper even if it provides no personal benefits.

There is considerable evidence that kin selection occurs among birds, squirrels, and other animals. The more closely the animals are related, the more likely they are to risk their lives for one another. Studies in a wide variety of cultures show the same pattern of helping among humans (Essock-Vitale & McGuire, 1985). For example, people in the United States are three times as likely to donate a kidney to a relative as to a nonrelative (Borgida, Conner, & Monteufel, 1992). (See "In Review: Helping Behavior" for a summary of the major reasons why people help and the conditions under which they are most likely to do so.)

empathy-altruism theory   A theory suggesting that people help others because they feel empathy toward them.

Helping Behavior

Theory	Basic Premise	Important Variables
Arousal:cost-reward	People help in order to reduce the unpleasant arousal caused by another person's distress. They attempt to minimize the costs of doing this.	Factors that affect the costs of helping and of not helping
Empathy-altruism	People sometimes help for utterly altruistic reasons. They are motivated by a desire to Increase another person's well-being.	The amount of empathy that one person feels for another
Evolutionary	People help relatives because it increases the chances that the helper's genes will survive in future generations.	The biological relationship between the helper and the recipient of help

FOCUS ON RESEARCH

Does Family Matter?

In and of themselves, the data on kidney donations do not confirm evolutionary theories of helping and altruism. The tendency to donate organs to relatives could also be due to the effects of empathy toward more familiar people, social pressure from family members, or other social influence processes. To control for the effects of some of these confounding variables, researchers have turned to the laboratory to study the role of evolutionary forces in helping behavior.

■ What was the researchers' question?

Eugene Burnstein, Christian Crandell, and Shinobu Kitayama (1994) wanted to know whether people faced with a choice of whose life to save will act in a manner consistent with the concept of kin selection. That is, would people be inclined to help relatives before nonrelatives, and would a relative's ability to produce offspring affect this tendency?

■ How did the researchers answer the question?

For ethical as well as practical reasons, Burnstein and his colleagues could not put people's lives in danger and then observe which (if any) of their relatives tried to save them. So instead, they used a simulation, or *analogue,* method. Specifically, they asked people to imagine a situation and then to say how they would respond if the situation were real.

The participants in this analogue experiment were 110 men and 48 women enrolled at universities in Japan and the United States. The first independent variable was the kind of help that was needed. Some participants were asked to imagine life-or-death situations in which there was time to save only one of three people who were asleep in separate rooms of a burning house. Other participants were asked to imagine everyday situations in which they had time to help only one of three people who each needed a small favor. The other independent variables were the characteristics of the people needing help in each situation—such as how closely they were related to the potential helper and their age, sex, and physical health. The dependent variable was the participants' choice of which person they would help first.

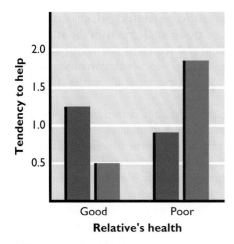

FIGURE 14.12

Kin Selection and Helping

In this analogue experiment, students said they would be more likely to save the life of a healthy relative than that of a sick one, but more likely to do a favor for the sick relative. Such results have been cited in support of the evolutionary approach to helping behavior (Burnstein, Crandell, & Kitayama, 1994).

■ What did the researchers find?

Consistent with evolutionary theory of kin selection, participants imagining the life-or-death situation said they would be much more likely to first save a close relative (such as their brother) than a more distant relative. They were also more likely to first save either relative than an unrelated friend. Was this simply because people tend to help closer relatives in any situation? Probably not, because genetic relatedness played a much smaller role in decisions about doing favors. Here, participants said that they would be only slightly more likely to help a close relative than a distant relative.

A relative's ability to produce offspring—and thus help family genes survive—also affected the participants' responses. For example, although participants said they were more willing to do a small favor for an elderly relative than a teenage relative, they also said they would be much more likely to save the life of the teenager. Similarly, they were more likely to do a favor for a sick relative than for a healthy one; but in a life-or-death situation, they chose to save the healthy relative more often than the sick one (see Figure 14.12). And overall, the participants said they were more likely to save the life of a female relative than a male relative, *unless* the female was past childbearing age. There were no substantial differences between the responses of students in the United States and those in Japan.

■ What do the results mean?

The results of this experiment generally support the concept of kin selection, which predicts that we tend to help closer relatives because it helps us in the genetic long run. Specifically, if we save the life of a relative who is able to father or produce offspring, we have really helped ourselves, because more of our genes will be present in the next generation. Evolutionary psychologists see data such as those obtained by Burnstein's research group as evidence that even today, kin selection affects the decisions people make when it comes to saving the life of another person. In short, they conclude there is an evolutionary basis for helping.

■ What do we still need to know?

Although these findings are consistent with the predictions of evolutionary theory, they must be interpreted with caution, and in light of the methods that were used to obtain them. Analogue studies give clues to behavior—and allow experimental control—in situations that approximate, but may not precisely duplicate, those outside the laboratory. They tend to be used when it would be unethical or impractical to expose people to "the real thing." However, we might question whether the students' responses might have been different if they were actually in the situations described in this analogue experiment. The researchers showed that kin selection *could* play a role in human helping behavior; they did not demonstrate that it actually does.

Moreover, this study does not enable us to predict the behavior of specific individuals in specific situations (Batson, 1998). For example, people sometimes risk their lives to save the lives of total strangers (Goffard, 1999). Like all behavior, helping and altruism depend on the interplay of many genetic and environmental factors—including interactions between particular people and particular situations. Future studies may tell us why and when people offer help to members of their family, and to nonrelatives as well.

---

cooperation Any type of behavior in which several people work together to attain a goal.

competition Any type of behavior in which individuals try to attain a goal for themselves while denying that goal to others.

Cooperation, Competition, and Conflict

Helping is one of the many ways in which people cooperate in order to accomplish their goals. **Cooperation** is any type of behavior in which people work together to attain a goal. For example, several law students might form a study group to help one another pass the bar exam. But people also compete with others for limited resources. Those same students might later try to outdo one another to be chosen for a single job opening at a top law firm. **Competition** exists whenever individuals try to attain a goal for themselves while denying that goal to others. Finally, there is **conflict,** which occurs when a person or group believes that another person or group interferes with the attainment of a goal. When the law students become attorneys and represent opposing parties in a trial, they will be in conflict with one another. One way in which psychologists have learned about all three of these phenomena is by studying social dilemmas (Gifford & Hine, 1997).

Social dilemmas are situations—usually occurring in large communities—in which an action that is most rewarding for each individual will, if adopted by all, become catastrophic for everyone. For instance, it might benefit a factory owner's immediate profit picture to dump toxic waste into a river; but if all factories do the same, the environment will eventually become uninhabitable for everyone. Similarly, during a drought, each homeowner is better off in the short run by watering the lawn as often as necessary to keep it from dying; but if everyone ignores local water restrictions, there will be no drinking water for anyone in the long run. Social dilemmas reflect inherent conflicts between the interests of the individual and those of the group and between short-term and long-term interests (Schroeder, 1995). Are people from collectivist cultures (which emphasize cooperation) less likely to act competitively or selfishly in social dilemma situations? This may be true in general, but interpersonal conflict in such situations still appears to some extent in all cultures (P. B. Smith & Bond, 1999).

Group Processes

■ What makes a good leader?

Although Western industrialized cultures tend to emphasize individuals over groups, the fact remains that most important decisions and efforts by governments and businesses in those cultures and elsewhere are made by groups, not individuals. Sometimes group processes are effective, as when a team of doctors, nurses, specialists, and two parents brought the McCaughey septuplets into the world on November 19, 1997. At other times, they can have disastrous results, as we will see later. For now, let's consider some of the social psychological processes that often occur in groups to alter the behavior of their members and the quality of their collective efforts.

Group Leadership

A good leader can help a group pursue its goals, but a poor one can get in the way of a group's functioning. What makes a good leader? Early research suggested that the personalities of good and bad leaders were about the same, but we now know that certain

A TEAM EFFORT How many people does it take to deliver a baby? Multiply your answer by seven, and you still won't come close to the number of medical professionals who, in 1997, worked as a well-organized team to ensure the healthy delivery of the McCaughey septuplets.

personality traits often distinguish effective from ineffective leaders. For example, using tests similar to those that measure the big-five traits described in Chapter 11, Robert Hogan and his colleagues (1994) found that effective leaders tend to score high on dominance, emotional stability, agreeableness, and conscientiousness. Other researchers have found that in general, effective leaders are intelligent, success oriented, and flexible (J. M. Levine & Moreland, 1998).

Having particular personality traits does not guarantee good leadership ability, however. People who are effective leaders in one situation may be ineffective in another (Yukl & Van Fleet, 1992). The reason is that effective leadership also depends on the characteristics of the group members, the task at hand, and most important, the interaction between these factors and the leader's style.

Two main styles of leadership have been identified. **Task-oriented** leaders provide very close supervision, lead by giving orders, and generally discourage group discussion (Yukl & Van Fleet, 1992). Their style may make them unpopular. In contrast, **person-oriented** leaders provide loose supervision, ask for group members' ideas, and are generally concerned with subordinates' feelings. They are usually well liked by those they lead.

Research on leadership effectiveness and gender provides one explanation as to why one leadership style is not invariably better than another. According to Alice Eagly and her associates, men and women in Western cultures tend to have different leadership styles (Eagly, Karau, & Makhijani, 1995). Overall, men and women are equally capable leaders, but men tend to be more effective when success requires a more task-oriented leader, and women are more effective when success requires a more person-oriented leader. One interpretation of these differences is that the gender-role learning processes described in Chapter 9 lead men and women to "specialize" in different leadership behaviors. This may be one reason some people do not like female leaders who act in a "masculine" manner or occupy leadership positions traditionally held by men. In certain circumstances, such responses create bias against female leaders, particularly among male members of the groups they lead (Eagly, Makhijani, & Klonsky, 1992).

Most contemporary theories of leadership are known as *contingency* theories (J. M. Levine & Moreland, 1998) because they suggest that leadership effectiveness is contingent, or dependent upon, factors such as the leader's relations with group members and the nature of the group's task. These theories note, for example, that task-oriented leaders tend to be most effective when the group is working under time pressure, when the task is unstructured, and when circumstances make it unclear as to what needs to be done first and how duties should be divided. People stranded in an elevator in a burning building, for example, need a task-oriented leader. Conversely, person-oriented leaders tend to be most effective when the task is structured and there are no severe time limits (Chemers, 1987). These people would be particularly successful, for example, in managing an office in which the workers know their jobs well.

Groupthink

The emphasis on group decisions in most large organizations is based on the belief that several people working together will make better decisions than will individuals working alone. As noted in Chapter 7, this belief is generally correct; yet under certain circumstances, groups have been known to make amazingly bad decisions (J. M. Levine & Moreland, 1998). Consider two examples. First, in the late 1930s, U.S. government leaders decided not to take special precautions to defend Hawaii's Pearl Harbor. The Japanese attack there on December 7, 1941, killed 2,500 people. Second, in 1986, administrators at the National Aeronautics and Space Administration (NASA) ignored engineers' warnings about the effects of cold weather and decided to launch the space shuttle *Challenger*. The spacecraft exploded seventy-three seconds after liftoff, killing all aboard. After analyzing these and other disastrous governmental decisions, Irving Janis (1989) proposed that they can be attributed to a phenomenon called **groupthink**. Groupthink occurs, he said, when group members are unable to realistically evaluate the options available to them or to fully consider the potential negative consequences of the option they are about to choose.

conflict A phenomenon occurring when a person or group believes that another person or group stands in the way of achieving a valued goal.

social dilemmas Situations in which actions that produce rewards for one individual will produce negative consequences if they are adopted by everyone.

task-oriented Referring to leaders who provide close supervision, lead by giving directives, and generally discourage group discussion.

person-oriented Referring to leaders who provide loose supervision, ask for group members' ideas, and are generally concerned with subordinates' feelings.

groupthink A pattern of thinking that over time renders group members unable to evaluate realistically the wisdom of various options and decisions.

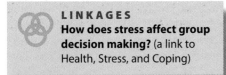

LINKAGES
How does stress affect group
decision making? (a link to
Health, Stress, and Coping)

Groupthink is particularly likely when three conditions exist: (1) the group is isolated from outside influences (J. C. Turner et al., 1992), (2) the group is working under time pressure or other intense stressors (Worchel & Shackelford, 1991), and (3) the leader is not impartial. This last condition appeared to play a crucial role in President John F. Kennedy's decision to support a disastrously unsuccessful invasion of Cuba by anti-Castro Cubans in 1961. Before the final decision was made, several advisers were told that Kennedy had made up his mind and it was time to "close ranks with the president." This situation created enormous pressure for conformity (May & Zelikow, 1997).

When these three conditions exist, groups tend to become close-minded and to rationalize their decision as the only reasonable one. They dismiss other options and quickly suppress any dissenting voices. As a result, the group becomes more and more certain that its decision cannot possibly be wrong. Although some researchers have questioned the prevalence and dangers of groupthink (Aldag & Fuller, 1993), most researchers agree that it does occur, at least under conditions similar to those originally identified by Janis (R. S. Baron, Kerr, & Miller, 1992).

Some psychologists have worked on developing techniques to help groups avoid groupthink. One is to designate someone to play the "devil's advocate," a person who constantly challenges the group's emerging decisions and offers alternatives (Janis, 1989; Risen, 1998). Another is to encourage the expression of diverse opinions by making them anonymous. Group members might sit at separate computers and send e-mail messages to the group about all the options that occur to them. These special systems hide the sender's identity, allowing the group to discuss the options through e-mail without knowing who is saying what. Research on this procedure suggests that it is effective in stimulating logical debate and making people less inhibited about disagreeing with the group (O'Brien, 1991).

active review Social Psychology

Linkages

As noted in Chapter 1, all of psychology's subfields are related to one another. Our discussion of how the presence of others affects motivation illustrates just one way in which the topic of this chapter, social psychology, is linked to the subfield of motivation and emotion (Chapter 8). The Linkages diagram shows ties to two other subfields as well, and there are many more ties throughout the book. Looking for linkages among subfields will help you see how they all fit together and help you better appreciate the big picture that is psychology.

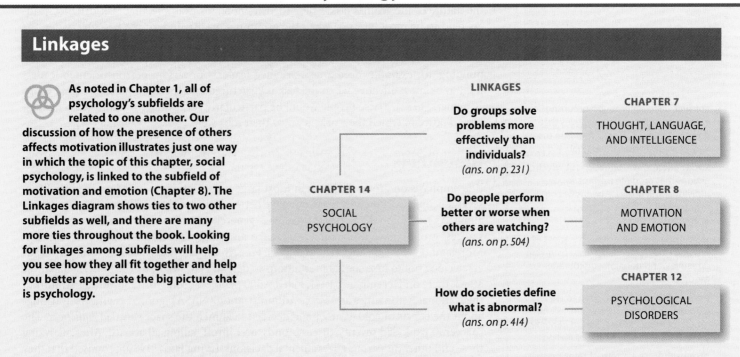

LINKAGES

Do groups solve
problems more
effectively than
individuals?
(ans. on p. 231)

CHAPTER 7
THOUGHT, LANGUAGE,
AND INTELLIGENCE

CHAPTER 14
SOCIAL
PSYCHOLOGY

Do people perform
better or worse when
others are watching?
(ans. on p. 504)

CHAPTER 8
MOTIVATION
AND EMOTION

How do societies define
what is abnormal?
(ans. on p. 414)

CHAPTER 12
PSYCHOLOGICAL
DISORDERS

Summary

Social cognition, the mental processes through which people perceive and react to others, is one aspect of *social psychology,* the study of how people influence and are influenced by other people. Through social cognition, each person creates a unique perception of reality.

SOCIAL INFLUENCES ON THE SELF

How do we compare ourselves to others?

People's social and cultural environments affect their thoughts and feelings about themselves, including their *self-esteem* and their *self-concept.* When people have no objective criteria by which to judge themselves, they look to others as the basis for *social comparison.* Such comparison can affect self-evaluation or self-esteem. Categories of people that are habitually used for social comparison are known as *reference groups.* Comparison to reference groups sometimes produces *relative deprivation,* which in turn can cause personal and social turmoil.

A person's *social identity* is formed from beliefs about the groups to which the person belongs. Social identity affects the beliefs we hold about ourselves, our self-concept. Social identity permits people to feel part of a larger group, engendering loyalty and sacrifice from group members, but also potentially creating bias and discrimination toward people who are not members of the group.

SOCIAL PERCEPTION

Do we perceive people and objects in similar ways?

Social perception concerns the processes by which people interpret information about others, form impressions of them, and draw conclusions about the reasons for their behavior. *Schemas,* the mental representations about people and social situations that we carry into social interactions, affect what we pay attention to, what we remember, and how we judge people and events.

First impressions are formed easily and quickly, in part because people apply existing schemas to their perceptions of others. First impressions change slowly, because people are "cognitive misers"; once we form an impression about another person, we try to maintain it because doing so simplifies the world. Schemas, however, can create *self-fulfilling prophecies,* leading us to act in ways that bring out behavior in others that is consistent with our expectations of them.

Attribution is the process of explaining the causes of people's behavior, including our own. Observers tend to attribute behavior to causes that are either internal or external to the actor. Attributions are also affected by biases that systematically distort one's view of behavior. The most common attributional biases are the *fundamental attribution error* (and its cousin, the ultimate attribution error), the *actor-observer bias,* and the *self-serving bias.* Personal and cultural factors can affect the extent to which people exhibit attributional biases.

ATTITUDES

Do attitudes always determine behavior?

An *attitude* is the tendency to respond positively or negatively to a particular object. Attitudes affect a wide range of behaviors. Most social psychologists see attitudes as composed of three components: cognitive (beliefs), affective (feelings), and behavioral (actions). However, it is often difficult to predict a specific behavior from a person's beliefs or feelings about an object. Cognitive theories suggest that the likelihood of attitude-behavior consistency depends on agreement of the person's thoughts and feelings, subjective norms, perceived control over the behavior, and prior direct experience with the attitude object.

Attitudes can be learned through modeling, as well as through classical or operant conditioning. They are also subject to the mere-exposure effect: All else being equal, people develop greater liking for a new object the more often they are exposed to it.

The effectiveness of a persuasive message in changing attitudes is influenced by the characteristics of the person who communicates the message, by its content, and by the audience receiving it. The *elaboration likelihood model* suggests that attitude change can occur via either the peripheral or the central route, depending on a person's ability and motivation to carefully consider an argument. Accordingly, different messages will produce attitude change under different circumstances. Another approach is to change a person's behavior, in the hope that attitudes will be adjusted to match the behavior. *Cognitive dissonance theory* holds that inconsistency between cognitions about attitudes and cognitions about behavior creates discomfort that often results in tension-reducing attitude change.

PREJUDICE AND STEREOTYPES

How does prejudice develop?

Stereotypes often lead to *prejudice* and *discrimination.* Motivational theories of prejudice suggest that some people have a need to dislike people who differ from themselves. This need may stem from the trait of authoritarianism, as well as from a strong social identity with one's in-group. In either case, feeling superior to members of out-groups helps these people to feel better about themselves. As a result, in-group members tend to discriminate against out-groups. Cognitive theories suggest that people categorize others into groups in order to reduce social complexity. Learning theories maintain that stereotypes, prejudice, and discriminatory behaviors can be learned from parents, peers, and the media.

The *contact hypothesis* proposes that intergroup contact can reduce prejudice and lead to more favorable attitudes toward the stereotyped group—but only if the contact occurs under specific conditions, such as equal status between groups. But even these conditions may not change unconscious social cognitions underlying prejudice and stereotyping.

INTERPERSONAL ATTRACTION

What factors affect who likes whom?

Interpersonal attraction is affected by many variables. Physical proximity is important because it allows people to meet. The situation in which they meet is important because positive or negative aspects of the situation tend to be associated with the other person. Characteristics of the other person are also important. Attraction tends to be greater when two people share similar attitudes and personal characteristics. Physical appearance plays a role in attraction; initially, attraction is strongest to those who are most physically attractive. But for long-term relationships, the *matching hypothesis* applies: People tend to choose others whose physical attractiveness is about the same as theirs.

Two key components of successful intimate relationships are interdependence and mutual commitment. Sternberg's triangular theory suggests that love is a function of three components: passion, intimacy, and commitment. Varying combinations of these three components create qualitatively different types of love. Marital satisfaction depends on communication, the perception that the relationship is equitable, the couple's ability to deal effectively with conflict and anger, and agreement on important issues in the marriage.

SOCIAL INFLUENCE

What social rules shape our behavior?

Norms establish the rules for what should and should not be done in a particular situation. One particularly powerful norm is reciprocity, the tendency to respond to others as they have acted toward you. *Deindividuation* is a psychological state in which people temporarily lose their individuality, their normal inhibitions are relaxed, and they may perform aggressive or illegal acts that they would not do otherwise.

A person's motivational state is affected by the presence of other people. By enhancing one's most likely behavior in a situation, the presence of others sometimes creates *social facilitation* (which improves performance) and sometimes creates *social impairment* (which interferes with performance). When people work in groups, they often exert less effort than when alone, a phenomenon called *social loafing.*

When behavior or beliefs change as the result of unspoken or implicit group pressure, *conformity* has occurred; when the change is the result of a request, *compliance* has occurred. People tend to follow the normative responses of others, and groups create norms when none already exist. People sometimes exhibit public conformity without private acceptance; at other times, the responses of others have an impact on private beliefs. People conform because they want to be right, because they want to be liked, and because they tend to be rewarded for doing so. People are most likely to conform when the situation is ambiguous, as well as when others in the group are in unanimous agreement. Up to a point, conformity usually increases as the number of people holding the majority view grows larger. Effective strategies for inducing compliance include the foot-in-the-door technique, the door-in-the-face procedure, and the low-ball approach.

OBEDIENCE

How far will people go to obey authority?

Obedience involves complying with an explicit demand from an authority figure. Research by Stanley Milgram indicates that obedience is likely even when obeying an authority appears to result in pain and suffering for another person.

Obedience declines when the status of the authority figure declines, as well as when others are observed to disobey. Some people are more likely to obey orders than others.

Because participants in Milgram's studies experienced considerable stress, the experiments have been questioned on ethical grounds. Nevertheless, his research showed that people do not have to be psychologically disordered to inflict pain on others.

AGGRESSION

Are people born aggressive?

Aggression is an act intended to harm another person. Freud saw aggression as due partly to death instincts. More recent theories attribute aggressive tendencies to genetic factors, brain dysfunctions, and hormonal influences. Learning is also important; people learn to display aggression by watching others and by being rewarded for aggressive behavior. There are wide cultural differences in the occurrence of aggression.

A variety of emotional factors play a role in aggression. The *frustration-aggression hypothesis* suggests that frustration can lead to aggression, particularly in the presence of cues that invite or promote aggression. Arousal from sources unrelated to aggression, such as exercise, can also make aggressive responses more likely, especially if aggression is already a dominant response in that situation. Research in *environmental psychology* suggests that factors such as high temperature and crowding increase the likelihood of aggressive behavior, particularly among people who are already angry.

ALTRUISM AND HELPING BEHAVIOR

What motivates people to help one another?

Humans often display **helping behavior** and **altruism.** There are three major theories of why people help others. According to the **arousal: cost-reward theory,** people help in order to reduce the unpleasant arousal they experience when others are in distress. Their specific reaction to a suffering person depends on the costs associated with helping or not helping. Helping behavior is most likely when the need for help is clear and when diffusion of responsibility is not created by the presence of other people—a phenomenon called the **bystander effect.** Environmental and personality factors also affect willingness to help. The **empathy-altruism theory** suggests that helping can be truly unselfish if the helper feels empathy for the person in need. Finally, evolutionary theory suggests that humans have an innate tendency to help others, especially relatives, because doing so increases the likelihood that family genes will survive.

Cooperation is any type of behavior in which people work together to attain a goal; *competition* exists whenever individuals try to attain a goal for themselves while denying that goal to others. Interpersonal *conflict* occurs when one person or group believes that another stands in the way of reaching some goal. Psychologists study conflict by observing behavior in *social dilemmas,* situations in which behavior that benefits individuals in the short run may spell disaster for an entire group in the long run.

GROUP PROCESSES

What makes a good leader?

Effective leaders tend to score high on dominance, emotional stability, agreeableness, and conscientiousness. In general, they are also intelligent, success oriented, and flexible. *Task-oriented* leaders provide close supervision, lead by giving orders, and generally discourage group discussion. In contrast, *person-oriented* leaders provide loose supervision, ask for group members' ideas, and are generally concerned with subordinates' feelings. Overall, men and women are equally capable leaders, but men tend to be more effective when success requires a more task-oriented leader, and women tend to be more effective when success requires a more person-oriented leader.

Groupthink occurs when group members are unable to realistically evaluate the options available to them or to fully consider the possible negative consequences of a contemplated decision. This pattern of thinking is most likely to occur when a group is isolated from outside forces, when it is working under time pressure or other intense stressors, and when it lacks a truly impartial leader.

Learn by Doing

Put It in Writing

A survey reveals that first-graders from various ethnic groups in a local school hold prejudiced attitudes toward one another. Imagine that you have been hired to develop a program to help these children become less prejudiced and more accepting of members of other ethnic groups. Write a one-page description of two or three classroom activities that would help you to accomplish this goal, and tell why you think they would do so. Do you think these activities could be successful in eliminating all prejudiced thinking in the children? Why or why not?

Personal Learning Activity

Research cited in this chapter suggests that the physical appearance of a partner tends to be more important to men, whereas a partner's intelligence tends to be more important to women. If that is true, what would you hypothesize about the qualities men versus women say they are looking for when they place ads for a partner in a personals column? Develop a research plan to test your hypothesis, and then collect some data by reading and analyzing at least a week's worth of personals ads in your local newspaper. Was your hypothesis supported? Did gender differences in the content of the ads hold true for homosexuals as well as heterosexuals? Write a brief report of your findings, and summarize what you think they can and cannot say about the factors that attract people to each other. *For additional projects, see the five Personal Learning Activities in the corresponding chapter of the study guide that accompanies this text.*

Step into Action

Courses

Social Psychology
Social Conflict
Marriage and Family
Social Cognition
Interpersonal Processes
Prejudice and Discrimination

Robert Cialdini, *Influence: Science and Practice* (Addison-Wesley, 1993) (summary of research on influence and how it is applied in everyday life)
Russell Geen and Edward Donnerstein (Eds.), *Human Aggression: Theory, Research, and Implications for Social Policy* (Academic Press, 1998) (readings on the origins of, and factors in, aggression)

Movies

Last of the Mohicans (reference groups)
Rosewood; A Patch of Blue (prejudice and discrimination)
Higher Learning (cultural diversity and stereotypes)

Books

D. A. Schroeder, L. A. Penner, J. F. Dovidio, and J. A. Piliavin, *The Psychology of Helping and Altruism* (McGraw-Hill, 1995) (an introduction to research)
Charles Stangor (Ed.), *Stereotypes and Prejudice: Essential Readings* (Psychology Press, 2000) (a collection of research articles on prejudice)

The Web

The World Wide Web is a good source of additional information about the science of psychology, provided you use it carefully and think critically about the information you find. The PsychAbilities web site that accompanies this text offers many resources relevant to this chapter. These resources include interactive NetLab exercises; Thinking Critically and Evaluating Research exercises; ACE chapter quizzes; recommended web links; and articles on current events, books, and movies. At http://college.hmco.com, select *Psychology* and then this textbook.

Review of Key Terms

Can you define each of the key terms in the chapter? Check your definitions against those on the pages listed in parentheses below or in the Glossary/Index at the end of the text.

actor-observer bias *(p. 491)*

aggression *(p. 512)*

altruism *(p. 518)*

arousal:cost-reward theory *(p. 519)*

attitude *(p. 493)*

attribution *(p. 490)*

bystander effect *(p. 519)*

cognitive dissonance theory *(p. 495)*

competition *(p. 523)*

compliance *(p. 505)*

conflict *(p. 524)*

conformity *(p. 505)*

contact hypothesis *(p. 498)*

cooperation *(p. 523)*

deindividuation *(p. 503)*

discrimination *(p. 497)*

elaboration likelihood model *(p. 494)*

empathy-altruism theory *(p. 521)*

environmental psychology *(p. 517)*

frustration-aggression
hypothesis *(p. 514)*

fundamental attribution error
(p. 491)

groupthink *(p. 525)*

helping behavior *(p. 518)*

matching hypothesis *(p. 500)*

norms *(p. 503)*

obedience *(p. 508)*

person-oriented (leaders) *(p. 525)*

prejudice *(p. 496)*

reference groups *(p. 487)*

relative deprivation *(p. 488)*

schemas *(p. 488)*

self-concept *(p. 487)*

self-esteem *(p. 487)*

self-fulfilling prophecy
(p. 490)

self-serving bias *(p. 492)*

social cognition *(p. 487)*

social comparison *(p. 487)*

social dilemmas *(p. 524)*

social facilitation *(p. 504)*

social identity *(p. 488)*

social impairment *(p. 504)*

social loafing *(p. 504)*

social perception *(p. 488)*

social psychology *(p. 487)*

stereotypes *(p. 496)*

task-oriented (leaders) *(p. 525)*

Multiple-Choice Self-Test

Select the best answer for each of the questions below. Then check your response against the Answer Key in the Appendix.

1. Jack took an entry-level job after completing college with honors and having one of his term papers published. Now Jack is depressed because the older people around him make more money than he does and are more advanced in their careers. Jack is experiencing

   a. cognitive dissonance.
   b. relative deprivation.
   c. social facilitation.
   d. a self-fulfilling prophecy.

2. When Alaa says, "I am a Muslim," he is describing his

   a. self-esteem.
   b. self-schema.
   c. social identity.
   d. social perception.

3. When Rowland first met Jacob, Jacob wasn't feeling well and threw up on Rowland's shoes. According to research on first impressions, we would expect Rowland to

   a. feel sorry for Jacob and thus have a positive first impression of him.
   b. develop a negative impression of Jacob because of the negative first experience with him.
   c. have an initial negative impression that will become positive later, no matter what Jacob does.
   d. have a positive first impression of Jacob because he is a male.

4. Gena is convinced that she won't like her blind date, Pat. When Pat arrives, he is outgoing and considerate, but Gena is short-tempered and rude to him. Soon Pat becomes irritable and ends the date early. Gina's prediction that she wouldn't have a good time came true due to

   a. cognitive dissonance.
   b. prejudice.
   c. a self-fulfilling prophecy.
   d. the fundamental attribution error.

5. "I earned an A on my history test because I studied hard and I'm smart, but I failed my philosophy test because the test was poorly worded and the teacher didn't like me." This statement is an example of

   a. actor-observer bias.
   b. the fundamental attribution error.
   c. a self-fulfilling prophecy.
   d. a self-serving bias.

6. Richard markets a new toothpaste by including a picture of an attractive celebrity in his ads. He is using the _____ route to try to achieve attitude change among consumers.

   a. central
   b. peripheral
   c. direct
   d. persuasive

7. Rachel and Matteus listen to a boring lecture. Afterward, Rachel is offered $100 and Matteus is offered $1 to tell the lecturer's next class that the lecture was interesting and fun. Both agree to do so. According to cognitive dissonance theory, we would expect real attitude change about the lecture to occur in

   a. Rachel, but not Matteus.
   b. Matteus, but not Rachel.
   c. both Rachel and Matteus.
   d. neither Rachel nor Matteus.

8. Lila does not like people with red hair because she believes that they are impulsive and not very bright. The best way to reduce Lila's prejudice against red-haired people would be to

   a. tell her about research showing that red-haired people do not differ from other people.
   b. arrange for Lila to supervise a group of red-haired people as they solve a problem.
   c. assign Lila to work with a group, which includes red-heads, to build a playground.
   d. put Lila on a committee led by a red-haired person.

9. According to research on interpersonal attraction, a good predictor of whether one person will like another person is

   a. similar attitudes.
   b. similar degrees of attraction.
   c. similar ways of dealing with anger.
   d. similar height and weight.

10. Georgio and Louisa share their thoughts, hopes, and daily worries. They plan to stay married throughout their lifetime, and they enjoy an active and satisfying sex life. According to Sternberg's theory, Georgio and Louisa are experiencing _____ love.

    a. consummate
    b. companionate
    c. temporary
    d. romantic

11. When Ashley laughed during her uncle's funeral, the other members of her family felt very uncomfortable. Ashley's laughter exemplified

    a. deindividuation.
    b. social loafing.
    c. social inhibition.
    d. a norm violation.

12. In Harper Lee's novel *To Kill a Mockingbird*, an angry mob tries to lynch a prisoner who is accused of assault. Attorney Atticus Finch stands in front of the jail, talking to the crowd, calling people by name, and reminding them of their families. Soon the mob disperses, no longer a faceless crowd but now a group of identifiable individuals. Atticus obviously understood the phenomenon of

    a. diffusion of responsibility.
    b. deindividuation.
    c. situational ambiguity.
    d. social facilitation.

13. Shawn's teacher doesn't keep track of her students' performance in groups, so Shawn does not put as much effort into his group project as he does into his individual project. Shawn is exhibiting

    a. a self-serving bias.
    b. social facilitation.
    c. social loafing.
    d. diffusion of responsibility.

14. Keyonna thought that the play she had just seen was boring, but everyone else seemed to like it; at the closing curtain, the audience gave the actors a standing ovation. Keyonna stood up and applauded, too, even though she didn't believe the actors deserved it. Keyonna's behavior in this situation is an example of

    a. conformity.
    b. compliance.
    c. obedience.
    d. a self-fulfilling prophecy.

15. Colleen knows she should take a day off from work to study for a big exam, but she also knows her boss won't like it. So she first asks for the entire week off. When the boss refuses, she asks for the one day off instead, and he agrees. Colleen used the _____ approach to gain her boss's compliance.

    a. foot-in-the-door
    b. door-in-the-face
    c. low-ball
    d. peripheral

16. Which of the following is *not* a major factor in determining whether or not a person will obey an order?

    a. the prestige of the authority figure giving the order
    b. personality characteristics of the person receiving the order
    c. the presence of another person who disobeys the order
    d. The gender of the person given the order

17. Leonard is very upset because he just learned that he failed his physics final exam and will not be able to graduate on time. When his roommate comes home and accidentally knocks over Leonard's glass of lemonade, Leonard becomes abusive, screaming at his roommate and throwing books and pillows at him. This is an example of the _____ theory of aggression.

    a. frustration-aggression
    b. generalized arousal
    c. authoritarian
    d. biological

18. According to the arousal:cost-reward theory, Ruth will be most likely to help a lost child she finds crying in the mall if she

    a. works with children every day.
    b. is upset by the crying and has the time to help.
    c. never shopped in that mall before.
    d. was lost in a mall as a small child herself.

19. Which of the following summarizes the evolutionary view of helping behavior?

    a. People feel good when they help others.
    b. People help others in order to improve the chance that at least some of their genes will survive in future generations.
    c. People are motivated to protect other individuals if the costs of helping are outweighed by the benefits.
    d. People learn to be helpful.

20. When groups are small, closely knit, isolated from outside influence, and headed by biased leaders, they often make poor decisions because they fail to consider them carefully enough. This phenomenon is called

    a. deindividuation.
    b. groupthink.
    c. social facilitation.
    d. social impairment

STATISTICS IN PSYCHOLOGICAL RESEARCH

Understanding and interpreting the results of psychological research depend on *statistical analyses,* the methods for describing and drawing conclusions from data. Chapter 1 introduced some terms and concepts associated with these analyses. *Descriptive statistics* are the numbers that psychologists use to describe and present their data. *Inferential statistics* are the mathematical procedures they use to draw conclusions from data and to make inferences about what the data mean. Here, we present more details about these statistical analyses that will help you to evaluate research results.

DESCRIBING DATA

To illustrate our discussion, let's imagine a hypothetical experiment on the effects of rewards on performance. The experimenter presents a set of mathematics problems to two groups of people. Each group must solve the problems within a fixed time. For each correct answer, the low-reward group is paid ten cents. The high-reward group gets one dollar. The hypothesis to be tested is the **null hypothesis,** the assertion that the independent variable manipulated by the experimenter will have *no effect* on the dependent variable measured by the experimenter. In this case, the null hypothesis is that the size of the reward (the independent variable) will not affect performance on the mathematics task (the dependent variable).

Assume that the experimenter has obtained a random sample of participants, assigned them randomly to the two groups, and done everything possible to avoid the confounds and other research problems discussed in Chapter 1. The experiment has been run, and the researcher now has the data, a list of the number of correct answers given by each participant in each group. Now comes the first task of statistical analysis. We must describe the data in a way that makes them easy to understand.

The Frequency Histogram

The simplest way to describe the data is to draw up something like Table 1, in which all the numbers are simply listed. After examining the table, you might notice that the high-reward group seems to have done better than the low-reward group. But the difference is not immediately obvious. It might be even harder to see if more participants had been involved or if the scores included three-digit numbers. A more satisfactory way of presenting the same data is in a picture-like graphic known as a **frequency histogram** (see Figure 1).

Construction of a histogram is simple. First, divide the scale for measuring the dependent variable (in this case, the number of correct solutions) into a number of categories, or "bins." The bins in our example are 1–2, 3–4, 5–6, 7–8, and 9–10. Next, sort the raw data into the appropriate bin. (For example, the score of a participant who had 5 correct answers would go into the 5–6 bin, a score of 8 would go into the 7–8 bin, and so on.) Finally, for each bin, count the number of scores in that bin, and draw a bar up to the height of that number on the vertical axis of the graph. The set of bars makes up the frequency histogram. Figure 1 shows a histogram comparing the scores of the high-reward group and the low-reward group. Now the difference between groups that was difficult to see in Table 1 becomes clearly visible. More people in the high-reward group obtained high scores than in the low-reward group.

null hypothesis A testable statement that the independent variable manipulated by an experimenter will have no effect on the dependent variable being measured by the experimenter.

frequency histogram A pictorial presentation of how often each possible score on a dependent variable occurs in a set of research data.

<table>
<tr><td colspan="2">

TABLE 1

A Simple Data Set

Here are the test scores obtained by thirteen participants performing under low-reward conditions and thirteen participants performing under high-reward conditions.

</td></tr>
</table>

Low Reward	High Reward
4	6
6	4
2	10
7	10
6	7
8	10
3	6
5	7
2	5
3	9
5	9
9	3
5	8

FIGURE 1

A Frequency Histogram

The height of each bar of a histogram represents the number of scores falling within each range of score values. The pattern formed by these bars gives a visual image of how research results are distributed.

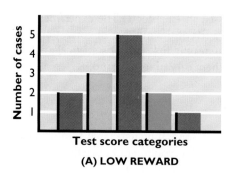

(A) LOW REWARD

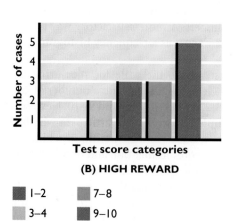

(B) HIGH REWARD

■ 1–2   ■ 7–8
■ 3–4   ■ 9–10
■ 5–6

Histograms and other "pictures" of data are useful for visualizing and better understanding the "shape" of research data. But in order to analyze data statistically, we need to use other ways of handling the numbers that make up these graphic presentations. For example, before we can tell whether two histograms are different statistically or just visually, the data they represent must be summarized using descriptive statistics.

Descriptive Statistics

The four basic categories of descriptive statistics do the following: (1) count the number of observations made; (2) summarize the typical value of a set of data; (3) summarize the spread, or variability, in a set of data; and (4) express the correlation between two sets of data, using the correlation coefficient described in Chapter 1.

N   The easiest statistic to compute, abbreviated as N, simply describes the number of observations that make up the data set. In Table 1, for example, $N = 13$ for each group, or 26 for the entire data set. Simple as it is, N plays a very important role in more sophisticated statistical analyses.

Measures of Central Tendency   It is apparent in Figure 1 that there is a difference in the pattern of scores between the two groups. But how much of a difference? What is the typical value, the *central tendency,* that represents each group's performance? There are three measures that capture this typical value: the mode, the median, and the mean. The *mode* is the value or score that occurs most frequently in the data set. The *median* is the halfway point in a set of data; half the scores fall above the median, and half fall below it. The *mean* is the arithmetic average. To find the mean, add the values of all the scores and divide by the number of scores (N).

Measures of Variability   The variability, or spread, or dispersion of a set of data is often just as important as its central tendency. This variability can be quantified by measures known as the *range* and the *standard deviation.* The range is simply the difference between the highest and the lowest values in a data set. For the data in Table 1, the range for the low-reward group is $9 - 2 = 7$; for the high-reward group, the range is $10 - 3 = 7$. The standard deviation, or SD, describes the average difference between each score and the mean of the data set.

The Normal Distribution   In most subfields in psychology, when researchers collect many measurements and plot their data in histograms, the pattern that results often resembles that shown for the low-reward group in Figure 1. That is, the majority of

Statistics can be valuable for describing research results, but critical thinking demands that we evaluate them carefully before drawing conclusions about what they mean. Knowing this pointy-haired executive's tendency toward uncritical thinking, you can bet that Dogbert's impressive-sounding restatement of the definition of *median* will win him an extension of his pricey consulting contract.

DILBERT reprinted by permission of United Feature Syndicate, Inc.

scores tend to fall in the middle of the distribution, while fewer and fewer scores occur as one moves toward the extremes. As more and more data are collected, and as smaller and smaller bins are used (perhaps containing only one value each), the histogram tends to smooth out until it resembles the bell-shaped curve known as the **normal distribution,** or *normal curve,* which is shown in Figure 2. When a distribution of scores follows a truly normal curve, its mean, median, and mode all have the same value. Furthermore, if the curve is normal, we can use its standard deviation to describe how any particular score stands in relation to the rest of the distribution.

The distribution of IQ scores shown in Figure 2 provides an example. They are distributed in a normal curve, with a mean, median, and mode of 100 and a standard deviation (SD) of 16. In such a distribution, half of the population will have an IQ above 100, and half will be below 100. The shape of the true normal curve is such that 68 percent of the area under it lies within one standard deviation above and below the mean. In terms of IQ, this means that 68 percent of the population has an IQ somewhere between 84 (100 minus 16) and 116 (100 plus 16). Of the remaining 32 percent of the population, half falls more than 1 SD above the mean, and half falls more than 1 SD below the mean. Thus, 16 percent of the population has an IQ above 116, and 16 percent scores below 84.

The normal curve is also the basis for percentiles. A **percentile score** indicates the percentage of people or observations that fall below a given score in a normal distribution. In Figure 2, for example, the mean score (which is also the median) lies at a point below which 50 percent of the scores fall. Thus, the mean of a normal distribution is at the 50th

FIGURE 2

The Normal Distribution

Many kinds of research data approximate the shape of the normal curve, in which most scores fall toward the center of the range.

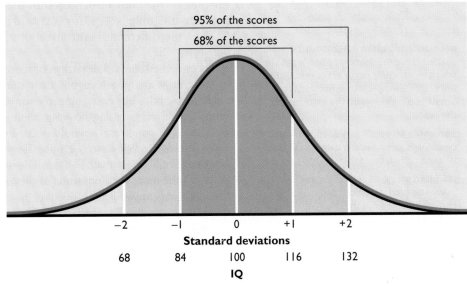

THE NORMAL DISTRIBUTION OF IQ

percentile. What does this mean for IQ? If you score 1 SD above the mean, your score is at a point above which only 16 percent of the population falls. This means that 84 percent of the population (100 percent minus 16 percent) must be below that score. So this IQ score is at the 84th percentile. A score at 2 SDs above the mean is at the 97.5 percentile, because 97.5 percent of the scores are below it in a normal distribution.

Scores may also be expressed in terms of their distance in standard deviations from the mean, producing what are called **standard scores.** A standard score of 1.5, for example, is 1.5 standard deviations from the mean.

INFERENTIAL STATISTICS

It can be hard to understand the meaning of research results summarized in descriptive statistics alone. Is a correlation between college grade-point averages and the eating of certain foods large enough to support the hypothesis that diet is important for mental functioning? Is the difference in the effects of two different kinds of psychotherapy large enough to recommend one over the other? The answers to questions such as these are based largely on the results of analyses that use inferential statistics.

Consider again the descriptive statistics from our rewards experiment. They tell us that the performances of the high- and low-reward groups differ, but there is some uncertainty. Is the difference large enough to be important? Does it represent a real effect or a fluke? The researcher would like to have some *measure of confidence* that the difference between groups did not occur by chance alone. **Inferential statistics** use certain rules to estimate the likelihood that a particular correlation or a particular difference between groups was due to chance. If that likelihood is small enough, the researcher can usually conclude that the correlation or difference is *statistically significant.*

Differences Between Means: The *t* Test

One of the most important tools of inferential statistics is the *t* test. It allows the researcher to ask how likely it is that the difference between two means occurred by chance rather than because of the independent variable. When the *t* test or another inferential statistic says that the probability of chance effects is small enough (usually less than 5 percent), the results are said to be statistically significant. Conducting a *t* test of statistical significance requires the use of three descriptive statistics.

The first component of the *t* test is the size of the observed effect, the difference between the means. Recall that the mean is calculated by summing a group's scores and dividing by the number of scores. In the example shown in Table 1, the mean of the high-reward group is 94/13, or 7.23, and the mean of the low-reward group is 65/13, or 5. Thus the difference between the means for the high- and low-reward groups is $7.23 - 5 = 2.23$.

Second, the standard deviation of scores in each group must be known. If the scores in the groups are quite variable, their standard deviations will be large, indicating that chance may have played a large role in producing the results. If the scores within each group are all very similar, however, their standard deviations will be small, which suggests that the same results would occur in the groups if the experiment were repeated. Thus, the *difference* between groups is more likely to be significant when each group's standard deviation is small. In Table 1, some people in the low-reward group actually did better on the math test than some in the high-reward group. If variability is high enough that the scores of two groups overlap, the difference between group means, though large, may not be statistically significant.

Third, we need to take the sample size, *N*, into account. The larger the number of participants or observations, the more likely it is that a given difference between means is significant. This is so because, with larger samples, random factors within a group will have less impact on the group's mean. The unusual performance of a few people who were sleepy or anxious or hostile, for example, will likely be canceled out by the scores of

normal distribution A smooth, bell-shaped curve representing a set of data in which most scores occur in the middle of the possible range, with fewer and fewer scores occurring toward the extremes of the range.

percentile score A way of stating what percentage of scores in a data set fall at or below a certain score.

standard score A way of stating how many standard deviations separate a particular score from the mean of all the scores in a data set.

inferential statistics A form of statistical analysis designed to provide a measure of confidence about how likely it is that a certain result appeared by chance.

the more representative majority of people. The same effect of sample size can be seen in coin tossing. If you toss a quarter five times, you might not be too surprised if heads come up 80 percent of the time. But if you get 80 percent heads after one hundred tosses, you might begin to suspect that this is probably not due to chance alone. Some other effect, perhaps some bias in the coin, is probably producing the results. For the same reason, a relatively small correlation coefficient—between diet and grades, say—might be statistically significant if it was based on 50,000 students. As the number of participants increases, it becomes less likely that the correlation reflects the influence of a few oddball cases.

To summarize, as the difference between the means gets larger, as N increases, and as standard deviations get smaller, t increases. This increase in t raises the researcher's confidence in the significance of the difference between means.

Beyond the *t* Test

Many experiments in psychology are considerably more complex than simple comparisons between two groups. They often involve three or more experimental and control groups. Some experiments also include more than one independent variable. For example, suppose we had been interested not only in the effect of reward size on performance but also in the effect of problem difficulty. We might then create six groups whose members would perform easy, moderate, or difficult problems under low- or high-reward conditions.

In an experiment like this, the results might be due to the size of the reward, the difficulty of the problem, or the combined effects (known as the *interaction*) of the two. Analyzing the size and source of these effects is typically accomplished through procedures known as *analysis of variance.* The details of analysis of variance are beyond the scope of this book, but note that, as in the *t* test, the statistical significance of each effect is influenced by differences between means, standard deviation, and sample size.

For more detailed information about how analysis of variance and other inferential statistics are used to understand and interpret the results of psychological research, consider taking courses in research methods and statistical or quantitative methods.

Chapter 1 Introduction to the Science of Psychology

1A Structuralists used introspection to study the elements of consciousness *(p. 5)*. **2B** A behaviorist uses functional analysis of behavior to see what benefits certain actions have *(p. 7)*. **3C** Cognitive psychologists investigate thoughts and information processing *(p. 9)*. **4C** Sue must compare her cats' behavior with that of other Abyssinians *(p. 19)*. **5C** A hypothesis is a specific, testable proposition about a phenomenon *(p. 23)*. **6B** Dr. McMarty should examine the data for patterns or relationships among the variables *(p. 22)*. **7C** Case studies are used to collect descriptive data *(p. 21)*. **8D** All of the answers are correct *(p. 22–23)*. **9D** Double-blind is an experimental procedure that helps prevent experimenter bias from confounding a study's results *(p. 25–26)*. **10A** The variable that is measured following the manipulation is the dependent variable *(p. 23)*. **11C** José cannot ethically use a true experiment to determine causality so he must use a quasi-experiment *(p. 26)*. **12B** The experimental group is the one that receives the special treatment *(p. 23)*. **13C** Statistical significance is determined when the result is larger than would be expected by chance alone *(p. 29)*. **14B** The closer the correlation coefficient is to -1.0 or +1.0, the stronger the relationship between the two variables *(p. 28)*. **15D** A correlation coefficient tells the degree to which two variables vary together, not whether a cause and effect relationship exists *(p. 28)*. **16A** Behaviorists say that people think and behave in ways that have previously been rewarded *(p. 9)*. **17A** Species-specific behaviors are instinctive *(p. 9)*. **18D** The four scientific goals in research are description, prediction, control, and explanation *(p. 20)*. **19A** Uncontrolled, sometimes uncontrollable, factors such as personality, time of day and room temperature are random variables *(p. 25)*. **20D** All are good reasons for ethical behavior *(p. 30)*.

Chapter 2 Biology and Behavior

1A The sensory system provides information about the environment *(p. 54)*. **2A** Without motor nerves to move his skeletal muscles, Kong's cousin cannot climb skyscrapers *(p. 46)*. **3D** The sympathetic nervous system is less active now that Kalli is not hurrying *(p. 47)*. **4A** The medulla, located in the hindbrain, helps to regulate heart rate, blood pressure, and breathing *(p. 47)*. **5B** Broca's area and Wernicke's area, both located in the left cerebral hemisphere, are responsible for comprehension of language *(p. 58)*. **6C** Both cerebral hemispheres are activated when a person is recognizing and naming people *(p. 53)*. **7C** Malfunctions of GABA systems contribute to Huntington's disease, and malfunctions of dopamine systems contribute to Parkinson's disease *(p. 43)*. **8A** Neurons secrete neurotransmitters across synapses and endocrine organs release hormones into the blood stream *(pp. 62–63)*. **9D** The right parietal lobe has been affected, causing George's foot to tingle *(p. 56)*. **10A** Some simple behaviors like reflexes occur automatically via the spinal cord and without instructions from the other portion of the central nervous system, the brain *(p. 48)* **11C** The somatic system carries information to and from the central nervous system *(p. 46)*. **12D** The sympathetic system of the autonomic nervous system has been activated *(p. 47)*. **13A** The cerebellum is that part of the hindbrain that controls finely coordinated movements *(p. 51)*. **14B** All the information going to and from the brain must travel through the intact spinal cord *(p. 46)*. **15D** If the reticular formation fibers in Lily's hindbrain were damaged, she would go into a coma *(p. 50)*. **16C** The sensory cortex in the occipital lobe receives information concerning vision *(p. 54)*. **17A** Damage to Broca's area creates difficulties in speaking *(p. 58)*. **18B** Defects in the hippocampus have been found in people with Alzheimer's disease *(p. 53)*. **19A** Glands release hormones such as cortisol into the bloodstream *(p. 63)*. **20B** The frontal lobe contains the motor cortex, and the right side of the brain controls the left side of the body *(p. 55)*.

Chapter 3 Sensation and Perception

1A The frequency of a sound wave determines pitch *(p. 84)*. **2B** Expecting a stimulus to occur lowers the response criterion *(p. 72)*. **3C** According to Weber's law, the lighter the objects being compared, the smaller the weight difference needed to detect a change in weight *(pp. 72–73)*. **4A** Kinesthesia gives us knowledge of the position of our body parts *(pp. 87, 91)*. **5D** This is an abbreviated version of the correct sequence *(p. 82)*. **6A** The described procedure defines absolute threshold *(p. 71)*. **7C** Saturation refers to the purity of color *(p. 77)*. **8D** The trichromatic theory proposes that combining three primary colors can produce any other color *(pp. 77–78)*. **9C** The sense of smell does not send its messages through the thalamus *(p. 85)*. **10B** People moving at the same speed, in a sense having a "common fate," are perceived as a group *(p. 95)*. **11A** Shanelle wants to be sure the children are dressed alike so that they will be perceived as a group *(p. 94)*. **12C** Interposition is the depth perception cue that operates on this basis *(p. 96)*. **13A** Bottom-up processing is the reaction to basic aspects of a stimulus *(pp. 101–102)*. **14B** Looming is a motion cue such that objects increasingly fill the retinal space as they get closer *(p. 97)*. **15C** As an object moves closer and increases the size of the retinal image, the perceived distance decreases at the same rate so the perceived size remains constant *(pp. 98–99)*. **16D** Both similarity and proximity are responsible for the fans' perception of a pattern such as spelling of a word *(pp. 94–95)*. **17A** Aparna's sensory systems automatically reacted to create afterimages, thus reflecting bottom-up processing *(p. 79)*. **18A** Covert orienting involves a shift of attention that isn't easily observed *(p. 106)*. **19D** Texture, smell, and temperature all contribute to food's flavor *(p. 85)*. **20B**. Gustation is the sense of taste *(p. 85)*.

Chapter 4 Consciousness

1B Zandra's exposure to Rembrandt's paintings caused her to like them more *(p. 118)*. **2B** Lisa's sensation of the watch on her arm occurs at the preconscious level of mental activity *(p. 117)*. **3A** In her altered state, Denisha's inhibitions are lessened and her perceptions are changed *(p. 121)*. **4B** People with narcolepsy suddenly fall asleep in the middle of a waking state *(pp. 124–125)*. **5B** Edie's success depends on her expectation that the messages will help her *(p. 119)*. **6A** Disruptions of your circadian rhythm can make you grouchy and less productive *(p. 126)*. **7B** According to Freud, unacceptable thoughts, feeling, and memories are kept in the unconscious to protect a person from anxiety *(p. 117)*. **8C** Hypnosis has been used to help people reduce nausea from chemotherapy, surgical bleeding, and pain *(p. 131)*. **9A** Norman is about to meditate *(p. 131)*. **10D** During REM sleep, mental activity, heart rate, and blood pressure increase while muscle tension decreases *(pp. 123–124)*. **11B** An antagonist is a molecule that fits into a receptor and blocks other neurotransmitters from binding *(pp. 132–133)*. **12C** Caffeine is a stimulant which does not cause hallucinations *(p. 136)*. **13C** Dissociation means a split in consciousness that allows the hypnotized person and hypnotist to share control *(p. 130)*. **14C** Cocaine increases norepinephrine activity in the central nervous system *(p. 135)*. **15A** Tolerance is a need for increasingly larger amounts of a drug to achieve the same effect *(p. 133)*. **16A** An agonist binds with a receptor and stimulates it, as the normal neurotransmitter would *(p. 137)*. **17B** Opiates relieve pain and cause sleep *(p. 136)*. **18A** Cocaine is a stimulant *(p. 135)*. **19C** Nightmares are frightening dreams that take place during REM sleep *(p. 125)*. **20D** Since alcohol's physiological effects involve dopamine, dopamine agonists can reduce cravings and withdrawal effects *(p. 134)*.

Chapter 5   Learning

1A When an organism stops responding to a repeated stimulus, habituation has occurred *(p. 153)*.   **2B** After repeated pairings with a stimulus that already triggers a reflexive response, the conditioned stimulus alone elicits the reflexive-like response *(pp. 146–147)*.   **3A** The green light should predict the presentation of the puff of air *(p. 147)*.   **4C** Extinction is the gradual disappearance of a conditioned response when the UCS is eliminated *(p. 148)*.   **5D** Reconditioning involves the repetition of the conditioning process after extinction *(p. 148)*.   **6C** For survival reasons, people are biologically prepared to link taste signals with illness *(p. 151)*.   **7D** Seeing a dog is enough to make Najla fearful *(p. 149)*.   **8D**. Najla has learned from the experience of watching others pet a dog *(p. 167)*.   **9C** Operant conditioning involves learning that behaviors have consequences *(p. 153)*.   **10C** Jodi is not going to tell her boss how she feels because she wants to "avoid" being fired *(p. 155)*.   **11D** A discriminitive stimulus signals that a reward will occur if a certain response is given *(p. 155)*.   **12D** Shaping is the process of reinforcing successive approximations to the target behavior *(p. 157)*.   **13B** A negative reinforcer increases a behavior that removes an unpleasant event or stimulus *(p. 154)*.   **14C** Punishment is most effective if it immediately follows the behavior *(p. 161)*.   **15A** People learn they are unable to control circumstances or outcomes *(pp. 164–165)*.   **16B** Jamey must exhibit a fixed number of behaviors while Susan must work a variable amount of time *(p. 159)*.   **17A** Kenyatta's grandmother mistakenly used a cognitive map of her own house *(p. 166)*.   **18A** Having been classically conditioned to a white lab rat, Albert now generalizes to other white, furry animals *(p. 149)*.   **19C** Leroy learned vicariously by watching what the consequences of Jared's behavior were *(p. 168)*.   **20D** Working in groups is an active learning method that improves students' recall of information *(p. 172)*.

Chapter 6   Memory

1C Implicit memories are not purposefully recalled but do influence behavior *(p. 181)*.   **2A** Episodic memories are of those events you witnessed or experienced *(p. 181)*.   **3B** Procedural memories involve how to do something or how to carry out a procedure *(p. 181)*.   **4B** Maintenance rehearsal is a method of keeping information in short-term memory by repeating it *(p. 182)*.   **5B** Unrehearsed information stays in short-term memory for about eighteen seconds *(p. 184)*.   **6C** Selective attention allows Reepal to focus on the most important information *(p. 184)*.   **7A** Chunking involves grouping information into meaningful units that can be stored *(p. 185)*.   **8C** Semantic memory contains general knowledge not linked to a specific event *(p. 181)*.   **9A** Due to the primacy effect, items at the beginning of a list are remembered best *(pp. 188–189)*.   **10B** Anterograde amnesia is the ability to form new long-term memories following a brain injury *(p. 203)*.   **11B** The answer options in multiple choice tests act as retrieval cues for information in long-term memory *(p. 189)*.   **12B** People sometimes remember material better when they are in the same place as when they learned it *(p. 190)*.   **13C** Semantic networks are links of related information. When a person recalls information from one node of the network, it can feel as if the person is very close to accessing the information needed in the next node *(pp. 190–191)*.   **14C** Constructed memory is a fabricated, but seemingly real, recollection *(pp. 191–193)*.   **15B** Research has shown that eye witnesses' confidence about their testimony is not always a reliable guide to their credibility *(pp. 195–196)*.   **16A** The decay of memories is most rapid immediately following the learning *(p. 198)*.   **17C** As Ebbinghaus discovered, relearning takes much less time than learning. This difference represents the savings from one learning to the next learning *(p. 197)*.   **18C** Proactive interference occurs when old information disrupts the learning of new information *(p. 198)*.   **19A** Since acetylcholine plays a prominent role in memory, the memory problems of Alzheimer's patients are related to the loss of neurons that use acetylcholine *(p. 202)*.   **20A** The method of loci involves mentally placing objects in various spots in a familiar location (loci) *(p. 205)*.

Chapter 7   Thought, Language, and Intelligence

1D Thinking is part of an information processing system that manipulates mental representations *(p. 215)*.   **2B** Cognitive maps are mental representations of familiar parts of your world *(p. 216)*.   **3B** Basing his strategy on an algorithm would require Clint to evaluate every possible move and countermove *(p. 219)*.   **4B** Mental models are clusters of propositions that represent people's understanding of how things work *(p. 218)*.   **5B** Setting aside a difficult problem, hoping for a solution to occur while working on something else, is called incubation *(p. 222)*.   **6D** Functional fixedness occurs when a person fails to use a familiar object in a novel way to solve a problem *(p. 225)*.   **7C** Confirmation bias is a strong tendency to confirm rather than refute the preferred hypothesis, even in the face of strong evidence against the hypothesis *(p. 225)*.   **8A** The gambler's fallacy has led Richard to believe that the probability of a random event will change over time *(p. 230)*.   **9C** Incorrect words or word endings are not likely to have been reinforced. They are overgeneralizations of a language rule the child has learned *(pp. 234–235)*.   **10A** A critical period is a limited window of opportunity for language learning. If the critical period is missed, normal language development will not occur *(p. 234)*.   **11A** Alfred Binet designed the first IQ test to identify children with special educational needs *(p. 236)*.   **12D** Formal reasoning is based on the rules of logic *(p. 219)*.   **13C** As a result of current scoring methods, an IQ score reflects how well a person performs relative to other people of the same age *(p. 239)*.   **14C** If the scores from this preemployment test predict future performance on the job, the test is valid *(p. 240)*.   **15A** A reliable test yields consistent and stable scores over time *(p. 240)*.   **16A** IQ tests appear to be most valid for assessing aspects of intelligence that are related to school work *(p. 241)*.   **17D** The highest correlation is likely to be found between the identical twins' scores *(pp. 241–242)*.   **18C** An IQ score between 50 and 70 reflects mild mental retardation. This individual will have difficulty with academic material and abstract reasoning *(p. 248)*.   **19B** The multiple intelligences approach focuses on abilities not measured by IQ tests *(p. 247)*.   **20A** Creative people are internally motivated, have a set of creative skills, use divergent thinking, and have expertise in the field of pursuit *(p. 228)*.

Chapter 8   Motivation and Emotion

1B The evolutionary approach suggests that adaptive behaviors that promote the survival of the species are inborn motivations to pass on genes *(p. 259)*.   **2A** Homeostasis is the tendency to maintain physiological systems at a steady, stable level by adjusting to changes *(p. 259)*.   **3D** Arousal theory states that people are motivated to behave in ways that maintain an individual, optimal level of arousal *(p. 260)*.   **4B** Incentive theory states that behavior is goal directed to obtain positive stimuli and avoid negative stimuli *(p. 260)*.   **5A** When stimulated, the ventromedial nucleus tells Ahmed that there is no need to eat *(p. 262)*.   **6A** The mere presence of others tends to increase food consumption *(264)*.   **7B** Although bulimics can maintain normal weight, they may experience dehydration and other symptoms *(pp. 265–266)*.   **8C** The Chicago survey found that people in the United States have sex less frequently and with fewer partners than was earlier believed *(p. 268)*.   **9C** Only men experience the refractory period *(p. 269)*.   **10B** Edwina will encourage her son to try difficult tasks, praise his efforts, and help him learn from his mistakes *(p. 275)*.   **11A** People with high achievement needs set realistic goals, actively seek success, and take risks *(p. 274)*.   **12A** Physiological needs, including those for food and water, come first in Maslow's hierarchy *(p. 278)*.   **13C** Jill's situation has both positive and negative features, so she is faced with an approach-avoidance conflict *(p. 279)*.   **14B** The sympathetic nervous system is involved in the fight-or-flight syndrome *(p. 282)*.   **15A** James's theory states that we experience emotions only by perceiving our physiological response to an event *(p. 284)*.   **16D** Transferred excitation occurs when arousal from an experience carries over to a different situation. This is consistent with Schachter's theory of emotion *(p. 287)*.   **17B** Cannon's theory maintains that emotional experience originates in the thalamus and simultaneously triggers physiological arousal and cognitive awareness *(p. 288)*.   **18D** As children grow up, they learn an emotional culture, which are rules that govern what emotions are appropriate, in what situations, and what expressions are allowed *(p. 292)*.   **19B** Human emotions are communicated mainly through facial movements and expressions *(p. 290)*.   **20B** In allowing Diane's emotional state to guide his behavior, Sam is using social referencing *(pp. 292–293)*.

Chapter 9   Human Development

1C Behavioral genetics researches nature vs nurture, heredity, and individual characteristics or differences *(p. 300)*.   **2D** Alcohol, drugs, and smoking are teratogens and potentially dangerous to the developing baby during pregnancy *(pp. 303–304)*.   **3B** Maternal smoking can cause respiratory difficulties and low birth weight in the newborn *(p. 304)*.   **4D** Newborns visually prefer novelty and shapes that resemble human faces *(p. 305)*.   **5C** With normal brain development, grasping and rooting reflexes should have disappeared by 6 months of age *(p. 306)*.   **6A** Assimilation is the process of taking in information that adds to an existing schema *(p. 308)*. **7B** Adriana is probably four to six years old; she is in the preoperational stage *(p. 313)*. **8B** Babies become upset and stare longer when natural physical laws are defied *(pp. 310–311)*. **9B** Young children may lack adequate memory encoding and storage processes *(p. 309)*. **10A** The easy baby adapts easily, fusses little, and calms quickly *(p. 319)*. **11B** Harlow's attachment studies demonstrate that infant monkeys form attachments based on contact comfort needs *(pp. 320–321)*. **12D** With ambivalent insecure attachment, the child sometimes prefers and sometimes rejects the caretaker *(p. 322)*. **13C** Authoritative parents are sympathetic but firm; permissive parents give lots of freedom *(p. 325)*. **14B** In North American cultures, males are usually encouraged to achieve, act independently, explore, and assume responsibility *(p. 328)*. **15C** Ludmilla is still confused about her identity *(p. 331)*. **16C** Asian American adolescents are less likely to engage in sexual activity *(p. 330)*. **17A** People at the Stage 1 (preconventional) level of moral reasoning are concerned with avoiding punishment *(p. 333)*. **18C** These changes occur mainly in middle adulthood *(pp. 335–336)*. **19A** Adults over sixty-five years of age are generally slower and less effective than younger ones at solving complex problems they have not seen before *(p. 336)*. **20B** Terminal drop is the decline in mental functioning that occurs in the months or years preceding death *(p. 339)*.

Chapter 10   Health, Stress, and Coping

1D Stressors include physical and psychological components that affect health *(p. 349)*. **2A** The more stressors Lila has, the more physical, psychological, and behavioral responses she will probably experience *(p. 352)*. **3D** Stressors are events and situations to which people must adjust or adapt *(p. 350)*. **4A** The first stage of the GAS, the alarm reaction, involves some version of the fight-or-flight syndrome *(p. 352)*. **5C** Exhaustion is the last stage of the GAS and represents a serious, progressive depletion of resources *(p. 353)*. **6B** Rumination is continuously thinking about negative events and it tends to intensify negative emotional states *(p. 355)*. **7B** Catastrophizing involves the exaggeration of negative consequences *(p. 355)*. **8D** Behavioral stress responses are changes in the way people look, act, or talk *(pp. 355–356)*. **9B** Flashbacks are associated with post-traumatic stress disorder *(p. 356)*. **10C** Stressors that are predictable have less impact than those that are unpredictable *(p. 358)*. **11C** Perceived control over stressful events helps reduce the negative effects *(p. 358)*. **12B** Laton is trying to improve the employees' social support networks *(p. 360)*. **13B** People who are impulsive or low on conscientiousness are more likely to die from accidents or violence *(p. 362)*. **14C** Natural killer cells of the immune system have antiviral properties and help prevent tumors *(p. 364)*. **15B** Cynical hostility is a risk factor in heart disease *(pp. 365–366)*. **16A** Smoking is not only related to cancer, it also aggravate many other dangerous illnesses *(p. 367)*. **17A** Personalizing the risk of danger to the individual should increase the likelihood of behavioral change *(p. 369)*. **18B** Being aware of a problem behavior and thinking about changing it occur during the contemplation stage of readiness to alter a health habit *(p. 369)*. **19A** Sayumi is using the coping strategy of cognitive restructuring or changing her thinking about an event or person *(pp. 370–371)*. **20C** Progressive relaxation trains a person to physically relax muscles, thus reducing heart rate and blood pressure *(p. 371)*.

Chapter 11   Personality

1B Personality is defined as a person's unique pattern of enduring psychological and behavioral characteristics *(p. 377)*. **2A** The id contains the life and death instincts, is impulsive and pleasure seeking *(p. 378)*. **3D** During the latency period, which lasts from about age five until puberty, an individual's focus is on education and social development *(p. 380)*. **4B** Displacement is deflecting an impulse from its original target to a less threatening one *(p. 379)*. **5A** Severe toilet training can lead to a fixation that is seen as sloppy, disorganized, and impulsive behavior in adulthood *(p. 380)*. **6D** Although based on a small, culturally biased sample and not scientifically derived, Freud's theory profoundly impacted psychology *(p. 382)*. **7B** Trait theory assumes that personality traits are relatively stable, consistent, and predictable *(p. 383)*. **8C** Allport believed that there are about seven central traits to personality *(pp. 383–384)*. **9D** Trait theorists have identified five (called "the big-five") cross-cultural factors that make up personality *(pp. 385–386)*. **10C** Trait theories describe personality but do not explain how personality develops *(p. 389)*. **11B** Twin studies suggest that there are genetic predispositions toward particular personality traits and temperament *(pp. 387–388)*. **12A** Internals expect events to be controlled mainly by their own efforts *(pp. 389–390)*. **13C** Reciprocal determinism is a mutually influential

interaction among cognitive patterns, the environment and behavior *(p. 390)*. **14D** Person variables and situation variables are important in explaining particular behaviors *(pp. 390–391)*. **15C** Personality represents patterns of thought, learned by interaction and observation, that guide actions *(p. 377)*. **16C** Conditions of worth are created when "people" are evaluated instead of their behavior *(p. 393)*. **17B** A preoccupation with perceived need for material things and a devaluation of what one does have, leads to a deficiency orientation *(p. 394)*. **18D** Unconscious needs, motives, and conflicts supposedly guide responses to the relatively unstructured stimuli of the projective test *(p. 400)*. **19C** Research has found that those rated as ill-tempered as children are more likely to be aggressive in adulthood *(p. 397)*. **20B** An objective test contains clear, specific questions or statements that can be scored and evaluated mathematically *(pp. 398–399)*.

Chapter 12   Psychological Disorders

1C Approximately 48% of the population in the United States have experienced a mental disorder at some point in their lives *(p. 409)*. **2C** The practical approach defines abnormality based on the content, context, and consequence of behavior *(p. 411)*. **3B** The medical model attributes abnormal behavior to the presence of biochemical, genetic, or other physical problem *(p. 412)*. **4D** Diathesis-stress model attributes abnormal behavior to biological, environmental, and psychological causes *(pp. 414–415)*. **5D** The global assessment of functioning is one evaluation axis of the *DSM IV (p. 416)*. **6A** Agoraphobia is the fear of being alone or away from the security of home *(p. 421)*. **7C** OCD involves an obsession with particular thoughts or images, which motivates repetitive, uncontrollable behaviors *(p. 422)*. **8A** Conversion disorder involves functional impairment with no physical cause *(p. 424)*. **9A** Severe pain in the absence of any physical problem is symptomatic of pain disorder *(p. 424)*. **10B** Dissociative identity disorder is a condition in which a person reports having more than one identity *(p. 426)*. **11B** Sleep changes and weight gain or loss are typical of major depressive disorder *(p. 427)*. **12B** Depressed women, certain ethnic groups, males over forty-five and living alone, and those who talk about suicide do tend to commit suicide *(pp. 428–429)*. **13A** Attribution is the process of explaining causes of own and other's behavior *(p. 432)*. **14C** Schizophrenia is characterized by abnormality in thinking, writing, speaking, affect, perception and attention, and personal identity *(p. 433)*. **15D** Thought broadcasting is a delusion in which patients believe that their thoughts can be heard by others *(p. 433)*. **16C** The most common symptoms of paranoid schizophrenia include delusions of grandeur or persecution, often with anger, anxiety, or jealousy *(p. 435)*. **17A** An impulsive, selfish, unscrupulous person with few morals or deep feelings might have an antisocial personality disorder *(p. 438)*. **18D** The more violent forms of antisocial personality disorder are associated with the experience of abuse in childhood *(pp. 438–439)*. **19A** A substance-related disorder is characterized by long-term drug/alcohol use that causes physical or psychological harm to the user or others *(p. 441)*. **20B** Children with autistic disorder usually show little attachment, poor eye contact, and asocial behavior *(p. 441)*.

Chapter 13   Treatment of Psychological Disorders

1C As a part of psychodynamic therapy, the client reports all feelings, thoughts, memories, and images that come to mind in free association *(p. 454)*. **2A** Gestalt therapy uses role playing, among other techniques, to help clients become more self-aware and self-accepting *(pp. 457–458)*. **3A** Licensed clinical psychologists generally hold a doctoral degree in clinical or counseling psychology *(p. 452)*. **4B** Psychoanalysis focuses on revealing and working through unconscious conflicts *(p. 454)*. **5A** Empathy involves an effort to perceive the client's view of reality *(p. 456)*. **6A** Carl Rogers developed client-centered therapy *(p. 456)*. **7C** By paraphrasing what Shanobi has said, her friend is responding in a manner consistent with reflection *(p. 456)*. **8A** Insight involves becoming aware of previously unconscious material *(p. 454)*. **9C** Behavioral therapists see compulsive behaviors as learned habits *(p. 458)*. **10C** Psychoanalysts today focus less on instincts and more on interpersonal relationships *(p. 455)*. **11C** Confidentiality is a critical aspect of therapy than can be violated only under special circumstances, as when the therapist must defend against a client's charge of malpractice. Neither an employer's request for information nor termination of therapy would justify the disclosure of such information *(p. 472)*. **12B** Community psychologists are concerned with promoting social changes that prevent psychological problems *(pp. 478–479)*. **13A** Flooding is a behavior therapy technique that places a client in a feared but harmless situation to extinguish the fear *(p. 461)*. **14D** Cognitive restructuring replaces stress-provoking thoughts with more constructive thoughts thereby using thoughts to change behavior *(pp. 463–464)*. **15B** ECT involves passing electric current through the brain to treat depression when other treatments have failed *(p. 473)*. **16A** The Dodo Bird Verdict suggests that theories of behavior and specific methods of treatment are irrelevant to the success of psychotherapy *(p. 467)*. **17A** One of the most important elements of success with any therapy is the client-therapist relationship which involves trust, intimate disclosure, and empathy *(p. 471)*. **18C** Neuroleptics are drugs that can reduce psychotic symptoms but can cause severe side effects *(p. 474)*. **19B** Anxiolytics are drugs that reduce anxiety and tension *(p. 475)*. **20C** Simultaneous treatment of several clients has many positive features, however, client improvement is not more rapid with this technique than with others *(p. 464)*.

Chapter 14   Social Psychology

1B Jack is experiencing relative deprivation, comparing himself to others around him *(p. 488)*. **2C** Alaa is describing his social identity as a Muslim *(p. 488)*. **3B** The first impression is formed quickly and is difficult to change *(p. 489)*. **4C** The change in the date's behavior was probably due to a self-fulfilling prophecy *(p. 490)*. **5D** A self-serving bias is the tendency to take credit for success and blame external causes for failures *(p. 492)*. **6B** In utilizing a celebrity to sell this product, Richard is taking the peripheral route to attitude change *(p. 494)*.

7B When cognitions and behavior are inconsistent, people feel uneasy and motivated to change attitudes to make them consistent with the behavior *(p. 495)*. **8C** The contact hypothesis suggests that stereotypes and prejudices can be reduced through cooperation and interdependence *(p. 498)*. **9A** People tend to like others who have attitudes similar to their own, especially attitudes about other people *(p. 500)*. **10A** Intimacy, commitment, and passion are characteristic of consummate love *(p. 502)*. **11D** Laughing during a funeral is an example of norm violation *(p. 503)*. **12B** Deindividuation occurs when people in a group temporarily lose their individuality and behave in ways they otherwise would not *(p. 503)*. **13C** Shawn is exhibiting social loafing by not putting in as much effort as other group members *(p. 504)*. **14A** Conformity results from unspoken group pressure *(p. 505)*. **15B** Colleen is attempting to use the door-in-the-face technique, first asking for an unrealistic favor, then a smaller one *(p. 508)*. **16D** The gender of the person giving the order is not a major factor determining whether someone else will obey the order or not *(pp. 510–511)*. **17A** Frustration produces a readiness to respond aggressively, which can later be environmentally triggered *(p. 514)*. **18B** Ruth will be most likely to help if she is upset and the cost of helping is not very high *(p. 519)*. **19B** According to the evolutionary view, people display helping behaviors to protect their gene pool's chances of survival in future generations *(p. 521)*. **20B** Groupthink is the deterioration over time of a group's ability to realistically evaluate options and their own decisions *(pp. 525–526)*.

REFERENCES

Abbott, B. B., Schoen, L. S., & Badia, P. (1984). Predictable and unpredictable shock: Behavioral measures of aversion and physiological measures of stress. *Psychological Bulletin, 96,* 45–71.

Abeles, N. (1985). Proceedings of the American Psychological Association, 1985. *American Psychologist, 41,* 633–663.

Abramis, D. J. (1994). Work role ambiguity, job satisfaction, and job performance: Meta-analyses and review. *Psychological Reports, 75,* 1411–1433.

Abramowitz, J. S. (1997). Effectiveness of psychological and pharmacological treatments for obsessive-compulsive disorder: A quantitative review. *Journal of Consulting and Clinical Psychology, 65,* 44–52.

Abrams, R. (1993). ECT technique: Electrode placement, stimulus type, and treatment frequency. In C. E. Coffey (Ed.), *The clinical science of electroconvulsive therapy* (pp. 17–28). Washington, DC: American Psychiatric Press.

Abrams, R. (1997). *Electroconvulsive therapy* (3rd ed.). New York: Oxford University Press.

Abrams, R. L., & Greenwald, A. G. (2000). Parts outweigh the whole (word) in unconscious analysis of meaning. *Psychological Science, 11,* 118–124.

Abreu, J. M. (1999). Conscious and unconscious African American stereotypes: Impact on first impression and diagnostic ratings by therapists. *Journal of Consulting and Clinical Psychology, 67,* 387–393.

Achenbach, T. M. (1997). *Empirically based assessment of child and adolescent psychopathology.* Thousand Oaks, CA: Sage.

Acitelli, L. K. (1992). Gender differences in relationship awareness and marital satisfaction among young married couples. *Personality and Social Psychology Bulletin, 18,* 102–110.

Acocella, J. (1998, April 6). The politics of hysteria. *New Yorker,* pp. 64–79.

Addis, M. E. (1997). Evaluating the treatment manual as a means of disseminating empirically validated psychotherapies. *Clinical Psychology: Science and Practice, 4,* 1–11.

Addis, M. E., & Krasnow, A. D. (2000). A national survey of practicing psychologists' attitudes toward psychotherapy treatment manuals. *Journal of Consulting and Clinical Psychology, 68,* 331–339.

Ader, D. N., & Johnson, S. B. (1994). Sample description, reporting, and analysis of sex in psychological research: A look at APA and APA division journals in 1990. *American Psychologist, 49,* 216–218.

Adler, T. (1993, March). Bad mix: Combat stress, decisions. *APA Monitor,* p. 1.

Adolphs, R., Tranel, D., & Damasio, A. R. (1998). The human amygdala in social judgment. *Nature, 393*(6684), 470–474.

Adorno, T. W., Frenkel-Brunswik, E., Levinson, D. J., & Sanford, R. N. (1950). *The authoritarian personality.* New York: Harper & Row.

Agarwal, D. P. (1997). Molecular genetic aspects of alcohol metabolism and alcoholism. *Pharmacopsychiatry, 30*(3), 79–84.

Agency for Healthcare Research and Quality (AHRQ). (1999). *Treatment of depression–newer pharmacotherapies* (Evidence Report/Technology Assessment, Number 7, Pub. No. 99—E014). Rockville, MD: Author.

Aggleton, J. F. (1993). The contribution of the amygdala to normal and abnormal emotional states. *Trends in Neuroscience, 16*(8), 328–333.

Agnew, C. R., Van Lange, P. A. M., Rusbult, C. E., & Langston, C. A. (1998). Cognitive interdependence: Commitment and the mental representation of close relationships. *Journal of Personality and Social Psychology, 74,* 939–954.

Ahima, R. S., & Flier, J. S. (2000). Leptin. *Annual Review of Physiology, 62,* 413–437.

Ahmed, A., & Ruffman, T. (1998). Why do infants make A not B errors in a search task, yet show memory for the location of hidden objects in a nonsearch task? *Developmental Psychology, 34,* 441–453.

Aiken, L. R. (1994). *Psychological testing and assessment* (8th ed.). Boston: Allyn & Bacon.

Ainsworth, M. D. S. (1989). Attachments beyond infancy. *American Psychologist, 44,* 709–716.

Ainsworth, M. D. S., & Marvin, R. S. (1995). On the shaping of attachment theory and research: An interview with Mary D. S. Ainsworth (Fall 1994). *Monographs of the Society for Research in Child Development, 60,* 3–21.

Ainsworth, M. D. S., Blehar, M. D., Waters, E., & Wall, S. (1978). *Patterns of attachment: A psychological study of the Strange Situation.* Hillsdale, NJ: Erlbaum.

Albee, G. (1968). Conceptual models and manpower requirements in psychology. *American Psychologist, 23,* 317–320.

Albee, G. W. (1985, February). The answer is prevention. *Psychology Today, 19,* 60–62.

Albert, M. S., Savage, C. R., Blazer, D., Jones, K., Berkman, L., & Seeman, T. (1995). Predictors of cognitive change in older persons: MacArthur studies of successful aging. *Psychology and Aging, 10,* 578–589.

Alberti, R. E., & Emmons, M. L. (1986). *Your perfect right: A guide to assertive living* (5th ed.). San Luis Obispo, CA: Impact Publishers.

Aldag, R. J., & Fuller, S. R. (1993). Beyond fiasco: A reappraisal of the groupthink phenomenon and a new model of group decision processes. *Psychological Bulletin, 113,* 533–552.

Alderete, E., Eskenazi, B., & Sholtz, R. (1995). Effect of cigarette smoking and coffee drinking on time to conception. *Epidemiology, 6*(4), 403–408.

Al-Kubaisy, T., Marks, I. M., Logsdail, S., Marks, M. P., Lovell, K., Sungur, M., & Araya, R. (1992). Role of exposure homework in phobia reduction: A controlled study. *Behavior Therapy, 23,* 599–621.

Allen, L. S., & Gorski, R. A. (1992). Sexual orientation and the size of the anterior commissure in the human brain. *Proceedings of the National Academy of Sciences of the United States of America, 89,* 7199–7202.

Allen, L. S., Hines, M., Shryne, J. E., & Gorski, R. A. (1989). Two sexually dimorphic cell groups in the human brain. *Journal of Neuroscience, 9,* 497–506.

Allison, D. B. et al. (1999). Annual deaths attributable to obesity in the United States. *Journal of the American Medical Association, 282,* 1530–1538.

Alloy, L. B., Abramson, L. Y., & Francis, E. L. (1999). Do negative cognitive styles confer vulnerability to depression? *Current Directions in Psychological Science, 8,* 128–132.

Allport, G. W. (1961). *Pattern and growth in personality.* New York: Holt, Rinehart & Winston.

Allport, G. W., & Odbert, H. S. (1936). Trait names: A psycholexical study. *Psychological Monographs, 47*(1, Whole No. 211).

Alston, J. H. (1920). Spatial condition of the fusion of warmth and cold in heat. *American Journal of Psychology, 31,* 303–312.

Altemeyer, B. (1988). *Right-wing authoritarianism.* Winnipeg: University of Manitoba Press.

Altemeyer, B. (1994). Reducing prejudice in right-wing authoritarians. In M. Zanna & J. Olson (Eds.), *The psychology of prejudice: The Ontario Symposium* (Vol. 7, pp. 131–148). Hillsdale, NJ: Erlbaum.

Altman, L. K. (2000, April 10). Company developing marijuana for medical uses. *New York Times* [On-line].

Aluja-Fabregat, A., & Torrubia-Beltri, R. (1998). Viewing of mass media violence, perception of violence, personality and academic achievement. *Personality and Individual Differences, 25,* 973–989.

Alvarez, F. J., Delrio, M. C., & Prada, R. (1995). Drinking and driving in Spain. *Journal of Studies on Alcohol, 56*(4), 403–407.

Amabile, T. M. (1996). *Creativity in context:* Update to "The Social Psychology of Creativity." Boulder, CO: Westview.

Amabile, T. M., Hennessey, B. A., & Grossman, B. S. (1986). Social influences on creativity: The effects of contracted-for reward. *Journal of Personality & Social Psychology, 50,* 14–23.

Amabile, T. M., Hill, K. G., Hennessey, B. A., & Tighe, E. M. (1994). The Work Preference Inventory: Assessing intrinsic and extrinsic motivational orientations. *Journal of Personality and Social Psychology, 66*(5), 950–967.

American Educational Research Association, American Psychological Association, & National Council on Measurement in Education. (1999). *Standards for Educational and Psychological Testing.* Washington, DC: American Educational Research Association.

American Psychiatric Association. (1993, April). Practice guide for major depressive disorder in adults. *American Journal of Psychiatry, 150*(Suppl.), 1–26.

American Psychiatric Association. (1994). *Diagnostic and statistical manual of mental disorders* (4th ed.). Washington, DC: Author.

American Psychiatric Association. (1999). Position statement on psychiatric treatment and sexual orientation. *American Journal of Psychiatry, 156,* 1131.

American Psychiatric Association. (2000). *Diagnostic and statistical manual of mental disorders* (4th ed., rev.). Washington DC: Author.

American Psychological Association. (1992). Ethical principles of psychologists and code of conduct. *American Psychologist, 47,* 1597–1611.

American Psychological Association. (1993). *Violence and youth: Psychology's response.* Washington: DC: Author.

American Psychological Association. (1996, December). *Task Force Report: On-line psychotherapy and counseling.* Washington, DC: Author.

American Psychological Association. (1998). *Directory survey.* Washington, DC: Author.

American Psychological Association. (2000). *1998–1999 Survey of Undergraduate Departments of Psychology.* Washington, DC: Author.

Andersen, S. M., & Berk, M. S. (1998). The social-cognitive model of transference: Experiencing past relationships in the present. *Current Directions in Psychological Science, 7,* 109–115.

Anderson, A. K., & Phelps, E. A. (2000). Expression without recognition: Contributions of the human amygdala to emotional communication. *Psychological Science, 11,* 106–111.

Anderson, B. L. (1992). Psychological interventions for cancer patients to enhance the quality of life. *Journal of Consulting and Clinical Psychology, 60,* 569–575.

Anderson, C. A. (1997). Effects of violent movies and trait hostility on hostile feelings and aggressive thoughts. *Aggressive Behavior, 23,* 161–178.

Anderson, C. A., & Anderson, K. P. (1998). Temperature and aggression: Paradox, controversy, and a (fairly) clear picture. In R. G. Geen & E. Donnerstein (Eds.), *Human aggression* (pp. 248–298). San Diego: Academic Press.

Anderson, C. A., & Dill, K. E. (2000). Video games and aggressive thoughts, feelings, and behavior in the laboratory and in life. *Journal of Personality and Social Psychology 78,* 772–790.

Anderson, C. A., Benjamin, A. J., & Bartholow, B. D. (1998). Does the gun pull the trigger?: Automatic priming effects of weapon pictures and weapon names. *Psychological Science, 9,* 308–314.

Anderson, C. A., Lindsay, J. J., & Bushman, B. J. (1999). Research in the psychological laboratory: Truth or triviality? *Current Directions in Psychological Science, 8,* 3–9.

Anderson, E. M., & Lambert, M. J. (1995). Short-term dynamically oriented psychotherapy: A review and meta-analysis. *Clinical Psychology Review, 9*(6), 503–514.

Anderson, J. R. (1990a). *The adaptive character of thought.* Hillsdale, NJ: Erlbaum.

Anderson, J. R. (1990b). *Cognitive psychology and its implications* (3rd ed.). New York: Freeman.

Anderson, J. R. (2000). *Cognitive psychology and its implications* (5th ed.). New York: Worth.

Andreasen, N. C., Arndt, S., Alliger, R., Miller, D., & Flaum, M. (1995). Symptoms of schizophrenia. *Archives of General Psychiatry, 52,* 341–351.

Andrews, B., Brewin, C., Ochera, J., Morton, J., Bekerian, D. A., Davies, G. M., & Mollon, P. (2000). The timing, triggers, and quality of recovered memories in therapy. *British Journal of Clinical Psychology, 39,* 11–26.

Angst, J., Angst, F., & Stassen, H. H. (1999). Suicide risks inpatients with major depressive disorder. *Journal of Clinical Psychiatry, 60*(Suppl. 2), 57–62.

Anonymous. (1998). Changed my life [Review of the book Smart Drugs II: The Next Generation: New Drugs and Nutrients to Improve Your Memory and Increase Your Intelligence (Smart Drugs Series, Vol. 2)] [On-line]. Available: www.amazon.com/exec/obidos/ASIN/0962741876/qid%3d969373168/002-6667371-3045655

Anrep, G. V. (1920). Pitch discrimination in the dog. *Journal of Physiology, 53,* 367–385.

Anthony, T., Cooper, C., & Mullen, B. (1992). Cross-racial facial identification: Five studies of sex differences in facial prominence. *Personality and Social Psychology Bulletin, 18,* 296–301.

Antoni, M. H., Cruess, D. G., Cruess, S., Lutgendorf, S., Kumar, M., Ironson, G., Klimas, N., Fletcher, M. A., & Schneiderman, N. (2000). Cognitive-behavioral stress management intervention effects on anxiety, 24-hr urinary norepinephrine output, and t-cytotoxic/suppressor cells over time among symptomatic HIV-infected gay men. *Journal of Consulting and Clinical Psychology, 68,* 31–45.

Antonuccio, D. O., Danton, W. G., & DeNelsky, G. Y. (1995). Psychotherapy versus medication for depression: Challenging the conventional wisdom with data. *Professional Psychology: Research and Practice, 26,* 574–585.

Appelle, S., Lynn, S. J., & Newman, L. (2000). Alien abduction experiences. In E. Cardena, S. J. Lynn, & S. Krippner (Eds.), *Varieties of anomalous experience: Examining the scientific evidence* (pp. 253–282). Washington, DC: American Psychological Association.

Appleton, W. S. (2000). *Prozac and the new antidepressants: What you need to know about Prozac, Zoloft, Paxil, Luvox, Wellbutrin, Effexor, Serzone, Vestra, Celexa, St. John's Wort, and others* (rev. ed.). New York: Plume Books.

Araque, A., Sanzgiri, R. P., Parpura, V., & Haydon, P. G. (1999). Astrocyte-induced modulation of synaptic transmission. *Canadian Journal of Physiology and Pharmacology, 77,* 699–706.

Archambault, C. M., Czyzewski, D., Cordua y Cruz, G. D., Foreyt, F. P., & Mariotto, M. J. (1989). Effects of weight cycling in female rats. *Physiology and Behavior, 46,* 417–421.

Archer, J. (2000). Sex differences between heterosexual partners: A meta-analytic review. *Psychological Bulletin, 126,* 651–680.

Arenberg, D. (1982). Changes with age in problem solving. In F. I. M. Craik & S. Trehub (Eds.), *Aging and cognitive processes* (pp. 221–236). New York: Plenum.

Arkes, H. R., & Ayton, P. (1999). The sunk cost and Concorde effects: Are humans less rational than lower animals? *Psychological Bulletin, 125,* 591–600.

Armstrong, M. S., & Vaughan, K. (1996). An orienting response model of eye movement desensitization. *Journal of Behavior Therapy and Experimental Psychiatry, 27,* 21–32.

Arndt, J., Greenberg, J., Pyszczynski, T., & Solomon, S. (1997). Subliminal exposure to death-related stimuli increases defense of the cultural worldview. *Psychological Science, 8,* 379–385.

Arner, P. (2000). Obesity: A genetic disease of adipose tissue? *British Journal of Nutrition, 83,* S9–S16.

Arnett, J. J. (1999). Adolescent storm and stress, reconsidered. *American Psychologist, 54,* 317–326.

Arnett, J. J. (2000). Emerging adulthood: A theory of development from the late teens through the twenties. *American Psychologist, 55,* 469–480.

Aronoff, J., Barclay, A. M., & Stevenson, L. A. (1988). The recognition of threatening stimuli. *Journal of Personality and Social Psychology, 54,* 647–655.

Aronson, E. (1990). Applying social psychology to desegregation and energy conservation. *Personality and Social Psychology Bulletin, 16,* 118–132.

Aronson, E. (1995). *The social animal* (7th ed.). New York: Freeman.

Aronson, E. (1999a). The power of self-persuasion. *American Psychologist, 54,* 875–884.

Aronson, E. (1999b). *The social animal* (8th ed.). New York: Worth Publishers/ Freeman.

Aronson, E., Wilson, T. D., & Akert, R. M. (1999). *Social psychology* (3rd ed.). New York: Longman.

Arterberry, M. E., Craton, L. G., & Yonas, A. (1993). Infants' sensitivity to motion-carried information for depth and object properties. In C. Granrud (Ed.), *Visual perception and cognition in infancy. Carnegie Mellon symposia on cognition* (pp. 215–234). Hillsdale, NJ: Erlbaum.

Asch, S. E. (1951). Effects of group pressure upon the modification and distortion of judgments. In H. Guetzkow (Ed.), *Groups, leadership, and men* (pp. 177–190). Pittsburgh: Carnegie Press.

Asch, S. E. (1955). Opinions and social pressure. *Scientific American, 193,* 31–35.

Asch, S. E. (1956). Studies of independence and conformity: A minority of one against a unanimous majority. *Psychological Monographs, 70,* 1–70.

Ashcraft, M. H. (1989). *Human memory and cognition.* Glenview, IL: Scott, Foresman.

Ashton, H. (1995). Protracted withdrawal from benzodiazepines: The post-withdrawal syndrome. *Psychiatric Annals, 25*(3), 174–179.

Aslin, R. N., Jusczyk, P. W., & Pisoni, D. B. (1998). Speech and auditory processing during infancy: Constraints on and precursors to language. In W. Damon (Ed.), *Handbook of child psychology* (5th ed., pp. 147–198). New York: Wiley.

Aspinwall, L. G., & Duran, R. E. F. (1999). Psychology applied to health. In A. Stec & D. Bernstein (Eds.), *Psychology: Fields of application.* Boston: Houghton Mifflin.

Aspinwall, L. G., & Taylor, S. E. (1992). Modeling cognition adaptation: A longitudinal investigation of the impact of individual differences and coping on college adjustment and performance. *Journal of Personality and Social Psychology, 63,* 989–1003.

Associated Press. (1997, October 22). Forty percent in senior classes fail at science. *Chicago Tribune.*

Associated Press. (1999, November 17). Stripes near Waldo mean slow down. *St. Petersburg Times.*

Atkinson, J. W., & Raynor, J. O. (1974). *Personality, motivation, and achievement.* Washington, DC: Hemisphere.

Ayllon, T. (1999). *How to use token economy and point systems* (2nd ed.) Austin, Texas: PRO-ED.

Ayllon, T., & Azrin, N. H. (1968*). The token economy: A motivational system for therapy and rehabilitation.* New York: Appleton-Century-Crofts.

Azar, B. (1996, November). Project explores landscape of midlife. *APA Monitor,* p. 26.

Azar, B. (2000). The debate over child care isn't over yet. *Monitor on Psychology, 31,* 32–34.

Bacharach, V. R., & Baumeister, A. A. (1998). Direct and indirect effects of maternal intelligence, maternal age, income, and home environment on intelligence of preterm, low-birth-weight children. *Journal of Applied Developmental Psychology, 19,* 361–375.

Backman, L., & Nilsson, L. (1991). Effects of divided attention on free and cued recall of verbal events and action events. *Bulletin of the Psychonomic Society, 29,* 51–54.

Baddeley, A. (1982). *Your memory: A user's guide.* New York: Macmillan.

Baddeley, A. (1992). Working memory. *Science, 255,* 556–559.

Baddeley, A. (1998) *Human memory: Theory and practice.* Boston: Allyn & Bacon.

Bagley, C., & Tremblay, P. (1998). On the prevalence of homosexuality and bisexuality, in a random community survey of 750 men aged 18 to 27. *Journal of Homosexuality, 36,* 1–18.

Bagwell, C. L., Newcomb, A. F., & Bukowski, W. M. (1998). Preadolescent friendship and peer rejection as predictors of adult adjustment. *Child Development, 69,* 140–153.

Bahrick, H. P., Bahrick, P. O., & Wittlinger, R. P. (1975). Fifty years of memory for names and faces: A cross-cultural approach. *Journal of Experimental Psychology: General, 104,* 54–75.

Bahrick, H. P., & Hall, L. K. (1991). Lifetime maintenance of high school mathematics content. *Journal of Experimental Psychology: General, 120,* 20–33.

Bahrick, H. P., Hall, L. K., & Berger, S. A. (1996). Accuracy and distortion in memory for high school grades. *Psychological Science, 7,* 265–271.

Bahrick, H. P., Hall, L. K., Noggin, J. P., & Bahrick, L. E. (1994). Fifty years of language maintenance and language dominance in bilingual Hispanic immigrants. *Journal of Experimental Psychology: General, 123,* 264–283.

Bailey, A. J. (1993). The biology of autism. *Psychological Medicine, 23,* 7–11.

Bailey, J. M., & Benishay, D. S. (1993). Familial aggregation of female sexual orientation. *American Journal of Psychiatry, 150,* 272–277.

Bailey, J. M., & Pillard, R. C. (1991). A genetic study of male sexual orientation. *Archives of General Psychiatry, 48,* 1089–1096.

Bailey, J. M., Bobrow, D., Wolfe, M., & Mikach, S. (1995). Sexual orientation of adult sons of gay fathers. *Developmental Psychology, 31*(1), 124–129.

Bailey, J. M., Dunne, M. P., & Nicholas, G. (2000). Genetic and environmental influences on sexual orientation and its correlates in an Australian twin sample. *Journal of Personality and Social Psychology, 78,* 524–536.

Baillargeon, R. (1992). A model of physical reasoning in infancy. In C. Rovee-Collier & L. P. Lipsett (Eds.), *Advances in infancy research.* Norwood, NJ: Ablex.

Baillargeon, R. (1994a). How do infants learn about the physical world? *Current Directions in Psychological Science, 3,* 133–139.

Baillargeon, R. (1994b). Physical reasoning in young infants: Seeking explanations for impossible events. *British Journal of Development Psychology, 12,* 9–33.

Baillargeon, R. (1995). Physical reasoning in infancy. In M. S. Gazzaniga (Ed.), *The cognitive neurosciences* (pp. 181–204). Cambridge, MA: MIT Press.

Baillargeon, R. (1998). Infants' understanding of the physical world. In M. Sabourin et al. (Eds.), *Advances in psychological science: Vol. 2. Biological and cognitive aspects* (pp. 503–529). Hove, England: Taylor & Francis.

Balaban, M. T. (1995). Affective influences on startle in five-month-old infants: Reactions to facial expressions of emotion. *Child Development, 66*(1), 28–36.

Baldessarini, R. J., & Tondo, L. (2000). Does lithium treatment still work? Evidence of stable responses over three decades. *Archives of General Psychiatry, 57,* 187–190.

Balestreri, R., Fontana, L., & Astengo, F. (1987). A double-blind placebo-controlled evaluation of the safety and efficacy of vinpocetine in the treatment of patients with chronic vascular senile cerebral dysfunction. *Journal of the American Geriatric Society, 35,* 425–430.

Ball, S. G., Buchwald, A. M., & Waddell, M. T. (1995). Depression and generalized anxiety symptoms in panic disorder: Implications for comorbidity. *Journal of Nervous and Mental Disorders, 183*(5), 304–308.

Balleine, B., & Dickinson, A. (1994). Role of cholecystokinin in the motivational control of instrumental action in rats. *Behavioral Neuroscience, 108*(3), 590–605.

Baltes, P. B. (1993). The aging mind: Potential and limits. *The Gerontologist, 33,* 580–594.

Baltes, P. B. (1994, August). *Life-span developmental psychology: On the overall landscape of human development.* Invited address presented at the annual meeting of the American Psychological Association, Los Angeles.

Bancroft, J. (1994). Homosexual orientation: The search for a biological basis. *British Journal of Psychiatry, 164,* 437–440.

Bancroft, J. (1997). *Researching sexual behavior: Methodological issues.* Bloomington, IN: Indiana University Press.

Bandura, A. (1965). Influence of a model's reinforcement contingencies on the acquisition of imitative responses. *Journal of Personality and Social Psychology, 1,* 589–595.

Bandura, A. (1983). Psychological mechanisms of aggression. In R. G. Geen & C. I. Donnerstein (Eds.), *Aggression: Theoretical and empirical reviews* (Vol. 1, pp. 1–40). New York: Academic Press.

Bandura, A. (1992). Self-efficacy mechanism in psychobiologic functioning. In R. Schwarzer (Ed.), *Self-efficacy: Thought control of action* (pp. 355–394). Washington, DC: Hemisphere.

Bandura, A. (1997). *Self-efficacy: The exercise of control.* New York: Freeman.

Bandura, A. (1999). Social cognitive theory of personality. In L. Pervin & O. John (Eds.), *Handbook of personality research* (2nd ed., pp. 154–196). New York: Guilford.

Bandura, A. (2000). Exercise of human agency through collective efficacy. *Current Directions in Psychological Science, 9,* 75–78.

Bandura, A., Blanchard, E. B., & Ritter, B. (1969). The relative efficacy of desensitization and modeling approaches for inducing behavioral, affective, and attitudinal changes. *Journal of Personality and Social Psychology, 13,* 173–199.

Bandura, A., Ross, D., & Ross, S. A. (1963). Imitation of film-mediated aggressive models. *Journal of Abnormal and Social Psychology, 66,* 3–11.

Banich, M. T., & Heller, W. (1998). Evolving perspectives on lateralization of function. *Current Directions in Psychological Science, 7,* 1–2.

Banich, M. T., Stolar, N., Heller, W., & Goldman, R. B. (1992). A deficit in right hemisphere performance after induction of a depressed mood. *Neuropsychiatry, Neuropsychology, and Behavioral Neurology, 5*(1), 20–27.

Banks, M. S., & Salapatek, P. (1983). Infant visual perception. In P. H. Mussen (Ed.), *Handbook of child psychology: Vol. 2. Infancy and developmental psychobiology.* New York: Wiley.

Banta, B. D. (1997). Cooperation and competition in peaceful societies. *Psychological Bulletin, 121,* 299–320.

Bar, M., & Biederman, I. (1998). Subliminal visual priming. *Psychological Science, 9,* 464–469.

Barclay, J. R., Bransford, J. D., Franks, J. J., McCarrell, N. S., & Nitsch, K. (1974). Comprehension and semantic flexibility. *Journal of Verbal Learning and Verbal Behavior, 13,* 471–481.

Bardo, M. T. (1998). Neuropharmacological mechanisms of drug reward: Beyond dopamine in the nucleus accumbens. *Critical Reviews of Neurobiology, 12*(1–2), 37–67.

Bargones, J. Y., & Werner, L. A. (1994). Adults listen selectively; infants do not. *Psychological Science, 5,* 170–174.

Barinaga, M. (1999, November 26). Learning visualized, on the double. *Science, 286,* 1661.

Barlow, D. H. (1988). *Anxiety and its disorders: The nature and treatment of panic and anxiety.* New York: Guilford.

Barnett, W. S. (1998). Long-term cognitive and academic effects of early childhood education of children in poverty. *Preventive Medicine: An International Devoted Practice & Theory, 27,* 204–207.

Barnier, A. J., & McConkey, K. M. (1998). Posthypnotic responding away from the hypnotic setting. *Psychological Science, 9,* 256–262.

Baron, M. (1997). Genetic linkage and bipolar affective disorder: Progress and pitfalls. *Molecular Psychiatry, 2,* 200–210.

Baron, R. A., & Byrne, D. (1994). *Social psychology: Understanding human interaction* (7th ed.). Boston: Allyn & Bacon.

Baron, R. A., & Richardson, DC (1994). *Human aggression* (2nd ed.) New York: Plenum.

Baron, R. S., Kerr, N. L., & Miller, N. (1992). *Group process, group decision, group action.* Pacific Grove, CA: Brooks/Cole.

Barrett, G. V., & Depinet, R. L. (1991). A reconsideration of testing for competence rather than for intelligence. *American Psychologist, 46,* 1012–1024.

Barrick, M. R., & Mount, M. K. (1991). The Big Five personality dimensions and job performance: A meta-analysis. *Personnel Psychology, 44,* 1–26.

Barsalou, L. W. (1993). Flexibility, structure, and linguistic vagary in concepts: Manifestations of a compositional system of perceptual symbols. In A. F. Collins, S. E. Gathercole, M. A. Conway, & P. E. Morris (Eds.), *Theories of memory* (pp. 29–101). Hove, England: Erlbaum.

Barsky, A. J., Wool, C., Barnett, M. C., & Cleary, P. D. (1994). Histories of childhood trauma in adult hypochondriacal patients. *American Journal of Psychiatry, 151,* 397–401.

Bartoshuk, L. M. (1991). Taste, smell, and pleasure. In R. C. Bollef (Ed.), *The hedonics of taste* (pp. 15–28). Hillsdale, NJ: Erlbaum.

Bartoshuk, L. M. (2000). Comparing sensory experiences across individuals: Recent psychophysical advances illuminate genetic variation in taste perception. *Chemical Senses, 25,* 447–460.

Bartoshuk, L. M., & Wolfe, J. M. (1990). Conditioned taste aversion in humans: Are there olfactory versions? *Chemical Senses, 15,* 551.

Baskin, D., Bluestone, H., & Nelson, M. (1981). Ethnicity and psychiatric diagnosis. *Journal of Clinical Psychology, 37,* 529–537.

Bass, E., & Davis, L. (1988). *The courage to heal: A guide for women survivors of child sexual abuse.* New York: Harper & Row.

Bates, E. (1993, March). *Nature, nurture, and language development.* Paper presented at the biennial meeting of the Society for Research in Child Development, New Orleans.

Batson, C. D. (1998). Altruism and prosocial behavior. In D. Gilbert, S. T. Fiske, & G. Lindzey (Eds.), *Handbook of social psychology* (Vol. 2, 4th ed., pp. 282–316). Boston: McGraw-Hill.

Batson, C. D., Sager, K., Garst, E., & Kang, M. (1997). Is empathy-induced helping due to self-other merging? *Journal of Personality and Social Psychology, 73,* 495–509.

Battaglia, G., Yeh, S. Y., & De Souza, E. B. (1988). MDMA-induced neurotoxicity: Parameters of degeneration and recovery of brain serotonin neurons. *Pharmacology, Biochemistry and Behavior, 29,* 269–274.

Baucom, D. H., Shoham, V., Mueser, K. T., Daiuto, A. D., & Stickle, T. R. (1998). Empirically supported couple and family interventions for marital distress and adult mental health problems. *Journal of Consulting and Clinical Psychology, 66,* 53–88.

Bauer, P. J. (1996). What do infants recall of their lives?: Memory for specific events by one- to two-year-olds. *American Psychologist, 51,* 29–41.

Baum, A., Gatchel, R. J., & Krantz, D. S. (1997) *Introduction to health psychology* (3rd ed.) New York: McGraw-Hill.

Baummeister, R. (1995). Self and identity: An introduction. In A. Tesser (Ed.), *Advanced social psychology* (pp. 51–98). New York: McGraw-Hill.

Baumeister, R. F. (1998). The self. In D. Gilbert, S. T. Fiske, & G. Lindzey (Eds.), *Handbook of social psychology* (Vol. 1, 4th ed., pp. 680–740). Boston: McGraw-Hill.

Baumeister, R. F. (2000). Gender differences in erotic plasticity: The female sex drive as socially flexible and responsive. *Psychological Bulletin, 126,* 347–374.

Baumeister, R. F., & Leary, M. R. (1995). The need to belong: Desire for interpersonal attachments as a fundamental human motivation. *Psychological Bulletin, 117*(3), 497–529.

Baumrind, D. (1971). Current patterns of parental authority. *Developmental Psychology Monographs, 4*(1, part 2).

Baumrind, D. (1986). *Familial antecedents of social competence in middle childhood.* Unpublished monograph, Institute of Human Development, University of California, Berkeley.

Baumrind, D. (1991). Effective parenting during the early adolescent transition. In P. A. Cowan & E. M. Hetherington (Eds.), *Family transition* (pp. 111–163). Hillsdale, NJ: Erlbaum.

Beardsley, R. S., Gardocki, G. J., Larson, D. B., & Hidalgo, J. (1988). Prescribing of psychotropic medication by primary-care physicians and psychiatrists. *Archives of General Psychiatry, 45,* 1117–1119.

Beatty, J. (1995). *Principles of behavioral neuroscience.* Dubuque: Brown and Benchmark.

Beauchamp-Turner, D. L., & Levinson, D. M. (1992). Effects of meditation on stress, health, and affect. Medical Psychotherapy: *An International Journal, 5,* 123–131.

Beck, A. T. (1967). *Depression: Clinical, experimental and theoretical aspects.* New York: Harper & Row.

Beck, A. T. (1976). *Cognitive therapy and the emotional disorders.* New York: International Universities Press.

Beck, A. T. (1995). Cognitive therapy: A 30-year retrospective. In S. O. Lilienfeld (Ed.), *Seeing both sides: Classic controversies in abnormal psychology* (pp. 303–311). Pacific Grove, CA: Brooks/Cole. (Original work published in 1991)

Beck, A. T., Brown, G., Berchick, R. J., Stewart, B. L., & Steer, R. A. (1990). Relationship between hopelessness and ultimate suicide: A replication with psychiatric outpatients. *American Journal of Psychiatry, 147,* 190–195.

Beck, A. T., & Emery, G. (1985). *Anxiety disorders and phobias: A cognitive perspective.* New York: Basic Books.

Beck, A. T., Sokol, L., Clark, D., Berchick, R., & Wright, F. (1992). A crossover study of focused cognitive therapy for panic disorder. *American Journal of Psychiatry, 149,* 778–783.

Beck, J. S., & Beck, A. T. (1995). *Cognitive therapy: Basics and beyond.* New York: Guilford Press.

Beck, M. (1992, December 7). The new middle age. *Newsweek,* pp. 50–56.

Becker, A. E., Grinspoon, S. K., Klibanski, A., & Herzog, D. B. (1999). Eating disorders. *New England Journal of Medicine, 340,* 1092–1098.

Begley, S. (1997, September 29). Hope for "snow babies." *Newsweek,* pp. 62–63.

Belin, P., Zatorre, R. J., Lafaille, P., Ahad, P., & Pike, B. (2000). Voice-selective areas in human auditory cortex. *Nature, 403,* 309–312.

Bell, B. E., & Loftus, E. F. (1989). Trivial persuasion in the courtroom: The power of (a few) minor details. *Journal of Personality and Social Psychology, 56,* 669–679.

Bell, P. A., Fisher, J. D., Baum, A., & Greene, T. (1996). *Environmental psychology* (4th ed.). Fort Worth, TX: Holt, Rinehart & Winston.

Belli, R. F., & Loftus, E. F. (1996). The pliability of autobiographical memory: Misinformation and the false memory problem. In D. C. Rubin (Ed.), *Remembering our past: Studies in autobiographical memory* (pp. 157–179). New York: Cambridge University Press.

Belsky, J., & Kelly, J. (1994). *The transition to parenthood.* New York: Dell.

Benecke, M. (1999). Spontaneous human combustion: Thoughts of a forensic biologist. *Skeptical Inquirer, 22,* 47–51.

Benedetti, F., & Amanzio, M. (1997). The neurobiology of placebo analgesia: From endogenous opioids to cholecystokinin. *Progress in Neurobiology, 52,* 109–125.

Benedetti, F., Arduino, C., & Amanzio, M. (1999) Somatotopic activation of opioid systems by target-directed expectations of analgesia. *Journal of Neuroscience, 19,* 3639–3648.

Benight, C. C., Swift, E., Sanger, J., Smith, A., & Zeppelin, D. (1999). Coping self-efficacy as a mediator of distress following a natural disaster. *Journal of Applied Social Psychology, 29,* 2443–2464.

Benjamin, K., Wilson, S. G., & Mogil, J. S. (1999). *Journal of Pharmacology & Experimental Therapeutics, 289,* 1370–1375.

Bennet, W. M. (1994). Marijuana has no medicinal value. *Hospital Practice, 29*(4), 26–27.

Bennett, H. L., Giannini, J. A., & Davis, H. S. (1985). Nonverbal response to intraoperational conversation. *British Journal of Anaesthesia, 57,* 174–179.

Ben-Shakhar, G., & Furedy, J. J. (1990) *Theories and applications in the detection of deception: A psychophysiological and international perspective.* New York: Springer-Verlag.

Benson, H. (1975). *The relaxation response.* New York: Morrow.

Berger, R., & Hannah, M. T. (Eds.), *Preventive approaches in couples therapy.* Bristol, PA: Brunner/Mazel.

Bergin, A. E. (1971). The evaluation of therapeutic outcomes. In A. E. Bergin & S. L. Garfield (Eds.), *Handbook of psychotherapy and behavior change: An empirical analysis* (pp. 217–270). New York: Wiley.

Berkowitz, L. (1994). Is something missing? Some observations prompted by the Cognitive-neoassociationist view of anger and emotional aggression. In L. R. Huesmann (Ed.), *Human aggression: Current perspectives* (pp. 35–60). New York: Plenum.

Berkowitz, L. (1998). Affective aggression: The role of stress, pain, and negative affect. In R. G. Geen & E. Donnerstein (Eds.), *Human aggression* (pp. 49–72). San Diego: Academic Press.

Berlin, L. J., Cassidy, J., & Belsky, J. (1995). Loneliness in young children and infant-mother attachment: A longitudinal study. *Merrill-Palmer Quarterly, 41,* 91–103.

Bernard, L. L. (1924). *Instinct.* New York: Holt, Rinehart & Winston.

Bernhardt, P. C. (1997). Influences of serotonin and testosterone in aggression and dominance: Convergence with social psychology. *Current Directions in Psychological Science, 6,* 44–48.

Bernstein, D. A. (1970). The modification of smoking behavior: A search for effective variables. *Behaviour Research and Therapy, 8,* 133–146.

Bernstein, D. A., Borkovec, T. D., & Hazlette-Stevens, H. (2000). *Progressive relaxation training: A manual for the helping professions* (2nd ed.) New York: Praeger.

Bernstein, D. M., & Roberts, B. (1995). Assessing dreams through self-report questionnaires: Relation with past research and personality. *Dreaming: Journal of the Association for the Study of Dreams, 5,* 13–27.

Bernstein, I. L. (1978). Learned taste aversions in children receiving chemotherapy. *Science, 200,* 1302–1303.

Berry, J. W., & Bennett, J. A. (1992). Cree conceptions of cognitive competence. *International Journal of Psychology, 27,* 73–88.

Berscheid, E., & Reis, H. T. (1998). Attraction and close relationships. In D. Gilbert, S. T. Fiske, & G. Lindzey (Eds.), *Handbook of social psychology* (Vol. 2, 4th ed., pp. 193–281). Boston: McGraw-Hill.

Bersoff, D. M. (1999). Why good people sometimes do bad things: Motivated reasoning and unethical behavior. *Personality & Social Psychology Bulletin, 25,* 28–39.

Best, D. (1992, June). *Cross-cultural themes in developmental psychology.* Paper presented at workshop on cross-cultural aspects of psychology. Western Washington University, Bellingham.

Best, J. B. (1999). *Cognitive psychology* (5th ed.). Belmont, CA: Brooks/Cole.

Beutler, L. E. (2000). David and Goliath: When empirical and clinical standards of practice meet. *American Psychologist, 55,* 997–1007.

Beyerstein, B. L. (1999). Pseudoscience and the brain: Tuners and tonics for aspiring superhumans. In S. Della Sala (Ed.), *Mind myths: Exploring popular assumptions about the mind and brain* (pp. 59–82). Chichester, England: Wiley.

Biaggio, M., Paget, T. L., & Chenoweth, M. S. (1997). A model for ethical management of faculty-student dual relationships. *Professional Psychology: Research and Practice, 28,* 184–189.

Bickman, L. (1999). Practice makes perfect and other myths about mental health services. *American Psychologist, 54,* 965–978.

Bickis, M., Kelly, I. W., & Byrnes, G. (1995). Crisis calls and temporal and lunar variables: A comprehensive study. *The Journal of Psychology, 129,* 701–711.

Biederman, I., Cooper, E. E., Fox, P. W., & Mahadevan, R. S. (1992). Unexceptional spatial memory in an exceptional memorist. *Journal of Experimental Psychology: Learning, Memory, and Cognition, 18,* 654–657.

Bierut, L. J., Heath, A. C., Bucholz, K. K., Dinwiddie, S. H., Madden, P. A., Statham, D. J., Dunne, M. P., & Martin, N. G. (1999). Major depressive disorder in a community-based twin sample: Are there different genetic and environmental contributions for men and women? *Archives of General Psychiatry, 56,* 557–563.

Binet, A., & Simon, T. (1905). Methodes nouvelles pour le diagnostic du niveau intellectuel des anormaux. *L'Annee Psychologique, 11,* 191–244.

Birnbaum, M. H., & Sotoodeh, Y. (1991). Measurement of stress: Scaling the magnitudes of life changes. *Psychological Science, 2,* 236–243.

Bittigau, P., & Ikonomidou, C. (1997). Glutamate in neurologic diseases. *Journal of Child Neurology, 12,* 471–485.

Bjork, R. A. (1998). Assessing our own competence: Heuristics and biases. In D. Gopher & A. Koriat (Eds.), *Attention and performance* (Vol. 17). Orlando: Academic Press.

Bjork, R. A., & Vanhuele, M. (1992). Retrieval inhibition and related adaptive peculiarities of human memory. *Advances in Consumer Research, 19,* 155–160.

Bjorklund, D. F., & Green, B. L. (1992). The adaptive nature of cognitive immaturity. *American Psychologist, 47,* 46–54.

Blackwell, B. (1973). Psychotropic drugs in use today. *Journal of the American Medical Association, 225,* 1637–1641.

Blagrove, M. (1996). Problems with the cognitive psychological modeling of dreaming. *Journal of Mind and Behavior, 17,* 99–134.

Blair, I. V., & Banaji, M. (1996). Automatic and controlled processes in stereotype priming. *Journal of Personality and Social Psychology, 70,* 1142–1163.

Blake, R. (1998). What can be "perceived" in the absence of visual awareness? *Current Directions in Psychological Science, 6,* 157–162.

Blakeslee, S. (2000). A decade of discovery yields a shock about the brain. *New York Times,* January 4.

Blanchard, J. (1999). The co-occurrence of substance use in other mental disorders: Editor's introduction. *Clinical Psychology Review, 20,* 145–148.

Blass, E. M. (1996). Mothers and their infants: Peptide-mediated physiological, behavioral and affective changes during suckling. *Regulatory Peptides, 66*(1–2), 109–112.

Blass, T. (2000). The Milgram paradigm 35 years later: Some things we know about obedience to authority. In T. Blass (Ed.), *Current perspectives on the Milgram paradigm.* Mahwah, N.J: Erlbaum.

Blazer, D. G., Kessler, R. C., McGonagle, K. A., & Swartz, M. S. (1994). The prevalence and distribution of major depression in a national community sample: The national comorbidity survey. *American Journal of Psychiatry, 151,* 979–986.

Blehar, M., & Rosenthal, N. (1989). Seasonal affective disorders and phototherapy. *Archives of General Psychiatry, 46,* 469–474.

Block, J. A. (1971). *Lives through time.* Berkeley: Bancroft Books.

Block, J. A. (1995). A contrarian view of the five-factor approach. *Psychological Bulletin, 117,* 187–215.

Block, R. I., & Ghoneim, M. M. (1993). Effects of chronic marijuana use on human cognition. *Psychopharmacology, 110*(1–2), 219–228.

Bloom, L. (1995). *The transition from infancy to language: Acquiring the power of expression.* New York: Cambridge University Press.

Blum, L. N., Nielsen, N. H., & Riggs, J. A. (1998). Alcoholism and alcohol abuse among women. *Journal of Women's Health, 7,* 861–871.

Blumberg, M. S., & Lucas, D. E. (1994). Dual mechanisms of twitching during sleep in neonatal rats. *Behavioral Neuroscience, 108*(6), 1196–1202.

Blume, E. S. (1998). *Secret survivors: Uncovering incest and its aftereffects in women.* New York: Ballantine.

Blundell, J. E., & Cooling, J. (2000). Routes to obesity: Phenotypes, food choices and activity. *British Journal of Nutrition, 83,* S33–S38.

Bodian, S. (1999). *Meditation for dummies.* Indianapolis: IDG Books Worldwide.

Bogartz, R. S., Shinskey, J. L., & Speaker, C. J. (1997). Interpreting infant looking: The event set x event set design. *Developmental Psychology, 33,* 408–422.

Bolles, R. C. (1975). *Theory of motivation* (2nd ed.). New York: Harper & Row.

Bond, G., Aiken, L., & Somerville, S. (1992). The Health Beliefs Model and adolescents with insulin-dependent diabetes mellitus. *Health Psychology, 11,* 190–198.

Booth, P. B., & Lindaman, S. (2000). Theraplay for enhancing attachment in adopted children. In H. G. Kaduson & C. Schaefer (Eds.), *Short-term play therapy for children.* New York: Guilford Press.

Borgida, E., Conner, C., & Monteufel, L. (1992). Understanding living kidney donors: A behavioral decision-making perspective. In S. Spacapan & S. Oskamp (Eds.), *Helping and being helped* (pp. 183–212). Newbury Park, CA: Sage.

Borkman, T. J. (1997). A selected look at self-help groups in the U.S. *Health and Social Care in the Community, 5,* 357–364.

Borman, W. C., Hanson, M. A., & Hedge, J. W. (1997). Personnel selection. *Annual Review of Psychology, 48,* 299–337.

Bosma, H, Marmot, M. G., Hemingway, H., Nicholson, A. C., Brunner, E., & Stansfeld, S. A. (1997). Low job control and risk of coronary heart disease in Whitehall II (prospective cohort) study. *British Medical Journal, 314,* 558–565.

Boss, P. (1999). *Ambiguous loss: Learning to live with unresolved grief.* Cambridge, MA: Harvard University Press.

Botwinick, J. (1961). Husband and father-in-law: A reversible figure. *American Journal of Psychology, 74,* 312–313.

Bouchard, T., & McGue, M. (1981). Familial studies of intelligence: A review. *Science, 212*(4498), 1055–1059.

Bouchard, T. J., Jr., Lykken, D. T., McGue, M., Segal, N. L., & Tellegen, A. (1990). Sources of human psychological differences: The Minnesota study of twins reared apart. *Science, 250,* 223–228.

Bouton, M., Mineka, S., & Barlow, D. (2001). A modern learning theory perspective on the etiology of panic disorder. *Psychological Review, 107.*

Bovasso, G. B., Eaton, W. W., & Armenian, H. K. (1999). The long-term outcomes of mental health treatment in a population-based study. *Journal of Consulting and Clinical Psychology, 67,* 529–538.

Bowden, C. L. (2000). Efficacy of lithium in mania and maintenance therapy of bipolar disorder. *Journal of Clinical Psychiatry, 61,* 35–40.

Bowden, C. L., Calabrese, J. R., McElroy, S. L., Gyulai, L., Wassef, A., Petty, F., Pope, H. G. Jr., Chou, J. C., Keck, P. E. Jr, Rhodes, L. J., Swann, A. C., Hirschfeld, R. M., & Wozniak, P. J. (2000). A randomized, placebo-controlled 12-month trial of divalproex and lithium in treatment of outpatients with bipolar I disorder. *Archives of General Psychiatry, 57,* 481–489.

Bower, G. H. (1975). Cognitive psychology: An introduction. In W. K. Estes (Ed.), *Handbook of learning and cognitive processes: Vol. 1.* Hillsdale, NJ: Erlbaum.

Bower, G. H. (1981). Mood and memory. *American Psychologist, 36,* 129–148.

Bower, J. E., Kemeny, M. E., Taylor, S. E., & Fahey, J. L. (1999). Cognitive processing, discovery of meaning, CD4 decline, and AIDS-related mortality among bereaved HIV-seropositive men. *Journal of Consulting and Clinical Psychology, 66,* 979–986.

Bowers, K. S., & Farvolden, P. (1996). Revisiting a century-old Freudian slip from suggestion to the truth repressed. *Psychological Bulletin, 119,* 355–380.

Bowers, W. A. (1989). Cognitive therapy with inpatients. In A. Freeman, K. M. Simon, L. E. Beutler, & H. Arkowitz (Eds.), *Comprehensive handbook of cognitive therapy.* New York: Plenum.

Bowlby, J. (1951). Maternal care and mental health. *World Health Organization Monograph 2*. Geneva: World Health Organization.

Bowlby, J. (1973). *Attachment and loss: Vol. 2*. Separation. New York: Basic Books.

Bowman, E. S., & Nurnberger, J. I. (1993). Genetics of psychiatry diagnosis and treatment. In D. L. Dummer (Ed.), *Current psychiatric therapy* (pp. 46–56). Philadelphia: Saunders.

Boyatzis, R. E. (1982). *The competent manager*. New York: Wiley.

Bozarth, M. A., & Wise, R. A. (1984). Anatomically distinct opiate receptor fields mediate reward and physical dependence. *Science, 224*, 516–518.

Bracken, B. A., & McCallum, R. S. (1998). *The universal nonverbal intelligence test*. Itasca, IL: Riverside Publishing Company.

Bradbury, T. N., Campbell, S. M., & Fincham, F. D. (1995). Longitudinal and behavioral analysis of masculinity and femininity in marriage. *Journal of Personality and Social Psychology, 68*, 328–341.

Bradley-Johnson, S., Graham, D. P., & Johnson, C. M. (1986). Token reinforcement on WISC-R performance for white, low-socioeconomic, upper and lower elementary-school-age students. *Journal of School Psychology, 24*, 73–79.

Bradshaw, G. L. (1993a). Why did the Wright brothers get there first? Part 1. *Chemtech, 23*(6), 8–13.

Bradshaw, G. L. (1993b). Why did the Wright brothers get there first? Part 2. *Chemtech, 23*(7), 16–22.

Brandimonte, M. A., Hitch, G. J., & Bishop, D. V. M. (1992). Influence of short-term memory codes on visual image processing: Evidence from image transformation tasks. *Journal of Experimental Psychology: Learning, Memory, and Cognition, 18*, 157–165.

Brandtstadter, J., & Renner, G. (1990). Tenacious goal pursuit and flexible goal adjustment: Explication and age-related analysis of assimilative and accommodative strategies of coping. *Psychology and Aging, 5*, 58–67.

Bransford, J. D., Brown, A. L., & Cocking, R. R. (Eds.). (1999). *How people learn: Brain, mind, experience, and school*. Washington, DC: National Academy Press.

Bransford, J. D., & Stein, B. S. (1993). *The ideal problem solver* (2nd ed.). New York: Freeman.

Braun, A. E., Balkin, T. J., & Wesensten, N. J. (1998). Dissociated pattern of activity in visual cortices and their projections during human rapid eye movement sleep. *Science, 279*, 91–95.

Bray, G. A., & Tartaglia, L. A. (2000). Medicinal strategies in the treatment of obesity. *Nature, 404*, 672–677.

Breggin, P. R. (1997). *Brain-Disabling Treatments in Psychiatry : Drugs, Electroshock, and the Role of the FDA* . New York: Springer.

Brehm, S. (1992). *Intimate relationships*. New York: McGraw-Hill.

Brehm, S., Kassin, S., & Fein, S. (1999). *Social psychology* (4th ed., Table 6.4). Boston: Houghton Mifflin.

Breier, A., Buchanan, R. W., Elkashef, A., Munson, R. C., Kirkpatrick, B., & Gellad, F. (1992). Brain morphology and schizophrenia: A magnetic resonance imaging study of limbic, prefrontal cortex, and caudate structures. *Archives of General Psychiatry, 49*, 921–926.

Breier, A., Su, T. P., Saunders, R., Carson, R. E., Kolachana, B. S., de Bartolomeis, A., Weinberger, D. R., Weisenfeld, N., Malhotra, A. K., Eckelman, W. C., & Pickar, D. (1997). Schizophrenia is associated with elevated amphetamine-induced synaptic dopamine concentrations: Evidence from a novel positron emission topography method. *Proceedings of the National Academy of Sciences, 94*, 2569–2573.

Brelsford, J. W. (1993). Physics education in a virtual environment. In *Proceedings of the 37th Annual Meeting of the Human Factors and Ergonomics Society*. Santa Monica, CA: Human Factors.

Bremner, J. D., Shobe, K. K., & Kihlstrom, J. F. (2000). False memories in women with self-reported childhood sexual abuse. *Psychological Science, 11* , 333–337.

Brener, N. D., Hassan, S. S., & Barrios, L. C. (1999). Suicidal ideation among college students in the United States. *Journal of Consulting and Clinical Psychology, 67*, 1004–1008.

Brennen, T., Baguley, T., Bright, J., & Bruce, V. (1990). Resolving semantically induced tip-of-the-tongue states for proper nouns. *Memory & Cognition, 18*, 339–347.

Brenner, R., Azbel, V., Madhusoodanan, S., & Pawlowska, M. (2000). *Clinical Therapeutics, 22*, 411–419.

Breuer, J., & Freud, S. (1896). *Studies on hysteria*. New York: Avon. (Reprinted in 1966)

Brewer, M. B., & Brown, R. J. (1998). Intergroup relations. In D. Gilbert, S. T. Fiske, & G. Lindzey (Eds.), *Handbook of social psychology* (Vol. 2, 4th ed., pp. 554–594). Boston: McGraw-Hill.

Brewer, W. F., & Treyens, J. C. (1981). Role of schemata in memory for places. *Cognitive Psychology, 13*, 207–230.

Brewerton, T. D., Lydiard, R. B., Herzog, D. B., & Brotman, A. W. (1995). Comorbidity of Axis I psychiatric disorders in bulimia nervosa. *Journal of Clinical Psychiatry, 56*(2), 77–80.

Brigham, C. C. (1923). *A study of American intelligence*. Princeton, NJ: Princeton University Press.

Bright, J. I., Baker, K. D., & Neimeyer, R. A. (1999). Professional and paraprofessional group treatments for depression: A comparison of cognitive-behavioral and mutual support interventions. *Journal of Consulting and Clinical Psychology, 67*, 491–501.

Brislin, R. (1993). *Understanding culture's influence on behavior*. Fort Worth: Harcourt, Brace, Jovanovich.

British Medical Association. (2000). *Acupuncture: Efficacy, safety, and practice*. London: Harwood Academic Publishers.

Brock, J. W., Farooqui, S. M., Ross, K. D., & Payne, S. (1994). Stress-related behavior and central norepinephrine concentrations in the REM sleep-deprived rat. *Physiology and Behavior, 55*(6), 997–1003.

Brock, T. C., Green, M. C., & Reich, D. A. (1998). New evidence of flaws in the *Consumer Reports* study of psychotherapy. *American Psychologist, 53*, 62–72.

Brody, J. E. (1998, September 15). Personal health: Teenagers and sex–Younger and more at risk. *New York Times* (Web Archive).

Brody, N., & Ehrlichman, H. (1998). *Personality psychology: The science of individuality*. Upper Saddle River, NJ: Prentice-Hall.

Bronstein, P., Duncan, P., Clauson, J., Abrams, C. L., Yannett, N., Ginsburg, G., & Milne, M. (1998). Preventing middle school adjustment problems for children from lower-income families: A program for aware parenting. *Journal of Applied Developmental Psychology, 19*, 129–152.

Brooks-Gunn, J. (1988). Antecedents and consequences of variations in girls' maturational timing. *Journal of Adolescent Health Care, 9*(5), 1–9.

Brooks-Gunn, J., Klebanov, P. K., & Duncan, G. J. (1996). Ethnic differences in children's intelligence test scores: Role of economic deprivation, home environment, and maternal characteristics. *Child Development, 67*, 396–408.

Brown, A. S. (1991). A review of the tip-of-the-tongue experience. *Psychological Bulletin, 109*, 204–233.

Brown, G. K., Beck, A. T., Steer, R. A., & Grisham, J. R. (2000). Risk factors for suicide in psychiatric outpatients: A 20-year prospective study. *Journal of Consulting and Clinical Psychology, 68*, 371–377.

Brown, G. W., & Moran, P. M. (1997). Single mothers, poverty and depression. *Psychological Medicine, 27*, 21–33.

Brown, J. (1958). Some tests of the decay theory of immediate memory. *Quarterly Journal of Experimental Psychology, 10*, 12–21.

Brown, J. R., & Dunn, J. (1996). Continuities in emotion understanding from three to six years. *Child Development, 67*, 789–802.

Brown, P. D., & O'Leary, K. D. (2000). Therapeutic alliance: Predicting continuance and success in group treatment for spouse abuse. *Journal of Consulting and Clinical Psychology, 68*, 340–345.

Brown, R., & McNeill, D. (1966). The "tip-of-the-tongue" phenomenon. *Journal of Verbal Learning and Verbal Behavior, 5*, 325–337.

Brownell, K. D., & Rodin, J. (1994). The dieting maelstrom: Is it possible and advisable to lose weight? *American Psychologist, 49*(9), 781–791.

Bruce, T. J., Spiegel, D. A., & Hegel, M. T. (1999). Cognitive-behavioral therapy helps prevent relapse and recurrence of panic disorder following Alpazolam discontinuation: A long-term follow-up of the Peoria and Dartmouth studies. *Journal of Consulting and Clinical Psychology, 67*, 151–156.

Bruck, M., Cavanagh, P., & Ceci, S. J. (1991). Fortysomething: Recognizing faces at one's 25th reunion. *Memory & Cognition, 19*, 221–228.

Brüning, J. C., Gautam, D., Burks, D. J., Gillette, J., Schubert, M., Orban, P. C., Klein, R., Krone, W., Müller-Wieland, D., & Kahn, C. R. (2000). Role of brain insulin receptor in control of body weight and reproduction. *Science, 289*, 2122.

Brunvald, J. H. (1989). Curses! Broiled again! *The hottest urban legends going*. New York: Norton.

Bryson, S. E., & Smith, I. M. (1998). Autism. *Mental Retardation & Developmental Disabilities Research Reviews, 4*, 97–103.

Bugental, D. B., & Goodnow, J. J. (1998). Socialization processes. In W. Damon & N. Eisenberg (Eds.), *Handbook of child psychology: Vol. 3. Social, emotional, and personality development* (5th ed., pp. 389–462). New York: Wiley.

Bui, K.-V. T, Peplau, L. A., & Hill, C. T. (1996). Testing the Rusbult model of relationship commitment and stability in a 15-year study of heterosexual couples. *Personality and Social Psychology Bulletin, 22*, 1244–1257.

Bullough, V. L. (1995, August). Sex matters. *Scientific American,* pp. 105–106.

Burac, J. A. (2001). *Development of autism: Perspectives from theory and research*. Hillsdale, NJ: Erlbaum.

Burchard, R. E. (1992). Coca chewing and diet. *Current Anthropology, 33*(1), 1–24.

Burger, J. M., & Petty, R. E. (1981). The low-ball compliance technique: Task or person commitment? *Journal of Personality and Social Psychology, 40,* 492–500.

Burish, T., & Jenkins, R. (1992). Effectiveness of biofeedback and relaxation training in reducing the side effects of cancer chemotherapy. *Health Psychology, 11,* 17–23.

Burke, K. C., Burke, J. K., Jr., Regier, D. A., & Rae, D. S. (1990). Age at onset of selected mental disorders in five community populations. *Archives of General Psychiatry, 47,* 511–518.

Burke, R. S., & Stephens, R. S. (2000). Social anxiety and drinking in college students: A social cognitive theory analysis. *Clinical Psychology Review, 19,* 513–530.

Burleson, B. R., Albrecht, T. L., & Sarason, I. G. (Eds.). (1994). *Communication of social support: Messages, interactions, relationships, and community.* Thousand Oaks, CA: Sage.

Burleson, M. H., Gregory, W. L., & Trevarthen, W. R. (1995). Heterosexual activity: Relationship with ovarian function. *Psychoneuroendocrinology, 20*(4), 405–421.

Burman, B., & Margolin, G. (1992). Analysis of the association between marital relationships and health problems: An interactional perspective. *Psychological Bulletin, 112,* 39–63.

Burnstein, E., Crandell, C., & Kitayama, S. (1994). Some Neo-Darwinian decision rules for altruism: Weighing cues for inclusive fitness as a function of the biological importance of the decision. *Journal of Personality and Social Psychology, 67,* 773–789.

Burr, D. C., Morrone, C., & Fiorentini, A. (1996). Spatial and temporal properties of infant colour vision. In F. Vital-Durand, J. Atkinson, J., & O. J. Braddick (Eds.), *Infant vision* (pp. 63–77). Oxford: Oxford University Press.

Burris, C. T., Branscombe, N. R., & Klar, Y. (1997). Maladjustment implications of group gender-role discrepancies: An ordered distinction model. *European Journal of Social Psychology, 27,* 675–685.

Burton, A. M., Wilson, S., Cowan, M., & Bruce, V. (1999). Face recognition in poor-quality video: Evidence from security surveillance. *Psychological Science, 10,* 243–248.

Bushman, B. J. (1998). Priming effects of media violence on the accessibility of aggressive constructs in memory. *Personality and Social Psychology Bulletin, 24,* 537–545.

Buss, A. H. (1995). *Personality: Temperament, social behavior, and the self.* Boston: Allyn & Bacon.

Buss, A. H. (1997). Evolutionary perspectives on personality traits. In R. Hogan, J. Johnson, & S. Briggs (Eds.), *Handbook of personality psychology* (pp. 345–366). San Diego: Academic Press.

Buss, D. M. (1995). The future of evolutionary psychology. *Psychological Inquiry, 6,* 81–87.

Buss, D. M. (1999). *Evolutionary psychology: The new science of the mind.* Boston: Allyn & Bacon.

Butler, R. (1998). Information seeking and achievement motivation in middle childhood and adolescence: The role of conceptions of ability. *Developmental Psychology, 35,* 146–163.

Cabanac, M., & Morrissette, J. (1992). Acute, but not chronic, exercise lowers the body weight set-point in male rats. *Physiology and Behavior, 52*(6) 1173–1177.

Cabeza, R., & Nyberg, L. (2000). Imaging cognition II: An empirical review of 275 PET and MRI studies. *Journal of Cognitive Neuroscience, 12,* 1–47.

Cacioppo, J. T., Berntson, G. G., & Petty, R. E. (1997). Persuasion. *Encyclopedia of human biology* (Vol. 6, pp. 679–690). San Diego: Academic Press.

Cacioppo, J. T., Malarkey, W. B., Kiecolt-Glaser, J. K., Uchino, B. N., Sgoutas-Emch, S. A., Sheridan, J. F., Berntson, G. G., & Glaser, R. (1995). Heterogeneity in neuroendocrine and immune responses to brief psychological stressors as a function of autonomic cardiac activation. *Psychosomatic Medicine, 57,* 154–164.

Cacioppo, J. T., Petty, R. E., & Crites, S. L. (1993). Attitude change. In V. S. Ramachandran (Ed.), *Encyclopedia of human behavior.* San Diego, CA: Academic Press.

Cacioppo, J. T., Poehlmann, K. M., Kiecolt-Glaser, J. K., Malarkey, W. B., Burleson, M. H., Berntson, G. G., & Glaser, R. (1998). Cellular immune responses to acute stress in female caregivers of dementia patients and matched controls. *Health Psychology, 17,* 182–189.

Cadoret, R. J., Yates, W. R., Troughton, E., Woodworth, G., & Stewart, M. A. (1995). Adoption study demonstrating two genetic pathways to drug abuse. *Archives of General Psychiatry, 52,* 42–52.

Cahill, L., & McGaugh, J. L. (1998). Mechanisms of emotional arousal and lasting declarative memory. *Trends in Neuroscience, 21,* 294–299.

Cahill, S. P., Carrigan, M. H., & Frueh, B. C. (1999). Does EMDR work? And if so, why?: A critical review of controlled outcome and dismantling research. *Journal of Anxiety Disorders, 13,* 5–33.

Cairns, R. B., Gariepy, J., & Hood, K. E. (1990). Development, microevolution, and social behavior. *Psychological Review, 97,* 49–65.

Calvert, G. A., Bullmore, E. T., Brammer, M. J., Campbell, R., Williams, S. C., McGuire, P. K., Woodruff, P. W., Iversen, S. D., & David, A. S. (1997). Activation of auditory cortex during silent lipreading. *Science, 276*(5312), 593–596.

Campbell, S. S., & Murphy, P. J. (1998). Extraocular circadian phototransduction in humans. *Science, 279,* 396–399.

Campfield, L. A., Smith, F. J., & Burn, P. (1998). Strategies and potential molecular targets for obesity treatment. *Science, 280*(5368), 1383–1387.

Campfield, L. A., Smith, F. J., Guisez, Y., Devos, R., & Burn, P. (1995). Recombinant mouse OB protein: Evidence for a peripheral signal linking adiposity and central neural networks. *Science, 269,* 546–549.

Campione, J. C., Brown, A. L., & Ferrara, R. A. (1982). Mental retardation and intelligence. In R. J. Sternberg (Ed.), *Handbook of human intelligence.* Cambridge: Cambridge University Press.

Campos, J. J. (1980). Human emotions: Their new importance and their role in social referencing. *Research and Clinical Center for Child Development, 1980–81 Annual Report,* 1–7.

Cann, A., & Ross, D. A. (1989). Olfactory stimuli as context cues in human memory. *American Journal of Psychology, 102,* 91–102.

Cannon, T. D. (1998). Neurodevelopmental influences in the genesis and epigenesis of schizophrenia: An overview. *Applied and Preventive Psychology, 7,* 47–62.

Cannon, T. D., Zorrilla, L. E., Shtasel, D., Gur, R. E., Gur, R. C., Marco, E. J., Moberg, P., & Price, A. (1994). Neuropsychological functioning in siblings discordant for schizophrenia and healthy volunteers. *Archives of General Psychiatry, 51,* 651–661.

Cannon, W. B. (1927/1987). The James-Lange theory of emotions: A critical examination and an alternative theory. Special issue: 100 years of the American Journal of Psychology. *American Journal of Psychology, 100*(3–4), 567–586.

Cannon, W. B., & Washburn, A. L. (1912). An explanation of hunger. *American Journal of Physiology, 29,* 444–454.

Cao, Y., Vikingstad, E. M., Huttenlocher, P. R., Towle, V. L., & Levin, D. N. (1994). Functional magnetic resonance studies of the reorganization of the human head sensorimotor area after unilateral brain injury in the perinatal period. *Proceedings of the National Academy of Sciences of the United States of America, 91,* 9612–9616.

Capron, C., & Duyme, M. (1989). Assessment of effects of socio-economic status on IQ in a full cross-fostering study. *Nature, 340,* 552–553.

Caramazza, A., & Hillis, A. E. (1991). Lexical organization of nouns and verbs in the brain. *Nature, 349,* 788–790.

Carey, G., & DiLalla, D. L. (1994). Personality and psychopathology: Genetic perspectives. *Journal of Abnormal Psychology, 103,* 32–43.

Carli, L. L., Ganley, R., & Pierce-Otay, A. (1991). Similarity and satisfaction in romantic relationships. *Personality and Social Psychology Bulletin, 17,* 419–426.

Carlson, M., Marcus-Newhall, A., & Miller, N. (1990). Effects of situational aggression cues: A quantitative review. *Journal of Personality and Social Psychology, 58,* 622–633.

Carlson, N. R. (1998). *Physiology of behavior.* Boston: Allyn & Bacon.

Carmichael, L. L., Hogan, H. P., & Walter, A. A. (1932). An experimental study of the effect of language on the reproduction of visually perceived form. *Journal of Experimental Psychology, 15,* 73–86.

Carnegie Task Force on Learning in the Primary Grades. (1996). *Years of promise: A comprehensive learning strategy for America's children.* New York: Carnegie Corporation.

Carraher, T. N., Carraher, D., & Schliemann, A. D. (1985). Mathematics in the streets and in the schools. *British Journal of Developmental Psychology, 3,* 21–29.

Carrigan, M. H., & Levis, D. J. (1999). The contributions of eye movements to the efficacy of brief exposure treatment for reducing fear of public speaking. *Journal of Anxiety Disorders, 13,* 101–118.

Carstensen, L. (1997, August). *Psychology and the aging revolution: Changes in social needs and social goals across the lifespan.* Paper presented at the annual convention of the American Psychological Association.

Carter, M. M., & Barlow, D. H. (1995). Learned alarms: The origins of panic. In W. T. O'Donohue & L. Krasner (Eds.), *Theories of behavior therapy: Exploring behavior change* (pp. 209–228). Washington, DC: American Psychological Association.

Carter, M. M., Hollon, S. D., Carson, R., & Shelton, R. C. (1995). Effects of a safe person on induced distress following a biological challenge in panic disorder with agoraphobia. *Journal of Abnormal Psychology, 104,* 156–163.

Cartwright, R. D. (1978). *A primer on sleep and dreaming.* Reading, MA: Addison-Wesley.

Carver, C. S., & Scheier, M. F. (1995). *Perspectives on personality.* (3rd ed.) Boston: Allyn & Bacon.

Carver, C. S., & Scheier, M. F. (2000). *Perspectives on personality* (4th ed.). Boston: Allyn & Bacon.

Casagrande, M., Violani, C., Lucidi, F., Buttinelli, E., & Bertini, M. (1996). Variations in sleep mentation as a function of time of night. *International Journal of Neuroscience, 85,* 19–30.

Caspi, A. (1998). Personality development across the life course. In W. Damon & N. Eisenberg (Eds.), *Handbook of child psychology: Vol. 3. Social, emotional, and personality development* (5th ed., pp. 311–388). New York: Wiley.

Caspi, A., & Silva, P. A. (1995). Temperamental qualities at age 3 predict personality traits in young adulthood: Longitudinal evidence from a birth cohort. *Child Development, 66,* 468–498.

Caspi, A., Begg, D., & Dickson, N., Harrington, H., Langley, J., Moffitt, T. E., & Silva, P. A. (1997). Personality differences predict health-risk behaviors in young adulthood: Evidence from a longitudinal study. *Journal of Personality and Social Psychology, 73,* 1052–1063.

Caspi, A., Bem, D. J., & Elder, G. H., Jr. (1989). Continuities and consequences of interactional styles across the life course. *Journal of Personality, 57,* 375–406.

Caspi, A., Henry, B., McGee, R. O., Moffitt, T. E., & Silva, P. A. (1995). Temperamental origins of child and adolescent behavior problems: From age 3 to Age 15. *Child Development, 66,* 55–68.

Cassel, E., & Bernstein, D. A. (2001). *Criminal behavior.* Boston: Allyn & Bacon.

Ceci, S. J., Huffman, M. L. C., Smith, E., & Loftus, E. F. (1994). Repeatedly thinking about a non-event: Source misattributions among preschoolers. *Consciousness and Cognition, 3,* 388–407.

Centers for Disease Control. (1998). *Violence: Suicide in the United States.* Atlanta: Centers for Disease Control.

Centers for Disease Control and Prevention. (1998). *Trends in the HIV & AIDS epidemic.* Washington, DC: U.S. Government Printing Office.

Centers for Disease Control and Prevention. (1999a). *Chronic diseases and their risk factors.* Washington, DC: U.S. Government Printing Office.

Centers for Disease Control and Prevention. (1999b). *HIV/AIDS surveillance report.* Atlanta, Georgia: National Center for HIV, STD, and TB Prevention.

Centers for Disease Control and Prevention. (1999c). Increases in unsafe sex and rectal gonorrhea among men who have sex with men–San Francisco, California, 1994–1997. *Journal of the American Medical Association, 281,* 696–697.

Centerwall, L. (1990). Controlled TV viewing and suicide in countries: Young adult suicide and exposure to television. *Social Psychiatry and Social Epidemiology, 25,* 149–153.

Cernoch, J. M., & Porter, R. H. (1985). Recognition of maternal axillary odors by infants. *Child Development, 56,* 1593–1598.

Chamberlin, J. (2000). Easing children's psychological distress in the emergency room. *Monitor on Psychology, 31,* 40–42.

Chambless, D. L. (1990). Spacing of exposure sessions in the treatment of agoraphobia and simple phobia. *Behavior Therapy, 21,* 217–229.

Chambless, D. L., & Hollon, S. D. (1998). Defining empirically supported therapies. *Journal of Consulting and Clinical Psychology, 66,* 7–18.

Champion, V., & Huster, G. (1995). Effect of interventions on stage of mammography adoption. *Journal of Behavioral Medicine, 18,* 159–188.

Chao, R. K. (1994). Beyond parental control and authoritarian parenting style: Understanding Chinese parenting through the cultural notion of training. *Child Development, 65,* 1111–1119.

Charlton, T., Gunter, B., & Coles, D. (1998). Broadcast television as a cause of aggression? Recent findings from a naturalistic study. *Emotional and Behavioural Difficulties, 3,* 5–13.

Chase, T. N. (1998). The significance of continuous dopaminergic stimulation in the treatment of Parkinson's disease. *Drugs, 55* (Suppl. 1), 1–9.

Chastain, G., & Thurber, S. (1989). The SQ3R study technique enhances comprehension of an introductory psychology textbook. *Reading Improvement, 26,* 94–96.

Chemers, M. M. (1987). Leadership processes: Intrapersonal, interpersonal, and societal influences. In C. Hendrick (Ed.), *Group processes.* Newbury Park, CA: Sage.

Chen, C., Shin-Ying, L., & Stevenson, H. W. (1995). Response style and cross-cultural comparisons of rating scales among East Asian and North American students. *Psychological Science, 6,* 170–175.

Chen, M., & Bargh, J. A. (1997). Nonconscious behavioral confirmation processes: The self-fulfilling consequences of automatic stereotype activation. *Journal of Experimental Social Psychology, 33,* 541–560.

Chen, M. S., Huber, A. B., Van Der Haar, M. E., Frank, M., Schnell, L., Spillmann, A. A., Christ, F., & Schwab, M. E. (2000). Nogo-A is a myelin-associated neurite outgrowth inhibitor and an antigen for monoclonal antibody IN-1. *Nature, 403,* 434–439.

Cheng, Y., Kawachi, I., Coakley, E. H., Schwartz, J., & Colditz, G. (2000). Association between psychosocial work characteristics and health functioning in American women: Prospective study. *British Medical Journal, 320,* 1432–1436.

Chisholm, K. (1997, June). Trauma at an early age inhibits ability to bond. *APA Monitor,* p. 11.

Choi, I., Nisbett, R. E., & Norenzayan, A. (1999). Causal attribution across cultures: Variation and universality. *Psychological Bulletin, 125,* 47–63.

Chomsky, N. (1965). *Aspects of the theory of syntax.* Cambridge, MA: MIT Press.

Choo, K. L., & Guilleminault, C. (1998). Narcolepsy and idiopathic hypersomnolence. *Clinical Chest Medicine, 19*(1), 169–181.

Chorney, M. L., Chorney, K., Sense, N., Owen, M. J., Daniels, J., McGuffin, P., Thompson, L. A., Detterman, D. K., Benbow, C. P., Lubinski, D., Eley, T. C., & Plomin, R. (1998). A quantitative trait locus (QTL) associated with cognitive ability in children. *Psychological Science, 9,* 159–166.

Christensen, K. A., Stephens, M. A. P., & Townsend, A. L. (1998). Mastery in women's multiple roles and well-being: Adult daughters providing care to impaired parents. *Health Psychology, 17,* 163–171.

Chu, J. (1994). Active learning in epidemiology and biostatistics. *Teaching and Learning in Medicine, 6,* 191–193.

Chugani, H. T., & Phelps, M. E. (1986). Maturational changes in cerebral function in infants determined by 18FDG positron emission tomography. *Science, 231,* 840–843.

Churchland, P. M. (1989). *A neurocomputational perspective: The nature of mind and the structure of science.* Cambridge, MA: MIT Press.

Cialdini, R. B. (1993). *Influence: Science and practice* (3rd ed.). New York: HarperCollins.

Cialdini, R. B. (1995). Principles and techniques of social influence. In A. Tesser (Ed.), *Advanced social psychology* (pp. 257–282). New York: McGraw-Hill.

Cialdini, R. B., & Trost, M. (1998). Social influence: Social norms, conformity, and compliance. In D. Gilbert, S. T. Fiske, & G. Lindzey (Eds.), *Handbook of social psychology* (Vol. 2, 4th ed., pp. 151–192). Boston: McGraw-Hill.

Cialdini, R. B., Baumann, D. J., & Kenrick, D. T. (1981). Insights from sadness: A three-step model of the development of altruism as hedonism. *Developmental Review, 1,* 207–223.

Cialdini, R. B., Brown, S. L., Lewis, C., & Neuberg, S. (1997). Reinterpreting the empathy-altruism hypothesis: When one into one equals oneness. *Journal of Personality and Social Psychology, 73,* 481–494.

Clancy, S. A., Schacter, D. L., McNally, R. J., & Pittman, R. K. (2000). False recognition in women reporting recovered memories of sexual abuse. *Psychological Science, 11,* 26–31.

Clapham, K., & Abramson, E. E. (1985). Aversive conditioning of junk food consumption: A multiple baseline study. *Addictive Behaviors, 10,* 437–440.

Clark, D. C., & Fawcett, J. (1992). Review of empirical risk factors for evaluation of the suicidal patient. In B. Bongar (Ed.), *Suicide: Guidelines for assessment, management, and treatment* (pp. 16–48). New York: Oxford University Press.

Clark, D. M., & Fairburn, C. G. (Eds.). (1997). *Science and practice of cognitive behavioural therapy.* New York: Oxford University Press.

Clark, D. M., Salkovskis, P. M., Ost, L.-G., Breitholtz, E., Koehler, K. A., Westling, B. E., Jeavons, A., & Gelder, M. (1997). Misinterpretation of body sensations in panic disorder. *Journal of Consulting and Clinical Psychology, 65,* 203–213.

Clark, E. V. (1983). Meanings and concepts. In P. H. Mussen, J. H. Flavell, & E. M. Markman (Eds.), *Handbook of child psychology: Vol. 3. Cognitive development* (4th ed., pp. 787–840). New York: Wiley.

Clark, L. A., Watson, D., & Reynolds, S. (1995). Diagnosis and classification of psychopathology: Challenges to the current system and future directions. *Annual Review of Psychology, 46,* 121–153.

Clark, M. (1994). Close relationships. In R. S. Wyer & T. K. Srull (Eds.), *Handbook of social cognition* (2nd ed.). Hillsdale, NJ: Erlbaum.

Clark, M. S., & Pataki, S. P. (1995). Interpersonal processes influencing attraction and relationships. In A. Tesser (Ed.), *Advanced social psychology* (pp. 283–332). New York: McGraw-Hill.

Clarke-Stewart, K. A. (1988). Parents' effects on children's development: A decade of progress? *Journal of Applied Developmental Psychology, 9,* 41–84.

Clarke-Stewart, K. A. (1989). Infant day care: Maligned or malignant? *American Psychologist, 44,* 266–273.

Clarke-Stewart, K. A., & Fein, G. G. (1983). Early childhood programs. In P. H. Mussen (Ed.), *Handbook of child psychology: Vol. 2. Infancy and developmental psychobiology.* New York: Wiley.

Clarkin, J. F., & Carpenter, D. (1995). Family therapy in historical perspective. In B. Bongar & L. E. Beutler (Eds.), *Comprehensive textbook of psychotherapy: Theory and practice* (pp. 205–227). New York: Oxford University Press.

Clay, R. A. (1996, December). Some elders thrive on working into late life. *APA Monitor*, p. 35.

Clay, R. A. (2000). APA task force considers changes to proposed ethics code. *Monitor on Psychology, 31*, 86–87.

Clay, R. A. (2000a). Psychotherapy *is* cost-effective. *Monitor on Psychology,* January, pp. 40–41.

Clay, R. A. (2000b). Often, the bells and whistles backfire. *Monitor on Psychology, 31*, 64–65.

Clendenen, V. I., Herman, C. P., & Polivy, J. (1995). Social facilitation of eating among friends and strangers. *Appetite, 23*, 1–13.

Clifton, R. K. (1992). The development of spatial hearing in human infants. In L. A. Werner & E. W. Rubel (Eds.), *Developmental psychoacoustics* (pp. 135–157). Washington, DC: American Psychological Association.

Clifton, R. K., Rochat, P., Litovsky, R., & Perris, E. (1991). Object representation guides infants' reaching in the dark. *Journal of Experimental Psychology: Human Perception and Performance, 17*, 323–329.

Cnattingius, S., Signorello, L. B., Anneren, G., Clausson, B., Ekbom, A., Ljunger, E., Blot, W. J., McLaughlin, J. K., Petersson, G., Rane, A., & Granath, F. (2000). Caffeine intake and the risk of first-trimester spontaneous abortion. *New England Journal of Medicine, 343*, 1839–1845.

CNN/Time. (1997). Poll: U.S. hiding knowledge of aliens. *CNN/Time* [On-line]. Available: www-cgi.cnn.com/US/9706/15/ufo.poll/index.html

Coccaro, E. F. (1989). Central serotonin and impulsive aggression. *British Journal of Psychiatry, 155*, 52–62.

Cofer, L. F., Grice, J., Palmer, D., Sethre-Hofstad, L., & Zimmermann, K. (1992, June 20–22). *Evidence for developmental continuity of individual differences in morningness-eveningness.* Paper presented at the annual meeting of the American Psychological Society, San Diego, CA.

Cohen, C. E. (1981). Person categories and social perception: Testing some boundaries of the processing effects of prior knowledge. *Journal of Personality and Social Psychology, 40*, 441–452.

Cohen, D., Nisbett, R. E., Bowdle, B. F., Schwarz, N. (1996). Insult, aggression, and the southern culture of honor: An "experimental ethnography." *Journal of Personality and Social Psychology, 70*, 945–960.

Cohen, J., & Servan-Schreiber, D. (1992). Context, cortex, and dopamine: A connectionist approach to behavior and biology in schizophrenia. *Psychological Review, 99*, 45–77.

Cohen, S., & Herbert, T. B. (1996). Health psychology: Psychological factors and physical disease from the perspective of human psychoneuroimmunology. In J. Spence, D. Foss, & J. Darley (Eds.), *Annual review of psychology* (Vol. 42). El Camino, CA: Annual Review, Inc.

Cohn, J. F., & Tronick, E. Z. (1983). Three-month-old infants' reaction to simulated maternal depression. *Child Development, 54*, 185–193.

Cole, K. N., Mills, P. E., Dale, P. S., & Jenkins, J. R. (1991). Effects of preschool integration for children with disabilities. *Exceptional Children, 58*, 36–45.

Coleman, D. (1992). Why do I feel so tired? Too little, too late. *American Health, 11*(4), 43–46.

Coley, R. L., & Chase-Lansdale, P. L. (1998). Adolescent pregnancy and parenthood: Recent evidence and future directions. *American Psychologist, 53*, 152–166.

Collins, G. (1997, May 30). Trial near in new legal tack in tobacco war. *New York Times*, p. A10.

Collins, W. A., Maccoby, E. E., Steinberg, L., Hetherington, E. M., & Bornstein, M. H. (2000). Contemporary research on parenting: The case for nature *and* nurture. *American Psychologist, 55*, 218–232.

Colombo, M., D'Amato, M. R., Rodman, H. R., & Gross, C. G. (1990). Auditory association cortex lesions impair auditory short-term memory in monkeys. *Science, 247*, 336–338.

Colwill, R. M. (1994). Associative representations of instrumental contingencies. *Psychology of Learning and Motivation, 31*, 1–72.

Compas, B. E., Haaga, D. A. F., Keefe, F. J., Leitenberg, H., & Williams, D. A. (1998). Sampling of empirically supported psychological treatments from health psychology: Smoking, chronic pain, cancer, and bulimia nervosa. *Journal of Consulting and Clinical Psychology, 66*, 89–112.

Conel, J. L. (1939/1967). *The postnatal development of the human cerebral cortex* (Vols. 1, 8). Cambridge, MA: Harvard University Press.

Connor, L. T., Balota, D. A., & Neely, J. H. (1992). On the relation between feeling of knowing and lexical decision: Persistent subthreshold activation of topic familiarity? *Journal of Experimental Psychology: Learning, Memory, and Cognition, 18*, 544–554.

Conrad, R. (1964). Acoustic confusions in immediate memory. *British Journal of Psychology, 55*, 75–84.

Consumer Reports (1995, November). *Mental health: Does therapy help?* pp. 734–739.

Contrada, R. J., Ashmore, R. D., Gary, M. L., Coups, E., Egeth, J. D., Sewell, A., Ewell, K., Goyal, T. M.., & Chasse, V. (2000). Ethnicity-related sources of stress and their effects on well-being. *Current Directions in Psychological Science, 9*, 136–139.

Cook, T., & Mineka, S. (1987). Second-order conditioning and overshadowing in the observational conditioning of fear in monkeys. *Behaviour Research and Therapy, 25*, 349–364.

Cookson, J., & Duffett, R. (1998) Fluoxetine: therapeutic and undesirable effects. *Hospital Medicine, 59*, 622–626

Cooper, L. A., Schacter, D. L., Ballesteros, S., & Moore, C. (1992). Priming and recognition of transformed three-dimensional objects: Effects of size and reflection. *Journal of Experimental Psychology: Learning, Memory, and Cognition, 18*, 43–57.

Cooper, M. L., Russell, M., Skinner, J. B., Frone, M. R., & Mudar, P. (1992). Stress and alcohol use: The moderating effects of gender, coping, and alcohol expectancies. *Journal of Abnormal Psychology, 101*, 139–152.

Cooper, R. M., & Zubek, J. P. (1958). Effects of enriched and restricted early environments on the learning ability of bright and dull rats. *Canadian Journal of Psychology, 12*, 159–164.

Coovert, M. D., & Reeder, G. D. (1990). Negativity effects in impression formation: The role of unit formation and schematic expectations. *Journal of Experimental Social Psychology, 26*, 49–62.

Copeland, J., & Snyder, M. (1995). When counselors confirm: A functional analysis. *Personality and Social Psychology Bulletin, 21*, 1210–1220.

Corbetta, M., Miezin, F. M., Dobmeyer, S., Shulman, G. L., & Petersen, S. E. (1991). Selective and divided attention during visual discriminations of shape, color, and speed: Functional anatomy by positron emission tomography. *Journal of Neuroscience, 11*, 2383–2402.

Coren, S. (1999). Psychology applied to animal training. In A. Stec & D. Bernstein (Eds.), *Psychology: Fields of application*. Boston: Houghton Mifflin.

Cork, R. C., Kihlstrom, J. F., & Hameroff, S. R. (1992). Explicit and implicit memory dissociated by anesthetic technique. *Society for Neuroscience Abstracts, 22*, 523.

Cornblatt, B., & Erlenmeyer-Kimling, L. E. (1985). Global attentional deviance in children at risk for schizophrenia: Specificity and predictive validity. *Journal of Abnormal Psychology, 94*, 470–486.

Cornelius, R. R. (1996). *The science of emotion*. Upper Saddle River, NJ: Prentice-Hall.

Corsini, R. J., & Wedding, D. (1995). *Current psychotherapies* (5th ed.). Itasca, IL: Peacock.

Coryell, W., Scheftner, W., Keller, M., Endicott, J., Maser, J., & Klerman, G. (1993). The enduring consequences of mania and depression. *American Journal of Psychiatry, 150*, 720–727.

Costa, P. T., Jr., & McCrae, R. (1992). *Revised NEO Personality Inventory: NEO PI and NEO Five-Factor Inventory* (NEO FFI: Professional Manual). Odessa, FL: Psychological Assessment Resources, Inc.

Costa, P. T., Jr., & McCrae, R. R. (1995). Primary traits of Eysenck's P-E-N system: Three- and five-factor solutions. *Journal of Personality and Social Psychology, 69*, 308–317.

Costa, P. T., Jr., & McCrae, R. R. (1997). In R. Hogan, J. A. Johnson, & S. R. Briggs (Eds.), Longitudinal stability of adult personality. *Handbook of personality psychology* (pp. 269–290). San Diego: Academic Press.

Costello, E., Costello, A., Edelbrock, C., Burns, B., Dulcan, M., Brent, D., & Janiszewski, S. (1988). Psychiatric disorders in pediatric primary care. *Archives of General Psychiatry, 45*, 1107–1116.

Cotanche, D. A. (1997). Hair cell regeneration in the avian cochlea. *Ann Otol Rhinol Laryngol Supplement, 168*, 9–15.

Cowan, N. (1988). Evolving concepts of memory storage, selective attention, and their mutual constraints within the human information-processing system. *Psychological Bulletin, 104*, 163–191.

Cowan, W. M. (1979). The development of the brain. *Scientific American, 241*, 112–133.

Cowey, A. (1994). Cortical visual areas and the neurobiology of higher visual processes. In M. J. Farah & G. Ratcliff (Eds.), *The neurophysiology of high-level vision: Collected tutorial essays* (pp. 3–31). Hillsdale, NJ: Erlbaum.

Craig, A. D., & Bushnell, M. C. (1994). The thermal grill illusion: Unmasking the burn of cold pain. *Science, 265,* 252–254.

Craig, A. D., Bushnell, M. C., Zhang, E. B. T., & Blomqvist, A. (1994). A thalamic nucleus specific for pain and temperature sensation. *Nature, 372,* 770–773.

Craik, F. I. M. (1994). Memory changes in normal aging. *Current Directions in Psychological Science, 3,* 155–158.

Craik, F. I. M., & Rabinowitz, J. C. (1984). Age differences in the acquisition and use of verbal information. In H. Bouma & D. G. Bouwhuis (Eds.), *Attention and performance* (Vol. 10, pp. 471–499). Hillsdale, NJ: Erlbaum.

Craik, F. I. M., Moroz, T. M., Moscovitch, M., Stuss, D. T., Winocur, G., Tulving, E., & Kapur, S. (1999). In search of the self: A positron emission topography study. *Psychological Science, 10,* 26–34.

Cramer, E. P. (1999). Hate crime laws and sexual orientation. *Journal of Sociology & Social Welfare, 26,* 5–24.

Crandall, C. S., Preisler, J. J., & Aussprung, J. (1992). Measuring life event stress in the lives of college students: The Undergraduate Stress Questionnaire (USQ). *Journal of Behavioral Medicine, 15,* 627–662.

Crawford, C. B., & Krebs, D. L. (Eds.). (1998). *Handbook of evolutionary psychology: Ideas, issues, and applications.* Mahwah, NJ: Erlbaum.

Crawford, H. J., Brown, A. M., & Moon, C. E. (1993). Sustained attentional and disattentional abilities: Differences between low and highly hypnotizable persons. *Journal of Abnormal Psychology, 102*(4), 534–543.

Crawford, M., & Marecek, J. (1989). Psychology reconstructs the female. *Psychology of Women Quarterly, 13,* 147–165.

Crews, F. (1996). The verdict on Freud. *Psychological Science, 7,* 63–67.

Crick, F., & Koch, C. (1998). Consciousness and neuroscience. *Cerebral Cortex, 8,* 97–107.

Crick, N. R., Casas, J. F., & Mosher, M. (1997). Relational and overt aggression in preschool. *Developmental Psychology, 33,* 579–588.

Crick, N. R., Werner, N. E., Casas, J. F., O'Brien, K. M., Nelson, D. A., Grotpeter, J. K., & Markon, K. (1999). Childhood aggression and gender: A new look at an old problem. In D. Bernstein (Ed.), *Nebraska Symposium on Motivation* (Vol. 44, pp. 75–141). Lincoln, Nebraska: University of Nebraska Press.

Critchley, E. M. (1991). Speech and the right hemisphere. *Behavioural Neurology, 4*(3), 143–151.

Croft, H., Settle, E., Jr, Houser, T., Batey, S. R., Donahue, R. M., & Ascher, J. A. (1999). A placebo-controlled comparison of the antidepressant efficacy and effects on sexual functioning of sustained-release bupropion and sertraline. *Clinical Therapeutics, 21,* 643–658.

Cronbach, L. J. (1990). *Essentials of psychological testing* (5th ed.). New York: Harper & Row.

Crosby, A. E., Cheltenham, M. P., & Sacks, J. J. (1999). Incidence of suicidal ideation and behavior in the United States, 1994. *Suicide & Life Threatening Behavior, 29,* 131–140.

Cross, S. E., & Madson, L. (1997). Models of the self: Self-construals and gender. *Psychological Bulletin, 122,* 5–37.

Cross, S. E., & Markus, H. R. (1999). The cultural constitution of personality. In L. Pervin & O. John (Eds.), *Handbook of personality research* (2nd ed., pp. 378–398). New York: Guilford.

Cross-National Collaborative Group. (1992). The changing rate of major depression: Cross-national comparisons. *Journal of the American Medical Association, 268,* 3098–3105.

Cruz, A., & Green, B. (2000). Thermal stimulation of taste. *Nature, 403,* 889–892.

Crystal, D. S., Chen, C., Fuligni, A. J., Stevenson, H. W., Hsu, C.-C., Ko, H.-J., Kitamura, S., & Kimura, S. (1994). Psychological maladjustment and academic achievement: A cross-cultural study of Japanese, Chinese, and American high school students. *Child Development, 65,* 738–753.

Csikszentmihalyi, M. (1999). If we are so rich, why aren't we happy? *American Psychologist, 54,* 821–827.

Culbertson, F. M. (1997). Depression and gender. An international review. *American Psychologist, 52,* 25–31.

Culp, R. E., Cook, A. S., & Housley, P. C. (1983). A comparison of observed and reported adult-infant interactions: Effects of perceived sex. *Sex Roles, 9,* 475–479.

Culver, R., Rotton, J., & Kelly, I. W. (1988). Moon mechanisms and myths: A critical appraisal of explanations of purported lunar effects on human behavior. *Psychological Reports, 62,* 683–710.

Cumsille, P. E., Sayer, A. G., & Graham, J. W. (2000). Perceived exposure to peer and adult drinking as predictors of growth in positive alcohol expectancies during adolescence. *Journal of Consulting and Clinical Psychology, 68,* 531–536.

Curim, I. S., & Sarin, R. K. (1992). Robustness of expected utility model in predicting individual choices. *Organizational Behavior and Human Decision Processes, 52,* 544–568.

Cusack, K., & Spates, C. R. (1999). The cognitive dismantling of eye movement desensitization and reprocessing (EMDR) treatment of posttraumatic stress disorder (PTSD). *Journal of Anxiety Disorders, 13,* 87–99.

Czeisler, C. A., Duffy, J. F., Shanahan, T. L., Brown, E. N., Mitchell, J. F., Rimmer, D. W., Ronda, J. M., Silva, E. J., Allan, J. S., Emens, J. S., Dijk, D-J., & Kronauer, R. E. (1999). Stability, precision, and near 24-hour period of the human circadian pacemaker. *Science, 284,* 2177–2181.

d'Ydewalle, G., & Rosselle, H. (1978). Text expectations in text learning. In M. M. Gruneberg, P. E. Morris, & R. N. Sykes (Eds.), *Practical aspects of memory.* Orlando, FL: Academic Press.

Dabbs, J. M., & Morris, R. (1990). Testosterone, social class, and antisocial behavior in a sample of 4462 men. *Psychological Science, 1,* 209–211.

Dabbs, J. M., Carr, T. S., Frady, R. L., & Riad, J. K. (1995). Testosterone, crime, and misbehavior among 692 male prison inmates. *Personality and Individual Differences, 18,* 627–633.

Dadds, M. R., Spence, S. H., Holland, D. E., Barrett, P. M., & Laurens, K. R. (1997). Prevention and early intervention for anxiety disorders: A controlled trial. *Journal of Consulting and Clinical Psychology, 65,* 627–635.

Dahlstrom, W. G. (1992). The growth in acceptance of the MMPI. *Professional Psychology: Research and Practice, 23,* 345–348.

Dale, P. S. (1976). *Language and the development of structure and function.* New York: Holt, Rinehart & Winston.

Dalton, S. (1997). *Overweight and Weight Management: the Health Professional's Guide to Understanding and Treatment.* Gaithersburg, MD: Aspen Publishers.

Daly, G., Hawi, Z., Fitzgerald, M., & Gill, M. (1999). Mapping susceptibility loci in attention deficit hyperactivity disorder: Preferential transmission of parental alleles at DAT1, DBH and DRD5 to affected children. *Molecular Biology, 4,* 192–196.

Daly, M., & Wilson, M. (1988). *Homicide.* New York: Aldine de Gruyter.

Damasio, A. R., Grabowski, T. J., Bechara, A., Damasio, H., Ponto, L. L. B., Parvizi, J., & Hichwa, R. D. (2000). Subcortical and cortical brain activity during the feeling of self-generated emotions. *Nature Neuroscience, 3,* 1049–1056.

Damos, D. (1992). *Multiple task performance.* London: Taylor & Francis.

Dark, V. J., & Benbow, C. P. (1993). Cognitive differences among the gifted: A review and new data. In D. K. Detterman (Ed.), *Current topics in human intelligence* (Vol. 3). Norwood, NJ: Ablex.

Darwin, C. E. (1872/1965). *The expression of emotions in man and animals.* Chicago: University of Chicago Press.

Dasgupta, A. M., Juza, D. M., White, G. M., & Maloney, J. F. (1995). Memory and hypnosis: A comparative analysis of guided memory, cognitive interviews, and hypnotic hypermnesia. *Imagination, Cognition, and Personality, 14*(2), 117–130.

Davanloo, H. (1999). Intensive short-term dynamic psychotherapy–central dynamic sequence: Phase of challenge. *International Journal of Short-Term Dynamic Psychotherapy, 13,* 237–262.

Davidson, J. K., & Moore, N. B. (1994). Guilt and lack of orgasm during sexual intercourse: Myth versus reality in college women. *Journal of Sex Education and Therapy, 20*(3), 153–174.

Davidson, J. M., Camargo, C. A., & Smith, E. R. (1979). Effects of androgen on sexual behavior in hypogonadal men. *Journal of Clinical Endocrinological Metabolism, 48,* 955–958.

Davidson, K., Hall, P., & MacGregor, M. (1996). Gender differences in the relation between interview-derived hostility scores and resting blood pressure. *Journal of Behavioral Medicine, 19,* 185–201.

Davidson, K., & Prkachin, K. (1997). Optimism and unrealistic optimism have an interacting impact on health-promoting behavior and knowledge changes. *Personality and Social Psychology Bulletin, 23,* 617–625.

Davies, C. (1999). Junior doctor is cleared in baby overdose death. *London Daily Telegraph,* April 21, p. 2.

Davies, R. J., & Stradling, J. R. (2000). The efficacy of nasal continuous positive airway pressure in the treatment of obstructive sleep apnea syndrome is proven. *American Journal of Respiratory Critical Care Medicine, 161,* 1775–1776.

Davis, J. D., Gallagher, R. J., Ladove, R. F., & Turansky, A. J. (1969). Inhibition of food intake by a humoral factor. *Journal of Comparative and Physiological Psychology, 67,* 407–414.

Davis, K. D., Taylor, S. J., Crawley, A. P., Wood, M. L., & Mikulis, D. J. (1997). Functional MRI of pain- and attention-related activations in the human cingulate cortex. *Journal of Neurophysiology, 77,* 3370–3380.

Davis, M. H., Luce, C., & Kraus, S. J. (1994). The heritability of characteristics associated with dispositional empathy. *Journal of Personality, 60,* 369–391.

Davis, R. A., & Moore, C. C. (1935). Methods of measuring retention. *Journal of General Psychology, 12,* 144–155.

Davison, G. C. (1998). Being bolder with the Boulder Model: The challenge of education and training in empirically supported treatments. *Journal of Consulting and Clinical Psychology, 66,* 163–167.

Davison, G. C., & Neale, J. M. (1990). *Abnormal psychology* (5th ed.). New York: Wiley.

Dawes, R. (1998). Behavioral judgment and decision making. In D. Gilbert, S. T. Fiske, & G. Lindzey (Eds.), *Handbook of social psychology* (Vol. 1, 4th ed., pp. 497–549). Boston: McGraw-Hill.

Dawes, R. M. (1994). *House of cards: Psychology and psychotherapy built on myth.* New York: Free Press.

Dawson-Basoa, M., & Gintzler, A. R. (1997). Involvement of spinal cord delta opiate receptors in the antinociception of gestation and its hormonal simulation. *Brain Research, 757,* 37–42.

De Benedittis, G., Lornenzetti, A., & Pieri, A. (1990). The role of stressful life events in the onset of chronic primary headache. *Pain, 40,* 65–75.

de Castro, J. M., & Goldstein, S. J. (1995). Eating attitudes and behaviors pre- and postpubertal females: Clues to the etiology of eating disorders. *Physiology and Behavior, 58*(1), 15–23.

De Houwer, A. (1995). Bilingual language acquisition. In P. Fletcher & B. MacWhinney (Eds.), *The handbook of child language* (pp. 219–250). Cambridge, MA: Blackwell Publishers.

de Rios, M. D. (1989). Power and hallucinogenic states of consciousness among the Moche: An ancient Peruvian society. In C. A. Ward (Ed.), *Altered states of consciousness and mental health: A cross-cultural perspective* (pp. 285–299). Newbury Park, CA: Sage.

de Silva, P. (1994). Psychological treatment of sexual problems. *International Review of Psychiatry, 6*(2–3), 163–173.

DeAngelis, T. (1995, February). Firefighters' PTSD at dangerous levels. *APA Monitor,* pp. 36–37.

DeBeurs, E., van Balkom, A. J. L. M., Lange, A., Koele, P., & van Dyck, R. (1995). Treatment of panic disorder with agoraphobia: Comparison of fluvoxamine, placebo, and psychological panic management combined with exposure and of exposure in vivo alone, *American Journal of Psychiatry, 152*(5), 683–691.

DeJongh, A., Ten Broeke, E., & Renssen, M. R. (1999). Treatment of specific phobias with eye movement desensitization and reprocessing (EMDR): Protocol, empirical status, and conceptual issues. *Journal of Anxiety Disorders, 13,* 69–85.

DeLoache, J. S., Miller, K. F., & Rosengren, K. S. (1997). The credible shrinking room: Very young children's performance with symbolic and nonsymbolic relations. *Psychological Science, 8,* 308–313.

Dement, W. (1960). The effect of dream deprivation. *Science, 131,* 1705–1707.

Dement, W., & Kleitman, N. (1957). Cyclic variations in EEG during sleep and their relation to eye movements, body motility and dreaming. *Electroencephalography and Clinical Neurophysiology, 9,* 673–690.

DeNeve, K. M. (2000). Happy as an extraverted clam? The role of personality for subjective well-being. *Current Directions in Psychological Science, 8,* 141–144.

Denmark, F., Russo, N. F., Frieze, I. H, & Sechzer, J. A. (1988). Guidelines for avoiding sexism in psychological research. *American Psychologist, 43,* 582–585.

DePaulo, B. M. (1994). Spotting lies: Can humans learn to do better? *Current Directions in Psychological Science, 3,* 83–86.

Derogowski, J. B. (1989). Real space and represented space: Cross-cultural perspectives. *Behavior and Brain Sciences, 12,* 51–73.

Derryberry, D., & Tucker, D. M. (1992). Neural mechanisms of emotion. *Journal of Consulting and Clinical Psychology, 60,* 329–338.

DeRubeis, R. J., & Crits-Christoph, P. (1998). Empirically supported individual and group psychological treatments for adult mental disorders. *Journal of Consulting and Clinical Psychology, 66,* 37–52.

DeRubeis, R. J., Gelfand, L. A., Tang, T. Z., & Simons, A. D. (1999). Medications versus cognitive behavior therapy for severely depressed outpatients: Mega-analysis of four randomized comparisons. *American Journal of Psychiatry, 156,* 1007–1013.

Deschaumes, M. C., Dittmar, A., Sicard, G., & Vernet, M. E. (1991). Results from six autonomic nervous system responses confirm "autonomic response specificity" hypothesis. *Homeostasis in Health and Disease, 33*(5–6), 225–234.

Deutsch, M., & Gerard, H. B. (1955). A study of normative and informative social influences on individual judgments. *Journal of Abnormal and Social Psychology, 51,* 629–636.

Devor, E. J. (1994). A developmental–genetic model of alcoholism: Implications for genetic research. *Journal of Consulting and Clinical Psychology, 62,* 1108–1115.

DeVries, R. (1969). Constancy of generic identity in the years three to six. *Monographs of the Society for Research in Child Development, 34*(3, Serial No. 127).

DeWitt, L. A., & Samuel, A. G. (1990). The role of knowledge-based function in music perception. *Journal of Experimental Psychology: General, 119,* 123–144.

DeWolff, M. S., & van IJzendoorn, M. H. (1997). Sensitivity and attachment: A meta-analysis on parental antecedents of infant attachment. *Child Development, 68,* 571–591.

Dhurandhar, N. V., Israel, B. A., Kolesar, J. M., Mayhew, G. F., Cook, M. E., & Atkinson, R. L. (2000). Increased adiposity in animals due to a human virus. *International Journal of Obesity 24,* 989–996.

Diamond, M. (1993). Homosexuality and bisexuality in different populations. *Archives of Sexual Behavior, 22,* 291–310.

Diener, E., & Diener, C. (1995). Most people are happy. *Psychological Science, 7,* 181–185.

Diener, E. (2000). Subjective well-being: The science of happiness and a proposal for a national index. *American Psychologist, 55,* 34–43.

Dijkstra, A., DeVries, H., & Bakker, M. (1996). Pros and cons of quitting, self-efficacy, and the stages of change in smoking cessation. *Journal of Consulting and Clinical Psychology, 64,* 758–763.

Dion, K. K. (1992). Stereotyping based on physical attractiveness. Issues and conceptual perspectives. In C. P. Herman, M. P. Zanna, & E. T. Higgins (Eds.), The Ontario Symposium: Vol. 3. *Physical appearance, stigma, and social behavior* (pp. 209–239). Beverly Hills, CA: Sage.

Dionne, V. E., & Dubin, A. E. (1994). Transduction diversity in olfaction. *Journal of Experimental Biology, 194,* 1–21.

Ditto, P. H., & Lopez, D. F. (1992). Motivated skepticism: Use of differential decision criteria for preferred and nonpreferred conclusions. *Journal of Personality and Social Psychology, 63,* 568–584.

Ditton, P. M. (1999). *Mental health and treatment of inmates and probationers* (Special Report NCJ 174463). Washington, DC: U.S. Department of Justice, Office of Justice Programs, Bureau of Justice Statistics.

Dixon, M., Brunet, A., & Lawrence, J.-R. (1990). Hynotizability and automaticity: Toward a parallel distributed processing model of hynotic responding. *Journal of Abnormal Psychology, 99,* 336–343.

Dodds, J. P., Nardone, A., Mercey, D. E., & Johnson, A. M. (2000). Increase in high risk sexual behaviour among homosexual men, London 1996–98: Cross sectional, questionnaire study. *British Medical Journal, 320,* 1510–1511.

Dodson, C., & Reisberg, D. (1991). Indirect testing of eyewitness memory: The (non)effect of misinformation. *Bulletin of the Psychonomic Society, 29,* 333–336.

Dollard, J., Doob, L., Miller, N., Mowrer, O. H., & Sears, R. R. (1939). *Frustration and aggression.* New Haven, CT: Yale University Press.

Domhoff, G. W. (1996). *Finding meaning in dreams: A quantitative approach.* New York: Plenum Press.

Domhoff, G. W. (1999). Drawing theoretical implications from descriptive empirical findings on dream content. *Dreaming 9,* 201–210.

Donnerstein, E. (1984a). Aggression. In A. S. Kahn (Ed.), *Social psychology.* Dubuque, IA: William C. Brown.

Donnerstein, E. (1984b). Pornography: Its effects on violence against women. In N. M. Malamuth & E. Donnerstein (Eds.), *Pornography and sexual aggression.* New York: Academic Press.

Donnerstein, E., & Linz, D. (1995). The mass media: A role in injury causation and prevention. *Adolescent Medicine: State of the Art Reviews, 6,* 271–284.

Donnerstein, E., Slaby, R. G., & Eron, L . D. (1995). The mass media and youth aggression. In L. Eron, J. Gentry, & P. Schlegel (Eds.), *Reason to hope: A psychosocial perspective on violence and youth* (pp. 219–250). Washington, DC: American Psychological Association.

Dooley, D. (2001). *Social research methods* (4th ed.). Upper Saddle River, NJ: Prentice Hall.

Dore, J. (1978). Conditions for the acquisition of speech acts. In I. Markova (Ed.), *The social context of language.* New York: Wiley.

Dordain, G., & Deffond, D. (1994). Pyridoxine neuropathies: Review of the literature. *Therapie, 49*(4), 333–337.

Dormehl, I. C., Jordaan, B., Oliver, D. W., & Croft, S. (1999). SPECT monitoring of improved cerebral blood flow during long-term treatment of elderly patients with nootropic drugs. *Clinical and Nuclear Medicine, 24,* 29–34.

Dovidio, J. F., & Gaertner, S. L. (1999). Reducing prejudice: Combating intergroup biases. *Current Directions in Psychological Science, 8,* 101–105.

Dovidio, J. F., & Penner, L. A. (2001). Helping and altruism. In G. Fletcher & M. Clark (Eds.), *Blackwell handbook of social psychology: Interpersonal processes* (pp. 162–195). Boston: Blackwell.

Dovidio, J. F., Allen, J., & Schroeder, D. A. (1990). The specificity of empathy-induced helping: Evidence for altruism. *Journal of Personality and Social Psychology, 59,* 249–260.

Dovidio, J. F., Gaertner, S. L., & Validzic, A. (1998). Intergroup bias: Status, differentiation, and a common in-group identity. *Journal of Personality and Social Psychology, 75,* 109–120.

Dovidio, J. F., Piliavin, J. A., Gaertner, S. L., Schroeder, D. A., & Clark, R. D., III (1991). The arousal: cost-reward model and the process of intervention: A review of the evidence. In M. Clark (Ed.), *Review of personality and social psychology: Vol. 12. Prosocial behavior* (pp. 86–118). Newbury Park, CA: Sage.

Downey-Lamb, M. M., & Woodruff-Pak, D. S. (1999). Early detection of cognitive deficits using eyeblink classical conditioning. *Alzheimer's Reports, 2,* 37–44.

Dowson, D. I., Lewith, G. T., & Machin, D. (1985). The effects of acupuncture versus placebo in the treatment of headache. *Pain, 21,* 35–42.

Dreyfus, H. L., & Dreyfus, S. E. (1988). Making a mind versus modeling the brain: Intelligence back at a branchpoint. In S. R. Graubard (Ed.), *The artificial intelligence debate.* Cambridge, MA: MIT Press.

Druckman, D., & Bjork, R. A. (1994). *Learning, remembering, believing: Enhancing human performance.* Washington, DC: National Academy Press.

Drummond, S. P. A., Brown, G. G., & Gillin, J. Christian (2000). Altered brain response to verbal learning following sleep deprivation. *Nature, 403,* 655–657.

Druss, B. G., Rosenheck, R. A., & Sledge, W. H. (2000). Health and disability costs of depressive illness in a major U.S. Corporation. *American Journal of Psychiatry, 157,* 1274–1278.

DuBois, D. L., Felner, R. D., Brand, S., Adan, A. M., & Evans, E. G. (1992). A prospective study of life stress, social support, and adaptation in early adolescence. *Child Development, 63,* 542–557.

Duchamp-Viret, P., Chaput, M. A., & Duchamp, A. (1999). Odor response properties of rat olfactory receptor neurons. *Science, 284,* 2171–2174.

Dujovne, V., & Houston, B. (1991). Hostility-related variables and plasma lipid levels. *Journal of Behavioral Medicine, 14,* 555–564.

Dumont, F., & Corsini, R. J. (2000). *Six therapists and one client.* New York: Springer.

Duncan, G. J., Brooks-Gunn, J., & Klebanov, P. K. (1994). Economic deprivation and early childhood development. *Child Development, 65,* 296–318.

Dunn, J. F., & Plomin, R. (1990). *Separate lives: Why siblings are so different.* New York: Basic Books.

Dunn, J. F., Brown, H., Slomkowski, C., Tesla, C., & Youngblade, L. (1991). Young children's understanding of other people's feelings and beliefs: Individual differences and their antecedents. *Child Development, 62,* 1352–1366.

Dunne, E., & Fitzpatrick, A. C. (1999). The views of professionals on the role of self-help groups in the mental health area. *Irish Journal of Psychological Medicine, 16,* 84–89.

Durand, V. M., & Barlow, D. H. (1997). *Abnormal psychology.* Pacific Grove, CA.

Dustman, R., Emmerson, R., Ruhling, R., Shearer, D., Seinhaus, L., Johnson, S., Bonekat, H., & Shigeoka, J. (1990). Age and fitness effects on EEG, ERPs, visual sensitivity, and cognition. *Neurobiology of aging, 11,* 193–200.

Dutton, D. G., & Aron, A. P. (1974). Some evidence for heightened sexual attraction under conditions of high anxiety. *Journal of Personality and Social Psychology, 30,* 510–517.

Dweck, C. S. (1998). The development of early self-conceptions: Their relevance for motivational processes. In J. Heckhausen & C. S. Dweck (Eds.), *Motivation and self-regulation across the life span.* New York: Cambridge University Press.

Dweck, C. S., Chiu, C., & Hong, Y. (1995). Implicit theories and their role in judgments and reactions: A world from two perspectives. *Psychological Inquiry, 6,* 267–285.

Eacott, M. J. (1999). Memory of events of early childhood. *Current Directions in Psychological Science, 8,* 46–49.

Eagly, A. H. (1996). Differences between women and men: Their magnitude, practical importance, and political meaning. *American Psychologist, 51,* 158–159.

Eagly, A. H., & Chaiken, S. (1998). In D. Gilbert, S. T. Fiske, & G. Lindzey (Eds.), *Handbook of social psychology* (Vol. 1, 4th ed., pp. 269–322). Boston: McGraw-Hill.

Eagly, A. H., & Wood, W. (1999). The origins of sex differences in human behavior: Evolved dispositions versus social roles. *American Psychologist, 54,* 408–423.

Eagly, A. H., Karau, S. J., & Makhijani, M. G. (1995). Gender and the effectiveness of leaders: A meta-analysis. *Psychological Bulletin, 117,* 125–145.

Eagly, A. H., Makhijani, M. G., & Klonsky, B. G. (1992). Gender and evaluation of leaders: A meta-analysis. *Psychological Bulletin, 111,* 3–22.

Eberhardt, J. L., & Fiske, S. T. (1998). Confronting racism: The problem and the response. In J. L. Eberhardt & S. T. Fiske (Eds.), *Confronting racism: The problem and the response* (pp. 1–2). Thousand Oaks, CA: Sage Publications.

Eccleston, C., & Crombez, G. (1999). Pain demands attention: A cognitive-affective model of the interruptive function of pain. *Psychological Bulletin, 125,* 356–366.

Echeburua, E., de Corral, P., Garcia Bajos, E., & Borda, M. (1993). Interactions between self-exposure and alprazolam in the treatment of agoraphobia without current panic: An exploratory study. *Behavioural and Cognitive Psychotherapy, 21,* 219–238.

Edwards, A. E., & Acker, L. E. (1972). A demonstration of the long-term retention of a conditioned GSR. *Psychosomatic Science, 26,* 27–28.

Ehlers, A. (1995). A 1-year prospective study of panic attacks: Clinical course and factors associated with maintenance. *Journal of Abnormal Psychology, 104,* 164–172.

Ehrlichman, H., & Halpern, J. N. (1988). Affect and memory: Effects of pleasant and unpleasant odors on retrieval of happy and unhappy memories. *Journal of Personality and Social Psychology, 55,* 769–779.

Eich, E. (1989). Theoretical issues in state dependent memory. In H. L. Roediger & F. I. M. Craik (Eds.), *Varieties of memory and consciousness.* Hillsdale, NJ: Erlbaum.

Eich, E., & Macaulay, D. (2000). Are real moods required to reveal mood-congruent and mood-dependent memory? *Psychological Science, 11,* 244–248.

Eich, E., & Metcalfe, J. (1989). Mood dependent memory for internal versus external events. *Journal of Experimental Psychology: Learning, Memory, and Cognition, 15,* 443–455.

Eich, J. E., Weingartner, H., Stillman, R. C., & Gillin, J. C. (1975). State dependent accessibility of retrieval cues in the retention of a categorized list. *Journal of Verbal Learning and Verbal Behavior, 14,* 408–417.

Eichelman, B. (1983). The limbic system and aggression in humans. *Neuroscience and Bio-behavioral Reviews, 7,* 391–394.

Eichorn, D. H., Clausen, J. A., Haan, N., Honzik, M. P., & Mussen, P. H. (1981). *Present and past in middle life.* New York: Academic Press.

Einhorn, H., & Hogarth, R. (1982). Prediction, diagnosis and causal thinking in forecasting. *Journal of Forecasting, 1,* 23–36.

Eisenberg, N. (1998). Introduction. In W. Damon & N. Eisenberg (Eds.), *Handbook of child psychology: Vol. 3. Social, emotional, and personality development* (5th ed., pp. 1–24). New York: Wiley.

Eisenberg, N., & Fabes, R. A. (1998). Prosocial development. In W. Damon & N. Eisenberg (Eds.), *Handbook of child psychology: Vol. 3. Social, emotional, and personality development* (5th ed., pp. 701–778). New York: Wiley.

Eisenberg, N., Cialdini, R. B., McCreath, H., & Shell, R. (1987). Consistency-based compliance: When and why do children become vulnerable? *Journal of Personality and Social Psychology, 52,* 1174–1181.

Eisenberg, N., Fabes, R. A., & Murphy, B. C. (1995). Relations of shyness and low sociability to regulation and emotionality. *Journal of Personality and Social Psychology, 68,* 505–518.

Eisenman, R. (1994). Conservative sexual values: Effects of an abstinence program on student attitudes. *Journal of Sex Education and Therapy, 20*(2), 75–78.

Ekman, P. (1993). Facial expression and emotion. *American Psychologist, 48,* 384–392.

Ekman, P. (1994). Strong evidence for universals in facial expressions: A reply to Russell's mistaken critique. *Psychological Bulletin, 115*(2), 268–287.

Ekman, P., & Davidson, R. J. (1993). Voluntary smiling changes regional brain activity. *Psychological Science, 4*(5), 342–345.

Ekman, P., Davidson, R. J., & Friesen, W. V. (1990). The Duchenne smile: Emotional expression and brain physiology II. *Journal of Personality and Social Psychology, 58,* 342–353.

Ekman, P., Friesen, W. V., & Ellsworth, P. (1972). *Emotion in the human face: Guidelines for research and a review of findings.* New York: Pergamon Press.

Ekman, P., Levenson, R. W., & Friesen, W. V. (1983). Autonomic nervous system activity distinguishes among emotions. *Science, 221,* 1208–1210.

Elkin, I. (1994). The NIMH treatment of depression collaborative research program: Where we began and where we are. In A. E. Bergin & S. L. Garfield (Eds.), *Handbook of psychotherapy and behavior change.* New York: Wiley.

Elkin, I. (1999). A major dilemma in psychotherapy outcome research: Disentangling therapists from therapies. *Clinical Psychology: Science and Practice, 6,* 10–32.

Elkin, I., Shea, T., Watkins, J., Imber, S., Sotsky, S., Collins, J., Glass, D., Pilkonis, P., Leber, W., Docherty, J., Fiester, S., & Perloff, M. (1989). National Institute of Mental Health treatment of depression collaborative research program. *Archives of General Psychiatry, 46,* 971–982.

Elkin, I., Yamaguchi, J. L., Arnoff, D. B., Glass, C. R., Sotsky, S. M., & Krupnick, J. L. (1999). "Patient-treatment fit" and early engagement in therapy. *Psychotherapy Research, 9,* 437–451.

Ellis, A. (1962). *Reason and emotion in psychotherapy.* New York: Lyle Stuart.

Ellis, A. (1993). Reflections on rational-emotive therapy. *Journal of Consulting and Clinical Psychology, 61,* 199–201.

Ellis, A. (1995). Rational emotive behavior therapy. In R. J. Corsini & D. Wedding (Eds.), *Current psychotherapies* (5th ed., pp. 162–196). Itasca, IL: Peacock.

Ellis, A. (1997). Using rational emotive behavior therapy techniques to cope with disability. *Professional Psychology: Research and Practice, 28,* 17–22.

Ellis, A. L., & Mitchell, R. W. (2000). Sexual orientation. In L. T. Szuchman & F. Muscarella (Eds.), *Psychological perspectives on human sexuality.* New York: Wiley.

Ellis, N. R. (1991). Automatic and effortful processes in memory for spatial location. *Bulletin of the Psychonomic Society, 29,* 28–30.

Engel, S. A. (1999). Using neuroimaging to measure mental representations: Finding color-opponent neurons in visual cortex. *Current Directions in Psychological Science, 8,* 23–27.

Engeland, H. V. (1993). Pharmacotherapy and behaviour therapy: Competition or cooperation? *Acta Paedopsychiatrica International Journal of Child and Adolescent Psychiatry, 56*(2), 123–127.

Engen, T., Gilmore, M. M., & Mair, R. G. (1991). Odor memory. In T. V. Getchell et al. (Eds.), *Taste and smell in health and disease.* New York: Raven Press.

Enns, C. Z. (1994). On teaching about the cultural relativism of psychological constructs. *Teaching of Psychology, 21,* 205–211.

Epping-Jordan, M. P., Watkins, S. S., Koob, G. F., & Markou, A. (1998). Dramatic decreases in brain reward function during nicotine withdrawal. *Nature, 393,* 76–79.

Epstein, L. H., Valoski, A., Wing., R. R., & McCurley, J. (1994). Ten-year outcomes of behavioral family-based treatment for childhood obesity. *Health Psychology, 13,* 373–383.

Erel, O., & Burman, B. (1995). Interrelatedness of marital relations and parent-child relations: A meta-analytic review. *Psychological Bulletin, 118,* 108–132.

Ericsson, K. A., & Charness, N. (1994). Expert performance: Its structure and acquisition. *American Psychologist, 49,* 725–747.

Ericsson, K. A., & Kintsch, W. (1995). Long-term working memory. *Psychological Review, 102*(2), 211–245.

Ericsson, K. A., & Polson, P. G. (1988). An experimental analysis of the mechanisms of a memory skill. *Journal of Experimental Psychology: Learning, Memory, & Cognition, 14,* 305–316.

Ericsson, K. A., & Simon, H. A. (1994). *Protocol analysis: Verbal reports as data* (rev. ed.). Cambridge, MA: MIT Press.

Ericsson, K. A., & Staszewski, J. (1989). Skilled memory and expertise: Mechanisms of exceptional performance. In D. Klahr & K. Kotovsky (Eds.), *Complex information processing: The impact of Herbert A. Simon.* Hillsdale, NJ: Erlbaum.

Erikson, E. H. (1968). *Identity: Youth and crisis.* New York: Norton.

Ernst, E. (2000). Herbal medicines: Where is the evidence? *British Medical Journal, 321,* 395–396.

Eron, L. D., Huesmann, L. R., Lefkowitz, M. M., & Walder, L. O. (1996). Does television violence cause aggression? In D. F. Greenberg (Ed.), *Criminal careers: Vol. 2. The international library of criminology, criminal justice and penology* (pp. 311–321). Aldershot, England: Dartmouth Publishing Company.

Essock-Vitale, S. M., & McGuire, M. T. (1985). Women's lives viewed from an evolutionary perspective: II. Patterns of helping. *Ethology and Sociobiology, 6,* 155–173.

Esterson, A. (1993). *Seductive mirage: An exploration of the work of Sigmund Freud.* Chicago: Open Court.

Evans, D. A., Hebert, L. E., Beckett, L. A., Scherr, P. A., Albert, M. S., Chown, M. J., Pilgrim, D. M., & Taylor, J. O. (1997). Education and other measures of socioeconomic status and risk of incident Alzheimer's disease in a defined population of older persons. *Archives of Neurology, 54,* 1399–1405.

Evans, G. W., Hygge, S., & Bullinger, M. (1995). Chronic noise and psychological stress. *Psychological Science, 6,* 333–338.

Evans, G. W., Wells, N. M., Chan, H.-Y. E., & Saltzman, H. (2000). Housing quality and mental health. *Journal of Consulting and Clinical Psychology, 68,* 526–530.

Everaerd, W., & Laan, E. (1994). Cognitive aspects of sexual functioning and dysfunctioning. *Sexual and Marital Therapy, 9,* 225–230.

Everett, S. A., Warren, C. W., Santelli, J. S., Kann, L., Collins, J. L., & Kolbe, L. J. (2000). Use of birth control pills, condoms, and withdrawal among U.S. high school students. *Journal of Adolescent Health, 27,* 112–118.

Eysenck, H. J. (1952). The effects of psychotherapy: An evaluation. *Journal of Consulting Psychology, 16,* 319–324.

Eysenck, H. J. (1961). The effects of psychotherapy. In H. J. Eysenck (Ed.), *Handbook of abnormal psychology.* New York: Basic Books.

Eysenck, H. J. (1966). *The effects of psychotherapy.* New York: International Science Press.

Eysenck, H. J. (1978). An exercise in mega-silliness. *American Psychologist, 33,* 517.

Eysenck, H. J. (1986). What is intelligence? In R. J. Sternberg & D. K. Detterman (Eds.), *What is intelligence? Contemporary viewpoints on its nature and definition.* Norwood, NJ: Ablex.

Eysenck, H. J. (1990a). Genetic and environmental contributions to individual differences: The three major dimensions of personality. *Journal of Personality, 58,* 245–261.

Eysenck, H. J. (1990b). Biological dimensions of personality. In L. A. Pervin (Ed.), *Handbook of personality: Theory and research.* (pp. 244–276). New York: Guilford.

Eysenck, H. J. (1994). A biological theory of intelligence. In D. K. Detterman (Ed.), *Current topics in human intelligence* (Vol. 4). Norwood, NJ: Ablex.

Eysenck, H. J., & Rachman, S. (1965). *The causes and cures of neurosis: An introduction to modern behavior therapy based on learning theory and the principle of conditioning.* San Diego: Knapp.

Faedda, G., Tondo, L., Teicher, M., Baldessarini, R., Gelbard, H., & Floris, G. (1993). Seasonal mood disorders: Patterns of seasonal recurrence in mania and depression. *Archives of General Psychiatry, 50,* 17–23.

Fagot, B. I. (1997). Attachment, parenting, and peer interactions of toddler children. *Developmental Psychology, 33,* 489–499.

Fairweather, G. W., & Fergus, E. O. (1993). *Empowering the mentally ill.* Austin: Fairweather.

False Memory Syndrome Foundation. (1997). Outcome of recent malpractice suits against therapists brought by former patients claiming negligent encouragement or implantation of false memories. *FMSF Newsletter, 6,* 7–9.

Farooqi, I. S., Jebb, S. A., Langmack, G., Lawrence, E., Cheetham, C. H., Prentice, A. M., Hughes, I. A., McCamish, M. A., & O'Rahilly, S. (1999). Effects of recombinant leptin therapy in a child with congenital leptin deficiency. *The New England Journal of Medicine, 341,* 879–884.

Fassler, D. G., & Dumas, L. S. (1997). *Help me, I'm sad: Recognizing, treating, and preventing childhood depression.* New York: Viking Press.

Faust, J., Olson, R., & Rodriguez, H. (1991). Same-day surgery preparation: Reduction of pediatric patient arousal and distress through participant modeling. *Journal of Consulting and Clinical Psychology, 59,* 475–478.

Federal Bureau of Investigation. (1999). *Crime in the United States—1998.* Washington, DC: U.S. Government Printing Office.

Federal Bureau of Investigation. (2000). *Crime in the United States—1999.* Washington, DC: U.S. Government Printing Office.

Feingold, A., & Mazzella, R. (1998). Gender differences in body image are increasing. *Psychological Science, 9,* 190–195.

Feist, J., & Feist, G. J. (1998). *Theories of personality* (4th ed.). Boston: McGraw-Hill.

Felten, D. L., Cohen, N., Ader, R., Felten, S. Y., Carlson, S. L., & Roszman, T. L. (1991). Central neural circuits involved in neural-immune interactions. In R. Ader (Ed.), *Psychoneuroimmunology* (2nd ed.). New York: Academic Press.

Fenson, L., Dale, P. S., Reznick, J. S., & Bates, E. (1994). Variability in early communicative development. *Monographs of the Society for Research in Child Development, 59,* 173.

Fenton, W. S., & McGlashan, T. H. (1991). Natural history of schizophrenia subtypes: 1. Longitudinal study of paranoid, hebephrenic, and undifferentiated schizophrenia. *Archives of General Psychiatry, 48,* 969–977.

Fenton, W. S., & McGlashan, T. H. (1994). Antecedent, symptoms progression, and long-term outcome of the deficit syndrome in schizophrenia. *American Journal of Psychiatry, 151,* 351–356.

Fernald, A. (1990, December). Cited by T. Adler, "Melody is the message" of infant-directed speech. *APA Monitor,* p. 9.

Fernández-Dols, J.-M., & Ruiz-Belda, M.-A. (1995). Are smiles a sign of happiness?: Gold medal winners at the Olympic Games. *Journal of Personality and Social Psychology, 69,* 1113–1119.

Festinger, L. (1954). A theory of social comparison processes. *Human Relations, 7,* 117–140.

Festinger, L. (1957). *A theory of cognitive dissonance.* Evanston, IL: Row, Petersen.

Festinger, L., & Carlsmith, J. M. (1959). Cognitive consequences of forced compliance. *Journal of Abnormal and Social Psychology, 58,* 203–210.

File, S. E., Fluck, E., & Fernandes, C. (1999). Beneficial effects of glycine (bioglycin) on memory and attention in young and middle-aged adults. *Journal of Clinical Psychopharmacology, 19,* 506–512.

Filipek, P. A., Accardo, P. J., Barancek, G. T., Cook, E. H., Jr., Dawson, G., Gordon, B., Gravel, J., Johnson, C. P., Kallen, R. J., Levy, S. E., Minshew, N. J., Prizanat, B. M., Rapin, I., Rogers, S. J., Stone, W. L., Teplin, S., Tuchman, R. F., & Volkmar, F. R. (1999). The screening and diagnosis of autistic spectrum disorders. *Journal of Autism and Developmental Disorders, 29,* 439–484.

Finer, N., James, W. P., Kopelman, P. G., Lean, M. E., & Williams, G. (2000). One-year treatment of obesity: A randomized, double-blind, placebo-controlled, multicentre study of orlistat, a gastrointestinal lipase inhibitor. *International Journal of Obesity and Related Metabolic Disorders, 24,* 306–313.

Fink, M. (1999). *Electroshock: Restoring the Mind.* New York: Oxford University Press.

Fischer, K. W., & Bidell, T. (1991). Constraining nativist inferences about cognitive capacities. In S. Carey & R. Gelman (Eds.), *The epigenesis of mind: Essays on biology and cognition* (pp. 199–235). Hillsdale, NJ: Erlbaum.

Fischer, P. J., & Breakey, W. R. (1991). The epidemiology of alcohol, drug, and mental disorders among homeless persons. *American Psychologist, 46,* 1115–1128.

Fischoff, B., & MacGregor, D. (1982). Subjective confidence in forecasts. *Journal of Forecasting, 1,* 155–172.

Fisher, C. D. (2000). Mood and emotion while working: Missing pieces of job satisfaction? *Journal of Organizational Behavior, 21,* 185–202.

Fisher, W. A., Fisher, J. D., & Rye, B. J. (1995). Understanding and promoting AIDS-preventive behavior: Insights from the theory of reasoned action. *Health Psychology, 14, 255*–264.

Fiske, A. P., Kitayama, S., Markus, H. R., & Nisbett, R. E. (1998). The cultural matrix of social psychology. In D. T. Gilbert, S. T. Fiske, & G. Lindzey (Eds.), *Handbook of social psychology* (Vol. 2, 4th ed., pp. 915–981). Boston: McGraw-Hill.

Fiske, S. T. (1995). Social cognition. In A. Tesser (Ed.), *Advanced social psychology* (pp. 149–194). New York: McGraw-Hill.

Fiske, S. T. (1998). Stereotyping, prejudice, and discrimination. In D. Gilbert, S. T. Fiske, & G. Lindzey (Eds.), *Handbook of social psychology* (Vol.2, 4th ed., pp. 357–414). Boston: McGraw-Hill.

Fitzgerald, T. E., Tennen, H., Affect, G. S., & Pransky, G. (1993). The relative importance of dispositional optimism and control appraisals in quality of life after coronary artery bypass surgery. *Journal of Behavioral Medicine, 16,* 25–43.

Flavell, J. E., Azrin, N., Baumeister, A., Carr, E., Dorsey, M., Forehand, R., Foxx, R., Lovaas, O. I., Rincover, A., Risley, T., Romanczyk, R., Russo, D., Schroeder, S., & Solnick, J. (1982). The treatment of self-injurious behavior. *Behavior Therapy, 13,* 529–554.

Flavell, J. H. (1996). Piaget's legacy. *Psychological Science, 7,* 200–203.

Flegal, K. M., Carroll, M. D., Kuczmarski, R. J., & Johnson, C. L. (1998). Overweight and obesity in the United States: prevalence and trends, 1960–1994. *International Journal of Obesity, 22,* 39–47.

Flynn, J. T. (1999). Searching for justice: The discovery of IQ gains over time. *American Psychologist, 54,* 5–20.

Foa, E. B., & Kozak, M. J. (1995). DSM-IV field trial: Obsessive-compulsive disorder. *American Journal of Psychiatry, 152,* 90–96.

Foa, E. B., Dancu, C. V., Hembree, E. A., Jaycox, L. H., Meadows, E. A., & Street, G. P. (1999). A comparison of exposure therapy, stress-inoculation training, and their combination for reducing posttraumatic stress disorder in female assault victims. *Journal of Consulting and Clinical Psychology, 67,* 194–200.

Foa, E. B., Franklin, M. E., Perry, K. J., & Herbert, J. D. (1996). Cognitive biases in generalized social phobia. *Journal of Abnormal Psychology, 105,* 433–439.

Folk, C. L., Remington, R. W., & Wright, J. H. (1994). The structure of attentional control: Contingent attentional capture by apparent motion, abrupt onset, and color. *Journal of Experimental Psychology: Human Perception and Performance, 20,* 317–329.

Folkman, S., & Lazarus, R. (1988). *Manual for the ways of coping questionnaire.* Palo Alto, CA: Consulting Psychologists Press.

Folkman, S., Lazarus, R. S., Gruen, R. J., & DeLongis, A. (1986). Appraisal, coping, health status, and psychological symptoms. *Journal of Personality and Social Psychology, 50,* 571–579.

Folkman, S., & Moskowitz, J. T. (2000). Stress, positive emotion, and coping. *Current Directions in Psychological Science, 9,* 115–118.

Ford, D. E., & Kamerow, D. B. (1989). Epidemiological study of sleep disturbances and psychiatric disorders: An opportunity for prevention? *Journal of the American Medical Association, 262,* 1479–1484.

Foreyt, J. P., Brunner, R. L., Goodrick, G. K., & Cutter, G. (1995). Psychological correlates of weight fluctuation. *International Journal of Eating Disorders, 17*(3), 263–275.

Foster, M. D. (2000). Positive and negative responses to personal discrimination: Does coping make a difference? *Journal of Social Psychology, 140,* 93–106.

Foulkes, D. (1985). *Dreaming: A cognitive-psychological analysis.* Hillsdale, NJ: Erlbaum.

Fowler, R. D. (2000). A lesson in taking our own advice. *Monitor on Psychology, 31,* 9.

Fowles, D. (1992). Schizophrenia: Diathesis-stress revisited. *Annual Review of Psychology, 43,* 303–336.

Fox, A. S., & Olster, D. H. (2000). Effects of intracerebroventricular leptin administration on feeding and sexual behaviors in lean and obese female zucker rats. *Hormones and Behavior, 37,* 377–387.

Foxhall, K. (2000). How will the rules on telehealth be written? *Monitor on Psychology, 31,* 38.

Fozard, J., Wolf, E., Bell, B., Farland, R., & Podolsky, S. (1977). Visual perception and communication. In J. Birren & K. Schaie (Eds.), *Handbook of the psychology of aging.* New York: Van Nostrand Reinhold.

Frances, A. J., Pincus, H. A., & Widiger, T. A. (1996). DSM-IV and international communication in psychiatric diagnosis. In Y. Honda, M. Kastrup, & J. E. Mezzich (Eds.), *Psychiatric diagnosis: A world perspective.* New York: Springer.

Frank, J. D., & Frank, J. B. (1991). *Persuasion and healing: A comparative study of psychotherapy* (3rd ed.). Baltimore, MD: Johns Hopkins University Press.

Frank, J. S. (1978). *Psychotherapy and the human predicament.* New York: Schocken Books.

Frank, L. G., Glickman, S. E., & Licht, P. (1991). Fatal sibling aggression, precocial development, and androgens in neonatal spotted hyenas. *Science, 252,* 702–704.

Frank, M. G., Ekman, P., & Friesen, W. V. (1993). Behavioral markers and recognizability of the smile of enjoyment. *Journal of Personality and Social Psychology, 64*(1), 83–93.

Frankenberg, W. K., & Dodds, J. B. (1967). The Denver developmental screening test. *Journal of Pediatrics, 71,* 181–191.

Frankmann, S. P., & Green, B. G. (1987). Differential effects of cooling on the intensity of taste. *Annals of the New York Academy of Science, 510,* 300–303.

Freedland, R. L., & Bertenthal, B. I. (1994). Developmental changes in interlimb coordination: Transition to hands-and-knees crawling. *Psychological Science, 5,* 26–32.

Freedman, J. L. (1992). Television violence and aggression: What psychologists should tell the public. In P. Suedfeld & P. E. Tetlock (Eds.), *Psychology and social policy.* New York: Hemisphere.

Freedman, J. L., & Fraser, S. C. (1966). Compliance without pressure: The foot-in-the-door technique. *Journal of Personality and Social Psychology, 4,* 195–202.

Freud, S. (1900). The interpretation of dreams. In J. Strachey (Ed.), *The standard edition of the complete psychological works of Sigmund Freud: Vol. 8.* London: Hogarth Press.

Fridlund, A., Sabini, J. P., Hedlund, L. E., Schaut, J. A., Shenker, J. I., & Knauer, M. J. (1990). Audience effects on solitary faces during imagery: Displaying to the people in your head. *Journal of Nonverbal Behavior, 14*(2), 113–137.

Fried, P. A., Watkinson, B., & Gray, R. (1992). A follow-up study of attentional behavior in 6-year-old children exposed prenatally to marijuana, cigarettes, and alcohol. *Neurotoxicity and Teratology, 14*(5), 299–311.

Friedman, H. S., Tucker, J. S., Schwartz, J. E., Martin, L. R., Tomlinson-Keasey, C., Wingard, D. L., & Criqui, M. H. (1995a). Childhood conscientiousness and longevity: Health behaviors and cause of death. *Journal of Personality and Social Psychology, 68,* 696–703.

Friedman, H. S., Tucker, J. S., Schwartz, J. E., Tomlinson-Keasey, C., Martin, L. R., Wingard, D. L., & Criqui, M. H. (1995b). Psychosocial and behavioral predictors of longevity: The aging and death of the "Termites." *American Psychologist, 50,* 69–78.

Friedman, M., & Rosenman, R. H. (1959). Association of specific overt behavior patterns with blood and cardiovascular findings: Blood cholesterol level, blood clotting time, incidence of arcus senilis, and clinical coronary artery disease. *Journal of the American Medical Association, 169,* 1286–1296.

Friedman, M., & Rosenman, R. H. (1974). *Type A behavior and your heart.* New York: Knopf.

Friedman, S. M., Daub, C., Cresci, K., & Keyser, R. (1999). A comparison of job satisfaction among nursing assistants in nursing homes and the Program of All-Inclusive Care for the Elderly (PACE). *Gerontologist, 39,* 434–439.

Fritzler, B. K., Hecker, J. E., & Losee, M. C. (1997). Self-directed treatment with minimal therapist contact: Preliminary findings for obsessive-compulsive disorder. *Behaviour Research and Therapy, 35,* 627–631.

Fritzsche, B., Finkelstein, M., & Penner, L. A. (2000). To help or not to help: Capturing individual's decision policies. *Social Behavior and Personality, 28,* 561–578.

Fulbright, R. K., Jenner, A. R., Mencl, W. E., Pugh, K. R., Shaywitz, B. A., Shaywitz, S. E., Frost, S. J., Skudlarski, P., Constable, R. T., Lacadie, C. M., Marchione, K. E., & Gore, J. C. (1999). The cerebellum's role in reading: a functional MR imaging study. *American Journal of Neuroradiology, 20,* 1925–1930.

Fuller, J. B., Morrison, R., Jones, L., Bridger, D., & Brown, V. (1999). The effects of psychological empowerment on transformational leadership and job satisfaction. *Journal of Social Psychology, 139,* 389–391.

Funder, D. C. (1993). Explaining traits. *Psychological Inquiry, 5,* 125–127.

Funder, D. C., & Colvin, C. R. (1997). Congruence of others' and self-judgments of personality. In R. Hogan, J. Johnson, & S. Briggs (Eds.), *Handbook of personality psychology* (pp. 617–648). San Diego: Academic Press.

Funtowicz, M. N., & Widiger, T. A. (1999). Sex bias in the diagnosis of personality disorders: An evaluation of DSM-IV criteria. *Journal of Abnormal Psychology, 108,* 195–201.

Furstenberg, F. F., Brooks-Gunn, J., & Chase-Lansdale, L. (1989). Teenaged pregnancy and childbearing. *American Psychologist, 44,* 313–320.

Gabrieli, J. D. E. (1998). Cognitive neuroscience of human memory. *Annual Review of Psychology, 49,* 87–115.

Gabrieli, J. D. E., Fleischman, D. A., Keane, M. M., Reminger, S. L., & Morrell, F. (1995). Double dissociation between memory systems underlying explicit and implicit memory in the human brain. *Psychological Science, 6,* 76–82.

Gaertner, S. L., Dovidio, J. F., & Bachman, B. A. (1997). Revisiting the contact hypothesis: The induction of a common group identity. *International Journal of Intercultural Relations, 20,* 271–290.

Galanter, E. (1962). Contemporary psychophysics. In R. Brown (Ed.), *New directions in psychology* (Vol. 1). New York: Holt, Rinehart, Winston.

Galatzer-Levy, R. M., Bachrach, H., Skolnikoff, A., & Waldron, S., Jr. (2000*). Does psychoanalysis work?* New Haven, CT: Yale University Press.

Gallagher, M. (1998, January 26). Day careless. *National Review,* pp. 37–41.

Gallagher, M., & Chiba, A. A. (1996). The amygdala and emotion. *Current Opinions in Neurobiology, 6*(2), 221–227.

Gallopin, T., Fort, P., Eggermann, E., Cauli, B., Luppi, P.-H., Rossier, J., Audinat, E., Mühlethaler, M., & Serafin, M. (2000). Identification of sleep-promoting neurons in vitro. *Nature, 404,* 992–995.

Galotti, K. M. (1999). *Cognitive psychology in and out of the laboratory* (2nd ed.). Belmont, CA: Brooks/Cole.

Ganchrow, J. R., Steiner, J. E., & Daher, M. (1983). Neonatal facial expressions in response to different qualities and intensities of gustatory stimuli. *Infant Behavior and Development, 6,* 189–200.

Gara, M. A., Woolfolk, R. L., Cohen, B. D., Goldston, R. B., Allen, L. A., & Novalany, J. (1993). Perception of self and other in major depression. *Journal of Abnormal Psychology, 102,* 93–100.

Garb, H. N. (1997). Race bias, social class bias, and gender bias in clinical judgment. *Clinical Psychology: Science and Practice, 4,* 99–120.

Garb, H. N., Florio, C. M., & Grove, W. M. (1998). The validity of the Rorschach and the Minnesota Multiphasic Personality Inventory: Results from meta-analyses. *Psychological Science, 9,* 402–404.

Garb, H. N., Florio, C. M., & Grove, W. M. (1999). The Rorschach controversy: Reply to Parker, Hunsley, and Hanson. *Psychological Science, 10,* 293–294.

Garcia, J., & Koelling, R. A. (1966). Relation of cue to consequences in avoidance learning. *Psychonomic Science, 4,* 123–124.

Garcia-Coll, C. T., Oh, W., & Hoffman, J. (1987). The social ecology: Early parenting of Caucasian American mothers. *Child Development, 58,* 955–963.

Gardner, H. (1993). *Multiple intelligences: The theory in practice.* New York: Basic Books.

Gardner, H. (1998). Are there additional intelligences? The case for naturalistic, spiritual, and existential intelligence. In J. Kane (Ed.), *Education, information, and transformation.* Englewood Cliffs, NJ: Prentice-Hall.

Gardner, R., Heward, W. L., & Grossi, T. A. (1994). Effects of response cards on student participation and academic achievement: A systematic replication with inner-city students during whole-class science instruction. *Journal of Applied Behavior Analysis, 27,* 63–71.

Garfield, S. L. (1998). Some comments on empirically supported treatments. *Journal of Consulting and Clinical Psychology, 66,* 121–125.

Garland, A. F., & Zigler, E. (1993). Adolescent suicide prevention: Current research and social policy implications. *American Psychologist, 48,* 169–182.

Garry, M., & Loftus, E. (1994). Pseudomemories without hypnosis. *International Journal of Clinical and Experimental Hypnosis, 42*(4), 363–373.

Gaster, B., & Holroyd, J. (2000). St. John's wort for depression: A systematic review. *Archives of Internal Medicine, 160,* 152–156.

Gawande, A. (1998, March 30). No mistake. *New Yorker.*

Gazzaniga, M. S., Fendrich, R., & Wessinger, C. M. (1994). Blindsight reconsidered. *Current Directions in Psychological Science, 3*(3), 93–95.

Gazzaniga, M. S., & LeDoux, J. E. (1978). *The integrated mind.* New York: Plenum.

Geary, D. C. (1999). Evolution and developmental sex differences. *Current Directions in Psychological Science, 8,* 115–120.

Geen, R. G. (1998a). Process and personal variables in affective aggression. In R. G. Geen & E. Donnerstein (Eds.), *Human aggression* (pp. 2–24). San Diego: Academic Press.

Geen, R. G. (1998b). Aggression and antisocial behavior. In D. Gilbert, S. T. Fiske, & G. Lindzey (Eds.), *Handbook of social psychology* (Vol. 2, 4th ed., pp. 317–356). Boston: McGraw-Hill.

Gelman, R., & Baillargeon, R. (1983). A review of some Piagetian concepts. In P. H. Mussen (Ed.), *Handbook of child psychology* (Vol. 3). New York: Wiley.

Gerbner, G., Morgan, M., & Signorielli, N. (1994). *Television violence profile No. 16: The turning point.* Philadelphia: Annenberg School for Communication.

Gerrard, M., Gibbons, F. X., & Bushman, B. J. (1996). Relation between perceived vulnerability to HIV and precautionary sexual behavior. *Psychological Bulletin, 119,* 390–409.

Gerschman, J. A., Reade, P. C., & Burrows, G. D. (1980). Hypnosis and dentistry. In G. D. Burrows & L. Dennerstein (Eds.), *Handbook of hypnosis and psychosomatic medicine.* Amsterdam: Elsevier.

Geschwind, N. (1979). Specializations of the human brain. *Scientific American, 241,* 180–199.

Gfeller, J. D. (1994). Hypnotizability enhancement: Clinical implications of empirical findings. *American Journal of Clinical Hypnosis, 37*(2), 107–116.

Gibson, E., Dembofsky, C. A., Rubin, S., & Greenspan, J. S. (2000). Infant sleep position practices 2 years into the "back to sleep" campaign. *Clinical Pediatrics, 39,* 285–289.

Gibson, E. J., & Walk, R. D. (1960). The visual cliff. *Scientific American, 202,* 64–71.

Gifford, R., & Hine, D. (1997). Toward cooperation in the commons dilemma. *Canadian Journal of Behavioural Science, 29,* 167–178.

Gilbert, D. T. (1998). Ordinary personology. In D. Gilbert, S. T. Fiske, & G. Lindzey (Eds.), *Handbook of social psychology* (Vol.2, 4th ed., pp. 89–150). Boston: McGraw-Hill.

Gilbert, D. T., & Malone, P. S. (1995). The correspondence bias. *Psychological Bulletin, 117,* 21–38.

Gilbert, D. T., & Wilson, T. D. (2000). Miswanting: Some problems in the forecasting of future affective states. In J. P. Forgas (Ed.), *Feeling and thinking: The role of affect in social cognition.* New York: Cambridge University Press.

Gilbert, S. (1997, August 20). Two spanking studies indicate parents should be cautious. *New York Times Magazine.*

Giles, T. R. (1990). Bias against behavior therapy in outcome reviews: Who speaks for the patient? *The Behavior Therapist, 13,* 86–90.

Gilligan, C. (1982). *In a different voice: Psychological theory and women's development.* Cambridge, MA: Harvard University Press.

Gilligan, C. (1993). Adolescent development reconsidered. In A. Garrod (Ed.), *Approaches to moral development: New research and emerging themes.* New York: Teachers College Press.

Gilman, A. G., Goodman, L. S., Rall, T. W., & Murad, F. (1985). *Goodman and Gilman's the pharmacological basis of therapeutics* (7th ed.). New York: Macmillan.

Gilovich, T. (1997). Some systematic biases of everyday judgment. *Skeptical Inquirer, 21,* 31–35.

Givens, B. (1995). Low doses of ethanol impair spatial working memory and reduce hippocampal theta activity. *Alcoholism Clinical and Experimental Research, 19*(3), 763–767.

Gladue, B. A. (1994). The biopsychology of sexual orientation. *Current Directions in Psychological Science, 3*(5), 150–154.

Glanzer, M., & Cunitz, A. (1966). Two storage mechanisms in free recall. *Journal of Verbal Learning and Verbal Behavior, 5,* 351–360.

Gleitman, L., & Landau, B. (1994). *The acquisition of the lexicon.* Cambridge, MA: MIT Press.

Glenmullen, J. (2000). *Prozac Backlash: Overcoming the Dangers of Prozac, Zoloft, Paxil, and Other Antidepressants with Safe, Effective Alternatives.* New York: Simon & Schuster.

Gleuckauf, R., & Quittner, A. (1992). Assertiveness training for disabled adults in wheelchairs: Self-report, role-play, and activity pattern outcomes. *Journal of Consulting and Clinical Psychology, 60,* 419–425.

Glicksohn, J. (1991). Altered sensory environments, altered states of consciousness, and altered-state cognition. *Journal of Mind and Behavior, 14*(1), 1–11.

Glod, M. (1998, April 27). Springer mania: Too hot for parents and teachers. *Washington Post*, pp. A1, A10.

Glover, J. A., Krug, D., Dietzer, M., George, B. W., & Hannon, M. (1990). "Advance" advance organizers. *Bulletin of the Psychonomic Society, 28*, 4–6.

Goffard, C. (1999). Seventeen-year-old pulls child from burning car. *St. Petersburg Times*, December 2, 3b.

Gold, M. S. (1994). The epidemiology, attitudes, and pharmacology of LSD use in the 1990s. *Psychiatric Annals, 24*(3), 124–126.

Goldberg, J. F., Harrow, M., & Grossman, L. S. (1995). Course and outcome in bipolar affective disorder: A longitudinal follow-up study. *American Journal of Psychiatry, 152*, 379–384.

Goldberg, L. R. (1995). What the hell took so long? Donald W. Fiske and the Big-Five factor structure. In P. E. Shrout & S. T. Fiske (Eds.), *Personality research, methods, and theory: A festschrift honoring Donald W. Fiske* (pp. 29–43). Hillsdale, NJ: Erlbaum.

Goldfried, M. R., Castonguay, L. G., Hayes, A. M., Drozd, J. F., & Shapiro, D. A. (1997). A comparative analysis of the therapeutic focus in cognitive-behavioral and psychodynamic-interpersonal sessions. *Journal of Consulting and Clinical Psychology, 65*, 720–748.

Goldman, M. S., Darkes, J., & Del Boca, F. K. (1999). Expectancy meditation of biopsychosocial risk for alcohol use and alcoholism. In I. Kirsch (Ed.), *How expectancies shape experience* (pp. 233–262). Washington, DC: American Psychological Association.

Goldman, M. S., Del Boca, F. K., & Darkes, J. (1999). Alcohol expectancy theory: The application of cognitive neuroscience. In K. Leonard & H. Blane (Eds.), *Psychological theories of drinking and alcoholism* (2nd ed., pp. 203–246). New York: Guilford.

Goldman-Rakic, P. S. (1987). Development of cortical circuitry and cognitive function. *Child Development, 58*, 601–622.

Goldstein, E. B. (1999). *Sensation and perception* (5th ed.). Pacific Grove, CA: Brooks/Cole.

Goldstein, I., Lue, T. F., Padma-Nathan, H., Rosen, R. C., Steers, W. D., & Wicker, P. A. (1998). Oral sildenafil in the treatment of erectile dysfunction: Sildenafil Study Group. *New England Journal of Medicine, 338*, 1397–1404.

Golomb, J., Kluger, A., De Leon, M. J., Ferris, S. H., Convit, A., Mittelman, M. S., Cohen, J., Rusinek, H., De Santi, S., & George, A. E. (1994). Hippocampal formation size in normal human aging: A correlate of delayed secondary memory performance. *Learning and Memory, 1*, 45–54.

Goodenough, F. L. (1932). Expression of the emotions in a blind-deaf child. *Journal of Abnormal and Social Psychology, 27*, 328–333.

Goodman-Gilman, A. G., Rall, T. W., Nies, A. S., & Taylor, P. (1990). *The pharmacological basis of therapeutics* (8th ed.). New York: Pergamon Press.

Goodwin, F. K., & Jamison, K. R. (Eds.). (1990). *Manic-depressive illness*. New York: Oxford University Press.

Goplerud, E. N. (1980). Social support and stress during the first year of graduate school. *Professional Psychology, 11*, 283–290.

Gorman, J. M., Liebowitz, M. R., Fyer, A. J., & Stein, J. (1989). A neuroanatomical hypothesis for panic disorder. *American Journal of Psychiatry, 146*, 148–161.

Gosling, S. D. (1998). Personality dimensions in spotted hyenas (*Crocuta crocuta*). *Journal of Comparative Psychology, 112*, 107–118.

Gosling, S. D., & John, O. P. (1999). Personality dimensions in nonhuman animals: A cross-species review. *Current Directions in Psychological Science, 8*, 69–75.

Gossop, M., Griffiths, P., Powis, B., & Strang, J. (1994). Cocaine; Patterns of use, route of administration, and severity of dependence. *British Journal of Psychiatry, 164*(5), 660–664.

Gottesman, I. I. (1991). *Schizophrenia genesis*. New York: Freeman.

Gottfried, A. W. (1997, June). Parents' role is critical to children's learning. *APA Monitor*, p. 24.

Gottlieb, G. (2000). Environmental and behavioral influences on gene activity. *Current Directions in Psychological Science, 9*, 93–97.

Gottman, J. M., Coan, J., Carrere, S., & Swanson, C. (1998). Predicting marital happiness and stability from newlywed interactions. *Journal of Marriage and the Family, 60*, 5–22.

Gould, E., Beylin, A., Tanapat, P., Reeves, A., & Shors, T. J. (1999). Learning enhances adult neurogenesis in the hippocampal formation. *Nature Neuroscience, 2*, 260–265.

Gould, R. A., Otto, M. W., Pollack, M. H., & Yap, L. (1997). Cognitive behavioral and pharmacological treatment of generalized anxiety disorder: A preliminary meta-analysis. *Behavior Therapy, 28*, 285–305.

Gourevitch, P. (1999) *We wish to inform you that tomorrow we will be killed with our families: Stories from Rwanda*. New York: Picador

Grady, D. (1998, October 13). High chlamydia rates found in teenagers. *New York Times* (Web Archive).

Graham, S. (1992). "Most of the subjects were white and middle class." *American Psychologist, 47*, 629–639.

Graham, S., & Weiner, B. (1996). Theories and principles of motivation. In D. C. Berliner & Robert C. Calfee (Eds.), *Handbook of educational psychology* (pp. 63–84). New York: Macmillan Library Reference.

Grandin, T. (1996). *Thinking in pictures: And other reports from my life with autism*. New York: Vintage Press.

Grassi, L., Rasconi, G., Pedriali, A., Corridoni, A., & Bevilacqua, M. (2000). Social support and psychological distress in primary care attenders. *Psychotherapy and Psychosomatics, 69*, 95–100.

Grencavage, L., & Norcross, J. C. (1991). Where are the commonalities among the therapeutic common factors? *Professional Psychology: Research and Practice, 21*, 372–378.

Green, A. I., & Patel, J. K. (1996). The new pharmacology of schizophrenia. *Harvard Mental Health Letter, 13*(6), 5–7.

Green, D. M., & Swets, J. A. (1966). *Signal detection theory and psychophysics*. New York: Wiley.

Green, E. J., Greenough, W. T., & Schlumpf, B. E. (1983). Effects of complex or isolated environments on cortical dendrites of middle-aged rats. *Brain Research, 264*(2), 233–240.

Green, J. P., & Lynn, S. J. (1995). Hypnosis, dissociation, and simultaneous task performance. *Journal of Personality and Social Psychology, 69*, 728–735.

Green, J. T., & Woodruff-Pak, D. S. (2000). Eyeblink classical conditioning: Hippocampal formation is for neutral stimulus associations as cerebellum is for association response. *Psychological Bulletin, 126*, 138–158.

Green, M. (1991). Visual search, visual strains, and visual architecture. *Perception and Psychophysics, 50*, 388–404.

Green, R. A., Cross, A. J., & Goodwin, G. M. (1995). Review of the pharmacology and clinical pharmacology of 3,4-methylenedioxymethamphetamine (MDMA or "ecstacy"). *Psychopharmacology, 119*, 247–260.

Greenberg, M. T, Lengua, L. J, Coie, J. D, Pinderhughes, E. E., Bierman, K., Dodge, K. A., Lochman, J. E., & McMahon, R. J. (1999). Predicting developmental outcomes at school entry using a multiple-risk model: Four American communities. *Developmental Psychology, 35*, 403–417.

Greenblatt, D., Harmatz, J., & Shader, R. I. (1993). Plasma alprazolam concentrations: Relation to efficacy and side effects in the treatment of panic disorder. *Archives of General Psychiatry, 50*, 715–732.

Greenfield, P. M. (1994). Video games as cultural artifacts. *Journal of Applied Developmental Psychology, 15*, 3–12.

Greenfield, P. M. (1995, Winter). Culture, ethnicity, race, and development: Implications for teaching theory and research. *Society for Research in Child Development Newsletter*, pp. 3ff.

Greenfield, P. M., Camaioni, L., Ercolani, P., Weiss, L., Lauber, B. A., & Perucchini, P. (1994). Cognitive socialization by computer games in two cultures: Inductive discovery or mastery of an iconic code? *Journal of Applied Developmental Psychology, 15*, 59–86.

Greenfield, P. M., & Childs, C. P. (1991). Developmental continuity in biocultural context. In R. Cohen & A. W. Siegel (Eds.), *Context and development* (pp. 135–159). Hillsdale, NJ: Erlbaum.

Greenwald, A. G., & Banaji, M. R. (1995). Implicit social cognition: Attitudes, self-esteem, and stereotypes. *Psychological Review, 102*, 4–27.

Greenwald, A. G., Klinger, M. R., & Schuh, E. S. (1995). Activation by marginally perceptible ("subliminal") stimuli: Dissociation of unconscious from conscious cognition. *Journal of Experimental Psychology: General, 124*(1), 22–42.

Greenwald, R. (1996). The information gap in the EMDR controversy. *Professional Psychology: Research and Practice, 27*, 67–72.

Greenwald, R. (1999). Eye movement desensitization and reprocessing (EMDR): New hope for children suffering from trauma and loss. *Clinical Child Psychology & Psychiatry, 3*, 279–287.

Greer, A. E., & Buss, D. M. (1994). Tactics for promoting sexual encounters. *Journal of Sex Research, 31*(3), 185–201.

Griffitt, W. B., & Guay, P. (1969). "Object" evaluation and conditioned affect. *Journal of Experimental Research in Personality, 4*, 1–8.

Grilo, C. M., Pogue-Geile, M. F. (1991). The nature of environmental influences on weight and obesity: A behavior genetic analysis. *Psychological Bulletin, 110*, 520–537.

Grinspoon, L. (1999). The future of medical marijuana. *Forsch Komplementarmed, 6,* 40–43.

Grinspoon, L., & Bakalar, J. B. (1995). Marijuana as medicine: A plea for reconsideration. *Journal of the American Medical Association, 273*(23), 1875–1876.

Grob, C., & Dobkins-de-Rios, M. (1992). Adolescent drug use in cross-cultural perspective. *Journal of Drug Issues, 22*(1) 121–138.

Groopman, J. (2000). Second opinion. *The New Yorker,* January 24, pp. 40–49.

Gross, J. J., & Levenson, R. W. (1997). Hiding feeling: The acute effects of inhibiting negative and positive emotion. *Journal of Abnormal Psychology, 106,* 95–103.

Groth-Marnat, G. (1997). *Handbook of psychological assessment* (3rd ed.). New York: Wiley.

Grunberg, N. E. (1994). Overview: Biological processes relevant to drugs of dependence, *Addiction, 89*(11), 1443–1446.

Grusec, J. E. (1991). Socialization of concern for others in the home. *Developmental Psychology, 27,* 338–342.

Grusec, J. E., & Goodnow, J. J. (1994). Impact of parental discipline methods on the child's internalization of values. *Developmental Psychology, 30,* 4–19.

Guerin, D. W., Gottfried, A. W., & Thomas, C. W. (1997). Difficult temperament and behaviour problems: A longitudinal study from 1. 5 to 12 years. *International Journal of Behavioral Development, 21,* 71–90.

Guevara, M. A., Lorenzo, I., Ramos, J., & Corsi–Cabrera, M. (1995). Inter- and intra-hemispheric EEG correlation during sleep and wakefulness. *Sleep, 18*(4), 257–265.

Guilford, J. P. (1959). Traits of creativity. In H. H. Anderson (Ed.), *Creativity and its cultivation.* New York: Harper & Row.

Guilford, J. P., & Hoepfner, R. (1971). *The analysis of intelligence.* New York: McGraw-Hill.

Guntheroth, W. G., & Spiers, P. S. (1992). Sleeping prone and the risk of sudden infant death syndrome. *Journal of the American Medical Association, 267,* 2359–2362.

Gur, R. E., Cowell, P. E., Latshaw, A., Turetsky, B. I., Grossman, R. I., Arnold, S. E., Bilker, W. B., & Gur, R. C. (2000). Reduced dorsal and orbital prefrontal gray matter volumes in schizophrenia. *Archives of General Psychiatry, 57,* 761–768.

Gura, T. (1999). Leptin not impressive in clinical trial. *Science, 286,* 881–882.

Guyton, A. C. (1991). *Textbook of medical physiology* (8th ed.) Philadelphia: Saunders.

Ha, H., Tan, E. C., Fukunaga, H., & Aochi, O. (1981). Naloxone reversal of acupuncture analgesia in the monkey. *Experimental Neurology, 73,* 298–303.

Haaga, D. A. (2000). Introduction to the special section on stepped care models in psychotherapy. *Journal of Consulting and Clinical Psychology, 68,* 547–548.

Haber, R. N. (1979). Twenty years of haunting eidetic imagery: Where's the ghost? *The Behavioral and Brain Sciences, 2,* 583–629.

Haberlandt, K. (1999). *Human memory: Exploration and application.* Boston: Allyn & Bacon.

Hackel, L. S., & Ruble, D. N. (1992). Changes in the marital relationship after the first baby is born: Predicting the impact of expectancy disconfirmation. *Journal of Personality and Social Psychology, 62,* 944–957.

Hacking, I. (1995). *Rewriting the soul: Multiple personality and the sciences of memory.* Princeton, NJ: Princeton University Press.

Hackman, J. R. (1998). Why don't teams work? In R. S. Tindale, J. Edwards, & E. J. Posavac (Eds.), *Applications of theory and research on groups to social issues.* New York: Plenum.

Haddock, G., & Zanna, M. P. (1998a). Affect, cognition, and the prediction of social attitudes. In W. Stroebe & M. Hewstone (Eds.), *European review of social psychology* (Vol. 10). New York: Wiley.

Haddock, G., & Zanna, M. P. (1998b) Authoritarianism, values, and the favorability and structure of antigay attitudes. In G. Herek (Ed.), *Stigma and sexual orientation: Understanding prejudice against lesbians, gay men, and bisexuals. Psychological perspectives on lesbian and gay issues.*

Haldeman, D. C. (1994). The practice and ethics of sexual orientation conversion therapy. *Journal of Consulting and Clinical Psychology, 62*(2), 221–227.

Halford, J. C., & Blundell, J. E. (2000). Pharmacology of appetite suppression. *Progress in Drug Research, 54,* 25–58.

Hall, C. C. I. (1997). Cultural malpractice: The growing obsolescence of psychology with the changing U.S. population. *American Psychologist, 52,* 642–651.

Hall, C. S., Lindzey, G., & Campbell, J. P. (1998). *Theories of personality* (4th ed.). New York: Wiley.

Hall, G. C. N., & Hirschman, R. (1991). Toward a theory of sexual aggression: A quadripartite model. *Journal of Consulting and Clinical Psychology, 59,* 662–669.

Hall, L. K., & Bahrick, H. P. (1998). The validity of metacognitive predictions of widespread learning and long-term retention. In G. Mazzoni & T. Nelson (Eds.), *Metacognition and cognitive neuropsychology: Monitoring and control processes* (pp. 23–36). Mahwah, NJ: Erlbaum.

Hall, R. C., Hoffman, R. S., Beresford, T. P., Wooley, B., et al. (1989). Physical illness encountered in patients with eating disorders. *Psychosomatics, 30,* 174–191.

Halpern, D. F. (1997). Sex differences in intelligence. *American Psychologist, 52,* 1091–1102.

Halverson, C. F., Jr., & Wampler, K. S. (1997). Family influences on personality development. In R. Hogan, J. Johnson, & S. Briggs (Eds.), *Handbook of personality psychology* (pp. 241–267). San Diego: Academic Press.

Hamilton, D. L., & Sherman, J. (1994). Social stereotypes. In R. S. Wyer & T. K. Srull (Eds.), *Handbook of social cognition* (2nd ed.). Hillsdale, NJ: Erlbaum.

Hamilton, W. D. (1964). The evolution of social behavior: Parts I and II. *Journal of Theoretical Biology, 7,* 1–52.

Hamm, A. O., Vaitl, D., & Lang, P. J. (1989). Fear conditioning, meaning, and belongingness: A selective association analysis. *Journal of Abnormal Psychology, 98,* 395–406.

Hammond, W. R., & Yung, B. (1993). Minority student recruitment and retention practices among schools of professional psychology: A national survey and analysis. *Professional Psychology: Research and Practice, 24,* 3–12.

Han, S., & Shavitt, S. (1994). Persuasion and culture: Advertising appeals in individualist and collectivist societies. *Journal of Experimental Social Psychology, 30,* 326–350.

Hancock, E. (1996, February). High control at work makes for a healthy heart. *Johns Hopkins Magazine,* p. 31.

Harackiewicz, J. M., & Elliot, A. J. (1993). Achievement goals and intrinsic motivation. *Journal of Personality and Social Psychology, 65*(5), 904–915.

Hare, R. D. (1993). *Without conscience: The disturbing world of the psychopaths among us.* New York: Pocket Books.

Harlow, H. F. (1949). The formation of learning sets. *Psychological Review, 56,* 51–65.

Harlow, H. F. (1959, June). Love in infant monkeys. *Scientific American,* 68–74.

Harmon-Jones, E., Brehm, J. W., Greenberg, J., Simon, L., & Nelson, D. E. (1996). Evidence that the production of negative consequences is not necessary to produce cognitive dissonance. *Journal of Personality and Social Psychology, 72,* 515–525.

Harper, R. C., Frysinger, J. D., Marks, J. X., & Zhang, R. B. (1988). Cardiorespiratory control during sleep. In P. J. Schwartz (Ed.), *The sudden infant death syndrome: Cardiac and respiratory mechanisms and interventions* (*Annals of the New York Academy of Sciences,* Vol. 533). New York: New York Academy of Sciences.

Harris, C. V., & Goetsch, V. L. (1990). Multi-component flooding treatment of adolescent phobia. In E. L. Feindler & G. R. Kalfus (Eds.), *Adolescent behavior therapy handbook* (Vol. 22). New York: Springer.

Harris, G. C., & Aston-Jones, G. (1995). Involvement of D2 dopamine receptors in the nucleus accumbens in opiate withdrawal syndrome. *Nature, 371,* 155–157.

Harris, J. R. (1995). Where is the child's environment? A group socialization theory of development. *Psychological Review, 102,* 458–489.

Harris, J. R. (1998). *The nurture assumption.* New York: Free Press.

Harris, J. R. (2000). Context-specific learning, personality, and birth order. *Current Directions in Psychological Science, 9,* 174–177.

Hart, D., & Yates, M. (1997). The interrelation of self and identity in adolescence: A developmental account. In R. Vasta (Ed.), *Annals of child development: Vol. 12. A research annual* (pp. 207–243), London: Jessica Kingsley Publishers.

Hartman, E., Baekeland, F., & Zwilling, G. (1972). Psychological differences between long and short sleepers. *Archives of General Psychiatry, 26,* 463–468.

Hartung, C. M., & Widiger, T. A. (1998). Gender differences in the diagnosis of mental disorders: Conclusions and controversies of DSM-IV. *Psychological Bulletin, 123,* 260–278.

Hartup, W. W, & Stevens, N. (1997). Friendships and adaptation in the life course. *Psychological Bulletin, 121,* 355–370.

Harvard Mental Health Letter. (1998a). Mood disorders: An overview—Part II, Vol. 14(7), pp. 1–5.

Harvard Mental Health Letter. (1998b). Mood disorders: An overview—Part III, Vol. 14(8), pp. 1–5.

Harwood, H., Fountain, D., & Livermore, G. (1998). *The Economic Costs of Alcohol and Drug Abuse in the United States, 1992.* Bethesda, MD: National Institute on Drug Abuse and the National Institute on Alcohol Abuse and Alcoholism. Publication No. 98–4327.

Hastie, R. (1986). Review essay: Experimental evidence on group accuracy. In B. Grofman & G. Owen (Eds.), *Information pooling and group decision making* (pp. 129–264). Greenwich, CT: JAI Press.

Hastie, R., Penrod, S. D., & Pennington, N. (1984). *Inside the jury.* Cambridge, MA: Harvard University Press.

Hatfield, E., & Rapson, R. L. (1995). *Love and sex: Cross-cultural perspectives.* Boston: Allyn & Bacon.

Hattori, M., Fujiyama A., Taylor, T. D., Watanabe, H., Yada, T., Park, H. S., Toyoda, A., Ishii, K., Totoki, Y., Choi, D.K., Soeda, E., Ohki, M., Takagi, T., Sakaki, Y., Taudien, S., Blechschmidt, K., Polley, A., Menzel, U., Delabar, J., Kumpf, K., Lehmann, R., Patterson, D., Reichwald, K., Rump, A., Schillhabel, M., & Schudy, A. (2000). The DNA sequence of human chromosome 21. *Nature, 405,* 311–319.

Hauptman, J., Lucas, C., Boldrin, M. N., Collins, H., & Segal, K. R. (2000). Orlistat in the long-term treatment of obesity in primary care settings. *Archives of Family Medicine, 9,* 160–167.

Hawkins, H. L., Kramer, A. R., & Capaldi, D. (1993). Aging, exercise, and attention. *Psychology and Aging, 7,* 643–653.

Hawkins, J. D., Catalano, R. F., Kosterman, R., Abbott, R., & Hill, K. G. (1999). Preventing adolescent health-risk behaviors by strengthening protection during childhood. *Archives of Pediatrics and Adolescent Medicine, 153,* 226–234.

Hayes, J. R. M. (1952). Memory span for several vocabularies as a function of vocabulary size. *Massachusetts Institute of Technology Acoustic Laboratory Progress Report.* Cambridge: MIT Press.

Hayflick, L. (1994). *How and why we age.* New York: Ballantine Books.

Hays, P. A. (1995). Multicultural applications of cognitive-behavior therapy. *Professional Psychology: Research and Practice, 26,* 309–315.

Hays, W. L. (1981). *Statistics* (3rd ed.). New York: Holt, Rinehart, Winston.

He, L. F. (1987). Involvement of endogenous opioid peptides in acupuncture analgesia. *Pain, 31,* 99–121.

Healy, D. J., Haroutunian, V., Powchik, P., Davidson, M., Davis, K. L., Watson, S. J., & Meador-Woodruff, J. H. (1998). AMPA receptor binding and subunit mRNA expression in prefrontal cortex and striatum of elderly schizophrenics. *Neuropsychopharmacology, 19,* 278–286.

Hebb, D. O. (1955). Drives and the C. N. S. (conceptual nervous system). *Psychological Review, 62,* 243–254.

Hegarty, J. D., Baldessarini, R. J., Tohen, M., Waternaux, C., & Oepen, G. (1994). One hundred years of schizophrenia: A meta-analysis of the outcome literature. *American Journal of Psychiatry, 151,* 1409–1416.

Heim, C., Newport, J., Heit, S., Graham, Y. P., Wilcox, M., Bonsall, R., Miller, A. H., & Nemeroff, C. B. (2000). Pituitary-adrenal and autonomic responses to stress in women after sexual and physical abuse in childhood. *Journal of the American Medical Association, 284,* 592–597.

Heine, S. J., & Lehman, D. R. (1997). Culture, dissonance, and self-affirmation. *Personality and Social Psychology Bulletin, 23,* 389–400.

Hejmadi, A., Davidson, R. J., & Rozin, P. (2000). Exploring Hindu Indian emotion expressions: Evidence for accurate recognition by Americans and Indians. *Psychological Science, 11,* 183–187.

Heller, W., Etienne, M. A., & Miller, G. A. (1995). Patterns of perceptual asymmetry in depression and anxiety: Implications for neuropsychological models of emotion and psychopathology. *Journal of Abnormal Psychology, 104*(2), 327–333.

Heller, W., Nitschke, J. B., & Miller, G. A. (1998). Lateralization in emotion and emotional disorders. *Current Directions in Psychological Science, 7,* 26–32.

Helmers, K. F., & Krantz, D. S. (1996). Defensive hostility, gender and cardiovascular levels and responses to stress. *Annals of Behavioral Medicine, 18,* 246–254.

Helmers, K. F., Krantz, D. S., Merz, C. N. B., Klein, J., Kop, W. J., Gottdiener, J. S., & Rozanski, A. (1995). Defensive hostility: Relationship to multiple markers of cardiac ischemia in patients with coronary disease. *Health Psychology, 14,* 202–209.

Helms, J. E. (1992). Why is there no study of cultural equivalence in standardized cognitive ability testing? *American Psychologist, 47,* 1083–1101.

Helson, R., & Moane, G. (1987). Personality change in women from college to midlife. *Journal of Personality and Social Psychology, 53,* 176–186.

Helzer, J. E., Canino, G. J., Yeh, E., Bland, R. C., Lee, C. K., Hwu, H., & Newman, S. (1990). Alcoholism—North America and Asia: A comparison of population surveys with the diagnostic interview schedule. *Archives of General Psychiatry, 47,* 313–319.

Hendrick, C., & Hendrick, S. (1986). A theory and method of love. *Journal of Personality and Social Psychology, 50,* 392–402.

Henkel, L. A., Franklin, N., & Johnson, M. K. (2000). Cross-modal source monitoring, confusion between perceived and imagined events. *Journal of Experimental Psychology: Learning, Memory and Cognition, 26,* 321–335.

Henker, B., & Whalen, C. K. (1989). Hyperactivity and attention deficits. *American Psychologist, 44,* 216–223.

Henry, W. P. (1998). Science, politics, and the politics of science: The use and misuse of empirically validated treatment research. *Psychotherapy Research, 8,* 126–140.

Hepburn, M. A. (1995). *TV violence: Myth and reality. Social Education, 59,* 309–311.

Herek, G. M. (Ed.). (1998). *Stigma and sexual orientation.* Thousand Oaks, CA: Sage.

Hergenhahn, B. R., & Olson, M. H. (1999). *An introduction to theories of personality* (5th ed.). Upper Saddle River, NJ: Prentice Hall.

Herness, M. S., & Gilbertson, T. A. (1999). Cellular mechanisms of taste transduction. *Annual Review of Physiology, 61,* 873–900.

Herrmann, D. J., & Searleman, A. (1992). Memory improvement and memory theory in historical perspective. In D. Herrmann, H. Weingartner, A. Searlman, & C. McEvoy (Eds.), *Memory improvement: Implications for memory theory.* New York: Springer-Verlag.

Herzog, D. B., Dorer, D. J., Keel, P. K., Selwyn, S. E., Ekeblad, E. R., Flores, A. T., Greenwood, D. N., Burwell, R. A., & Keller, M. B. (1999). Recovery and relapse in anorexia and bulimia nervosa: A 7.5-year follow-up study. *Journal of the American Academy of Child and Adolescent Psychiatry, 38,* 829–837.

Herzog, D. B., Greenwood, D. N., Dorer, D. J., Flores, A. T., Ekeblad, E. R., Richards, A., Blais, M. A., & Keller, M. B. (2000). Mortality in eating disorders: A descriptive study. *International Journal of Eating Disorders, 28,* 20–26.

Hesse, J., Mogelvang, B., & Simonsen, H. (1994). Acupuncture versus metropolol in migraine prophylaxis: A randomized trial of trigger point inactivation. *Journal of Internal Medicine, 235,* 451–456.

Hetherington, E. M., & Clingempeel, W. G. (1992). Coping with marital transitions. *Monographs of the Society for Research in Child Development, 57*(2–3, Serial No. 227).

Hettinger, T. P., Frank, M. E., & Myers, W. E. (1996). Are the tastes of polycose and monosodium glutamate unique? *Chemical Senses, 21*(3), 341–347.

Heyman, R. E., & Neidig, P. H. (1999). A comparison of spousal aggression prevalence rates in U.S. army and civilian representative samples. *Journal of Consulting and Clinical Psychology, 67,* 239–242.

Heymsfield, S. B., Greenberg, A. S., Fujioa, K., Dixon, R. M., Kushner, R., Hunt, T., Lubina, J. A., Patane, J., Self, B., Hunt, P., & McCamish, M. (1999). Recombinant leptin for weight loss in obese and lean adults. *Journal of the American Medical Association, 282,* 1568–1575.

Hilgard, E. R. (1965). *Hypnotic susceptibility.* New York: Harcourt, Brace & World.

Hilgard, E. R. (1977). *Divided consciousness: Multiple controls in human thought and action.* New York: Wiley.

Hilgard, E. R. (1979). *Personality and hypnosis: A study of imaginative involvement.* Chicago: University of Chicago Press.

Hilgard, E. R. (1980). Consciousness in contemporary psychology. *Annual Review of Psychology, 31,* 1–26.

Hilgard, E. R. (1992). Divided consciousness and dissociation. *Consciousness and Cognition, 1,* 16–31.

Hilgard, E. R., & Marquis, D. G. (1936). Conditioned eyelid responses in monkeys, with a comparison of dog, monkey, and man. *Psychological Monographs, 47,* 186–198.

Hilgard, E. R., Morgan, A. H., & MacDonald, H. (1975). Pain and dissociation in the cold pressor test: A study of "hidden reports" through automatic key-pressing and automatic talking. *Journal of Abnormal Psychology, 84,* 280–289.

Hill, C. T., & Peplau, L. A. (1998). Premarital predictors of relationship outcomes: A 15-year follow-up of the Boston Couples Study. In T. N. Bradbury (Ed.), *The developmental course of marital dysfunction* (pp. 237–278). New York: Cambridge University Press.

Hill, J. O., & Peters, J. C. (1998). Environmental contributions to the obesity epidemic. *Science, 280,* 1371–1374.

Hill, T., Lewicki, P., Czyzewska, M., & Boss, A. (1989). Self-perpetuating biases in person perception. *Journal of Personality and Social Psychology, 57,* 373–386.

Hilliard, R. B., Henry, W. P., & Strupp, H. H. (2000). An interpersonal model of psychotherapy: Linking patient and therapist developmental history, therapeutic process, and types of outcome. *Journal of Consulting and Clinical Psychology, 68,* 125–133.

Hilton, H. (1986). *The executive memory guide.* New York: Simon & Schuster.

Hinsz, V. B. (1990). Cognitive and consensus processes in group recognition memory performance. *Journal of Personality and Social Psychology, 59,* 705–718.

Hiroto, D. S. (1974). Locus of control and learned helplessness. *Journal of Experimental Psychology, 102,* 187–193.

Hirouchi, M., Oka, M., Itoh, Y., Ukai, Y., & Kimura, K. (2000). Role of metabotropic glutamate receptor subclasses in modulation of adenylyl cyclase activity by a nootropic NS-105. *European Journal of Pharmacology, 387,* 9–17.

Hirschfeld, J. A. (1995). The "Back-to-Sleep" campaign against SIDS. *American Family Physician, 51,*(3), 611–612.

Hirschfeld, R. M., Allen, M. H., McEvoy, J. P., Keck, P. E. Jr, & Russell, J. M. (1999). Safety and tolerability of oral loading divalproex sodium in acutely manic bipolar patients. *Journal of Clinical Psychiatry, 60,* 815–818.

Hirsch-Pasek, K., Treiman, R., & Schneiderman, M. (1984). Brown and Hanlon revisited: Mothers' sensitivity to ungrammatical forms. *Journal of Child Language, 11,* 81–88.

Ho, D. Y., & Chiu, C. (1998). Component ideas of individual, collectivism, and social organization. In U. Kim, C. Kagitcibasi, & H. C. Triandis (Eds.), *Individualism and collectivism: Theory, method, and applications.* Thousand Oaks, CA: Sage.

Hobson, J. A. (1997). Dreaming as delirium: A mental status analysis of our nightly madness. *Seminar in Neurology, 17,* 121–128.

Hobson, J. A., & Stickgold, R. (1994). Dreaming: A neurocognitive approach. *Consciousness and Cognition, 3,* 1–15.

Hobson, J. A., Pace-Schott, E. F., Stickgold, R., & Kahn, D. (1998). To dream or not to dream? Relevant data from new neuroimaging and electrophysiological studies. *Current Opinions in Neurobiology, 8,* 239–244.

Hoffman, D. (1999). When the nuclear alarms went off, he guessed right. *International Herald Tribune*, February 11, p. 2.

Hofstadter, D. (1995). *Fluid concepts and creative analogies.* New York: Basic Books.

Hogan, R. J., Curphy, G. J., & Hogan, J. (1994). What we know about leadership: Effectiveness and personality. *American Psychologist, 49,* 493–504.

Hogarth, R. M., & Einhorn, H. J. (1992). Order effects in belief updating: The belief adjustment model. *Cognitive Psychology, 24,* 1–55.

Holahan, C. J., Moos, R. H., Holahan, C. K., & Brennan, P. L. (1997). Social context, coping strategies, and depressive symptoms: An expanded model with cardiac patients. *Journal of Personality and Social Psychology, 72,* 918–928.

Holden, C. (1996). Small refugees suffer the effects of early neglect. *Science, 274,* 1076–1077.

Holden, C. (1998). New clues to alcoholism risk. *Science, 280,* 1348–1349.

Holman, B. R. (1994). Biological effects of central nervous system stimulants. *Addiction, 89*(11), 1435–1441.

Holmes, D. S. (1984). Meditation and somatic arousal reduction: A review of the experimental evidence. *American Psychologist, 39,* 1–10.

Holmes, D. S. (1991). *Abnormal psychology.* New York: HarperCollins.

Holway, A. H., & Boring, E. G. (1941). Determinants of apparent visual size with distance variant. *American Journal of Psychology, 54,* 21–37.

Hong, Y., Morris, M. W., Chiu, C., & Benet-Martinez, V. (2000). Multicultural minds: A dynamic constructivist approach to culture and cognition. *American Psychologist, 55,* 709–720.

Honts, C. R., & Quick , B. D. (1995). The polygraph in 1996: Progress in science and the law. *North Dakota Law Review, 71,* 997–1020.

Hood, B. M., Willen, J. D., & Driver, J. (1998). Adult's eyes trigger shifts of visual attention in human infants. *Psychological Science, 9,* 131–134.

Hooker, E. (1993). Reflections of a 40-year exploration: A scientific view on homosexuality. *American Psychologist, 48,* 450–453.

Hopf, H. C., Muller, F. W., & Hopf, N. J. (1992). Localization of emotional and volitional facial paresis. *Neurology, 42*(10), 1918–1923.

Hoptman, M. J., & Davidson, R. J. (1994). How and why do the two cerebral hemispheres interact? *Psychological Bulletin, 116,* 195–219.

Horgan, J. (1996, December). Why Freud isn't dead. *Scientific American,* pp. 106–111.

Horne, J. A. (1988). *Why we sleep: The functions of sleep in humans.* Oxford: Oxford University Press.

Horney, K. (1937). *Neurotic personality of our times.* New York: Norton.

Horowitz, L. M., Rosenberg, S. E., & Bartholomew, K. (1993). Interpersonal problems, attachment styles, and outcome in brief dynamic psychotherapy. *Journal of Consulting and Clinical Psychology, 61,* 549–560.

Houpt, T. R. (1994). Gastric pressure in pigs during eating and drinking. *Physiology and Behavior, 56*(2), 311–317.

House, J. S., Landis, K. R., & Umberson, D. (1988). Structures and processes of social support. *Annual Review of Sociology, 14,* 293–318.

Howard, D. V. (1983). *Cognitive psychology.* New York: Macmillan.

Howard-Pitney, B., LaFramboise, T., Basil, M., September, B., & Johnson, M. (1992). Psychological and social indicators of suicide ideation and suicide attempts in Zuni adolescents. *Journal of Consulting and Clinical Psychology, 60,* 473–476.

Howe, M. L. (1995, March). *Differentiating cognitive and sociolinguistic factors in the decline of infantile amnesia.* Paper presented at the biennial meeting of the Society for Research in Child Development, Indianapolis.

Hoy, A. W. (1999). Psychology applied to education. In A. M. Stec & D. A. Bernstein (Eds.), *Psychology: The fields of application.* Boston: Houghton Mifflin.

Hoyert, D. L., Kochanek, K. D., & Murphy, S. L. (1999). *Deaths: Final data for 1997. National Vital Statistics Report.* Hyattsville, MD: National Center for Health Statistics. DHHS Publication No. (PHS) 99–1120.

Hoyle, R. H. (1993). Interpersonal attraction in the absence of explicit attitudinal information. *Social Cognition, 11,* 309–320.

Hu, S., Patatucci, A. M. L., Patterson, C., Li, L., Fulker, D. W., Cherny, S. S., Kruglyak, L., & Hamer, D. H. (1995). Linkage between sexual orientation and chromosome Xq28 in males but not females. *Nature Genetics, 11,* 248–256.

Huang, L., & Li, C. (2000). Leptin: A multifunctional hormone. *Cell Research, 10,* 81–92.

Hubble, M. A., Duncan, B. L., & Miller, S. D. (Eds.). (1999). *The heart and soul of change: What works in psychotherapy.* Washington, DC: American Psychological Association.

Hubel, D. H., & Wiesel, T. N. (1979). Brain mechanisms of vision. *Scientific American, 241,* 150–162.

Hudson, J. A., & Sheffield, E. G. (1998). Deja vu all over again: Effects of reenactment on toddlers' event memory. *Child Development, 69,* 51–67.

Hudson, W. (1960). Pictorial depth perception in subcultural groups in Africa. *Journal of Social Psychology, 52,* 183–208.

Huesmann, L. R. (1995). *Screen violence and real violence: Understanding the link.* Auckland, NZ: Media Aware.

Huesmann, L. R. (1998). The role of social information processing and cognitive schema in the acquisition and maintenance of habitual aggressive behavior. In R. G. Geen & E. Donnerstein (Eds.), *Human aggression.* San Diego: Academic Press.

Huesmann, L. R., & Eron, L. D. (1986). *Television and the aggressive child: A cross-national comparison.* Hillsdale, NJ: Erlbaum.

Huesmann, L. R., Moise, J., Podolski, C., & Eron, L. (1997, April). *Longitudinal relations between early exposure to television violence and young adult aggression: 1977–1992.* Paper presented at the annual meeting of the Society for Research in Child Development. Washington, DC.

Hughes, J. R., Higgins, S. T., & Bickel, W. K. (1994). Nicotine withdrawal versus other drug withdrawal syndromes: Similarities and dissimilarities. *Addiction, 89*(11), 1461–1470.

Hull, C. L. (1951). *Essentials of behavior.* New Haven, CT: Yale University Press.

Humphreys, L. G. (1984). General intelligence. In C. R. Reynolds & R. T. Brown (Eds.), *Perspectives on bias in mental testing.* New York: Plenum.

Hunsley, J., & Bailey, J. M. (1999). The clinical utility of the Rorschach: Unfulfilled promises and an uncertain future. *Psychological Assessment, 11,* 266–277.

Hunsley, J., & Rumstein-McKean, O. (1999). Improving psychotherapeutic services via randomized trials, treatment manuals, and component analysis designs. *Journal of Clinical Psychology, 55,* 1507–1517.

Hunt, E. (1983). On the nature of intelligence. *Science, 219,* 141–146.

Hunt, M. (1982). *The universe within.* New York: Simon & Schuster.

Hunt, R., & Rouse, W. B. (1981). Problem solving skills of maintenance trainees in diagnosing faults in simulated power plants. *Human Factors, 23,* 317–328.

Hunter, E. J. (1979). *Combat casualties who remain at home.* Paper presented at Western Regional Conference of the Inter University Seminar, "Technology in Combat." Naval Postgraduate School, Monterey, CA.

Hunter, J. N. (1997). Needed: A ban on the significance test. *Psychological Science, 8,* 3–7.

Hunter, M. A., & Ames, E. W. (1988). A multifactor model of infants' preferences for novel and familiar stimuli. In C. Rovee-Collier & L. P. Lipsitt (Eds.), *Advances in infancy research* (Vol. 5, pp. 69–91). Norwood, NJ: Ablex.

Hunter, R. H. (1995). Benefits of competency-based treatment programs. *American Psychologist, 50,* 509–513.

Hurt, H., Brodsky, N. L., Betancourt, L., & Braitman, L. E. (1995). Cocaine-exposed children: Follow-up through 30 months. *Journal of Developmental and Behavioral Pediatrics, 16*(1), 29–35.

Huston, A. C., & Wright, J. C. (1989). The forms of television and the child viewer. In G. Comstock (Ed.), *Public communication and behavior* (Vol. 2). San Diego, CA: Academic Press.

Huttenlocher, P. R. (1990). Morphometric study of human cerebral cortex development. *Neuropsychologia, 28,* 517–527.

Hyde, J. S. (1986). Gender differences in aggression. In J. S. Hyde & M. C. Linn (Eds.), *The psychology of gender: Advances through meta-analysis.* Baltimore: Johns Hopkins University Press.

Hyde, J. S. (1994). Can meta-analysis make feminist transformations in psychology? *Psychology of Women Quarterly, 18,* 451–462.

Hyde, J. S., & Durik, A. M. (2000). Gender differences in erotic plasticity–Evolutionary or sociocultural forces? Comment on Baumeister (2000). *Psychological Bulletin, 126,* 375–379.

Hyman, I. A. (1995). Corporal punishment, psychological maltreatment, violence, and punitiveness in America: Research, advocacy, and public policy. *Applied and Preventive Psychology, 4,* 113–130.

Hyman, I. E., Jr. (2000). The memory wars. In U. Neisser & I. E. Hyman Jr. (Eds.), *Memory observed* (2nd ed., pp. 374–379). New York: Worth.

Hyman, I. E., Jr., & Loftus, E. F. (1998). Errors in autobiographical memory. *Clinical Psychology Review, 18,* 933–948.

Iacono, W. G., & Lykken, D. T. (1997). The validity of the lie detector: Two surveys of scientific opinion. *Journal of Applied Psychology, 82,* 426–433.

Igalens, J., & Roussel, P. (2000). A study of the relationships between compensation package, work motivation, and job satisfaction. *Journal of Organizational Behavior, 20,* 1003–1025.

Ilgen, D. R., & Pulakos, E. D. (Eds.). (1999). *The changing nature of performance: Implications for staffing, motivation, and development.* San Francisco, CA: Jossey-Bass.

Inciardi, J. A., Surratt, H. L., & Saum, C. A. (1997). *Cocaine-exposed infants: Social, legal, and public health issues.* Thousand Oaks, CA: Sage.

Ingram, R. E., Miranda, J., & Segal, Z. V. (1998). *Cognitive vulnerability to depression.* New York: Guilford Press.

International Association for the Evaluation of Education Achievement. (1999). *Trends in mathematics and science achievement around the world.* Boston: Lynch School of Education, Boston College.

Ironson, G., Wynings, C., Schneiderman, N., Baum, A., Rodriguez, M., Greenwood, D., Benight, C., Antoni, M., LaPerriere, A., Huang, H. B . S., Klimas, N., & Fletcher, M. A. (1997). Posttraumatic stress symptoms, intrusive thoughts, loss, and immune function after Hurricane Andrew. *Psychosomatic Medicine, 59,* 128–141.

Irvin, J. E., Bowers, C. A., Dunn, M. E., & Wang, M. C. (1999). Efficacy of relapse prevention: A meta-analytic review. *Journal of Consulting and Clinical Psychology, 67,* 563–570.

Irwin, M., Daniels, M., Smith, T., Bloom, E., & Weiner, H. (1987). Impaired natural killer cell activity during bereavement. *Brain, Behavior, and Immunity, 1,* 98–104.

Iversen, L. L., & Snyder, S. H. (2000). *The science of marijuana.* Oxford, England: Oxford University Press.

Iwahashi, K., Matsuo, Y., Suwaki, H., Nakamura, K., & Ichikawa, Y. (1995). CYP2E1 and ALDH2 genotypes and alcohol dependence in Japanese. *Alcoholism Clinical and Experimental Research, 19*(3), 564–566.

Izard, C. E. (1977). *Human emotions.* New York: Plenum.

Izard, C. E. (1993). Organizational and motivational functions of discrete emotions. In M. Lewis & J. M. Haviland (Eds.), *Handbook of emotions.* New York: Guilford.

Jacob, S., & McClintock, M. K. (2000). Psychological state and mood effects of steroidal chemosignals in women and men. *Hormones and Behavior, 37,* 57–78.

Jacobson, N. S., & Hollon, S. D. (1996). Cognitive-behavior therapy versus pharmacotherapy: Now that the jury's returned its verdict, it's time to present the rest of the evidence. *Journal of Consulting and Clinical Psychology, 64,* 74–80.

Jacobson, N. S., Christensen, A., Prince, S. E., Cordova, J., & Eldridge, K. (2000). Integrative behavioral couples therapy: An acceptance-based, promising new treatment for couple discord. *Journal of Consulting and Clinical Psychology, 68,* 351–355.

Jaffee, S., & Hyde, J. S. (2000). Gender differences in moral orientation: A meta-analysis. *Psychological Bulletin, 126,* 703–726.

Jagger, C., Clarke, M., & Stone, A. (1995). Predictors of survival with Alzheimer's disease: A community-based study. *Psychological Medicine, 25,* 171–177.

Jahnke, J. C., & Nowaczyk, R. H. (1998). *Cognition.* Upper Saddle River, NJ: Prentice-Hall.

James, W. (1890). *Principles of psychology.* New York: Holt.

James, W. (1892). *Psychology: briefer course.* New York: Holt.

Jancke, L., & Kaufmann, N. (1994). Facial EMG responses to odors in solitude and with an audience. *Chemical Senses, 19*(2), 99–111.

Janig, W. (1996). Neurobiology of visceral afferent neurons: Neuroanatomy, functions, organ regulations and sensations. *Biological Psychology, 5,* 29–51.

Janis, I. L. (1989). *Crucial decisions: Leadership in policy making and crisis management.* New York: Free Press.

Janowiak, J. J., & Hackman, R. (1994). Meditation and college students' self-actualization and rated stress. *Psychological Reports, 75*(2), 1007–1010.

Janowitz, H. D. (1967). Role of gastrointestinal tract in the regulation of food intake. In C. F. Code (Ed.), *Handbook of physiology: Alimentary canal 1.* Washington, DC: American Physiological Society.

Jensen, J. P., Bergin, A. E., & Greaves, D. W. (1990). The meaning of eclecticism: New survey and analysis of components. *Professional Psychology: Research and Practice, 21,* 124–130.

Jensen, M., & Karoly, P. (1991). Control beliefs, coping efforts, and adjustment to chronic pain. *Journal of Consulting and Clinical Psychology, 59,* 431–438.

Jhanwar, U. M., Beck, B., Jhanwar, Y. S., & Burlet, C. (1993). Neuropeptide Y projection from the arcuate nucleus to the parvocellular division of the paraventricular nucleus: Specific relation to the ingestion of carbohydrate. *Brain Research, 631*(1), 97–106.

Johnson, J., & Vickers, Z. (1993). Effects of flavor and macronutrient composition of food servings on liking, hunger and subsequent intake. *Appetite, 21*(1), 25–39.

Johnson, J. G., Cohen, P., Dohrenwend, B. P., Link, B. G., & Brook, J. S. (1999). A longitudinal investigation of social causation and social selection processes involved in the association between socioeconomic status and psychiatric disorders. *Journal of Abnormal Psychology, 108,* 490–499.

Johnson, J. M., Seikel, J. A., Madison, C. L., & Foose, S. M. (1997). Standardized test performance of children with a history of prenatal exposure to multiple drugs/cocaine. *Journal of Communication Disorders, 30,* 45–73.

Johnson, J. S., & Newport, E. L. (1989). Critical period effects in second language learning. *Cognitive Psychology, 21,* 60–99.

Johnson, M. A., Dziurawiec, S., Ellis, H., & Morton, J. (1991). Newborns' preferential tracking of face-like stimuli and its subsequent decline. *Cognition, 4,* 1–19.

Johnson, W. R., & Neal, D. (1998). Basic skills and the black-white earnings gap. In C. Jencks & M. Phillips (Eds.), *The black-white test score gap* (pp. 480–497). Washington, DC: Brookings Institute Press.

Johnson-Laird, P. N. (1983). *Mental models.* Cambridge: Cambridge University Press.

Johnston, K. (1988). Adolescents' solutions to dilemmas in fables: Two moral orientations. In C. Gilligan, J. V. Ward, J. M. Taylor, & B. Bardige (Eds.), *Mapping the moral domain: A contribution to psychological theory and education.* Cambridge, MA: Harvard University Press.

Jones, E. E. (1982). Psychotherapists' impressions of treatment outcome as a function of race. *Journal of Clinical Psychology, 38,* 722–731.

Jones, G. V. (1990). Misremembering a common object: When left is not right. *Memory & Cognition, 18,* 174–182.

Jones, L. V., & Appelbaum, M. I. (1989). Psychometric methods. *Annual Review of Psychology, 40,* 23–44.

Jordan, N. C., Huttenlocher, J., & Levine, S. C. (1992). Differential calculation abilities in young children from middle- and low-income families. *Developmental Psychology, 28,* 644–653.

Jorgensen, R. S., Johnson, B. T., Kolodziej, M. E., & Schreer, G. E. (1996). Elevated blood pressure and personality: A meta-analytic review. *Psychological Bulletin, 120,* 293–320.

Josephson, W. L. (1987). Television violence and children's aggression: Testing the priming, social script, and disinhibition predictions. *Journal of Personality and Social Psychology, 53,* 882–890.

Joy, J. E., Watson, S. J., Jr., & Benson, J. A., Jr. (1999). *Marijuana and medicine: Assessing the science base.* Washington, DC: National Academy Press.

Julien, R. M. (1995). *A primer of drug action* (7th ed.). New York: Freeman.

Julien, R. M. (1997) *A Primer of Drug Action: A Concise, Nontechnical Guide to the Actions, Uses, and Side Effects of Psychoactive Drugs* (8th ed.). New York: Freeman.

Jung, C. G. (1916). *Analytical psychology.* New York: Moffat.

Jung, C. G. (1933). *Psychological types.* New York: Harcourt, Brace and World.

Just, N., & Alloy, L. B. (1997). The response styles theory of depression: Tests and an extension of the theory. *Journal of Abnormal Psychology, 106,* 221–229.

Kagan, J. R., & Snidman, N. (1991). Temperamental factors in human development. *American Psychologist, 46,* 856–862.

Kagan, J. R., Snidman, N., Arcus, D., & Resnick, J. S. (1994). *Galen's prophecy: Temperament in human nature.* New York: Basic Books.

Kahen, V., Katz, L. F., & Gottman, J. M. (1994). Linkages between parent-child interaction and conversations of friends. *Social Development, 3,* 238–254.

Kahn, D. A. (1995). New strategies in bipolar disorder: Part II. Treatment. *Journal of Practical Psychiatry and Behavioral Health, 3,* 148–157.

Kahneman, D., & Tversky, A. (1984). Choices, values, and frames. *American Psychologist, 29,* 341–356.

Kales, A., & Kales, J. (1973). Recent advances in the diagnosis and treatment of sleep disorders. In G. Usdin (Ed.), *Sleep research and clinical practice.* New York: Brunner/Mazel.

Kalichman, S. C., Cherry, C., & Browne-Sperling, F. (1999). Effectiveness of a video-based motivational skills-building HIV risk-reduction intervention for inner-city African American men. *Journal of Consulting and Clinical Psychology, 67,* 959–966.

Kanki, B. J., & Foushee, H. C. (1990). Crew factors in the aerospace workplace. In S. Oskamp & S. Spacepan (Eds.), *People's reactions to technology* (pp. 18–31). Newbury Park, CA: Sage.

Kanner, B. (1995). *Are you normal?* New York: St. Martin's Press.

Kaplan, M. F. (1987). The influencing process in group decision making. In C. Hendrick (Ed.), *Group processes.* Newbury Park, CA: Sage.

Kaplan, M. F., & Miller, C. E. (1987). Group decision making and normative vs. informational influence: Effects of type of issue and assigned decision rule. *Journal of Personality and Social Psychology, 53,* 306–313.

Kapur, N. (1999). Syndromes of retrograde amnesia: A conceptual and empirical synthesis. *Psychological Bulletin, 125,* 800–825.

Kapur, S., & Mann, J. J. (1993). Antidepressant action and the neurobiologic effects of ECT: Human studies. In C. E. Coffey (Ed.), *The clinical science of electroconvulsive therapy.* Washington, DC: American Psychiatric Press.

Karau, S. J., & Williams, K. D. (1997). The effects of group cohesiveness on social loafing and social compensation. *Group Dynamics, 1,* 156–168.

Karni, A., Tanne, D., Rubenstein, B. S., Askenasy, J. J. M., & Sagi, D. (1994). Dependence on REM sleep of overnight improvement of a perceptual skill. *Science, 265,* 679–682.

Karon, B. P., & Widener, A. J. (1997). Repressed memories and World War II: Lest we forget. *Professional Psychology: Research and Practice, 28*(4), 338–340.

Kashani, J. H., Orvaschel, H., Rosenberg, T. K., & Reid, J. C. (1989). Psychopathology in a community sample of children and adolescents: A developmental perspective. *Journal of the American Academy of Child and Adolescent Psychiatry, 28,* 701–706.

Kass, S. (1999). Frequent testing means better grades, studies find. *APA Monitor, 30,* 10.

Kassin, S. M., Rigby, S., & Castillo, S. R. (1991). The accuracy-confidence correlation in eyewitness testimony: Limits and extensions of the retrospective self-awareness effect. *Journal of Personality and Social Psychology, 61,* 698–707.

Kastenbaum, R., Kastenbaum, B. K., & Morris, J. (1989). Strengths and preferences of the terminally ill: Data from the National Hospice Demonstration Study.

Kato, S., Wakasa, Y., & Yamagita, T. (1987). Relationship between minimum reinforcing doses and injection speed in cocaine and pentobarbital self-administration in crab-eating monkeys. *Pharmacology, Biochemistry, and Behavior, 28,* 407–410.

Katzell, R. A., & Thompson, D. E. (1990). Work motivation: Theory and practice. *American Psychologist, 45,* 144–153.

Kauffman, N. A., Herman, C. P., & Polivy, J. (1995). Hunger–induced finickiness in humans. *Appetite, 24,* 203–218.

Kaufman, L., & Kaufman J. H. (2000). Explaining the moon illusion. *Proceedings of the National Academy of Sciences of the United States of America, 97,* 500–505.

Kaufman, M. H. (1997). The teratogenic effects of alcohol following exposure during pregnancy, and its influence on the chromosome constitution of the pre-ovulatory egg. *Alcohol and Alcoholism, 32,* 113–128.

Kavanagh, D. J. (1992). Recent developments in expressed emotion in schizophrenia. *British Journal of Psychiatry, 160,* 601–620.

Kawachi, I., Colditz, G. A., & Stone, C. B. (1994). Does drinking coffee increase the risk of coronary heart disease? Results from a meta-analysis. *British Heart Journal, 72*(3), 269–275.

Kaye, W. H., Klump, K. L., Frank, G. K., & Strober, M. (2000). Anorexia and bulimia nervosa. *Annual Review of Medicine, 51,* 299–313.

Kazdin, A. E. (1977). *The token economy: Review and evaluation.* New York: Plenum.

Kazdin, A. E. (1994). *Behavior modification in applied settings* (5th ed.). Pacific Grove, CA: Brooks/Cole.

Kazdin, A. E., & Weisz, J. R. (1998). Identifying and developing empirically supported child and adolescent treatments. *Journal of Consulting and Clinical Psychology, 66,* 19–36.

Keating, D. P. (1990). Adolescent thinking. In S. S. Feldman & G. R. Elliott (Eds.), *At the threshold: The developing adolescent* (pp. 4–89). Cambridge, MA: Harvard University Press.

Kee, M., Hill, S. M., & Weist, M. D. School-based behavior management of cursing, hitting, and spitting in a girl with profound retardation. *Education and Treatment of Children, 22,* 171–178.

Keefe, F. J., & France, C. R. (1999). Pain: Biopsychosocial mechanisms and management. *Current Directions in Psychological Science, 8,* 137–141.

Keeling, P. J., & Roger, A. J. (1995). The selfish pursuit of sex. *Nature, 375,* 283.

Keesey, R. E., & Powley, T. L. (1986). The regulation of body weight. *Annual Review of Psychology, 37,* 109–133.

Keinan, G., Friedland, N., & Ben-Porath, Y. (1987). Decision making under stress: Scanning of alternatives under physical threat. *Acta Psychologica, 64,* 219–228.

Keller, M. B., McCullough, J. P., Klein, D. N., Arnow, B., Dunner, D. L., Gelenberg, A. J., Markowitz, J. C., Nemeroff, C. B., Russell, J. M., Thase, M. E., Trivedi, M. H., Zajecka, J., Blalock, J. A., Borian, F. E., DeBattista, C., Fawcett, J., Hirschfeld, R. M. A., Jody, D. N., Keitner, G., Kocsis, J. H., Koran, L. M., Kornstein, S. G., Manber, R., Miller, I., Ninan, P. T., Rothbaum, B., Rush, A. J., Schatzberg, A. F., & Vivian, D. . (2000). A comparison of nefazodone, the cognitive behavioral-analysis system of psychotherapy, and their combination for the treatment of chronic depression. *The New England Journal of Medicine, 342,* 1462–1470.

Kelley, K. W. (1985). Immunological consequences of changing environmental stimuli. In G. P. Moberg (Ed.), *Animal stress.* Bethesda, MD: American Physiological Society.

Kellman, P. J., & Banks, M. S. (1998). Infant visual perception. In W. Damon, D. Kuhn, & R. Siegler (Eds.), *Handbook of child psychology: Vol. 2. Cognition, language and perception* (5th ed., pp. 103–146). New York: Wiley.

Kelly, T. H., Foltin, R. W., Emurian, C. S., & Fischman, M. W. (1990). Multidimensional behavioral effects of marijuana. *Progress in Neuro-Psychopharmacology and Biological Psychiatry, 14,* 885–902.

Kelter, D., & Buswell, B. N. (1996). Evidence for the distinctiveness of embarrassment, shame, and guilt: A study of recalled antecedents and facial expressions of emotion. *Cognition and Emotion, 10,* 117–125

Kemble, E. D., Filipi, T., & Gravlin, L. (1985) Some simple classroom experiments on cerebral lateralization. *Teaching of Psychology, 12,* 81–83.

Kemeny, M. E., & Dean, L. (1995). Effects of AIDS-related bereavement on HIV progression among New York City gay men. *AIDS Education and Prevention, 7,* 36–47.

Kendall, P. C. (1999). Clinical significance. *Journal of Consulting and Clinical Psychology, 67,* 283–284.

Kendall, P. C., & Chambless, D. L. (Eds.). (1998) Special section: Empirically supported psychological therapies. *Journal of Consulting and Clinical Psychology, 66,* 3–167.

Kendler, K. S., & Diehl, N. S. (1993). The genetics of schizophrenia: A current genetic-epidemiologic perspective. *Schizophrenia Bulletin, 19,* 87–112.

Kendler, K. S., Heath, A. C., Neale, M. C., Kessler, R. C., & Eaves, L. J. (1992). A population-based twin study of alcoholism in women. *Journal of the American Medical Association, 268,* 1877–1882.

Kendler, K. S., Kessler, R. C., Walters, E. E., MacLean, C., Neale, M. C., Heath, A. C., & Eaves, L. J. (1995). Stressful life events, genetic liability, and onset of an episode of major depression in women. *American Journal of Psychiatry, 152,* 833–842.

Kendler, K. S., Neale, M. C., Kessler, R. C., Heath, A. C., & Eaves, L. J. (1992). Major depression and generalized anxiety disorder: Same genes (partly) different environments? *Archives of General Psychiatry, 49,* 716–722.

Kendler, K. S., Thorton, L. M., & Gardner, C. O. (2000). Stressful life events and previous episodes in the etiology of major depression in women: An evaluation of the "kindling" hypothesis. *American Journal of Psychiatry, 157,* 1243–1251.

Kenrick, D. T. (1994). Evolutionary social psychology: From sexual selection to social cognition. In M. Zanna (Ed.), *Advances in experimental social psychology* (Vol. 26, pp. 75–122). San Diego, CA: Academic Press.

Kenrick, D. T., Neuberg, S. L., & Cialdini, R.B. (1999). *Social psychology: Unraveling the mystery.* Boston: Allyn & Bacon.

Kenrick, D. T., Groth, G., Trost, M., & Sadalla, E. K. (1993). Integrating evolutionary and social exchange perspectives on relationships: Effects of gender, self-appraisal, and involvement level on mate selection. *Journal of Personality and Social Psychology, 64,* 951–969.

Kent, S., Rodriguez, F., Kelley, K. W., & Dantzer, R. (1994). Reduction in food and water intake induced by microinjection of interleukin-1b in the ventromedial hypothalamus of the rat. *Physiology and Behavior, 56*(5), 1031–1036.

Kernberg, O. (1976). *Object relations theory and clinical psychoanalysis.* New York: Jason Aronsen.

Kerr, M. P., & Payne, S. J. (1994). Learning to use a spreadsheet by doing and by watching. *Interacting with Computers, 6,* 3–22.

Kessler, R. C. (1997). The effects of stressful life events on depression. In J. T. Spence, J. M. Darley, & D. J. Foss (Eds.), *Annual Review of Psychology, 48,* 191–214.

Kessler, R. C., Berglund, P. A., Zhao, S., Leaf, P. J., Kouzis, A. C., Bruce, M. L., Friedman, R. M., Grossier, R. C., Kennedy, C., Narrow, W. E., Kuehnel, T. G., Laska, E. M., Manderscheid, R. W., Rosenheck, R. A., Santoni, T. W., & Schneier, M. (1996). The 12-month prevalence and correlates of serious mental illness. In R. W. Manderscheid & M. A. Sonnenschein (Eds.), *Mental health, United States, 1996* (DHHS Publication No. [SMA] 96-3098, pp. 59–70). Washington, DC: U.S. Government Printing Office.

Kessler, R. C., McGonagle, K. A., Zhao, S., Nelson, C. B., Hughes, M., Eshleman, S., Wittchen, H. U., & Kendler, K. S. (1994). Lifetime and 12-month prevalence of DSM-III-R psychiatric disorders in the United States. *Archives of General Psychiatry, 51,* 8–19.

Kety, S. S., Wender, P. H., Jacobsen, B., Ingraham, L. J., Jansson, L., Faber, B., & Kinney, D. K. (1994). Mental illness in the biological and adoptive relatives of schizophrenic adoptees. *Archives of General Psychiatry, 51,* 442–455.

Kiecolt-Glaser, J. K., & Glaser, R. (1992). Psychoneuroimmunology: Can psychological interventions modulate immunity? *Journal of Consulting and Clinical Psychology, 60,* 569–575.

Kiecolt-Glaser, J. K., Page, G. G., Marucha, P. T., MacCallum, R. C., & Glaser, R. (1998). Psychological influences on surgical recovery: Perspectives from psychoneuroimmunology. *American Psychologist, 53,* 1209–1218.

Kiesler, D. J. (1996). *Contemporary interpersonal theory and research.* New York: Wiley.

Kihlstrom, J. F. (1999). The psychological unconscious. In L. Pervin & O. John (Eds.), *Handbook of personality* (pp. 424–442). New York: Guilford.

Kilbey, M. M. (1999). One academic's viewpoint on prescription privileges. *APA Monitor*, December, p. 11.

Killen, J. D., Fortmann, S. P., Davis, L., & Varady, A. (1997). Nicotine patch and self-help video for cigarette smoking cessation. *Journal of Consulting and Clinical Psychology, 65,* 663–672.

Kimble, G. A. (1999). Functional behaviorism: A plan for unity in psychology. *American Psychologist, 54,* 981–988.

Kimmel, A. J. (1998). In defense of deception. *American Psychologist, 53,* 803–805.

King, J., & Pribram, K. H. (Eds.). (1995). *The scale of conscious experience: Is the brain too important to be left to specialists to study?* Mahwah, NJ: Erlbaum.

Kinsbourne, M., & Cook, J. (1971). Generalized and lateralized effects of concurrent verbalization on a unimanual skill. *Quarterly Journal of Experimental Psychology, 23,* 341–345.

Kinsey, A. C., Pomeroy, W. B., & Martin, C. E. (1948). *Sexual behavior in the human male.* Philadelphia: Saunders.

Kinsey, A. C., Pomeroy, W. B., Martin, C. E., & Gebhard, P. H. (1953). *Sexual behavior in the human female.* Philadelphia: Saunders.

Kircher, J. C., Horowitz, S. W., & Raskin, D. C. (1988). Meta-analysis of mock crime studies of the control question polygraph technique. *Law and Human Behavior, 12,* 79–90.

Kirsch, I. (1994a). Defining hypnosis for the public. *Contemporary Hypnosis, 11*(3), 142–143.

Kirsch, I. (1994b). Clinical hypnosis as a nondeceptive placebo: Empirically derived techniques. *American Journal of Clinical Hypnosis, 37*(2), 95–106.

Kishioka, S., Miyamoto, Y., Fukunaga, Y., Nishida, S., & Yamamoto, H. (1994). Effects of a mixture of peptidase inhibitors (Amastatin, Captopril and Phosphoramidon) on met enkephalin, beta-endorphin, dynorphin (1–13) and electroacupuncture-induced antinociception in rats. *Japanese Journal of Pharmacology, 1994, 66,* 337–345.

Kitano, H., Chi, I., Rhee, S., Law, C., & Lubben, J. (1992). Norms and alcohol consumption: Japanese in Japan, Hawaii, and California. *Journal of Studies on Alcohol, 53,* 33–39.

Kitayama, S., & Markus, H. R. (1992, May). *Construal of self as cultural frame: Implications for internationalizing psychology.* Paper presented to the Symposium on Internationalization and Higher Education, Ann Arbor.

Kitayama, S., Markus, H. R., Matsumoto, H., & Norasakkunkit, V. (1997). Individual and collective processes in the construction of the self: Self-enhancement in the United States and self-criticism in Japan. *Journal of Personality and Social Psychology, 72,* 1245–1267.

Kjellberg, A., Landstrom, U., Tesarz, M., Soderberg, L., & Akerlund, E. (1996). The effects of nonphysical noise characteristics, ongoing task and noise sensitivity on annoyance and distraction due to noise at work. *Journal of Environmental Psychology, 16,* 123–136.

Klahr, D., & Simon, H. (1999). Studies of scientific discovery: Complementary approaches and convergent findings. *Psychological Bulletin, 125,* 524–543.

Klaus, M. H., & Kennell, J. H. (1976). *Maternal infant bonding: The impact of early separation or loss on family development.* St. Louis: Mosby.

Klein, D. C., & Seligman, M. E. P. (1976). Reversal of performance deficits and perceptual deficits in learned helplessness and depression. *Journal of Abnormal Psychology, 85,* 11–26.

Klein, D. N. (1993). False suffocation alarms, spontaneous panics, and related conditions: An integrative hypothesis. *Archives of General Psychiatry, 50,* 306–316.

Klein, J. G. (1991). Negativity effects in impression formation: A test in the political arena. *Personality and Social Psychology Bulletin, 17,* 412–418.

Klein, M. (1975). *The writings of Melanie Klein: Vol. 3.* London: Hogarth Press.

Klein, R. A. (1999). Treating fear of flying with virtual reality exposure therapy. In L. VandeCreek & T. L. Jackson (Eds.), *Innovations in clinical practice: A sourcebook, Vol. 17.* Sarasota, FL: Professional Resource Press.

Kleinknecht, R. A. (1991). *Mastering anxiety: The nature and treatment of anxious conditions.* New York: Plenum.

Kleinknecht, R. A. (1994). Acquisition of blood, injury, and needle fears and phobias. *Behaviour Research and Therapy, 32,* 817–823.

Kleinknecht, R. A. (2000). Social phobia. In M. Hersen & M. K. Biaggio (Eds.), *Effective brief therapies: A clinician's guide.* New York: Academic Press.

Kleinknecht, R. A., Dinnel, D. L., Tanouye-Wilson, S., & Lonner, W. (1994). Cultural variation in social anxiety and phobia: A study of Taijin Kyofusho. *The Behavior Therapist, 17,* 175–178.

Kleinman, A. (1991, April). *Culture and DSM-IV: Recommendations for the introduction and for the overall structure.* Paper presented at the National Institute of Mental Health–sponsored Conference on Culture and Diagnosis, Pittsburgh, PA.

Klepp, K.-I., Kelder, S. H., & Perry, C. L. (1995). Alcohol and marijuana use among adolescents: Long-term outcomes of the class of 1989 study. *Annals of Behavioral Medicine, 17,* 19–24.

Klerman, G. L., & Weissman, M. M. (Eds.). (1993). *New applications of interpersonal therapy.* Washington, DC: American Psychiatric Press.

Klesges, R. C., Haddock, C. K., Lando, H., & Talcott, G. W. (1999). Efficacy of forced smoking cessation and an adjunctive behavioral treatment on long-term smoking rates. *Journal of Consulting and Clinical Psychology, 67,* 952–958.

Klich, N. R., & Feldman, D. C. (1992). The role of approcal and achievement needs in feedback-seeking behavior. *Journal of Managerial Issues, 4*(4), 554–570.

Kline, S., & Groninger, L. D. (1991). The imagery bizarreness effect as a function of sentence complexity and presentation time. *Bulletin of the Psychonomic Society, 29,* 25–27.

Kling, K. C., Hyde, J. S., Showers, C. J., & Buswell, B. N. (1999). Gender differences in self-esteem: A meta-analysis. *Psychological Bulletin, 125,* 470–500.

Klonoff-Cohen, H. S., & Edelstein, S. L. (1995). A case-control study of routine death scene sleep position in sudden infant death syndrome in Southern California. *Journal of the American Medical Association, 273*(10), 790–794.

Klosko, J. S., Barlow, D. H., Tassinari, R., & Cerny, J. A. (1990). A comparison of alprazolam and behavior therapy in treatment of panic disorder. *Journal of Consulting and Clinical Psychology, 58,* 77–84.

Kluger, A. N., & DeNisi, A. (1998). Feedback interventions: Toward the understanding of a double-edged sword. *Current Directions in Psychological Science, 7,* 67–72.

Kohlberg, L., & Gilligan, C. (1971). The adolescent as a philosopher: The discovery of the self in a postconventional world. *Daedalus, 100,* 1051–1086.

Köhler, W. (1924). *The mentality of apes.* New York: Harcourt Brace.

Kohut, H. (1984). Selected problems of self-psychological theory. In J. D. Lichtenberg & S. Kaplan (Eds.), *Reflections on self psychology* (pp. 387–416). Hillsdale, NJ: Erlbaum.

Kok, M. R., & Boon, M. E. (1996). Consequences of neural network technology for cervical screening: increase in diagnostic consistency and positive scores. *Cancer, 78,* 112–117.

Kondo, T., & Raff, M. (2000). Oligodendrocyte precursor cells reprogrammed to become multipotential CNS stem cells. *Science, 289,* 1754–1757.

Koob, G. F., & Bloom, F. E. (1988). Cellular and molecular mechanisms of drug dependence. *Science, 242,* 715–723.

Koob, G. F., Roberts, A. J., Schulteis, G., Parsons, L. H., Heyser, C. J., Hyytia, P., Merlo-Pich, E., & Weiss, F. (1998). Neurocircuitry targets in ethanol reward and dependence. *Alcohol: Clinical and Experimental Research, 22*(1), 3–9.

Koopmans, J. R., & Boomsma, D. I. (1996). Familial resemblance in alcohol use: Genetic or cultural transmission? *Journal of Studies in Alcoholism, 57,* 19–28.

Kopelman, P. G. (2000). Obesity as a medical problem. *Nature, 404,* 635–43.

Koppenaal, L., & Glanzer, M. (1990). An examination of the continuous distractor task and the "long-term recency effect." *Memory & Cognition, 18,* 183–195.

Kordower, J. H., Freeman, T. B., Snow, B. J., Vingerhoets, F. J. G., Mufson, E. J., Sanberg, P. R., Hauser, R. A., Smith, D. A., Nauert, G. M., Perl, D. P., & Olanow, C. W. (1995). Neuropathological evidence of graft survival and striatal reinnervation after the transplantation of fetal mesencephalic tissue in a patient with Parkinson's disease. *The New England Journal of Medicine, 332,* 1118–1124.

Kornhaber, M., Krechevsky, M., & Gardner, H. (1990). Engaging intelligence. *Educational Psychologist, 25,* 177–199.

Korteling, J. (1991). Effects of skill integration and perceptual competition on age-related differences in dual-task performance. *Human Factors, 33,* 35–44.

Kosslyn, S. M. (1976). Can imagery be distinguished from other forms of internal representation? Evidence from studies of information retrieval times. *Memory & Cognition, 4,* 291–297.

Krakauer, J. (1997). *Into thin air.* New York: Villard.

Krantz, D., & Durel, L. (1983). Psychobiological substrates of the Type A behavior pattern. *Health Psychology, 2,* 393–411.

Krantz, D., Contrada, R., Hill, D., & Friedler, E. (1988). Environmental stress and biobehavioral antecedents of coronary heart disease. *Journal of Consulting and Clinical Psychology, 56,* 333–341.

Kranzler, H. R., & Anton, R. F. (1994). Implications of recent neuropsychopharmacologic research for understanding the etiology and development of alcoholism. *Journal of Consulting and Clinical Psychology, 62,* 1116–1126.

Kraus, S. J. (1995). Attitudes and the prediction of behavior: A meta-analysis of the empirical literature. *Personality and Social Psychology Bulletin, 21,* 58–75.

Krauzlis, R. J., & Lisberger, S. G. (1991). Visual motion commands for pursuit eye movements in the cerebellum. *Science, 253,* 568–571.

Kristof, N. D. (1997, August 17). Where children rule. *New York Times Magazine.*

Krosnick, J. A., Betz, A. L., Jussim, L. J., & Lynn, A. R. (1992). Subliminal conditioning of attitudes. *Personality and Social Psychology Bulletin, 18,* 152–162.

Krueger, J. (1998). Enhancement bias in descriptions of self and others. *Personality and Social Psychology Bulletin, 24,* 505–516.

Krueger, J., Ham, J. J., & Linford, K. M. (1996). Perceptions of behavioral consistency: Are people aware of the actor-observer effect? *Psychological Science, 7,* 259–264.

Kruger, J., & Dunning, D. (1999) Unskilled and unaware of it: How difficulties in recognizing one's own incompetence lead to inflated self-assessments. *Journal of Personality & Social Psychology, 77,* 1121–1134.

Krykouli, S. E., Stanley, B. G., Seirafi, R. D., & Leibowitz, S. F (1990). Stimulation of feeding by galanin: Anatomical localization and behavioral specificity of this peptide's effects in the brain. *Peptides, 11*(5), 995–1001.

Kulynych, J. J., & Stromberg, C. (1998). Legal Update #11: Telecommunication in psychological practice. *Register Report, 24*(1/2), 9–18.

Kunkel, D., Wilson, B. J., Linz, D., Potter, J., Donnerstein, E., Smith, S. L., Blumenthal, E., & Gray, T. (1996). *The national television violence study.* Studio City, CA: Mediascope.

Kunz, P. R., & Woolcott, M. (1976). Season's greetings: From my status to yours. *Social Science Research, 5,* 269–278.

Kurtz, L. F. (1997). *Self-help and support groups: A handbook for practitioners.* Thousand Oaks, CA: Sage.

Kushner, M. G., Thuras, P., Kaminski, J., Anderson, N., Neumeyer, B., & Mackenzie, T. (2000). Expectancies for alcohol to affect tension and anxiety as a function of time. *Addictive Behaviors, 25,* 93–98.

Kutchins, H., & Kirk, S. A. (1997). *Making us crazy: The psychiatric bible and the creation of mental disorders.* New York: Free Press.

Kwan, M., Greenleaf, W. J., Mann, J., Crapo, L., & Davidson, J. M. (1983). The nature of androgen action on male sexuality: A combined laboratory-self-report study on hypogonadal men. *Journal of Clinical Endocrinology and Metabolism, 57,* 557–562.

Kwan, V. S. Y., Bond, M. H., & Singelis, T. M. (1997). Pancultural explanations for life satisfaction: Adding relationship harmony to self-esteem. *Journal of Personality and Social Psychology, 73,* 1038–1051.

Laan, E., Everaerd, W., Van Aanhold, M. T., & Rebel, M. (1993). Performance demand and sexual arousal in woman. *Behavior Research and Therapy, 31,* 25–36.

LaBerge, S. (1993). Lucid dreaming. In M. Carskadon (Ed.), *Encyclopedia of sleep and dreaming* (pp. 338–341). New York: Macmillan.

Labouvie-Vief, G. (1982). Discontinuities in development from childhood. In T. M. Field, A. Huston, H. C. Quay, L. Troll, & G. E. Finley (Eds.), *Review of human development.* New York: Wiley.

Labouvie-Vief, G. (1992). A new-Piagetian perspective on adult cognitive development. In R. J. Sternberg & C. A. Berg (Eds.), *Intellectual development.* New York: Cambridge University Press.

Lacayo, A. (1995). Neurologic and psychiatric complications of cocaine abuse. *Neuropsychiatry, Neuropsychology, and Behavioral Neurology, 8*(1), 53–60.

LaFromboise, T. D., Foster, S., & James, A. (1996). *Ethics in multicultural counseling.* Thousand Oaks, CA: Sage.

Lagerspetz, K. M. J., & Lagerspetz, K. Y. H. (1983). Genes and aggression. In E. C. Simmel, M. E. Hahn, & J. K. Walters (Eds.), *Aggressive behavior: Genetic and neural approaches.* Hillsdale, NJ: Erlbaum.

LaGreca, A. M., Silverman, W. K., Vernberg, E. M., & Prinstein, M. J. (1996). Symptoms of posttraumatic stress in children after Hurricane Andrew: A prospective study. *Journal of Consulting and Clinical Psychology, 64,* 712–723.

Lahey, B. B., Applegate, B., Barkley, R., Garfinkel, B., McBurnett, K., Kerdyk, L., Greenhill, L., Hynd, G., Frick, P., Newcorn, J., Biederman, J., Ollendick, T., Hart, E., Perez, D., Waldman, I., & Shaffer, D. (1994). DSM-IV Field Trials for oppositional defiant disorder and conduct disorder in children and adolescents. *American Journal of Psychiatry, 151,* 1163–1171.

Lahey, B. B., Loeber, R., Hart, E. L., Frick, P. J., & Applegate, B. (1995). Four-year longitudinal study of conduct disorder in boys: Patterns and predictors of persistence. *Journal of Abnormal Psychology, 104,* 83–93.

Lamar, J. (2000). Suicides in Japan reach a record high. *British Medical Journal, 321,* 528.

Lamb, M. E. (1976). Parent-infant interaction in 8-month-olds. *Child Psychiatry and Human Development, 7,* 56–63.

Lambert, N. M. (1999). Developmental trajectories in psychology: Applications to education and training. *American Psychologist, 54,* 991–1002.

Lambert, M. J., & Bergin, A. E. (1994). The effectiveness of psychotherapy. In A. E. Bergin & S. L. Garfield (Eds.), *Handbook of psychotherapy and behavior change* (4th ed.). New York: Wiley.

Landau, B. (1986). Early map use as an unlearned ability. *Cognition, 22,* 201–223.

Landrine, H. (1991). Revising the framework of abnormal psychology. In P. Bronstein & K. Quina (Eds.), *Teaching a psychology of people.* Washington, DC: American Psychological Association.

Landrine, H., & Klonoff, E. (1992). Culture and health-related schemas: A review and proposal for interdisciplinary integration. *Health Psychology, 11,* 267–276.

Landsdale, M., & Laming, D. (1995). Evaluating the fragmentation hypothesis: The analysis of errors in cued recall. *Acta Psychologica, 88,* 33–77.

Lang, P. J. (1995). The emotion probe: Studies of motivation and attention. *American Psychologist, 50*(5), 372–385.

Lang, P. J., & Melamed, B. G. (1969). Avoidance conditioning therapy of an infant with chronic ruminative vomiting. *Journal of Abnormal Psychology, 74,* 1–8.

Langlois, J. H., Kalakanis, L., Rubenstein, A. J., Larson, A., Hallam, M., & Smoot, M. (2000). Maxims or myths of beauty: A meta-analytic and theoretical review. *Psychological Bulletin, 126,* 390–423.

Lapchak, P. A., Araujo, D. M., Hilt, D. C., Sheng J., & Jiao, S. (1997). Adenoviral vector-mediated GDNF gene therapy in a rodent lesion model of late stage Parkinson's disease. *Brain Research, 777,* 153–160.

Lara, M. E., & Klein, D. N. (1999). Psychosocial processes underlying the maintenance and persistence of depression: Implications for understanding chronic depression. *Clinical Psychology Review, 19,* 533–570.

Larson, J. R., Jr., Christensen, C., Franz, T. M., & Abbott, A. S. (1998). Diagnosing groups: The pooling, management, and impact of shared and unshared case information in team-based medical decision making. *Journal of Personality and Social Psychology, 75,* 93–108.

Larson, R. W., & Verma, S. (1999). How children and adolescents spend time across the world: Work, play, and developmental opportunities. *Psychological Bulletin, 125,* 701–736.

Latané, B. (1981). The psychology of social impact. *American Psychologist, 36,* 343–356.

Latané, B., & Rodin, J. (1969). A lady in distress: Inhibiting effects of friends and strangers on bystander intervention. *Journal of Experimental Social Psychology, 5,* 189–202.

Lau, M. A., Pihl, R. O., & Peterson, J. B. (1995). Provocation, acute alcohol intoxication, cognitive performance, and aggression. *Journal of Abnormal Psychology, 104,* 150–155.

Laughery, K. R. (1999). Modeling human performance during system design. In E. Salas (Ed.), *Human/technology interaction in complex systems* (Vol. 9, pp. 147–174). Stamford, CT: JAI Press.

Laumann, E. O., Gagnon, J. H., Michael, R. T., & Michaels, S. (1994). *The social organization of sexuality: Sexual practices in the United States.* Chicago: University of Chicago Press.

Laumann, E. O., Paik, A., Rosen, R. C. (1999). Sexual dysfunction in the United States: Prevalence and predictors. *Journal of the American Medical Association, 281,* 537–544.

Law, D. J., Pellegrino, J. W., & Hunt, E. B. (1993). Comparing the tortoise and the hare: Gender differences and experience in dynamic spatial reasoning tasks. *Psychological Science, 4,* 35–40.

Lawford, B. R., Young, R. M., Rowell, J. A., Qualichefski, J., Fletcher, B. H., Syndulko, K., Ritchie, T., & Noble, E. P. (1995). Bromocriptine in the treatment of alcoholics with the D2 dopamine receptor A1 allele. *Nature Medicine, 1*(4), 337–341.

Lawless, H. T., & Engen, T. (1977). Associations to odors: Interference, memories and verbal learning. *Journal of Experimental Psychology, 3,* 52–59.

Lazarus, A. A. (1971). *Behavior therapy and beyond.* New York: McGraw-Hill.

Lazarus, R. S., & Folkman, S. (1984). *Stress, appraisal, and coping.* New York: Springer-Verlag.

Lazarus, R. S., Opton, E. M., Nomikos, M. S., & Rankin, M. O. (1965). The principle of short-circuiting of threat: Further evidence. *Journal of Personality, 33,* 622–635.

LeDoux, J. E. (1995). Emotion: Clues from the brain. *Annual Review of Psychology, 46,* 209–235.

LeDoux, J. E. (1996). *The emotional brain.* New York: Simon & Schuster.

Lee, V. E., Brooks-Gunn, J., & Schnur, E. (1988). Does Head Start work? A 1-year follow-up comparison of disadvantaged children attending Head Start, no preschool, and other preschool programs. *Developmental Psychology, 24,* 210–222.

Lee, M. C., Schiffman, S. S., & Pappas, T. N. (1994). Role of neuropeptides in the regulation of feeding behavior: A review of cholecystokinin, bombesin, neuropeptide Y, and galanin. *Neuroscience and Biobehavioral Reviews, 18*(3), 313–323.

Lefcourt, H. M., Davidson, K., Prkachin, K. M., & Mills, D. E. (1997). Humor as a stress moderator in the prediction of blood pressure obtained during five stressful tasks. *Journal of Research in Personality, 31,* 523–542.

Legerstee, M., Anderson, D., & Schaffer, A. (1998). Five- and eight-month-old infants recognize their faces and voices as familiar and social stimuli. *Child Development, 69,* 37–50.

Lehman, H. E. (1967). Schizophrenia: IV. Clinical features. In A. M. Freedman, H. I. Kaplan, & H. S. Kaplan (Eds.), *Comprehensive textbook of psychiatry.* Baltimore: Williams & Wilkins.

Leibel, R. L., Rosenbaum, M., & Hirsch, J. (1995). Changes in energy expenditure resulting from altered body weight. *New England Journal of Medicine, 332*(10), 621–628.

Leigh, B. C., Schafer, J., & Temple, M. T. (1995). Alcohol use and contraception in first sexual experiences. *Journal of Behavioral Medicine. 18*(1), 81–95.

Leippe, M. R., Manion, A. P., & Romanczyk, A. (1992). Eyewitness persuasion: How and how well do fact finders judge the accuracy of adults' and children's memory reports? *Journal of Personality and Social Psychology, 63,* 181–197.

Lennard, A. L., & Jackson, G. H. (2000). Stem cell transplantation. *British Medical Journal, 321,* 433–437.

Lenneberg, E. H. (1967). *Biological foundations of language.* New York: Wiley.

Leonard, B. E. (1992). *Fundamentals of psychopharmacology.* New York: Wiley.

Leonhardt, D. (2000). Makes sense to test for common sense. Yes? No? *New York Times,* May 24, 2000.

Lepore, S. J. (1995a). Measurement of chronic stressors. In S. Cohen, R. C. Kessler, & L. U. Gordon (Eds.), *Measuring stress: A guide for health and social scientists.* New York: Oxford University Press.

Lepore, S. J. (1995b). Cynicism, social support, and cardiovascular reactivity. *Health Psychology, 14,* 210–216.

LeVay, S. (1991). A difference in hypothalamic structure between heterosexual and homosexual men. *Science, 253,* 1034–1037.

Levenson, R. W., & Ruef, A. M. (1992). Empathy: A physiological substrate. *Journal of Personality and Social Psychology, 63,* 234–246.

Levenson, R. W., Ekman, P., & Friesen, W. V. (1990). Voluntary facial action generates emotion-specific autonomic nervous system activity. *Psychophysiology, 27*(4), 363–384.

Levenson, R. W., Ekman, P., Heider, K., & Friesen, W. V. (1992). Emotion and autonomic nervous system activity in the Minangkabau of West Sumatra. *Journal of Personality and Social Psychology, 62*(6), 972–988.

Leventhal, T., & Brooks-Gunn, J. (2000). The neighborhoods they live in: The effects of neighborhood residence on child and adolescent outcomes. *Psychological Bulletin, 126,* 309–337.

Levine, J. M., & Moreland, R. L. (1998). Small groups. In D. Gilbert, S. T. Fiske, & G. Lindzey (Eds.), *Handbook of social psychology* (Vol. 2, 4th ed., pp. 415–469). Boston: McGraw-Hill.

Levine, M. W., & Schefner, J. M. (1981). *Fundamentals of sensation and perception.* Reading, MA: Addison-Wesley.

Levine, R. V., Martinez, T. M., Brase, G., & Sorenson, K. (1994). Helping in 36 U.S. cities. *Journal of Personality and Social Psychology, 67,* 69–82.

Levine, R., Sato, S., Hashimoto, T., & Verna, J. (1995). Love and marriage in eleven cultures. *Journal of Cross-Cultural Psychology, 26,* 554–571.

Levine, S. (1999). In a loud and noisy world, baby boomers pay the consequences. *International Herald Tribune,* February 1.

Levinthal, C. F. (1996). *Drugs, behavior, and modern society.* Boston: Allyn & Bacon.

Levy, R. L., Cain, K. C., Jarrett, M., & Heitkemper, M. M. (1997). The relationship between daily life stress and gastrointestinal symptoms in women with irritable bowel syndrome. *Journal of Behavioral Medicine, 20,* 177–194.

Levy-Shiff, R. (1994). Individual and contextual correlates of marital change across the transition to parenthood. *Developmental Psychology, 30,* 591–601.

Lewicki, P. (1992). Nonconscious acquisition of information. *American Psychologist, 47,* 796–801

Lewinsohn, P. M., & Rosenbaum, M. (1987). Recall of parental behavior by acute depressives, remitted depressives, and nondepressives. *Journal of Personality and Social Psychology, 52,* 611–619.

Lewis, C. E., Jacobs Jr., D. R., McCreath, H., Kiefe, C. I., Schreiner, P. J., Smith, D. E., & Williams, O. D. (2000). Weight gain continues in the 1990s: 10-year trends in weight and overweight from the CARDIA study. *American Journal of Epidemiology, 151,* 1172–1181.

Lewis, M., & Goldberg, S. (1969). Perceptual-cognitive development in infancy: A generalized expectancy model as a function of the mother-infant interaction. *Merrill-Palmer Quarterly, 15,* 81–100.

Lewontin, R. (1976). Race and intelligence. In N. J. Block & G. Dworkin (Eds.), *The IQ controversy: Critical readings.* New York: Pantheon.

Ley, R. (1994). The "suffocation alarm" theory of panic attacks: A critical commentary. *Journal of Behavior Therapy and Experimental Psychiatry, 25,* 269–273.

Liberman, R. P., Wallace, C. J., Blackwell, G., Kopelowicz, A., Vaccaro, J. V., & Mintz, J. (1998). Skills training versus psychosocial occupational therapy for persons with persistent schizophrenia. *American Journal of Psychiatry, 155,* 1087–1091.

Lichstein, K. L., & Riedel, B. W. (1994). Behavioral assessment and treatment of insomnia: A review with an emphasis on clinical application. *Behavior Therapy, 25,* 659–688.

Lichtenstein, P., Holm, N. V., Verkasalo, P. K., Iliadou, A., Kaprio, J., Koskenvuo, M., Pukkala, E., Skytthe, A., & Hemminki, K. (2000). Environmental and heritable factors in the causation of cancer–Analyses of cohorts of twins from Sweden, Denmark, and Finland. *The New England Journal of Medicine, 343,* 78–85.

Lickey, M., & Gordon, B. (1991). *Medicine and mental illness: The use of drugs in psychiatry.* San Francisco: Freeman.

Lieberman, A., & Pawl, J. (1988). Clinical applications of attachment theory. In J. Bellsky & T. Nezworski (Eds.), *Clinical applications of attachment.* Hillsdale, NJ: Erlbaum.

Lieberman, M. A., & Tobin, S. (1983). *The experience of old age.* New York: Basic Books.

Liebert, R. M., & Spiegler, M. D. (1994). *Personality: Strategies and issues.* Pacific Grove, CA: Brooks/Cole.

Liebert, R. M., & Sprafkin, J. (1988). *The early window: Effects of television on children and youth* (3rd ed.). New York: Pergamon Press.

Liepert, J., Bauder, H., Miltner, W. H. R., Taub, E., & Weiller, C. (2000). Treatment-induced cortical reorganization after stroke in humans. *Stroke, 31* , 1210.

Lilienfeld, S. O., Garb, H. N., & Wood, J. M. (2000). The scientific status of projective techniques. *Psychological Science in the Public Interest, 1,* 27–66.

Lilienfeld, S. O., Lynn, S. J., Kirsch, I., Chaves, J. F., Sarbin, T. R., Ganaway, G. K., & Powell, R. A. (1999). Dissociative identity disorder and the sociocognitive model: Recalling the lessons of the past. *Psychological Bulletin, 125,* 507–523.

Lilienfeld, S. O., & Marino, L. (1999). Essentialism revisited: Evolutionary theory and the concept of mental disorder. *Journal of Abnormal Psychology, 108,* 400–411.

Lillywhite, A. R., Wilson, S. J., & Nutt, D. J. (1994). Successful treatment of night terrors and somnambulism with paroxetine. *British Journal of Psychiatry, 16,* 551–554.

Lin, L., Umahara, M., York, D. A., & Bray, G. A. (1998). Beta-casomorphins stimulate and enterostatin inhibits the intake of dietary fat in rats. *Peptides, 19,* 325–331.

Lin, S., Thomas, T. C., Storlien, L. H., & Huang, X. F. (2000). Development of high fat diet-induced obesity and leptin resistance in C57BI/6J mice. *International Journal of Obesity Related Metabolic Disorders, 24,* 639–646.

Lindsey, K. P., & Paul, G. L. (1989). Involuntary commitments to public mental institutions: Issues involving the overrepresentation of blacks and assessment of relevant functioning. *Psychological Bulletin, 106,* 171–183.

Linz, D., Donnerstein, E., & Penrod, S. (1987). The findings and recommendations of the Attorney General's Commission on Pornography: Do the psychological facts fit the political fury? *American Psychologist, 42,* 946–953.

Littlewood, R. (1992). Psychiatric diagnosis and racial bias: Empirical and interpretative approaches. *Social Science & Medicine, 34,* 141–149.

Liu, C., Weaver, D. R., Jin, X., Shearman, L. P., Pieschl, R. L., Gribkoff, V. K., & Reppert, S. M. (1997). Molecular dissection of two distinct actions of melatonin on the suprachiasmatic circadian clock. *Neuron, 19,* 91–102.

Liu, L. G. (1985). Reasoning counterfactually in Chinese: Are there any obstacles? *Cognition, 21,* 239–270.

Liu, Y., Gao, J.-H., Liu, H.-L., & Fox, P. (2000). The temporal response of the brain after eating revealed by functional MRI. *Nature, 405,* 1058–1062.

Loeber, R., & Stouthamer-Loeber, M. (1998). Development of juvenile aggression and violence. Some common misconceptions and controversies. *American Psychologist, 53,* 242–259.

Loehlin, J. C. (1992). *Genes and environment in personality development.* Newbury Park, CA: Sage.

Loewenstein, G. (1994). The psychology of curiosity: A review and reinterpretation. *Psychological Bulletin, 116*(1), 75–98.

Loftus, E. F. (1992). When a lie becomes memory's truth: Memory distortion after exposure to misinformation. *Psychological Science, 3,* 121–123.

Loftus, E. F. (1993). The reality of repressed memories. *American Psychologist, 48,* 518–537.

Loftus, E. F. (1997a). Memory for a past that never was. *Current Directions in Psychological Science, 6,* 60–65.

Loftus, E. F. (1997b). Repressed memory accusations: Devastated families and devastated patients. *Applied Cognitive Psychology, 11,* 25–30.

Loftus, E. F. (1998). The price of bad memories. *Skeptical Inquirer, 22,* 23–24.

Loftus, E. F., & Ketcham, K. (1991). *Witness for the defense.* New York: St. Martin's Press.

Loftus, E. F., & Ketcham, K. (1994). *The myth of repressed memory: False memories and allegations of sexual abuse.* New York: St. Martin's Press.

Loftus, E. F., & Palmer, J. C. (1974). Reconstruction of automobile destruction: An example of the interaction between language and memory. *Journal of Verbal Learning and Verbal Behavior, 13,* 585–589.

Loftus, T. M., Jaworsky, D. E., Frehywot, G. L., Townsend, C. A., Ronnett, G. V., Lane, M. D., & Kuhajda, F. P. (2000). Reduced food intake and body weight in mice treated with fatty acid synthase inhibitors. *Science, 288,* 2379–2381.

Logue, A. W. (1985). Conditioned food aversion in humans. *Annals of the New York Academy of Sciences, 104,* 331–340.

Lohr, J. M., Lilienfeld, S. O., Tolin, D. F., & Herbert, J. D. (1999). Eye movement desensitization and reprocessing: An analysis of specific versus nonspecific treatment factors. *Journal of Anxiety Disorders, 13,* 185–207.

London Daily Telegraph. (1998, September 19). "'Cat' that turned out to be a clock."

Long, J. C., Knowler, W. C., Hanson, R. L., Robin, R. W., Urbanek, M., Moore, E., Bennett, P. H., & Goldman, G. (1998). Evidence for genetic linkage to alcohol dependence on chromosomes 4 and 11 from an autosome-wide scan in an American Indian population. *American Journal of Medical Genetics, 81,* 216–221.

Longo, N., Klempay, S., & Bitterman, M. E. (1964). Classical appetitive conditioning in the pigeon. *Psychonomic Science, 1,* 19–20.

Lopez, S. R. (1989). Patient variable biases in clinical judgment: Conceptual overview and methodological considerations. *Psychological Bulletin, 106,* 184–203.

Lord, C. G. (1997). *Social psychology.* Fort Worth: Harcourt, Brace.

Löw, K., Crestani, F., Keist, R., Benke, D., Brunig, I., Benson, J. A., Fritschy, J. M., Rulicke, T., Bluethmann, H., Mohler, H., & Rudolph, U. (2000). Molecular and neuronal substrate for the selective attenuation of anxiety. *Science, 290,* 131–134.

Luborsky, L. (1972). Another reply to Eysenck. *Psychological Bulletin, 78,* 406–408.

Luborsky, L. (1997). The core conflictual relationship theme: A basic case formulation method. In T. D. Eells (Ed.), *Handbook of psychotherapy case formulation* (pp. 58–83). New York: Guilford.

Luborsky, L., Singer, B., & Luborsky, L. (1975). Comparative studies of psychotherapies: Is it true that everyone has won and all must have prizes? *Archives of General Psychiatry, 32,* 995–1008.

Luchins, A. S. (1942). Mechanization in problem solving: The effect of Einstellung. *Psychological Monographs, 54*(6, Whole No. 248).

Lue, T. F. (2000). Drug Therapy: Erectile Dysfunction. *The New England Journal of Medicine, 342,* 1802–1813.

Luntz, B. K., & Widom, C. S. (1994). Antisocial personality disorder in abused and neglected children grown up. *American Journal of Psychiatry, 151,* 670–674.

Luria, Z. (1992, February). *Gender differences in children's play patterns.* Paper presented at University of Southern California, Los Angeles.

Lutsky, N. (1995). When is "obedience" obedience? Conceptual and historical commentary. *Journal of Social Issues, 51,* 55–65.

Lutz, D. J., & Sternberg, R. J. (1999). Cognitive development. In M. H. Bornstein & M. E. Lamb (Eds.), *Developmental psychology: An advanced textbook* (4th ed.) Mahwah, NJ: Erlbaum.

Lydiard, R. B., Steiner, M., Burnham, D., & Gergel, I. (1998). Efficacy studies of paroxetine in panic disorder. *Psychopharmacology Bulletin, 34,* 175–182.

Lykken, D. T. (1992). Why (some) Americans believe in the lie detector while others believe in the guilty knowledge test. *Integrative Physiological and Behavioral Science, 26,* 214–222.

Lykken, D. T. (1998). *A tremor in the blood: Uses and abuses of the lie detector.* Cambridge, MA: Perseus Publishing.

Lykken, D. T. (1999). *Happiness: What studies on twins show us about nature, nurture, and the happiness set point.* New York: Golden Books.

Lynam, D. R. (1996). The early identification of chronic offenders: Who is the fledgling psychopath? *Psychological Bulletin, 120,* 209–234.

Lynn, S. J., & Rhue, J. W. (1986). The fantasy-prone person: Hypnosis, imagination, and creativity. *Journal of Personality and Social Psychology, 51,* 404–408.

Lynn, S. J., Lock, T. G., Myers, B., & Payne, D. G. (1997). Recalling the unrecallable: Should hypnosis be used to recover memories in psychotherapy? *Current Directions in Psychological Science, 6,* 79–83.

Lynn, S. J., Myers, B., & Malinoski, P. (in press). Hypnosis, pseudomemories, and clinical guidelines: A sociocognitive perspective. In J. D. Read & D. S. Lindsay (Eds.), *Recollections of trauma: Scientific studies and clinical practice.* New York: Plenum.

Lyons, W. E., Mamounas, L. A., Ricaurte, G. A., Coppola, V., Reid, S. W., Bora, S. H., Wihler, C., Koliatsos, V. E., & Tessarollo, L. (1999). Brain-derived neurotrophic factor-deficient mice develop aggressiveness and hyperphagia in conjunction with brain serotonergic abnormalities. *Proceedings of the National Academy of Science U S A, 96,* 15239–15244.

Lyubomirsky, S., & Nolen-Hoeksema, S. (1995). Effects of self-focused rumination on negative thinking and interpersonal problem solving. *Journal of Personality and Social Psychology, 69,* 176–190.

Lyubomirsky, S., & Ross, L. (1997). Hedonic consequences of social comparison: A contrast of happy and unhappy people. *Journal of Personality and Social Psychology, 73,* 1141–1157.

MacAndrew, C., & Edgerton, R. B. (1969). *Drunken comportment.* Chicago: Aldine.

MacArthur Foundation. (1999). *Research network on successful midlife development.* Vero Beach, FL: The John D. and Catherine T. MacArthur Foundation.

MacDonald, M., & Bernstein, D. A. (1974). Treatment of a spider phobia with in vivo and imaginal desensitization. *Journal of Behavior Therapy and Experimental Psychiatry, 5,* 47–52.

Mack, A., & Rock, I. (1998). *Inattentional blindness.* Cambridge, MA: MIT Press.

Madden, T. J., Ellen, P. S., & Ajzen, I. (1992). A comparison of the theory of planned behavior and the theory of reasoned action. *Personality and Social Psychology Bulletin, 18,* 3–9.

Maddux, J. E. (1993). Social cognitive models of health and exercise behavior: An introduction and review of conceptual issues. *Journal of Applied Sport Psychology, 5,* 116–140.

Maddux, J. E., & DuCharme, K. A. (1997). Behavioral intentions in theories of health behavior. In D. S. Gochman (Ed.), *Handbook of health behavior research: Vol. 1: Personal and social determinants* (pp. 133–151). New York: Plenum.

Magavi, S. S., Leavitt, B. R., & Macklis, J. D. (2000). Induction of neurogenesis in the neocortex of adult mice. *Nature, 405,* 951–955.

Mahesh Yogi, M. (1994). *Science of being and art of living.* New York: NAL/Dutton.

Mahrer, A. R., & Nadler, W. P. (1986). Good moments in psychotherapy: A preliminary review, a list, and some promising research avenues. *Journal of Consulting and Clinical Psychology, 54,* 10–15.

Maier, S. F., & Watkins, L. R. (2000). The immune system as a sensory system: Implications for psychology. *Current Directions in Psychological Science, 9,* 98–102.

Major, B., Sciacchtinano, A. M., & Crocker, J. (1993). In-group versus out-group comparisons and self-esteem. *Personality and Social Psychology Bulletin, 19,* 711–721.

Malamuth, N. M. (1998). The confluence model as an organizing framework for research on sexually aggressive men: Risk moderators, imagined aggression, and pornography consumption. In R. G. Geen & E. Donnerstein (Eds.), *Human aggression* (pp. 230–247). San Diego: Academic Press.

Malamuth, N. M., & Check, J. V. P. (1983). Sexual arousal to rape depictions: Individual differences. *Journal of Abnormal Psychology, 92,* 55–67.

Malamuth, N. M., Heavy, C., & Linz, D. (1993). Predicting men's antisocial behavior against women: The interaction model of sexual aggression. In N. G. Hall & R. Hirschman (Eds.), *Sexual aggression: Issues in etiology and assessment, treatment and policy* (pp. 63–97). New York: Hemisphere.

Malamuth, N. M., Sockloskie, R. J., Koss, M. P., & Tanaka, J. S. (1991). Characteristics of aggressors against women: Testing a model using a national sample of college students. *Journal of Consulting and Clinical Psychology, 59,* 670–681.

Malarkey, W. B., Kiecolt-Glaser, J. K., Pearl, D., & Glaser, R. (1994). Hostile behavior during marital conflict alters pituitary and adrenal hormones. *Psychosomatic Medicine, 56,* 41–51.

Malatesta, C. Z., & Izard, C. E. (1984). The ontogenesis of human social signals: From biological imperative to symbol utilization. In N. A. Fox & R. J. Davidson (Eds.), *The psychobiology of affective development* (pp. 161–206). Hillsdale, NJ: Erlbaum.

Malenka, R. C., & Nicoll, R. A. (1999). Long-term potentiation—a decade of progress? *Science, 285,* 1870–1874.

Malgrange, B., Rigo, J. M., Van de Water, T. R., Staecker, H., Moonen, G., & Lefebvre, P. P. (1999). Growth factor therapy to the damaged inner ear: Clinical prospects. *International Journal of Pediatric Otorhinolaryngology, 49* (Suppl 1), S19–S25.

Manderscheid, R., & Barrett, S. (Eds.). (1987). *Mental health, United States, 1987* (National Institute of Mental Health, DHHS Pub. No. ADM 87–1518). Washington, DC: U.S. Government Printing Office.

Manfield, P. (Ed.). (1998). *Extending EMDR: A casebook of innovative applications.* New York: Norton.

Manji, H. K., Bowden, C. L., & Belmaker, R. H. (Eds.). (2000). *Bipolar medications: Mechanisms of action.* Washington, DC: American Psychiatric Press.

Mann, K., Roschke, J., Nink, M., Aldenhoff, J., Beyer, J., Benkert, O., & Lehnert, H. (1992). Effects of corticotropin-releasing hormone administration in patients suffering from sleep apnea syndrome. *Society for Neuroscience Abstracts, 22,* 196.

Mannuzza, M., Schneider, F. R., Chapman, T. F., Liebowitz, M. R., Klein, D. F., & Fyer, A. J. (1995). Generalized social phobia. *Archives of General Psychiatry, 52,* 230–237.

Mansfield, P. K., Voda, A., & Koch, P. B. (1995). Predictors of sexual response changes in heterosexual midlife women. *Health Values, 19*(1), 10–20.

Marcus, G. F. (1996). Why do children say "breaked"? *Current Directions in Psychological Science, 5,* 81–85.

Markman, E. M. (1994). Constraints children place on word meanings. In P. Bloom (Ed.), *Language acquisition: Core readings.* Hemel Hempstead: Harvester Wheatsheaf.

Markowitz, J. C., & Swartz, H. A. (1997). Case formulation in interpersonal psychotherapy of depression. In T. D. Eells (Ed.), *Handbook of psychotherapy case formulation* (pp. 192–222). New York: Guilford.

Markus, H. R., & Kitayama, S. (1991). Culture and the self: Implications for cognition, emotion, and motivation. *Psychological Review, 98,* 224–253.

Markus, H. R., & Kitayama, S. (1997). Culture and the self: Implications for cognition, emotion, and motivation. In L. A. Peplau & S. Taylor (Eds.), *Sociocultural perspectives in social psychology* (pp. 157–216). Upper Saddle River, NJ: Prentice-Hall.

Markus, H. R., Kitayama, S., & Heiman, R. J. (1996). Culture and "basic" psychological principles. In E. T. Higgins & A. W. Kruglanski (Eds.), *Social psychology: Handbook of basic principles* (pp. 857–913). New York: Guilford.

Marmar, C. R. (1990). Psychotherapy process research: Progress, dilemmas, and future directions. *Journal of Consulting and Clinical Psychology, 58,* 265–272.

Marshall, W. L. (1989). Pornography and sex offenders. In D. Zillmann & J. Bryant (Eds.), *Pornography: Research advances and policy considerations.* Hillsdale, NJ: Erlbaum.

Martin, B., & Hoffman, J. (1990). Conduct disorders. In M. Lewis & S. M. Miller (Eds.), *Handbook of developmental psychopathology.* New York: Plenum.

Martin, D. J., Garske, J. P., & Davis, M. K. (2000). Relation of the therapeutic alliance with outcome and other variables: A meta-analytic review. *Journal of Consulting and Clinical Psychology, 68,* 438–450.

Martin, S. (1999). Revision of ethics code calls for stronger former client sex rule. *APA Monitor,* July/August, p. 44.

Martindale, C. (1981). *Cognition and consciousness.* Homewood, IL: Dorsey Press.

Martindale, C. (1991). *Cognitive psychology: A neural-network approach.* Pacific Grove, CA: Brooks/Cole.

Marzuk, P. M., Tardiff, K., Leon, A. C., Hirsch, C. S., Stajic, M., Portera, L., Hartwell, N., & Iqbal, I. (1995). Fatal injuries after cocaine use as a leading cause of death among young adults in New York City. *New England Journal of Medicine, 332*(26), 1753–1757.

Masand, P., Popli, A. P., & Welburg, J. B. (1995). Sleepwalking. *American Family Physician, 51*(3), 649–653.

Maslach, C., & Goldberg, J. (1998). Prevention of burnout: New perspectives. *Applied and Preventive Psychology, 7,* 63–74.

Masling, J., & Bornstein, R. F. (1991). Perception without awareness and electrodermal responding: A strong test of subliminal psychodynamic activation effects. *Journal of Mind and Behavior, 12,* 33–47.

Maslow, A. H. (1943). A theory of human motivation. *Psychological Review, 50,* 370–396.

Maslow, A. H. (1954). *Motivation and personality.* New York: Harper.

Maslow, A. H. (1962). *Toward a psychology of being.* Princeton, NJ: Van Nostrand.

Maslow, A. H. (1970). *Motivation and personality* (2nd ed.). New York: Harper & Row.

Maslow, A. H. (1971). *The farther reaches of human nature.* New York: McGraw-Hill.

Mason, N. S., & Chaney, J. M. (1996). Bulimia nervosa in undergraduate women: Factors associated with internalization of the sociocultural standard of thinness. *Applied and Preventive Psychology, 5,* 249–259.

Mason, R. T., Fales, H. M., Jones, T. H., Pannell, L. K., Chinn, J. W., & Crews, D. (1989). Sex pheromones in snakes. *Science, 245,* 290–293.

Masters, J. C., Burish, T. G., Hollon, S. D., & Rimm, D. C. (1987). *Behavior therapy: Techniques and empirical findings* (3rd ed.). San Diego: Harcourt Brace Jovanovich.

Masters, W. H., & Johnson, V. E. (1966). *Human sexual response.* Boston: Little, Brown.

Matlin, M. W. (1998). *Cognition* (4th ed.). Ft. Worth: Harcourt Brace College Publishers.

Matson, J., Sevin, J., Fridley, D., & Love, S. (1990). Increasing spontaneous language in autistic children. *Journal of Applied Behavior Analysis, 23,* 227–223.

Matsumoto, D., and Ekman, P. (1989). American-Japanese cultural differences in intensity ratings of facial expressions of emotion. *Motivation and Emotion, 13,* 143–157.

Matthies, E., Hoeger, R., & Guski, R. (2000). Living on polluted soil: Determinants of stress symptoms. *Environment and Behavior, 32,* 270–286.

Maupin, H. E., & Fisher, J. R. (1989). The effects of superior female performance and sex-role orientation in gender conformity. *Canadian Journal of Behavioral Science, 21,* 55–69.

Mayer, D. J., & Price, D. D. (1982). A physiological and psychological analysis of pain: A potential model of motivation. In D. W. Pfaff (Ed.), *The physiological mechanisms of motivation.* New York: Springer-Verlag.

Mayer, F. S., & Sutton, K. (1996). *Personality: An integrative approach.* Upper Saddle River, NJ: Prentice-Hall.

May, E. R., & Zelikow, P. D. (Eds.). (1997). *The Kennedy tapes: Inside the White House during the Cuban Missile Crisis.* New York: Belknap Press.

McAdams, D. P. (1997). A conceptual history of personality psychology. In R. Hogan, J. Johnson, & S. Briggs (Eds.), *Handbook of personality psychology* (pp. 4–40). San Diego: Academic Press.

McAuley, E. (1992). The role of efficacy cognitions in the prediction of exercise behavior in middle-aged adults. *Journal of Behavioral Medicine, 15,* 65–88.

McBride, T. D., Calsyn, R. J., Morse, G. A., Klinkenberg, W. D., & Allen, G. A. (1998). Duration of homeless spells among severely mentally ill individuals—A survival analysis. *Journal of Community Psychology, 26,* 473–490.

McCartney, K., Harris, M., & Bernieri, F. (1990). Growing up and growing apart: A developmental meta-analysis of twin studies. *Psychological Bulletin, 107,* 226–237.

McCarty, M. F. (1995). Optimizing exercise for fat loss. *Medical Hypotheses, 44*(5), 325–330.

McClelland, D. C. (1958). Risk-taking in children with high and low need for achievement. In J. W. Atkinson (Ed.), *Motives in fantasy, action, and society.* Princeton, NJ: Van Nostrand.

McClelland, D. C. (1985). Human motivation. Glenview, IL: Scott, Foresman.

McCloskey, M. (1983). Naive theories of motion. In D. Gentner & K. Stevens (Eds.), *Mental models.* Hillsdale, NJ: Erlbaum.

McCrae, R. R., & Costa, P. T., Jr. (1997). Personality trait structure as a human universal. *American Psychologist, 52,* 509–516.

McCrae, R. R., & John, O. (1992). An introduction to the five-factor model and its applications. *Journal of Personality, 60,* 175–215.

McDougall, W. (1908). *An introduction to social psychology.* London: Methuen.

McEwen, B. S. (1991). Steroid-hormones are multifunctional messengers to the brain. *Trends in Endocrinology and Metabolism, 2,* 62–67.

McEwen, B. S. (1994). How do sex and stress hormones affect nerve cells? *Annals of the New York Academy of Science, 743,* 1–18.

McEwen, B. S. (1998). Protective and damaging effects of stress mediators. *New England Journal of Medicine, 338,* 171–179.

McEwen, B. S., & Seeman, T. (1999). Protective and damaging effects of mediators of stress: Elaborating and testing concepts of allostasis and allostatic load. *Annals of the New York Academy of Sciences, 896,* 30–47.

McGarvey, R. (1989, February). Recording success. *USAIR Magazine,* pp. 94–102.

McGee, H. (1999). Taking stock of new flavours. *Nature, 400,* 17–18.

McGehee, D. S., Heath, M. J. S., Gelber, S., Devay, P., &Role, L. W. (1995). Nicotine enhancement of fast excitation synaptic transmissions in CNS by presynaptic receptors. *Science, 269,* 5231, 1692–1696.

McGlashan, T. H., & Hoffman, R. E. (2000). Schizophrenia as a disorder of reduced synaptic connectivity. *Archives of General Psychiatry, 57,* 637–648.

McGlynn, F. D., Moore, P. M., Lawyer, S., & Karg, R. (1999). Relaxation training inhibits fear and arousal during in vivo exposure to phobia-cue stimuli. *Journal of Behavior Therapy and Experimental Psychiatry, 30,* 155–168.

McGregor, I., Newby-Clark, I. R., & Zanna, M. P. (1999). "Remembering" dissonance: Simultaneous accessibility of inconsistent cognitive elements moderates epistemic discomfort. In E. Harmon-Jones & J. Mills, Judson (Eds.), *Cognitive dissonance: Progress on a pivotal theory in social psychology.* (pp. 325–335) American Psychological Association, Washington, DC, USA 1999.

McGue, M. (1992). When assessing twin concordance, use the probandwise not the pairwise rate. *Schizophrenia Bulletin, 18,* 171–176.

McGue, M. (1999). The behavioral genetics of alcoholism. *Current Directions in Psychological Science, 8,* 109–115.

McGue, M., Pickens, R., & Svikis, D. (1992). Sex and age effects on the inheritance of alcohol problems: A twin study. *Journal of Abnormal Psychology, 101,* 3–17.

McGuire, M. T., Wing, R. R., Klem, M. L., Lang., W., & Hill, J. O. (1999). What predicts weight regain in a group of successful weight losers? *Journal of Consulting and Clinical Psychology, 67,* 177–185.

McGuire, P. A. (1998, November). California enacts drug-training law for psychologists. *APA Monitor,* p. 24.

McIntosh, D. N., Silver, R. C., & Wortman, C. B. (1993). Religion's role in adjustment to a negative life event: Coping with the loss of a child. *Journal of Personality and Social Psychology, 65,* 812–821.

McIntosh, J. L. (1992). Suicide of the elderly. In B. Bonger (Ed.), *Suicide: Guidelines for assessment, management, and treatment.* New York: Oxford University Press.

McKenna, J. J., Thoman, E. B., Anders, T. F., Sadeh, A., Schechtman, V. L., & Glotzbach, S. F. (1993). Infant-parent co-sleeping in an evolutionary perspective: Implications for understanding infant sleep development and the sudden infant death syndrome. *Sleep, 16*(3), 263–282.

McLaughlin, C. S., Chen, C., Greenberger, E., & Biermeier, C. (1997). Family, peer, and individual correlates of sexual experience among Caucasian and Asian-American late adolescents. *Journal of Research on Adolescence, 7,* 33–53.

McLeod, J. D., Kessler, R. C., & Landis, K. R. (1992). Speed of recovery from major depressive episodes in a community sample of married men and women. *Journal of Abnormal Psychology, 101,* 277–286.

McLoyd, V. C. (1998). Socioeconomic disadvantage and child development. *American Psychologist, 53,* 185–204.

McMahon, P. (2000). Oregon man leads life without frills, leaves $9 million to charities, children. *USA Today,* January 31, p. 4A.

McMullin, R. E. (2000). *The new handbook of cognitive therapy techniques.* New York: Norton.

McNeilly, M. D., Robinson, E. L., Anderson, N. B., Pieper, C. F., Shah, A., Toth, P. S., Martin, P., Jackson, D., Saulter, T. D., White, C., Kuchibatla, M., Collado, S. M., & Gerin, W. (1995). Effects of racist provocation and social support on cardiovascular reactivity in African American women. *International Journal of Behavioral Medicine, 2,* 321–338.

McPhail, T. L., & Penner, L. A. (1995, August). *Can similarity moderate the effects of aversive racism?* Paper presented at the 103rd annual meeting of the American Psychological Association, New York.

Medin, D. L., & Ross, B. H. (1997). *Cognitive psychology* (2nd ed.). Fort Worth, TX: Harcourt Brace Jovanovich.

Meeus, W. H., & Raaijmakers, Q. A. W. (1995). Obedience in modern society. *Journal of Social Issues, 51,* 155–176.

Mehle, T. (1982). Hypothesis generation in an automobile malfunction inference task. *Acta Psychologica, 52,* 87–116.

Mehta, S. I. (1995). A method for instant assessment and active learning. *Journal of Engineering Education, 84,* 295–298.

Meichenbaum, D. H. (1977). *Cognitive behavior modification: An integrative approach.* New York: Plenum.

Meichenbaum, D. H. (1995). Cognitive-behavioral therapy in historical perspective. In B. Bongar & L. E. Beutler (Eds.), *Comprehensive textbook of psychotherapy: Theory and practice* (pp. 140–158). New York: Oxford University Press.

Meins, E., Fernyhough, C., Russell, J., & Clark-Carter, D. (1998). Security of attachment as a predictor of symbolic and mentalising abilities: A longitudinal study. *Social Development, 7,* 1–24.

Melzack, R., & Wall, P. D. (1965). Pain mechanisms: A new theory. *Science, 150,* 971–979.

Menaker, M., & Vogelbaum, M. A. (1993). Mutant circadian period as a marker of suprachiasmatic nucleus function. *Journal of Biological Rhythms, 8,* 93–98.

Mendl, M. (1999). Performing under pressure: Stress and cognitive function. *Applied Animal Behaviour Science, 65,* 221–244.

Menini, A., Picco, C., & Firestein, S. (1995, February 2). Quantal-like current fluctuations induced by odorants in olfactory receptor cell. *Nature, 373,* 435–437.

Merzenich, M. (1998). Long-term change of mind. *Science, 282,* 1062–1063.

Mesquita, B., & Frijda, N. H. (1992). Cultural variations in emotions: A review. *Psychological Bulletin, 112,* 179–204.

Metzinger, T. (Ed.). (2000). *Neural correlates of consciousness: Empirical and conceptual questions.* Cambridge, MA: MIT Press.

Meyer, B. H. F. L., Ehrhardt, A. A., Rosen, L. R., & Gruen, R. S. (1995). Prenatal estrogens and the development of homosexual orientation. *Developmental Psychology, 31*(1), 12–21.

Meyer, J. D., & Salovey, P. (1997). What is emotional intelligence? In P. Salovey & D. Sluyter (Eds.), *Emotional development and emotional intelligence.* New York: Basic Books.

Meyer, R. G. (1975). A behavioral treatment of sleepwalking associated with test anxiety. *Journal of Behavior Therapy and Experimental Psychiatry, 6,* 167–168.

Meyers, C., & Jones, T. B. (1993). *Promoting active learning: Strategies for the college classroom.* San Francisco: Jossey-Bass.

Michael, R. T, Wadsworth, J., Feinleib, J., Johnson, A. M., Laumann, E. O, & Wellings, K. (1998). Private sexual behavior, public opinion, and public health policy related to sexually transmitted diseases: A US-British comparison. *American Journal of Public Health, 88,* 749–754.

Mikelson, K. D., Kessler, R. C., & Shaver, P. R. (1997). Adult attachment in a nationally representative sample. *Journal of Personality and Social Psychology, 72,* 1092–1106.

Miklowitz, D. J., & Alloy, L. B. (1999). Psychosocial factors in the course and treatment of bipolar disorder: Introduction to the special section. *Journal of Abnormal Psychology, 108,* 555–557.

Mikulincer, M. (1995). Attachment style and the mental representation of the self. *Journal of Personality and Social Psychology, 69,* 1203–1215.

Milberger, S., Biederman, J., Faraone, S. V., & Chen, L. (1997). Further evidence of an association between attention-deficit/hyperactivity disorder and cigarette smoking: Findings from a high-risk sample of siblings. *American Journal on Addictions, 6,* 205–217.

Milgram, S. (1963). Behavioral study of obedience. *Journal of Abnormal and Social Psychology, 67,* 371–378.

Milgram, S. (1965). Some conditions of obedience and disobedience to authority. *Human Relations, 18,* 57–76.

Milgram, S. (1974). *Obedience to authority.* New York: Harper & Row.

Milgram, S. (1977, October). Subject reaction: The neglected factor in the ethics of experimentation. *Hastings Center Report,* pp. 19–23.

Millar, S. (1994). *Understanding and representing space theory and evidence from studies with blind and sighted children.* New York: Oxford University Press.

Miller, B. (1998). Hinckley loses appeal on leave. *Washington Post,* April 15, p. B3.

Miller, G. A. (1956). The magical number seven, plus or minus two: Some limits on our capacity to process information. *Psychological Review, 63,* 81–97.

Miller, G. A. (1991). *The science of words.* New York: Scientific American Library.

Miller, G. A., Heise, G. A., & Lichten, W. (1951). The intelligibility of speech as a function of the context of the test materials. *Journal of Experimental Psychology, 41,* 329–335.

Miller, J. G. (1999). Cultural psychology: Implications for basic psychological theory. *Psychological Science, 10,* 85–91.

Miller, J. G., & Bersoff, D. M. (1994). Cultural influences on the moral status of reciprocity and the discounting of endogenous motivation. *Personality and Social Psychology Bulletin, 20,* 592–607.

Miller, K. F., Smith, C. M., Zhu, J., & Zhang, H. (1995). Preschool origins of cross-national differences in mathematical competence: The role of number-naming systems. *Psychological Science, 6,* 56–60.

Miller, L. K. (1999). The savant syndrome: Intellectual impairment and exceptional skill. *Psychological Bulletin, 125,* 31–46.

Miller, L. T., & Vernon, P. A. (1997). Developmental changes in speed of information processing in young children. *Developmental Psychology, 33,* 549–554.

Miller, N. E. (1959). Liberalization of basic S-R concepts: Extensions to conflict behavior, motivation, and social learning. In S. Koch (Ed.), *Psychology: A study of science* (Vol. 2, pp. 196–292). New York: McGraw-Hill.

Miller, N. E., Bailey, C. U., & Stevenson, J. A. F. (1930). Decreased hunger but increased food intake resulting from hypothalmic lesions. *Science, 112,* 256–259.

Millon, T., & Davis, R. D. (1996). *Disorders of personality. DSM-IV and beyond* (2nd ed.). New York: Wiley.

Milner, B. (1966). Amnesia following operation on temporal lobes. In C. W. M. Whitty & O. L. Zangwill (Eds.), *Amnesia.* London: Butterworth.

Milner, D. (1983). *Children and race.* Beverly Hills, CA: Sage.

Minshew, N. J., Payton, J. B., & Sclabassi, R. J. (1986). Cortical neurophysiologic abnormalities in autism. *Neurology, 36*(Suppl. 1), 194.

Miranda, J., & Green, B. L. (1999). The need for mental health services research focusing on poor young women. *Journal of Mental Health Policy and Economics, 2,* 73–89.

Mischel, W. (1999). *Introduction to personality* (6th ed.). Fort Worth, TX: Harcourt.

Mischel, W., & Shoda, Y. (1995). A cognitive-affective system of personality: Reconceptualizing situations, dispositions, dynamics, and influences. *Psychological Review, 90,* 394–402.

Mischel, W., & Shoda, Y. (1998). Reconciling dynamics and dispositions. *Annual Review of Psychology, 49,* 229–258.

Mishina, T. M. (1999). Russian group therapies mirror culture. *Psychology International, 10,* 1, 4–5.

Miyake, K., Chen, S., & Campos, J. J. (1985). Infant temperament, mother's mode of interaction, and attachment in Japan: An interim report. In I. Bretherton & E. Waters (Eds.), Growing points of attachment theory and research. *Monographs of the Society for Research in Child Development, 50*(1–2, Serial No. 209).

Moergen, S., Merkel, W., & Brown, S. (1990). The use of covert sensitization and social skills training in the treatment of an obscene telephone caller. *Journal of Behavior Therapy and Experimental Psychiatry, 21,* 269–275.

Mogenson, G. J. (1976). Neural mechanisms of hunger: Current status and future prospects. In D. Novin, W. Wyrwicka, & G. Bray (Eds.), *Hunger: Basic mechanisms and clinical applications.* New York: Raven.

Mokdad, A. H., Serdula, M. K., Dietz, W. H., Bowman, B. A., Marks, J. S., & Koplan, J. P. (2000). The continuing epidemic of obesity in the United States. *Journal of the American Medical Association, 284,* 1650–1651.

Moldin, S. O., & Gottesman, I. I. (1997). At issue: Genes, experience, and chance in schizophrenia—positioning for the 21st century. *Schizophrenia Bulletin, 23,* 547–561.

Molloy, D. W., Guyett, G. H., Wilson, D. B., Duke, R., Rees, L., & Singer, J. (1991). Effect of tetrahydroaminoacridine on cognition, function and behaviour in Alzheimer's disease. *Canadian Medical Association Journal, 144,* 29–34.

Molsa, P. K., Marttila, R. J., & Rinne, U. K. (1995). Long-term survival and predictors of mortality in Alzheimer's disease and multi-infarct dementia. *Acta Neurologica Scandinavica, 91,* 159–164.

Monane, M., Leichter, D., & Lewis, O. (1984). Physical abuse in psychiatrically hospitalized children and adolescents. *Journal of the American Academy of Child and Adolescent Psychiatry, 23,* 653–658.

Mondadori, C. (1996). Nootropics: Preclinical results in the light of clinical effects; comparison with tacrine. *Critical Reviews in Neurobiology, 10,* 357–370.

Monroe, S. M., Thase, M., & Simons, A. (1992). Social factors and psychobiology of depression: Relations between life stress and rapid eye movement sleep latency. *Journal of Abnormal Psychology, 101,* 528–537.

Monroe, S. M., Rohde, P., Seeley, J. R., & Lewinsohn, P. M. (1999). Life events and depression in adolescence: Relationship loss as a prospective risk factor for first onset of major depressive disorder. *Journal of Abnormal Psychology, 108,* 606–614.

Monteith, M. J., Sherman, J. W., & Devine, P. G. (1998). Suppression as a stereotype control strategy. *Personality & Social Psychology Review, 2,* 63–82.

Monteith, M. J., Zuwerink, J. R., & Devine, P. G. (1994). Prejudice and prejudice reduction: Classic challenges and contemporary approaches. In P. G. Devine, D. L. Hamilton, & T. M. Ostrom (Eds.), *Social cognition: Impact on social psychology* (pp. 324–346). San Diego, CA: Academic Press.

Moon, C., Cooper, R. P., & Fifer, W. P. (1993). Two-day-olds prefer their native language. *Infant Behavior and Development, 16,* 495–500.

Moore, R. Y. (1997). Circadian rhythms: Basic neurobiology and clinical applications. *Annual Review of Medicine, 48,* 253–266.

Moran, D. R. (2000). *Is active learning for me?* Poster presented at APS Preconvention Teaching Institute, Denver, June, 2000.

Morgan, C. D., & Murray, H. A. (1935). A method for investigating fantasy: The thematic apperception test. *Archives of Neurology and Psychiatry, 34,* 289–306.

Morganstern, J., Labouvie, E., McCrady, B. S., Kahler, C. W., & Frey, R. M. (1997). Affiliation with Alcoholics Anonymous after treatment: A study of its therapeutic effects and mechanism of action. *Journal of Consulting and Clinical Psychology, 65,* 768–777.

Morin, C. M., Kowatch, R. A., Barry, T., & Walton, E. (1993). Cognitive-behavior therapy for late-life insomnia. *Journal of Consulting and Clinical Psychology, 61,* 137–146.

Morrill, A. C., Ickovics, J. R., Golubchikov, V. V., Beren, S. E., & Rodin, J. (1996). Safer sex: Social and psychological predictors of behavioral maintenance and change among heterosexual women. *Journal of Consulting and Clinical Psychology, 64,* 819–828.

Morris, J. S., Friston, K. J., Buchel, C., Frith, C. D., Young, A. W., Calder, A. J., & Dolan, R. J. (1998). A neuromodulatory role for the human amygdala in processing emotional facial expressions. *Brain, 121,* 47–57.

Morris, M. W., & Peng, K. (1994). Culture and cause: American and Chinese attributions for social and physical events. *Journal of Personality and Social Psychology, 67,* 949–971.

Mortimer, R. G., Goldsteen, K., Armstrong, R. W., & Macrina, D. (1988). Effects of enforcement, incentives, and publicity on seat belt use in Illinois. *University of Illinois, Dept. of Health & Safety Studies, Final Report to Illinois Dept. of Transportation* (Safety Research Report 88–11).

Moscovici, S. (1985). Social influence and conformity. In G. Lindzey & E. Aronson (Eds.), *The handbook of social psychology* (Vol. 2, 3rd ed.). New York: Random House.

Motowidlo, S. J., Borman, W. C., & Schmidt, M. J. (1997). A theory of individual differences in task and contextual performance. *Human Performance, 10,* 71–83.

Mroczek, D. K., & Kolarz, C. M. (1998). The effect of age on positive and negative affect: A developmental perspective on happiness. *Journal of Personality and Social Psychology, 75,* 1333–1349.

Muir, J. L. (1997). Acetylcholine, aging, and Alzheimer's disease. *Pharmacological and Biochemical Behavior, 56*(4), 687–696.

Mulder, H. E., Van Olphen, A. F., Bosman, A., & Smoorenburg, G. F. (1992). Phoneme recognition by deaf individuals using the multichannel nucleus cochlear implant. *Acta Otolaryngology, 112,* 946–955.

Mullen, B. (1986). Atrocity as a function of lynch mob composition: A self-attention perspective. *Personality and Social Psychology Bulletin, 12,* 187–197.

Munroe, R. H., & Munroe, R. L. (1994). Behavior across cultures: Results from observational studies. In W. J. Lonner & R. S. Malpass (Eds.), *Psychology and culture.* Boston: Allyn & Bacon.

Muris, P., & Merckelbach, H. (1999). Traumatic memories, eye movements, phobia, and panic: A critical note on the proliferation of EMDR. *Journal of Anxiety Disorders, 13,* 209–223.

Murray, B. (1996, February). Psychology remains top college major. *APA Monitor* (pp. 1, 42).

Murray, B. (2000). Learning from real life. *APA Monitor, 31,* 72–73.

Murray, E. A., & Mishkin, M. (1985). Amygdalectomy impairs crossmodal association in monkeys. *Science, 228,* 604–606.

Murray, H. A. (1938). *Explorations in personality.* New York: Oxford University Press.

Murray, H. A. (1971). *Thematic Apperception Test.* Cambridge: Harvard University Press.

Murray, J. A., & Terry, D. (1999). Parental reactions to infant death: The effects of resources and coping strategies. *Journal of Social and Clinical Psychology, 18,* 341–369.

Myers, B. J. (1987). Mother-infant bonding as a critical period. In M. H. Bornstein (Ed.), *Sensitive periods in development: Interdisciplinary perspectives.* Hillsdale, NJ: Erlbaum.

Myers, D. G. (2000a). The funds, friends, and faith of happy people. *American Psychologist, 55,* 56–67.

Myers, D. G. (2000b). *The American paradox: Spiritual hunger in an age of plenty.* New Haven, CT: Yale University Press.

Myers, D. G., & Diener, E. (1995). Who is happy? *Psychological Science, 6,* 10–19.

Myers, M. G., Reeves, R. A., Oh, P. I., & Joyner, C. D. (1996). Overtreatment of hypertension in the community? *American Journal of Hypertension, 9,* 419–425.

Nadel, L., & Jacobs, W. J. (1998). Traumatic memory is special. *Current Directions in Psychological Science, 7,* 154–157.

Nader, K., Schafe, G. E., & Le Doux, J. E. (2000). Fear memories require protein synthesis in the amygdala for reconsolidation after retrieval. *Nature, 406,* 722–726.

Naëgelé, B., Thouvard, V., Pépin, J.-L., Lévy, P., Bonnet, C., Perret, J. E., Pellat, P., & Feuerstein, C. (1995). Deficits of cognitive functions in patients with sleep apnea syndrome. *Sleep, 18*(1), 43–52.

Nash, A. J., & Fernandez, M. (1996). P300 and allocation of attention in dual-tasks. *International Journal of Psychophysiology, 23,* 171–180/*Psychological Inquiry, 6,* 314–318.

Nash, M., Drake, S., Wiley, S., Khalsa, S., & Lynn, S. (1986). Accuracy of recall by hypnotically age-regressed subjects. *Journal of Abnormal Psychology, 95,* 298–300.

Nathan, P. J. (1999). The experimental and clinical pharmacology of St. John's Wort (Hypericum perforatum L.). *Molecular Psychiatry, 4,* 333–388.

National Advisory Mental Health Council. (1996). Basic behavioral science research for mental health: Vulnerability and resilience. *American Psychologist, 51,* 22–28.

National Cancer Institute. (1994). *National Cancer Institute fact book, 1994.* Washington, DC: U.S. Department of Health and Human Services.

National Center for Education Statistics. (1998). *Digest of Education Statistics, 1998.* Washington, DC: United States Department of Education.

National Center for Health Statistics. (1997) *Youth Risk Behavior Survey.* Washington, DC: Centers for Disease Control and Prevention

National Center for Health Statistics. (1999). *Healthy people 2000, Review 1998–99.* Hyattsville, Maryland: U.S. Public Health Service.

National Center for Health Statistics. (2000). *Trends in pregnancies and pregnancy rates by outcome: Estimates for the United States, 1976–1996.* Washington, DC: Centers for Disease Control and Prevention.

National Computer Systems. (1992). *Catalog of assessment instruments, reports, and services.* Minneapolis: NCS.

National Institute for Occupational Safety and Health. (1999). *Stress at Work.* Washington, DC: NIOSH Publication No. 99–101.

National Institute of Mental Health. (1995). *Medications.* Washington, DC: USDHHS.

National Institute of Mental Health. (1998a). *Genetics and mental disorders: Report of the National Institute of Mental Health's genetics workgroup.* Rockville, MD: Author.

National Institute of Mental Health. (1998b). *Mental illness in America: The National Institute of Mental Health agenda.* Washington, DC: NIMH.

National Institute on Alcohol Abuse and Alcoholism. (1998, May 13). News release.

National Institute on Alcohol Abuse and Alcoholism. (2000). *Tenth special report to the U.S. Congress on alcohol and health.* Washington, DC: National Institutes of Health (Publication No. 00–1583).

National Institute on Drug Abuse. (1997). *Research report: Heroin addiction and abuse.* Washington, DC: National Institute on Drug Abuse.

National Institute on Drug Abuse. (2000). Facts about MDMA (Ecstacy). *NIDA Notes, 14* [On-line]. Available: http://165.122.78.61/NIDA_Notes/NNVol14N4/tearoff.html

National Science Foundation. (1997). *Survey of doctorate recipients.* Washington, DC: National Academy Press.

National Science Foundation. (1998). *Summary report on doctorate recipients from United States universities.* Washington, DC: National Academy Press.

National Task Force on the Prevention and Treatment of Obesity. (2000). Dieting and the development of eating disorders in overweight and obese adults. *Archives of Internal Medicine, 160,* 2581–2589.

Needham, A., & Baillargeon, R. (1999). Effects of prior experience on 4. 5 month-old infants' object segregation. *Infant Behavior & Development, 21,* 1–24.

Neher, A. (1991). Maslow's theory of motivation: A critique. *Journal of Humanistic Psychology, 31,* 89–112.

Neisser, U. (1998). *The rising curve: Long-term gains in I. Q. and related measures.* Washington, DC: American Psychological Association.

Neisser, U. (2000a). Memorists. In U. Neisser & I. E. Hyman Jr. (Eds.), *Memory observed* (2nd ed., pp. 475–478). New York: Worth.

Neisser, U. (2000b). Snapshots or benchmarks? In U. Neisser & I. E. Hyman Jr. (Eds.), *Memory observed* (2nd ed., pp. 68 –74). New York: Worth.

Neisser, U., Boodoo, G., Bouchard, T. J., Boykin, A. W., Brody, N., Ceci, S. J., Halpern, D. F., Loehlin, J. C., Perloff, R., Sternberg, R. J., & Urbina, S. (1996). Intelligence: Knowns and unknowns. *American Psychologist, 51,* 77–101.

Nelson, C. A. (1999). Neural plasticity and human development. *Current Directions in Psychological Science, 8,* 42–45.

Nelson, D. L. (1999). Implicit memory. In D. E. Morris & M. Gruneberg (Eds.), *Theoretical aspects of memory.* London: Routledge.

Nelson, K. (1986). Event knowledge and cognitive development. In K. Nelson (Ed.), *Event knowledge: Structure and function in development.* Hillsdale, NJ: Erlbaum.

Nemeroff, C. B. (1998). Psychopharmacology of affective disorders in the 21st century. *Biological Psychiatry, 44,* 517–525.

Neugarten, B. L. (1977). Personality and aging. In J. E. Birren & K. W. Schaie (Eds.), *Handbook of the psychology of aging.* New York: Van Nostrand Reinhold.

Neumann, C. S., Grimes, K., Walker, E. F., & Baum, K. (1995). Developmental pathways to schizophrenia: Behavioral subtypes. *Journal of Abnormal Psychology, 104,* 558–566.

Neville, H. A., Heppner, M. J., Louie, C. E., Thompson, C. E., Brooks, L., & Baker, C. E. (1996). The impact of multicultural training on white racial identity attitudes and therapy competencies. *Professional Psychology: Research and Practice, 27,* 83–89.

Newcombe, N. S., & Fox, N. A. (1994). Infantile amnesia: Through a glass darkly. *Child Development, 65,* 31–40.

Newcombe, N. S., Drummey, A. B., Fox, N. A., Lie, E., & Ottinger-Alberts, W. (2000). Remembering early childhood: How much, how, and why (or why not). *Current Directions in Psychological Science, 9,* 55–58.

Newport, E. L., & Meier, R. (1985). The acquisition of American Sign Language. In D. I. Slobin (Ed.), *The cross-linguistic study of language acquisition.* Hillsdale, NJ: Erlbaum.

Newsome, J. T. (1999). Another side to caregiving: Negative reactions to being helped. *Current Directions in Psychological Science, 8,* 183–187.

Newsome, J. T., & Schulz, R. (1998). Caregiving from the recipient's perspective: Negative reactions to being helped. *Health Psychology, 17,* 172–181.

NICHD Early Child Care Research Network (1997). The effects of infant child care on infant-mother attachment security: Results of the NICHD Study of Early Child Care. *Child Development, 68,* 860–879.

NICHD Early Child Care Research Network (1998). Early child care and self-control, compliance and problem behavior at 24 and 36 months. *Child Development, 69,* 1145–1170.

NICHD Early Child Care Research Network (1999). Chronicity of maternal depressive symptoms, maternal sensitivity, and child functioning at 36 months. *Developmental Psychology, 35,* 1297–1310.

Nicholson, A. N., Pascoe, P. A., Spencer, M. B., Stone, B. M., Roehis, T., & Roth, T. (1986). Sleep after transmeridian flights. *Lancet, 2,* 1205–1208.

Nicholson, I. R., & Neufeld, R. W. J. (1993). Classification of the schizophrenias according to symptomatology: A two factor model. *Journal of Abnormal Psychology, 102,* 259–270.

Nickell, J. (1997, January/February). Sleuthing a psychic sleuth. *Skeptical Inquirer, 21,* 18–19.

Nickell, J. (2001). Exorcism! Driving out the nonsense. *Skeptical Inquirer, 25,* 20–24.

Nickerson, R. A., & Adams, M. J. (1979). Long-term memory for a common object. *Cognitive Psychology, 11,* 287–307.

Nielsen Media. (1990). *1990 report on television.* New York: Nielsen Media, Inc.

Nietzel, M. T., & Bernstein, D. A. (1987). *Introduction to clinical psychology* (2nd ed.). New York: Prentice-Hall.

Nietzel, M. T., Bernstein, D. A., & Milich, R. (1998). *Introduction to clinical psychology* (5th ed.). Englewood Cliffs, NJ: Prentice-Hall.

Nietzel, M. T., Speltz, M. L., McCauley, E. A., & Bernstein, D. A. (1998). *Abnormal psychology.* Boston: Allyn & Bacon.

Nigg, J. T. (2000). On inhibition/disinhibition in developmental psychopathology: Views from cognitive and personality psychology and a working inhibition taxonomy. *Psychological Bulletin, 126,* 220–246.

NIH Consensus Conference (1998). Acupuncture. *Journal of the American Medical Association 280,* 1518–1524.

Nilsson, G. (1996, November). Some forms of memory improve as people age. *APA Monitor,* p. 27.

Nisbett, R. E., Peng, K., Choi, I., & Norenzayan, A. (2001). Culture and systems of thought: Holistic vs. analytic cognition. *Psychological Review, 108.*

Noble, H. B. (2000). Outgrowth of new field of tissue engineering. *New York Times,* January 25.

Nolan, R. P., Spanos, N. P., Hayward, A. A., & Scott, H. A. (1995). The efficacy of hypnotic and nonhypnotic response-based imagery for self-managing recurrent headache. *Imagination, Cognition, and Personality, 14*(3), 183–201.

Nolen-Hoeksema, S. (1990). *Sex differences in depression.* Stanford, CA: Stanford University Press.

Nolen-Hoeksema, S., Larson, J., & Grayson, C. (1999). Explaining gender differences in depression. *Journal of Personality and Social Psychology, 77,* 1061–1072.

Nolen-Hoeksma, S., Morrow, J., & Fredrickson, N. (1993). Response styles and the duration of episodes of depressed mood. *Journal of Abnormal Psychology, 102,* 20–28.

Noll, R. B. (1994). Hypnotherapy for warts in children and adolescents. *Journal of Developmental and Behavioral Pediatrics, 15*(3), 170–173.

Norenzayan, A., & Nisbet, R. E. (2000). Culture and causal cognition. *Current Directions in Psychological Science, 9,* 132–135.

Northcut, T. B., & Heller, N. R. (Eds.). (1999). *Enhancing psychodynamic therapy with cognitive-behavioral techniques.* Northvale, NJ: Jason Aronson.

Novak, M. A. (1991, July). Psychologists care deeply about animals. *APA Monitor,* p. 4.

Nowinski, J. (1999) Self-help groups for addictions. In B.S. McCrady & E. E. Epstein (Eds.), *Addictions: A comprehensive guidebook*. New York: Oxford University Press.

Nurnberger, J. (1993). Genotyping status report for affective disorder. *Psychiatric Genetics, 3,* 207–214.

O'Brien, T. L. (1991, September 2). Computers help thwart "groupthink" that plagues meetings. *Chicago Sun Times.*

O'Conner, E. P., & Kratochwill, T. R. (1999). Self-help interventions: The reported practices of school psychologists. *Professional Psychology: Research and Practice, 30,* 147–153.

O'Farrell, T. J., & Murphy, C. M. (1995). Marital violence before and after alcoholism treatment. *Journal of Consulting and Clinical Psychology, 63,* 256–262.

O'Leary, K. D., Malone, J., & Tyree, A. (1994). Physical aggression in early marriage: Prerelationship and relationship effects. *Journal of Consulting and Clinical Psychology, 62,* 594–602.

Oatley, K. (1993). Those to whom evil is done. In R. S. Wyer & T. K. Srull (Eds.), *Toward a general theory of anger and emotional aggression: Advances in social cognition,* Vol. VI. Hillsdale, NJ: Erlbaum.

Oden, M. H. (1968). The fulfillment of promise: 40-year follow-up of the Terman gifted group. *Genetic Psychology Monographs, 17,* 3–93.

Offenbach, S., Chodzko-Zajko, W., & Ringel, R. (1990). Relationship between physiological status, cognition, and age in adult men. *Bulletin of the Psychonomics Society, 28,* 112–114.

Öhman, A., & Soares, J. F. (1994). "Unconscious anxiety": Phobic responses to masked stimuli. *Journal of Abnormal Psychology, 103*(2), 231–240.

Öhman, A., Dimberg, U., & Öst, L. G. (1985). Animal and social phobias: A laboratory model. In S. Reiss & R. R. Bootzin (Eds.), *Theoretical issues in behavior therapy.* Orlando, FL: Academic Press.

Oldenberg, P.-A., Zheleznyak, A., Fang, Y.-F., Lagenaur, C. F., Gresham, H. D., & Lindberg, F. P. (2000). Role of CD47 as a marker of self on red blood cells. *Science, 288,* 2051–2054.

Olds, J. (1973). Commentary on positive reinforcement produced by electrical stimulation of septal areas and other regions of rat brain. In E. S. Valenstein (Ed.), *Brain stimulation and motivation: Research and commentary.* Glenview, IL: Scott, Foresman.

Olds, J., & Milner, P. (1954). Positive reinforcement produced by electrical stimulation of septal areas and other regions of the rat brain. *Journal of Comparative and Physiological Psychology, 47,* 419–427.

Oliner, S. P., & Oliner, P. M. (1988). *The altruistic personality: Rescuers of Jews in Nazi Europe.* New York: Free Press.

Olio, K. A. (1994). Truth in memory. *American Psychologist, 49,* 442–443.

Olney, J. W., Wozniak, D. F., & Farber, N. B. (1997). Excitotoxic neurodegeneration in Alzheimer's disease: New hypothesis and new therapeutic strategies. *Archives of Neurology, 54,* 1234–1240.

Olson, G. M., & Sherman, T. (1983). Attention, learning, and memory in infants. In P. H. Mussen (Ed.), *Handbook of child psychology: Vol. 2. Infancy and developmental psychobiology.* New York: Wiley.

Olson, J. M., & Zanna, M. P. (1993). Attitudes and attitude change. In L. W. Porter & M. R. Rosenzweig (Eds.), *Annual review of psychology* (Vol. 44, pp. 117–154). Palo Alto, CA: Annual Reviews Inc.

O'Neill, H. (2000). After rape, jail—a friendship forms. *St. Petersburg Times,* September 24, pp. 1A, 14A.

Ones, D. S., Viswesvaran, C., & Schmidt, F. L. (1993). Comprehensive meta-analysis of integrity test validities: Findings and implications for personnel selection and theories of job performance. *Journal of Applied Psychology, 78,* 679–703.

Ones, D. S., & Viswesvaran, C. (1996). Bandwidth-fidelity dilemma in personality measurement for personnel selection. *Journal of Organizational Behavior, 17,* 609–626.

Oppel, S. (2000). Managing ABCs like a CEO. *St. Petersburg Times,* March 5, 1A, 12–13A.

Orne, M. T., & Evans, F. J. (1965). Social control in the psychological experiment: Antisocial behavior and hypnosis. *Journal of Personality and Social Psychology, 1,* 189–200.

Orne, M. T., Sheehan, P. W., & Evans, F. J. (1968). Occurrence of posthypnotic behavior outside the experimental setting. *Journal of Personality and Social Psychology, 9,* 189–196.

Ornitz, E. M. (1989). Autism: At the interface of sensory and information processing. In G. Dawson (Ed.), *Autism: Nature, diagnosis, and treatment.* New York: Guilford.

Ortmann, A., & Hertwig, R. (1997). Is deception acceptable? *American Psychologist, 52,* 746–747.

Oskamp, S., & Schultz, P. W. (1998). *Applied social psychology* (2nd ed.). Upper Saddle River, NJ: Prentice-Hall.

Öst, L.-G. (1978). Behavioral treatment of thunder and lightning phobia. *Behavior Research and Therapy, 16,* 197–207.

Öst, L.-G. (1992). Blood and injection phobia: Background and cognitive, physiological and behavioral variables. *Journal of Abnormal Psychology, 101,* 68–74.

Öst, L.-G., Hellström, K., & Kåver, A. (1992). One- versus five-session exposure in the treatment of needle phobia. *Behavior Therapy, 23,* 263–282.

Ouimette, P. C., Finney, J. W., & Moos, R. H. (1997). Twelve-step and cognitive-behavioral treatment for substance abuse: A comparison of treatment effectiveness. *Journal of Consulting and Clinical Psychology, 65,* 230–240.

Overmier, J. B., & Seligman, M. E. P. (1967). Effects of inescapable shock upon subsequent escape and avoidance learning. *Journal of Comparative and Physiological Psychology, 63,* 23–33.

Overton, D. A. (1984). State dependent learning and drug discriminations. In L. L. Iverson, S. D. Iverson, & S. H. Snyder (Eds.), *Handbook of psychopharmacology* (Vol. 18). New York: Plenum.

Overton, P. G., Richards, C. D., Berry, M. S. & Clark, D. (1999). Long-term potentiation at excitatory amino acid synapses on midbrain dopamine neurons. *Neuroreport, 10,* 221–226.

Paik, H., & Comstock, G. (1994). The effects of television violence on antisocial behavior: A meta-analysis. *Communication Research, 21,* 516–546.

Paivio, S. C., & Greenberg, L. S. (1995). Resolving "unfinished business": Efficacy of experiential therapy using empty-chair dialogue. *Journal of Consulting and Clinical Psychology, 63,* 419–425.

Palmer, S. E. (1999). *Vision science: Photons to phenomenology.* Cambridge, MA: MIT Press.

Palmisano, M., & Herrmann, D. (1991). The facilitation of memory performance. *Bulletin of the Psychonomic Society, 29,* 557–559.

Paloutzian, R. F., & Kirkpatrick, L. A. (1995). Introduction: The scope of religious influences on personal and societal well-being. *Journal of Social Issues, 51,* 1–11.

Pan, H. S., Neidig, P. H., & O'Leary, K. D. (1994). Predicting mild to severe husband-to-wife physical aggression. *Journal of Consulting and Clinical Psychology, 62,* 975–981.

Pantev, C., Oostenveld, R., Engelien, A., Ross, B., Roberts, L. E., & Hoke, M. (1998). Increased auditory cortical representation in musicians. *Nature, 392,* 811–814.

Paoletti, M. G. (1995). Biodiversity, traditional landscapes and agroecosystem management. *Landscape and Urban Planning, 31*(1–3), 117–128.

Papp, L., Klein, D., Martinez, J., Schneier, F., Cole, R., Liebowitz, M., Hollander, E., Fryer, A., Jordan, F., & Gorman, J. (1993). Diagnostic and substance specificity of carbon monoxide-induced panic. *American Journal of Psychiatry, 150,* 250–257.

Parke, R. D. (1996). *Fatherhood.* Cambridge, MA: Harvard University Press.

Parke, R. D., & O'Neil, R. (2000). The Influence of Significant Others on Learning about Relationships: From Family to Friends. In R. S. L. Mills & S. Duck (Eds.), *The Developmental Psychology of Personal Relationships.* New York: Wiley.

Parkes, C. M. P., & Weiss, R. S. (1983). *Recovery from bereavement.* New York: Basic Books.

Parnas, J., Cannon, T., Jacobsen, B., Schulsinger, H., Schulsinger, F., & Mednick, S. (1993). Lifetime DSM-III-R diagnostic outcomes in the offspring of schizophrenic mothers. *Archives of General Psychiatry, 50,* 707–714.

Patrick, C. J., Cuthbert, B. N., & Lang, P. J. (1994). Emotion in the criminal psychopath: Fear imaging processing. *Journal of Abnormal Psychology, 103,* 523–534.

Patterson, D. R., Goldberg, M. L., & Ehde, D. M. (1996). Hypnosis in the treatment of patients with severe burns. *American Journal of Clinical Hypnosis, 38,* 200–212.

Pauk, W., & Fiore, J. P. (2000). *Succeed in college!* Boston: Houghton Mifflin.

Paul, G. L. (1969). Behavior modification research: Design and tactics. In C. M. Franks (Ed.), *Behavior therapy: Appraisal and status* (pp. 29–62). New York: McGraw-Hill.

Paul, G. L. (2000). Milieu therapy. In A. E. Kazdin (Ed.), *The encyclopedia of psychology.* Washington, DC: American Psychological Association.

Paul, G. L., & Lentz, R. J. (1977). *Psychosocial treatment of chronic mental patients: Milieu versus social learning programs.* Cambridge, MA: Harvard University Press.

Paul, G. L., Stuve, P., & Cross, J. V. (1997). Real-world inpatient programs: Shedding some light—A critique. *Applied and Preventive Psychology, 6,* 193–204.

Paulhus, D. L., Trapnell, P. D., & Chen, D. (1999). Birth order effects on personality and achievement within families. *Psychological Science, 10,* 482–488.

Paus, T., Zijdenbos, A., Worsley, K., Collins, D. L., Blumenthal, J., Giedd, J. N., Rapoport, J. L., & Evans, A. C. (1999). Structural maturation of neural pathways in children and adolescents: in vivo study. *Science, 283,* 1908–1911.

Pavlov, I. P. (1927). *Conditioned reflexes.* Oxford: Oxford University Press.

Penfield, W., & Rasmussen, T. (1968). *The cerebral cortex of man: A clinical study of localization of function.* New York: Hafner.

Peng, K., & Nisbett, R. E. (1999). Culture, dialectics, and reasoning about contradiction. *American Psychologist, 54,* 741–754.

Pennebaker, J. W. (1993). Putting stress into words: Health, linguistic, and therapeutic implications. *Behaviour Research and Therapy, 31,* 539–548.

Pennebaker, J. W. (1995). *Emotion, disclosure, and health.* Washington, DC: American Psychological Association.

Pennebaker, J. W., & Chew, C. H. (1985). Deception, electrodermal activity, and inhibition of behavior. *Journal of Personality and Social Psychology, 49,* 1427–1433.

Pennebaker, J. W., & O'Heeron, R. C. (1984). Confiding in others and illness rate among spouses of suicide and accidental death victims. *Journal of Abnormal Psychology, 93,* 473–476.

Pennebaker, J. W., Colder, M., & Sharp, L. K. (1990). Accelerating the coping process. *Journal of Personality and Social Psychology, 58,* 528–537.

Penner, L. A., & Craiger, J. P. (1992b). The weakest link: The performance of individual group members. In R. W. Swezey & E. Salas (Eds.), *Teams: Their training and performance* (pp. 57–74). Norwood, NJ: Ablex.

Penner, L. A., Dovidio, J., & Albrecht, T. L. (2001). Helping victims of loss and trauma: A social psychological perspective. In J. Harvey & E. Miller (Eds.), *Loss and trauma: General and close relationship perspectives* (pp. 62–85). Philadelphia: Brunner Routledge.

Penner, L. A., & Finkelstein, M. A. (1998). Dispositional and structural determinants of volunteerism. *Journal of Personality and Social Psychology, 74,* 525–537.

Penner, L. A., Fritzsche, B. A., Craiger, J. P., & Friefeld, T. R. (1995). Measuring the prosocial personality. In J. Butcher & C. D. Spielberger (Eds.), *Advances in personality assessment* (Vol. 10, pp. 147–163). Hillsdale, NJ: Erlbaum.

Penner, L. A., Knoff, H., Batchshe, G., Nelson, D. L., & Spielberger, C. D. (Eds.). (1994). *Contributions of psychology to science and math education.* Washington, DC: American Psychological Association.

Perls, F. S. (1969). *Ego, hunger and aggression: The beginning of Gestalt therapy.* New York: Random House.

Perls, F. S., Hefferline, R. F., & Goodman, P. (1951). *Gestalt therapy.* New York: Julian Press.

Peroutka, S. J., Newman, H., & Harris, H. (1988). The subjective effects of 3,4–methylenedioxymethamphetamine in recreational users. *Neuropharmacology, 1*(4), 273–277.

Persons, J. B., & Silberschatz, G. (1998). Are results of randomized controlled trials useful to psychotherapists? *Journal of Consulting and Clinical Psychology, 66,* 126–135.

Pervin, L. A. (1996). The science of personality. New York: Wiley.

Pervin, L. A., & John, O. P. (1997). *Personality: Theory and research* (7th ed.). New York: Wiley.

Peterson, A., Compas, B., Brooks-Gunn, J., Stemmler, M., Ey, S., & Grant, K. (1993). Depression in adolescence. *American Psychologist, 48,* 155–168.

Peterson, A. C. (1987, September). Those gangly years. *Psychology Today,* pp. 28–34.

Peterson, C., & Barrett, L. C. (1987). Explanatory style and academic performance among university freshmen. *Journal of Personality and Social Psychology, 53,* 603–607.

Peterson, C., Maier, S. F., & Seligman, M. E. (1993). *Learned helplessness: A theory for the age of personal control.* New York: Oxford University Press.

Peterson, C., & Seligman, M. E. P. (1984). Causal explanations as a risk factor for depression: Theory and evidence. *Psychological Review, 91,* 347–374.

Peterson, C., Seligman, M. E. P., Yurko, K. H., Martin, L. R., & Friedman, H. S. (1998). Catastrophizing and untimely death. *Psychological Science, 9,* 127–130.

Peterson, L. R., & Peterson, M. J. (1959). Short-term retention of individual verbal items. *Journal of Experimental Psychology, 58,* 193–198.

Petrie, K. J., Booth, R. J., Pennebaker, J. W., & Davison, K. P. (1995). Disclosure of trauma and immune response to a Hepatitis B vaccination program. *Journal of Consulting and Clinical Psychology, 63,* 787–792.

Petrill, S. A., Plomin, R., Berg, S., Johansson, B., Pederson, N. L., Ahern, F., & McClearn, G. E. (1998). The genetic and environmental relationship between general and specific cognitive abilities in twins age 80 and older. *Psychological Science, 9,* 183–189.

Pettigrew, T. F. (1979). The ultimate attribution error: Extending Allport's cognitive analysis of prejudice. *Personality and Social Psychology Bulletin, 5,* 461–476.

Pettigrew, T. F. (1997). Generalized intergroup contact effects on prejudice. *Personality and Social Psychology Bulletin, 23,* 173–185.

Petty, R. E., & Wegener, D. T. (1998). Attitude change: Multiple roles for persuasion variables. In D. Gilbert, S. T. Fiske, & G. Lindzey (Eds.), *Handbook of social psychology* (Vol.1, 4th ed., pp. 323–390). Boston: McGraw-Hill.

Peyron, C., Faraco, J., Rogers, W., Ripley, B., Overeem, S., Charnay, Y., Nevsemalova, S., Aldrich, M., Reynolds, D., Albin, R., Li, R., Hungs, M., Pedrazzoli, M., Padigaru, M., Kucherlapati, M., Fan, J., Maki, R., Lammers, G. J., Bouras, C., Kucherlapati, R., Nishino, S., & Mignot, E. (2000). A mutation in a case of early onset narcolepsy and a generalized absence of hypocretin peptides in human narcoleptic brains. *Nature Medicine, 6,* 991–997.

Pezdek, K., Finger, K., & Hodge, D. (1997). Planting false childhood memories: The role of event plausibility. *Psychological Science, 8,* 437–441.

Phares, E. J. (1991). *Introduction to personality* (3rd ed.). New York: Harper-Collins.

Phelps, E. A., O'Connor, K. J., Cunningham, W. A., Funayama, E. S., Gatenby, J. C., Gore, J. C., & Banaji, M. R. (2000). Performance on indirect measures of race evaluation predicts amygdala activation. *Journal of Cognitive Neuroscience, 12,* 729–738.

Phillips, D. P. (1983). The impact of media violence on U.S. homicides. *American Sociological Review, 48,* 560–568.

Phillips, D. P., & Cartensen, L. L. (1986). Clustering of teenage suicides after television news stories about suicide. *New England Journal of Medicine, 315,* 685–689.

Phillips, N. A. (2000). Female sexual dysfunction: Evaluation and treatment. *American Family Physician, 62,* 127–136, 141–142.

Phillips, R. L., Ernst, R. E., Brunk, B., Ivanova, N., Mahan, M. A., Deanehan, J. K., Moore, K. A., Overton, G. C., & Lemischka, I. R. (2000). The genetic program of hematopoietic stem cells *Science, 288,* 1635–1640.

Phinney, J. S. (1990). Ethnic identity in adolescents and adults: A review of research. *Psychological Bulletin, 108,* 499–514.

Phinney, J. S. (1996). When we talk about American ethnic groups, what do we mean? *American Psychologist, 51,* 918–927.

Piaget, J. (1952). *The origins of intelligence in children.* New York: International Universities Press.

Pierce, G., Sarason, I., & Sarason, B. (1991). General and specific support expectations and stress as predictors of perceived supportiveness: An experimental study. *Journal of Personality and Social Psychology, 63,* 297–307.

Pike, A., & Plomin, R. (1996). Importance of nonshared environmental factors for childhood and adolescent psychopathology. *Journal of the American Academy of Child and Adolescent Psychiatry, 35,* 560–570.

Piliavin, J. A., Dovidio, J. F., Gaertner, S. L., & Clark, R. D., III (1981). *Emergency intervention.* New York: Academic Press.

Pillard, R. C., & Bailey, J. M. (1998). Human sexual orientation has a heritable component. *Human Biology, 70,* 347–365.

Pillemer, D. B. (1998). What is remembered about early childhood events? *Clinical Psychology Review, 18,* 895–915.

Pinel, J. P. J. (1993). *Biopsychology.* Boston: Allyn & Bacon.

Plomin, R. (1989). Environment and genes: Determinants of behavior. *American Psychologist, 44,* 105–111.

Plomin, R. (1994). *Genetics and experience: The developmental interplay between nature and nurture.* Newbury Park, CA: Sage.

Plomin, R. (1997). Let's not give away DNA. *APA Monitor, 28,* 30.

Plomin, R., & Caspi, A. (1999). Behavioral genetics and personality. In L. Pervin & O. John (Eds.) *Handbook of personality research* (2nd ed.). New York: Guilford.

Plomin, R., Chipuer, H. M., & Loehlin, J. C. (1990). Behavioral genetics and personality. In L. A. Pervin (Ed.), *Handbook of personality: Theory and research* (pp. 225–243). New York: Guilford Press.

Plomin, R., DeFries, J. C., McClearn, G. E., & Rutter, M. (2000). *Behavioral Genetics* (4th ed.). New York: Freeman.

Plous, S. (1996). Attitudes toward the use of animals in psychological research and education: Results from a national survey of psychologists. *American Psychologist, 51,* 1167–1180.

Plutchik, R., & Conte, H. R. (Eds). (1997). *Circumplex models of personality and emotions.* Washington, DC: American Psychological Association.

Pollack, I. (1953). The assimilation of sequentially coded information. *American Journal of Psychology, 66,* 421–435.

Pollack, V. (1992). Meta-analysis of subjective sensitivity to alcohol in sons of alcoholics. *American Journal of Psychiatry, 149,* 1534–1538.

Polusny, M. A., & Follette, V. M. (1995). Long-term correlates of child sexual abuse: Theory and review of the empirical literature. *Applied and Preventive Psychology, 4,* 143–166.

Polusny, M. A., & Follette, V. M. (1996). Remembering childhood abuse: A national survey of psychologists' clinical practices, beliefs, and personal experiences. *Professional Psychology: Research and Practice, 27,* 41–52.

Pomerleau, C. S., & Pomerleau, O. F. (1992). Euphoriant effects of nicotine in smokers. *Psychopharmacology, 108,* 460–465.

Poole, D. A., Lindsay, D. S., Memon, A., & Bull, R. (1995). Psychotherapy and the recovery of memories of childhood sexual abuse: U.S. and British practitioners' opinions, practices, and experiences. *Journal of Consulting and Clinical Psychology, 63,* 426–437.

Pope, H. G., Jr., Hudson, J. I., Bodkin, J. A., & Oliva, P. (1998). Questionable validity of "dissociative amnesia" in trauma victims: Evidence from prospective studies. *British Journal of Psychiatry, 172,* 210–215.

Pope, H. G., Jr., & Yurgelun-Todd, D. (1996). The residual cognitive effects of heavy marijuana use in college students. *Journal of the American Medical Association, 275,* 521–527.

Pope, K. S. (in press). Pseudoscience, cross-examination, and scientific evidence in the recovered memory controversy. *Psychology, Public Policy, and Law.*

Pope-Davis, D. B., Reynolds, A. L., Dings, J. G., & Nielson, D. (1995). Examining multicultural counseling competencies of graduate students in psychology. *Professional Psychology: Research and Practice, 26,* 322–329.

Porges, S. W., Doussard, R. J. A., & Maita, A. K. (1995). Vagal tone and the physiological regulation of emotion. *Monographs of the Society for Research on Child Development, 59*(2–3), 167–186, 250–283.

Porkka-Heiskanen, T., Strecker, R. E., Thakkar, M., Bjorkum, A. A., Greene, R. W., & McCarley, R. W. (1997). Adenosine: A mediator of the sleep-inducing effects of prolonged wakefulness. *Science, 276,* 1265–1268.

Porte, H. S., & Hobson, J. A. (1996). Physical motion in dreams: One measure of three theories. *Journal of Abnormal Psychology, 105,* 329–335.

Porter, R. H. (1998/1999). Olfaction and human kin recognition. *Genetica, 104,* 259–263.

Porter, S., Yuille, J. C., & Lehman, D. R. (1999). The nature of real, implanted, and fabricated memories for emotional childhood events: Implications for the recovered memory debate. *Law & Human Behavior, 23,* 517–537.

Posener, J. A., DeBattista, C., Williams, G., H., Kraemer, H. C., Kalehzan, B. M., & Schatzberg, A. F. (2000). 24-hour monitoring of cortisol and corticotropin secretion in psychotic and nonpsychotic major depression. *Archives of General Psychiatry, 57,* 755–760.

Posner, M. I., & Peterson, S. E. (1990). The attention system of the human brain. *Annual Review of Neurosciences, 13,* 24–42.

Posner, M. I., & Raichle, M. E. (1994). *Images of mind.* New York: Scientific American Books.

Potter, P. T., & Zautra, A. J. (1997). Stressful life events' effects on rheumatoid arthritis disease activity. *Journal of Consulting and Clinical Psychology, 65,* 319–323.

Powch, I. G., & Houston, B. K. (1996). Hostility, anger-in, and cardiovascular activity in White women. *Health Psychology, 15,* 200–208.

Pratkanis, A. R. (1992). The cargo-cult science of subliminal persuasion. *Skeptical Inquirer, 16,* 260–273.

Pratkanis, A. R., & Aronson, E. (1991). *Age of propaganda: The everyday use and abuse of persuasion.* New York: Freeman.

Pratkanis, A. R., Eskenazi, J., & Greenwald, A. G. (1994). What you expect is what you believe (but not necessarily what you get): A test of the effectiveness of self-help audiotapes. *Basic and applied social psychology, 15,* 251–276.

Preciado, J. (1994). The empirical basis of behavior therapy applications with Hispanics. *The Behavior Therapist, 17,* 63–65.

Prentice-Dunn, S., & Rogers, R. W. (1989). Deindividuation and the self-regulation of behavior. In P. B. Paulus (Ed.), *Psychology of group influence* (2nd ed.). Hillsdale, NJ: Erlbaum.

Prescott, J. W. (1996). The origins of human love and violence. *Pre- and Peri-Natal Psychology Journal, 10,* 143–188.

Price, R. (1992). Psychosocial impact of job loss on individuals and families. *Current Directions in Psychological Sciences,* 1–11.

Prior, M. (1999). Resilience and coping: The role of individual temperament. In E. Frydenberg (Ed.), *Learning to cope: Developing as a person in complex societies.* New York: Oxford University Press.

Prochaska, J. O. (1994). Strong and weak principles for progressing from precontemplation to action on the basis of twelve problem behaviors. *Health Psychology, 13,* 47–51.

Prochaska, J. O., DiClemente, C., & Norcross, J. (1992). In search of how people change: Application to addictive behaviors. *American Psychologist, 47,* 1102–1114.

Pryor, T. (1995). Diagnostic criteria for eating disorders: DSM-IV revisions. *Psychiatric Annals, 25*(1), 40–45.

Quintana, S. M. (1998). Children's developmental understanding of ethnicity and race. *Applied and Preventive Psychology, 7,* 27–45.

Quintana, S. M., & Bernal, M. E. (1995). Ethnic minority training in counseling psychology: Comparisons with clinical psychology and proposed standards. *The Counseling Psychologist, 23*(1), 102–121.

Quitkin, F. M., Rabkin, J. G., Gerald, J., Davis, J. M., & Klein, D. F. (2000). Validity of clinical trials of antidepressants. *American Journal of Psychiatry, 157,* 327–337.

Rabasca, L. (1999a). High marks for psychologists who prescribe. *APA Monitor,* September, p. 21.

Rabasca, L. (1999b). Behavioral interventions can cut the use of restraints. *APA Monitor,* July/August, p. 27.

Rada, J. B., & Rogers, R. W. (1973). *Obedience to authority: Presence of authority and command strength.* Paper presented at the annual convention of the Southeastern Psychological Association.

Radecki, T. E. (1990, April-June). Cartoon monitoring. *National Coalition on Television Violence News,* p. 9.

Radvansky, G. A. (1999). Aging, memory, and comprehension. *Current Directions in Psychological Science, 8,* 49–53.

Raguram, R., & Bhide, A. (1985). Patterns of phobic neurosis: A retrospective study. *British Journal of Psychiatry, 147,* 557–560.

Raine, A., Brennan, P., & Mednick, S. (1994). Birth complications combined with early maternal rejection at age 1 year predispose to violent crime at age 18 years. *Archives of General Psychiatry, 51,* 984–988.

Raine, A., Lencz, T., Bihrle, S., LaCasse, L., & Colletti, P. (2000). Reduced prefrontal gray matter volume and reduced autonomic activity in antisocial personality disorder. *Archives of General Psychiatry, 57,* 119–127.

Raine, A., Venables, P., & Williams, M. (1990). Relationships between central and autonomic measures of arousal at age 15 years and criminality at age 24 years. *Archives of General Psychiatry, 47,* 1003–1007.

Ramachandran, V. S. (1988, August). Perceiving shape from shading. *Scientific American,* pp. 76–83.

Ramey, C. T., & Ramey, S. L. (1998). Early intervention and early experience. *American Psychologist, 53,* 109–121.

Ramey, C. T, Campbell, F. A., Burchinal, M., Skinner, M. L., Gardner, D. M., & Ramey, S. L. (2000). Persistent effects of early childhood education on high-risk children and their mothers. *Applied Developmental Science, 4,* 2–14.

Ramey, S. L. (1999). Head Start and preschool education: Toward continued improvement. *American Psychologist, 54,* 344–346.

Ranta, S., Jussila, J., & Hynynen, M. (1990). Recall of awareness during cardiac anaesthesia: Influence of feedback information to the anaesthesiologists. *Acta Aneasthesiolgia Scandinavica, 40,* 554–560.

Rapee, R., Brown, T., Antony, M., & Barlow, D. (1992). Response to hyperventilation and inhalation of 5. 5% carbon dioxide-enriched air across DSM-III anxiety disorders. *Journal of Abnormal Psychology, 101,* 538–552.

Raskin, D. C. (1986). The polygraph in 1986: Scientific, professional and legal issues surrounding applications and acceptance of polygraph evidence. *Utah Law Review 1986,* 29–74.

Ratcliff, R., & McKoon, G. (1989). Memory models, text processing, and cue-dependent retrieval. In H. L. Roediger & F. I. M. Craik (Eds.), *Varieties of memory and consciousness.* Hillsdale, NJ: Erlbaum.

Ratner, C. (1994). The unconscious: A perspective from sociohistorical psychology. *Journal of Mind and Behavior, 15*(4), 323–342.

Rattenborg, N., Lima, S. L., & Amlaner, C. J. (1999). Half-awake to the risk of predation. *Nature, 397,* 397–398.

Reber, A. S. (1992). The cognitive unconscious: An evolutionary perspective. *Consciousness and Cognition: An International Journal, 1*(2), 93–133.

Redd, W. H. (1984). Psychological intervention to control cancer chemotherapy side effects. *Postgraduate Medicine, 75,* 105–113.

Reed, S. K. (2000) *Cognition* (5th ed.). Belmont, CA: Wadsworth.

Reedy, M. N. (1983). *Personality and aging.* In D. S. Woodruff & J. E. Birren (Eds.), Aging: Scientific perspectives and social issues (2nd ed.). Monterey, CA: Brooks/Cole.

Reeve, J. M. (1996). *Understanding motivation and emotion.* New York: Harcourt, Brace, Jovanovich.

Regier, D. A., Farmer, M. E., Rae, D. S., Myers, J. K., Kramer, M., Robins, L. N., George, L. K., Karno, M., & Locke, B. Z. (1993). One-month prevalence of mental disorders in the United States and sociodemographic characteristics: The Epidemiologic Catchment Area study. *Acta Psychiatrica Scandinavica, 88,* 35–47.

Regier, D. A., Narrow, W., Rae, D., Manderscheid, R., Locke, B., & Goodwin, F. (1993). The de facto U.S. mental and addictive disorders service system: Epidemiologic catchment area prospective 1-year prevalence rates of disorders and services. *Archives of General Psychiatry, 50*, 85–94.

Reich, T., Edenberg, H. J., Goate, A., Williams, J. T., Rice, J. P., Van Eerdewegh, P., Foroud, T., Hesselbrock, V., Schuckit, M. A., Bucholz, K., Porjesz, B., Li, T. K., Conneally, P. M., Nurnberger, J. I., Jr., Tischfield, J. A., Crowe, R. A., Cloninger, C. R., Wu, W., Shears, S., Carr, K., Crose, C., Willig, C., & Begleiter, H. (1998). Genome-wide search for genes affecting the risk for alcohol dependence. *American Journal of Medical Genetics, 81*, 207–215.

Reinisch, J. M., Ziemba-Davis, M., & Sanders, S. A. (1991). Hormonal contributions to sexually dimorphic behavioral development in humans. *Psychoneuroendocrinology, 16*, 213–278.

Reisberg, D. (1997). *Cognition: Exploring the science of the mind.* New York: Norton.

Reisenzein, R. (1983). The Schachter theory of emotion: Two decades later. *Psychological Bulletin, 94*, 239–264.

Reiss, A. J., & Roth, J. A. (1993). *Understanding and preventing violence.* Washington, DC: National Academy Press.

Reitman, D., & Drabman, R. S. (1999). Multifaceted uses of a simple timeout record in the treatment of a noncompliant 8-year-old boy. *Education and Treatment of Children, 22*, 136–145.

Rendall, D., Cheney, D. L., & Seyfarth, R. M. (2000). Proximate factors mediating "contact" calls in adult female baboons (*Papio cynocephalus ursinus*) and their infants. *Journal of Comparative Psychology, 114*, 36–46.

Rescorla, L. A. (1981). Category development in early language. *Journal of Child Language, 8*, 225–238.

Rescorla, R. A. (1968). Probability of shock in the presence and absence of CS in fear conditioning. *Journal of Comparative and Physiological Psychology, 66*, 1–5.

Resnick, M. (1997). Protecting adolescents from harm: Findings from the National Longitudinal Study of Adolescent Health. *Journal of the American Medical Association, 278*, 823–832.

Reynolds, C. F. III, Frank, E., Perel, J. M. Imber, S. D., Cornes, C., Miller, M. D., Mazumdar, S., Houck, P. R., Dew, M. A., Stack, J. A., Pollock, B. G., & Kupfer, D. J. (1999). Nortriptyline and interpersonal psychotherapy as maintenance therapies for recurrent major depression: A randomized controlled trial in patients older than 59 years. *Journal of the American Medical Association, 281*, 39–45.

Rheingold, H., & Cook, K. (1975). The contents of boys' and girls' rooms as an index of parents' behavior. *Child Development, 46*, 459–463.

Rhodewalt, F., & Zone, J. B. (1989). Appraisal of life change, depression, and illness in hardy and nonhardy women. *Journal of Personality and Social Psychology, 56*, 81–88.

Rice, G., Anderson, C., Risch, N., & Ebers, G. (1999). Male homosexuality: absence of linkage to microsatellite markers at Xq28. *Science, 284*, 665–667.

Rice, M. E. (1997). Violent offender research and implications for the criminal justice system. *American Psychologist, 52*, 414–423.

Richards, J. M., Beal, W. E., Seagal, J. D., & Pennebaker, J. W. (2000). Effects of disclosure of traumatic events on illness behavior among psychiatric prison inmates. *Journal of Abnormal Psychology*, 109, 156–160

Richards, P. S., & Bergin, A. E. (Eds.). (2000). *Handbook of Psychotherapy and Religious Diversity.* Washington, DC: American Psychological Association.

Richardson, P. H., & Vincent, C. A. (1986). Acupuncture for the treatment of pain: A review of evaluative research. *Pain, 24*, 15–40.

Richardson-Klavehn, A., & Bjork, R. A. (1988). Measures of memory. *Annual Review of Psychology, 39*, 475–543.

Rickels, K., Schweizer, E., Weiss, S., & Zavodnick, S. (1993). Maintenance drug treatment of panic disorder. II: Short- and long-term outcome after drug taper. *Archives of General Psychiatry, 50*, 61–68.

Ridley, M. (2000). *Genome: The Autobiography of a Species in 23 Chapters.* New York: HarperCollins.

Riedel, W. J., & Jolles, J. (1996). Cognition enhancers in age-related cognitive decline. *Drugs and Aging, 8*, 245–274.

Riger, S. (1992). Epistemological debates, feminist voices: Science, social values, and the study of women. *American Psychologist, 47*, 730–740.

Riggio, R. E. (1989). *Introduction to industrial/organizational psychology.* Glenview, IL: Scott, Foresman.

Rinn, W. E. (1984). The neuropsychology of facial expressions: A review of the neurological and psychological mechanisms for producing facial expressions. *Psychological Bulletin, 95*, 52–77.

Rioux, S. (1998). *The motivational basis of organizational citizenship behavior.* Unpublished doctoral dissertation, University of South Florida.

Ripple, C. H., Gilliam, W. S., Chanana, N., & Zigler, E. (1999). Will fifty cooks spoil the broth?: The debate over entrusting Head Start to the states. *American Psychologist, 54*, 327–343.

Rips, L. J. (1994). *The psychology of proof: Deductive reasoning in human thinking.* Cambridge, MA: MIT Press.

Risen, J. (1998). CIA seeks "curmudgeon" to signal its mistakes. *New York Times,* July 7.

Rittenhouse, C. D., Stickgold, R., & Hobson, J. A. (1994). Constraint on the transformation of characters, objects, and settings in dream reports. *Consciousness and Cognition, 3*(1), 100–113.

Robbins, J. (2000). Virtual reality finds a real place as a medical aid. *New York Times,* July 4.

Robbins, S. P. (1998). *Organizational Behavior: Concepts, Controversies, Applications.* Upper Saddle River, NJ: Prentice Hall.

Robbins, T. L. (1995). Social loafing on cognitive tasks: An examination of the "sucker effect." *Journal of Business and Psychology, 9*, 337–342.

Robbins, T. W., & Everitt, B. J. (1999). Interaction of the dopaminergic system with mechanisms of associative learning and cognition: Implications for drug abuse. *Psychological Science, 10*, 199–202.

Roberts, B. W., & DelVecchio, W. F. (2000). The rank-order consistency of traits from childhood to old-age: A quantitative review of longitudinal studies. *Psychological Bulletin, 126*, 3–25.

Robertson, I. H., & Murre, J. M. J. (1999). Rehabilitation of brain damage: Brain plasticity and principles of guided recovery. *Psychological Bulletin, 125*, 544–575.

Robertson, J., & Robertson, J. (1971). Young children in brief separation: A fresh look. *Psychoanalytic Study of the Child, 26*, 264–315.

Robins, L. N., & Regier, D. A. (Eds.). (1991). *Psychiatric disorders in America: The Epidemiologic Catchment Area study.* New York: Free Press.

Robins, L. N., Helzer, J. E., Weissman, M. M., Orvaschel, H., Gruenberg, E., Burke, J. D., Jr., & Regier, D. A. (1984). Lifetime prevalence of specific psychiatric disorders in three sites. *Archives of General Psychiatry, 41*, 949–958.

Robins, R. W., Gosling, S. D., & Craik, K. H. (1999). An empirical analysis of trends in psychology. *American Psychologist, 54*, 117–128.

Robinson, J. H., & Pritchard, W. S. (1995). "The scientific case that nicotine is addictive": Reply. *Psychopharmacology, 117*(1), 16–17.

Rock, I. (1978). *An introduction to perception.* New York: Macmillan.

Rock, I. (1983). *The logic of perception.* Cambridge, MA: MIT Press.

Rodier, P. M. (2000). The early origins of autism. *Scientific American, 282*, 56–63.

Rodriguez de Fonseca, F., Carrera, M. R. A., Navarro, M., Koob, G. F., & Weiss, F. (1997). Activation of corticotropin-releasing factor in the limbic system during cannabinoid withdrawal. *Science, 276*, 2050–2054.

Roediger, H. L., III, Guynn, M. J., & Jones, T. C. (1995). Implicit memory: A tutorial review. In G. d'Ydewalle, P. Eelen, & P. Bertelson (Eds.), *International perspectives on psychological science: Vol. 2. The state of the art* (pp. 67–94). Hove, UK: Erlbaum.

Roediger, H. L., III, & McDermott, K. B. (1995). Creating false memories: Remembering words not presented in lists. *Journal of Experimental Psychology: Learning, Memory, and Cognition, 21*, 803–814.

Roediger, H. L., & McDermott, K. B. (2000). Tricks of memory. *Current Directions in Psychological Science, 9*, 123–127.

Roffwarg, H. P., Hermann, J. H., & Bowe-Anders, C. (1978). The effects of sustained alterations of waking visual input on dream content. In A. M. Arkin, J. S. Antrobus, & S. J. Ellman (Eds.), *The mind in sleep.* Hillsdale, NJ: Erlbaum.

Roffwarg, H. P., Muzio, J. N., & Dement, W. C. (1966). Ontogenetic development of the human sleep-dream cycle. *Science, 152*, 604–619. (Revised 1969.)

Rogelberg, S. G., & Luong, A. (1998). Nonresponse to mailed surveys: A review and guide. *Current Directions in Psychological Science, 7*, 60–65.

Rogers, C. R. (1942). *Counseling and psychotherapy.* Boston: Houghton Mifflin.

Rogers, C. R. (1951). *Client-centered therapy.* Boston: Houghton Mifflin.

Rogers, C. R. (1961). *On becoming a person.* Boston: Houghton Mifflin.

Rogers, C. R. (1970). *Carl Rogers on encounter groups.* New York: Harper & Row.

Rogers, C. R. (1980). *A way of being.* Boston: Houghton Mifflin.

Rogers, J., Madamba, S. G., Staunton, D. A., & Siggins, G. R. (1986). Ethanol increases single unit activity in the inferior olivary nucleus. *Brain Research, 385*, 253–262.

Rogers, S. J. (1998). Empirically supported comprehensive treatments for young children with autism. *Journal of Clinical Child Psychology, 27*, 168–179.

Rogers, S. M., & Turner, C. F. (1991). Male-male sexual contact in the U.S.A.: Findings from five sample surveys, 1970–1990. *Journal of Sex Research, 28*, 491–519.

Rogers, T. B. (1995). *The psychological testing enterprise: An introduction.* Belmont, CA: Wadsworth.

Rogge, R. D., & Bradbury, T. N. (1999). Till violence do us part: The differing roles of communication and aggression in predicting adverse marital outcomes. *Journal of Consulting and Clinical Psychology, 67,* 340–351.

Rogoff, B., & Waddell, K. J. (1982). Memory for information organized in a scene by children from two cultures. *Child Development,* 53, 1224–1228.

Rohan, M. J., & Zanna, M. P. (1996). *Value transmission in families.* In C. Seligman, J. M. Olson, & M. P. Zanna (Eds.), *The psychology of values: The Ontario symposium* (Vol. 8, pp. 253–276). Mahwah, NJ: Erlbaum.

Rolls, E. T., Critchley, H. D., Browning, A., & Hernadi, I. (1998). The neurophysiology of taste and olfaction in primates, and umami flavor. *Annals of the New York Academy of Science, 855,* 426–437.

Roorda, A., & Williams, D. R. (1999). The arrangement of the three cone classes in the living human eye. *Nature 397,* 520–522.

Rosch, E. (1975). Cognitive representations of semantic categories. *Journal of Experimental Psychology: General, 104,* 192–223.

Rosch, E., Mervis, C. B., Gray, W. D., Johnson, D. M., & Boyes-Braem, P. (1976). Basic objects in natural categories. *Cognitive Psychology, 8,* 382–439.

Rosen, B. C., & D'Andrade, R. (1959). The psychosocial origins of achievement motivation. *Sociometry, 22,* 188–218.

Rosen, G. M. (1999). Treatment fidelity and research on eye movement desensitization and reprocessing (EMDR). *Journal of Anxiety Disorders, 13,* 173–184.

Rosen, R. (1991). *The healthy company.* Los Angeles: J. P. Tarcher.

Rosenbaum, M., & Bennett, B. (1986). Homicide and depression. *American Journal of Psychiatry, 143,* 367–370.

Rosenbaum, R. S., Priselac, S. K., Black, S. E., Gao, F., Nadel, L., & Moscovitch, M. (2000). Remote spatial memory in an amnesic person with extensive bilateral hippocampal lesions. *Nature Neuroscience, 3,* 1044–1048.

Rosenfarb, I. S., Goldstein, M. J., Mintz, J., & Nuechterlein, K. H. (1995). Expressed emotion and subclinical psychopathology observable within the transactions between schizophrenic patients and their family members. *Journal of Abnormal Psychology, 104,* 259–267.

Rosenfeld, J. P. (1995). Alternative views of Bashore and Rapp's (1993) alternatives to traditional polygraphy: A critique. *Psychological Bulletin, 117*(1), 159–166.

Rosenstock, I. M. (1974). Historical origins of the health belief model. *Health Education Monographs, 2,* 328–335.

Rosenthal, R. R. (1966). *Experimenter effects in behavioral research.* New York: Appleton-Century-Crofts.

Rosenthal, R. (1996). *Initial report task force on statistical inference.* Washington, DC: Science Directorate of the American Psychological Association.

Rosenzweig, M. R., & Bennett, E. L. (1996). Psychobiology of plasticity: Effects of training and experience on brain and behavior. *Behavioural Brain Research, 78,* 57–65.

Ross, C. A. (1997). *Dissociative identity disorder: Diagnosis, clinical features, and treatment of multiple personality.* New York: Wiley.

Ross, C. A., Anderson, G., Fleisher, W. P., & Norton, G. R. (1991). The frequency of multiple personality disorder among psychiatric inpatients. *American Journal of Psychiatry, 148,* 1717–1720.

Ross, L., & Nisbett, R. E. (1991). *The person and the situation: Perspectives of social psychology.* New York: McGraw-Hill.

Ross, S. I., & Jackson, J. M. (1991). Teachers' expectations for Black males' and Black females' academic achievement. *Personality and Social Psychology Bulletin, 17,* 78–82.

Rossini, E. D., & Morretti, R. J. (1997). Thematic Apperception Test (TAT) interpretation: Practice recommendations from a survey of clinical psychology doctoral programs accredited by the American Psychological Association. *Professional Psychology: Research and Practice, 28,* 393–398.

Rothbart, M. K., & Lewis, S. (1994). Cognitive processes and intergroup relations: A historical perspective: In P. G. Devine, D. L. Hamilton, & T. M. Ostrom (Eds.), *Social cognition: Impact on social psychology* (pp. 347–382). San Diego, CA: Academic Press.

Rothbart, M. K., Ahadi, S. A., & Evans, D. E. (2000). Temperament and personality: Origins and outcomes. *Journal of Personality and Social Psychology,* 78, 122–135.

Rothbaum, B. O., & Hodges, L. F. (1999). The use of virtual reality exposure in the treatment of anxiety disorders. *Behavior Modification, 23,* 507–525.

Rothbaum, B. O., Hodges, L. F., Alarcon, R., Ready, D., Shahar, F., Graap, K., Pair, J., Hebert, P., Gotz, D., Wills, B., & Baltzall, D. (1999). Virtual reality exposure therapy for PTSD Vietnam veterans: A case study. *Journal of Traumatic Stress, 12,* 263–271.

Rothbaum, B. O., Hodges, L. F., Kooper, R., & Opdyke, D. (1995). Effectiveness of computer-generated virtual reality graded exposure in the treatment of acrophobia. *American Journal of Psychiatry, 152,* 626–628.

Rottenstreich, Y., & Tversky, A. (1997). Unpacking, repacking, and anchoring: Advances in support theory. *Psychological Review, 104,* 406–415.

Rotter, J. B. (1982). *The development and application of social learning theory.* New York: Praeger.

Rotter, J. B. (1990). Internal versus external control of reinforcement: A case history of a variable. *American Psychologist, 45,* 489–493.

Rotton, J. (1990). Individuals under stress. In C. E. Kimble (Ed.), *Social psychology: Living with people.* New York: W. C. Brown.

Rotton, J., & Kelly, I. W. (1985). Much ado about the full moon: A meta-analysis of lunar-lunacy research. *Psychological Bulletin, 97,* 286–306.

Rouéché, B. (1986, December 8). Cinnabar. *The New Yorker.*

Rovee-Collier, C. (1993). The capacity for long-term memory in infancy. *Current Directions in Psychological Science, 2,* 130–135.

Rovee-Collier, C. (1999). The development of infant memory. *Current Directions in Psychological Science, 8,* 80–85.

Rowe, D. C. (1997). Genetics, temperament, and personality. In R. Hogan, J. Johnson, & S. Briggs (Eds.), *Handbook of personality psychology* (pp. 367–386). San Diego: Academic Press.

Rowe, D. C., Almeida, D. M., & Jacobson, K. C. (1999). School context and genetic influences on aggression in adolescence. *Psychological Science, 10,* 277–280.

Rowe, D. C., Jacobson, K. C., Van den Oord, E. J. C. G. (1999). Genetic and environmental influences on vocabulary IQ: Parental education level as moderator. *Child Development, 70,* 1151–1162.

Rozin, P. (1982). "Taste-smell confusions" and the duality of the olfactory sense. *Perception and Psychophysics, 31,* 397–401.

Rozin, P. (1996). Sociocultural influences on human food selection. In E. D. Capaldi (Ed.), *Why we eat what we eat: The psychology of eating* (pp. 233–263). Washington, DC: American Psychological Association.

Rubin, E. (1915). Synsoplevede figure. Copenhagen; Gyldendalske.

Rubin, K. H., Bukowski, W., & Parker, J. G. (1998). Peer interactions, relationships, and groups. In W. Damon & N. Eisenberg (Eds.), *Handbook of child psychology: Vol. 3. Social, emotional, and personality development* (5th ed., pp. 619–700). New York: Wiley.

Rubinstein, S., & Caballero, B. (2000). Is Miss America an undernourished role model? *Journal of the American Medical Association, 283,* 1569.

Ruble, D. N., & Martin, C. L. (1998). Gender development. In W. Damon & N. Eisenberg (Eds.), *Handbook of child psychology: Vol. 3. Social, emotional, and personality development* (5th ed., pp. 933–1016). New York: Wiley.

Rudman, L. A., Greenwald, A. G., Mellott, D. S., & Schwartz, J. L. K. (1999). Measuring the automatic components of prejudice: Flexibility and generality of the Implicit Association Test. *Social Cognition, 17,* 437–465.

Rumelhart, D. E., & McClelland, J. L. (1986). *Parallel distributed processing: Explorations in the microstructure of cognition: Vol. 1. Foundations.* Cambridge, MA: Bradford.

Rusbult, C. E., & Van Lange, P. A. M. (1996). Interdependence processes. In E. T. Higgins & A. W. Kruglanski (Eds.), *Social psychology: Handbook of basic principles* (pp. 564–596). New York: Guilford.

Rusbult, C. E., Verette, J., Whitney, G. A., Slovik, L. F., & Lipkus, I. (1991). Accommodation processes in close relationships: Theory and preliminary empirical evidence. *Journal of Personality and Social Psychology, 60,* 53–78.

Russell, J. A. (1991). Culture and the categorization of emotions. *Psychological Bulletin, 110,* 426–450.

Russell, J. A. (1994). Is there universal recognition of emotion from facial expression? A review of the cross-cultural studies. *Psychological Bulletin, 155*(2), 102–141.

Russell, J. A. (1995). Facial expressions of emotion: What lies beyond minimal universality? *Psychological Bulletin, 118,* 379–391.

Rutkowski, G. K., Gruder, C. L., & Romer, D. (1983). Group cohesiveness, social norms, and bystander intervention. *Journal of Personality and Social Psychology, 44,* 545–552.

Rutter, M. L. (1997). Nature-nurture integration. The example of antisocial behavior. *American Psychologist, 52,* 390–398.

Rutter, M., & Schopler, E. (1992). Classification of pervasive developmental disorders: Some concepts and practical considerations. *Journal of Autism and Developmental Disorders, 22,* 459–482.

Ryan, R. H., & Geiselman, R. E. (1991). Effects of biased information on the relationship between eyewitness confidence and accuracy. *Bulletin of the Psychonomic Society, 29,* 7–9.

Rymer, R. (1992, April 23). A silent childhood. *The New Yorker,* pp. 41–81.

Rymer, R. (1993). *Genie: A scientific tragedy.* New York: HarperCollins.

Rynders, J., & Horrobin, J. (1980). Educational provisions for young children with Down's syndrome. In J. Gottlieb (Ed.), *Educating mentally retarded persons in the mainstream* (pp. 109–147). Baltimore: University Park Press.

Saarni, C., Mummer, D. L., & Campos, J. J. (1998). Emotional development: Action, communication, and understanding. In W. Damon & N. Eisenberg (Eds.), *Handbook of child psychology: Vol. 3. Social, emotional, and personality development* (5th ed., pp. 237–310). New York: Wiley.

Sachs, J. (1967). Recognition memory for syntactic and semantic aspects of connected discourse. *Perception and Psychophysics, 2,* 437–442.

Sack, R. L., Hughes, R. J., Edgar, D. M., & Lewy, A. J. (1997). Sleep-promoting effects of melatonin: At what dose, in whom, under what conditions, and by what mechanisms? *Sleep, 20,* 908–915.

Sackeim, H. A. (1985, June). The case for ECT. *Psychology Today,* pp. 36–40.

Sacks, O. (1985). *The man who mistook his wife for a hat.* New York: Summit Books.

Sacks, O. (1992, July 27). The landscape of his dreams. *The New Yorker.*

Sagi, A., van IJzendoorn, M. H., Aviezer, O., Donnell, F., & Mayseless, O. (1994). Sleeping out of home in a kibbutz communal arrangement: It makes a difference for infant-mother attachment. *Child Development, 65,* 992–1004.

Sakairi, Y. (1992). Studies on meditation using questionnaires. *Japanese Psychological Review, 35*(1), 94–112.

Saks, M. J. (1992). Obedience versus disobedience to legitimate versus illegitimate authorities issuing good versus evil directives. *Psychological Science, 3,* 221–223.

Salloum, I. M., Cornelius, J. R., Thase, M. E., Daley, D. C., Kirisci, L., & Spotts, C. (1998). Naltrexone utility in depressed alcoholics. *Psychopharmacological Bulletin, 34,* 111–115.

Salovey, P., Mayer, J. D., & Rosenhan, D. L. (1991). Mood and helping: Mood as a motivator of helping and helping as a regulator of mood. In M. S. Clark (Ed.), *Review of personality and social psychology: Vol. 12. Prosocial behavior* (pp. 215–237). Newbury Park, CA: Sage.

Salovey, P., Rothman, A. J., & Rodin, J. (1998). Health behavior. In D. Gilbert, S. T. Fiske, & G. Lindzey (Eds.), *Handbook of social psychology* (Vol. 2, 4th ed., pp. 684–732). Boston: McGraw-Hill.

Salzer, M. S., Rappaport, J., & Segre, L. (1999). Professional appraisal of professionally led and self-help groups. *American Journal of Orthopsychiatry, 69,* 536–540.

Samuel, S. E., & Gorton, G. E. (1998). National survey of psychology internship directors regarding education for prevention of psychologist-patient sexual exploitation. *Professional Psychology: Research and Practice, 29,* 86–90.

Sanchez-Ramos, J., Song, S., Cardozo-Pelaez, F., Hazzi, C., Stedeford, T., Willing, A., Freeman, T. B., Saporta, S., Janssen, W., Patel, N., Cooper, D. R., & Sanberg, P. R. (2000). Adult bone-marrow stromal cells differentiate into neural cells *in vitro. Experimental Neurology, 164,* 247–256.

Sanders, M. R., Markie-Dadds, C., Tully, L. A., & Bor, W. (2000). The triple p-positive parenting program: A comparison of enhanced, standard, and self-directed behavioral family intervention for parents of children with early onset conduct problems. *Journal of Consulting and Clinical Psychology, 68,* 624–640.

Sanderson, W. C., Rapee, R. M., & Barlow, D. H. (1989). The influence of an illusion of control on panic attacks induced via inhalation of 5. 5 carbon dioxide-enriched air. *Archives of General Psychiatry, 46,* 157–162.

Sandin, R. H., Enlund, G., Samuelsson, P., & Lennmarken, C. (2000). Awareness during anaesthesia: a prospective case study. *Lancet, 355,* 707–711.

Sanna, L. J. (1992). Self-efficacy theory: Implications for social facilitation and social loafing. *Journal of Personality and Social Psychology, 62,* 774–786.

Sarason, B. R., Sarason, I. G., & Gurung, R. A. R. (1997). Close personal relationships and health outcomes: A key to the role of social support. In S. Duck (Ed.), *Handbook of personal relationships* (pp. 547–573). New York: Wiley.

Sarason, I. G., Sarason, B. R., Keefe, D. E., Hayes, B. E., & Shearin, E. N. (1986). Cognitive interference: Situational determinants and traitlike characteristics. *Journal of Personality and Social Psychology, 51,* 215–226.

Sarason, I. G., Johnson, J., & Siegel, J. (1978). Assessing impact of life changes: Development of the life experiences survey. *Journal of Clinical and Consulting Psychology, 46,* 932–946.

Sato, T. (1997). Seasonal affective disorder and phototherapy: A critical review. *Professional Psychology: Research and Practice, 28,* 164–169.

Saudino, K. J. (1998). Moving beyond the heritability question: New directions in behavioral genetic studies of personality. *Current Directions in Psychological Science, 6,* 86–89.

Savelkoul, M., Post, M. W. M., de Witte, L. P., & van den Borne, H. B. (2000). Social support, coping, and subjective well-being in patients with rheumatic diseases. *Patient Education and Counseling, 39,* 205–218.

Savin-Williams, R. C., & Demo, D. H. (1984). Developmental change and stability in adolescent self-concept. *Developmental Psychology, 20,* 1100–1110.

Saxe, L., & Ben-Shakhar, G. (1999). Admissibility of polygraph tests: The application of scientific standards post-Daubert. *Psychology, Public Policy, and Law, 5,* 203–223.

Sayers, J. (1991). *Mother of psychoanalysis.* New York: Norton.

Scarr, S. (1998). How do families affect intelligence? Social environmental and behavior genetic prediction. In J. J. McArdle, R. W. Woodcock, et al. (Eds), *Human cognitive abilities in theory and practice* (pp. 113–136). Mahwah, NJ: Erlbaum.

Scarr, S., & Carter-Saltzman, L. (1982). Genetics and intelligence. In R. Sternberg (Ed.), *Handbook of human intelligence.* Cambridge, England: Cambridge University Press.

Scarr, S., & Weinberg, R. A. (1976). IQ test performance of black children adopted by white families. *American Psychologist, 31,* 726–739.

Schachar, R., & Logan, G. (1990). Impulsivity and inhibitory control in normal development and childhood psychopathology. *Developmental Psychology, 26,* 710–720.

Schacter, D. L. (1999). The seven sins of memory: Insights from psychology and cognitive neuroscience. *American Psychologist, 54,* 182–203.

Schacter, D. L., & Cooper, L. A. (1993). Implicit and explicit memory for novel visual objects: Structure and function. *Journal of Experimental Psychology: Learning, Memory, and Cognition, 19*(5), 995–1009.

Schacter, D. L., Chiu, C.-Y. P., & Ochsner, K. N. (1993). Implicit memory: A selective review. *Annual Review of Neuroscience, 16,* 159–182.

Schacter, D. L., Cooper, L. A., Delaney, S. M., Peterson, M. A., & Tharan, M. (1991). Implicit memory for possible and impossible objects: Constraints on the construction of structural descriptions. *Journal of Experimental Psychology: Learning, Memory, and Cognition, 17,* 3–19.

Schacter, D. L., Norman, K. A., & Koutstaal, W. (1998). The cognitive neuroscience of constructive memory. *Annual Review of Psychology, 49,* 289–318.

Schachter, S., & Singer, J. (1962). Cognitive, social and physiological determinants of emotional state. *Psychological Review, 69,* 379–399.

Schafer, J., & Brown, S. A. (1991). Marijuana and cocaine effect expectancies and drug use patterns. *Journal of Consulting and Clinical Psychology, 59,* 558–565.

Schaefer, J., Sykes, R., Rowley, R., & Baek, S. (1988, November*). Slow country music and drinking.* Paper presented at the 87th annual meetings of the American Anthropological Association, Phoenix, AZ.

Schaffer, C. E., Davidson, R. J., & Saron, C. (1983). Frontal and parietal EEG asymmetry in depressed and non-depressed subjects. *Biological Psychiatry, 18,* 753–762.

Schaie, K. W. (1993). The Seattle longitudinal study of adult intelligence. *Current Directions in Psychological Science, 2*(6), 171–175.

Schaie, K. W., & Willis, S. L. (1999). Theories of everyday competence and aging. In V. L. Bengston & W. K. Schaie (Eds.), *Handbook of theories of aging.* New York: Springer.

Scharff, J. S., & Scharff, D. E. (1998). *Object relations individual psychotherapy.* Northvale, NJ: Jason Aronson.

Scheerer, M., Rothmann, R., & Goldstein, K. (1945). A case of "idiot savant": An experimental study of personality organization. *Psychological Monognomics, 58*(4).

Scheier, M. F., Carver, C. S., & Bridges, M. W. (1994). Distinguishing optimism from neuroticism (and trait anxiety, self-mastery, and self-esteem): A reevaluation of the Life Orientation Test. *Journal of Personality and Social Psychology, 67,* 1063–1078.

Scheier, M. F., Matthews, K. A., Owens, J. F., Magovern, G. J., Lefebvre, R. C., Abbott, R. A., & Carver, C. S. (1989). Dispositional optimism and recovery from coronary artery bypass surgery: The beneficial effects on physical and psychological well-being. *Journal of Personality and Social Psychology, 57,* 1024–1040.

Schenck, C. H., & Mahowald, M. W. (1992). Motor dyscontrol in narcolepsy: Rapid eye movement (REM) sleep without atonia and REM sleep behavior disorder. *Annals of Neurology, 32*(1), 3–10.

Schiffman, S. S., Graham, B. G., Sattely-Miller, & Warwick, Z. (1999). Orosensory perception of dietary fat. *Current Directions in Psychological Science, 7,* 137–143.

Schloss, P., & Williams, D. C. (1998). The serotonin transporter: A primary target for antidepressant drugs. *Journal of Psychopharmacology, 12,* 115–121.

Schmidt, N. B., Lerew, D. R., & Jackson, R. J. (1997). The role of anxiety sensitivity in the pathogenesis of panic: Prospective evaluation of spontaneous panic attacks during acute stress. *Journal of Abnormal Psychology, 106,* 355–364.

Schmidt, N. B., Lerew, D. R., & Jackson, R. J. (1999). Prospective evaluation of anxiety sensitivity in the pathogenesis of panic: Replication and extension. *Journal of Abnormal Psychology, 108,* 532–537.

Schmolck, H., Buffalo, E. A., Squire, L. R. (2000). Memory distortions over time: Recollections of the O. J. Simpson trial verdict after 15 and 32 months. *Psychological Science, 11*, 39–47.

Schnabel, T. (1987). Evaluation of the safety and side effects of antianxiety agents. *American Journal of Medicine, 82* (Suppl. 5A), 7–13.

Schneider, B. (1985). Organizational behavior. *Annual Review of Psychology, 36*, 573–611.

Schneider, W., & Bjorklund, D. F. (1998). *Memory*. In W. Damon, D. Kuhn, & R. Siegler (Eds.), *Handbook of child psychology: Vol. 2. Cognition, language and perception* (5th ed., pp. 467–521). New York: Wiley.

Schnurr, P. P., Ford, J. D., Friedman, M. J., Green, B. L., Dain, B. J., & Sengupta, A. (2000). Predictors and outcomes of posttraumatic stress disorder in World War II veterans exposed to mustard gas. *Journal of Consulting and Clinical Psychology, 68*, 258–268.

Schreiber, G. B., Robins, M., Striegel-Moore, R., Obarzanek, E., Morrison, J. A., & Wright, D. J. (1996). Weight modification efforts reported by black and white preadolescent girls: National Heart, Lung, and Blood Institute Growth and Health Study. *Pediatrics, 98*, 63–70.

Schroeder, D. A. (1995). An introduction to social dilemmas. In D. Schroeder (Ed.), *Social dilemmas: Perspectives on individuals and groups* (pp. 1–13). Westport, CT: Praeger.

Schroeder, D. A., Penner, L. A., Dovidio, J. F., & Piliavin, J. A. (1995). *The psychology of helping and altruism: Problems and puzzles.* New York: McGraw-Hill.

Schuckit, M. A. (1998). Biological, psychological, and environmental predictors of alcoholism risk: A longitudinal study. *Journal of Studies in Alcoholism, 59*, 485–494.

Schulteis, G., Ahmed, S. H., Morse, A. C., Koob, G. F., & Everitt, B. J. (2000). Conditioning and opiate withdrawal. *Nature, 405*, 1013–1014.

Schultz, D. P., & Schultz, S. E. (1998). *Psychology and work today* (7th ed.). Upper Saddle River, NJ: Prentice-Hall.

Schultz, D. P., & Schultz, S. E. (2000). *A history of modern psychology*. (7th ed.). Fort Worth, TX: Harcourt Brace.

Schultz, D. P., & Schultz, S. E. (2001). *Theories of Personality.* Pacific Grove, CA: Brooks Cole.

Schulz, R. (1978). *The psychology of death, dying, and bereavement.* Reading, MA: Addison-Wesley.

Schulz-Hardt, S., Frey, D., Luthgens, C., & Moscovici, S. (2000). Biased information search in group decision making. *Journal of Personality and Social Psychology, 78*, 665–669.

Schwartz, B., & Reisberg, D. (1991). *Learning and memory.* New York: Norton.

Schwartz, C., Kagan, J., & Snidman, N. (1995, May). *Inhibition from toddlerhood to adolescence.* Paper presented at the annual meeting of the American Psychiatric Association, Miami.

Schwartz, M. W., Woods, S. C., Porte Jr., D., Seeley R. J., & Baskin, D. G. (2000). Central nervous system control of food intake. *Nature 404*, 661–671.

Schwarz, N. (1999). Self-reports: How the questions shape the answers. *American Psychologist, 54*, 93–105.

Schwender, D., Klasing, D., Daunderer, M., Maddler, C., Poppel, E., & Peter, K. (1995). Awareness during general anesthetic: Definition, incidence, clinical relevance, causes, avoidance, and medicolegal aspects. *Anaesthetist, 44*, 743–754.

Scribner, S. (1977). Modes of thinking and ways of speaking: Culture and logic reconsidered. In P. N. Johnson-Laird & P. C. Wason (Eds.), *Thinking: Readings in cognitive science.* Cambridge: Cambridge University Press.

Seamon, J. G., Ganor-Stern, D., Crowley, M. J., & Wilson, S. M. (1997). A mere exposure effect for transformed three-dimensional objects: Effects of reflection, size, or color changes on affect and recognition. *Memory and Cognition, 25*, 367–374.

Seamon, J. G., Williams, P. C., Crowley, M. J., Kim, I. J., Langer, S. A., Orne, P. J., & Wishengrad, D. L. (1995). The mere exposure effect is based on implicit memory: Effects of stimulus type, encoding conditions, and number of exposures on recognition and affect judgements. *Journal of Experimental Psychology: Learning, Memory, and Cognition, 21*(3), 711–721.

Searle, L. V. (1949). The organization of hereditary maze-brightness and maze-dullness. *Genetic Psychology Monographs, 39*, 279–325.

Sears, R. (1977). Sources of satisfaction of the Terman gifted men. *American Psychologist, 32*, 119–128.

Sedikides, C., Campbell, W. K., Reeder, G., & Elliot, A. J. (1998). The self-serving bias in relational context. *Journal of Personality and Social Psychology, 74*, 378–386.

Seeley, R. J., Kaplan, J. M., & Grill, H. J. (1995). Effect of occluding the pylorus on intraoral intake: A test of the gastric hypothesis of meal termination. *Physiology and Behavior, 58*(2), 245–249.

Segal, N. L. (1993). Twin, sibling, and adoption methods: Tests of evolutionary hypotheses. *American Psychologist, 48*, 943–956.

Segal, Z. V., Gemar, M., & Williams, S. (2000). Differential cognitive response to a mood challenge following successful cognitive therapy or pharmacotherapy for unipolar depression. *Journal of Abnormal Psychology, 108*, 3–10.

Segall, M. H., Dasen, P. R., Berry, J. W., & Poortinga, Y. H. (1990). *Human behavior in global perspective: An introduction to cross-cultural psychology.* Elmwood, NY: Pergamon Press.

Segerstrom, S. C., Taylor, S. E., Kemeny, M. E., & Fahey, J. L. (1998). Optimism is associated with mood, coping and immune change in response to stress. *Journal of Personality & Social Psychology, 74*, 1646–1655.

Seligman, M. E. P. (1971). Phobias and preparedness. *Behavior Therapy, 2*, 307–320.

Seligman, M. E. P. (1975). *Helplessness: On depression, development, and death.* San Francisco: Freeman.

Seligman, M. E. P. (1991). *Learned optimism.* New York: Knopf.

Seligman, M. E. P. (1995). *What You Can Change and What You Can't: The Complete Guide to Successful Self-Improvement.* New York: Fawcett.

Seligman, M. E. P., & Csikszentmihalyi, M. (2000). Positive psychology: An introduction. *American Psychologist, 55*, 5–14.

Seligman, M. E. P., Castellon, C., Cacciola, J., Shulman, P., Luborsky, L., Ollove, M., & Downing, R. (1988). Explanatory style change during cognitive therapy for unipolar depression. *Journal of Abnormal Psychology, 97*, 13–18.

Seligman, M. E. P., & Schulman, P. (1986). Explanatory style as a predictor of productivity and quitting among life insurance agents. *Journal of Personality and Social Psychology, 50*, 832–838.

Sell, R. L., Wells, J. A., & Wypij, D. (1995). The prevalence of homosexual behavior and attraction in the United States, the United Kingdom, and France: Results of national population-based samples. *Archives of Sexual Behavior, 24*(3), 235–248.

Selman, R. L. (1981). The child as a friendship philosopher. In S. R. Asher & J. M. Gottman (Eds.), *The development of children's friendships.* New York: Cambridge University Press.

Selye, H. (1956). *The stress of life.* New York: McGraw-Hill.

Selye, H. (1974). *The general adaptation syndrome.* In H. Selye, Stress without distress. New York: HarperCollins.

Selye, H. (1976). *The stress of life* (2nd ed.). New York: McGraw-Hill.

Seppa, N. (1997, June). Children's TV remains steeped in violence. *APA Monitor*, p. 36.

Serpell, R. (1994). The cultural construction of intelligence. In W. J. Lonner & R. S. Malpass (Eds.), *Psychology and culture.* Boston: Allyn & Bacon.

Servan-Schreiber, E., & Anderson, J. R. (1990). Learning artificial grammars with competitive chunking. *Journal of Experimental Psychology: Learning, Memory, and Cognition, 16*, 592–608.

Service, R. F. (1994, October 14). Neuroscience: Will a new type of drug make memory-making easier? *Science, 266*, 218–219.

Sevcik, R. A., & Savage-Rumbaugh, E. S. (1994). Language comprehension and use by great apes. *Language and Communication, 14*, 37–58.

Shadish, W. R., Cook, T. D., & Campbell, D. T. (in press). *Experimental and quasi-experimental designs for generalized causal inference.* Boston: Houghton Mifflin.

Shadish, W. R., Matt, G. E., Navarro, A. M., & Phillips, G. (2000). The effects of psychological therapies under clinically representative conditions: A meta-analysis. *Psychological Bulletin, 126*, 512–529.

Shaffer, D. R. (1999). *Developmental psychology*: Childhood and adolescence. Pacific Grove, CA: Brooks/Cole.

Shalev, A. Y., Peri, T., Brandes, D., Freedman, S., Orr, S. P., & Pitman, R. K. (2000). Auditory startle response in trauma survivors with posttraumatic stress disorder: A prospective study. *American Journal of Psychiatry, 157*, 255–261.

Shand, M. A. (1982). Sign-based short-term memory coding of American Sign Language and printed English words by congenitally deaf signers. *Cognitive Psychology, 14*, 1–12.

Shapiro, D. E., & Schulman, C. E. (1996). Ethical and legal issues in e-mail therapy. *Ethics and Behavior, 6*, 107–124.

Shapiro, D. H., & Walsh, R. N. (Eds.). (1984). *Meditation: Classical and contemporary perspectives.* New York: Aldine.

Shapiro, F. (1989a). Eye movement desensitization: A new treatment for posttraumatic stress disorder. *Journal of Behavior Therapy and Experimental Psychiatry, 20*, 211–217.

Shapiro, F. (1989b). Efficacy of the eye movement desensitization procedure in the treatment of traumatic memories. *Journal of Traumatic Stress, 2*, 199–223.

Shapiro, F. (1991). Eye movement desensitization and reprocessing procedure: From EMD to EMD/R—A new treatment model for anxiety and related traumata. *The Behavior Therapist, 15*, 133–135.

Shapiro, F. (1995). *Eye movement desensitization and reprocessing: Basic principles, protocols, and procedures.* New York: Guilford.

Shapiro, F. (1996). Eye movement desensitization and reprocessing (EMDR): Evaluation of controlled PTSD research. *Journal of Behavior Therapy and Experimental Psychiatry, 27,* 209–218.

Shapiro, F. (1999). Eye movement desensitization and reprocessing (EMDR): Accelerated information processing and affect-driven constructions. *Crisis Intervention and Time-Limited Treatment, 4,* 145–157.

Shaver, P. R., & Clark, C. L. (1996). Forms of adult romantic attachment and their cognitive and emotional underpinnings. In G. G. Noam & K. W. Fischer (Eds.), *Development and vulnerability in close relationships: The Jean Piaget symposium series* (pp. 29–58). Mahwah, NJ: Erlbaum.

Sher, K. J., Walitzer, K., Wood, P., & Brent, E. (1991). Characteristics of children of alcoholics: Putative risk factors, substance use and abuse, and psychopathology. *Journal of Abnormal Psychology, 100,* 427–448.

Sher, K. J., Wood, M. D., Wood, P. K., & Raskin, G. (1996). Alcohol outcome expectancies and alcohol use: A latent variable cross-lagged panel study. *Journal of Abnormal Psychology, 105,* 561–574.

Sherif, M. (1937). An experimental approach to the study of attitudes. *Sociometry, 1,* 90–98.

Sherin, J. E., Shiromani, P. J., McCarley, R. W., & Saper, C. B. (1996). Activation of ventrolateral preoptic neurons during sleep. *Science, 271,* 216–219.

Sherman, S. J. (1980). On the self-erasing nature of errors of prediction. *Journal of Personality and Social Psychology, 39,* 211–221.

Sherman, J. W., & Bessenoff, G. R. (1999). Stereotypes as source-monitoring cues: On the interaction between episodic and semantic memory. *Psychological Science, 10,* 106–110.

Sherwin, B. B., & Gelfand, M. M. (1987). The role of androgen in the maintenance of sexual functioning in oophorectomized women. *Psychosomatic Medicine, 49,* 397–409.

Sherwin, B. B., Gelfand, M. M., & Brender, W. (1985). Androgen enhances sexual motivation in females: A prospective crossover study of sex steroid administration in the surgical menopause. *Psychosomatic Medicine, 47,* 339–351.

Shiffman, S., Engberg, J. B., Paty, J. A., & Perz, W. G. (1997). A day at a time: Predicting smoking lapse from daily urge. *Journal of Abnormal Psychology, 106,* 104–116.

Shiloh, S. (1996). Genetic counseling: A developing area of interest for psychologists. *Professional Psychology: Research and Practice, 27,* 475–486.

Shimamura, A. P., Berry, J. M., Mangels, J. A., Rusting, C. L., & Jurica, P. J. (1995). Memory and cognitive abilities in university professors: Evidence for successful aging. *Psychological Science, 6,* 271–277.

Shin, L. M., Kosslyn, S. M., McNally, R. J., Alpert, N. M., Thompson, W. L., Rauch, S. L., Macklin, M. L., & Pitman, R. K. (1997). Visual imagery and perception in posttraumatic stress disorder: A positron emission tomographic investigation. *Archives of General Psychiatry, 54,* 233–241.

Shlomo, A. (1999). *Culturally competent family therapy: A general model.* Westport, CT: Praeger.

Shneidman, E. S. (1987). A psychological approach to suicide. In G. VandenBos & B. K. Bryant (Eds.), *Cataclysms, crises, and catastrophes: Psychology in action. The master lectures, Vol. 6* (pp. 147–183). Washington, DC: American Psychological Association.

Shreeve, J. (1993, June). Touching the phantom. *Discover,* pp. 35–42.

Shweder, R. A., Much, N. C., Mahapatra, M., & Park, L. (1994). The "big three" of morality (autonomy, community, and divinity), and the "big three" explanations of suffering, as well. In A. Brandt & P. Rozin (Eds.), *Morality and health.* Stanford, CA: Stanford University Press.

Siegal, M. (1997). *Knowing children: Experiments in conversation and cognition* (2nd ed.). Hove, England: Psychology Press/Erlbaum/Taylor & Francis.

Siegel, J. M., & Rogawski, M. A. (1988). A function for REM sleep: Regulation of noradrenergic receptor sensitivity. *Brain Research Review, 13,* 213–233.

Siegler, R. S. (1994). Cognitive variability: A key to understanding cognitive development. *Current Directions in Psychological Science, 3,* 1–4.

Siegler, R. S. (1995). Children's thinking: How does change occur? In W. Schneider & F. Weinert (Eds.), *Memory performance and competencies: Issues in growth and development.* Hillsdale, NJ: Erlbaum.

Silbert, M. H., & Pines, A. M. (1984). Pornography and sexual abuse of women. *Sex Roles, 10,* 857–868.

Silver, E. (1995). Punishment or treatment? Comparing the lengths of confinement of successful and unsuccessful insanity defendants. *Law and Human Behavior, 19,* 375–388.

Silver, E., Cirincione, C., & Steadman, H. J. (1994). Demythologizing inaccurate perceptions of the insanity defense. *Law and Human Behavior, 18,* 63–70.

Silver, R. L., & Wortman, C. B. (1980). Coping with undesirable life events. In J. Garber & M. E. P. Seligman (Eds.), *Human helplessness: Theory and applications* (pp. 279–340). New York: Academic Press.

Silverman, K., Evans, A. M., Strain, E. C., & Griffiths, R. R. (1992). Withdrawal syndrome after the double-blind cessation of caffeine consumption. *New England Journal of Medicine, 327,* 1109–1114.

Simons, D. J., & Levin, D. T. (1997). Failure to detect changes to attended objects. *Investigative Ophthalmology and Visual Science, 38,* S747.

Simonton, D. K. (1999). Creativity and genius. In L. Pervin & O. John (Ed.), *Handbook of personality research* (2nd ed., pp. 629–652). New York Guilford.

Sims, J. H., & Baumann, D. D. (1972). The tornado threat: Coping styles of the north and south. *Science, 17,* 1386–1392.

Simpson, J. A., & Kenrick, D. T. (1997). *Evolutionary social psychology.* Mahwah, NJ: Erlbaum.

Simpson, J. A., Rholes, W. S., & Nelligan, J. S. (1992). Support seeking and support giving within couples in an anxiety-provoking situation: The role of attachment styles. *Journal of Personality and Social Psychology, 62,* 434–446.

Simpson, S., Hurtley, S. M., & Marx, J. (2000). Immune cell networks. *Science, 290,* 79.

Sinclair, R. C., Hoffman, C., Mark, M. M., Martin, L. L., & Pickering, T. L. (1994). Construct accessibility and the misattribution of arousal. *Psychological Science, 5*(1), 15–19.

Sinha, M. K., & Caro, J. F. (1998). Clinical aspects of leptin. *Vitamins and Hormones, 54,* 1–30.

Sinha, R., & Parsons, O. A. (1996). Multivariate response patterning of fear and anger. *Cognition and Emotion, 10,* 173–198.

Sinton, C. M., & McCarley, R. W. (2000) Neuroanatomical and neurophysiological aspects of sleep: Basic science and clinical relevance. *Seminars in Clinical Neuropsychiatry, 5,* 6–19.

Sirvio, J. (1999). Strategies that support declining cholinergic neurotransmission in Alzheimer's disease patients. *Gerontology, 45,* 3–14.

Skinner, B. F. (1961). *Cumulative record* (3rd ed.). Englewood Cliffs, NJ: Prentice-Hall.

Slamecka, N. J., & McElree, B. (1983). Normal forgetting of verbal lists as a function of their degree of learning. *Journal of Experimental Psychology: Learning, Memory, and Cognition, 9,* 384–397.

Slater, A., Mattock, A., Brown, E., & Bremner, J. G. (1991). Form perception at birth. *Journal of Experimental Child Psychology, 51,* 395–406.

Sleek, S. (1999, February). Programs aim to attract minorities to psychology. *APA Monitor,* p. 47.

Slomkowski, C., & Dunn, J. (1996). Young children's understanding of other people's beliefs and feelings and their connected communication with friends. *Developmental Psychology, 32,* 442–447.

Slutske, W. S., Heath, A. C., Dinwiddie, S. H., Madden, P. A., Bucholz, K. K., Dunne, M. P., Statham, D. J., & Martin, N. G. (1998). Common genetic risk factors for conduct disorder and alcohol dependence. *Journal of Abnormal Psychology, 107,* 363–374.

Small, B. J., & Bäckman, L. (1999). Time to death and cognitive performance. *Current Directions in Psychological Science, 8,* 168–172.

Small, G. W., Rabins, P. V., Barry, P. P., Buckholtz, N. S., DeKosky, S. T., Ferris, S. H., Finkel, S. I., Gwyther, L. P., Khachaturian, Z. S., Lebowitz, B. D., McRae, T. D., Morris, J. C., Oakley, F., Schneider, L. S., Streim, J. E., Sunderland, T., Teri, L. A., & Tune, L. E. (1997). Diagnosis and treatment of Alzheimer's disease and related disorders: Consensus statement of the American Association for Geriatric Psychiatry, the Alzheimer's Association, and the American Geriatrics Society. *Journal of American Medical Association, 278,* 1363–1371.

Smith, A. P., & Maben, A. (1993). Effects of sleep deprivation, lunch, and personality on performance, mood, and cardiovascular function. *Physiology and Behavior, 54*(5), 967–972.

Smith, B. W., Pargament, K. I., Brant, C., & Oliver, J. M. (2000). Noah revisited: Religious coping by church members and the impact of the 1993 Midwest flood. *Journal of Community Psychology, 28,* 169–186.

Smith, E. (1998). Mental representation and memory. In D. Gilbert, S. T. Fiske, & G. Lindzey (Eds.), *Handbook of social psychology* (Vol. 1, 4th ed., pp. 391–445). Boston: McGraw-Hill.

Smith, E., & Mackie, D. (2000). *Social Psychology.* Philadelphia: Taylor & Francis.

Smith, E. E. (2000). Neural bases of human working memory. *Currents Directions on Psychological Science, 9,* 45–49.

Smith, H. S., & Cohen, L. H. (1993). Self-complexity and reactions to a relationship breakup. *Journal of Clinical and Social Psychology, 12,* 367–384.

Smith, J. (1993). *Understanding stress and coping.* New York: Macmillan.

Smith, M. L., Glass, G. V., & Miller, T. I. (1980). *The benefits of psychotherapy.* Baltimore: Johns Hopkins University Press.

Smith, M. U., & DiClemente, R. J. (2000). STAND: A peer educator training curriculum for sexual risk reduction in the rural South. Students Together Against Negative Decisions. *Preventive Medicine, 30,* 441–449.

Smith, P., & Yule, W. (1999). Eye movement desensitization and reprocessing. In W. Yule (Ed.) *Posttraumatic stress disorders: Concepts and therapy.* Chichester, England: Wiley.

Smith, P. B., & Bond, M. (1999). *Social psychology across cultures.* Boston: Allyn & Bacon.

Smith, S., & Freedman, D. G. (1983, April). *Mother-toddler interaction and maternal perception of child temperament in two ethnic groups: Chinese-American and European-American.* Paper presented at the meeting of the Society for Research in Child Development, Detroit, MI.

Smith, S. L., & Donnerstein, E. (1998). Harmful effects of exposure to media violence: Learning of aggression, emotional desensitization, and fear. In R. G. Geen & E. Donnerstein (Eds.), *Human aggression* (pp. 230–247). San Diego: Academic Press.

Smith, S. M., Vela, E., & Williamson, J. E. (1988). Shallow input processing does not induce environmental context-dependent recognition. *Bulletin of the Psychonomic Society, 26,* 537–540.

Smith, S. S., O'Hara, B. F., Persico, A. M., Gorelick, D. A., Newlin, D. B., Vlahov, D., Solomon, L., Pickens, R., & Uhl, G. R. (1992). Genetic vulnerability to drug abuse. The D2 dopamine receptor Taq i B1 restriction fragment length polymorphism appears more frequently in polysubstance abusers. *Archives of General Psychiatry, 49,* 723–727.

Smith, T. W. (1992). Hostility and health: Current status of a psychosomatic hypothesis. *Health Psychology, 11,* 139–150.

Smyth, J. M., Stone, A. A., Hurewitz, A., & Kaell, A. (1999). Effects of writing about stressful experiences on symptom reduction in patients with asthma or rheumatoid arthritis. *Journal of the American Medical Association, 281,* 1304–1309.

Snarey, J. (1987). A question of morality. *Psychological Bulletin, 97,* 202–232.

Snowden, L. R., & Cheung, F. (1990). Use of inpatient mental health services by members of ethnic minority groups. *American Psychologist, 45,* 347–355.

Snyder, M., & Cantor, N. (1998). Understanding personality and social behavior: A functionalist strategy. In D. Gilbert, S. T. Fiske, & G. Lindzey (Eds.), *Handbook of social psychology,* Vol. 1 (4th ed., pp. 635–679). Boston: McGraw-Hill.

Soken, N. H., & Pick, A. D. (1992). Intermodal perception of happy and angry expressive behaviors by seven-month-old infants. *Child Development, 63,* 787–795.

Solomon, A. (1998, January 12). Anatomy of melancholy. *New Yorker,* pp. 46–61.

Solomon, R. L. (1980). The opponent-process theory of acquired motivation: The costs of pleasure and the benefits of pain. *American Psychologist, 35,* 691–712.

Solomon, R. L., Kamin, L. J., & Wynne, L. C. (1953). Traumatic avoidance learning: The outcomes of several extinction procedures with dogs. *Journal of Abnormal and Social Psychology, 48,* 291–302.

Solso, A. L. (1987). *Inside the Russian mind.* Unpublished manuscript.

Sommer, R. (1999). Applying environmental psychology. In D. A. Bernstein & A. M. Stec (Eds.), *The psychology of everyday life.* Boston: Houghton Mifflin.

Sorce, J., Emde, R., Campos, J., & Klinnert, M. (1981, April). *Maternal emotional signaling: Its effect on the visual cliff behavior of one-year-olds.* Paper presented at the meetings of the Society for Research in Child Development, Boston, MA.

Sorrentino, R. M., & Roney, C. J. R. (2000). *The uncertain mind: Individual differences in facing the unknown.* Philadelphia: Psychology Press.

Spanagel, R., & Weiss, F. (1999). The dopamine hypothesis of reward: past and current status. *Trends in Neuroscience, 22,* 521–527.

Spangler, G., Fremmer-Bombik, E., & Grossman, K. (1996). Social and individual determinants of infant attachment security and disorganization. *Infant Mental Health Journal, 17,* 127–139.

Spangler, W. (1992). Validity of questionnaire and TAT measures of need for achievement: Two meta-analyses. *Psychological Bulletin, 112,* 140–154.

Spanos, N. P. (1996). *Multiple identities and false memories: A sociocognitive perspective.* Washington, DC: American Psychological Association.

Spanos, N. P., Burnley, M. C. E., & Cross, P. A. (1993). Response expectancies and interpretations as determinants of hypnotic responding. *Journal of Personality and Social Psychology, 65*(6), 1237–1242.

Spelke, E. S., Breinlinger, K., Macomber, J., & Jacobson, K. (1992). Origins of knowledge. *Psychological Review, 99,* 605–632.

Sperry, L. (1999). *Cognitive behavior therapy of DSM-IV personality disorders : Highly effective interventions for the most common personality disorders.* Bristol, PA: Bruner/Mazel.

Sperry, R. W. (1968). Hemisphere deconnection and unity in conscious awareness. *American Psychologist, 23,* 723–733.

Spiegel, D. (Ed.). (1994). *Dissociation: Culture, mind, and body.* Washington, DC: American Psychiatric Press.

Spiegel, D. A., & Bruce, T. J. (1997). Benzodiazepines and exposure-based cognitive behavior therapies for panic disorder: Conclusions from combined treatment trials. *American Journal of Psychiatry, 151,* 876–881.

Spielman, A. J., Saskin, P., & Thorpy, M. J. (1987). Treatment of chronic insomnia through restriction of time in bed. *Sleep, 10,* 45–56.

Spitzer, R. L., Skodol, A. E., Gibbon, M., & Williams, J. B. W. (1983). *Psychopathology: A casebook,* New York: McGraw-Hill.

Sporer, S. L., Penrod, S., Read, D., & Cutler, B. (1995). Choosing, confidence, and accuracy: A meta-analysis of the confidence-accuracy relation in eyewitness testimony. *Psychological Bulletin, 118,* 315–327.

Springer, K., & Belk, A. (1994). The role of physical contact and association in early contamination sensitivity. *Developmental Psychology, 30*(6), 864–868.

Squire, L. R. (1986). Mechanisms of memory. *Science, 232,* 1612–1619.

Sramek, J. J., & Cutler, N. R. (1999). Recent developments in the drug treatment of Alzheimer's disease. *Drugs & Aging, 14,* 359–373.

St. Clair, M. (1999). *Object relations and self-psychology: An introduction.* Pacific Grove, CA: Brooks/Cole.

St. Lawrence, J. S. (1993). African-American adolescents' knowledge, health-related attitudes, sexual behavior, and contraceptive decisions: Implications for the prevention of adolescent HIV infection. *Journal of Consulting Clinical Psychology, 61,* 104–112.

St. Lawrence, J. S., Eldridge, G. D., Shelby, M. C., Little, C. E., Brasfield, T. L., & O'Bannon, R. E., III (1997). HIV risk reduction for incarcerated women: A comparison of brief interventions based on two theoretical models. *Journal of Consulting and Clinical Psychology, 65,* 504–509.

Staddon, J. E. R., & Ettinger, R. H. (1989). *Learning: An introduction to the principles of adaptive behavior.* San Diego: Harcourt Brace Jovanovich.

Stanley, B. G., Willett, V. L., Donias, H. W., & Ha-Lyen, H. (1993). The lateral hypothalamus: A primary site mediating excitatory aminoacid-elicited eating. *Brain Research, 630*(1–2), 41–49.

Stanton-Hicks, M., & Salamon, J. (1997). Stimulation of the central and peripheral nervous system for the control of pain. *Journal of Clinical Neurophysiology, 14,* 46–62.

Stasser, G., Stewart, D., & Wittenbaum, G. M. (1995). Expert roles and information exchange during discussion: The importance of knowing who knows what. *Journal of Experimental Social Psychology, 31,* 244–265.

Statistical Abstracts of the United States (1997). Washington, DC: National Data Book.

Statistics Canada (1998). *Causes of Death, 1995.* Ottawa: Ministry of Industry, Science, and Technology, Health Statistics Division.

Steadman, H. J. (1993). *Reforming the insanity defense: An evaluation of pre- and post-Hinckley reforms.* New York: Guilford.

Stec, A. M., & Bernstein, D. A. (Eds.). (1999). *Psychology: Fields of application.* Boston: Houghton Mifflin.

Steele, C. M. (1997). A threat in the air: How stereotypes shape intellectual identity and performance. *American Psychologist, 52,* 613–629.

Steele, T. D., McCann, U. D., & Ricaurte, G. A. (1994). 3,4-methylenedioxymethamphetamine (MDMA, ecstacy): Pharmacology and toxicology in animals and humans. *Addiction, 89*(5), 539–51.

Stein, D. M., & Lambert, M. J. (1995). Graduate training in psychotherapy: Are therapy outcomes enhanced? *Journal of Consulting and Clinical Psychology, 63,* 182–196.

Stein, E. (1999). *The Mismeasure of Desire: The Science, Theory and Ethics of Sexual Orientation.* New York: Oxford University Press.

Stein, K. D., Goldman, M. S., & Del Boca, F. K. (2000). The influence of alcohol expectancy priming and mood manipulation on subsequent alcohol consumption. *Journal of Abnormal Psychology, 109,* 106–115.

Steinberg, L. (1990). Autonomy, conflict, and harmony in the family relationship. In S. S. Feldman & G. R. Elliott (Eds.), *At the threshold: The developing adolescent* (pp. 255–276). Cambridge, MA: Harvard University Press.

Steinberg, L., Dornbusch, S. M., & Brown, B. B. (1992). Ethnic differences in adolescent achievement: An ecological perspective. *American Psychologist, 47,* 723–729.

Steinberg, L., Lamborn, S. D., Darling, N., Mounts, N. S., & Dornbusch, S. M. (1994). Over-time changes in adjustment and competence among adolescents from authoritative, authoritarian, indulgent, and neglectful families. *Child Development, 65,* 754–770.

Stephens, R. S., Roffman, R. A., & Simpson, E. E. (1994). Treating adult marijuana dependence: A test of the relapse prevention model. *Journal of Consulting and Clinical Psychology. 62*(1), 92–99.

Steriade, M., & McCarley, R. W. (1990). *Brainstem control of wakefulness and sleep.* New York: Plenum.

Stern, J., & Stern, M. (1992). Chiles (New Mexico). *The New Yorker,* p. 68.

Stern, K., & McClintock, M. K. (1998). Regulation of ovulation by human pheromones. *Nature 392,* 177–179.

Stern, Y., Tang, M. X, Denaro, J., & Mayeux, R. (1995). Increased risk of mortality in Alzheimer's disease patients with more advanced educational and occupational attainment. *Annals of Neurology, 37,* 590–595.

Sternberg, R. J. (1985). *Beyond IQ: A triarchic theory of human intelligence.* Cambridge, England: Cambridge University Press.

Sternberg, R. J. (1988a). *The triarchic mind.* New York: Cambridge Press.

Sternberg, R. J. (1988b). Triangulating love. In R. J. Sternberg & M. L. Barnes (Eds.), *The psychology of love.* New Haven: Yale University Press.

Sternberg, R. J. (1989). Domain generality versus domain specificity: The life and impending death of a false dichotomy. *Merrill-Palmer Quarterly, 35,* 115–130.

Sternberg, R. J. (1996). *Successful intelligence.* New York: Simon & Schuster.

Sternberg, R. J. (1999). Ability and expertise: It's time to replace the current model of intelligence. *American Educator,* Spring 1999, pp. 10–51.

Sternberg, R. J., & Kaufman, J. C. (1998). Human abilities. *Annual Review of Psychology, 49,* 479–502.

Sternberg, R. J., & Lubert, T. I. (1992). Buy low and sell high: An investment approach to creativity. *Current Directions in Psychological Science, 1*(1), 1–5.

Sternberg, R. J., & O'Hara, L. A. (1999). Creativity and intelligence (pp. 251–272). In R. J. Sternberg et al. (Eds), *Handbook of creativity.* New York: Cambridge University Press.

Sternberg, R. J., & Williams, W. M. (1997). Does the graduate record examination predict meaningful success of graduate training of psychologists? A Case Study. *American Psychologist, 52,* 630–641.

Sternberg, R. J., Wagner, R. K., Williams, W. M., & Horvath, J. A. (1995). Testing common sense. *American Psychologist, 50,* 912–927.

Stevens, A. (1996). *Private myths: Dreams and dreaming.* Cambridge, MA: Harvard University Press.

Stevens, R. (1999). Personal communication, April 21.

Stevenson, H. (1992). A long way from being number one: What we can learn from East Asia. *Washington, DC: Federation of Behavior, Psychological and Cognitive Sciences.*

Stickgold, R., Rittenhouse, C. D., & Hobson, J. A. (1994). Dream splicing: A new technique for assessing thematic coherence in subjective reports of mental activity. *Consciousness and Cognition, 3*(1), 114–128.

Stoff, D. M., Breiling, J., & Maser, J. D. (Eds.). (1997). *Handbook of antisocial behavior.* New York: Wiley.

Stokes, P. E. (1998). Ten years of fluoxetine. *Depression and Anxiety, 8,* 1–4.

Stoleru, S., Gregoire, M. C., Gerard, D., Decety, J., Lafarge, E., Cinotti, L., Lavenne, F., Le Bars, D., Vernet-Maury, E., Rada, H., Collet, C., Mazoyer, B., Forest, M. G., Magnin, F., Spira, A., & Comar, D. (1999). Neuroanatomical correlates of visually evoked sexual arousal in human males. *Archives of Sexual Behavior, 28,* 1–21.

Stone, J., Wiegand, A. W., Cooper, J., & Aronson, E. (1997). When exemplification fails: Hypocrisy and the motive for self-integrity. *Journal of Personality and Social Psychology, 72,* 54–65.

Strain, E. C., Mumford, G. K., Silverman, K., & Griffiths, R. R. (1994). Caffeine dependence syndrome: Evidence from case histories and experimental evaluations. *Journal of the American Medical Association, 272*(13), 1043–1048.

Strang, J., Witten, J., & Hall, W. (2000). Improving the quality of the cannabis debate: Defining the different domains. *British Medical Journal, 320,* 108–110.

Streissguth, A. P., Barr, H. M., Bookstein, F. L., Sampson, P. D., & Olson, H. C. (1999). The long-term neurocognitive consequences of prenatal alcohol exposure: A 14-year study. *Psychological Science, 10,* 186–190.

Strongman, K. T., & Kemp, S. (1991). Autobiographical memory for emotion. *Bulletin of the Psychonomic Society, 29,* 195–198.

Stroop, J. R. (1935). Studies of interference in serial verbal reactions. *Journal of Experimental Psychology, 18,* 643–662.

Suarez, E., Williams, R., Kuhn, C., Zimmerman, E., & Schanberg, S. (1991). Biobehavioral basis of coronary-prone behavior in middle-aged men. Part ii: Serum cholesterol, the Type A behavior pattern, and hostility as interactive modulators of physiological reactivity. *Psychosomatic Medicine, 53,* 528–537.

Sue, D. W., Bingham, R. P., Porché-Burke, L., & Vasquez, M. (1999). The diversification of psychology: A multicultural revolution. *American Psychologist, 54,* 1061–1069.

Sue, S. (1998). In search of cultural competence in psychotherapy and counseling. *American Psychologist, 53,* 440–448.

Sue, S. (1999). Science, ethnicity, and bias: Where have we gone wrong? *American Psychologist, 54,* 1070–1077.

Sue, S., & Okazaki, S. (1990). Asian-American educational achievements: A phenomenon in search of an explanation. *American Psychologist, 45,* 913–920.

Suh, E., Diener, E., & Fujita, F. (1996). Events and subjective well-being: Only recent events matter. *Journal of Personality and Social Psychology, 70,* 1091–1102.

Suh, E., Diener, E., Oishi, S., & Triandis, H. C. (1998). The shifting basis of life satisfaction judgments across cultures: Emotions versus norms. *Journal of Personality and Social Psychology, 74,* 482–493.

Sullivan, J. W., & Horowitz, F. D. (1983). The effects of intonation on infant attention: The role of the rising intonation contour. *Journal of Child Language, 10,* 521–534.

Sullivan, P. F. (1995). Mortality in anorexia nervosa. *American Journal of Psychiatry, 152,* 1073–1074.

Suls, J., & Fletcher, B. (1985). The relative efficacy of avoidant and nonavoidant coping strategies: A meta-analysis. *Health Psychology, 4,* 249–288.

Suls, J., & Wan, C. K. (1993). The relationship between trait hostility and cardiovascular reactivity: A quantitative review and analysis. *Psychophysiology, 30,* 1–12.

Summala, H., & Mikkola, T. (1994). Fatal accidents among car and truck drivers: Effects of fatigue, age, and alcohol consumption. *Human Factors, 36*(2), 315–326.

Suzdak, P. D., Glowa, J. R., Crawley, J. N., Schwartz, R. D., Skolnick, P., & Paul, S. M. (1986). A selective imidazobenzodiazepine antagonist of ethanol in the rat. *Science, 234,* 1243–1247.

Swaab, D. E., & Hofman, M. A. (1990). An enlarged suprachiasmatic nucleus in homosexual men. *Brain Research, 537,* 141–148.

Swaab, D. E., & Hofman, M. A. (1995). Sexual differentiation of the human hypothalamus in relation to gender and sexual orientation. *Trends in Neuroscience, 18*(6), 264–270.

Swaab, D. F., Zhou, J.-N., Fodor, M., & Hofman, M. A. (1997). Sexual differentiation of the human hypothalamus: Differences according to sex, sexual orientation, and transsexuality. In L. Ellis & L. Ebertz (Eds.), *Sexual orientation: Toward biological understanding.* Westport CT: Praeger.

Swan, G. E. (1996, December). Some elders thrive on working into late life. *APA Monitor,* p. 35.

Swan, G. E., & Carmelli, D. (1996). Curiosity and mortality in aging adults: A 5-year follow-up of the Western Collaborative Group Study. *Psychology and Aging, 11,* 449–453.

Swann, W. B., Jr., Stein-Seroussi, A., & Giesler, R. B. (1992). Why people self-verify. *Journal of Personality and Social Psychology, 62,* 392–401.

Sweller, J., & Gee, W. (1978). Einstellung: The sequence effect and hypothesis theory. *Journal of Experimental Psychology: Human Learning and Memory, 4,* 513–526.

Swets, J. A. (1992). The science of choosing the right decision threshold in high-stakes diagnostics. *American Psychologist, 47,* 522–532.

Swets, J. A., Dawes, R. M., & Monahan, J. (2000). Psychological science can improve diagnostic decisions. *Psychological Science in the Public Interest, 1,* 1–26.

Swindle, R., Jr., Heller, K., Pescosolido, B., & Kikuzawa, S. (2000). Responses to nervous breakdowns in America over a 40-year period: Mental health policy implications. *American Psychologist, 55,* 740–749.

Swithers, S. E., & Hall, W. G. (1994). Does oral experience terminate ingestion? *Appetite, 23*(2), 113–138.

Szasz, T. S. (1987). *Insanity: The idea and its consequences.* New York: Wiley.

Szatmari, P., Jones, M. B., Zwaigenbaum, L., & MacLean, J. E. (1998). Genetics of autism: Overview and new directions. *Journal of Autism and Developmental Disorders, 28,* 351–368.

Tagliabue, J. (1999, January 28). Devil gets his due, but Catholic church updates exorcism rites. *International Herald Tribune,* p. 6.

Takahashi, J., Palmer, T. D., & Gage, F. H. (1999). Retinoic acid and neurotrophins collaborate to regulate neurogenesis in adult-derived neural stem cell cultures. *Journal of Neurobiology, 38,* 65–81.

Takayama, H., Ray, J., Raymon, H. K., Baird, A., Hogg, J., Fisher, L. J., & Gage, F. H. (1995). Basic fibroblast growth factor increases dopaminergic graft survival and function in a rat model of Parkinson's disease. *Nature Medicine, 1,* 54–64.

Takei, N., Sham, P., O'Callaghan, E., Murray, G. K., Glover, G., & Murray, R. M. (1994). Prenatal exposure to influenza and the development of schizophrenia: Is the effect confined to females? *American Journal of Psychiatry, 151,* 117–119.

Tanaka-Matsumi, J., & Higginbotham, H. N. (1994). Clinical application of behavior therapy across ethnic and cultural boundaries. *The Behavior Therapist, 17,* 123–126.

Tanda, G., Pontieri, F. E., & Di Chiara, G. (1997). Cannabinoid and heroin activation of mesolimbic dopamine transmission by a common mu1 opioid receptor mechanism. *Science, 276,* 2048–2050.

Tannen, D. (1994). *Gender and discourse.* New York: Oxford University Press.

Tanner, J. M. (1978). *Foetus into man: Physical growth from conception to maturity.* London: Open Books, 1978.

Tartaglia, L. A., Dembski, M., Weng, X., Deng, N., Culpepper, J., Devos, R., Richards, G., Campfield, L. A., Clark, F. T., Deeds, J., Muir, C., Sanker, S., Moriarty, A., Moore, K. J., Smutko, J. S., Mays, G. G., Woolf, E. A., Monroe, C. A., & Tepper, R. I. (1996). Identification and expression cloning of a leptin receptor, OB-R. *Cell, 83,* 1263–1271.

Task Force on Promotion and Dissemination of Psychological Procedures. (1995). Training in and dissemination of empirically validated psychological treatments: Report and recommendations. *Clinical Psychologist, 48,* 3–23.

Tasker, F., & Golombok, S. (1995). Adults raised as children in lesbian families. *American Journal of Orthopsychiatry, 65*(2), 203–215.

Taub, A. (1998). Thumbs down on acupuncture. *Science, 279,* 159.

Taubes, G. (1998). Weight increases worldwide? *Science, 280,* 1368.

Taylor, R. L., & Richards, S. B. (1991). Patterns of intellectual differences of Black, hispanic, and White children. *Psychology in the Schools, 28,* 5–8.

Taylor, S. E. (1998a). *Health psychology* (4th ed.). New York: McGraw-Hill.

Taylor, S. E. (1998b). The social being in social psychology. In D. Gilbert, S. T. Fiske, & G. Lindzey (Eds.), *Handbook of social psychology* (Vol.1, 4th ed., pp. 58–95). Boston: McGraw-Hill.

Taylor, S. E., & Armor, D. A. (1996). Positive illusions and coping with adversity. *Journal of Personality, 64,* 873–898.

Taylor, S. E., & Aspinwall, L. G. (1996). Mediating processes in psychosocial stress: Appraisal, coping, resistance, and vulnerability. In H. B. Kaplan (Ed.), *Perspectives on psychosocial stress.* New York: Academic Press.

Taylor, S. E., & Lobel, M. (1989). Social comparison activity under threat: Downward evaluation and upward contacts. *Psychological Review, 96.*

Taylor, S. E., Kemeny, M. E., Reed, G. M., Bower, J. E., & Gruenewald, T. L. (2000a). Psychological resources, positive illusions, and health. *American Psychologist, 55,* 99–109.

Taylor, S. E., Klein, L. C., Lewis, B. P., Gruenewald, T. L., Gurung, R. A. R., & Updegraff, J. A. (2000b). Biobehavioral responses to stress in females: Tend-and-befriend, not fight-or-flight. *Psychological Review.*

Taylor, S. E., Repetti, R. L., & Seeman, T. (1997). Health psychology: What is an unhealthy environment and how does it get under the skin? *Annual Review of Psychology, 48,* 411–447.

Taylor, S. P., & Hulsizer, M. R. (1998). Psychoactive drugs and human aggression. In R. G. Geen & E. Donnerstein (Eds.), *Human aggression* (pp. 139–167). San Diego: Academic Press.

Teigen, K. H. (1994). Yerkes-Dodson: A law for all seasons. *Theory and Psychology, 4*(4), 525–547.

Teitelbaum, P. (1957). Random and food-directed activity in hyperphagic and normal rats. *Journal of Comparative and Physiological Psychology, 50,* 386–490.

Tellegen, A., Lykken, D. T., Bouchard, T. J., Wilcox, K. J., Segal, N. L., & Rich, S. (1988). Personality similarity in twins reared apart and together. *Journal of Personality and Social Psychology, 54,* 1031–1039.

Ter Riet, G., Kleijnen, J., & Knipschild, P. (1990). Acupuncture and chronic pain: A criteria-based meta-analysis. *Journal of Clinical Epidemiology, 43,* 1191–1199.

Terman, L. M. (1916). *The measurement of intelligence.* Boston: Houghton Mifflin.

Terman, L. M., & Oden, M. H. (1947). *The gifted child grows up: Vol. 4. Genetic studies of genius.* Stanford, CA: Stanford University Press.

Terman, L. M., & Oden, M. H. (1959). *The gifted group at midlife.* Stanford, CA: Stanford University Press.

Tesser, A. (1993). The importance of heritability in psychological research: The case of attitudes. *Psychological Review, 100,* 129–142.

Thelen, E. (1995). Motor development: A new synthesis. *American Psychologist, 50,* 79–95.

Thom, A., Sartory, G., & Jöhren, P. (2000). Comparison between one-session psychological treatment and benzodiazepine in dental phobia. *Journal of Consulting and Clinical Psychology, 68,* 378–387.

Thomas, A., & Chess, S. (1977). *Temperament and development.* New York: Brunner/Mazel.

Thomas, E. L., & Robinson, H. A. (1972). *Improving reading in every class: A sourcebook for teachers.* Boston: Allyn & Bacon.

Thompson, J. K. (1996a). Eating disorders: Introduction. In J. K. Thompson (Ed.), *Body image, eating disorders, and obesity* (pp. 173–176). Washington, DC: American Psychological Association.

Thompson, J. K. (1996b). Introduction: Assessment and treatment of binge eating disorder. In J. K. Thompson (Ed.), *Body image, eating disorders, and obesity* (pp. 1–22). Washington, DC: American Psychological Association.

Thompson, J. K., Heinberg, L. J., Altabe., M., Tantleff-Dunn, S. (1999). *Exacting beauty: Theory, assessment and treatment of body image disturbance.* Washington, DC: American Psychological Association.

Thompson, R. A. (1998). Early sociopersonality development. In W. Damon & N. Eisenberg (Eds.), *Handbook of child psychology: Vol. 3. Social, emotional, and personality development* (5th ed., pp. 25–104). New York: Wiley.

Thompson, S. C., Sobolow-Shubin, A., Galbraith, M. E., Schwankovksy, L., & Cruzen, D. (1993). Maintaining perceptions of control: Finding perceived control in low control circumstances. *Journal of Personality and Social Psychology, 64,* 293–304.

Thompson, W. G. (1995). Coffee: Brew or bane. *American Journal of the Medical Sciences, 308*(1), 49–57.

Thomson, C. P. (1982). Memory for unique personal events: The roommate study. *Memory & Cognition, 10,* 324–332.

Thoresen, C., & Powell, L. (1992). Type A behavior pattern: New perspectives on theory, assessment, and intervention. *Journal of Clinical and Consulting Psychology, 60,* 595–604.

Thorndike, E. L. (1898). Animal intelligence: An experimental study of the associative processes in animals. *Psychological Monographs, 2*(Whole No. 8).

Thorndike, E. L. (1905). *The elements of psychology.* New York: Seiler.

Thorndike, R. L., Hagan, E., & Sattler, J. (1986). *Stanford-Binet* (4th ed.). Chicago: Riverside.

Thorpe, G. L., & Olson, S. L. (1997). *Behavior therapy: Concepts, procedures, and applications* (2nd ed.). Boston: Allyn & Bacon.

Tidwell, M. C. O., Reis, H. T., & Shaver, P. R. (1996). Attachment, attractiveness, and social interaction: A diary study. *Journal of Personality and Social Psychology, 71,* 729–745.

Tiihonen, J., Kuikka, J., Bergstrom, K., Hakola, P., Karhu, J., Ryynänen, O.-P., & Föhr, J. (1995). Altered striatal dopamine re-uptake site densities in habitually violent and non-violent alcoholics. *Nature Medicine, 1*(7), 654–657.

Tinbergen, N. (1989). *The study of instinct.* Oxford: Clarendon.

Todorov, C., Freeston, M. H., & Borgeat, F. (2000). On the pharmacotherapy of obsessive-compulsive disorder: is a consensus possible? *Canadian Journal of Psychiatry, 45,* 257–262.

Tolman, E. C., & Honzik, C. H. (1930). Introduction and removal of reward and maze performance in rats. *University of California Publication in Psychology, 4,* 257–275.

Tomasello, M. (2000). Culture and cognitive development. *Current Directions in Psychological Science, 9,* 37–40.

Toni, N., Buchs, P. A., Nikonenko, I., Bron, C. R., & Muller, D. (1999). LTP promotes formation of multiple spine synapses between a single axon terminal and a dendrite. *Nature, 402,* 421–425.

Trabasso, T. R., & Bower, G. H. (1968). *Attention in learning.* New York: Wiley.

Tremblay, A., & Bueman, B. (1995). Exercise-training, macronutrient balance and body weight control. *International Journal of Obesity, 19*(2), 79–86.

Tremblay, R. E., Pagani-Kurtz, L., Mâsse, L., Vitaro, F., & Pihl, R. O. (1995). A bimodal preventive intervention for disruptive kindergarten boys: Its impact through mid-adolescence. *Journal of Consulting and Clinical Psychology, 63,* 560–568.

Tremblay, R. E., Pihl, R. O., Vitaro, F., & Dobkin, P. (1994). Predicting early onset of male antisocial behavior from preschool behavior. *Archives of General Psychiatry, 51,* 732–739.

Triandis, H. C. (1964). Cultural influences upon cognitive processes. In L. Berkowitz (Ed.), *Advances in experimental social psychology.* New York: Academic Press.

Triandis, H. C. (1994). *Culture and social behavior.* New York: McGraw-Hill.

Triandis, H. C. (1996). The psychological measurement of cultural syndromes. *American Psychologist, 51,* 407–415.

Triandis, H. C. (1997). Cross-cultural perspectives on personality. In R. Hogan, J. Johnson, & S. Briggs (Eds.), *Handbook of personality psychology* (pp. 439–464). San Diego: Academic Press.

Triandis, H. C. (1998). Vertical and horizontal individualism and collectivism: Theory and research implications for international management. In J. L. C. Cheng, R. B. Peterson, et al. (Eds.), *Advances in international comparative management*. Stamford, CT: JAI Press.

Trierweiler, S. J., Neighbors, H. W., Munday, C., Thompson, E. E., Binion, V. J., & Gomez, J. P. (2000). Clinician attributions associated with the diagnosis of schizophrenia in African American and non-African American patients. *Journal of Consulting and Clinical Psychology, 68,* 171–175.

Tronick, E. Z. (1989). Emotions and emotional communication in infants. *American Psychologist, 44,* 112–119.

Tronick, E. Z., Morelli, G. A., & Ivey, P. K. (1992). The Efe forager infant and toddler's pattern of social relationships: Multiple and simultaneous. *Developmental Psychology, 28,* 568–577.

Trope, Y., Cohen, O., & Alfieri, T. (1991). Behavior identification as a mediator of dispositional inference. *Journal of Personality and Social Psychology, 61,* 873–883.

Trower, P. (1995). Adult social skills: State of the art and future directions. In W. O'Donohue & L. Krasner (Eds.), *Handbook of psychological skills training: Clinical techniques and applications* (pp. 54–80). Boston: Allyn & Bacon.

Tryon, R. C. (1940). Genetic differences in maze-learning ability in rats. *Yearbook of the National Society for the Study of Education, 39,* 111–119.

Tseng, W., Kan-Ming, M., Li-Shuen, L., Guo-Qian, C., Li-Wah, O., & Hong-Bo, Z. (1992). Koro epidemics in Guangdong China. Journal of Nervous and Mental Disease, 180, 117–123.

Tsuang, M. T., Stone, W. S., & Faraone, S. V. (2000). Toward reformulating the diagnosis of schizophrenia. *American Journal of Psychiatry, 157,* 1041–1950.

Tulving, E. (1983). *Elements of episodic memory.* Oxford: Oxford University Press.

Tulving, E. (1995). Organization of memory: Quo vadis? In M. S. Gazzaniga (Ed.), *The Cognitive Neurosciences,* pp. 839–853. Cambridge, MA: MIT Press.

Tulving, E., & Psotka, J. (1971). Retroactive inhibition in free recall: Inaccessibility of information available in the memory store. *Journal of Experimental Psychology, 87,* 1–8.

Turiel, E. (1998). The development of morality. In W. Damon & N. Eisenberg (Eds.), *Handbook of child psychology: Vol. 3. Social, emotional, and personality development* (5th ed., pp. 863–932). New York: Wiley.

Turkheimer, E., & Waldron, M. (2000). Nonshared environment: A theoretical, methodological, and quantitative review. *Psychological Bulletin, 126,* 78–108.

Turner, A. M., & Greenough, W. T. (1985). Differential rearing effects on rat visual cortex synapses: I. Synaptic and neuronal density and synapses per neuron. *Brain Research, 329,* 195–203.

Turner, C. F., Miller, H. G., & Rogers, S. M. (1998). Survey measurement of sexual behaviors: Problems and progress. In J. Bancroft (Ed.), *Researching Sexual Behavior.* Bloomington: Indiana University Press.

Turner, J. C. (1987). *Rediscovering the social group: A self-categorization theory.* New York: Basil Blackwell.

Turner, J. C. (1991). *Social influence.* Pacific Grove, CA: Brooks/Cole.

Turner, M. E., Pratkanis, A. R., Probasco, P., & Leve, C. (1992). Threat, cohesion, and group effectiveness: Testing a social identity maintenance prospective on groupthink. *Journal of Personality and Social Psychology, 63,* 781–796.

Tversky, A., & Kahneman, D. (1974). Judgment under uncertainty: *Heuristics and biases. Science, 185,* 1124–1131.

Tversky, A., & Kahneman, D. (1981). The framing of decisions and the psychology of choice. *Science, 211,* 453–458.

Tversky, A., & Kahneman, D. (1991). Loss aversion in riskless choice: A reference dependent model. *Quarterly Journal of Economics, 106,* 1039–1061.

Tversky, A., & Kahneman, D. (1993). Probabilistic reasoning. In A. Goldman (Ed.), *Readings in philosophy and cognitive science* (pp. 43–68). Cambridge, MA: MIT Press.

Tversky, B., & Tuchin, M. (1989). A reconciliation of the evidence on eyewitness testimony: Comments on McCloskey and Zaragoza. *Journal of Experimental Psychology: General, 118,* 86–91.

U.S. Census Bureau. (2000). *Current Population Survey: Poverty Highlights, 1999.* Washington, DC: U.S. Government Printing Office.

U.S. Department of Health and Human Services. (1996). *Physical Activity and Health: A Report of the Surgeon General.* Atlanta: Centers for Disease Control and Prevention, 1996.

U.S. Department of Health and Human Services. (1997, September 9). Substance Abuse and Mental Health Services Administration news release.

U.S. Department of Health and Human Services. (2000). *National health and nutrition examination survey, 1999.* Washington, DC: National Center for Health Statistics.

U.S. Department of Health and Human Services. (2000). *Reducing tobacco use: A report of the Surgeon General.* Atlanta, GA: Centers for Disease Control and Prevention.

U.S. Department of Justice. (1997). *Lifetime likelihood of going to state or federal prison.* Washington, DC: Bureau of Justice Statistics.

U.S. Department of Justice. (1998). *Alcohol and crime: An analysis of national data on the prevalence of alcohol involved in crime.* Washington, DC: Author.

U.S. Department of Justice. (1999). *Eyewitness evidence: A guide for law enforcement.* Washington, DC: National Institute of Justice.

U.S. Surgeon General. (1999). *Mental health: A report of the surgeon general.* Rockville, MD: U.S. Department of Health and Human Services.

Uchino, B. N., Uno, D., & Holt-Lunstad, J. (1999). Social support, physiological processes, and health. *Current Directions in Psychological Science, 8,* 145–148.

Uhl, G. R., Sora, I., & Wang, Z. (1999). *Proceedings of the National Academy of Sciences, 96,* 7752–7755.

Valenza, E., Simion, F., Assia, V. M., & Umilta, C. (1996). Face preference at birth. *Journal of Experimental Psychology: Human Perception and Performance, 22,* 892–903.

Vallacher, R. R., & Novak, A. (1997). The emergence of dynamical social psychology. *Psychological Inquiry, 8,* 73–99.

Van Bezooijen, R., Otto, S. A., & Heenan, T. A. (1983). Recognition of vocal expression of emotion: A three-nation study to identify universal characteristics. *Journal of Cross-Cultural Psychology, 14,* 387–406.

van IJzendoorn, M. H. (1995). Adult attachment representations, parental responsiveness, and infant attachment: A meta-analysis on the predictive validity of the Adult Attachment Interview. *Psychological Bulletin, 117,* 387–403.

Van Sickel, A. D. (1992). Clinical hypnosis in the practice of anesthesia. *Nurse Anesthesiologist, 3,* 67–74.

Vattano, F. (2000). *The mind: Video teaching modules* (2nd ed.). Fort Collins, CO: Colorado State University and Annenberg/CPB.

Velligan, D. I., Bow-Thomas, C. C., Huntzinger, C., Ritch, J., Ledbetter, N., Prihoda, T. J., & Miller, A. L. (2000). Randomized controlled trial of the use of compensatory strategies to enhance adaptive functioning in outpatients with schizophrenia. *American Journal of Psychiatry, 157,* 1317–1328.

Vernet, M. E., Robin, O., & Dittmar, A. (1995). The ohmic perturbation duration, an original temporal index to quantify electrodermal responses. *Behavioural Brain Research, 67*(1), 103–107.

Vincent, C. A., & Richardson, P. H. (1986). The evaluation of therapeutic acupuncture: Concepts and methods. *Pain, 24,* 1–13.

Voegtlin, T., & Verschure, P. F. (1999). What can robots tell us about brains? A synthetic approach towards the study of learning and problem solving. *Review of Neuroscience, 10,* 291–310.

Vohs, K. D., Bardone, A. M., Joiner, T. E., Jr., Abramson, L. Y., & Heatherton, T. F. (1999). Perfectionism, perceived weight status, and self-esteem interact to predict bulimic symptoms: A model of bulimic symptom development. *Journal of Abnormal Psychology, 108,* 695–700.

Vokey, J. R., & Read, J. D. (1985). Subliminal messages: Between the devil and the media. *American Psychologist, 40,* 1231–1239.

Volz, H. P., & Laux, P. (2000). Potential treatment for subthreshold and mild depression: A comparison of St. John's wort extracts and fluoxetine. *Comprehensive Psychiatry, 41,* 133–137.

Volz, J. (2000). Successful aging: The second 50. *APA Monitor, 31,* 24–28.

Von Wright, J. M., Anderson, K., & Stenman, U. (1975). Generalization of conditioned GSRs in dichotic listening. In P. M. A. Rabbitt & S. Dornic (Eds.), *Attention and performance V.* New York: Academic Press.

Vygotsky, L. S. (1991). Genesis of the higher mental functions. In P. Light, S. Sheldon, & M. Woodhead (Eds.), *Learning to think: Child development in social context* (Vol. 2, pp. 32–41). London: Routledge.

Vyse, S. A. (1997). *Believing in magic: The psychology of superstition.* New York: Oxford University Press.

Waagenaar, W. (1986). My memory: A study of autobiographical memory over six years. *Cognitive Psychology, 18,* 225–252.

Waagenaar, W. A. (1989). *Paradoxes of gambling behavior.* Hillsdale, NJ: Erlbaum.

Wade, C. (1988, April). *Thinking critically about critical thinking in psychology.* Paper presented at the annual meeting of the Western Psychological Association, San Francisco, CA.

Wade, W. A., Treat, T. A., & Stuart, G. L. (1998). Transporting an empirically supported treatment for panic disorder to a service clinic setting: A benchmarking strategy. *Journal of Consulting & Clinical Psychology, 66,* 231–239.

Wakefield, J. C. (1999). Evolutionary versus prototype analyses of the concept of disorder. *Journal of Abnormal Psychology, 108,* 374–399.

Walberg, H. J. (1987). Studies show curricula efficiency can be attained. *NASSP Bulletin, 71,* 15–21.

Walker, E. F., & Diforio, D. (1998). Schizophrenia: A neural diathesis-stress model. *Psychological Review, 104,* 667–685.

Walker, L. (1991). The feminization of psychology. *Psychology of Women Newsletter of Division, 35,* 1, 4.

Walker, L. J. (1989). A longitudinal study of moral reasoning. *Child Development, 60,* 157–166.

Wallace, R. K., & Benson, H. (1972). The physiology of meditation. *Scientific American, 226,* 84–90.

Wallen, K., & Lovejoy, J. (1993). Sexual behavior: Endocrine function and therapy. In J. Schulkin (Ed.), *Hormonal pathways to mind and brain.* New York: Academic Press.

Waller, N. G., & Shaver, P. R. (1994). The importance of nongenetic influences on romantic love styles: A twin-family study: *Psychological Science, 3,* 268–274.

Walsh, W., & Banaji M. (1997). The collective self. In J. Snodgrass & R. Thompson (Eds.), *The self across psychology: Self-recognition, self-awareness, and the self* (pp. 193–214). New York: New York Academy of Sciences.

Wang, X., Merzenich, M. M., Sameshima, K., & Jenkins, W. M. (1995). Remodelling of hand representation in adult cortex determined by timing of tactile stimulation, *Nature, 378,* 71–75.

Warburton, D. M. (1995). Effects of caffeine on cognition and mood without caffeine abstinence. *Psychopharmacology, 119,* 66–70.

Ward, C. (1994). Culture and altered states of consciousness. In W. J. Lonner & R. S. Malpass (Eds.), *Psychology and culture.* Boston: Allyn & Bacon.

Ward, L. M. (1997). Involuntary listening aids hearing. *Psychological Science, 8,* 112–118.

Warner, L., Kessler, R., Hughes, M., Anthony, J., & Nelson, C. (1995). Prevalence and correlates of drug use and dependence in the United States. *Archives of General Psychiatry, 52,* 219–229.

Watanabe, S., Sakamoto, J., & Wakita, M. (1995). Pigeons' discrimination of paintings by Monet and Picasso. *Journal of Experimental Analysis of Behavior, 63,* 165–174.

Watanabe, T., & Sugita, Y. (1998). REM sleep behavior disorder (RBD) and dissociated REM sleep. *Nippon Rinsho, 56*(2), 433–438.

Waterman, A. S. (1982). Identity development from adolescence to adulthood: An extension of theory and a review of research. *Developmental Psychology, 18,* 341–358.

Watson, J. B. (1913). Psychology as the behaviorist views it. *Psychological Review, 20,* 158–177.

Watson, J. B. (1919). *Psychology from the standpoint of a behaviorist.* Philadelphia: Lippincott.

Watson, J. B. (1925). *Behaviorism.* London: Kegan Paul, Trench, Trubner.

Watson, M. W. (1981). The development of social roles: A sequence of social-cognitive development. *New Directions for Child Development, 12,* 33–41.

Watson, R. I. (1963). *The great psychologists: From Aristotle to Freud.* Philadelphia: Lippincott.

Watt, N. F., & Saiz, C. (1991). Longitudinal studies of premorbid development of adult schizophrenics. In E. F. Walker (Ed.), *Schizophrenia: A life-course in developmental perspective.* San Diego, CA: Academic Press.

Wearden, A. J., Tarrier, N., Barrowclough, C., Zastowny, T. R., & Rahill, A. A. (2000). A review of expressed emotion research in health care. *Clinical Psychology Review, 20,* 633–666.

Webb, W. B. (1968). *Sleep: An experimental approach.* New York: Macmillan.

Weber, R. J. (1992). *Forks, phonographs, and hot air balloons: A field guide to inventive thinking.* New York: Oxford University Press.

Wechsler, D. (1939). *The measurement of adult intelligence.* Baltimore: Williams & Wilkins.

Wechsler, D. (1949). *The Wechsler Intelligence Scale for Children.* New York: Psychological Corporation.

Weekes, J. R., Lynn, S. J., Green, J. P., & Brentar, J. T. (1992). Pseudomemory in hypnotized and task-motivated subjects. *Journal of Abnormal Psychology, 101,* 356–360.

Weeks, D., & Weeks, J. (1995). *Eccentrics: A study of sanity and strangeness.* New York: Villard.

Wehr, T. A., Sack, D., Rosenthal, N., Duncan, W., & Gillian, J. C. (1983). Circadian rhythm disturbances in manic-depressive illness. *Federation Practitioner, 42,* 2809–2814.

Weiler, B. L., & Widom, C. S. (1996). Psychopathy and violent behavior in abused and neglected young adults. *Criminal Behaviour & Mental Health, 6,* 253–271.

Weinberg, J., & Levine, S. (1980). Psychobiology of coping in animals: The effects of predictability. In S. Levine & H. Ursin (Eds.), *Coping and health.* New York: Plenum.

Weinberg, R. A., Scarr, S., & Waldman, I. D. (1992). The Minnesota transracial adoption study: A follow-up of IQ test performance at adolescence. *Intelligence, 16,* 117–135.

Weiner, B. (1993). On sin versus sickness: A theory of perceived responsibility and social motivation. *American Psychologist, 48*(9), 957–965.

Weinstein, D. (1999). Who Are You? *Sunday Telegraph Magazine,* July 24, 24–26.

Weiskrantz, L. (1997). *Consciousness lost and found: A neuropsychological exploration.* Oxford, England: Oxford University Press.

Weiss, B., & Weisz, J. R. (1995). Relative effectiveness of behavioral versus nonbehavioral child psychotherapy. *Journal of Consulting and Clinical Psychology, 63,* 317–320.

Weiss, D. S., Marmar, C. R., Metzler, T. J., & Ronfeldt, H. M. (1995). Predicting symptomatic distress in emergency services personnel. *Journal of Consulting and Clinical Psychology, 63,* 361–368.

Weiss, S., & Moore, M. (1990). Cultural differences in the perception of magazine alcohol advertisements by Israeli Jewish, Moslem, Druze, and Christian high school students. *Drug and Alcohol Dependence, 26,* 209–215.

Weissman, M. M., Bland, R., Joyce, P. R., Newman, S., Wells, J. E., & Wittchen, H. U. (1993). Sex differences in rates of depression: Cross-national perspectives. *Journal of Affective Disorders, 29,* 77–84.

Weist, R. M. (1989). Time concepts in language and thought: Filling the Piagetian void from two to five years. In I. Levin & D. Zakay (Eds.), *Time and human cognition.* Amsterdam: Elsevier Science Publishers.

Weisz, J. R., & Jensen, P. S. (1999). Efficacy and effectiveness of psychotherapy and pharmacotherapy with children and adolescents. *Mental Health Services Research, 1,* 125–157.

Weisz, J. R., Weiss, B., Han, S. S., Granger, D. A., & Morton, T. (1995). Effects of psychotherapy with children and adolescents revisited: A meta-analysis of treatment outcome studies. *Psychological Bulletin, 117,* 450–468.

Wells, G. L., & Bradfield, A. L. (1999). Distortions in eyewitness' recollections: Can the postidentification-feedback effect be moderated? *Psychological Science, 10,* 138–144.

Wells, G. L., Malpass, R. S., Lindsay, R. C. L., Fisher, R. P., Turtle, J. W., & Fulero, S. M. (2000). From the lab to the police station: A successful application of eyewitness research. *American Psychologist, 55,* 581–598.

Weltzin, T. E., Bulik, C. M., McConaha, C. W., & Kaye, W. H. (1995). Laxative withdrawal and anxiety in bulimia nervosa. *International Journal of Eating Disorders, 17*(2), 141–146.

Wertheimer, M. (1987). *A brief history of psychology* (3rd ed.). New York: Holt, Rinehart & Winston.

Westen, D. (1998). The scientific legacy of Sigmund Freud: Toward a psychodynamically informed psychological science. *Psychological Bulletin, 124,* 333–371.

Westen, D., & Gabbard, G. O. (1999). Psychoanalytic approaches to personality. In L. Pervin & O. John (Eds.), *Handbook of personality research* (2nd ed., pp. 57–101). New York: Guilford.

Weston, C., & Went, F. (1999). Speaking up for yourself: Description and evaluation of an assertiveness training program for people with learning disabilities. *Mental Handicap, 27,* 110–115.

Whalen, P. J. (1998). Fear, vigilance, and ambiguity: Initial neuroimaging studies of the human amygdala. *Current Directions in Psychological Science, 7,* 177–188.

Whimbey, A. (1976). *Intelligence can be taught.* New York: Bantam.

Whisman, M. A. (1999). Marital dissatisfaction and psychiatric disorders: Results from a national comorbidity study. *Journal of Abnormal Psychology, 108,* 701–706.

Whitam, F. L., Diamond, M., & Martin, J. (1993). Homosexual orientation in twins: A report on 61 pairs and three triplet sets. *Archives of Sexual Behavior, 22*(3), 187–206.

Whitbourne, S. K., Zuschlag, M. K., Elliot, L. B., & Waterman, A. D. (1992). Psychosocial development in adulthood: A 22-year sequential study. *Journal of Personality and Social Psychology, 63,* 260–271.

White, F. J. (1998). Nicotine addiction and the lure of reward. *Nature Medicine, 4,* 659–660.

White, M. (1987). *The Japanese educational challenge: A commitment to children.* New York: Free Press.

Wickens, C. D. (1989). Attention and skilled performance. In D. Holding (Ed.), *Human skills* (pp. 71–105). New York: Wiley.

Wickens, C. D. (1992). *Engineering psychology and human performance* (2nd ed.). New York: HarperCollins.

Wickens, C. D., & Carswell, C. M. (1997). Information processing. In G. Salvendy (Ed.), *Handbook of human factors and ergonomics* (2nd ed., pp. 89–122). New York: Wiley Interscience.

Wickens, C. D., Gordon, S. E., & Liu, Y. (1998). *An introduction to human factors engineering.* New York: Longman.

Wickens, C. D., Stokes, A., Barnett, B., & Hyman, F. (1992). The effects of stress on pilot judgment in a MIDIS simulator. In O. Svenson & J. Maule (Eds.), *Time pressure and stress in human judgment and decision making.* New York: Plenum.

Wickramasekera, I., Davies, T. E., & Davies, S. M. (1996). Applied psychophysiology: A bridge between the biomedical model and the biopsychosocial model in family medicine. *Professional Psychology: Research and Practice, 27,* 221–233.

Widiger, T. A. (1997). The construct of mental disorder. *Clinical Psychology: Science and Practice, 4,* 262–266.

Widom, C. S. (1989). The cycle of violence. *Science, 244,* 160–166.

Widom, C. S. (2000). *Childhood Victimization: Early Adversity, Later Psychopathology.* Washington, DC: National Institute of Justice Journal.

Wiebe, D. J., & Smith, T. W. (1997). Personality and health: Progress and problems in psychomatics. In R. Hogan, J. Johnson, & S. Briggs (Eds.), *Handbook of personality psychology* (pp. 891–918). San Diego: Academic Press.

Wiedenfeld, S., O'Leary, A., Bandura, A., Brown, S., Levine, S., & Raska, K. (1990). Impact of perceived self-efficacy in coping with stressors on components of the immune system. *Journal of Personality and Social Psychology, 59,* 1082–1094.

Wiertelak, E. P., Maier, S. F., & Watkins, L. R. (1992). Cholecystokinin antianalgesia: Safety cues abolish morphine analgesia. *Science, 256,* 830–833.

Wigfield, A., & Eccles, J. S. (2000). Expectancy-value theory of achievement motivation. *Contemporary Educational Psychology, 25,* 68–81.

Wiggins, J. S. (1997). In defense of traits. In R. Hogan, J. Johnson, & S. Briggs (Eds.), *Handbook of personality psychology* (pp. 97–118). San Diego: Academic Press.

Wiggins, J. S., & Trapnell, P. D. (1997). Personality structure: The return of the Big Five. In R. Hogan, J. Johnson, & S. Briggs (Eds.), *Handbook of personality psychology* (pp. 737–766). San Diego: Academic Press.

Williams, J. E., & Best, D. L. (1990). *Measuring stereotypes: A multination study* (rev. ed.). Newbury Park, CA: Sage.

Williams, K. D., & Sommer, K. L. (1997). Social ostracism by coworkers: Does rejection lead to loafing or compensation? *Personality and Social Psychology Bulletin, 23,* 693–706.

Williams, L. M. (1994). What does it mean to forget child sexual abuse? A reply to Loftus, Garry, and Feldman (1994). *Journal of Consulting and Clinical Psychology, 62,* 1182–1186.

Williams, T. J., Pepitone, M. E., Christensen, S. E., Cooke, B. M., Huberman, A. D., Breedlove, T. J., Jordan, C. I., & Breedlove, S. M. (2000). Finger length patterns and human sexual orientation. *Nature, 404,* 455–456.

Willis, S. L., & Schaie, K. W. (1999). Intellectual functioning in midlife. In S. L. Willis & J. D. Reid (Eds.), *Life in the middle: Psychological and social development in middle age.* San Diego: Academic Press.

Wills, T. A. (1991). Similarity and self-esteem in downward comparison. In J. M. Suls & T. A. Wills (Eds.), *Social comparison: Contemporary theory and research* (pp. 23–50). Hillsdale, NJ: Erlbaum.

Wilson, D. L., Silver, S. M., Covi, W. G., & Foster, S. (1996). Eye movement desensitization and reprocessing: Effectiveness and autonomic correlates. *Journal of Behaviour Therapy and Experimental Psychiatry, 27,* 219–229.

Wilson, G. T. (1985). Limitations of meta-analysis in the evaluation of the effects of psychological therapy. *Clinical Psychology Review, 5,* 35–47.

Wilson, G. T. (1995). Behavior therapy. In R. J. Corsini & D. Wedding (Eds.), *Current psychotherapies* (5th ed., pp. 197–228). Itasca, IL: Peacock.

Wilson, G. T. (1997). Dissemination of cognitive behavioral treatments: Commentary. *Behavior Therapy, 28,* 473–475.

Wilson, G. T., Loeb, K. L., Walsh, B. T., Labouvie, E., Petkova, E., Liu, X., & Waternaux, C. (1999). Psychological versus pharmacological treatments of bulimia nervosa: Predictors and processes of change. *Journal of Consulting and Clinical Psychology, 67,* 451–459.

Wilson, G. T., Nathan, P. E., O'Leary, K. D., & Clark, L. A. (1996). *Abnormal psychology.* Boston: Allyn & Bacon.

Wilson, W. J. (1997). *When work disappears: The world of the new urban poor.* New York: Vintage Books.

Winn, P. (1995). The lateral hypothalamus and motivated behavior: An old syndrome reassessed and a new perspective gained. *Current Directions in Psychological Science, 4,* 182–187.

Winokur, G., Coryell, W., Keller, M., Endicott, J., & Leon, A. (1995). A family study of manic-depressive (Bipolar I) disease. *Archives of General Psychiatry, 52,* 367–373.

Winson, J. (1990, November). The meaning of dreams. *Scientific American,* pp. 86–96.

Winter, D. G. (1996). *Personality: Analysis and interpretation of lives.* New York: McGraw-Hill.

Winzelberg, A. J., Eppstein, D., Eldredge, K. L., Wilfley, D., Dasmahapatra, R., Dev, P., & Taylor, C. B. (2000). Effectiveness of an internet-based program for reducing risk factors for eating disorders. *Journal of Consulting and Clinical Psychology, 68,* 346–350.

Wise, R. A. (1996). Neurobiology of addiction. *Current Opinions in Neurobiology, 6*(2), 243–251.

Wise, R. A. (1998). Drug-activation of brain reward pathways. *Drug & Alcohol Dependence, 51,* 13–22.

Wiseman, R., West, D., & Stemman, R. (1996, January/February). Psychic crime detectives: A new test for measuring their successes and failures. *Skeptical Inquirer, 21,* 38–58.

Witt, S. D. (1997). Parental influence on children's socialization to gender roles. *Adolescence, 32,* 253–259.

Wittchen, H. U., Zhao, S., Kessler, R. C., & Eaton, W. W. (1994). DSM-III-R: Generalized anxiety disorder in the national comorbidity survey. *Archives of General Psychiatry, 51,* 355–364.

Wittenbaum, G. M., & Stasser, G. (1996). Management of information in small groups. In J. L. Nye & A. M. Brower (Eds.), *What's social about cognition? Social cognition in small groups* (pp. 3–28). Newbury Park, CA: Sage.

Woelk, H. (2000). Comparison of St. John's wort and imipramine for treating depression: Randomised controlled trial. *British Medical Journal, 321,* 536–539.

Wolf, A. M., & Colditz, G. A. (1998). Current estimates of the economic cost of obesity in the United States. *Obesity Research, 6,* 97–106.

Wolpe, J. (1958). *Psychotherapy by reciprocal inhibition.* Stanford, CA: Stanford University Press.

Wong, M. M., & Csikszentmihalyi, M. (1992). *Journal of Personality and Social Psychology, 60,* 154–164.

Wong, S. E., Martinez-Diaz, J. A., Massel, H. K., Edelstein, B. A., Wiegand, W., Bowen, L., & Liberman, R. P. (1993). Conversational skills training with schizophrenic inpatients: A study of generalization across settings and conversants. *Behavior Therapy, 24,* 285–304.

Wood, W., Wong, F. Y., & Chachere, G. (1991). Effects of media violence on viewers' aggression in unconstrained social interaction. *Psychological Bulletin, 109,* 371–383.

Woodall, K. L., & Matthews, K. A. (1993). Changes in and stability of hostile characteristics: Results from a 4-year longitudinal study of children. *Journal of Personality and Social Psychology, 64,* 491–499.

Woodbury, D., Schwarz, E. J., Prockop, D. J., & Black, I. B. (2000). Adult rat and human bone marrow stromal cells differentiate into neurons. *Journal of Neuroscience Research, 61,* 364–370.

Woods, S. C., Schwartz, M. W., Baskin, D. G., & Seeley, R. J. (2000). Food intake and the regulation of body weight. *Annual Review of Psychology, 51,* 255–277.

Woods, S. C., Seeley, R. J., Porte, D., Jr., & Schwartz, M. W. (1998). Signals that regulate food intake and energy homeostasis. *Science, 280,* 1378–1383.

Woodworth, R. S., & Schlosberg, H. (1954). *Experimental psychology.* New York: Holt.

Woolfolk-Hoy, A. (1999). Psychology applied to education. In A. Stec & D. Bernstein (Eds.), *Psychology: Fields of application.* Boston: Houghton Mifflin.

Woolley, J. D. (1997). Thinking about fantasy: Are children fundamentally different thinkers and believers from adults? *Child Development, 68,* 991–1011.

Worchel, S., & Shackelford, S. L. (1991). Groups under stress: The influence of group structure and environment on process and performance. *Personality and Social Psychology Bulletin, 17,* 640–647.

Worchel, S., Cooper, J., Goethals, G., & Olson, J. (2000). *Social psychology.* Belmont, CA: Wadsworth.

World Health Organization (1998). *Communicable Disease Surveillance and Response.* Geneva, Switzerland: WHO.

Worthington, J. J. 3rd, Pollack, M. H., Otto, M. W., McLean, R. Y., Moroz, G., & Rosenbaum, J. F. (1998). Long-term experience with clonazepam in patients with a primary diagnosis of panic disorder. *Psychopharmacology Bulletin, 34,* 199–205.

Wren, C. S. (1998, September 22). For crack babies, a future less bleak. *New York Times* (Web Archive).

Wren, C. S. (1999, February 24). U. N. Drug Board Urges Research on Marijuana as Medicine. *New York Times* [On-line].

Wright, G. N., & Phillips, L. D. (1980). Cultural variation in probabilistic thinking: Alternative ways of dealing with uncertainty. *International Journal of Psychology, 15,* 239–257.

Wright, W. F., & Bower, G. H. (1992). Mood effects on subjective probability. *Organizational Behavior and Human Decision Processes, 52,* 276–291.

Wu, H. W., Cacioppo, J. T., Glaser, R., Kiecolt-Glaser, J. K., & Malarkey, W. B. (1999). Chronic stress associated with spousal caregiving of patients with Alzheimer's dementia is associated with downregulation of B-lymphocyte GH mRNA. *Journals of Gerontology, 54A,* M212–M215.

Wurtman, R. J., & Wurtman, J. J. (1995). Brain serotonin, carbohydrate-craving, obesity and depression. *Obesity Research, 3*(Suppl. 4), 477S–480S.

Wynn, K., & Chiang, W.-C. (1998). Limits to infants' knowledge of objects: The case of magical appearance. *Psychological Science, 9,* 448–455.

Yakimovich, D., & Saltz, E. (1971). Helping behavior: The cry for help. *Psychonomic Science, 23,* 427–428.

Yalom, I. D. (1995). *The theory and practice of group therapy* (4th ed.). New York: Basic Books.

Yantis, S. (1993). Stimulus-driven attentional capture. *Current Directions in Psychological Science, 2,* 156–161.

Yates, J. F., Lee, J. W., & Shinotsuka, H. (1992*). Cross-national variation in probability judgment.* Paper presented at the 33rd annual meeting of the Psychonomic Society, St. Louis.

Yates, J. F., Zhu, Y., Ronis, D. L., Wang, D. F., Shinotsuka, H., & Masanao, T. (1989). Probability judgment accuracy: China, Japan, and the United States. *Organizational Behavior and Human Decision Processes, 43,* 145–171.

Yerkes, R. M. (Ed.). (1921). Psychological examining in the U.S. Army. *Memoirs of the National Academy of Sciences,* No. 15.

Yesavage, J. A., Leirer, V. O., Denari, M., & Hollister, L. E. (1985). Carry-over effects of marijuana intoxication on aircraft pilot performance: A preliminary report. *American Journal of Psychiatry, 142,* 1325–1329.

York, J. L., & Welte, J. W. (1994). Gender comparisons of alcohol consumption in alcoholic and nonalcoholic populations. *Journal of Studies on Alcohol, 55*(6), 743–750.

Young, A. W., Aggleton, J. P., Hellawell, D. J., & Johnson, M. (1995). Face processing impairments after amygdalotomy. *Brain, 118*(1), 15–24.

Young, M. E. (1995). On the origin of causal theories. *Psychonomic Bulletin & Review, 2,* 83–104.

Yukl, G., & Van Fleet, D. D. (1992). Theory and research on leadership in organizations. In M. D. Dunnette & L. M. Hough (Eds.), *Handbook of industrial and organizational psychology* (Vol. 3, 2nd ed., pp. 147–198). Palo Alto, CA: Consulting Psychologists Press.

Yutrzenka, B. A. (1995). Making a case for training in ethnic and cultural diversity in increasing treatment efficacy. *Journal of Consulting and Clinical Psychology, 63,* 197–206.

Zadra, A., & Donderi, D. C. (2000). Nightmares and bad dreams: Their prevalence and relationship to well-being. *Journal of Abnormal Psychology, 109,* 273–281.

Zahn-Waxler, C., Radke-Yarrow, M., Wagner, E., & Chapman, M. (1992). Development of concern for others. *Developmental Psychology, 28,* 1038–1047.

Zahrani, S. S., & Kaplowitz, S. A. (1993). Attributional biases in individualistic and collectivist cultures: A comparison of Americans with Saudis. *Social Psychology Quarterly, 56*(3), 223–233.

Zajonc, R. B. (1965). Social facilitation. *Science, 149,* 269–274.

Zajonc, R. B. (1998). Emotions. In D. Gilbert, S. T. Fiske, & G. Lindzey (Eds.), *Handbook of social psychology* (Vol. 1, 4th ed., pp. 591–634). Boston: McGraw-Hill.

Zald, D. H., & Pardo, J. V. (1997). Emotion, olfaction, and the human amygdala: Amygdala activation during aversive olfactory stimulation. *Proceedings of the National Academy of Sciences of the United States of America, 94* (8), 4119–4124.

Zhang, Y., Proenca, R., Maffei, M., Barone, M., Leopold, L., & Friedman, J. M. (1994). Positional cloning of the mouse obese gene and its human homologue. *Nature, 372,* 425–432.

Zhou, J.-N., Hofman, M. A., Gooren, L. J. G., & Swaab, D. F. (1995). A sex difference in the human brain and its relation to transsexuality. *Nature, 378,* 68–70.

Zigler, E. F., & Seitz, V. (1982). Social policy and intelligence. In R. J. Sternberg (Ed.), *Handbook of human intelligence* (pp. 586–641). Cambridge, England: Cambridge University Press.

Zigler, E. F., Taussig, C., & Black, K. (1992). Early childhood intervention: A promising preventive for juvenile delinquency. *American Psychologist, 47,* 997–1006.

Zillmann, D. (1988). Cognition-excitation interdependencies in aggressive behavior. *Aggressive Behavior, 14,* 51–64.

Zillmann, D. (1996). Sequential dependencies in emotional experience and behavior. In R. D. Kavanaugh, B. Zimmerberg, & S. Fein (Eds.), *Emotion: Interdisciplinary perspectives* (pp. 243–272). Mahwah, NJ: Erlbaum.

Zillmann, D., Katcher, A. H., & Milavsky, B. (1972). Excitation transfer from physical exercise to subsequent aggressive behavior. *Journal of Experimental Social Psychology, 8,* 247–259.

Zimbardo, P. G. (1973). The psychological power and pathology of imprisonment. *Catalog of Selected Documents in Psychology, 3,* 45.

Zimmerman, M., Reischl, T., Seidman, E., Rappaport, J., Toro, P., & Salem, D. (1991). Expansion strategies of a mutual help organization. *American Journal of Community Psychology, 19,* 251–279.

Zinbarg, R. E., & Barlow, D. H. (1996). Structure of anxiety and the anxiety disorders: A hierarchical model. *Journal of Abnormal Psychology, 105,* 181–193.

Zoellner, L. A., Foa, E. B., Brigidi, B. D., & Przeworski, A. (2000). Are trauma victims susceptible to "false memories"? *Journal of Abnormal Psychology, 109,* 517–524.

Zsambok, C. E., & Klein, G. (1997). *Naturalistic decision making.* Hillsdale, NJ: Erlbaum.

Zubin, J., & Spring, B. (1977). Vulnerability—A new view of schizophrenia. *Journal of Abnormal Psychology, 86,* 103–126.

Zuckerman, M. (1984). Sensation seeking: A comparative approach to a human approach. *The Behavioral and Brain Sciences, 7,* 413–471.

Zuckerman, M. (1990). Some dubious premises in research and theory on racial differences. *American Psychologist, 45,* 1297–1303.

Zuckerman, M. (1993). Out of sensory deprivation and into sensation seeking: A personal and scientific journey. In G. G. Brannigan & M. R. Merrens (Eds.), *The undaunted psychologist: Adventures in research* (pp. 45–57). Philadelphia: Temple University Press.

Zuckerman, M. (1996). "Conceptual clarification" or confusion in "The study of sensation seeking" by J. S. H. Jackson and M. Maraun. *Personality and Individual Differences, 21,* pp. 111–114.

Zuckerman, M. (1999). *Vulnerability to psychopathology: A biosocial model.* Washington, DC: American Psychological Association.

Zungu-Dirwayi, N., Hugo, F., van Heerden, B. B., & Stein, D. J. (1999). Are musical obsessions a temporal lobe phenomenon? *Journal of Neuropsychiatry & Clinical Neurosciences, 11,* 398–400.

CREDITS

CREDITS (continued from copyright page)

TEXT CREDITS

Chapter 1: **p. 3** *Figure 1.1* From *American Journal of Psychology*. Copyright © 1961 by the Board and Trustees of the University of Illinois. Used with permission of the University of Illinois Press. **p. 17** *Table 1.3* Table from, "Persuasion and Culture: Advertising Appeals in Individualistic and Collectivistic Societies," by S. Han and S. Shavitt, in *Journal of Experimental Social Psychology*, Volume 30, 326–350, copyright © 1994 by Academic Press, reproduced by permission of the publisher.

Chapter 2: **p. 56** *Figure 2.10* From *The Cerebral Cortex of Man* by Wilder Penfield and Theodore Rasmussen. Copyright © 1950; copyright renewed © 1978 by Theodore Rasmussen. Reprinted by permission of The Gale Group. **p. 261** *Figure 2.13* Reprinted by permission of the publisher from *The Postnatal Development of the Human Cerebral Cortex, Volumes I–VIII* by Jesse LeRoy Conel, Cambridge, Mass.: Harvard University Press, Copyright © 1939, 1975 by the President and Fellows of Harvard College.

Chapter 3: **p. 81** *Table 3.2* M. W. Levine, *Fundamentals of Sensation and Perception*, Third Edition. Copyright © 2000 Oxford University Press. Reprinted by permission of the author. **p. 93** *Figure 3.18* From Gardner, M. (1970). "Of Optical Illusions from Figures that are Undecidable to Hot Dogs that Float." *Scientific American*, 222 (May), 124, 127. Reprinted by permission of Martin Gardner. **p. 101** *Figure 3.24 Journal of Social Psychology*, 52, pp. 183–208. Reprinted with permission of the Helen Dwight Reid Educational Foundation. Published by Heldref Publications, 1319 Eighteenth St., NW, Washington, DC 20036-1802. Copyright © 1960. **p. 104** *Figure 3.28* Reprinted from *Cognition*, 4, M.A. Johnson, S. Dziurawiec, H. Ellis, and J. Morton, "Newborns' Preferential Tracking of Face-Like Stimuli and Its Subsequent Decline," pp. 1–19, copyright © 1991, with permission from Elsevier Science.

Chapter 4: **p. 118** *Figure 4.2* D.L. Schacter, L.A. Cooper, S.M. Delaney, M.A. Peterson, and M. Tharan's article "Implicit Memory for Possible and Impossible Objects: Constraints on the Construction of Structural Descriptions," (1991) from *Journal of Experimental Psychology: Learning, Memory, and Cognition*, 17, 3–19. Copyright © 1991 by the American Psychological Association. Reprinted with permission. **p. 123** *Figure 4.3* Horne, J.A., *Why We Sleep: The Functions of Sleep in Humans and Other Mammals*. Copyright © 1988 James Horne. Reprinted by permission of Oxford University Press. **p. 124** *Figure 4.4* Adapted by permission of the author from *A Primer of Sleep and Dreaming* by Rosalind Cartwright. **p. 130** *Figure 4.6* Reprinted by permission of the author from *Hypnotic Age Susceptibility* by Ernest R. Hilgard. Copyright © 1965. Published by Harcourt, Brace, Jovanovich, Inc.

Chapter 5: **p. 156** *Figure 5.8* From: *The Psychology of Learning and Memory* by Hintzman. Copyright © 1978 W.H. Freeman and Company. Used with permission of the author. **p. 159** *Figure 5.10* Adapted with permission from *Teaching Machines*, by B.F. Skinner. Copyright © 1961.

Chapter 6: **p. 185** *Figure 6.3* From *Cognitive Psychology: Memory, Language, and Thought* by Darlene V. Howard. © 1983 by Darlene V. Howard. Reprinted by permission of the author. **p. 187** *Figure 6.5* Figure from, "Long-Term Memory for a Common Object," by R.S. Nickerson and M.J. Adams from *Cognitive Psychology*, Volume 11, 287–307, copyright © 1979 by Academic Press, reproduced by permission of the publisher. **p. 199** *Figure 6.13* Tulvin and Psotka, "Retroactive Inhibition in Free Recall: Inaccessibility of Information Available in the Memory Store," *Journal of Experimental Psychology*, 87, pp. 1–8, 1971. Copyright © 1971 by the American Psychological Association. Reprinted with permission.

Chapter 7: **p. 238** *Figure 7.8* Simulated items similar to those in the *Wechsler Intelligence Scales for Adults and Children*. Copyright © 1949, 1955, 1974, 1981, 1991 by The Psychological Corporation, a Harcourt Assessment Company. Reproduced by permission. All rights reserved. **p. 249** *Figure 7.13* Reprinted with permission from Robert J. Sternberg, "Testing for Practical and Creative Intelligence," *New York Times*, November 8, 1997.

Chapter 8: **p. 263** *Figure 8.3* Adapted with permission from Schwartz, M.W., Woods, S.C., Porte Jr., D., Seeley, R.J. and Baskin, D.G. (2000). Central nervous system control of food intake. *Nature 404*, 661–671. **p. 269** *Figure 8.4* Adapted from W.H. Masters and V.E. Johnson, *Human Sexual Response*, p. 5 (Boston: Little, Brown & Company, 1966). Reprinted by permission from Masters and Johnson Institute. **p. 291** *Figure 8.12* From "Voluntary Facial Action Generates Emotion-Specific Autonomic Nervous System Activity," by R.W. Levenson, P. Ekman, and W.V. Friesen, *Psychophysiology*, 1990, 24, 363–384. Copyright © 1990 the Society for Psychophysiological Research. Reprinted with permission of Cambridge University Press.

Chapter 9: **p. 310** *Figure 9.5* Baillargeon, R., "A model of physical reasoning in infancy." From C. Rovee-Collier and L.P. Lipsitt (eds.), *Advances in infancy research*. Copyright © 1992. Reprinted by permission from ABLEX Publishing Corporation. **p. 336** *Figure 9.8* Reprinted with permission.

Chapter 10: **p. 351** *Table 10.2* C.S. Crandall, J.J. Preisler, and J. Aussprung, "Measuring life event stress in the lives of college students: The Undergraduate Stress Questionnaire (USQ)" from the *Journal of Behavioral Medicine*, 15, 627–662. Copyright © 1992 by Plenum Publishing Corporation. Reprinted by permission of Plenum Publishing Corporation and C.S. Crandall. **p. 353** *Figure 10.2* "The General Adaptation Syndrome," from *Stress without Distress* by Hans Selye, M.D. Copyright © 1974 by Hans Selye, M.D. Reprinted by permission of HarperCollins Publishers, Inc. **p. 358** *Figure 10.4* Adapted from Lazarus, Option, Nornikos, and Rankin, *Journal of Personality*, 33:4. Copyright © Blackwell Publishers. Reprinted with permission.

Chapter 11: **p. 378** *Figure 11.1* From *Personality Strategies and Issues* by R.M. Liebert and M.D. Spiegler. Copyright © 1987, 1982, 1978, 1974, 1970 The Dorsey Press; © 1994, 1990 Brooks/Cole Publishing Company, Pacific Grove, CA 93950, a division of International Thomson Publishing Inc. By permission of the publisher. **p. 384** *Figure 11.2* Reprinted by special permission of the publisher, Psychological Assessment Resource, Inc., Odessa, Florida 33556, from the Structured Interview of Reported Symptoms by Richard Rogers, Ph.D., Copyright © 1986, 1992 by PAR, Inc. Further reproduction is prohibited without permission of PAR, Inc. **p. 385** *Figure 11.3* From "The Causes and Cures of Neurosis: An Introduction to Modern Behavior Therapy Based on Learning Theory and the Principle of Conditioning" by H.J. Eysenck and S. Rachman. © 1965 by Edits. **p. 390** *Figure 11.4* Reprinted from *Journal of Behavior Therapy and Experimental Psychiatry*, 13, A. Bandura, "The Assessment and Predictive Generality of Self-Precepts of Efficacy," pp. 195–199. Copyright © 1982 with permission from Elsevier Science. **p. 399** *Figure 11.5* From Minnesota Multiphasic Personality Inventory-2 Profile for Clinical Scales. Copyright © by the Regents of the University of Minnesota 1942, 1943 (renewed 1970), 1989. All rights reserved. "MMPI-2" and "Minnesota Multiphasic Personality Inventory-2" are trademarks owned by the University of Minnesota.

Chapter 13: **p. 461** *Figure 13.1* Reprinted with permission of the author from Matson, J., Sevin, J., Fridley, and Love, S. (1990). "Increasing Spontaneous Language in Autistic Children," *Journal of Applied Behavior Analysis*, 23, pp. 227–233.

Chapter 14: **p. 501** *Figure 14.5* Kenrick, D.T., Groth, G., Trost, M. & Sadalla, E.K. (1993), "Integrating Evolutionary and Social Exchange Perspectives on Relationships: Effects of Gender, Self-Appraisal, and Involvement Level on Mate Selection," *Journal of Personality and Social Psychology*, 64, pp. 951–969. Copyright © 1993 by the American Psychological Association. Reprinted with permission. **p. 509** *Figure 14.8* Adapted with permission from S. Milgram, "Behavioral Study of

Obedience," from *Journal of Abnormal and Social Psychology*, 67, No. 4, p. 376. Copyright © 1963. **p. 518** *Figure 14.11* Figure from, "Temperature and Aggression: Paradox, Controversy, and a (fairly) Clear Picture," by C.A. Anderson, and K.P. Anderson, in *Human Aggression*, edited by R.G. Green and E. Donnerstein. Copyright © 1998 by Academic Press. Reprinted by permission of the publisher.

PHOTO CREDITS

Chapter 1: p. 4 © Kevin Horan/Tony Stone Images *(left)*; © Frank Siteman/Index Stock Imagery *(right)*. **p. 5** Archives of the History of American Psychology—The University of Akron. **p. 7** The Ferdinand Hamburger Archives of The Johns Hopkins University. **p. 9** Thomas McAvoy/Timepix. **p. 12** © Dana White/PhotoEdit. **p. 14** © Zigy Kaluzny/Stone. **p. 15** Courtesy of Wellesley College Archives, photo by Partridge *(top)*; Courtesy of Wilberforce University, Archives and Special Collections *(bottom)*. **p. 16** © Chip Hires/Liaison Agency. **p. 21** © David Young-Wolff/PhotoEdit. **p. 22** © Allen Stephens/Liaison Agency. **p. 25** © Willie L. Hill, Jr./Stock Boston. **p. 30** © A. Ramey/PhotoEdit. **p. 31** © The New Yorker Collection 1981 Charles Addams from cartoonbank.com. All Rights Reserved.

Chapter 2: p. 43 © Markel/Gamma-Liaison. **p. 48** © Maria Melin/Liaison Agency. **p. 50** D.N. Levin, H. Xiaoping, K.K. Tan, S. Galhotra, C.A. Palizzare, G.T.Y. Chen, R.N. Beck, C.T. Chen, M.D. Cooper, J.F. Mullan, J. Hekmatpanah, and J.-P. Spire (1989). The Brain: Integrated three-dimensional display of MR and PET images. Radiology, 172: 783–789 *(left)*; © Manfred Kage/Peter Arnold, Inc. *(right)*. **p. 52** © Bachmann/The Image Works. **p. 57** THE FAR SIDE © FARWORKS, INC. All rights reserved. **p. 58** © Bob Daemmrich/Stock Boston.

Chapter 3: p. 73 © David R. Frazier/Photo Researchers. **p. 76** © Omikron/Photo Researchers. **p. 78** © Michael Simpson/Index Stock Imagery. **p. 79** Reprinted by permission from Nature. Roorda, A. & Williams, D.R. (1999). The arrangement of the three cone classes in the living human eye. *Nature 397*, 520–522. Copyright 1999 Macmillan Magazines Ltd. **p. 80** Vienot, Brettel, Mollon—MNHN, CNRS. **p. 83** AP/Wide World Photos. **p. 87** L.M. Bartoshuk and V.B. Duffy. **p. 88** © Billy Hustace/Stone. **p. 89** © Alain Evrard/Photo Researchers. **p. 90** Reuters/MIKE BLAKE/Archive Photos. **p. 95** THE FAR SIDE © FARWORKS, INC. All rights reserved. **p. 97** AP/Wide World Photos. **p. 98** © David Young-Wolff/PhotoEdit **p. 99** From MIND SIGHTS by Shepard © 1990 by Roger N. Shepard. Used with permission by W.H. Freeman and Company. **p. 103** Miami Herald. **p. 105** © PhotoEdit.

Chapter 4: p. 115 © David Welling/Animals Animals. **p. 117** Permission granted by International Creative Management Inc. Copyright © 1986 by Berke Breathed. Cartoon first appeared in The Washington Post. **p. 120** AP/Wide World Photos **p. 122** Jacques Jangoux/Photo Researchers *(top)*; Nathan Benn/NGS Image Collection *(bottom)*. **p. 125** © Bob Daemmrich/The Image Works. **p. 126** © David Young-Wolff/PhotoEdit *(top)*; AP/Wide World Photo *(bottom)*. **p. 129** © David Parker/Photo Researchers. **p. 131** © Grant Mason/Manni Mason's Pictures. **p. 133** The William H. Helfand Collection, New York. **p. 135** © Barry King/Liaison Agency.

Chapter 5: p. 148 © Tom Stack & Assoc. **p. 151** © Steven Needham/Envision. **p. 154** Nina Leen/Timepix. **p. 156** © Frank Lotz Miller/Black Star. **p. 157** © The New Yorker Collection 1993 Tom Cheney from cartoonbank.com. All Rights Reserved. **p. 158** © Rick Smolan/Stock Boston. **p. 159** Courtesy of The Lincoln Electric Company. **p. 161** Lang, P.J., & Malamed, B.G. (1969). Avoidance conditioning therapy of an infant with chronic ruminative vomiting. Journal of Abnormal Psychology, 74, 1–8. **p. 167** Kohler, W. 1976. The Mentality of Apes. London: Routledge and Kegan Paul. **p. 168** © Paul Chesley/Tony Stone Images *(top)*; Albert Bandura/Stanford University *(bottom)*. **p. 171** © Charles Gupton/Stock Boston. **p. 172** © Rhoda Sidney/PhotoEdit.

Chapter 6: p. 181 © Mary Kate Denny/Tony Stone Images. **p. 184** © Frank Siteman/Stock Boston. **p. 187** Franco Magnani, 1700 El Camino Real, Rue 21 Sp. 16, South San Francisco, CA 94080-1281 *(left)*; Photo by S. Schwartzenberg, © Exploratorium, www.exploratorium.edu *(right)*. **p. 190** © Jeff Dunn/Index Stock Imagery. **p. 192** William F. Brewer, in Brewer, W. F., & Treyens, J. C. (1981), Role of schemata in memory for places. Cognitive Psychology, 13, 207–230. **p. 196** © Paul Conklin. **p. 199** © Laurence Monneret/Tony Stone Images. **p. 203** Courtesy of Prof. Dominique Muller.

Chapter 7: p. 215 © Frank Siteman/PhotoEdit. **p. 217** © Steve Starr/Stock Boston. **p. 219** © Paul Howell/Liaison Agency. **p. 221** CALVIN AND HOBBES © Watterson. Reprinted with permission of UNIVERSAL PRESS SYNDICATE. All rights reserved. **p. 229** © Tim Boyle/Liaison Agency. **p. 231** AP/Wide World

Photos. **p. 233** © Joe McNally/Corbis Sygma. **p. 234** © Michael Grecco/Stock Boston. **p. 235** Dr. Ronald H. Cohn/Gorilla Foundation/Koko.org. **p. 241** © The New Yorker Collection 1998 J. B. Handelsman from cartoonbank.com. All Rights Reserved. **p. 250** Fraser Hale/St. Petersburg Times.

Chapter 8: p. 258 AP/Wide World Photos. **p. 260** Harlow Primate Laboratory, University of Wisconsin. **p. 262** © Richard Howard. **p. 264** © Peter Menzel/Stock Boston. **p. 265** AP/Wide World Photos. **p. 272** AP/Wide World Photos. **p. 275** Reprinted by permission of the publishers from Henry A. Murray, Thematic Apperception Test, Cambridge, Mass.: Harvard University Press, © 1943 by the President and Fellows of Harvard College, © 1971 by Henry A. Murray *(top)*; © The New Yorker Collection 1993 Al Ross from cartoonbank.com. All Rights Reserved *(bottom)*. **p. 276** © Walter Hodges/Tony Stone Images. **p. 282** From The Neurological Examination 4th ed., by R.N. DeJong. New York: Lipincott/Harper & Row, 1979. **p. 287** © Bob Daemmrich/Stock Boston. **p. 290** © Reuters/Antonio Guevara/Archive Photos *(top)*; © Eastcott/Momatiuk/Woodfin Camp *(bottom left)*; © Rick Smolan/Stock Boston *(bottom right)*.

Chapter 9: p. 300 © Les Stone/Corbis Sygma. **p. 302** © C. Salvador/Corbis Sygma. **p. 303** Photo Lennart Nilsson/Albert Bonniers Forlag AB, Behold Man, Little, Brown and Company. **p. 305** Nelson, C. A. (1987). The recognition of facial expressions in the first two years of life: Mechanisms of development. Child Development, 58, 889–909. **p. 306** © Petit Format/J. DaCunha/Photo Researchers. **p. 308** © George Zimbel/Monkmeyer. **p. 309** Courtesy of Carolyn Rovee-Collier. **p. 312** Reprinted with special permission of King Features Syndicate. **p. 313** © Pedrick/The Image Works. **p. 317** © Laima Druskis/Stock Boston. **p. 318** © Bob Daemmrich. **p. 319** © Amy C. Etra/PhotoEdit. **p. 321** Harlow Primate Library, University of Wisconsin. **p. 322** © Michael Newman/PhotoEdit. **p. 327** © Bill Aron/PhotoEdit. **p. 328** © Jeff Greenberg/Photo Researchers. **p. 332** © Mary Kate Denny/PhotoEdit. **p. 337** © Ken Coleman/PhotoEdit. **p. 338** © Bob Daemmrich/Stock Boston. **p. 339** © David J. Sams/Stock Boston *(top)*; Reuters/Joe Skipper/Archive Photos *(bottom)*.

Chapter 10: p. 351 © Reuters/Allen Fredrickson/Archive Photos. **p. 355** Reprinted with special permission of King Features Syndicate. **p. 357** © David Alan Harvey/Woodfin Camp. **p. 360** © Lauren Greenfield/Corbis Sygma. **p. 365** © Esbin-Anderson/The Image Works. **p. 368** © Huntly Hersch/Index Stock Imagery *(top)*; © Farley/Monkmeyer *(bottom)*. **p. 370** Courtesy of American Psychological Association. **p. 371** © Leslie O'Shaughnessy/Medical Images.

Chapter 11: p. 380 © Bob Daemmrich/Stock Boston. **p. 381** Mary Evans Picture Library. **p. 383** © John Neubauer/PhotoEdit. **p. 386** © Robert Caputo/AURORA. **p. 391** THE FAR SIDE © FARWORKS, INC. All rights reserved *(top)*; © Titan Sports/Corbis Sygma *(bottom left)*; © Andy King/Corbis Sygma *(bottom right)*. **p. 393** AP/Wide World Photos. **p. 396** AP/Wide World Photos. **p. 401** © The New Yorker Collection 1999 J.C. Duffy from cartoonbank.com. All Rights Reserved *(top)*; © Charlotte Miller *(bottom)*.

Chapter 12: p. 410 © Dana White/PhotoEdit. **p. 411** © Grox-J. M. News/Sipa Press. **p. 412** © J.L. Dugast/Corbis Sygma. **p. 413** Culver Pictures. **p. 424** Photo reproduced with permission of Susan Mineka. **p. 426** Photofest. **p. 431** © Dan McCoy/Rainbow. **p. 434** © Grunnitus/Monkmeyer. **p. 438** FBI/Liaison Agency. **p. 441** © Bob Daemmrich/The Image Works. **p. 444** Reuters/Montana Dept. of Justice/Archive Photos.

Chapter 13: p. 453 Stock Montage. **p. 454** Photograph © Edmund Engelman. **p. 455** © Charles Gupton/Tony Stone Images. **p. 457** Michael Rougier/Timepix. **p. 460** Georgia Tech photo by Gary Meek. **p. 462** © Rick Friedman/Black Star. **p. 463** Courtesy, Albert Ellis, Institute for Rational-Emotive Therapy. **p. 471** © Bill Aron/PhotoEdit. **p. 473** © Will & Deni McIntyre/Photo Researchers. **p. 477** © The New Yorker Collection 2000 Frank Cotham from cartoonbank.com. All Rights Reserved. **p. 479** © Joseph Sohm; ChromoSohm Inc./Corbis.

Chapter 14: p. 489 Michael Newman/PhotoEdit. **p. 490** DILBERT reprinted by permission of United Feature Syndicate, Inc. **p. 492** © Peter Ginter/Material World. **p. 494** © Sean Sprague/Stock Boston. **p. 499** © J. Marshall/The Image Works. **p. 500** © Michelle Bridwell/PhotoEdit. **p. 502** © Myrleen Ferguson/PhotoEdit. **p. 505** AP/Wide World Photos. **p. 507** © Jonathan Nourok/PhotoEdit. **p. 509** From the film OBEDIENCE copyright 1965 by Stanley Milgram and distributed by Penn State Media Sales. Permission granted by Alexandra Milgram. **p. 510** John Chiasson/Liaison Agency. **p. 514** © AFP/Corbis. **p. 519** © Ellen Senisi/The Image Works. **p. 520** © Benali/Liaison Agency. **p. 524** © Najlah Feanny/Saba.

Appendix: p. A-3 DILBERT reprinted by permission of United Feature Syndicate, Inc.

Key terms, which appear in **boldface,** are followed by their definitions.

Rods   *Photoreceptors in the retina that allow sight even in dim light, but that cannot discriminate colors,* 75, 76, 79

Role theory   *A theory proposing that hypnotized people act in accordance with a social role that demands compliance,* 130

Sampling   *The process of selecting participants who are members of the population that the researcher wishes to study,* 26

Satiety   *The condition of no longer wanting to eat,* 261. See also **Hunger**

Saturation   *The purity of a color,* 77, 78

Schemas   *Basic units of knowledge that organize past experience and provide a framework for understanding future experience,* 308
   constructive memory and, 194–195
   in infancy and childhood, 308–309
   social perception and, 488–489, 490

Schemas   *Mental representations of what we know and expect about the world,* 102–103, 194–195, 217, 218

Schizophrenia   *A pattern of severely disturbed thinking, emotion, perception, and behavior that*